rary and Archives Canada Cataloguing in Publication

audon, Kenneth C., 1944–

Management information systems: managing the digital firm / Kenneth C. Laudon, Jane P. Laudon; Canadian adaptation by Mary Elizabeth Brabston.—3rd Canadian ed.

Includes bibliographical references and index.
ISBN 0-13-197388-6

1. Management information systems. 2. Information technology—Management. I. Laudon, Jane Price II. Brabston, Mary Elizabeth, 1948– III. Title.

T58.6.L38 2007   658.4'038   C2005-905433-6

ISBN 0-13-197388-6

Vice-President, Editorial Director: Michael J. Young
Editor-in-Chief: Gary Bennett
Acquisitions Editor: Laura Paterson Forbes
Marketing Manager: Eileen Lasswell
Developmental Editor: Eleanor MacKay
Production Editor: Laura Price
Copy Editor: Nicole Mellow
Proofreader: Shirley Corriveau
Production Coordinator: Deborah Starks
Permissions and Photo Researcher: Sandy Cooke
Indexer: Belle Wong
Layout: Bill Renaud
Director: Julia Hall
and Interior Design: Anthony Leung
Images: Young man and women using mobile phones, Ingram Publishing/Alamy; Binary Hallway, Steven Puetzer/Masterfile.

11 10 09 08 07

nd bound in the United States of America.

Third Canadian Edition

Management Information Systems

Managing the Digital Firm

Kenneth C. Laudon
New York University

Jane P. Laudon
Azimuth Information Systems

Canadian adaptation by
Mary Elizabeth Brabston
I. H. Asper School of Business
University of Manitoba

PEARSON
Prentice
Hall

Toronto

For
Erica and Elisabeth
-K.C.L. AND J.P.L.

For my parents,
Donald and Mary Jane Brabston
-M.E.B.

About the Authors

Kenneth C. Laudon is a Professor of Information Systems at New York University's Stern School of Business. He holds a B.A. in Economics from Stanford and a Ph.D. from Columbia University. He has authored twelve books dealing with electronic commerce, information systems, organizations, and society. Professor Laudon has also written over forty articles concerned with the social, organizational, and management impacts of information systems, privacy, ethics, and multimedia technology.

Professor Laudon's current research is on the planning and management of large-scale information systems and multimedia information technology. He has received grants from the National Science Foundation to study the evolution of national information systems at the Social Security Administration, the IRS, and the FBI. A part of this research is concerned with computer-related organizational and occupational changes in large organizations, changes in management ideology, changes in public policy, and understanding productivity change in the knowledge sector.

Ken Laudon has testified as an expert before the United States Congress. He has been a researcher and consultant to the Office of Technology Assessment (United States Congress) and to the Office of the President, several executive branch agencies, and Congressional Committees. Professor Laudon also acts as an in-house educator for several consulting firms and as a consultant on systems planning and strategy to several Fortune 500 firms.

At NYU's Stern School of Business, Ken Laudon teaches courses on Managing the Digital Firm, Information Technology and Corporate Strategy, Professional Responsibility (Ethics), and Electronic Commerce and Digital Markets. Ken Laudon's hobby is sailing and he is a veteran Newport to Bermuda Race captain.

Jane Price Laudon is a management consultant in the information systems area and the author of seven books. Her special interests include systems analysis, data management, MIS auditing, software evaluation, and teaching business professionals how to design and use information systems.

Jane received her Ph.D. from Columbia University, her M.A. from Harvard University, and her B.A. from Barnard College. She has taught at Columbia University and the New York University Graduate School of Business. She maintains a lifelong interest in Oriental languages and civilizations.

The Laudons have two daughters, Erica and Elisabeth.

About the Canadian Adapter

Mary Elizabeth Brabston is a tenured Associate Professor of Management Information Systems at the University of Manitoba's I.H. Asper School of Business. Dr. Brabston has also taught at the Copenhagen Business School as a visiting professor. Prior to the Asper School, Dr. Brabston taught at the University of Tennessee at Chattanooga. Dr. Brabston received her doctorate at Florida State University. A native of Alabama in the United States, Dr. Brabston became a Canadian citizen in 2003. Having spent her life working as a banker, political staffer, development officer, and academic, Dr. Brabston brings a comprehensive view to her analysis of how information systems can help organizations achieve their potential—and the challenges associated with doing so. Dr. Brabston's teaching and research interests focus on strategic planning and applications of information systems and information resource management, as well as electronic commerce design, use, and implementation. Her work has appeared in such publications as the Journal of Computing and Information Technology, Journal of Computer Information Systems, Journal of Information Systems Education, and Human Relations.

Brief Contents

Contents

Chapter 3

Information Systems, Organizations, Management, and Strategy   65

Chapter 6

Managing Data Resources   191

Opening Case: Better Data Help Virgin Mobile Australia Win the Customer Wars   192

Chapter 9   Information Systems Security and Control   **300**

Opening Case: Wesfarmers Outsources to a Managed Security Service   301

PART III   Systems Development and Management   338

Chapter 10   Systems Development   339

Chapter 11   Information Resource Management   378

Chapter 12   Managing Global Systems   413

PART IV   Applications for the Digital Firm   442

Chapter 13   Electronic Business and Electronic Commerce   443

Chapter 14   Enterprise Applications and Business Process Integration   476

Chapter 15   Enhancing Decision Making in the Digital Firm   510

Opening Case: Daimler's Bremen Plant Optimizes Deliveries with DSS   511

Preface

Management Information Systems: Managing the Digital Firm, Third Canadian Edition, is based on the premise that knowledge about information systems is essential for creating successful, competitive firms, managing global corporations, adding business value, and providing useful products and services to customers.

One of the central questions facing managers today is how to optimize their firms' returns on their information systems investments. In Canada alone, capital expenditures for computing and telecommunications equipment and services will amount to an estimated $65 billion in 2005. Accordingly, one goal of this book is to help managers make better decisions about technology and achieve the maximum value from their information technology investments. We accomplish this goal in part by describing how contemporary real-world managers and firms make these decisions and in part by providing analytic concepts that are useful when making decisions. This book provides an introduction to management information systems (MIS) that undergraduate and MBA students will find vital to their professional success regardless of their major area or concentration.

Digital Integration of the Enterprise: The Emerging Digital Firm

A continuing stream of information technology innovations, from the Internet to wireless networks to digital phone and cable systems, is transforming the business world. These innovations enable entrepreneurs and innovative traditional firms to create new business models, destroy old business models, disrupt entire industries, build new business processes, and transform the day-to-day conduct of business.

The growth of the Internet, the globalization of trade, and the rise of information economies have raised the importance of information technologies and systems in business and management. It is essential that business students understand how information technologies are changing business firms and markets today and how they will likely change in the near-term future as digital technologies continue to evolve.

For example, companies are relying on Internet and networking technology to conduct more of their work electronically, seamlessly linking factories, offices, and sales forces around the globe. Leading-edge firms, such as Nortel, Bombardier, and Nygård, are extending these networks to suppliers, customers, and other groups outside the organization so they can react instantly to customer demands and market shifts.

Ultimately, these changes are leading to fully digital firms where all internal business processes and relationships with customers and suppliers are digitally enabled. In digital firms, information to support business decisions is available anytime and anywhere in the organization. Accordingly, we have changed the subtitle of this text to *Managing the Digital Firm*.

New to the Third Canadian Edition

This edition has been totally rewritten to teach managers how to optimize the return on investments in information technologies and systems. Throughout the text, chapter contents and case studies describe how information systems contribute to better management decisions, more efficient business processes, and higher firm profitability. Each chapter identifies the organizational and managerial factors that help the firm benefit from its information technology investments. This edition also highlights new opportunities for improving business performance from leading-edge technologies that are transforming computing and communications. The following features and content reflect this new direction.

New Chapter on IT Infrastructure and Platforms

A completely new chapter on information technology (IT) infrastructure and platforms (Chapter 5) replaces the chapter on hardware and software in previous editions. Instead of focusing on how hardware and software work, this new chapter provides an overview of the technology and service components of IT infrastructure and the most important trends in hardware and software platforms. The chapter examines the capabilities of major technology vendors as well as key technologies to help managers make intelligent choices about the appropriate technology platforms and services for their firms. Additional material, primarily technical in nature, can be found on the Companion Website for Chapter 5.

New Chapter on Telecommunications, Networks, and the Internet

Earlier editions treated telecommunications and the Internet as separate topics. This is no longer valid. The Internet has become the dominant networking standard for voice and data communication, and the distinctions between providers of voice, cable, and Internet services are disappearing. We have created a new chapter on telecommunications, networks and the Internet (Chapter 7) that deals with the impact of the convergence of computing and communications technologies and the emergence of Internet technology for integrating voice, video, and data communication in a single network.

New Chapter on the Wireless Revolution

Wireless technology has created a whole new platform for delivering products and communicating with customers and suppliers. We believe wireless systems have become so pervasive and powerful that the topic merits its own chapter (Chapter 8). This chapter features in-depth discussion of technologies for wireless networking and wireless applications. Included in our coverage are cellular systems and network generations, wireless data networks and Internet access (Bluetooth, Wi-Fi, WiMax, and emerging broadband services), wireless networking standards, m-commerce, radio-frequency identification (RFID) systems, and other applications where wireless technology is having its greatest impact.

Newly Revised Chapter on Information Systems Security and Control

In previous editions, security and control was one of the last chapters in the text. This topic has become so important that we've positioned it much earlier as Chapter 9 in the part on information technology. The chapter has also been fully rewritten to provide in-depth coverage of Internet security; wireless security challenges; new legal obligations such as PIPEDA and Sarbanes-Oxley for safeguarding the accuracy, security, and privacy of information systems; the organizational, management, and technical framework for an up-to-date security policy; and computer forensics.

New Chapter on Enterprise Applications and Business Process Integration

A new full chapter (Chapter 14) is dedicated to supply chain management, customer relationship management, enterprise systems, and new system platforms for delivering enterprise-wide services. It explains how these applications work, how they provide value for the business, and the challenges of developing and using them successfully.

Newly Revised Chapter on Knowledge Management Systems

Knowledge management systems are another core enterprise application and one of the fastest-growing software applications in business today. Our newly revised chapter (Chapter 16) provides in-depth coverage of leading-edge, enterprise-wide knowledge management systems for capturing, distributing, and applying organizational knowledge. The chapter shows how companies are using these enterprise-wide knowledge management systems along with knowledge work systems and intelligent techniques to improve organizational performance and management decision making.

New Management Opportunities, Challenges, and Solutions Section

We have replaced the "Management Challenges" section with a new section called "Management Opportunities, Challenges, and Solutions" at the end of each chapter to give more attention to relevant management issues. This section highlights opportunities as well as challenges and provides solution guidelines for addressing the challenges.

Management Opportunities, Challenges, and Solutions

Opportunities

Throughout your managerial career, you will face decisions on how to use networking technology and services to enhance the performance of your firm. You should be aware of the challenges in trying to implement these decisions and how they can be addressed.

Firms have an opportunity to bring about radical reductions in the cost of data and voice communication and to use networking and Internet technology in new ways as parts of new business models. The business value of these technologies cannot be underestimated.

Management Challenges

Telecommunications and networking technologies present challenges as well as opportunities for organizations. Three stand out: loss of management control over information systems, the need for organizational change, and the difficulty of ensuring infrastructure scalability and reliability.

Loss of Management Control Managing information systems technology and corporate data are more difficult in a distributed networked environment because of the lack of a single, central point where needed management can occur. Distributed client/server networks, peer-to-peer computing networks, mobile wireless networks, and Internet computing have created new independent sources of computing power. End

New Leading-Edge Topics

In addition to new chapters and features that we have already described, this edition includes up-to-date treatment of the following topics:

- Wi-Fi, WiMax, and EV-DO wireless networks (Chapter 8)
- Wi-Fi security issues (Chapter 9)
- Radio-frequency identification (RFID) systems (Chapter 8)
- Internet telephony (VoIP) (Chapter 7)
- Digital convergence (convergence of telecommunications and computing) (Chapters 5 and 7)
- Computer forensics (Chapter 9)

- Grid computing, edge computing, and autonomic computing (Chapter 5)
- Web services and service-oriented architecture (Chapter 5)
- Nanotechnology (Chapter 5)
- 3G cellular networks (Chapter 8)
- Wireless sensor networks (Chapter 8)
- Information systems implications of PIPEDA, Sarbanes-Oxley, and other government regulations (Chapters 4 and 9)
- Business intelligence (Chapter 15)
- Strategic information systems for business ecosystems (Chapter 3)

Expanded Treatment of Outsourcing

Chapter 12, "Managing Global Systems," features an expanded discussion of the challenges of managing international outsourcing and global teams. Chapter 5, "IT Infrastructure and Platforms," includes a detailed discussion of hardware and software outsourcing.

New Hands-On Guide to MIS

The Companion Website for the third Canadian edition features a new Hands-On Guide to MIS. This guide provides students with hands-on knowledge they can apply to their MIS student projects and in the workplace. The "Hands-On Guide" includes helpful how-to instructions on how to solve a case study problem, how to design and normalize a relational database, how to use entity/relationship diagrams, and how to write structured query language (SQL) queries.

Hallmark Features of this Text

Management Information Systems: Managing the Digital Firm, Third Canadian Edition, has many unique features designed to create an active, dynamic learning environment.

Integrated Framework for Describing and Analyzing Information Systems

An integrated framework portrays information systems as being composed of management, organization, and technology elements. This framework is used throughout the text to describe and analyze information systems and information system problems and is reinforced in the student projects and case studies.

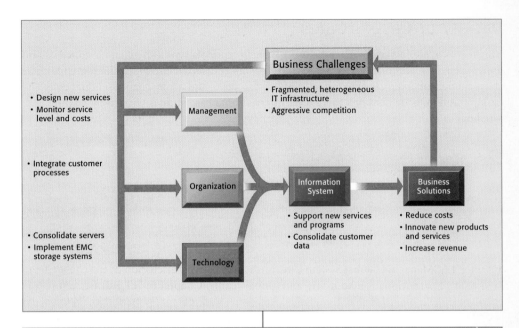

A special diagram accompanying each chapter-opening case graphically illustrates how management, organization, and technology elements work together to create an information systems solution to the business challenges discussed in the case.

Real-World Examples from Domestic and International Organizations

Real-world examples drawn from business and public organizations are used throughout the text to illustrate text concepts. More than 200 companies around the world are discussed in long and short case studies and within the body of each chapter.

Content and products. NTT DoCoMo, the wireless arm of Nippon Telegraph and Telephone Company, offers Internet-enabled cell phone users services for email and for accessing Web sites formatted for tiny screens. Subscribers can check train schedules, obtain movie listings, browse restaurant guides, purchase tickets on Japan Airlines, trade stocks, view new cartoons, and read Japan's largest daily newspaper. Menus of services can be tailored to individual subscribers' interests. Some of these services are free. Those that aren't are bundled and charged to subscribers' monthly telephone bills.

Banking and financial services. Scotiabank offers wireless alerts about changes in stock trading information on digital cell phones that support text messaging. Thailand's Bank of Asia offers a mobile service called ASIA M-Banking. Enrolled customers can check account balances, transfer funds between savings and other accounts, and pay their mobile phone and Internet usage charges using a Web-enabled mobile phone. They can complete these banking transactions anywhere at any time without having to visit a bank branch. Seoul-based Infobank offers a secure wireless platform for mobile phone users interested in securities trading.

Chapter concepts are illustrated with examples from real-world companies.

Variety of Case Studies

This text provides a variety of case studies to help students synthesize chapter concepts and apply their new knowledge to real-world problems and scenarios. Every chapter contains a short chapter-opening case, two short Window On cases, and a long chapter-ending case. The Companion Website contains three long international case studies written by leading MIS scholars.

WINDOW ON MANAGEMENT

Deutsche Bank Ties Business Continuity Planning to the Business

Deutsche Bank AG is one of the world's largest banks, with 65 400 employees serving 21 million customers in 74 different countries, including Canada. It has investment banking and asset management businesses throughout Europe, the Pacific Rim, and the Americas. Management is dedicated to protecting the interests of customers, employees, partners, regulators, and shareholders against loss of revenue and reputation, and the company has always treated business continuity planning very seriously.

The bank has a global business continuity and disaster recovery program which addresses data backup and recovery and procedures for minimizing changes in operational, financial, and credit risk exposures. Operational risk focuses on the firm's ability to maintain communications with customers and keep mission-critical systems up and running. Financial risk deals with the firm's ability to continue generating revenue and obtaining adequate financing. Credit risk occurs when investments erode from lack of liquidity in the broader market.

Every six months, Deutsche Bank New York offices test their disaster recovery plan, practicing what they would do if their computer centres went down. The company's data are always backed up on tape. Prior to September 11, 2001, Deutsche Bank had two computer centres: one in the World Trade Center and one in New Jersey. Tragically, Deutsche Bank lost two employees and its New York offices in the World Trade Center terrorist attacks, but the remaining employees were back working within a few days because the company was so well prepared. "One of our data centres was affected, but all applications were recovered from the second site in New Jersey almost immediately," according to Tony Kerrison, Deutsche Bank's head of enterprise services.

tion computer centre or from bank offices where information systems staff work.

Seow's team organizes and conducts interviews with heads of Deutsche Bank businesses to identify what is most critical to them—revenue loss, loss of reputation, loss of customer confidence, or violations of government regulations. Each business then identifies the processes required to minimize the identified risks.

Deutsche Bank has classified critical processes into two major categories: processes for business survival and processes critical to crisis support. Business survival processes are those required for Deutsche Bank to meet its business objectives. An example would be ensuring that traders in money markets and foreign exchange can work continuously because their business is a major revenue stream for the bank. (Deutsche Bank trading amounts to billions of dollars every day.) Deutsche Bank has a trading room in its DRC for this purpose, along with backup back office operations to support trading activity.

An example of processes critical to crisis support is human resources because it looks after staff welfare and staff counselling. Corporate communications are also important in the event of a crisis, but marketing, for example, would receive less priority in a crisis situation.

Seow's group is responsible for ensuring that appropriate processes and resources are in place so that the bank can respond effectively if a catastrophic event occurs. Deutsche Bank's business continuity planning revolves around planning for various scenarios that could affect its operations to make sure business can continue. Worst-case events could be a

Each chapter contains two Window On boxes (Window On Management, Window On Organizations, or Window On Technology) that present real-world examples illustrating the management, organization, and technology issues in the chapter.

Variety of Hands-On Projects

Companion Website Running Case Study The Companion Website contains a running case study that accompanies each chapter in the text. The case study provides students with the opportunity to problem solve in an ongoing real-world business scenario. Students learn about a simulated company called Dirt Bikes Canada, and then apply their information systems knowledge to problems facing this growing company. Examples of running case projects include the following:

- Performing a competitive analysis for Dirt Bikes (Chapter 3)
- Redesigning Dirt Bikes' database for customer relationship management (Chapter 6)
- Analyzing the return on investment for a new employee training system for Dirt Bikes (Chapter 11)
- Analyzing Dirt Bikes' supply chain management (Chapter 14)
- Identifying opportunities for knowledge management at Dirt Bikes (Chapter 16)

Developing a Web Site Privacy Policy

Software requirements: Web browser software

Word processing software

Electronic presentation software (optional)

Dirt Bikes's management wants to make sure it has policies and procedures in place to protect the privacy of visitors to its Web site. You have been asked to develop Dirt Bikes's Web site privacy policy. The TRUSTe Web site (www.truste.org) has Model Privacy Policy Disclosures in its Resources for businesses that you can download and review to help you draft Dirt Bikes's privacy policy. You can also examine specific companies' privacy policies by searching for Web site privacy policy on Yahoo! or using another search engine.

Prepare a report for management that addresses the following issues:

1. How much data should Dirt Bikes collect on visitors to its Web site? What information could it discover by tracking visitors' activities at its Web site? What value would this information provide the company? What are the privacy problems raised by collecting such data?

2. Should Dirt Bikes use cookies? What are the advantages of using cookies for both Dirt Bikes and its Web site visitors? What privacy issues do they create for Dirt Bikes?

3. Should Dirt Bikes join an organization such as TRUSTe to certify it has adopted approved privacy practices? Why or why not?

The Companion Website for each chapter contains a project requiring students to use application software, Web tools, or analytical skills to solve a problem that Dirt Bikes Canada has encountered. Each assignment lists the software tools that students will need to use to solve the problem and the questions students need to answer.

You will find the complete running case project and any required files at **www.pearsoned. ca/laudon**.

Hands-On Application Software Exercises Each chapter features a hands-on application software exercise for which students can solve problems using spreadsheet, database, Web page development, or electronic presentation software. Some of these exercises require students to use these application software tools in conjunction with Web activities. The application software exercises include business problems dealing with supply chain management (Chapter 2), capital budgeting (Chapter 11), customer relationship management (Chapter 14), and product pricing (Chapter 15).

Application Software Exercise:
Database Exercise: Building a Relational Database for a Small Business

Sylvester's Bike Shop, located in Vancouver, British Columbia, sells road, mountain, hybrid, leisure, and children's bicycles. Currently, Sylvester's purchases bikes from three suppliers, but plans to add new suppliers in the near future. This rapidly growing business needs a database system to manage this information.

Initially, the database should house information about suppliers and products. The database will contain two tables: a supplier table and a product table. The reorder level refers to the number of items in inventory that triggers a decision to order more items to prevent a stockout. (In other words, if the number of units of a particular inventory falls below the reorder level, the item should be reordered.) The user should be able to perform several queries and produce several managerial reports based on the data contained in the two tables.

Using the information found in the tables on the Companion Website for Chapter 6, develop a simple relational database for Sylvester's. Once you have developed the database, perform the following activities.

1. Prepare a report that identifies the five most expensive bicycles. The report should list the bicycles in descending order from most expensive to least expensive, the quantity on hand for each, and the markup percentage for each.

2. Prepare a report that lists each supplier, its products, the quantities on hand, and associated reorder levels. The report should be sorted alphabetically by supplier. Within each supplier category, the products should be sorted alphabetically.

3. Prepare a report listing only the bicycles that are low in stock and need to be reordered. The report should provide supplier information for the items identified.

4. Write a brief description of how the database could be enhanced to further improve management of the business. What tables or fields should be added? What additional reports would be useful?

Students can use their application software skills to solve real-world business problems based on chapter concepts.

The application exercises are included in each chapter, at **www.pearsoned.ca/laudon**, along with the required data files and complete instructions.

E-Commerce and E-Business Projects The hands-on electronic commerce or electronic business projects give students the opportunity to use Web research tools and interactive software at various company Web sites to solve specific business problems related to chapter concepts. These projects encourage critical-thinking skills as students explore business resources on the Internet.

Electronic Commerce Project: Comparing Online Storefront Hosting Services

You would like to set up a Web site to sell towels, linens, pottery and tableware from Portugal and are examining services for hosting small business Internet storefronts. Your Web site should be able to take secure credit card payments and to calculate shipping costs and taxes. Initially you would like to display photos and descriptions of 40 different products. Visit Yahoo! Canada's Geocities Web hosting service (**ca.geocities.yahoo.com**) and Webserve.ca, and compare the range of e-commerce hosting services they offer to small businesses, their capabilities, and costs. Also examine the tools they provide for creating an e-commerce site. Compare both of these services and decide which of the two you would use if you were actually establishing a Web store. Write a small report indicating your choice and explaining the strengths and weaknesses of both.

Students are presented with the problem of setting up a small business Internet storefront to sell housewares from Portugal. To create an effective Web site, students will need to examine e-commerce tools, ensure their site attracts consumers, and ensure it handles online purchases securely.

Comprehensive Projects A long comprehensive project for each part of the text can be found on the Companion Website. These four projects require students to apply text concepts to demanding problems that they might encounter as firms become more digitally integrated and Internet enabled. The projects include the following:

· Analyzing business processes for an enterprise system (Part One project)
· Creating a new Internet business (Part Two project)
· Redesigning business processes (Part Three project)
· Designing an enterprise information portal (Part Four project)

Web Sites of Interest

Every chapter contains a list of additional Web sites that students can access to discover more about information systems or about the chapter topics. Some of these Web sites will be useful references for instructors as well. Students may find that they continue to refer to some of these Web sites long after the course is over.

Attention to Functional Business Applications of MIS

The "Make IT Your Business" section on the Companion Website for each chapter shows how the topics in each chapter specifically relate to the major functional areas of business: finance and accounting, human resources, manufacturing and production, and sales and marketing. This section also directs students to pages in the chapter where functional business examples can be found.

Overview of the Text

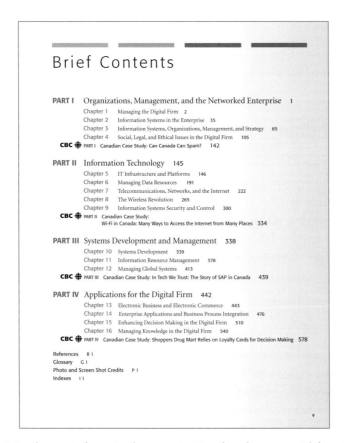

Part One introduces students to the organizational and managerial foundations of systems, their strategic role, and the organizational and management changes driving electronic business and the emerging digital firm. Chapters in Part One provide an extensive introduction to real-world systems, focusing on their relationships to organizations, management, business processes, and important ethical and social issues.

Part Two provides the technical foundation for understanding information systems and for making wise information technology choices. Chapters in Part Two describe major components of information technology infrastructure: hardware and software platforms and services, data storage and management technology, and telecommunications services and technologies, including the Internet technology. Concluding this section are full chapters on wireless technology (Chapter 8) and security and control (Chapter 9).

Part Three focuses on the process of developing and managing systems in organizations. Chapter 10 describes how companies use new information systems to redesign their organizations and business processes and the role of new technologies such as Web services for rapid application development and digital integration. Chapter 11 explains how information systems departments work and how successful systems depend on understanding the business value of systems and managing system-related change. Chapter 12 deals with developing and managing international information systems, including the special challenges and opportunities posed by offshore outsourcing.

Part Four describes the role of information systems in enhancing business processes and management decision making across the enterprise. Chapter 13 describes the many e-business and e-commerce applications used by firms today. An entire chapter (Chapter 14) is devoted to enterprise applications because they have been so widely used for digital integration to improve organizational performance. Chapter 15 describes decision-support and executive support systems that enhance firm performance by helping managers and employees make better decisions. Another full chapter (Chapter 16) deals with knowledge management systems because in an information economy much of a firm's value depends on its ability to create and manage knowledge.

Flexibility of Chapter Order The chapters in the text are placed in a logical order for a typical introductory MIS class. However, many instructors prefer to teach the material in a different order. We have attempted to be flexible and to have most chapters "stand on their own" without previous material necessary to teach a particular chapter. For example, Part Two (technology) could be taught before Part One (organizational issues). Chapter Four (ethics) could be taught at the end of the course, and so forth.

Chapter Outline

Each chapter contains the following:

- An opening case describing a real-world organization to establish the theme and importance of the chapter
- A diagram analyzing the opening case in terms of the management, organization, and technology model used throughout the text
- A series of chapter objectives written in easy-to-understand language for students
- A concluding section on management opportunities, challenges, and solutions related to the chapter theme
- A chapter summary keyed to the learning objectives
- A list of key terms that students can use to review concepts
- Review questions for students to test their comprehension of chapter material
- Discussion questions raised by the broader themes of the chapter
- An application software exercise requiring students to use application software tools to develop solutions to real-world business problems based on chapter concepts
- An electronic commerce or electronic business project
- A group project to develop teamwork and presentation skills
- A list of additional Web sites related to the chapter content
- A chapter-ending long case study illustrating important themes and concepts presented in the chapter

Companion Website (www. pearsoned.ca/laudon)

Management Information Systems: Managing the Digital Firm, Third Canadian Edition, is supported by an excellent Companion Website at **www.pearsoned.ca/laudon** that truly reinforces and enhances the text material. You will find the following items available to both students and instructors:

Interactive Study Guide. An Interactive Study Guide will help students review skills and check their mastery of chapter concepts with a variety of self-test questions. Students can send their answers to an electronic grader and receive instant feedback

Glossary. An alphabetical listing of all key terms and definitions found in the text permits students to study the glossary and search for any term using the "Find" function of their web browsers.

Management Decision Problem. A Management Decision Problem is also provided for each chapter. Management Decision Problems provide opportunities to apply chapter concepts to additional real-world, management decision making scenarios. These problems can be used for practical group learning or individual learning both in an outside of the classroom.

Dirt Bikes Canada Running Case. The Dirt Bikes Canada Running Case accompanies each chapter and provides students with the opportunity to practice their problem-solving skills using a real-world business scenario.

Additional Cases. Additional cases provide students with further opportunities to apply their understanding of the concepts and principles presented in the text.

Additional Topics. Students will find brand new material on specific topics, as well as material that has been moved from the hard copy of the text on the Companion Website. These topics are found under the chapter in which they are first discussed. Faculty and students will find this material at **www.pearsoned.ca/laudon**.

We don't know where the future will take us in terms of new trends or futurist views. Certainly, the trend toward ubiquitous computing—the anytime/any place/any device view—may mean that ubiquitous computing is in fact the next era. If so, computing will be built into our glasses, cars, refrigerators and televisions—perhaps even the clothes we wear. It will certainly be interesting to see what the future holds in computing.

 Additional material on categorizing computer systems by Mary Brabston (University of Manitoba) can be found on the Companion Website.

Technology Drivers of Infrastructure Evolution

The changes in IT infrastructure we have just described have resulted from developments in computer processing, memory chips, storage devices, telecommunications and networking hardware and software, and software design that have exponentially increased computing power while exponentially reducing costs. Let's look at the most important developments.

The Additional Topics icons direct students to further information on the Companion Website.

CBC/Pearson Education Canada Video Library for MIS. The CBC and Pearson Education Canada have combined their experience in global reporting and academic publishing to create a special set of videos to supplement the textbook. The library consists of four/five video segments that supplement the part-ending Canadian Case Studies in the book.

Web Destinations. The Companion Website also includes links to all the Web sites described at the ends of the chapters in the book.

Hands-On Guide to MIS. The new Hands-On Guide to MIS provides students with hands-on knowledge they can apply in their MIS student projects and in the workplace.

Instructor's Resources

The following resources are available to aid instructors:

Instructor's Resource CD-ROM The Instructor's Resource CD-ROM contains a rich collection of materials to facilitate the teaching of the course. Some of the material presented on the CD-ROM can olso be downloaded from a secure password-protected instructor's area of the Companion Website. The CD-ROM includes the following items:

Instructor's Manual The Instructor's Manual features answers or notes to all the questions in the textbook—namely the questions in the "Window On" boxes, the Review and Discussion Questions, the Application Software Exercises, the Electronic Business Projects, Group Projects, and case studies. The Instructor's Resource Manual also features an in-depth lecture outline, teaching ojectives, and teaching suggestions.

Pearson TestGen A comprehensive testbank of various types of questions has been prepared to accompany the new edition. The questions are rated by difficulty level, and the answers are referenced by section. The testbank is presented in a special computerized format known as Pearson TestGen. It enables instructors to view and edit the existing question, add questions, generate tests, and print the tests in a variety of formats. Powerful search and sort functions make it easy to locate questions and arrange them in any order desired. TestGen also enables instructors to administer tests on a local area network, have the tests graded electronically, and have the results prepared in electronic or printed reports. Issued on the Instructor's Resource CD-ROM, the Pearson TestGen is compatible with IBM or Macintosh systems.

PowerPoint Slides Electronic colour slides are available in Microsoft PowerPoint. The slides illuminate and build on key concepts in the text.

Image Library The Image Library is an impressive resource to help instructors create vibrant lecture presentations. Almost every figure, table and photo in the text is provided and organized by chapter for convenience. These images can be easily imported into Microsoft PowerPoint to create new presentations or to add to existing ones.

International Case Studies The International Case Studies, written by leading MIS scholars, will enable students further opportunity to synthesize chapter concepts and apply their knowledge to real-world problems and scenarios.

WebCT www.prenhall.com/webct
   Gold Level customer support, available exclusively to adopters of Pearson Education courses, is provided free of charge on adoption and provides priority assistance, training discounts, and dedicated technical support.

Blackboard www.prenhall.com/blackboard
   Pearson Education's abundant online content combined with Blackboard's popular tools and interface result in robust Web-based courses that are easy to implement, manage, and use—taking your courses to new heights in student interaction and learning.

CourseCompass www.prenhall.com/coursecompass
   CourseCompass is a dynamic, interactive online course management tool powered exclusively for Pearson Education by Blackboard. This exciting product allows you to teach market-leading Pearson Education content in an easy-to-use customizable format.

Blackboard
www.blackboard.com

CourseCompass

Acknowledgments

The production of any book involves valued contributions from a number of persons. I would like to thank all of my editors for encouragement, insight, and strong support during the production of this edition. Eleanor MacKay is an outstanding editor who guided the development of this edition with a skilled and creative hand. I thank Eileen Lasswell for her superb marketing work.

I thank Jennifer Mix, Gary Bennett, and Laura Forbes for their roles as acquisitions editors in managing this project. Laura Price is commended for the production/manufacturing of this text. Finally, I thank Nicole Mellow for her work in ensuring that the manuscript is accurate and easy to understand.

One of our goals was to write a book that was authoritative, synthesized diverse views in the MIS literature, and helped define a common academic field. A large number of leading scholars in the field were contacted and assisted us in this effort. Reviewers for the third Canadian edition include the following :

David Chan (University of Toronto)

Danny I. Cho (Brock University)

Malcolm Ferrier (British Columbia Institute of Technology)

Rebecca Grant (University of Victoria)

M. Gordon Hunter (University of Lethbridge)

Dennis Kira (Concordia University)

Sherrie Y. X. Komiak (Memorial University of Newfoundland)

Francisco B. P. Moro (University of Windsor)

Leighann Neilson (University of Guelph)

Ken Sekhon (Camosun College)

Roy Sinn (Langara College)

Maryann Sullivan (Algonquin College)

It is our hope that this group endeavour contributes to a shared vision and understanding of the MIS field.

A Great Way to Learn and Instruct Online

The Pearson Education Canada Companion Website is easy to navigate and is organized to correspond to the chapters in this textbook. Whether you are a student in the classroom or a distance learner you will discover helpful resources for in-depth study and research that empower you in your quest for greater knowledge and maximize your potential for success in the course.

[www.pearsoned.ca/laudon]

PEARSON Prentice Hall

Jump to...   http://www.pearsoned.ca/laudon   Home Search Help Profile

Companion Website

Home >

Companion Website

Management Information Systems: Managing the Digital Firm, Third Canadian Edition, by Laudon, Laudon, and Brabston

Student Resources

The modules in this section provide students with tools for learning course material. These modules include:

- Self-Study Questions
- Flashcard Glossary
- Making IT Your Business
- Dirt Bikes Running Case
- Additional Cases
- Hands-On Guide to MIS
- International Resources

In the quiz modules students can send answers to the grader and receive instant feedback on their progress through the Results Reporter. Coaching comments and references to the textbook may be available to ensure that students take advantage of all available resources to enhance their learning experience.

Instructor Resources

A link to the protected Instructor's Central site provides instructors with additional teaching tools. Downloadable PowerPoint Presentations and an Instructor's Manual are just some of the materials that may be available in this section. Where appropriate, this section will be password protected. To get a password, simply contact your Pearson Education Canada Representative or call Faculty Sales and Services at 1-800-850-5813.

PART I

Organizations, Management, and the Networked Enterprise

Part I   Canadian Case Study

Can Canada Can Spam?

Chapter 1

Managing the Digital Firm

OBJECTIVES

After reading this chapter, you will be able to:

1. Explain why information systems are so important today for business and management.

2. Evaluate the role of information systems in today's competitive business environment.

3. Assess the impact of the Internet and Internet technology on business and government.

4. Define an information system from both a technical and business perspective, and distinguish between computer literacy and information systems literacy.

5. Identify the major management challenges to developing and using information systems.

Opening Case: DaimlerChrysler's Agile Supply Chain

DaimlerChrysler includes the Chrysler Group, the Mercedes and Smart Passenger Car Group, and the Commercial Vehicles unit. It operates 104 plants in 37 countries, using 14 000 different suppliers and 13 000 sales outlets in 200 countries. The auto industry is known for very tough competition and fickle customers, so survival increasingly depends on being able to bring new models more quickly to market as economically as possible.

To deal with these challenges, DaimlerChrysler studied every step in the vehicle production and sales process, starting with vehicle design and ending with service and repair. DaimlerChrysler then developed a series of information systems that automated and streamlined all transactions with suppliers. An Integrated Volume Planning system gathers sales data to send back to production planning systems and suppliers so that they can adjust deliveries of parts and production to make exactly the right amount of vehicle models that are actually selling in dealer showrooms.

A Global Supplier Portal provides a common interface and system platform to handle every type of interaction between DaimlerChrysler and its suppliers. About 6000 DaimlerChrysler suppliers registered for this portal use it to interact with DaimlerChrysler's various business groups. DaimlerChrysler also uses the portal internally to share information among different divisions and business units.

At the earliest stages of car design, the Chrysler Group and 3400 of its suppliers use a Web-enabled system called Powerway to track parts through nine quality control "gates" before they are certified for use on production lines. In the past, quality specialists used to store thousands of pieces of paper in hundreds of binders to deal with quality issues that surfaced with the thousands of companies that design Chrysler's parts. For example, if a drive train was an eighth of an inch too short, it could take up to three weeks to notify the supplier, fix the problem, and incorporate the corrected part back into the design process. Powerway replaces paper-based processes with digital links to supplier systems. It helps Chrysler identify potential design and engineering problems before physical parts are actually constructed, so any issues can be rapidly resolved. That in turn helps Chrysler design new cars much faster—and remain competitive.

Sources: Tracy Mayor, "The Supple Supply Chain," *CIO Magazine*, August 15, 2004; Larry Gould, "Effectively Managing Inventory in the Supply Chain," *Automotive Design & Production*, **www.autofieldguide.com**, accessed September 3, 2004; and **www.daimlerchrysler.com**, accessed September 3, 2004.

DaimlerChrysler's information systems use both technology and knowledge of the business to enable the company and its suppliers to respond instantly to changes in the marketplace or other events. These information systems give DaimlerChrysler the agility to monitor and react to data as events unfold, and they are intimately linked with systems of suppliers and related companies. Managers can "see into" these systems and, when necessary, make adjustments on the fly to keep manufacturing and delivery processes aligned with customer needs.

The agility exhibited by DaimlerChrysler is part of the transformation of business firms throughout the world into fully digital firms. These digital firms use the Internet and networking technology to make data flow seamlessly among different parts of the organization; streamline the flow of work; and create electronic links with customers, suppliers, and other organizations.

As a manager, you will need to know how information systems can make your business more competitive, efficient, and profitable. In this chapter, we begin our investigation of information systems and organizations by describing information systems from both technical and behavioural perspectives and by examining the changes they are bringing to organizations and management.

1.1 Why Information Systems?

We are in the midst of a swiftly moving river of technology and business innovations that is transforming the global business landscape. An entirely new Internet business culture is emerging with profound implications for the conduct of business. You can see this every day by observing how business people work using high-speed Internet connections for email and information gathering, portable computers connected to wireless networks, cellular telephones connected to the Internet, and hybrid handheld devices delivering phone, Internet, and computing power to an increasingly mobile and global workforce.

The emerging Internet business culture has created a set of expectations that we all share. We have all come to expect online options for purchasing goods and services, we expect our business colleagues to be available by e-mail and cell phone, and we expect to be able to communicate with our vendors, customers, and employees any time of day or night over the Internet. We even expect our business partners around the world to be "fully connected." Internet culture is global.

In this text and in the business world, you will often encounter the term *information technology*. **Information technology** (abbreviated **IT**) refers to all of the computer-based information systems used by organizations and their underlying technologies. Briefly, information technologies and systems are revolutionizing the operation of firms, industries, and markets. The main objective of this book is to describe the nature of this transformation and to help you as a future manager take advantage of the emerging opportunities.

Why Information Systems Matter

We start by examining why information systems and IT are so important. There are four reasons why IT will make a difference to you as a manager throughout your career.

Capital Management Information technology has become the largest component of capital investment for firms in many industrialized societies. In 2004, the information and communications technology (ICT) sector of the Canadian economy contributed $64 billion to the Canadian GDP, representing 5.4 percent of Canadian output, up from 4 percent in 1997. The ICT sector has grown at twice the rate of GDP growth since 1997. These figures do not include expenditures that leave Canada, primarily going to the U.S. for additional ICT spending. Looking at business use of the Internet, more than 90 percent of businesses in Canada use the Internet for some purpose, including simply accessing the Internet. The percentage of large businesses using the Internet is higher (by 10 percent) than small businesses.

As managers, many of you will work for firms that use information systems intensively and make large investments in information technology. You will certainly want to know how to invest this money wisely. If you make wise choices, your firm can outperform competitors. If you make poor choices, you will be wasting valuable capital. This book is dedicated to helping you make wise decisions about IT and information systems.

Foundation of Doing Business In Canada, 566 000 workers are employed in the ICT sector, a 4.2 percent rate of growth between 1997 and 2003, compared to 2.3 percent across all other sectors of the Canadian economy. Employees in the ICT sector earned an average of $53 335 in 2004, 45 percent more than the economy-wide average of $36 700. Unfortunately, Canadian companies and individuals also import ICT goods, creating a trade deficit in the ICT sector of $21.7 billion, a 16.5 percent increase since 1997. Computer equipment alone accounts for 41 percent of this trade deficit (Canadian ICT Sector Profile, 2005). These figures illustrate how important the ICT sector has become. Indeed, in many industries, survival and even existence without extensive use of information systems is inconceivable. Obviously, all of e-commerce would be impossible without substantial IT investments, and firms such as Baystreet, Amazon, eBay, Google, E*Trade, or the world's largest online university, the University of Phoenix, simply would not exist. Today's service industries—finance, insurance, and real estate as well as personal services such as travel, medicine, and education—could not operate without IT. Similarly, retail firms such as Hudson's Bay Company and Wal-Mart and manufacturing firms such as Bombardier and General Motors require IT to survive and prosper. Just like offices, telephones, filing cabinets, and efficient tall buildings with elevators were once part of the foundation for business in the twentieth century, information technology is a crucial part of the foundation for business in the twenty-first century.

There is a growing interdependence between a firm's ability to use information technology and its ability to implement corporate strategies and achieve corporate goals (see Figure 1-1). What a business would like to do in five years often depends on what its systems will be able to do. Increasing market share, becoming the high-quality or low-cost

information technology (IT)

FIGURE 1-1   *The interdependence between organizations and information systems.*

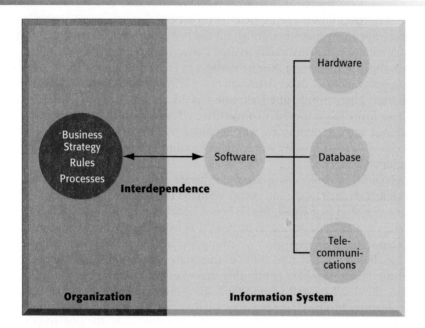

In contemporary systems, there is a growing interdependence between a firm's information systems and its business capabilities. Changes in strategy, rules, and business processes increasingly require changes in hardware, software, databases, and telecommunications. Often, what the organization would like to do depends on what its systems will permit it to do.

producer, developing new products, and increasing employee productivity depend more and more on the kinds and quality of information systems in an organization. The more you understand this relationship, the more valuable you will be as a manager.

Productivity   Today's managers have very few tools at their disposal for achieving significant gains in productivity. IT is one of the most important tools along with innovations in organization and management, and in fact, these innovations need to be linked together. A substantial and growing body of research reported throughout this book suggests investment in IT plays a critical role in increasing the productivity of firms and entire nations (Zhu et al., 2004). Firms that invested wisely in information technology experienced continued growth in productivity and efficiency.

Strategic Opportunity and Advantage   If you want to take advantage of new opportunities in markets, develop new products, and create new services, chances are quite high you will need to make substantial investments in IT to realize these new business opportunities. If you want to achieve a strategic advantage over your rivals, to differentiate yourself from your competitors, IT is one avenue for achieving these advantages along with changes in business practices and management. We talk more about IT contributions to competitive strategy in Chapter 3. These advantages might not last forever, but then again most strategic advantages throughout history are short-lived. However, a string of short-lived competitive advantages is a foundation for long-term advantages in business.

How Much Does IT Matter?

In May 2003, Nicholas Carr, an editor at *Harvard Business Review*, wrote an article titled "IT Doesn't Matter," which stirred significant debate in the business community. Carr's argument in a nutshell is that because every firm can purchase IT in the marketplace, because any advantage obtained by one company can easily be copied by another company, and because IT is now a commodity based on standards (such as the Internet) that all companies can freely use, it is no longer a differentiating factor in organizational performance.

Carr argued that no firm can use IT to achieve a strategic edge over its competitors any more than it could with electricity, telephones, or other infrastructure. Therefore, Carr concludes, firms should reduce spending on IT, follow rather than lead IT in their industry, reduce risks by preparing for computer outages and security breaches, and avoid deploying IT in new ways.

Most management information system (MIS) experts disagree. As we discuss later in this chapter and subsequent chapters throughout the book, research demonstrates that there is considerable variation in firms' ability to use IT effectively. Many highly adept firms continually obtain superior returns on their investment in IT while less adept firms do not.

Copying innovations of other firms can be devilishly difficult, with much being lost in the translation. There is only one Dell, one Wal-Mart, one Amazon, and one eBay, and each of these firms has achieved a competitive advantage in its industry based in large part on unique ways of organizing work enabled by IT that have been very difficult to copy. If copying were so easy, we would expect to find much more powerful competition for these market leaders.

Although falling prices for hardware and software and new computing and telecommunications standards such as the Internet have made the application of computers to business much easier than in the past, this does not signal the end of innovation or the end of firms developing strategic advantages using IT. Far from the end of innovation, commoditization often leads to an explosion in innovation and new markets and products. For example, the abundance and availability of materials such as wood, glass, and steel during the last century made possible a continuing stream of architectural innovation.

Likewise, the development of standards and lowering costs of computer hardware made possible new products and services such as the Apple iPod and iTunes, the Sony Walkman portable music player, RealMedia online streaming music, and the entire online content industry. Entirely new businesses and business models have emerged for the digital distribution of music, books, journals, and films.

Carr is surely correct in stating that not all investments in IT work out or have strategic value. Some are needed just to stay in business, to comply with government reporting requirements, and to satisfy the needs of customers and vendors. Perhaps the more important questions are how much does IT make a difference, and where can it best be deployed to make a competitive difference?

We make a major effort in this book to suggest ways you as a manager and potential entrepreneur can use information technology and systems to create differentiation from your competitors and strategic advantage in the marketplace. As we describe throughout, to achieve any measure of "success," investment in IT must be accompanied by significant changes in business operations and processes and changes in management culture, attitudes, and behaviour. Without these changes, investment in IT can be a waste of precious investor resources.

Why IT Now? Digital Convergence and the Changing Business Environment

A combination of information technology innovations and a changing domestic and global business environment makes the role of IT in business even more important for managers than just a few years ago. The Internet revolution is not something that happened and then burst, but instead has turned out to be an ongoing, powerful source of new technologies with significant business implications for much of this century.

There are five factors to consider when assessing the growing impact of IT in business firms both today and over the next ten years.

- Internet growth and technology convergence
- Transformation of the business enterprise
- Growth of a globally connected economy
- Growth of knowledge- and information-based economies
- Emergence of the digital firm

These changes in the business environment, summarized in Table 1-1, pose a number of new challenges and opportunities for business firms and their managements.

TABLE 1-1   *The Changing Contemporary Business Environment*

INTERNET GROWTH AND TECHNOLOGY CONVERGENCE

New business technologies with favourable costs

E-business, e-commerce, and e-government

Rapid changes in markets and market structure

Increased obsolescence of traditional business models

TRANSFORMATION OF THE BUSINESS ENTERPRISE

Flattening

Decentralization

Flexibility

Location independence

Low transaction and coordination costs

Empowerment

Collaborative work and teamwork

GLOBALIZATION

Management and control in a global marketplace

Competition in world markets

Global workgroups

Global delivery systems

RISE OF THE INFORMATION ECONOMY

Knowledge- and information-based economies

New products and services

Knowledge as a central productive and strategic asset

Time-based competition

Shorter product life

Turbulent environment

Limited employee knowledge base

EMERGENCE OF THE DIGITAL FIRM

Digitally enabled relationships with customers, suppliers, and employees

Core business processes accomplished using digital networks

Digital management of key corporate assets

Agile sensing and responding to environmental changes

The Internet and Technology Convergence   One of the most frequently asked questions by investors, journalists, and business entrepreneurs is, "What's the next big thing?" As it turns out, the next big thing is in front of us. We are in the midst of a networking and communications revolution driven by the growth of the Internet, Internet-based technologies, and new business models and processes that leverage the new technologies.

Although "digital convergence" was predicted a decade ago, it is now an undeniable reality. Four massive industries are moving toward a common platform: the computer hardware and software industry, the consumer electronics industry, the communications industry (traditional and wireless telephone networks), and the content industry (movies, music, text, and research industries). Although each industry has its favoured platform, the outlines of the future are clear: a world of near universal, online, on-demand, and personalized information services from text messaging on cell phones, to games, education, and entertainment.

The Internet is bringing about a convergence of technologies, roiling markets, entire industries, and firms in the process. Traditional boundaries and business relationships are breaking down, even as new ones spring up. Telephone networks are merging into the Internet, and cellular phones are becoming Internet access devices. Handheld storage devices such as iPods are emerging as potential portable game and entertainment centres. The Internet-connected personal computer is moving toward a new role as home entertainment control centre.

Traditional markets and distribution channels are weakening and new markets are being created. For instance, the markets for music CDs and video DVDs and the music and video store industries are undergoing rapid change. New markets for online streaming media and for music and video downloads have materialized.

Today, networking and the Internet are nearly synonymous with doing business. Firms' relationships with customers, employees, suppliers, and logistic partners are becoming digital relationships. As a supplier, you cannot do business with Hudson's Bay Company, Wal-Mart, or most national retailers unless you adopt their well-defined digital technologies. As a consumer, you will increasingly interact with sellers in a digital environment. As an employer, you will be interacting more electronically with your employees and giving them new digital tools to accomplish their work.

So much business is now enabled by or based upon digital networks that we use the terms *electronic business* and *electronic commerce* frequently throughout this text. **Electronic business**, or **e-business**, designates the use of Internet and digital technology to execute all of the activities in the enterprise. E-business includes activities for the internal management of the firm and for coordination with suppliers and other business partners. It also includes **electronic commerce**, or **e-commerce**. E-commerce is the part of e-business that deals with the buying and selling of goods and services electronically with computerized business transactions using the Internet, networks, and other digital technologies. It also encompasses activities supporting those market transactions, such as advertising, marketing, customer support, delivery, and payment.

The technologies associated with e-commerce and e-business have also brought about similar changes in the public sector. Governments on all levels are using Internet technology to deliver information and services to citizens, employees, and businesses with which they work. **E-government** is the application of the Internet and related technologies to digitally enable government and public sector agencies' relationships with citizens, businesses, and other arms of government. In addition to improving delivery of government services, e-government can make government operations more efficient and also empower citizens by giving them easier access to information and the ability to network electronically with other citizens. For example, citizens in some provinces can apply for unemployment benefits online, and the Internet has become a powerful tool for instantly mobilizing interest groups for political action and fund-raising.

Transformation of the Business Enterprise Along with rapid changes in markets and competitive advantage are changes in the firms themselves. The Internet and new markets are changing the cost and revenue structure of traditional firms and are hastening the demise of traditional business models.

Experts believe that 50 to 70 percent of travel sales will be online within a decade. Realtors have had to reduce commissions on home sales because of competition from Internet real estate sites. The business model of traditional local telephone companies, and the value of their copper-based networks, is rapidly declining as millions of consumers switch to cellular and Internet telephones.

The Internet and related technologies make it possible to conduct business across firm boundaries almost as efficiently and effectively as it is to conduct business within the firm. This means that firms are no longer limited by traditional organizational boundaries or physical locations in how they design, develop, and produce goods and services. It is possible to maintain close relationships with suppliers and other business partners at great distances and outsource work that firms formerly did themselves to other companies.

For example, Cisco Systems does not manufacture the networking products it sells; it uses other companies, such as Flextronics, for this purpose. Cisco uses the Internet to

electronic business (e-business)

electronic commerce (e-commerce)

e-government

transmit orders to Flextronics and to monitor the status of orders as they are shipped. Montreal-based Bombardier uses information systems to provide their employees with access to new material, revisions, updates and information on service-related subjects, including service bulletins and airworthiness directives for more than 700 Bombardier business aircraft currently enrolled in its in-house computer integrated maintenance management system (CIMMS). Bombardier customers have around-the-clock access to their aircraft maintenance tracking information through an expanded suite of services on a secure Bombardier Internet site. In addition to these changes, there has also been a transformation in the management of the enterprise. The traditional business firm was—and still is—a hierarchical, centralized, structured arrangement of specialists who typically relied on a fixed set of standard operating procedures to deliver a mass-produced product (or service). The new style of business firm is a flattened (less hierarchical), decentralized, flexible arrangement of generalists who rely on nearly instant information to deliver mass-customized products and services uniquely suited to specific markets or customers.

The traditional management group relied—and still relies—on formal plans, a rigid division of labour, and formal rules. The new manager relies on informal commitments and networks to establish goals (rather than formal planning), a flexible arrangement of teams and individuals working in task forces, and a customer orientation to achieve coordination among employees. The new manager appeals to the knowledge, learning, and decision making of individual employees to ensure proper operation of the firm. Once again, information technology makes this style of management possible.

Globalization   A growing percentage of the North American economy—and other advanced industrial economies in Europe and Asia—depends on imports and exports. Foreign trade, both exports and imports, accounts for more than 25 percent of the goods and services produced in North America, and even more in countries such as Japan and Germany. Companies are also distributing core business functions in product design, manufacturing, finance, and customer support to locations in other countries where the work can be performed more cost effectively. The success of firms today and in the future depends on their ability to operate globally.

Information systems provide the communication and analytic power that firms need to conduct trade and manage businesses on a global scale. Controlling the far-flung global corporation—communicating with distributors and suppliers, operating around the clock in different national environments, coordinating global work teams, and servicing local and international reporting needs—is a major business challenge that requires powerful information system responses.

Globalization and information technology also bring new threats to domestic business firms. Because of global communication and management systems, customers now can shop in a worldwide marketplace, obtaining price and quality information reliably 24 hours a day (see Figure 1-2). To become competitive participants in international markets, firms need powerful information and communication systems.

Rise of the Information Economy   Canada, the United States, Japan, Germany, and other major industrial powers are being transformed from industrial economies to knowledge- and information-based service economies while manufacturing has been moving to lower-wage countries. In a knowledge- and information-based economy, knowledge and information are key ingredients in creating wealth.

The knowledge and information revolution began at the turn of the twentieth century and has gradually accelerated. Within the last 25 years in Canada, the number of white-collar workers employed in offices has surpassed the number of farm workers, service workers, and blue-collar workers employed in manufacturing for the first time in history. Today most people no longer work on farms or in factories but instead are found in sales, education, health care, banks, insurance firms, and law firms; they also provide business services, such as copying, computer programming, or making deliveries. These jobs primarily involve working with, distributing, or creating new knowledge and information.

In knowledge- and information-based economies, the market value of many firms is based largely on intangible assets, such as proprietary knowledge, information, unique

FIGURE 1-2 *The Orbitz travel reservations Web site.*

At the Orbitz Web site, visitors can make online reservations for airlines, hotels, rental cars, cruises, and vacation packages and obtain information on travel and leisure topics. These online travel services are supplanting traditional travel agencies.

business methods, brands, and other "intellectual capital." Physical assets, such as buildings, machinery, tools, and inventory, now account for less than 20 percent of the market value of many public firms in the United States (Lev 2001).

Knowledge and information provide the foundation for valuable new products and services, such as credit cards, overnight package delivery, or worldwide reservation systems. **Knowledge- and information-intense products**, such as computer games, require a great deal of knowledge to produce, and knowledge is used more intensively in the production of traditional products as well. In the automobile industry, for instance, both design and production now rely heavily on knowledge and information technology.

Emergence of the Digital Firm All of the changes we have just described, coupled with equally significant organizational redesign, have created the conditions for a fully digital firm. The **digital firm** can be defined along several dimensions. A digital firm is one in which nearly all of the organization's *significant business relationships* with customers, suppliers, and employees are digitally enabled and mediated. *Core business processes* are accomplished through digital networks spanning the entire organization or linking multiple organizations.

Business processes refer to the set of logically related tasks and behaviours that organizations develop over time to produce specific business results and the unique manner in which these activities are organized and coordinated. Developing a new product, generating and fulfilling an order, creating a marketing plan, and hiring an employee are examples of business processes, and the ways organizations accomplish their business processes can be a source of competitive strength. (A detailed discussion of business processes can be found in Chapter 2.)

Key corporate assets—intellectual property, core competencies, and financial and human assets—are managed through digital means. In a digital firm, any piece of information required to support key business decisions is available at any time and anywhere in the firm.

Digital firms sense and respond to their environments far more rapidly than traditional firms, giving them more flexibility to survive in turbulent times. Digital firms offer extraordinary opportunities for more global organization and management. By digitally enabling and streamlining their work, digital firms have the potential to achieve unprecedented levels of profitability and competitiveness. DaimlerChrysler, described earlier,

knowledge- and information-intense products

digital firm

business processes

illustrates some of these qualities. Electronically integrating key business processes with suppliers has made this company much more agile and adaptive to customer demands and changes in its supplier network.

Figure 1-3 illustrates a digital firm making intensive use of Internet and digital technology for electronic business. Information can flow seamlessly among different parts of the company and between the company and external entities—its customers, suppliers, and business partners. More and more organizations are moving toward this digital firm vision.

A few firms, such as Nygård, Cisco Systems, or Dell Computers, are close to becoming fully digital firms, using the Internet to drive every aspect of their business. In most other companies, a fully digital firm is still more vision than reality, but this vision is driving them toward digital integration. Firms are continuing to invest heavily in information systems that integrate internal business processes and build closer links with suppliers and customers.

The Window on Organizations describes such a digital firm in the making. Cemex, a world-leading global cement and construction materials firm, has achieved impressive results through ruthless focus on operational excellence. Management took an enterprise-wide view of its business processes and developed a series of information systems to turn the company into a lean, efficient, agile machine that could instantly respond to changes in customer orders, weather, and other last-minute events.

FIGURE 1-3   *Electronic business and electronic commerce in the emerging digital firm.*

THE EMERGING DIGITAL FIRM
ELECTRONIC BUSINESS

ELECTRONIC COMMERCE

Factories
• Just-in-time production
• Continuous inventory replenishment
• Production planning

Customers
• Online marketing
• Online sales
• Built-to-order products
• Customer service
• Sales force automation

Remote offices and work groups
• Communicate plans and policies
• Group collaboration
• Electronic communication
• Scheduling

Business partners
• Joint design
• Outsourcing

Suppliers
• Procurement
• Supply chain management

Companies can use Internet technology for e-commerce transactions with customers and suppliers, for managing internal business processes, and for coordinating with suppliers and other business partners. E-business includes e-commerce as well as the management and coordination of the enterprise.

WINDOW ON ORGANIZATIONS

Cemex: A Digital Firm in the Making

Cemex, based in Monterrey, Mexico, is a 98-year-old company that sells cement and ready-mix concrete products. It has 53 plants around the globe in countries including the United States, Spain, Egypt, Colombia, and the Philippines, and is the world's third largest cement and concrete manufacturer. Cemex also purchases supplies from Canada and received an $18 million loan from Export Development Canada to increase the level of Canadian supply to the company (Pettigrew 2005).

The concrete business is an asset-intensive, low-efficiency business with unpredictable demand. Cemex dispatchers used to take orders for 8000 grades of mixed concrete and forwarded them to six regional mixing plants, each with its own fleet of trucks. Customers routinely changed half of their orders, sometimes only hours before delivery, and these orders might have to be rerouted because of weather, traffic jams, or problems with building permits. Cemex's phone lines were often jammed as customers, truckers, and dispatchers tried to get orders straight. Many orders were lost.

Lorenzo Zambrano, a grandson of the founder of the company, took over the business in 1985 and decided to apply information technology to these problems. He and Cemex chief information officer Gelacio Iniguez developed a series of systems that would enable Cemex to manage unforecastable demand better than its competitors.

Zambrano and Iniguez used ideas gleaned from visits to U.S. companies such as Federal Express, Exxon, and Houston's 911 emergency dispatch system to see how other organizations anticipated demand for their services. They developed a system linking Cemex delivery trucks to a global positioning system satellite to help dispatchers monitor the location, direction, and speed of every vehicle. This information helps Cemex send the right truck to deliver a specific grade of cement or redirect deliveries when prompted by last-minute changes.

The company has reduced average delivery time from three hours to 20 minutes, realizing huge savings in fuel, maintenance, and personnel costs. Cemex now uses 35 percent fewer trucks to deliver the same amount of cement. Customers are willing to pay premium prices to Cemex because they do not have to keep work crews idle waiting for cement deliveries to show up.

Cemex's production facilities previously operated independently, without precise knowledge of customer demand. A satellite communications system called CemexNet now electronically links all the firm's production facilities and coordinates them from a central clearinghouse. Dispatchers know the exact location, speed, and direction of all vehicles at all times and can quickly select the most optimal arrangement of trucks and mixing plant locations to fill an order.

Customers, distributors, and suppliers can use the Internet to place orders directly, check shipment delivery times, and review payment records without having to telephone a customer service representative. Zambrano and his managers now have access to almost every detail about Cemex operations within 24 hours while competitors are working with month-old data.

Zambrano developed a sophisticated executive information system that enables him to monitor closely from his laptop computer operations in the 35 countries where Cemex operates. If a region is coloured green, it is doing well. Yellow signals a potential problem, and red indicates a real problem. Zambrano can then systematically dig down to find out the details of any area of interest. At that level of detail, he can even read the e-mail exchanges about a production problem at an individual plant. Sometimes Zambrano will send an e-mail about production issues to plant workers to let them know he is watching.

Cemex uses a sophisticated scheduling system to expedite cement delivery. Cemex manages deliveries and all of its manufacturing and production processes from a highly computerized control room. The company is moving toward a digital firm organization.

Cemex's profit margins are higher than its bigger rivals, Zurich-based Holcim Limited and Paris-based Lafarge SA, even as the company has expanded from a provincial Mexican cement maker to an international powerhouse. In addition to maximizing operational efficiency, Cemex saves by using petroleum coke for half of its fuel needs. Petroleum coke, also known as pet coke, is the blackened leftover from the oil-refining process. In the cement industry, energy accounts for up to 40 percent of operating costs.

Cemex also designed software to make it easier for company executives and plant managers to keep tabs on power use. Managers use the software to plan each month's energy consumption, ensuring that conveyors, electric grinders, and other equipment run mainly during hours of off-peak electricity rates. As a result, Cemex cut its energy bills by 17 percent in the past four years.

Cemex's productivity has outpaced all of its major rivals in Mexico, and production output has grown sixfold since 1985. In an industry known for tough price competition and thin profit margins, Cemex revenue has grown at a rate of 9 percent over the past decade.

To Think About: How did digital technology transform the way Cemex ran its business? It has been said that Cemex has refocused efforts from managing assets to managing information. Explain. To what extent is Cemex a digital firm?

Sources: Andrew Rowsell-Jones, "The Best of Both Worlds," *CIO Australia*, July 12, 2004; John Lyons, "Expensive Energy? Burn Other Stuff, One Firm Decides," *Wall Street Journal*, September 1, 2004; www.cemex.com, accessed September 2, 2004; John Lyons, "Cemex Cements Its Position with Agreement to Buy RMC," *Wall Street Journal*, September 28, 2004; Pierre Pettigrew, Address at a Plenary Hosted by the Canadian Chamber of Commerce in Northern Mexico on a New Approach to Business Development, available, http://w01.international.gc.ca/minpub/Publication.asp?publication_id=379348&Language=E, accessed July 19, 2005; and Melba Newsome, "The Cement Mixer," *Context*, December 2001/January 2002.

1.2 Perspectives on Information Systems

Information systems can be best be understood by looking at them from both a technology and a business perspective.

What Is an Information System?

An **information system** can be defined technically as a set of interrelated components that collect (or retrieve), process, store, and distribute information to support decision making and control in an organization. In addition to supporting decision making, coordination, and control, information systems may also help managers and workers analyze problems, visualize complex subjects, and create new products.

Information systems contain information about significant people, places, and things within the organization or in the environment surrounding it. By **information**, we mean data that have been shaped into a form that is meaningful and useful to human beings. **Data**, in contrast, are streams of raw facts representing events occurring in organizations or the physical environment before they have been organized and arranged into a form that people can understand and use.

A brief example contrasting information and data may prove useful. Supermarket checkout counters ring up millions of pieces of data, such as product identification numbers or the cost of each item sold. These pieces of data can be totalled and analyzed to provide meaningful information, such as the total number of bottles of dish detergent sold at a particular store, which brands of dish detergent were selling the most rapidly at that store or sales territory, or the total amount spent on that brand of dish detergent at that store or sales region (see Figure 1-4).

Three activities in an information system produce the information that organizations need to make decisions, control operations, analyze problems, and create new products or services. These activities are input, processing, and output (see Figure 1-5). **Input** captures or collects raw data from within the organization or from its external environment. **Processing** converts this raw input into a more meaningful form. **Output** transfers the processed information to the people who will use it or to the activities for which it will be used. Information systems also require **feedback**, which is output that is returned to appropriate members of the organization to help them evaluate or correct the input stage.

information system
information
data
input
processing
output
feedback

FIGURE 1-4 *Data and information.*

Data

331 Brite Dish Soap 1.29
863 BL Hill Coffee 4.69
173 Meow Cat .79
331 Brite Dish Soap 1.29
663 Country Ham 3.29
524 Fiery Mustard 1.49
113 Ginger Root .85
331 Brite Dish Soap 1.29

Information

Sales Region: Maritimes
Store: Superstore #122

ITEM NO.	DESCRIPTION	UNITS SOLD
331	Brite Dish Soap	7156

YTD SALES
$ 9,231.24

An information system contains information about an organization and its surrounding environment. Three basic activities—input, processing, and output—produce the information organizations need. Feedback is output returned to appropriate people or activities in the organization to evaluate and refine the input. Environmental actors such as customers, suppliers, competitors, stockholders, and regulatory agencies interact with the organization and its information systems.

In DaimlerChrysler's Integrated Volume Planning system, raw input consists of vehicle identification number, model, colour, and optional features of cars ordered from dealers. DaimlerChrysler's computers store these data and process them to anticipate how many new vehicles to manufacture for each model, colour, and option package. The output would consist of orders to suppliers specifying the quantity of each part or component that was needed and the exact date each part was to be delivered to DaimlerChrysler's

FIGURE 1-5 *Functions of an information system.*

Raw data from a supermarket checkout counter can be processed and organized to produce meaningful information such as the total unit sales of dish detergent or the total sales revenue from dish detergent for a specific store or sales territory.

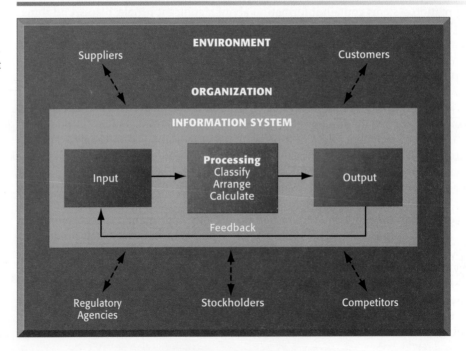

production facilities to produce the vehicles that customers have ordered. The system provides meaningful information such as what models, colours, and options are selling in which locations; the most popular models and colours; and which dealers sell the most cars and trucks.

Our interest in this book is in formal, organizational computer-based information systems, such as those designed and used by DaimlerChrysler and its suppliers. **Formal systems** rest on accepted and fixed definitions of data and procedures for collecting, storing, processing, disseminating, and using these data. The formal systems we describe in this text are structured; that is, they operate in conformity with predefined rules that are relatively fixed and not easily changed. For instance, DaimlerChrysler's Integrated Volume Planning system would require unique numbers or codes for identifying each vehicle part or component and each supplier.

Informal information systems (such as office gossip networks) rely, by contrast, on unstated rules of behaviour. There is no agreement on what is information or on how it will be stored and processed. These systems are essential for the life of an organization, but an analysis of their qualities is beyond the scope of this text.

Formal information systems can be either computer based or manual. Manual systems use paper-and-pencil technology. These manual systems serve important needs, but they are not the subject of this text. **Computer-based information systems (CBIS)**, in contrast, rely on computer hardware and software technology to process and disseminate information. From this point on, when we use the term *information systems*, we are referring to computer-based information systems—formal organizational systems that rely on computer technology.

The Window on Technology describes some of the typical technologies used in computer-based information systems today. United Parcel Service (UPS) invests heavily in information systems technology to make its business more efficient and customer-oriented. It uses an array of information technologies including bar-code scanning systems, wireless networks, large mainframe computers, handheld computers, the Internet, and many different pieces of software for tracking packages, calculating fees, maintaining customer accounts, and managing logistics.

formal systems
computer-based information systems (CBIS)

WINDOW ON TECHNOLOGY

UPS Competes Globally with Information Technology

United Parcel Service (UPS) started out in 1907 in a closet-sized basement office. Jim Casey and Claude Ryan, two teenagers from Seattle with two bicycles and one phone, promised the "best service and lowest rates." UPS has used this formula successfully for more than 90 years and is now the world's largest ground and air package-distribution company.

Today UPS delivers more than 13.6 million parcels and documents each day in more than 200 countries and territories. The firm has been able to maintain leadership in small-package delivery services despite stiff competition from FedEx and Airborne Express by investing heavily in advanced information technology. During the past decade, UPS has poured billions of dollars into technology and systems to boost customer service while keeping costs low and streamlining operations.

Using a handheld computer called a Delivery Information Acquisition Device (DIAD), a UPS driver can automatically capture customers' signatures along with pickup, delivery, and time-card information. The driver then places the DIAD into the UPS truck's vehicle adapter, an information-transmitting device that

is connected to the cellular telephone network. Package tracking information is then transmitted to UPS' computer network for storage and processing in UPS' main computers in Mahwah, New Jersey, and Alpharetta, Georgia. From there, the information can be accessed worldwide to provide proof of delivery to customers or to respond to customer queries.

Through its automated package tracking system, UPS can monitor packages throughout the delivery process. At various points along the route from sender to receiver, bar-code devices scan shipping information on the package label; the information is then fed into the central computer. Customer service representatives can check the status of any package from desktop computers linked to the central computers and are able to respond immediately to inquiries from customers. UPS customers can also access this information from the company's Web site using their own computers or wireless devices such as pagers and cell phones.

Anyone with a package to ship can access the UPS Web site to track packages, check delivery routes, calculate shipping rates, determine time in transit, and schedule a pickup. Businesses anywhere can use the Web site to arrange UPS shipments and bill the shipments to the company's UPS account number or to a credit card. The data collected at the UPS Web site are transmitted to the UPS central computer and then back to the customer after processing. UPS also provides tools that enable customers such Cisco Systems to embed UPS functions, such as tracking and cost calculations, into their own Web sites so that they can track shipments without visiting the UPS site.

A capability called UPS Campus Ship allows employees in multiple offices of a business to process and ship from their computers and have shipping procedures controlled by a central administrator set up by the business. Morris, Schneider and Prior LLC, a top law firm serving the financial services industry, uses this capability to track and control shipping costs. This firm is constantly sending time-sensitive documents from three different locations to clients throughout the United States. UPS tools automate the allocation and reporting of this firm's shipping costs and even itemize and detail shipping expenses for each client.

Information technology helps UPS reinvent itself and keep growing. UPS is now leveraging its decades of expertise managing its own global delivery network to manage logistics and supply chain management for other companies. It created a UPS Supply Chain Solutions division that provides a complete bundle of standardized services to subscribing companies at a fraction of what it would cost to develop their own systems and infrastructure. These services include supply chain design and management, freight forwarding, customs brokerage, mail services, multimodal transportation, and financial services, in addition to logistics services. The UPS supply chain management division, located online at www.upslogistics.ca, also provides important information for shippers, such as the recent shutdown and reopening of the port of Vancouver due to a local cartage strike.

Birkenstock Footprint Sandals is one of many companies benefiting from these services. Birkenstock's German plants pack shoes in crates that are bar-coded with their U.S. destination. UPS contracts with ocean carriers in Rotterdam to transport the shoe crates across the Atlantic to New Jersey ports instead of routing them through the Panama Canal to Birkenstock's California warehouses. UPS trucks whisk each incoming shipment to a UPS distribution hub and, within hours, to 3000 different retailers. By handing this work over to UPS, Birkenstock has cut the time to get its shoes to stores by half. Along the way, UPS uses bar-code scanning to keep track of every shipment until the merchant signs off on it. UPS also handles Internet orders for Jockey International, laptop repairs for Toshiba America, and X-ray machine installation in Europe for Philips Medical Systems.

To Think About: What are the inputs, processing, and outputs of UPS' package tracking system? What technologies are used? How are these technologies related to UPS' business strategy? How do UPS' systems provide value for the company and its customers? What would happen if these technologies were not available?

Sources: Dean Foust, "Big Brown's New Bag," and "Online Extra: UPS's Eskew on 'the Next Logical Step,' " *BusinessWeek,* July 19, 2004; Galen Gruman, "UPS vs. FedEx: Head-to-Head on Wireless " and "New Technologies Hit Mainstream," *CIO Magazine,* June 1, 2004; "Paper Trail," *RoundUPS,* Fall 2004; www.upslogistics.ca; and Todd R. Weiss, "UPS Delivers New Package Check-in System for Customers," *Computerworld,* April 9, 2003.

Using a handheld computer called a Delivery Information Acquisition Device (DIAD), UPS drivers automatically capture customers' signatures along with pickup, delivery, and time-card information. UPS information systems use these data to track packages while they are being transported.

Although computer-based information systems use computer technology to process raw data into meaningful information, there is a sharp distinction between a computer and a computer program on the one hand, and an information system on the other. Electronic computers and related software programs are the technical foundation, the tools and materials, of modern information systems. Computers provide the equipment for storing and processing information. Computer programs, or software, are sets of operating instructions that direct and control computer processing. Knowing how computers and computer programs work is important when designing solutions to organizational problems, but computers are only part of an information system.

A house is an appropriate analogy. Houses are built with hammers, nails, and wood, but these do not make a house. The architecture, design, setting, landscaping, and all of the decisions that lead to the creation of these features are part of the house and are crucial for solving the problem of putting a roof over one's head.

Computers and programs are the hammer, nails, and lumber of CBIS, but alone they cannot produce the information a particular organization needs. To understand information systems, you must understand the problems they are designed to solve, their architectural and design elements, and the organizational processes that lead to these solutions.

It Isn't Just Technology: A Business Perspective on Information Systems

Managers and business firms invest in information technology and systems because they provide real economic value to the business. The decision to develop or maintain an information system assumes that the returns on this investment will be superior to other investments in buildings, machines, or other assets. These superior returns will be expressed as increases in productivity, as increases in revenues (which will increase the firm's stock market value), or perhaps as superior long-term strategic positioning of the firm in certain markets (which produce superior revenues in the future).

There are also situations in which firms invest in information systems to cope with governmental regulations or other environmental demands. For instance, one of the major ways firms can comply with the reporting requirements of the recent U.S. Sarbanes-Oxley Act (for more on the importance of this act to Canadian business, see Chapter 9) is to develop a document management system that can trace the flow of virtually all material documents it uses (see Chapter 16).

In some cases, firms must invest in information systems simply because these investments are required to stay in business. For instance, some small banks may be forced to invest in automatic teller machine (ATM) networks or offer complex banking services requiring large technology investments simply because it is a "cost of doing business." Nevertheless, it is assumed that most information systems investments will be justified by favourable returns.

We can see that from a business perspective, an information system is an important instrument for creating value for a firm. Information systems enable a firm to increase its revenue or decrease its costs by providing information that helps managers make better decisions or that improves the execution of business processes. For example, the information system for analyzing supermarket checkout data illustrated in Figure 1-4 can increase firm profitability by helping managers make better decisions on which products to stock and promote in retail supermarkets and, as a result, increase business value.

Every business has an information value chain, illustrated in Figure 1-6, in which raw information is systematically acquired and then transformed through various stages that add value to that information. The value of an information system to a business, as well as the decision to invest in any new information system, is, in large part, determined by the extent to which the system will lead to better management decisions, more efficient business processes, and higher firm profitability. Although there are other reasons why systems are developed, their primary purpose is to contribute to corporate value.

The business perspective calls attention to the organizational and managerial nature of information systems. An information system represents an organizational and management solution, based on information technology, to a challenge posed by the environment. Every chapter in this book begins with short case study that illustrates this concept. A diagram at the beginning of each chapter illustrates the relationship between a changing business environment and resulting management and organizational decisions to use IT as a solution to challenges generated by the business environment.

To fully understand information systems, a manager must understand the broader organization, management, and information technology dimensions of systems (see Figure 1-7) and their power to provide solutions to challenges and problems in the business environment. We refer to this broader understanding of information systems, which encompasses an understanding of the management and organizational dimensions of systems as well as the technical dimensions of systems, as **information systems literacy**. Information systems literacy includes a behavioural as well as a technical approach to studying information systems. **Computer literacy**, in contrast, focuses primarily on knowledge of information technology.

information systems literacy
computer literacy

FIGURE 1-6   *The business information value chain.*

From a business perspective, information systems are part of a series of value-adding activities for acquiring, transforming, and distributing information that managers can use to improve decision making, enhance organizational performance, and, ultimately, increase firm profitability.

Review the diagram at the beginning of the chapter that reflects this expanded definition of an information system. The diagram shows how DaimlerChrysler's production and supplier systems solve the business challenge presented by a fierce array of competitors and rapidly changing consumer preferences. These systems create value for DaimlerChrysler by making its production, supply chain, and quality control processes more efficient and cost effective. The diagram also illustrates how management, technology, and organizational elements work together to create the systems.

FIGURE 1-7   *Information systems are more than computers.*

Using information systems effectively requires an understanding of the organization, management, and information technology shaping the systems. An information system creates value for the firm as an organizational and management solution to the challenges posed by the environment.

Each chapter of this text begins with a similar diagram to help you analyze the chapter-opening case. You can use this diagram as a starting point for analyzing any information system or information system problem you encounter.

Dimensions of Information Systems

We now examine each of the dimensions of information systems—organizations, management, and information technology.

Organizations   Information systems are an integral part of organizations. Indeed, for some companies, such as credit reporting firms, without an information system, there would be no business. The key elements of an organization are its people, structure, business processes, politics, and culture. We introduce these components of organizations here and describe them in greater detail in Chapters 2 and 3.

Organizations are composed of different levels and specialties. Their structures reveal a clear-cut division of labour. Experts are employed and trained for different functions. The major **business functions**, or specialized tasks performed by business organizations, consist of sales and marketing, manufacturing and production, finance and accounting, and human resources (see Table 1-2).

Chapter 2 provides more detail on these business functions and the ways in which they are supported by information systems. Each of the four parts of this text concludes with a *Make IT Your Business* section showing how chapter topics relate to each of these functional areas. The section also provides page numbers in each chapter where these functional examples can be found.

An organization coordinates work through a structured hierarchy and through its business processes, which we defined earlier. The hierarchy arranges people in a pyramid structure of rising authority and responsibility. The upper levels of the hierarchy consist of managerial, professional, and technical employees while the lower levels consist of operational personnel.

Most organizations' business processes include formal rules that have been developed over a long time for accomplishing tasks. These rules guide employees in a variety of procedures, from writing an invoice to responding to customer complaints. Some of these procedures have been formalized and written down, but others are informal work practices, such as a requirement to return telephone calls from coworkers or customers, that are not formally documented. Many business processes are incorporated into information systems, such as how to pay a supplier or how to correct an erroneous bill.

Organizations require many different kinds of skills and people. In addition to managers, **knowledge workers** (such as engineers, architects, or scientists) design products or services and create new knowledge, and **data workers** (such as secretaries, bookkeepers, or clerks) process the organization's paperwork. **Production or service workers** (such as machinists, assemblers, or packers) actually produce the organization's products or services.

Each organization has a unique *culture*, or fundamental set of assumptions, values, and ways of doing things, that has been accepted by most of its members. Parts of an organization's culture can always be found embedded in its information systems. For

TABLE 1-2   *Major Business Functions*

Function	Purpose
Sales and marketing	Selling the organization's products and services
Manufacturing and production	Producing products and services
Finance and accounting	Managing the organization's financial assets and maintaining the organization's financial records
Human resources	Attracting, developing, and maintaining the organization's labour force; maintaining employee records

business functions
knowledge workers
data workers
production or service workers

instance, the United Parcel Service's concern with placing service to the customer first is an aspect of its organizational culture that can be found in the company's package tracking systems.

Different levels and specialties in an organization create different interests and points of view. These views often conflict. Conflict is the basis for organizational politics. Information systems come out of this cauldron of differing perspectives, conflicts, compromises, and agreements that are a natural part of all organizations. In Chapter 3, we examine these features of organizations and their role in the development of information systems in greater detail.

Management Management's job is to make sense out of the many situations faced by organizations, make decisions, and formulate action plans to solve organizational problems. Managers perceive business challenges in the environment; they set the organizational strategy for responding to those challenges; and they allocate the human and financial resources to coordinate the work and achieve success. Throughout, they must exercise responsible leadership. The business information systems described in this book reflect the hopes, dreams, and realities of real-world managers.

But managers must do more than manage what already exists. They must also create new products and services and even recreate the organization from time to time. A substantial part of management responsibility is creative work driven by new knowledge and information. Information technology can play a powerful role in redirecting and redesigning the organization. Chapter 3 describes managerial activities, and Chapter 15 discusses management decision making in detail.

It is important to note that managerial roles and decisions vary at different levels of the organization. **Senior managers** make long-range strategic decisions about what products and services to produce. **Middle managers** carry out the programs and plans of senior management. **Operational managers** are responsible for monitoring the firm's daily activities. All levels of management are expected to be creative and to develop novel solutions to a broad range of problems. Each level of management has different information needs and information system requirements.

Technology Information technology is one of many tools managers use to cope with change. **Computer hardware** is the physical equipment used for input, processing, and output activities in an information system. It consists of the following: the computer processing unit; various input, output, and storage devices; and physical media to link these devices together.

Computer software consists of the detailed, preprogrammed instructions that control and coordinate the computer hardware components in an information system. Chapter 5 describes the contemporary software and hardware platforms used by firms today in detail.

Storage technology includes both the physical media for storing data, such as magnetic disk, optical disc, or tape, and the software governing the organization of data on these physical media. More detail on data organization and access methods can be found in Chapter 6.

Communications technology, consisting of both physical devices and software, links the various pieces of hardware and transfers data from one physical location to another. Computers and communications equipment can be connected in networks for sharing voice, data, images, sound, or even video. A **network** links two or more computers to share data or resources such as a printer.

The world's largest and most widely used network is the **Internet**. The Internet is an international network of networks that are both commercial and publicly owned. The Internet connects hundreds of thousands of different networks from more than 200 countries around the world. More than 600 million people working in science, education, government, and business use the Internet to exchange information or business transactions with other organizations around the globe. Chapter 7 provides more detail on networks and Internet technology.

The Internet is extremely elastic. If networks are added or removed, or if failures occur in parts of the system, the rest of the Internet continues to operate. Through special

senior managers

middle managers

operational managers

computer hardware

computer software

storage technology

communications technology

network

Internet

communication and technology standards, any computer can communicate with virtually any other computer linked to the Internet using ordinary telephone lines.

The Internet has created a new "universal" technology platform on which to develop all sorts of new products, services, strategies, and business models. This same technology platform has internal uses, providing the connectivity to link different systems and networks within the firm. Internal corporate networks based on Internet technology are called **intranets**. Private intranets extended to authorized users outside the organization are called **extranets**, and firms use extranets to coordinate their activities with other firms for making purchases, collaborating on design, and other interorganizational work. Some of DaimlerChrysler's systems for coordinating with suppliers are based on extranets.

Because it offers so many new possibilities for doing business, the Internet capability known as the **World Wide Web (WWW)** is of special interest to organizations and managers. The World Wide Web is a system with universally accepted standards for storing, retrieving, formatting, and displaying information in a networked environment. Information is stored and displayed as electronic "pages" that can contain text, graphics, animations, sound, and video. These Web pages can be linked electronically to other Web pages, regardless of where they are located, and viewed by any type of computer. By clicking on highlighted words or buttons on a Web page, you can link to related pages to find additional information, software programs, or still more links to other points on the Web. The Web can serve as the foundation for new kinds of information systems such as UPS's Web-based package tracking system or Cemex's Web system for entering customer orders and checking shipments described in this chapter's Window On boxes.

All of the Web pages maintained by an organization or individual are called a **Web site**. Businesses have created Web sites with stylish typography, colourful graphics, push-button interactivity, and often sound and video to disseminate product information widely, to "broadcast" advertising and messages to customers, to collect electronic orders and customer data, and, increasingly, to coordinate far-flung sales forces and organizations on a global scale (see Figure 1-8).

FIGURE 1-8   *The DaimlerChrysler Extended Enterprise Network Web site.*

DaimlerChrysler's Extended Enterprise Network is an extranet for suppliers to access a series of internal company applications. Internet technology standards make it possible for DaimlerChrysler to link to the systems of many different companies.

intranets

extranets

World Wide Web (WWW)

Web site

In Chapters 4 and 7, we describe the Web and other Internet capabilities in greater detail. We also discuss relevant features of Internet technology throughout the text because it affects so many aspects of information systems in organizations.

All of these technologies represent resources that can be shared throughout the organization and constitute the firm's **information technology (IT) infrastructure**. The IT infrastructure provides the foundation, or *platform*, on which the firm can develop its specific information systems. Each organization must carefully design and manage its information technology infrastructure so that it has the set of technology services it needs for the work it wants to accomplish with information systems. Chapters 5 through 9 of this text examine each major technology component of information technology infrastructure and show how they all work together to create the technology platform for the organization.

Now look at the case about UPS' package tracking system in the Window on Technology and identify the organization, management, and technology elements. The organization element anchors the package tracking system in UPS' sales and production functions (the main product of UPS is a service—package delivery). It specifies the required procedures for identifying packages with both sender and recipient information, taking inventory, tracking the packages en route, and providing package status reports for UPS customers and customer service representatives. The system must also provide information to satisfy the needs of managers and workers. UPS drivers need to be trained in both package pickup and delivery procedures and in how to use the package tracking system so that they can work efficiently and effectively. UPS customers may need some training to use UPS in-house package tracking software or the UPS Web site.

UPS' management is responsible for monitoring service levels and costs and for promoting the company's strategy of combining low-cost, superior service. Management decided to use automation to increase the ease of sending a package using UPS and of checking its delivery status, thereby reducing delivery costs and increasing sales revenues.

The technology supporting this system consists of handheld computers, bar-code scanners, wired and wireless communications networks, desktop computers, UPS's central computer, storage technology for the package delivery data, UPS in-house package tracking software, and software to access the World Wide Web. The result is an information system solution to the business challenge of providing a high level of service with low prices in the face of mounting competition.

Complementary Assets and Organizational Capital   Awareness of the organizational and managerial dimensions of information systems can help us understand why some firms achieve better results from their information systems than others. Studies of returns from information technology investments show that there is considerable variation in the returns firms receive (see Figure 1-9). Some firms invest a great deal and receive a great deal (quadrant 2); others invest an equal amount and receive few returns (quadrant 4). Still other firms invest little and receive much (quadrant 1) while others invest little and receive little (quadrant 3). These results suggest that investing in information technology does not by itself guarantee good returns. What accounts for this variation among firms?

The answer lies in the concept of complementary assets. Information technology investments alone cannot make organizations and managers more effective unless they are accompanied by supportive values, structures, and behaviour patterns in the organization and other complementary assets. **Complementary assets** are those assets required to derive value from a primary investment (Teece 1988). For instance, to realize value from automobiles requires substantial complementary investments in highways, roads, gasoline stations, repair facilities, and a legal regulatory structure to set standards and control drivers.

Recent research on business information technology investment indicates that firms that support their technology investments with investments in complementary assets, such as new business processes, management behaviour, organizational culture, and training, receive superior returns while those firms failing to make these complementary investments receive few or no returns on their information technology investments

information technology (IT) infrastructure

complementary assets

FIGURE 1-9   *Variation in returns on information technology investment.*

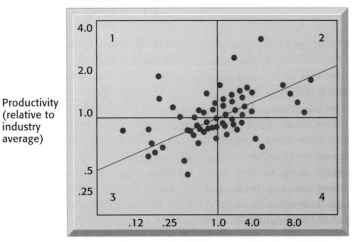

IT Capital Stock (relative to industry average)

Although, on average, investments in information technology produce returns far above those returned by other investments, there is considerable variation across firms.

Source: Based on Erik Brynjolfsson and Lorin M. Hitt, "Beyond Computation: Information Technology, Organizational Transformation and Business Performance." *Journal of Economic Perspectives* 14, no. 4 (Fall 2000). Used with permission of the American Economic Association.

(Brynjolfsson 2003; Brynjolfsson and Hitt 2000; Davern and Kauffman 2000; Laudon 1974). These investments in organization and management are also known as **organizational and management capital**.

Table 1-3 lists the major complementary investments that firms need to make to realize value from their information technology investments. Some of this investment involves tangible assets, such as buildings, machinery, and tools. However, the value of investments in information technology depends to a large extent on complementary investments in management and organization.

TABLE 1-3   *Complementary Social, Managerial, and Organizational Assets Required to Optimize Returns from Information Technology Investments*

Organizational assets	Supportive organizational culture that values efficiency and effectiveness
	Efficient business processes
	Decentralized authority
	Distributed decision-making rights
	Strong IS development team
Managerial assets	Strong senior management support for technology investment and change
	Incentives for management innovation
	Teamwork and collaborative work environments
	Training programs to enhance management decision skills
	Management culture that values flexibility and knowledge-based decision making
Social assets	The Internet and telecommunications infrastructure
	IT-enriched educational programs raising labour force computer literacy
	Standards (both government and private sector)
	Laws and regulations creating fair, stable market environments
	Technology and service firms in adjacent markets to assist implementation

organizational and management capital

Key organizational complementary investments include a supportive business culture that values efficiency and effectiveness, efficient business processes, decentralization of authority, highly distributed decision rights, and a strong information system (IS) development team.

Important managerial complementary assets are strong senior management support for change, incentive systems that monitor and reward individual innovation, an emphasis on teamwork and collaboration, training programs, and a management culture that values flexibility and knowledge.

Important social investments (not made by the firm but by the society at large, other firms, governments, and other key market actors) are the Internet and the supporting Internet culture, educational systems, network and computing standards, regulations and laws, and the presence of technology and service firms.

Throughout the book, we emphasize a framework of analysis that considers technology, management, and organizational assets and their interactions. Perhaps the single most important theme in this book, reflected in case studies, vignettes, and exercises, is that managers need to consider the broader organization and management dimensions of information systems to understand current problems as well as to derive substantial above-average returns from their information technology investments. As you will see throughout the text, firms that can address these related dimensions of IT investment are, on average, richly rewarded.

1.3 Contemporary Approaches to Information Systems

Multiple perspectives on information systems show that the study of information systems is a multidisciplinary field. No single theory or perspective dominates. Figure 1-10 illustrates the major disciplines that contribute problems, issues, and solutions in the study of information systems. In general, the field can be divided into technical and behavioural approaches. Information systems are sociotechnical systems. Though they are composed of machines, devices, and "hard" physical technology, they require substantial social, organizational, and intellectual investments to make them work properly.

Technical Approach

The technical approach to information systems emphasizes mathematically based models to study information systems, as well as the physical technology and formal capabilities of these systems. The disciplines that contribute to the technical approach are computer science, management science, and operations research.

Computer science is concerned with establishing theories of computability, methods of computation, and methods of efficient data storage and access. Management science emphasizes the development of models for decision-making and management practices. Operations research focuses on mathematical techniques for optimizing selected parameters of organizations, such as transportation, inventory control, and transaction costs.

Behavioural Approach

An important part of the information systems field is concerned with behavioural issues that arise in the development and long-term maintenance of information systems. Issues such as strategic business integration, design, implementation, utilization, and management cannot be explored usefully with the models used in the technical approach. Other behavioural disciplines contribute important concepts and methods.

For instance, sociologists study information systems with an eye toward how groups and organizations shape the development of systems and also how systems affect individuals, groups, and organizations. Psychologists study information systems with an interest in how human decision makers perceive and use formal information. Economists study

FIGURE 1-10   *Contemporary approaches to information systems.*

The study of information systems deals with issues and insights contributed from technical and behavioural disciplines.

information systems with an interest in what impact systems have on control and cost structures within the firm and within markets.

The behavioural approach does not ignore technology. Indeed, information systems technology is often the stimulus for a behavioural problem or issue. But the focus of this approach is generally not on technical solutions. Instead, it concentrates on changes in attitudes, management and organizational policy, and behaviour.

Approach of This Text: Sociotechnical Systems

Throughout this book, you will find a rich story with four main actors: suppliers of hardware and software (the technologists); business firms making investments and seeking to obtain value from technology; managers and employees seeking to achieve business value (and other goals); and the contemporary legal, social, and cultural context (the firm's environment). Together these actors produce what we call *management information systems*.

The study of **management information systems (MIS)** began in the 1970s to focus on the use of computer-based information systems in business firms and government agencies (Laudon 1974; Davis and Olson 1985). MIS combines the work of computer science, management science, and operations research with a practical orientation toward developing system solutions to real-world problems and managing information technology resources. It is also concerned with behavioural issues surrounding the development, use, and impact of information systems, which are typically discussed in the fields of sociology, economics, and psychology. The study of information systems has just started to influence other disciplines (Baskerville and Myers 2002) through concepts such as the information processing view of the firm. Today some scholars often refer to MIS (the discipline, as opposed to the type of information systems discussed in Chapter 15) as the management *of* information systems.

Our experience as academics and practitioners leads us to believe that no single approach effectively captures the reality of information systems. The successes and failures of information are rarely all technical or all behavioural. Our best advice to students is to understand the perspectives of many disciplines. Indeed, the challenge and excitement of the information systems field is that it requires an appreciation and tolerance of many different approaches.

The view we adopt in this book is best characterized as the **sociotechnical view** of systems. In this view, optimal organizational performance is achieved by jointly optimizing

management information systems (MIS)

sociotechnical view

both the social and technical systems used in production (Mumford, 2000 and 1997; Williams and Edge 1996).

Adopting a sociotechnical systems perspective helps to avoid a purely technological approach to information systems. For instance, the fact that information technology is rapidly declining in cost and growing in power does not necessarily or easily translate into productivity enhancement or bottom-line profits. The fact that a firm has recently installed an enterprise-wide financial reporting system does not necessarily mean that it will be used or will be used effectively. Likewise, the fact that a firm has recently introduced new business procedures and processes does not necessarily mean employees will be more productive in the absence of investments in new information systems to enable those processes.

In this book, we stress the need to optimize the firm's performance as a whole. Both the technical and behavioural components need attention. This means that technology must be changed and designed to fit organizational and individual needs. At times, the technology may have to be "de-optimized" to accomplish this fit. For instance, mobile phone users adapt this technology to their personal needs, and as a result, manufacturers quickly seek to adjust the technology to conform to user expectations (Lee 2003; Sawyer and Allen 2003; Bautsch 2001). Organizations and individuals must also be changed through training, learning, and planned organizational change to allow the technology to operate and prosper (Lamb et al. 2004; Orlikowski and Baroudi 1991; Orlikowski 1992). Figure 1-11 illustrates this process of mutual adjustment in a sociotechnical system.

1.4   Learning to Use Information Systems: New Opportunities with Technology

Although information systems are creating many exciting opportunities for both businesses and individuals, they are also a source of new problems, issues, and challenges for managers. In this course, you will learn about both the challenges and opportunities information systems pose, and you will be able to use information technology to enrich your learning experience.

The Challenge of Information Systems: Key Management Issues

Although information technology is advancing at a blinding pace, there is nothing easy or mechanical about developing and using information systems. There are five major challenges confronting managers:

FIGURE 1-11   *A sociotechnical perspective on information systems.*

In a sociotechnical perspective, the performance of a system is optimized when both the technology and the organization mutually adjust to one another until a satisfactory fit is obtained.

1. *The information systems investment challenge: How can organizations obtain business value from their information systems?* Earlier in this chapter, we described the importance of information systems as investments that produce value for the firm. We showed that not all companies realize good returns from information systems investments. It is obvious that one of the greatest challenges facing managers today is ensuring that their companies do indeed obtain meaningful returns on the money they spend on information systems. It is one thing to use information technology to design, produce, deliver, and maintain new products. It is another thing to make money doing it. How can organizations obtain a sizable payoff from their investment in information systems? How can management ensure that information systems contribute to corporate value?

   Senior management can be expected to ask these questions: How can we evaluate our information systems investments as we do other investments? Are we receiving the return on investment from our systems that we should? Do our competitors get more? Far too many firms still cannot answer these questions. Their executives are likely to have trouble determining how much they actually spend on technology or how to measure the returns on their technology investments. Most companies lack a clear-cut decision-making process for deciding which technology investments to pursue and for managing those investments (Hartman 2002).

2. *The strategic business challenge: What complementary assets are needed to use information technology effectively?* Despite heavy information technology investments, many organizations are not realizing significant business value from their systems, because they lack—or fail to appreciate—the complementary assets required to make their technology assets work. The power of computer hardware and software has grown much more rapidly than the ability of organizations to apply and use this technology. To benefit fully from information technology, realize genuine productivity, and become competitive and effective, many organizations actually need to be redesigned. They will have to make fundamental changes in employee and management behaviour, develop new business models, retire obsolete work rules, and eliminate the inefficiencies of outmoded business processes and organizational structures. New technology alone will not produce meaningful business benefits.

3. *The globalization challenge: How can firms understand the business and system requirements of a global economic environment?* The rapid growth in international trade and the emergence of a global economy call for information systems that can support both producing and selling goods in many different countries. In the past, each regional office of a multinational corporation focused on solving its own unique information problems. Given language, cultural, and political differences among countries, this focus frequently resulted in chaos and the failure of central management controls. To develop integrated, multinational, information systems, businesses must develop global hardware, software, and communications standards; create cross-cultural accounting and reporting structures; and design transnational business processes.

4. *The information technology infrastructure challenge: How can organizations develop an information technology infrastructure that can support their goals when business conditions and technologies are changing so rapidly?* Many companies are saddled with expensive and unwieldy information technology platforms that cannot adapt to innovation and change. Their information systems are so complex and brittle that they act as constraints on business strategy and execution. Meeting new business and technology challenges may require redesigning the organization and developing a new IT infrastructure.

   Creating the IT infrastructure for a digital firm is an especially formidable task. Most companies are crippled by fragmented and incompatible computer hardware, software, telecommunications networks, and information systems that prevent information from flowing freely between different parts of the organization. Although Internet standards are solving some of these connectivity problems, creating data and computing platforms that span the enterprise—and, increasingly, link the enterprise to external business partners—is rarely as seamless as promised. Many organizations are still struggling to integrate their islands of information and technology. Chapters 5 through 9 provide more detail on IT infrastructure issues.

5. *Ethics and security: The responsibility and control challenge: How can organizations ensure that their information systems are used in an ethically and socially responsible manner? How can we design information systems that people can control and understand?* Although information systems have provided enormous benefits and efficiencies, they have also created new ethical, legal, and social problems and challenges. Chapter 4 is devoted entirely to ethical and social issues raised by information systems, such as threats to individual privacy and intellectual property rights, computer-related health problems, computer crimes, and elimination of jobs. A major management challenge is to make informed decisions that are sensitive to the negative consequences of information systems as well to the positive ones.

Managers face an ongoing struggle to maintain security and control. Today, the threat of unauthorized penetration or disruption of information systems has never been greater. Information systems are so essential to business, government, and daily life that organizations must take special steps to ensure their security, accuracy, and reliability. A firm invites disaster if it uses systems that can be disrupted or accessed by outsiders, that do not work as intended, or that do not deliver information in a form that people can correctly use. Information systems must be designed so that they are secure, function as intended, and so that humans can control the process. Chapter 9 treats these issues in detail.

Managers will need to ask: Can we apply high-quality assurance standards to our information systems, as well as to our products and services? Can we develop systems with tight security that are still easy to use? Can we design information systems that respect people's rights of privacy while still pursuing our organization's goals? Should information systems monitor employees? What do we do when an information system designed to increase efficiency and productivity eliminates jobs?

This text is designed to provide future managers with the knowledge and understanding required to deal with these challenges. To further this objective, each succeeding chapter concludes with a Management Opportunities, Challenges, and Solutions section that outlines the key issues which managers need to understand.

Integrating Text with Technology: New Opportunities for Learning

In addition to the changes in business and management that we have just described, we believe that information technology creates new opportunities for learning that can make the MIS course more meaningful and exciting. We have provided a series of hands-on projects and a student Web site for integrating the text with leading-edge technology.

Application software exercises require students to use spreadsheet, database, Web browser, and other application software in hands-on projects related to chapter concepts. Students can apply the application software skills they have learned in other courses to real-world business problems. You can find these exercises following the Discussion Questions at the end of each chapter, and both the exercises and their data files can be found on the Companion Website.

A running case study based on a simulated company called Dirt Bikes Canada enables students to learn about a specific business and develop information system solutions for that business. The Companion Website for each chapter of the text contains a running case scenario and project where students can apply their analytical skills and chapter concepts. Many of these projects require extensive use of the Web or spreadsheet and database software. For each chapter, you will also find an Electronic Commerce or Electronic Business project for which you can use Web research and interactive software at various company Web sites to solve specific business problems. The project is described at the end of each chapter after the running case and additional details can be found on the Companion Website for that chapter.

As you read each chapter of the text, you can visit the Companion Website and use the Internet for additional interactive learning and management problem solving. You will find an Internet Connection margin note in every chapter directing you to Web sites for which we have provided additional exercises and projects related to the concepts and organizations described in that particular chapter. A graded online Interactive Study Guide contains questions to help you review what you have learned and test your mastery of chapter concepts. Also at the Laudon Companion Website are links to additional online case studies and international resources.

Longer, comprehensive projects conclude each major section of the text. These projects require students to apply what they have learned to more demanding problems, such as analyzing enterprise system requirements, developing an Internet business model, designing a corporate knowledge intranet, and redesigning business processes for a new system. Some of these projects require use of the Web. All of these projects can be found on the Companion Website.

Summary

1. **Explain why information systems are so important today for business and management.**

   Information systems are a part of the foundation for conducting business today. In many industries, survival and even existence without extensive use of IT is inconceivable, and IT plays a critical role in increasing productivity. Although information technology has become more of a commodity, when coupled with complementary changes in organization and management, it can provide the foundation for new products, services, and ways of conducting business that provide firms with a strategic advantage. Information technology has become the largest component of capital investment for firms in many industrialized societies.

2. **Evaluate the role of information systems in today's competitive business environment.**

   Information systems have become essential for helping organizations deal with changes in global economies and the business enterprise. Information systems provide firms with communication and analytic tools for conducting trade and managing businesses on a global scale. Information systems are the foundation of new knowledge-based products and services in knowledge economies and help firms manage their knowledge assets. Information systems make it possible for businesses to adopt more flexible arrangements of employees and management that can coordinate with other organizations across great distances. Organizations are trying to become more competitive and efficient by transforming themselves into digital firms where nearly all core business processes and relationships with customers, suppliers, and employees are digitally enabled. The Internet is bringing about a convergence of technologies that is further widening the use of information systems in business and transforming industries and business models.

3. **Assess the impact of the Internet and Internet technology on business and government.**

   The Internet provides global connectivity and a flexible platform for the seamless flow of information across the enterprise and between the firm and its customers and suppliers. It is the primary technology infrastructure for electronic commerce, electronic business, and the emerging digital firm. In electronic commerce (e-commerce), businesses can exchange electronic purchase and sale transactions with each other and with individual customers. Electronic business (e-business) uses Internet and other digital technology for organizational communication and coordination, collaboration with business partners, and the management of the firm, as well as for electronic commerce transactions. Digital firms use Internet technology intensively to manage their internal processes and relationships with customers, suppliers, and other external entities. E-government uses the Internet and intranets to improve delivery of government services, make internal operations more efficient, and empower citizens to network electronically with other citizens.

4. **Define an information system from both a technical and business perspective, and distinguish between computer literacy and information systems literacy.**

   An information system collects, stores, and disseminates information from an organization's environment and internal operations to support organizational functions and decision making, communication, coordination, control, analysis, and visualization. Information systems transform raw data into useful information through three basic activities: input, processing, and output, with feedback to adjust the system. From a business perspective, an information system creates economic value for the firm as an organizational and management solution, based on information technology, to a challenge posed by the environment. The information system is part of a series of value-adding activities for acquiring, transforming, and distributing information to improve management decision making, enhance organizational performance, and, ultimately, increase firm profitability.

Information systems are rooted in organizations; they are an outcome of organizational structure, culture, politics, workflows, and standard operating procedures. They are instruments for organizational change and value creation, making it possible to recast these organizational elements into new business models and redraw organizational boundaries. Managers are problem solvers who are responsible for analyzing the many challenges confronting organizations and for developing strategies and action plans. Information systems are one of their tools, delivering the information required for solutions. Information systems both reflect management decisions and serve as instruments for changing the management process. Information systems cannot make managers and organizations more effective unless they are accompanied by complementary assets such as new

or changed business processes, changes in organizational culture, or changes in management behaviour.

Information systems literacy requires an understanding of the organizational and management dimensions of information systems as well as the technical dimensions addressed by computer literacy. Information systems literacy draws on both technical and behavioural approaches to studying information systems. Both perspectives can be combined into a sociotechnical approach to systems.

5. ***Identify the major management challenges to developing and using information systems.***

There are five key management challenges in developing and using information systems: 1. obtaining business value from information systems; 2. providing appropriate complementary assets to use information technology effectively; 3. understanding the system requirements of a global business environment; 4. creating an information technology infrastructure that is flexible enough to support changing organizational goals; and 5. designing systems that people can control, understand, and use in a socially and ethically responsible manner.

Key Terms

Business functions,   19
Business processes,   10
Communications technology,   20
Complementary assets,   22
Computer-based information systems
    (CBIS),   15
Computer hardware,   20
Computer literacy,   17
Computer software,   20
Data,   13
Data workers,   19
Digital firm,   10
E-government,   8
Electronic business (e-business),   8
Electronic commerce (e-commerce),   8

Extranets,   21
Feedback,   13
Formal systems,   15
Information,   13
Information system,   13
Information systems literacy,   17
Information technology (IT),   4
Information technology (IT)
    infrastructure,   22
Input,   13
Internet,   20
Intranets,   21
Knowledge- and information-intense
    products,   10

Knowledge workers,   19
Management information systems (MIS),   25
Middle managers,   20
Network,   20
Operational managers,   20
Organizational and management capital,   23
Output,   13
Processing,   13
Production or service workers,   19
Senior managers,   20
Sociotechnical view,   25
Storage technology,   20
Web site,   21
World Wide Web (WWW),   20

Review Questions

1. *List and describe four reasons why information systems are so important for business today.*

2. *Describe five technology and business trends that have enhanced the role of information systems in today's competitive business environment.*

3. *Describe the capabilities of a digital firm. Why are digital firms so powerful? What are the four principal systems driving the movement toward digital firms?*

4. *What is an information system? Distinguish a computer, a computer program, and an information system. What is the difference between data and information?*

5. *What activities convert raw data to usable information in information systems? What is their relationship to feedback?*

6. *What is the purpose of an information system from a business perspective? What role does it play in the business information value chain?*

7. *What is information systems literacy? How does it differ from computer literacy?*

8. *What are the organizational, management, and technology dimensions of information systems?*

9. *What are the Internet and the World Wide Web? How have they changed the roles played by information systems in organizations?*

10. *Why do some firms obtain greater value from their information systems than others? What role do complementary assets and organizational and management capital play?*

11. *Distinguish between a behavioural and a technical approach to information systems in terms of the questions asked and the answers provided. What major disciplines contribute to an understanding of information systems?*

12. *What are the key management challenges involved in developing, operating, and maintaining information systems today?*

Discussion Questions

1. *Information systems are too important to be left to computer specialists. Do you agree? Why or why not?*

2. *As computers become faster and cheaper and the Internet becomes more widely used, most of the problems we have with information systems will disappear. Do you agree? Why or why not?*

Application Software Exercise:
Database Exercise: Adding Value to Information for Management Decision Making

Effective information systems add value to data to create meaningful information for management decisions that improve business performance. At the Companion Website for Chapter 1, you can find a Store and Regional Sales Database with raw data on weekly store sales of computer equipment in various sales regions. The database includes fields for store identification number, sales region number, item number, item description, unit price, units sold, and the weekly sales period when the sales were made. Develop some reports and queries to make this information more useful for management. Modify the database table, if necessary, to provide all of the information you require. Here are some questions you might consider:

1. Which are the best-performing stores and sales regions?
2. What are the best-selling products?
3. Which stores and sales regions sell the most of which products?
4. When are the strongest and weakest selling periods? For which stores? Which sales regions? Which products?
5. How can your company improve sales in the weakest store and sales region? (Answers will vary.)

Electronic Commerce Project: Analyzing Shipping Costs

You are the shipping clerk of a small firm that prints, binds, and ships popular books for a midlevel publisher. Your production facilities are located in Quebec City, Quebec (Postal code G1R 2W7). Your customers' warehouses are located in Richmond, British Columbia (V5T 1A5); Winnipeg, Manitoba (R3T 5V4); Don Mills, Ontario (M3C 2T8); Montreal, Quebec (H3B 4W5); and Halifax, Nova Scotia (E3C 1H9). The production facility operates 250 days per year. Your books are usually shipped in one of two sized packages:

(A) Height: 9 inches, Length: 13, Width: 17 inches, Weight: 45 lbs.

(B) Height: 10 inches, Length: 6, Width: 12 inches, Weight: 16 lbs.

The company ships about four of the A boxes to each of the warehouses on an average day and about eight B boxes daily.

Your task is to select the best shipper for your company. Compare three shippers, such as DHL Express Canada (**www.dhl.ca**), UPS (**www.ups.com**), and Canada Post (**www.canadapost.ca**). Consider not only costs but also issues such as delivery speed, pickup schedules, drop-off locations, tracking ability, and ease of use of the Web site. Which service did you select? Explain why.

Group Project: Analyzing a Business System

In a group with three or four classmates, find a description in a computer or business magazine of an information system used by an organization. Look for information about the company on the Web to gain further insight into the company, and prepare a brief description of the business.

Describe the system you have selected in terms of its inputs, processes, and outputs; how feedback is used; and its organization, management, and technology features and the importance of the system to the company. If possible, use electronic presentation software to present your analysis to the class.

Web Sites of Interest

There are many interesting Web sites to enhance your learning about information systems. You can search the Web yourself, or just try the following sites to add to what you have already learned.

Pearson Education Canada Laudon, Laudon, and Brabston Companion Website **www.pearsoned.ca/laudon**
The Web site that supports this text. You should bookmark this site on your computer.

Gartner Group **www.gartner.com**
A wealth of research information on a wide variety of management information systems topics.

Information Technology Association of Canada **www.itac.ca**
A Web site for professionals that includes Canadian e-commerce case studies and a lot of information about IT careers and job skills.

CASE STUDY:
Gold Medal Information Technology for the Olympics

The European Union's lowest-tech country, Greece, successfully met the massive information requirements of the Athens 2004 Olympics. How did the Greeks do it?

Organizers of the 2004 Games in Athens had to ensure that information was fed instantaneously to thousands of reporters and Olympic officials in almost zero response times. SchlumbergerSema, the information technology (IT) systems provider that took over from IBM as Olympic sponsor after the Sydney 2000 Games, managed this biannual project.

Ironically, the precedence for failure had already been set by Atlanta, the city that Athens lost to for the 1996 Olympics. In the memory of media personnel, the 1996 Games are etched as "the Glitch Games" because of an information blackout that caused horrible delays in competition results reaching reporters. In the case of Athens 2004, reporters expected to encounter real blackouts. "It's true; here you see power outages very often," said Claude Philipps, SchlumbergerSema's chief technology integrator for the 2004 Summer Games. "[Greek organizers] took this seriously... There is a diesel generator in every venue." Considering the crucial role of IT in the Games, the Greek organizers had to eliminate any risk of blackouts.

SchlumbergerSema, the 14.3 billion dollar company with offices in New York, Paris, and The Hague, managed the development and operation of computing systems for the 2004 Summer Olympics in Athens. The company made an early start and had completed half of the necessary software applications 20 months before the Games were due to begin. It tested these applications and trained the nearly 4000 people needed to run them in its Athens Integration Test Laboratory opened in 2002.

SchlumbergerSema's work for the Athens Games was part of an IT contract that it called the world's largest. The company agreed to handle every detail of IT work for six successive Olympic Games, a project that began with the 2002 Winter Games in Salt Lake City and will end with the London Summer Games in 2012. "We act as a global inte-

grator, pulling together a team of 10 to 12 technology companies. We provide the key applications. We provide the hardware. And we operate the systems during the Games," said Philipps.

The task was much larger this time around than in Salt Lake City. While the Salt Lake Organizing Committee handed out 89 000 accreditations for 78 sporting events spanning 10 different venues, the Athens 2004 Organizing Committee for the Olympic Games' (ATHOC) provided 200 000 accreditations for 300 events in 37 venues. SchlumbergerSema calculated that the 2004 Games would require two to three times more "IT power" than the Salt Lake 2002 Winter Games, their first assignment as official sponsor. For Athens, they provided 10 000 computers, 450 servers, 2000 fax machines and copiers, and 2000 printers, plus a workforce of nearly 4000 (3500 of whom were volunteers).

These machines, networked with optical fibre and tied to the Internet, ran two types of applications: Games Management Systems (GMS), which handled organizational tasks including accreditation, accommodations, health services, and transportation; and Info Diffusion Systems (IDS), which provided journalists, officials, public Web sites, sponsors, and television commentators with results, statistics, and other important information related to the events themselves.

Developing the IDS tools was a greater challenge than developing the GMS. "GMS is an important piece, but the most important piece is the real-time results systems," said Philipps. "If they fail, two to three billion people across the world will not be happy." For the benefit of commentators, the systems must send distances, times, scores, and other results across the network as soon as the data become available. According to Philipps, when a runner crosses the finish line, the person's time will reach commentators' desktops no more than three-tenths of a second later.

In addition to building the applications and laying down all the hardware needed to run them, including redundant machines, hubs, routers, and networking cable, SchlumbergerSema spent more than 200 000 hours testing the systems at the Athens Integration Test Lab. How much did all this cost? About $500 million, which seems reasonable considering how much the company spent on the Salt Lake City Games. Although the Salt Lake City project was, at most, half the size of the Athens project, it cost about $450 million. In at least one sense, SchlumbergerSema's Olympian task is very much like any other IT project: It gets easier the second time around.

The 1998 Winter Olympics in Nagano, Japan, had just ended, but Dave Busser, the chief information officer of the Salt Lake Organizing Committee (SLOC), was already on the phone to the world's leading technology companies, trying to put together the massive array of computer and telephone equipment needed to run the Salt Lake City Games in 2002. He would need the next four years to get all the right hardware and software in place and tested, drawing on the expertise of 17 different technology companies and spending roughly $450 million.

"It's one of the biggest projects you can imagine," Busser told PC Magazine. "And the deadline for getting it all done was absolutely not going to change." Busser and his team did get it done, and the games had few, if any, high-tech mishaps.

A wide area high speed network comprising almost 50 000 kilometres of optical fibre spanned the 2002 Games' 41 venues. "It was the largest in Utah," Busser continued. "And probably, on any given day, the largest private network in the U.S." The network connected over 5000 Gateway desktops and laptops, 500 to 600 servers from Gateway and Sun, myriad printers from Xerox and Kodak, and the requisite timing devices and scoreboards from Seiko.

Then there was the official Web site of the games, which was visited by more than 15 million unique users over the course of the Games. The site was hosted and operated by MSNBC, with Qwest providing the network access and various peripheral applications. "It was the largest single-event Web site in history," said Busser. And then there was the telephone equipment. The committee relied on 14 000 desk phones, 10 000 mobile phones, and 7000 two-way radios. More than 2300 people were needed to operate all this technology. Half were volunteers and half were employees of SLOC or the various technology companies supplying equipment.

What was SLOC's massive network of machines used for? Some systems handled organizational duties, tending to everything from transportation around the city to accreditation at the various athletic venues to hotel accommodations. Others systems managed the competitions themselves, keeping track of the athletes' performances and supplying television commentators with up-to-the-minute information. Still other components served as information kiosks for members of the media and visitors to the Games.

The machines installed at the athletic venues were the most important and had to be incredibly fast so television commentators could have the latest data at their fingertips. "Data had to be delivered almost in real time," said Busser.

"We agreed to deliver the result data to the commentators in 300 milliseconds." The infrastructure also had to be reliable. Systems at each venue could tap into a central data centre through the SLOC wide area network but were also designed to operate on their own and have access to backup data. "We could have lost our primary data centre, and the events would still go on. Supporting athletic competition was our first priority."

Failures are always possible, as any IT manager will tell you, but Busser and his team spent weeks and weeks trying to ensure mishaps would be kept to a minimum. "We did over 100 000 hours of testing and conducted two comprehensive technical rehearsals where we actually tested all of our operational procedures," said Busser. "When the real thing started, we didn't have a couple of weeks to work through the bugs. We didn't have that grace period. Everything had to work on day one."

According to Busser, everything did work on day one and continued to work through the Salt Lake City Games. Gateway, which supplied all the PCs for the Games as well as technical support for those PCs, is in agreement. SchlumbergerSema moved from Salt Lake City to Athens without a real break. Before Atlanta, IBM had run the Olympics' information technology for years without a glitch.

In 2003 ATOS Origin acquired SchlumbergerSema, including the Olympics contract. ATOS Origin is in the throes of a major testing program that will prove whether its IT systems are as fit as the athletes who will compete in the winter Olympics in Torino in 2006.

ATOS Origin is carrying out lengthy testing in preparation for Torino, including user acceptance tests of its commentator information systems, resilience tests of the GMS and IDS systems, a multi-sport test that simulates the games to discover the overall performance of the systems, and ongoing 'homologation' tests designed to ensure that systems and interfaces meet user requirements. "As we have only one chance to get it right, we test, test and test again our systems and applications under intense conditions. After these tests are complete, the next step is the technical rehearsals which will take place in October and are designed to assess whether the technology, people and processes are all ready," said Philips.

ATOS set up operations in Beijing in October 2004, four years before the 2008 Olympics. The China Olympics should present many of the same challenges as the Athens Games in terms of infrastructure and being perceived as "low tech."

Vancouver will host the XXI Olympic Winter Games from 12 to 28 February 2010, a project that will generate up to $10 billion in revenue. The mountain events will take place in Whistler, which will also host the 2010 Paralympic Winter Games from 12 to 21 March 2010. It will be interesting to see if SchlumbergerSema continues to grab the gold for their Olympic IT performance.

Sources: Cade Metz, "Athens Apps Up and Running," *PC Magazine*, December 23, 2002, available **www.pcmag.com/print_article/ 0,3048,a=35110,00.asp**, accessed June 8, 2003; Cade Metz, "Olympian Technology Powers the Games," *PC Magazine*, February 22, 2002, available **www.pcmag.com/print_article/0,3048,a=23111,**

00.asp, accessed June 8, 2003; John Hadoulis, "Fixing Games Glitches Before They Happen," *Athens News*, April 4, 2003, available **www.invgr.com/olympics_schlumbergersema_glitches.htm**, accessed June 8, 2003; "Olympics Testing Labs Opened," *eWeek*, November 11, 2002, available **www.eweek.com/**, accessed June 8, 2003; David Aponovich, "No Medal, But IT Integrator Still Scores at Salt Lake Games," *CIO Update*, February 27, 2002, available **www. cioupdate.com/news/article.php/10493_981721**, accessed June 8, 2003; *MCN Direct Newswire*, "Atos Origin warms up for winter Olympics," available **www.conferencepage.com/mcndirect/ issues2005/mcndirect280605.asp**., accessed. July 19, 2005; and **www.atosorigin.com**, accessed July 19, 2005.

CASE STUDY QUESTIONS

1. What were the obstacles to implementing the information systems for the Athens Olympic games? Will these be the same obstacles for the Vancouver games?

2. How do you think the Internet and the World Wide Web have changed the Olympics? What impact have they had on fans of the Olympics?

3. What features or characteristics does the Olympics infrastructure have to exhibit in order to deliver the data required by SchlumbergerSema and ATOS Origin?

4. Do you think the Olympics should award long-term contracts like the SchlumbergerSema/ATOS Origin contract? Why or why not?

Chapter 2

Information Systems in the Enterprise

OBJECTIVES

After completing this chapter, you will be able to:

1. Evaluate the role played by the major types of systems in a business and their relationship to each other.

2. Describe the information systems supporting the major business functions: sales and marketing, manufacturing and production, finance and accounting, and human resources.

3. Analyze the relationship between organizations, information systems, and business processes.

4. Explain how enterprise applications promote business process integration and improve organizational performance.

5. Assess the challenges posed by information systems in the enterprise and propose management solutions.

Opening Case: Fast Fashion, Hot Systems

In the fast-paced world of fashion retailing, nothing seems more important than time to market. Instead of the traditional four clothing fashion seasons (spring, summer, autumn, and winter), styles now change once a month or even faster. Some women's clothing store chains get a delivery of new styles twice a month. Welcome to the world of Speed Chic.

A number of companies have adopted this strategy, including Sweden's H&M, TopShop in the United Kingdom, and Spain's Zara and Mango. Mango/MNG Holding SL is based outside Barcelona, with more than 700 women's boutique stores in 72 countries. It is known for an eclectic mix of body-hugging styles. Mango began its expansion into North America with the opening of five stores in Canada in 2005. Mango believes its approach to "fast fashion" will help it move into the North American market.

Bringing out a steady stream of trendy new merchandise requires flexibility and speed from design through production and delivery to the store shelf. Once garments roll off production lines, Mango's proprietary inventory replenishment system determines exactly which pieces should be sent to which stores.

Four times each year, Mango's designers meet to discuss important new trends for each of its main collections. Each collection consists of five or six smaller collections. Design teams meet each week to adjust for changing trends. After clothing and accessories styles have been decided, Mango's product management and distribution team assigns them personalities, such as trendy, dressy, or suitable for hot weather.

Once items have been classified, they are sent to one of Mango's 731 stores, each of which is classified by traits such as the climate where the shop is located or whether large or small sizes sell best. Mango's inventory replenishment system makes sure the merchandise is sent to compatible shops.

The system transmits order data to a large distribution machine on the ground floor of Mango headquarters, which is surrounded by a rotating ring of cardboard boxes on hooks. Bar-coded clothes that have just arrived from factories are scanned and placed into one of 466 store-specific slots. They then are boxed and shipped to retail stores. Mango can add new items to its stores once a week, about six times more frequently than the typical American clothing chain. Retail store managers can adjust store plans daily based on input from regional supervisors and headquarters.

Mango is not the only fashion retailer making use of a wide variety of information technologies. Canadian fashion company Nygård pioneered the use of technology in the 1980s by moving toward paperless processes. Nygård's Winnipeg-based facility is electronically connected to its biggest customers' cash registers. "This system receives a download of the retailer's weekly point-of-sale data and generates re-orders automatically based on sales," Chairman Peter Nygård says. "Items are delivered to customers on a just-in-time basis, compared to the traditional eight-week turnaround for most other manufacturers. Nygård also receives its raw materials in the same manner." Nygård says it has moved to a Web-based purchase order (PO) system.

According to Nygård, eliminating the manual system saves the company more than 1000 person-hours each month, as well as reduces miscommunications and clerical errors. The company says it expects a two-year return on investment (ROI). "The new system has reduced the time it takes to issue a payment from weeks to minutes, eliminated 90 percent of the company's manual PO processes, and dramatically improved the quality of its supplier communications," Nygård lists. The company also says developer productivity has increased by 35 to 50 percent.

Sources: Erin White, "For Retailer Mango, Frenzied 'Fast Fashion' Proves Sweet," *Wall Street Journal*, May 28, 2004; Cecilie Rohwedder, "Making Fashion Faster," *Wall Street Journal*, February 28, 2004; Hanna Aronovich, "Ready Made Couture," *U.S. Business Review*, March 2005.

Mango has a core of designers and production facilities that can churn out new fashion styles at lightning speed. But Mango would not be able stock its stores so quickly with hot fashion trends without its powerful information systems. These information systems support finely tuned business processes that organize merchandise based on style and customer tastes to drive inventory replenishment. Similarly, Nygård uses its information systems from the design table through ordering, manufacturing, distributing, and accounting for all its products.

As a manager, you will want to know exactly how information systems can help your company. You will need to understand which types of information systems are available to businesses and what systems can do for business.

In this chapter, we first look at different ways of classifying information systems based on the organizational level, business functions, and business processes they support. We then briefly examine enterprise applications, which consist of enterprise systems, supply chain management systems, customer relationship management systems, and knowledge management systems. These enterprise applications span the entire firm, integrating information from multiple functions and business processes to enhance the performance of the organization as a whole.

2.1   Major Types of Systems in Organizations

Because there are different interests, specialties, and levels in an organization, there are different kinds of systems. No single system can provide all the information an organization needs. Figure 2-1 illustrates one way to depict the kinds of systems found in an organization. In the illustration, the organization is divided into strategic, management, and operational levels and then is further divided into functional areas such as sales and marketing, manufacturing and production, finance and accounting, and human resources. Systems are developed to serve these different organizational interests (Anthony 1965).

Different Kinds of Systems

Three main categories of information systems serve different organizational levels: operational-level systems, management-level systems, and strategic-level systems. **Operational-level systems** support operational managers by keeping track of the elementary activities and transactions of the organization, such as sales, receipts, cash deposits, payroll, credit decisions, and the flow of materials in a factory. The principal purpose of systems at this level is to answer routine questions and to track the flow of transactions through the organization. How many parts are in inventory? What happened to Mr. Williams's payment? To answer these kinds of questions, information generally must be easily available, current, and accurate. Examples of operational-level systems include a system to record bank deposits

FIGURE 2-1   *Types of information systems.*

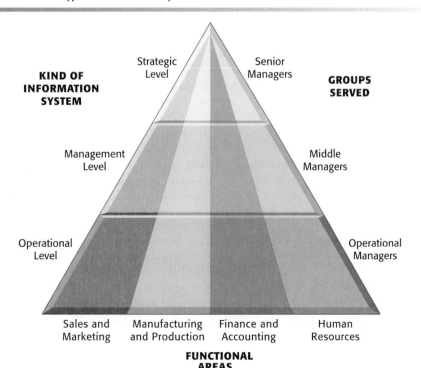

Organizations can be divided into strategic, management, and operational levels and into four major functional areas: sales and marketing, manufacturing and production, finance and accounting, and human resources. Information systems serve each of these levels and functions.

operational-level systems

from automatic teller machines or one that tracks the number of hours worked each day by employees on a factory floor.

Management-level systems serve the monitoring, controlling, decision-making, and administrative activities of middle managers. The principal question addressed by such systems is this: Are things working well? Management-level systems typically provide periodic reports rather than instant information on operations. An example is a relocation control system that reports on the total moving, house-hunting, and home financing costs for employees in all company divisions, noting wherever actual costs exceed budgets.

Some management-level systems support nonroutine decision making. They tend to focus on decisions for which information requirements are not always clear. These systems often answer "what-if" questions: What would be the impact on production schedules if we were to double sales in the month of December? What would happen to our return on investment if a factory schedule were delayed for six months? Answers to these questions frequently require new data from outside the organization as well as data from inside that cannot be easily drawn from existing operational-level systems.

Strategic-level systems help senior management tackle and address strategic issues and long-term trends, both in the firm and in the external environment. Their principal concern is matching changes in the external environment with existing organizational capability. What will employment levels be in five years? What are the long-term industry cost trends, and where does our firm fit in? What products should we be making in five years?

Information systems also serve the major business functions, such as sales and marketing, manufacturing and production, finance and accounting, and human resources. A typical organization has operational-, management-, and strategic-level systems for each functional area. For example, the sales function generally has a sales system on the operational level to record daily sales figures and process orders. A management-level system tracks monthly sales figures by sales territory and reports on territories where sales exceed or fall below anticipated levels. A system to forecast sales trends over a five-year period serves the strategic level. We first describe the specific categories of systems serving each organizational level and their value to the organization. Then we show how organizations use these systems for each major business function.

Four Major Types of Systems

Figure 2-2 shows the specific types of information systems that correspond to each organizational level. The organization has executive support systems (ESS) at the strategic level; management information systems (MIS) and decision-support systems (DSS) at the management level; and transaction processing systems (TPS) at the operational level. Systems at each level in turn are specialized to serve each of the major functional areas. Thus, the typical systems found in organizations are designed to assist workers or managers at each level and in the functions of sales and marketing, manufacturing and production, finance and accounting, and human resources.

Table 2-1 summarizes the features of the four types of information systems. It should be noted that each of the different systems may have components that are used by organizational levels and groups other than their main constituencies. A secretary may find information on an MIS, or a middle manager may need to extract data from a TPS.

Transaction Processing Systems Transaction processing systems **(TPS)** are the basic business systems that serve the operational level of the organization. A transaction processing system is a computerized system that performs and records the daily routine transactions necessary to conduct business. Examples are sales order entry, hotel reservation systems, payroll, employee record keeping, and shipping. The Parks Canada campsite reservation system discussed in the chapter-ending case study is an example of a TPS.

At the operational level, tasks, resources, and goals are predefined and highly structured. The decision to grant credit to a customer, for instance, is made by a lower-level

management-level systems
strategic-level systems
transaction processing systems (TPS)

FIGURE 2-2   *The four major types of information systems.*

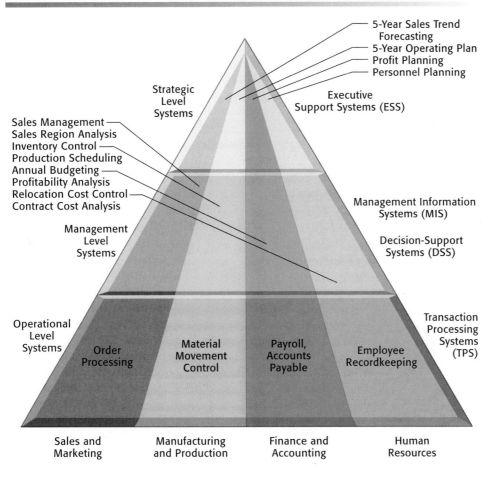

This figure provides examples of TPS, DSS, MIS, and ESS, showing the level of the organization and business function that each supports.

FUNCTIONAL AREAS

supervisor according to predefined criteria. All that must be determined is whether the customer meets the criteria.

Figure 2-3 depicts a payroll TPS, which is a typical accounting transaction processing system found in most firms. A payroll system keeps track of the money paid to employees.

TABLE 2-1   *Characteristics of Information Processing Systems*

TYPE OF SYSTEM	INFORMATION INPUTS	PROCESSING	INFORMATION OUTPUTS	USERS
ESS	Aggregate data; external, internal	Graphics; simulations; interactive	Projections; responses to queries	Senior managers
DSS	Low-volume data or massive databases optimized for data analysis; analytic models and data analysis tools	Interactive; simulations; analysis	Special reports; decision analyses; responses to queries	Professionals; staff managers
MIS	Summary transaction data; high-volume data; simple models	Routine reports; simple models; low-level analysis	Summary and exception reports	Middle managers
TPS	Transactions; events	Sorting; listing; merging; updating	Detailed reports; lists; summaries	Operations personnel; supervisors

FIGURE 2-3 *A symbolic representation for a payroll TPS.*

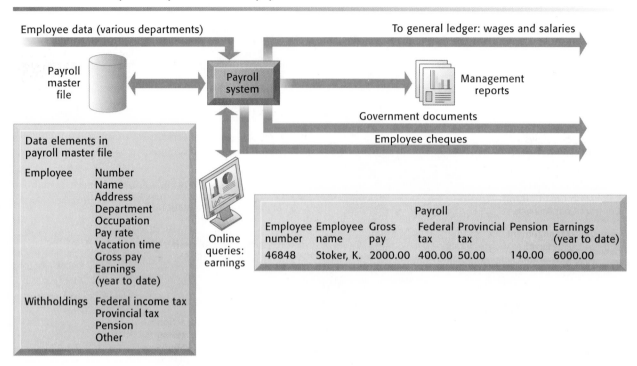

A payroll system is a typical accounting TPS that processes transactions such as employee time cards and changes in employee salaries and deductions. It keeps track of money paid to employees, withholding tax, and paycheques.

The master file is composed of discrete pieces of information (such as a name, address, or employee number) called data elements. Data are keyed into the system, updating the data elements. The elements in the master file are combined in different ways to make up reports of interest to management and government agencies and to send paycheques to employees. These TPS can generate other report combinations of existing data elements.

Other typical TPS applications are identified in Figure 2-4. The figure shows that there are five functional categories of TPS: sales/marketing, manufacturing/production, finance/accounting, human resources, and other types of TPS that are unique to a particular industry. The United Parcel Service (UPS) package tracking system described in Chapter 1 is an example of a manufacturing TPS. UPS sells package delivery services; the TPS system keeps track of all of its package shipment transactions.

Transaction processing systems are often so central to a business that TPS failure for a few hours can lead to a firm's demise and perhaps that of other firms linked to it. Imagine what would happen to UPS if its package tracking system were not working! What would the airlines do without their computerized reservation systems?

Managers need TPS to monitor the status of internal operations and the firm's relations with the external environment. TPS are also major producers of information for the other types of systems. (For example, the payroll system illustrated here, along with other accounting TPS, supplies data to the company's general ledger system, which is responsible for maintaining records of the firm's income and expenses and for producing reports such as income statements and balance sheets.)

Management Information Systems In Chapter 1, we define management information systems as the study of information systems in business and management. The term management information systems (MIS) also designates a specific category of information systems serving management-level functions. **Management information systems (MIS)** serve the management level of the organization, providing managers with reports and often online access to the organization's current performance and historical records. Typically, MIS are oriented almost exclusively to internal, not envi-

management information systems (MIS)

FIGURE 2-4   *Typical applications of TPS.*

TYPE OF TRANSACTION PROCESSING SYSTEM					
	Sales/ marketing systems	Manufacturing/ production systems	Finance/ accounting systems	Human resources systems	Other types (e.g., university)
Major functions of system	Customer service Sales management Promotion tracking Price changes Dealer communications	Scheduling Purchasing Shipping/receiving Operations	General ledger Billing Cost accounting	Personnel records Benefits Compensation Labour relations Training	Admissions Grade records Course records Alumni records
Major application systems	Sales order information system Sales commission system Sales support system	Machine control systems Purchase order systems Quality control systems	General ledger Payroll Accounts receivable/payable Funds management systems	Employee records Benefit systems Employee skills inventory	Registration system Student transcript system Curriculum class control systems Alumni benefactor system

There are five functional categories of TPS: sales/marketing, manufacturing/production, finance/accounting, human resources, and other types of systems specific to a particular industry. Within each of these major functions are subfunctions. For each of these subfunctions (e.g., sales management) there is a major application system.

ronmental or external, events. MIS primarily serve the functions of planning, controlling, and decision making at the management level. Generally, they depend on underlying transaction processing systems for their data.

MIS summarize and report on the company's basic operations. The basic transaction data from TPS are compressed, filtered, or summarized and are usually presented in long reports that are produced on a regular schedule. Figure 2-5 shows how typical MIS transform transaction-level data from inventory, production, and accounting into MIS files that are used to provide managers with reports. Figure 2-6 shows a sample report from this system.

MIS usually serve managers primarily interested in weekly, monthly, and yearly results, although some MIS enable managers to drill down to see daily or hourly data if required. MIS generally provide answers to routine questions that have been specified in advance and have a predefined procedure for answering them. For instance, MIS reports might list the total pounds of lettuce used this quarter by a fast-food chain or, as illustrated in Figure 2-6, compare total annual sales figures for specific products to planned targets. These systems are generally not flexible and have little analytical capability. Most MIS use simple routines such as summaries and comparisons, as opposed to sophisticated mathematical models or statistical techniques.

Decision-Support Systems Decision-support systems (DSS) also serve the management level of the organization. DSS help managers make decisions that are unique, rapidly changing, and not easily specified in advance. They address problems where the procedure for arriving at a solution may not be fully predefined. Although DSS use internal information from TPS and MIS, they often bring in information from external sources, such as current stock prices or product prices of competitors.

Clearly, by design, DSS have more analytical power than other systems. They use a variety of models to analyze data, or they condense large amounts of data into a form in which they can be analyzed by decision makers. DSS are designed so that users can work

decision-support systems (DSS)

FIGURE 2-5   *How management information systems obtain their data from the organization's TPS.*

In the system illustrated by this diagram, three TPS supply summarized transaction data to the MIS reporting system at the end of the time period. Managers gain access to the organizational data through the MIS, which provide them with the appropriate reports.

with them directly; these systems explicitly include user-friendly software. DSS are interactive; the user can change assumptions, ask new questions, and include new data.

A DSS for assessing patients' health under long-term care has been implemented in Ontario. Patients receiving health care at home or in nursing homes can be assessed using standardized categories developed at the University of Waterloo and the University of Alberta in conjunction with MED e-care Healthcare Solutions, Inc., a Toronto-based software development firm (www.mede-care.com). Once patients have been assessed with the DSS, their records can be transmitted electronically from one agency to another as needed, such as when a patient moves from home health care to a nursing home. Patients can be assessed repeatedly to determine how they are responding to treatment over time. Among the data elements that are assessed in the minimum data set standard categories (MDS) are cognitive abilities, memory, depression, history of falls, pressure ulcers, and incontinence. Patient care can be planned before the patient even arrives at the nursing home by using these assessment tools. MED e-care is also partnering with other Canadian firms, such as

FIGURE 2-6   *A sample MIS report.*

This report showing summarized annual sales data was produced by the MIS in Figure 2-5.

Consolidated Consumer Products Corporation Sales by Product and Sales Region: 2005

PRODUCT CODE	PRODUCT DESCRIPTION	SALES REGION	ACTUAL SALES	PLANNED	ACTUAL versus PLANNED
4469	Carpet Cleaner	Central	4,066,700	4,800,000	0.85
		Atlantic	3,778,112	3,750,000	1.01
		Prairies	4,867,001	4,600,000	1.06
		Western	4,003,440	4,400,000	0.91
		TOTAL	16,715,253	17,550,000	0.95
5674	Room Freshener	Central	3,676,700	3,900,000	0.94
		Atlantic	5,608,112	4,700,000	1.19
		Prairies	4,711,001	4,200,000	1.12
		Western	4,563,440	4,900,000	0.93
		TOTAL	18,559,253	17,700,000	1.05

Momentum Software, based in Winnipeg, Manitoba, to provide its MDS software to nursing homes throughout North America. Figure 2-7 illustrates the type of DSS now being developed. By using MDS and other standards being developed for patient assessment, many vendors can develop a variety of DSS tools for long-term care applications.

Other types of DSS are less model-driven, focusing instead on extracting useful information to support decision making from massive quantities of data. For example, Intrawest—the largest ski operator in North America—collects and stores vast amounts of customer data from its Web site, call centre, lodging reservations, ski schools, and ski equipment rental stores. It uses special software to analyze these data to determine the value, revenue potential, and loyalty of each customer so managers can make better decisions on how to target their marketing programs. The system segments customers into seven categories based on needs, attitudes, and behaviours, ranging from "passionate experts" to "value-minded family vacationers." The company then emails video clips that would appeal to each segment to encourage more visits to its resorts.

Sometimes you will hear DSS referred to as *business intelligence systems* because they focus on helping users make better business decisions. You will learn more about them in Chapter 15.

Executive Support Systems Senior managers use **executive support systems (ESS)** to help them make decisions. ESS serve the strategic level of the organization. They address nonroutine decisions requiring judgment, evaluation, and insight because there is no agreed-on procedure for arriving at a solution.

ESS are designed to incorporate data about external events, such as new tax laws or competitors, but they also draw summarized information from internal MIS and DSS. They filter, compress, and track critical data, displaying the data of greatest importance to senior managers. For example, the CEO of Leiner Health Products, the largest manufacturer of private-label vitamins and supplements in the United States, has ESS that provide, on his desktop, a minute-to-minute view of the firm's financial performance as measured by working capital, accounts receivable, accounts payable, cash flow, and inventory.

ESS employ the most advanced graphics software and can present graphs and data from many sources. Often the information is delivered to senior executives through a **portal**, which uses a Web interface to present integrated personalized business content. You will learn more about other applications of portals in Chapters 13, 14, and 16.

Unlike the other types of information systems, ESS are not designed primarily to solve specific problems. Instead, ESS provide a generalized computing and communications capacity that can be applied to a changing array of problems. Although many DSS are designed to be highly analytical, ESS tend to make less use of analytical models.

Questions ESS assist in answering include the following: In what business should we be? What are our competitors doing? What new acquisitions would protect us from

FIGURE 2-7 *DSS for assessing and monitoring patients.*

It is used daily by health care professionals responsible for providing health care to patients who require long-term care.

Patient Data

Direct Access Storage   Remote PC Running DSS Application   Reports for Patient Health Care Plan

PC

Reports

executive support systems (ESS)

portal

FIGURE 2-8   *Model of a typical executive support system.*

This system pools data from diverse internal and external sources and makes them available to executives in an easy-to-use form.

cyclical business swings? Which units should we sell to raise cash for acquisitions? Figure 2-8 illustrates a model of ESS. It consists of workstations with menus, interactive graphics, and communications capabilities that can be used to access historical and competitive data from internal corporate systems and external databases such as Dow Jones News/Retrieval or Ipsos-Reid, the Canadian polling firm. Because ESS are designed to be used by senior managers who often have little, if any, direct contact or experience with computer-based information systems, they incorporate easy-to-use graphic interfaces. More details on leading-edge applications of DSS and ESS can be found in Chapter 15.

Relationship of Systems to One Another

Figure 2-9 illustrates how the systems serving different levels in the organization are related to one another. TPS are typically a major source of data for other systems while ESS are primarily a recipient of data from lower-level systems. The other types of systems may exchange data with each other as well. Data may also be exchanged among systems serving different functional areas. For example, an order captured by a sales system may be transmitted to a manufacturing system as a transaction for producing or delivering the product specified in the order or to MIS for financial reporting.

FIGURE 2-9   *Interrelationships among systems.*

The various types of systems in the organization have interdependencies. TPS are major producers of information that is required by the other systems, which, in turn, produce information for other systems. These different types of systems have been loosely coupled in most organizations.

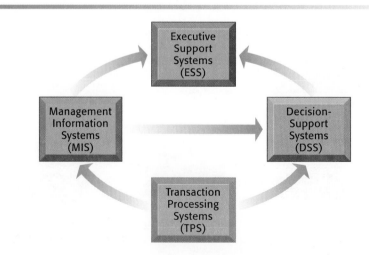

It is definitely advantageous to integrate these systems so that information can flow easily between different parts of the organization and provide management with an enterprise-wide view of how the organization is performing as a whole. But integration costs money, and integrating many different systems is extremely time consuming and complex. This is a major challenge for large organizations, which are typically saddled with hundreds, even thousands of different applications serving different levels and business functions. Each organization must weigh its needs for integrating systems against the difficulties of mounting a large-scale systems integration effort. Section 2.3 and Chapter 14 treat this issue in greater detail.

2.2   Systems From a Functional Perspective

Information systems can be classified by the specific organizational function they serve as well as by organizational level. We now describe typical information systems that support each of the major business functions and provide examples of functional applications for each organizational level.

Sales and Marketing Systems

The sales and marketing function is responsible for selling the organization's products or services. Marketing is concerned with identifying the customers for the firm's products or services, determining what customers need or want, planning and developing products and services to meet their needs, and advertising and promoting these products and services. Sales is concerned with contacting customers, selling the products and services, taking orders, and following up on sales. **Sales and marketing information systems** support these activities.

Table 2-2 shows that information systems are used in sales and marketing in a number of ways. At the strategic level, sales and marketing systems monitor trends affecting new products and sales opportunities, support planning for new products and services, and monitor the performance of competitors. At the management level, sales and marketing systems support market research, advertising and promotional campaigns, and pricing decisions. They analyze sales performance and the performance of the sales staff. At the operational level, sales and marketing systems assist in locating and contacting prospective customers, tracking sales, processing orders, and providing customer service support.

Review Figure 2-6. It shows the output of a typical sales information system at the management level. The system consolidates data about each item sold (such as the product code, product description, and price) for further management analysis. Company managers examine these sales data to monitor sales activity and buying trends.

Manufacturing and Production Systems

The manufacturing and production function is responsible for actually producing the firm's goods and services. Manufacturing and production systems deal with the planning,

TABLE 2-2   *Examples of Sales and Marketing Information Systems*

SYSTEM	DESCRIPTION	ORGANIZATIONAL LEVEL
Order processing	Enter, process, and track orders	Operational
Pricing analysis	Determine prices for products and services	Management
Sales trend forecasting	Prepare five-year sales forecasts	Strategic

sales and marketing information systems

Information systems can guide the actions of machines and equipment to help pharmaceutical and other types of firms monitor and control the manufacturing process.

development, and maintenance of production facilities; the establishment of production goals; the acquisition, storage, and availability of production materials; and the scheduling of equipment, facilities, materials, and labour required to fashion finished products. **Manufacturing and production information systems** support these activities.

Table 2-3 shows some typical manufacturing and production information systems arranged by organizational level. Strategic-level manufacturing systems deal with the firm's long-term manufacturing goals, such as where to locate new plants or whether to invest in new manufacturing technology. At the management level, manufacturing and production systems analyze and monitor manufacturing and production costs and resources. Operational manufacturing and production systems deal with the status of production tasks.

Most manufacturing and production systems use some sort of inventory system, as illustrated in Figure 2-10. Data about each item in inventory, such as the number of units depleted because of a shipment or purchase or the number of units replenished by reordering or returns, are either scanned or keyed into the system. The inventory master file contains basic data about each item, including the unique identification code for each item, a description of the item, the number of units on hand, the number of units on order, and the reorder point (the number of units in inventory that triggers a decision to reorder to prevent a stockout). Companies can estimate the number of items to reorder, or they can use a formula for calculating the least expensive quantity to reorder called the *economic order quantity*. The system produces reports that give information about such things as the number of each item available in inventory, the number of units of each item to reorder, or items in inventory that must be replenished.

Product life cycle management (PLM) systems are one type of manufacturing and production system that have become increasingly valuable in the automotive, aerospace, and consumer products industries. PLM systems are based on a data repository that organizes every piece of information that goes into making a particular product, such as formula cards, packaging information, shipping specifications, and patent data. Once all these data are available, companies can select and combine the data they need to serve specific functions. For example, designers and engineers can use the data to determine which parts are needed for a new design while retailers can use the data to determine shelf height and how materials should be stored in warehouses.

For many years, engineering-intensive industries have used **computer-aided design (CAD)** systems to automate the modelling and design of their products. This sophisticated graphics software enables users to create a digital model of a part, a product, or a structure and make changes to the design on the computer without having to build physical prototypes. PLM software goes beyond CAD software to include not only automated modelling and design capabilities but also tools to help companies manage and automate

manufacturing and production information systems

product life cycle management (PLM) systems

computer-aided design (CAD)

TABLE 2-3 *Examples of Manufacturing and Production Information Systems*

SYSTEM	DESCRIPTION	ORGANIZATIONAL LEVEL
Machine control	Control the actions of machines and equipment	Operational
Production planning	Decide when and how many products should be produced	Management
Facilities location	Decide where to locate new production facilities	Strategic

FIGURE 2-10 *Overview of an inventory system.*

Shipment and order data

Inventory
Control
System

Inventory
master
file

**Data elements in
inventory master file:**

Item code
Description
Units on hand
Units on order
Reorder point

Online
queries

Management
reports

This system provides information
about the number of items available in inventory to support manufacturing and production activities.

**Inventory Status Report
Report Date: 1/14/2005**

Item Code	Description	Units on Hand	Units on Order
6361	Fan belt	10,211	0
4466	Power cord	55,710	88,660
9313	Condenser	663	10,200
8808	Paint sprayer	11,242	0

materials sourcing, engineering change orders, and product documentation, such as test
results, product packaging, and post-sales data. The Window on Organizations describes
how these systems are providing new sources of value.

WINDOW ON ORGANIZATIONS

Product Life Cycle Management Systems: Faster Products, Faster Processes

What if there were a way to determine automatically the feasibility of a new product's design? What if all the information
related to that product—the marketing plan, design criteria,
product specifications, testing data, and packaging data— were
immediately available to make sure that the design could be
easily manufactured and sold? What if this information were
instantly available to designers, engineers, suppliers, marketing
staff, and anyone else involved in the development and rollout
of a new product? Enter product life cycle management (PLM)
systems.

Nissan Diesel Motor Company, established in 1950, manufactures trucks and buses. Its product line includes a wide
range of light-, medium-, and heavy-duty vehicles, buses and
bus chassis, engines, vehicle components, and special-purpose
engines. The company has distributors in nearly 60 countries
around the world.

Developing a truck model generates vast amounts of data to
manage and involves more components and complex assembly
combinations than developing passenger cars. Like other truck
manufacturers, Nissan Diesel Motor Company faced a challenge in keeping this complex product data organized. It
turned to IBM and Dassault Systems' ENOVIA Product Life
Cycle Management product for a solution

Nissan Diesel uses ENOVIA's Digital Mock-Up (DMU)
Navigator to manage and connect truck component data as a
vehicle is developed from design to manufacturing. DMU simulates Nissan Diesel's manufacturing processes, so the com-

pany can detect errors during early states of production planning. This tool also manages truck components so that engineers can easily search for and work on parts. ENOVIA links
product data and processes so that each Nissan development
team member can share comprehensive and up-to-date product information throughout the entire development cycle. This
management system configuration has shortened Nissan's cycle
time for creating a vehicle layout by 90 percent.

Waters Corporation is a leading supplier of high-performance liquid chromatography instrumentation, thermal analysis, and mass spectrometry products that provide fundamental
data on the composition of natural products and synthetic
chemical mixtures, as well as the physical properties of materials. The company introduces several new products each year.
Waters implemented mySAP Product Lifecycle Management
software to help those involved in designing, maintaining, and
manufacturing products share information more easily.

Waters had maintained data separately for product development and production, making it difficult to find out materials costs early in the development cycle. The company migrated
120 000 different files and pieces of data from its old systems to
mySAP PLM to define the mechanical, electrical, and software
components of its products.

Waters designers begin with a concept and move through
the engineering design phases to a preliminary version of the
product. After additional testing and design work, the product
is moved to prerelease/preproduction status. The mySAP PLM

software moves all supporting documents and bills of material for the product from one stage to another. It also introduces product data to manufacturing engineers and other specialists as product data and configurations are being created. As these configurations and data stabilize, marketing staff can view them to see what data and configurations will be introduced into the marketplace.

Jostens, known for its custom high school class rings, graduation announcements, and yearbooks, adopted UGS Corporation's PLM software to help it manage its vast array of product details. The company signs about 5000 to 10 000 new agreements to produce class rings for schools each year. Each school has a specific mascot and other features that have to be designed into the rings. Once those parts of the rings are designed, students select additional features they want, such as an etching of an activity. That means many thousands of customized rings must be developed and tracked. The UGS PLM software reduces the time required to produce the moulds for the rings.

Loewen, a Canadian specialty wood window manufacturer based in Steinbach, Manitoba, has standard products that, when combined with special features and designs, create more

than 4.3 trillion potential options. To speed up design and production, the company needed to find a better way to manage this vast amount of product data. PLM software automatically determines the feasibility of a new product's design and enables multiple designers to work simultaneously on the same project and share design information with potential customers. The system enables engineers to know automatically which parts work together, while production groups can use the data to achieve savings by consolidating materials and orders. Loewen hopes that PLM will increase productivity by 30 percent while saving as much as $183,000 per year.

To Think About: How do project life cycle management systems provide value for these companies? Should every company that manufactures products use this software? Explain your answer.

Sources: Debra D'Agostino, "PLM: The Means of Production," *eWeek*, February 7, 2004; Beth Bacheldor, "Deeper Than Designs," *Information Week*, August 9, 2004, and "Product Life-Cycle Management Market Ramps Up," *Information Week*, July 19, 2004; and Dassault Systems, "Nissan Diesel Develops Vehicle Configuration Management System with PLM Solutions from IBM and Dassault Systems," July 12, 2004.

Finance and Accounting Systems

The finance function is responsible for managing the firm's financial assets, such as cash, stocks, bonds, and other investments, to maximize the return on these financial assets. The finance function is also in charge of managing the capitalization of the firm (finding new financial assets in stocks, bonds, or other forms of debt). To determine whether the firm is getting the best return on its investments, the finance function must obtain a considerable amount of information from sources external to the firm.

The accounting function is responsible for maintaining and managing the firm's financial records—receipts, disbursements, depreciation and payroll—to account for the flow of funds in a firm. Finance and accounting share related problems—how to keep track of a firm's financial assets and fund flows. They provide answers to questions such as: What is the current inventory of financial assets? What records exist for disbursements, receipts, payroll, and other fund flows?

Table 2-4 shows some of the typical **finance and accounting information systems** found in large organizations. Strategic-level systems for the finance and accounting function establish long-term investment goals for the firm and provide long-range forecasts of the firm's financial performance. At the management level, information systems help managers oversee and control the firm's financial resources. Operational systems in finance and accounting track the flow of funds in the firm through transactions and records such as paycheques, payments to vendors, securities reports, and receipts. Review Figure 2-3, which illustrates a payroll system, a typical accounting transaction processing system found in all businesses with employees.

finance and accounting information systems

TABLE 2-4 *Examples of Finance and Accounting Information Systems*

SYSTEM	DESCRIPTION	ORGANIZATIONAL LEVEL
Accounts receivable	Tracks money owed the firm	Operational
Budgeting	Prepares short-term budgets	Management
Profit planning	Plans long-term profits	Strategic

Human Resources Systems

The human resources function is responsible for attracting, developing, and maintaining the firm's workforce. **Human resources information systems** support activities such as identifying potential employees, maintaining complete records on existing employees, and creating programs to develop employees' talents and skills.

Strategic-level human resources systems identify personnel requirements (skills, educational level, types of positions, number of positions, and cost) for meeting the firm's long-term business plans. At the management level, human resources systems help managers monitor and analyze the recruitment, allocation, and compensation of employees. Human resources operational systems track the recruitment and placement of the firm's employees (see Table 2-5).

Figure 2-11 shows how human resources systems can be accessed through the Internet. Figure 2-12 illustrates a typical human resources transaction processing system for employee record keeping. It maintains basic employee data, such as the employee's name, age, sex, marital status, address, educational background, salary, job title, date of hire, and date of termination. The system can produce a variety of reports, such as lists of newly hired employees, employees who have been terminated or are on leaves of absence, employees classified by job type or educational level, or employee job performance evaluations. These systems are typically designed to provide data that can satisfy federal and provincial record-keeping requirements for Equal Employment Opportunity (EEO) and other purposes.

TABLE 2-5   *Examples of Human Resources Information Systems*

SYSTEM	DESCRIPTION	ORGANIZATIONAL LEVEL
Training and development	Tracks employee training, skills, and performance appraisals	Operational
Compensation analysis	Monitors the range and distribution of employee wages, salaries, and benefits	Management
Human resources planning	Plans the long-term labour force needs of the organization	Strategic

FIGURE 2-11   *Best Software's human resources and payroll management software.*

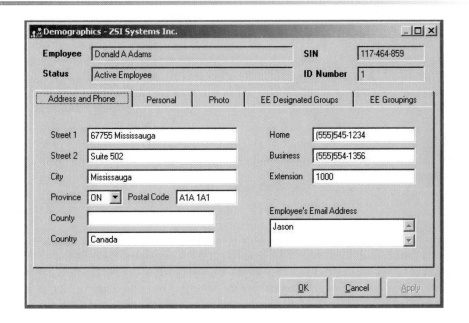

Best Software's ABRA Suite software for human resources and payroll management includes online tools to view and change employment and payroll information. Human resources information systems reduce administrative costs, provide faster service to employees, and help firms manage their workforce.

human resources information systems

FIGURE 2-12 *An employee record-keeping system.*

This system maintains data on the firm's employees to support the human resources function.

Data elements in employee master file:

Employee: Number
Name
Address
Department
Age
Marital status
Sex
Salary
Educational background
Job title
Date of hire
Date of termination
Termination reason

Termination Report			
Date	Name	Number	Reason
11/12/2004	John Hansen	29433	Position eliminated
12/1/2004	Patricia Carlyle	14327	Retired
1/12/2005	Ellen Quimby	21224	Left company

2.3 Integrating Functions and Business Processes: Introduction to Enterprise Applications

One of the major challenges facing firms today is putting together the information stored in the systems we have just described to make information flow across the enterprise. Electronic commerce, electronic business, and intensifying global competition are forcing firms to focus on speed to market, improved customer service, and more efficient execution. The flow of information and work needs to be orchestrated so that the organization can perform like a well-oiled machine. These changes require powerful new systems that can integrate information from many different functional areas and organizational units and coordinate firm activities with those of suppliers and other business partners.

Business Processes and Information Systems

The new digital firm business environment requires companies to think more strategically about their business processes, which we introduced in Chapter 1. Business processes refer to sets of logically related activities for accomplishing a specific business result. Business processes also refer to the unique ways in which organizations and management coordinate these activities. A company's business processes can be a source of competitive strength if they enable the company to innovate or execute better than its rivals. Business processes can also be liabilities if they are based on outdated ways of working that impede organizational responsiveness and efficiency.

Some business processes support the major functional areas of the firm; others are cross-functional. Table 2-6 describes some typical business processes for each of the functional areas.

Many business processes are cross-functional, transcending the boundaries between sales, marketing, manufacturing, and research and development. These cross-functional processes cut across the traditional organizational structure, grouping employees from different functional specialties to complete a piece of work. For example, the order fulfillment process at many companies requires cooperation among the sales function (receiving the

TABLE 2-6 *Examples of Functional Business Processes*

FUNCTIONAL AREA	BUSINESS PROCESS
Manufacturing and production	Assembling the product Checking for quality Producing bills of materials
Sales and marketing	Identifying customers Making customers aware of the product Selling the product
Finance and accounting	Paying creditors Creating financial statements Managing cash accounts
Human resources	Hiring employees Evaluating employees' job performance Enrolling employees in benefits plans

order, entering the order), the accounting function (credit checking and billing for the order), and the manufacturing function (assembling and shipping the order). Figure 2-13 illustrates how this cross-functional process might work. Information systems support these cross-functional processes as well as processes for the separate business functions.

Systems for Enterprise-Wide Process Integration

Today's firms are finding that they can become more flexible and productive by coordinating their business processes more closely and, in some cases, integrating these processes so they focus on efficient management of resources and customer service. **Enterprise applications** are designed to support organization-wide process coordination and integration. These enterprise applications consist of enterprise systems, supply chain management systems, customer relationship management systems, and knowledge management systems. Each of these enterprise applications integrates a related set of functions and business processes to enhance the performance of the organization as a whole.

Generally, these more contemporary systems take advantage of corporate intranets and Web technologies that enable the efficient transfer of information within the firm and to

FIGURE 2-13   *The order fulfillment process.*

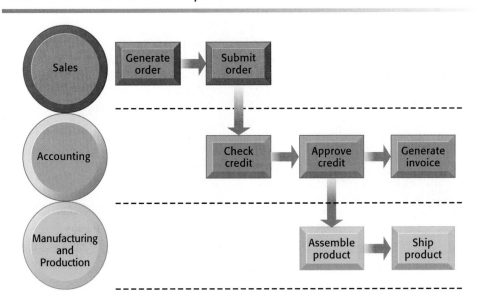

Generating and fulfilling an order is a multi-step process involving activities performed by the sales, manufacturing and production, and accounting functions.

enterprise applications

partner firms. These systems are inherently cross-level, cross-functional, and business-process oriented. Figure 2-14 shows that the architecture for these enterprise applications encompasses processes spanning the entire organization and, in some cases, extending beyond the organization to customers, suppliers, and other key business partners.

Enterprise systems create an integrated organization-wide platform to coordinate key internal processes of the firm. Information systems for supply chain management (SCM) and customer relationship management (CRM) can help coordinate processes for managing the firm's relationships with its suppliers and customers. Knowledge management systems enable organizations to better manage processes for capturing and applying knowledge and expertise. Collectively, these four systems represent the areas in which corporations are digitally integrating their information flows and making major information system investments.

Overview of Enterprise Applications

We next look briefly at each of the major enterprise applications to see how they fit into the overall information architecture of the enterprise. We examine enterprise systems and systems for supply chain management and customer relationship management in greater detail in Chapter 14 and cover knowledge management applications in Chapter 16.

Overview of Enterprise Systems A large organization typically has many different kinds of information systems that support different functions, organizational levels, and business processes. Most of these systems were built around different functions, business units, and business processes that do not "talk" to each other and thus can-

FIGURE 2-14   *Enterprise application architecture.*

Enterprise applications automate processes that span multiple business functions and organizational levels and may extend outside the organization.

FIGURE 2-15   *Traditional view of systems.*

In most organizations today, separate systems built over a long period of time support discrete business processes and discrete segments of the business value chain. The organization's systems rarely include vendors and customers.

not automatically exchange information. Managers might have a hard time assembling the data they need for a comprehensive, overall picture of the organization's operations. For instance, sales personnel could not tell at the time they place an order whether the items that were ordered were in inventory; customers could not track their orders; and manufacturing could not communicate easily with finance to plan for new production. This fragmentation of data in hundreds of separate systems could have a negative impact on organizational efficiency and business performance. Figure 2-15 illustrates the traditional arrangement of information systems.

Enterprise systems, also known as *enterprise resource planning (ERP) systems*, solve this problem by providing a single information system for organization-wide coordination and integration of key business processes. Information that was previously fragmented in different systems can seamlessly flow throughout the firm so that it can be shared by business processes in manufacturing, accounting, human resources, and other areas of the firm. Discrete business processes from sales, production, finance, and logistics can be integrated into company-wide business processes that flow across organizational levels and functions. Figure 2-16 illustrates how enterprise systems work.

The enterprise system collects data from various key business processes in manufacturing and production, finance and accounting, sales and marketing, and human resources and stores the data in a single comprehensive data repository where they can be used by other parts of the business. Managers emerge with more precise and timely information for coordinating the daily operations of the business and a firm-wide view of business processes and information flows.

enterprise systems

FIGURE 2-16   *Enterprise systems.*

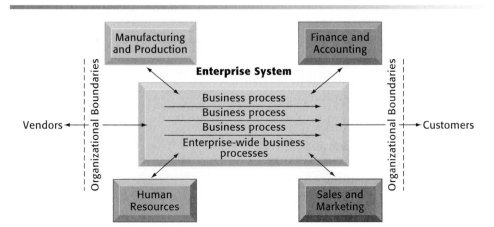

Enterprise systems integrate the key business processes of an entire firm into a single software system that enables information to flow seamlessly throughout the organization. These systems focus primarily on internal processes but may include transactions with customers and vendors.

For example, when a sales representative in Brussels enters a customer order, the data flows automatically to others in the company who need to see it. The factory in Hong Kong receives the order and begins production. The warehouse checks its progress online and schedules the shipment date. The warehouse can check its stock of parts and replenish whatever the factory has depleted. The enterprise system stores production information where it can be accessed by customer service representatives to track the progress of the order through every step of the manufacturing process. Updated sales and production data automatically flow to the accounting department. The system transmits information for calculating the salesperson's commission to the payroll department. The system also automatically recalculates the company's balance sheets, accounts receivable and payable ledgers, cost-centre accounts, and available cash. Corporate headquarters in London can view up-to-the-minute data on sales, inventory, and production at every step of the process, as well as updated sales and production forecasts and calculations of product cost and availability. Chapter 14 provides more detail on these types of enterprise system capabilities.

Overview of Supply Chain Management Systems

Supply chain management (SCM) systems are more outward facing, focusing on helping the firm manage its relationship with suppliers to optimize the planning, sourcing, manufacturing, and delivery of products and services. These systems provide information to help suppliers, purchasing firms, distributors, and logistics companies coordinate, schedule, and control business processes for procurement, production, inventory management, and delivery of products and services.

Supply chain management systems are one type of **interorganizational system** because they automate the flow of information across organizational boundaries. A firm using a supply chain management system would exchange information with its suppliers about availability of materials and components, delivery dates for shipments of supplies, and production requirements. It might also use the system to exchange information with its distributors about inventory levels, the status of orders being fulfilled, or delivery dates for shipments of finished goods. You will find examples of other types of interorganizational information systems throughout this text because these systems make it possible for firms to link electronically to customers and to outsource their work to other companies.

Table 2-7 describes how firms can benefit from supply chain management systems. The ultimate objective is to get the right amount of their products from their source to their point of consumption with the least amount of time and with the lowest cost. Supply chain management systems can be built using intranets, extranets, or special supply chain management software.

The supply chain management systems used by the Alberta Gaming and Liquor Commission (AGLC) are described in the Window on Technology. The AGLC needed to manage its distribution activities to cut costs and boost efficiency. It implemented a new system for warehouse management and transportation management by contracting with another company to provide those services. These systems enable the AGLC to reduce inventory levels while avoiding stockouts.

TABLE 2-7   *How Information Systems Facilitate Supply Chain Management*

INFORMATION FROM SUPPLY CHAIN MANAGEMENT SYSTEMS HELPS FIRMS:
Decide when and what to produce, store, and move
Rapidly communicate orders
Track the status of orders
Check inventory availability and monitor inventory levels
Reduce inventory, transportation, and warehousing costs
Track shipments
Plan production based on actual customer demand
Rapidly communicate changes in product design

supply chain management (SCM) systems

interorganizational system

WINDOW ON TECHNOLOGY

AGLC Supplies Liquor Efficiently

Eight years of prohibition in Alberta came to an end when 51 000 Albertans signed a plebiscite urging the Alberta government to allow the legal sale of liquor in the province. The first two of Alberta's legal liquor stores opened in 1924. The government operated these liquor stores, closely monitored by the newly formed Alberta Liquor Control Board (ALCB).

Subsequently, the Liquor Control Act was amended many times to allow the sale of liquor in clubs and canteens, cold beer stores, and self-serve liquor stores, and the minimum legal age for drinking was reduced from 21 to 18 years. In 1993, liquor retailing was privatized. In 1996, The Alberta Gaming and Liquor Commission (AGLC) was created by combining the responsibilities and operations of the Alberta Liquor Control Board, Alberta Lotteries, the Alberta Gaming Commission, Alberta Lotteries and Gaming, and the Gaming Control Branch.

Today there are more than 1100 private liquor retail outlets in Alberta, employing more than 4000 people—a 300 percent growth rate since privatization. In addition, liquor sales have almost doubled in the 12 years since privatization. When liquor retailing in Alberta was privatized, the AGLC ceased to provide warehousing, transportation, and logistics-related systems. The AGLC turned to the Tibbett and Britten Group Americas (TBGA) for these important services.

TBGA established a subsidiary company, Connect Logistics Services, in 1994 to serve the alcohol beverage industry, and in particular, the ALCB, now the AGLC. (In 2004, Tibbett & Britten became part of Exel.) Retailers, licensed establishments, and producers and distributors of spirits, wine, coolers, and imported beer products receive a complete range of supply chain services—such as bonded warehousing (in St. Albert, Alberta and Vancouver, British Columbia), retail and on-premise delivery, demand forecasting and inventory replenishment, and order management (via its call centre and the Internet). The demand management services area (DMS) is operated by a specialist TBGA team, working with Connect Logistics, dedicated to helping manufacturers and retailers achieve better balanced and timed deployment of inventory.

With the appointment of TBGA to operate the distribution facility in St. Albert, Alberta, DMS took on the task of designing and implementing the demand planning and replenishment processes. DMS makes inventory management more economical and effective by synchronising strategic, operational, and tactical planning.

Through DMS, businesses can forecast demand more accurately—down to the level of "by item by shipping point"—by identifying and analyzing marketing factors, seasonality aspects, and other conditions driving sales. They can then respond proactively to changes in demand: supply can be procured on a priority basis and products can be deployed dynamically within the supply chain. This in turn maximizes sales and

customer satisfaction, and investment costs of buffer stocks or risking stock-outs can be avoided.

"What-if" situations can be explored through the use of advanced tools and proven planning processes, thus saving money and resources from being wasted on less-than-optimal solutions. By developing a single plan and implementing it across an entire supply chain, businesses can meet customer requirements consistently and also reduce costs, in spite of the varying complexities of the chain or demand.

To handle its 40 000 square metre warehouse, Connect Logistics hired all the existing government employees, and most are still employed there. At the start of the contract, there were a number of major changes in the industry that Connect Logistics had to orchestrate; about 200 government-run stores were replaced by more than 1100 smaller independent retailers. The positive outcome for the AGLC was that it was able to offer a larger variety of products. Alcohol consumption has not increased (even though revenues have doubled) generally in Alberta; however, consumers now have a wider choice of more than 13 000 products—up from 3300 in 1994.

Following the success in Alberta, Connect Logistics won the British Columbia Liquor Distribution Branch (BCLDB) contract in 1996 to operate that province's Agent Stocking Program in a 16 500 square metre bonded warehouse for importers, agents, and distributors dealing with import products in quantities beyond the capacities of government warehouses.

At the Alberta site, products from more than 210 agents, representing producers from around the world, are received and shipped to 1500 licensees and retail stores. Approximately 17 million cases pass through the site each year, and more than 11 000 SKUs are in stock at any given time. One hundred and eighty team members work in the warehouse five days a week, in two shifts.

The stock in the warehouse is held on a consignment basis; that is, the agent or producer has ownership until it is shipped to the retailer or licensed establishment. Either the agents can manage their own inventory levels in the Connect warehouse, or Connect's sister company, Supply Logistics, can manage their inventory.

Seven unmanned automated storage and retrieval (ASRS) cranes service a 21 000-pallet, high-bay area where products are stored. Another area that has conventional pallet racking and block stacking provides a further 16 000 pallet positions. All order assemblers use Vocollect, voice-picking technology, and at case level, they spot-check with radio frequency terminals prior to dispatch. The Alberta team holds a near-perfect order fulfillment record.

Connect Logistics manages physical distribution, which is subcontracted to local carriers. Specific routes are put out to tender annually, and at present, 13 carriers service Connect's customers in Alberta and make deliveries to all outlets serving alcoholic beverages, such as hotels, bars, stores, and restaurants that wish to deal directly with the distribution centre.

Consumers, agents, government, and licensees have all enjoyed various benefits with the steady improvements that have occurred over the years. With more efficient systems, customer service has been enhanced and the cost of operations reduced. Connect Logistics has also installed Manugistics, a demand-planning software system, and J.D. Edwards 7.3 (now a part of Oracle), an order and warehouse management system.

As well, a freight auditing system and a Web-based ordering and information inquiry system have been introduced by Connect at www.liquorconnect.com. Licensees and retailers can now place orders from an online catalogue. The system also helps agents monitor their inventory levels online.

Based on historical sales, the DMS developers built forecasting models that included lead times and ordering parameters in the software to establish warehouse safety stocks. They took vendor promotional activity into consideration and shared

seasonal forecasts with manufacturers in their effort to synchronize demand with production. Through software integration, businesses can replenish orders generated from sales data captured by the warehouse system.

As a result, the DMS demand planning and replenishment processes have permitted distillers and manufacturers to reduce costs, improve service to retail outlets, and reduce inventory levels on specific SKUs by up to 25 percent.

To Think About: How did these supply chain management systems change the way the Alberta AGLC worked? What value did they provide?

Sources: "Case Study: Canada–Alberta LGC," www.tibbett-britten.com/cs/algc-can.php, accessed July 8, 2005; "Case Study: North America: Demand Management Services (DMS)," www.tibbett-britten.com/cs/dms-na.php, accessed July 8, 2005; "History of Gaming in Alberta," www.gaming.gov.ab.ca/who/gaming_history.asp, accessed September 21, 2005; "A Short History of Liquor Regulations in Alberta 1924–2005," www.aglc.gov.ab.ca/liquor/liquor_general/liquor_history.asp, accessed September 21, 2005; "Before and After Privatization," www.gaming.gov.ab.ca/who/before_after.asp, accessed September 21, 2005.

Overview of Customer Relationship Management Systems

Instead of treating customers as exploitable sources of income, businesses are now viewing them as long-term assets to be nurtured through customer relationship management. **Customer relationship management (CRM) systems** focus on coordinating all of the business processes surrounding the firm's interactions with its customers in sales, marketing, and service to optimize revenue, customer satisfaction, and customer retention. The ideal CRM system provides end-to-end customer care from receipt of an order through product delivery.

In the past, a firm's processes for sales, service, and marketing were highly compartmentalized, and these departments did not share much essential customer information. Some information on a specific customer might be stored and organized in terms of that person's account with the company. Other pieces of information about the same customer might be organized by products that were purchased. There was no way to consolidate all of this information to provide a unified view of a customer across the company. CRM systems try to solve this problem by integrating the firm's customer-related processes and consolidating customer information from multiple communication channels—telephone, email, wireless devices, or the Web—so that the firm can present one coherent face to the customer (see Figure 2-17).

Good CRM systems provide data and analytical tools for answering questions such as these: What is the value of a particular customer to the firm over his or her lifetime? Who are our most loyal customers? (It can cost six times more to sell to a new customer than to an existing customer.) Who are our most profitable customers? What do these profitable customers want to buy? Firms can then use the answers to these questions to acquire new customers, provide better service and support to existing customers, customize their offerings more precisely to customer preferences, and provide ongoing value to retain profitable customers (see Figure 2-18).

Overview of Knowledge Management Systems

The value of a firm's products and services is based not only on its physical resources but also on intangible knowledge assets. Some firms can perform better than others because they have better knowledge about how to create, produce, and deliver products and services. This firm knowledge is difficult to imitate, unique, and can be leveraged into long-term strategic benefit.

customer relationship management (CRM) system

FIGURE 2-17   *Customer relationship management (CRM).*

Customer relationship management systems examine customers from a multifaceted perspective. These systems use a set of integrated applications to address all aspects of the customer relationship, including customer service, sales, and marketing.

Knowledge management systems collect all relevant knowledge and experience in the firm and make it available wherever and whenever it is needed to support business processes and management decisions. They also link the firm to external sources of knowledge.

Knowledge management systems support processes for acquiring, storing, distributing, and applying knowledge, as well as processes for creating new knowledge and integrating it into the organization. They include enterprise-wide systems for managing and distributing documents, graphics, and other digital knowledge objects, systems for creating corporate knowledge directories of employees with special areas of expertise, office systems for distributing knowledge and information, and knowledge work systems to facilitate knowledge creation. Other knowledge management applications are expert systems that codify the knowledge of experts in information systems that can be used by other members of the organization and tools for knowledge discovery that recognize patterns and important relationships in large pools of data. Table 2-8 provides examples of knowledge management systems, and Chapter 16 describes these knowledge management applications in detail.

knowledge management systems

FIGURE 2-18   *Results of using customer relationship management software.*

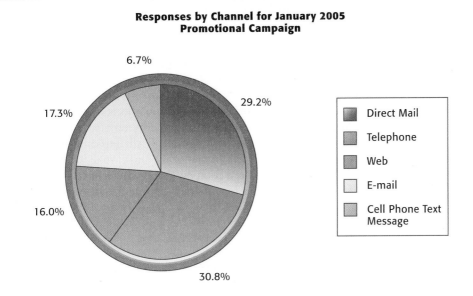

Responses by Channel for January 2005 Promotional Campaign

- 6.7%
- 29.2%
- 17.3%
- 16.0%
- 30.8%

Legend:
- Direct Mail
- Telephone
- Web
- E-mail
- Cell Phone Text Message

Customer relationship management software provides a single point through which users can manage and evaluate marketing campaigns across multiple channels, including email, direct mail, telephone, the Web, and wireless messages.

TABLE 2-8 *Knowledge Management Systems in the Organization*

ORGANIZATIONAL PROCESS	ROLE OF KNOWLEDGE MANAGEMENT SYSTEMS
Acquiring knowledge	Knowledge discovery systems can find patterns or relationships in vast quantities of data while other intelligent techniques can find solutions to problems that are too complex to be solved by humans. Knowledge work systems provide knowledge workers with graphics, analytical, communication, and document management tools, as well as access to internal and external sources of data to help them generate new ideas. Knowledge networks provide online directories of employees with special areas of expertise.
Storing knowledge	Knowledge repositories collect documents and digital media containing knowledge from internal and external sources in a single location. Expert systems can elicit and incorporate expertise from human experts and embed it in software systems that can be accessed by other members of the organization.
Distributing knowledge	Office systems and communication tools can distribute documents and other forms of information among information and knowledge workers and link offices to other business units inside and outside the firm. Group collaboration systems can help employees access and work simultaneously on the same document from many different locations and coordinate their activities.
Applying knowledge	Organizational knowledge can be incorporated into management decision making through decision-support systems and incorporated into important business processes by being captured by key application systems, including enterprise applications.

Management Opportunities, Challenges, and Solutions

Organizations still need different types of information systems serving various organizational levels, functions, and business processes, and they increasingly need systems providing enterprise-wide integration. These needs create both opportunities and challenges.

Opportunities

Businesses face extraordinary opportunities to apply information systems throughout the firm to achieve higher levels of productivity, earnings, and, ultimately, higher share prices. Today information systems support virtually all levels and functions in the firm. In addition, they enhance decision making of both managers and employees, providing information where and when it is needed in a format that is easily integrated into everyday business life. But there are challenges to achieving these objectives.

Management Challenges

Integration and the Whole Firm View In the past, information systems were built to serve the narrow interests of different business functions (such as marketing, finance, or operations) or to serve a specific group of decision makers (such as middle managers). The problem with this approach is that it results in the building of thousands of systems that cannot share information with one another and it makes it difficult for managers to obtain the information they need to operate the whole firm. Building systems that serve specific interests in the firm but can also be integrated to provide firm-wide information is a challenge.

Management and Employee Training With so many systems in a large business firm, and with fairly high employee turnover typical of the last few years, training people how to use existing systems and learn new systems is a major challenge. Obviously, without training or when training is limited, employees and managers cannot use information systems to maximum advantage, and the result can be a low return on investment in systems.

Accounting for the Cost of Systems and Managing Demand for Systems As the cost of information falls because of the power of information technology, demands for information and technology services proliferate throughout the firm. Unfortunately, if employees and managers believe information services are free, their demands will be infinite. One of the challenges facing business managers is understanding which systems are truly necessary and truly productive with high returns on investment and which systems are merely conveniences that cost a great deal but deliver little.

Solution Guidelines

A number of solutions exist to the challenges we have just described.

Inventorying the Firm's Information Systems for a 360-Degree View of Information You should develop a list of firm-wide information requirements to get a 360-degree view of the most important information needs for your company as a whole. Once you have this list developed, examine how your existing systems— most developed to service specific groups and levels in the firm—provide this information to corporate-wide systems. You will need to inventory your firm's existing information systems and those under construction. (Many firms have no idea of all the systems in their firm or what information they contain.) Identify each system, and understand which group or level in the firm benefits from the system.

Employee and Management Education Systems are usually not obvious or self-taught for most people. You will need to ensure that you understand how much training is required to support new systems, and budget accordingly. Once you have an inventory of just the major systems in a firm that are used every day by thousands of employees, try to identify how they learn to use the systems, how effective their training is, and how well they use the systems. Do they exploit all the potential value built into the systems?

Accounting for the Costs and Benefits of Information Systems To manage the demand for information services, you will need a specific accounting system. It is worthwhile to examine the methods used in your industry and by industry competitors to account for their information systems budgets. Your system should use some method for charging the budgets of various divisions, departments, and groups that directly benefit from a system. And there are other services that should be charged to any group because they are a part of the firm's general IT infrastructure (described in Chapter 5) and serve everyone. For instance, you would not want to charge various groups for Internet or intranet services because they are services provided to everyone in the firm. However, you would want to charge the manufacturing division for a production control system because it benefits that division exclusively. Equally important, management should prioritize which systems most deserve funding and corporate attention.

Summary

1. **Evaluate the role played by the major types of systems in a business and their relationship to each other.**

   There are four major types of information systems in contemporary organizations. Operational-level systems are transaction processing systems (TPS) that track the flow of the daily routine transactions that are necessary to conduct business. Management-level systems (MIS and DSS) provide the management control level with reports and access to the organization's current performance and historical records. Most MIS reports condense information from TPS and are not highly analytical. Decision-support systems (DSS) support management decisions when these decisions are unique, rapidly changing, and not specified easily in advance. They have more advanced analytical models and data analysis capabilities than MIS and often draw on information from external as well as internal sources. Executive support systems (ESS) support the strategic level by providing data of greatest importance to senior management decision makers, often in the form of graphs and charts delivered via portals. They have limited analytical capabilities but can draw on sophisticated graphics software and many sources of internal and external information.

   The various types of systems in the organization exchange data with one another. TPS are a major source of data for other systems, especially MIS and DSS. ESS primarily receive data from lower-level systems. Today's business environment calls for more integration among systems than in the past, but integration is not easy to achieve.

2. **Describe the information systems supporting the major business functions: sales and marketing, manufacturing and production, finance and accounting, and human resources.**

   At each level of the organization information systems support the major functional areas of the business. Sales and marketing systems help the firm identify customers for the firm's products or services, develop products and services to meet customers' needs, promote the products and services, sell the products and services, and provide ongoing customer support. Manufacturing and production systems deal with the planning, development, and production of products and services, and controlling the flow of production. Finance and accounting systems keep track of the firm's financial assets and fund flows. Human resources systems maintain employee records; track employee skills, job performance, and training; and support planning for employee compensation and career development.

3. **Analyze the relationship between organizations, information systems, and business processes.**

   Business processes refer to the manner in which work activities are organized, coordinated, and focused to produce a specific business result. They also represent unique ways in which organizations coordinate work, information, and knowledge and the ways in which management chooses to coordinate work. Managers need to pay attention to business processes because they determine how well the organization can execute, and thus are a potential source of strategic success or failure. Although each of the major business functions has its own set of business processes, many other business processes are cross-functional, such as order fulfillment. Information systems can help organizations achieve great efficiencies by automating parts of these processes or by helping organizations rethink and streamline them. Firms can become more flexible and efficient by coordinating and integrating their business processes to improve management of resources and customer service.

4. **Explain how enterprise applications promote business process integration and improve organizational performance.**

   Enterprise applications, such as enterprise systems, supply chain management systems, customer relationship management systems, and knowledge management systems, are designed to support organization-wide process coordination and integration so that the organization can operate more efficiently. They span multiple functions and business processes and may be tied to the business processes of other organizations. Enterprise systems integrate the key internal business processes of a firm into a single software system so that information can flow throughout the organization, improving coordination, efficiency, and decision making. Supply chain management systems help the firm manage its relationship with suppliers to optimize the planning, sourcing, manufacturing, and delivery of products and services. Customer relationship management uses information systems to coordinate all of the business processes surrounding the firm's interactions with its customers to optimize firm revenue and customer satisfaction. Knowledge management systems enable firms to optimize the creation, sharing, and distribution of knowledge to improve business processes and management decisions.

5. **Assess the challenges posed by information systems in the enterprise and propose management solutions.**

   The array of information systems available can help businesses achieve higher levels of productivity and financial worth. Management challenges include the tension between developing systems that can serve specific interests in the firm and provide organization-wide information, the need for management and employee training to use systems properly, and the need to prioritize which systems most merit corporate attention and funding. Solutions include inventorying the firm's information systems to establish organization-wide information needs, employee and management training, and establishing a system for accounting for information systems.

Key Terms

Computer-aided design (CAD), 46
Customer relationship management (CRM) system, 56
Decision-support systems (DSS), 41
Enterprise applications, 51
Enterprise systems, 53
Executive support systems (ESS), 43
Finance and accounting information systems, 48

Human resources information systems, 49
Interorganizational systems, 54
Knowledge management systems, 57
Management information systems (MIS), 40
Management-level systems, 38
Manufacturing and production information systems, 46
Operational-level systems, 37

Portal, 43
Product life cycle management (PLM) systems, 46
Sales and marketing information systems, 45
Strategic-level systems, 38
Supply chain management (SCM) systems, 54
Transaction processing systems (TPS), 38

Review Questions

1. *Identify and describe the three levels of the organizational hierarchy. Which types of information systems serve each level?*

2. *List and briefly describe the major types of systems in organizations.*

3. *What are the five types of TPS in business organizations? What functions do they perform? Give examples of each.*

4. *What are the characteristics of MIS? How do MIS differ from TPS? From DSS?*

5. *What are the characteristics of DSS? How do they differ from those of MIS and ESS?*

6. *Describe the relationship between TPS, MIS, DSS, and ESS.*

7. *List and describe the information systems serving each of the major functional areas of a business.*

8. *What is a business process? Give two examples of processes*

for functional areas of the business and one example of a cross-functional process.

9. *Why are organizations trying to integrate their business processes? What are the four key enterprise applications for organization-wide process integration?*

10. *What are enterprise systems? How do they change the way an organization works?*

11. *What are supply chain management systems? How do they benefit businesses?*

12. *What are customer relationship management systems? How do they benefit businesses?*

13. *What is the role of knowledge management systems in the enterprise? What organizational processes are supported by knowledge management applications?*

14. *What are the challenges posed by the existence of various types of information systems in the enterprise? How can these challenges be addressed?*

Discussion Questions

1. *How could information systems be used to support the order fulfillment process illustrated in Figure 2-13? What are the most important pieces of information these systems should capture? Explain your answer.*

2. *Adopting an enterprise application is a key business decision as well as a technology decision. Do you agree? Why or why not? Who should make this decision?*

Application Software Exercise:
Spreadsheet Exercise: Improving Supply Chain Management

You run a company that manufactures aircraft components. You have many competitors who are trying to offer lower prices and better service to customers, and you are trying to determine if you can benefit from better supply chain management. At the Companion Website, you can find a spreadsheet file that contains a list of all of the items that your firm has ordered from its suppliers during the past three months. The fields in the spreadsheet file include vendor name, vendor identification number, purchaser's order number, item identification number and item description (for each item ordered from the vendor), cost

per item, number of units of the item ordered, total cost of each order, vendor's accounts payable terms, promised shipping date, promised transit time, and actual arrival date for each order.

Prepare a recommendation of how you can use the data in this spreadsheet database to improve your supply chain management. You may wish to consider ways to identify preferred suppliers or other ways of improving the movement and production of your products. Some criteria you might consider include the supplier's track record for on-time deliveries, suppliers offering the best accounts payable terms, and suppliers offering lower pricing when the same item can be provided by multiple suppliers. Use your spreadsheet software to prepare reports and, if appropriate, graphs to support your recommendations.

Electronic Business Project: Planning Transportation Logistics

The MapQuest (**www.mapquest.com**) and Rand McNally (**www.randmcnally.com**) Web sites illustrate emerging capabilities of geographic software on the World Wide Web. They include interactive capabilities for planning a trip, as well as a service offering maps of cities around the world, down to the street level. The software on the sites can calculate the distance between two points and provide itemized driving directions to any location. You can also click maps of your starting and ending locations to see detailed street maps and places of interest.

You have just started working as a dispatcher for Cross-Country Transport, a new trucking and delivery service based in Regina, Saskatchewan. Your first assignment is to plan a delivery of office equipment and furniture from Quebec City, Quebec (at the corner of Avenue Turcotte and Rue Beaucage)

to Richmond, British Columbia (corner of Blundell and CooperRoads). To guide your trucker, you need to know the distance between the two cities and the most efficient route between them. The distance is too long to drive in one day, given that the driver will drive for only 10 hours a day. Therefore, you also need to plan one or more stopovers. Use both sites to plan this trip, and select the one you would use in the future, considering ease of use, cost (if any), clarity of the maps, and the driving instructions.

Which service did you decide to use, and why? What changes would you suggest to the developers of that site? Consider all aspects of the site, including ease of viewing the route, help planning stopovers, time of route segments, and so forth.

Group Project: Describing Management Decisions and Systems

With a group of three or four other students, find a description of a senior manager of a corporation in *Canadian Business, Business Week, Forbes, Fortune,* or other business magazines. Write a description of the kinds of decisions this manager has to make and suggest an executive support system or decision-

support system that might be useful for this executive. Describe the data provided by the system and how that system would support decisions. If possible, use presentation software to present your findings to the class.

Web Sites of Interest

There are many interesting sites to enhance your learning about how information systems are categorized and how they support organizations. You can search the Web yourself, or just try the following sites to add to what you have already learned.

Brint **www.brint.com**
Search for interesting articles on a variety of business and technology topics.

Tech Tutorials **www.techtutorials.net**
Offers free tutorials on a variety of PC applications.

ComputerWorld and *ComputerWorld Canada*
www.computerworld.com and **www.itworldcanada.com/Pages /Docbase/BrowsePublication.aspx?Publication=Computer World&lid=Publication_ComputerWorld**
The leading computer periodical for IS managers.

Computing Canada **www.itbusiness.ca**
Canada's leading computer periodical; the site also hosts other Canadian computer-related periodicals.

CASE STUDY:
New Ways to Make Reservations with Parks Canada

In recent years, more and more travellers wish to make their reservations online. Many travellers go online to search for hotels to stay in and book reservations. The desire for online booking finally hit campers, too. According to Andrew Campbell, Information Management and chief information officer for Parks Canada, campers in Canada began demanding an online campsite reservation system for Parks Canada by the early 2000s.

In early 2004, Tri-Media's interactive arm (then known as e-commatrix.com) won a 10-year, $10 million joint contract, with three other partners, to develop a national campground reservation system and to maintain the system's infrastructure for Parks Canada. Andrew Campbell of Parks Canada says, "The system provides visitors with a new way to plan their trip to a national park of Canada, and to enjoy the breathtaking scenery, outstanding wildlife viewing, and wonderful recreational opportunities they provide."

The new and improved system was to replace the earlier individual campground reservation services offered by some national parks; campers can now make reservations in multiple campgrounds by making just one toll-free phone call or visiting one Web site. This facility is much better than the U.S. National Parks Reservation Service, through which campers can make only one park reservation at a time.

The Parks Canada project was part of the Government Online initiative, a federal endeavor to put most government services on line. This project was aimed to design, develop, and manage a bilingual, self-contained Web and call centre reservation and commerce system for Parks Canada. From the summer of 2005, those planning to camp at a national park of Canada campground could reserve a campsite online or through a national call centre well ahead of time.

With the new system, campers can make guaranteed reservations of campsites in campgrounds of their choice to make sure that they will not be disappointed when they actually arrive at the campgrounds. This also ensures shorter line-ups at the park gates. For those who prefer not to make reservations and thus save on reservation fees, campsites will still be available on a first-come, first-served basis.

The project's specifications were quite detailed and mandated by strict Government of Canada guidelines. Specifications included implementation of call centre service for the management of reservation calls and to help desk functionality; a local park operator point-of-sale interface; a local park management financial interface; a Government of Canada management interface, including procedures, reporting and reconciliation; customer relationship management functionality that would allow end users to self-manage their profiles and contact methods; and functionality that would allow government officials to manage, analyze and track usage from a Web-based interface. The project also included a marketing and public relations campaign that would promote the use and acceptance of this new service for increased user fees. The increase in the user fees would, of course, help to pay for development and maintenance of the new reservation system.

As in most system development projects, there were numerous obstacles and challenges. The system needed to support Parks Canada's management team in producing a service, technology, and communication effort that would both manage and unify the varying needs and biases of the country's park directors. Historically, the park directors have run isolated, independent systems and have proven to be cynical or averse to participating in centralized or national campaigns. Development of a fully bilingual system provided its own challenges—particularly when attempting to deliver such a system in a short time frame. Having the system pay for itself through pay-per-use fees was a challenge, too— both figuring out how much to charge for the service per use, and selling users on paying the fee.

The new system would have to meet the Government of Canada's very strict privacy and security guidelines as well as the guidelines on database modelling and data schemas (see Chapter 6). The government also has stringent guidelines on brand usage and presentation, as well as World Wide Web Consortium usability standards to ensure that those who are disabled can still use the Web site. The Web site and its associated call centre must also be available to remote areas of the country where even telephone service is considered "advanced" technology, such as some of the national parks themselves.

Parks Canada contracted with Tri-Media because of their experience in working in collaborative settings and success in delivering integrated marketing and technology solutions. Tri-Media partnered with a call centre operator and consultant and another interactive marketing agency to provide the new system.

Tri-Media also supported Parks Canada as needed to design, install, and test wireless and satellite communication infrastructures to enable remote parks that didn't have this infrastructure to communicate with the centralized system.

The project was delivered in the four month timeline demanded. At peak times during the 2004 pilot season, the system supported more than 2000 simultaneous transactions from around the world. During the 2005 season, simultaneous user volumes reached upwards of 5000.

The new system handles reservations for 16 national parks from coast to coast, with two more to come online in 2006. The system will enhance visitor services by providing a pre-trip planning tool and by eliminating the stress of uncertainty and the disappointment of arriving too late at a campground to get a campsite. Campers will be able to make arrangements and decisions based on their individual needs, desired trip outcomes, and site availability.

With this service, campsite reservations will be easy to make and can be standardized at all participating national park campgrounds. Campers can make a reservation using the Internet service, which is accessible 24 hours a day or by using a toll-free number to reach the call centre. The call centre is open 12 hours a day and also offers a TTY number. The per use fee is $11, with a $9 fee for cancellations or changes. Commercial tour groups and other groups can also use the system to make campsite reservations.

The success and acceptance of this primarily Web-based program, created by Canadians has resulted in Tri-Media being awarded additional work, including the management of Parks Canada's toll-free information lines and fulfillment services and the sale and fulfillment of park passes.

Sources: "National Campground Reservation Service," **www.tri-media.com/en/experience/case_study_archive/details.php?id=21**, accessed July 11, 2005; "Campground Reservation Service: Frequently Asked Questions," **www.pc.gc.ca/voyage-travel/reserve/faq_E.asp**, accessed July 11, 2005; "Full Implementation of the New Campground Reservation Service in National Parks of Canada," **http://pc.gc.ca/apps/cp-nr/release_e.asp?id=860&andor1=nr**, February 18, 2005, accessed July 11, 2005.

CASE STUDY QUESTIONS

1. What is Parks Canada's competitive strategy? Who are Parks Canada's competitors?

2. How did Parks Canada address the challenges they faced in implementing the online reservation system?

3. What other information systems should Parks Canada implement? Why?

4. How would you categorize the new reservation system, based on the various classifications we examined in this chapter?

5. What additional functionalities or types of systems should Parks Canada add to their reservation system?

Chapter 3

Information Systems, Organizations, Management, and Strategy

OBJECTIVES

After completing this chapter, you will be able to:

1. Identify and describe important features of organizations that managers need to understand in order to develop and use information systems successfully.

2. Evaluate the impact of information systems on organizations.

3. Assess how information systems support the activities of managers in organizations.

4. Analyze how information systems support various business strategies for competitive advantage.

5. Assess the challenges posed by strategic information systems and propose management solutions.

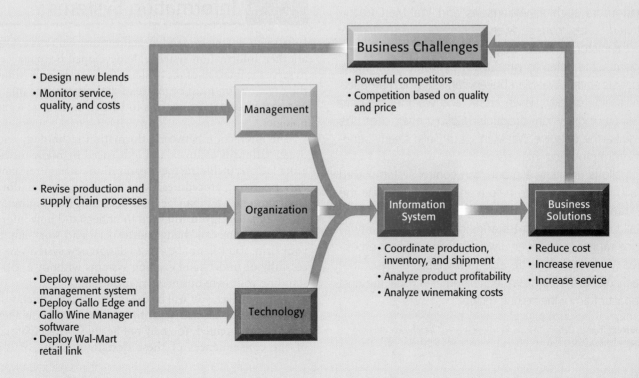

- Design new blends
- Monitor service, quality, and costs

- Revise production and supply chain processes

- Deploy warehouse management system
- Deploy Gallo Edge and Gallo Wine Manager software
- Deploy Wal-Mart retail link

Management

Organization

Technology

Business Challenges

- Powerful competitors
- Competition based on quality and price

Information System

- Coordinate production, inventory, and shipment
- Analyze product profitability
- Analyze winemaking costs

Business Solutions

- Reduce cost
- Increase revenue
- Increase service

Opening Case: Gallo Winery Leads by Blending Business with Technology

E.&J. Gallo Winery is the largest wine producer in the world, selling 65 million cases of wine in 2003. Despite its leadership position, Gallo must be concerned about the taste of its wines, price, and service. It has other large competitors, including Inniskillin, Allied Domecq, Kendall Jackson, Beringer Blass, Robert Mondavi, and Mission Hill, all of whom offer good quality wines at low prices.

How does Gallo manage to maintain its market leadership? The answer is by continually finding new ways to master the art and science of winemaking and by paying close attention to the distribution and marketing of wine worldwide. Gallo manages its production processes and relationships with suppliers very carefully.

To make sure shoppers know exactly where to find Gallo products, it implemented a product accountability system at its regional distribution centres. A complex warehouse management system coordinates production, component replenishment, inventory, and shipment, integrating with Gallo's order and transportation management systems. This system helped shorten the order-to-door cycle by 10 days. All orders are electronic, and payment is received electronically. Gallo's distributors know exactly what they are going to get by eligibility, product, and place.

To further support close relationships with distributors and retailers, a system called Gallo Edge helps retail customers such as Albertsons and Wal-Mart in the United States manage wine placement and profitability in their stores. Gallo Edge analyzes Wal-Mart's data about Gallo sales to produce a by-bottle profitability analysis so that Wal-Mart buyers can see which products are selling quickly, which aren't, and whether they are making money on products. Gallo never sees the results—the data are Wal-Mart's, but Gallo clearly benefits from providing this service.

Gallo is updating a production control system called Gallo Wine Manager to help management evaluate the relationship between wine taste and costs. Because Gallo sells 95 different brands of wine in a variety of price ranges, from everyday table wine to very expensive wine, it wants to be able to understand the cost of each blend. This system lets winemakers see the cost impact of any winemaking recipe.

Sources: Thomas Claburn, "Recipe for a Better Winery," *Information Week*, September 20, 2004; and **www.gallo.com**, accessed September 26, 2004.

The E.&J. Gallo Winery vignette illustrates the interdependence of business environments, organizational culture, management strategy, and the development of information systems. Gallo developed a series of systems to increase service and operational efficiency in response to competitive pressures from its surrounding environment, but this systems effort could not succeed without a significant amount of organizational and management change. New information systems have changed the way Gallo and its customers run their businesses and make management decisions.

As a manager, you will need to know how to use information systems strategically and how systems can help you make better decisions. This chapter explains some things you need to know about the relationship between organizations, management, information systems, and business strategy. First, we introduce the features of organizations that you will need to understand when you design, develop, and operate information systems. Next, we survey the role of management in organizations and see where information systems have had an impact. Finally, we examine the problems firms face from competition and the ways in which information systems can provide competitive advantage.

3.1 Organizations and Information Systems

Information systems and organizations influence one another. Information systems are developed by managers to serve the interests of the business firm. At the same time, the organization must be aware of and open to the influences of information systems to benefit from new technologies.

The interaction between information technology and organizations is complex and influenced by many mediating factors, including the organization's structure, standard operating procedures, politics, culture, surrounding environment, and management decisions (see Figure 3-1). As a manager, you will need to understand how information systems can change both social and work life in your firm. You will not be able to design new systems successfully or understand existing systems without understanding your own business organization.

As a manager, you will be the one to decide which systems will be developed, what they will do, and how they will be implemented. You may not be able to anticipate all of the consequences of these decisions. Some of the

FIGURE 3-1 *The two-way relationship between organizations and information technology.*

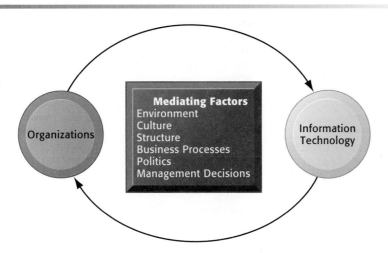

The complex two-way relationship is mediated by many factors, not the least of which are the decisions made—or not made—by managers. Other factors mediating the relationship include the organizational culture, structure, politics, business processes, and environment.

changes that occur in business firms because of new information technology (IT) investments cannot be foreseen and have results that may or may not meet your expectations. Who would have imagined ten years ago, for instance, that email and instant messaging would become a dominant form of business communication and that many managers would be inundated with more than 200 email messages each day (Walker 2004)? A technology introduced to boost productivity may actually wind up lowering it.

What Is an Organization?

An **organization** is a stable, formal social structure that takes resources from the environment and processes them to produce outputs. This technical definition focuses on three elements of an organization. Capital and labour are primary production factors provided by the environment. The organization (the firm) transforms these inputs into products and services in a production function. The products and services are consumed by environments in return for supply inputs (see Figure 3-2).

An organization is more stable than an informal group (such as a group of friends that meets every Friday for lunch) in terms of longevity and routine. Organizations are formal legal entities with internal rules and procedures that must abide by laws. Organizations are also social structures because they are a collection of social elements, much as a machine has a structure—a particular arrangement of valves, cams, shafts, and other parts.

This definition of organizations is powerful and simple, but it is not very descriptive or even predictive of real-world organizations. A more realistic behavioural definition of an organization is that it is a collection of rights, privileges, obligations, and responsibilities that are delicately balanced over a period of time through conflict and conflict resolution (see Figure 3-3).

organization

FIGURE 3-2 *The technical microeconomic definition of the organization.*

In the microeconomic definition of organizations, capital and labour (the primary production factors provided by the environment) are transformed by the firm through the production process into products and services (outputs to the environment). The products and services are consumed by the environment, which supplies additional capital and labour as inputs in the feedback loop.

FIGURE 3-3   *The behavioural view of organizations.*

The behavioural view of organizations emphasizes group relationships, values, and structures.

In this behavioural view of the firm, people who work in organizations develop cus-
tomary ways of working; they gain attachments to existing relationships; and they make
arrangements with subordinates and superiors about how work will be done, the amount
of work that will be done, and under what conditions work will be done. Most of these
arrangements and feelings are not discussed in any formal rulebook.

How do these definitions of organizations relate to information systems technology? A
technical view of organizations encourages us to focus on how inputs are combined to
create outputs when technology changes are introduced into the company. The firm is
seen as infinitely malleable, with capital and labour substituting for each other quite easily. But the more realistic behavioural definition of an organization suggests that developing new information systems, or redeveloping old ones, involves much more than a technical rearrangement of machines or workers—some information systems change the
organizational balance of rights, privileges, obligations, responsibilities, and feelings that
have been established over a long period of time.

Changing these elements can take a long time, be very disruptive, and require more
resources to support training and learning. For example, the length of time required to
implement a new information system effectively can be much longer than anticipated
simply because there is a lag between implementing a technical system and teaching
employees and managers how to use it.

Technological change requires changes in who owns and controls information; who
has the right to access and update that information; and who makes decisions about
whom, what, when, and how. This more complex view forces us to look at the way work is
designed and the procedures used to achieve outputs.

The technical and behavioural definitions of organizations are not contradictory.
Indeed, they complement each other: The technical definition tells us how thousands of
firms in competitive markets combine capital, labour, and information technology while
the behavioural model takes us inside the individual firm to see how that technology
affects the organization's inner workings. Section 3.2 describes how each of these definitions of organizations can help explain the relationships between information systems
and organizations.

Some features of organizations are common to all organizations; others distinguish one
organization from another. Let us look first at the features common to all organizations.

Common Features of Organizations

You might not think that Air Canada, Apple Computer, and the St. Johns, Newfoundland,
Police Department have much in common, but they do. In some respects, all modern organizations are alike because they share the characteristics that are listed in Table 3-1. German
sociologist Max Weber was the first to describe these "ideal-typical" characteristics of organizations in 1911. He called organizations **bureaucracies** that have certain "structural" features.

bureaucracies

TABLE 3-1 *Structural Characteristics of All Organizations*

Clear division of labour

Hierarchy

Explicit rules and procedures

Impartial judgments

Technical qualifications for positions

Maximum organizational efficiency

According to Weber, all modern bureaucracies have clear-cut divisions of labour and specialization. Organizations arrange specialists in a hierarchy of authority in which everyone is accountable to someone and authority is limited to specific actions. Authority and action are further limited by abstract rules or procedures (standard operating procedures, or SOPs) that are interpreted and applied to specific cases. These rules create a system of impartial and universal decision making; everyone is treated equally. Organizations try to hire and promote employees on the basis of technical qualifications and professionalism (not personal connections). The organization is devoted to the principle of efficiency: maximizing output while minimizing inputs.

According to Weber, bureaucracies are prevalent because they are the most efficient form of organization. Other scholars have supplemented Weber, identifying additional features of organizations. All organizations develop business processes (routines), politics, and cultures.

Routines and Business Processes All organizations, including business firms, become very efficient over time because individuals in the firm develop **routines** for producing goods and services. Routines—sometimes called *standard operating procedures*—are precise rules, procedures, and practices that have been developed to cope with virtually all expected situations. As employees learn these routines, they become highly productive and efficient, and the firm is able to reduce its costs over time as efficiency increases. For instance, when you visit a doctor's office, receptionists have a well-developed set of routines for gathering basic information from you; nurses have a different set of routines for preparing you for an interview with a doctor; and the doctor has a well-developed set of routines for diagnosing you.

Business processes, which we described in Chapters 1 and 2, are collections of such routines. A business firm in turn is a collection of business processes (see Figure 3-4). By analyzing business processes and individual routines, you can achieve a very clear understanding of how a business actually works. Moreover, by conducting a business process analysis, you will also begin to understand how to change the business to make it more efficient or effective. Throughout this book, we examine business processes to understand how they might be changed or replaced by using information technology to achieve greater efficiency and higher levels of customer service.

Organizational Politics People in organizations occupy different positions with different specialties, concerns, and perspectives. As a result, they naturally have divergent viewpoints about how resources, rewards, and punishments should be distributed. These differences matter to both managers and employees, and they result in political struggle for resources, competition, and conflict within every organization. Political resistance is one of the great difficulties of bringing about organizational change—especially the development of new information systems. Virtually all large information systems investments by a firm that bring about significant changes in strategy, business objectives, business processes, and procedures become politically charged events. Managers who know how to work with the politics of an organization will be more successful than less skilled managers in implementing new information systems. Throughout this book, you will find many examples where internal politics defeated the best-laid plans for an information system.

routines

FIGURE 3-4   *Routines, business processes, and firms.*

All organizations are composed of individual routines and behaviours, a collection of which make up a business process. A collection of business processes make up the business firm. New information system applications require that individual routines and business processes change to achieve high levels of organizational performance.

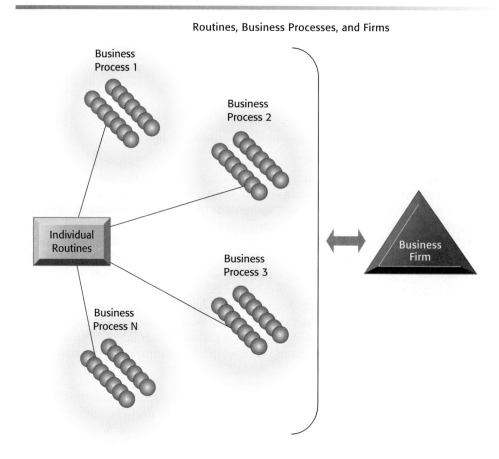

Routines, Business Processes, and Firms

Organizational Culture All organizations have bedrock, unassailable, unquestioned (by the members) assumptions that define their goals and products. **Organizational culture** is this set of fundamental assumptions about what products the organization should produce, how it should produce them, where, and for whom. Generally, these cultural assumptions are taken totally for granted and are rarely publicly announced or spoken about (Schein 1985). Business processes—the actual way business firms produce value—are usually embedded in the organization's culture.

You can see organizational culture at work by looking around your university or college. Some bedrock assumptions of university life are that professors know more than students, students attend college to learn, and classes follow a regular schedule. Organizational culture is a powerful unifying force that restrains political conflict and promotes common understanding, agreement on procedures, and common practices. If we all share the same basic cultural assumptions, agreement on other matters is more likely.

At the same time, organizational culture is a powerful constraint on change, especially technological change. Most organizations will do almost anything to avoid making changes in basic assumptions. Any technological change that threatens commonly held cultural assumptions usually meets a great deal of resistance. However, there are times when the only sensible way for a firm to move forward is to employ a new technology that directly opposes an existing organizational culture. When this situation occurs, the technology is often stalled while the culture slowly adjusts. You will find many examples in later chapters that describe the difficulties of changing the culture of a business to implement a new information system.

organizational culture

Unique Features of Organizations

Although all organizations do have common characteristics, no two organizations are identical. Organizations have different structures, goals, constituencies, leadership styles, tasks, and surrounding environments.

Different Organizational Types One important way in which organizations differ is in their structure or shape. The differences among organizational structures are characterized in many ways. Mintzberg's classification, described in Table 3-2, identifies five basic kinds of organizations (Mintzberg 1979).

The kind of information systems you find in a business firm—and the nature of problems with these systems—often reflects the type of organization. For instance, in a professional bureaucracy such as a hospital it is not unusual to find parallel patient record systems operated by the administration, another by doctors, and another by other professional staff such as nurses and social workers. In small entrepreneurial firms, you will often find poorly designed systems, developed in a rush, that often outgrow their usefulness quickly. In huge multidivisional firms operating in hundreds of locations, you will often find there is no single integrating information system, but instead each locale or division has its own set of information systems.

Organizations and Environments Organizations reside in environments from which they draw resources and to which they supply goods and services. Organizations and environments have a reciprocal relationship. On the one hand, organizations are open to and dependent on the social and physical environment that surrounds them. Without financial and human resources—people willing to work reliably and consistently for a set wage, or revenue from customers— organizations could not exist. Organizations must respond to legislative and other requirements imposed by government, as well as the actions of customers and competitors. On the other hand, organizations can influence their environments. For example, business firms form alliances with other businesses to influence the political process; they advertise to influence customer acceptance of their products.

Figure 3-5 illustrates the role of information systems in helping organizations perceive changes in their environments and also in helping organizations to act on their

TABLE 3-2 Organizational Structures

ORGANIZATIONAL TYPE	DESCRIPTION	EXAMPLES
Entrepreneurial structure	Young, small firm in a fast-changing environment. It has a simple structure and is managed by an entrepreneur serving as its single chief executive officer.	Small start-up business
Machine bureaucracy	Large bureaucracy existing in a slowly changing environment, producing standard products. It is dominated by a centralized management team and centralized decision making.	Midsize manufacturing firm
Divisionalized bureaucracy	Combination of multiple machine bureaucracies, each producing a different product or service, all topped by one central headquarters.	Very large firms, such as Power Corporation
Professional bureaucracy	Knowledge-based organization where goods and services depend on the expertise and knowledge of professionals. Dominated by department heads with weak centralized authority.	Law firms, school systems, hospitals
Adhocracy	Task force organization that must respond to rapidly changing environments. Consists of large groups of specialists organized into short-lived multidisciplinary teams with weak central management.	Consulting firms, such as the Rand Corporation

FIGURE 3-5 *Environments and organizations have a reciprocal relationship.*

Environments shape what organizations can do, but organizations can influence their environments and decide to change environments altogether. Information technology plays a critical role in helping organizations perceive environmental change and in helping organizations act on their environment.

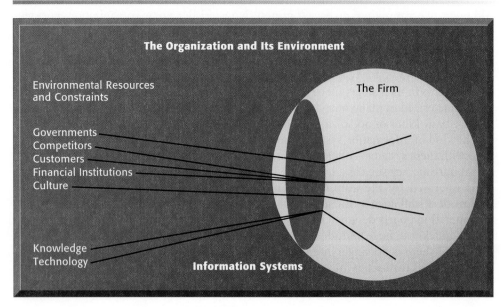

environments. Information systems are key instruments for environmental scanning, helping managers identify external changes that might require an organizational response.

Environments generally change much faster than organizations. The main reasons for organizational failure are an inability to adapt to a rapidly changing environment and a lack of resources—particularly among young firms—to sustain even short periods of troubled times (Freeman et al. 1983). New technologies, new products, and changing public tastes and values (many of which result in new government regulations) put strains on any organization's culture, politics, and people. Most organizations do not cope well with large environmental shifts. The inertia built into an organization's standard operating procedures, the political conflict raised by changes to the existing order, and the threat to closely held cultural values typically inhibit organizations from making significant changes. It is not surprising that only 10 percent of the Fortune 500 companies in 1919 still exist today.

Other Differences among Organizations Organizations have different shapes or structures for many other reasons. They differ in their ultimate goals and the types of power used to achieve them. Some organizations have coercive goals (e.g., prisons); others have utilitarian goals (e.g., businesses). Still others have normative goals (e.g., universities, religious groups). Organizations also serve different groups or have different constituencies, some primarily benefiting their members, others benefiting clients, stockholders, or the public. The nature of leadership differs greatly from one organization to another—some organizations may be more democratic or authoritarian than others. Another way organizations differ is by the tasks they perform and the technology they use. Some organizations perform primarily routine tasks that could be reduced to formal rules that require little judgment (such as manufacturing auto parts) while others (such as consulting firms) work primarily with nonroutine tasks.

As you can see in Table 3-3, the list of unique features of organizations is longer than the common features list. It stands to reason that information systems will have different effect on different types of organizations. Different organizations in different circumstances experience different effects from the same technology. Only by close analysis of a specific organization can a manager effectively design and manage information systems.

The Window on Organizations shows how unique environments, culture, and organizational characteristics have affected Internet use and electronic commerce in Canada and Mexico, even in comparison with the country that adjoins them both, the United

States. Canada is more affluent than Mexico, with a high percentage of its population using the Internet. However, that does not necessarily translate into a high rate of online purchasing because consumers are heavily taxed and remain partial to bricks-and-mortar stores. Mexico's government is actively trying to promote Internet use, but a high percentage of its citizens live below the poverty line and inexpensive telecommunications services are not widely available.

TABLE 3-3 *Summary of Salient Features of Organizations*

COMMON FEATURES	UNIQUE FEATURES
Formal structure	Organizational type
Routines	Environments
Politics	Goals
Culture	Power
	Constituencies
	Function
	Leadership
	Tasks
	Technology

 # WINDOW ON ORGANIZATIONS

Variations in North American E-Commerce

Internet shopping IS flourishing in the United States, but it is not equally popular in other countries. Here, we examine e-commerce in Canada and Mexico to see some of the differences in online shopping within North America.

Canada is definitely a major user of the Internet, with more users per capita than the U.S. About 71 percent of Canadian adults use the Internet, compared to 68 percent in the U.S. About 35 percent of Canadian households using the Internet do so through high-speed connections. In addition, 51 percent of Canadian Internet users do their banking through the Internet, compared to only 33 percent of U.S. Internet users. About 3.2 million Canadian households engaged in e-commerce in 2003. Yet Canadians use the Internet much less than Americans for retail shopping. The reasons for this situation are unclear.

Canadian retail companies have responded accordingly, investing less in e-commerce Web sites than their U.S. counterparts. One famous department store organization, the Hudson's Bay Company (HBC), operates some of the most popular Canadian department store brands, including The Bay, Zellers, and Home Outfitters. However, its Web site (hbc.com) offers less than 10 percent of its bricks-and-mortar products online. Moreover, consumers seem primarily interested in online sale items, so hbc.com makes marked-down items its primary focus. Michael LeBlanc, HBC's coordinator of Web sites, believes its online strategy is successful for increasing Hudson's Bay's physical store traffic. He points out,

for example, that the company offers its Web customers the ability to pick up purchases at one of HBC's bricks-and-mortar stores.

Robert Sartor, the CEO of the Forzani Group, the owner of seven sporting goods brands, believes that one reason for Canadians' lower interest in online shopping is that Canadians are taxed more heavily than are Americans, leaving Canadians with less disposable income. Moreover, e-commerce shopping usually leaves the shopper "having to pay for shipping and handling online, and if you return it, you have to pay that again," according to Sartor. Forzani has successfully used the Internet to build an email list to support its bricks-and-mortar stores. However, its attempt at online selling failed. In 1999, Forzani built an e-commerce enterprise but closed it after one and one-half years because it had generated too little growth. "At the rate of growth we were seeing," explains Sartor, "it'd be 12, 13, 14 years before we got the returns we're used to."

Nor are Canadian consumers doing their purchasing on foreign Web sites. In 2003, nearly 70 percent of Canadian purchases over the Internet were spent at domestic Web sites.

E-commerce challenges in Mexico stem from different sources. Per capita income is one-fourth that of the U.S., and distribution of that income is very uneven, with more than 40 percent of the population below the poverty line. Mexico has an undeveloped telecommunications infrastructure, limited investment in information technology by small and medium-sized businesses, unreliable logistics and delivery systems, and limited online payment options. As well, high-speed access to the Internet is very expensive.

A much smaller percentage of Mexicans (about 20 percent) use credit cards for purchases than in Canada and the United States, and they have less disposable income for shopping. Only about 9 million people in Mexico have PCs (out of a population of 106 million!), and more than half of these PC owners have Internet access. As of 2003, Mexico had over 12 million Internet users, most of whom are under 35 years old.

Nevertheless, interest in e-commerce and the Internet is high, and Internet use is increasing. According to Pyramid Research, close to $50 billion is being spent on Internet e-commerce in Mexico, making it one of the leading countries in Latin America for online business. Currently, more than 4 million Mexicans do their banking online. Local online retail sites and online Web sites for bricks-and-mortar retailers are being developed. One active Mexican online retailer is Sanborns, and its Web site is supported by more than 100 stores.

Mexico's business community strongly backs Internet business. Mexico's political and business leadership would like to use the Internet to catch up with more advanced countries. The government of Mexico wants to make Mexico a digital economy. It is actively trying to promote the development of an information technology industry in Mexico along with a regulatory framework for e-commerce. Mexico's e-commerce law recognizes electronic contracts and makes sure consumer protection laws apply to the online world.

To Think About: What organizational factors explain why Canada and Mexico have had such different experiences adopting e-commerce?

Sources: Bob Tedeschi, "E-Commerce Report," *New York Times*, January 26, 2004; CBC Business News, "Shopping on the Web Up 25%: StatsCan," September 23, 2004; Eastern Michigan University, "Best Prospects in the ICT Market," revised April 24, 2004; and "The World Fact Book: Mexico," www.cia.gov, accessed September 25, 2004.

Organizing the IT Function

Given that there are many types of business firms, there are many ways in which the IT function is organized within the firm. In the typical firm, the formal organizational unit responsible for information technology services is called the **information systems department.** The information systems department is responsible for maintaining the hardware, software, data storage, and networks that comprise the firm's IT infrastructure. We describe IT infrastructure in detail in Chapter 5.

The information systems department consists of specialists, such as programmers, systems analysts, project leaders, and information systems managers (see Figure 3-6). **Programmers** are highly trained technical specialists who write the software instructions for computers. **Systems analysts** are the principal liaisons between the information systems groups and the rest of the organization. It is the systems analyst's job to translate business problems and requirements into information requirements and systems. **Information systems managers** are leaders of teams of programmers and analysts, project managers, physical facility managers, telecommunications managers, and heads of office system groups. They are also managers of computer operations and data entry staff. Also external specialists, such as hardware vendors and manufacturers, software firms, and consultants frequently participate in the day-to-day operations and long-term planning of information systems.

In many companies, the information systems department is headed by a **chief information officer (CIO)**. The role of the CIO is a senior management position that oversees the use of information technology in the firm.

End users are representatives of departments outside of the information systems group for whom applications are developed. These users play an increasingly large role in the design and development of information systems.

In the early years of computing, the information systems group was composed mostly of programmers, who performed very highly specialized but limited technical functions. Today, a growing proportion of staff members are systems analysts and network specialists, with the information systems department acting as a powerful change agent in the organization. The information systems department suggests new business strategies and new information-based products and services and coordinates both the development of the technology and the planned changes in the organization.

In the past, firms generally developed their own software and managed their own computing facilities. Today, many firms are turning to external vendors to provide these

information systems department

programmers

systems analysts

information systems managers

chief information officer (CIO)

end users

FIGURE 3-6   *Information technology services.*

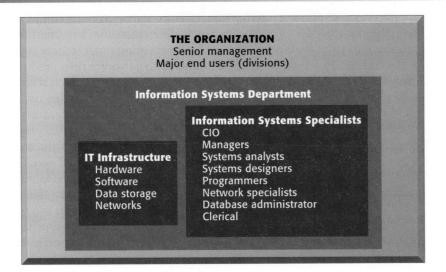

Many types of specialists and groups are responsible for the design and management of the organization's information technology infrastructure.

services (see Chapters 5, 7, and 10) and are using their information systems departments to manage these service providers.

3.2   How Information Systems Affect Organizations and Business Firms

Information systems have become integral, online, interactive tools deeply involved in the minute-to-minute operations and decision making of large organizations. Over the last decade, information systems have fundamentally altered the economics of organizations and greatly increased the possibilities for organizing work. Theories and concepts from economics and sociology help us understand the changes brought about by IT.

Economic Impacts

From the point of view of economics, IT changes both the relative costs of capital and the costs of information. Information technology can be viewed as a production factor that can be substituted for traditional capital and labour. As the cost of information technology decreases, it is substituted for labour, which historically has been a rising cost. Hence, information technology should result in a decline in the number of middle managers and clerical workers as information technology substitutes for their labour.

As the cost of information technology decreases, it substitutes for other forms of capital such as buildings and machinery, which remain relatively expensive. Hence, over time we should expect managers to increase their investments in IT because of its declining cost relative to other capital investments.

IT also obviously affects the cost and quality of information and changes the economics of information. Information technology helps firms contract in size because it can reduce transaction costs—the costs incurred when a firm buys on the marketplace what it cannot make itself. According to **transaction cost theory**, firms and individuals seek to economize on transaction costs, much as they do on production costs. Using markets is expensive (Coase 1937; Williamson 1985) because of costs such as locating and communicating with distant suppliers, monitoring contract compliance, buying insurance, obtaining information on products, and so forth. Traditionally, firms have tried to reduce transaction costs through vertical integration, by getting bigger, hiring more employees, and buying their own suppliers and distributors, as both General Motors and Ford used to do.

transaction cost theory

Information technology, especially the use of networks, can help firms lower the cost of market participation (transaction costs), making it worthwhile for firms to contract with external suppliers instead of using internal sources. For instance, by using computer links to external suppliers, Chrysler Corporation can achieve economies by obtaining more than 70 percent of its parts from other companies. Information systems make it possible for companies such as Cisco Systems and Dell Computer to outsource their production to contract manufacturers such as Flextronics instead of making their products themselves.

Figure 3-7 shows that as transaction costs decrease, firm size (the number of employees) should shrink because it becomes easier and cheaper for the firm to contract for the purchase of goods and services in the marketplace rather than to make the product or offer the service itself. Firm size can stay constant or contract even if the company increases its revenues. Information technology also can reduce internal management costs. According to **agency theory**, the firm is viewed as a "nexus of contracts" among self-interested individuals rather than as a unified, profit-maximizing entity (Jensen and Meckling 1976). A principal (owner) employs "agents" (employees) to perform work on his or her behalf. However, agents need constant supervision and management; otherwise, they will tend to pursue their own interests rather than those of the owners. As firms grow in size and scope, agency or coordination costs rise because owners must expend more and more effort supervising and managing employees.

By reducing the costs of acquiring and analyzing information, information technology permits organizations to reduce agency costs because it becomes easier for managers to oversee a greater number of employees. Figure 3-8 shows that by reducing overall management costs, information technology enables firms to increase revenues while shrinking the number of middle managers and clerical workers. We have seen examples in earlier chapters where information technology expanded the power and scope of small organizations by enabling them to perform coordinating activities such as processing orders or keeping track of inventory with very few clerks and managers.

Organizational and Behavioural Impacts

Theories based on the sociology of complex organizations also provide some understanding about how and why firms change with the implementation of new IT applications.

IT Flattens Organizations Large, bureaucratic organizations, which primarily developed before the computer age, are often inefficient, slow to change, and less competitive than newly created organizations. Some of these large organizations have

FIGURE 3-7 *The transaction cost theory of the impact of information technology on the organization.*

Firms traditionally grew in size to reduce transaction costs. IT potentially reduces the costs for a given size, shifting the transaction cost curve inward, opening up the possibility of revenue growth without increasing size, or even revenue growth accompanied by shrinking size.

agency theory

FIGURE 3-8 *The agency cost theory of the impact of information technology on the organization.*

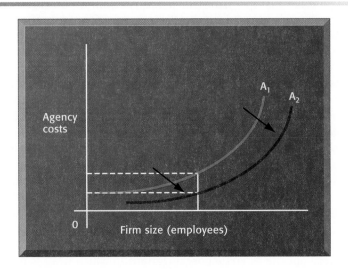

As firms grow in size and complexity, traditionally they experience rising agency costs. IT shifts the agency cost curve down and to the right, enabling firms to increase size while lowering agency costs.

downsized, reducing the number of employees and the number of levels in their organizational hierarchies.

Behavioural researchers have theorized that information technology facilitates flattening of hierarchies by broadening the distribution of information to empower lower-level employees and increase management efficiency (see Figure 3-9). IT pushes decision-making rights lower in the organization because lower-level employees receive the information they need to make decisions without supervision. (This empowerment is also possible because of the higher educational levels of the workforce, which give employees the capabilities to make intelligent decisions.) Second, because managers can now receive so much more accurate information on time, they become much faster at making decisions, so fewer managers are required. IT also enables managers who push decisions lower to monitor, track, and control those decisions through information distribution and controls built into the systems. Management costs decline as a percentage of revenues, and

FIGURE 3-9 *Flattening organizations.*

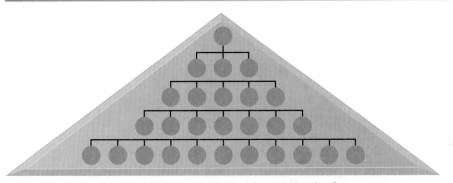

A traditional hierarchical organization with many levels of management

An organization that has been "flattened" by removing layers of management

Information systems can reduce the number of levels in an organization by providing managers with information to supervise larger numbers of workers and by giving lower-level employees more decision-making authority.

the hierarchy becomes much more efficient (Drucker 1988; Bresnahan, Brynjolffson, and Hitt 2000; Laudon and Marr 1995; Malone 1997).

These changes mean that the management span of control has also been broadened, enabling high-level managers to manage and control more workers spread over greater distances. Many companies have eliminated thousands of middle managers as a result of these changes.

Post-industrial Organizations and Virtual Firms

Post-industrial theories based more on history and sociology than economics also support the notion that IT should flatten hierarchies. In post-industrial societies, authority increasingly relies on knowledge and competence, and not merely on formal positions. Hence, the shape of organizations should flatten because professional workers tend to be self-managing, and decision making should become more decentralized as knowledge and information become more widespread throughout the firm (Drucker 1988). Information technology may encourage task force-networked organizations in which groups of professionals come together—face to face or electronically—for short periods of time to accomplish a specific task (e.g., designing a new automobile); once the task is accomplished, the individuals join other task forces.

More firms may operate as **virtual organizations** in which work is no longer tied to geographic location. Virtual organizations use networks to link people, assets, and ideas. They can ally with suppliers, customers, and, sometimes, even competitors to create and distribute new products and services without being limited by traditional organizational boundaries or physical locations. For example, Calyx and Corolla is a networked virtual organization selling fresh flowers directly to American customers, bypassing traditional florists. The firm takes orders over the telephone or from its Web site and transmits them to grower farms, which ship flowers using FedEx directly to customers. Canadian Facility Management & Design, a Canadian magazine that publishes six times a year, is run almost as a virtual corporation. The publisher is in Etobicoke, the art director in Markham, circulation management is in North Toronto, and the editor is in Hamilton.

Who makes sure that self-managed teams do not head off in the wrong direction? Who decides which person works on which team and for how long? How can managers evaluate the performance of someone who is constantly rotating from team to team? How do people know where their careers are headed? New approaches for evaluating, organizing, and informing workers are required, and not all companies can make virtual work effective.

Increasing Flexibility of Organizations

Information technology helps companies organize in more flexible ways, increasing their ability to sense and respond to changes in the marketplace and to take advantage of new opportunities. Information systems can give both large and small organizations additional flexibility to overcome some of the limitations posed by their size.

Small organizations can use information systems to acquire some of the muscle and reach of larger organizations. They can perform coordinating activities, such as processing bids or keeping track of inventory, and many manufacturing tasks with very few managers, clerks, or production workers.

Large organizations can use information technology to achieve some of the agility and responsiveness of small organizations. One aspect of this phenomenon is **mass customization**, which is the ability to offer individually tailored products or services using the same production resources as mass production. Information systems can make the production process more flexible so that products can be tailored to each customer's unique set of requirements (Zipkin 2001). Software and computer networks can be used to tightly link the plant floor with orders, design, and purchasing and to finely control production machines so products can be produced in greater variety and can be easily customized with no added cost for small production runs.

For example, the Lands' End Web site enables users to order jeans, dress pants, chinos, and shirts custom-tailored to their own specifications. Customers enter their measurements into a form on the Web site, which then transmits each customer's specifications over a network to a computer that develops an electronic made-to-measure pattern for

virtual organizations

mass customization

that customer. The individual patterns are then transmitted electronically to a manufacturing plant where they are used to drive fabric-cutting equipment (Ives and Piccoli 2003). There are almost no extra production costs because the process does not require additional warehousing, production overruns, and inventories, and the cost to the customer is only slightly higher than that of a mass-produced garment.

A related trend is micromarketing, in which information systems can help companies pinpoint tiny target markets for these finely customized products and services—as small as individualized "markets of one." We discuss micromarketing in more detail in section 3.4.

Understanding Organizational Resistance to Change Throughout this book, you will find many case studies that describe resistance to new systems in the organization and the difficulties that managers face in getting their firms to change rapidly. Our previous discussion of business processes suggests one powerful reason why there is resistance to IT applications: Many IT investments require changes in personal, individual routines. These changes can be painful for those involved and require retraining and additional effort on the part of the employee who may or may not be compensated for this effort.

Another behavioural approach views information systems as the outcome of political competition between organizational subgroups for influence over the organization's policies, procedures, and resources (Keen 1981; Kling 1980; Laudon 1974; Laudon 1986). Information systems inevitably become bound up in organizational politics because they influence access to a key resource—namely, information. Information systems can affect who does what to whom, when, where, and how in an organization. Because information systems potentially change an organization's structure, culture, politics, and work, there is often considerable resistance to them when they are introduced.

Because organizational resistance to change is so powerful, many information technology investments flounder and do not increase productivity. Indeed, research on project implementation failures demonstrates that the most common reason for failure of large projects to reach their objectives is not the failure of the technology, but organizational and political resistance to change. Figure 3-10 illustrates these competing arenas for managing change. Chapter 11 treats this issue in detail. Therefore, as a manager involved in future IT investments, your ability to work with people and organizations is just as important as your technical awareness and knowledge.

The Internet and Organizations

The Internet, especially the World Wide Web, is beginning to have an important impact on the relationships between firms and external entities, and even on the organization of business processes inside a firm. The Internet increases the accessibility, storage, and dis-

FIGURE 3-10   *Organizational resistance and the mutually adjusting relationship between technology and the organization.*

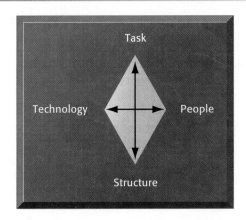

Implementing information systems has consequences for task arrangements, structures, and people. According to this model, to implement change, all four components must be changed simultaneously.

Source: Reprinted by permission of James G. March.

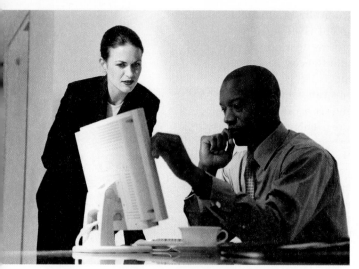

A corporate chief executive learns how to use a new computer system. Senior managers' time is very limited, so they require systems that are extremely easy to use.

tribution of information and knowledge for organizations. In essence, the Internet is capable of dramatically lowering the transaction and agency costs facing most organizations. For instance, brokerage firms and banks can now deliver their internal-operations procedures manuals to their employees at distant locations by posting them on the corporate Web site, saving millions of dollars in distribution costs. A global sales force can receive nearly instant price product information updates using the Web or instructions from management sent by email. Vendors of some large retailers can access retailers' internal Web sites directly for up-to-the-minute sales information and to initiate replenishment orders instantly.

Businesses are rapidly rebuilding some of their key business processes based on Internet technology and making this technology a key component of their IT infrastructures. If prior networking is any guide, there will be simpler business processes, fewer employees, and much flatter organizations than in the past.

3.3   The Impact of IT on Management Decision Making

One of the most important contributions of information technology and systems to business firms is the reduction in information uncertainty and the resulting improvement in decision making. Over the last decade, IT has directly contributed to an improvement in the quality of information flowing to management and employee decision makers.

Prior to the development of the Internet and corporate-wide enterprise information systems (described in Chapters 2, 14, and 15), business decision makers had limited, delayed, and inaccurate knowledge of customers, sales, inventories, and business processes such as delivery, order fulfillment times, and order entry. This meant decisions were made using information that was at best approximate and often wrong. In this environment, as a reaction to the information uncertainty, the solution was to double up people, increase production buffers of spare parts, and build very large warehouses to store excess production.

Significant investments in IT, which are chronicled throughout this book, have lifted the fog of uncertainty and replaced it with a much more precise, timely, and accurate level of decision making that was unimaginable a few years ago. These trends toward more real-time information and decision making will accelerate as new wireless communications technologies and mobile computing platforms extend their reach.

How IT Affects Management Decision Making

Although almost everyone believes IT has contributed to better management decision making, there have actually been few large-scale quantitative studies on this topic. The positive impact of IT on management decision making is typically inferred from productivity measures and the overall performance of the firm (profitability), along with its stock market share price.

The role of a manager is very complex and involves a great deal more than simply decision making. In Chapter 15, we review in detail the process of decision making, the types of decisions managers make (**structured decisions** versus **unstructured decisions**), and the stages of the decision-making process. In this chapter, it is important to understand the breadth of the management role and the various approaches to understanding exactly how IT supports managers.

structured decisions

unstructured decisions

The Role of Managers in Organizations

Managers play key roles in organizations. Their responsibilities range from making decisions, to writing reports, to attending meetings, to arranging birthday parties. We can better understand managerial functions and roles by examining classical and contemporary models of managerial behaviour.

Classical Descriptions of Management The **classical model of management**, which describes what managers do, has been largely unquestioned since the 1920s. Henri Fayol and other early writers first described the five classical functions of managers as planning, organizing, coordinating, deciding, and controlling. This description of management activities dominated management thought for a long time, and it is still popular today.

But these terms actually describe formal managerial functions and are unsatisfactory as a description of what managers actually do. The terms do not address what managers do when they plan, decide things, and control the work of others. We need a refined understanding of how managers actually behave.

Behavioural Models Contemporary behavioural scientists have observed that managers do not behave as the classical model of management led us to believe. Kotter (1982), for example, describes the morning activities of the president of an investment management firm.

7:35 A.M. Richardson arrives at work, unpacks her briefcase, gets some coffee, and begins making a list of activities for the day.

7:45 A.M. Bradshaw (a subordinate) and Richardson converse about a number of topics and exchange pictures recently taken on summer vacations.

8:00 A.M. They talk about a schedule of priorities for the day.

8:20 A.M. Wilson (a subordinate) and Richardson talk about some personnel problems, cracking jokes in the process.

8:45 A.M. Richardson's secretary arrives, and they discuss her new apartment and arrangements for a meeting later in the morning.

8:55 A.M. Richardson goes to a morning meeting run by one of her subordinates. Thirty people are there, and Richardson reads during the meeting.

11:05 A.M. Richardson and her subordinates return to the office and discuss a difficult problem. They try to define the problem and outline possible alternatives. She lets the discussion roam away from and back to the topic again and again. Finally, they agree on a next step.

In this example, it is difficult to determine which activities constitute Richardson's planning, coordinating, and decision making. **Behavioural models** state that the actual behaviour of managers appears to be less systematic, more informal, less reflective, more reactive, less well organized, and much more frivolous than students of information systems and decision making generally expect it to be.

Observers find that managerial behaviour actually has five attributes that differ greatly from the classical description: First, managers perform a great deal of work at an unrelenting pace—studies have found that managers engage in more than 600 different activities each day, with no break in their pace. Second, managerial activities are fragmented; most activities last for less than nine minutes, and only 10 percent of the activities exceed one hour in duration. Third, managers prefer speculation, hearsay, gossip—they want current, specific, and ad hoc information (printed information often will be too old). Fourth, they prefer oral forms of communication to written forms because oral media provide greater flexibility, require less effort, and bring a faster response. Fifth, managers give high priority to maintaining a diverse and complex Web of contacts that acts as an informal information system and helps them execute their personal agendas and short- and long-term goals.

classical model of management

behavioural models

Analyzing managers' day-to-day behaviour, Mintzberg found that it could be classified into 10 managerial roles. **Managerial roles** are expectations of the activities that managers should perform in an organization. Mintzberg found that these managerial roles fell into three categories: interpersonal, informational, and decisional.

Interpersonal Roles   Managers act as figureheads for the organization when they represent their companies to the outside world and perform symbolic duties, such as giving out employee awards, in their **interpersonal role**. Managers act as leaders, attempting to motivate, counsel, and support subordinates. Managers also act as liaisons between various organizational levels; within each of these levels, they serve as liaisons among the members of the management team. Managers provide time and favours, which they expect to be returned.

Informational Roles   In their **informational role**, managers act as the nerve centres of their organizations, receiving the most concrete, up-to-date information and redistributing it to those who need to be aware of it. Managers are therefore information disseminators and spokespersons for their organizations.

Decisional Roles   Managers make decisions. In their **decisional role**, they act as entrepreneurs by initiating new kinds of activities; they handle disturbances arising in the organization; they allocate resources to staff members who need them; and they negotiate conflicts and mediate between conflicting groups in the organization.

Table 3-4, based on Mintzberg's role classifications, is one look at where systems can and cannot help managers. The table shows that information systems do not yet contribute to some important areas of management life. These areas will provide great opportunities for future systems efforts.

managerial roles

interpersonal roles

informational roles

decisional roles

Models of Decision Making

It is simplistic to think that organizations are composed of individual managers acting as rational decision makers and making decisions in a vacuum. The real business world is rarely like this. In fact most managers are members of a team of decision makers, working in

TABLE 3-4 *Managerial Roles and Supporting Information Systems*

ROLE	BEHAVIOUR	SUPPORT SYSTEMS
Interpersonal Roles		
Figurehead	→	None exist
Leader	Interpersonal →	None exist
Liaison	→	Electronic communication systems
Informational Roles		
Nerve centre	→	Management information systems, ESS
Disseminator	Information →	Mail, office systems
Spokesperson	processing →	Office and professional systems, workstations
Decisional Roles		
Entrepreneur	Decision →	None exist
Disturbance handler	making →	None exist
Resource allocator	→	DSS systems
Negotiator	→	None exist

Source: Kenneth C. Laudon and Jane P. Laudon; and Mintzberg, 1971.

a specific firm with a specific culture and set of political alliances and conflicts. The decisions that come out of an organization are the result of these many different forces and influences. A number of models attempt to describe how business people in firms make decisions. Some of these models focus on individual decision making while others focus on decision making in groups.

One place to start thinking about decision making is to consider the rational individual model. Individual models of decision making assume that human beings are in some sense rational. The **rational model** of human behaviour is built on the idea that people engage in basically consistent, rational, value-maximizing calculations. According to this model, an individual identifies goals, ranks all possible alternative actions by their contributions to those goals, and chooses the alternative that contributes most to those goals (Simon 1947).

Critics of this model show that in fact people cannot specify all of the alternatives, and most individuals do not have singular goals and are unable to rank all alternatives and consequences. Many decisions are so complex that calculating the **choice** (even if done by computer) is virtually impossible. Instead of searching through all alternatives, people tend to choose the first available alternative that moves them toward their ultimate goal. In making policy decisions, people choose policies most like the previous policy (Lindblom 1959). Finally, some scholars point out that decision making is a continuous process in which final decisions are always being modified.

Other research has found that humans differ in how they maximize their values and in how they use frames of reference to interpret information and make choices. Tversky and Kahneman (1981) show that humans have built-in biases that can distort decision making. They show that humans are very poor at assessing risk, almost always overestimating the probability of unlikely events and underestimating the likelihood of probable events. For instance, people are much more likely to fear shark attacks at the beach and much less likely to fear having a car accident driving to the beach. People can be manipulated into choosing alternatives that they might otherwise reject simply by changing the frame of reference (Tversky and Kahneman 1981). These biases can affect the way information systems are designed and used for management decision making.

Decision making often is not performed by a single individual but by entire groups or organizations. **Organizational models of decision making** take into account the structural and political characteristics of an organization. Bureaucratic, political, and even "garbage can" models have been proposed to describe how decision making takes place in organizations.

According to **bureaucratic models of decision making**, an organization's most important goal is the preservation of the organization. The reduction of uncertainty is another major goal. Policy tends to be incremental, only marginally different from the past, because radical policy departures involve too much uncertainty. These models depict organizations generally as not choosing or deciding in a rational sense. Rather, according to bureaucratic models, whatever organizations do is the result of routines and existing business processes honed over years of active use.

Organizations rarely change these routines and business processes because they may have to change personnel and incur risks (who knows if the new techniques work better than the old ones?). Although senior management and leaders are hired to coordinate and lead the organization, they are effectively trapped by the organization's standard business processes and existing solutions. Some organizations do, of course, change; they learn new ways of behaving, and they can be led. But all of these changes require a long time. Look around and you will find many organizations doing pretty much what they did 10, 20, or even 30 years ago. Most business firms that you know about now and do business with every day will not exist in 10 years. About half of all new firms fail in five years, and only 17 percent of the Fortune 500 of 1955 still exists (Starbuck 1983).

In **political models of decision making**, what an organization does is a result of political bargains struck among key leaders and interest groups. Organizations do not come up with solutions that are chosen to solve some problem. They reach compromises that reflect the conflicts, the major stakeholders, the diverse interests, the unequal power, and the confusion that constitute politics.

rational model
choice
organizational models of decision making
bureaucratic models of decision making
political models of decision making

Implications for the Design and Understanding of Information Systems

To deliver genuine benefits, information systems must be developed with a clear understanding of the organization in which they will be used and exactly how they can contribute to managerial decision making. In our experience, the central organizational factors to consider when planning a new system are the following:

- The environment in which the organization must function
- The structure of the organization: hierarchy, specialization, routines, and business processes
- The organization's culture and politics
- The type of organization and its style of leadership
- The principal interest groups affected by the system and the attitudes of workers who will be using the system
- The kinds of tasks, decisions, and business processes that the information system is designed to assist

Systems should be developed to support individual, group, and organizational decision making. Information systems developers should design systems that have the following characteristics:

- They are flexible and provide many options for handling data and evaluating information.
- They are capable of supporting a variety of styles, skills, and knowledge as well as keeping track of many alternatives and consequences.
- They are sensitive to the organization's bureaucratic and political requirements.

3.4 Information Systems and Business Strategy

Certain types of information systems have become especially critical to firms' long-term prosperity and survival. These systems, which are powerful tools for staying ahead of the competition, are called *strategic information systems.*

What Is a Strategic Information System?

Strategic information systems change the goals, operations, products, services, or environmental relationships of organizations to help them gain an edge over competitors. Systems that have these effects may even change the business of organizations. For instance, The Bank of Montreal transformed its core business from traditional banking services, such as customer chequing and savings accounts and loans, to electronic commerce, money management, and financial information services, providing online access to individuals and businesses to handle their financial record keeping, cash management, and investment information and transactions. The Bank of Montreal provides online services that include point-of-sale automobile financing; recruiting and hiring their own employees; consumer financing for small- to medium-sized businesses, permitting the companies' customers to finance purchase of their products and services immediately; and wireless services for cellular phone- and personal digital assistant-using bank customers. The Bank of Montreal also developed the first *virtual bank* in Canada (Ray, 2000; Baroudi, 2000).

Strategic information systems should be distinguished from strategic-level systems for senior managers that focus on long-term, decision-making problems. Strategic information systems can be used at all organizational levels and are more far-reaching and deep rooted than the other kinds of systems we have described. Strategic information systems profoundly alter the way a firm conducts its business or the very business of the firm itself. As

strategic information systems

we will see, organizations may need to change their internal operations and relationships with customers and suppliers in order to take advantage of new information technology.

Traditional models of strategy are being modified to accommodate the impact of digital firms and new information flows. Before the emergence of the digital firm, business strategy emphasized competing head-to-head against other firms in the same marketplace. Today, the emphasis is increasingly on exploring, identifying, and occupying new market niches before competitors; understanding the customer value chain better; and learning faster and more deeply than competitors.

Business strategy is a set of activities and decisions firms make that determine the following:

- Products and services the firm produces
- Industries in which the firm competes
- Competitors, suppliers, and customers of the firm
- Long-term goals of the firm

Strategies often result from a conscious strategic planning process in which nearly all small to large firms engage at least once a year. This process produces a document called the strategic plan, and the managers of the firm are given the task of achieving the goals of the strategic plan. But firms have to adapt these plans to changing environments. Where firms end up is not necessarily where they planned to be. Nevertheless, strategic plans are useful interim tools for defining what the firm will do until the business environment changes.

Thinking about strategy usually takes place at three different levels:

- **Business.** A single firm producing a set of related products and services
- **Firm.** A collection of businesses that make up a single, multidivisional firm
- **Industry.** A collection of firms that make up an industrial environment or ecosystem

Information systems and technologies play a crucial role in corporate strategy and strategic planning at each of these three different levels. Just about any substantial information system—a supply chain system, customer relationship system, or enterprise management system—can have strategic implications for a firm. As we pointed out in Chapter 1, and again in Chapter 5, what the firm wants to do in the next five years will be shaped in large part by what its information systems enable it to do. IT and the ability to use IT effectively will shape what the firm makes or provides customers, how it makes the product and service, how it competes with others in its industry, and how it cooperates with other firms and logistic partners.

To understand how IT fits into the strategic thinking process, it is useful to consider the three levels of business strategy (the business, the firm, and the industry). At each level of strategy, IT plays an important role.

Business-Level Strategy: The Value Chain Model

At the business level of strategy, the key question is, "How can we compete effectively in this particular market?" The market might be light bulbs, utility vehicles, or cable television, or the business may be a service firm providing travel or financial services. The most common generic strategies at this level are (1) become the low-cost producer, (2) differentiate your product or service, and/or (3) change the scope of competition by either enlarging the market to include global markets or narrowing the market by focusing on small niches not well served by your competitors. Digital firms provide new capabilities for supporting business-level strategy by managing the supply chain, developing efficient customer "sense and response" systems, and participating in value webs to deliver new products and services to market.

Leveraging Technology in the Value Chain
At the business level, the most common analytical tool is value chain analysis. The **value chain model** highlights specific activities in the business where competitive strategies can best be applied (Porter

business strategy

value chain model

1985) and where information systems are most likely to have a strategic impact. The value chain model identifies specific, critical leverage points where a firm can use information technology most effectively to enhance its competitive position. Exactly where can it obtain the greatest benefit from strategic information systems—what specific activities can be used to create new products and services, enhance market penetration, lock in customers and suppliers, and lower operational costs? This model views the firm as a series or chain of basic activities that add a margin of value to a firm's products or services. These activities can be categorized as either primary activities or support activities.

Primary activities are most directly related to the production and distribution of the firm's products and services that create value for the customer. Primary activities include inbound logistics, operations, outbound logistics, sales and marketing, and service. Inbound logistics includes receiving and storing materials for distribution to production. Operations transforms inputs into finished products. Outbound logistics entails storing and distributing finished products. Sales and marketing includes promoting and selling the firm's products. The service activity includes maintenance and repair of the firm's goods and services.

Support activities make the delivery of the primary activities possible and consist of organization infrastructure (administration and management), human resources (employee recruiting, hiring, and training), technology (improving products and the production process), and procurement (purchasing input).

Organizations have competitive advantage when they provide more value to their customers or when they provide the same value to customers at a lower price. An information system could have a strategic impact if it helps the firm provide products or services at a lower cost than competitors or if it provides products and services at the same cost as competitors but with greater value. The value activities that add the most value to products and services depend on the features of each particular firm.

The firm's value chain can be linked to the value chains of its partners, including suppliers, distributors, and customers. Figure 3-11 illustrates the activities of the firm value chain and the industry value chain, showing examples of strategic information systems

FIGURE 3-11   *The firm value chain and the industry value chain.*

Illustrated are various examples of strategic information systems for the primary and support activities of a firm and its value partners that would add a margin of value to a firm's products or services.

primary activities

support activities

that could be developed to make each of the value activities more cost effective. A firm can achieve a strategic advantage by providing value, not only through its internal value chain processes but also through powerful, efficient ties to industry value partners.

Digitally enabled networks can be used not only to purchase supplies but also to closely coordinate production of many independent firms. For instance, the Italian casual wear company Benetton uses subcontractors and independent firms for labour-intensive production processes, such as tailoring, finishing, and ironing, while maintaining control of design, procurement, marketing, and distribution. Benetton uses computer networks to provide independent businesses and foreign production centres with production specifications so that they can efficiently produce the items needed by Benetton retail outlets (Camuffo, Romano, and Vinelli 2001).

Internet technology has made it possible to extend the value chain so that it ties together all the firm's suppliers, business partners, and customers into a value web. A **value web** is a collection of independent firms that use information technology to coordinate their value chains to produce a product or service for a market. It is more customer driven and operates in a less linear fashion than the traditional value chain. Nygård, featured in the opening case for Chapter 2, uses IT to manage its value web.

Figure 3-12 shows that this value web synchronizes the business processes of customers, suppliers, and trading partners among different companies in an industry or related industries. These value webs are flexible and adaptive to changes in supply and demand. Relationships can be bundled or unbundled in response to changing market conditions. A company can use this value web to maintain long-standing relationships with many customers over long periods or to respond immediately to individual customer transactions. Firms can accelerate time to market and to customers by optimizing their value web relationships to make quick decisions on who can deliver the required products or services at the right price and location.

Businesses should try to develop strategic information systems for both the internal value chain activities and the external value activities that add the most value. A strategic analysis might, for example, identify sales and marketing activities for which information systems could provide the greatest boost. The analysis might recommend a system to

FIGURE 3-12   *The value web.*

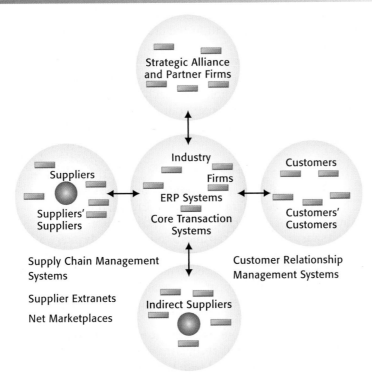

The value web is a networked system that can synchronize the value chains of business partners within an industry to respond rapidly to changes in supply and demand.

Strategic Alliance and Partner Firms

Suppliers

Industry Firms

Customers

ERP Systems

Suppliers' Suppliers

Core Transaction Systems

Customers' Customers

Supply Chain Management Systems

Customer Relationship Management Systems

Supplier Extranets

Net Marketplaces

Indirect Suppliers

value web

reduce marketing costs by targeting marketing campaigns more efficiently or by providing information for developing products more finely attuned to a firm's target market. A series of systems, including some linked to systems of other value partners, might be required to create a strategic advantage.

Value chains and value webs are not static. From time to time, they may have to be redesigned to keep pace with changes in the competitive landscape (Fine et al. 2002). Companies may need to reorganize and reshape their structural, financial, and human assets and recast systems to tap new sources of value.

We now show how information technology at the business level helps the firm reduce costs, differentiate products, and serve new markets.

Information Systems Products and Services Firms can use information systems to create unique new products and services that can be easily distinguished from those of competitors. Strategic information systems for **product differentiation** can prevent the competition from responding in kind so that firms with these differentiated products and services no longer have to compete on the basis of cost.

Many of these information technology-based products and services have been created by financial institutions. Citibank developed automatic teller machines (ATMs) and bank debit cards in 1977. Citibank ATMs were so successful that Citibank's competitors were forced to counter with their own ATM systems. Major banking institutions, such as the Bank of Montreal, continue to innovate by providing online electronic banking services so that customers can do most of their banking transactions using home computers linked to proprietary networks or the Internet. These banks have recently launched new account aggregation services that enable customers to view all of their accounts, including their credit cards, investments, online travel rewards, and even accounts from competing banks, from a single online source. Some companies, such as ING Direct and NetBank, have used the Web to set up virtual banks offering a full array of banking services without any physical branches. (Customers mail in their deposits and use designated ATMs to obtain cash.)

Computerized reservation systems such as American Airlines's SABRE system started out as a powerful source of product differentiation for the airline and travel industries. These traditional reservation systems are now being challenged by new travel services with which consumers can make their own airline, hotel, and car reservations directly on the Web, bypassing travel agents and other intermediaries.

Manufacturers and retailers are starting to use information systems to create products and services that are custom-tailored to fit the precise specifications of individual customers. Dell Computer Corporation sells directly to customers using assemble-to-order manufacturing. Individuals, businesses, and government agencies can buy computers directly from Dell, customized with the exact features and components they need. They can place their orders directly using a toll-free telephone number or Dell's Web site. Once Dell's production control receives an order, it directs an assembly plant to assemble the computer using components from an on-site warehouse based on the configuration specified by the customer.

Systems to Focus on Market Niche A business can create new market niches by identifying a specific target for a product or service that it can serve in a superior manner. Through **focused differentiation**, the firm can provide a specialized product or service for this narrow target market better than competitors.

An information system can give companies a competitive advantage by producing data for finely tuned sales and marketing techniques. These systems treat existing information as a resource that the organization can mine to increase profitability and market penetration. Information systems enable companies to analyze customer buying patterns, tastes, and preferences closely so that they efficiently pitch advertising and marketing campaigns to smaller and smaller target markets.

The data come from a range of sources—credit card transactions, demographics, purchases from checkout counter scanners at supermarkets and retail stores, and information collected when people access and interact with Web sites. Sophisticated software tools can

product differentiation

focused differentiation

find patterns in these large pools of data and infer rules from them that can be used to guide decision making. Analysis of these data can drive one-to-one marketing where personal messages can be created based on individualized preferences. Contemporary customer relationship management (CRM) systems feature analytical capabilities for this type of intensive data analysis (see Chapters 2 and 14).

For example, Sears Roebuck continually analyzes purchase data from its 60 million past and present credit card users to target appliance buyers, gardening enthusiasts, and mothers-to-be with special promotions. The company might mail customers who purchase a washer and dryer a maintenance contract and annual contract renewal forms.

The Window on Technology shows how the hotel industry is trying to wring more value out of its customer data. Hotel chains are aggressively recruiting business travelers to sign up with their customer loyalty programs to capture more detailed data about their repeat customers. The customer data they had been collecting through their reservation systems was not sufficiently reliable or detailed for them to develop targeted customer profiles for marketing. The hotels believe the data is key to their growth. More examples of customer data analysis can be found in Chapters 6, 14, and 15.

The cost of acquiring a new customer has been estimated to be five times that of retaining an existing customer. By carefully examining transactions of customer purchases and activities, firms can identify profitable customers and win more of their business. Likewise, companies can use these data to identify nonprofitable customers. Companies that skillfully use customer data focus on identifying their most valued customers and use data from a variety of sources to understand these customers' needs (Reinartz and Kumar 2002; Davenport et al. 2001; Clemons and Weber 1994).

Supply Chain Management and Efficient Customer Response Systems
Digital firms have the capabilities to go far beyond traditional strategic systems for taking advantage of digital links with other organizations. A powerful business-level strategy available to digital firms involves linking the value chains of vendors and suppliers to the firm's value chain (Kopczak and Johnson 2003). Digital firms can carry integration of value chains further by linking the customer's value chain to the firm's value chain in an efficient customer response system. Firms using systems to link with customers and suppliers can reduce their inventory costs while responding rapidly to customer demands.

By keeping prices low and shelves well stocked using a legendary inventory replenishment system, Wal-Mart has become the leading retail business in North America. Wal-Mart's continuous replenishment system sends orders for new merchandise directly to suppliers as soon as consumers pay for their purchases at the cash register. Point-of-sale terminals record the bar code of each item passing the checkout counter and send a purchase transaction directly to a central computer at Wal-Mart headquarters. The computer collects the orders from all Wal-Mart stores and transmits them to suppliers. Suppliers can also access Wal-Mart's sales and inventory data using Web technology.

Because the system can replenish inventory with lightning speed, Wal-Mart does not need to spend much money on maintaining large inventories of goods in its own warehouses. The system also enables Wal-Mart to adjust purchases of store items to meet customer demands. Competitors, such as Sears, have been spending 24.9 percent of sales on overhead. But by using systems to keep operating costs low, Wal-Mart pays only 16.6 percent of sales revenue for overhead. (Operating costs average 20.7 percent of sales in the retail industry.)

Wal-Mart's continuous inventory replenishment system uses sales data captured at the checkout counter to transmit orders to restock merchandise directly to its suppliers. The system enables Wal-Mart to keep costs low while fine-tuning its merchandise to meet customer demands.

WINDOW ON TECHNOLOGY

Hotel Loyalty Programs Become Competitive Weapons

Hotels have traditionally used customer loyalty programs to provide incentives for repeat customers. Now they are promoting them even more aggressively, especially for business travellers. Why? The answer lies in the data.

Growing awareness of customer relationship management techniques has made hotels realize they can profit even more than in the past by collecting and analyzing detailed data about their guests. According to Robert Mandelbaum, a hotel analyst with PKF Consulting in Atlanta, the hotel chains are "desperate for data.... Hotels need information about their guests and especially about business travellers." Encouraging guests to sign up for customer loyalty programs is "the easiest way to get that information."

Guests signing up for Wyndham Hotels' frequent-guest program provide information about their choice of bed, whether they prefer to relax with a soda or a glass of wine after checking in, the airline frequent flyer program to which they belong, as well as their addresses, email addresses, and phone numbers. Those who sign up online are automatically registered for a monthly "Wyndham News by Request" email notice of special members-only offers and program updates. Guests who refuse to sign up for such programs do not receive as much preferential treatment as those that do.

The same type of service is offered to loyalty card members of other hotel chains. Toronto-based Fairmont Hotels offers three different levels of free "club" membership. Membership entitles members to benefits such as discounted or free high-speed Internet access, free local calls, free newspapers, and so on. Those who do not sign up pay extra for these services. Similarly, Hilton HHonors loyalty program members are allowed to check out late while nonmembers who check out late have to pay for an additional day.

The hotels use this detailed data to better serve their guests, and they also use it to develop targeted sales and marketing campaigns for enlarging their market share. Until recently, these data collection efforts have been woefully inadequate. According to Robert Burke, of Egroup Communications of Miami, which manages email databases for the lodging industry, the U.S. hotel industry had collected data on only about 10 percent of its business travellers. The databases were incomplete or disorganized so that the hotels really knew very little about their guests.

One exception is the Hilton Hotel chain. It spent $50 million on a customer information system called OnQ, which contains 7.5 million profiles of active guests in every property across the eight hotel brands owned by Hilton, including Hilton, Doubletree, Embassy Suites, Hampton Inn, Hilton Garden Inn, Hilton Grand Vacations, and Homewood Suites. In combination with Hilton's HHonors frequent-guest program, the system can recognize the same customer whether that person is checking into a $79 room at Hampton Inn or a $540 suite at the Hilton Hawaiian Village in Honolulu.

OnQ was largely custom-developed for Hilton. It includes a property management system and a hotel-owner reporting module, as well as Hilton's customer relationship management applications. All the pieces are integrated with a central reservation system, a sales force automation tool, an older revenue management system, a financial and human resources application from PeopleSoft (now Oracle) enterprise software, and Hilton's e-commerce site. The system is delivered as an information technology service to the 52 hotels directly owned by Hilton and hotels that are operated as Hilton franchises. The franchisees license the software for about three-fourths of a percent of their annual revenue.

OnQ makes it easier to match customer reservations with records of customer profiles in the Hilton database. Employees at the front desk tapping into the system can instantly search through 180 million records to find out customer preferences and their past experiences with Hilton so they can give these guests exactly what they want. Before this system was implemented, only two out of every 10 guest reservations could be matched to an existing customer profile. OnQ is now matching 4.7 out of every 10 guest reservations, and it will eventually be able to match six out of 10.

One of the main ways OnQ provides value is by establishing the value of each customer to Hilton, based on personal history and on predictions about the value of that person's future business with Hilton. OnQ can also identify customers who are clearly not profitable. Extra attention to profitable customers appears to be paying off. The rate of accommodation at Hilton Hotels instead of rival hotels has soared to 61 percent from 41 percent two years ago. OnQ will be further put to the test as Hilton opens additional hotels.

To Think About: Why are frequent-guest programs so important for the hotel industry? How do they provide value? To what extent can OnQ provide the Hilton chain with a competitive advantage? Explain your answer.

Sources: Tony Kontzer, "Data-Driven," *Information Week,* August 2, 2004; and Christopher Elliott, "Hotels Get Pushy About Their Loyalty Programs," *New York Times,* June 1, 2004.

Wal-Mart's continuous replenishment system is an example of efficient supply chain management, which we introduced in Chapter 2. Supply chain management systems can not only lower inventory costs, but they also can deliver the product or service more rapidly to the customer. Supply chain management can thus be used to create **efficient customer response systems** that respond to customer demands more efficiently. An efficient customer response system directly links consumer behaviour to distribution, production and supply chains. Wal-Mart's continuous replenishment system provides this type of efficient customer response. Dell Computer Corporation's assemble-to-order system, described earlier, is another example of an efficient customer response system.

The convenience and ease of using these information systems raise **switching costs** (the cost—lost time and expenditure—of switching from one supplier or system to a competing supplier or system), which discourages customers from going to competitors. An example of a company using an efficient customer response system to raise switching costs is Source Medical, the Canadian arm of Allegiance Corporation, which began as American Health Corporation and later became Baxter International, eventually becoming Allegiance Corporation, a division of Cardinal Health. Baxter's original "stockless inventory" and ordering system, still in use by Allegiance and Source Medical, uses supply chain management to create an efficient customer response system. Participating hospitals become unwilling to switch to another supplier because of the system's convenience and low cost. Source Medical is the largest hospital supplier in Canada. When hospitals want to place an order, they do not need to call a salesperson or send a purchase order— they simply use a PC with Internet access on-site to order from the full Source Medical supply catalogue. The system generates shipping, billing, invoicing, and inventory information, and the online response provides customers with an estimated delivery date. With nine regional customer-facing distribution warehouses from Vancouver to St. John's along with local warehousing closer to their customers, Source Medical can make daily deliveries of its products, often within hours of receiving an order.

Source Medical delivery personnel no longer drop off their cartons at loading docks to be placed in hospital storerooms. Instead, they deliver orders directly to the hospital corridors, dropping them at nursing stations, operating rooms, and supply closets. This delivery system has created, in effect, a "stockless inventory," with Source Medical serving as the hospitals' warehouse.

Figure 3-13 compares stockless inventory with the just-in-time supply method and traditional inventory practices. While just-in-time inventory enables customers to reduce their inventories by ordering only enough material for a few days at a time, stockless inventory enables them to eliminate their inventories entirely. All inventory responsibilities shift to the distributor, which manages the supply flow. Stockless inventory is a powerful instrument for locking in customers, thus giving the supplier a decided competitive advantage. Information systems can also raise switching costs by making product support, service, and other interactions with customers more convenient and reliable (Vandenbosch and Dawar 2002).

Supply chain management and efficient customer response systems are two examples of how emerging digital firms can engage in business strategies not available to traditional firms. Both types of systems require network-based information technology infrastructure investment and software competence to make customer and supply chain data flow seamlessly among different organizations. Both types of strategies have greatly enhanced the efficiency of individual firms and even the economy as a whole by moving toward a demand-pull production system and away from the traditional supply-push economic system in which factories were managed on the basis of 12-month official plans rather than on near-instantaneous customer purchase information. Chapter 14 provides more detail on this topic. Figure 3-14 illustrates the relationships between supply chain management, efficient customer response, and the various business-level strategies.

Firm-Level Strategy and Information Technology

A business firm is typically a collection of businesses. Often, the firm is organized financially as a collection of strategic business units, and the returns to the firm are directly tied to strategic business unit performance. Information systems can improve the overall performance of these business units by promoting synergies and core competencies. The idea

efficient customer response systems

switching costs

FIGURE 3-13 *Stockless inventory compared to traditional and just-in-time supply methods.*

The just-in-time supply method reduces inventory requirements of the customer, whereas stockless inventory enables the customer to eliminate inventories entirely. Deliveries are made daily, sometimes directly to the departments that need the supplies.

driving synergies is that when the output of some units can be used as inputs to other units, or two organizations can pool markets and expertise. These relationships can lower costs and generate profits. Recent bank and financial firm mergers throughout the world, such as the mergers of Toronto Dominion Bank and Canada Trust, JPMorgan Chase and Bank One Corporation, Bank of America and FleetBoston Financial Corporation, Deutsche Bank and Bankers Trust, and Citicorp and Travelers Insurance, occurred precisely for this purpose.

One use of information technology in these synergy situations is to tie together the operations of disparate business units so that they can act as a whole. For example, the Hudson's Bay Company's (HBC) acquisition of K-Mart's operations provided HBC with additional retail outlets. Merging with Bank One provided JPMorgan Chase with a massive network of retail branches in the Midwest and Southwest. Information systems would help the merged banks lower retailing costs and increase cross-marketing of financial products.

Enhancing Core Competencies A second concept for firm-level strategy involves the notion of core competency. The argument is that the performance of all business units can increase insofar as these business units develop, or create, a central core of competencies. A **core competency** is an activity for which a firm is a world-class leader. Core competencies may involve being the world's best miniature parts designer, the best package delivery service, or the best thin-film manufacturer. In general, a core competency relies on knowledge that is gained over many years of experience and from having a first-class research organization or simply key people who follow the literature and stay abreast of new external knowledge.

Any information system that encourages the sharing of knowledge across business units enhances competency. These systems might encourage or enhance existing competencies and help employees become aware of new external knowledge; these systems might also help a business leverage existing competencies to related markets.

core competency

FIGURE 3-14 *Business-level strategy.*

Efficient customer response and supply chain management systems are often interrelated, helping firms lock in customers and suppliers while lowering operating costs. Other types of systems can be used to support product differentiation, focused differentiation, and low-cost producer strategies.

Industry-Level Strategy and Information Systems: Competitive Forces and Network Economics

Firms together comprise an industry, such as automotive, telephone, television broadcasting, and forest products industries, to name a few. The key strategic question at this level of analysis is, "How and when should we compete with as opposed to cooperate with others in the industry?" While most strategic analyses emphasize competition, a great deal of money can be made by cooperating with other firms in the same industry or firms in related industries. For instance, firms can cooperate to develop industry standards in a number of areas; they can cooperate by working together to build customer awareness and by working collectively with suppliers to lower costs (Shapiro and Varian 1999). The principal concepts for analyzing strategy at the industry level are information partnerships, the competitive forces model, business ecosystems, and network economics.

Information Partnerships Firms can form information partnerships and even link their information systems to achieve unique synergies. In an **information partnership**, both companies can join forces to gain a strategic advantage without actually merging by sharing information (Konsynski and McFarlan 1990). Air Canada has an arrangement with Canadian Imperial Bank of Commerce (CIBC) to award one airmile in its frequent flyer program for every dollar spent using a CIBC Aerogold credit card. Air Canada benefits from increased customer loyalty, and CIBC gains new credit card subscriptions and a highly credit-worthy customer base for cross marketing. Air Canada has also allied with Primus Canada, awarding five frequent flyer airmiles for each dollar of long distance billing when a customer spends over $15 a month.

These partnerships help firms gain access to new customers, creating new opportunities for cross-selling and targeting products. Companies that have been traditional competitors may find these alliances to be mutually advantageous. Source Medical offers its customers medical and office supplies from competitors through its electronic ordering channel.

The Competitive Forces Model In Porter's **competitive forces model**, which is illustrated in Figure 3-15, a firm faces a number of external threats and opportunities that affect an organization's strategy and ability to compete: the threat of new

information partnership
competitive forces model

entrants into its market, the pressure from substitute products or services, the bargaining power of customers, the bargaining power of suppliers, and the positioning of traditional industry competitors (Porter 1985). The nature of the players in an industry and their relative bargaining power determine **industry structure** and the overall profitability of doing business in the industry's specific environment.

Competitive advantage can be achieved by enhancing the firm's ability to deal with customers, suppliers, substitute products and services, and new entrants to its market, which in turn may change the balance of power between a firm and other competitors in the industry in the firm's favour.

How can information systems be used to achieve strategic advantage at the industry level? By working with other firms, industry participants can use information technology to develop industry-wide standards for exchanging information or business transactions electronically (see Chapters 5, 7, and 8), which force all market participants to subscribe to similar standards. Earlier we described how firms can benefit from value webs with complementary firms in the industry. These efforts increase efficiency at the industry level as well as at the business level—making product substitution less likely and perhaps raising entry costs—thus discouraging new entrants. Also, industry members can build industry-wide, IT-supported consortia, symposia, and communications networks to coordinate activities concerning government agencies, foreign competition, and competing industries.

An example of industry-level cooperation can be found in Exostar, an electronic marketplace shared by major aerospace and defense firms for procurement and for cooperation on joint development projects. These companies can raise the industry's productivity by working together to create an integrated supply chain.

In the age of the Internet, the traditional competitive forces are still at work, but competitive rivalry has become much more intense (Porter 2001). Internet technology is based on universal standards that any company can use, making it easy for rivals to compete on price alone and for new competitors to enter the market. Because information is available to everyone, the Internet raises the bargaining power of customers, who can quickly find the lowest-cost provider on the Web. Profits have been dampened. Some industries, such as the travel industry and the financial services industry, have been more affected than others. Table 3-5 summarizes some of the potentially negative impacts of the Internet on business firms.

However, contrary to Porter's somewhat negative assessment, the Internet also creates new opportunities for building brands and developing very large and loyal customer bases that are willing to pay a premium for that brand, such as Yahoo!, eBay, Amazon, Google, and many others. In addition, as with all IT-enabled business initiatives, some

FIGURE 3-15 *Porter's competitive forces model.*

Various forces affect an organization's ability to compete and therefore greatly influence a firm's business strategy. There are threats from new market entrants and from substitute products and services. Customers and suppliers wield bargaining power. Traditional competitors constantly adapt their strategies to maintain their market positioning.

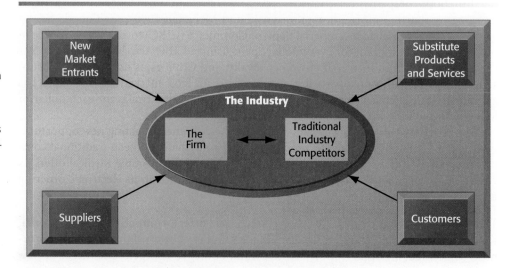

industry structure

TABLE 3-5 *Impact of the Internet on Competitive Forces and Industry Structure*

COMPETITIVE FORCE	IMPACT OF THE INTERNET
Substitute products or services	Enables new substitutes to emerge with new approaches to meeting needs and performing functions.
Customers' bargaining power	Availability of global price and product information shifts bargaining power to customers.
Suppliers' bargaining power	Procurement over the Internet tends to raise bargaining power over suppliers. Suppliers can also benefit from reduced barriers to entry and from the elimination of distributors and other intermediaries standing between them and their users.
Threat of new entrants	The Internet reduces barriers to entry, such as the need for a sales force, access to channels, and physical assets. It provides a technology for driving business processes that makes other things easier to do.
Positioning and rivalry among existing competitors	Widens the geographic market, increasing the number of competitors, and reduces differences among competitors. Makes it more difficult to sustain operational advantages. Puts pressure to compete on price.

firms are far better at using the Internet than other firms, which creates new strategic opportunities for the successful firms.

Business Ecosystems: Keystone and Niche Firms The Internet and the emergence of digital firms call for some modification of the industry competitive forces model. The traditional Porter model assumes a relatively static industry environment; relatively clear-cut industry boundaries; and a relatively stable set of suppliers, substitutes, and customers, with the focus on industry players in a market environment. Instead of participating in a single industry, some of today's firms are much more aware that they participate in industry sets—collections of industries that provide related services and products (see Figure 3-16). **Business ecosystem** is another term for these loosely coupled but interdependent networks of suppliers, distributors, outsourcing firms, transportation service firms, and technology manufacturers (Iansiti and Levien 2004).

The concept of a business ecosystem builds on the idea of the value web described earlier, the main difference being that cooperation takes place across many industries rather than many firms. For instance, both Microsoft and Wal-Mart provide platforms composed of information systems, technologies, and services that thousands of other firms in

FIGURE 3-16   *An ecosystem strategic model.*

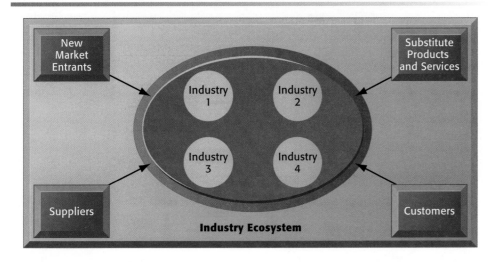

The digital firm era requires a more dynamic view of the boundaries among industries, firms, customers, and suppliers, with competition occurring among industry sets in a business ecosystem. In the ecosystem model, multiple industries work together to deliver value to the customer. IT plays an important role in enabling a dense network of interactions among the participating firms.

business ecosystem

different industries use to enhance their own capabilities. Microsoft has estimated that more than 40 000 firms use its Windows platform to deliver their own products, support Microsoft products, and extend the value of Microsoft's own firm. Wal-Mart's order entry and inventory management system is a platform used by thousands of suppliers to obtain real-time access to customer demand, track shipments, and control inventories (as described in the chapter-opening case).

Business ecosystems can be characterized as having one or a few keystone firms that dominate the ecosystem and create the platforms used by other niche firms. Keystone firms in the Microsoft ecosystem would include Microsoft and technology producers such as Intel and IBM. Niche firms include thousands of software application firms, software developers, service firms, networking firms, and consulting firms that both support and rely on Microsoft products.

Alternatively, it is equally possible to think of ecosystems at the industry level. The computer chip, automobile, aircraft, and medical device industries can be usefully seen as industrial sets or ecosystems that involve the cooperation of multiple industries to function efficiently or even survive. For instance, the medical device industry relies on a university research community for innovative designs and research, on the microprocessor industry for sensors and controls, and on the precision machining industry for production.

Information technology plays a powerful role in establishing business ecosystems. Obviously, many firms use information systems to develop into keystone firms by building IT-based platforms that other firms can use. For example, eBay has created a platform for auctions and online stores used by over 400 000 small businesses every day (see Figure 3-17). Amazon.com and portals such as Yahoo! have created online store business platforms used by Fortune 500 firms such as Dell (and thousands of smaller firms) to sell directly to the public. In the digital firm era, we can expect greater emphasis on the use of IT to build industry ecosystems because the costs of participating in these ecosystems will fall and the benefits to all firms will increase rapidly as the platform grows (see the following discussion of network economics).

Individual firms should consider how their investments in IT will enable them to become profitable niche players in larger ecosystems created by keystone firms. For instance, in making decisions about which products to build or which services to offer, a firm should consider the existing business ecosystems these products are related to and how it might use IT to enable participation in these larger ecosystems.

FIGURE 3-17   *The eBay Web site.*

The eBay Web site provides a platform for more than 400 000 small and large businesses to operate online storefronts and auctions. A massive information system powers this business ecosystem.

Network Economics A final strategic concept useful at the industry level is **network economics**. In traditional economics—the economics of factories and agriculture—production experiences diminishing returns. The more any given resource is applied to production, the lower the marginal gain in output, until a point is reached where the additional inputs produce no additional outputs. This is the law of diminishing returns, and it is the foundation for most of modern economics.

In some situations, the law of diminishing returns does not work. For instance, in a network, the marginal costs of adding another participant are about zero while the marginal gain is much larger. The larger the number of subscribers in a telephone system or the Internet, the greater the value to all participants because each user can interact with more people (see Chapters 5 and 7 for more detailed discussions of network economics). It is no more expensive to operate a television station with 1000 subscribers than a station with 10 million subscribers. And the value of a community of people grows with size while the cost of adding new members is inconsequential.

Network economics plays an underlying role in the ecosystem model described earlier insofar as participants in the ecosystem gain value as the ecosystem grows in power. From this network economics perspective, information technology can be strategically useful. Internet sites can be used by firms to build communities of users—like-minded customers who want to share their experiences. These communities can build customer loyalty and enjoyment and build unique ties to customers. The giant online auction site eBay and iVillage, an online community for women, are two examples. Both businesses are based on networks of millions of users, and both companies have used the Web and Internet communication tools to build communities. The more people offering products on eBay, the more valuable is the eBay site to everyone because more products are listed and more competition among suppliers lowers prices. Network economics can also provide strategic benefits to commercial software vendors. The value of their software and complementary software products increases as more people use them, and there is a larger installed base to justify continued use of the product and vendor support (Gallaugher and Wang 2002).

Management Opportunities, Challenges, and Solutions

We have seen that the relationship between information systems and organizational performance is very complex, providing managers with both opportunities and challenges.

Opportunities

Business firms face a continuing stream of IT-enabled opportunities to lower their transaction and agency costs and to harness the power of the new information technologies that appear regularly to develop unique products, services, and processes. Clearly, some firms will excel in learning how to use the technology, and because of this fact there are opportunities for strategic competitive advantages at all three levels—business, firm, and industry.

Management Challenges

Some firms achieve better organizational performance and strategic advantage with systems, but not without significant hurdles.

Sustainability of Competitive Advantage The competitive advantages strategic systems confer do not necessarily last long enough to ensure long-term profitability. Because competitors can retaliate and copy strategic systems, competitive advantage is not always sustainable. Markets, customer expectations, and technology change; globalization has made these changes even more rapid and unpredictable

network economics

(Eisenhardt 2002). The Internet can make competitive advantage disappear very quickly because virtually all companies can use this technology. Classic strategic systems, such as American Airlines's SABRE computerized reservation system, Citibank's ATM system, and FedEx's package tracking system, benefited by being the first in their industries. Then rival systems emerged. Information systems alone cannot provide an enduring business advantage. Systems originally intended to be strategic frequently become tools for survival, required by every firm to stay in business (these systems are known as strategic necessities), or they may inhibit organizations from making the strategic changes essential for future success.

Difficulties of Managing System-Related Change Bringing about change through new information technology and systems is slowed considerably by the natural inertia of organizations. Of course, organizations can and do change, but the process is more complicated and much slower than is typically anticipated.

Solution Guidelines

Strategic information systems often change the organization as well as its products, services, and operating procedures, driving the organization into new behavioural patterns. Using technology for strategic benefit requires careful planning and management.

Performing a Strategic Systems Analysis Managers interested in using information systems for competitive advantage will need to perform a strategic systems analysis. To identify the types of systems that would provide a strategic advantage to their firms, managers should ask the following questions:

1. What is the structure of the industry in which the firm is located?
   - What are some of the competitive forces at work in the industry? Are there new entrants to the industry? What is the relative power of suppliers, customers, and substitute products and services over prices?
   - Is the basis of competition quality, price, or brand?
   - What are the direction and nature of change within the industry? From where are the momentum and change coming?
   - How is the industry currently using information technology? Is the organization behind or ahead of the industry in its application of information systems?
2. What are the business, firm, and industry value chains for this particular firm?
   - How is the company creating value for the customer—through lower prices and transaction costs or higher quality? Are there any places in the value chain where the business could create more value for the customer and additional profit for the company?
   - Does the firm understand and manage its business processes using the best practices available? Is it taking maximum advantage of supply chain management, customer relationship management, and enterprise systems?
   - Does the firm leverage its core competencies?
   - Is the industry supply chain and customer base changing in ways that benefit or harm the firm?
   - Could the firm benefit from strategic partnerships and value webs?
   - Where in the value chain would information systems provide the greatest value to the firm?

Managing Strategic Transitions Adopting the kinds of strategic systems described in this chapter generally requires changes in business goals, relationships with customers and suppliers, internal operations, and information architecture. These sociotechnical changes, affecting both social and technical elements of the organization, can be considered **strategic transitions**—a movement between levels of sociotechnical systems.

These changes often entail blurring of organizational boundaries, both external and internal. Suppliers and customers must become intimately linked and may share each other's responsibilities. Managers will need to devise new business processes for coordinating their firms' activities with those of customers, suppliers, and other organizations. The organizational change requirements surrounding new information systems are so important that they merit attention throughout this text. Chapters 10 and 11 examine organizational change issues in great detail.

strategic transitions

Summary

1. **Identify and describe important features of organizations that managers need to understand in order to develop and use information systems successfully.**

    Managers need to understand certain essential features of organizations to develop and use information systems successfully. All modern organizations are hierarchical, specialized, and impartial. They use explicit routines to maximize efficiency. All organizations have their own cultures and politics arising from differences in interest groups. Organizations differ in goals, groups served, social roles, leadership styles, incentives, surrounding environments, and types of tasks performed. These differences create varying types of organizational structures, and they also help explain differences in organizations' use of information systems.

2. **Evaluate the impact of information systems on organizations.**

    Information systems and the organizations in which they are used interact with and influence each other. The introduction of a new information system will affect organizational structure, goals, work design, values, competition between interest groups, decision making, and day-to-day behaviour. At the same time, information systems must be designed to serve the needs of important organizational groups and will be shaped by the organization's structure, tasks, goals, culture, politics, and management. Information technology can reduce transaction and agency costs, and these changes have been accentuated in organizations using the Internet. The information systems department is the formal organizational unit that is responsible for the organization's information systems function. Organizational characteristics and managerial decisions determine the role this group will actually play.

3. **Assess how information systems support the activities of managers in organizations.**

    Several different models of what managers actually do in organizations show how information systems can be used for managerial support. Early classical models of managerial activities stress the functions of planning, organizing, coordinating, deciding, and controlling. Contemporary research looking at the actual behaviour of managers has found that managers' real activities are highly fragmented, variegated, and brief in duration, with managers moving rapidly and intensely from one issue to another. Managers spend considerable time pursuing personal agendas and goals, and contemporary managers shy away from making grand, sweeping policy decisions. Decision making can also take place at the individual or group level. Individual models of decision making assume that human beings can rationally choose alternatives and consequences based on the priority of their objectives and goals. Organizational models of decision making illustrate that real decision making in organizations takes place in arenas where many psychological, political, and bureaucratic forces are at work.

    Information technology provides new tools for managers to carry out both their traditional and newer roles, enabling them to monitor, plan, and forecast with more precision and speed than ever before and to respond more rapidly to the changing business environment. Information systems have been most helpful to managers by providing support for their roles in disseminating information, providing liaisons between organizational levels, and allocating resources. However, some managerial roles cannot be supported by information systems, and information systems are less successful at supporting unstructured decisions.

4. **Analyze how information systems support various business strategies for competitive advantage.**

    Businesses can use strategic information systems to gain an edge over competitors. These systems change organizations' goals, business processes, products, services, or environmental relationships, driving them into new forms of behaviour.

    Information systems can be used to support strategy at the business, firm, and industry levels. At the business level of strategy, information systems can be used to help firms become the low-cost producers, differentiate products and services, or serve new markets. Information systems can also be used to lock in customers and suppliers using efficient customer response and supply chain management applications. Value chain analysis is useful at the business level to highlight specific activities in the business where information systems are most likely to have a strategic impact.

At the firm level, information systems can be used to achieve new efficiencies or to enhance services by tying together the operations of disparate business units so that they can function as a whole or promote the sharing of knowledge across business units.

At the industry level, systems can promote competitive advantage by facilitating cooperation with other firms in the industry, creating consortiums or communities for sharing information, exchanging transactions, or coordinating activities. The competitive forces model, information partnerships, business ecosystems, and network economics are useful concepts for identifying strategic opportunities for systems at the industry level.

5. *Assess the challenges posed by strategic information systems and propose management solutions.*

Information systems are closely intertwined with an organization's structure, culture, and business processes. New systems disrupt established patterns of work and power relationships, so there is often considerable resistance to them when they are introduced. The complex relationship between information systems, organizational performance, and decision making must be carefully managed.

Implementing strategic systems often requires extensive organizational change and a transition from one sociotechnical level to another. These changes are called *strategic transitions* and are often difficult and painful to achieve. Moreover, not all strategic systems are profitable, and they can be expensive to build. Many strategic information systems are easily copied by other firms so that strategic advantage is not always sustainable.

Key Terms

Agency theory, 76
Behavioural models, 81
Bureaucracies, 68
Bureaucratic models of decision making, 83
Business ecosystem, 95
Business strategy, 85
Chief information officer (CIO), 74
Choice, 83
Classical model of management, 81
Competitive forces model, 93
Core competency, 92
Decisional roles, 82
Efficient customer response systems, 91
End users, 74
Focused differentiation, 88

Industry structure, 94
Information partnership, 93
Information systems department, 74
Information systems managers, 74
Informational roles, 82
Interpersonal roles, 82
Managerial roles, 82
Mass customization, 78
Network economics, 97
Organization (behavioural definition), 67
Organization (technical definition), 67
Organizational culture, 70
Organizational models of decision making, 83
Political models of decision making, 83
Primary activities, 86

Product differentiation, 88
Programmers, 74
Rational model, 83
Routines, 69
Strategic information systems, 84
Strategic transitions, 99
Structured decisions, 80
Support activities, 86
Switching costs, 91
Systems analysts, 74
Transaction cost theory, 75
Unstructured decisions, 80
Value chain model, 85
Value web, 87
Virtual organizations, 78

Review Questions

1. *What is an organization? Compare the technical definition of organizations with the behavioural definition.*

2. *What features do all organizations have in common? In which ways can organizations differ?*

3. *How are information technology services delivered in organizations? Describe the role played by programmers, systems analysts, information systems managers, and the chief information officer (CIO).*

4. *Describe the major economic theories that help explain how information systems affect organizations.*

5. *Describe the major behavioural theories that help explain how information systems affect organizations.*

6. *Why is there considerable organizational resistance to the introduction of information systems?*

7. *Compare the descriptions of managerial behaviour in the classical and behavioural models.*

8. *Which specific managerial roles can information systems*

support? Where are information systems particularly strong in supporting managers, and where are they weak?

9. *Compare individual and organizational models of decision making.*

10. *What is the impact of the Internet on organizations and the process of management?*

11. *Describe appropriate models for analyzing strategy at the business level and the types of strategies and information systems that can be used to compete at this level.*

12. *Describe appropriate strategies for the firm level and how information systems can help companies compete at this level.*

13. *How can the competitive forces model, information partnerships, business ecosystems, and network economics be used to identify strategies at the industry level?*

14. *How have the value chain and competitive forces models*

changed as a result of the Internet and the emergence of digital firms?

15. *Describe the management challenges posed by the role of information systems in organizations, and suggest some solutions.*

Discussion Questions

1. *It has been said that there is no such thing as a sustainable strategic advantage. Do you agree? Why or why not?*

2. *It has been said that the advantage that leading-edge* retailers such as Dell and Wal-Mart have over their competition isn't technology; it's their management. Do you agree? Why or why not?

Application Software Exercise:
Database Exercise: Using a Database for Strategic Business Development

The Queen's Inn is a small three-story hotel on the Atlantic Ocean in St. Johns, Newfoundland, a popular vacation spot. Ten rooms overlook side streets, 10 rooms have bay windows that offer limited views of the ocean, and the remaining 10 rooms in the front of the hotel face the ocean. Room rates are based on room choice, length of stay, and number of guests per room. Room rates are the same for one to four guests. Fifth and sixth guests must pay an additional $20 charge each per day. Guests staying for seven days or more receive a 10 percent discount on their daily room rates.

Business has grown steadily during the past 10 years. Now totally renovated, the hotel uses a romantic weekend package to attract couples, a vacation package to attract young families, and a weekday discount package to attract business travellers. The owners currently use a manual reservation and bookkeeping system, which has caused many problems. Sometimes two families have been booked in the same room at the same time.

Management does not have immediate data about the hotel's daily operations and income.

Use the information provided in this description and in the database tables at the Companion Website for Chapter 3 to develop reports that would provide information to help management make the business more competitive and profitable. The database and related queries should be designed to make it easy to identify information, such as the average length of stay per room type, the average number of visitors per room type, and the base income per room (i.e., length of visit multiplied by the daily rate) during a specified period of time.

After identifying the preceding information, write a brief report describing what the database information reveals about the current business situation. For example, what is the strongest customer base? Which specific business strategies might be pursued to increase room occupancy and revenue? How could the database be improved to provide better information for strategic decisions?

Electronic Commerce Project: Configuring and Pricing an Automobile

Your current seven-year-old car has tried your patience one too many times, and you decide to purchase a new automobile. You have been interested in a Ford family car and want to investigate the Ford Taurus (if you are personally interested in another car, domestic or foreign, investigate that one instead). Go to Microsoft Network's (MSN) Canadian Autos Web site (**en.autos.sympatico.msn.ca**), and begin your investigation. Locate the Ford Taurus. Research the various automobiles available in that model and determine which you would prefer. Explore full details about the specific car, including pricing, standard features, and options. Locate and read at least two reviews if possible. Explore the features for locating a vehicle in inventory and purchasing directly. Finally, explore the other capabilities of the MSN Autos site for financing.

Having recorded or printed the information you need from the MSN Autos site for your purchase decision, surf to the Web site of the manufacturer, in this case Ford (**www.ford.ca**). Compare the information available on this Web site for the Ford Taurus. Be sure to check the price and any incentives being offered (which may disagree with what you found at MSN). Next, find a dealer on the Ford site so that you can view the car before making your purchase decision. Explore the other features of this Web site.

Finally, visit a third site, Cars4U.com, and research the car you have selected as you did on MSN. Compare the information you find at this site with the information provided by MSN and the auto manufacturer site, and try to locate the lowest price for the car you want in a local dealer's inventory. Which site would you use to purchase your car? Why? Also, suggest improvements for the MSN Autos, Ford, and Cars4U Web sites.

Group Project: Identifying Opportunities for Strategic Information Systems

With a group of three or four students, select a company described in the *Globe and Mail*, *The Financial Post*, *Canadian Business*, *Fortune*, *Forbes*, or another business publication. Visit the company's Web site to find additional information about that company and to see how the firm is using the Web. On the basis of this information, analyze the business. Include a description of the organization's features, such as important business processes, culture, structure, and environment, as well as its business strategy. Suggest strategic information systems appropriate for that particular business, including those based on Internet technology, if appropriate. If possible, use electronic presentation software to present your findings to the class.

Web Sites of Interest

There are many interesting Web sites to enhance your learning about how information systems affect organizations and how they can be used to support an organization's strategy. You can search the Web yourself, or just try the following sites to add to what you have already learned.

Harvard Business Review **www.hbr.com**
A must-read for business majors. Includes articles on a variety of business issues, including strategic information systems.

Source Medical **www.sourcemedical.com**
The Canadian spinoff of Baxter Healthcare's medical products distribution operation is a well-organized Web site for the casual viewer. Source Medical's customers access part of their Web site (not available to the general public) to find out what they need to know about Canada's largest medical products distributor.

Knowledge Management Magazine article about the attention economy **www.kmmagazine.com/xq/asp/sid.0/articleid. 258E7641-A0F4-47A3-AC63-5C00E2BC8478/qx/display.htm**
Tom Davenport, a leading management scholar, proposes a new way to add or lose value in an organization—the ability to manage attention

CASE STUDY:
Telus Enhances Strategic Performance Through Internal Performance

Telus, the leading telecommunications company in Canada, became what it is today by amalgamating several large corporate entities. This brought together 25 000 employees from multiple organizations, which meant Telus's senior officers had to find ways to centralize and optimize performance metrics to oversee employee productivity.

Breakthrough business intelligence (BI) is about deploying applications to large numbers of front-line workers and their managers. "Revenues were down across the industry, and with deregulation, executives needed to see better productivity," says Kevin Lam, manager of business performance at Telus, recalling how things looked in the wake of the 1999 megamerger with BC Telecom. "Centrally, we needed an overall picture of performance; but we also needed a way to help our field force—thousands of front-line employees—become more effective."

Information Builders and iWay Software together came up with a BI solution to track, measure, and report on employee efficiency by obtaining information from a variety of back-end applications and data sources. Senior management, concerned by the downward spiralling of the telecommunication industry, kept demanding that internal operations had to be vastly improved. According to Lam, what they needed was a Web-based reporting application that would centralize Telus' productivity metrics and simplify analytic activities.

"It used to be 'OK, we'll measure you on how many widgets you do,'" Lam says. "But using a single dimension could drive the wrong performance and encourage the wrong culture, especially if the goal becomes customer satisfaction." A comprehensive scorecard model that Telus delivers to employees via a secure dashboard provides multidimensional views of all the factors affecting employee performance.

"If you want to spike productivity, measure people," Lam explains. "But the catch is: can you sustain it?" Some studies show that after a quick 5-percent increase, productivity can then fall below original levels. "We had to make sure metrics were fair, complete, audited, and communicated well, which means a cultural change, not just new technology adoption," Lam says.

The employee scorecard application that delivers substantial business value was created by Telus in association with Information Builders' Consulting. Since this employee information is important to a number of Telus managers, it has been made available online in a user-friendly scorecard format. Telus business analysts access this scorecard information on a daily basis. With managers keeping a close eye on employee performance, there has been a significant improvement in the way employees work.

As mentioned earlier, it was the large number of mergers that created the need for centralization of information. "Each of the firms that Telus amalgamated had its own systems and processes," Lam says. "We found ourselves in a situation where we needed to access information from a lot of different systems."

Telus also urgently needed a Web-based reporting solution. The rapid growth of the company made management realize the importance of a more effective reporting infrastructure. Information Builders' Consulting was given the contract to come up with an integrated solution to access multiple data stores, with a variety of reporting options using Web-based service applications.

Information Builders and iWay Software provided Telus with the technology to build a business intelligence application to track the productivity of about 3000 field service personnel. WebFOCUS software was selected for its Web-reporting capabilities, information delivery environment, and intuitive dashboard interface and iWay software was selected for its broad data access, integration, and extraction, transformation, and loading (ETL) capabilities.

"We needed to get a handle on the productivity level of our individual field service employees so we could measure their output and, ultimately, drive efficiency," explains Lam. "If each employee was averaging 10 units of work per day, would it be possible to expect 10.5 units? Could we bring about a 5 percent productivity gain? We thought it was a reasonable assumption, but we needed business intelligence technology to track day-to-day performance and gauge our success."

Information Builders' Consulting, together with internal developers at Telus, designed, developed, tested, and deployed the BI solution. They created the entire BI infrastructure in about six months. Using ETL technology from iWay Software, they gathered field-service information from such applications as Siebel, SAP, and Microsoft Access and combined data sources, such as DB2, SAP BW, FOCUS, Informix, and various types of flat files, into an enterprise data warehouse. WebFOCUS also helped the developers create a self-service reporting and analysis solution to access data in the warehouse as well as live data from production information systems. "The tools are easy to work with," says Lam. "Our business analysts were able to use them on their own soon after we brought in the software."

Working in the background, the iWay software populates the enterprise data warehouse with current field-service information while WebFOCUS extracts data from the warehouse and other sources to create reports and distribute information over the Telus intranet. In a simple manner, iWay can take the data required for the scorecard from various types of transactional and database systems and consolidate them in the enterprise data warehouse. Without worrying about the source, users see a seamless interface, get the fields they need filled in and the reports written.

Scheduled performance reports, now emailed to about 100 business managers, are also available in a secure version on the company intranet. Through an electronic scorecard interface, authorized users can create their own reports and drill down into the data. The reports contain evaluations of employee performance in common field-service tasks, for example, the installation and repair of voice and data services. The data from employees' scorecards are automatically rolled up into manager-level scorecards so that the managers can compare overall productivity against corporate and industry benchmarks.

Scorecard information is available to managers through a Web browser, and they can also create reports in Microsoft Excel, Adobe PDF, and HTML formats. "The system enables managers to obtain the information they need," Lam says. "They can break down reports by day, week, month, and year. For example, they can create productivity reports, find out how much overtime their employees are clocking, and slice the data in many other precise ways."

When individual measures of employee performance can be consolidated, accountability can be encouraged throughout the organization, which, in turn, improves employee efficiency and also causes employee contributions to be recognized. According to Lam, this is the driving force behind the regional productivity gains of one to two million dollars per month. The data in the scorecards enable managers to conduct meaningful performance reviews with employees and provide details for root cause analysis. The organization itself is then able to identify areas where operational improvements can be achieved. Data can help compare each staff member's performance with team averages and general quality-of-service benchmarks.

Telus has quickly recovered the costs of implementing BI technology, totalling just under $1 million, including outlays for hardware, software, licensing, and labour. "The solution paid for itself in a single month of productivity gains," says Lam. "We have demonstrated its ability to increase the efficiency and performance of our field service employees, provide superior information to managers and staff, and deliver better service to our customers."

The solution was showcased as one of Telus's major successes at a recent CEO meeting. "The system was spotlighted in our company review because it was one of the first of its kind to reveal this level of individual performance detail to the front line," Lam says. "It shows individual contributions, reveals how long activities are taking, and delivers information we can use to identify further improvements."

The value of the employee scorecard solution is being increasingly recognized throughout the organization and is now regarded as an enterprise standard not only for Telus' field forces but for other parts of the organization as well. By reusing the WebFOCUS front-end and the iWay back-end, Telus's developers have been able to create performance measures for all of its business units. Lam explained that when Telus rolled out the system three years ago, it was a challenge to link the company's strategy to its operations, such as its effort to measure what employees were doing to maintain corporate customer satisfaction goals.

The original application, to track the performance of Telus field forces, has expanded to track contracts and customer orders. Telus has not yet finished determining the uses for the new technologies it has added to its arsenal.

Sources: Information Builders, "WebFOCUS and iWay Deliver Front-Line Efficiency Improvements at Telus, Boosting Productivity by More Than $1 Million per Month With Web-Based Employee Scorecard," **www.informationbuilders.com/applications/Telus.html**, accessed. July 14, 2005; Eric Rogge, "Move in Sync," *Information Week*, April 1, 2005, **http://informationweek.bizintelligencepipeline.com/160403492**, accessed July 14, 2005; Marc L. Songini, "Information Builders to help measure the enterprise," *Computerworld*, May 27, 2004, **www.computerworld.co.nz/news.nsf/0/B0094887E52EC9A1CC256EA00068A2A4?OpenDocument&More=KnowledgeMgt**, accessed July 14, 2005.

CASE STUDY QUESTIONS

1. Analyze Telus using the value chain and competitive forces models.

2. What role do information systems play in Telus' business strategy? How do systems provide value for Telus?

3. What management, organization, and technology factors hinder Telus from achieving the goals of its business strategy? What management, organization, and technology factors help Telus achieve its goals?

4. Do you think Telus' business strategy will work? Why or why not?

Chapter 4

Social, Legal, and Ethical Issues in the Digital Firm

OBJECTIVES

After completing this chapter, you will be able to:

1. Analyze the ethical, social, and political issues that are raised by information systems.

2. Identify the main moral dimensions of an information society and specific principles for conduct that can be used to guide ethical decisions.

3. Evaluate the impact of contemporary information systems and the Internet on the protection of individual privacy and intellectual property.

4. Assess how information systems have affected everyday life.

5. Identify the principal management challenges posed by the ethical and social impact of information systems and propose management solutions.

- Secure IT
- Promote ethical standards
- Prosecute those who violate the law

- Develop and maintain security controls

- Develop and enforce ethics codes
- Update security continuously

Management

Organization

Technology

Business Challenges

- Higher ethical standards
- Opportunities and challenges from new technology

Information System

- Provide means to track hackers and spies

Business Solutions

- Keep confidential material in-house
- Prosecute law breakers

Opening Case: Israel's Trojan Horse Corporate Scandal

What began as a family feud and a minor computer hacking incident has exploded into one of the biggest business scandals in Israel. Its repercussions have reached into the highest levels of the corporate world and the shock has rocked even the most secure among business moguls. Some of the most elite institutions, such as a high-tech company trading in New York, have been accused of using illicit spyware in corporate espionage.

The affected comprise a wide range—a cigarette importer, the Ace hardware chain, Hewlett-Packard Company, a popular TV entertainment reporter, who complained that his computer had been broken into to get celebrity phone numbers, and so on.

The scandal has exposed the ugly side of the Israeli business world—a dangerous combination of dog-eat-dog competition in a small market, technology that is extremely sophisticated, and a long tradition of secrecy associated with the Israeli military forces. This has caused major security software makers to scramble to bring their products up to date to fight this type of cybercrime.

The police accidentally discovered this problem when author Amnon Jacont found on the Internet excerpts of the book he was still writing. He realized his computer had been invaded when more and more of his computer's contents were getting onto the Internet and even his banking information was being stolen. In his complaint to the police, he named his stepdaughter's ex-husband Michael Haephrati as a possible suspect.

As Jacont said in a newspaper interview, Haephrati had become "vengeful and obsessive" after his marriage failed. When the police found surveillance software, a Trojan horse program, on Jacont's machine, Nir Nateev, head of the police computer and cybercrime department in Tel Aviv said, it triggered an international investigation by British, German, and American authorities. "We never saw this in the past," Nateev said. "They were very, very, very surprised by the size of the case and helped us a lot in this."

Investigations revealed that Haephrati had sold customized copies of his Trojan horse program to three Israeli private investigators who employed this technology to conduct business espionage for their clients. Subsequently, Haephrati and his wife Ruth, who reportedly have residences in London and Germany, were arrested in London; they are currently awaiting extradition hearings and will be tried in Israel.

The scandal could have "unpleasant consequences" for foreign investment, according to Sever Plocker, a leading Israeli economic commentator, who says, "People don't like to invest in countries where companies do some very unethical things," he said. "I think it is bad for Israel, bad for the image of Israel, and nothing to be proud about."

When the police lifted the gag order, the "Trojan horse" scandal, named after the monitoring software secretly planted on the corporate computers, was splashed across the front pages of newspapers around the world. Twenty-two people have been arrested, with more arrests in the works.

Nearly a hundred computers have been confiscated by the police. "It's getting bigger every day," said Nateev. "In the end, there will be dozens [of companies] involved."

Understandably, the business world was shaken by the scandal and fears that foreign investment could be drastically affected, as predicted by the country's central bank chief, American economist Stanley Fischer. According to Amir Barnea, a business professor at the Interdisciplinary Center (a prestigious Israeli university), the hyper-competitive business atmosphere in a tiny market of seven million people was the root cause of this scandal. "Unfortunately, some managers may lose the distinction between a legitimate fight for survival and doing illegal acts," he said.

Israel has a history of its military units being the development sources of its high technology, with a tendency towards deep secrecy and independent thinking. This is probably why such a scandal arose. It is significant that this country has some of the top computer security companies in the world.

Victims of the scandal were lured into installing spyware into their computers when some of its versions arrived by email as confidential documents. Then, the spyware proceeded to record every keystroke and collect business documents and email information on the victim's PC; this information was subsequently transmitted to a server computer registered in London, England.

According to Robert Sandilands, the head of the virus research lab for Authentium Inc., a Florida security firm, "This was not designed very well. This does not seem to be the work of an experienced virus writer."

Senior executives from three prominent private investigation firms, among them a former top military investigator, a retired Shin Bet security agent, and former police officers, are some of those suspected of involvement. Those arrested include 11 private investigators, for engaging in industrial espionage, and eight senior executives from some of Israel's leading companies, such as Cellcom, YES, Pelephone, Meir Car Imports, and Tami-4, a mineral water retailer.

Those implicated in the scandal are some of Israeli top companies—Amdocs Ltd., a business-software maker that trades on the New York Stock Exchange; Cellcom, a phone carrier; and three subsidiaries of the Bezeq phone monopoly: a long-distance carrier, a cell phone provider, and a satellite TV firm. These companies, however, claim that they did not have any knowledge of the wrongful methods used by the investigators hired by them.

Lawyers for the suspects said their clients acknowledged ordering the private investigators to gather information on their rivals but did not know that the information was obtained illegally. Police dismissed the claim, asserting that the information obtained for the companies was valuable to the extent that the victims lost competitive bids and thousands of customers as a result of the espionage.

"The software is totally legal," said Ofir Katz Neriah, the lawyer for one of the suspects. "The question is if the use that my client made of the software was illegal—and the answer is definitely not."

Reports say that some of the alleged victims are Hewlett-Packard and the Ace hardware chain, as well as the Globes business daily, Strauss-Elite food group, the HOT cable company, and the Bezeq parent company. There is evidence to connect the Israeli industrial espionage affair with similar cases across Europe, according to the police. Police say they cannot identify these companies to the public since they have "yet to inform them of the espionage."

The Trojan horse is just one of the many new tactics that are part of the rapidly growing pandemic of high-tech espionage, as Ira Winkler, author of the book *Spies Among Us*, says. He points out that, as in most instances, the Israeli Trojan horse case was broken by tracing the source to a vengeful relative. "Never underestimate the stupidity of criminals."

Sources: "Israeli 'Trojan Horse' Scandal Widens," Associated Press, June 1, 2005, **www.msnbc.msn.com/id/8064757/**, accessed July 15, 2005; Yaakov Katz, "Trojan Horse Also Hit Major International Firms," *The Jewish Post*, May 30, 2005, **www.jpost.com/servlet/Satellite?pagename=JPost/JPArticle/ ShowFull&cid=1117333096614**, accessed July 15, 2005; Josef Federman, "Scandal Jolts Israel's Industrial Elite," *The Winnipeg Free Press*, June 2, 2005.

Creating a Trojan horse is not illegal, but using it is illegal as well as unethical. Not only is the programmer who sold the Trojan horse software guilty of a criminal act, but so are the private investigation firms that bought the software and used it for their clients to spy on unsuspecting companies. The investigation firms' clients, who undoubtedly knew that this critical, confidential information was being gathered, are also culpable.

This case shows that information systems raise new and often perplexing ethical and legal challenges. You will want to know what these ethical and legal challenges are and how you should deal with them as a manager and as an individual. You will also want to understand their impact on society as a whole. This chapter helps you by describing the major ethical, legal, and social issues raised by information systems and by providing guidelines for analyzing ethical issues on your own.

4.1 Understanding Social, Legal, and Ethical Issues Related to Systems

In the last five years, we have witnessed arguably one of the most ethically challenging periods for business. Table 4-1 provides a small sample of cases demonstrating failed ethical judgment by senior and middle managers in the past few years. These lapses in management ethical and business judgment occurred across a broad spectrum of industries.

In today's new legal environment, managers who violate the law and are convicted will most likely spend time in prison. Although in the past business firms would often pay for the legal defense of their employees enmeshed in civil charges and criminal investigations, now firms are encouraged to cooperate with prosecutors to reduce charges against the entire firm for obstructing investigations. These developments mean that, more than ever, managers and employees will have to judge for themselves what constitutes proper legal and ethical conduct.

Although these major instances of failed ethical and legal judgment were not masterminded by information systems departments, financial reporting information systems were instrumental in many of these frauds. In many cases, the perpetrators of these crimes artfully used financial reporting information systems to bury their decisions from public scrutiny in the vain hope they would never be caught. We deal with the issue of control in financial reporting and other information systems in Chapter 9. In this chapter, we talk about the ethical dimensions of these and other actions based on the use of information systems.

TABLE 4-1 *Recent Examples of Failed Ethical Judgment by Managers*

Enron	Top three executives and several middle managers criminally indicted for misstating earnings using illegal accounting schemes. Bankruptcy declared in 2001.
WorldCom	Second-largest U.S. telecommunications firm. Chief executives indicted for improperly inflating revenue by billions using illegal accounting methods. Bankruptcy declared in July 2002 with $50 billion in debts; CEO Bernie Ebbers sentenced to 25 years in prison.
Merrill Lynch	Indicted for assisting Enron in the creation of financial vehicles that had no business purpose, enabling Enron to misstate its earnings.
Parmalat	Italy's eighth-largest industrial group indicted for misstating over $6 billion in revenues, earnings, and assets over several years; senior executives indicted for embezzlement.
Bristol-Myers Squibb	Pharmaceutical firm agreed to pay a fine of $183 million for misstating its revenues by $1.8 billion and inflating its stock value.
Government of Canada	Sponsorship scandal, wherein the government apparently paid marketing firms friendly to the government for services that were either not needed or not provided. The investigation is ongoing.

Ethics refers to the principles of right and wrong that individuals, acting as free moral agents, use to make choices to guide their behaviours. Information systems raise new ethical questions for both individuals and societies because they create opportunities for intense social change and thus threaten existing distributions of power, money, rights, and obligations. Like other technologies, such as steam engines, electricity, telephones, and radio, information technology can be used to achieve social progress, but it can also be used to commit crimes and threaten cherished social values. The development of information technology will produce benefits for many and costs for others.

Ethical issues with respect to information systems have been given new urgency by the rise of the Internet and electronic commerce. Internet and digital firm technologies make it easier than ever to assemble, integrate, and distribute information, unleashing new concerns about the appropriate use of customer information, the protection of personal privacy, and the protection of intellectual property.

Other pressing ethical issues raised by information systems include establishing accountability for the consequences of information systems, setting standards to safeguard system quality that protects the safety of the individual and society, and preserving values and institutions considered essential to the quality of life in an information society.

When using information systems, it is essential to ask: What is the ethical and socially responsible course of action?

A Model for Thinking about Ethical, Social, and Political Issues

Ethical, social, and political issues are closely linked. The ethical dilemma you may face as a manager of information systems typically is reflected in social and political debate. One way to think about these relationships is given in Figure 4-1. Imagine society as a more or less calm pond on a summer day, a delicate ecosystem in partial equilibrium with individuals and with social and political institutions. Individuals know how to act in this pond because social institutions (e.g., family, education, organizations) have developed well-honed rules of behaviour, and these rules are backed by laws developed in the political sector that prescribe behaviour and promise sanctions for violations. Now toss a rock into the centre of the pond. But imagine instead of a rock that the disturbing force is a powerful shock of new information technology and systems hitting a society more or less at rest. What happens? Ripples, of course.

Suddenly individual actors are confronted with new situations often not covered by the old rules. Social institutions cannot respond overnight to these ripples—it may take years to develop etiquette, expectations, social responsibility, politically correct attitudes, or

ethics

FIGURE 4-1   *The relationship between ethical, social, and political issues in an information society.*

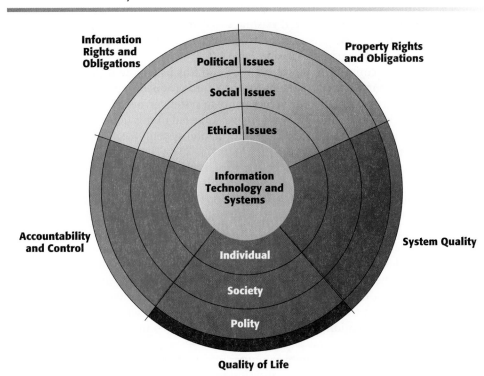

The introduction of new information technology has a ripple effect, raising new ethical, social, and political issues that must be dealt with on the individual, social, and political levels. These issues have five moral dimensions: information rights and obligations, property rights and obligations, system quality, quality of life, and accountability and control.

approved rules. Political institutions also require time before developing new laws and often require the demonstration of real harm before they act. In the meantime, you may have to act. You may be forced to act in a legal grey area.

We can use this model to illustrate the dynamics that connect ethical, social, and political issues. This model is also useful for identifying the main moral dimensions of the information society, which cut across various levels of action—individual, social, and political.

Five Moral Dimensions of the Information Age

The major ethical, social, and political issues raised by information systems include the following moral dimensions:

- *Information rights and obligations.* What **information rights** do individuals and organizations possess with respect to information about themselves? What can they protect? What obligations do individuals and organizations have concerning this information?

- *Property rights and obligations.* How will traditional intellectual property rights be protected in a digital society in which tracing and accounting for ownership are difficult and ignoring property rights is easy?

- *Accountability and control.* Who can and will be held accountable and liable for the harm done to individual and collective information and property rights?

- *System quality.* What standards of data and system quality should we demand to protect individual rights and the safety of society?

- *Quality of life.* What values should be preserved in an information- and knowledge-based society? Which institutions should we protect from violation? Which cultural values and practices are supported by the new information technology?

We explore these moral dimensions in detail in section 4.3.

information rights

Key Technology Trends That Raise Ethical Issues

Ethical issues long preceded information technology. Nevertheless, information technology has heightened ethical concerns, taxed existing social arrangements, and made some laws obsolete or severely crippled. There are four key technological trends responsible for these ethical stresses and they are summarized in Table 4-2.

The doubling of computing power every 18 months has made it possible for most organizations to use information systems for their core production processes. As a result, our dependence on systems and our vulnerability to system errors and poor data quality have increased. Social rules and laws have not yet adjusted to this dependence. Standards for ensuring the accuracy and reliability of information systems (see Chapter 10) are not universally accepted or enforced.

Advances in data storage techniques and rapidly declining storage costs have been responsible for the multiplying databases on individuals—employees, customers, and potential customers—maintained by private and public organizations. These advances in data storage have made the routine violation of individual privacy both cheap and effective. Already massive data storage systems are cheap enough for regional and even local retailing firms to use in identifying customers.

Advances in data analysis techniques for large pools of data are a third technological trend that heightens ethical concerns because companies and government agencies are able to find out a lot of detailed personal information about individuals. With contemporary data management tools (see Chapter 6) companies can assemble and combine the myriad pieces of information about individuals stored on computers much more easily than in the past.

Think of all the ways you generate computer information about yourself—credit card purchases, telephone calls, magazine subscriptions, video rentals, mail-order purchases, banking records, and local, provincial, and federal government records (including court and police records). Put together and mined properly, this information could reveal not only your credit information but also your driving habits, your tastes, your associations, and your political interests.

Companies with products to sell purchase relevant information from these sources to help them more finely target their marketing campaigns. Chapters 3 and 6 describe how companies can analyze large pools of data from multiple sources to rapidly identify buying patterns of customers and suggest individual responses. The use of computers to combine data from multiple sources and create electronic dossiers of detailed information on individuals is called **profiling**.

For example, hundreds of Web sites allow DoubleClick (www.doubleclick.net), an Internet advertising broker, to track the activities of their visitors in exchange for revenue from advertisements based on visitor information DoubleClick gathers. DoubleClick uses this information to create a profile of each online visitor, adding more detail to the profile as the visitor accesses an associated DoubleClick site. Over time, DoubleClick can create a detailed dossier of a person's spending and computing habits on the Web that can be sold to companies to help them target their Web ads more precisely.

profiling

TABLE 4-2 *Technology Trends That Raise Ethical Issues*

TREND	IMPACT
Computing power doubles every 18 months	More organizations depend on computer systems for critical operations.
Rapidly declining data storage costs	Organizations can easily maintain detailed databases on individuals.
Data analysis advances	Companies can analyze vast quantities of data gathered on individuals to develop detailed profiles of individual behaviour.
Networking advances and the Internet	Copying data from one location to another and accessing personal data from remote locations are much easier.

New data analysis technology called **nonobvious relationship awareness (NORA)** has given both government and the private sector even more powerful profiling capabilities. NORA can take information about people from many disparate sources, such as employment applications, telephone records, customer listings, and "wanted" lists, and correlate relationships to find obscure hidden connections that might help identify criminals or terrorists (see Figure 4-2).

NORA technology scans data and extracts information as the data are being generated so that it could, for example, instantly discover a man at an airline ticket counter who shares a phone number with a known terrorist before that person boards an airplane. The technology is considered a valuable security tool but it does have privacy implications because it can provide such a detailed picture of the activities and associations of a single individual (Barrett and Gallagher 2004).

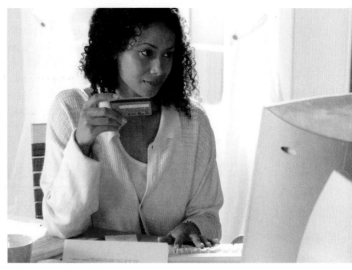

Credit card purchases can make personal information available to market researchers, telemarketers, and direct-mail companies. Advances in information technology facilitate the invasion of privacy.

Last, advances in networking, including the Internet, promise to greatly reduce the costs of moving and accessing large quantities of data and open the possibility of mining large pools of data remotely using small desktop machines. These advances permit an invasion of privacy on a scale and with a precision heretofore unimaginable. If computing and networking technologies continue to advance at the same pace as in the past, by 2023 large organizations will be able to devote the equivalent of a contemporary desktop personal computer to monitoring each of the 350 million individuals who will then be living in North America (Farmer and Mann 2003).

The development of global digital superhighway communication networks widely available to individuals and businesses poses many ethical and social concerns. Who will

FIGURE 4-2   *Nonobvious relationship awareness (NORA)*

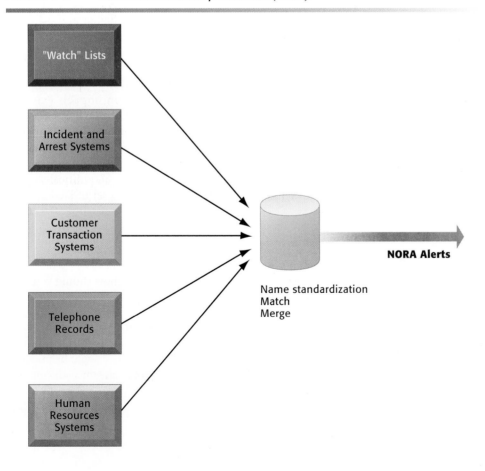

NORA technology can take information about people from disparate sources and find obscure, nonobvious relationships. It might discover, for example, that an applicant for a job at a casino shares a telephone number with a known criminal and issue an alert to the hiring manager.

nonobvious relationship awareness (NORA)

account for the flow of information over these networks? Will you be able to trace information collected about you? What will these networks do to the traditional relationships between family, work, and leisure? How will traditional job designs be altered when millions of "employees" become subcontractors using mobile offices for which they themselves must pay?

In the next section, we consider some ethical principles and analytical techniques for dealing with these kinds of ethical and social concerns.

4.2 Ethics in an Information Society

Ethics is a concern of humans who have freedom of choice. Ethics is about individual choice: When faced with alternative courses of action, what is the correct moral choice? What are the main features of ethical choice?

Basic Concepts: Responsibility, Accountability, and Liability

Ethical choices are decisions made by individuals who are responsible for the consequences of their actions. **Responsibility** is a key element of ethical action. Responsibility means that you accept the potential costs, duties, and obligations for the decisions you make. **Accountability** is a feature of systems and social institutions: It means that mechanisms are in place to determine who is responsible for an action. Systems and institutions in which it is impossible to find out who took what action are inherently incapable of ethical analysis or ethical action. Liability extends the concept of responsibility further to the area of laws.

Liability is a feature of political systems in which a body of laws is in place that permits individuals to recover the damages done to them by other actors, systems, or organizations. **Due process** is a related feature of law-governed societies and is a process in which laws are known and understood, and there is an ability to appeal to higher authorities to ensure that the laws are applied correctly.

These basic concepts form the underpinning of an ethical analysis of information systems and those who manage them. First, as discussed in Chapter 3, information technologies are filtered through social institutions, organizations, and individuals. Systems do not have impacts by themselves. Whatever information system impacts exist are products of institutional, organizational, and individual actions and behaviours. Second, responsibility for the consequences of technology falls clearly on the institutions, organizations, and individual managers who choose to use the technology. Using information technology in a socially responsible manner means that you can and will be held accountable for the consequences of your actions. Third, in an ethical, political society, individuals and others can recover damages done to them through a set of laws characterized by due process.

Ethical Analysis

When confronted with a situation that seems to present ethical issues, how should you analyze it? The following five-step process should help.

1. *Identify and clearly describe the facts.* Find out who did what to whom, and where, when, and how. In many instances, you will be surprised at the errors in the initially reported facts, and often you will find that simply getting the facts straight helps define the solution. It also helps to get the opposing parties involved in an ethical dilemma to agree on the facts.

2. *Define the conflict or dilemma, and identify the higher-order values involved.* Ethical, social, and political issues always reference higher values. The parties to a dispute all

responsibility
accountability
liability
due process

claim to be pursuing higher values (e.g., freedom, privacy, protection of property, and the free enterprise system). Typically, an ethical issue involves a dilemma: two diametrically opposed courses of action that support worthwhile values. For example, the chapter-ending case study illustrates two competing values: the need to protect citizens from terrorist acts and the need to protect individual privacy.

3. *Identify the stakeholders.* Every ethical, social, and political issue has stakeholders: players in the game who have an interest in the outcome, who have invested in the situation, and who usually have vocal opinions (Smith 2003). Find out the identity of these groups and what they want. This information will be useful later when designing a solution.

4. *Identify the options that you can reasonably take.* You may find that none of the options satisfy all the interests involved, but that some options do a better job than others. Sometimes arriving at a good or ethical solution may not always be a balancing of consequences to stakeholders.

5. *Identify the potential consequences of your options.* Some options may be ethically correct but disastrous from other points of view. Other options may work in one instance but not in other similar instances. Always ask yourself, "What if I choose this option consistently over time?"

Candidate Ethical Principles

Once your analysis is complete, what ethical principles or rules should you use to make a decision? What higher-order values should inform your judgment? Although you are the only one who can decide which among many ethical principles you will follow, and how you will prioritize them, it is helpful to consider some ethical principles with deep roots in many cultures that have survived throughout recorded history.

1. Do unto others as you would have them do unto you (the Golden Rule). Putting yourself into the place of others, and thinking of yourself as the object of the decision, can help you think about fairness in decision making.

2. If an action is not right for everyone to take, it is not right for anyone (**Immanuel Kant's Categorical Imperative**). Ask yourself, "If everyone did this, could the organization, or society, survive?"

3. If an action cannot be taken repeatedly, it is not right to take at all (**Descartes' rule of change**). This is the slippery-slope rule: An action may bring about a small change now that is acceptable, but if repeated would bring unacceptable changes in the long run. In the vernacular, it might be stated as "once started down a slippery path, you may not be able to stop."

4. Take the action that achieves the higher or greater value (the **Utilitarian Principle**). This rule assumes you can prioritize values in a rank order and understand the consequences of various courses of action.

5. Take the action that produces the least harm, or the least potential cost (**Risk Aversion Principle**). Some actions have extremely high failure costs of very low probability (e.g., building a nuclear generating facility in an urban area) or extremely high failure costs of moderate probability (speeding and automobile accidents). Avoid these high-failure-cost actions, and pay greater attention to high-failure-cost potential of moderate to high probability.

6. Assume that virtually all tangible and intangible objects are owned by someone else unless there is a specific declaration otherwise. (This is the **ethical "no free lunch" rule**.) If something someone else has created is useful to you and has value, then you should assume the creator wants compensation for this work.

Although these ethical rules cannot be guides to action, actions that do not easily pass these rules deserve some very close attention and a great deal of caution. The appearance of unethical behaviour may do as much harm to you and your company as actual unethical behaviour.

Immanuel Kant's Categorical Imperative

Descartes' rule of change

Utilitarian Principle

Risk Aversion Principle

ethical "no free lunch" rule

Professional Codes of Conduct

When groups of people claim to be professionals, they take on special rights and obligations because of their special claims to knowledge, wisdom, and respect. Professional codes of conduct are promulgated by professional associations such as the Canadian Medical Association (CMA), the Canadian Bar Association (CBA), the Association of Information Technology Professionals (AITP), the Canadian Information Processing Society (CIPS), and the Association of Computing Machinery (ACM). These professional groups take responsibility for the partial regulation of their professions by determining entrance qualifications and competence. Codes of ethics are promises by professions to regulate themselves in the general interest of society. For example, avoiding harm to others, honouring property rights (including intellectual property), and respecting privacy are among the General Moral Imperatives of the ACM's Code of Ethics and Professional Conduct (ACM 1993).

Some Real-World Ethical Dilemmas

Information systems have created new ethical dilemmas in which one set of interests is pitted against another. For example, many of the large telephone companies use information technology to reduce the size of their workforce. Voice recognition software reduces the need for human operators by enabling computers to recognize a customer's responses to a series of computerized questions. Many companies monitor what their employees are doing on the Internet to prevent them from wasting company resources on nonbusiness activities (see the Window on Management in chapter 7).

In each of these two instances, you can find competing values at work, with groups lined up on either side of a debate. A company may argue, for example, that it has a right to use information systems, such as voice recognition software, to increase productivity and reduce the size of its workforce to lower costs and stay in business. Employees displaced by information systems may argue that employers have some responsibility for their welfare. Business owners might feel obligated to monitor employee email and Internet use to minimize drains on productivity (Jackson, Dawson and Wilson, 2003; Urbaczewski and Jessup 2002). See Figure 4-3 for an example of monitoring software. Employees might believe they should be able to use the Internet for short personal tasks in place of the telephone. A close analysis of the facts can sometimes produce compromised solutions that give each side "half a loaf." Try to apply some of the principles of ethical analysis described to each of these cases. What is the right thing to do?

FIGURE 4-3 *SurfControl monitoring software.*

SurfControl offers tools for tracking Web and email activity and for filtering unauthorized email and Web site content. The benefits of monitoring employee email and Internet use should be balanced with the need to respect employee privacy.

4.3 The Moral Dimensions of Information Systems

In this section, we take a closer look at the five moral dimensions of information systems first described in Figure 4-1. In each dimension we identify the ethical, social, and political levels of analysis and use real-world examples to illustrate the values involved, the stakeholders, and the options chosen.

Information Rights: Privacy and Freedom in the Internet Age

Privacy is the claim of individuals to be left alone, free from surveillance or interference from other individuals or organizations, including the state. Claims to privacy are also involved at the workplace: Millions of employees are subject to electronic and other forms of high-tech surveillance (Ball 2001). Information technology and systems threaten individual claims to privacy by making the invasion of privacy cheap, profitable, and effective.

The claim to privacy is protected in the Canadian, U.S., and German constitutions in a variety of different ways and in other countries through various statutes. In Canada, the claim to privacy is protected primarily by the right to be secure against unreasonable search or seizure found in the Charter of Rights and Freedoms. In addition, on April 13, 2000, Parliament passed the Personal Information Protection and Electronic Documents Act (PIPEDA), Canada's modern privacy law. PIPEDA establishes the following principles to govern the collection, use, and disclosure of personal information: accountability, identifying the purposes for the collection of personal information, obtaining consent, limiting collection, limiting use, disclosure and retention, ensuring accuracy, providing adequate security, making information management policies readily available, providing individuals with access to information about themselves, and giving individuals a right to challenge an organization's compliance with these principles.

PIPEDA further provides for the Privacy Commissioner to receive complaints concerning contraventions of the principles, conduct investigations, and attempt to resolve such complaints. Unresolved disputes relating to certain matters can be taken to the Federal Court for resolution. This act complements the 1983 Privacy Act, which imposes rules on how federal government departments and agencies collect, use, and disclose personal information.

Every Canadian province and territory has enacted legislation parallel to the federal *Privacy Act* and the *Access to Information Act*. These laws prevent the unnecessary distribution of one's personal information and guarantee access to unrestricted government information.

Some of the provincial laws apply only to information held by the public sector. "Public sector" organizations under the privacy laws include public or private companies that are regulated by the government, such as financial institutions, air transportation companies, and broadcast media. The only province with a privacy law governing the private sector is Quebec. Right now Quebec is the only province with privacy laws for the private sector that meet European Union standards. That's significant for international trade, which increasingly concerns information, not hard products. By the way, the United States doesn't meet those standards either.

Due process has become a key concept in defining privacy. Due process requires that a set of rules or laws exist that clearly define how information about individuals will be treated and what appeal mechanisms are available. Perhaps the best statement in Canada of due process in record keeping is given by the *Canadian Standards Association's Model Privacy Code*. Published in March 1996, the Code establishes 10 basic principles for all organizations that collect or use personal information. Retailers, direct marketers, financial institutions, telecommunications companies, product manufacturers, service providers, schools, universities, hospitals, personnel departments, and government agencies are potential users.

privacy

By choosing to adopt the voluntary Code, organizations demonstrate that they are following fair, nationally accepted principles. The Code is also an important resource for consumers, employees, patients, and other "data subjects," says Professor Jim Savary, former vice-president of Policy and Issues at the Consumers' Association of Canada. "The Code is a vehicle for challenging an organization's behaviour. You can refer to these principles if you are uneasy about the information you are asked to supply or how it will be used."

The ten practices in the Code are:

- Accountability
- Identifying purposes
- Consent
- Limiting collection
- Limiting use, disclosure, and retention
- Accuracy
- Safeguards
- Openness
- Individual access
- Challenging compliance

Most North American and European privacy law is based on a regime called Fair Information Practices (FIP) first set forth in a report written in 1973 by a U.S. government advisory committee (U.S. Department of Health, Education, and Welfare, 1973). **Fair Information Practices (FIP)** is a set of principles governing the collection and use of information about individuals. Fair Information Practices preceded but are similar to the *Model Privacy Code* in Canada. The five Fair Information Practices principles are shown in Table 4-3.

FIP principles are based on the notion of a "mutuality of interest" between the record holder and the individual. The individual has an interest in engaging in a transaction, and the record keeper—usually a business or government agency—requires information about the individual to support the transaction. Once gathered, the individual maintains an interest in the record, and the record may not be used to support other activities without the individual's consent.

Fair Information Practices form the basis of 16 U.S. statutes listed in Table 4-4 that set forth the conditions for handling information about individuals in such areas as credit reporting, education, financial records, newspaper records, cable communications, electronic communications, and even video rentals. Knowledge of these laws is important to any organization engaging in trade with American organizations. The U.S. Privacy Act of 1974 is the most important of these laws, regulating the federal government's collection, use, and disclosure of information. Most federal privacy laws apply only to the federal

Fair Information Practices (FIP)

TABLE 4-3 *U.S. Federal Trade Commission Fair Information Practice Principles*

1. *Notice/Awareness (core principle):* Web sites must disclose their information practices before collecting data. Includes identification of collector; uses of data; other recipients of data; nature of collection (active/inactive); voluntary or required status; consequences of refusal; and steps taken to protect confidentiality, integrity, and quality of the data.

2. *Choice/Consent (core principle):* There must be a choice regime in place allowing consumers to choose how their information will be used for secondary purposes other than supporting the transaction, including internal use and transfer to third parties.

3. *Access/Participation:* Consumers should be able to review and contest the accuracy and completeness of data collected about them in a timely, inexpensive process.

4. *Security:* Data collectors must take responsible steps to assure that consumer information is accurate and secure from unauthorized use.

5. *Enforcement:* There must be in place a mechanism to enforce FIP principles. This can involve self-regulation, legislation giving consumers legal remedies for violations, or federal statutes and regulations.

TABLE 4-4 *Federal Privacy Laws in the United States*

GENERAL FEDERAL PRIVACY LAWS

Freedom of Information Act of 1966 as Amended (5 USC 552)

Privacy Act of 1974 as Amended (5 USC 552a)

Electronic Communications Privacy Act of 1986

Computer Matching and Privacy Protection Act of 1988

Computer Security Act of 1987

Federal Managers Financial Integrity Act of 1982

PRIVACY LAWS AFFECTING PRIVATE INSTITUTIONS

Fair Credit Reporting Act of 1970

Family Educational Rights and Privacy Act of 1974

Right to Financial Privacy Act of 1978

Privacy Protection Act of 1980

Cable Communications Policy Act of 1984

Electronic Communications Privacy Act of 1986

Video Privacy Protection Act of 1988

The Health Insurance Portability and Accountability Act of 1996 (HIPAA)

Children's Online Privacy Protection Act of 1998 (COPPA)

Financial Modernization Act (Gramm-Leach-Bliley Act) of 1999

government. Only credit, banking, cable, and video rental industries have been regulated by U.S. privacy law.

In the United States, privacy law is enforced by individuals who must sue agencies or companies in court to recover damages. Canada and European countries define privacy in a similar manner to that in the United States, but they have chosen to enforce their privacy laws by creating privacy commissions or data protection agencies to pursue complaints brought by citizens.

The European Directive On Data Protection In Europe, privacy protection is much more stringent than in the United States. Unlike the U.S., European countries, just like Canada, do not allow businesses to use personally identifiable information without consumers' prior consent. On October 25, 1998, the European Commission's Directive on Data Protection went into effect, broadening privacy protection in European Union (EU) nations. The directive requires companies to inform people when they collect information about them and disclose how it will be stored and used. Customers must provide their informed consent before any company can legally use data about them, and they have the right to access that information, correct it, and request that no further data be collected. **Informed consent** can be defined as consent given with knowledge of all the facts needed to make a rational decision. EU member nations must translate these principles into their own laws and cannot transfer personal data to countries such as the United States that do not have similar privacy protection regulations.

The PIPEDA, passed by Parliament in 1999, places Canada in accord with the European Directive on Data Protection, permitting Canadians to continue to do business with European companies. PIPEDA requires consent from consumers before a company can collect or distribute information about them.

Internet Challenges to Privacy Internet technology has posed new challenges for the protection of individual privacy. Information sent over this vast network of networks may pass through many different computer systems before it reaches its final destination. Each of these systems is capable of monitoring, capturing, and storing communications that pass through it.

informed consent

It is possible to record many online activities, including which online newsgroups or files a person has accessed, which Web sites and Web pages he or she has visited, and what items that person has inspected or purchased over the Web. Much of this monitoring and tracking of Web site visitors occurs in the background without the visitor's knowledge. Tools to monitor visits to the World Wide Web have become popular because they help organizations determine who is visiting their Web sites and how to better target their offerings. (Some firms also monitor the Internet usage of their employees to see how they are using company network resources.) Web retailers now have access to software that lets them "watch" the online shopping behaviour of individuals and groups while they are visiting a Web site and making purchases. The commercial demand for this personal information is virtually insatiable.

Web sites can learn the identities of their visitors if the visitors voluntarily register at the site to purchase a product or service or to obtain a free service, such as information. Web sites can also capture information about visitors without their knowledge using cookie technology.

Cookies are tiny files deposited on a computer hard drive when a user visits certain Web sites. Cookies identify the visitor's Web browser software and track visits to the Web site. When the visitor returns to a site that has stored a cookie, the Web site software will search the visitor's computer, find the cookie, and know what that person has done in the past. It may also update the cookie, depending on the activity during the visit. In this way, the site can customize its contents for each visitor's interests. For example, if you purchase a book on the Amazon.com Web site and return later from the same browser, the site will welcome you by name and recommend other books of interest based on your past purchases. DoubleClick, introduced earlier in this chapter, uses cookies to build its dossiers with details of online purchases and to examine the behaviour of Web site visitors. Figure 4-4 illustrates how cookies work.

Web sites using cookie technology cannot directly obtain visitors' names and addresses. However, if a person has registered at a site, that information can be combined with cookie data to identify the visitor. Web site owners can also combine the data they have gathered from cookies and other Web site monitoring tools with personal data from other sources such as offline data collected from surveys or paper catalogue purchases to develop very detailed profiles of their visitors.

There are now even more subtle and surreptitious tools for surveillance of Internet users. Marketers use Web bugs as another tool to monitor online behaviour. **Web bugs** are tiny graphic files embedded in email messages and Web pages that are designed to monitor who is reading the email message or Web page and transmit that information to another computer. Other **spyware** can secretly install itself on an Internet user's computer

FIGURE 4-4   *How cookies identify Web visitors.*

Cookies are written by a Web site on a visitor's hard drive. When the visitor returns to that Web site, the Web server requests the ID number from the cookie and uses it to access the data stored by that server on that visitor. The Web site can then use these data to display personalized information.

User

1. Windows XP
   IE
   jdoe123@aol.com
2. Cookie
3. 931032944 Previous buyer
4. Welcome back, Jane Doe!

Server

1. The Web server reads the user's Web browser and determines the operating system, browser name, version number, Internet address, and other information.
2. The server transmits a tiny text file with user identification information called a cookie, which the user's browser receives and stores on the user's computer hard drive.
3. When the user returns to the Web site, the server requests the contents of any cookie it deposited previously in the user's computer.
4. The Web server reads the cookie, identifies the visitor, and calls up data on the user.

cookies

Web bugs

spyware

by piggybacking on larger applications. Once installed, the spyware calls out to Web sites to send banner ads and other unsolicited material to the user, and it can also gather information and report the user's movements on the Internet to other computers without the owner's knowledge.

Google has been using tools to scan the contents of messages received by users of its free Web-based email service called Gmail. Ads that users see when they read their email are related to the subjects of these messages. Google's service offers users 1 gigabyte of storage space—far more than any of its competitors—but privacy advocates find the practice offensive (Hansell 2004).

The U.S. has allowed businesses to gather transaction information generated in the marketplace and then use that information for other marketing purposes without obtaining the informed consent of the individual whose information is being used. U.S. e-commerce sites are largely content to publish statements on their Web sites informing visitors about how their information will be used. Some have added *opt-out* selection boxes to these information policy statements. An **opt-out** model of informed consent permits the collection of personal information until the consumer specifically requests that the data not be collected. Privacy advocates would like to see wider use of an **opt-in** model of informed consent in which a business is prohibited from collecting any personal information unless the consumer specifically takes action to approve information collection and use. Prior to the enactment of PIPEDA, Canadian companies did what American companies did—use the opt-out model as their primary modus operandi. Today, most Canadian companies use the opt-in model so they have explicit consent to collect this type of data.

The online industry has preferred self-regulation to privacy legislation for protecting consumers. In 1998, the online industry formed the Online Privacy Alliance to encourage self-regulation and to develop a set of privacy guidelines for its members. The group promotes the use of online seals, such as that of TRUSTe, certifying Web sites that adhere to certain privacy principles (see Figure 4-5). Members of the advertising network industry, including DoubleClick, Atlas DMT, ValueClick, and 24/7 Real Media, have created an additional industry association called the Network Advertising Initiative (NAI) to develop its own privacy policies to help consumers opt out of advertising network programs and provide consumers redress from abuses.

In general, however, most Internet businesses do little to protect the privacy of their customers, and consumers do not do as much as they should to protect themselves. Many companies with Web sites do not have privacy policies. Of the companies that do post

FIGURE 4-5   *The TRUSTe seal of approval.*

Web sites are starting to post their privacy policies for visitors to review. The TRUSTe seal designates Web sites that have agreed to adhere to TRUSTe's established privacy principles of disclosure, choice, access, and security.

opt-out

opt-in

privacy polices on their Web sites, about half do not monitor their sites to ensure they adhere to these policies. The vast majority of online customers claim they are concerned about online privacy, but less than half read the privacy statements on Web sites (Laudon and Traver 2004).

Technical Solutions In addition to legislation, new technologies are available to protect user privacy during interactions with Web sites. Many of these tools are used for encrypting email, for making email or surfing activities appear anonymous, for preventing client computers from accepting cookies, or for detecting and eliminating spyware.

There are now tools to help users determine the kind of personal data that can be extracted by Web sites. The **Platform for Privacy Preferences**, known as **P3P**, enables automatic communication of privacy policies between an e-commerce site and its visitors. P3P provides a standard for communicating a Web site's privacy policy to Internet users and for comparing that policy to the user's preferences or to other standards such as the FTC's new FIP guidelines or the European Directive on Data Protection. Users can use P3P to select the level of privacy they wish to maintain when interacting with the Web site.

The P3P standard allows Web sites to publish privacy policies in a form that computers can understand. Once it is codified according to P3P rules, the privacy policy becomes part of the software for individual Web pages (see Figure 4-6). Users of recent versions of Microsoft Internet Explorer Web browsing software can access and read the P3P site's privacy policy and a list of all cookies coming from the site. Internet Explorer enables users to adjust their computers to screen out all cookies or let in selected cookies based on specific levels of privacy. For example, the "medium" level accepts cookies from first-party host sites that have opt-in or opt-out policies but rejects third-party cookies that use personally identifiable information without an opt-in policy.

However, P3P only works with Web sites of members of the World Wide Web Consortium who have translated their Web site privacy policies into P3P format. The technology will display cookies from Web sites that are not part of the consortium, but users will not be able to obtain sender information or privacy statements. Many users may also need to be educated about interpreting company privacy statements and P3P levels of privacy.

Ethical Issues The ethical privacy issue in this information age is as follows: Under what conditions should I (you) invade the privacy of others? What legitimates intruding into others' lives through unobtrusive surveillance, through market research, or by whatever means? Do we have to inform people that we are eavesdropping? Do we have to inform people that we are using credit history information for employment screening purposes?

FIGURE 4-6   *The P3P standard.*

P3P enables Web sites to translate their privacy policies into a standard format that can be read by the user's Web browser software. The user's Web browser software evaluates the Web site's privacy policy to determine whether it is compatible with the user's privacy preferences.

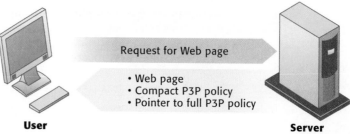

Request for Web page

- Web page
- Compact P3P policy
- Pointer to full P3P policy

User   **Server**

1. The user with P3P Web browsing software requests a Web page.
2. The Web server returns the Web page along with a compact version of the Web site's policy and a pointer to the full P3P policy. If the Web site is not P3P compliant, no P3P data are returned.
3. The user's Web browsing software compares the response from the Web site with the user's privacy preferences. If the Web site does not have a P3P policy or the policy does not match the privacy levels established by the user, it warns the user or rejects the cookies from the Web site. Otherwise, the Web page loads normally.

Platform for Privacy Preferences (P3P)

Social Issues The social issue of privacy concerns the development of expectations of privacy, or privacy norms, as well as public attitudes. In what areas of life should we as a society encourage people to think they are in private territory as opposed to public view? For instance, should we as a society encourage people to develop expectations of privacy when using electronic mail, cellular telephones, bulletin boards, the postal system, the workplace, or the street? Should expectations of privacy be extended to criminal conspirators?

Political Issues The political issue of privacy concerns the development of statutes that govern the relations between record keepers and individuals. Should we permit the RCMP or CSIS to monitor email at will to apprehend suspected criminals and terrorists (see the chapter-ending case study). To what extent should e-commerce sites and other businesses be allowed to maintain personal data about individuals?

Property Rights: Intellectual Property

Contemporary information systems have severely challenged existing law and social practices that protect private intellectual property. **Intellectual property** is considered to be intangible property created by individuals or corporations. Information technology has made it difficult to protect intellectual property because computerized information can be so easily copied or distributed on networks. Intellectual property is subject to a variety of protections under three different legal traditions: trade secret, copyright, and patent law.

Trade Secrets Any intellectual work product—a formula, device, pattern, or compilation of data—used for a business purpose can be classified as a **trade secret**, provided it is not based on information in the public domain. Trade secret law has arisen out of the broad "duty of good faith" and the principle of equity that whoever "has received information in confidence shall not take unfair advantage of it." The Supreme Court of Canada has stated that the test for whether there has been a breach of confidence consists of three elements:

1. The information conveyed must be confidential (that is, it must not be public knowledge);
2. The information must have been communicated in confidence;
3. The information must have been misused by the party to whom it was communicated.

As trade secret law in Canada is a matter of provincial jurisdiction, the drafting and interpretation of agreements that contain trade secret provisions must be carried out by a lawyer in the province that governs the agreement in question. Similarly, the assessment of whether a breach of confidence has occurred must be carried out by a lawyer in the province that governs the obligation of confidence. In general, trade secret laws grant a monopoly on the ideas behind a work product, but it can be a very tenuous monopoly.

Software that contains novel or unique elements, procedures, or compilations can be included as a trade secret. Trade secret law protects the actual ideas in a work product, not only their manifestation. To make this claim, the creator or owner must take care to bind employees and customers with nondisclosure agreements and to prevent the secret from falling into the public domain.

The limitation of trade secret protection is that although virtually all software programs of any complexity contain unique elements of some sort, it is difficult to prevent the ideas in the work from falling into the public domain when the software is widely distributed.

Copyright **Copyright** is a statutory grant that protects creators of intellectual property from having their work copied by others for any purpose for a period of at least 50 years. The Copyright Office registers copyrights and enforces copyright law in Canada. Parliament has extended copyright protection to books, periodicals, lectures, dramas, musical compositions, maps, drawings, artwork of any kind, and motion pictures. The intent behind copyright laws has been to encourage creativity and authorship by ensuring

intellectual property

trade secret

copyright

that creative people receive the financial and other benefits of their work. Most industrial nations have their own copyright laws, and there are several international conventions and bilateral agreements through which nations coordinate and enforce their laws.

Copyright law in Canada is one of the principal means of protecting computer software in Canada. Canadian copyright law is governed by the Copyright Act, which protects original literary, artistic, musical, and dramatic works. Computer software is protected in Canada as a literary work. Canadian copyright comes into existence automatically, and in the case of software, it comes into existence at the time the software was created and continues until the end of the calendar year in which the *author* of the software dies (regardless of whether the author has sold or assigned the copyright in the software or not) and continues for an additional period of 50 years following the end of that calendar year.

"Moral" rights are also protected under Canadian copyright law. Moral rights in Canada include the right of the author of a piece of software to be associated with the software by name or pseudonym and the right to remain anonymous. They also include the author's right to the integrity of the software (that is, the author's right to stop the software from being distorted, mutilated or modified, to the prejudice of the author's honour or reputation, or from being used in association with a product, service, cause, or institution).

Moral rights remain with the *author* of a piece of software, even where the software, or the copyright in the software, has been sold or assigned; regardless of whether the author created the software in the employ of someone else, or created it under contract, or otherwise.

Copyright protection is clear-cut: It protects against copying of entire programs or their parts. Damages and relief are readily obtained for infringement. The drawback to copyright protection is that the underlying ideas behind a work are not protected, only their manifestation in a work. A competitor can use your software, understand how it works, and develop new software that follows the same concepts without infringing on a copyright.

"Look and feel" copyright infringement lawsuits are precisely about the distinction between an idea and its expression. Most of this type of copyright infringement has occurred in the United States. For instance, in the early 1990s, Apple Computer sued Microsoft Corporation and Hewlett-Packard Inc. for infringement of the *expression* of Apple's Macintosh interface. Among other claims, Apple claimed that the defendants copied the expression of overlapping windows. The defendants counterclaimed that the idea of overlapping windows can only be expressed in a single way and, therefore, was not protectable under the "merger" doctrine of copyright law. When ideas and their expression merge, the expression cannot be copyrighted. In general, courts appear to be following the reasoning of a 1989 U.S. case—*Brown Bag Software* vs. *Symantec Corp.*—in which the court dissected the elements of software alleged to be infringing. The court found that neither similar concept, function, general functional features (e.g., drop-down menus), nor colours are protected by copyright law (*Brown Bag* vs. *Symantec Corp.*, 1992).

Patents A **patent** grants the owner an exclusive monopoly on the ideas behind an invention for between 17 and 20 years. The intent behind patent law is to ensure that inventors of new machines, devices, or methods receive the full financial and other rewards of their labour and yet still make widespread use of the invention possible by providing detailed diagrams for those wishing to use the idea under license from the patent's owner. The granting of a patent is determined by the Patent Office and relies on court rulings.

The key concepts in patent law are originality, novelty, and invention. The Canadian Patent Office does not accept applications for software patents because software is considered to fall under Canadian copyright law. In the United States, the U.S. Patent Office did not routinely issue patents on software until a 1981 Supreme Court decision that held that computer programs could be a part of a patentable process. Since that time, hundreds of U.S. software patents have been granted, and thousands await consideration.

The strength of patent protection is that it grants a monopoly on the underlying concepts and ideas of software. The difficulty is passing stringent criteria of nonobviousness (e.g., the work must reflect some special understanding and contribution), originality, and novelty as well as years of waiting to receive protection.

patent

Challenges to Intellectual Property Rights Contemporary information technologies, especially software, pose severe challenges to existing intellectual property regimes and, therefore, create significant ethical, social, and political issues. Digital media differ from books, periodicals, and other media in terms of ease of replication; ease of transmission; ease of alteration; difficulty classifying a software work as a program, book, or even music; compactness—making theft easy; and difficulties in establishing uniqueness.

The proliferation of electronic networks, including the Internet, has made it even more difficult to protect intellectual property. Before widespread use of networks, copies of software, books, magazine articles, or films had to be stored on physical media, such as paper, computer disks, or videotape, creating some hurdles to distribution. Using networks, information can be more widely reproduced and distributed. A study conducted by the International Data Corporation for the Business Software Alliance found more than one-third of the software worldwide was counterfeit or pirated, and the Business Software Alliance reported $29 billion in yearly losses from software piracy (Geitner 2004; Lohr 2004).

The Internet was designed to transmit information freely around the world, including copyrighted information. With the World Wide Web in particular, you can easily copy and distribute virtually anything to thousands and even millions of people around the world, even if they are using different types of computer systems. Information can be illicitly copied from one place and distributed through other systems and networks even though these parties do not willingly participate in the infringement.

Individuals have been illegally copying and distributing digitized MP3 music files on the Internet. Napster provided software and services that enabled users to locate and share digital music files, including those protected by copyright. In February 2001, a U.S. federal district court ruled that Napster had to stop listing all copyrighted files without permission on its central index. The company was forced to declare bankruptcy. (It eventually became a Web site selling only legal music downloads.)

Major entertainment industry groups subsequently filed suit to block illegal file sharing on other Web sites, such as Madster, Grokster, Kazaa, and Morpheus. However, these sites, as well as software and services for file trading over the Web, such as Gnutella, cannot be so easily regulated, so copyrighted music continues to be traded for free. Illegal file sharing is so widespread that it is threatening the viability of the music recording industry. (More detail on this topic can be found in the case study concluding Chapter 13.) As more and more homes adopt high-speed Internet access, illegal file sharing of videos will pose similar threats to the motion picture industry. However, in a June 2005 decision, the U.S. Supreme Court ruled that companies that build businesses with the active intent of encouraging copyright infringement should be held liable for their customers' illegal actions. Because of this ruling against Grokster in a suit brought by MGM, a major producer/distributor of music, movies, and videos, other similar Web sites are now also constrained from this type of business when the site itself either encourages copyright infringement or the sole purpose of the site is copyright infringement. While the Napster and Grokster cases were in the U.S. courts, they affect this type of business globally.

The manner in which information is obtained and presented on the Web further challenges intellectual property protections. Web pages can be constructed from bits of text, graphics, sound, or video that may come from many different sources. Each item may belong to a different entity, creating complicated issues of ownership and compensation (see Figure 4-7). Web sites use a capability called **framing** to let one site construct an on-screen border around content obtained by linking to another Web site. The first site's border and logo stay on-screen, making the content of the new Web site appear to be offered by the previous Web site.

Mechanisms are being developed to sell and distribute books, articles, and other intellectual property on the Internet, and the American **Digital Millennium Copyright Act (DMCA)** of 1998 is providing some copyright protection. The DMCA implemented a World Intellectual Property Organization (WIPO) treaty that makes it illegal to circumvent technology-based protections of copyrighted materials. Internet service providers (ISPs) are required to take down sites of copyright infringers that they are hosting once they are notified of the problem. The 1998 act went further than the WIPO treaty

framing
Digital Millennium Copyright Act
(DMCA)

FIGURE 4-7 *Who owns the pieces? Anatomy of a Web page.*

Web pages are often constructed with elements from many different sources, clouding issues of ownership and intellectual property protection.

LOGO
artist, design firm, or Web site publisher

TEXTUAL CONTEXT
writer or newspaper publisher

PHOTOGRAPH
freelance photographer, wire service, photo agency, photo library, or newspaper publisher

ARTICLE EXCERPT
writer or newspaper publisher

BUSINESS
stock exchanges, wire service, or database publisher

COLUMN
writer, syndication service, or newspaper publisher

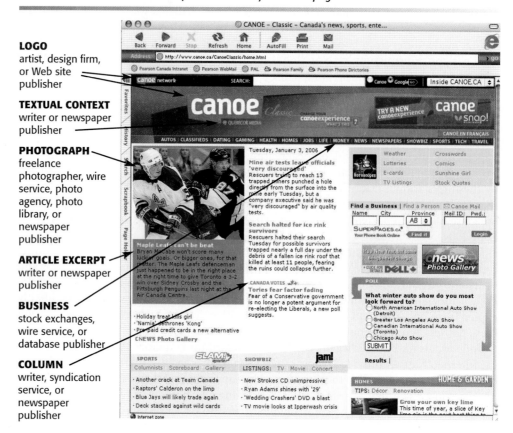

requirements by including the making of copies of computer programs for computer maintenance, allowing the making of digital works for preservation purposes, and providing federal protection for industrial design in vessel hulls. Database protection was left out at the last moment because it was a very contentious item.

What effect did the DMCA have on Canadian copyright legislation? The DMCA set the agenda for copyright discussions in Canada on:

- Technological tampering—"devices" or "conduct"
- ISP liability
- Library provisions to be examined
- Database protection

The Speech from the Throne in the fall of 2002 looked to establish policy which would bring Canada into alignment with WIPO and which would also look at some other long-term aims of copyright legislation in Canada. Compliance with WIPO would include short-term goals of technological measures protection and digital rights management as well as the liability of the Internet service provider when copyright is infringed by its users. The government also plans to look at the blank recording levy—a levy incorporated in the price of blank media that is aggregated and split among various recording industry publishers, artists, etc.—that is currently in place and to examine the fair use part of the Copyright Act and whether it could or should be expanded. In the medium term, Canadian lawmakers will be looking at the duration of copyright and whether it should be increased to life plus 70 as has just taken place in the United States. And finally in the longer term, protection of native folklore and oral histories will be examined.

Ethical Issues The central ethical issue concerns the protection of intellectual property such as software, digital books, digital music, or digitized video. Should I (you) copy for my own use a piece of software or other digital content material protected by trade secret, copyright, and/or patent law? Is there continued value in protecting intellectual property when it can be so easily copied and distributed over the Internet?

Social Issues There are several property-related social issues raised by new information technology. Most experts agree that the current intellectual property laws are breaking down in the Information Age. The vast majority of Americans report in surveys that they routinely violate some minor laws—everything from speeding to taking paper clips from work to copying books and software. The ease with which software and digital content can be copied contributes to making us a society of lawbreakers. These routine thefts threaten to reduce the speed with which new information technologies can and will be introduced and, therefore, threaten further advances in productivity and social well-being.

Political Issues The main property-related political issue concerns the creation of new property protection measures to protect investments made by creators of new software, digital books, and digital entertainment. Microsoft and 1400 other software and information content firms are represented by the Software and Information Industry Association (SIIA), which lobbies for new laws and enforcement of existing laws to protect intellectual property around the world. (SIIA was formed on January 1, 1999, from the merger of the Software Publishers Association [SPA] and the Information Industry

---

TABLE 4-5 *Employee Usage Guidelines for [Organization]*

Purpose Software will be used only in accordance with its license agreement. Unless otherwise provided in the license, any duplication of copyrighted software, except for backup and archival purposes by software manager or designated department, is a violation of copyright law. In addition to violating copyright law, unauthorized duplication of software is contrary to [organization's] standards of conduct. The following points are to be followed to comply with software license agreements:

1. All users must use all software in accordance with its license agreements and the [organization's] software policy. All users acknowledge that they do not own this software or its related documentation and, unless expressly authorized by the software publisher, may not make additional copies except for archival purposes.

2. [Organization] will not tolerate the use of any unauthorized copies of software or fonts in our organization. Any person illegally reproducing software can be subject to civil and criminal penalties, including fines and imprisonment. All users must not condone illegal copying of software under any circumstances and anyone who makes, uses, or otherwise acquires unauthorized software will be appropriately disciplined.

3. No user will give software or fonts to any outsiders including clients, customers, and others. Under no circumstances will software be used within [organization] that has been brought in from any unauthorized location under [organization's] policy, including, but not limited to, the Internet, the home, friends, and colleagues.

4. Any user who determines that there may be a misuse of software within the organization will notify the Certified Software Manager, department manager, or legal counsel.

5. All software used by the organization on organization-owned computers will be purchased through appropriate procedures.

I have read [organization's] software code of ethics. I am fully aware of our software compliance policies and agree to abide by them. I understand that violation of any above policies may result in my termination.

EMPLOYEE SIGNATURE

DATE

Published by the SPA Anti-Piracy. You are given permission to duplicate and modify this policy statement so long as attribution to the original document comes from SPA Anti-Piracy.

Association [IIA].) The SIIA runs an antipiracy hotline for individuals to report piracy activities and educational programs to help organizations combat software piracy. SIIA has also published guidelines for employee use of software. At the SIIA Web site (www.siia.net), there is a "Canadian Section" with its own board of Canadian executives and online forms for reporting piracy. The SIIA has developed model Employee Usage Guidelines for software, described in Table 4-5.

Allied against SIIA are a host of groups and millions of individuals who believe that antipiracy laws cannot be enforced in the digital age and that software should be free or be paid for on a voluntary basis (shareware software). According to these groups, greater social benefit results from the free distribution of software.

Accountability, Liability, and Control

Along with privacy and property laws, new information technologies are challenging existing liability law and social practices for holding individuals and institutions accountable. If a person is injured by a machine controlled, in part, by software, who should be held accountable and, therefore, liable? Should a public bulletin board or an electronic service such as America Online permit the transmission of pornographic or offensive material (as broadcasters), or should they be held harmless against any liability for what users transmit (as is true of common carriers such as the telephone system)? What about the Internet? If you outsource your information processing, can you hold the external vendor liable for injuries done to your customers? Some real-world examples may shed light on these questions.

Computer-Related Liability Problems During the weekend of March 15, 2002, tens of thousands of Bank of America customers in California, Arizona, and Nevada were unable to access their paycheques and social security payments that had just been deposited electronically. Cheques bounced. Withdrawals were blocked because of insufficient funds. Because of an operating error at the bank's computer centre in Nevada, a batch of direct deposit transactions was not processed. The bank lost track of money that should have been credited to customers' accounts, and it took days to rectify the problem (Carr and Gallagher 2002). Who is liable for any economic harm caused by this system failure to individuals or businesses that could not access their full account balances in this period?

On November 28, 2000, a double failure in Sprint Canada's network shut down trading on Vancouver's Canadian Venture Exchange for more than two hours. Three hundred thousand Rogers@Home cable customers were left without service recently when a rodent chewed through cables that were exposed during routine repairs. In November 1998, a railway backhoe operator accidentally cut an AT&T Canada fibre cable along the rail line between Toronto and Windsor, crashing computers, knocking out phone lines, and generally disrupting communications in southern Ontario. The main branch of the Bank of Nova Scotia was computerless.

These cases reveal the difficulties faced by information systems executives who ultimately are responsible for any harm done by systems developed by their staffs. In general, as computer software is part of a machine, and the machine injures someone physically or economically, the producer of the software and the operator can be held liable for damages. If the software acts like a book by storing and displaying information, then courts have been wary of holding software authors liable. In general, it is very difficult (if not impossible) to hold software producers liable for their software products when those products act like a book, regardless of the physical or economic harm that results. Historically, print publishers, books, and periodicals have not been held liable (the exception being instances of fraud or defamation) because of fears that liability claims would interfere with rights guaranteeing freedom of expression.

What about software as service? ATM machines are a service provided to bank customers. Should this service fail, customers will be inconvenienced and perhaps harmed economically if they cannot access their funds in a timely manner. Should liability protections be extended to software publishers and operators of defective financial, accounting, simulation, or marketing systems?

Software is very different from books. Software users may develop expectations of infallibility about software; software is less easily inspected than a book, and it is more difficult to compare with other software products for quality; software claims to perform a task rather than describe a task like a book; and people come to depend on services essentially based on software. Given the centrality of software to everyday life, the chances are excellent that liability law will extend its reach to include software even when the software merely provides an information service.

Telephone systems have not been held liable for the messages transmitted because they are regulated common carriers. In return for their right to provide telephone service, they must provide access to all, at reasonable rates, and achieve acceptable reliability. But broadcasters and cable television systems are subject to a wide variety of federal and local constraints on content and facilities. Organizations can be held liable for offensive content on their Web sites; and online services such as America Online might be held liable for postings by their users.

Ethical Issues The central liability-related ethical issue raised by new information technologies is whether individuals and organizations that create, produce, and sell systems (both hardware and software) are morally responsible for the consequences of their use (see Johnson and Mulvey 1995). If the providers are liable, under what conditions are they liable? What liabilities (and responsibilities) should the user assume, and what should the provider assume?

Social Issues The central liability-related social issue concerns the expectations that society should allow to develop around service-providing information systems. Should individuals (and organizations) be encouraged to develop their own backup devices to cover likely or easily anticipated system failures, or should organizations be held strictly liable for system services they provide? If organizations are held strictly liable, what impact will this have on the development of new system services? Can society permit networks and bulletin boards to post libellous, inaccurate, and misleading information that will harm many persons? Or should information service companies become self-regulating and self-censoring?

Political Issues The leading liability-related political issue is the debate between information providers of all kinds (from software developers to network service providers), who want to be relieved of liability as much as possible (thereby maximizing their profits), and service users (individuals, organizations, and communities), who want organizations to be held responsible for providing high-quality system services (thereby maximizing the quality of service). Service providers argue they will withdraw from the marketplace if they are held liable while service users argue that only by holding providers liable can they guarantee a high level of service and compensation to injured parties. Should legislation impose liability or restrict liability on service providers? This fundamental cleavage is at the heart of numerous political and judicial conflicts.

System Quality: Data Quality and System Errors

The debate over liability and accountability for unintentional consequences of system use raises a related but independent moral dimension: What is an acceptable, technologically feasible level of system quality? At what point should system managers say, "Stop testing, we've done all we can to perfect this software. Ship it!" Individuals and organizations may be held responsible for avoidable and foreseeable consequences, which they have a duty to perceive and correct. And the grey area is that some system errors are foreseeable and correctable only at very great expense, an expense so great that pursuing this level of perfection is not feasible economically—no one could afford the product.

For example, although software companies try to debug their products before releasing them to the marketplace, they knowingly ship buggy products because the time and cost of fixing all minor errors would prevent these products from ever being released (Rigdon 1995). What if the product was not offered on the marketplace? Would social welfare as a whole not advance and perhaps even decline? Carrying this further, just what is the responsibility of a producer of computer services—should it withdraw the product that can never be perfect, warn the user, or forget about the risk (let the buyer beware)?

Three principal sources of poor system performance are (1) software bugs and errors, (2) hardware or facility failures caused by natural or other causes, and (3) poor input data quality. Chapter 9 discusses why zero defects in software code of any complexity cannot be achieved and why the seriousness of remaining bugs cannot be estimated. Hence, there is a technological barrier to perfect software, and users must be aware of the potential for catastrophic failure. The software industry has not yet arrived at testing standards for producing software of acceptable but not perfect performance (Collins et al. 1994).

This topic is explored in the Window on Technology, which describes how software contributed to the radiation poisoning of 28 patients at Panama's National Cancer Institute. As you read this case, try to determine what factors allowed this terrible tragedy to occur. How much was the software responsible? How much were "people" factors responsible? To whom should blame be assigned?

Although software bugs and facility catastrophe are likely to be widely reported in the press, by far the most common source of business system failure is data quality. Few companies routinely measure the quality of their data, but studies of individual organizations report data error rates ranging from 0.5 to 30 percent (Redman 1998).

Ethical Issues The central quality-related ethical issue that information systems raise is at what point should we release software or services for consumption by others? At what point can we conclude that our software or service achieves an economically and technologically adequate level of quality? What are we obliged to know about the quality of our software, its procedures for testing, and its operational characteristics?

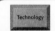

WINDOW ON TECHNOLOGY

When Software Kills: What Happened at Panama's National Cancer Institute

Victor Garcia feels lucky to be alive. He was one of 28 patients at the National Cancer Institute of Panama who received excessive doses of gamma ray radiation for cancer treatments in November 2000. Since then, 21 of these patients have died, and the International Atomic Energy Agency (IAEA) believes at least five of these deaths were caused by radiation poisoning.

The three Panamanian medical physicists who used the software to figure out the dose of radiation for these patients were charged with second-degree murder. Under Panamanian law, they may be held responsible because they introduced changes in the software that guided the radiation therapy machine used on these patients. How could this tragedy have happened?

Before administering radiation treatment, a physician devises a treatment plan that determines what dose of radiation can be safely targeted at a cancerous tumour. The plan also specifies where to place metal shields known as "blocks" to protect noncancerous areas. Using this plan, a medical physicist inputs information on the size, shape, and location of the blocks into software for guiding radiation machines. The software creates a three-dimensional picture of how the dose will be distributed and calculates how long the radiation treatment should last.

The Panamanian medical physicists were following a doctor's instructions to be more protective of pelvic organs by adding a fifth block to the four blocks ordinarily used on cancer patients. However, the radiation machine software, which was created by Multidata Systems International of St. Louis, Missouri, was designed for treatments only when four or fewer blocks are prescribed.

Olivia Saldana, one of the Panamanian physicists, tried to make the software work for a fifth block. She entered the dimensions of all five blocks as a single composite shape. Although it looked like the system could work with this composite shape, the software miscalculated appropriate doses. Patients were subjected to 20 to 50 percent more radiation than they should have received.

Multidata insists that it did nothing wrong. Multidata's software manual stated it is "the responsibility of the user" to verify the results of the software's calculations. Had the hospital verified the radiation doses by manually checking the software's calculations or by testing the dosages in water before irradiating patients, the staff would have found out about the overdoses before they were administered.

Unfortunately, National Cancer Institute physicists did not always manually verify the results of the software calculations. Three radiation physicists were working overtime to treat more than 100 patients per day because the hospital was understaffed. The IAEA found that the hospital examined only the functioning of the hardware. It had no quality assurance program for the software or for its results. Consequently, physicists were not required to tell anyone they had changed the way they entered data into the system, and no one questioned the software's results.

By 1997, the hospital staff was so worried about radiation overdoses that it reported to the Panamanian Ministry of Health that "overexposure of radiation therapy patients due to human error" would be a risk unless conditions at the hospital improved.

Independent experts not associated with the case assert that the software that controls medical equipment and other life-critical devices should be designed to pause or shut down if told to execute a task it is not programmed to perform. When the IAEA investigated the National Cancer Institute incident in May 2001, it found other ways to get the software to miscalculate treatment times. Every time investigators treated one, two, or four blocks of varying shapes as a single block, the software miscalculated the treatment times.

The IAEA investigating team and a team from the M. D. Anderson Cancer Center in Houston found Multidata's manual did not describe precisely how to digitize coordinates of shield-

ing blocks. The report also noted that the manual did not provide specific warnings against data entry approaches that are different from the standard procedure described.

Examiners from the U.S. Food and Drug Administration (FDA) who inspected Multidata in May 2001 found that Multidata had received at least six complaints about calculation errors related to the software's inability to handle certain types of blocks correctly. The examiners reported that Multidata had been aware of this failure since at least September 1992 but had not taken any corrective action. In 2003, Multidata signed a consent decree with the FDA that it would not make or sell software for radiation therapy devices in the U.S. although it can sell its products abroad.

To Think About: What management, organization, and technology factors were responsible for the excess radiation doses at Panama's National Cancer Institute? Who was responsible for the malfunctioning of the system? Was an adequate solution developed for this problem? Explain your answer.

Sources: Deborah Gage and John McCormick, "We Did Nothing Wrong," *Baseline Magazine*, March 2004; and "FDA Seeks Injunction against Multidata Systems Intl.," *FDA News*, May 7, 2003.

Social Issues The leading quality-related social issue once again deals with expectations: As a society, do we want to encourage people to believe that systems are infallible, that data errors are impossible? Do we instead want a society where people are openly skeptical and questioning of the output of machines, where people are at least informed of the risk? By heightening awareness of system failure, do we inhibit the development of all systems, which in the end contributes to social well-being?

Political Issues The leading quality-related political issue concerns the laws of responsibility and accountability. The Standards Council of Canada sets Canadian standards, including the international ISO 9000 and ISO 14000 standards. Many of these standards relate to computing and information systems, but penalties for failure to abide by the standards are unclear or nonexistent. Should industry associations be encouraged to develop industry-wide standards of quality? Or should Parliament wait for the marketplace to punish poor system quality, recognizing that in some instances this will not work (e.g., if all retail grocers maintain poor quality systems, customers will have no alternatives)?

Quality of Life: Equity, Access, and Boundaries

The negative social costs of introducing information technologies and systems are beginning to mount along with the power of the technology. Many of these negative social consequences are not violations of individual rights or property crimes. Nevertheless, these negative consequences can be extremely harmful to individuals, societies, and political institutions. Computers and information technologies potentially can destroy valuable elements of our culture and society even while they bring us benefits. If there is a balance of good and bad consequences of using information systems, who do we hold responsible for the bad consequences? Next, we briefly examine some of the negative social consequences of systems, considering individual, social, and political responses.

Balancing Power: Centre Versus Periphery An early fear of the computer age was that huge, centralized mainframe computers would centralize power at corporate headquarters and in the nation's capital, resulting in a Big Brother society, as was suggested in George Orwell's novel *1984*. The shift toward highly decentralized computing, coupled with an ideology of empowerment of thousands of workers, and the decentralization of decision making to lower organizational levels have reduced fears of power centralization in institutions. Yet much of the empowerment described in popular business magazines is trivial. Lower-level employees may be empowered to make minor decisions, but the key policy decisions may be as centralized as in the past.

Rapidity of Change: Reduced Response Time to Competition
Information systems have helped to create much more efficient national and international markets. The now-more-efficient global marketplace has reduced the normal social buffers that permitted businesses many years to adjust to competition. Time-based competition has an ugly side: The business you work for may not have enough time to respond to global competitors and may be wiped out in a year, along with your job. We stand the risk of developing a "just-in-time society" with "just-in-time jobs" and "just-in-time" workplaces, families, and vacations.

Maintaining Boundaries: Family, Work, and Leisure
Parts of this book were produced on trains, planes, and on vacations and during what otherwise

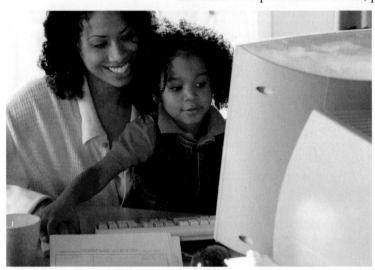

Although some people enjoy the convenience of working at home, the "do anything anywhere" computing environment can blur the traditional boundaries between work and family time.

might have been "personal" time. The danger of ubiquitous computing, telecommuting, nomad computing, and the "do anything anywhere" computing environment is that it might actually come true. If so, the traditional boundaries that separate work from family and just plain leisure will be weakened. Although authors have traditionally worked just about anywhere (typewriters have been portable for nearly a century), the advent of information systems, coupled with the growth of knowledge-work occupations, means that more and more people will be working when traditionally they would have been playing or communicating with family and friends. The work umbrella now extends far beyond the eight-hour day.

Weakening these institutions poses clear-cut risks. Family and friends historically have provided powerful support mechanisms for individuals, and they act as balance points in a society by preserving private life, providing a place for people to collect their thoughts, think in ways contrary to their employer, and dream.

Dependence and Vulnerability
Today, our businesses, governments, schools, and private associations, such as churches, are incredibly dependent on information systems and are, therefore, highly vulnerable if these systems should fail. With systems now as ubiquitous as the telephone system, it is startling to remember that there are no regulatory or standard-setting forces in place similar to telephone, electrical, radio, television, or other public-utility technologies. The absence of standards and the critical nature of some system applications will probably call forth demands for national standards and perhaps regulatory oversight.

Computer Crime and Abuse
New technologies, including computers, create new opportunities for committing crime by creating new valuable items to steal, new ways to steal them, and new ways to harm others. **Computer crime** is the commission of illegal acts through the use of a computer or against a computer system. Computers or computer systems can be the object of the crime (destroying a company's computer centre or a company's computer files), as well as the instrument of a crime (stealing computer lists by illegally gaining access to a computer system using a home computer). Simply accessing a computer system without authorization or with intent to do harm, even by accident, is now a federal crime. Chapter 9 provides more detail on this topic.

Computer abuse is the commission of acts involving a computer that may not be illegal but that are considered unethical. One widespread form of abuse is *spamming*, in which thousands and even hundreds of thousands of unsolicited email and electronic

computer crime
computer abuse

messages are sent out. **Spam** is junk email sent by an organization or individual to a mass audience of Internet users who have expressed no interest in the product or service being marketed. Spammers tend to market pornography, fraudulent deals and services, outright scams, and other products not widely approved in most civilized societies.

Spamming has been growing because it only costs a few cents to send thousands of messages advertising wares to Internet users. Hundreds of CDs can be purchased on the Web that offer spammers millions of email addresses harvested by software robots that read message boards, chat rooms, and Web sites, or spammers can use their own harvesting tools for this purpose. These minuscule costs make spamming worthwhile if only one recipient in 100,000 email messages sent makes a purchase (see Figure 4-8).

Some countries have passed laws to outlaw spamming or to restrict its use. Spamming is more tightly regulated in Europe than in the United States. On May 30, 2002, the European Parliament passed a ban on unsolicited commercial messaging. Electronic marketing can be targeted only to people who have given prior consent. In the United States, it is still legal if it does not involve fraud and the sender and subject of the email are properly identified.

The Window on Management shows that most U.S. efforts to control spamming are through legislation and technical means. Members of the Direct Marketing Association and other companies believe that regulating spam, rather than banning it altogether, would still allow legitimate businesses to use email for direct-marketing purposes. Other major interest groups, however, have lobbied against antispam legislation, believing it would harm legitimate email marketing and put e-commerce at a disadvantage. The spamming problem is a serious one because spam messages clog the Internet and affect business productivity.

The Canadian government has been very aggressive in implementing computer crime legislation. There are basically two sections in the Canadian Criminal Code, Sections 342.1 and 430, that define computer crime. Section 342.1 is itself divided into two parts. The first part deals with most of the items that would traditionally be considered computer crime. It defines unlawful entry into systems, interception of transmissions, as well as mandating a harsh 10-year prison sentence for violation of these laws. The second part defines data or computer programs, to give written documentation as to what kind of materials would qualify under the statute. Section 430 criminalizes the actual destruction, alteration, or interruption of data or data transmission. It does not set specific sentences, but one assumes they would be similar in nature to Section 342.1. Other related codes

FIGURE 4-8 *Spam filtering software.*

Spam consists of unsolicited email messages, which can be bothersome, offensive, and even a drain on office worker productivity. Spam filtering software such as McAfee's SpamKiller blocks suspicious email.

that more generally refer to the misuse of telecommunications include Section 184, the unlawful interception of telecommunications; Section 326, theft of telecommunications; and Section 327, possession of a device to intercept telecommunications.

The item, however, that truly distinguishes the Canadian government from others who try to enforce computer crime laws is the clear definition of a jurisdictional boundary for computer crime. All sections pertaining to such events fall under the mandate of the Royal Canadian Mountain Police (RCMP), specifically the Information Technology Security Branch (ITSB). In consultation with the Treasury Board Secretariat (TSB) and Communications Security Establishment (CSE), the ITSB is responsible for the information technology security of all of Canada. The ITSB's primary role is to educate the government on security matters by running seminars, printing documents, and providing consultation; however, they also work with local law enforcement officials to crack down on computer crime.

The ITSB is composed of three branches. The Security Evaluation and Inspection Team's (SEIT) primary function is to set up, secure, and be a consulting organization for any computers and networks set up by the government of Canada. The Computer Investigative Support Unit (CISU) is the legal branch of the RCMP. They provide legal counsel, acquire warrants, and direct the prosecution of computer criminals. Finally, the Counter Technical Intrusion Unit (CTIU) is responsible for performing periodic sweeps of governmental computer systems, assisting local police, and performing technical evaluations in cases of communications theft.

Employment: Trickle-Down Technology and Reengineering Job Loss

Reengineering work (see Chapter 10) is typically hailed in the information systems community as a major benefit of new information technology. It is much less frequently noted that redesigning business processes could potentially cause millions of middle-level managers and clerical workers to lose their jobs. One economist has raised the possibility that we will create a society run by a small "high tech elite of corporate professionals...in a nation of the permanently unemployed" (Rifkin 1993).

Other economists are much more sanguine about the potential job losses. They believe relieving bright, educated workers from reengineered jobs will result in these workers moving to better jobs in fast-growth industries. Missing from this equation are unskilled, blue-collar workers and older, less well educated middle managers. It is not clear that these groups can be retrained easily for high-quality (high-paying) jobs. Careful planning and sensitivity to employee needs can help companies redesign work to minimize job losses.

Equity and Access: Increasing Racial and Social Class Divisions

Does everyone have an equal opportunity to participate in the digital age? Will the social, economic, and cultural gaps that exist in most societies be reduced by information systems technology? Or will the divisions be increased, permitting the wealthy to become even better off relative to others?

WINDOW ON MANAGEMENT

Can the Spamming Monster Be Tamed?

Email may have made the Internet the most socially interactive medium in history, but spam is turning it into the most cluttered. Spam now accounts for 65 percent of email traffic worldwide, and that percentage is even higher in some countries (80 percent in Korea). According to International Data Center research, spam volume jumped to 8.5 billion messages daily in 2004. If spam keeps growing at its current rate, the Internet will soon become unusable.

Spam costs for businesses are very high because of the computing and network resources consumed by billions of unwanted email messages and the time consumed in trying to deal with them. Estimates are that far more than 50 percent—some estimates as high as 80 percent—of all email messages received today are spam. A great deal of spam email uses subject lines that conceal the real purpose of the messages. Most messages take only a few seconds for the recipient to delete, but some messages use subject headings that require recipients to read the messages quickly to see if they are worthwhile.

According to Nucleus Research, the average worker receives 13.3 spam messages per day, which take six and one half minutes to review and process, amounting to 1.4 percent of each worker's productive time. Assuming an hourly pay rate of $30 and 2,080 hours of work a year, Nucleus calculates spam costs businesses $874 each year in lost productivity for every office worker with an email account. Multiplying that number by 16 million workers amounts to $14 billion in wasted productivity in Canada alone. According to consulting firm mi2g Limited, which focuses on risk management, worldwide spam caused more damage than the worldwide losses from computer viruses and worms ($8.5 billion).

Spam continues to defy most legal and technical efforts to eliminate it. Spammers can easily switch back and forth among free email accounts to broadcast their messages, disguising their true email addresses. Many spam messages are sent from one country while another country hosts the spam Web site. There are legitimate business and personal uses for email, and many businesses using direct marketing do not wish to see email regulated.

Most corporate networks use spam filters, as do many Internet service providers. Individuals can purchase filtering software from companies such as Brightmail, MailFrontier, or Sendmail or use the filtering capabilities of major email software. These tools block suspicious email before it enters a recipient's email inbox. Another technique for avoiding spam is to block any messages sent from computers or email addresses known to be used by spammers.

However, spam filters can block legitimate messages, and many spammers skirt around filters by continually changing their accounts, creating false return addresses, or using cryptic phrases that most filters won't catch. Nevertheless, antispam systems appear to be a good investment. An International Data Center study found that antispam systems in a typical company with 5000 email users halved the amount of time employees spent on email, saving the company US $783,000.

The U.S. CAN-SPAM Act of 2003, which went into effect on January 1, 2004, does not outlaw spamming but does ban deceptive email practices by requiring commercial email messages to display an accurate subject line, identify the true sender, and offer recipients an easy way to remove their names from email lists. Experts believe the CAN-SPAM Act will have little impact. Although it makes it easier to know who sends spam, it overrides stronger state statutes, some of which outlaw spam, and it has little impact on spammers based abroad. According to John Mozena, vice president of the antispam advocacy group Coalition Against Unsolicited Commercial Email, unsolicited email can't be regulated in the same manner as regular postal service mail or telemarketing because there is no additional cost to the marketer to send emails to people who haven't opted out.

So far, this has been the case. A few people have been prosecuted under the law, but the flow of unsolicited junk email is as strong as ever, with spammers turning to instant messaging as a new channel for their activities. A Consumer Reports study surveying more than 2000 email users found that 47 percent were receiving more spam three months after the law went into effect than before.

The question is: What will it take to stop spamming abuses, or will Internet users remain prey to the spamming monster?

To Think About: Is spamming an important management issue? Why or why not? How should this problem be handled?

Sources: Sudhir Chowdhary, "Festival Blues: India Inc. Grapples with Spam," *ZDNet India*, December 20, 2004; Daniel Nasaw, "Federal Law Fails to Lessen Flow of Junk Email," *Wall Street Journal*, August 10, 2004; Saul Hansell, "Junk Email and Fraud Are Focus of Crackdown," *New York Times*, August 25, 2004, "4 Rivals Near Agreement on Ways to Fight Spam," *New York Times*, June 23, 2004; Laurie J. Flynn, "Internet Giants File 7 Suits Aimed at Stopping Spam," *New York Times*, October 29, 2004; Brent Staples, "The Battle Against Junk Mail and Spyware on the Web," *New York Times*, January 3, 2004; Thomas Claburn, "Anti-Spam Technologies Prove Their Value," *Information Week*, April 26, 2004; Thomas Claburn, "Turning the Tide," *Information Week*, January 17, 2005; G. Patrick Pawling "Turning Drains into Gains," *Cisco IQ Magazine*, First Quarter 2004; Pui-Wing Tam, "Fruitcake Debutantes Defined by O, and Other Spam Tricks," *Wall Street Journal*, May 28, 2004; and Saul Hansell, "Totaling Up the Bill for Spam," *New York Times*, July 28, 2003.

These questions have not yet been fully answered because the impact of systems technology on various groups in society has not been thoroughly studied. What is known is that information, knowledge, computers, and access to these resources through educational institutions and public libraries are inequitably distributed along ethnic and social class lines, as are many other information resources. Several studies have found that certain ethnic and income groups are less likely to have computers or online Internet access even though computer ownership and Internet access have soared in the past five years. Although the gap is narrowing, higher-income families in each ethnic group are still more likely to have home computers and Internet access than lower-income families in the same group (Lenhart et al. 2003).

A similar **digital divide** exists in schools, with schools in high-poverty areas likely to have fewer computers, fewer high-quality educational technology programs, or slower or little Internet access available for their students. Left uncorrected, the digital divide could lead to a society of information haves, computer literate and skilled, versus a large group

digital divide

of information have-nots, computer illiterate and unskilled. Public interest groups want to narrow this digital divide by making digital information services—including the Internet—available to virtually everyone just as basic telephone service is now.

Health Risks: RSI, CVS, and Technostress

The most important occupational disease today is **repetitive stress injury (RSI).** RSI occurs when muscle groups are forced through repetitive actions often with high-impact loads (such as tennis) or tens of thousands of repetitions under low-impact loads (such as working at a computer keyboard).

The single largest source of RSI is computer keyboards. The most common kind of computer-related RSI is **carpal tunnel syndrome (CTS)**, in which pressure on the median nerve through the wrist's bony structure, called the carpal tunnel, produces pain. The pressure is caused by constant repetition of keystrokes: In a single shift, a data entry clerk or secretary may perform 23 000 keystrokes. Symptoms of carpal tunnel syndrome include numbness, shooting pain, inability to grasp objects, and tingling. Millions of workers have been diagnosed with carpal tunnel syndrome.

RSI is avoidable. Designing workstations for a neutral wrist position (using a wrist rest to support the wrist), proper monitor stands, and footrests all contribute to proper posture and reduced RSI. New, ergonomically correct keyboards are also an option. These measures should be backed by frequent rest breaks and rotation of employees to different jobs.

Repetitive stress injury (RSI) is the leading occupational disease today. The single largest cause of RSI is computer keyboard work.

RSI is not the only occupational illness computers cause. Back and neck pain, leg stress, and foot pain also result from poor ergonomic designs of workstations. **Computer vision syndrome (CVS)** refers to any eyestrain condition related to computer display screen use. Its symptoms, which are usually temporary, include headaches, blurred vision, and dry and irritated eyes.

The newest computer-related malady is **technostress**, which is stress induced by computer use. Its symptoms include aggravation, hostility toward humans, impatience, and fatigue. According to experts, humans working continuously with computers come to expect other humans and human institutions to behave like computers, providing instant response, attentiveness, and an absence of emotion. Technostress is thought to be related to high levels of job turnover in the computer industry, high levels of early retirement from computer-intense occupations, and elevated levels of drug and alcohol abuse.

The incidence of technostress is not known but it is thought to be in the millions and growing rapidly. Computer-related jobs now top the list of stressful occupations based on health statistics in several industrialized countries.

To date, the role of radiation from computer display screens in occupational disease has not been proved. Video display terminals (VDTs) emit nonionizing electric and magnetic fields at low frequencies. These rays enter the body and have unknown effects on enzymes, molecules, chromosomes, and cell membranes. Long-term studies are investigating low-level electromagnetic fields and birth defects, stress, low birth weight, and other diseases. All manufacturers have reduced display screen emissions since the early 1980s, and European countries such as Sweden have adopted stiff radiation emission standards.

The computer has become a part of our lives—personally as well as socially, culturally, and politically. It is unlikely that the issues and our choices will become easier as information technology continues to transform our world. The growth of the Internet and the information economy suggests that all the ethical and social issues we have described will be heightened further as we move into the first digital century.

repetitive stress injury (RSI)

carpal tunnel syndrome (CTS)

computer vision syndrome (CVS)

technostress

Management Opportunities, Challenges, and Solutions

The ethical and social implications of information systems are now more far-reaching than ever, affecting individuals who use information systems as well as managers and employees in business firms.

Opportunities

Managers have the opportunity to create an ethical business environment that is within the law, and it is their responsibility to do so. Doing the right thing with information systems in the long term will always lead to a stronger, more reliable organization. This may not mean that management actions will always make employees, shareholders, or customers happy, but these actions should be the result of a careful ethical analysis using the principles we have outlined in this chapter.

Management Challenges

Technology can be a double-edged sword. It has been the source of many benefits, but it also has created new opportunities for breaking the law or taking benefits away from others, raising the following management challenges.

Understanding the Moral Risks of New Technology Rapid technological change means that the choices facing individuals also rapidly change, and the balance of risk and reward and the probabilities of apprehension for wrongful acts change as well. In this environment, it is important for management to conduct an ethical and social impact analysis of new technologies as they emerge. Managers might take each of the moral dimensions described in this chapter and briefly speculate on how a new technology affects each dimension. There may not always be right answers for how to behave, but there should be management awareness of the moral risks of new technology.

Establishing Corporate Ethics Policies that Include Information Systems Issues As a manager, you will be responsible for developing, enforcing, and explaining corporate ethics policies. Historically, corporate management has paid much more attention to financial integrity and personnel policies than to the information systems area. But based on what you will have learned after reading this chapter, it is clear your corporation should have an ethics policy in the information systems (IS) area covering such issues as privacy, property, accountability, system quality, and quality of life. The challenge will be in educating non-IS managers about the need for these policies, as well as educating your workforce.

Solution Guidelines

Some corporations have developed far-reaching corporate IS codes of ethics, including BC Hydro, Nortel, FedEx, IBM, and American Express. Most firms, however, have not developed these codes of ethics, leaving their employees unsure about expected correct behaviour. There is some dispute concerning a general code of ethics versus a specific information systems code of ethics. As managers, you should strive to develop an IS-specific set of ethical standards for each of the five moral dimensions:

- *Information rights and obligations.* A code should cover topics such as employee email and Internet privacy, workplace monitoring, treatment of corporate information, and policies on customer information.
- *Property rights and obligations.* A code should cover topics such as software licenses, ownership of firm data and facilities, ownership of software created by employees on company hardware, and software copyrights. Specific guidelines for contractual relationships with third parties should be covered as well.

- *System quality.* The code should describe the general levels of data quality and system error that can be tolerated, with detailed specifications left to specific projects. The code should require that all systems attempt to estimate data quality and system error probabilities.

- *Quality of life.* The code should state that the purpose of systems is to improve the quality of life for customers and for employees by achieving high levels of product quality, customer service, and employee satisfaction and human dignity through proper ergonomics, job and workflow design, and human resources development.

- *Accountability and control.* The code should specify a single individual responsible for all information systems, and reporting to this individual should be others who are responsible for individual rights, the protection of property rights, system quality, and quality of life (e.g., job design, ergonomics, and employee satisfaction). Responsibilities for control of systems, audits, and management should be clearly defined. The potential liabilities of systems officers and the corporation should be detailed in a separate document.

Summary

1. *Analyze the ethical, social, and political issues that are raised by information systems.*

   Information technology has raised new possibilities for behaviour for which laws and rules of acceptable conduct have not yet been developed. Information technology is introducing changes that create new ethical issues for societies to debate and resolve. Increasing computing power, storage, and networking capabilities— including the Internet—can expand the reach of individual and organizational actions and magnify their impact. The ease and anonymity with which information can be communicated, copied, and manipulated in online environments are challenging traditional rules of right and wrong behaviour. Ethical, social, and political issues are closely related. Ethical issues confront individuals who must choose a course of action, often in a situation in which two or more ethical principles are in conflict (a dilemma). Social issues spring from ethical issues as societies develop expectations in individuals about the correct course of action. Political issues spring from social conflict and are mainly concerned with using laws that prescribe behaviour to create situations in which individuals behave correctly.

2. *Identify the main moral dimensions of an information society and specific principles for conduct that can be used to guide ethical decisions.*

   The moral dimensions of information systems center on information rights and obligations, property rights and obligations, accountability and control, system quality, and quality of life. Six ethical principles are available to judge conduct. These principles are derived independently from several cultural, religious, and intellectual traditions that include the Golden Rule, Immanuel Kant's Categorical Imperative, Descartes' rule of change, the Utilitarian Principle, the Risk Aversion Principle, and the ethical "no free lunch" rule. These principles should be used in conjunction with an ethical analysis to guide decision making. The ethical analysis involves identifying the facts, values, stakeholders, options, and consequences of actions. Once completed, you can consider which ethical principle to apply to a situation to arrive at a judgment.

3. *Evaluate the impact of contemporary information systems and the Internet on the protection of individual privacy and intellectual property.*

   Contemporary information systems technology, including Internet technology, challenges traditional regimens for protecting individual privacy and intellectual property. Data storage and data analysis technology enable companies to easily gather personal data about individuals from many different sources and analyze these data to create detailed electronic profiles about individuals and their behaviours. Data flowing over the Internet can be monitored at many points. The activities of Web site visitors can be closely tracked using cookies and other Web monitoring tools. Not all Web sites have strong privacy protection policies, and they do not always allow for informed consent regarding the use of personal information. The online industry prefers self-regulation to governments tightening privacy protection legislation.

   Traditional copyright laws are insufficient to protect against software piracy because digital material can be copied so easily. Internet technology also makes intellectual property even more difficult to protect because digital material can be copied easily and transmitted to many different locations simultaneously over the Internet. Web pages can be constructed easily using pieces of content from other Web sites without permission.

4. *Assess how information systems have affected everyday life.*

Although computer systems have been sources of efficiency and wealth, they have some negative impacts. Errors in large computer systems are impossible to eradicate totally. Computer errors can cause serious harm to individuals and organizations, and existing laws and social practices are often unable to establish liability and accountability for these problems. Less serious errors are often attributable to poor data quality, which can cause disruptions and losses for businesses. Jobs can be lost when computers replace workers or tasks become unnecessary in reengineered business processes. The ability to own and use a computer may be exacerbating socioeconomic disparities among different racial groups and social classes. Widespread use of computers increases opportunities for computer crime and computer abuse. Computers can also create health problems such as repetitive stress injury, computer vision syndrome, and technostress.

5. *Identify the principal management challenges posed by the ethical and social impact of information systems and propose management solutions.*

The main management challenges posed by the ethical and social impact of information systems are the need to understand the moral risks of new technology and the difficulty of establishing corporate ethics policies that address information systems issues. For each of the five moral dimensions of information systems, corporations should develop a corporate ethics policy statement to guide individuals and to encourage appropriate decision making. The policy areas are as follows:

- *Individual information rights.* Spell out corporate privacy and due process policies.
- *Property rights.* Clarify how the corporation will treat property rights of software owners.
- *System quality.* Identify methodologies and quality standards to be achieved.
- *Quality of life.* Identify corporate policies on family, computer crime, decision making, vulnerability, job loss, and health risks.
- *Accountability and control.* Clarify who is responsible and accountable for corporate information.

Key Terms

Accountability, 112
Carpal tunnel syndrome (CTS), 134
Computer abuse, 130
Computer crime, 130
Computer vision syndrome (CVS), 134
Cookies, 118
Copyright, 121
Descartes' rule of change, 113
Digital divide, 133
Digital Millennium Copyright Act
   (DMCA), 123
Due process, 112
Ethical "no free lunch" rule, 113

Ethics, 108
Fair Information Practices (FIP), 116
Framing, 123
Immanuel Kant's Categorical Imperative, 113
Information rights, 109
Informed consent, 117
Intellectual property, 121
Liability, 112
Nonobvious relationship awareness
   (NORA), 111
Opt-in, 119
Opt-out, 119
Platform for Privacy Preferences (P3P), 120

Patent, 122
Privacy, 115
Profiling, 110
Repetitive stress injury (RSI), 134
Responsibility, 112
Risk Aversion Principle, 113
Spam, 131
Spyware, 118
Technostress, 134
Trade secret, 121
Utilitarian Principle, 113
Web bugs, 118

Review Questions

1. *In what ways are ethical, social, and political issues connected? Give some examples.*

2. *What are the key technological trends that heighten ethical concerns?*

3. *What are the differences between responsibility, accountability, and liability?*

4. *What are the five steps in an ethical analysis?*

5. *Identify and describe six ethical principles.*

6. *What is a professional code of conduct?*

7. *What are meant by privacy and fair information practices?*

8. *How is the Internet challenging the protection of individual privacy?*

9. *What role can informed consent, legislation, industry self-regulation, and technology tools play in protecting individual privacy of Internet users?*

10. *What are the three different regimes that protect intellectual property rights? What challenges to intellectual property rights does the Internet pose?*

11. *Why is it so difficult to hold software services liable for failure or injury?*

12. *What is the most common cause of system quality problems?*

13. *Name and describe four quality of life impacts of computers and information systems.*

14. *What is technostress, and how would you identify it?*

15. *Name three management actions that could reduce RSI injuries.*

Discussion Questions

1. *Should producers of software-based services, such as ATMs, be held liable for economic injuries suffered when their systems fail?*

2. *Should companies be responsible for unemployment caused by their information systems? Why or why not?*

Application Software Exercise
Word Processing and Web Page Development Tool Exercise:
Creating a Simple Web site

Build a simple Web site of your own design for a business using the Web page creation function of Microsoft Word, Microsoft FrontPage, or a Web page development tool of your choice. Your Web site should include a home page with a description of your business and at least one picture or graphic. From the home page, you must be able to link to a second Web page and, from there, link to a third Web page. Make the home page long enough so that when you arrive at the bottom of the page, you can no longer see the top. Include a link back to the top. Also include a link to one of the secondary Web pages. On the secondary page, include a link to the top of that page and a link back to the top of the home page. Also include a link to the third page, which should contain a link to its own top and a link back to the top of the home page. Finally, on one of the secondary pages, include another picture or graphic, and on the other page, include an object that you create using Microsoft Excel or other spreadsheet software.

On at least one page, use a logo that you create. What would be the difference if you used the trademark or logo of an established company? What permissions would you need to obtain to do so? The Companion Website for Chapter 4 includes instructions for completing this project. If you have tested every function and all work to your satisfaction, save the pages you have created for submission to your instructor.

Electronic Commerce Project: Using Internet Newsgroups for Online Market Research

You are producing hiking boots that you are selling through a few stores. You think your boots are more comfortable than those of your competitors. You believe you can undersell many of your competitors if you can significantly increase your production and sales. You would like to use the Internet discussion groups interested in hiking, climbing, and camping to both sell your boots and to make them well known. Visit Google's Usenet archives (groups.google.com), which store discussion postings from many thousands of newsgroups. Through this site, you can locate all relevant newsgroups and search them by keyword, author's name, forum, date, and subject. Choose a message and examine it carefully, noting all the information you can obtain, including information about the author.

1. How could you use these newsgroups to market your boots?

2. What ethical principles might you be violating if you use these messages to sell your boots? Do you think there are ethical problems in this type of newsgroup use? Explain your answer.

3. Decide whether you want to use the newsgroups to locate Web sites on the topic being searched (hiking, climbing, or camping) for the hiking boots industry. Examine the various sites to determine whether there are other ways to draw potential buyers to the Web site you may decide to establish.

4. Next go to Yahoo.ca to search for the hiking boots industry, and locate sites that will help you develop other new ideas for contacting potential customers.

5. Given what you have learned in this and previous chapters, prepare a plan to use newsgroups and other alternative methods to begin attracting visitors to your site.

Group Project: Developing a Corporate Ethics Code

With three or four of your classmates, develop a corporate ethics code on privacy that addresses both employee privacy and the privacy of customers and users of a corporate Web site. Be sure to consider email privacy and employer monitoring of work sites, as well as corporate use of information about employees concerning their off-job behaviour (e.g., lifestyle, marital arrangements, and so forth). If possible, use electronic presentation software to present your ethics code to the class.

CASE STUDY:
Security versus Privacy: Does Terrorism Change the Debate?

Discussions on many levels are underway in most countries, including Canada, the U.S., England, and Spain, about the kind of country in which their citizens want to live and the balance between public safety and private freedom. Is the government's collection of so much information on each of us more dangerous than the possible benefits? Are we willing to give up some of our freedom and privacy if we believe our safety depends on it?

People want technology both for convenience and protection, and so most are now tolerant of increasingly prevalent surveillance cameras and collection of personal data by government and private corporations. There are around 300 million cameras in use around the world. These cameras are already being used in Great Britain and the U.S. to monitor bridges, tunnels, airports, and border crossings, as well as activities in stores, banks, and garages. In Great Britain, an estimated 2.5 million closed-circuit television cameras are being used so that the average Londoner is probably photographed 300 times a day. London systems record every vehicle that enters the city to better control traffic and so police can plan emergency routes when needed. This information is also shared with intelligence agencies to help protect citizens and solve crimes. When four bombs were set off in the London Underground subway system and on a bus in July 2005, police were able within days to identify the four bombers based on camera footage taken at King's Cross subway station.

Computers record immigration and visa applications—the U.S. database for visa applications already contains 50 million records, most with photographs. Law enforcement organizations are also now using this database. According to Miles Matthews, a senior U.S. Justice Department official, "It's not just useful for terrorism. It's drug trafficking, money laundering, a variety of frauds, not to mention domestic crimes."

Large databases of medical records are being created so that "if you're brought to an emergency room anywhere in the world, your medical records pop up in 30 seconds," explains Ben Schneiderman, a University of Maryland expert on new computing techniques. The U.S. federal government's Centers for Disease Control and Prevention is creating a computerized network to collect and analyze health data from eight major cities, including doctors' reports, emergency room visits, and medication sales to watch out for clusters of symptoms associated with both terrorist attacks and major natural disease outbreaks.

These surveillance activities generate massive amounts of data, and information systems technology is now capable of storing and transmitting this data. Jeffrey Ullman, a former Stanford University database researcher, claims that if all of these data were collected, a digital dossier of every person in the U.S. would require only "a couple terabytes (trillion characters) of well-defined information." One estimate projects that by 2023 a corporation will be able to devote one PC to monitoring every U.S. citizen in the population, estimated to be at more than 325 million people by then.

In May 2003, President George W. Bush ordered U.S. intelligence agencies to purchase as much satellite imagery as possible from private companies because satellite photos from all over the world are of such high quality that they can be used for domestic and foreign surveillance. The U.S. is also planning to increase its own surveillance satellites under a program called Future Imagery Architecture. The United States is coming closer to being able to monitor all movements of people everywhere. The Central Intelligence Agency (CIA) has been spending about $35 million annually since 1999 to improve its own technology in its enormous electronic archives. For example, it is improving face-recognition software to help track specific people through photographs and videos.

Since the September 11, 2001 terrorist attacks, Canadians and Americans have been asked to place more trust in law enforcement and intelligence agencies. The Bush administration argues that Americans can even trust these agencies to exercise broad new powers. The U.S. Congress overwhelmingly approved an extension of such powers when it passed the USA Patriot Act in October 2001 with almost no opposition. This law automatically expires in October 2005, but President Bush is asking the U.S. Congress to make it permanent.

This 342-page act gave law enforcement officials broader authority to conduct electronic surveillance and wiretaps and tightened oversight of financial activities to prevent money laundering that might benefit terrorists. It changed provisions of the Foreign Intelligence Surveillance Act passed in 1978 by allowing the Federal Bureau of Investigation (FBI) to share information gathered in terrorism investigations with local law enforcement agencies so that it could potentially be used for criminal prosecution. The Patriot Act enabled federal prosecutors to seek wiretap and surveillance authority and to obtain client records from financial institutions without evidence of criminal activity. (A federal judge ruled this part of the act unconstitutional in late September 2004.) Civil liberties groups and hundreds of communities have objected to this legislation.

In her annual report to Parliament in 2004, Canada's privacy commissioner, Jennifer Stoddart, urged that the increased collection of Canadians' personal information to combat terrorism poses a grave threat to civil liberties. Stoddart urged that "we must ensure the privacy rights of individuals are not lost or submerged in the chorus of voices calling for more security, more data, and more information about all of us." The report came just days after British Columbia's privacy commissioner concluded that British Columbians' personal information needs greater safeguards from the reach of the USA Patriot Act.

On December 13, 2003, the U.S. Congress and President Bush granted the FBI additional powers through passage and signing of the Intelligence Authorization Act, which funds all the intelligence activities of the federal government. This statute defines financial institutions to include travel agencies, car dealerships, real estate and insurance agents, casinos, hotels, and even the U.S. Postal Service. Under its provisions, the FBI can obtain personal data from all of these organizations without obtaining court approval and without the person's knowledge.

The FBI has been using a tool called Carnivore to eavesdrop on communication flowing through the Internet. Carnivore software, stored on the computers of Internet service providers (ISPs), inspects all the headers of the millions of email messages passing through an ISP's computer system to identify those of criminal or terrorist suspects falling under court orders. Carnivore then selects those messages and contents for FBI agents to review.

Privacy watchdogs view the system as "the electronic equivalent of listening to everybody's phone calls to see if it's the phone call you should be monitoring." FBI Director Robert Mueller defended the practice at a June 2003 American Civil Liberties Union (ACLU) meeting. "In our free and exceptionally open society, there is no guarantee that there will never be another terrorist attack. And therefore we must thoroughly investigate every threat, whether at home or abroad, carefully—carefully—observing the constitutional rights of all," he said.

On March 12, 2004, the FBI, the Department of Justice, and the Drug Enforcement Administration filed a proposal to require major Internet service providers to modify their networks to facilitate further electronic eavesdropping by law enforcement officials. The proposal gives law enforcement agencies easy access to all forms of switched Internet communications, including new Internet-based telephone services, instant messaging systems, and high-capacity Internet communications provided by cable systems and the telephone network.

The U.S. government is combining surveillance data from multiple sources into massive databases. The Transportation Security Administration (TSA) had been using a computer system implemented in 1996 called Computer Assisted Passenger Prescreening System (CAPPS) to profile airline passengers to identify those who are high risk. It tags unusual behaviour such as purchasing one-way airline tickets with cash.

CAPPS problems included inaccurate or out-of-date data and mix-ups as to the people on the high-risk list. Names written in alphabets other than the Roman alphabet, such as Japanese, Russian, or Arabic, could be written in English in many different ways. Moreover, the same name could be written differently, for example, by omitting a middle initial. Senator Edward Kennedy of Massachusetts was stopped from boarding airplanes five times between March 1 and April 6, 2004 because his name resembled an alias used by a suspected terrorist who had been barred from flying on airlines in the U.S.

The TSA developed a more sophisticated approach called CAPPS II. In addition to evaluating such travel-related behaviour and looking for passenger names on watch lists, CAPPS II gave transportation agencies access to numerous public and private databases when a passenger books a flight. It matched passenger names, addresses, phone numbers, dates of birth, and photo IDs from airline passenger lists against data from credit-reporting agencies, and then it scanned law enforcement and intelligence files to determine whether the person was a security risk.

In June 2004 TSA dropped CAPPS II in response to criticism from the U.S. Congress and privacy advocates. In its place TSA proposed a system called Secure Flight, which has many of the same features as CAPPS II. Secure Flight also matches passenger data against commercial databases, but it does not use the computer routines developed for CAPPS II that tried to determine if passengers not on watch lists should be singled out for scrutiny.

In December 2001, Parliament passed Bill C-36, the Anti-Terrorism Act of Canada. These new anti-terrorist measures provide new investigative tools that can be used against terrorist groups, including measures that take the investigatory powers currently in the Criminal Code and in Bill C-24 that make it easier to use electronic surveillance against criminal organizations. One of these new measures eliminates the need to demonstrate that electronic surveillance is a last resort in the investigation of terrorists. The legislation extends the period of validity of a wiretap authorization from the previous 60 days to up to one year when police are investigating a terrorist group offence. A Superior Court judge will still have to approve the use of electronic surveillance to ensure that these powers are used appropriately.

The American Defense Advanced Research Projects Agency (DARPA) has been working on a number of projects that would create massive databases that capture transactional data from many different sources. A project called Combat Zones That See (CTS) would record and analyze the movement of every vehicle in a foreign city using software to identify vehicles by size, colour, shape, license plate, or drivers' and passengers' faces. Its goal is to help the U.S. military protect its troops overseas. Its founding document states that the program "aspires to build the world's first multi-camera surveillance system that uses automatic analysis of live video" to study vehicle movement "and significant events across an extremely large area."

MATRIX, which stands for Multistate Anti-Terrorism Information Exchange, is a massive database developed by a private company called Seisint and funded and managed by the Department of Homeland Security and several state governments. MATRIX was launched in 2002 to help investigators establish patterns and links for profiling crime and terrorism suspects. The database includes 4 billion records with data on criminal histories, federal terrorist watch lists, drivers' licenses, vehicle registrations, and incarcerations as well as credit histories, pilot licenses, aircraft ownership, boat ownership, property ownership, and other public and commercial data. So far, only five states have signed on to MATRIX—Florida, Connecticut, Michigan, Ohio, and Pennsylvania. Eleven others have withdrawn from the project.

The construction of massive databases of personal information has alarmed both government officials and privacy watchdogs. Marc Rotenberg, the executive director of the Electronic Privacy Information Center (EPIC), describes the problem: "What seems to be small-scale, discrete systems end up being combined into large databases." Although the public has no problem with the collection of most of this "small" data independently, weaving it all together can become a massive invasion of privacy, he believes. A June 2004 report by a bipartisan Technology and Privacy Advisory Committee appointed by Secretary of Defense Donald Rumsfeld to evaluate Pentagon programs for data mining called for restrictions on federal agency searches of personally identifiable information to safeguard privacy when fighting terrorism.

There are also technical problems with assembling and analyzing gigantic pools of data. Although information technology enables the creation of these massive databases, it has not solved the problems of integrating disparate sources of information and of arriving at valid conclusions. Massive databases can produce very unreliable results because they become very difficult to examine. Piotr Indyk, a Massachusetts Institute of Technology (MIT) database researcher, points out that as the amount of data collected rapidly increases, the number of chance correlations also increases so that the number of logically valid but actually useless solutions grows just as rapidly.

Data in very large data repositories can be very unreliable. Information systems specialists often use the term GIGO, meaning "garbage in, garbage out." Think of the problems in your own financial records, from misspellings to digital transposition to misidentification to outdated records. According to Larry English of Information Impact, a database consulting firm, "It is routine to find in large customer databases defective records—records with at least one major error or omission—at a rate of at least 20 to 35 percent." Moreover, research using a massive database requires both an "unusually smart analyst," Ullman points out, and an accurate model of what the analyst is looking for.

Even a 1 percent error rate in searching for terrorists using so much data would produce millions of false alarms, requiring an immense amount of wasted investigators' time while wrongly labelling and greatly disturbing many innocent people. "A 99 percent hit rate is great for advertising, but terrible for spotting terrorism" is the explanation given by Gene Spafford, the director of Purdue University's Center for Education and Research in Information Assurance and Security. In addition, further tightening identification criteria would result in many terrorists and criminals being missed, including, for example, many of those who hijacked the 9/11 planes or who were involved in the London bombings, but who had previously lived quiet, seemingly normal lives.

So far, thousands of intercepted phone calls, email, messages, documents, and other messages collected for terror surveillance have proved too massive to analyze. Three years after the September 11 attacks, more than 120 000 hours of potentially valuable terrorism-related recordings had not yet been translated by the FBI because the agency did not have enough linguists trained in Arabic and other languages.

Although consumers balk at businesses intruding on their privacy, they are more supportive of government agencies collecting personal information to fight terrorism. A Harris Poll conducted in February 2003 revealed that 84 percent of those polled favoured stronger document and physical security for travellers, and 44 percent supported expanded government monitoring of cell phones and email. According to Columbia University professor Alan Westin, who conducted the poll, "how to put a system in place to protect us from [both] terrorism and invasions of privacy is something we are just barely beginning to understand."

Sources: Eric Lichtblau, "F.B.I. Said to Lag on Translations of Terror Tapes," *New York Times*, September 28, 2004; Reuters, "Judge Rules Against Patriot Act Provision," September 29, 2004; Matthew L. Wald, "U.S. Wants Air Traveler Files for Security Test," *New York Times*, September 22, 2004; Rachel L. Swarns, "Senator? Terrorist? A Watch List Stops Kennedy at Airport," *The New York Times*, August 20, 2004; Ryan Singel, "Secure Flight Gets Wary Welcome," *Wired News*, August 27, 2004; Sebastian Rupley, "FBI Petitions for Broad Wiretapping Rights," *PC Magazine*, March 15, 2004; Robert Pear, "Panel Urges New Protection on Federal 'Data Mining,' " *New York Times*, May 17, 2004; Brian Bergstein, "Terrorist Scoring System Sparked Investigations and Arrests," *Information Week*, May 20, 2004; Brian Gail Repsher Emery, "Patriot Games," and Andy Sullivan, "U.S. to Force Airlines to Provide Traveler Data," Yahoo! News, March 17, 2 004; Sara Kehaulani Goo, "Northwest Gave U.S. Data on Passengers," *Washington Post*, January 18, 2004; Matthew L. Wald, "Privacy Issues Slow Updated Airlines Security," *New York Times*, May 11, 2004; Heather MacDonald, "The 'Privacy' Jihad," *Wall Street Journal*, April 1, 2004; Larry Greenemeier, "Lawmakers Want Info," *Information Week*, February 25, 2004; Joe Sharkey, "When Flying Is Truly the Only Way to Go," *New York Times*, May 25, 2004; Matthew L. Wald, "Privacy Issue Delays Change in Airport Screening System," *New York Times*, February 13, 2004; Meg Mitchell Moore, "Serving Up Your Customers," *CSO Magazine*, January 2004; Jeffrey Rosen, "How to Protect America, and Your Rights," *New York Times*, February 6, 2004; Ethan Bronner, "Collateral Damage," *New York Times*, February 22, 2004; Andrew P. Napolitano, "Repeal the Patriot Act," *Wall Street Journal*, March 5, 2004; David E. Sanger, "President Urging Wider U.S. Powers in Terrorism Law," *New York Times*, September 11, 2003; Adam Clymer, "In Fight for Privacy, States Set Off Sparks," *New York Times*, July 6, 2003; Sean Marciniak, "Web Privacy Services Complicate Work of Federal Investigators," *Wall Street Journal*, July 3, 2003; Michael J. Sniffen, "Pentagon Developing System to Track Every Vehicle in a City," **www.security-focus.com**, July 1, 2003; "Pentagon Tool Records Every Breath," **http://australianit.news.com.au**, June 3, 2003; Jeff Milchen,

"Fighting Terror Without Losing Our Freedom," *Baltimore Sun*, June 22, 2003; Randall Edwards, "CAPPS II Faces Scrutiny Before Funding," **www.fce.com**, June 19, 2003; Jane Black, "Privacy: For Every Attack, a Defense," *Business Week*, July 22, 2003; "Putting the Blinders Back on Big Brother," *BusinessWeek Online*, March 27, 2003; "Mueller Defends FBI at Civil Liberties Meeting," **www.cnn.com**, June 13, 2003; Eric Lichtblau, "Administration Plans Defense of Terror Law," *New York Times*, August 19, 2003; Jesse J. Holland, "Ashcroft Pushes Anti-Terror Law Expansion," Associated Press, June 5, 2003; Dan Farmer and Charles C. Mann, "Give Me Duquesne Minus 7, for a Nickel," *Technology Review*, May 2003; "Surveillance Nation," *Technology Review*, April 2003; James Bamford, "Big Brother Is Tracking You, Without a Warrant," *New York Times*, May 18, 2003; Jane Black, "At Justice, NSEERS Spells Data Chaos," *BusinessWeek Online*, May 2, 2003; Ann Davis, "Why a 'No Fly List' Aimed at Terrorists Delays Others," *Wall Street Journal*, April 22, 2003; Charles Lewis and Adam Mayle, "Justice Department Drafts Sweeping Expansion of Anti-Terrorism Act," **www.publicintegrity.org**, February 7, 2003; Farhad Manjoo, "Please Step to the Side, Sir," **www.salon.com**, April 10, 2003; Matt Welch, "Get Ready for PATRIOT II," **www.alternet.org**, April 2, 2003; Kevin Poulsen, "FBI Seeks Internet Telephony Surveillance," *BusinessWeek Online*, March 28, 2003; T. C. Webster, "Government to 'Save' Digital History," **www.worldnetdaily.com**, March 4, 2003; Matthew Brezezinski, "Fortress American," *New York Times*, February 23, 2003; Jennifer S. Lee, "State Department Link Will Open Visa Database to Police Officers," *New York Times*, January 31, 2003; and William J. Broad and Judith Miller, "Health Data Monitored for Bioterror Warning," *New York Times*, January 27, 2003; EPIC USA Patriot Act page, available **www.epic.org/terrorism/usapatriot**, accessed July 16, 2005; "Royal Assent of Bill C-36, The Anti-Terrorism Act," available **http://canada.justice.gc.ca/en/news/nr/2001/doc_28217.html**, accessed July 16, 2005.

CASE STUDY QUESTIONS

1. Do the increased surveillance power and capability of the U.S. government present an ethical dilemma? What about Canada's new surveillance capability provided by the Anti-Terrorism Act? Explain your answer.

2. Apply an ethical analysis to the issue of the U.S. government's use of information technology to ensure public safety and U.S. citizens' privacy rights. Do you think that Canada's Privacy Commissioner is correct that this poses a "grave threat to civil liberties"? Is that true for Canadians, or only Americans?

3. What are the ethical, social, and political issues raised by the U.S. government creating massive databases to collect personal data on individuals and profile them? What about the photo technology that enables law enforcement to track and/or identify people such as the London bombers?

4. How effective are electronic eavesdropping and massive databases as terrorism and crime-prevention tools? Explain your answer.

5. State your views on ways to solve the problems of collecting the key data the U.S. and Canadian governments need to combat terrorism without interfering with individual privacy.

CBC ⊛ Part I CANADIAN CASE STUDY:
Can Canada Can Spam?

With a chorus of Vikings singing "Spam spam spam spam," Eric Idle, Graham Chapman, and Terry Jones of the British comedy group Monty Python, revealed their loathing for the mystery meat mixture. Because of the popularity of this very funny comedy skit, the junk email that we all receive in massive doses on a daily basis is called "spam."

During World War II, spam was one of the few meats exempted from rationing. When this continued long after the war was over, people got sick of spam. The Monty Python sketch was thus created to lament the ubiquitous presence of spam on every menu. The word "spam" later came to be used to describe junk mail with advertising messages that flooded Usenet newsgroups and individuals' emails. "Spamming" referred to the repetitive and unwanted presence of these emails. The makers of Spam, Hormel, even though always supportive of Monty Python's skit, were not thrilled about the association of their product with unwanted emails. However, they released a special Spam issue for the Broadway premiere of Eric Idle's hit musical Spamalot.

So, what is this email called spam? According to **www.whatis.com**, even though spam is considered unsolicited junk email by users of the Internet, to the sender it is merely a form of bulk mail sent to those on distribution lists obtained from companies that specialize in creating these lists. Spammers expect only a fraction of the millions of their list members to respond positively to their offers.

Spam is somewhat like telemarketing calls, but it costs the user to a certain extent because everyone has to pay for the cost of maintaining the Internet. Spamming has become a significant problem for all Internet users.

Let's look at the statistics on spam. As recently as 2002, email traffic reports indicated that spam amounted to only about 10 percent of email volume. By the end of 2004—only two years later—spam accounted for 80 percent of email volume. The phenomenal growth of spamming has forced companies that offer Internet services to factor it into their pricing. The cost of spamming has to be borne not only by organizations that conduct business electronically but also by individuals that use the Internet for personal communication.

In Canada, Internet users received an average of 79 unsolicited emails per week in 2004 (The Canadian inter@ctive Reid Report 2004). Surveys among email users have revealed that 53 percent of users have become leery of emails and 22 percent use email less frequently overall.

But the threat from spam goes beyond draining users' resources and taking up bandwidth on the Internet. Greater dangers that can be delivered by spam include spyware, viruses, phishing, and botnets, as well as a host of other threatening technologies. MessageLabs, which keeps tabs on the spam invasion, reported seeing 18 million phishing emails in 2004. Phishing is email fraud whereby the perpetrator sends emails that appear to come from well known and trustworthy Web sites in an attempt to gather personal and financial information from the recipient. A phishing expedition, like the fishing expedition it is named for, is a speculative venture: the phisher puts out the bait hoping to lure at least a few of the prey that encounter it. Web sites that are frequently spoofed by phishers include PayPal, eBay, MSN, Yahoo, BestBuy, and America Online. Banks and other financial institutions are also frequently spoofed by phishers.

Often, spam delivers spyware—software that collects personal information about users and may sometimes even alter their computer's operation without their knowledge or consent. According to a 2004 study, 89 percent of users infected by spyware had not been aware of the presence of the spyware in their computers.

Spam has thus undermined users' confidence in the Internet as a safe means of communication and business transactions. Therefore, in May 2004, the Minister of Industry introduced the "Antispam Action Plan for Canada" to combat spamming. A task force was set up to implement the action plan within a year. This task force, led by Industry Canada, comprises experts and key persons from the three groups mainly affected by spam: businesses, consumers, and Internet service providers.

The first challenge the task force faced was to determine how effective current Canadian legislation is with regard to spam. In Canada, we have watched with bemused interest that the U.S.–touted "CanSpam" Act has not reduced spam at all. Maintaining the balance among privacy, freedom of expression, and stopping spam is not easy, as the American attempts to thwart spam have shown. Interestingly, many of those involved in the task force on spam felt that existing Canadian legislation—when properly and diligently enforced—could greatly reduce the volume of spam. The Personal Information Protection and Electronic Documents Act (PIPEDA), the Competition Act, and the Criminal Code of Canada should all be used to reduce spam.

PIPEDA prohibits the release of personal information, such as email addresses, without consent and specifies that any information can only be used for its intended purpose, requiring consent for additional uses, such as spam. The Competition Act deals with deceptive and misleading representations, something much of spam contains. Finally, the Criminal Code of Canada prohibits unauthorized access to computer systems and networks, fraud, and harming data; these laws should address the issue of viruses, Trojan horses, spyware, and phishing. It is also possible that the Telecommunications Act has provisions that apply to sending spam wirelessly through a short message service (SMS) network.

Yet, the overall enforcement of these and other Canadian laws that apply to spam has been limited. The agencies responsible for enforcing these laws have limited resources and competing priorities. They also frequently do not have the technical expertise to track down, investigate, and prosecute spam perpetrators. Determining who has jurisdiction is another challenge: is jurisdiction established by the location of the spammer, the location of the Internet servers delivering the spam, or the location of the users that receive the spam?

The task force on spam then compared existing Canadian law related to spam with similar laws in several countries: the United States, Australia, the United Kingdom, France, and the European Union, all of which have spam laws. In doing so, they identified gaps in Canadian law and have proposed new legislation to address these gaps.

What has been done so far to fight spam? Two cases have been heard by the Privacy Commissioner of Canada under the jurisdiction of PIPEDA. In the first case, Michael Geist received two email solicitations to purchase season tickets from a community football team. The team's office had obtained his email address from university and law firm Web sites. He filed a complaint with the Privacy Commissioner after he received the second email, which was sent after Geist requested that he not be sent any more emails.

The Office of the Privacy Commissioner found that a business address, such as that found on the law firm's Web site, is, in fact, personal information and therefore protected by PIPEDA. This information can be gathered and used without consent—but only for its intended purpose, not to solicit through email.

In the second case, Suzanne Morin received email solicitations at her business email address. Her email address was collected from an online professional association's membership directory. She filed a complaint with the Privacy Commissioner, who again found that the solicitation at her business address represented a violation of personal information use in contravention of the Act. In both cases, the organizations, a community football team and a marketing company, apologized for their actions, removed the email addresses from their email marketing lists, and amended their internal practices in accordance with the Commissioner's findings.

Only one such case has been heard so far by the Competition Bureau. Performance Marketing Ltd. made false claims about two weight-loss patches, Zyapex and Dyapex. The claims were made in emails. Performance Marketing Ltd. failed to enforce its own anti-spam policy, leading to its affiliates using spam to sell these products. The Competition Bureau's Project FairWeb, aimed at combating misleading and deceptive advertising on the Internet, pursued the case. In a consent agreement issued in December 2004, Performance Marketing agreed to ensure that spam will not be used as a vehicle for marketing its products. The company will also post a notice on its Web site correcting the claims and provide a full refund to the purchasers of the diet patches.

Unfortunately, where spam is concerned, these three cases only represent the tip of the iceberg. Every day, spammers think up new ways to spam. Immediately after the devastation of Hurricane Katrina in late August 2005, spammers masquerading as charitable organizations started firing off spam, simply including the word "Katrina" in their subject lines. Commtouch, an anti-spam technology company, reported that these spam emails used subject lines such as: "Claim your stock car racing gift Katrina," "Enter now for a complimentary trip to Maui Katrina," "Today's Headlines: Hurricane Katrina slams into Gulf coast; dozens are dead," and "Instantly Track Katrina's Progress."

According to Commtouch, while some spam may have masqueraded as messages relating to Katrina, the real spam content for August 2005—based on 1.5 billion spam messages—was similar to those of other months. Pharmaceuticals lead the list of spam content (29 percent), followed by financing schemes (21 percent), and sex enhancers (14 percent). Commtouch's spam detection centre identified almost 28 million new spam in that same month, averaging almost a million per day. Believe it or not, that is a slight decrease from the previous month. Still, it was a 38-percent increase over August 2004. Mirapoint, a competitor of Commtouch, found that pornography was the third highest subject of spam. Another competitor, Clearswift, found that gambling-related spam increased 1500 percent over the previous year—presumably caused by the popularity of poker shows on reality television.

As the CBC video for this case relates, there is now more junk email than legitimate email. It takes about 1.5 seconds, at a minimum, to delete a spam message, costing businesses around the world billions of dollars a year, at the rate of about $1000 per employee per year. Other studies show that spam does not cost so much but is still expensive. Some Web sites even host spam cost calculators, such as Computer Mail Services, Inc. (**www.cmsconnect.com**). Still these statistics do not even count the cost of losing an important message in all the spam you are deleting—something everyone has probably done at one time or another. It is estimated that most spam comes from 200 big spammers, while the rest represents a sort of "cottage industry" of spammers.

All of this—cost, threats to computers, bandwidth reduction—has resulted in the rise of the anti-spam industry. In Canada alone, there are more than 700 businesses involved in anti-spam and anti-virus activities. Fighting spam and viruses has become a $1.5 billion industry. The more spam is blocked, the more creative the spammers become—and the more creative the anti-spammers must become. That is why Carleton University received a $10 million grant to teach students how to combat viruses and spam so that their graduates could find jobs in the industry doing exactly that.

What can individuals do to thwart spam? Do not give out your email address over the Internet without knowing how it will be used. Ensure that Web sites you deal with have privacy policies, and check to see what their policies say they do with your data. Use spam filters provided by your Internet service provider, and download and use spam filters on your own computer.

The problem with any spam filter is that it will actually do one of two things: either permit too much spam to get through to your email or send too much legitimate email to your spam folder, where you can only retrieve it after sifting through all the real spam. Various Web sites post reviews and comparisons of the most popular spam filter programs; check out these reviews, and then pick a spam filter.

But what about organizations? What can they do to fight spam? The advice for organizations is similar to that for individuals. Aggressive filtering of spam helps. Running other

software to thwart viruses, spyware, and other technologies, such as Web bugs (see Chapter 4), helps, too. Most businesses today will probably have to make computer security a priority. For spammers, it is too easy to get in and dump viruses and a host of other threats inside a company's computers. Organizations that make security a top priority and instill that focus throughout the organization will find it easier to survive the spam era than those that ignore the threat.

Sources: The Canadian inter@ctive Reid Report, Fourth Quarter Winter 2004, cited by "What is Spam?" Industry Canada, **http://3-com.ic.gc.ca/epic/internet/inecic-ceac.nsf/en/h_gv00170e.html**, accessed October 2, 2005; "Commtouch Reports August Spam Trends: Spammers Seek to Profit from Katrina," **www.commtouch.com//Site/News_Events/pr_content.asp?news_id=449&cat_id=1**, accessed October 2, 2005; "What is Spam?" Industry Canada, **http://3-com.ic.gc.ca/epic/internet/inecic-ceac.nsf/en/h_gv00170e.html**, accessed October 2, 2005; "The Cost of Spam," **www.cmsconnect.com/Marketing/spamcalc.htm**, accessed October 2, 2005; Enid Burns, "The Deadly Duo: Spam and Viruses, August 2005," **www.clickz.com/stats/sectors/email/print.php/3549111**, accessed October 2, 2005; "Stopping Spam: Creating a Stronger, Safer Internet," May 2005, **http://e-com.ic.gc.ca/epic/internet/inecic-ceac.nsf/vwapj/stopping_spam_May2005.pdf/$file/stopping_spam_May2005.pdf**, accessed October 2, 2005; "Spam Intercepts," **www.messagelabs.com/portal/server.pt?space=CommunityPage&cached=true&parentname=CommunityPage&parentid=2&in_hi_userid=5882&control=SetCommunity&CommunityID=454&PageID=0**, accessed October 2, 2005; "Spam (Monty Python," September 30, 2005, **http://en.wikipedia.org/wiki/Spam_(Monty_Python)**, accessed October 2, 2005; and "Average Global Ratio of Spam in Email Scanned by MessageLabs," **www.messagelabs.com/portal/server.pt/gateway/PTARGS_0_0_453_454_-454_43/http%3B/0120-0176-CTC1%3B8080/publishedcontent/publish/_dotcom_libraries_en/files/monthly_reports/messagelabs_intelligence_report__spam_intercepts_timeline_july_2005_us_5.pdf**, accessed October 2, 2005.

Video Resource

"The Spammed (Life of the Spammed)," Venture 910 (January 18, 2004).

CASE STUDY QUESTIONS

1. Do you think Canada differs in the amount of spam that is sent from Canadian computers? That is received on Canadian computers? Why, or why not?

2. Why would someone send spam? Give at least three different, unrelated reasons to send spam.

3. Why has spam become such a cost to both individuals and organizations? Can you calculate the cost to business of spam? What factors and costs would go into your calculation?

4. Why is it so easy for spammers to avoid prosecution?

5. What can organizations do to stop spam? What can lawmakers do to stop spam?

PART II

Information Technology

Chapter 5

IT Infrastructure and Platforms

OBJECTIVES

After completing this chapter, you will be able to:

1. Define IT infrastructure and describe the components and levels of IT infrastructure.

2. Identify and describe the stages of IT infrastructure evolution.

3. Identify and describe the technology drivers of IT infrastructure evolution.

4. Assess contemporary computer hardware platform trends.

5. Assess contemporary software platform trends.

6. Evaluate the challenges of managing IT infrastructure and management solutions.

Opening Case: Hong Kong's New World Telecommunications Prospers with a New IT Infrastructure

New World Telecommunications is a Hong Kong–based telecommunications company that offers international calling services to 1.1 million subscribers. It also provides telecommunications services to businesses, such as private leased lines, Internet telephone, Internet-based virtual private networks, high-speed frame-relay data transmission, and online data centres.

New World's market is one of cutthroat competition. Its ability to deliver its services competitively depends on a flexible IT infrastructure that can provide uninterrupted and smooth access to data and the ability to support new services in a very short time. New World had been storing its data on different servers, each of which required license fees and some fragmentation of data. To keep its business running and reduce maintenance costs, New World needed to integrate its storage and servers. The company also needed to integrate its customer relationship management, billing, and operational support systems so that, for example, a corporate customer could log on to a Web portal to view service usage, maintain account information, and monitor network performance.

New World Telecommunications enlisted storage vendor EMC to manage its 400-gigabyte production and billing data as well as 80 gigabytes of customer data that resided on six Sun Solaris servers and a Hewlett-Packard (HP) Unix server. EMC updated New World's storage infrastructure to an automated storage area network (SAN) to make it easier to access data from many different servers across the enterprise.

New World was using different brands of servers: Sun, HP, and Compaq Tru64. EMC helped the company centralize its data across all these different brands of servers. New World also consolidated servers so that processing work was transferred from 107 to 70 machines.

By adopting this new infrastructure, New World has reduced system administration costs by 25 percent and has considerably enhanced its flexibility in providing new products and services. In the past, it would take the company nearly three weeks to roll out new market programs. In Hong Kong's fiercely competitive telecommunications business, three weeks seems like an eternity. According to Samuel Poon, New World's director of information technology, "Now we're able to launch a new program within two or three days."

Sources: Raoul LeBlond and Ben Worthen, "Taking IT to the Next Level," *CIO Asia*, January 2004 and **www.nwt-009.com**, accessed September 10, 2004.

New World Telecommunications enhanced its efficiency and competitiveness by better selection and management of its hardware and software technology. The company consolidated servers, updated its storage technology, and implemented software that could integrate its key business systems. These investments gave the company a more flexible IT infrastructure for meeting current and future business needs.

As a manager, you will face many decisions about investments in hardware, software, and other elements of IT infrastructure that are necessary for your firm to conduct its business. These investments may even give your firm new capabilities to surge ahead of competitors. This chapter provides an overview of the technology and service components of IT infrastructure and the most important trends in hardware and software platforms. We look at the capabilities of major technology vendors as well as the technologies themselves to help managers make intelligent choices about the appropriate technology platform for their firm. If you would like a more introductory discussion of hardware and software or a review of basic hardware and software concepts, you can find this information at the Companion Website for Chapter 5.

The Computer System

A **computer** is a physical device that receives data from users as input, processes the data according to stored instructions, and outputs the processed information. A contemporary computer system consists of a central processing unit, primary storage, secondary storage, input devices, output devices, and communications devices (see Figure 5-1).

The central processing unit manipulates data into a more useful form and controls the other parts of the computer system. Primary storage temporarily stores data and program instructions while secondary storage devices (magnetic and optical disks, magnetic tape) store data and programs even when the computer is not turned on. Input devices, such as a keyboard or mouse, convert data and instructions into electronic form for input into the computer. Output devices, such as printers and video display terminals, convert electronic data produced by the computer system and display them in a form that people can understand. Communications devices provide connections between the computer and communications networks. Buses are circuitry paths for transmitting data and signals among the parts of the computer system.

In order for information to flow through a computer system and be in a form suitable for processing, all symbols, pictures, or words must be reduced to a string of binary digits. A binary digit is called a **bit** and represents either a 0 or a 1. In the computer, the presence of an electronic or magnetic signal means 1, and its absence signifies 0. Digital computers operate directly with binary digits, either singly or strung together to form bytes. A string of 8 bits that the computer stores as a unit is called a **byte**. Each byte can be used to store a decimal number, a symbol, a character, or part of a picture.

The CPU and Primary Storage

The **central processing unit** (CPU) is the part of the computer system where the manipulation of symbols, numbers, and characters occurs, and it controls the other parts of the computer system. Located near the CPU is **primary storage** (sometimes called primary or main memory), where data and program instructions are stored temporarily during

FIGURE 5-1   *Hardware components of a computer system.*

A contemporary computer system is composed of six major components. The central processing unit manipulates data and controls the other parts of the computer system; primary storage temporarily stores data and program instructions during processing; secondary storage stores data and instructions permanently; input devices convert data and instructions from their input form for processing in the computer; output devices present data in a form that people can understand; and communications devices control the transfer of information to and from different computers on communications networks.

computer

bit

byte

central processing unit (CPU)

primary storage

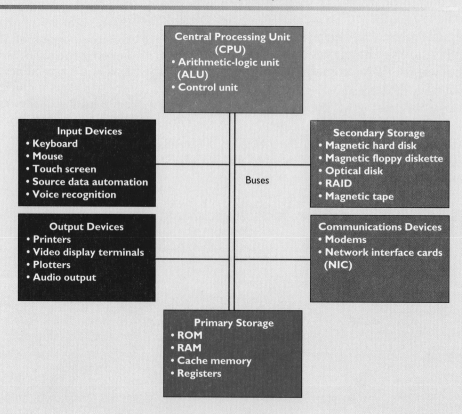

processing while the computer is on. Buses provide pathways for transmitting data and signals between the CPU, primary storage, and the other devices in the computer system. The characteristics of the CPU and primary storage are very important in determining a computer's speed and capabilities.

Primary storage has three functions: it stores all or part of the software program that is being executed; it stores the operating system programs that manage the operation of the computer; and it stores data that the program is using. Internal primary storage is often called **RAM**, or **random access memory**. It is called RAM because it can directly access any randomly chosen location in the same amount of time.

Primary memory is divided into storage locations called *bytes*. Each location contains a set of eight binary switches or devices, each of which can store one bit of information. The set of eight bits found in each storage location is sufficient to store one letter, one digit, or one special symbol (such as $). Each byte has a unique address, similar to a mailbox, indicating where it is located in RAM. The computer can remember where the data in all of the bytes are located simply by keeping track of these addresses. Computer storage capacity is measured in bytes. Table 5-1 lists the primary measures of computer storage capacity and processing speed.

Primary storage is composed of *semiconductors*, which are integrated circuits made by printing thousands and even millions of tiny transistors on small silicon chips. There are several different kinds of semiconductor memory used in primary storage. RAM is used for short-term storage of data or program instructions. RAM is *volatile*: Its contents will be lost when the computer's electric supply is disrupted by a power outage or when the computer is turned off. **ROM**, or **read-only memory**, can only be read from; it cannot be written to and is non-volatile; its contents are present even when the computer is turned off. ROM chips come from the manufacturer with programs already burned in, or stored, although some ROM chips can be updated electronically. ROM is used in general-purpose computers to store important or frequently used programs.

Computer Processing

The processing capability of the CPU plays a large role in determining the amount of work that a computer system can accomplish.

Microprocessors and Processing Power

Contemporary CPUs use semiconductor chips called **microprocessors**, which integrate all of the memory, logic, and control circuits for an entire CPU onto a single chip. The speed

---

TABLE 5-1 Key Measures of Computer Storage Capacity and Processing Speed

TIME	ABBREVIATION	SECONDS
Millisecond	ms	1/1 000
Microsecond	mus	1/1 000 000
Nanosecond	ns	1/1 000 000 000
Picosecond	ps	1/1 000 000 000 000

STORAGE CAPACITY	ABBREVIATION	NUMBER OF BYTES
Byte	B	1*
Kilobyte	KB	1 000**
Megabyte	MB	1 000 000
Gigabyte	GB	1 000 000 000
Terabyte	TB	1 000 000 000 000

* String of eight bits
** Actually 1024 bytes

random access memory (RAM)
read-only memory (ROM)
microprocessors

and performance of a computer's microprocessors help determine a computer's processing power and are based on the number of bits that can be processed at one time (*word length*), the amount of data that can be moved between the CPU, primary storage, and other devices (data bus width), and cycle speed, measured in **megahertz**. (Megahertz is abbreviated **MHz** and stands for millions of cycles per second).

Microprocessors can be made faster by using **reduced instruction set computing (RISC)** in their design. Conventional chips, based on complex instruction set computing, have several hundred or more instructions hard-wired into their circuitry, and they may take several cycles to execute a single instruction. If the seldom-used instructions are eliminated, the remaining instructions can execute much faster. RISC computers have only the most frequently used instructions embedded in them. A RISC CPU can execute most instructions in a single machine cycle and sometimes multiple instructions at the same time. RISC technology is often used in scientific and workstation computing. A variety of faster chips with additional features such as security or lower power requirements are being developed by chip manufacturers such as IBM, Intel, and AMD.

Connections to the Central Computer Unit

All *peripheral* devices (located outside the central computer unit) must be connected in some way to the central computer unit, usually through a **port**. Ports determine which devices can be used based on their connectors and *drivers* (software that manages the interface between the peripheral device and the central computer unit), as well as which cables can be used for the connection.

There are many different kinds of ports. Most keyboards and computer mice use a *PS/2* port while display screens use a video display port found on the graphics adapter card in the central computer unit. Microphone and headset/speaker ports are found on sound cards. Other ports can be used by a variety of devices. A **serial port** sends a signal along the cable one bit at a time while a **parallel port** sends the signal, multiple bits at a time, much faster than the serial connection.

Recent technology has sped up port connections. **Firewire**, also known as IEEE1824, is available on all newer Apple computers and is now becoming available on PCs as well; it can transfer data much faster than older ports. **Universal serial bus (USB)** ports are available on most computers today. USB technology permits up to 128 devices to be "daisy-chained" through only 1 USB port by use of USB hubs. USB ports and hubs can also provide power to peripheral devices, adding convenience as well as speed. Finally, *wireless ports* permit laptops and hand-held computers to be *synchronized* with desktop computers without using cables. They can also connect computers on a network as we will see in Chapter 7.

Additional material on computer systems and how they actually process information and the various types of storage, input, and output technologies by Mary Brabston (University of Manitoba) can be found on the Companion Website.

megahertz (MHz)

reduced instruction set computing (RISC)

port

serial port

parallel port

Firewire

universal serial bus (USB)

5.1 | IT Infrastructure

In Chapter 1, we defined *information technology (IT) infrastructure* as the shared technology resources that provide the platform for the firm's specific information system applications. IT infrastructure includes investment in hardware, software, and services—such as consulting, education, and training—that are shared across the entire firm or across entire business units in the firm. For instance, a firm's investment in thousands of new desktop computers networked together and linked to the Internet is an infrastructure investment because it serves many groups, goals, and business initiatives.

Supplying Canadian firms with IT infrastructure and services is a $54.8 billion dollar industry when telecommunications, networking equipment, and telecommunications services (Internet, telephone, and data transmission) are included (Nasscom Newsline

2005). Investments in infrastructure account for between 25 and 35 percent of information technology expenditures in large firms (Weill et al. 2002).

A firm's IT infrastructure provides the foundation for serving customers, working with vendors, and managing internal firm business processes (see Figure 5-2). In this sense, IT infrastructure defines the capabilities of the firm today and in the near term of, say, three to five years (the length of time it takes to make a significant change in the firm's IT infrastructure). For instance, if you want to provide customers with a daily balance of cell phone charges on a Web site, and if you plan to use this capability as a strategic differentiating feature of your firm, this service implies certain infrastructure capabilities. If you are a bank and want to sell banking services anywhere in Canada or the world to all your customers, whether they have car loans, home loans, brokerage accounts, or just chequing accounts, you will need an infrastructure that crosses these different lines of business and operates on a global-enterprise-wide basis. As Figure 5-2 illustrates, business strategy, IT strategy, and IT itself all influence each other in what is called a *recursive* relationship; separately and together, they influence the IT services and infrastructure that the firm will provide to support customer services, supplier services, and enterprise services.

Defining IT Infrastructure

There are two ways of defining IT infrastructure: as *technology* or as *services clusters*. We will briefly discuss these two definitions here, but as you continue reading this text, keep these definitions, and the impact IT infrastructure has at various organizational levels, in mind to help you to see how infrastructure does in fact add value to organizations.

In the technology-based definition, IT infrastructure is like the plumbing or electrical systems in a building: a set of physical devices and software applications that are required

FIGURE 5-2   *Connection between the firm, IT infrastructure, and business capabilities.*

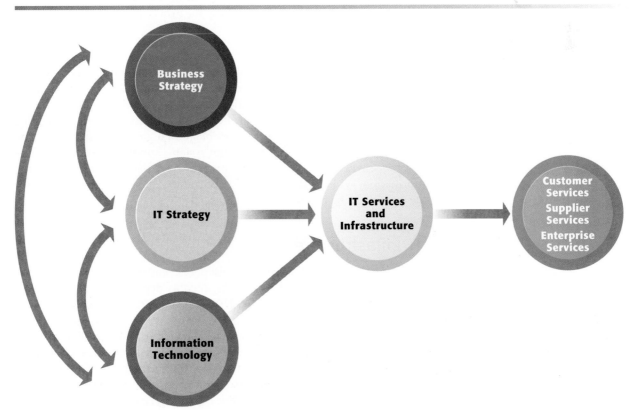

The services a firm is capable of providing to its customers, suppliers, and employees are a direct function of its IT infrastructure. Ideally, this infrastructure should support the firm's business and information systems strategy. New information technologies have a powerful impact on business and IT strategies, as well as the services that can be provided to customers.

to operate the entire enterprise. Capacity and speed are two of the main components of value found in this perspective.

But an even more useful *service-based* definition focuses on the services provided by all this hardware and software. In this definition, IT infrastructure is a set of firm-wide services budgeted by management that comprise both human and technical capabilities (Weill et al. 2002). These services include the following:

- Computing platforms used to provide computing services that connect employees, customers, and suppliers into a coherent digital environment, including large mainframes, desktop and laptop computers, personal digital assistants (PDAs), and Internet appliances.

- Telecommunications services that provide data, voice, and video connectivity to employees, customers, and suppliers.

- Data management services that store and manage corporate data and provide capabilities for analyzing the data.

- Application software services that provide enterprise-wide capabilities such as enterprise resource planning, customer relationship management, supply chain management, and knowledge management systems that are shared by all business units.

- Physical facilities management services that develop and manage the physical installations required for computing, telecommunications, and data management services.

- IT management services that plan and develop the infrastructure, coordinate with the business units for IT services, manage accounting for IT expenditures, and provide project management services.

- IT standards services that provide the firm and its business units with policies that determine which information technologies will be used, when, and how.

- IT education services that provide training in system use to employees and offer managers training in how to plan for and manage IT investments.

- IT research and development services that provide the firm with research on potential future IT projects and investments that could help the firm differentiate itself in the marketplace.

This "service platform" perspective makes it easier to understand the business value provided by infrastructure investments. For instance, the real business value of a fully loaded Pentium 4 PC operating at 2 gigahertz that costs about $1700 or a high-speed Internet connection is hard to understand without knowing who will use it and how it will be used. When we look at the services provided by these tools, however, their value becomes more apparent: The new PC makes it possible for a high-cost employee making $100 000 a year to connect to all the company's major systems and the Internet. The high-speed Internet service saves this employee about one hour per day in reduced wait time for Internet information. Without this PC and Internet connection, the value of this one employee to the firm might be cut in half.

Levels of IT Infrastructure

Firm infrastructure is organized at three major levels: public, enterprise, and business unit (see Figure 5-3). There may be other lower levels, such as departments or individual employees, but for now, we focus on these three. The value of IT infrastructure is different for each level, but significant value is added at each level.

All firms are dependent on public IT infrastructure, which includes the Internet, the public switched telephone network, industry-operated networks, and other IT support facilities such as cable systems and cellular networks. Without the public IT infrastructure, the firm could not operate any interorganizational systems or obtain external data, so the value the public IT infrastructure adds is this capability, enabling the organization to be competitive, efficient, and effective.

Enterprise-wide infrastructure includes services such as email, a central corporate Web site, corporate-wide intranets, and an increasing array of enterprise-wide software

FIGURE 5-3   *Levels of IT infrastructure.*

Shares/Centrally Coordinated Infrastructure

Corporate HQ IT

Business Unit 1 — Local IT

Business Unit 2 — Local IT

Order processing
Production systems
Transaction systems
Customer data
Vendor data

Enterprise-side Infrastructure

E-mail
Corporate Web site
Enterprise systems

Public Infrastructure

Internet
Telephone networks
Industry networks

IT infrastructure exists at three different levels: public, enterprise, and business unit. Each level of infrastructure provides a set of IT services and capabilities.

applications (see Chapter 14). The value of enterprise-wide IT infrastructure is evident in the increase in the ability to communicate and in decreasing response time and time to market.

Business units also have their own infrastructure that is uniquely suited to their line of business, such as specialized production software and systems, customer and vendor systems, and local order entry and other transaction systems. The local business unit IT infrastructure permits each diverse business unit to focus on only those technologies and applications it needs, such as a supply chain management system for commodity goods. The value of the local business IT infrastructure is found in this ability to focus and use customized systems.

In multiunit businesses, typical of most large firms, a central corporate infrastructure is also used to manage the entire enterprise, receive reports from business units, and exercise central oversight.

Figure 5-3 raises some interesting questions: What, for instance, should be handled by enterprise infrastructure and what should be handled by local business units? How much should local business units be charged (and on what basis) for use of enterprise architecture? Local business units may have unique demands that an enterprise-wide infrastructure may not address.

Evolution of IT Infrastructure: 1950–2005

The IT infrastructure in organizations today is an outgrowth of more than 50 years of evolution in computing platforms. We have identified five stages in this evolution, each representing a different configuration of computing power and infrastructure elements (see Figure 5-4). The five eras are automated special-purpose machines, general-purpose mainframe and minicomputer computing, personal computers, client/server networks, and enterprise and Internet computing.

These eras do not necessarily end for all organizations at the same time, and the technologies that characterize one era may also be used in another era for other purposes. For example, some companies still run traditional mainframe or minicomputer systems. Mainframe computers today are used as massive servers supporting large Web sites and corporate enterprise applications. More detail on infrastructure history and the types of computers, including supercomputers, can be found on the Companion Website for Chapter 5.

FIGURE 5-4 *Eras in IT infrastructure evolution.*

Illustrated here are the typical computing configurations characterizing each of the five eras of IT infrastructure evolution.

Stages in IT Infrastructure Evolution

Electronic
Accounting
Machine
(1930–1950)

Mainframe/
Minicomputer
(1950–present)

Personal
Computer
(1981–present)

Client Server
(1983–present)

Enterprise
Internet
(1992–present)

Enterprise
Server

Internet

Electronic Accounting Machine Era: 1930–1950 The first era of business computing used specialized machines that could sort computer cards into bins, accumulate totals, and print reports (Da Cruz 2004). Although the electronic accounting machine was an efficient processor of accounting tasks, the machines were large and cumbersome. There were no programmers, and a human machine operator was the operating system, controlling all system resources.

General-Purpose Mainframe and Minicomputer Era: (1950 To Present)

The first commercial all-electronic vacuum tube computers appeared in the early 1950s with the introduction of the UNIVAC computers and the IBM 700 Series. Not until 1959 with the introduction of the IBM 1401 and 7090 transistorized machines did widespread commercial use of **mainframe** computers begin in earnest. In 1965, the general-purpose commercial mainframe computer truly came into its own with the introduction of the IBM 360 series. The 360 was the first commercial computer with a powerful operating system that could provide time sharing, multitasking, and virtual memory in more advanced models.

Mainframe computers eventually became powerful enough to support thousands of online remote terminals connected to the centralized mainframe using proprietary communication protocols and proprietary data lines. The first airline reservation systems appeared in 1959 and became the prototypical online, real-time interactive computing system that could scale to the size of an entire nation.

IBM dominated mainframe computing from 1965 onward and still dominates this $33 billion global market in 2004. Today IBM mainframe systems can work with a wide variety of different manufacturers' computers and multiple operating systems on client/server networks and networks based on Internet technology standards.

The mainframe era was a period of highly centralized computing under the control of professional programmers and systems operators (usually in a corporate data centre), with most elements of infrastructure provided by a single vendor, the manufacturer of the hardware and the software. This pattern began to change with the introduction of **minicomputers** produced by Digital Equipment Corporation (DEC) in 1965. DEC minicomputers (PDP-11 and later the VAX machines) offered powerful machines at far lower prices than IBM mainframes, making possible decentralized computing, customized to the specific needs of individual departments or business units rather than time sharing on a single huge mainframe.

Personal Computer Era: (1981 To Present)

Although the first truly personal computers (PCs) appeared in the 1970s (the Xerox Alto, MIT's Altair, and the Apple I and II, to name a few), these machines had only limited distribution to computer enthusiasts. The appearance of the IBM PC in 1981 is usually credited as the beginning of the PC era because this machine was the first to become widely adopted in American businesses. At first using the DOS operating system, a text-based command language, and later the Microsoft Windows operating system, the **Wintel PC** computer (Windows operating system software on a computer with an Intel microprocessor) became the standard desktop personal computer. Today, 95 percent of the world's estimated 1 billion computers use the Wintel standard.

Proliferation of PCs in the 1980s and early 1990s launched a spate of personal desktop productivity software tools—word processors, spreadsheets, electronic presentation software, and small data management programs—that were very valuable to both home and corporate users. These PCs were standalone systems until PC operating system software in the 1990s made it possible to link them into networks.

Client/Server Era (1983 To Present)

In **client/server computing**, desktop or laptop computers called **clients** are networked to powerful **server** computers that provide the client computers with a variety of services and capabilities. Computer processing work is split between these two types of machines. The client is the user point of entry while the server typically processes and stores shared data, serves up Web pages, or manages network activities. The term *server* refers to both the software application and the physical computer on which the network software runs. The server could be a mainframe, but today server computers typically are more powerful versions of personal computers, based on inexpensive Intel chips and often using multiple processors in a single computer box.

mainframe

minicomputers

Wintel PC

client/server computing

clients

server

The simplest client/server network consists of a client computer networked to a server computer, with processing split between the two types of machines. This is called a *two-tiered client/server architecture*. While simple client/server networks can be found in small businesses, most corporations have more complex, **multitiered** (often called **N-tier**) **client/server architectures** in which the work of the entire network is balanced over several different levels of servers, depending on the kind of service being requested (see Figure 5-5).

For instance, at the first level, a **Web server** will serve a Web page to a client in response for a request for service. Web server software is responsible for locating and managing stored Web pages. If the client requests access to a corporate system (a product list or price information, for instance), the request is passed along to an **application server**. Application server software handles all application operations between a user and an organization's back-end business systems. The application server may reside on the same computer as the Web server or on its own dedicated computer. Chapters 6 and 7 provide more detail on other pieces of software that are used in multitiered client/server architectures for e-commerce and e-business.

Client/server computing enables businesses to distribute computing work across a series of smaller, inexpensive machines that cost much less than minicomputers or centralized mainframe systems. The result is an explosion in computing power and applications throughout the firm.

Novell Netware was the leading technology for client/server networking at the beginning of the client/server era. Today Microsoft is the market leader, with its **Windows** operating systems (Windows Server, Windows XP, Windows 2000), dominating 78 percent of the local area network market.

Enterprise Internet Computing Era (1992 To Present) The success of the client/server model posed a new set of problems for corporations. Many large firms found it difficult to integrate all of their local area networks (LANs) into a single, coherent corporate computing environment. Applications developed by local departments and divisions in a firm, or in different geographic areas, could not communicate easily with one another and share data.

In the early 1990s, firms turned to networking standards and software tools that could integrate disparate networks and applications throughout the firm into an enterprise-wide infrastructure. As the Internet developed into a trusted communications environment after 1995, business firms began seriously using the *Transmission Control Protocol/ Internet Protocol (TCP/IP)* networking standards (which work together and are most

FIGURE 5-5   *A multitiered client/server network (N-tier).*

Client   Internet   Web Server   Application Server

Sales
Production
Accounting
HR
Systems

Data

multitiered (N-tier) client/server architectures

Web server

application server

Windows

In a multitiered client/server network, client requests for service are handled by different levels of servers.

frequently linked as we have indicated here) to tie their disparate networks together. We discuss TCP/IP in detail in Chapter 7.

The resulting IT infrastructure links different pieces of computer hardware and smaller networks into an enterprise-wide network so that information can flow freely across the organization and between the firm and other organizations. It can link different types of computer hardware, including mainframes, servers, PCs, mobile phones, and other handheld devices, and it includes public infrastructures such as the telephone system, the Internet, and public network services.

The enterprise infrastructure also requires software that can link disparate applications and enable data to flow freely among different parts of the business. Chapter 2 describes how enterprise applications can perform this function. Other solutions for enterprise integration include enterprise application integration software, Web services, and outsourcing to external vendors that provide hardware and software for a comprehensive enterprise infrastructure. We discuss these solutions in detail in section 5.4 and in Chapter 14.

The enterprise era promises to bring about a truly integrated computing and IT services platform for the management of global enterprises to deliver critical business information painlessly and seamlessly to decision makers when and where they need it to create customer value. This could be everything from getting inventory data to the mobile salesperson in the customer's office, to helping a customer at a call centre with a problem customer, or providing managers with precise up-to-the-minute information on company performance.

That is the promise, but the reality is wrenchingly difficult and awesomely expensive. Most firms have a huge, tangled web of hardware systems and software applications inherited from the past. This situation makes achieving this level of enterprise integration a difficult, long-term process that can last perhaps as long as a decade and cost large companies hundreds of millions of dollars. Table 5-2 compares each era on the infrastructure dimensions introduced.

We don't know where the future will take us in terms of new trends or futurist views. Certainly, the trend toward ubiquitous computing—the anytime/any place/any device view—may mean that ubiquitous computing is in fact the next era. If so, computing will be built into our glasses, cars, refrigerators and televisions—perhaps even the clothes we wear. It will certainly be interesting to see what the future holds in computing.

 Additional material on categorizing computer systems by Mary Brabston (University of Manitoba) can be found on the Companion Website.

Technology Drivers of Infrastructure Evolution

The changes in IT infrastructure we have just described have resulted from developments in computer processing, memory chips, storage devices, telecommunications and networking hardware and software, and software design that have exponentially increased computing power while exponentially reducing costs. Let's look at the most important developments.

Moore's Law and Microprocessing Power In 1965, Gordon Moore, the Chairman Emeritus of Intel Corporation, the world's leading chip maker, wrote in *Electronics* magazine that since the first microprocessor chip was introduced in 1959, the number of components on a chip with the smallest manufacturing costs per component (generally transistors) had doubled each year. This assertion became the foundation of **Moore's Law**. Moore later reduced the rate of growth to a doubling every two years (Tuomi 2002).

This law would later be interpreted in multiple ways. There are at least three variations of Moore's Law, none of which Moore ever stated: (1) the power of microprocessors doubles every 18 months (Gates 1996); (2) computing power doubles every 18 months; and (3) the price of computing falls by half every 18 months.

There is reason to believe the exponential growth in the number of transistors and the power of processors coupled with an exponential decline in computing costs will continue in the future. Chip manufacturers continue to miniaturize components. Intel has recently changed its manufacturing process from 0.13-microncomponent size (a micron is a millionth of a metre), introduced in 2002, to a newer 90-nanometre process in 2004

Moore's Law

TABLE 5-2 *Stages in the IT Infrastructure Evolution*

INFRASTRUCTURE DIMENSION	ELECTRONIC ACCOUNTING MACHINE ERA (1930–1950)	MAINFRAME ERA (1959 TO PRESENT)	PC ERA (1981 TO PRESENT)	CLIENT/SERVER ERA (1983 TO PRESENT)	ENTERPRISE ERA (1992 TO PRESENT)
SIGNATURE FIRM(S)	IBM Burroughs NCR	IBM	Microsoft/Intel Dell HP IBM	Novell Microsoft	SAP Oracle PeopleSoft
HARDWARE PLATFORM	Programmable card sorters	Centralized mainframe	Wintel computers	Wintel computers	Multiple: • Mainframe • Server • Client
OPERATING SYSTEM	Human operators	IBM 360 IBM 370 Unix	DOS/Windows Linux IBM 390	Windows 3.1 Windows Server Linux	Multiple: • Unix/Linux • OS 390 • Windows Server
APPLICATION AND ENTERPRISE SOFTWARE	None; application software created by technicians	Few enterprise-wide applications; departmental applications created by in-house programmers	No enterprise connectivity; boxed software	Few enterprise-wide applications; boxed software applications for workgroups and departments	Enterprise-wide applications linked to desktop and departmental applications: • mySAP • Oracle E-Business Suite • PeopleSoft Enterprise One
NETWORKING/ TELECOMMUNICATIONS	None	Vendor-provided: • Systems Network Architecture (IBM) • DECNET (Digital) • AT&T voice	None or limited	Novell NetWare Windows 2003 Linux AT&T voice	LAN Enterprise-wide area network (WAN) TCP/IP Internet standards-enabled
SYSTEM INTEGRATION	Vendor-provided	Vendor-provided	None	Accounting and consulting firms Service firms	Software manufacturer Accounting and consulting firms System integration firms Service firms
DATA STORAGE AND DATABASE MANAGEMENT	Physical card management	Magnetic storage Flat files Relational databases	DBase II and III Access	Multiple database servers with optical and magnetic storage	Enterprise database servers
INTERNET PLATFORMS	None	Poor to none	None at first Later browser-enabled clients	None at first Later: • Apache server • Microsoft IIS	None in the early years Later: • Intranet- and Internet-delivered enterprise services • Large server farms

(a nanometre is a billionth of a metre). With a size of about 50 nanometres, today's transistors should no longer be compared to the size of a human hair but rather to the size of a virus, the smallest form of organic life.

By using nanotechnology, Intel believes it can shrink the size of transistors down to the width of several atoms. **Nanotechnology** uses individual atoms and molecules to create computer chips and other devices that are thousands of times smaller than current technologies permit. IBM and other research labs have created transistors from nanotubes and other electrical devices (IBM 2004) and have developed a manufacturing process that could produce nanotube processors economically (see Figure 5-6). Other new technologies include strained silicon, 300-millimetre production wafers (which decrease the costs of production), and denser interconnections among components.

While the first Pentium microprocessors operated at 75 megahertz, today's Pentiums are available with 3-gigahertz speed. However, increasing processor speeds at the same exponential rate as in the past may no longer be possible. As processor speeds increase, heat is generated that cannot be dissipated with air fans.

Another brake on future increases in microprocessor speed is more market-oriented: Most consumers may not need vast increases in microprocessor speed but instead are more interested in low power consumption for longer battery life and low weight to increase laptop and handheld computer portability. For this reason, Intel and other firms are designing the next generation of chips to be less power hungry and lower in weight even if they are the same or even slower speed. Other options include putting multiple processors on a single chip.

FIGURE 5-6   *Examples of nanotubes.*

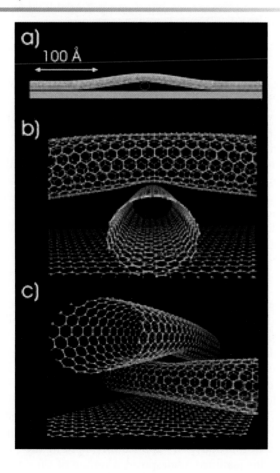

Nanotubes are tiny tubes about 10 000 times thinner than a human hair. They consist of rolled up sheets of carbon hexagons. Discovered in 1991 by researchers at NEC, they have potential use as minuscule wires or in ultra-small electronic devices and are very powerful conductors of electrical current.

nanotechnology

The Law of Mass Digital Storage
A second technology driver of IT infrastructure change is the Law of Mass Digital Storage. The world produces as much as 5 exabytes of unique information per year (an exabyte is a billion gigabytes, or 10^{18} bytes). The amount of digital information is roughly doubling every year (Lyman and Varian 2003). Almost all of this information growth involves magnetic storage of digital data, and printed documents account for only 0.003 percent of the annual growth.

Fortunately, the cost of storing digital information is falling at an exponential rate of 100 percent a year. PC hard drive capacity—beginning with a Seagate 506 in 1980 that had 5 megabytes of storage—has grown at a compound annual growth rate of 25 percent in the early years to more than 60 percent a year since 1990. Today's PC hard drives have storage densities approaching 1 gigabyte per square inch and total capacities of over 200 gigabytes.

From 1980 to 1990, hard disk drive capacities for PCs grew at the rate of 25 percent annual compound growth, but after 1990, growth accelerated to more than 65 percent each year.

Metcalfe's Law and Network Economics
Moore's Law and the Law of Mass Storage help us understand why computing resources are now so readily available. But why do people want more computing and storage power? The economics of networks and the growth of the Internet provide some answers.

Robert Metcalfe—inventor of Ethernet local area network technology—claimed in 1970 that the value or power of a network grows exponentially as a function of the number of network members. Metcalfe and others point to the *increasing returns to scale* that network members receive as more and more people join the network. As the number of members in a network grows linearly, the value of the entire system grows exponentially and continues to grow forever as the number of members increases. Demand for information technology has been driven by the social and business value of digital networks, which rapidly multiply the number of actual and potential links among network members. We discuss Metcalfe's Law in greater detail in Chapter 7.

Declining Communications Costs and the Internet
A fourth technology driver transforming IT infrastructure is the rapid decline in the costs of communication and the exponential growth in the size of the Internet. An estimated 1.1 billion people worldwide now have Internet access (including more than 20.5 million in Canada) (Internet World Stats 2005), and more than 51 percent of all Canadian companies have Web sites. Figure 5-7 illustrates the exponentially declining cost of communication both over the Internet and over telephone networks (which increasingly are based on the Internet). As communication costs fall toward a very small number and approach 0, utilization of communication and computing facilities explodes.

To take advantage of the business value associated with the Internet, firms must greatly expand their Internet connections, including wireless connectivity, and greatly expand the power of their client/server networks, desktop clients, and mobile computing devices. There is every reason to believe these trends will continue.

Standards and Network Effects
Today's enterprise infrastructure and Internet computing would be impossible—now and in the future—without agreements among manufacturers and widespread consumer acceptance of **technology standards**. Technology standards are specifications that establish the compatibility of products and the ability to communicate in a network (Stango 2004).

Technology standards unleash powerful economies of scale and result in price declines as manufacturers focus on the products built to a single standard. Without these economies of scale, computing of any sort would be far more expensive than is currently the case. Table 5-3 describes important standards that have shaped IT infrastructure.

Beginning in the 1990s, corporations started moving toward standard computing and communications platforms. The Wintel PC with the Windows operating system and Microsoft Office desktop productivity applications became the standard desktop and mobile client computing platform. Widespread adoption of Unix as the enterprise server operating system of choice made possible the replacement of proprietary and expensive

technology standards

FIGURE 5-7 *Exponential declines in Internet communications costs.*

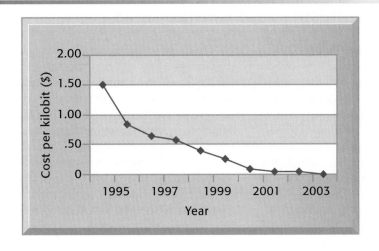

One reason for the growth in the Internet population is the rapid decline in Internet connection and overall communication costs. The cost per kilobit of Internet access has fallen exponentially since 1995. Digital Subscriber Line (DSL) and cable modems now deliver a kilobit of communication for a retail price of around 2 cents.

Source: Authors

mainframe infrastructure. In telecommunications, the Ethernet standard enabled PCs to connect together in small local area networks (LANs; see Chapter 7), and the TCP/IP standard enabled these LANs to be connected into firm-wide networks, and ultimately, to the Internet.

TABLE 5-3 *Some Important Standards in Computing.*

STANDARD	SIGNIFICANCE
American Standard Code for Information Interchange (ASCII)(1958)	Made it possible for computer machines from different manufacturers to exchange data; later used as the universal language linking input and output devices such as keyboards and mice to computers. Adopted by the American National Standards Institute in 1963.
Common Business Oriented Language (COBOL) (1959)	An easy-to-use software language that greatly expanded the ability of programmers to write business-related programs and reduced the cost of software. Sponsored by the Defense Department in 1959.
Unix (1969–1975)	A powerful multitasking, multiuser, portable operating system initially developed at Bell Labs (1969) and later released for use by others (1975). It operates on a wide variety of computers from different manufacturers. Adopted by Sun, IBM, HP, and others in the 1980s and became the most widely used enterprise-level operating system.
Transmission Control Protocol/Internet Protocol (TCP/IP) (1974)	Suite of communications protocols and a common addressing scheme that enables millions of computers to connect together in one giant global network (the Internet). Later, it was used as the default networking protocol suite for local area networks and intranets. Developed in the early 1970s for the U.S. Department of Defense.
Ethernet (1973)	A network standard for connecting desktop computers into local area networks that enabled the widespread adoption of client/server computing and local area networks and further stimulated the adoption of personal computers.
IBM/Microsoft/Intel Personal Computer (1981)	The standard Wintel design for personal desktop computing based on standard Intel processors and other standard devices, Microsoft DOS, and later Windows software. The emergence of this standard, low-cost product laid the foundation for a 25-year period of explosive growth in computing throughout all organizations around the globe. Today, more than 1 billion PCs power business and government activities every day.
World Wide Web (1989–1993)	Standards for storing, retrieving, formatting, and displaying information as a worldwide web of electronic pages incorporating text, graphics, audio, and video enables the creation of a global repository of billions of Web pages by 2004.

5.2   Infrastructure Components

IT infrastructure today is composed of seven major components. Figure 5-8 illustrates these different but related infrastructure components and the major vendors within each component category. From the point of view of the firm, these components constitute investments that must be coordinated with one another to provide the firm with a coherent infrastructure. To understand the value of providing advanced IT infrastructure, one only has to look at the research and development funding flowing into this important segment of the economy. In 2004, the information and communications technologies (ICT) sector reached 40 percent of total Canadian private sector research and development funding (Industry Canada 2005).

In the past, technology vendors were often in competition with one another, offering purchasing firms a mixture of incompatible, proprietary, partial solutions. But increasingly, vendors have been forced by large customers to cooperate in strategic partnerships with one another. For instance, a hardware and services provider such as IBM cooperates with all the major enterprise software providers, has strategic relationships with system integrators (often accounting firms), and promises to work with whichever database products its client firms wish to use (even though it sells its own database management

FIGURE 5-8   *The IT infrastructure ecosystem.*

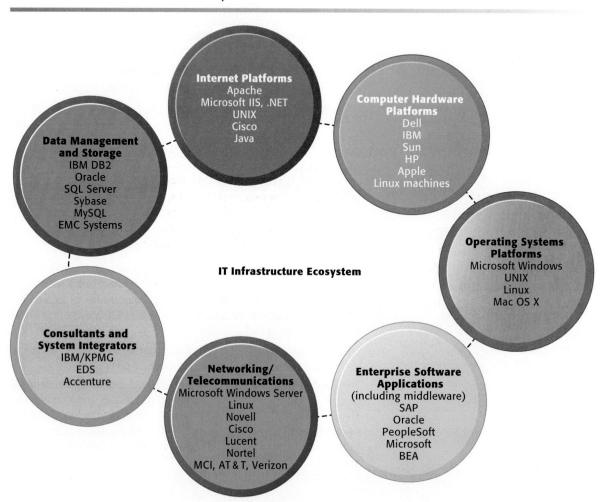

There are seven major components that must be coordinated to provide the firm with a coherent IT infrastructure. Listed here are major technologies and suppliers for each component.

software called DB2). Let's examine the size and dynamics of each of these infrastructure components and their markets.

Computer Hardware Platforms

This component includes client machines (desktop PCs, mobile computing devices such as PDAs and laptops) and server machines. The client machines use primarily Intel or AMD microprocessors.

The server market is more complex, using mostly Intel or AMD processors in the form of blade servers in racks, but this market also includes Sun SPARC microprocessors and IBM PowerPC chips specially designed for server use. **Blade servers** are ultrathin comput-

ers consisting of a circuit board with processors, memory, and network connections that are stored in racks. They take up less space than traditional box-based servers. Secondary storage may be provided by a hard drive in each blade server or by external, very large mass-storage drives. A large group of servers can be connected to form **server farms**, which are used by commercial vendors for their subscribers to conduct activities requiring heavy use of servers, such as e-commerce.

A blade server is a thin, modular processing device that is intended for a single dedicated application (such as serving Web pages) that can be easily inserted into a space-saving rack with many similar servers.

The marketplace for computer hardware has increasingly become concentrated in top firms such as IBM, HP, Dell, and Sun Microsystems, which produce 90 percent of the machines, and three chip producers, Intel, AMD, and IBM, which account for over 90 per cent of the processors sold in 2004. The industry has collectively settled on Intel as the standard processor (with AMD catching up), with major exceptions in the server market for Unix and Linux machines, which might use SUN or IBM Unix processors.

Mainframes have not disappeared. The mainframe market has actually grown steadily over the last decade although the number of providers has dwindled to one: IBM. IBM has also repurposed its mainframe systems so they can be used as giant servers for massive enterprise networks and corporate Web sites. A single IBM mainframe can run up to 17 000 instances of Linux or Windows server software and is capable of replacing thousands of smaller blade servers.

Operating System Platforms

At the client level, 95 percent of PCs and 45 percent of handheld devices use some form of Microsoft Windows operating system (such as Windows XP, Windows 2000, or Windows CE). In contrast, in the server marketplace, more than 85 percent of the corporate servers in North America use some form of the **Unix** operating system or **Linux**, an inexpensive and robust open-source relative of Unix. Although Microsoft Windows Server 2003 is capable of providing enterprise-wide operating system and network services, it is generally not used when there are more than 3000 client computers in a network.

Unix and Linux constitute the backbone of corporate infrastructure throughout much of the world because they are scalable, reliable, and much less expensive than mainframe operating systems. By scalable, we mean that it is easy to add additional machines, memory, storage, or networking hardware, compared to other operating systems. By reliable, we mean that computers that use Unix and Linux are less likely to crash or receive viruses than computers with other operating systems. (The fact that Unix and Linux are less likely to attract viruses may only be due to their smaller market share on individual PCs.) Computers running Unix and Linux can also run on many different types of processors. Unix is not very user-friendly and is command-driven, that is, users input commands in

blade servers
server farms
Unix
Linux

program sentence structure. Linux is much more user-friendly, particularly with add-ons that permit Windows-like input. The major providers of Unix operating systems are IBM, HP, and Sun, each with slightly different and partially incompatible versions.

Although Windows continues to dominate the client marketplace, many corporations have begun to explore Linux as a low-cost desktop operating system provided by commercial vendors such as Red Hat Linux and Linux-based desktop productivity suites such as Sun's StarOffice.

Linux is also available in free versions downloadable from the Internet as **open-source software**. Open-source software is described more fully later, but in essence it is software that allows free access to its program code, allowing a worldwide community of programmers to modify the program code to make improvements or fix errors. It is available for free.

Enterprise Software Applications

In addition to software for applications used by specific groups or business units, Canadian firms must spend their technology dollars on software for enterprise applications that are treated as components of IT infrastructure. The largest providers of enterprise application software are SAP, followed by Oracle, PeopleSoft, and J.D. Edwards. PeopleSoft recently purchased J.D. Edwards and then in turn was purchased by Oracle (Directions Magazine 2003). SAP and PeopleSoft promise to provide software that works with any hardware or operating system; Oracle applications run only on Oracle databases (although they are compatible with all operating systems and hardware platforms). It remains to be seen if Oracle will refocus the J.D. Edwards and PeopleSoft enterprise application software packages to run only on Oracle databases. Also included in this category is middleware software supplied by vendors such as BEA for achieving firm-wide integration by linking the firm's existing application systems. We describe both types of software in detail in section 5.4.

Microsoft is attempting to move into the lower ends of this market by focusing on small and medium-sized businesses. There are more than 1 million businesses in Canada (Industry Canada 2005), and most have not yet developed enterprise applications. In general, most large firms already have implemented enterprise applications and have developed long-term relationships with their providers. Once a firm decides to work with an enterprise vendor, switching can be difficult and costly, though not impossible.

Data Management and Storage

There are few choices for enterprise database management software, which is responsible for organizing and managing the firm's data so that it can be efficiently accessed and used. Chapter 6 describes this software in detail. The leading database software providers are IBM (DB2), Oracle, Microsoft (SQL Server), and Sybase (Adaptive Server Enterprise), which supply more than 90 percent of the database software marketplace. A growing new entrant is MySQL, a Linux open-source relational database product available for free on the Internet and increasingly supported by HP and others in a move designed to prevent Microsoft from monopolizing the small and medium-sized firm database market with its SQL Server product.

The physical data storage market is dominated by EMC Corporation for large-scale systems and a small number of PC hard disk manufacturers led by Seagate, Maxtor, and Western Digital. In addition to traditional disk arrays and tape libraries, large firms are turning to network-based storage technologies. **Storage area networks (SANs)** connect multiple storage devices on a separate high-speed network dedicated to storage. The SAN creates a large central pool of storage that can be rapidly accessed and shared by multiple servers.

The amount of new digital information in the world is doubling every three years, driven in part by e-commerce and e-business and by statutes and regulations requiring firms to invest in extensive data storage and management facilities (such as the Personal

open-source software

storage area networks (SANs)

Information Protection and Electronic Documents Act of Canada (PIPEDA) and the U.S. Sarbanes-Oxley Act of 2002). Consequently, the market for digital data storage devices has been growing at more than 15 percent annually over the last five years.

Networking/Telecommunications Platforms

Revenues for the information and communications technology (ICT) sector in Canada were estimated at $130.2 billion in 2003 (Industry Canada 2005). Chapter 7 is devoted to an in-depth description of the enterprise networking environment, including the Internet. Windows Server 2003, Windows 2000 Server, and Windows NT are predominantly used as local area network operating systems, followed by Novell, Linux, and Unix. Large enterprise-wide area networks primarily use some variant of Unix. Nearly all local area networks, as well as wide area enterprise networks, use the TCP/IP protocol suite as a standard (see Chapter 7).

The leading networking hardware providers are Cisco, Lucent, Nortel, and Juniper Networks. Telecommunications platforms are typically provided by telecommunications/telephone services companies that offer voice and data connectivity, wide area networking, and Internet access. Leading telecommunications service vendors include Primus, MCI, AT&T, and regional telephone companies such as Sasktel. As we discuss in Chapters 7 and 8, this market is exploding with new providers of cellular wireless, Wi-Fi, Wireless Application Protocol (WAP), and Internet telephone services.

Internet Platforms

Internet platforms overlap with and must relate to the firm's general networking infrastructure and hardware and software platforms. Nevertheless, in most corporations, Internet expenditures are separated out from general IT infrastructure expenditures.

Internet-related infrastructure expenditures are for hardware, software, and management services to support a firm's Web site, including Web hosting services, and for intranets and extranets. A **Web hosting service** maintains a large Web server, or series of servers, and provides fee-paying subscribers with space to maintain their Web sites. This category of technology expenditures is growing by approximately 10 percent per year. Companies such as Montreal-based CGI offer these services.

The Internet revolution of the late 1990s led to a veritable explosion in server computers, with many firms collecting thousands of small servers to run their Internet operations. Since then there has been a steady push toward server consolidation, reducing the number of server computers by increasing the size and power of each. The Internet hardware server market has become increasingly concentrated in the hands of Dell, HP/Compaq, and IBM as prices have fallen dramatically.

The major Web software application development tools and suites are supplied by Microsoft (FrontPage and the Microsoft.NET family of development tools used to create Web sites using Active Server Pages for dynamic content), Sun (Sun's Java is the most widely used tool for developing interactive Web applications on both the server and client sides), and a host of independent software developers, including Macromedia (Dreamweaver and Flash), media software (Real Media), and text tools (Adobe Acrobat). Developed at IBM's research centre in Don Mills, Ontario, Websphere is the leading software development tool for large corporate Web sites. Chapter 7 describes the components of the firm's Internet platform in greater detail.

Consulting and System Integration Services

Although 20 years ago it might have been possible for a large firm to implement all of its own IT infrastructure, this is far less common today simply because even large firms do not have the staff, the skills, the budget, or the necessary experience. Implementing new infrastructure requires (as noted in Chapters 1 through 3) significant changes in business processes and procedures, training and education, and software integration.

Web hosting service

Software integration means ensuring the new infrastructure works with the firm's older, so-called legacy systems and ensuring the new elements of the infrastructure work with one another. **Legacy systems** are generally older transaction processing systems created for mainframe computers that continue to be used to avoid the high cost of replacing or redesigning them. Replacing these systems is cost prohibitive and generally not necessary if these older systems can be integrated into a contemporary infrastructure.

Most companies in the past relied on their accounting firms to provide consulting and system integration services simply because the accounting firms were the only ones that truly understood a company's business processes and had the expertise to change its software. However, in the United States, accounting firms have been prohibited by law from providing these services and, as a result, have split off consulting services into separate entities, such as Accenture (formerly part of Arthur Andersen) and KPMG Consulting (split off from the KPMG accounting firm and now part of IBM). In Canada, the accounting firms have not been forced to spin off their consulting departments, but three out of the four top firms have done so. Canadian public accounting firms can still offer consulting services, except in the case of a publicly traded client.

Consulting and systems integration have become a lucrative market that can greatly expand the revenues of computer hardware and enterprise software vendors. IBM's consulting services revenues now equal its hardware revenues, and for enterprise software firms such as Oracle and SAP, consulting, integration, and maintenance revenue exceed the revenues from software sales.

5.3   Contemporary Hardware Platform Trends

Although the cost of computing per se has fallen exponentially, the cost of the IT infrastructure has not followed suit, but rather has expanded as a percentage of corporate revenues and budgets. Why? The cost of computing services, like consulting and systems integration, has risen dramatically, the cost of software remains high, and the intensity of computing and communicating has increased as other costs have declined. For instance, employees now use much more sophisticated applications, requiring more powerful and expensive hardware of many different types (laptop, desktop, handheld, and tablet computers).

Firms also face a number of other challenges. They need to integrate information stored in different applications, on different platforms (telephone, legacy systems, intranet, Internet sites, desktop, and mobile devices). We cover mobile commerce and wireless technologies in Chapter 8.

Firms also need to build resilient infrastructure that can withstand huge increases in peak loads and routine assaults from hackers and viruses. Because customer and employee expectations for service are increasing, firms need to increase their service levels to meet customer demands.

Each of the trends in hardware and software platforms we now describe seeks to address some or all of these challenges.

The Integration of Computing and Telecommunications Platforms

Arguably the most dominant theme in hardware platforms today is the convergence of telecommunications and computing platforms to the point where, increasingly, computing takes place over the network. You can see this convergence at several levels.

At the client level, communication devices such as cell phones are taking on functions of handheld computers while handheld PDAs are taking on cell phone functions. For instance, the Palm Treo 600 digital handheld integrates phone, camera, and handheld computer in one device. Soon full-length films and short commercials will be distributed over cell-phone-like devices. Television, radio, and video are moving toward all-digital production and distribution. There is little doubt that personal computers of some sort

legacy systems

will be the core of the home entertainment centre and the mobile personal entertainment centre of the next five years as a storage device and operating system.

At the server and network level, the growing success of Internet telephone systems (now the fastest-growing type of telephone service) demonstrates how historically separate telecommunications and computing platforms are converging toward a single network—the Internet. Chapter 7 describes the convergence of computing and telecommunications in greater depth.

Other major trends in hardware platforms described here are based in large part on computing over high-capacity networks. The network in many respects is becoming the source of computing power, enabling business firms to expand their computing power greatly at very little cost.

The Palm Treo 600 combines a mobile phone, email, personal organizer, Web access, and camera all in one device. The convergence of computing and communications technologies has turned cell phones into mobile computing platforms.

Grid Computing

Grid computing involves connecting geographically remote computers into a single network to create a virtual supercomputer by combining the computational power of all computers on the grid. Grid computing takes advantage of the fact that most computers use their central processing units on average only 25 percent of the time for the work they have been assigned, leaving these idle resources available for other processing tasks. Grid computing was impossible until high-speed Internet connections enabled firms to connect remote machines economically and move enormous quantities of data.

Grid computing requires software programs to control and allocate resources on the grid, such as open-source software provided by Globus Alliance (www.globus.org) or other private providers such as Groove Networks (www.groove.net). Client software communicates with a server software application. The server software breaks data and application code into chunks that are then parceled out to the grid's machines. The client machines can perform their traditional tasks while running grid applications in the background.

The business case for using grid computing involves cost savings, speed of computation, and agility. For example, Royal Dutch/Shell Group is using a scalable grid computing platform that improves the accuracy and speed of its scientific modeling applications to find the best oil reservoirs. This platform, which links 1024 IBM servers running Linux, in effect creates one of the largest commercial Linux supercomputers in the world. The grid adjusts to accommodate the fluctuating data volumes that are typical in this seasonal business. Royal Dutch/Shell Group claims the grid has enabled the company to cut processing time for seismic data while improving output quality and helping its scientists pinpoint problems in finding new oil supplies.

In another example, in Quebec, researchers are developing a grid application to forecast the local weather. Hopefully, this application will improve the forecasts of Environment Canada, which uses a Montreal-based supercomputer for that purpose with accuracy to approximately a 50-square kilometre grid. The Quebec project would let those who want more detailed local weather forecasting take the Environment Canada data, merge it with data from local barometers and other gauges, and create precise weather forecasts for areas as small as one square kilometre (Akin 2001).

On-Demand Computing (Utility Computing)

On-demand computing refers to firms off-loading peak demand for computing power to remote, large-scale data processing centres. In this manner, firms can reduce their investment in IT infrastructure by investing just enough to handle average processing loads and paying for only as much additional computing power as the market demands. Another term for on-demand computing is **utility computing**, which suggests that firms purchase

grid computing
on-demand computing
utility computing

computing power from central computing utilities and pay only for the amount of computing power they use, much as they would pay for electricity.

IBM is investing $12 billion to bring this vision to reality and has created on-demand computing centres around the world where businesses can experiment with these concepts. HP's Adaptive Enterprise offers similar capabilities.

In addition to lowering the cost of owning hardware resources, on-demand computing gives firms greater agility when using technology. On-demand computing shifts firms from having a fixed infrastructure capacity toward a highly flexible infrastructure, some of it owned by the firm, and some of it rented from giant computer centres owned by IBM, HP, or others. This arrangement frees firms to launch entirely new business processes that they would never attempt with a fixed infrastructure.

For example, the Canadian Imperial Bank of Commerce (CIBC) outsources a significant portion of its infrastructure to Hewlett-Packard's Adaptive Computing Center. HP provides support for 28 000 CIBC email users, 41 000 desktop PCs, 4500 automatic teller machines (ATMs), and 10 000 point-of-sale terminals. CIBC management believed that it was more cost-effective to outsource this portion of its infrastructure and focus on banking rather than operating its own IT infrastructure for these functions (HP 2004).

In another example, specialty food and gift specialist Harry and David uses IBM's On Demand services to deal with an annual traffic surge before the gift-giving season. About 65 percent of annual sales takes place between mid-November and late December. Rather than purchase enough infrastructure to handle this peak load, Harry and David rent this capacity when they need it (Shankland 2003; IBM 2004).

Additional examples of value from on-demand computing can be found in the Window on Management. Qantas Airways contracted with IBM for a flexible on-demand computing arrangement to lower operational costs and help it remain competitive against other carriers. Ford Motor Company Europe switched to an IBM on-demand service for its help desk. Both companies pay IBM a basic fee for an anticipated level of service and then pay IBM additional fees if they use more computing resources than planned.

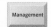 **WINDOW ON MANAGEMENT**

On-Demand Computing at Qantas Airways and Ford Motor Company Europe

Qantas Airways is the leading airline in Australia, flying to about 140 destinations in Australia and 33 other countries. Although recent profits have been strong, the company faces cost pressures from high fuel prices and lower levels of global airline traffic since 2000. Moreover, two-thirds of the international airlines flying to Australia are owned or subsidized by their governments, and Qantas must try to keep prices in line with its competition. Keeping costs low and service to customers high are very big priorities.

When Qantas decided to replace its 30-year-old data centre, it had a choice: It could build a new one to be maintained in-house, or it could outsource its IT infrastructure. IBM Global Services offered an arrangement for on-demand computing with flexible pricing. In May 2004, Qantas signed a 10-year contract with IBM worth more than $558 million for these services.

Qantas CIO Fiona Baliour believes that airlines no longer obtain a competitive advantage because they possess information technology. The advantage lies in "how they use it.

Running IT at a low unit cost becomes a competitive advantage" says Baliour. On-demand computing with IBM enables Qantas to better match its IT infrastructure to actual business needs and to "get out of the capital investment cycle." Qantas is able to predict its computing requirements by looking at how it is filling aircraft seats.

Qantas's arrangement with IBM covers primarily the infrastructure and systems that support its core applications. Most of Qantas's 450 Unix servers, which had been running at less than 50 percent of capacity, will be replaced by Linux servers at IBM's hosting centre in Sydney, Australia. The contract established a baseline usage of computing resources that is less than half of what Qantas was paying for fixed IT costs. Qantas can adjust its usage upward or downward, depending on business conditions, and should be ensured fast response times for its processing.

Qantas will continue to develop its own software applications while IBM will handle change management for application development and maintenance and the migration of applications from testing to production status. IBM will also provide Qantas with services for information system procurement and security and a service desk for resolving issues with all the providers of its IT services.

Qantas awarded a $615 million outsourcing contract to Telstra Corporation to convert its telecommunications infrastructure into a network based on the Internet Protocol (IP) and to provide data, voice, and desktop services.

Outsourcing much of Qantas's IT infrastructure to IBM has not only reduced fixed costs for information technology but has also freed its new employees to pursue technology-modernization projects that may have higher value. By outsourcing to IBM and Telstra, Qantas was able to cut its information systems staff from 900 to 700 people. IBM believes the travel industry is especially well suited for on-demand computing because travel companies are looking for ways to shift their focus from IT operations to core business issues.

Another company that has benefited from IBM's on-demand computing is Ford Motor Company Europe. Ford Motor Company is the world's second largest car and truck manufacturer, with 350 000 employees across the globe. Ford Motor Company Europe has a Company to Dealer Systems Division that is responsible for infrastructure and application support to its European dealer network.

Ford's lines of business, which are the "customers" of Ford's Company to Dealer Systems (CDS), wanted wore variable and immediate support. CDS maintained an automated help desk service that was fixed in price and capabilities, with little flexibility to address constantly changing dealer application needs.

Ford worked with IBM Business Consulting Services/AMS to design a "pay-as-you-go" help desk solution hosted and staffed by IBM. Computing resources for the help desk are allocated based on a quarterly computer capacity plan reflecting the estimated volume of calls, user registrations, and application launches. IBM bills Ford for usage over the capacity plan at a premium to encourage efficient planning.

This on-demand arrangement has made Ford's CDS a more responsive provider of IT Services, adding to retail customer satisfaction and to Ford Europe's brand reputation. By using efficient demand forecasting and capacity planning, combined with on-demand computing services, Ford Europe is saving 10 percent per help desk call.

To Think About: What are the management benefits of on-demand computing for these companies? How do IBM's on-demand services provide value for them?

Sources: Tony Kontzer, "Airline Taps IBM for Flexible Pricing Deal," *Information Week*, May 24, 2004 and "Qantas Airways Hand over IT Management to IBM, *Information Week*, May 17, 2004; "Case Studies: Ford Motor Company Europe—Company to Dealer Systems," www.ibm.com, accessed September 10, 2004; and Qantas Corporate Communication, "Qantas Faces Significant Challenges," August 19, 2004.

Autonomic Computing

Computer systems have become so complex that some experts believe they may not be manageable in the future. With operating systems, enterprise, and database software weighing in at millions of lines of code, and large systems encompassing many thousands of networked devices, the problem of managing these systems is very immense (Kephardt and Chess 2003).

It is estimated that one-third to one-half of a company's total IT budget is spent preventing or recovering from system crashes. About 40 percent of these crashes are caused by operator error. The reason is not that operators are not well trained or do not have the right capabilities. Rather, it is because the complexities of today's computer systems are too difficult to understand, and IT operators and managers are under pressure to make decisions about problems in seconds.

Today, the consequences of an outage are far more serious than in the past. For example, eBay loses millions of dollars every time there is an outage of any significant duration. Therefore, firms must spend extraordinary resources to ensure systems do not fail. You can find out more about the impact of system outages and preventive measures in Chapter 9.

One approach to dealing with this problem from a computer hardware perspective is to employ autonomic computing. **Autonomic computing** is an industry-wide effort to develop systems that can configure themselves, optimize and tune themselves, heal themselves when broken, and protect themselves from outside intruders and self-destruction. Imagine, for instance, a desktop PC that could know it was invaded by a computer virus. Instead of blindly allowing the virus to invade, the PC would identify and eradicate the virus or, alternatively, turn its workload over to another processor and shut itself down before the virus destroyed any files.

autonomic computing

By choosing the word *autonomic*, IBM is making an analogy with the autonomic nervous system. The autonomic nervous system controls lower-level but vital functions of the human body without raising them to a conscious level. The vision of autonomic computing is that it will free system administrators from many of today's routine system management and operational tasks so administrators can devote more of their IT skills to fulfilling the needs of their core businesses (Ganek and Corbi 2003).

Table 5-4 describes the four dimensions of autonomic computing. Currently, the bare outlines of some of these capabilities are already present in desktop operating systems. For instance, virus and firewall protection software can detect viruses on PCs, automatically defeat the viruses, and alert operators. These programs can be updated automatically as the need arises by connecting to an online virus protection service such as McAfee. Other key elements of autonomic computing are still missing but are sure to be on the agenda of research centres in the next decade. Without progress toward self-managing systems, the management resources required to operate a large-scale computing environment may be cost prohibitive.

Edge Computing

Edge computing is a multitier, load-balancing scheme for Web-based applications in which significant parts of Web site content, logic, and processing are performed by smaller, less expensive servers located nearby the user. In this sense, edge computing is another technique like grid computing and on-demand computing for using the Internet to share the workload experienced by a firm across many computers located remotely on the network.

Figure 5-9 illustrates the components of edge computing. There are three tiers in edge computing: the local client; the nearby edge computing platform, which consists of servers positioned at any Internet service provider; and enterprise computers located at the firm's main data centre. The edge computing platform is owned by a service firm such as Akamai, which employs about 15 000 edge servers around the world.

In an edge platform application, requests from the user client computer are initially processed by the edge servers. Presentation components such as static Web page content, reusable code fragments, and interactive elements gathered on forms are delivered by the edge server to the client. Database and business logic elements are delivered by the enterprise computing platform.

There are four main business benefits to edge computing:

edge computing

- Technology costs are lowered because the firm does not need to purchase infrastructure at its own data centre to handle all of the requests from customers and can instead focus on building infrastructure to contain corporate databases and business logic.

TABLE 5-4 *Four Aspects of Self-Management as They Are Now and Would Be with Autonomic Computing.*

CONCEPT	CURRENT COMPUTING	AUTONOMIC COMPUTING
Self-configuration	Corporate data centres have multiple vendors and and platforms. Installing, configuring, and integrating systems is time consuming and error prone.	Automated configuration of components and systems follows high-level policies. Rest of system adjusts automatically and seamlessly.
Self-optimization	Systems have hundreds of manually set, nonlinear tuning parameters, and their number increases with each release.	Components and systems continually seek opportunities to improve their own performance and efficiency.
Self-healing	Problem determination in large, complex systems can take a team of programmers weeks.	System automatically detects, diagnoses, and repairs localized software and hardware problems.
Self-protection	Detection of and recovery from attacks and cascading failures is manual.	System automatically defends against malicious attacks or cascading failures. It uses early warning to anticipate and prevent systemwide failures.

FIGURE 5-9   *Edge computing platform.*

Edge computing involves the use of the Internet to balance the processing load of enterprise platforms across the client and edge computing platform.

- Service levels are enhanced because response time of Web-based applications is reduced. Local client computers can be served with most static and dynamic content immediately, and customer response time is dramatically reduced.

- Flexibility of the firm is enhanced because it can respond to business opportunities quickly without going through a lengthy infrastructure acquisition cycle by making use of service provider platforms that already exist.

- Resilience is increased because seasonal or even daily spikes in the workload can be shared across the Web, and failure in edge nodes will not disable the entire system.

5.4   Contemporary Software Platform Trends

To play a useful role in the firm's information technology infrastructure, computer hardware requires computer software. Chapter 1 defined computer *software* as the detailed instructions that control the operation of a computer system. Selecting appropriate software for the organization is a key management decision. A software **program** is a series of statements or instructions to the computer. The process of writing or coding programs is termed *programming,* and individuals who specialize in this task are called *programmers* or coders.

There are two major types of software: system software and application software. Each kind performs a different function. **System software** is a set of generalized programs that manage the computer's resources, such as the central processor, communications links, and peripheral devices. Programmers who write system software are called *system programmers.* One of the major parts of system software is the **operating system** which manages and controls the activities of the computer.

program
system software
operating system

Application software describes the programs that are written for or by users to apply the computer to a specific task. Software for processing an order or generating a mailing list is application software. Programmers who write application software are called *application programmers*. Today most programmers can write both system and application software.

The types of software are interrelated and can be thought of as a set of nested boxes, each of which must interact closely with the other boxes surrounding it. Figure 5-10 illustrates this relationship. The system software surrounds and controls access to the hardware. Application software must work through the system software in order to operate. End users work primarily with application software. Each type of software must be specially designed for a specific machine to ensure its compatibility. For more on security software, see Chapter 9.

A software platform is an underlying computer system on which application programs can run. On PCs, for example, Windows XP and the Mac OS X are two different platforms. Historically, most application programs had to be written to run on a particular platform. Each platform provided a different application program interface. Thus, a PC program would have to be written to run on the Windows XP platform and then again to run on the Mac OS X platform. Today new open or standards-conforming interfaces allow many programs to run on, or interoperate, with different platforms through mediating or "broker" programs. There are four major themes in contemporary software platform evolution:

- Linux and open-source software
- Java
- Web services and service-oriented architecture
- Software outsourcing

The Rise of Linux and Open-Source Software

Open-source software is software produced by a community of several hundred thousand programmers around the world. According to the leading open-source professional association, OpenSource.org, open-source software is free and can be modified by users. Works derived from the original code must also be free, and the software can be redistributed by

Additional material on various types of software by Mary Brabston (University of Manitoba) can be found on the Companion Website.

FIGURE 5-10   *The major types of software.*

The relationship between system software, application software, and users can be illustrated by a series of nested boxes. System software—consisting of operating systems, language translators, and utility programs (such as disk optimization or security programs)—controls access to the hardware. Application software, such as programming languages and "fourth-generation" languages, must work through the system software to operate. The user interacts primarily with the application software.

SYSTEM SOFTWARE

Operating System

Schedules computer events
Allocates computer resources
Monitors events

Language Translators

Interpreters
Compilers

Utility Programs

Routine operations (e.g., sort, list, print)
Manage data (e.g., create files, merge files)

APPLICATION SOFTWARE

Programming languages
Assembly language

FORTRAN   PASCAL
COBOL   C
BASIC   Fourth-generation languages and PC software tools

application software

the user without additional licensing. Open-source software is by definition not restricted to any specific operating system or hardware technology, although most open-source software is currently based on a Linux or Unix operating system (Open Source Development Lab 2004). A related free software movement supported by the Free Software Foundation supports similar goals of making software freely available without the restrictions of copyright or patent law (which we explain in Chapter 4).

Open-source software is based on the premise that it is superior to commercially produced proprietary software because thousands of programmers around the world working for no pay can read, perfect, distribute, and modify the source code much faster, and with more reliable results, than small teams of programmers working for a single software company. Of course, it could also be true that a formal testing program could make proprietary software more reliable. The jury is still out on this judgment.

Although it may seem that contributors to open-source software receive nothing in return, in fact they receive respect, prestige, and access to a network of knowledgeable programmers (who in turn can be tapped for solutions, or even employment). Although the process of software improvement may seem chaotic or unorganized, in fact these are self-organizing communities of dedicated professionals who have a well-defined organizational structure and a set of business processes (or procedures) for getting the work done. The open-source movement has been evolving for more than 30 years and has demonstrated after many years of effort that it can produce commercially acceptable, high-quality software.

Now thousands of open-source programs are available from hundreds of Web sites. The range of open-source software extends from operating systems to office suites, browsers, and games. Several large software companies are converting some of their commercial programs to open source. IBM, for instance, is handing over its Java-based database program called Cloudscape to the Apache Software Foundation, an open-source group. Novell is investing heavily in open-source companies that sell versions of open-source server software.

Few complain about the cost of open-source software, which can result in the savings of millions of dollars for large corporations (see Table 5-5).

Linux Perhaps the most well known open-source software is Linux, an operating system related to Unix. Linux was created by the Finnish programmer Linus Torvalds and was first posted on the Internet in August 1991. Linux is now the world's fastest-growing client and server operating system. Linux was installed in nearly 3 percent of new shipments of PCs in 2004, and this number is expected to grow to over 20 percent of new PC shipments by 2010 (Bulkeley 2002).

Applications for the Linux operating system are also rapidly increasing. Many of these applications are embedded in cell phones, PDAs, and other handheld devices (Open Source Development Lab 2004). Although Linux is currently a small but rapidly growing

TABLE 5-5 *Proprietary and Open-Source Software Pricing Comparison*

PROPRIETARY SOFTWARE	OPEN-SOURCE SOFTWARE EQUIVALENT
Microsoft Windows XP Professional Edition $400	Linux free
Microsoft Office $650	Open Office $0 StarOffice 7 $85
Microsoft Outlook $150	Mozilla browser with email $16
Microsoft SQL server $2799	MySQL server edition $1995

Sources: Lisa Vaas, "Microsoft Pitches New Low-Cost, Entry-Level Database Edition," *eWeek*, February 24, 2005, available **www.eweek.com/article2/0%2C1759%2C1769335%2C00.asp**, accessed April 9, 2005; Open Office Web site, available **www.openoffice.ca**, accessed April 21, 2005; Mozilla Web site, available **www.mozilla.org**, accessed April 21, 2005; Staples Canada Web site, available **www.staples.ca**, accessed April 9, 2005; MySQL Web site, available **www.mysql.com**, accessed April 9, 2005.

presence on the desktop, it plays a major role in the back-office running Web servers and local area networks. Linux is the most rapidly growing LAN server.

IBM, HP, Intel, Dell, and Sun have made Linux a central part of their offerings to corporations. More than two dozen countries in Asia, Europe, and Latin America have adopted open-source software and Linux (Lohr 2003). Cost is a major driver. For example, Morgan Stanley is replacing 4000 servers running Windows NT with much cheaper machines running Linux for an estimated five-year cost saving of $122 million (Kerstetter 2003).

Cost played an important role in the decisions to adopt Linux in the Canadian cities of Calgary and Toronto. Both cities, described in the Window on Technology, have very low technology budgets and are under pressure to seek out no-frills solutions. The city of Calgary found that adopting Linux not only reduced software purchase costs, but it also created additional savings by cutting down on computer processing time.

The rise of open-source software, particularly Linux and the applications it supports at the client and server level, has profound implications for corporate software platforms: cost reduction, reliability and resilience, and integration because Linux works on all the major hardware platforms from mainframes to servers to clients. Linux has the potential to break Microsoft's monopoly of the desktop. Sun's StarOffice has an inexpensive Linux-based version that competes with Microsoft's Office productivity suite. However, this transition will take many years because of the sunk costs of billions of spreadsheets, Word documents, and PowerPoint presentations, many of which will not be easily converted to Linux office suites.

WINDOW ON TECHNOLOGY

Technology

Two Canadian Cities Go For Linux

"Downward budget pressure" convinced the Canadian city of Calgary to take a hard look at Linux. Like other municipal governments, Calgary was on the receiving end of budget cuts that left it searching for low-cost technology solutions.

In the fall of 2002, Calgary had about 140 Unix servers, with 60 percent of them running the Sun Solaris version of Unix, 25 percent running HP's Tru64 Unix and the rest running other operating systems. According to Dan Ryan, Calgary's manager of infrastructure and desktop management, "Unix was so expensive because everything was proprietary—both the hardware and the software." As these servers aged and required replacement, Calgary found it did not have the money to upgrade to another expensive environment.

Ryan and his team started investigating Linux. They found out that both HP and IBM had invested heavily in making sure their products could support Linux and that Oracle had become certified on commercial Red Hat Linux. Calgary uses Oracle database products extensively. Ryan was further sold on Linux when he learned that many other large organizations, including DaimlerChrysler, the U.S. Department of Defense, and the U.S. Postal Service, had started using Linux.

To test Linux capabilities, Calgary ran four pilot projects over a three-month period in 2003. The first two projects were led by HP, and the remaining two were performed by Calgary's information systems staff who were versed in Unix but learned enough Linux to take on these projects.

One application tested Calgary's tax installment plan running on Linux. This application has about 175 000 records in its file for residents who pay property taxes once a month. Running on a Unix computer, this application took about 73 minutes to process. In the test, the same application took only 31 minutes running on an Intel computer with two CPUs and the Linux operating system.

Another test used the application for Calgary's annual tax account balance, which handles 330 000 property tax records. This application took about 60 hours to process on a computer with eight CPUs running Unix. Running on a Linux-based Intel computer with two CPUs, the application took only 13.5 hours.

From these tests, Ryan learned that Linux could improve computer performance as well as lower costs. As a result of adopting Linux, Calgary's capital and operating costs have dropped by 75 percent. Calgary used to pay over $650 000 for equipment maintenance on its Unix servers. By the end of 2004, it will pay less than $150 000 to maintain its Linux computers. These savings mean that Ryan does not have to wait as long to replace Calgary's computer systems.

Toronto's Children's Services Division (CSD) is reporting similar benefits from Linux. CSD has 62 branches, a main office, and remote locations, including 58 day-care centres. This organization has a small information technology budget of approximately $2 million per year, which is tiny compared to other city departments. CSD, like other Toronto departments, has some autonomy in technology decisions, and it is allowed to purchase the hardware and software that it believes is best for its purposes.

CSD's service and support costs were escalating as old PCs neared the end of their useful life cycle. The division investigated purchasing new PCs running Microsoft Windows XP but the cost was prohibitive—about $1600 to purchase each PC plus an additional hundred dollars per machine to license Windows XP. The Children's Services Division instead installed Red Hat Linux version 7.3 on about 450 desktop computers at a cost of about $250 per machine.

The transition to Linux was not difficult for the division because it uses inexpensive desktop machines with no floppy disk drives or hard drives. All data and software are stored on a central server networked to these desktop clients, so users have no opportunity to install unauthorized software. Everything is centrally maintained.

By installing Linux, the division does not need to worry about licensing operating systems—Linux is almost free. If there is a problem, CSD's information systems staff can turn to the open-source community supporting Linux. To help them, CSD staff typically find many other users who have already dealt with the same issue. Hardware and software are so easy to maintain that the division needs only six information systems staff members to support 450 users.

On the negative side, CSD did have to spend more time and money training its staff on Linux, and not all software is yet compatible with Linux.

By reducing maintenance at the desktop, CSD saves in human resources and can use its technology budget for other purposes including new Sun servers and data storage services.

To Think About: Is Linux a good choice for these government organizations? Why or why not? How does Linux provide value? Would private business firms obtain similar benefits? What are the business and technology issues that should be addressed when making that decision?

Sources: Patricia Pickett, "City of Calgary Moves to Linux," *ComputerWorld Canada*, March 5, 2004; Kathleen Sibley, "A Tale of Two Open Source Cities," www.itbusiness.ca, accessed April 30, 2004; Ryan B. Patrick, "City Rolls Out Desktop Linux," www.opencitygov.org, accessed September 10, 2004.

Java Is Everywhere

Java is an operating system-independent, processor-independent, object-oriented programming language that has become the leading interactive programming environment for the Web. If an object moves on the Web or takes input from the user, a Java applet is likely behind it.

Java was created by James Gosling and the Green Team at Sun Microsystems in 1992 as a programming environment to support interactive cable television content delivery. Widespread use of Java did not occur until 1995 when large numbers of people started using the World Wide Web and Internet. Nearly all Web browsers come with a Java platform built in. More recently, the Java platform has migrated into cellular phones, automobiles, music players, game machines, and finally, into set-top cable television systems serving interactive content and pay-per-view services.

Java software is designed to run on any computer or computing device, regardless of the specific microprocessor or operating system the device uses. A Macintosh PC, an IBM PC running Windows, a Sun server running Unix, and even a smart cellular phone or personal digital assistant can share the same Java application. For each of the computing environments in which Java is used, Sun has created a Java Virtual Machine that interprets Java programming code for that machine. In this manner, the code is written once and can be used on any machine for which there exists a Java Virtual Machine.

Java is particularly useful in network environments such as the Internet. Here, Java is used to create miniature programs called *applets* that are designed to reside on centralized network servers. The network delivers to client computers only the applets required for a specific function. With Java applets residing on a network, a user can download only the software functions and data that he or she needs to perform a particular task, such as analyzing the revenue from one sales territory. The user does not need to maintain large software programs or data files on his or her desktop machine.

Java is also a very robust language that can handle text, data, graphics, sound, and video, all within one program if needed. Java enables PC users to manipulate data on networked systems using Web browsers, reducing the need to write specialized software. A **Web browser** is an easy-to-use software tool with a graphical user interface for displaying Web pages and for accessing the Web and other Internet resources. Microsoft's Internet Explorer, Mozilla, and Netscape Navigator are examples of Web browsers. At the

Java

Web browser

enterprise level, Java is being used for more complex e-commerce and e-business applications that require communication with an organization's back-end transaction processing systems.

The rapid deployment of Java was hindered in the past because of disagreements between Sun Microsystems and Microsoft over Java standards. In an effort to promote widespread adoption of the Java technology, Sun had embarked on an open licensing program. Beginning in August 1995, Sun entered into license and distribution agreements with major platform manufacturers, including Apple, DEC, Fujitsu, Hewlett-Packard, IBM, Microsoft, Netscape, Novell, SCO, Siemens, and Silicon Graphics.

Shortly thereafter, Microsoft began introducing variations to the standard Java Virtual Machine and created its own proprietary version of Java that was incompatible with standard Java. Sun filed a series of antitrust lawsuits against Microsoft to halt these actions. In April 2004, under pressure from major customers such as General Motors, Microsoft and Sun entered into a 10-year-long agreement that settled Sun's antitrust lawsuits. Microsoft agreed to stop distributing the Microsoft Java Virtual Machine it had developed for its proprietary version of Java and to cooperate with Sun in the development of new technologies, including Java.

Software for Enterprise Integration

Without doubt, the single most urgent software priority for Canadian firms is integration of existing legacy software applications with newer Web-based applications into a coherent single system that can be rationally managed. In the past, business firms typically developed their own custom software and made their own choices about their software platform (all of the various pieces of software that need to work together). This strategy produced hundreds of thousands of computer programs that frequently could not communicate with other software programs, were difficult and expensive to maintain, and were nearly impossible to change quickly as business models changed.

One solution is to replace isolated systems that cannot communicate with enterprise applications for customer relationship management, supply chain management, knowledge management, and enterprise systems, which integrate multiple business processes. Chapter 14 provides a detailed description of these enterprise applications and their roles in digitally integrating the enterprise.

Not all firms can jettison all of their legacy systems to convert to enterprise-wide platforms. These existing legacy mainframe applications are essential to daily operations and are very risky to change, but they can become more useful if their information and business logic can be integrated with other applications.

Some integration of legacy applications can be achieved by using special software called **middleware** to create an interface or bridge between two different systems. Middleware is software that connects two otherwise separate applications, enabling them to communicate with each other and to exchange data.

Firms may choose to write their own software to connect one application to another, but increasingly they are purchasing **enterprise application integration (EAI) software** packages to connect disparate applications or application clusters. This software enables multiple systems to exchange data through a single software hub rather than developing countless custom software interfaces to link each system (see Figure 5-11). WebMethods, Tibco, CrossWorlds, SeeBeyond, BEA, and Vitria are leading enterprise application integration software vendors.

Web Services and Service-Oriented Architecture

Enterprise application integration software tools are product specific, meaning that they can work only with certain pieces of application software and operating systems. For example, one EAI tool to connect a specific piece of sales order entry software to manufacturing, shipping, and billing applications might not work with another vendor's order entry software. Web services provide a standardized alternative for dealing with integration.

middleware

enterprise application integration (EAI) software

FIGURE 5-11 *Enterprise application integration (EAI) software versus traditional integration.*

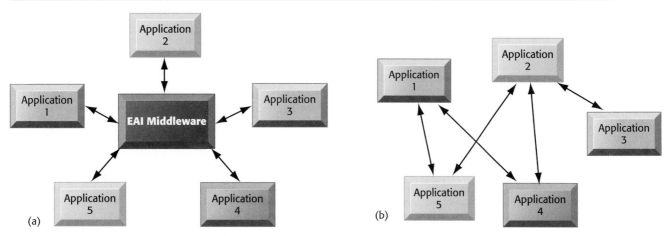

EAI software (a) uses special middleware that creates a common platform with which all applications can freely communicate with each other. EAI requires much less programming than traditional point-to-point integration (b).

Web services refer to a set of loosely-coupled software components that exchange information with each other using standard Web communication standards and languages. They can exchange information between two different systems regardless of the operating systems or programming languages on which the systems are based. They can be used to develop open standard Web-based applications linking systems of two different organizations, and they can also be used to create applications that link disparate systems within a single company. Web services are not tied to any one operating system or programming language, and different applications can use them to communicate with each other in a standard way without time-consuming custom coding.

The foundation technology for Web services is **XML**, which stands for **eXtensible Markup Language**. This language was developed in 1996 by the World Wide Web Consortium (W3C, the international body that oversees the development of the Web) as a more powerful and flexible markup language than Hypertext Markup Language (HTML) for Web pages. **Hypertext Markup Language (HTML)** is a page description language for specifying how text, graphics, video, and sound are placed on a Web page document. While HTML is limited to describing how data should be presented in the form of Web pages, XML can perform presentation, communication, and storage of data. In XML, a number is not simply a number; the XML *tag* specifies whether the number represents a price, a date, or a postal code. Table 5-6 illustrates some sample XML statements.

By tagging selected elements of document content for their meanings, XML makes it possible for computers to manipulate and interpret their data automatically and perform operations on the data without human intervention. Web browsers and computer programs, such as order processing or enterprise resource planning (ERP) software, can follow programmed rules for applying and displaying the data. XML provides a standard format for data exchange, enabling Web services to pass data from one process to another.

Web services communicate through XML messages over standard Web protocols. **SOAP**, which stands for **Simple Object Access Protocol**, is a set of rules for structuring messages that enables applications to pass data and instructions to one another. **WSDL** stands for **Web Services Description Language**; it is a common framework for describing the tasks performed by a Web service and the commands and data it will accept so that it can be used by other applications. **UDDI**, which stands for **Universal Description, Discovery, and Integration**, enables a Web service to be listed in a directory of Web services so that it can be easily located. Companies discover and locate Web services through this directory much as they would locate services in the yellow pages of a telephone book. Using these protocols, a software application can connect freely to other applications without custom programming for each different application with which it wants to communicate. Everyone shares the same standards.

Web services
eXtensible Markup Language (XML)
Hypertext Markup Language (HTML)
Simple Object Access Protocol (SOAP)
Web Services Description Language (WSDL)
Universal Description, Discovery, and Integration (UDDI)

TABLE 5-6 *Examples of XML*

PLAIN ENGLISH	XML
Subcompact	\<AUTOMOBILETYPE="Subcompact">
4 passenger	\<PASSENGERUNIT="PASS">4\</PASSENGER>
$16,800	\<PRICE CURRENCY="USD">$16,800\</PRICE>

The collection of Web services that are used to develop a firm's software systems constitutes what is known as a service-oriented architecture. A **service-oriented architecture (SOA)** is a set of self-contained services that communicate with each other to create a working software application. Business tasks are accomplished by executing a series of these services. Software developers reuse these services in other combinations to assemble other applications as needed.

Dollar Rent A Car's systems use Web services to link its online booking system with Southwest Airlines' Web site. Although both companies' systems are based on different technology platforms, a person booking a flight on SouthwestAir.com can reserve a car from Dollar without leaving the airline's Web site. Instead of struggling to get Dollar's reservation system to share data with Southwest's information systems, Dollar used Microsoft.NET Web services technology as an intermediary. Reservations from Southwest are translated into Web services protocols, which are then translated into formats that can be understood by Dollar's computers.

Other car rental companies have linked their information systems to airline companies' Web sites before. But without Web services, these connections had to be developed one at a time. Web services provide a standard way for Dollar's computers to "talk" to other companies' information systems without having to build special links to each one. Dollar is now expanding its use of Web services to link directly to the systems of a small tour operator and a large travel reservation system as well as a wireless Web site for mobile phones and PDAs. It does not have to write new software code for each new partner's information systems or each new wireless device (see Figure 5-12).

Virtually all major software vendors such as IBM, Microsoft, Sun, and HP provide tools and entire platforms for building and integrating software applications using Web services. IBM includes Web service tools in its WebSphere e-business software platform, and Microsoft has incorporated Web services tools in its Microsoft.NET platform.

Businesses such as Federal Express publish the Web services they offer to customers, describing each service using Web service description language (WSDL). FedEx customers, such as Kingston, Ontario's Swyrich Corporation, can then incorporate these Web services into their own systems such as a Web site.

Software Outsourcing

Today most business firms continue to operate their legacy systems that continue to meet a business need and that would be extremely costly to replace. But they will purchase most of their new software applications from external sources. Figure 5-13 illustrates the universal use of open-source software for Canadian organizations.

There are three external sources for software: software packages from a commercial software vendor, software services from an application service provider, and outsourcing custom application development to an outside software firm, often offshore firms in low-wage areas of the world.

Software Packages and Enterprise Software
We have already described software packages for enterprise applications as one of the major types of software components in contemporary IT infrastructures. A **software package** is a prewritten commercially available set of software programs that eliminates the need for a firm to write its own software programs for certain functions, such as payroll processing or order handling.

service-oriented architecture (SOA)

software package

FIGURE 5-12   *How Dollar Rent A Car uses Web services.*

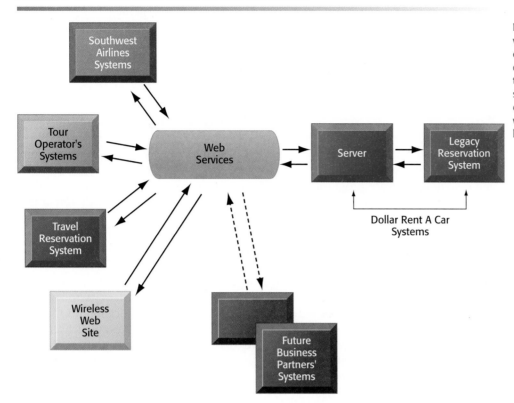

Dollar Rent A Car uses Web services to provide a standard intermediate layer of software to "talk" to other companies' information systems. Dollar Rent A Car can use this set of Web services to link to other companies' information systems without having to build a separate link to each firm's systems.

Enterprise application software vendors such as SAP, PeopleSoft, and Oracle have developed powerful software packages that can support the primary business processes of a firm worldwide from warehousing, customer relationship management, supply chain

FIGURE 5-13   *Canadian development and use of open-source software (OSS) by sector.*

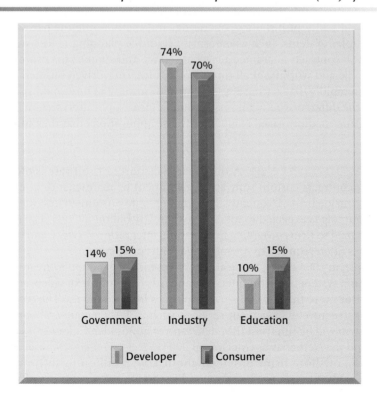

OSS developers and consumers are almost equally represented in each sector. These statistics may point to a similar level of OSS sophistication in government, industry, and education.

Source: www.e-cology.ca. Reprinted with permission of e-Cology Corporation.

management, and finance to human resources. Somewhat like the "software in a box" purchased with a personal computer, these large-scale enterprise software systems provide a single, integrated, worldwide software system for firms at a cost much less than they would pay if they developed it themselves. These systems are so complex and require so much experience that very few corporations have the expertise required to develop these packages. Chapter 14 is devoted to a discussion of the benefits and risks of enterprise systems.

Application Service Providers A second external source of software is online application service providers (ASPs). An **application service provider (ASP)** is a business that delivers and manages applications and computer services from remote computer centres for multiple users using the Internet or a private network. Instead of buying and installing software programs, subscribing companies can rent the same functions from these services. Users pay for the use of this software either on a subscription or per-transaction basis.

The ASP's solution combines package software applications and all of the related hardware, system software, network, and other infrastructure services that the customer otherwise would have to purchase, integrate, and manage independently. The ASP customer interacts with a single entity instead of an array of technologies and service vendors.

The time-sharing services of the 1970s, which ran applications such as payroll on their computers for other companies, were an earlier version of this application hosting. But today's ASPs run a wider array of applications than these earlier services and deliver many of these software services over the Web. In Web-based services, servers perform the bulk of the processing and the only essential program needed by users is a desktop computer running either client software or a Web browser.

Large and medium-sized businesses are using ASPs for enterprise systems, sales force automation, or financial management, and small businesses are using them for functions such as invoicing, tax calculations, electronic calendars, and accounting. ASP vendors are starting to provide tools to integrate the applications they manage with clients' internal systems or with applications hosted by different vendors (McDougall 2004). In addition, enterprise software vendors such as SAP and PeopleSoft have developed ASP versions of their enterprise software packages (such as www.mysap.com) for small and medium-sized firms that do not want to run this enterprise software on their own servers.

Some companies find it much easier to rent software from the ASP firm and avoid the expense and difficulty of installing, operating, and maintaining the hardware and software for complex systems, such as enterprise resource planning (ERP) systems (Walsh 2003). The ASP contracts guarantee a level of service and support to ensure that the software is available and working at all times. Today's Internet-driven business environment is changing so rapidly that getting a system up and running in three months instead of six could mean the difference between success and failure. Application service providers also enable small and medium-sized companies to use applications that they otherwise could not afford.

Software Outsourcing A third external source of software is **outsourcing**, in which a firm contracts custom software development or maintenance of existing legacy programs to outside firms, frequently firms that operate offshore in low-wage areas of the world. Outsourcing is expected to total more than $61 billion in 2005. The largest expenditure here is paid to firms providing middleware, integration services, and other software support that is often required to operate larger enterprise systems.

For example, in 2004 Dow Chemical hired IBM for $1.35 billion to create an integrated communication system based on Internet standards to handle text, video, and voice communications for more than 50 000 Dow employees in 63 countries. The contract extends to other infrastructure management services, such as LAN, email, and application support. The system will be run from IBM data centres in Boulder, Colorado, as well as Brazil, Singapore, and the Netherlands (McDougal 2004).

In the U.S., offshore firms provided about US $8 billion in software services in 2004, which is about 2 percent of the combined U.S. software plus software services

application service provider (ASP)

outsourcing

budget (around US $400 billion). In Canada, however, Statistics Canada and PriceWaterhouseCoopers, in separate reports, reported that Canadian corporate CEOs were less likely to outsource jobs to low-wage countries than their global counterparts (Beauchesne 2005). Even so, up until recently, this type of software development involved lower-level maintenance, data entry, and call centre operations, but with the growing sophistication and experience of offshore firms, particularly in India, more and more new program development is taking place offshore. Chapter 10 discusses more on outsourcing, and Chapter 12 discusses offshore software outsourcing in greater detail.

Management Opportunities, Challenges, and Solutions

The objective of infrastructure management is to provide a coherent and balanced set of computer-based services to customers, employees, and suppliers. To attain this objective, firms must deal with a series of issues:

- Cost of IT infrastructure
- Integration of information, applications, and platforms
- Flexibility to respond to business environments
- Resilience
- Service levels

Let's look more closely at infrastructure trends, opportunities, and challenges.

Trends

Computer technology changes at an incredibly fast rate. Managers today must stay current on trends in hardware and software and the uses of computing technology. The following are just three of the trends that are shaping the future of computing.

Any-Platform Movement Microsoft's .NET approach to computing may or may not be the solution to attempts to reach cross-platform nirvana, but .NET does draw attention to the growing need for cross-platform utilization of resources. Users want to be able to access their email and files from wherever they are. Current developments include *pocket* or *palm* editions of applications, such as word processing or even SAP. But what is needed is the ability to *synchronize* all locations and platforms an individual uses so that they are the same, or so that the data and files on each machine can be accessed from any other type of device. Developments in this area are just beginning but hold promise for the future.

Capacity Planning Managers and information systems specialists need to pay more attention to hardware capacity planning than they did in the past. **Capacity planning** is the process of predicting when a computer hardware system will become saturated. It considers factors such as the maximum number of users that the system can accommodate at one time, the impact of existing and future software applications, and performance measures such as minimum response time for processing business transactions. Capacity planning ensures that the firm has enough computing power for its current and future needs. For example, the Nasdaq Stock Market performs ongoing capacity planning to identify peaks in the volume of stock trading transactions and to ensure it has enough computing capacity to handle large surges in volume when trading is very heavy.

Although capacity planning is performed by information system specialists, input from business managers is essential. Business managers need to determine acceptable levels of computer response time and availability for the firm's mission-critical systems to maintain the level of business performance they expect. New applications, mergers and acquisitions, and changes in business volume will all affect computer workload and must be taken into account when planning hardware capacity.

capacity planning

E-Everything There is a trend today to take whatever data and applications an organization has and move it to the Web. From supply chain and customer relationship management systems, to transaction processing systems, companies are taking their applications and their associated databases and transforming them into e-systems—systems available through Web interfaces, mostly common Web browsers. This provides easy-to-use access for anyone anywhere with access to an Internet connection and authorization to access the application or data. Movements such as e-government and e-learning are part of this trend. The Hudson Bay Company's recent investments in moving their supply chain management and customer relationship management systems to the Web are also part of this trend. These investments permitted HBC to combine the loyalty cards for their various businesses, such as The Bay, Zellers, and Home Outfitters, enabling customers to earn points at all HBC businesses on one loyalty card.

Opportunities

There is a continuous increase in the power of information technology. This means that new business models and processes can be invented around new technologies as they appear. Firms that have the capability and knowledge to manage their IT infrastructures to take advantage of these opportunities will reap enormous benefits.

Management Challenges

Creating and managing a coherent IT infrastructure raises multiple challenges: making wise infrastructure investments, dealing with scalability and technology change, and management and governance.

Making Wise Infrastructure Investments IT infrastructure is a major capital investment for the firm. If too much is spent on infrastructure, it lies idle and constitutes a drag on the firm's financial performance. If too little is spent, important business services cannot be delivered, and the firm's competitors (who spent just the right amount) will outperform the under-investing firm. How much should the firm spend on infrastructure? This question is not easy to answer.

A related question is whether a firm should purchase its own IT infrastructure components or rent them from external suppliers. As we discussed earlier, a major trend in computing platforms—both hardware and software—is to outsource to external providers. The decision either to purchase your own IT assets or rent them from external providers is typically called the *rent versus buy* decision.

Choosing and Coordinating Infrastructure Components Firms today create IT infrastructures by choosing combinations of vendors, people, and technology services and fitting them together so they function as a coherent whole. When each element of infrastructure is driven by somewhat different forces, accomplishing this task is a major management job. For instance, changes in law may mandate vast increases in data storage and retrieval, but the existing hardware platform may be incapable of supporting the additional computing demand.

Dealing with Infrastructure Change As firms grow, they can quickly outgrow their infrastructure. As firms shrink, they can get stuck with excessive infrastructure purchased in better times. How can a firm remain flexible when most of the investments in IT infrastructure are fixed cost purchases and licenses? How well does the infrastructure scale? **Scalability** refers to the ability of a computer, product, or system to expand to serve a large number of users without breaking down.

How can the infrastructure be changed, and over what time frame? Because the firm's digital infrastructure permeates every nook and cranny of the firm, and therefore directly affects how employees perform on a daily basis, any change in this infrastructure would seem to have to occur slowly, guided by some vision (business or technology based) or understanding of the future requirements for infrastructure. Left to constituent business units, or a single chief information officer and his or her staff, chaos could rein or, alternatively, bold techno-

scalability

logically advanced plans may come and go without any real change. Who will supply this vision or understanding needed for long-term, stable evolution?

Management and Governance A long-standing issue among information system managers and CEOs has been the question of who will control and manage the firm's IT infrastructure. Should departments and divisions have the responsibility for making their own information technology decisions or should IT infrastructure be centrally controlled and managed? What is the relationship between central information systems management and business unit information systems management? How will infrastructure costs be allocated among business units? Each organization will need to arrive at answers based on its own needs.

Solution Guidelines

There are no formulas or easy answers to these questions, and each firm arrives at a different set of decisions based on the firm's history, current financial condition, and its strategy. The following guidelines will be helpful.

Perhaps the single most frequent question that CIOs ask (often prodded by their boards of directors) is, "Are we spending too much on IT infrastructure?" In some companies, the opposite question is more common: "Are we spending enough on IT to keep up with our competitors?" As it turns out, there is no single, simple answer, no formula for getting it right. But there are several ways to approach the issue and several rules of thumb.

A Competitive Forces Model for IT Infrastructure Figure 5-14 illustrates a competitive forces model (not the competitive forces model developed and espoused by Porter which we introduced in Chapter 3) you can use to address the question of how much your firm should spend on IT infrastructure.

Market Demand for your Firm's Services Make an inventory of the services you currently provide to customers, suppliers, and employees. Most firms do not have such an inventory. Survey each group, or hold focus groups to find out if the services you currently offer are meeting the needs of each group. For example, are customers complaining of slow responses to their queries about price and availability? Are employees complaining about the difficulty of finding the right information for their jobs? Are suppliers complaining about the difficulties of discovering your production requirements?

Your Firm's Business Strategy Analyze your firm's five-year business strategy, and try to assess what new services and capabilities will be required to achieve strategic goals.

Your Firm's IT Strategy, Infrastructure, and Cost Examine your firm's information technology plans for the next five years, and assess its alignment with the firm's business plans. Make an inventory of existing IT infrastructure costs. Many firms do not know the total cost of their existing IT infrastructure. You will want to perform a total cost of ownership analysis (see page 185). If your firm has no IT strategy, you will need to devise one that takes into account the firm's five-year strategic plan.

Information Technology Assessment Is your firm behind the technology curve or at the "bleeding edge" of information technology? Both situations are to be avoided. Clearly, you do not want to spend resources on advanced technologies that are still experimental, often expensive, and sometimes unreliable. You want to spend on technologies for which standards have been established and suppliers of IT are competing on cost, not design, and where there are multiple suppliers. On the other hand, you do not want to put off investment in new technologies, allowing your competitors time to develop new business models and capabilities and experience using the new technologies.

Competitor Firm Services Benchmark your service levels to customers, suppliers, and employees against those of your competitors. Establish quantitative and qualitative

FIGURE 5-14 *Competitive forces model for IT infrastructure.*

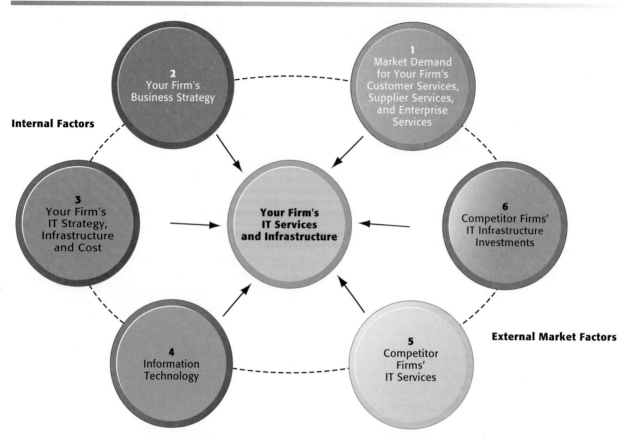

There are six factors you can use to answer the question, "How much should our firm spend on IT infrastructure?"

measures of service for your firm and your competitors, and try to assess what services they offer customers, suppliers, and employees. If your firm has significant shortfalls in service levels to any of these groups, your firm is at a competitive disadvantage. Look for ways your firm can excel at service levels.

Competitor Firm IT Infrastructure Investments   Benchmark your expenditures for IT infrastructure against your competitors. Although some firms regard their IT expenditures as a competitive secret, you can find out information on public companies' IT investments in their public securities filings when those expenditures affect a firm's financial results. Many companies are quite public about their innovative expenditures on IT, and you can impute the level of expenditures based on your research in the trade and professional literature.

It is not necessarily the case that you should spend as much as, or more than, your competitors. Perhaps your firm has discovered much less expensive ways of providing services, and this can lead to a cost advantage. Alternatively, your firm may be spending far less than competitors and experiencing commensurate poor performance and losing market share.

After completing this analysis, you should have a good idea of how much you and your competitor firms are spending on IT infrastructure, what you are receiving in return, and how your competitive position might be improved.

Starting Out Small

Before embarking on a large-scale infrastructure project, it may be useful to experiment with new technologies on a smaller scale. These projects should concentrate on infrastructure improvements that can be easily implemented and where the return on investment (ROI) is very clear.

Total Cost of Ownership of Technology Assets

In benchmarking your firm's expenditures on IT infrastructure with that of your competitors, you will need to consider a wide range of costs. The actual cost of owning technology resources includes the original cost of acquiring and installing hardware and software, as well as ongoing administration costs for hardware and software upgrades, maintenance, technical support, training, and even utility and real estate costs for running and housing the technology. The **total cost of ownership (TCO)** model can be used to analyze these direct and indirect costs to help firms determine the actual cost of specific technology implementations. Table 5-7 describes the most important TCO components to consider in a TCO analysis.

When all these cost components are considered, the TCO for a PC might run up to three times the original purchase price of the equipment. Hidden costs for support staff, downtime, and additional network management can make distributed client/ server architectures—especially those incorporating handheld computers and wireless devices—more expensive than centralized mainframe architectures.

Hardware and software acquisition costs account for only about 20 percent of TCO, so managers must pay close attention to administration costs to understand the full cost of the firm's hardware and software. It is possible to reduce some of these administration costs through better management. The investment bank Morgan Stanley estimates that businesses spent $160 billion between 2000–2002 on unnecessary technology expenditures (Phillips 2002). Many large firms are saddled with redundant, incompatible hardware and software because their departments and divisions have been allowed to make their own technology purchases. These information technology infrastructures are excessively unwieldy and expensive to administer.

These firms could reduce their TCO through greater centralization and standardization of their hardware and software resources. Companies could reduce the size of the information systems staff required to support their infrastructure if the firm minimizes the number of different computer models and pieces of software that employees are allowed to use. In a centralized infrastructure, systems can be administered from a central location and troubleshooting can be performed from that location (David, Schuff, and St. Louis 2002).

total cost of ownership (TCO)

TABLE 5-7 *Total Cost of Ownership (TCO) Cost Components*

INFRASTRUCTURE COMPONENT	COST COMPONENTS
HARDWARE ACQUISITION	Purchase price of computer hardware equipment, including computers, terminals, storage, and printers
SOFTWARE ACQUISITION	Purchase or license of software for each user
INSTALLATION	Cost to install computers and software
TRAINING	Cost to provide training for information systems specialists and end users
SUPPORT	Cost to provide ongoing technical support, help desks, and so forth
MAINTENANCE	Cost to upgrade the hardware and software
INFRASTRUCTURE	Cost to acquire, maintain, and support related infrastructure, such as networks and specialized equipment (including storage backup units)
DOWNTIME	Cost of lost productivity if hardware or software failures cause the system to be unavailable for processing and user tasks
SPACE AND ENERGY	Real estate and utility costs for housing and providing power for the technology

Summary

1. Define IT infrastructure and describe the components and levels of IT infrastructure.

IT infrastructure is the shared technology resources that provide the platform for the firm's specific information system applications. IT infrastructure includes hardware, software, and services that are shared across the entire firm. Major IT infrastructure components include computer hardware platforms, operating system platforms, enterprise software platforms, networking and telecommunications platforms, database management software, Internet platforms, and consulting services and systems integrators. There are three different levels of IT infrastructure: public, enterprise, and business unit.

You can better understand the business value of IT infrastructure investments by viewing IT infrastructure as a platform of services as well as a set of technologies.

2. Identify and describe the stages of IT infrastructure evolution.

There are five stages of IT infrastructure evolution. IT infrastructure in the earliest stage consisted of specialized "electronic accounting machines" that were primitive computers used for accounting tasks. IT infrastructure in the mainframe era (1950 to present) consists of a mainframe performing centralized processing that could be networked to thousands of terminals and eventually some decentralized and departmental computing using networked minicomputers. The personal computer era (1981 to present) in IT infrastructure has been dominated by the widespread use of stand-alone desktop computers with office productivity tools. The predominant infrastructure in the client/server era (1983 to present) consists of desktop or laptop clients networked to more powerful server computers that handle most of the data management and processing. The enterprise Internet computing era (1992 to present) is defined by large numbers of PCs linked into local area networks and growing use of standards and software to link disparate networks and devices linked into an enterprise-wide network so that information can flow freely across the organization.

3. Identify and describe the technology drivers of IT infrastructure evolution.

A series of technology developments has driven the continuing transformation of IT infrastructure. Moore's Law deals with the exponential increase in processing power and decline in the cost of computer technology, stating that every 18 months the power of microprocessors doubles and the price of computing falls by half. The Law of Mass Digital Storage deals with the exponential decrease in the cost of storing data, stating that the number of kilobytes of data that can be stored on mag-

netic media for \$1 roughly doubles every 15 months. Metcalfe's Law helps explain the mushrooming use of computers by showing that a network's value to participants grows exponentially as the network takes on more members. Also driving exploding computer use is the rapid decline in costs of communication and growing agreement in the technology industry to use computing and communications standards.

4. Assess contemporary computer hardware platform trends.

Contemporary hardware and software platform trends address the overwhelming need to reduce IT infrastructure costs, to integrate information across platforms, and to provide a higher level of flexibility and service to the firm and its customers. The integration of computing and telecommunications platforms, grid computing, edge computing, and on-demand computing demonstrate that, increasingly, computing is taking place over a network. Grid computing involves connecting geographically remote computers into a single network to create a computational grid that combines the computing power of all the computers on the network with which to attack large computing problems. Edge computing balances the processing load for Web-based applications by distributing parts of the Web content, logic, and processing among multiple servers. On-demand computing also depends on networks for firms to purchase additional processing power from large computer service firms and to have that power delivered when they need it over a network. In autonomic computing, computer systems have capabilities for automatically configuring and repairing themselves.

5. Assess contemporary software platform trends.

Contemporary software platform trends include the growing use of Linux, open-source software, and Java; software for enterprise integration; and software outsourcing. Open-source software is produced and maintained by a global community of programmers and is downloadable for free. Linux is a powerful, resilient open-source operating system that can run on multiple hardware platforms and is used widely to run Web servers. Java is an operating-system- and hardware-independent programming language that is the leading interactive programming environment for the Web.

Software for enterprise integration includes enterprise applications and middleware such as enterprise application integration (EAI) software and Web services. Unlike EAI software, Web services are loosely-coupled software components based on open Web standards that are not product-specific and can work with any application software and operating system. They can be used as components of Web-based applications linking the systems of two different organizations or to link disparate systems of a single company. Companies are purchasing their new software applications from outside sources, including application software packages, by outsourcing custom application development to an external vendor (that may be offshore), or by renting software services from an application service provider.

6. ***Evaluate the challenges of managing IT infrastructure and management solutions.***

    Major infrastructure challenges include making wise infrastructure investments, choosing and coordinating infrastructure components, dealing with infrastructure change, and agreeing on infrastructure management and governance. Solution guidelines include using a competitive forces model to determine how much to spend on IT infrastructure and where to make strategic infrastructure investments, starting out new infrastructure initiatives with small experimental pilot projects, and establishing the total cost of ownership (TCO) of information technology assets. The total cost of owning technology resources includes not only the original cost of computer hardware and software but also costs for hardware and software upgrades, maintenance, technical support, and training.

Key Terms

Application server, 156
Application service provider (ASP), 180
Application software, 172
Autonomic computing, 169
Bit, 148
Blade servers, 163
Byte, 148
Capacity planning, 181
Central processing unit (CPU), 148
Clients, 155
Client/server computing, 155
Computer, 148
Edge computing, 170
Enterprise application integration (EAI) software, 176
eXtensible Markup Language (XML), 177
Firewire, 150
Grid computing, 167
Hypertext Markup Language (HTML), 177
Java, 175
Legacy systems, 166
Linux, 163

Mainframe, 155
Megahertz (MHz), 150
Microprocessors, 149
Middleware, 176
Minicomputers, 155
Moore's Law, 157
Multitiered (N-tier) client/server architectures, 156
Nanotechnology, 159
On-demand computing, 167
Open-source software, 164
Operating system, 171
Outsourcing, 180
Parallel port, 150
Port, 150
Primary storage, 148
Program, 171
Random access memory (RAM), 149
Read-only memory (ROM), 149
Reduced instruction set computing (RISC), 150
Scalability, 182
Serial port, 150

Server, 155
Server farms, 163
Service-oriented architecture (SOA), 178
Simple Object Access Protocol (SOAP), 177
Software package, 178
Storage area networks (SANs), 164
System software, 171
Technology standards, 160
Total cost of ownership (TCO), 185
Universal Description, Discovery, and Integration (UDDI), 177
Universal serial bus (USB), 150
Unix, 163
Utility computing, 167
Web browser, 175
Web hosting service, 165
Web server, 156
Web services, 177
Web Services Description Language (WSDL), 177
Windows, 156
Wintel PC, 155

Review Questions

1. *Define IT infrastructure from both a technology and a services perspective. Which services does IT infrastructure comprise?*

2. *Name and describe the different levels of IT infrastructure.*

3. *List each of the eras in IT infrastructure evolution, and describe their distinguishing characteristics.*

4. *Define and describe the following: Web server, application server, multitiered client/server architecture.*

5. *What are Moore's Law and the Law of Mass Digital Storage? What aspects of infrastructure change do they help explain?*

6. *How do network economics, declining communications costs, and technology standards affect IT infrastructure and the use of computers?*

7. *List and describe the components of IT infrastructure that firms need to manage.*

8. *Compare grid computing and edge computing.*

9. *How can businesses benefit from on-demand computing and autonomic computing?*

10. *Define and describe open source software and Linux. How can they benefit businesses?*

11. *What is Java? Why is it important today?*

12. *What is the difference between enterprise application integration software and Web services? What role is played by XML in Web services?*

13. *Name and describe the three external sources for software.*

14. *Name and describe the management challenges posed by IT infrastructure.*

15. *How would using a competitive forces model help firms with infrastructure investments?*

16. *How would calculating the total cost of ownership (TCO) of technology assets help firms make infrastructure investments?*

Discussion Questions

1. Why is selecting computer hardware and software for the organization an important management decision? What management, organization, and technology issues should be considered when selecting computer hardware and software?

2. Should organizations use application service providers (ASPs) for all their software needs? Why or why not? What management, organization, and technology factors should be considered when making this decision?

Application Software Exercise
Spreadsheet Exercise: Evaluating Computer Hardware and Software Options

You have been asked to obtain pricing information on hardware and software for an office of 30 people. Using the Internet, get pricing for 30 PC desktop systems (monitors, computers, and keyboards) manufactured by IBM, Dell, and Compaq as listed at their respective corporate Web sites. (For the purposes of this exercise, ignore the fact that desktop systems usually come with preloaded software packages.) Also obtain pricing on 15 monochrome desktop printers manufactured by Hewlett-Packard and by Xerox.

After pricing the desktop systems and printers, obtain pricing on 30 copies of Microsoft's Office XP or Office 2003, the most recent versions of Corel's WordPerfect Office and IBM's Lotus SmartSuite application packages, and on 30 copies of Microsoft Windows XP Professional Edition. The application software suite packages come in various versions, so be sure that each package contains programs for word processing, spreadsheet analysis, database analysis, graphics preparation, and email.

Prepare a spreadsheet showing your research results for the desktop systems, for the printers, and for the software. Use your spreadsheet software to determine the desktop system, printer, and software combination that will offer both the best performance and pricing per worker. Because every two workers will share one printer (15 printers/30 systems), assume only

half a printer cost per worker in the spreadsheet. Assume that your company will take the standard warranty and service contract offered by each product's manufacturer.

Each desktop system must satisfy the minimum specifications shown in the following table:

MINIMUM DESKTOP SPECIFICATIONS

Processor speed	2 GHz
Hard drive	60 GB
RAM	512 MB
CD-ROM speed	48 speed
Monitor (diagonal measurement)	17 inches

Each desktop printer must satisfy the minimum specifications shown in the following table:

MINIMUM MONOCHROME PRINTER SPECIFICATIONS

Print speed	12 pages per minute
Print resolution	600 x 600
Network ready?	Yes
Maximum price/unit	$1000

Electronic Business Project:
Planning and Budgeting for Outsourcing to an Application Service Provider

The Foremost Composite Materials Company is planning to implement a customer relationship management (CRM) system that could be accessed over the Internet by its sales representatives from around the world. Rather than re-invent the wheel, management has decided to use an application service provider specializing in CRM systems to provide this service for its sales force. You are to evaluate at least two application service providers who sell or lease online CRM systems and provide management with a proposal assessing the two vendors and their software and making a recommendation as to which vendor you would choose.

The firm has fifteen sales representatives, each of whom is responsible for a global region (e.g., Northern Europe, Southern Europe, Africa), and has at most 250 customers. In addition to the CRM system being available to the sales force, management will also want access to the system, which should provide management with a variety of reports regarding individual, representative, and regional sales. Two vendors you want to be sure to include in your review are Salesforce.com and Siebel Systems (**www.siebel.com**).

Group Project: Evaluating Server Operating Systems

Form a group with three or four of your classmates. One should research and compare the capabilities and costs of Linux versus the most recent version of the Windows operating system for servers. Another group should research and compare the capabilities and cost of Linux versus Unix. Each group should present its findings to the class, using electronic presentation software if possible.

Web Sites of Interest

There are many interesting Web sites to enhance your learning about hardware and software. You can search the Web yourself or try the following Web sites to add to what you have already learned.

Tom's Hardware **www.tomshardware.com**
The latest news on hardware testing and comparisons of different hardware brands.

Whatis.com **www.whatis.com**
An up-to-date combination of a dictionary and an encyclopedia of hardware, software, and applications.

Informit **www.informit.com**
For the real "techie" in the class—an excellent Web site for staying up-to-date with the latest developments in hardware.

Red Hat Corporation **www.redhat.com**
Linux vendor offering software and support for this open-source operating system.

CASE STUDY:
Direct Wines Ages Wine, Not IT

As the UK population consumes increasing amounts of wine, suppliers are fighting hard to increase their share of the retail market. Reading, England-based Direct Wines Ltd. specializes in quality wines from smaller producers and has grown into the world's largest mail-order supplier of wines. Founder Tony Laithwaite began importing French wines and selling them from a rented railway arch in 1969. When *The Sunday Times* published an expose in 1973 on some of the dirty tricks of the British wine trade, Laithwaite wrote a letter to *The Times* to distance himself from those bad practices. His letter drew a huge response from readers, and the newspaper established The Sunday Times Wine Club with Laithwaite's help. Today, Direct Wines ships more than 30 million bottles of wine through Laithwaite's (**www.laithwaites.co.uk**) and The Sunday Times Wine Club (**www.stwc.co.uk**). Direct Wines 2003 revenues were more than $465 million. Direct Wines supplies wines to more than 700 000 customers at least once every six months and mass mails to 500 000 customers every month.

The key to Direct Wines' success is efficient fulfillment: getting the right product to the right customer at the right time. "Customer service is our most critical success factor," said Michael Bennett, IT director at Direct Wines. "Even the best products in the world count for very little unless customer orders are fulfilled promptly and accurately." But with more than 700 employees, the 33-year-old company was finding it hard to coordinate all of the activities along their supply chain through customer order fulfillment. Their supply chain encompasses the wine distributors from whom they buy, the wine they offer for sale, their warehouses and distribution centres (one warehouse is run by a third party),

transportation facilities and equipment, and shipping right to their customers' doors. For example, Direct Wines would order wines from a supplier using computers; record the purchase, arrival, and storage of the wine in their warehouse; record the order of the wine from the customer; bill the customer; and ship to the customer—all using their computer systems.

Direct Wines IT Director Michael Bennett said: "We had acquired new sytems as we went along, some packages, and some bespoke IT, all on different platforms, and while this was perfectly adequate to running the business, it did create additional problems... The required integration of multiple systems was proving increasingly difficult... We needed a better way of matching product to customer demand, not only to meet the customer's needs, but the requirements of our own organization for planning, warehousing, and inventory management... There was no consistency of data, and this required excessive manual checking."

If those computers could "talk" to each other, sharing data, then most of these steps would be processed by computer with little human intervention or chance for human error. In addition, inventory statistics, accounts payable, and accounts receivable could be kept current, and reports on exceptions prepared automatically for management.

Until recently, Direct Wines used different systems to manage different parts of its business. These disparate systems were hard to maintain and upgrade. As is typical, no one decision could be made; rather, many decisions were required to update Direct Wines' information technology and systems. Customer data would be housed in one system, vendor data in another, inventory data in still another, and so on. Recognizing the need to update their systems, Direct Wines decided to integrate their information systems.

First, the decision was made to move to SAP's R/3 enterprise wide system. SAP is the world's leading vendor of enterprisewide systems. SAP software permits data to move from purchasing to receiving to inventory to factory floor to warehousing to distribution, ordering, and billing with almost no human intervention. This system is not only more efficient; it is also more accurate since the potential for human error is reduced. Direct Wines uses a range of SAP modules, including logistics, materials management, planning, sales and distribution, and purchase orders. Direct Wines then decided to run the new SAP system on a Hewlett-Packard Unix platform with a variety of hardware servers, tape libraries, and switches (see Chapter 7 on telecommunications) to standardize Direct Wines' hardware.

The increased storage requirements of the new SAP R/3 enterprise-wide system led Direct Wines to implement a storage area network as well, partnering Hewlett-Packard with Prestige Systems, and then Novasoft, another Direct Wines solutions provider, to design and implement the storage area network (SAN). Finally, Direct Wines decided to implement SAP R/3 using an Oracle database. Oracle is the leading enterprise-wide database management software in the world (see Chapter 6 for more discussion on databases).

SAP's systems use what SAP calls "best practices" for operation. This means that SAP has mapped the best practices of its leading customers and has developed SAP to work the way these companies operate. Implementing SAP R/3, therefore, meant that Direct Wines had to change some of its business processes so that the new system could integrate all of the data. The SAP R/3 implementation, which took seven months, was expected to result in more consolidated information that would help Direct Wines relate supply to demand and fulfill customer orders more quickly and more effectively. Better planning and improved inventory management should result in fewer substitutions and should reduce

inventory by 10 percent. Direct Wines gets a competitive advantage from being able to fill their orders efficiently and without substitution. The new enterprise-wide system should help them attain this goal.

Sources: "Direct Wines Limited," Hoovers Online, available **www.hoovers.com/direct-wines/--ID__102549--/free-co-fact sheet.xhtml**, accessed February 18, 2005; "Direct Wines," SPSS, Inc., available **www.spss.com/success/template_view.cfm?Story_ID=66**, accessed February 18, 2005; "Direct Wines—A Case Study," QAS Customer Case Studies, available **www.qas.com/uk/customers/casestudy.asp?Organisation= DirectWines&Type=Retail**, accessed February 18, 2005; "Delivering the Drink," *e.logistics magazine*, January/February 2004, available **www.elogmag.com/magazine/31/delivering-drink.shtml**, accessed February 17, 2005; "Case Study: Direct Wines Grows with SAP," *The Retail Bulletin*, available **www.theretailbulletin.com/print.php?id=3066**, accessed February 17, 2005.

CASE STUDY QUESTIONS:

1. What problems do you think Direct Wines experienced from using a variety of different systems and platforms?

2. How did hardware fit in with and support Direct Wines' strategy? Do the changes in hardware and software at Direct Wines mean that the role of information technology changed?

3. Why did Direct Wines choose to standardize their platform? What were the main strengths of the new platform?

4. Why did Direct Wines decide to implement SAP R/3? What changes do you think Direct Wines would have to make while implementing SAP R/3?

5. What benefits would Direct Wines achieve from use of a storage area network?

6. What business and technology issues did Direct Wines face when making these changes?

Chapter 6

Managing Data Resources

OBJECTIVES

After reading this chapter, you will be able to:

1. Describe basic file organization concepts and the problems of managing data resources in a traditional file environment.
2. Describe how a database management system organizes information, and compare the principal database models.
3. Apply important database design principles.
4. Evaluate new database trends.
5. Identify the challenges and key management decisions posed by data resource management.

- Design new services
- Monitor service level and costs

- Provide services to customers

- Design data warehouse using Oracle 9i Designer and Warehouse Builder
- Implement data warehouse using Oracle 9i DBMS

Management

Organization

Technology

Business Challenges
- Isolated corporate systems
- Aggressive competition

Information System
- Consolidate data
- Monitor daily performance
- Analyze customer data

Business Solutions
- Reduce costs
- Innovate new products and services
- Increase revenue

Opening Case: Better Data Help Virgin Mobile Australia Win the Customer Wars

Virgin Mobile Australia is a major player in the Australian mobile phone industry. It had grown aggressively by pioneering new products and services, including a pre-paid service that did not require a contract, free voice mail, and billing all calls by the second. Other competitors followed suit, leaving Virgin Mobile Australia wondering how it could maintain its competitive lead. The answer lay in making better use of the company's data.

Senior management wanted a better picture of Virgin Mobile's customer base and how well the company was operating. This was no easy task. Virgin Mobile Australia had many different systems, each with different pieces of data that could solve only part of the puzzle. It had an enterprise system, a customer relationship management system, and systems for prepaid cell phone service as well as monthly billable cell phone service. The company needed to develop a single enterprise-wide view of the data in all of these systems to produce "one version of the truth."

The company created a data warehouse that reorganized the data from all of these systems in a massive database in order to produce the company-wide information management required. The data warehouse runs on Oracle 9i database management software and was developed using Oracle 9i Designer to define the system's data model and Oracle 9i Warehouse Builder to design the data warehouse. The data warehouse reached one terabyte in 2005 and it is used by more than 70 users.

With the data warehouse, Virgin Mobile Australia can pull data from multiple systems together to obtain an integrated view of its customers and services. Every morning, Virgin Mobile executives can check indicators such as the number of new connections made the previous day, the demographic profile of new customers, and the handsets they purchased. Management can also find out the performance of each store and point-of-sale campaign, consumer reaction to new products and services, and customer attrition rates.

Most important, the warehouse provides data for monitoring customer usage in terms of the total minutes used each month and the revenue generated by each customer. Average revenue-per-user (ARPU) is a key performance indicator for this company to measure its success. All of this information helps Virgin Mobile

react quickly to changes in a very dynamic market and improve its profitability.

Sources: Lynn Tryba, "Winning with a Warehouse," *Profit Magazine,* February 2004; and "Virgin Mobile Uses Business Intelligence to Achieve Rapid Expansion," www.oracle.com, accessed May 17, 2004.

Virgin Mobile Australia's experience illustrates how much information system effectiveness depends on how data are stored, organized, and accessed. Inability to locate and assemble essential business data would have impaired Virgin Mobile's organizational performance. Proper delivery of information depends not only on the capabilities of computer hardware and software but also on the organization's ability to manage data as an important resource.

As a manager, you will want to make sure your company's data are organized so that they can be easily accessed and used. This chapter introduces you to the technologies for managing data as a resource. We also describe the managerial and organizational issues and key decisions that must be addressed to use data resources effectively.

6.1 Organizing Data in a Traditional File Environment

An effective information system provides users with accurate, timely, and relevant information. Accurate information is free of errors. Information is timely when it is available to decision makers when it is needed. Information is relevant when it is useful and appropriate for the types of work and decisions that require it.

Contemporary systems store data that can provide useful information in computer files. When the files are properly arranged and maintained, users can easily store, access, modify, and retrieve the information they need. Despite the use of excellent hardware and software, many organizations have inefficient information systems because of poor file management. We will start by looking at the traditional methods organizations have used to arrange data in computer files and the problems they pose.

File Organization Terms and Concepts

A computer system organizes data in a hierarchy that starts with bits and bytes and progresses to fields, records, files, and databases (see Figure 6-1). A bit represents the smallest

FIGURE 6-1   *The data hierarchy.*

A computer system organizes data in a hierarchy that starts with the bit, which represents either a 0 or a 1. Bits can be grouped to form a byte to represent one character, number or symbol. Bytes can be grouped to form a field, and related fields can be grouped to form a record. Related records can be collected to form a file, and related files can be organized into a database.

unit of data a computer can handle. A group of bits, called a byte, represents a single character, which can be a letter, a number, or another symbol. A grouping of characters into a word, a group of words, or a complete number (such as a person's name or age) is called a **field**. (Note that not all numbers are considered numeric; for example, a person's social insurance number is actually considered to be a text field because no arithmetic calculations are conducted on it.) A group of related fields, such as the student's name, the course taken, the date, and the grade, comprises a **record**; a group of records of the same type is called a **file**.

For example, the student records in Figure 6-1 could constitute a course file. A group of related files makes up a **database**. The student course file illustrated in Figure 6-1 could be grouped with files on students' personal histories and financial backgrounds to create a student database.

A record describes an entity. An **entity** is a person, place, thing, or event on which we store and maintain information. An order is a typical entity in a sales order file, which maintains information on a firm's sales orders. Each characteristic or quality describing a particular entity is called an **attribute**. For example, order number, order date, order amount, item number, and item quantity would each be an attribute of the entity order. The specific values that these attributes can have can be found in the fields of the record describing the entity order (see Figure 6-2). In this illustration ORDER represents an *entity class* or *entity type*, a group of similar entities about which we collect information (attributes). The particular set of values for Order number, Order date, Item number, and Quantity shown in Figure 6-2 are for a single occurrence of that entity type, and this is called an *instance* of that entity.

Every record in a file should contain at least one field that uniquely identifies that record so that the record can be retrieved, updated, or sorted. This identifier field is called a **key field**. An example of a key field is the order number for the order record illustrated in Figure 6-2 or an employee number or social security number for a personnel record (containing employee data, such as the employee's name, age, address, job title, and so forth).

Problems with the Traditional File Environment

In most organizations, systems tended to grow independently and not according to some grand plan. Each functional area tended to develop systems in isolation from other

FIGURE 6-2 *Entities and attributes.*

This record describes the entity called ORDER and its attributes. The specific values for Order number, Order date, Item number, and Quantity for this particular order are an instance of the entity ORDER and represent the fields for this particular record. Order number is the key field because each order is assigned a unique identification number.

functional areas. Accounting, finance, manufacturing, human resources, and sales and marketing all developed their own systems and data files. Figure 6-3 illustrates the traditional approach to information processing.

Each application, of course, required its own files and its own computer program to operate. For example, the human resources functional area might have a personnel master file, a payroll file, a medical insurance file, a pension file, a mailing list file, and so forth until tens, perhaps hundreds, of files and programs existed. In the company as a whole, this process led to multiple master files created, maintained, and operated by separate divisions or departments. As this process goes on for five or ten years, the organization is saddled with hundreds of programs and applications that are very difficult to maintain and manage. The resulting problems are data redundancy and inconsistency, program-data dependence, inflexibility, poor data security, and an inability to share data among applications.

Data Redundancy and Inconsistency **Data redundancy** is the presence of duplicate data in multiple data files so that the same data are stored in more than one

FIGURE 6-3 *Traditional file processing.*

The use of a traditional approach to file processing encourages each functional area in a corporation to develop specialized applications. Each application requires a unique data field that is likely to be a subset of the master file. These subsets lead to data redundancy and inconsistency, processing inflexibility, and wasted storage resources.

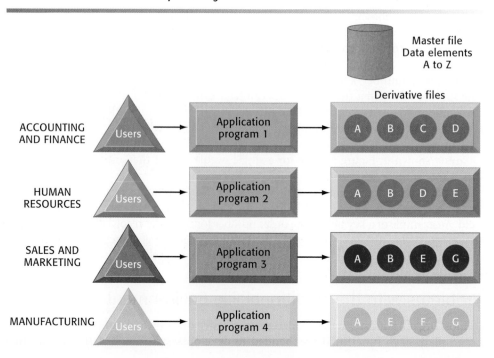

place or location. Data redundancy occurs when different divisions, functional areas, and groups in an organization independently collect the same piece of data and store it independently of each other. Data redundancy wastes storage resources and also leads to **data inconsistency**, where the same attribute may have different values. For example, in instances of the entity ORDER illustrated in Figure 6-2, the quantity of an item ordered may be updated in some systems but not in others, or some systems may show a different value for Quantity than others. Because it is collected and maintained in so many different places, the same attribute, Item number, may also have different names in different systems throughout the organization. Some systems might use Item number, and others might use Product number, for example.

Additional confusion might result from using different coding systems to represent values for an attribute. For instance, the sales, inventory, and manufacturing systems of a clothing retailer might use different codes to represent clothing size. One system might represent clothing size as "extra large" while another might use the code "XL" for the same purpose. The resulting confusion would make it difficult for companies to create customer relationship management, supply chain management, or enterprise systems that integrate data from different sources.

Program-Data Dependence **Program-data dependence** refers to the coupling of data stored in files and the specific programs required to update and maintain those files so that changes in programs require changes to the data. Every traditional computer program has to describe the location and nature of the data with which it works. In a traditional file environment, any change in a software program could require a change in the data accessed by that program. If the original data file were changed, then other programs that required that data would no longer work properly. These changes could cost millions of dollars to implement properly.

Lack of Flexibility A traditional file system can deliver routine scheduled reports after extensive programming efforts, but it cannot deliver ad hoc reports or respond to unanticipated information requirements in a timely fashion. The information required by ad hoc requests is somewhere in the system but may be too expensive to retrieve. Several programmers might have to work for weeks to put together the required data items in a new file.

Poor Security Because there is little control or management of data, access to and dissemination of information may be out of control. Management may have no way of knowing who is accessing or even making changes to the organization's data. Maintaining security and control over multiple databases in multiple locations is more difficult than maintaining security and control over one database.

Lack of Data Sharing and Availability The lack of control over access to data in this confused environment does not make it easy for people to obtain information. Because pieces of information in different files and different parts of the organization cannot be related to one another, it is virtually impossible for information to be shared or accessed in a timely manner. Information cannot flow freely across different functional areas or different parts of the organization. If users find different values of the same piece of information in two different systems, they may not want to use these systems because they cannot trust the accuracy of their data.

6.2 The Database Approach to Data Management

Database technology can cut through many of the problems a traditional file organization creates. A more rigorous definition of a **database** is a collection of data organized to serve many applications efficiently by centralizing the data and controlling redundant data.

data inconsistency
program-data dependence
database

Rather than storing data in separate files for each application, data are stored so as to appear to users as being stored in only one location. A single database services multiple applications. For example, instead of a corporation storing employee data in separate information systems and separate files for personnel, payroll, and benefits, the corporation could create a single common human resources database. Figure 6-4 illustrates the database concept.

Database Management Systems

A **database management system** (**DBMS**) is simply the software that permits an organization to centralize data, manage them efficiently, and provide access to the stored data by application programs. The DBMS acts as an interface between application programs and the physical data files. When the application program calls for a data item, such as gross pay, the DBMS finds this item in the database and presents it to the application program. Using traditional data files, the programmer would have to specify the size and format of each data element used in the program and then tell the computer where they were located. A DBMS eliminates most of the data definition statements found in traditional programs.

The DBMS relieves the programmer or end user from the task of understanding where and how the data are actually stored by separating the logical and physical views of the data. The *logical view* presents data as they would be perceived by end users or business specialists while the *physical view* shows how data are actually organized and structured on physical storage media. The database management software makes the physical database available for different logical views presented for various application programs. The logical description of the entire database showing all the data elements and relationships among them is called the **conceptual schema** while

database management system (DBMS)

conceptual schema

FIGURE 6-4   *The contemporary database environment.*

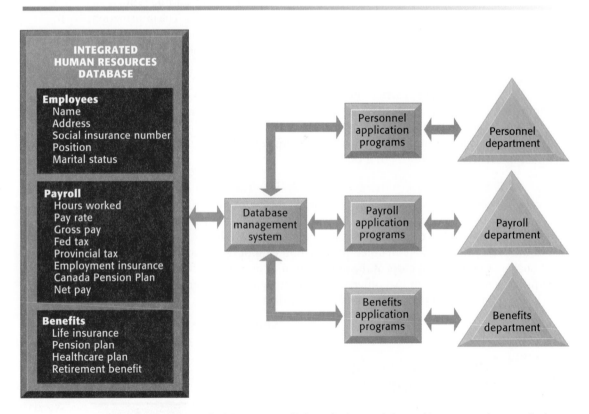

A single human resources database serves multiple applications and also enables a corporation to easily draw together all the information for various applications. The database management system acts as the interface between the application programs and the data.

the specifications of how data from the conceptual schema are stored on physical media is termed the *physical schema* or *internal schema*. The specific set of data from the database, or *view*, that is required by each user or application program is termed the **subschema**. For example, for the human resources database illustrated in Figure 6-4, an employee retirement benefits program might use a subschema consisting of the employee's name, address, social insurance number, pension plan, and retirement benefits data.

A database management system has three components:

1. A data definition language
2. A data manipulation language
3. A data dictionary

The **data definition language** is the formal language programmers use to specify the structure of the content of the database. The data definition language defines each data element as it appears in the database before that data element is translated into the forms required by application programs.

Most DBMS have a specialized language called a **data manipulation language** that is used in conjunction with some conventional third- or fourth-generation programming languages to manipulate the data in the database. This language contains commands that permit end users and programming specialists to extract data from the database to satisfy information requests and develop applications.

The most prominent data manipulation language today is **structured query language**, or **SQL**. End users and information systems specialists can use SQL as an interactive query language to access data from databases, and SQL commands can be embedded in application programs written in conventional programming languages.

The third element of a DBMS is a **data dictionary**. This is an automated or manual file that stores definitions of data elements and data characteristics, such as usage, physical representation, ownership (who in the organization is responsible for maintaining the data), authorization, and security. Many data dictionaries can produce lists and reports of data use, groupings, program locations, and so on.

Figure 6-5 illustrates a sample data dictionary report that shows the size, format, meaning, and uses of a data element in a human resources database. A **data element** represents a field. In addition to listing the standard name (AMT-PAY-BASE), the dictionary lists the names that reference this element in specific systems and identifies the individuals, business functions, programs, and reports that use this data element.

By creating an inventory of data contained in the database, the data dictionary serves as an important data management tool. For instance, business users could consult the dictionary to find out exactly what pieces of data are maintained for the sales or marketing function or even to determine all the information maintained by the entire enterprise. The dictionary could supply business users with the name, format, and specifications required to access data for reports. Technical staff could use the dictionary to determine what data elements and files must be changed if a program is changed.

Most data dictionaries are entirely passive; they simply report. More advanced types are active; changes in the dictionary can be automatically used by related programs. For instance, to change a data field from numeric to text, one could simply enter the change in the dictionary without having to modify and recompile all application programs using that data field.

In an ideal database environment, the data in the database are defined only once and used for all applications whose data reside in the database, thereby eliminating data redundancy and inconsistency. Application programs, which are written using a combination of the data manipulation language of the DBMS and a conventional programming language, request data elements from the database. Data elements called for by the application programs are found and delivered by the DBMS. The programmer does not have to specify in detail how or where the data are to be found.

subschema
data definition language
data manipulation language
structured query language (SQL)
data dictionary
data element

FIGURE 6-5 *Sample data dictionary report.*

The sample data dictionary report for a human resources database provides helpful information, such as the size of the data element, which programs and reports use it, and which group in the organization is the owner responsible for maintaining it. The report also shows some of the other names that the organization uses for this piece of data.

```
NAME:  AMT-PAY-BASE
FOCUS NAME:  BASEPAY
PC NAME:  SALARY

DESCRIPTION:  EMPLOYEE'S ANNUAL SALARY

SIZE:  9 BYTES
TYPE:  N  (NUMERIC)
DATE CHANGED:  01/01/04
OWNERSHIP:  COMPENSATION
UPDATE SECURITY:  SITE PERSONNEL
ACCESS SECURITY:  MANAGER, COMPENSATION PLANNING AND RESEARCH
                  MANAGER, JOB EVALUATION SYSTEMS
                  MANAGER, HUMAN RESOURCES PLANNING
                  MANAGER, SITE EQUAL OPPORTUNITY AFFAIRS
                  MANAGER, SITE BENEFITS
                  MANAGER, CLAIMS PAYING SYSTEMS
                  MANAGER, QUALIFIED PLANS
                  MANAGER, SITE EMPLOYMENT/EEO
BUSINESS FUNCTIONS USED BY: COMPENSATION
                           HR PLANNING
                           EMPLOYMENT
                           INSURANCE
                           PENSION

PROGRAMS USING: PI01000
                PI02000
                PI03000
                PI04000
                PI05000

REPORTS USING:  REPORT 124 (SALARY INCREASE TRACKING REPORT)
                REPORT 448 (GROUP INSURANCE AUDIT REPORT)
                REPORT 452 (SALARY REVIEW LISTING)
                PENSION REFERENCE LISTING
```

How a DBMS Solves the Problems of the Traditional File Environment A DBMS can reduce data redundancy and inconsistency by minimizing isolated files in which the same data are repeated. The DBMS may not enable the organization to eliminate data redundancy entirely, but it can help control redundancy. Even if the organization maintains some redundant data, using a DBMS eliminates data inconsistency because the DBMS can help the organization ensure that every occurrence of redundant data has the same values. The DBMS uncouples programs and data, enabling data to stand on their own. Access and availability of information can be increased and program development and maintenance costs can be reduced because users and programmers can perform ad hoc queries of data in the database. The DBMS enables the organization to centrally manage data, their use, and security.

The Window on Organizations illustrates some of the benefits of a DBMS for information management. Procter & Gamble had to manage massive amounts of product data for its more than 300 brands. Because these data were stored in 30 separate repositories, the company could not easily bring together information about the company's various products and their components, degrading operational efficiency. Management of these data improved once P&G created a common set of technical standards for all its products and organized its data in a single global database.

Types of Databases

Contemporary DBMS use different database models to keep track of entities, attributes, and relationships. Each model has certain processing advantages and certain business advantages.

Relational DBMS The most popular type of DBMS today for PCs as well as for larger computers and mainframes is the **relational DBMS**. The relational data model

relational DBMS

WINDOW ON ORGANIZATIONS

Organization

A Database Helps Proctor & Gamble Manage Product Information

Procter & Gamble (P&G) is one of the largest consumer goods companies in the world, with more than $43 billion in annual sales. P&G sells more than 300 brands worldwide, including major brands such as Tide, Mr. Clean, Ivory Soap, Crest, Pringles, Pampers, Clairol, and Prell. P&G has five global business units in more than 80 countries, including research and development and contract manufacturing operations. The Canadian business unit was ranked one of the top 50 "Best Employers" in Canada for 2005 by Hewitt Associates.

The fundamental product development process at P&G begins with the creation of a set of technical specifications for a product, raw material, packaging material, piece of artwork, or analytical and process standards. Each P&G product has its own set of technical standards and specifications. For example, the formula card (equivalent to a list of ingredients or instructions) for a single size and fragrance of one Olay product defines technical standards for 30 raw material specifications, 20 test methods, three packaging standards, eight packaging material standards, four artwork standards, manufacturing instructions, a set of quality acceptance criteria, one process standard, two additional formula cards tied to the same packaging standard, and 15 substitute ingredient standards for producing a product in a different location.

Because P&G is a global company with some products tailored to regional markets and consumer tastes, P&G has many functionally similar products with significant variations in actual specifications for different regions. There were no global data standards or "pick lists" across all P&G divisions. Consequently, P&G has more than 600 000 specifications and a mountain of product data to manage.

These data used to be stored in 30 separate data repositories, preventing information sharing among researchers and raising material acquisition costs. For example, P&G had perhaps 12 different sets of specifications for blue dye, and it was placing 12 different orders for the same blue dye to the same supplier at 12 different prices. One large P&G business unit was using more than 50 different types of adhesives around the world with scores of suppliers, even though the specifications for several adhesives were identical with different commercial names and only three adhesive types were needed to meet all global needs.

P&G made the management of product information easier by cataloguing the technical standards for all of its products and organizing them in a single global database called the Corporate Standards System (CSS). The system is based on eMatrix from MatrixOne, a provider of product life cycle management software. This database is now available to 8200 P&G employees and will be made available to some suppliers and contract manufacturers.

The database organizes any and every piece of information that goes into making a particular product. Once this information is in the database, data can be analyzed from many different perspectives to deliver information to serve specific functions. For instance, designers and engineers can use the data to design a new product or improve an old one. Purchasing can use the data to consolidate materials orders. The data even help retailers determine the proper shelf height for storing an item.

P&G's investment in the database is producing returns. With all product data in one place, P&G can obtain a unified company-wide picture of what materials it needs and use this information to consolidate purchases to secure better prices. This information helped P&G cut down on total adhesive use and develop new processes for applying adhesives more economically.

The database also enables P&G researchers who need constant access to standards to work more efficiently and facilitates reuse of technical standards that have already been defined. A researcher in one facility may have already defined a technical standard for a hair-colouring gel while another researcher may be working on a similar product or a product that may interact with that brand of hair colour. The second researcher will be able to reuse the colouring product's technical standards and know precisely how an ingredient in that product might react with other ingredients. In heavily regulated industries such as health and beauty products, ingredients and their proportions must be exact. Precision and consistency among technical standards are critical.

In the case of dyes for bottled products, the database stores a pre-approved palette of colours for bottles. When P&G's research and development group is working on new products, it can use this information without repeating a study to show that there is no problem with using that dye in a new product.

The CSS is being enhanced to create more structured data from technical standards that can be easily shared with more groups in the company. Specification data will be delivered to users through specialized interfaces that are tailored for specific business needs. The CSS will define and catalogue technical standards for any new product, whether that product was developed internally or through an acquisition.

To Think About: How does P&G's CSS database provide value for the company? What management, organization, and technology issues had to be addressed when developing this database?

Sources: Lafe Low, "They Got It Together," *CIO Magazine*, February 15, 2004; Deborah D'Agostino, "PLM: The Means of Production," *eWeek*, February 27, 2004; "Procter & Gamble Awarded Enterprise Value Award by *CIO Magazine* for Work with MatrixOne on Innovative Product Lifecycle Management Application," *MatrixOne*, February 23, 2004; and "Procter & Gamble," www.matrixone.com, accessed May 20, 2004; "Best Employers in Canada," Hewitt Associates, available http://was4.hewitt.com/best employers/canada/best.htm, accessed April 13, 2005.

represents all data in the database as simple two-dimensional tables called relations. Tables may be referred to as files. Information in more than one file can be easily extracted and combined.

Figure 6-6 shows a supplier table and a part table. In each table, the rows represent unique records, and the columns represent fields, or the attributes that describe the entities. The correct term for a row or record in a relation is **tuple**. Often a user needs information from a number of relations to produce a report. Here is the strength of the relational model: It can relate data in any one file or table to data in another file or table as long as both tables share a common data element.

To demonstrate, suppose we wanted to find in the relational database in Figure 6-6 the names and addresses of suppliers who could provide us with part number 137 or part number 152. We would need information from two tables: the supplier table and the part table. Note that these two files have a shared data element: Supplier_Number.

In a relational database, three basic operations, as shown in Figure 6-7, are used to develop useful sets of data: select, project, and join. The *select* operation creates a subset consisting of all records in the file that meet stated criteria. Select creates, in other words, a subset of rows that meet certain criteria. In our example, we want to select records (rows) from the part table where the part number equals 137 or 152. The *join* operation combines relational tables to provide the user with more information than is available in individual tables. In our example, we want to join the now-shortened part table (only parts numbered 137 or 152 will be presented) and the supplier table into a single new resultant table.

The *project* operation creates a subset consisting of columns in a table, permitting the user to create new tables (also called views) that contain only the information required. In our example, we want to extract from the new resultant table only the following columns: Part_Number, Supplier_Number, Supplier_Name, and Supplier_Address (see Figure 6-7).

Leading mainframe relational database management systems include IBM's DB2 and Oracle from the Oracle Corporation. DB2, Oracle, and Microsoft SQL Server are used as DBMS for midrange computers. Microsoft Access is a PC relational database management system, and Oracle Lite is a DBMS for handheld computing devices.

Hierarchical and Network DBMS You can still find older systems that are based on a hierarchical or network data model. The **hierarchical DBMS** is used to model one-to-many relationships, presenting data to users in a treelike structure. Within each record, data elements are organized into pieces of records called segments. To the user, each record

---

FIGURE 6-6   *The relational data model.*

Each table is a relation, each row is a tuple representing a record, and each column is an attribute representing a field. These relations can easily be combined and extracted to access data and produce reports, provided that any two share a common data element. In this example, the PART and SUPPLIER files share the data element Supplier_Number.

tuple
hierarchical DBMS

FIGURE 6-7 *The three basic operations of a relational DBMS.*

Project selected columns

The select, project, and join operations enable data from two different tables to be combined and only selected attributes to be displayed.

looks like an organizational chart with one top-level segment called the root. An upper segment is connected logically to a lower segment in a parent–child relationship. A parent segment can have more than one child, but a child can have only one parent.

Figure 6-8 shows a hierarchical structure that might be used for a human resources database. The root segment is Employee, which contains basic employee information such as name, address, and identification number. Immediately below it are three child segments: Compensation (containing salary and promotion data), Job Assignments (containing data about job positions and departments), and Benefits (containing data about beneficiaries and benefit options). The Compensation segment has two children below it: Performance Ratings (containing data about employees' job performance evaluations) and Salary History (containing historical data about employees' past salaries). Below the Benefits segment are child segments for Pension, Life Insurance, and Health, containing data about these benefit plans.

While hierarchical structures depict one-to-many relationships, **network DBMS** depict data logically as many-to-many relationships. In other words, parents can have multiple children, and a child can have more than one parent. A typical many-to-many relationship for a network DBMS is the student–course relationship (see Figure 6-9).

network DBMS

FIGURE 6-8 *A hierarchical database for a human resources system.*

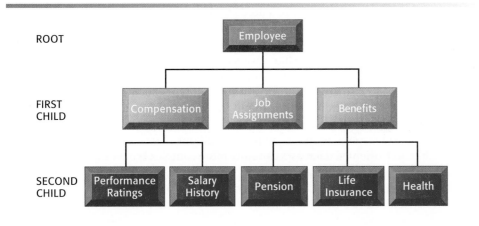

The hierarchical database model looks like an organizational chart or family tree. It has a single root segment (Employee) connected to lower level segments (Compensation, Job Assignments, and Benefits). Each subordinate segment, in turn, may connect to other subordinate segments. Here, Compensation connects to Performance Ratings and Salary History. Benefits connects to Pension, Life Insurance, and Health. Each subordinate segment is the child of the segment directly above it.

FIGURE 6-9 *The network data model.*

This illustration of a network data model showing the relationship the students in a university have to the courses they take represents an example of logical many-to-many relationships.

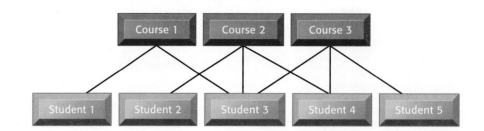

There are many courses in a university and many students. A student takes many courses, and a course has many students.

Hierarchical and network DBMS are considered outdated and are no longer used for building new database applications. They are much less flexible than relational DBMS and do not support ad hoc, English language–like inquiries for information. All paths for accessing data must be specified in advance and cannot be changed without a major programming effort. For instance, if you queried the human resources database illustrated in Figure 6-8 to find out the names of the employees with the job title of administrative assistant, you would discover that there is no way the system can find the answer in a reasonable amount of time. This path through the data was not specified in advance.

Relational DBMS, in contrast, have much more flexibility in providing data for ad hoc queries, combining information from different sources, and providing capability to add new data and records without disturbing existing programs and applications. However, these systems can be slowed down if they require many accesses to the data stored on disk to carry out the select, join, and project commands. Selecting one part number from among millions, one record at a time, can take a long time. Of course, the database can be tuned to speed up prespecified queries.

Hierarchical DBMS can still be found in large legacy systems that require intensive high-volume transaction processing. Banks, insurance companies, and other high-volume users continue to use reliable hierarchical databases, such as IBM's Information Management System (IMS) developed in 1969. As relational products acquire more muscle, firms will shift away completely from hierarchical DBMS, but this will happen over a long period of time.

Object-Oriented Databases Conventional database management systems were designed for homogeneous data that can be easily structured into predefined data fields and records organized in rows and columns. But many applications today and in the future will require databases that can store and retrieve not only structured numbers and characters but also drawings, images, photographs, voice, and full-motion video. Conventional DBMS are not well suited to handling graphics-based or multimedia applications. For instance, design data in a computer-aided design (CAD) database consist of complex relationships among many types of data. Manipulating these kinds of data in a relational system requires extensive programming to translate these complex data structures into tables and rows. An **object-oriented DBMS**, however, stores the data and procedures that act on those data as objects that can be automatically retrieved and shared.

Object-oriented database management systems (OODBMS) are becoming popular because they can be used to manage the various multimedia components or Java applets used in Web applications, which typically integrate pieces of information from a variety of sources. OODBMS also are useful for storing data types such as recursive data. (An example would be parts within parts as found in manufacturing applications.) Finance and trading applications often use OODBMS because they require data models that must be easy to change to respond to new economic conditions.

Although object-oriented databases can store more complex types of information than relational DBMS, they are relatively slow compared with relational DBMS for processing large numbers of transactions. Hybrid **object-relational DBMS** systems are now available to provide capabilities of both object-oriented and relational DBMS. A hybrid approach

object-oriented DBMS

object-relational DBMS

can be accomplished in three different ways: by using tools that offer object-oriented access to relational DBMS, by using object-oriented extensions to existing relational DBMS, or by using a hybrid object-relational database management system, now offered by all the major DBMS vendors.

6.3   Creating a Database Environment

To create a database environment, you must understand the relationships among the data, the type of data that will be maintained in the database, how the data will be used, and how the organization will need to change to manage data from a company-wide perspective. Increasingly, database design will also have to consider how the organization can share some of its data with its business partners (Jukic, Jukic, and Parameswaran 2002). We now describe important database design principles and the management and organizational requirements of a database environment.

Designing Databases

To create a database, you must go through two design exercises: a conceptual design and a physical design. The conceptual, or logical, design of a database is an abstract model of the database from a business perspective while the physical design shows how the database is actually arranged on direct-access storage devices. Logical design requires a detailed description of the business information needs of the actual end users of the database. Ideally, database design will be part of an overall organizational data-planning effort (see Chapter 10).

The conceptual database design describes how the data elements in the database are to be grouped. The design process identifies relationships among data elements and the most efficient way of grouping data elements together to meet information requirements. The process also identifies redundant data elements and the groupings of data elements required for specific application programs. Groups of data are organized, refined, and streamlined until an overall logical view of the relationships among all the data elements in the database emerges.

To use a relational database model effectively, complex groupings of data must be streamlined to minimize redundant data elements and awkward many-to-many relationships. The process of creating small, stable, yet flexible and adaptive data structures from complex groups of data is called **normalization**. Figures 6-10 and 6-11 illustrate this process.

In the particular business modelled here, an order can have more than one part, but each part is provided by only one supplier. If we build a relation called ORDER with all the fields included here, we would have to repeat the name and address of the supplier for every part on the order, even though the order is for parts from a single supplier. This relationship contains what are called *repeating data groups* because there can be many parts on a single order to a given supplier. A more efficient way to arrange the data is to break down ORDER into smaller relations, each of which describes a single entity. If we

normalization

FIGURE 6-10   *An unnormalized relation for ORDER.*

ORDER

Order_Number	Part_Quantity	Part_Number	Part_Description	Unit_Price	Supplier_Number	Supplier_Name	Supplier_Address	Order_Date	Delivery_Date

An unnormalized relation contains repeating groups. For example, there can be many parts and suppliers for each order. There is only a one-to-one correspondence between Order_Number, Order_Date, and Delivery_Date.

FIGURE 6-11   *A normalized relation for ORDER.*

After normalization, the original relation ORDER has been broken down into four smaller relations. The relation ORDER is left with only three attributes and the relation ORDERED_PART has a combined, or concatenated, key consisting of Order_Number and Part_Number.

go step by step and normalize the relation ORDER, we emerge with the relations illustrated in Figure 6-11. You can find out more about normalization, entity-relationship diagramming, and database design in the *Hands-On Guide to Management Information Systems* (on the Companion Website).

If a database has been carefully considered, with a clear understanding of business information needs and usage, the database model will most likely be in some normalized form. Many real-world databases are not fully normalized because this may not be the most efficient or cost-effective way to meet business requirements.

Database designers document their data model with an **entity-relationship diagram**, illustrated in Figure 6-12. This diagram illustrates the relationship between the entities ORDER, ORDERED_PART, PART, and SUPPLIER. The boxes represent entities. The lines connecting the boxes represent relationships. A line connecting two entities that ends in two short marks designates a one-to-one relationship. A line connecting two entities that ends with a crow's foot topped by a short mark indicates a one-to-many relationship. Figure 6-12 shows that one ORDER can contain many ORDERED_PARTs. Each PART can be ordered many times and can appear many times in a single order. Each PART can have only one SUPPLIER, but many PARTs can be provided by the same SUPPLIER.

Distributing Databases
Database design also considers how the data are to be distributed. Information systems can be designed with a centralized database that is used by a single central processor or by multiple processors in a client/server network. Alternatively, the database can be distributed. A **distributed database** is one that is stored in more than one physical location.

There are two main methods of distributing a database (see Figure 6-13). In a *partitioned* database, parts of the database are stored and maintained physically in one location, and other parts are stored and maintained in other locations (see Figure 6-13a) so that each remote processor has the necessary data to serve its local area. Changes in local files can be justified with the central database on a batch basis, often at night. Another strategy is to *replicate* (that is, duplicate in its entirety) the central database (Figure 6-13b) at all remote locations. For example, Lufthansa Airlines replaced its centralized mainframe database with a replicated database to make information more immediately available to flight dispatchers. Any change made to Lufthansa's Frankfurt DBMS is automatically replicated in New York and Hong Kong. This strategy also requires updating the central database during off-hours.

Distributed systems reduce the vulnerability of a single, massive central site. They increase service and responsiveness to local users and often can run on smaller, less

entity-relationship diagram

distributed database

FIGURE 6-12   *An entity-relationship diagram.*

Order_Number
Order_Date
Delivery_Date

ORDER

belongs
to   includes

Order_Number
Part_Number
Part_Quantity

ORDERED_
PART

is
ordered   contains

Part_Number
Part_Description
Unit_Price
Supplier_Number

PART

provides   is supplied
by

Supplier_Number
Supplier_Name
Supplier_Address

SUPPLIER

This diagram shows the relationships between the entities ORDER, ORDERED_PART, PART, and SUPPLIER that might be used to model the database in Figure 6-11.

expensive computers. Distributed systems, however, depend on high-quality telecommunications lines, which themselves are vulnerable. Moreover, local databases can sometimes depart from central data standards and definitions, and they pose security problems by widely distributing access to sensitive data. Database designers need to weigh these factors in their decisions.

Ensuring Data Quality

A good database design and data model are not enough to guarantee that the database will deliver the information the organization needs. Data that are inaccurate, untimely, or inconsistent with other sources of information can create serious operational and financial problems for businesses. When faulty data go unnoticed, they can lead to incorrect decisions,

FIGURE 6-13   *Distributed databases.*

(a) Partitioned
database

Central
database

Host CPU

Remote
CPU   Remote
                    CPU

Remote database
partition A   Remote database
                    partition B

(b) Duplicate
database

Central
database

Host CPU

Remote
CPU   Remote
                    CPU

Remote database
duplicate   Remote database
                    duplicate

There are alternative ways of distributing a database. The central database can be partitioned (a) so that each remote processor has the necessary data to serve its own local needs. The central database also can be replicated (b) at all remote locations.

product recalls, and even financial losses. The Gartner Group believes that customer data degrades at a rate of 2 percent per month, making poor data quality a major obstacle to successful customer relationship management implementation (Klau 2003).

Some of these data quality problems are caused by redundant and inconsistent data produced by a traditional file environment. During the database design effort, data-describing entities such as a customer, product, or order should be named and defined consistently for all business areas using the database. If a database is properly designed and enterprise-wide data standards established, duplicate or inconsistent data elements should be minimal.

Most data quality problems, however, such as misspelled names, transposed numbers, or incorrect or missing codes, stem from errors during data input. The incidence of these errors is rising as companies move their businesses to the Web and allow customers and suppliers to enter data into their Web sites that directly update internal systems.

Before a new database is in place, organizations need to identify and correct their faulty data and establish better routines for editing once the database is in operation. Analysis of data quality often begins with a **data quality audit**, which is a structured survey of the accuracy and level of completeness of the data in an information system. Data quality audits can be performed by surveying entire data files, surveying samples from data files, or surveying end users for their perceptions of data quality.

Data cleansing, also known as *data scrubbing*, consists of activities for detecting and correcting data in a database or file that are incorrect, incomplete, improperly formatted, or redundant. Data cleansing not only corrects data but also enforces consistency among different sets of data that originated in separate information systems. Specialized data-cleansing software can automatically survey data files, correct errors in the data, and integrate the data in a consistent company-wide format.

6.4 Database Trends

Organizations are installing powerful data analysis tools and data warehouses to make better use of the information stored in their databases and are taking advantage of database technology linked to the World Wide Web. Let's explore these developments.

Multidimensional Data Analysis

Sometimes managers need to analyze data in ways that traditional database models cannot represent. For example, a company selling four different products—nuts, bolts, washers, and screws—in the East, West, and Central regions might want to know actual sales by product for each region and might also want to compare them with projected sales. This analysis requires a multidimensional view of data.

To provide this type of information, organizations can use either a specialized multidimensional database or a tool that creates multidimensional views of data in relational databases. Multidimensional analysis enables users to view the same data in different ways using multiple dimensions. Each aspect of information—product, pricing, cost, region, or time period—represents a different dimension. So, a product manager could use a multidimensional data analysis tool to learn how many washers were sold in the East in June, how that compares with the previous month and the previous June, and how it compares with the sales forecast. Another term for multidimensional data analysis is **online analytical processing (OLAP)**.

Figure 6-14 shows a multidimensional model that could be created to represent products, regions, actual sales, and projected sales. A matrix of actual sales can be stacked on top of a matrix of projected sales to form a cube with six faces. If you rotate the cube 90 degrees one way, the face showing will be product versus actual and projected sales. If you rotate the cube 90 degrees again, you can see region versus actual and projected sales. If you rotate 180 degrees from the original view, you can see projected sales and product versus region. Cubes can be nested within cubes to build complex views of data.

data quality audit

data cleansing

online analytical processing (OLAP)

FIGURE 6-14 *Multidimensional data model.*

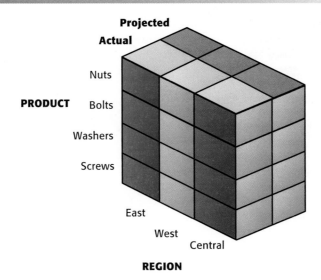

The view that is showing is product versus region. If you rotate the cube 90 degrees, the face that will be showing is product versus actual and projected sales. If you rotate the cube 90 degrees again, you can see region versus actual and projected sales. Other views are possible. The ability to rotate the data cube is the main technique for multidimensional reporting. It is sometimes called "slice and dice."

Data Warehouses and Data Mining

Decision makers need concise, reliable information about current operations, trends, and changes. What has been immediately available at most firms is current data only (historical data were available through special information system reports that took a long time to produce). Data often are fragmented in separate operational systems, such as sales or payroll, so that different managers make decisions from incomplete knowledge bases. Users and information systems specialists may have to spend inordinate amounts of time locating and gathering data (Watson and Haley 1998). Data warehousing addresses this problem by integrating key operational data from around the company in a form that is consistent, reliable, and easily available for reporting.

What Is a Data Warehouse? A **data warehouse** is a massive database that stores current and historical data of potential interest to managers throughout the company. The data originate in many core operational systems and external sources, including Web site transactions, each with different data models. They may include legacy systems, relational or object-oriented DBMS applications, and systems based on hypertext markup language (HTML) or extensible markup language (XML) documents. The data from these diverse applications are copied into the data warehouse database as often as needed—hourly, daily, weekly, or monthly. The data are standardized into a common data model and consolidated so that they can be used across the enterprise for management analysis and decision making. The data are available for anyone to access as needed but cannot be altered.

Figure 6-15 illustrates the data warehouse concept. The data warehouse must be carefully designed by both business and technical specialists to ensure it can provide the right information for critical business decisions. The firm may need to change its business processes to benefit from the information in the warehouse (Cooper, Watson, Wixom, and Goodhue 2000).

Companies can build enterprise-wide data warehouses in which a central data warehouse serves the entire organization, or they can create smaller, decentralized warehouses called data marts. A **data mart** is a subset of a data warehouse in which a summarized or highly focused portion of the organization's data is placed in a separate database for a specific population of users. For example, a company might develop marketing and sales data marts to deal with customer information. A data mart typically focuses on a single subject area or line of business, so it usually can be constructed more rapidly and at lower cost than an enterprise-wide data warehouse. However, complexity, costs, and management problems will arise if an organization creates too many data marts.

data warehouse
data mart

FIGURE 6-15   *Components of a data warehouse.*

A data warehouse extracts current and historical data from operational systems inside the organization. These data are combined with data from external sources and reorganized into a central database designed for management reporting and analysis. The information directory provides users with information about the data available in the warehouse.

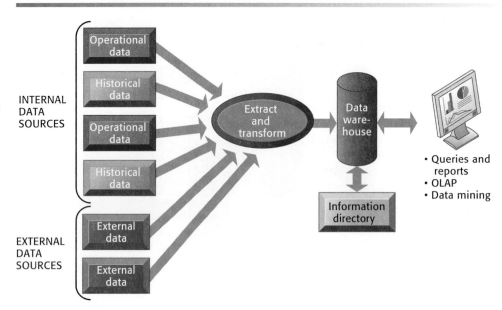

The Window on Technology describes some of the technical issues that must be addressed when creating a data warehouse. Both HSBC Bank Canada and Axfood had collected massive amounts of customer data that they wanted to analyze immediately to make better marketing, pricing, and inventory decisions. As you read this case, pay attention to the benefits that can be provided by large data warehouses and the technology issues that need to be addressed to make them effective.

Data Mining A data warehouse system provides a range of ad hoc and standardized query tools, analytical tools, and graphical reporting facilities, including tools for OLAP and data mining. **Data mining** uses a variety of techniques to find hidden patterns and relationships in large pools of data and to infer rules from them that can be used to predict future behaviour and guide decision making (Fayyad et al. 2002, Hirji 2001). Data mining is often used to provide information for targeted marketing in which personalized or individualized messages can be created based on individual preferences, and there are many other data-mining applications in both business and scientific work. These systems can perform high-level analyses of patterns or trends, but they can also drill down to provide more detail when needed. Table 6-1 describes how some organizations are benefiting from data mining, and Chapter 15 provides more detail on how data mining is being used to guide business decision making.

Data mining requires changes in typical business processes to be able to capture the data efficiently as close to the source as possible (e.g., during the actual transaction), to store the data in a secure, reliable database environment capable of handling massive amounts of data and analytical processing, and to access the data from a variety of locations in a variety of formats, easily readable and understandable by research analysts. These changes may be hard to make, but without them, the value of the data warehouse and the data mining itself will not be maximized.

Data mining is both a powerful and profitable tool, but it poses challenges to the protection of individual privacy. Data-mining technology can combine information from many diverse sources to create a detailed "data image" about each of us—our income, our driving habits, our hobbies, our families, and our political interests. The question of whether companies should be allowed to collect such detailed information about individuals is explored in Chapter 4.

Enterprise-wide systems, such as SAP, can be used for both data warehousing and data mining. Siebel Systems, a leading vendor of customer relationship management (CRM)

data mining

TABLE 6-1   *How Businesses Are Using Data Mining*

ORGANIZATION	DATA-MINING APPLICATION
Disco S.A.	Disco, an Argentine supermarket chain, uses data mining to analyze purchasing patterns of more than 1.5 million customers who participate in a frequent-buyer program in more than 200 stores.
Bank of Montreal	Bank of Montreal uses data mining to better understand their customers by using various query tools, a statistical package, and in-house developed analytics. One set of analytics sends prompts to an account manager, indicating that a specific bank customer has changed their banking patterns and that the manager should follow up with that customer. This data mining leads to retaining business and customers and even obtaining new business from those customers.
Lillian Vernon Corporation	Lillian Vernon, a catalogue company, mines data from its Web site as well as from its catalogue sales to determine which products sell best. By analyzing its Web visitor data, it found that men were more likely to visit its Web site than to flip through a paper catalogue. Lillian Vernon now places products that appeal to men prominently on its Web site.
Red Robin Restaurants	Greenwood Village, a chain based in Colorado, uses OLAP and data mining to analyze the menus for its 87 corporate restaurants and more than 100 franchise locations. By analyzing the price, cost, and quality of each item in all the meals the restaurants serve, Red Robin can identify the menu items that offer both high volume and high profit margin.
Samsung Electronics America	Samsung analyzes data from 10 000 resellers to identify orders that went to competitors. It found that for its computer monitors sold to the health care industry, one competitor was responsible for 40 percent of the lost deals.

software, has data mining applications, as does Oracle, the leading database vendor, with its Oracle Data Miner software. SAS Institute and SPSS, Inc. also provide data mining applications with their other software. IBM has also entered this arena with its WebFountain Advanced Text Analytic Solutions, while RMSI also focuses on data warehousing and data mining applications. While most vendors of data mining software are generalists, there are suppliers of data mining applications that specialize in a particular type of data. For example, Canada's United Bioinformatica licenses a variety of data mining software solutions to mine terabytes of genetic data for medical research purposes.

Benefits of Data Warehouses Data warehouses not only offer improved information, they also make it easy for decision makers to obtain this information. They even include the ability to model and remodel the data. It has been estimated that 70 percent of the world's business information resides on mainframe databases, many of which support older legacy systems. Many of these legacy systems are critical production applications that support the company's core business processes. As long as these systems can efficiently process the necessary volume of transactions to keep the company running, firms are reluctant to replace them, thereby avoiding disrupting critical business functions and high system replacement costs. Many of these legacy systems use hierarchical DBMS or even older nondatabase files in which information is difficult for users to access. Data warehouses enable decision makers to access data as often as they need without affecting the performance of the underlying operational systems. Many organizations are making access to their data warehouses even easier by using Web technology.

WINDOW ON TECHNOLOGY

Large Data Warehouses: When Bigger Is Better

Until a few years ago, a data warehouse or transactional database that held 1 terabyte (TB) of data was considered big. Today a "big" database holds tens of terabytes. The data warehouses used by HSBC Bank Canada and Axfood are examples, and they provide special benefits.

At HSBC Bank Canada, managers need to consolidate and analyze data across their numerous applications and banking products. They need to understand which customers are profitable, which customers are not profitable, and which products are profitable. They needed to maximize the relationships that exist between different product offerings and customers. HSBC Bank Canada needed a simple system that was scalable for their growing market and contained sophisticated data analysis tools. They implemented IBM's AS/400 architecture, using IBM's DB2 database management system, Trillium Software, RODIN, and business objects. HSBC used DB2 to house their data warehouse, and they cleaned their data using Trillium Software. They used RODIN to manage the data warehouse.

Today HSBC Bank Canada has many applications for customer relationship management and cross selling to customers. They know the present and future value of each customer to the bank and can use the information in a real-time environment while dealing with customers. Reports and analyses that previously took weeks now take only minutes to prepare, and analysis can now be done on a household, not just on an individual's account. Branch marketing employees can also access their portion of the data warehouse to support their own customers. Sales campaigns are now focused on the most appropriate customer segments, leading to increased sales from those campaigns.

Axfood, a major grocery chain with hundreds of retail stores throughout Scandinavia, also wanted instant analysis of its customer data. It already held a 20 percent market share, but the retail food industry is fiercely competitive, with razor-thin profit margins and many perishable goods with a limited shelf life. Axfood management believed its company could strengthen its leadership position in the Nordic retail food market by offering unique products combined with superior convenience and service. Axfood is based in Stockholm, Sweden, has 8 000 employees, and generates about $5 billion in annual revenue.

Like many other retail chains, Axfood had been gathering point-of-sale data about customer purchases and analyzing the data to make decisions about what items to stock in its stores. But its data-warehousing technology was not up to the task. The company was using two data warehouses for this purpose, one running on an Oracle DBMS and the other on Microsoft

SQL Server. These warehouses could support only weekly analyses of all the point-of-sale data and could not scale to handle Axfood's growing volume of data. Axfood's management had determined that by 2005 it would need 10 terabytes of storage.

Axfood's management wanted to know which products customers decided to buy within an hour of the actual purchase. If its hundreds of retail outlets experienced a sudden run on a particular brand of paper towels, for example, Axfood could replenish store shelves by the next day. Accurate and up-to-date customer purchase data would also help Axfood minimize excess inventory by enabling it to stock its shelves with items customers were sure to buy. "This level of responsiveness is the only way to maintain customer loyalty," states Axfood's data architect. "By having a better grasp on customer buying activities, we could make more targeted purchasing decisions, which would ultimately save us money and generate more revenue."

Axfood management determined that it could reduce the total cost of ownership of its technology assets for data management if it consolidated its data warehousing on a single platform. It selected IBM's DB2 Universal Database Enterprise Server Edition running on an IBM server, with 2.3 terabytes of storage. The IBM server met Axfood's requirements for a high level of performance and availability. It is large enough to host other applications besides the data warehouse, enabling Axfood to get a higher return on its hardware investment. This platform is more scalable, cost-effective, and easier to manage than the Oracle and Microsoft systems and can easily support Axfood's data management and storage needs.

Axfood's DB2 data warehouse uses DataStage from Ascential Software to extract, transform, and load sales data into the DB2 database, which stores and consolidates all the merchandise, stock, and purchase data.

Once the Axfood data warehouse is at full capacity, the company should recoup all the costs of its investment within two to three years. The data warehouse has helped transform Axfood into a much more agile and proactive company where the products customers want are instantly available on store shelves when and where they need them.

To Think About: How do large data warehouses provide value for a business? What special technology challenges do they pose?

Sources: Marianne Kolbasuk McGee, "Bigger and Better," *Information Week*, March 22, 2004; "Axfood Transforms Inventory Management Process with DB2 Data Warehouse," www.ibm.com, accessed May 17, 2004; "HSBC Bank Canada: AS/400 Data Warehouse Case Study," available www.coglinmill.com/pdf_files/rodrefhsbc.pdf, accessed April 14, 2005.

Databases and the Web

Database technology plays an important role in making organizations' information resources available on the World Wide Web. We now explore the role of hypermedia databases on the Web and the growing use of Web sites to access information stored in conventional databases inside the firm.

The Web and Hypermedia Databases Web sites store information as interconnected pages that contain text, sound, video, and graphics by using a hypermedia database. The **hypermedia database** approach to information management stores chunks of information in the form of nodes connected by links the user specifies (see Figure 6-16). The nodes can contain text, graphics, sound, full-motion video, or executable computer programs. Searching for information does not have to follow a predetermined organization scheme. Instead, a user can branch instantly to related information in any kind of relationship the author establishes. The relationship between records is less structured than in a traditional DBMS. The hypermedia database approach enables users to access topics on a Web site in whichever order they wish.

Linking Internal Databases to the Web A series of middleware and other software products has been developed to help users gain access to organizations' legacy data through the Web. For example, a customer with a Web browser might want to search an online retailer's database for pricing information. Figure 6-17 illustrates how that customer might access the retailer's internal database over the Web. The user would access the retailer's Web site over the Internet using Web browser software on his or her client PC. The user's Web browser software would request data from the organization's database, using HTML commands to communicate with the Web server. Because many back-end databases cannot interpret commands written in HTML, the Web server would pass these requests for data to special software that would translate HTML commands into SQL so that they could be processed by the DBMS working with the database. In a client/server environment, the DBMS resides on a special dedicated computer called a **database server**. The DBMS receives the SQL requests and provides the required data. The middleware transfers information from the organization's internal database back to the Web server for delivery in the form of a Web page to the user.

Figure 6-17 shows that the middleware working between the Web server and the DBMS could be an application server running on its own dedicated computer (see

FIGURE 6-16   *A hypermedia database.*

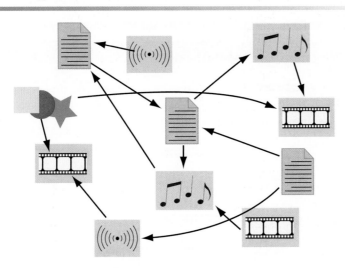

In a hypermedia database, users can choose their own paths to move from node to node. Each node can contain text, graphics, sound, full-motion video, or executable programs.

hypermedia database

database server

FIGURE 6-17   *Linking internal databases to the Web.*

Users can access an organization's internal database through the Web using their desktop PCs and Web browser software.

Client with Web browser | Internet | Web server | Application server | Database server | Database

Chapter 5). The application server software handles all application operations, including transaction processing and data access, between browser-based computers and a company's back-end business applications or databases. The application server takes requests from the Web server, runs the business logic to process transactions based on those requests, and provides connectivity to the organization's back-end systems or databases. Alternatively, the software for handling these operations could be a custom program or a series of software scripts. *Common Gateway Interface (CGI)* is a specification for transferring information between a Web server and a program designed to accept and return data. The program could be written in any programming language, including C, C++, Perl, Java, or Visual Basic.

There are a number of advantages to using the Web to access an organization's internal databases. Web browser software is extremely easy to use, requiring much less training than even user-friendly database query tools. The Web interface requires no changes to the internal database. Companies leverage their investments in older systems because it costs much less to add a Web interface in front of a legacy system than to redesign and rebuild the system to improve user access. Not only companies, but many organizations of all kinds can use this technology (see Figure 6-18).

Accessing corporate databases through the Web is creating new efficiencies and opportunities, and, in some cases, it is even changing the way business is being done. Some companies have created new businesses based on access to large databases through the Web. Others are using Web technology to provide employees with integrated firm-wide views of information. Table 6-2 describes some of these applications of Web-enabled databases.

FIGURE 6-18   *The ThomasNet.com Web database interface.*

The ThomasNet.com Web site links to a database of more than 170 000 companies, 400 000 products, thousands of online catalogues, and millions of CAD drawings searchable by product. More organizations are using the Web to provide and interface to internal databases.

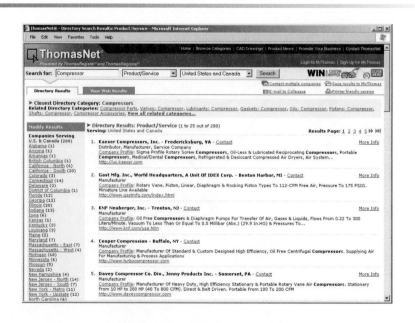

TABLE 6-2 *Examples of Web-Enabled Databases*

ORGANIZATION	USE OF WEB-ENABLED DATABASE
Domania.com	Home price database of 27 million past real estate sales.
Internet Movie Database	Web site linked to a massive database that includes summaries, cast information, and actor biographies for almost every film ever released.
iGo.com	Web site linked to a giant relational database housing information about batteries and peripherals for computers and other portable electronic devices. Visitors can immediately find online information about each electronic device and the batteries and parts it uses and can place orders for these parts over the Web.
Canadian Archaeological Association	The Canadian Archaeological Radiocarbon Database contains more than 30 000 records of archaeologically-related radiocarbon dates. This data is available to anyone—student, amateur archaeologist, or researcher—from the association's Web site.

Management Opportunities, Challenges, and Solutions

Effectively managing the organization's data resources requires much more than simply selecting a logical database model. The database is an organizational discipline, a method, not just a tool or technology. It requires organizational and conceptual change. Management commitment and understanding are essential.

Opportunities

Firms have become acutely aware of how much organizational performance can be improved by making better use of their data, as the examples in this chapter and other chapters of the text so clearly illustrate. This is why so many companies are investing in data mining and customer relationship management technology.

Management Challenges

It has been very difficult for organizations to manage their data effectively. A true database environment requires an organization to change the way it defines and uses data and typically represents a very large investment.

Organizational Obstacles to a Database Environment

Implementing a database requires widespread organizational change in the role of information (and information managers), the allocation of power at senior levels, the ownership and sharing of information, and patterns of organizational agreement, such as departmental boundaries. A database management system (DBMS) challenges the existing power arrangements in an organization and for that reason often generates political resistance. In a traditional file environment, each department constructed files and programs to fulfill its specific needs. Now, with a database, files and programs must be developed that take into account the whole organization's interest in data. Although the organization has spent the money on hardware and software for a database environment, it may not reap the benefits it should if it is unwilling to make the requisite organizational changes.

Cost/Benefit Considerations Designing a database to serve the enterprise can be a lengthy and costly process. In addition to the cost of DBMS software, related hardware, and data modelling, organizations should anticipate heavy expenditures for integrating, merging, and standardizing data from different systems and functional areas. Despite the clear advantages of the DBMS, the short-term costs of developing a DBMS often appear to be as great as the benefits. It may take time for the database to provide value.

Solution Guidelines

The critical elements for creating a database environment are (1) data administration, (2) data-planning and modelling methodology, (3) database technology and management, and (4) users. This environment is depicted in Figure 6-19.

Data Administration Database systems require that the organization recognize the strategic role of information and begin actively to manage and plan for information as a corporate resource. This means that the organization must develop a **data administration** function with the power to define information requirements for the entire company and with direct access to senior management. The chief information officer (CIO) becomes the primary advocate in the organization for database systems.

Data administration is responsible for the specific policies and procedures through which data can be managed as an organizational resource. These responsibilities include developing information policy, planning for data, overseeing logical database design and data dictionary development, and monitoring how information systems specialists and end-user groups use data.

The fundamental principle of data administration is that all data are the property of the organization as a whole. Data cannot belong exclusively to any one business area or organizational unit. All data should be available to any group that requires them to fulfill its mission. An organization needs to formulate an **information policy** that specifies its rules for sharing, disseminating, acquiring, standardizing, classifying, and inventorying information throughout the organization. Information policy lays out specific procedures and accountabilities, specifying which organizational units share information, where

FIGURE 6-19   *Key organizational elements in the database environment.*

For a database management system to flourish in any organization, data administration functions and data-planning and modelling methodologies must be coordinated with database technology and management. Resources must be devoted to train end users to use databases properly.

data administration

information policy

information can be distributed, and who is responsible for updating and maintaining the information. Although data administration is a very important organizational function, it has proved very challenging to implement.

Data-Planning and Modelling Methodology The organizational interests served by the DBMS are much broader than those in the traditional file environment; therefore, the organization requires enterprise-wide planning for data. Enterprise analysis, which addresses the information requirements of the entire organization (as opposed to the requirements of individual applications), is needed to develop databases. The purpose of enterprise analysis is to identify the key entities, attributes, and relationships that constitute the organization's data. These techniques are described in greater detail in Chapter 10.

Database Technology, Management, and Users Databases require new software and a new staff specially trained in DBMS techniques, as well as new data management structures. Most corporations develop a database design and management group within the corporate information systems division that is responsible for defining and organizing the structure and content of the database and maintaining the database. In close cooperation with users, the design group establishes the physical database, the logical relationships among elements, and the access rules and procedures. The functions it performs are called **database administration**.

A database serves a wider community of users than traditional systems. Relational systems with fourth-generation query languages permit employees who are not computer specialists to access large databases. In addition, users include trained computer specialists. To optimize access for nonspecialists, more resources must be devoted to training end users.

database administration

Summary

1. *Describe basic file organization concepts and the problems of managing data resources in a traditional file environment.*

A computer system organizes data in a hierarchy that starts with bits and bytes and progresses to fields, records, files, and databases. Traditional file management techniques make it difficult for organizations to keep track of all of the pieces of data they use in a systematic way and to organize these data so that they can be easily accessed. Different functional areas and groups were allowed to develop their own files independently. Over time, this traditional file management environment creates problems such as data redundancy and inconsistency, program-data dependence, inflexibility, poor security, and lack of data sharing and availability.

2. *Describe how a database management system organizes information, and compare the principal database models.*

A database management system (DBMS) consists of software that permits centralization of data and data management so that businesses have a single consistent source for all their data needs. A single database services multiple applications. A DBMS includes a data definition language, a data manipulation language, and a data

dictionary capability. The most important feature of the DBMS is its ability to separate the logical and physical views of data. The user works with a logical view of data. The DBMS retrieves information so that the user does not have to be concerned with its physical location.

The principal types of databases today are relational DBMS and object-oriented DBMS. Relational systems are very flexible for supporting ad hoc requests for information and for combining information from different sources. They support many-to-many relationships among entities. Relational DBMS are efficient for storing alphanumeric data that can be organized into structured fields and records, which are represented by attributes and tuples in two-dimensional tabular models. This flexibility was not possible with the older hierarchical and network database models. Object-oriented DBMS can store graphics and other types of data in addition to conventional text data to support multimedia applications. Organizations should use the DBMS that is best suited for their data model.

3. *Apply important database design principles.*

Designing a database requires both a logical design and a physical design. The logical design models the database from a business perspective. The organization's data model should reflect its key business processes and decision-making requirements. The process of creating small, stable, flexible, and adaptive data structures from complex groups of data when designing a relational database is termed *normalization*. Database design also considers whether a complete database or portions of the database can be distributed to more than one location to increase responsiveness and reduce vulnerability and costs. There are two major types of distributed databases: replicated databases and partitioned databases.

4. *Evaluate new database trends.*

Powerful tools are available to analyze the information in databases and to take advantage of information resources on the World Wide Web. Multidimensional data analysis, also known as online analytical processing (OLAP), can represent relationships among data as a multidimensional structure, which can be visualized as cubes of data and cubes within cubes of data, enabling more sophisticated data analysis. Data can be more conveniently analyzed across the enterprise by using a data warehouse, in which current and historical data are extracted from many different operational systems and consolidated for management decision making. Data mining analyzes large pools of data, including the con-

tents of data warehouses, to find patterns and rules that can be used to predict future behaviour and guide decision making. Hypermedia databases enable data to be stored in nodes linked together in any pattern the user establishes and are used for storing information at Web sites. Conventional databases can be linked to the Web to facilitate user access to an organization's internal data.

5. *Identify the challenges and key management decisions posed by data resource management.*

Developing a database environment requires much more than selecting database technology. It requires a formal information policy governing the maintenance, distribution, and use of information in the organization. The organization must also develop a data administration function and a data-planning methodology. Data planning may need to be performed to make sure that the organization's data model delivers information efficiently for its business processes and enhances organizational performance. There is political resistance in organizations to many key database concepts, especially the sharing of information that has been controlled exclusively by one organizational group. Creating a database environment is a long-term endeavour requiring large up-front investments and organizational change.

Key Terms

Attribute, 193
Conceptual schema, 196
Data administration, 214
Data cleansing, 206
Data definition language, 197
Data dictionary, 197
Data element, 197
Data inconsistency, 195
Data manipulation language, 197
Data mart, 207
Data mining, 208
Data quality audit, 206
Data redundancy, 194

Data warehouse, 207
Database, 193
Database (rigorous definition), 195
Database administration, 215
Database management system (DBMS), 196
Database server, 211
Distributed database, 204
Entity, 193
Entity-relationship diagram, 204
Field, 193
File, 193
Hierarchical DBMS, 200
Hypermedia database, 211

Information policy, 214
Key field, 193
Network DBMS, 201
Normalization, 203
Object-oriented DBMS, 202
Object-relational DBMS, 202
Online analytical processing (OLAP), 206
Program-data dependence, 195
Record, 193
Relational DBMS, 198
Structured query language (SQL), 197
Subschema, 197
Tuple, 200

Review Questions

1. *Why is file management important for overall system performance?*

2. *List and describe each of the components in the data hierarchy.*

3. *Define and explain the significance of entities, attributes, and key fields.*

4. *List and describe the problems of the traditional file environment.*

5. *Define a database and a database management system.*

6. *Name and briefly describe the three components of a DBMS.*

7. *What is the difference between a logical and a physical view of data?*

8. *List some benefits of a DBMS and the solutions it provides for the problems of a traditional file environment.*

9. *Describe the principal types of databases and the advantages and disadvantages of each.*

10. *What is normalization? How is it related to the features of a well-designed relational database?*

11. *What is a distributed database, and what are the two main ways of distributing data?*

12. *Why are data quality audits and data cleansing essential?*

13. Describe the capabilities of online analytical processing (OLAP) and data mining.

14. What is a data warehouse? How can it benefit organizations?

15. What is a hypermedia database? How does it differ from a traditional database? How is it used for the Web?

16. How can users access information from a company's internal databases through the Web?

17. What are the challenges of a database environment? What are the four key organizational elements for creating a database environment?

Discussion Questions

1. It has been said that you do not need database management software to create a database environment. Discuss this statement.

2. To what extent should end users be involved in the selection of a database management system and database design?

Application Software Exercise:
Database Exercise: Building a Relational Database for a Small Business

Sylvester's Bike Shop, located in Vancouver, British Columbia, sells road, mountain, hybrid, leisure, and children's bicycles. Currently, Sylvester's purchases bikes from three suppliers, but plans to add new suppliers in the near future. This rapidly growing business needs a database system to manage this information.

Initially, the database should house information about suppliers and products. The database will contain two tables: a supplier table and a product table. The reorder level refers to the number of items in inventory that triggers a decision to order more items to prevent a stockout. (In other words, if the number of units of a particular inventory falls below the reorder level, the item should be reordered.) The user should be able to perform several queries and produce several managerial reports based on the data contained in the two tables.

Using the information found in the tables on the Companion Website for Chapter 6, develop a simple relational database for Sylvester's. Once you have developed the database, perform the following activities.

1. Prepare a report that identifies the five most expensive bicycles. The report should list the bicycles in descending order from most expensive to least expensive, the quantity on hand for each, and the markup percentage for each.

2. Prepare a report that lists each supplier, its products, the quantities on hand, and associated reorder levels. The report should be sorted alphabetically by supplier. Within each supplier category, the products should be sorted alphabetically.

3. Prepare a report listing only the bicycles that are low in stock and need to be reordered. The report should provide supplier information for the items identified.

4. Write a brief description of how the database could be enhanced to further improve management of the business. What tables or fields should be added? What additional reports would be useful?

Electronic Commerce Project: Searching Online Databases

The Internet is a valuable source of databases where users can search for services and products in areas or countries that are far from their own locations. Your company is located in Saskatoon, Saskatchewan, and manufactures office furniture of various types. You have recently acquired several new customers in Australia, and a study you commissioned indicates that with a presence there, you could greatly increase your sales. Moreover, your study indicates that you could do even better if you actually manufactured many of your products locally (in Australia). First, you need to set up an office in Melbourne to establish a presence, and then you need to begin importing from Canada. You then can plan to start producing locally.

You will soon be travelling to the area to make plans to actually set up an office, and you want to meet with organizations that can help you with your operation. You will need to engage people or organizations that offer many services necessary for you to open your office, including lawyers, accountants, import-export experts, telecommunications equipment and support, and even trainers who can help you to prepare your future employees to work for you. List the companies you would contact to interview on your trip to determine if they can help you with these and any other functions you think vital to establishing your office. Start by searching for Canadian government advice on doing business in Australia; you may wish to start with

Strategis (**strategis.ic.gc.ca/engdoc/main.html**). Then try the following online databases to locate companies that you would like to meet with during your coming trip: Australian Business Register (**abr.business.gov.au**), Australia Trade Now (**australiatradenow.com**), and the Nationwide Business Directory of Australia (**www.nationwide.com.au**). If neces-sary, you should also try search engines such as Yahoo! (**www.yahoo.ca**) and Google (**www.google.ca**).

Rate the databases you used for accuracy of name, completeness, ease of use, and general helpfulness. What does this exercise tell you about database design?

Group Project: Creating Company-Wide Data Standards

An industrial supply company wants to create a data ware-house from which management can obtain a single corporate-wide view of critical sales information to identify best-selling products in specific geographic areas, key customers, and sales trends. The company's sales and product information are stored in two different systems: a divisional sales system run-ning on a UNIX server and a corporate sales system running on an IBM mainframe. Management would like to create a single standard format that consolidates data from both sys-tems in the data warehouse. The following format has been proposed.

Product_ID	Product_Description	Cost_Per_Unit	Units_Sold	Sales_Region	Division	Customer_ID

Following are sample reports from the two systems that would supply the data for the data warehouse.

MECHANICAL PARTS DIVISION SALES SYSTEM

Prod._No.	Product_Description	Cost_Per_Unit	Units_Sold	Sales_Region	Customer_ID
60231	4″ steel bearing	5.28	900 245	Eastern	Anderson
85773	SS assembly unit	12.45	992 111	Western	Kelly Industries

CORPORATE SALES SYSTEM

Product_ID	Product_Description	Unit_Cost	Units_Sold	Sales_Territory	Division
60231	Bearing, 4″	5.28	900 245	Prairies	Parts
85773	SS assembly unit	12.02	992 111	Maritimes	Parts

1. What business problems are created by not having these data in a single standard format?

2. How easy would it be to create a database with a single standard format that could store the data from both systems? Identify the problems that would have to be addressed.

3. Should the problems be solved by database specialists or general business managers? Who should have the authority to finalize a single company-wide format for this information in the data warehouse? Explain your position.

4. If possible, use electronic presentation software to present your findings to the class.

Web Sites of Interest

There are many interesting Web sites to enhance your learning about database software. You can search the Web yourself or try the following sites to add to what you have already learned.

Oracle Corporation **www.oracle.ca**
The Canadian arm of one of the world's major database/ERP companies.

Microsoft Access **www.microsoft.com/office/access**
Web site of MS Access, the most popular desktop database software.

IBM's DB2 **http://www-3.ibm.com/software/data**
Web site of DB2, one of the most popular mainframe database applications.

CASE STUDY:
Database Woes Plagues Homeland Security and Law Enforcement In Canada and the U.S.

The World Trade Center and Pentagon terrorist attacks on September 11, 2001, have focused attention worldwide, and particularly in North America, on the need for accurate information about terrorist activities to prevent similar catastrophes in the future. Much of the information necessary to combat future terrorist attacks, as well as to fight domestic crime, is stored in databases of literally thousands of federal, state, and local organizations. Bringing together these data to make them useful for fighting terrorism and crime has proven to be an immense task. We will begin our discussion by looking at what the U.S. has done to integrate these databases and end by looking at what Canada has done and how much cooperation it takes between Canada and the U.S. to be successful in this endeavour.

To begin with, the new U.S. Department of Homeland Security (DHS) comprises 22 agencies, each with its own computer systems and hardware. One major reason for creating this new department was to bring together the data stored in agency systems to collect, analyze, and distribute information about suspected terrorist activities. But the task is actually much larger than that because these 22 agencies represent only a few of the federal government's 146 agencies with law enforcement responsibilities.

Each of these agencies in turn has numerous databases, most of which are incompatible and technically archaic. They have different computing platforms, data names, data definitions, data sizes, and data files. They do not share their data with state and local agencies, which are vital for tracking potential terrorists and their activities. Ben Gianni, the vice president for homeland security of Computer Sciences Corporation, estimates that a project to connect the data from all of these agencies would take at least five years and cost a minimum of $15 billion.

When the FBI tried to create the huge Integrated Automated Fingerprint Identification System (IAFIS) in the late 1990s, for example, it had to integrate two already-existing but dissimilar systems, the FBI's IAFIS and the Immigration and Naturalization Service's Automated Biometric Identification (IDENT) System. While the IAFIS stored 10 rolled prints for each person, IDENT stored only two flat prints. For an interim solution, the FBI had to develop custom software to exchange fingerprinting data from the two systems. Two fingerprints from IAFIS were added to IDENT, while workstations for using 10 rolled prints were also being designed. Second a study had to be undertaken to determine how to capture the 10 prints more rapidly. Ultimately, the FBI developed a fast transaction type that retrieves an individual's criminal history without displaying the fingerprints. Fingerprint matching can be done later if needed.

The same data in different systems, even within the same organization, usually have different names, codes, and formats. So, for example, over the years, the FBI had created five critical but independent investigative application systems,

each storing its data differently. These databases are considered the backbone of the FBI systems. The FBI was not made part of the DHS, remaining part of the Department of Justice (DOJ), but it needs to collect and analyze accurate and timely criminal information to deal with terrorism and criminal activity.

The FBI is buried under an immense amount of paperwork and continues to rely on paper as its chief information management tool. Its computer systems are antiquated. For example, the FBI has five investigative application systems, but these systems could be viewed only using very old-fashioned green IBM 3270 terminals. Many agents could not access the Internet from their desks because of security concerns. Moreover, although the agents need to search these data, the technology allowed only single-word searches. So, for example, after the terrorist attacks of September 11, agents could search on such words as flight or school but could not search for phrases such as *flight school*. In fact, the FBI has no enterprise-wide architecture but rather has separate databases for more than 50 applications, which are written in various languages and run on disparate systems.

Agents required security clearances to access much of the data, but security clearance often took up to eight months to obtain. Because of its secretive culture, the FBI has had a mind-set to keep information to itself, a problem highlighted by and after September 11. In the past, when the FBI had to store its own information, it often overlooked key areas. For example, after September 11, the FBI needed data on foreign students, including obvious information such as their current schools and locations, but it had not collected it. So, it turned to the INS, but this agency did not even have a computer system to collect such data. Ultimately, the FBI had to contact all U.S. colleges and universities to ask them for the required information.

In November 2000, Congress allocated $472 million to update the FBI's systems. The FBI has already installed 21 000 desktop computers, more than 3000 printers, and nearly 1500 scanners. In addition, it has linked 622 FBI offices with high-speed data connections. Perhaps the single most important software project involves creating the Virtual Case File (VCF) system linking 31 FBI databases through a single Web portal. "We are now focused on implementing a data warehousing capability that can bring together our information into databases that can be accessed by agents throughout the world," observes FBI director Robert Mueller. FBI field agents can access the VCF system using a standard Web browser to search the entire FBI data warehouse. Instead of faxing or mailing pertinent information about a suspected terrorist from one office to another, FBI agents have electronic access to the files, which could also be shared with the Central Intelligence Agency (CIA), the National Security Agency, and local police departments. A system is being built to automate and scan all paper-based information into a relational database that can be mined.

In May 2002, the FBI's investigative guidelines were updated to allow agents to surf the Web and to use commercial data services and email. (Formerly, agents could not receive emails directly; the email messages were received elsewhere and were printed out and then handed to the agents, creating serious delays.)

The FBI is also working to communicate more openly with state and local law enforcement agencies. It is opening its National Law Enforcement Online (LEO) system to other law enforcement agencies to distribute information on terrorism. The FBI is also improving its National Crime Information Center (NCIC), its repository of 17 criminal records databases that contains mug shots and thumbprints.

The U.S. Immigration and Naturalization Service (INS) is another federal organization with serious database problems. The INS estimates that there are about 500 million people entering the United States each year, an immense volume that requires a huge system to track. However, aside from its lack of information on foreign students, after September 11, the INS could not even locate 45 percent of the aliens the FBI wanted to question about terrorism, according to a General Accounting Office (GAO) assessment report of November 2002. The report said the INS had even lost track of 4334 aliens from countries where al-Qaeda is known to operate.

The primary reason for the problems is the failure of the INS to maintain a database system that is both integrated and current. It has more than 16 separate database systems to capture data on aliens, including a Non-Immigrant Information System, an Asylum Prescreening System, a Student Exchange Visitor Information System, an Arrival Departure Information System, a Student and Schools System, a Deportable Alien Control System, and a Refugees, Asylum, and Parole System. According to the GAO report, "INS does not update all databases that contain alien address information [recorded when they entered the country] and does not have the ability to update address information in NIIS [the Non-Immigrant Information System]." Its databases do not even distinguish between aliens with the same names. Late in 2002, the INS formed a task force to find ways to centralize and improve its alien address systems.

The United States still lacks an accurate, up-to-date watch list of suspected terrorists and their supporters that could be the most essential tool for combating international terrorism. In September 2003, the White House, Central Intelligence Agency, FBI, and Department of Homeland Security agreed to set up a Terrorist Screening Center (TSC) as an interagency body to create, maintain, and control a master terrorist database. The TSC would be run by the FBI using the State Department's watch list, known as TIPOFF, as the backbone of a new database that would integrate all other existing databases on terrorism into a new state-of-the-art system.

To create the master watch list, TSC staff members would cleanse the data, weeding out duplications, obsolete records, and people who in the past had been wrongfully identified as terrorists or who shared the same last name as suspected terrorists. Data on fingerprints, distinguishing scars, birthmarks, credit card accounts, and other details would be employed to help distinguish harmless namesakes from serious suspects.

The TSC opened in Crystal City, Virginia, on December 1, 2003. The FBI Counterintelligence Division had announced to law enforcement agencies across the United States that the TSC was open for business as the single point of contact for assistance in identifying people with possible terrorist connections. The FBI cautioned, however, that TSC's initial capabilities were "limited."

On December 22, 2003, the FBI attaché to the American embassy in Paris informed French police that al-Qaeda planned to hijack an Air France jet and crash it somewhere in the United States. The French government grounded three flights and detained six passengers whose names matched the FBI watch list. All were mistaken identities, including a child whose name matched that of a Tunisian terrorist leader. The TSC was never consulted when U.S. intelligence picked up the information about the potential Air France hijacking, including the names of the suspected terrorists.

An October 1, 2004 report by the inspector general for the Department of Homeland Security (DHS), pointed out that the U.S. government had failed to consolidate all of its terrorist watch lists as of that date—three years after the September 11 attacks, partly because the DHS did not play a sufficiently strong leadership role in the project. The report further noted that although TSC had started integrating the various watch lists, it had trouble hiring enough analysts with high security clearances. The integrated terrorist database that was envisioned is still months and possibly years away.

What about the Canadian response, not only to prevent terrorism on our soil, but also to assist our neighbour in combating terrorism?

The Canada Customs and Revenue Agency is developing a massive surveillance database that officials will maintain on passengers to Canada. Quickly passed through Parliament, Bill S-23 established a database to hold detailed personal information on every air traveller arriving in Canada, foreigners and citizens alike.

This database is called the Advance Passenger Information/ Passenger Name Record, nicknamed the "Big Brother" database by the federal Privacy Commissioner. The federal privacy commissioner, George Radwanski, says the database will include "every destination you travel to, who you travel with, how you pay for your ticket, how long you stay, how many pieces of baggage you check each time, even your dietary preferences." This data will be kept for six years and could be used for "virtually anything the government deems appropriate—routine income tax audit or investigation purposes, data matches with other departments, criminal investigation 'fishing expeditions.'" Internal government documents reveal plans to expand its use to bus and rail travel as well. The latest version of the Public Safety Act also would permit the police to screen airline passenger lists, not only for terrorists, but for anyone wanted for any crime punishable by five years in jail or more.

The Auditor General of Canada has released a blistering report on how well Canada is progressing in terms of developing appropriate databases for our own homeland security and then integrating our databases with those of the U.S. According to a news release from her office, the Auditor General found:

- the government did not have a management framework that would guide investment, management, and development decisions and allow it to direct complementary actions in separate agencies or to make choices between conflicting priorities.

- the government as a whole failed to achieve improvements in the ability of security information systems to communicate with each other. Consequently, needed improvements will be delayed by several years. Moreover, even as the government was launching programs that would create new needs for fingerprint identification, projects that would have helped it to deal with the increased demand were not included in the initiative.

- deficiencies in the way intelligence is managed across the government. A lack of coordination has led to gaps in intelligence coverage as well as duplication. The government as a whole did not adequately assess intelligence lessons learned from critical incidents such as September 11 or develop and follow up on improvement programs. Individual agencies have created new coordinating mechanisms, but some departments are still not participating in them.

- gaps and inconsistencies in the watch lists used to screen visa applicants, refugee claimants, and travellers seeking to enter Canada. There is no overall quality control of this vital function, which is spread over several departments and agencies. No one monitors delays in the entry or the quality of the data on watch lists.

- security clearances are issued without checking applicants for criminal association. Transport Canada is not provided with all the information available to police and therefore has issued restricted area clearances to many individuals whose reliability must be questioned. Unless air transportation workers with access to aircraft are reliable, spending on passenger and cargo security will be of reduced value.

Unfortunately, this is much the same story as the U.S. experience with developing and integrating these immense databases to aid in the fight against terrorism. Organizational boundaries and a lack of willingness to share information are hindering these efforts worldwide. Privacy issues, different between countries, continents, and cultures, also hinder these efforts. And there are myriad ethical issues involved in this effort—not only privacy but profiling and security of the data.

What, if any, obligations does Canada have to its allies around the world, not just in the U.S., to share this information? It is difficult for any country to integrate all of its law enforcement, transportation, shipping, and foreign intelligence databases. Integrating and sharing that information

gleaned from myriad databases with another country is a logistical nightmare. So in fact the main difficulty in integrating data from so many varied sources may not be the ethical issues, but the technical ones as well as the overwhelming costs involved.

Sources: John Mintz, "DHS Blamed for Failure to Combine Watch Lists," *The Washington Post*, October 2, 2004; Robert Black, Gary Fields, and Jo Wrighton, "U.S. 'Terror' List Still Lacking," *Wall Street Journal*, January 2, 2004; Ted Bridis, "Review: FBI Computer Upgrades Inadequate," Associated Press, May 10, 2004; Christopher Whitcomb, "The Needle in the Database," *New York Times*, May 14, 2004; Larry Dignan, "A Fort Knox for Data," *Baseline*, January 16, 2004; Alex Salkever, "Spooks, Sleuths, and Data Sharing," *Business Week*, May 25, 2004; Larry Barrett, "FBI: Under the Gun," *Baseline*, September 10, 2003; Dan Verton, "FBI Has Made Major Progress, Former IT Chief Says," *Computerworld*, April 21, 2003, "FBI Begins Knowledge Management Face-Lift," *Computerworld*, April 21, 2003, and "Database Woes Thwart Counterterrorism Work," *Computerworld*, December 2, 2002; Judith Lamont, "Law Enforcement Gains Ground in Data Integration and Analysis," *KMWorld*, March 2003; Jennifer A. Lee, "Threats and Responses: Law Enforcement; State Department Link Will Open Visa Database to Police Officers," *New York Times*, January 31, 2003; Debbie Gage, "FBI Bureaucracy Hobbies Tech Adoption," *Baseline*, September 11, 2002; Debbie Gage and John McCormick, "The Disconnected Cop," *Baseline*, September 10, 2002; "NYPD Base Case," *Baseline*, September 10, 2002; Sean Gallagher, "Gotcha! Extending Existing Systems," *Baseline*, September 10, 2002; Doug Brown, "How Homeland Security Budgets Technology," *Baseline*, September 9, 2002; Andrew Coyne, "Hamas is OK, It's You We're Not Sure Of," *The National Post*, November 15, 2002, available **www.privcom.gc.ca/media/ np_021115_e.asp**, accessed April 17, 2005; "National Security in Canada – The 2001 Anti-Terrorism Initiative," Office of the Auditor General, available **www.oag-bvg.gc.ca/domino/reports.nsf/ html/20040303ce.html**, accessed April 17, 2005

CASE STUDY QUESTIONS

1. Briefly summarize the problems and major issues in this case.

2. Describe the major data management problems involved in bringing together and integrating the data needed to combat terrorism, in particular integrating the databases between allied countries.

3. What management, organization, and technology issues need to be addressed to solve these problems?

4. Suppose you are a consultant to the Canadian federal government. Based on what you have read in this chapter, suggest and describe several approaches you might recommend for solving this problem.

5. Describe the ethical and legal challenges involved in creating, maintaining, integrating, and sharing these databases, not only within a single country, but across national borders. Are there any solutions to these challenges?

Chapter 7

Telecommunications, Networks, and the Internet

OBJECTIVES

After reading this chapter, you will be able to:

1. Describe the features of contemporary corporate network infrastructure and key networking technologies.

2. Evaluate alternative transmission media, types of networks, and network services.

3. Assess the role of the Internet and the World Wide Web in the firm's information technology infrastructure.

4. Identify and describe the most important tools for communication and e-business.

5. Identify and describe the challenges posed by networking and the Internet, and propose management solutions.

- Develop network-based business processes
- Develop technology strategy and standards

- Revise teaching methods
- Develop new collaboration processes among teachers, students, and parents

- Develop Web site
- Install IP telephony
- Install multiservice network

Business Challenges
- Declining revenue
- Increasing demand for services

Management

Organization

Technology

Information System
- Consolidate voice and data communication
- Provide online learning

Business Solutions
- Increase service
- Reduce cost

Opening Case: Okanagan-Skaha School District Does More with Less Using Networking and the Internet

The Okanagan-Skaha School District in Penticton, British Columbia, is in an area blessed with "beaches, peaches, and wine." It is also an area where tax revenues and school budgets have been declining for several years while demand for information access and support services continues to grow. School administrators realized that the district's 19 schools, serving more than 8000 students, had to do more with less. How could this be done? The answer: Use networking and the Internet to cut operational costs while expanding programs to schools and the community.

The school district had been using an expensive public telephone network and an aging data network that had cobbled together many different hardware and operating system platforms. Working with Cisco Systems and Boardwalk Communications, the school district standardized desktop hardware and operating system software and replaced its outdated data and telephone networks with a multiservice network that can run voice, data, and video applications using the Internet Protocol (IP). The cities of Penticton and Summerfield built a private municipal fibre-optic backbone to support the district's new network.

The network supports Voice over IP (VoIP) telephones that enable teachers to send computerized phone messages to parents and students. This technology converts each teacher's classroom computer into a telephone that can transmit voice data in the form of packets over a data network based on the Internet Protocol. Using just a handset and a microphone, teachers can make calls from their computers without having to make a special trip to the administration office. This IP telephony system reduced the number of phone lines needed by the district from 150 to 25 and provided a uniform system for voice mail and systems administration, saving the district about $74 000 per year.

Teachers have developed Web sites for collaborating with students and parents. For example, physics instructor Dan Bergstrom uses software to demonstrate difficult scientific concepts so that students can make observations, take measurements, and manipulate the data to understand what is actually going on. Lecture notes are linked to lab notes, homework questions, and test questions. Students and teachers can access the district's network and all of its applications from wherever they are, using a Web browser program.

The new learning environment helps students learn responsibility and time management. Each class has a Web site with its course schedule, rules and expectations, and dates for tests and assignments.

Sources: Howard Baldwin, "Thinking Big," *Cisco IQ Magazine*, First Quarter 2004; "Okanagan-Skaha School District and Cisco Solutions Empower Teachers, Students and Parents," **www.cisco.com**, accessed April 27, 2004.

The Okanagan-Skaha School District was hampered by outdated networking technology, which prevented it from operating efficiently. By installing a multiservice network based on Internet technology that could handle voice, data, and video, the district realized multiple benefits. The network is simpler to administer, reduced communication costs, and provided a platform for multimedia Web sites where students could learn more effectively.

As more and more companies rely on telecommunications and the Internet to run their businesses, it is important to understand exactly how this technology can improve business performance and provide value. This chapter introduces the most important networking concepts and technologies used in business. We identify the key decisions and challenges you will face as a manager in implementing and using networking and the Internet.

7.1 Telecommunications and Networking in Today's Business World

We are in the midst of a networking and communications revolution driven by new Internet-based technologies, new business models, and processes that leverage the new technologies. This networking revolution shows no sign of abating. Until about 1990, all business communication was accomplished primarily through the postal system or telephone system as voice or fax traffic. Today a great deal of this communication takes place using computers and email, the Internet, cellular telephones, and mobile computers connected to wireless networks.

In 2004 an estimated 76 percent of private sector organizations and 99.89 percent of public sector organizations used email (Statistics Canada, 2005). Email is the number one use of the Internet by households in Canada. Figure 7-1 shows that Canadian companies in the various communications services industries generated $38 billion in revenues in 2003. Worldwide, telecommunications

FIGURE 7-1 *Industry Canada estimates of revenues generated in the Canadian communications industry from 1998–2003.*

Communications Service Industries Key Players

Wireless Providers

Bell & Partners*   Paging
TELUS Mobility   Companies
Rogers Wireless   e.g. PageNet
Microcell   Canada
Telecommunications

Wireless Carriers

Incumbents
Major Telephone Companies:
  Bell Canada
  TELUS
  Aliant
  MTS
  SaskTel

Independent Telephone
Companies:
  e.g. Thunder Bay Telephone

Overseas Carrier:
  e.g. Teleglobe

Competitors
e.g. Allstream Inc. (formerly
  AT&T Canada)
Call-Net (Sprint Canada)
FCI Broadband (formerly
  Futureway Communications)

Broadcast Distribution

Cable Providers
  Rogers Communications
  Shaw Communications
  Cogeco Cable
  Vidéotron Ltée
  Persona Cable
  EastLink Communications

Direct-to-Home (DTH)
  e.g. Bell Expressvu, StarChoice

Multi-point Distribution Systems
  e.g. Look Communications

$8.2 Billion

$23.1 Billion

2003 Revenues $38.0 Billion

$5.4 Billion

$1.3 Billion

Resellers, Satellite & Other Telecommunications

Resellers
  e.g. Primus Telecommunications

Satellite
  e.g. Telesat Canada, Globalstar,
  Mobile Satellite Ventures

*Bell & Partners includes Bell Mobility, Aliant Mobility, SaskTel Mobility and MTS Mobility.

Canadian companies in the various communications services industries generated $38 billion in revenues in 2003.

Source: Statistics Canada, *Survey of Telecommunications Service Providers* (April 2004) and CRTC, *Broadcast Distribution Statistical and Financial Summaries* (April 2004). Reproduced with the permission of the Minister of Public Works and Government Services, 2006.

equipment and services spending hit $2.2 trillion in 2004 and will expand to more than $3 trillion by 2007. There are more than 50 million communications services subscribers in Canada, counting both businesses and households (see Figure 7-2).

Today, networking and the Internet are now nearly synonymous with doing business. To this extent, nearly all business has become "e-business" insofar as the business is enabled by or based on digital networks.

The Business Telecommunications Environment

Understanding the telecommunications environment for businesses turns out to be a very complicated task (Figure 7-3). The purpose of business telecommunications is to make it possible for employees, customers, and suppliers to communicate whenever necessary to accomplish their work. A telecommunications environment provides *connectivity on demand* by providing communication channels for text, voice, and video images. In practice this is not so simple. Figure 7-3 illustrates the complexity of providing text, voice, and video connectivity to business firms.

The network infrastructure for a large corporation consists of many different kinds of networks for both data and voice communication. At the centre of the corporate networking infrastructure is a collection of local area networks (LANs) linked to other local

FIGURE 7-2   *Industry Canada compilation of the number of subscribers to communications services from 1998–2003.*

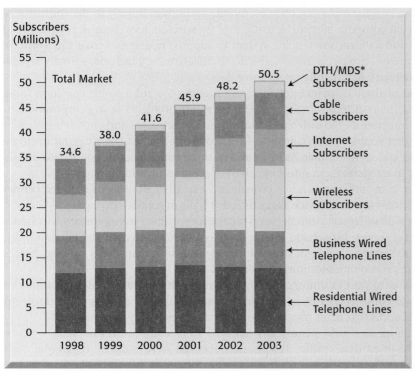

*Direct-to-Home (DTH) and Multipoint Distribution Systems (MDS).

There are more than 50 million communications services subscribers in Canada, counting both businesses and households.

Source: Industry Canada compilations based on Statistics Canada, *Survey of Telecommunications Service Providers* and CRTC, *Broadcast Distribution Statistical and Financial Summaries* (April 2004). Reproduced with the permission of the Minister of Public Works and Government Services, 2006.

FIGURE 7-3   *Corporate network infrastructure.*

Today's corporate network infrastructure is a collection of many different networks from the public switched telephone network; to the Internet; to corporate local area networks linking workgroups, departments, or office floors.

area networks and to firm-wide corporate networks. A series of servers supports a corporate Web site, a corporate intranet, and perhaps an extranet. Some of these servers link to other large computers supporting back-end systems. The infrastructure also supports a mobile sales force using cell phones; mobile employees linking to the company Web site or internal company networks using mobile wireless local area networks (Wi-Fi networks); and a videoconferencing system to support managers across the world. In addition to these computer networks, the firm's infrastructure includes a totally separate telephone network that handles most voice data.

Most of these disparate networks are moving toward a single common foundation based on Internet technologies. One of the major problems facing corporations today is how to integrate all the different communication networks and channels into a coherent system that enables information to flow from one part of the corporation to another, from one system to another. As more and more communication systems become digital, it is easier to integrate them into a coherent telecommunications system.

Today many different vendors provide some or all of a business's required **connectivity**. However, very few can provide all the different types of connectivity needed—text, video and voice. A wide variety of technologies is required, everything from ordinary telephone service to Internet service, broadband Internet service, wireless Internet, and wireless cell phones. One of the largest challenges you will face as a business manager is making choices about your firm's telecommunications environment.

One way to start examining and understanding a firm's telecommunications environment is to consider that there are two fundamentally different types of telecommunications networks that firms use: telephone networks and computer networks.

Telephone networks historically handled voice communication, and computer networks handled data traffic. Telephone networks were built by telephone companies throughout the twentieth century using voice transmission technologies (hardware and software), and these companies almost always operated as regulated monopolies throughout the world. This situation changed beginning in the mid-1980s. Telephone networks today offer much more than voice service, including standard and high-speed Internet, wireless telephone, and even video on demand services similar to residential cable systems.

Computer networks were originally built by computer companies seeking to transmit data between distributed workstations. Today these networks have largely been replaced by the Internet and local area networks in offices and buildings, which provide mostly data connectivity but which have expanded to include Internet telephony and limited video services.

These historically different telecommunications networks are slowly merging into a single digital network using shared Internet-based standards and equipment. Business managers like you will need to navigate this very complex environment and make the right decisions and investments and choose the right vendors. This chapter can help clarify your thinking and improve your decision making.

Networking and Communications Trends

The telecommunications revolution is enabled by new digital technologies, facilitated by market-oriented regulatory policies worldwide, and financed by global capital investment exceeding $2.2 trillion in worldwide expenditures in 2004. There are seven major trends in telecommunications that you should know:

- Rapid technological innovation has resulted in a proliferation of new hardware devices and new alternatives for business communications, from cell phones with Internet access to Wi-Fi wireless local area networks (described in the following chapter).

- Continuing telecommunications deregulation has encouraged competition, lowered prices in long-distance telephone service, and created many alternatives for local phone service such as wireless, cable, and Internet telephones.

- Distinctions between telephone, cable television, Internet, and satellite telecommunication providers have blurred as each type of network supplier seeks to provide video, voice, and data connectivity in a single network. For instance, telephone companies are

connectivity

moving into video delivery and cable channel programming using their digital subscriber lines into the house.

• Growing dominance of Internet technologies in voice, video, and data communications.

• Rapid growth in "last-mile" high-speed broadband connections to homes and businesses. Today, more than half of Canadian Internet users have broadband access provided by telephone and cable TV companies. In Korea, more than 90 percent of the Internet population has broadband access (Vara 2004).

• Rapid growth in wireless telephone, wireless computer networks, and mobile Internet devices.

• Growing scope of communication-intense services and products, such as Internet telephony and cell phone photography.

Deregulation of the Telecommunications Industry This revolution in telecommunications technology and services was facilitated by a regulatory environment that sought to break up old monopolies, encourage new market entrants, and reduce barriers to competition. The U.S. led the movement toward deregulation.

In the U.S. the Telecommunications Act of 1996 unleashed even more competition than the divestiture of the American Telephone and Telegraph (AT&T) Company into a long distance company and seven independent regional telephone companies (Regional Bell Operating companies, known as RBOCs). The Telecommunications Act of 1996 permitted long-distance companies to offer local service and required RBOCs to lease local last-mile lines to competitors at a deeply discounted rate. The act also allowed RBOCs to enter the long-distance market. In Canada, at first, most telephone companies were owned by provincial governments; today most local service is provided by Crown corporations while long distance service is offered by a large number of vendors, including the Crown corporations offering local service.

The combined impact of technological change and deregulation created a much more complex, diverse, and competitive telecommunications environment. Table 7-1 illustrates the complexity of today's telecommunications environment and the options available to business firms and individuals as a result of deregulation and new technologies. New entrants have poured into local communications markets—from wireless cell phones and networks for wireless Internet access to long-distance carriers, Voice Over Internet Protocol (VoIP) Internet telephone service providers, and cable companies.

TABLE 7-1   *Telephone Industry Firms Services Provided*

LONG DISTANCE CARRIERS	
Primus	Local, long distance, Internet telephone, data backup, 800 service, and Web services
CABLE TELEPHONE PROVIDERS	
Bell Canada	Long distance, wireless, high-speed Internet access, Internet telephone, high-speed data networks, dedicated Web hosting
Shaw Communications	Cable TV, digital cable TV, high-speed Internet access, Internet telephone
PURE WIRELESS PROVIDERS	
Rogers Communications	Wireless voice service, text messaging, picture and video messaging, email, mobile Web access, downloadable games, wireless Internet access
Telus	Wireless voice service, text messaging, picture and video messaging, email, mobile Web access, downloadable games, wireless Internet access, Web hosting
INTERNET TELEPHONY (VoIP) PROVIDERS	
Vonage (Private)	Internet telephone voice and fax services

Prior to all of these new technologies, telecommunications decisions were comparatively simple. There were few choices for telephone service, and for data communications, managers chose IBM, Digital Equipment (now a part of Hewlett-Packard), or another networking/computer firm. Now managers must make decisions that involve comparing many competitors and many different technologies, all of which promise to provide effortless connectivity.

The Business Value of Telecommunications and Networking

The reason behind the explosion in email, instant messages, wireless computing, wireless Internet, and cell phones is very clear: businesses and managers derive extraordinary business value from participating in communications networks. According to Metcalfe's Law, which we mentioned in Chapter 5, the more people participating in a network, the greater its value.

Robert Metcalfe was the inventor of Ethernet, the most widely installed local area network technology. Metcalfe argued that networks in general—and by inference, the Internet specifically—would grow exponentially because the value of the network to individuals grows exponentially as the network adds members (see Figure 7-4). In a simple two-person (two-node) network, each person can talk to one other, and there are two communication paths (Person A→Person B and Person B→Person A). With three nodes, there are six communication links (ab, ba, ac, ca, bc, and cb). Each communication link can be thought of as adding value. In the case of Internet business use, millions of businesspeople are available nearly instantly online, and the value of participating in high-speed digital networks for every participant has grown exponentially as the cost of joining the Internet has plummeted.

Other business value impacts of the telecommunications revolution are as follows:

- Declining transaction costs. It becomes less and less expensive to purchase, sell, and bargain in both digital and traditional markets as networking becomes less expensive and more powerful.

- Declining agency costs. The costs of managing falls as managers are able to monitor the performance of employees and markets remotely over networks.

- Increased agility. Managers and firms can respond more rapidly to changing business environment conditions.

FIGURE 7-4   *Metcalfe's Law.*

According to Metcalfe's Law, the value of participating in a network grows exponentially as the network adds more members.

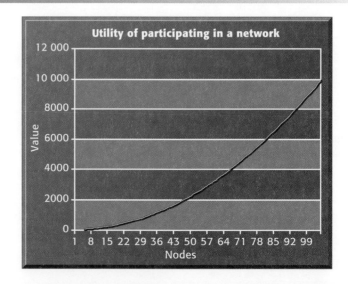

- Higher quality management decisions. Managers are more likely to make the right decisions based on correct and timely information.

- Declining geographic barriers. Coffee growers in Central America now use the Internet to obtain the best prices from large wholesale buyers in Canada, eliminating local middlemen and brokers.

- Declining temporal barriers. Some goods such as software can be produced around the clock, seven days a week. For instance, software production workers in India come to work in the morning to work on software projects handed off by Canadian software workers who have just finished their day.

7.2 Contemporary Networking Infrastructure

Now that we have sketched the outlines of the broad business telecommunications environment, we will examine more closely computer networks and networking technologies.

Networks and Corporate Infrastructure

In its simplest form, a network consists of two or more connected computers. Figure 7-5 illustrates the major hardware, software, and transmission components used in a simple network: computers, network interfaces, a connection medium, network operating system software, and either a hub or a switch. Each computer on the network contains a **network interface card** (**NIC**). Most personal computers today have this card built into the motherboard. The connection medium for linking network components can be a telephone wire, coaxial cable, or radio signal in the case of cell phone and wireless local area networks (WLANs and Wi-Fi networks).

FIGURE 7-5   *Components of a simple network.*

Illustrated here is a very simple network, consisting of computers, network operating system software, cable (wiring) to connect the devices, network interface cards, switches, and a router. In this illustration, the network operating system (NOS) resides on a dedicated server.

network interface card (NIC)

The **network operating system (NOS)** routes and manages communications on the network and coordinates network resources. It can reside on every computer in the network, or it can reside primarily on a dedicated server for all the applications on the network. Microsoft Windows Server 2003, along with the server versions of Windows 2000, Linux, and Novell NetWare, is the most widely used network operating system.

Most networks also contain a switch or a hub acting as a connection point between the computers. **Hubs** are very simple devices that connect network components, sending a packet of data to all other connected devices. A **switch** has more intelligence than a hub and can filter and forward data to a specified destination. Switches are used within individual networks. To communicate with another network, the network would use a device called a router. A **router** is a special communications processor used to route packets of data through different networks, ensuring that the message sent gets to the correct address.

Key Digital Networking Technologies

Contemporary digital networks and the Internet are based on three key technologies: client/server computing, the use of packet switching, and the development of widely used communications standards (the most important of which is Transmission Control Protocol/Internet Protocol [TCP/IP]) for linking disparate networks and computers.

Client/Server Computing
In Chapter 5, we introduced client/server computing in which client computers are connected in a network with one or more server computers. Client/server computing is a distributed computing model in which some of the processing power is located within small, inexpensive client computers under user control and resides literally on desktops, laptops, or in handheld devices. This is known as **distributed processing**. These powerful clients are linked to one another through a network that is controlled by a network server computer. The server sets the rules of communication for the network and provides every client with an address so it can be found by others on the network.

Client/server computing has largely replaced centralized mainframe computing in which most of the processing takes place on a central large mainframe computer. Client/server computing has extended computing to departments, workgroups, factory floors, and other parts of the business that could not be served by a centralized architecture. The Internet is the largest implementation of client/server computing.

Packet Switching
Packet switching is a method of slicing digital messages into parcels called packets, sending the packets along different communication paths as the paths become available, and then reassembling the packets once they arrive at their destinations (see Figure 7-6). Prior to the development of packet switching, computer networks used leased, dedicated telephone circuits to communicate with other computers in remote locations. In circuit-switched networks, such as the telephone system, a complete point-to-point circuit is assembled, and then communication can proceed. These dedicated circuit-switching techniques were expensive and wasted available communications capacity—the circuit was maintained regardless of whether any data were being sent.

Packet switching makes much more efficient use of the communications capacity of a network. In packet-switched networks, messages are first broken down into small fixed bundles of data called packets. There are many different packet sizes, depending on the communications standard being used. The packets include information for directing the packet to the right address and for checking transmission errors along with the data.

Data are gathered from many users, divided into small packets, and transmitted over various communications channels using routers. Each packet travels independently through these networks. Packets of data originating at one source can be routed through many different paths and networks before being reassembled into the original message when they reach their destinations.

Packet switching does not require a dedicated circuit but can make use of any spare capacity that is available. If some lines are disabled or too busy, the packets can be sent over any available line that eventually leads to the destination point.

network operating system (NOS)

hubs

switch

router

distributed processing

packet switching

FIGURE 7-6 *Packed-switched networks and packet communications.*

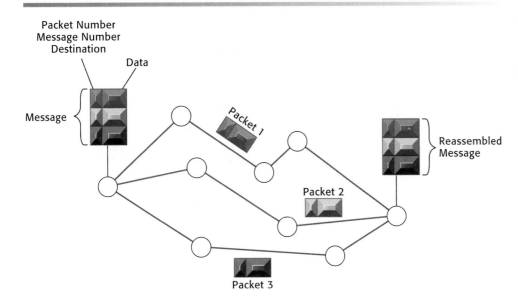

Data are grouped into small packets, which are transmitted independently over various communication channels and reassembled at their final destination.

TCP/IP and Connectivity A typical telecommunications network consists of diverse hardware and software components that need to work together to transmit information. Different components in a network can communicate with each other only by adhering to a common set of rules called protocols. A **protocol** is a set of rules and procedures governing transmission of information between two points in a network. In the past, many diverse proprietary and incompatible protocols often forced business firms to purchase computing and communications equipment from a single vendor. But today corporate networks are increasingly using a single, common, worldwide standard called **Transmission Control Protocol/Internet Protocol (TCP/IP)**.

TCP/IP provides a universally agreed-on method for breaking up digital messages into packets, routing them to the proper addresses, and then reassembling them into coherent messages. TCP/IP was developed during the early 1970s to support the U.S. Department of Defense Advanced Research Projects Agency (DARPA) efforts to help scientists transmit data among different types of computers over long distances.

TCP/IP uses a suite of protocols, the main ones being TCP and IP. *TCP* refers to the Transmission Control Protocol (TCP), which handles the movement of data between computers. TCP establishes a connection between the computers, sequences the transfer of packets, and acknowledges the packets sent. *IP* refers to the Internet Protocol (IP), which is responsible for the delivery of packets and includes the disassembling and reassembling of packets during transmission. Figure 7-7 illustrates the four-layer reference model for TCP/IP.

1. Application layer. Enables client application programs to access the other layers and defines the protocols that applications use to exchange data. One of these application protocols is the Hypertext Transfer Protocol (HTTP) that is used to transfer Web page files.

2. Transport layer. Responsible for providing the application layer with communication and packet services. This layer includes TCP and other protocols.

3. Internet layer. Responsible for addressing, routing, and packaging data packets called IP datagrams. The Internet Protocol (IP) is one of the protocols used in this layer.

4. Network interface layer. At the bottom of the reference model, the network interface layer is responsible for placing packets on and receiving them from the network medium, which could be any networking technology.

Two computers using TCP/IP can communicate even if they are based on different hardware and software platforms. Data sent from one computer to the other passes

protocol

Transmission Control Protocol/Internet Protocol (TCP/IP)

This figure illustrates the four layers of the TCP/IP reference model for communications.

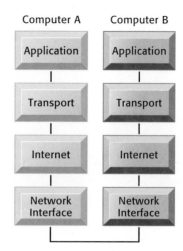

downward through all four layers, starting with the sending computer's application layer and passing through the network interface layer. After the data reach the recipient host computer, they travel up the layers and are reassembled into a format the receiving computer could use. If the receiving computer finds a damaged packet, it asks the sending computer to retransmit it. This process is reversed when the receiving computer responds.

Open Systems Interconnection (OSI) reference model is another network connectivity model developed by the International Standards Organization for linking different types of computers and networks. Like TCP/IP, OSI enables a computer connected to a network to communicate with any other computer on the same network or a different network, regardless of the manufacturer. OSI divides the telecommunications process into seven layers.

Physical Transmission Media

Networks can use different kinds of physical transmission media, including twisted wire, coaxial cable, fibre optics, and media for wireless transmission. Each has advantages and limitations. A wide range of speeds is possible for any given medium depending on the software and hardware configuration. Typically, the faster any given medium is, the more expensive it is.

Twisted Wire **Twisted wire**, also known as twisted pair wire, consists of strands of copper wire twisted in pairs and is an older type of transmission medium. Many of the telephone systems in buildings had twisted wires installed for analog communication, but they can be used for digital communication as well.

An *analog signal* is represented by a continuous waveform that passes through a communications medium and has been used for voice communication. A *digital signal* is a discrete, rather than a continuous, waveform. It transmits data coded into two discrete states: 1 bits and 0 bits, which are represented as on–off electrical pulses. Computers use digital signals, so if one wants to use the analog telephone system to send digital data, a device called a **modem** is required to translate digital signals into analog form (see Figure 7-8). *Modem* stands for modulation/demodulation.

Although twisted wire is low in cost and usually is already in place, it can be relatively slow and noisy for transmitting data. There are limits to the amount of data that ordinary twisted wire can carry, but new software and hardware used by local telephone companies have raised twisted-wire transmission capacity, to make it useful for high-speed connectivity to the Internet, to speeds up to one megabit per second (Mbps), or 1 million bits per second.

Open Systems Interconnection (OSI) reference model

twisted wire

modem

FIGURE 7-8   *Functions of the modem.*

Digital   Analog   Digital

A modem is a device that translates digital signals from a computer into analog form so that they can be transmitted over analog telephone lines. The modem also is used to translate analog signals back into digital form for the receiving computer.

Coaxial Cable **Coaxial cable**, similar to that used for cable television, consists of thickly insulated copper wire, which can transmit a larger volume of data than twisted wire. Cable is commonly used for local area networks because it is a faster, more interference-free transmission medium, capable of speeds up to 200 Mbps.

Fibre Optics and Optical Networks **Fibre-optic cable** consists of strands of clear glass fibre, each the thickness of a human hair, which are bound into cables. Data are transformed into pulses of light, which are sent through the fibre-optic cable by a laser device at rates varying from 500 kilobits to several trillion bits per second in experimental settings. Fibre-optic cable is considerably faster, lighter, and more durable than wire media and is well suited to systems requiring transfers of large volumes of data. However, fibre-optic cable is more difficult to work with, more expensive, and harder to install.

Until recently, fibre-optic cable had been used primarily as the high-speed network backbone while twisted wire and coaxial cable were used to connect the backbone to individual businesses and households. A **backbone** is the part of a network that handles the major traffic. It acts as the primary path for traffic flowing to or from other networks. Now, local cable companies are bringing fibre all the way into the basements of buildings so they can provide a variety of new services to businesses and eventually residential customers.

These **optical networks** can transmit all types of traffic—voice, data, and video—over fibre cables and provide the massive bandwidth for new types of services and software. Using optical networks, on-demand video, software downloads, and high-quality digital audio can be accessed using set-top boxes and other information appliances without severe degradation in quality or delays.

Optical networks can boost capacity by using **dense wavelength division multiplexing (DWDM)**. **Multiplexing** enables a single communications channel to simultaneously carry data transmissions from multiple sources. (This can be accomplished by dividing a high-speed channel into multiple channels of slower speeds or by assigning each transmission source a very small slice of time for using a high-speed channel.) DWDM boosts transmission capacity by using many different colours of light, or different wavelengths, to carry separate streams of data over the same fibre strand at the same time. DWDM combines up to 160 wavelengths per strand and can transmit up to 6.4 terabits per second (Tbps) over a single fibre. This technology will enable communications service providers to add transmission capacity to an existing fibre-optic network without having to lay more fibre-optic cable. Before wavelength division multiplexing, optical networks could use only a single wavelength per strand.

Wireless Transmission Much of the recent growth in communications and networking services is based on wireless technologies that use radio frequencies or infrared signals to send data between communications devices without using wires. Common technologies for wireless data transmission include microwave transmission, communication satellites, pagers, cellular telephones, personal communication services (PCS), personal digital assistants (PDAs), smart phones, and mobile data networks. Personal computers using wireless Wi-Fi network interface cards can connect to corporate networks and the Internet in locations where a Wi-Fi transmitter has been installed. Wireless transmission has become so important to corporations that we devote the next chapter to this topic.

coaxial cable
fibre-optic cable
backbone
optical networks
dense wavelength division multiplexing (DWDM)
multiplexing

Transmission Speed The total amount of digital information that can be transmitted through any telecommunications medium is measured in bits per second (bps). One signal change, or cycle, is required to transmit one or several bits; therefore, the transmission capacity of each type of telecommunications medium is a function of its frequency. The number of cycles per second that can be sent through that medium is measured in **hertz**—one hertz is equal to one cycle of the medium.

The range of frequencies that can be accommodated on a particular telecommunications channel is called **bandwidth**. The bandwidth is the difference between the highest and lowest frequencies that can be accommodated on a single channel. The greater the range of frequencies, the greater the bandwidth, and the greater the channel's transmission capacity. Table 7-2 compares the transmission speeds and relative costs of the major types of transmissions media.

Types of Networks

There are many different kinds of networks and ways of classifying them. One way of looking at networks is in terms of their geographic scope (see Table 7-3).

Local Area Networks The first computer networks appeared in the early 1960s and consisted of display terminals linked to a mainframe computer within the same building. Researchers at Xerox Palo Alto Research Center (PARC) invented the first local area network late in that decade to connect desktop machines into a coherent computing facility. These networks enabled desktop machines to share printers, communicate with one another, and store files on a central desktop machine called a server.

Today most people in corporations connect to other employees and groups using local area networks. A **local area network (LAN)** is designed to connect personal computers and other digital devices within a half mile or 500-metre radius. LANs typically connect a few computers in a small office, all the computers in one building, or all the computers in several buildings in close proximity. LANs interconnected within multiple buildings or a geographic area such as a school campus or military base create a **campus area network (CAN)**.

TABLE 7-2   *Typical Speeds and Costs of Telecommunications Transmission Media*

MEDIUM	SPEED	COST
Twisted wire	Up to 100 Mbps	Low
Microwave	Up to 200+ Mbps	High
Satellite	Up to 200+ Mbps	High
Coaxial cable	Up to 200 Mbps	High
Fibre-optic cable	Up to 6+ Tbps	High

Mbps = megabits per second
Gbps = gigabits per second
Tbps = terabits per second

TABLE 7-3   *Types of Networks*

TYPE	AREA
Local area network (LAN)	Up to 500 metres; an office or floor of a building
Campus area network (CAN)	Up to 1000 metres; a college campus or corporate facility
Metropolitan area network (MAN)	A city or metropolitan area
Wide area network (WAN)	Transcontinental or global area

hertz
bandwidth
local area network (LAN)
campus area network (CAN)

LANs can link to long-distance wide area networks (WANs, described later in this section) and other networks around the world by using the Internet.

Review Figure 7-5, which could serve as a model for a small LAN that might be used in an office. One computer is a dedicated network file server, providing users with access to shared computing resources in the network, including software programs and data files. The server determines who gets access to what and in which sequence. The router connects the LAN to other networks, which could be the Internet or another corporate network, so that the LAN can exchange information with networks external to it. The most common LAN operating systems are Windows, Linux, and Novell. Each of these network operating systems supports TCP/IP as their default networking protocol.

Ethernet is the dominant LAN standard at the physical network level, specifying the physical medium to carry signals between computers, access control rules, and a standardized frame or set of bits used to carry data over the system. Originally, Ethernet supported a data transfer rate of 10 Mbps. Newer versions, such as Fast Ethernet and Gigabit Ethernet, support data transfer rates of 100 Mbps and 1 Gbps, respectively, and are used in network backbones.

The LAN illustrated in Figure 7-5 uses a client/server architecture where the network operating system resides primarily on a single file server and the server provides much of the control and resources for the network. Alternatively, LANs may use a **peer-to-peer** architecture. A peer-to-peer network treats all processors equally and is used primarily in small networks with 10 or fewer users. The various computers on the network can exchange data by direct access and can share peripheral devices without going through a separate server.

In LANs using the Windows Server 2003 family of operating systems, the peer-to-peer architecture is called the *workgroup network model* in which a small group of computers can share resources, such as files, folders, and printers over the network without a dedicated server. The Windows *domain network model*, in contrast, uses a dedicated server to manage the computers in the network.

Larger LANs have many clients and multiple servers, with separate servers for specific services, such as storing and managing files and databases (file servers or database servers), managing printers (print servers), storing and managing email (mail servers), or storing and managing Web pages (Web servers).

Sometimes LANs are described in terms of the way their components are connected together, or their **topology**. There are three major LAN topologies: star, bus, and ring (see Figure 7-9).

In a star topology, all devices on the network connect to a single hub. Figure 7-9 illustrates a simple **star network** in which all network components connect to a single hub. All network traffic flows through the hub. In an *extended star*, multiple layers or hubs are organized into a hierarchy.

In a bus topology, one station transmits signals, which travel in both directions along a single transmission segment. All of the signals are broadcast in both directions to the entire network. All machines on the network receive the same signals, and software installed on the clients enables each client to listen for messages addressed specifically to it. **Bus networks** are the most common Ethernet topology.

A ring topology connects network components in a closed loop. Messages pass from computer to computer in only one direction around the loop, and only one station at a time may transmit. **Ring networks** are used primarily in older LANs using Token Ring networking software.

Metropolitan and Wide Area Networks

Wide area networks (WANs) span broad geographical distances—entire regions, states, continents, or the entire globe. The most universal and powerful WAN is the Internet. Computers connect to a WAN through public networks, such as the telephone system, private cable systems, or through leased lines or satellites. A **metropolitan area network (MAN)** is a network that spans a metropolitan area, usually a city and its major suburbs. Its geographic scope falls between a WAN and a LAN. MANs sometimes provide Internet connectivity for local area networks in a metropolitan region.

peer-to-peer

topology

star network

bus networks

ring networks

wide area networks (WANs)

metropolitan area network (MAN)

FIGURE 7-9 *Network topologies.*

The three basic network topologies are the bus, star, and ring.

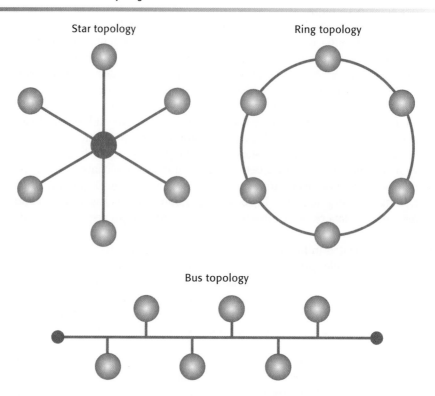

Broadband Network Services and Technologies

Broadband means high-speed and can designate either a single communications medium that can transmit multiple channels of data simultaneously or other technologies that enable high-speed transmission. A number of network services and technologies are available to companies that need high-speed transmission or access to the Internet.

FIGURE 7-10 *IP video conference locations on K-Net's network.*

broadband

This map of Canada shows the urban sites with video conferencing connections and facilities that now have Quality of Service (QoS) for their video and audio traffic over the Kuhkenah Network (K-Net) of Smart First Nations.

Source: Cal Kenny, Kuhkenah Network Multimedia Producer, Sioux Lookout, ON.

Frame relay is a shared network service that is faster and less expensive than packet switching and can achieve transmission speeds ranging from 56 kilobits per second (Kbps) to more than 40 Mbps. Frame relay packages data into frames similar to packets but takes advantage of higher-speed, more reliable digital circuits that require less error checking than packet switching. The major telecommunications carriers provide frame relay services. Many organizations use frame relay services in their international data communication networks.

A technology called **asynchronous transfer mode (ATM)** can handle many types of network traffic and provides transmission speeds ranging from 1.5 Mbps up to more than 9 Gbps. Like frame relay, ATM takes advantage of high-bandwidth digital circuits, parceling information into fixed 53-byte cells, of which 48 bytes are for data and 5 are for header information. ATM can pass data between computers from different vendors and is popular for transmitting data, video, and audio over the same network. Many telecommunications carriers and large enterprise backbone networks use ATM.

Integrated services digital network (ISDN) is an international standard for dial-up network access that integrates voice, data, image, and video services in a single link. Although ISDN cannot match the transmission capacity of frame relay or ATM, it is a dial-up service working on local telephone lines, where subscribers pay only for what they use (in addition to a small monthly fee). There are two levels of ISDN service: basic rate ISDN (which can transmit 128 Kbps) and primary rate ISDN (which can transmit at 1.5 Mbps).

Other high-capacity services include digital subscriber line technologies, cable modems, and T-1 lines. Like ISDN, **digital subscriber line (DSL)** technologies also operate over existing copper telephone lines to carry voice, data, and video, but they have higher transmission capacities than ISDN. There are several categories of DSL. Asymmetric digital subscriber lines (ADSLs) support a transmission rate of 1.5 to 9 Mbps when receiving data and up to 640 Kbps when sending data. Symmetric digital subscriber lines (SDSLs) support the same transmission rate for sending and receiving data at up to 3 Mbps.

Cable modems are modems designed to operate over cable TV lines. They can provide high-speed access to the Web or corporate intranets of up to 4 Mbps. However, cable modems use a shared line so that transmission slows down if there are a large number of local users sharing the cable line. This problem can be solved by increasing the capacity of the local cable.

Firms that have large amounts of data to move across the continent or around the world, or data that have high security or guaranteed service level requirements, often lease high-speed data lines from communication providers, typically long-distance telephone companies. These lines are designated as **T lines**, which range from T-1 to T-4. A T-1 line offers up to twenty-four 64-Kbps channels that can support a total data transmission rate of 1.544 Mbps. Each of these 64-Kbps channels can be configured to carry voice or data traffic. A T-3 line offers delivery at 45 Mbps, and a T-4 line (although rarely used) can deliver up to 274 Gbps. Leasing a T-1 line costs about $750 per month while a T-3 line costs around $3500 per month. Table 7-4 summarizes these network services.

7.3 The Internet

The Internet is the most well known and largest implementation of client/server computing and internetworking, linking hundreds of thousands of individual networks all over the world, which in turn service 600 million individual PCs or host computers. The word *Internet* derives from the word **internetworking** or the linking of separate networks, each of which retains its own identity, into an interconnected network. In Canada, 64.2% of all households access the Internet from home. The World Wide Web is the most popular service provided by the Internet, providing users access to over 8 billion Web pages containing text, graphics, audio, video, and other objects.

frame relay

asynchronous transfer mode (ATM)

integrated services digital network (ISDN)

digital subscriber line (DSL)

cable modems

T lines

internetworking

TABLE 7-4 *Broadband Network Services*

SERVICE	DESCRIPTION	BANDWIDTH
Frame relay	Packages data into frames for high-speed transmission over reliable circuits that require less error checking than packet switching	56 Kbps to 40+ Mbps
Asynchronous transfer mode (ATM)	Parcels data into uniform 53-byte cells for high-speed transmission; can transmit data, video, and audio over the same network	1.5 Mbps to 9+ Gbps
Integrated services digital network (ISDN)	Dial-up network access standard that can integrate voice, data, and video services	Basic rate ISDN: 128 Kbps Primary rate ISDN: 1.5 Mbps
Digital subscriber line (DSL)	Series of technologies for high-capacity transmission over copper wire	ADSL: Up to 9 Mbps for receiving and up to 640 Kbps for sending data SDSL: Up to 3 Mbps for both sending and receiving
Cable modem	Service for high-speed transmission of data over cable TV lines that are shared by many users	Up to 4 Mbps
T lines	Dedicated lines for high-speed data transmission and Internet connection	T-1: 1.544 Mbps T-3: 45 Mbps

Technically, the Internet is a global information system defined by three characteristics (Federal Networking Council 1995):

- A network composed of computers and other devices that are logically linked together by a unique address space based on the Internet Protocol
- A network where network devices (computers, routers, hubs, and other equipment) are able to support communications using TCP/IP or other compatible protocols
- A network that provides high-level services layered on a communication and network infrastructure

The incredible success of the Internet as the world's most extensive, public communications system—one that rivals the global telephone system in reach and range—results from a number of design factors. Table 7-5 describes four design factors that have made the Internet a nearly universal communications system.

This gigantic network of networks began in the early 1970s as a U.S. Department of Defense network to link scientists and university professors around the world. Today, individuals connect to the Internet in two ways. Most homes connect to the Internet by subscribing to an Internet service provider. An **Internet service provider (ISP)** is a commercial organization with a permanent connection to the Internet that sells temporary connections to retail subscribers. These connections can be provided by telephone lines, cable lines, or wireless connections. America Online, Yahoo!, and Microsoft Network (MSN) are ISPs in addition to being content portals. Internet service providers in Canada generated more than $1.5 billion in revenue in 2003. Individuals also connect to the Internet through their business firms, universities, or research centres that have designated Internet domains, such as www.ibm.com.

Internet Addressing, Architecture, and Governance

The Internet is based on the TCP/IP networking protocol suite described earlier in this chapter. Every computer on the Internet is assigned a unique **Internet Protocol (IP) address**, which currently is a 32-bit number represented by four strings of numbers, each a maximum of three digits long and ranging from 0 to 255. For instance, the IP address of www.microsoft.com is 207.46.250.119.

Internet service provider (ISP)

Internet Protocol (IP) address

TABLE 7-5 *Internet Success Design Factors*

DESIGN FACTOR	SIGNIFICANCE
Hourglass layered architecture	The Internet can be viewed as an hourglass in which the network technology and higher-level user services such as the Web are separated. Users do not have to be concerned with the details of network hardware or configurations; developers are not restricted in evolving new technologies by fears of interrupting user services.
End-to-end architecture	The network provides a very basic level of message transport to computers at the edge or end of the network while intelligence and processing power is located in or close to the devices attached at the edge of the network.
Scalability	The Internet's design enables it to support a growing volume of communications per device and growing numbers of devices without changes in network principles or design.
Distributed design and decentralized control	Except for the allocation of address blocks and top-level domain management, control of the network—such as how data packets are routed through the Internet—is distributed among thousands of local network operations and hundreds of other participants (such as local ISPs and campus and metropolitan network operators).

Source: Based on "The Internet's Coming of Age," National Research Council, Washington, D.C., 2000.

As described previously, when a user sends a message to another user on the Internet, the message is first decomposed into packets using the TCP protocol. Each packet contains its destination address. The packets are then sent from the client to the network server, and from there onto as many other servers as necessary to arrive at a specific computer with a known address. At the destination address, the packets are reassembled into the original message.

The Domain Name System Because it would be incredibly difficult for Internet users to remember strings of 12 numbers, a **Domain Name System (DNS)** converts IP addresses to domain names. The **domain name** is the English-like name that corresponds to the unique 32-bit numeric Internet Protocol (IP) address for each computer connected to the Internet. DNS servers maintain a database containing IP addresses mapped to their corresponding domain names. To access a computer on the Internet, users need only specify its domain name.

The DNS has a hierarchical structure (see Figure 7-11). At the top of the DNS hierarchy is the root domain. The child domain of the root is called a top-level domain, and the child domain of a top-level domain is called is a second-level domain. Top-level domains are two- and three-character names you are familiar with from surfing the Web, such as .com, .edu, .gov, and the various country codes such as .ca for Canada or .it for Italy. Second-level domains have two parts, designating a top-level name and a second-level name—such as buy.com, nyu.edu, or amazon.ca. A host name at the bottom of the hierarchy designates a specific computer on either the Internet or a private network.

The most common top-level domains (TLDs) currently available and officially sanctioned are shown in the list on page 240. Countries also have top-level domain names such as .uk, .au, and .fr (United Kingdom, Australia, and France, respectively). The most popular Canadian TLD is .ca, including organizations that are for-profit, not-for-profit, government, education, and so on. Some Canadian organizations choose to use the generic TLDs, such as Air Canada (www.aircanada.com) and Royal Bank (www.rbc.com). Much of this choice is driven by the original purpose of the top level domain names; country identifiers were to identify Web sites located outside of the U.S. However, the United States also has a country identifier top level domain name (.us). Many companies headquartered outside the U.S. felt use of the .com top level domain gave the U.S. an unfair advantage, so they applied for and received .com domain names.

Domain Name System (DNS)

domain name

FIGURE 7-11   *The Domain Name System.*

The Domain Name System is a hierarchical system with a root domain, top-level domains, second-level domains, and host computers at the third level.

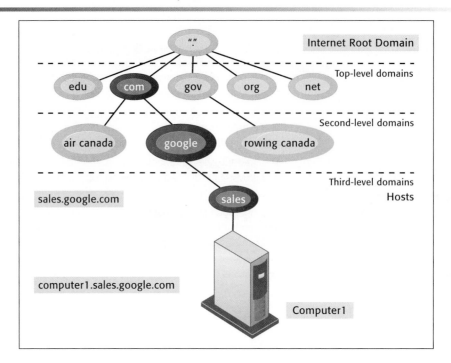

Also shown in the following list are recently approved top-level domains. In the near future, this list will expand to include many more types of organizations and industries. The list of proposed new TLDs is: .asia, .cat (or .ctl or .catala), .jobs, .mail (or .tmail or .mta), .mobi (or .mbl), .post, .tel, .travel, and .xxx.

.aero	Aviation
.biz	Business organizations
.com	Commercial organizations/businesses
.coop	Cooperative organizations
.edu	Educational institutions
.gov	U.S. government agencies
.info	Open TLD names
.int	International organizations
.mil	U.S. Department of Defense
.museum	Museums
.name	Personal
.net	Network computers
.org	Nonprofit organizations and foundations
.pro	Professional organizations

Limitations on IP Addresses: IPv4 and IPv6 How many unique addresses are there on the Internet if 600 million people are connected? The Internet addressing convention described earlier is called Internet Protocol version 4 (IPv4). This "dotted quad" addressing scheme (a 32-bit string of numbers organized into four sets of numbers ranging from 0 to 255) contains up to 4 billion addresses (2 to the 32nd power).

Because many corporations and governments have been given large blocks of millions of IP addresses to accommodate current and future workforces, and because of the Internet's population growth, the world is running out of available IP addresses using this scheme. A new version of the IP addressing schema being developed is called Internet

Protocol version 6 (IPv6) and contains 128-bit addresses (2 to the power of 128), or over a quadrillion possible unique addresses (National Research Council 2000).

Internet Architecture Internet data traffic courses over transcontinental high-speed backbone networks that generally operate today in the range of 45 Mbps to 2.5 Gbps (Figure 7-12). These trunk lines are typically owned by long-distance telephone companies (called network service providers) or by national governments. Local connection lines are owned by regional telephone and cable television companies that connect retail users in homes and businesses to the Internet. The regional networks lease access to ISPs, private companies, and government institutions.

Internet Governance No one "owns" the Internet, and it has no formal management organization per se. However, worldwide Internet policies are established by a number of different organizations and government bodies including the following:

- The Internet Architecture Board (IAB), which helps define the overall structure of the Internet
- The Internet Corporation for Assigned Names and Numbers (ICANN), which assigns IP addresses
- The Internet Network Information Center (InterNIC), which assigns domain names
- The Internet Engineering Steering Group (IESG), which oversees standards setting with respect to the Internet
- The Internet Engineering Task Force (IETF), which forecasts the next step in the growth of the Internet, keeping watch over its evolution and operation
- The Internet Society (ISOC), which is a consortium of corporations, government agencies, and nonprofit organizations that monitors Internet policies and practices
- The World Wide Web Consortium (W3C), which sets Hypertext Markup Language (HTML) and other programming standards for the Web

FIGURE 7-12   *Internet network architecture.*

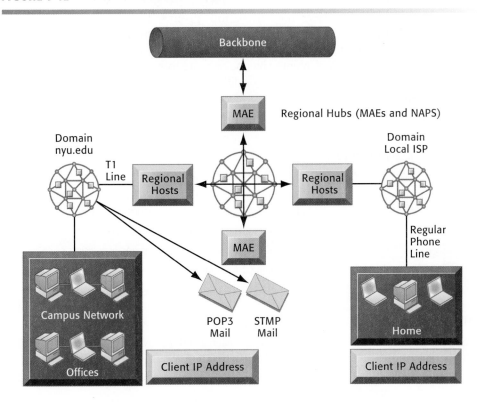

The Internet backbone connects to regional networks, which in turn provide access to Internet service providers, large firms, and government institutions. Network access points (NAPs) and metropolitan area exchanges (MAEs) are hubs where the backbone intersects regional and local networks and where backbone owners connect with one another.

Although none of these organizations has actual control over the Internet and how it functions, they can and do influence government agencies, major network owners, and ISPs. In addition to these professional bodies, the Internet must also conform to the laws of the sovereign nation-states in which it operates as well as the technical infrastructures that exist within the nation-state. Although in the early years of the Internet and the Web very little legislative or executive interference occurred, this situation is changing as the Internet plays a growing role in the distribution of information and knowledge, including content that some find objectionable.

Each organization pays for its own networks and local Internet connection services, a part of which is paid to the long-distance trunk line owners through monthly charges for telephone and Internet services. Consequently, the costs of email and other Internet connections tend to be far lower than equivalent voice, postal, or overnight delivery, making the Internet a very inexpensive communications medium. It is also a very fast method of communication, with messages arriving anywhere in the world in a matter of seconds, or after a minute or two at most.

Internet Services

The Internet is based on client/server technology. Individuals using the Internet control what they do through client applications on their computers, such as Web browser software. All the data, including email messages and Web pages, are stored on servers. A client uses the Internet to request information from a particular Web server on a distant computer, and the server sends the requested information back to the client over the Internet. Chapters 5 and 6 described how Web servers can also work with application servers and database servers to access information from an organization's internal information systems applications and their associated databases.

Client platforms today include not only PCs and other computers but also cell phones, small handheld digital devices, and other information appliances. An **information appliance** is a device, such as an Internet-enabled cell phone or a TV Internet receiver for Web access and email, that has been customized to perform a few specialized computing tasks well with minimal user effort. People increasingly rely on these easy-to-use specialized information appliances to connect to the Internet.

A client computer connecting to the Internet has access to a variety of services. These services include email, electronic discussion groups (Usenet newsgroups and LISTSERVs), chatting and instant messaging, **Telnet**, **File Transfer Protocol (FTP)**, and the World Wide Web. Table 7-6 provides a brief description of these services.

Each Internet service is implemented by one or more software programs. All of the services may run on a single server computer, or different services may be allocated to different machines. A single disk may store the data for these services, or multiple disks may store data

TABLE 7-6 *Major Internet Services*

CAPABILITY	FUNCTIONS SUPPORTED
Email	Person-to-person messaging; document sharing
Usenet newsgroups	Discussion groups on electronic bulletin boards
LISTSERVs	Discussion groups using email mailing list servers
Chatting and instant messaging	Interactive conversations
Telnet	Logging on to one computer system and doing work on another
FTP	Transferring files from computer to computer
World Wide Web	Retrieving, formatting, and displaying information (including text, audio, graphics, and video) using hypertext links

information appliance
Telnet
File Transfer Protocol (FTP)

for each type, depending on the amount of information being stored. Figure 7-13 illustrates one way that these services might be arranged in a multitiered client/server architecture.

The Internet and Business Value

The Internet is very different from any other networking technology developed in the past (see Table 7-7). Its unique features translate directly into business value for all businesses whether they are small or large.

In addition to lowering transaction and agency costs, the Internet creates value for businesses by enabling digital markets that are more efficient than traditional markets. In digital markets, firms can interact directly with consumers, creating the possibility for developing new products and services and customizing existing products. Companies can use email, chat, instant messaging, and electronic discussion groups to create ongoing dialogues with their customers and use the information they have gathered to tailor communication and products precisely to the needs of each individual (see Chapter 13). For all of these reasons, the Internet and Internet technology have become the primary infrastructure for electronic business, electronic commerce, and the digital firm.

The World Wide Web

The World Wide Web (the Web) is the most popular Internet service. It is a system with universally accepted standards for storing, retrieving, formatting, and displaying information using a client/server architecture. Web pages are formatted using hypertext with embedded links that connect documents to one another and that also link pages to other objects such as sound, video, or animation files. When you click a graphic and a video clip plays, you have clicked a hyperlink.

The Web was invented in the period from 1989 to 1991 by Dr. Tim Berners-Lee and his associates at the European Particle Physics Laboratory, better known as CERN. Information shared on the Web remained text-based until 1993, when Marc Andreessen and others at the National Center for Supercomputing Applications (NCSA) at the University of Illinois created a Web browser with a graphical user interface (GUI) called Mosaic that made it possible to view documents on the Web graphically—using coloured backgrounds, images, and even primitive animations. In 1994, Andreessen and Jim Clark founded Netscape, which created the first commercial browser, Netscape Navigator. In August 1995, Microsoft Corporation released its own browser, called Internet Explorer (IE), which is now the dominant Web browser.

FIGURE 7-13   *Client/server computing on the Internet.*

Client computers running Web browsers and other software can access an array of services on servers over the Internet. These services may all run on a single server or on multiple specialized servers.

TABLE 7-7 *Seven Unique Features of Internet Technology*

TECHNOLOGY FEATURE	BUSINESS SIGNIFICANCE
Ubiquity—Internet/Web technology is available everywhere: at work, at home, and elsewhere by using mobile devices, anytime.	The marketplace is extended beyond traditional boundaries and is removed from a temporal and geographic location. Shopping can take place anywhere in a market space. Customer convenience is enhanced and shopping costs reduced.
Global reach—The technology reaches across national boundaries, around the earth	Commerce is enabled across cultural and national boundaries seamlessly and without modification. The market space includes potentially billions of consumers and millions of businesses worldwide.
Universal standards—There is one set of technology standards, namely Internet standards.	One set of technical media standards exists across the globe. Training on applications using Internet technology is greatly reduced, not only reducing costs, but enabling individuals using this technology to be more mobile across business units and companies as well as countries.
Richness—It is possible to transmit video, audio, and text messages.	Video, audio, and text marketing messages can be integrated into a single marketing message and consumer experience. Companies can interact with their customers, building loyalties and reducing costs for many customer services.
Interactivity—The technology works through interaction with the user.	Businesses can engage consumers in a dialogue that dynamically adjusts the experience for each individual consumer and makes the consumer a co-participant in the process of delivering goods to market. The costs of interacting with customers can be reduced since physical interaction may not be necessary.
Information density—The technology reduces information costs and raises quality.	Information processing, information storage, and communication costs drop dramatically while currency, accuracy, and timeliness improve greatly. Information becomes plentiful, cheap, and accurate. Providing users and customers with more information can again build loyalty and reduce overall costs of serving customers.
Personalization/Customization—The technology enables personalized messages to be delivered to individuals as well as groups.	Businesses can personalize marketing messages and customize products and services based on individual consumer characteristics and preferences. Once again, this builds customer loyalty, but it also enables what is termed mass customization, meaning that a company can use mass production processes to develop products for a market as small as one individual.

Hypertext Web pages are based on a standard Hypertext Markup Language (HTML), which formats documents and incorporates dynamic links to other documents and pictures stored in the same or remote computers (see Chapter 5). Web pages are accessible through the Internet because Web browser software operating your computer can request Web pages stored on an Internet host server using the **Hypertext Transfer Protocol (HTTP)**. HTTP is the communications standard used to transfer pages on the Web. For example, when you type a Web address in your browser such as www.statcan.ca, your browser sends an HTTP request to the statcan.ca server requesting the home page of stat-can.ca, the main Statistics Canada Web site.

HTTP is the first set of letters at the start of every Web address, followed by the domain name, which specifies the organization's server computer that is storing the document. Most companies have a domain name that is the same as or closely related to their official corporate name. The directory path and document name are two more pieces of information within the Web address that help the browser track down the requested page. Together, the address is called a **Uniform Resource Locator (URL)**. When typed into a browser, a URL tells the browser software exactly where to look for the information. For example, in the following URL: http://www.canada.com/national/index.html, *http* names the protocol used to display Web pages, *www.canada.com* is the domain name, *national* is the directory path that identifies where on the domain Web server the page is stored, *index.html* is the document name, and *html* is the name and type of format it is in (it is an HTML page).

Hypertext Transfer Protocol (HTTP)

Uniform Resource Locator (URL)

Web Servers A Web server is software for locating and managing stored Web pages. It locates the Web pages requested by a user client on the computer where they are stored and delivers the Web pages to the user's computer. The most common Web server in use today is Apache HTTP Server, which controls 67 percent of the market. Apache is an open source product that is free of charge and can be downloaded from the Web (Figure 7-14). Microsoft's product Internet Information Services is the second most commonly used Web server with a 22 percent market share.

Server applications usually run on dedicated computers, although they can all reside on a single computer in small organizations. Chapters 5 and 6 describe how Web servers can also work with application servers and database servers to access information from an organization's internal information systems applications and their associated databases.

A typical Web site is a collection of Web pages linked to a **home page**—a text and graphical screen display that usually welcomes the user and provides a brief description of the organization that has established the Web site. Most home pages offer a way to contact the organization or individual. The person in charge of an organization's Web site is called a **Web master**.

Searching for Information on the Web Locating information on the Web is a critical function. Billions of Web pages exist, and this number will quickly double. No comprehensive catalogue of Web sites is available. The principal methods of locating information on the Web are Web site directories, search engines, intelligent agents, and broadcast or "push" technology.

Search Engines and Web site Directories   Several companies have created directories of Web sites and their addresses, providing search tools for finding information. Yahoo! is an example. People or organizations submit sites of interest, which then are classified and ranked by human experts. To search the Yahoo! directory, you enter one or more keywords and then you see a list of categories and sites with those keywords in the title.

Other search tools do not require Web sites to be preclassified and will search Web pages automatically. These tools, called **search engines**, can find Web sites that may be little known. Search engines contain software that looks for Web pages containing one or more of the search terms, then they display matches ranked by a method that usually involves the location and frequency of the search terms. These search engines create indexes of the Web pages they visit. The search engine software then locates Web pages of interest by searching through these indexes.

Some search engines are more comprehensive or current than others, depending on how their components are tuned, and some also classify Web sites by subject categories. Some search engines, such as AltaVista, seek to visit every Web site in existence, read the contents of the home page, identify the most common words or keywords, and create a huge database of domain names with keywords. Sometimes the search engines will only read the metatags and other keyword sections of the home page. The program that search

FIGURE 7-14   Major Web server providers.

Web server software providers

Other, 6%
Netscape Enterprise, 3%
Zeus, 2%
Microsoft, 22%
Apache HTTP, 67%

This figure illustrates the market share of each of the major Web server software providers.

Source: Based on data from Netcraft Web Server Survey, July 2004, **www.serverwatch.internet.com /netcraft**.

home page
Web master
search engines

engines unleash on the Web to perform this indexing function is called a *spider* or *crawler*. Because search engines do not always overlap, users may miss a page on one search engine but pick it up on another.

Google has become overwhelmingly the most popular Web search tool and is used for about 55 percent of all searches on the Web through its site. Google works by sending "crawlers" across the Internet and using its 10 000 computers to update its index of about 3 billion Web pages. Google software indexes and ranks sites based on relevance measured by how prominently the user's search terms appear on the pages that include them, the number of users who access these pages, and the number of outside links to a particular page. Google can be limited to a country and foreign language (see Figure 7-15), providing even more customized searches and easier reading.

Specialized search engines are also available to help users easily locate specific types of information. For example, PubMed specializes in searches for articles in medical journals. Some Web sites for locating information such as Yahoo! and Google have become so popular and easy to use that they also serve as portals for the Internet (see Chapter 13).

Search engines are no longer simply search engines but instead have transformed themselves into major shopping tools by offering search-related advertising. When users enter a search term at Google, MSN Search, Yahoo!, or any of the other sites serviced by these search engines, they receive two types of listings: sponsored links, for which advertisers have paid to be listed (usually at the top of the search results page) and unsponsored search results. For firms that pay the search engine companies $2 billion a year for sponsored links, this feature represents a powerful new marketing tool called **search-based advertising** that precisely matches consumer interest and timing with an advertising message.

Although the major search engines are used for locating general information of interest to users, they have also become a crucial tool within e-commerce sites. Customers can more easily search for the product information they want with the help of an internal search program; the difference is that within Web sites, the search engine is limited to finding matches from that one site.

Intelligent Agent Shopping Bots   Chapter 16 details the capabilities of software agents with built-in intelligence that can gather or filter information and perform other tasks to assist users. The Web crawler and spider software for searching the Web that we mentioned earlier is one type of intelligent software agent. **Shopping bots** are another type of intelligent agent software for searching the Internet for shopping information.

FIGURE 7-15   *Google search engine.*

Google is the most popular search engine in any country and almost any language. It offers search-based advertising. The listings displayed under "Liens commerciaux" (Sponsored Links) are links paid by advertisers. The unbiased results of the search are displayed under "Web."

search-based advertising

shopping bots

FIGURE 7-16   *Froogle, Google's shopping bot.*

Froogle features a shopping bot that can search Internet retailers for price and availability of products specified by the user.

Shopping bots can help people interested in making a purchase filter and retrieve information about products of interest, evaluate competing products according to criteria the users have established, and negotiate with vendors for price and delivery terms (Kocas 2002–2003; Maes, Guttman, and Moukas 1999). Many of these shopping agents search the Web for pricing and availability of products specified by the user and return a list of sites that sell the item along with pricing information and a purchase link. Table 7-8 compares various types of electronic commerce agents.

Broadcast and Push Technology   Instead of spending hours surfing the Web, users can have the information in which they are interested delivered automatically to their desktops through **push technology**. This technology enables a computer to broadcast information of interest directly to the user, rather than having the user "pull" content from Web sites.

Special client software enables the user to specify the categories of information he or she wants to receive, such as news, sports, financial data, and so forth, and how often this information should be updated. After finding the kind of information requested, push server programs serve it to the push client. The streams of information distributed through push technology are known as channels. Using push technology to transmit

push technology

TABLE 7-8   *Examples of Electronic Commerce Agents*

AGENT	DESCRIPTION
MySimon	Real-time shopping bot that searches more than 1000 affiliated and unaffiliated merchants in 90 categories
Froogle	Shopping bot service powered by Google that looks for the lowest prices of products for sale on the Web
BizRate	Provides comparison shopping information, including customer reviews, for millions of products and thousands of online stores
BestBookBuys.com	Shopping bot that searches 26 online bookstores to help users find the lowest prices for titles they specify
PricingCentral.com	Price comparison shopping portal that indexes price search engines and shopping bots into a comprehensive directory
Valuefind	Searches for the best deal from retail vendors and auctions; users can limit the search to a specific Web site

information to a select group of individuals is one example of **multicasting**. (LISTSERVs sending email to members of specific mailing lists is another.)

Push technology is the foundation of new content services for both computers and mobile devices. New online content services, such as the LATimes.com's NewsDirect, are using push technology to provide paid subscribers with news articles customized to their interests. Online marketplaces and exchanges can use push services to alert buyers about price changes and special deals. Companies are using internal push channels to broadcast important information, such as price updates or new competitor products, on their own private networks.

Web Logs (Blogs)   **Web logs**, also called **blogs**, are personal journals that are frequently updated and intended for general public consumption and posted on the Web. Blogs generally represent the personality of the author or reflect the purpose of the Web site that hosts the blog. The main characteristics of a blog are its journal form and informal style, and there is typically a new entry every day. Many blogs syndicate their content to subscribers of the blog using **Resource Description Framework Site Summary (RSS)**, a method of describing news or other Web content that is available for distribution or subscription from an online publisher to Web users. RSS is an extension of XML. Today companies are even hosting blogs about their products and services.

The Semantic Web   Most of the Web's content today is designed for humans to read and for computers to display, not for computer programs to analyze and manipulate. Search engines can discover when a particular term or keyword appears in a Web document, but they do not really understand its meaning or how it relates to other information on the Web. The **semantic Web** is a collaborative effort led by the World Wide Web Consortium to make Web searching more efficient by reducing the amount of human involvement in searching for and processing Web information. Tim Berners-Lee wrote the road map for the Semantic Web in 1998.

Although the semantic Web is still in its infancy, it could eventually bring additional structure to the meaningful content of Web pages so that the machines could make more sense of the Web and data in Web pages could be processed automatically. Two important technologies for developing the semantic Web are Extensible Markup Language (XML), which we introduced in Chapter 5, and the Resource Description Framework (RDF). RDF goes beyond XML to describe data in terms of objects and their interrelationships. Once data on the Web have specific meanings and rules for reasoning about them, agent technology could be harnessed to unleash software agents roaming from page to page to automatically carry out sophisticated tasks for users.

One prototype application is the semantic Web environmental directory (SWED) in the United Kingdom. Instead of centralizing the storage, management, and ownership of information about environmental organizations and projects, SWED continually harvests data and uses these data to create the directory (Frauenfelder 2004).

Intranets and Extranets

Organizations can use Internet networking standards and Web technology to create private networks called intranets. We introduced intranets in Chapter 1, explaining that an intranet is an internal organizational network that provides access to data across the enterprise. It uses the existing company network infrastructure along with Internet connectivity standards and software developed for the World Wide Web. Intranets can create networked applications that run on many different kinds of computers throughout the organization, including mobile handheld computers and wireless remote access devices.

While the Web is available to anyone, an intranet is private and is protected from public visits by **firewalls**—security systems with specialized software to prevent outsiders from entering private networks. Intranet software technology is the same as that of the World Wide Web. Intranets use HTML to program Web pages and to establish dynamic, point-and-click hypertext links to other pages. The Web browser and Web server software used for intranets are the same as those on the Web. A simple intranet can be created by linking a

multicasting

Web logs (blogs)

RDF Site Summary (RSS)

semantic Web

firewalls

client computer with a Web browser to a computer with Web server software using a TCP/IP network with software to keep unwanted visitors out. Since most employees already know how to use Web browsers, intranets save money by providing a low-cost, easy-to-use, standardized interface to the company's data, policies, employee directories, and other needed information and applications—all without the need for additional training.

Extranets A firm can create an extranet to allow authorized vendors and customers to have limited access to its internal intranet. For example, authorized buyers could link to a portion of a company's intranet from the public Internet to obtain information about the costs and features of the company's products. The company can use firewalls to ensure that access to its internal data is limited and remains secure; firewalls can also authenticate users, making sure that only authorized users can access the extranet.

Both intranets and extranets reduce transaction and agency costs by providing additional connectivity for coordinating disparate business processes within the firm and for linking electronically to customers and suppliers. Private industrial networks are based on extranets because they are so useful for linking organizations with suppliers, customers, or business partners. Extranets often are employed for collaborating with other companies for supply chain management, product design and development, and training efforts.

Next-Generation Networks and Internet2

The public Internet was not originally designed to handle massive quantities of data flowing through hundreds of thousands of networks. Experimental national research networks (NRNs) are developing high-speed, next-generation networks to address this problem. These private networks do not replace the public Internet, but they do provide test beds for leading-edge technology for research institutions, universities, and corporations that may eventually migrate to the public Internet. These national research networks include CANARIE in Canada, 6NET in Europe, the Asia Pacific Advanced Network (APAN), and **Internet2** and Next-Generation Internet (NGI) in the U.S.

CANARIE is a consortium that was formed in 1993, led by the private sector, to facilitate the development of Canada's communication's infrastructure and to stimulate next-generation products, applications, and services. CANARIE is the Canadian equivalent of Internet2 and NGI. There are currently 140 members of CANARIE with 21 representatives serving as board members. CANARIE has deployed the various versions of CA*net, the national backbone for Canada with one "drop" per province. CA*net is the foundation for "innovation infrastructure" by interconnecting regional networks, universities, and schools to promote an "innovation culture" through advanced applications, such as tele-learning, grids, and so forth. Today, CA*net has evolved to CA*net4, which is based on optical networking technologies to promote the fastest speeds available over the Internet, primarily for research and education purposes.

CANARIE, Internet2 and NGI are all NRN consortia representing more than 200 universities, private businesses, and government agencies that are working on a new, robust, high-bandwidth version of the Internet. The advanced networks created and in use by NRN members provide an environment in which new technologies can be tested and enhanced. Several new networks have been established, including CA*net4 (Canada's most advanced high-speed network), Abilene, and vBNS (a WorldCom/National Science Foundation partnership). Abilene is a proving ground for high-bandwidth technologies. The cross-country backbone is 10 gigabits per second, with the goal of offering 100 megabits per second of connectivity between every Abilene connected desktop.

CA*net4, Abilene, and vBNS (short for very high performance backbone network service) are high-performance backbone networks with bandwidths ranging from 2.5 Gbps to 9.6 Gbps that interconnect the gigaPoPs used by their members to access the network. A *gigaPoP* is a regional gigabit point of presence, or point of access, to the host high-speed network supporting data transfers at the rate of 1 Gbps or higher (see Figure 7-17).

NRN research groups are developing and implementing new quality of service technologies that will enable the Internet to provide different levels of service, depending on the type and importance of the data being transmitted. Today's Internet transmissions are considered

Internet2

FIGURE 7-17 *The CA*net4 infrastructure.*

CA*net4 Infrastructure

The CA*net4 infrastructure describes how this advanced Internet infrastructure works, not only across Canada but also with links to the U.S.

Source: Courtesy of Canarie.ca, **www.canarie.ca/about/downloads.html**.

"best effort"—packets of data arrive when they arrive without any regard to the priority of their contents. Different types of packets could be assigned different levels of priority as they travel over the network. For example, packets for applications such as video-conferencing, which must arrive simultaneously without any break in service, would receive higher priority than email messages, which do not have to be delivered instantaneously.

Other NRN projects include the development of more effective routing practices; standardized middleware that incorporates identification, authentication, and security services that today are often handled as a part of applications running on the Internet; and advanced applications for distributed computation, virtual laboratories, digital libraries, distributed learning, and tele-immersion.

The most recent effort to revitalize the Internet is called PlanetLab. It is a grassroots group of nearly 100 computer scientists at academic institutions backed by leading high-tech companies such as Intel and Hewlett-Packard. PlanetLab researchers are building an experimental overlay network on top of the Internet using computers called smart nodes attached to traditional Internet routers. Each smart node runs software that divides the machine's resources among many users, vastly increasing processing power, data storage capacity, and the ability to track data and programs flowing over the Internet. The smart nodes could be used to create a much smarter and more flexible network than today's Internet that could potentially monitor itself for damaging computer viruses, relieve bottlenecks automatically, and make users' personal computer programs and files portable to any Internet-connected terminal (Roush 2003).

7.4 Technologies and Tools for Communicating and E-Business

Internet technology is the source of the principal tools used today in business for communication and coordination.

Email, Chat, Instant Messaging, and Electronic Discussions

Email enables messages to be exchanged from computer to computer, eliminating costly long-distance telephone charges while expediting communication between different parts of the organization. In addition to providing electronic messaging, email software has capabilities for routing messages to multiple recipients, forwarding messages, and attaching text documents or multimedia files to messages. Although some organizations operate their own internal electronic mail systems, a great deal of email today is sent through the Internet.

Chatting and Instant Messaging Many employees now communicate interactively using **chat** or instant messaging tools. Chatting enables two or more people who are simultaneously connected to the Internet to hold live, interactive conversations. Chat groups are divided into channels, and each is assigned its own topic of conversation. The first generation of chat tools was for written conversations in which participants typed their remarks using their keyboard and read responses on their computer screen. Chat systems now feature voice and even video chat capabilities.

Instant messaging is a type of chat service that enables participants to create their own private chat channels. The instant messaging system alerts the user whenever someone on his or her private list is online so that the user can initiate a chat session with other individuals. A number of competing instant messaging systems exist for consumers, including Yahoo! Messenger, MSN Messenger, and AOL Instant Messenger. Some of these systems can provide voice-based instant messages so that a user can click a Talk button and have an online conversation with another person. Companies concerned with security are building proprietary instant messaging systems using tools such as Lotus Sametime. Many online retail businesses offer chat services on their Web sites to attract visitors, to encourage repeat purchases, and to improve customer service (see Figure 7-18).

Electronic Discussion Groups **Usenet** newsgroups are worldwide discussion groups posted on Internet electronic bulletin boards on which people share information and ideas on a defined topic, such as radiology or rock bands. Anyone can post messages on these bulletin boards for others to read. Many thousands of groups exist that discuss almost every conceivable topic.

Another type of forum, **LISTSERV**, enables discussions to be conducted through predefined groups but uses email mailing list servers instead of bulletin boards for

---

FIGURE 7-18 *L.L.Bean Web site's online chat feature.*

The L.L.Bean Web site provides online chat capabilities to answer visitors' questions and to help them find items for which they are looking.

email

chat

instant messaging

Usenet

LISTSERV

communication. If you find a LISTSERV topic you are interested in, you can subscribe. From then on, through email, you will receive all messages sent by other subscribers concerning that topic. You can, in turn, send a message to your LISTSERV, and it will automatically be broadcast to the other subscribers.

Groupware, Teamware, and Electronic Conferencing

Groupware provides capabilities for supporting enterprise-wide communication and collaborative work. Individuals, teams, and workgroups at different locations in the organization can use groupware for writing and commenting on group projects, sharing ideas and documents, conducting electronic meetings, tracking the status of tasks and projects, scheduling, and sending email. Any group member can review the ideas of other group members at any time and add to them, or individuals can post a document for others to comment on or edit. Commercial groupware products such as Lotus Notes and OpenText's LiveLink, which were originally based on proprietary networks, have been enhanced to integrate with the Internet or private intranets. Groove is a new groupware tool based on **peer-to-peer computing**, which enables people to work directly with other people over the Internet without going through a central server so that they can share processing tasks.

Teamware is similar to groupware, but features simpler Internet tools for building and managing work teams. Although teamware application development capabilities are not as powerful as those provided by sophisticated groupware products, teamware enables companies to implement collaboration applications easily that can be accessed using Web browser software. Documentum eRoom and Lotus Team Workplace are examples of commercial teamware products.

Electronic Conferencing Tools A growing number of companies are using Internet conferencing tools to stage meetings, conferences, and presentations online. Web conferencing and collaboration software provides a virtual conference table where participants can view and modify documents and slides or share their thoughts and comments using chat, audio, or video. The current generation of these tools from Lotus, Microsoft, and WebEx work through a standard Web browser. These forms of electronic conferencing are growing in popularity because they reduce the need for face-to-face meetings, saving travel time and cost.

Internet Telephony

Hardware and software have been developed for **Internet telephony**, enabling companies to use Internet technology for telephone voice transmission over the Internet or private networks. (Internet telephony products sometimes are called IP telephony products.) **Voice over IP (VoIP)** technology uses the Internet Protocol (IP) to deliver voice information in digital form using packet switching, avoiding the tolls charged by local and long-distance telephone networks (see Figure 7-19). Calls that would ordinarily be transmitted over public telephone networks would travel over the corporate network based on the Internet Protocol or the public Internet. IP telephony calls can be made and received with a desktop computer equipped with a microphone and speakers or with a VoIP-enabled telephone.

Early VoIP systems would drop voice packets or deliver them late, causing voice conversations to be choppy or garbled. As the technology matures, these performance problems are being resolved. VoIP networks pose some additional security issues, which are described in Chapter 9.

Although there are up-front investments required for an IP phone system, VoIP can reduce communication and network management costs by 20 to 30 percent. In addition to lowering long-distance costs and eliminating monthly fees for private lines, an IP network provides a single infrastructure for running voice, data, and video applications. Companies no longer have to maintain separate networks for each or provide support services and personnel for each different type of network. Businesses can use this technology for applications such as Internet conference calls using video, for Web sites that enable users to reach a live customer service representative by clicking a link on a Web

groupware

peer-to-peer computing

teamware

Internet telephony

Voice over IP (VoIP)

FIGURE 7-19   *How IP telephony works.*

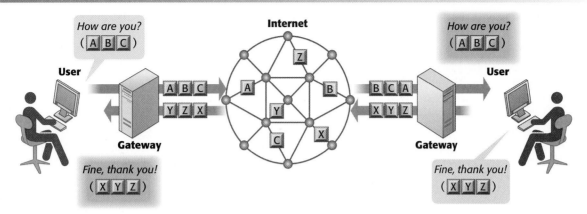

An IP phone call digitizes and breaks up a voice message into data packets that may travel along different routes before being reassembled at their final destination. A processor nearest the call's destination, called a gateway, arranges the packets in the proper order and directs them to the telephone number of the receiver or the IP address of the receiving computer.

page, or for unified messaging. **Unified messaging** systems combine voice mail, email, and faxes so they can all be obtained from one system.

Another advantage of VoIP is its flexibility. Phones can be added or moved to different offices without rewiring or reconfiguring the network. If a phone needs to be added or moved in a traditional telephone network, some additional cabling might be required and the firm would have to pay the telecommunications vendor to do the installation. With VoIP, users merely plug in their VoIP-enabled phones to the IP network at the new locations. Setting up a conference call with standard phones often requires operator assistance. With VoIP, a conference call can be arranged by a simple click and drag operation on the computer screen to select the names of the conferees. Voice and email can be combined into a single directory. The Window on Organizations details why more and more businesses are adopting this technology.

unified messaging

WINDOW ON ORGANIZATIONS

Organization

Internet Telephones: Why Not?

Allied Domecq is the world's second-largest publicly traded company for international spirits, wine, and quick-service restaurants, with nearly 12 000 employees and 50 businesses worldwide. Its brands include Courvoisier, Kahlua, Beefeater Gin, and the Dunkin' Donuts and Baskin-Robbins food chains.

Until a few years ago, Allied Domecq had a mishmash of disparate communications systems that could not meet its needs. Mark Whittle, senior manager for global communications at Domecq's Windsor, Canada, unit, used to say, "We had trouble getting data across our computer room, let alone North America." While modernizing its network infrastructure, the company decided to start using VoIP. Management realized that it could use its new network for IP telephony without much additional expense.

Domecq's Windsor, Ontario, computer centre supports IP telephony services for six smaller sites in sales and marketing, which include California, Florida, Chicago, and New York.

Consolidating each site's individual contracts for network maintenance and telephone systems produced savings. Besides reducing long-distance fees, the VoIP network eliminated service and travel fees and travel charges that telecommunications companies typically charge to add lines, create new extensions, or change the phone system. Domecq's various North American business units realized time savings for their own employees responsible for administering the traditional telephone networks. Some of these employees spent 15 to 20 percent of their time on this task. The VoIP network freed up their time so they could focus on more important business initiatives.

Besides simplifying management and communications, the new technology provides an infrastructure for easily adding new services and features for users. A manager can use the system to send a single message to all users simultaneously. When 100 executives moved after Domecq's spirits division was reorganized, very few changes had to be made to provide them with telephone service. No new wiring was required. They merely picked up their phones and moved to a new desk.

Canada's Maritime Steel and Foundries Ltd. has used a VoIP system from 3Com for more than four years. Maritime Steel has five divisions in three cities: Alberton on Prince Edward Island and New Glasgow and Dartmouth in Nova Scotia. Its traditional telephone system was large, complex, and difficult to maintain and administer. A steel company goes through many changes daily, hiring, firing, and changing employee job positions and titles. The communications system has to be flexible in order to accomodate these changes. It might cost $200 for a telecommunications specialist to visit each site to make such changes.

Sean Green, Maritime's manager of information systems, wanted a system that is easy to administer. By using VoIP, he now spends very little time taking care of Maritime's telephone needs. The system can be administered from a Web page, which Green can access anywhere he is working. Creating a new extension for an employee, for example, only takes about ten seconds. The system further eases communication by transferring voice into data. Voice messages can be turned into Wav files (Windows' digital audio format) and accessed by the recipient as audible email. With this feature, Maritime's executives can bring up a Web page anywhere in the world and access all their messages, including voice. Maritime's system paid for itself within two years.

U.S. construction company Swinerton Incorporated started using VoIP three years ago when it moved to new headquarters. Swinerton had been building more cubicles and spending money for the telephone provider to add more lines and move telephones around. Swinerton lacked sufficient internal staff to support a conventional phone system, so it purchased a system for $284 000 from NEC Corporation that included a server, 220 phones, two operator consoles, a voice mail system, management software, and training. Managers can control the system and make changes to phones and user accounts in many different locations from a single console.

Swinerton's VoIP service isn't quite as reliable as the conventional telephone system. Now and then a NEC handset fails. Larry Mathews, Swinerton's director of information technology, observes that a VoIP system is "only going to be as reliable as your data network," and users are accustomed to conventional telephones that always work. VoIP telephones may perform more like computers, which need to be rebooted from time to time and are vulnerable to hackers, computer viruses, and other security risks. If IP voice traffic isn't properly secured, it could be intercepted, copied, or redirected. Nevertheless, Swinerton is so pleased with the system that it installed 700 VoIP lines in offices from Houston to Oakland, California, and Seattle.

To Think About: How does VoIP technology provide value for businesses? What management, organization, and technology issues would have to be addressed to convert from a conventional telephone system to one using VoIP?

Sources: Susan Maclean, "Dialing IP for Increased Productivity," IT Focus, January 1, 2004, available www.itworldcanada.com/Pages/Docbase/View Article.aspx?ID=idgml-cff3cab6-db73-426b-82a8-7afcd1fd0aff &title=Dialling%20IP%20for%20increased%20productivity, accessed April 24, 2005; and David M. Ewalt, "The New Voice Choice," *Information Week*, March 1, 2004.

Telecommunications and cable companies such as Bell Canada, Primus Telecommunications, Rogers Communications, and Shaw Communications are starting to offer Internet calling services for consumers. Industry analysts predict an increase in VoIP phones shipped to businesses worldwide and cable companies offering Internet phone service will steal a growing percentage of residential phone lines from regional telephone companies over the next decade. The majority of long-distance phone calls in China use VoIP, and China's new local phone systems are also being built with this infrastructure (Ewalt 2004; Grant 2004; Ramstad and Brown 2004).

Virtual Private Networks

Internet technology can also reduce communication costs by enabling companies to create virtual private networks as low-cost alternatives to private WANs. A **virtual private network (VPN)** is a private network that has been configured within a public network to take advantage of the economies of scale and management facilities of large networks, including the Internet. The VPN provides the organization with the same capabilities at a much lower cost than owned or leased lines that can be used only by one organization. Although some VPNs run over proprietary networks open only to subscribers, many companies are turning to VPNs based on the Internet Protocol (IP) that run over the public Internet.

A virtual private network based on the Internet Protocol provides a secure connection between two points across the Internet, enabling private communications to travel

virtual private network (VPN)

securely over the public infrastructure (see Figure 7-20). VPNs based on the Internet Protocol provide substantial savings over non-IP networks while providing more bandwidth, more flexible network designs, and the ability to link more easily to remote and international offices. VPNs also provide a network infrastructure for combining voice and data networks.

Several competing protocols are used to protect data transmitted over the public Internet, including Point-to-Point Tunneling Protocol (PPTP). In a process called *tunneling*, packets of data are encrypted and wrapped inside IP packets so that non-IP data can travel securely through the Internet. By adding this wrapper around a network message to hide its content, organizations can create a private connection that travels through the public Internet.

Internet-based VPNs can be used in countries where private networks are not easily available. For example, CVG International, a subsidiary of the Corporation Venezolana de Guayana that markets products from Guyana, uses an Internet VPN from Equant to link offices in Miami, Venezuela, and Rotterdam. By using this VPN service for interoffice communications and communications with affiliated companies, CVG is cutting telecommunications costs. VPNs are also useful for building extranets because businesses can operate their own IP VPNs and give partners access over the public Internet. ISPs provide VPN services, or companies can create and manage their own VPNs.

7.5   The Internet in Canada

Although the Internet was developed in the U.S. and the World Wide Web was developed by a Brit in Switzerland (who now resides in Massachusetts in the U.S.), Canada has a history of both research and development in Internet technologies. There are many organizations in Canada working to further enhance the Internet globally and promote its access and speed locally.

FIGURE 7-20   *A virtual private network using the Internet.*

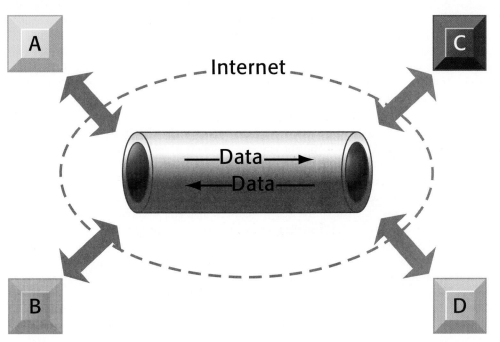

This VPN is a private network of computers linked using a secure "tunnel" connection over the Internet. It protects data transmitted over the public Internet by encoding the data and "wrapping" them within the IP. By adding a wrapper around a network message to hide its content, organizations can create a private connection that travels through the public Internet.

Many Canadian universities have Internet innovation research centres. CANARIE is the prime mover among government entities; CANARIE continues to receive federal funding even though it is a private-sector organization.

Like other countries around the globe, including the U.S., the more rural areas within Canada have much less access, particularly high-speed access, to the Internet. If you look at Figure 7-17, you will see that the northern half of Canada has no gigaPoP presence. High speed access from our less populated areas, primarily rural and frequently populated by Aboriginal peoples, is expensive and difficult to find. While the federal government is determined to provide Internet access to all schools in Canada, their progress in providing broadband access to rural areas is slow.

Even with this obstacle, Canada still ranks in the top 20 percent of countries in the world in what *The Economist* calls *e-readiness* (The 2005 E-Readiness Rankings, 2005) These rankings are based on a weighted collection of almost 100 quantitative and qualitative criteria, organized into six categories: connectivity and technical infrastructure (25 percent), business environment (20 percent), consumer and business adoption (20 percent), legal and policy environment (15 percent), social and cultural environment (15 percent), and supporting e-services (5 percent).

Canadian domain names (ending in .ca) were originally approved by one individual, a university computing staff member. Today Canadian domain names can be registered from a number of organizations, each offering a different price and different services in their registration packages.

WINDOW ON MANAGEMENT

Monitoring Employees on Networks: Unethical or Good Business?

Email use has exploded as millions of people the world over turn to it for speedy, convenient, and inexpensive business and personal communications. Not surprisingly, the use of email for personal reasons at the workplace has also grown, as has the use of the Web for personal business at work. A number of studies have concluded that at least 25 percent of employee online time is spent on non-work-related Web surfing, and perhaps as many as 90 percent of employees receive or send personal email at work.

Many companies have begun monitoring their employees' use of email and the Internet. A study by the American Management Association concluded that more than 75 percent of large U.S. companies are recording and reviewing employee communications and activities on the job, including email, Internet connections, and computer files. Joke emails are also a contentious issue, but Internet users are split. About the same proportion agree they often receive joke emails that they consider inappropriate (37 percent), as those who agree they look forward to receiving joke emails at work (35 percent). Nonetheless, joke or not, those emails are not related to work. The supervisor's legal right to spy on you is well-nigh unassailable. "It has always been cause for dismissal if you're not using company time to do company work," explains Paul Kent-Snowsell, a Vancouver lawyer who specializes in Internet cases.

Managers worry about the loss of time and employee pro-

ductivity when employees are focusing on personal rather than company business. If personal traffic on company networks is too high, it can also clog the company's network so that business work cannot be performed. Some employees at Xerox in the U.S. had sent so much junk and pornography email while on the job that the company's email system shut down. Too much time on personal business—on the Internet or not—can mean lost revenue or overcharges to clients. Some employees may be charging time they spend trading their personal stocks online or pursuing other personal business to clients, thus overcharging the clients.

When employees use email or the Web at employer facilities or with employer equipment, anything they do, including anything illegal, carries the company name. Therefore, the employer can be held liable. Management may fear that racist, sexually explicit, or other potentially offensive material accessed or traded by their employees could result in adverse publicity and even lawsuits for the firm. Even if the company is not found to be liable, responding to lawsuits could cost the company tens of thousands of dollars. Companies also fear email leakages of trade secrets or strategies.

Companies have the legal right to monitor what employees are doing with company equipment during business hours. The question is whether electronic surveillance is an appropriate tool for maintaining an efficient and positive workplace.

Some companies try to bank all personal activities on corporate networks—zero tolerance. Others block employee access to specific Web sites or limit personal time on the Web using software that enables IT departments to track the Web sites employees visit, the amount of time employees spend at these sites, and the files they download. Some firms have fired employees who have stepped out of bounds.

The Canada Customs and Revenue Agency (CCRA) employs nearly 25 000 workers with Internet access. The CCRA uses Websense software to automate the agency's Internet access policy. The CCRA wanted to prevent access to inappropriate sites using decision-making intelligence while permitting specific groups of workers to access sites specific to their job function—for example, enabling the CCRA's customs inspectors to access firearms import sites. Websense can also bar Web-based email sites (e.g., Hotmail or Google) and can restrict online surfing to a specific time period, such as lunch time or after hours.

No solution is problem free, but most believe companies should write and communicate corporate policies on employee email and Internet use to their employees. The policies should include explicit ground rules that state, by position or level, under what circumstances employees can use company facilities for email or Internet use. The policies should also inform employees whether these activities are monitored and explain why.

The rules should be tailored to specific business needs and organizational cultures. For example, although some companies may exclude all employees from visiting sites that have explicit sexual material, law firm or hospital employees may require access to these sites. Investment firms will need to allow many of their employees access to investment sites. A company dependent on widespread information sharing, innovation, and independence could very well find that monitoring creates more problems than it solves.

To Think About: Should managers monitor employee email and Internet usage? Why or why not? Describe an effective email and Web use policy for a company.

Sources: Chris Wood, Brenda Branswell, and Amy Cameron, "Who's Watching You?", *Maclean's*, available www.readersdigest.ca/debate.html?a =v&di=139&printer_version=1, accessed April 26, 2005; "Websense in Use at Canada Customs and Revenue Agency," available ww2.websense.com /docs/CaseStudies/Canada%20Customs%20and%20Revenue%20 Agency.pdf, accessed April 27, 2005; Riva Richmond, "It's 10 A.M. Do You Know Where Your Workers Are?" *Wall Street Journal*, January 12, 2004; Eric Zoeckler, "Issues to Ponder Before E-Monitoring Workers," *Suohamish County Business Journal*, July 2004; Olga Kharif, "Ever-Sharper Eyes Watch You Work," *Business Week*, July 22, 2003; Jason Gertzen, "Company Spy," *Milwaukee Journal-Sentinel*, May 17, 2003; and Laurie Willis, "More Companies Keeping Tabs on Employees," *San Francisco Chronicle*, May 13, 2003.

Management Opportunities, Challenges, and Solutions

Opportunities

Throughout your managerial career, you will face decisions on how to use networking technology and services to enhance the performance of your firm. You should be aware of the challenges in trying to implement these decisions and how they can be addressed.

Firms have an opportunity to bring about radical reductions in the cost of data and voice communication and to use networking and Internet technology in new ways as parts of new business models. The business value of these technologies cannot be underestimated.

Management Challenges

Telecommunications and networking technologies present challenges as well as opportunities for organizations. Three stand out: loss of management control over information systems, the need for organizational change, and the difficulty of ensuring infrastructure scalability and reliability.

Loss of Management Control Managing information systems technology and corporate data are more difficult in a distributed networked environment because of the lack of a single, central point where needed management can occur. Distributed client/server networks, peer-to-peer computing networks, mobile wireless networks, and Internet computing have created new independent sources of computing power. End users may be collecting, storing, and disseminating data and software that do not meet corporate standards.

Another consequence of placing computing power and networking resources in the hands of employees is the surging use of the Web and email for nonbusiness purposes. This practice is draining productivity and business performance, prompting many organizations to monitor employee use of networks and the Internet. The Window on Management explores the ethical implications of employee monitoring. When you read this case, pay attention to the ethical dilemma raised by workplace monitoring.

Organizational Change Requirements Leading-edge telecommunications technology and the Internet cannot make organizations more effective unless underlying organizational issues are fully addressed. Old ways of doing business must also be changed to work effectively with the Internet and related network technologies. These changes in corporate culture and organizational structure are not easy to make. It took several years of hard work and large financial investments for IBM to make its business processes Web enabled and to convince disparate business units to adopt a "one IBM" mind-set in which everyone uses common tools (Kanter 2001).

Scalability, Reliability, and Security Companies that intensively use communications technology require plentiful bandwidth and storage capacity for transmitting and maintaining all of the data generated by electronic commerce and electronic business transactions. Network infrastructures must be able to handle current e-commerce demands and scale rapidly to meet future demands while providing high levels of performance and availability for mission-critical applications.

Security is of paramount importance for firms with extensive networking and firms that conduct electronic transactions with individuals or other businesses outside organizational boundaries. Networks present end users, hackers, and thieves with many points of access and opportunities to steal or modify data in networks. Systems linked to the Internet are even more vulnerable because the Internet was designed to be available to everyone. Chapter 9 discusses Internet security issues in greater detail.

Solution Guidelines

Careful planning and management are essential for meeting these challenges.

Developing a Strategic Networking Plan A strategic networking plan is a good first step. The plan should describe how communications services and technology could enhance your firm's competitive position. Your analysis should identify the most critical areas where new network-based applications could make a large difference in performance. What areas need improvement? What communications services does your firm need? Do these services need to be integrated? How many different locations and users in the organization require access to communications services and networks? What is the anticipated frequency and volume of communications? What types of networks does your firm need to accomplish its business goals? Does the firm need long-distance networks, local area networks, or public networks such as the Internet? What level of availability and reliability do networks have to maintain? How much is your firm willing to spend to achieve this level of service?

Managing the Change To gain the full benefit of any new technology, organizations must carefully plan for and manage the changes. Business processes may need to be reengineered to accompany infrastructure changes (see Chapter 3). Management must address the organizational issues that arise from shifts in staffing, function, power, and the organizational culture that result when a new information technology infrastructure is implemented. Data administration (see Chapter 6) becomes even more important when networks link many different applications, business areas, and computing devices.

Summary

1. **Describe the features of a contemporary corporate network infrastructure and key networking technologies.**

   A contemporary corporate network infrastructure relies on both public and private infrastructures to support the movement of information across diverse technological platforms. It includes the traditional telephone system, mobile cellular communication, wireless local area networks, videoconferencing systems, a corporate Web site, intranets, extranets, and an array of local and wide area networks, including the Internet. This collection of networks evolved from two fundamentally different types of networks: telephone networks and computer networks.

   A simple network consists of two or more connected computers. Basic network components include computers, network interfaces, a connection medium, network operating system software, and either a hub or a switch.

   Contemporary networks have been shaped by the rise of client/server computing, the use of packet switching, and the adoption of TCP/IP as a universal communications standard for linking disparate networks and computers. Client/server networks have distributed much of the organization's computing power to the desktop and factory floor. Packet switching makes more efficient use of network communications capacity by breaking messages into small packets that are sent independently among different paths in a network and then reassembled at their destination. Protocols provide a common set of rules that enable communication among diverse components in a telecommunications network. TCP/IP is a suite of protocols that has become the dominant model of achieving connectivity among different networks and computers. It is the connectivity model used in the Internet.

2. **Evaluate alternative transmission media, types of networks, and network services.**

   The principal physical transmission media are twisted copper telephone wire; coaxial copper cable; fibre-optic cable; and wireless transmission using microwave, satellite, low-frequency radio waves, or infrared waves. The choice of transmission medium depends on the distance and volume of communication required by the organization and the organization's financial resources. Twisted wire enables companies to use existing wiring for telephone systems for digital communication, although it is relatively slow. Fibre-optic and coaxial cable are used for high-volume transmission but are expensive to install. Microwave and satellite are used for wireless communication over long distances. The transmission capacity of a medium, known as the bandwidth, is determined by the range of frequencies it can accommodate.

   There are different types of networks and network services available to organizations. Network selection and design should be based on the organization's information requirements and the distance required for transmission. Local area networks (LANs) connect PCs and other digital devices together within a 500-metre radius and are used today for many corporate computing tasks. Network components may be connected together using a star, bus, or ring topology. Wide area networks (WANs) span broad geographical distances, ranging from several miles to continents, and are private networks that are independently managed. Metropolitan area networks (MANs) span a single urban area while campus area networks (CANs) span a campus of buildings or a military base.

   A number of network services are available to organizations requiring high-bandwidth transmission. Frame relay is a shared network service with transmission speeds ranging from 56 Kbps to more than 40 Mbps; it relies on digital circuits that require less error checking than packet switching. Asynchronous transfer mode (ATM) provides transmission speeds of 1.5 Mbps to more than 9 Gbps, parcelling data into fixed 53-byte cells. ATM can pass data between computers from different vendors and is popular for transmitting data, video, and audio over the same network. Integrated services digital network (ISDN) is an international standard for dial-up network access that uses existing local telephone lines to integrate voice, data, image, and video services. Basic rate ISDN can transmit data at a rate of 128 Kbps.

   Digital subscriber line (DSL) technologies, cable modems, and T-1 lines are often used for high-capacity Internet connections. Like ISDN, DSL technologies also operate over existing copper telephone lines to carry voice, data, and video, but they have higher transmission capacities than ISDN. Asymmetric digital subscriber line (ADSL) supports a transmission rate of 1.5 to 9 Mbps when receiving data and up to 640 Kbps when sending data. Symmetric digital subscriber line (SDSL) supports the same transmission rate for sending and receiving data of up to 3 Mbps.

   Cable modems, which operate over cable TV lines, can provide high-speed access to the Web or corporate intranets at speeds of up to 4 Mbps. T lines are high-speed data lines leased from communications providers. A T-1 line supports a data transmission rate of 1.544 Mbps.

3. **Assess the role of the Internet and the World Wide Web in a firm's information technology infrastructure.**

   The Internet is a worldwide network of networks that uses the client/server model of computing and the TCP/IP network reference model. Every computer on the Internet is assigned a unique numeric IP address. The Domain Name System (DNS) converts IP addresses to domain names so that users only need to specify a domain name to access a computer on the Internet instead of typing in the numeric IP address. No one owns the Internet and it has no formal management organization. However, worldwide Internet policies are established by organizations and government bodies such as the Internet Architecture Board and the World Wide Web Consortium. The Internet must also conform to the laws of the sovereign nation-states in which it operates, as well as the technical infrastructures that exist within the nation-state.

The Internet's global reach and connectivity, scalability, distributed design, universal standards, richness, and interactivity have made it the primary infrastructure for electronic business and electronic commerce. Major Internet services include email, Usenet, LISTSERV, chatting, instant messaging, Telnet, FTP, and the World Wide Web.

The World Wide Web provides a universal set of standards for storing, retrieving, and displaying information in a client/server environment, enabling users to link to information resources housed on many different computer systems around the world. Web pages are based on Hypertext Markup Language (HTML) and can display text, graphics, video, and audio. Web site directories, search engines, and push technology can help users locate the information they need on the Web. Web technology and Internet networking standards provide the connectivity and interfaces for internal private intranets and private extranets that be accessed by many different kinds of computers inside and outside the organization.

4. *Identify and describe the most important tools for communication and e-business.*

The principal applications for communication are email, chatting, instant messaging, Usenet newsgroups, and LISTSERV services. These tools reduce time and cost when firms must manage organizational activities and communicate with many employees. Groupware, teamware, and electronic conferencing software provide tools to support communication and collaboration when people work together in groups or work teams, often in different locations. Firms are also starting to realize economies by using Internet telephony, which enables Internet technology to be used for telephone voice transmission. Internet technology can also reduce communication costs by enabling companies to create virtual private networks (VPNs) as low-cost alternatives to private WANs.

5. *Identify and describe the challenges posed by networking and the Internet, and propose management solutions.*

Challenges posed by networking and the Internet include loss of management control over information systems; the need for organizational change; and the difficulty of ensuring infrastructure scalability and reliability. Solutions include developing a strategic networking plan and carefully managing the business and organizational changes associated with intensive networking and the Internet.

Key Terms

Asynchronous transfer mode (ATM),   237
Backbone,   233
Bandwidth,   234
Broadband,   236
Bus networks,   235
Cable modems,   237
Campus area network (CAN),   234
Chat,   251
Coaxial cable,   233
Connectivity,   226
Dense wavelength division multiplexing (DWDM),   233
Digital subscriber line (DSL),   237
Distributed processing,   230
Domain name,   239
Domain Name System (DNS),   239
Email,   251
Fibre-optic cable,   233
File Transfer Protocol (FTP),   242
Firewalls,   248
Frame relay,   237
Groupware,   252
Hertz,   234
Home page,   245
Hubs,   230

Hypertext Transfer Protocol (HTTP),   244
Information appliance,   242
Instant messaging,   251
Integrated services digital network (ISDN),   237
Internet Protocol (IP) address,   238
Internet service provider (ISP),   238
Internet telephony   252
Internet2,   249
Internetworking,   237
LISTSERV,   251
Local area network (LAN),   234
Metropolitan area network (MAN),   235
Modem,   232
Multicasting,   248
Multiplexing,   233
Network interface card (NIC),   229
Network operating system (NOS),   230
Open Systems Interconnection (OSI) reference model,   232
Optical networks,   233
Packet switching,   230
Peer-to-peer,   235
Peer-to-peer computing,   252
Protocol,   231
Push technology,   247

RDF Site Summary (RSS),   248
Ring networks,   235
Router,   230
Search engines,   245
Search-based advertising,   246
Semantic Web,   248
Shopping bots,   246
Star network,   235
Switch,   230
T lines,   237
Teamware,   252
Telnet,   242
Topology,   235
Transmission Control Protocol/Internet Protocol (TCP/IP),   231
Twisted wire,   232
Unified messaging,   253
Uniform Resource Locator (URL),   244
Usenet,   251
Virtual private network (VPN),   254
Voice over IP (VoIP),   252
Web logs (blogs),   248
Web master,   245
Wide area networks (WANs),   235

Review Questions

1. Describe the features of a contemporary corporate telecommunications infrastructure and a simple network.

2. Describe seven major trends in telecommunications.

3. What is the business value of telecommunications and networking? What role is played by Metcalfe's Law?

4. Name and describe the three technologies that have shaped contemporary telecommunications systems.

5. Name the different types of physical transmission media and compare them in terms of speed and cost.

6. What is a local area network (LAN)? What are the components of a typical LAN? What are the functions of each component?

7. Name and describe the principal network topologies.

8. Define the following: WAN, MAN, modem, protocol, optical network, and bandwidth.

9. List and describe the various broadband network services.

10. What are the features that define the Internet? How is the Internet governed? How does it provide business value?

11. Explain how the domain name and IP addressing system works.

12. List and describe the principal Internet services.

13. List and describe alternative ways of locating information on the Web.

14. What are intranets and extranets? How do they provide value to businesses?

15. Describe the capabilities of next-generation networks, including Internet2? How do they differ from those of the existing public Internet? What benefits can they provide?

16. Name and describe the principal technologies and tools that support communication and electronic business.

17. What are Internet telephony and virtual private networks? How do they provide value to businesses?

18. Describe the challenges posed by networking and the Internet and some ways to address them.

Discussion Questions

1. Network design is a key business decision as well as a technology decision. Why?

2. A fully integrated IT infrastructure is essential for business success. Do you agree? Why or why not?

Application Software Exercise:
Spreadsheet Exercise: Analyzing Web Site Visitors

Your firm, Marina Clothiers, makes casual pants, shirts, and other clothes for both men and women. Your firm has been attempting to increase the number of online customers by placing advertising banners for your Web site at other Web sites. When users click on these banner ads, they automatically are transported to your Web site. Data from your advertising campaign are summarized in the weekly marketing trends reports (MTR) produced by your Web site analysis software, which appears on the Companion Website for Chapter 7.

- Visitors are the number of people who visited your Web site by clicking on a banner ad for your site that was placed on an affiliated Web site.

- Shoppers are the number of visitors referred by banner ads who reached a page in your Web site designated as a shopping page.

- Attempted buyers are the number of potential buyers referred by banner ads who reached a Web site designated as a page for summarizing and paying for purchases.

- Buyers are the number of buyers referred by banner ads who actually placed an order from your Web site.

- Source indicates the specific Web site from which visitors came to your Web site.

In trying to increase the number of online customers, you must determine your Web site's success in converting visitors to actual buyers. You must also look at the abandonment rate—the percentage of attempted buyers who abandon your Web site just as they were about to make a purchase. Low-conversion rates and high-abandonment rates are indicators that a Web site is not very effective. You also must identify likely Web site partners for a new advertising campaign. Use the MTR with your spreadsheet software to help you answer the following questions. Include a graphics presentation to support your findings:

1. What are the total number of visitors, shoppers, attempted buyers, and buyers at your Web site?

2. Which sources provided the highest conversion rate to buyers at your Web site—that is, the percentage of visitors from a previous site who become buyers on your site? What is the average conversion rate for your Web site?

3. Which sources provided the highest abandonment rate at your Web site—that is, the percentage of attempted buyers who abandoned their shopping cart

at your Web site before completing a purchase? What is the average abandonment rate for your Web site?

4. On which Web sites (or types of Web sites) should your firm purchase more banner ads?

Electronic Commerce Project: Using Web Search Engines for Business Research

You have heard that fuel cells might be an inexpensive way to provide electricity for your house, but you do not know anything about fuel cells. You decide that you want to research the topic to learn what fuel cells are and how they can be used for generating electricity for your house. Use the following four search engines to obtain that information:

Yahoo!, AltaVista, Google, and Ask Jeeves. If you wish, try some other search engines as well. Compare the volume and quality of information you find with each search tool. Which tool is the easiest to use? Which produced the best results for your research? Why?

Group Project: Identifying Strategic Opportunities for Networking Technology

With a group of two or three of your fellow students, describe in detail the ways that telecommunications technology can provide a firm with competitive advantage. Use the companies described in the chapters you have read so far to illustrate the points you make, or select from business or computer magazines examples of other companies using telecommunications. If possible, use electronic presentation software to present your findings to the class.

Web Sites of Interest

There are many interesting Web sites to enhance your learning about networking and the Internet. You can search the Web yourself or try the following Web sites to add to what you have already learned.

World Wide Web Consortium **www.w3.org**
One of the World Wide Web coordinating bodies. Find out what the Web may be like in the future.

Canadian Legislation **www.parl.gc.ca/LEGISINFO/**
Parliament's site to search for bills that have been submitted to Parliament. See what Parliament may be planning for regulating telecommunications in Canada.

Search Networking **www.searchnetworking.com**
A terrific site to find answers to questions about telecommunications.

Coast Software **www.coast.ca**
Canadian company specializing in Web management tools for the enterprise.

Google **www.google.ca**
The most popular search engine; you can download a host of tools, including a Photo editor, a toolbar, and a desktop search engine, and open a GMail account.

Hobbes' Internet Timeline **http://upword.dns2go.com/hobbe.html**
A detailed history of the Internet from the 1950s to 2000.

Wired News **www.wired.com/news**
News about a host of Internet technologies.

DoCoMo **www.nttdocomo.com**
Information about I-Mode and Japan's NTT DoCoMo company and network.

CASE STUDY:
The Canadian Trucking Industry Moves to the Internet

It's 1996. The World Wide Web is three years old, but the Internet hasn't reached Gore Bay, Ontario, on Manitoulin Island in Georgian Bay. Who would think that one of the first Canadian trucking companies to make use of the Internet would be located in a town that had no Internet access? But that's what happened.

Manitoulin Transport (MT) is a less-than-truckload (LTL) trucking company with 35 terminals across Canada. Started as a small business in 1953, MT now provides common carrier service all across Canada and in the 48 contiguous United States. Today MT is Canada's largest freight management provider, with more direct Canadian service points

than any other LTL carrier in North America. MT operates 400 tractors and uses over 100 owner-operators. MT also provides logistics support and custom brokerage.

Management at MT decided the best way to expand their customer base and grow their business was to move several functions, one at a time, to the Internet by establishing a Web presence. But first, how to get Internet access on Manitoulin Island? MT partnered with Ontario Northland IT Solutions to provide Internet access, not just to MT but all residents on the island, using a Web server set up at MT. Once the access was available, MT could begin developing its Web applications one by one.

Once the decision to move several applications to the Internet was made, MT hired an independent contractor to create its Web site. After the initial start-up, though, all maintenance, upgrades, and new applications were done in-house. MT found that its customers were slow to move to the Internet, but after a brief learning curve, MT discovered that it was their small- to medium-sized customers that used the Web site; most of the larger customers preferred using their pre-existing electronic data interchange (EDI) systems themselves. In addition, MT found that customers that enjoyed MT's phone-based customer service also needed education and training to enable them to give up that "lifeline" to the company.

Coordinating trucking traffic between customers and MT's 35 terminals is essential to the company's business. Like most transportation companies in 1996, customers call the home office to make their reservations, inquire about pickup and delivery times and the status of their shipments, and inquire about their bills. To maximize their support for this function, MT first developed an online freight tracking system in 1997. The freight tracking system permitted customers to obtain a report on the status and location of their shipments in real time by entering an identification number or waybill number on the system's Web page. This one application reduced customer wait times online, improving customer service and customer satisfaction, and reduced the workload on MT customer service representatives by about 200 calls per day.

The freight tracking system was so successful that MT examined other areas to see where the use of information technology and the Internet could help. MT equipped their 60 sales staff with laptop computers utilizing Lotus Notes groupware so they can update their information daily while on the road. "The technology lets them stay out of the office and make sales instead of doing paperwork," notes Myles McLeod, MT's vice-president of finance.

Since those first two Web-based applications, MT has expanded their Internet focus many times over. Manitoulin's electronic pickup feature is a fast and convenient way to manage freight. This Internet-based system utilizes an easy-to-navigate interface which can be accessed from anywhere in North America. By simply entering the shipper and consignee information and some shipment details, a pickup request can be generated by the shipper, consignee, or freight forwarder. MT has placed downloadable forms on its Web site for bills of lading, credit applications, viewers for their forms, rules and regulations for both Canadian and U.S. tariff laws, and customs forms for both Canada and the U.S. MT can also bill electronically, emailing invoices to customers instead of mailing them.

The MT Web development staff also created a customized home page for their customers. Dubbed MT Direct, the Web site allows a customer to create a customized account with its own home page and permits the customer to grant access through sub-accounts to various parties associated with their own business, such as their own customers, shippers, traffic and supply chain analysts, and their own accounts receivable and payable departments. MT Direct also provides secure access to advanced features, such as advanced shipment notices, transit reports, Internet pickups, and electronic bills of lading.

Reports that can be accessed through MT Direct can be formatted according to the customer's preferences, in HTML, PDF, PCL, TIFF, CSV, RTF, XLS, or 123 formats—a wide variety of viewing and formats, some of which also allow for manipulation or downloading of shipping statistics and data into the customer's own computer files. The entire procedure of conversion and email can be scheduled by customers to run at their choice of dates and times; this is done automatically. No intervention from Manitoulin personnel, other than submitting the initial report request, can mean less errors and protected privacy of customers' information.

MT has begun beta testing Internet-based solutions providing seamless integration between their customer's procurement systems and MT's systems. This technology-driven solution will link their customers' order systems with MT's pickup, delivery, and tracing systems to help expedite the shipping process, monitor freight movement cycles, and reduce errors.

MT also participates in a B2B network (see Chapter 13), allowing MT to post available truck space and secure loads, reducing deadheading, wherein empty or almost empty trucks are on the road.

In addition to these customer- and sales-focused applications, MT has also installed satellite navigation in many of its trucks to track their location and to communicate with their drivers. "This is a very time-sensitive business," says McLeod, "and there is a very fine line between making a profit on a shipment and losing money. Our goal is to keep the trucks loaded all the time, and the e-business tools help us in that regard." MT is also looking at land-based wireless technologies to handle communication with the whole fleet.

MT is not the only Canadian trucking company making use of the Internet and the Web. Montreal-based Empress Truck Rental and Leasing leases more than 400 trucks to its customers and provides maintenance on those trucks as well. Empress sells its trucks after the leases run out, so maintenance is an especially important factor in the company's success. The maintenance department must be able to obtain a variety of parts on short notice. Using the Internet, Empress can locate these parts and arrange for timely shipping.

Like MT, Empress started slowly on the Web, first establishing a simple contact Web site. Empress was also automating its materials procurement process and though they could expand this type of service to their customers through a professionally-developed Web site and e-commerce applications. Empress' renovated Web site enables automatic mileage update for maintenance purposes without human intervention from either end; customers can advise Empress of their mileage through the Web site. The Web site also allows for maintenance scheduling, replacement truck reservation, and online confirmation of transactions. Empress also uses their Web site as an advertising site, supplanting their monthly advertisements in trade magazines.

Another Canadian trucking company to make the move to the Web is Trimac Transport, headquartered in Calgary, Alberta. Trimac provides highway transport of commodities to customers throughout North America. Trimac also operates a third-party logistics company, Trimac Logistics, offering full logistic services. Since the mid-1990s, about the same time as MT and Empress were moving to the Web, Trimac began to implement a variety of Internet-based technologies. These included EDI transactions, satellite tracking of shipments, a shop maintenance system, and an enterprise resource planning (ERP) system (see Chapter 14). Trimac has also implemented a freight tracking system similar to MT's so their customers can log on and find out where their shipments are. To implement these technologies, Trimac has simply bought third-party systems and integrated them with their existing systems.

The trucking industry is about as traditional as an industry can be. Its processes are very similar—even between companies—and most of the processes are fairly routine. As recently as the mid 1990s, most of these processes were paper-based or had only recently been automated to a mainframe computer environment. As these three Canadian trucking companies—each with a different focus and market niche—show, even in very traditional industries, the Internet and the Web have changed the way business is conducted. The Internet and the Web have also changed the way customers view their vendors' businesses.

Sources: Gordon Arnaut, "On a Roll with High-Tech Trucks," November 18, 2002, available **www.globetechnology.com/einsider/**

robmagazine/stories/roll.html, accessed April 28, 2005; "Manitoulin—Transport Online Tracking (Canada)", available **www.beepknowledgesystem.org/ShowCase.asp?CaseTitleID=28 5&CaseID=649**, accessed April 28, 2005; "E-Commerce and the Canadian Trucking Industry—Handbook," available **www.tc.gc.ca/pol/en/report/E-commerce/HandbookEn /menu.htm**, accessed April 28, 2005; and **www.manitoulintransport.com**, accessed May 2, 2005.

CASE STUDY QUESTIONS:

1. Evaluate the trucking industry using the competitive forces and value chain models.

2. What is Manitoulin Transport's business strategy? What role do networking and the Internet play in this strategy?

3. What management, organization, and technology issues do Manitoulin Transport, Empress Trucking, and Trimac Transport face in running their businesses? What role do telecommunications and the Internet play in solving these challenges?

4. How effectively has Manitoulin Transport used information systems and the Internet to meet its business strategy goals and maintain a competitive edge?

Chapter 8

The Wireless Revolution

OBJECTIVES

After reading this chapter, you will be able to:

1. Identify the principal wireless transmission media and devices, cellular network standards, generations of mobile networking technology, and mobile computing standards for Internet access.

2. Describe the major standards for wireless networks and wireless Internet access.

3. Evaluate the role of m-commerce in business, and describe the most important m-commerce applications.

4. Assess the business value of wireless technology, and describe important wireless applications in business.

5. Identify and describe the challenges posed by wireless technology, and propose management solutions.

Opening Case: Toronto Healthcare Goes Wireless

Canada's publicly funded healthcare system faces greater pressure than ever to meet the needs of Canadians and to minimize costs. Hospitals across Canada must find ways to serve their patients—their market—more efficiently. This is particularly true in Ontario and in Toronto, a diverse city of more than 4 million people.

Hospital Logistics Inc. (HLI) is the logistics and supply chain management arm for the University Health Network. Serving seven Toronto hospitals in total, the HLI warehouse is located in Oakville, Ontario. It was formed by a partnership between University Health Network, a group of several Toronto hospitals, and ThiINC, a Toronto-based company that designs systems to manage healthcare supply chains. Hospital Logistics' mandate was to streamline inventory, ordering, and distribution of medical supplies at the Network's member hospitals.

The new HLI system uses Intermec radio-frequency (RF) hardware for warehouse operations and Intermec mobile computers in the hospitals themselves. The new system is part of a strategy to outsource much of these hospitals' supply chains. The system starts at the hospital supply carts and storage closets. Each ward has them, and their supplies are counted every day. Routinely used consumables are stocked in predetermined quantities. During each shift, a hospital worker makes the rounds with an Intermec mobile computer to take inventory. The Intermec mobile computer includes both wireless (RF-based) and wired configurations. Because radio waves can interfere with some hospital equipment, wired configurations are used inside hospitals.

The worker scans the bar-code label on the cart or shelf, identifying the location of the items, and then scans items from the computer's pull-down menu, entering the on-hand amount. A software application from TECSYS (a supply chain management software company) suggests the required amount for the item. The worker can then either choose that quantity or override the suggestion and order a different amount. When inventory checking is complete, the worker docks the Intermec mobile computer in its cradle, and the collected and ordering data is sent to Hospital Logistics through either a DSL line or a virtual private network, depending on the location. Shipments now frequently arrive the same day, instead of two to three days after the order is placed.

At the HLI warehouse, workers use an Intermec 802.11b RF system to transmit data across the warehouse, providing a wireless connection between the host computer and the stock pickers' handheld devices. Stock pickers receive the orders on their handhelds and can relay order status back to the host computer. The host computer then prints out a packing list. Since HLI maintains more than 2500 SKUs of goods, the new system greatly simplifies getting the right products to the right cart in each hospital.

The efficiency of this system helps minimize costs. The technology itself saves hospital worker and warehouse worker time. Hospitals can maintain lower inventory levels since replenishment is easy and quick. With better information about the costs associated with medical supplies, consolidation can also drive down costs by leveraging prices. There is a further savings through consolidating carrying costs. Wireless networking at the warehouse and mobile computing at both the hospital and warehouse save costs for Toronto healthcare; these savings have implications for other hospitals and healthcare consortia.

Sources: "Canadian Hospitals Make Healthy Changes with Intermec," available **www.torwug.org/CaseStudies/Local/Intermec_hospitals.asp**, accessed May 4, 2005; "Hospital Logistics, Inc. Customer Case Studies," available **www.tecsys.com/resources/casestudies/hli.shtml**, accessed May 4, 2005.

Wireless networking is changing the way Toronto hospitals serve their patients, and it is changing the way that other organizations and businesses work. Therefore, it is important for you to understand how this technology works, its benefits and challenges, and how it can provide business value. In this chapter, you will learn about the technologies for wireless networking, different types of wireless networks and networking standards, and m-commerce and other applications where wireless is having its greatest impact. We will also identify the key decisions and challenges you will face as a manager in implementing and using this technology.

8.1 The Wireless Computing Landscape

We are at the edge of a wireless revolution that is transforming computing and information systems. Until very recently, using a computer meant going to where the computer was located and logging on. If the computer was networked to another computer or the Internet, that connection was wired, and our ability to use computers was limited to those wired locations.

We still use tethered computer systems, but increasingly we are turning to wireless devices—cell phones, wireless handhelds, laptops with wireless Internet connections—to communicate and to obtain information and data. In the future, it is even more likely that we'll be using some form of wireless technology.

The Wireless Revolution

By most accounts, the wireless revolution is still at the beginning stage. But already, it is changing the way businesses produce and communicate their products, how they sell them, and even how they define them.

Mobile phones are cheaper, more powerful, and nearly ubiquitous. Usage has exploded, with an average of 186 million new subscribers added every year. In 2002, the number of mobile phones worldwide surpassed the number of fixed-line phones (see Figure 8-1), and 1.8 billion or more global users are anticipated by 2007. Today more than 63 percent of Canadian inhabitants have cell phones, with even higher percentages in Western Europe (85% of the population) and some Asian nations (67% in Japan, 75% in Korea). China is emerging as a mobile giant, counting over 300 million subscribers today and 575 million predicted by 2010 (*eMarketer* 2002).

Today's mobile phones are not just for voice communication—they have become mobile platforms for delivering digital data. With faster computer chips, compression technology, and wireless networks, cell phones are finding new uses as mobile information appliances for recording and downloading photos, video, music, and games and for accessing the Internet. Already cell phones have screens that display 65 000 colours, compared to 256 colours just a few years ago. Mobile phones are also emerging as alternatives to cash or credit cards as people use them to transmit payments to scanners on cash registers and vending machines.

Anytime, anywhere Internet access will soon be within reach. An array of technologies has emerged to provide high-speed wireless access to the Internet for PCs and other wireless handheld devices as well as for cell phones. These new high-speed services have extended Internet access to numerous locations that could not be covered by traditional wired Internet services. Even more powerful wireless transmission technologies are under development.

As they become woven together, wireless technologies will create a foundation for other innovations. Consequently, businesses of all sizes are devoting more of their resources to wireless devices, services, and applications. According to International Data

FIGURE 8-1 *Mobile versus fixed-line subscribers worldwide.*

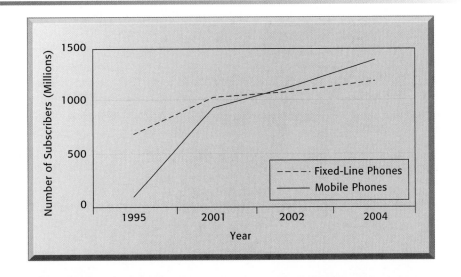

Mobile phone use is surpassing fixed-line use and will continue to grow very rapidly.

Sources: International Telecommunications Union, 2002 and 2003, and authors.

Corporation, worldwide wireless infrastructure and mobile network spending will grow from $38.8 billion in 2002 to $49 billion by 2007 (IDC 2003).

Businesses will increasingly use wireless networks and applications to cut costs, increase flexibility, and create new products and services. Loblaw, one of Canada's biggest food distributors, is testing radio frequency identification (RFID) technology to help them track goods, decreasing out-of-stock conditions on store shelves and cutting down on incidents of theft between suppliers' and stores'. Doctors are prescribing medications using wireless handhelds as they walk down hospital halls. Real estate agents use Palm smart phones to access all the available data on a house as they are showing it to prospective buyers. TransAlta, a Calgary, Alberta, power generation company, is deploying wireless local area networks at several generating plants to let field maintenance workers outfitted with handhelds link with back-end equipment and repair databases, ordering systems, and a new mobile workflow application. The implications for organizational productivity and performance are truly astounding.

The Business Value of Wireless Networking

Exactly how do the wireless innovations we have just described provide value for businesses? Chapter 7 described the business value provided by telecommunications and networking. Wireless networks for voice and data further amplify that value by providing anytime, anywhere communication and access to information, including the information resources of the Internet.

Wireless communication helps businesses stay more easily in touch with customers, suppliers, and employees and provides more flexible arrangements for organizing work. Companies can save on wiring offices and conference rooms by using wireless networks because they do not have to put cables through walls. Wireless networks also make additions, moves, and changes to offices and personnel much easier to implement.

A number of studies have shown that wireless networking increases worker productivity and output. If important data and people are accessible anywhere and anytime, workers spend less time trying to establish contact with people or to access information (Intel 2004; Sandsmark 2002).

For example, Intel studied the work habits and productivity of more than 100 of its employees who were upgraded to notebook computers that could access wireless LANs and the Internet. By taking advantage of wireless connectivity for tasks such as searching for files, copying documents, sending email, or scheduling meetings, employees realized a productivity gain of more than two hours per week, representing 5 percent of a typical 40-hour work week and nearly 100 hours of additional productivity per employee per year. If the average cost per employee was $100 000 per year, the annual benefit per employee would be $5000. The cost savings from using this technology more than paid for Intel's first-year cost of the new mobile devices.

Continuously connected wireless mobile systems actually changed the way Intel employees worked in the following ways:

- Employees made productive use of formerly wasted slices of time between larger tasks. Without a wireless notebook, an extra five minutes would have been insufficient to allow an employee to plug in, start up the system, connect to a remote network, and do useful work.

- Work locations became more flexible, with mobile employees believing they had more control over their work locations. They were able to select workplaces and times optimized to the task at hand—for example, working outside normal hours to support employees or partners in other parts of the world or finishing a piece of work while commuting.

- Wireless mobility allowed workers to reallocate their working time around professional and personal obligations.

Wireless technology has also been the source of new products, services, and sales channels in a variety of industries:

- Automotive manufacturers can build telematics as a value-added technology with their luxury cars. **Telematics** services combine wireless communication with tracking capabilities of a **global positioning system (GPS)**, a worldwide satellite navigational system. OnStar is an example. This optional telematics service is available in cars from General Motors (GM), Subaru, Volkswagen, Audi, and Isuzu. It has capabilities for on-board navigation, email, stolen vehicle tracking, accident assistance, and information services such as news, stock quotes, and local traffic and road condition reports, using GPS technology to track the exact location of the vehicle on the road.

- Airlines, airports, hotels, restaurants, and coffee shops such as Starbucks are equipping their spaces with hotspots for wireless Internet access to provide additional services and value to their customers.

- Safeway in the United Kingdom gave customers wireless Palm handheld devices and software to order products, increasing customer service. The wireless system also created a new low-cost channel to deliver coupons and special offers.

Inexpensive mobile devices make communication and Internet access available to groups that cannot afford conventional telephone or Internet service. For example, in China more than 300 million users use mobile phones, which is more than the number of fixed telephone lines in existence. In Africa, there are twice as many cellular telephones as fixed lines, and by 2008 mobile phones will outnumber fixed phones by four to one (Quadir 2003). Fast declining costs promise to make high-speed wireless communication even more affordable, with tremendous benefits for business, education, medicine, government, and social services.

Wireless Transmission Media and Devices

Wireless transmission sends signals through air or space without being tied to a physical line. All wireless media rely on various parts of the electromagnetic spectrum, as illustrated in Figure 8-2. Some types of wireless transmission, such as **microwave** or infrared, by nature occupy specific spectrum frequency ranges (measured in megahertz [MHz]). Other types of wireless transmissions, such as cellular telephones and paging devices, have been assigned a specific range of frequencies by national regulatory agencies and international agreements. Each frequency range has characteristics that have helped determine the specific function or data communications niche assigned to it.

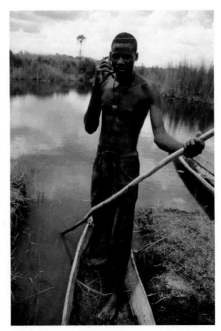

Mobile phones provide an inexpensive way of communicating and accessing information for people in Africa and other countries without extensive fixed phone lines or high PC usage and ownership.

Microwave systems, both terrestrial and celestial, transmit high-frequency radio signals through the atmosphere and are widely used for high-volume, long-distance, point-to-point communication. Microwave signals follow a straight line and do not bend with the curvature of the earth; therefore, long-distance terrestrial transmission systems require that transmission stations be positioned about 37 miles apart, adding to the expense of microwave.

This problem can be solved by bouncing microwave signals off communication **satellites**, enabling them to serve as relay stations for microwave signals transmitted from terrestrial stations. Communication satellites are cost-effective for transmitting large quantities of data over very long distances. Satellites are typically used for communications in large, geographically dispersed organizations that would be difficult to tie together through cabling media or terrestrial microwave transmission.

telematics

global positioning system (GPS)

microwave

satellites

Each telecommunications transmission medium or device occupies a different frequency range, measured in megahertz, on the electromagnetic spectrum.

For instance, Amoco uses satellites for real-time data transfer of oil field exploration data gathered from searches of the ocean floor. Using geosynchronous satellites, exploration ships transfer these data to central computing centres in the United States for use by researchers in Houston, Tulsa, and suburban Chicago. Figure 8-3 illustrates how this system works.

Conventional communication satellites move in stationary orbits approximately 35 000 kilometres above the earth. A newer satellite medium, the low-orbit satellite, travels much closer to the earth and is able to pick up signals from weaker transmitters. Low-orbit satellites also consume less power and cost less to launch than conventional satellites.

Devices for Wireless Transmission A range of alternative wireless devices is available for individuals requiring remote access to corporate systems and mobile communication and computing power. These devices include pagers, email handhelds, personal digital assistants (PDAs), cellular telephones, and smart phones. Personal computers are also starting to be used in wireless transmission, and Section 8.2 provides a detailed description of the technology for wireless computing.

FIGURE 8-3   *Amoco's satellite transmission system.*

Satellites help Amoco transfer seismic data between oil exploration ships and research centres in the United States.

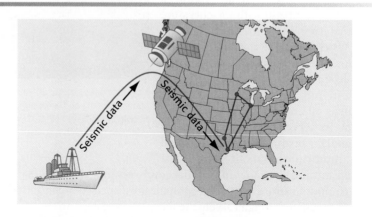

Paging systems, which beep when the user receives a short alphanumeric message, have been used for communicating with mobile workers. A more popular method of wireless text messaging is through **email handhelds**, such as the BlackBerry Handheld, which operate on a variety of wireless data network services. These devices include a small display screen and a keypad for typing short messages. Newer versions of these devices have an organizer, Web and voice transmission features, and can integrate with corporate applications. Email wireless handhelds are popular in the legal, financial, real estate, and other industries where there is a need to keep in constant touch with clients and the office.

Interestingly, the BlackBerry has led to the term *crackberry*, meaning someone who is so addicted to their BlackBerry (or other handheld device) that they constantly check it for email and messages, even when in meetings or while eating or watching the television. Supposedly, crackberry syndrome leads to increased stress due to constantly being connected and therefore always on call.

Cellular telephones (cell phones) work by using radio waves to communicate with radio antennas (towers) placed within adjacent geographic areas called cells. A telephone message is transmitted to the local cell by the cellular telephone and passed from antenna to antenna—cell to cell—until it reaches the cell of its destination, where it is transmitted to the receiving telephone. As a cellular signal travels from one cell into another, a computer that monitors signals from the cells switches the conversation to a radio channel assigned to the next cell. The radio antenna cells normally cover eight-mile hexagonal cells, although their radius is smaller in densely populated localities.

Older cellular systems are analog and newer cellular systems are digital. These digital cellular systems are capable of sending and receiving short text messages. **Short message service (SMS)** is a text message service used by a number of digital cell phone systems to send and receive short alphanumeric messages less than 160 characters in length. Like email, SMS messages can be forwarded and stored for later retrieval.

Personal digital assistants (PDAs) are small, handheld computers capable of entirely digital communications transmission. The handheld device includes applications such as an electronic scheduler, address book, memo pad, and expense tracker. More advanced models display, compose, send, and receive email messages and provide wireless access to the Internet. Some have built-in digital cameras and voice communication capabilities.

Higher-speed cellular networks and the Internet have spawned a new class of digital communication appliances that combine the functionality of a PDA with that of a digital cell phone. These **smart phones** can handle voice transmission and email; save addresses; store schedules; access a private corporate network; and access information from the Internet. Some have embedded digital cameras. Smart phones include Web browser software that enables digital cellular phones to access Web pages formatted to send text or other information that is suitable for tiny screens. To handle this growing mass of information on cell and smart phones, Zi Corporation, headquartered in Calgary, Alberta, has developed a number of applications to read handwriting on smart phone screens and to search all applications and data on the phone. Another Zi product predicts what the user is entering into the phone, learning by previous data entry what the user may be entering, thereby saving the user time in data entry.

Cellular Network Standards and Generations

Digital cellular service uses several different competing standards that do not interoperate with each other. This means that digital cellular handsets cannot work on networks that use another wireless standard.

In Europe and much of the rest of the world outside North America, the standard is **GSM**, short for **Global System for Mobile Communication**. Three out of four of the world's estimated 2 billion cell phones are GSM, including most of China, the world's largest cell phone market. The system's strength is its international roaming capability. Users have seamless same-number roaming in more than 170 countries. Most GSM systems outside North America operate in the 900-MHz and 1.8-GHz frequency bands. (In North America, they operate in the 1.9-GHz band.) The bandwidth is divided among

paging systems
email handhelds
cellular telephones (cell phones)
short message service (SMS)
personal digital assistants (PDAs)
smart phones
Global System for Mobile Communication (GSM)

users based on time division multiple access (TDMA) in which each user is allocated a portion of time on the frequency.

In the United States, GSM is not the standard because the Federal Communications Commission (FCC) permitted open competition in cell phone technology, resulting in multiple incompatible standards. This situation limits roaming and contributes to the high prices of North American cell phones.

There are GSM cell phone systems in the United States and Canada, including Rogers Communications, T-Mobile, VoiceStream, Cingular, and AT&T. However, the major standard in North America is **Code Division Multiple Access (CDMA)**, which is the system used by Sprint, Verizon, and MCI. CDMA was developed by the military during World War II. It transmits over several frequencies, occupies the entire spectrum, and randomly assigns users to a range of frequencies over time. In general, CDMA is cheaper to implement, is more efficient in its use of the spectrum, and provides higher quality throughput of voice and data than GSM. Because of its inherent efficiency, implementing CDMA and a standard called wide-band CDMA (WCDMA) is the long-term objective even of existing GSM systems.

Cellular Generations Another challenge for wireless cellular systems is the move from the historically slow and inefficient circuit-switched phone networks of the past to higher speed, cellular, digital packet-switched networks. This transition involves over $250 billion in worldwide investment in what are called **3G networks** (third-generation cellular networks).

The first generation (1G) of cellular networks, originating in the early 1980s, were analog based. They supported voice communication and were limited in capacity. Second-generation (2G) cellular networks appeared about 10 years later using digital circuit-switched networks. 2G systems provide better voice quality and global roaming capabilities and can support simple data services such as SMS. Although 2G systems are used primarily for voice, they can support data transmission at rates ranging from 9.6 to 14.4 kilobits per second (Kbps). This transmission speed is still too slow for comfortable Internet access.

Third-generation (3G) cellular networks are based on packet-switched technology to achieve greater efficiencies and higher transmission speeds than dedicated circuit-switched networks. 3G networks have speeds ranging from 144 Kbps for mobile users in, say, a car, to over 2 Mbps for stationary users. This is sufficient transmission capacity for video, graphics, and other rich media, in addition to voice, making 3G networks suitable for wireless broadband Internet access and always-on data transmission. If 3G networks live up to their promise, they will be able to handle email, instant messaging, and Web browsing as effortlessly as current wired technologies.

Although wireless carriers have invested in 3G technology, it is still not in wide use. In the meantime, those interested in high-speed Internet access and data transmission are turning to an interim solution called **2.5G networks**. These networks are packet-switched, use many existing infrastructure elements, and have data transmission rates ranging from 50 to 144 Kbps. A 2.5G service called **General Packet Radio Service (GPRS)** transports data over GSM wireless networks and improves wireless Internet access. 2.5 G also improves data transmission rates for CDMA. Table 8-1 summarizes these cellular generations.

Code Division Multiple Access (CDMA)

3G networks

2.5G networks

General Packet Radio Service (GPRS)

TABLE 8-1 *Wireless Cellular Generations*

GENERATION	CAPACITY	DESCRIPTION
1G	Low	Analog circuit-switched networks for voice communication
2G	10–19 Kbps	Digital circuit-switched wireless networks, primarily for voice communication; limited data transmission capability
2.5G	50–144 Kbps	Interim step toward 3G in North America; slower speed
3G	144 Kbps–2+ Mbps fixed	High-speed, mobile networks supporting video and other rich media, always on for email, browsing, instant messaging

Mobile Wireless Standards for Web Access

There are also competing standards governing the way wireless mobile devices access the Internet and the World Wide Web. **Wireless Application Protocol (WAP)** is a system of protocols and technologies that enables cell phones and other wireless devices with tiny display screens, low-bandwidth connections, and minimal memory to access Web-based information and services. WAP uses **Wireless Markup Language (WML)**, which is based on Extensible Markup Language (XML; see Chapter 5), and is optimized for tiny displays.

A person with a WAP-compliant phone uses the built-in microbrowser to make a request in WML. A **microbrowser** is an Internet browser with a small file size that can work with the low-memory constraints of handheld wireless devices and the low bandwidth of wireless networks. The request is passed to a WAP gateway, which retrieves the information from an Internet server in either standard Hypertext Markup Language (HTML) format or WML. The gateway translates HTML content back into WML so that the WAP client can receive it. The complexity of the translation process can affect the speed of information delivery. WAP supports most wireless network standards and operating systems for handheld computing devices.

I-mode is a wireless service offered by Japan's NTT DoCoMo mobile phone network that uses a different set of standards. Instead of using WAP, I-mode uses compact HTML to deliver content, making it easier for businesses to convert their HTML Web sites to mobile service. I-mode uses packet switching, which enables users to be connected constantly to the network and content providers to broadcast relevant information to users. (WAP users have to dial in to see if a site has changed.) I-mode can handle colour graphics not available on WAP handsets as well as video, although WAP is being modified to handle colour graphics (see Figure 8-4).

8.2 Wireless Computer Networks and Internet Access

The Institute of Electrical and Electronics Engineers (IEEE) has established a hierarchy of complementary standards for wireless computer networks. These standards include IEEE 802.15 for the personal area network (Bluetooth), IEEE 802.11 for the local area

FIGURE 8-4   *Wireless Application Protocol (WAP) versus I-mode.*

WAP and I-mode use alternative standards for accessing information from the wireless Web.

Wireless Application Protocol (WAP)
Wireless Markup Language (WML)
microbrowser
I-mode

TABLE 8-2 *Global Wireless Network Standards*

TYPE OF NETWORK	STANDARD
Personal area network (PAN)	IEEE 802.15 (Bluetooth)
Local area network (LAN)	IEEE 802.11 (Wi-Fi)
Metropolitan area network (MAN)	IEEE 802.16 (WiMax)
Wide area network (WAN)	IEEE 802.20 (proposed)

network (LAN) (Wi-Fi), 802.16 for the metropolitan area network (MAN) (WiMax), and the proposed 802.20 standard for the wide area network (WAN). Table 8-2 summarizes these standards.

Bluetooth

Bluetooth is the popular name for the 802.15 wireless networking standard, which is useful for creating small **personal area networks (PANs).** It can link up to eight devices within a 10-metre area using low-power, radio-based communication and can transmit up to 722 Kbps in the 2.4-gigahertz (GHz) band. The name Bluetooth comes from the 10th-century Danish King Harald Blatan (Bluetooth). Ericsson, the Scandinavian mobile handset company, was the first to develop this specification.

Wireless phones, pagers, computers, printers, and computing devices using Bluetooth can communicate with each other and even operate each other without direct user intervention (see Figure 8-5). For example, a person could highlight a telephone number on a wireless PDA and automatically activate a call on a digital phone, or that person could direct a notebook computer to send a document file wirelessly to a printer. Bluetooth can connect wireless keyboards and mice to PCs or cell phone ear pieces to a cell phone without wires. Bluetooth has low power requirements, making it appropriate for battery-powered handheld computers, cell phones, or PDAs. By 2006, 80 percent of mobile phones and 70 percent of PDAs will be Bluetooth-enabled.

FIGURE 8-5   *A Bluetooth network (PAN).*

Bluetooth enables a variety of devices, including cell phones, PDAs, wireless keyboards and mice, PCs, and printers, to interact wirelessly with each other within a small 10-metre area. In addition to the links shown, Bluetooth can be used to network similar devices to send data from one PC to another, for example.

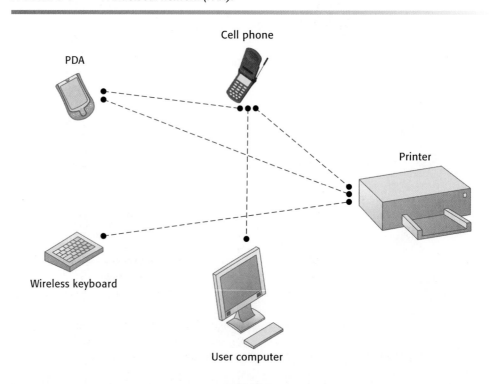

Bluetooth

personal area networks (PANs)

Although Bluetooth lends itself to home networking, it has uses in large corporations. A Coca-Cola bottling company in Australia equipped field sales and marketing staff with Bluetooth-enabled laptop computers and Bluetooth-enabled phones. Bluetooth enabled the laptop to connect to the mobile phone's data network so that employees could be connected to the Internet, company network, email, and client information anywhere and any time. Both United Parcel Service (UPS) and Federal Express equipped their delivery drivers with Bluetooth-enabled handhelds to expedite their work. You can find out more about these companies' use of Bluetooth in the chapter-ending case study.

Wi-Fi

The IEEE set of standards for wireless LANs is the 802.11 family, also known as **Wi-Fi** (for wireless fidelity). There are three standards in this family: 802.11a, 802.11b, and 802.11g.

The 802.11a standard can transmit up to 54 Mbps in the unlicensed 5-GHz frequency range and has an effective distance of 10 to 30 metres. The **802.11b** standard can transmit up to 11 Mbps in the unlicensed 2.4-GHz band and has an effective distance of 30 to 50 metres, although this range can be extended outdoors by using tower-mounted antennas. The 802.11g standard, which was recently finalized, can transmit up to 54 Mbps in the 2.4-GHz range.

Because 802.11b and 802.11g operate in the 2.4-GHz frequency, products developed for either of these two standards are compatible. Products designed for the 802.11a specification will not work with either 802.11b or 802.11g because 802.11a uses a different frequency band.

The 802.11b standard has been the most widely used standard for creating wireless LANs and providing wireless Internet access. However, 802.11g may become more popular in the next few years, and dual-band systems capable of handling 802.11b and 802.11g are expected to proliferate.

A Wi-Fi system can operate in two different modes. In *infrastructure mode,* wireless devices communicate with a wired LAN using access points. An **access point** is a box consisting of a radio receiver/transmitter and antennas that links to a wired network, router, or hub. Each access point and its wireless devices are known as a basic service set (BSS).

In ad-hoc mode, also known as peer-to-peer mode, wireless devices communicate with each other directly and do not use an access point. Most Wi-Fi communication uses infrastructure mode. (Ad-hoc mode is used for very small LANs in the home or small business office.)

Figure 8-6 illustrates an 802.11 wireless LAN operating in infrastructure mode that connects a small number of mobile devices to a larger wired LAN. Most wireless devices are client machines. The servers that the mobile client stations need to use are on the wired LAN. The access point controls the wireless stations and acts as a bridge between the main wired LAN and the wireless LAN. (A *bridge* connects two or more LANs based on the same protocol while a *gateway* connects two or more LANs based on different technologies.) The access point also controls the wireless stations.

Mobile wireless stations often need an add-in card called a wireless network interface card (NIC) that has a built-in radio and antenna. **Wireless NICs** can be credit-card-size cards that snap into the PCMCIA card slot on a PC or external adapters that plug into the PC's universal serial bus (USB) port. Newer laptop PCs come equipped with chips that can receive Wi-Fi signals.

Wi-Fi and Wireless Internet Access
The 802.11 standard can also be used to provide wireless access to the Internet using a broadband connection. In this instance, an access point plugs into an Internet connection, which could come from a cable TV line or a digital subscriber line (DSL) telephone service. Computers within a range of the access point would be able to use it to link wirelessly to the Internet.

Wi-Fi networking costs have declined so that a simple wireless Wi-Fi network can be set up for a few hundred dollars. Computer makers are making wireless capability a standard feature of their hardware. Intel now sells Centrino microprocessor and accessory chips for notebook computers that have specialized Wi-Fi capabilities (the accessory chips include a Wi-Fi transmitter) and smaller power consumption requirements.

Wi-Fi

802.11b

access point

wireless NICs

FIGURE 8-6   *An 802.11 wireless LAN.*

Mobile laptop computers equipped with wireless network interface cards link to the wired LAN by communicating with the access point. The access point uses radio waves to transmit network signals from the wired network to the client adapters, which convert them to data that the mobile device can understand. The client adapter then transmits the data from the mobile device back to the access point, which forwards the data to the wired network.

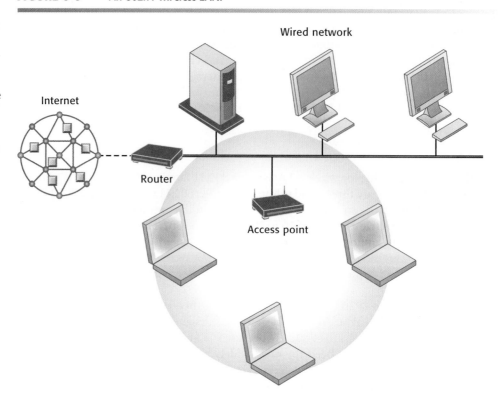

Benefits of Wi-Fi Large corporations and small businesses are using Wi-Fi networks to create low-cost wireless LANs and to provide Internet access from conference rooms and temporary workstations. Wi-Fi hotspots are springing up in hotels, airport lounges, libraries, fast food restaurants, and college campuses to provide mobile access to the Internet.

Hotspots typically consist of one or more access points positioned on a ceiling, wall, or other strategic spot in a public place to provide maximum wireless coverage for a specific area. Users in range of a hotspot can then access the Internet from their laptops. Some hotspots are free or do not require any additional software to use; others may require activation and the establishment of a user account by providing a credit card number over the Web.

Air Canada has installed Wi-Fi from Bell (called Bell Access Zone) in its Maple Leaf Lounges, and Via Rail has installed Wi-Fi in their business lounges, too. American Airlines is partnering with T-Mobile, along with Delta Air Lines and United Airlines, to install Wi-Fi services at the gates of several major airports. American Airlines also uses Wi-Fi for curbside check-in, baggage handling, and cargo package racking. Because 75 percent of its employees do not have a fixed workplace, American sees many other opportunities for integrating mobile computing into its business.

Passengers will also be able to use Wi-Fi services during their airline flights. Lufthansa Airlines and other airlines are starting to equip their jet airplanes with a Wi-Fi service called Connexion supplied by Boeing so that passengers with laptop computers can log on to the Internet while they are in flight.

Wi-Fi is very popular in South Korea. Hotels, restaurants, universities, and other public facilities have Wi-Fi hotspots, and thousands of college students use Wi-Fi on campus for research, course work, and downloading and listening to music.

Companies such as McDonald's in the U.S. and Starbucks are offering customers Wi-Fi services in many of their retail outlets. They will receive some revenue from their fees for Wi-Fi services, but their primary motivation for deploying the technology is to encourage customers to spend more time in their stores, purchase more food, or select their establishments over other competitors.

hotspots

For Starbucks, providing Wi-Fi hotspots provides special management benefits. The Window on Management shows how Starbucks' managers use the Wi-Fi networks in stores under their supervision to link to the Starbucks corporate network. This setup enables them to work with corporate systems on-site instead of having to travel to Starbucks' regional headquarters to use a computer. The time savings enable them to focus on store operations and employee management.

Many free public hotspots are available in Canada and other countries. For example, Pete's Peanut Pub in Calgary offers free Wi-Fi access. Wialess.com in St. Albans outside London has wired pubs and bars. Café chain Beugo has partnered with Broadscape to offer free Wi-Fi service to compete with Starbucks and Costa Coffee, where users must pay for Wi-Fi services. Other businesses around Europe are wiring numerous public gathering places where professionals and students are likely to congregate.

Over 4000 Starbucks cafes worldwide have Wi-Fi networks providing customers with wireless Internet access. These networks also provide managers with wireless access to Starbucks' private corporate network.

Wi-Fi Challenges Wi-Fi is clearly helping individual companies extend their networking to new areas and obtain Internet services at a very low cost. The challenge facing the technology industry as a whole, however, is how to transform Wi-Fi from a wireless hit-or-miss phenomenon into a sustainable business.

Right now, users cannot freely roam from hotspot to hotspot if these hotspots use different Wi-Fi network services. Unless the service is free, users would need to log on to separate accounts for each service, each with its own fees. All of the hotspots, some public, some private, need to be transformed into interoperable, dependable networks with billing systems, roaming agreements, and technical standards that will enable users to plug into hotspots at will. Some question whether commercial Wi-Fi services can flourish when so many free hotspots are available to mobile users.

One of the major drawbacks of Wi-Fi is its weak security features, which make these wireless networks vulnerable to intruders. Because the range of a Wi-Fi network can extend beyond the confines of the building where it is being used, an outsider may be able to penetrate the network, obtain a free Internet connection, and even gain access to the resources on the computers of legitimate network users. We provide more detail about Wi-Fi security issues in Chapter 9.

Another drawback of Wi-Fi networks is susceptibility to interference from nearby systems operating in the same spectrum. There is no way to control additional new devices in the same area that might cause interference, such as wireless phones, microwave ovens, or other wireless LANs.

WINDOW ON MANAGEMENT

Management

Wi-Fi: Starbucks' Solution To Go

From one Seattle coffee bean store in 1971, Starbucks has grown into the world's number one specialty coffee chain, with about 6500 outlets in 25 countries, including Canada. Starbucks shops can be found on street corners, in airport terminals, in supermarkets, and in office buildings. In 2001, the company started to provide wireless Internet access in its stores, and now more than 4000 Starbucks coffee houses around the world have Wi-Fi service. As this chapter is being written, Starbucks announced that it will offer Wi-Fi service in many of its Canadian outlets, starting with 140 stores in Ontario. By the time you are reading this, Starbucks should be available not only in Ontario, but also in British Columbia, Alberta, Saskatchewan, and Manitoba.

In the U.S., Deutche Telekom's T-Mobile USA unit is footing much of the cost of building these Wi-Fi wireless networks in the hope of acquiring subscribing Starbucks customers. In Canada, Bell Canada will be Starbucks' Wi-Fi provider.

To use the T-Mobile Hotspot service at Starbucks, customers need to activate a T-Mobile Hotspot account. Then, using a Wi-Fi-enabled laptop computer, Tablet PC, Pocket PC, or other Wi-Fi-enabled PDA, customers can launch their Web browsers from a participating Starbucks store and log on to the Internet.

Starbucks benefits in several ways. According to Ken Lombard, Starbucks' president of Music and Entertainment, "The convenience and reliability of T-Mobile Hotspot is bringing customers in frequently and keeping them in the stores longer." Internal research shows that T-Mobile Hotspot subscribers visit Starbucks more often, an average of eight times per month, and spend more time in the stores than non-Wi-Fi customers. The average time spent on the Internet at a Starbucks store lasts approximately one hour. Nearly 90 percent of T-Mobile Internet use at Starbucks occurs after 9 a.m., increasing business during non-peak hours.

The Wi-Fi networks could add to Starbucks' profits by enabling more sales per minute, reducing the time for clearing credit card sales at the cash register and delivering interactive training to local stores from a central server. The networks may even generate new sources of revenue, such as selling music downloads and even entertainment videos in Starbucks cafés.

In addition to boosting revenue, Starbucks' Wi-Fi networks are helping Starbucks improve the internal management of the business. Starbucks managers are using the service to create wireless local are networks (WLANs) to help run store operations and to give them wireless access to the company's private corporate network and systems. Starbucks has started equipping its district managers with Wi-Fi-enabled laptop computers to take advantage of these networks.

Lisa Jansen, who oversees 10 Starbucks stores in the Willamette Valley area near Portland, Oregon, previously had to go to a store, review its operations, develop a list of items on which to follow up, and drive as far as 37 kilometres to Starbucks' regional headquarters to file reports and send email. Then she would head out to another store and do the same thing. Now, instead of running her business from a cubicle in regional headquarters, Jansen can do her work sitting at a table in one of the stores she supervises. She saves 45 minutes of driving time twice a day, or up to 10 hours a week.

With the newfound time, Jansen can spend more time in stores to observe customers being served and their reactions to the service. She can see whether employees are following Starbucks' cash-handling policies and procedures and can determine whether each customer transaction is completed within the company's three-minute benchmark. If a store needs a new umbrella, she can order it on the spot. If a particular type of coffee has been selling well, she can send an electronic message to restock before the store's inventory runs out.

Artie Dohler, manager for several Starbucks stores in the New York Times Square district, has been able to increase the number of employees he manages from 100 to 115 and to improve their training. He uses the time he saves with wireless networking to interact more frequently with his employees. He works with them to taste and evaluate the coffees they serve and watches them introduce themselves or the store's products to customers. In 2001, Dohler's employee turnover rate was 117 percent, meaning he had to train a whole new staff each year. Since then, he has been able to reduce that turnover rate to 66 percent.

By implementing Wi-Fi, Starbucks has been able to increase the presence of district managers by 25 percent without adding any extra staff. With productivity gains like these, one can see why Lovina McMurchy, director of Starbucks' New Ventures Group, calls Starbucks' Wi-Fi networks a "great strategic asset."

Apparently, Canadians thirst for more than coffee at their local coffee houses. An Ipsos-Reid survey, commissioned by Bell Canada, found that 71 percent of respondents were likely or somewhat likely to use Wi-Fi services in coffee shops or other locales. Once consistent, reliable service is available throughout Canada at most coffee shops and fast food restaurants, usage should increase significantly, representing a new niche for Canadian computing.

To Think About: How does Wi-Fi provide value for Starbucks? Why is Starbucks so late in offering Wi-Fi service in their Canadian stores? What management, organization, and technology issues did Starbucks have to address when installing Wi-Fi networks in its stores?

Sources: Susan Rush, "Starbucks Brews Up More Wi-Fi," *Wireless Week*, July 7, 2004; "More than 3100 Wi-Fi Hotspots in Starbucks Stores," www.geekzone.com, accessed July 19, 2004; Tom Steinert-Threlkeld, "Make Mine 'To Stay,'" *Baseline Magazine*, April 2003; Tischelle George, "Starbucks' Data to Go," *Information Week*, January 20, 2003; and Rick Anderson, "Business: Starbucks: Just Getting Started," *Seattle Weekly*, April 30–May 6, 2003; Susan Rush, "Starbucks Canada Brews Wi-Fi," *Wireless Week*, October 7, 2005.

WiMax and EV-DO

A surprisingly large number of areas in North America and throughout the world do not have access to Wi-Fi or fixed broadband connectivity. Traditional DSL can reach only about 5 kilometres from the central telephone office switch, leaving many urban and suburban areas without DSL connections. Many older cable networks cannot handle high-speed broadband. The range of Wi-Fi systems is not more than 91 metres from the base station, making it difficult for rural groups that don't have cable or DSL service to find wireless access to the Internet.

The IEEE developed a new family of standards known as WiMax to deal with these problems. **WiMax**, which stands for worldwide interoperability for microwave access, is the popular term for IEEE Standard 802.16, known as the "Air Interface for Fixed Broadband Wireless Access Systems." WiMax has a wireless access range of up to 50 kilometres, compared to 91 metres for Wi-Fi and nine metres for Bluetooth, and a data transfer rate of up to 75 Mbps. The 802.16 specification also has robust security and quality of service features to support voice and video.

WiMax antennas will be able to beam high-speed Internet connections to rooftop antennas of homes and businesses that are kilometres away. The technology can provide long-distance broadband wireless access to rural areas and other locations that are not currently served while avoiding the steep installation costs of the traditional wired infrastructure. The 802.16a standard supports use of frequencies ranging from 2 to 11 GHz, which include both licensed and unregulated bands.

Intel is bringing out WiMax-enabled versions of its Centrino chip, and Nokia will have a WiMax cell phone in 2005. WiMax technology should be broadly available in 2006.

EV-DO and Wireless Cellular Access In addition to 3G networks for mobile phones, major cellular carriers are upgrading their networks to provide anytime, anywhere broadband access for PCs and other devices. Verizon's service, called BroadBand Access, uses a technology called **EV-DO**, which stands for evolution data optimized. EV-DO provides wireless access to the Internet over a cellular network at an average speed of 300 to 500 Kbps. Although it has a wider range of coverage than Wi-Fi, it will not work in "dead spots" where regular cell phone systems have weak signals, including deep inside buildings.

To use this service, Verizon subscribers install specific software and insert a special card into their laptops. The card has a mini antenna that connects the laptop to the Verizon Wireless network and establishes an Internet connection. Verizon is also starting to extend EV-DO service to PDAs and cell phones and expects the service to be available in every major U.S. metropolitan area by the end of 2005. Bell Canada plans to roll out their own EV-DO network in 2005 and 2006.

Over time, cell phones, wireless PDAs, and laptops will be able to switch from one type of network to another, moving from Wi-Fi to WiMax to cellular networks. Cell phone makers Nokia, LG Electronics, and Samsung are adding Wi-Fi capabilities to their phones. Motorola's CN620 clamshell mobile device combines Wi-Fi and GSM cellular technology. Hewlett-Packard's iPaq H6315 Pocket PC handheld supports Wi-Fi, Bluetooth, and GSM/GPRS cellular service. It will automatically connect to the fastest-available network and allows voice and data services to be used simultaneously.

Hewlett-Packard's HP6315 Pocket PC handheld supports Wi-Fi, Bluetooth, and cellular service. Users will be able to switch from one type of network to another to find the fastest service as they move from place to place.

FIGURE 8-7 *WiMax technology.*

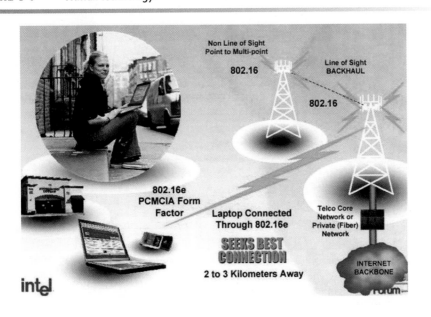

WiMax is a standards-based technology that provides high-speed wireless communication for metropolitan area networks (MANs). It can be used for "last mile" broadband connections to home or office, for creating wireless hotspots, and for providing high-speed enterprise connectivity for businesses.

8.3 M-Commerce and Mobile Computing

We have already described how Wi-Fi wireless network technology can be used to access the Internet from an untethered PC or handheld computing device. Wi-Fi offers some mobility for Internet access, but users can access the Web only if they are in range of their wireless networks. This type of wireless computing, in which users move from wireless hotspot to wireless hotspot to gain network or Internet access, is sometimes referred to as **nomadic computing**.

Mobile computing, in contrast, enables Internet-enabled cell phones, PDAs, and other wireless computing devices to access digital information on the Internet from any location. The use of the Internet for purchasing goods and services as well as for transmitting messages using wireless mobile devices is called m-commerce (see chapter 13 for more information). Although m-commerce represents a small fraction of total e-commerce transactions, revenue is steadily growing (see Figure 8-8).

M-Commerce Services and Applications

Table 8-3 describes the most popular categories of m-commerce services and applications for mobile computing. Location-based applications are of special interest because they take advantage of the unique capabilities of mobile technology. Whenever a user is connected to the Internet by a wireless device (cell phone, PDA, handheld), the transmission technology can be leveraged to determine that person's location and beam location-specific services or product information. For example, drivers could use this capability to obtain local weather data and traffic information along with alternate route suggestions and descriptions of nearby restaurants.

Instead of focusing on how to bring a customer to a Web site, marketing strategies will shift to finding ways to bring the message directly to the customer at the point of need (Kenny and Marshall 2000). Figure 8-9 illustrates how personalization can be extended by the ubiquitous Internet and m-commerce.

FIGURE 8-8 *Global m-commerce revenue 2000–2005.*

M-commerce sales represent a small fraction of total e-commerce sales, but that percentage is steadily growing.

Source: Copyright 2005. Jupitermedia Corporation. All rights reserved.

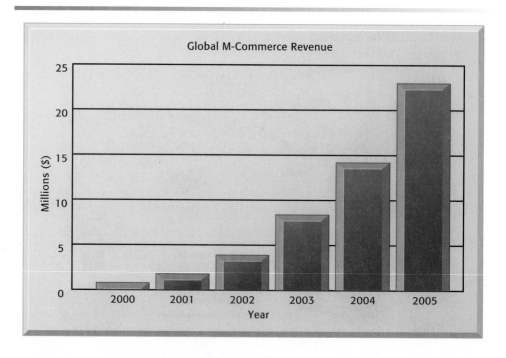

nomadic computing

mobile computing

TABLE 8-3 *M-Commerce Services and Applications for Mobile Computing.*

M-COMMERCE SERVICE	APPLICATIONS
Information-based services	Instant messaging, email, searching for a movie or restaurant using a cell phone or handheld PDA
Transaction-based services	Purchasing stocks, concert tickets, music, or games; searching for the best price on an item using a cell phone and buying it in a physical store or on the Web
Personalized services	Services that anticipate what a customer wants based on that person's location or data profile, such as updated airline flight information or beaming coupons for nearby restaurants

M-commerce applications have taken off for services that are time-critical, that appeal to people on the move, or that accomplish a task more efficiently than other methods. They are especially popular in Europe, Japan, South Korea, and other countries where fees for conventional Internet usage are very expensive. Here are some examples:

Mobile bill payment. Sumit Mobile Systems, working with mobile providers, banks, and utility companies, provides a service for people in Shanghai, China, to pay their utility bills by cell phone. Most people in China do not have chequing accounts and very few have credit cards, so bills must be paid by standing in a long line at a bank. The Sumit Smartpay system flashes a message on a subscriber's cell phone when a payment is due. The user then types in a secret number to authorize the payment from his or her bank

FIGURE 8-9   *Customer personalization with the ubiquitous Internet.*

Target	Platform	When	Content and Service
Traveller	Computer-equipped car	Whenever car is moving	Provide maps, driving directions, weather reports, ads for nearby restaurants and hotels.
Parent	Cell phone	During school days	Notify about school-related closings: Hello, Caroline. Your children's school is closing early. Press 1 for closure reason Press 2 for weather reports Press 3 for traffic reports
Stockbroker	Pager	During trading days. Notify if unusually high trading volume.	Summary portfolio analysis showing changes in positions for each holding.

Companies can use mobile wireless devices to deliver new value-added services directly to customers at any time and in any place, extending personalization and deepening relationships.

account (Manuel 2003). In Dublin, mPARK is a parking payment system, whereby car owners can pay for their parking in designated city-centre locations, using their mobile phone account as payment. Parking transactions are then billed to the driver's credit card or mobile phone account.

Content and products. NTT DoCoMo, the wireless arm of Nippon Telegraph and Telephone Company, offers Internet-enabled cell phone users services for email and for accessing Web sites formatted for tiny screens. Subscribers can check train schedules, obtain movie listings, browse restaurant guides, purchase tickets on Japan Airlines, trade stocks, view new cartoons, and read Japan's largest daily newspaper. Menus of services can be tailored to individual subscribers' interests. Some of these services are free. Those that aren't are bundled and charged to subscribers' monthly telephone bills.

Banking and financial services. Scotiabank offers wireless alerts about changes in stock trading information on digital cell phones that support text messaging. Thailand's Bank of Asia offers a mobile service called ASIA M-Banking. Enrolled customers can check account balances, transfer funds between savings and other accounts, and pay their mobile phone and Internet usage charges using a Web-enabled mobile phone. They can complete these banking transactions anywhere at any time without having to visit a bank branch. Seoul-based Infobank offers a secure wireless platform for mobile phone users interested in securities trading.

Wireless advertising. The cable television History Channel worked with Enpocket, a mobile marketing technology provider, to send 100 000 selected wireless users text messages promoting its special "Barbarians" show. An Enpocket survey of message recipients found that 88 percent received the message, 18 percent watched "Barbarians," and 12 percent forwarded the message to a friend. Because of this success, the History Channel decided to use wireless text messaging to promote more shows (Cho 2004).

Location-based services. Vodafone Italy, which has offered mobile services since 1995 to 19 million customers, started offering location-based services in mid-2002. Vodafone customers can access relevant traffic information, calculate itineraries, and search for nearby gas stations, hotels, restaurants, and health-care centres. In London, Zingo offers a service for using a mobile phone to hail nearby taxicabs. A mobile phone call to a specified telephone number connects to the closest available taxi driver. The caller speaks directly to the driver to confirm the details of the trip.

Games and entertainment. Rogers Wireless and MobiTV are offering mobile television in Canada, providing Rogers Wireless customers with real-time access to live television programming including exclusive Toronto Blue Jays content, news, sports and entertainment programming via Rogers Wireless' mobile Internet service. The service is expected to be commercially available in the second quarter. Korean mobile phone users can view an array of TV programs, store hours of digital music on their phones, and download video clips. Many mobile phone services offer downloadable digital games and ring tones (digitized melodies that play on mobile phones).

Accessing Information from the Wireless Web

Although cell phones, PDAs, and other handheld mobile devices can access the Web at any time and from any place, the amount of information that they can actually handle at one time is very limited. Until 3G broadband service comes into widespread use, these devices will not be able to transmit or receive large amounts of data. The information must also fit onto small display screens.

Some Web sites have been specifically designed for m-commerce. They feature Web pages with very few graphics and just enough information to fit on a small mobile handheld screen. Special **wireless portals** (also known as mobile portals) feature content and services optimized for mobile devices to steer users to the information they are most likely to need. They typically offer a variety of features, links to other wireless sites, the ability to select content to be pushed to the user's device, and a point of entry for anyone to send the user a message.

For example, the wireless portal of the Canadian government provides access to selected government information and services, such as Canadian government news releases, estimated waiting times for crossing the Canadian–U.S. land border, currency exchange rates and a currency converter, passport office locations and phone numbers, economic statistics, contact information for Canadian Members of Parliament, and Canadian government employee phone numbers (see Figure 8-10). Microsoft's wireless portal provides access to news from MSNBC, sports from ESPN, movie times, local traffic reports, restaurant listings, yellow pages, and stock market reports, as well as capabilities for managing email messages and instant messaging.

Voice portals accept voice commands for accessing Web content, email, and other electronic applications from a cell phone or standard telephone. Sophisticated voice recognition software processes the requests, and responses are translated back into speech for the customer. For example, AOLbyPhone provides voice access to weather forecasts, movie show times, sports scores, top news stories, stock prices, financial news, and business and residential directories. Users can also listen and reply to any email using their own voice. Bell Mobility offers a voice portal powered by Nuance so their Voicenet customers can listen to their email and other Web content including news, weather, and sports by using voice commands. The service is the first of its kind in Canada and is being offered in English and French to PCS (digital) and analog customers throughout Bell Mobility's coverage area.

Digital Payment Systems and M-Commerce

With a Wi-Fi connection, you can take advantage of all existing forms of Internet payment—the fact that you are connected wirelessly should have no impact. However, m-commerce requires special digital payment systems geared to the types of transactions that are taking place using cell phones, PDAs, and other small handheld devices. These transactions are mainly small and frequent purchases for items such as soft drinks, sports scores, newspapers, mobile games, or concert tickets amounting to $10 or less that are not well-suited to credit card billing. (For purchases below this amount, the charges levied by payment processors and banks make credit cards too expensive.)

Micropayment systems are working well in Europe and Asia, where mobile operators and Internet service providers (ISPs) handle small payments by adding them up and presenting

FIGURE 8-10   *The government of Canada's wireless portal.*

The government of Canada's wireless portal is a quick and easy single point of access to selected government information and services for mobile users.

wireless portals
voice portals

them on a single bill such as the mobile telephone bill. Examples are Vodafone's mPay bill in Europe and mONEPayment in Austria. Mobile phone bills can be used to pay for ring tones, logs, java games, and parking. In London, you can buy Virgin Cola using a Virgin Mobile phone by simply dialing a number on the vending machine (the cost of the drink is simply charged to your cell phone account). A mobile micropayment system from Finland's Sonera enables users in Helsinki to pay for parking using their mobile phones and have the payment amount invoiced on their mobile phone bills. In Japan, NTT DoCoMo handles the billing for millions of small purchases made by its I-mode subscribers.

NTT DoCoMo customers can also use a new stored payment system for their purchases. Special cell phones are equipped with a smart card computer chip that can store electronic cash. To pay, a person merely needs to wave the cell phone within a few inches of a special display in stores, restaurants, and near vending machines. There is no need to dial any special numbers. When the smart card chip runs out of cash, it can be recharged by slipping the phone into a slot of a machine found in offices and convenience stores and inserting money into the machine (Kageyama 2004).

In both North America and Europe, the micropayment services just described are based on a "walled garden" model in which individual service providers run their own separate payment systems. What is needed to help m-commerce take off is more interoperability achieved by having all the players agree on a common, secure platform for wireless m-commerce payments. To become widely adopted, a universal m-commerce payment system requires the backing of most of the major stakeholders in payment systems—consumers, vendors, phone equipment manufacturers, wireless service providers, and financial industry participants.

Several noteworthy interoperability initiatives have appeared. In March 2003, a consortium called Mobile Payment Services Association (MPSA) was founded by leading global wireless service providers Vodafone PLC, T-Mobile, Orange SA, and Telefonica Moviles SA to offer a single, simple way of paying for goods and services by mobile phone across the European continent. MPSA rebranded itself under the name Simpay in June 2003, and other wireless service providers are likely to join. Simpay works with a number of mobile phone systems, enabling customers to make purchases through mobile operator-managed payment accounts either online or in physical stores. Along similar lines, four of Austria's top five national communications operators, including T-Mobile, Hutchinson, One, and Telering, offer a single m-payment interface to merchants.

Mobile Wallets   In Chapter 13, we describe the value of digital wallets that store online shoppers' personal information and credit card numbers to expedite the purchase process. A few companies have started offering **mobile wallets (m-wallets)** that perform the same functions for wireless m-commerce transactions.

Deutsche Telecom's wireless service users in Germany and the United Kingdom can use the T-Mobile mobile wallet to enter all their personal data just once, and then when they make purchases from vendors in the Deutsche Telecom network, the mobile wallet automatically fills in the blanks on the order form. Some Nokia cell phone models include a mobile wallet capability for securely storing sensitive information.

M-Commerce Challenges

The number of Wi-Fi hotspots for wireless Internet access has been mushrooming in many countries because the technology combines high-speed Internet access with a measure of flexibility and mobility. Rollout of m-commerce services, however, has proved more problematic. Keyboards and screens on cell phones are still tiny and awkward to use. The data transfer speeds on second-generation cellular networks are very slow compared to dial-up and high-speed Internet connections for PCs. Each second waiting for data to download costs the customer money. Most Internet-enabled phones have limited memory and power supplies.

Web content for wireless devices is primarily in the form of text with few graphics. For mobile commerce to become popular and successful, more Web sites need to be designed

mobile wallets (m-wallets)

specifically for small wireless devices, and these wireless devices need to be more Web friendly. M-commerce will benefit from 3G networks and other cellular broadband services and from interoperable payment systems.

8.4 Wireless Technology in the Enterprise

In addition to m-commerce, mobile applications have permeated many other areas of business, creating new efficiencies and ways of working. In this section, we present examples of where mobile and wireless technologies are having their greatest impact.

Wireless Applications for Customer Relationship Management

Major customer relationship management (CRM) vendors have enhanced their products to provide mobile support for sales and service activities. A growing number of sales professionals work outside the office and require up-to-date customer records and account information to help them close deals. The ability to deliver this information on the spot helps mobile sales staff act decisively at the point of customer interaction.

For example, Siebel System's Siebel Sales Wireless enables sales professionals to access customer account records and related information such as order status or recent service issues at any time or location. They can also enter the most current account and business deal information data into their wireless devices to update the Siebel corporate customer database. The system will alert representatives to important events using wireless messaging.

Field service workers benefit from wireless applications that provide real-time access to critical information while they are servicing customers. Wireless CRM applications provide access to critical customer and service information while service representatives are working with clients. For example, a field service technician might use a wireless handheld to obtain information about the service history for a piece of equipment that must be fixed or whether parts required to fix the equipment are available. Some wireless CRM tools include capabilities for reporting field service staff time, expenses, parts availability, and details for follow-on work. Canadian Research in Motion, manufacturer of the BlackBerry, now offers Microsoft CRM for the BlackBerry mobile device.

Pitney Bowes, a large vendor of postage meters and mailing systems, uses a wireless customer relationship management application for its global mailing systems division, in which 1500 employees service its machines designed for low-volume distribution of mail. This system links Pitney Bowes' field service representatives to the company's call centre and service applications and enables them to access data from multiple back-end systems.

Figure 8-11 illustrates how this system works. When a customer calls to place a field service request, Siebel CRM software identifies the product needing repair, selects the field service representative to dispatch, and messages that technician's wireless device with the service request. The technician then acknowledges receipt of the order. Messages from the technicians' handhelds are routed to Antenna's wireless gateways, which translate the data into XML format and forward them over a frame relay or virtual private network (VPN) to Pitney Bowes' computer centre for use by Siebel Systems' CRM field service software, which automatically updates inventory, billing, call centre, and other back-end applications.

The system delivers customer and service history data instantly to the field service technician's handheld. It also tells the technician whether the work is covered by contract or is billable and feeds data for billable work into Pitney Bowes' billing system. If parts are required, the Siebel field service application determines if the part is in stock and sends information on these parts to a legacy inventory application that is linked to the company's SAP supply chain management system. Information from this system has enabled Pitney Bowes's field service staff to solve problems faster and complete more service calls per day (Songini 2004).

FIGURE 8-11   *Pitney Bowes' wireless CRM system.*

The application uses Pocket PC PDAs, RIM 957s wireless email handhelds and other wireless handhelds, field service software from CRM vendor Siebel Systems, cellular wireless data service from Cingular Wireless, and Antenna SmartClient and Antenna A3 middleware to link field workers using wireless handhelds to Siebel CRM software and Pitney Bowes' back-end system.

Wireless Supply Chain Management and Radio Frequency Identification (RFID)

Contemporary supply chain management (SCM) systems are a fertile area for mobile wireless technology because of the need to provide simultaneous, accurate information about demand, supply, production, and logistics as goods move among supply chain partners. SCM software vendors include capabilities for mobile support and wireless capture of data on movements of goods and other events.

The mySAP supply chain management software offers a number of mobile capabilities. Manufacturing employees can view work instructions on wireless handheld devices anywhere on the factory floor. Supervisors can use wireless handhelds to call up data from process control systems to monitor production-line behaviour.

A firm that needs to ship out goods can use mySAP SCM to create a shipment order and tender it to a selected freight forwarder. The forwarder can access this tendering application from a mobile device and accept, reject, or modify the planned order. If the forwarder rejects the tender or does not reply within an anticipated time frame, the supply chain management software triggers a text message alert to the logistics manager's mobile phone to expedite the search for another forwarder.

The mySAP SCM also uses mobile technology for warehouse management tasks such as picking, packing, unpacking, freight loading and unloading checks, and inventory queries. Some of these activities use radio frequency identification technology (RFID) technology. RFID technology is a powerful tool for supply chain management

Radio Frequency Identification (RFID)
Radio frequency identification (RFID) systems provide a powerful technology for tracking the movement of goods throughout the supply chain. RFID systems use tiny tags with embedded microchips containing data about an item and its location to transmit radio signals over a short distance to special RFID readers. The RFID readers then pass the data over a network to a computer for processing. Unlike bar codes, RFID tags do not need line-of-sight contact to be read.

The transponder, or RFID tag, is electronically programmed with information that can uniquely identify an item, such as an electronic identification code plus other information about the item, such as its location, where and when it was made, or its status during production. Embedded in the tag is a microchip for storing the data. The rest of the tag is an antenna that transmits data to the RFID reader.

The reader unit consists of an antenna and radio transmitter with a decoding capability attached to a stationary or handheld device. The reader emits radio waves in ranges anywhere from 2.54 centimetres to 30 metres, depending on its power output, the radio frequency employed, and surrounding environmental conditions. When a RFID tag comes within the range of the reader, the tag is activated and starts sending data. The reader captures these data, decodes them, and sends them back over a wired or wireless

radio frequency identification (RFID)

FIGURE 8-12 *How RFID works.*

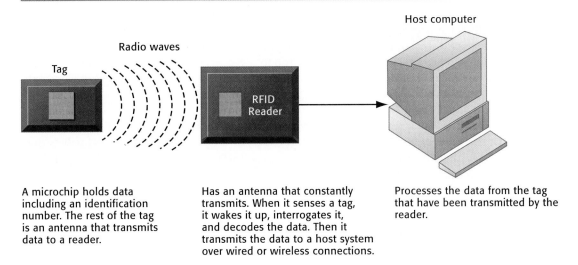

Radio waves

Tag

Host computer

RFID
Reader

A microchip holds data including an identification number. The rest of the tag is an antenna that transmits data to a reader.

Has an antenna that constantly transmits. When it senses a tag, it wakes it up, interrogates it, and decodes the data. Then it transmits the data to a host system over wired or wireless connections.

Processes the data from the tag that have been transmitted by the reader.

RFID uses low-powered radio transmitters to read data stored in a tag at distances ranging from 2.5 cm to 30 metres. The reader captures the data from the tag and sends them over a network to a host computer for processing.

network to a host computer for further processing (see Figure 8-12). Both RFID tags and antennas come in a variety of shapes and sizes.

RFID tags are categorized as either active or passive. Active RFID tags are powered by an internal battery and the tag data can be rewritten and modified. These tags might be used, for example, when manufacturing a part to give a machine a set of instructions and have the machine report its performance to the tag. The tag would capture these data so that they are added to the history of the tagged part. Active tags generally have a longer read range, but they are larger in size, cost more, and have a shorter operational life (up to 10 years) than passive tags. Automated toll-collection systems use active RFID tags.

Passive RFID tags do not have a separate power source and obtain their operating power from the radio frequency energy transmitted by the RFID reader. They are smaller, lighter, and less expensive than active tags with a virtually unlimited operational lifetime. They also have shorter read ranges than active tags and require a higher-powered reader. Passive tags are usually read-only and are programmed with data that cannot be modified.

RFID systems operate in a number of unlicensed frequency bands worldwide. Low-frequency systems (30 kilohertz to 500 kilohertz) have short reading ranges (centimetres to a few metres) and lower system costs. Low-frequency systems are often used in security, asset tracking, or animal identification applications. High-frequency RFID systems (850 MHz to 950 MHz and 2.4 GHz to 2.5 GHz) offer reading ranges that can extend beyond 27 metres and have high reading speeds. High-frequency RFID applications include railroad car tracking or automated toll collection for highways or bridges.

A RFID tag with an integrated circuit will never be as inexpensive as a bar code label, and RFID systems will not supplant bar codes entirely. However, RFID systems will become popular where bar codes or other optical technologies are not effective.

In inventory control and supply chain management, RFID can capture and manage more detailed information about items in warehouses or in production than bar-coding systems. If a large number of items are shipped together, RFID can track each pallet, lot, or even unit item in the shipment. Manufacturers using RFID will be able to track the production history of each product, for better understanding of product defects and successes.

The real savings from RFID come from the way it can improve an entire business process. Data from suppliers can be carried on tags and uploaded into the receiving company's enterprise system or supply chain management system the moment a component is delivered. RFID systems can give suppliers, manufacturers, distributors, and retailers much more detailed and real-time data for control over inventory, shipping, and other logistics. RFID could even change the way invoices are paid by triggering an electronic payment to the shipper once a tagged pallet enters a retailer's warehouse.

RFID has been available for decades, but widespread use was held back by the expense of the tags, which ranged from just under $1.50 to $28.00 each. Now the cost of a tag has dropped to about 25 cents and could drop to 5–8 cents within a few years. At these prices for tags, RFID becomes cost-effective for many organizations, including the University Health Network discussed in the beginning of the chapter, Home Depot, Delta Airlines, Federal Express, and Unilever.

The top 100 suppliers to Wal-Mart stores and thousands of suppliers to the U.S. Department of Defense are required to use passive RFID tags on cases and pallets they ship to these organizations. Wal-Mart expects RFID-tagged shipments will help it track and record inventory flow.

Coors UK, Scottish & Newcastle, and other large British brewing companies are using RFID to improve tracking of kegs that are shipped out and returned. Breweries lose on average 5 to 6 percent of their kegs each year, and RFID tracking has cut those losses in half (Hellweg 2004). Toyota's Ontario Parts Centre is the size of 17 football fields and manages more than 250 000 transactions every day. The Parts Centre uses RFID tracking to manage their inventory with warehouse management software. With approximately 450 associates, almost every employee has a radio frequency computer on their forklift, tugger, pole, bench, or cart.

Boeing Company and Airbus S.A.S., the world's largest airplane makers, are requiring more than 2000 of their suppliers to begin RFID tagging of aircraft and engine parts. Seventy percent of the purchase orders that Airbus receives from its customers contain incorrect part numbers and pricing data. If parts for Airbus planes had RFID tags, they could be scanned to generate accurate replacement orders, saving Airbus as much as $500 million per year. RFID tagging of Boeing airplane parts would provide more accurate information than that which mechanics enter manually, preventing unapproved parts from being used in finished products. This application of RFID could save Boeing $125 million per year in Federal Aviation Administration fines and part replacement time (Kontzer 2004).

Steep costs and extensive planning and preparation are required for successful deployment of RFID. A Forrester Research study estimated that a supplier that was required by Wal-Mart to implement RFID technology might spend $9.1 million in start-up and maintenance fees for one year (Overby 2004). In addition to installing RFID readers and tagging systems, these companies may need to upgrade their hardware and software to process the massive amounts of data produced by RFID systems—transactions that could add up to tens or hundreds of terabytes.

Special middleware is required to filter, aggregate, and prevent RFID data from overloading business networks and system applications. The middleware translates RFID data into formats that applications can use. Applications will need to be redesigned to accept massive volumes of RFID-generated data and to share those data with other applications. Major enterprise software vendors, including SAP, Oracle, and PeopleSoft (now a part of Oracle), now offer RFID-ready versions of their supply chain management applications.

Privacy activists have objected to RFID technology applications that could lead to more tracking and monitoring of individual behaviour. They fear it could someday enable marketers, the government, or insurers to compile details about individuals' shopping habits or even enable people's movements to be tracked. The Window on Organizations explores this topic.

Wireless in Health Care

Another area in which wireless technology is having a major impact is health care. Health care systems have been hampered by inefficiencies from paper-based processes and gaps between information systems. Many hospitals have wired networks but still have problems getting essential information to the right place at the right time because most physicians and nurses are rarely in one place for long.

WINDOW ON ORGANIZATIONS

Does RFID Threaten Privacy?

German retailer Metro AG has been an early and vigorous adopter of RFID technology. It is implementing a wireless inventory tracking system for 250 stores, 10 central warehouses, and 100 of its biggest suppliers, representing 65 percent of its sales in Germany. Metro expects to bring all of its approximately 800 German stores onto the system by the end of 2007. Gerd Wofram, Metro's project manager, believes the cost of this system will be offset by the savings it produces for both Metro and its suppliers, including Procter & Gamble, Gillette Company, and Kraft Foods.

Under Metro's system, suppliers will attach RFID tags to pallets and cases of goods supplied to certain stores and warehouses. As these tagged containers move in and out of Metro warehouses and stores, they will be tracked by RFID readers. By tracking supply and inventory more precisely, the RFID system will enable Metro to cut down on lost, stolen, or damaged products, ensure shelves are stocked, and eventually reduce staff. If all goes well, Metro could reduce its inventory carrying costs by up to 20 percent.

So far, so good. But when Metro tried to bring RFID closer to the customer, it unleashed a storm of controversy. Metro also uses RFID microchips in its Payback customer loyalty cards and RFID tags on CDs and DVDs for theft protection and for controlling customer previews of age-restricted DVDs. (Without a loyalty card as a key, customers can preview only the equivalent of G-rated films.) No RFID readers are in the stores tracking customers.

Nevertheless, Metro's move into RFID technology alarmed privacy activists. Katherine Albrecht, founder and director of Consumers Against Supermarket Privacy Invasion and Numbering (CASPIAN), which opposes marketing data collection, questioned the use of RFID in Metro loyalty cards. She warned that the identifying serial numbers in the store's RFID tags could not be deleted, so that the tags could be used to track customer whereabouts after they have taken their purchases home. Metro claimed the technology to erase the serial number from RFID tags would soon be available.

For many companies, privacy is still not an issue because they are not using RFID to track individual items—only pallets or shipping containers containing items. It is only when stores start RFID tagging individual items that privacy issues come into play. Once the price of RFID tags drops to 5 cents or less, companies will use them on individual consumer items, but that remains several years away.

If these companies want to please their customers, however, they will need to start thinking about how they will handle the privacy issue once RFID becomes cost-effective at the package level. Mark Roberti, editor of *RFID Journal*, recommends that businesses develop RFID privacy policies as they gradually implement this technology.

Some organizations are already looking for positive ways to deal with the RFID privacy issue. U.K. department store Marks & Spencer tested RFID tagging of in-store merchandise. It used throwaway paper RFID tags called Intelligent Labels that were attached to, but not embedded in, men's suits, shirts, and ties. Each tag contained a unique number that pointed to an entry in a database detailing product characteristics such as style, size, and colour. The tag numbers were not scanned when customers purchased the items, so no personal information was associated with them.

Before implementing this system, Marks & Spencer discussed the project with Katherine Albrecht of CASPIAN and with the United Kingdom's National Consumer Council. When Marks & Spencer heard the concerns of members of these organizations about RFID tags embedded in products that customers would take home, it decided to use removable tags.

In Singapore, the Alexander Hospital's Department of Emergency Medicine is running a pilot program in which emergency room (ER) patients are tracked using RFID tags. This system must manage a situation in which patients are admitted and discharged very quickly and move in unpredictable patterns around the ER. The RFID system was designed to reduce the time staff spend tracking down people. To maintain privacy, all personally identifiable information (patient names and contact numbers) can be accessed only by designated staff using individual passwords. The department keeps the patient tracking data only for 21 days, as required by the Ministry of Health.

To Think About: How does RFID technology threaten individual privacy? Should retailers have a RFID privacy policy? Why or why not? What issues should the privacy policy address? Does the potential use of RFID conflict with Canadian privacy legislation at the federal and/or provincial level?

Sources: Thomas Claburn, "Watching Out," *Information Week*, February 16, 2004; Karen J. Delaney, "Inventory Tool to Launch in Germany," *Wall Street Journal*, January 12, 2004; and Steve Ulfelder, "Raising an RFID Ruckus," *NewsFactor Top Tech News*, October 7, 2003.

Mobile technology can provide some solutions. Hospitals are installing wireless LANs in emergency rooms and treatment areas and are equipping staff with Wi-Fi-enabled laptop computers or wireless PDAs and smart phones. Table 8-4 provides examples of the efficiencies and improvements in patient care that result from using wireless technology.

TABLE 8-4 *Examples of Wireless Health Care Applications*

WIRELESS APPLICATION	DESCRIPTION
Electronic medical record (EMR) retrieval	Health care professionals can use wireless handhelds to enter and view medical records, including diagnostic information in real time. They can review data immediately and update patient records while making their rounds.
Wireless note taking for patient charts	Doctors and nurses can enter data electronically into wireless PDAs, smart phones, or laptops.
Lab test results	Doctors and nurses can immediately obtain data about lab tests from a wireless PDA, smart phone, or laptop.
Prescription generation	Health care professionals can use a mobile phone, wireless laptop, or handheld to send a prescription to a pharmacy, reducing delays and errors.
Medical databases	Health care professionals can check drug references and other medical information wherever they are working by connecting wirelessly to medical databases.

Wireless Sensor Networks and Pervasive Computing

Innovations in wireless technology are pushing computing into every facet of life, including cars, homes, office buildings, tools, and factories. A mesh of these technologies will provide connections anywhere and any time, making computing devices an even more integral part of our everyday lives. Computers will become increasingly embedded in our natural movements and interactions with our environments. This phenomenon is known as **pervasive computing**.

One example is the use of wireless sensor networks. **Wireless sensor networks (WSNs)** are networks of interconnected wireless devices that are embedded into the physical environment to provide measurements of many points over large spaces. They are based on devices with built-in processing, storage, and radio frequency sensors and antennas. The devices are linked into an interconnected network where data are routed seamlessly among all the nodes and forwarded to a computer for analysis.

These networks require no external infrastructure and can range from hundreds to thousands of nodes. Because wireless sensor devices are placed in the field for years at a time without any maintenance or human intervention, they must have very low power requirements and batteries capable of lasting for long periods of time—years.

Sensor networks typically have a tiered architecture such as that used by the wireless security system illustrated in Figure 8-13. This particular wireless sensor network consists of a hierarchy of nodes, starting with low-level sensors and progressing toward nodes for high-level data aggregation, analysis, and storage. Lower-level sensors for monitoring events such as doors opening and closing, motion, and breakage of windows and doors are complemented by a small group of more advanced sensors placed in key locations, such as cameras and acoustic and chemical detectors. Both simple and complex data are routed over a network to an automated facility that provides continuous building monitoring and control.

Wireless sensor networks are valuable in areas such as monitoring environmental changes, monitoring traffic or military activity, protecting property, efficiently operating and managing machinery and vehicles, establishing security perimeters, monitoring supply chain management, or detecting chemical, biological, or radiological material.

Wireless Sensor Network Standards and ZigBee Standards are being developed for this form of wireless computing. The 802.15.4 standard provides a specification of the radio frequency channel and signalling protocol to be used. Atop 802.15.4 is the **ZigBee** protocol that handles application-level communication between devices. Standard 802.15.4 determines which radio hardware to use while ZigBee determines the content of messages transmitted by each node in the network.

pervasive computing

wireless sensor networks (WSNs)

ZigBee

FIGURE 8-13   A wireless sensor network.

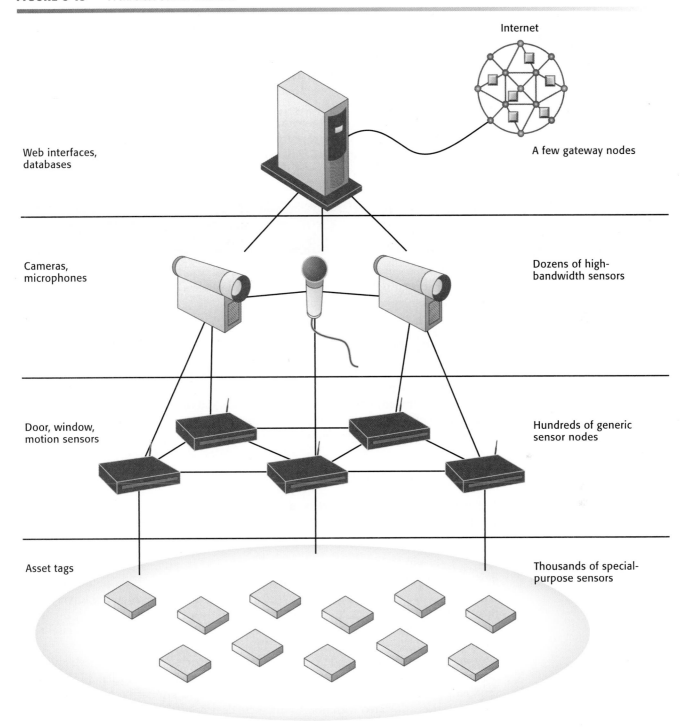

Internet

Web interfaces,
databases

A few gateway nodes

Cameras,
microphones

Dozens of high-
bandwidth sensors

Door, window,
motion sensors

Hundreds of generic
sensor nodes

Asset tags

Thousands of special-
purpose sensors

This wireless sensor network for a security system illustrates the hierarchical organization of wireless sensor networks. Each level handles different types of sensing.

Source: From Jason Hill, Mike Horton, Ralph King, and Lakshman Krishnamurthy, "The Platforms Enabling Wireless Sensor Networks," *Communications of the ACM* 47, no. 6 (June 2004).

Andover Controls Corporation, which has installed 100 000 building-control systems worldwide, is working with Goodman Manufacturing to use ZigBee sensors to cut energy consumption. The sensors monitor motion and temperature in rooms, tracking whether an air conditioner is on, whether someone is in the room, and the temperature. The data are passed from sensor to sensor to a computer that monitors the temperature or equipment. If air-conditioning has made a room too cold, the system could turn off that air conditioner.

The U.S. Department of Energy hired Honeywell International to use ZigBee sensors to reduce energy costs by up to 15 percent in steel, aluminum, and six other industries. Honeywell installed sensors at companies such as ExxonMobil, Alcoa, and Dow Chemical to track energy loss from piping systems and to monitor the use of gases in production processes. The network of sensors monitors the amount of gas constantly, enabling companies to eliminate leaks or wasted energy almost immediately. This application could save up to 256 trillion BTUs per year, more than the amount of natural gas used by Washington state in 2003. ZigBee has yet to capture the Canadian marketplace, but its advantages should mean movement into these same types of industries shortly in Canada.

Management Opportunities, Challenges, and Solutions

Some businesses will benefit from incorporating wireless technology into their business strategy; others may not. Before investing heavily in wireless technology, firms must address a series of technology and organizational issues.

Opportunities

Wireless technology gives firms more flexibility and the ability to innovate in unexpected ways. Wireless systems support business processes that are not limited by time or location, extending the company's reach and saving employees and customers substantial amounts of time. This set of technologies provides a new channel for connecting with customers. It can be a source of exciting new products and services.

Management Challenges

The main challenges posed by wireless technology deal with managing this technology, integrating it into the firm's information technology (IT) infrastructure, and maintaining security and privacy.

Integrating Wireless Technology into the Firm's IT Infrastructure

A large enterprise may have hundreds of wireless access points and many thousands of wireless devices to configure and monitor, similar to a desktop environment. It will be a challenge to integrate this new network infrastructure with the firm's existing infrastructure and applications, and central coordination and oversight are required.

Some companies have found that the savings they expected from using wireless did not materialize because of unexpected costs. Gains in productivity and efficiency from equipping employees with wireless mobile computing devices must be balanced against increased costs associated with integrating these devices into the firm's IT infrastructure and providing technical support. Other cost components include fees for wireless air time, end-user training, help-desk support, and software for special applications.

Although the cost per wireless PDA for a corporate employee is around $375, the total cost of ownership (TCO) for each device is much higher, running from $1250 to $3750, according to various consultant estimates. Costs are higher if a mobile device has extra processing power and runs many different applications and if mobile devices need to be integrated into back-end systems such as enterprise applications.

Not only does a firm have to build their wireless infrastructure, they must also develop information systems for the wireless environment they have built. Applications that take advantage of wireless technologies require much more complexity, including access and security, than typical wired applications.

Maintaining Security and Privacy Maintaining security and privacy poses special challenges for users of wireless technology. Wi-Fi security is not well-developed, making Wi-Fi systems especially vulnerable to penetration from outsiders (see Chapter 9). Wireless systems are easily susceptible to interference from other devices in the same bandwidth and to intrusion from outsiders.

One of the unique benefits of wireless technology is its location-tracking capability. However, this same capability worries privacy advocates who fear the technology could be abused to monitor where users are going and what they are doing every minute. We have already described some of these privacy issues in our discussion of RFID technology. Wireless PDAs, mobile phones, or automobiles with telematics features raise similar concerns.

Solution Guidelines

Here are some guidelines for managing mobile technology in the enterprise.

- *Identify areas in which wireless can provide value.* Once the value of wireless technology has been established, management should rank the areas where mobile connectivity will provide the greatest value to the company, quantifying likely benefits, costs, and risks. The areas where net benefits are highest and risks lowest or least likely to occur would be the first for wireless technology investments.

- *Create a management framework for wireless technology.* Firms need to establish a framework for managing their mobile technology and integrating it into their IT infrastructure. Special corporate policies are necessary for wireless usage, including security, end-user responsibilities, and wireless standards for hardware, software, and networking infrastructure. Limiting the number of different mobile hardware, software, and network vendors will help reduce the total cost of ownership (TCO). Management of wireless technology can also be improved by using special system management tools for downloading software, monitoring usage, and controlling security (see Chapter 9).

- *Use a pilot program before full-scale rollout of wireless systems.* It is very important to test wireless systems on a small scale before launching them throughout the organization. A pilot program allows employees to gain experience while providing feedback to improve the program. Once the wireless system has been fully launched, the firm should monitor progress using the indicators it has established to measure productivity and innovation.

Summary

1. ***Identify the principal wireless transmission media and devices, cellular network standards, generations of mobile networking technology, and mobile computing standards for Internet access.***

    Technologies and devices for wireless transmission include microwave transmission, communication satellites, pagers, email handhelds, personal digital assistants (PDAs), cellular telephones, and smart phones. Personal computers are also starting to be used in wireless transmission.

    Microwave systems, both terrestrial and celestial, transmit high-frequency radio signals through the atmosphere and are widely used for high-volume, long-distance, point-to-point communication. Communication satellites serve as relay stations for microwave signals transmitted from terrestrial stations.

    Major cellular standards include code division multiple access (CDMA), which is used primarily in North America, and global system for mobile communication (GSM), which is the standard in Europe and much of the rest of the world.

    Cellular networks have evolved from slow-speed (1G) analog networks to high-speed high-bandwidth digital packet-switched third-generation (3G) networks with speeds ranging from 144 Kbps to over 2 Mbps for data transmission. Second-generation (2G) cellular networks are digital circuit-switched networks used primarily for voice transmission, but they can also transmit data at rates ranging from 9.6 to 14.4 Kbps. 2.5G networks are packet-switched, use many existing infrastructure elements, and have data transmission rates ranging from 50 to 144 Kbps.

Alternative standards governing the way wireless mobile devices access the Internet and the World Wide Web include Wireless Application Protocol (WAP) and I-mode.

2. *Describe the major standards for wireless networks and wireless Internet access.*

The Institute of Electrical and Electronics Engineers (IEEE) has established a hierarchy of complementary standards for wireless computer networks. These include Bluetooth (802.15) for small personal area networks (PANs), Wi-Fi (802.11) for local area networks (LANs), and WiMax (802.16) for metropolitan area networks (MANs).

Bluetooth can link up to eight devices within a 10-metre area using low-power, radio-based communication and can transmit up to 722 Kbps in the 2.4-GHz band. Wireless phones, keyboards, computers, printers, and PDAs using Bluetooth can communicate with each other and even operate each other without direct user intervention.

The most popular of the 802.11 standards is currently 802.11b, which can transmit up to 11 Mbps in the unlicensed 2.4-GHz band and has an effective distance of 30 to 50 metres, although this range can be extended outdoors by using tower-mounted antennas. The 802.11b standard has been the most widely used standard for creating wireless LANs and providing broadband wireless Internet access. However, 802.11b is vulnerable to penetration by outsiders and interference from other wireless devices in the same frequency spectrum.

WiMax has a wireless access range of up to 50 kilometres and a data transfer rate of up to 75 Mbps, making it suitable for providing broadband Internet access in areas lacking DSL and cable lines. The 802.16 specification also has robust security and quality of service features to support voice and video.

Major cellular carriers are also upgrading their networks to provide wireless broadband access to the Internet at an average speed of 300 to 500 Kbps. Verizon's service, called BroadBand Access, uses a technology called EV-DO to provide Internet access over a cellular network.

3. *Evaluate the role of m-commerce in business, and describe the most important m-commerce applications.*

M-commerce uses the Internet for purchasing goods and services as well as for transmitting messages using wireless mobile devices. It is especially well-suited for location-based applications, such as finding local hotels and restaurants, monitoring local traffic and weather, and providing personalized location-based marketing. Mobile phones and handhelds are being used for mobile bill payment, banking, securities trading, transportation schedule updates, and digital music and game downloads.

Wireless portals (mobile portals) feature content and services optimized for mobile devices to steer users to the information they are most likely to need. Voice portals accept voice commands for accessing Web content, email, and other electronic applications from a cell phone or standard telephone.

M-commerce requires special digital payment systems that can handle micropayments, because most m-commerce purchases today are for very small amounts. Mobile wallets (m-wallets) expedite purchases by storing online shoppers' personal information and credit card numbers.

M-commerce represents a tiny fraction of all online purchases because wireless mobile devices cannot display merchandise very well. Mobile phones have tiny keyboards, small screens, and slow data transfer speeds (9.6 to 14.4 Kbps). M-commerce will benefit from interoperable payment systems for wireless devices and faster wireless networks to support more data-rich communication.

4. *Assess the business value of wireless technology, and describe important wireless applications in business.*

Wireless technology increases productivity and worker output by providing anytime, anywhere communication and access to information, including the information resources of the Internet. Wireless communication helps businesses stay in touch more easily with customers, suppliers, and employees and provides more flexible arrangements for organizing work.

Mobile applications are having a significant impact on customer relationship management (CRM), supply chain management (SCM), and health care. Mobile CRM applications provide additional support for sales and service activities at the point of customer interaction.

Mobile wireless technology facilitates supply chain management by capturing data on the movement of goods as these events take place and by providing detailed, immediate information as goods move among supply chain partners. Radio frequency identification (RFID) systems provide a powerful technology for this purpose. These systems use tiny tags that have embedded microchips that contain data about an item and its location. The tags transmit radio signals over a short distance to special RFID readers. The RFID readers then pass the data over a network to a computer for processing.

Mobile technology is improving health care by delivering essential information to physicians and nurses who constantly move from place to place and capturing patient information for electronic record systems at the point of creation.

Wireless sensor networks (WSNs) are networks of interconnected wireless devices with some processing and radio-transmitting capability that are embedded into the physical environment to provide measurements of many points over large spaces. Wireless sensor networks are valuable for monitoring environmental changes, traffic patterns, security incidents, or supply chain events.

5. **Identify and describe the challenges posed by wireless technology, and propose management solutions.**

The principal challenges posed by wireless technology are maintaining security and privacy and integrating this technology into the firm's IT infrastructure.

Solutions include identifying the areas in which wire-less can provide the greatest value, creating an appropriate framework for managing wireless technology, and using a pilot program before full-scale rollout of wireless systems. Key management decisions deal with establishing the business value of wireless technology, selecting appropriate wireless technologies and standards, and identifying the necessary changes in business processes to make wireless technology work.

Key Terms

2.5G networks, 272
3G networks, 272
802.11b, 275
Access point, 275
Bluetooth, 274
Cellular telephones (cell phones), 271
Code Division Multiple Access (CDMA), 272
Email handhelds, 271
EV-DO, 279
General Packet Radio Service (GPRS), 272
Global positioning system (GPS), 269
Global System for Mobile Communication (GSM), 271

Hotspots, 276
I-mode, 273
Microbrowser, 273
Microwave, 269
Mobile computing, 280
Mobile wallets (m-wallets), 284
Nomadic computing, 280
Paging systems, 271
Personal area networks (PANs), 274
Personal digital assistants (PDAs), 271
Pervasive computing, 290
Radio frequency identification (RFID), 286
Satellites, 269

Short message service (SMS), 271
Smart phones, 271
Telematics, 269
Voice portals, 283
Wi-Fi, 275
WiMax, 278
Wireless Application Protocol (WAP), 273
Wireless Markup Language (WML), 273
Wireless NICs, 275
Wireless portals, 283
Wireless sensor networks (WSNs), 290
ZigBee, 290

Review Questions

1. How does wireless technology provide business value?

2. Name and describe the principal wireless transmission media and devices.

3. List and describe the major cellular network standards and cellular network generations.

4. What is Bluetooth? Describe its capabilities. For what types of applications is it best suited?

5. What is Wi-Fi? Describe the 802.11b standard for wireless networking. How does it work?

6. What are the benefits and challenges of using Wi-Fi?

7. What is WiMax? How does it differ from Wi-Fi?

8. What is EV-DO? How does it differ from WiMax and Wi-Fi?

9. Compare the WAP and I-mode standards for wireless access to the Web.

10. What is the difference between nomadic computing and mobile computing?

11. List and describe the most important types of m-commerce services and applications.

12. How do wireless portals and voice portals help users access information on the Web?

13. Describe the payment systems for m-commerce. What role is played by mobile wallets?

14. What are some of the barriers to m-commerce?

15. How can wireless technology support customer relationship management and supply chain management?

16. What is RFID? How does it work? How does it provide value to businesses?

17. What are wireless sensor networks? How do they work? What applications use them?

18. Describe the challenges posed by wireless technology and some ways to address them.

Discussion Questions

1. Should all major retailing and manufacturing companies switch to RFID? Why or why not?

2. Is wireless technology a threat to privacy? Explain your answer.

Application Software Exercise:
Spreadsheet Exercise: Comparing Wireless Services

You would like to equip your sales force of 35 based in Edmonton, Alberta, with mobile phones that have capabilities for voice transmission, text messaging, and taking and sending photos. Use the Web to select a wireless service provider that provides nationwide service as well as good service in your home area. Examine the features of the mobile handsets offered by each of these vendors. Assume that each of the 35 salespeople will need to spend three hours per day during business hours (8 AM to 6 PM) on mobile voice communication, send 30 text messages per day, and five photos per week. Use your spreadsheet software to determine the wireless service and handset that will offer both the best pricing per user over a two-year period. For the purposes of this exercise, you do not need to consider corporate discounts.

Electronic Business Project: Identifying Wi-Fi Hotspots for Nomadic Computing

Your company has a sales force of 15 representatives, and your customers are concentrated in Vancouver and Victoria, British Columbia; and Seattle, Washington. Your sales representatives are constantly on the road, and you are looking for a way to provide them with Internet email and Web access so that they can easily communicate throughout the day with corporate headquarters as they meet with clients and travel from one meeting to another. Use Web sites such as **www.wifinder.com**, **www.hotspot-locations.com**, and **www.wi-fizone.org** to determine which commercial hotspots would be the most appropriate for your sales force and the commercial network services that these hotspots use. Then, research the Web sites of two or three commercial networks that seem most appropriate to discover more about their pricing and services. Finally, use **www.wifinder.com** and **www.wififreespot.com** to determine how many free public hotspots are available in these cities. Are there enough for your company to rely on these hotspots, or should you use a commercial Wi-Fi system? If so, which one?

Group Project: Comparing Mobile Internet Access Systems

Form a group with three or four of your classmates. Select mobile devices with Internet access from two different vendors, such as Palm, BlackBerry, Nokia, and Motorola. Your analysis should consider the purchase cost of each device, any additional software required to make it Internet enabled, the cost of wireless Internet services, and what Internet services are available for each device. You should also consider other capabilities of each device, including the ability to integrate with existing corporate or PC applications. Which device would you select? What criteria would you use to guide your selection? If possible, use electronic presentation software to present your findings to the class.

Web Sites of Interest

There are many interesting Web sites to enhance your learning about wireless computing and telecommunication. You can search the Web yourself or try the following sites to add to what you have already learned.

Primus Telecommunications **www.primus.ca**
One of Canada's more inventive wireless providers; Primus offers long distance service for cell phones as well as Internet service and VoIP service

Zi Corporation **www.zicorp.com**
Calgary-based company offering a variety of interesting applications for cell and smart phones

Palm Source Corporation **www.palmsource.com**
Home Web site of the Palm operating system used by many PDAs

PalmOne Corporation **www.palmone.com/ca**
Canadian home Web site of the PDA device company selling Palm devices

Microsoft Corporation Mobile Pocket PC **www.microsoft.com/windowsmobile/pocketpc/ppc/**
Home of the operating system that challenges Palm devices; similar interface to MS Windows XP

CASE STUDY:
UPS versus FEDEX: Two Competitors, Two Wireless Strategies

FedEx Corporation (FedEx) and United Parcel Service, Incorporated (UPS) are industry leaders in air and ground package distribution and specialized transportation and logistics services. The companies compete on a global scale and have established strongholds on particular aspects of the shipping business. UPS achieved its status primarily on the strength of its time-definite ground delivery of packages and documents. FedEx traditionally attributes its success and reputation to its unmatched performance in overnight deliveries. UPS delivers an average of over 13 million packages each day. FedEx averages approximately 5 million daily deliveries, but surpasses UPS in air deliveries, 3.1 million to 2 million. The two rivals have grown from very different beginnings to occupy their current standings in the marketplace. As technological advances enable UPS and FedEx to carry their respective businesses to greater heights, the evolution of the technology has them walking a fine line between fanning the flames of competition and growing side by side.

Nearly a century old, UPS has grown from a two-man, two-bicycle operation in Seattle, Washington, that promised the "best service and lowest rates" into a 355 000-employee corporate giant with a delivery fleet of 88 000 ground vehicles and nearly 600 airplanes. The fleet services 1.8 million shipping customers daily, bringing deliveries to 6.1 million consignees. UPS first expanded to Europe in 1975. In 2003, UPS revealed a $750 million improvement initiative for its package sorting and delivery systems. By 2007, UPS expects this initiative to result in a $750 million annual reduction in operating costs, mostly as a result of productivity improvements and more efficient driving routes.

UPS counts global reach, technology systems, customer relationships, brand equity, and e-commerce capabilities among its competitive strengths. The company's growth strategies include building on its status as the leader in domestic package operations, continuing to expand internationally, offering comprehensive supply chain solutions to businesses that seek to outsource such a complicated business component, and backing up the core delivery service with a strong portfolio of e-commerce solutions. UPS.com fields more than 9 million requests for package tracking each day, and the Web site receives 115 million hits overall on a daily basis.

FedEx Corporation is the parent company of the various operating companies under the FedEx name, which include FedEx Express, FedEx Ground, FedEx Freight, FedEx Trade Networks, and FedEx Services. FedEx Express, the corporation's time-certain express delivery service, was founded in 1971. The corporation as a whole employs 216 500 workers and contractors, and 134 000 of those employees serve FedEx Express as it provides delivery services to 214 countries using 53 500 drop-off locations, 643 aircraft, and 48 000 road vehicles. FedEx Ground recently began a six-year, $1.8 billion expansion initiative that by 2009 will double the company's capacity to process ground packages, currently at 2.5 million daily.

The growth strategies of FedEx include increasing high-tech and high-value-added business goods, globalization, acceleration of the supply chain, and continued expansion of Internet and e-commerce solutions. The corporation views its brand as a strong business asset and uses it to provide customers with an integrated set of business solutions, including those available from FedEx.com.

As UPS and FedEx continue to jockey for position in each other's strongest market domains, it is clear that the two companies take different approaches to the same goal. Both, like any company that is seeking to grow, look to increase the efficiency of their operations. Improved efficiency generally results from cutting costs of business processes and extending the usefulness and capabilities of resources beyond current expectations. One of the most important ways that UPS and FedEx have improved their businesses since the late 1980s is through the use of wireless technologies. But each company has taken a different approach to the implementation of such technologies.

FedEx acts more like a start-up business, jumping at the chance to adopt the latest and greatest applications as soon as they prove to be economical and effective for both the company and its customers. UPS, on the other hand, adheres to a more measured schedule of new technology rollouts, generally waiting from 5 to 7 years between major initiatives. This approach enables UPS to revamp its systems with uniform upgrades that can replace segments of the old systems in phases.

Their approaches, however, are not diametrically opposite. UPS is willing to make intermediate technology changes to take advantage of opportunities while FedEx tries to makes sure its adoptions have long-term viability and support its critical priorities. And regardless of approach, FedEx and UPS have determined that wireless technologies have a major impact on their key business processes, especially package pickup and delivery transactions and the physical packaging and sorting of packages.

Fifteen years ago, deploying wireless technology generally required contracting with a technology vendor to develop proprietary systems. These systems were costly because they had to be developed from the ground up, and neither company had the existing infrastructure or bandwidth to support wireless technology at the outset. These days, UPS and FedEx have taken advantage of wireless solutions based on global standards. Both companies use the Bluetooth short-range wireless specification, 802.11b wireless LANs, and general packet radio service (GPRS) cellular networks to varying degrees. The fact that these technologies are available off the shelf translates to greatly reduced development costs, easier maintenance, better capacity and security, and lower implementation costs.

For companies such as FedEx and UPS, reducing the time required to make every delivery by even one second can have an enormous impact on the cost of doing business across the board. Wireless technology has become the driving force behind making such improvements in efficiency possible. Not surprisingly, both companies have devoted sums in excess of $125 million to wireless initiatives. Wireless technology brings UPS and FedEx as close as they can come to having real-time data available for their operations. Putting wireless handheld devices in the hands of delivery personnel enables these workers to complete their tasks more quickly and provide an elevated level of customer service.

At UPS, drivers carry a handheld unit called a delivery information acquisition device (DIAD). The current version of the device is the DIAD IV, which, like its predecessor, the DIAD III, can connect to UPS operations centres directly using digital cellular technology and cellular transmitters in the delivery trucks. Therefore, information from pickup and delivery transactions that are gathered by personnel in the field can be transmitted to the company's global network almost immediately.

UPS plans to augment the power of its handheld units by adding Bluetooth capabilities. The upgrade will enable the devices to connect the handhelds to the trucks and to run applications, such as credit card transaction processing, in areas where an adequate GPRS cellular signal is not available. John Killeen, the director of global network services for UPS, admits that the full scope of Bluetooth's usefulness to the new DIADs is not apparent yet, but the reasonable cost and potential of the implementation make it worthwhile. UPS is also looking to improve customer service by adding global positioning satellite (GPS) tracking technology to the DIAD IV units. This type of tracking would facilitate services such as rerouting packages that are already in transit by the most economical route.

The FedEx equivalent of UPS' DIAD is the PowerPad. Like their counterparts at UPS, FedEx drivers use the handheld PowerPad to scan packages for pickup and delivery information. The method that FedEx uses to transmit this data to headquarters differs slightly, however. FedEx had previously equipped its vehicles with cellular transmitters for this purpose. When the company rolled out the PowerPad handhelds, it decided to keep the cellular transmitters and have the handhelds upload their data to the transmitters using Bluetooth. Because drivers previously had to dock their handheld units physically in the transmitters to transmit data to home base, the PowerPad with Bluetooth still provides FedEx with significant time and cost savings ($25 million per year) even though it does not provide a direct connection to the company's central systems.

The PowerPad units have other time-saving features as well. For example, FedEx drivers can lock and unlock drop boxes using an infrared signal from the PowerPad instead of a key. Because infrared signals require that the communicating devices line up to each other's apertures unimpeded, FedEx would like to improve this time-saving measure further by using a Bluetooth signal instead of the infrared signal. First, FedEx must address issues related to how much it would cost to deploy and maintain Bluetooth in the drop boxes. Taking the technology another step further, FedEx hopes that using Bluetooth in its drop boxes will eventually permit drivers to pass by empty drop boxes without having to check them.

Again, there are technology challenges to overcome: a drop box could be "silent" because it is empty or because the battery in its Bluetooth transmitter is dead. Other plans for the future of the PowerPad include making it 802.11b-enabled to maintain compatibility with Microsoft operating systems and adding information look-up and retrieval features so that delivery personnel can provide customers with better and more detailed information on topics such as packaging rules and regulations, supplies, and rates.

FedEx and UPS are also seeing the benefits of wireless technology in their sorting facilities and distribution centres. The main hubs for FedEx, in Memphis, Tennessee, and UPS, in Louisville, Kentucky, are tremendous facilities that process millions of packages every day. For both companies, lowering the cost of sorting these packages at their main hubs and smaller centres is an important business consideration. To collect package data during sorting, UPS and FedEx both use a portable ring scanner, which consists of a finger-mounted bar code reader that is connected to a terminal. The user wears the terminal on his or her forearm.

UPS will soon complete the rollout of a new scanning unit that places the terminal on the user's waist. Employees prefer this location because it results in less physical stress over the course of a workday. Additionally, the new scanners will use Bluetooth for communication between the finger-mounted bar code scanner and the waist-mounted terminal. Workers at UPS sorting facilities scan packages as they load them onto trucks. It was not unusual for the cables connecting the two pieces of the old scanners to get caught and break during the loading process. The new scanners will reduce UPS maintenance costs by 30 percent, spare parts costs by 35 percent, and downtime by 35 percent. Also, once turned on, the scanners are in an always-on mode and do not have to be triggered for each bar code read, as the old ring scanners did. The scanners can also transmit data to the company system in real time, so UPS inventory systems can flag issues and report more quickly to customers. (The old systems stored the data and transmitted them in periodic batches.) During the next four years, 55 000 scanners will be rolled out to about 1700 facilities.

FedEx has not yet found the need to replace its current ring scanner model. Despite the company's interest in increasing its volume of ground package shipping, smaller packages, such as envelopes, still account for the majority of the business. Therefore, FedEx requires fewer people to handle boxes, uses fewer ring scanners than UPS, and is not adversely affected by the costs associated with the equipment. FedEx also has found a problem with implementing Bluetooth because it runs on the same frequency as the 802.11b network that the company installed only three years ago, creating signal interference. UPS avoided this problem by upgrading its new scanning system all at once and designing devices and access points to use time-division multiplexing to alternate between 802.11b and Bluetooth so signals don't conflict.

Other wireless technology areas that UPS and FedEx are considering include radio frequency identification (RFID) and global positioning system (GPS) applications. RFID tags would replace bar code scanning entirely while GPS would enable precise tracking of drivers, vehicles, and packages in the field. Even though several industries have begun using RFID for shipping and supply chain management, for now, it remains cost-prohibitive for companies such as UPS and FedEx. They have many customers who operate on small budgets. Although having these customers print their own bar codes is quite reasonable, asking them to create RFID tags requires a much heavier investment. However, according to Winn Stephenson, FedEx Services' senior vice president of IT for technology services, adoption of RFID seems inevitable; it is just a matter of timing.

One significant challenge that remains for UPS and FedEx is designing applications that conform to the narrower bandwidth that is characteristic of wireless networks and that provide fault tolerance for disconnects. Despite these issues, both companies would insist that the dynamic transfer of data that wireless connectivity provides has them poised to continue as industry leaders.

Sources: Galen Gruman, "UPS vs. FedEx: Head-to-Head on Wireless" and "New Technologies Hit Mainstream," *CIO Magazine,* June 1, 2004; "RFID Adoption Survey: Current and Future Plans," *CIO Magazine,* June 30, 2004, Dean Foust, "Big Brown's New Bag" *Business* Week, July 19, 2004; Robert Carter, "Six Degrees of Preparation," *Optimize Magazine* 22 (January 2004); Mark Samuels, "UPS Wireless Plan Reaches Europe," VNU, **www.vnunet.com** June 30, 2004; United Parcel Service, Inc., 10-K Report, **www.ups.com**, FedEx Corporation 10-K Report, **www.fedex.com**.

CASE STUDY QUESTIONS

1. Analyze UPS and FedEx using the competitive forces and value chain models.

2. How are wireless technologies related to the core information systems and business strategies of UPS and Fed Ex? How do these technologies provide value to companies?

3. How do the implementations of wireless technology reflect the organizational differences between UPS and FedEx? Which wireless strategy is more effective? Explain your answer.

4. How will wireless technologies help UPS and FedEx in the future?

5. Both UPS and FedEx conduct business around the world. How does this impact their ability to implement and upgrade their wireless technologies? Does this apply to Canada as well?

Chapter 9

Information Systems Security and Control

OBJECTIVES

After completing this chapter, you will be able to:

1. Analyze why information systems need special protection from destruction, error, and abuse.

2. Assess the business value of security and control.

3. Evaluate elements of an organizational and managerial framework for security and control.

4. Evaluate the most important tools and technologies for safeguarding information resources.

5. Identify the challenges posed by information systems security and control, and propose management solutions.

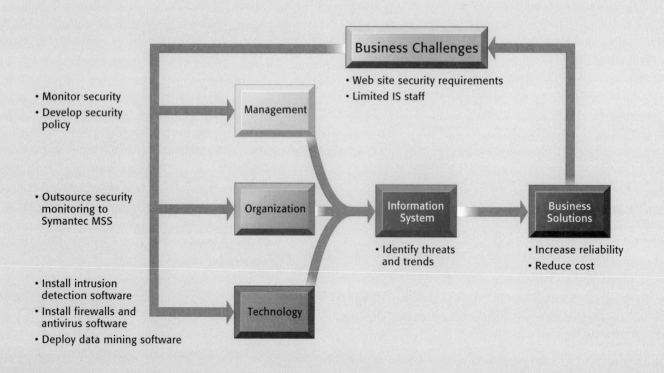

- Monitor security
- Develop security policy

- Outsource security monitoring to Symantec MSS

- Install intrusion detection software
- Install firewalls and antivirus software
- Deploy data mining software

Management

Organization

Technology

Business Challenges
- Web site security requirements
- Limited IS staff

Information System
- Identify threats and trends

Business Solutions
- Increase reliability
- Reduce cost

Opening Case: Wesfarmers Outsources to a Managed Security Service

Wesfarmers Limited is a diversified Australian holding company for businesses in home improvement retailing, chemical and fertilizer production, building materials, industrial and safety product distribution, rail transport, and forest products harvesting, milling, and processing. Its subsidiaries include companies such as Bunnings, Blackwoods, and Kleenheat Gas.

Wesfarmers had to pay more attention to the security of its information systems when it set up an Internet banking site in early 2003 for its Landmark division supplying financial services and products for agribusinesses. People could access the Wesfarmers Landmark Web site 24 hours a day, seven days a week. Wesfarmers had already invested heavily in firewalls, intrusion detection systems, antivirus software, and other security software, but it did not have sufficient information systems staff and resources for round-the-clock monitoring of infrastructure security.

Wesfarmers decided to outsource the management of its information systems security to Symantec's Managed Security Services, which now manages Wesfarmers' security environment remotely from an operations centre in North Ryde, Australia. The service provides real-time security monitoring, enhanced reporting, and complete management of Wesfarmers' network using intrusion detection software, and it monitors Wesfarmers' firewalls. Symantec identified ways to improve Wesfarmers' security and to better manage vulnerabilities that could potentially threaten its network.

Symantec demonstrated a unique and highly cost-effective solution that uses best-practice processes and procedures. A key feature is the ability to log on to an online security portal and retrieve real-time reports that can immediately alert the company to potential risks.

Wesfarmers subsequently sold Landmark, but it decided to keep the Symantec monitoring service because it provides so many benefits. Symantec can analyze the data the system collects while it is monitoring Wesfarmers' network to identify trends and threats over time.

Data from Symantec's security monitoring logs for Wesfarmers are put in a data-mining process to identify intruders who keep coming back. And because Symantec constantly tracks new security threats around the world, it can take protective action on vulnerabilities to head off trouble.

Sources: Karen Dearne, "Wesfarmers Trusts Security to Specialists," *Australian IT News*, February 10, 2004, and "Wesfarmers Limited Protects Its Resources with Symantec Managed Security Services," **www.riptech.com/region/au_nz**, accessed June 19, 2004; and **www.symantec.com**, accessed October 4, 2004.

Wesfarmers' experience illustrates the need for organizations to take special measures to protect their information systems to ensure their continued operation. Network disruptions, unauthorized users, software failures, hardware failures, natural disasters, employee errors, and terrorist attacks can prevent information systems from running properly or running at all.

Computer systems play such a critical role in business, government, and daily life that firms need to make security and control a top priority. **Security** refers to the policies, procedures, and technical measures used to prevent unauthorized access, alteration, theft, or physical damage to information systems. **Controls** consist of all the methods, policies, and organizational procedures that ensure the safety of the organization's assets, the accuracy and reliability of its accounting records, and operational adherence to management standards. Let us look at how information systems can be controlled and made secure so that they serve the purposes for which they are intended.

9.1 System Vulnerability and Abuse

Before computer automation, data about individuals or organizations were maintained and secured as paper records dispersed in separate business or organizational units. Information systems concentrate data in computer files that can potentially be accessed by large numbers of people and by groups outside of the organization.

When large amounts of data are stored in electronic form, they are vulnerable to many more kinds of threats than when they exist in manual form. Through communications networks, information systems in different locations can be interconnected. The potential for unauthorized access, abuse, or fraud is not limited to a single location but can occur at any access point in the network. Many students think that denial of service attacks, spoofing, and phishing can't harm them because they are only students. These types of crimes do not distinguish between companies, company executives, employees, and students—they simply attack. Everyone who uses a computer today needs to be aware of these problems and prepared to meet them head on.

Why Systems Are Vulnerable

Figure 9-1 illustrates the most common threats against contemporary information systems. They can stem from technical, organizational, and environmental factors compounded by poor management decisions. In the multitier client/server computing environment illustrated here, vulnerabilities exist at each layer and in the communications between the layers. Users at the client layer can cause harm by introducing errors or by accessing systems without authorization. It is possible to access data flowing over networks, steal valuable data during transmission, or alter messages without authorization. Radiation can disrupt a network at various points as well. Intruders can launch denial of service attacks or malicious software to disrupt the operation of Web sites. Those capable of penetrating corporate systems can destroy or alter corporate data stored in databases or files.

Systems malfunction if computer hardware breaks down, is not configured properly, or is damaged by improper use or criminal acts. Errors in programming, improper installation, or unauthorized changes cause computer software to fail. Computer systems can also be disrupted by power failures, floods, fires, or other natural disasters.

Domestic or offshore outsourcing to another company adds to system vulnerability because valuable information will reside on networks and computers outside the organization's control. Without strong safeguards, valuable data could be lost, destroyed, or could fall into the wrong hands, revealing important trade secrets or information that violate personal privacy. Some worry that outsourcing application development to offshore companies might provide opportunities for programmers to insert hidden code that would later enable someone to gain control over an application or its data (Schmerken 2004 and Fitzgerald 2004).

Internet Vulnerabilities Large public networks such as the Internet are more vulnerable than internal networks because they are virtually open to anyone. The Internet is so huge that when abuses do occur, they can have a widespread impact. When the Internet becomes part of the corporate network, the organization's information systems are even more vulnerable to actions from outsiders.

Computers that are constantly connected to the Internet by cable modems or digital subscriber lines (DSL) are more open to penetration by outsiders because they use fixed Internet addresses where they can be easily identified. (With dial-up service, a temporary Internet address is assigned for each session.) A fixed Internet address creates a fixed target for hackers.

Telephone service based on Internet technology (see Chapter 7) can be more vulnerable than the switched voice network if it does not run over a secure private network. Most Voice over IP (VoIP) traffic over the public Internet is not encrypted, so anyone with a network can listen in on conversations. Hackers can intercept conversations to obtain

FIGURE 9-1   *Contemporary security challenges and vulnerabilities.*

The architecture of a Web-based application typically includes a Web client, a server, and corporate information systems linked to databases. Each of these components presents security challenges and vulnerabilities. Floods, fires, power failures, and other electrical problems can cause disruptions at any point in the network.

security

controls

credit card and other confidential personal information or shut down voice service by flooding servers supporting VoIP with bogus traffic.

Vulnerability has also increased from widespread use of email and instant messaging (IM). Email can contain attachments that serve as springboards for malicious software or unauthorized access to internal corporate systems. Employees may use email messages to transmit valuable trade secrets, financial data, or confidential customer information to unauthorized recipients. Popular instant messaging applications for consumers do not use a secure layer for text messages, so they can be intercepted and read by outsiders during transmission over the public Internet. IM activity over the Internet can in some cases be used as a back door to an otherwise secure network. (IM systems designed for corporations, such as IBM's SameTime, include security features.)

Wireless Security Challenges Wireless networks using radio-based technology are even more vulnerable to penetration because radio frequency bands are easy to scan. Although the range of Wi-Fi networks is only several hundred feet, it can be extended up to one-fourth of a mile using external antennae. Local area networks (LANs) that use the 802.11b (Wi-Fi) standard can be easily penetrated by outsiders armed with laptops, wireless cards, external antennae, and freeware hacking software. Hackers can use these tools to detect unprotected networks, monitor network traffic, and, in some cases, gain access to the Internet or to corporate networks.

Wi-Fi transmission technology uses spread spectrum transmission in which a signal is spread over a wide range of frequencies. The particular version of spread spectrum transmission used in the 802.11 standard was designed to make it easier for stations to find and hear one another. The *service set identifiers (SSID)* identifying the access points in a Wi-Fi network are broadcast multiple times and can be picked up fairly easily by intruders' sniffer programs (see Figure 9-2). Wireless networks in many locations do not have basic protections against **war driving**, in which eavesdroppers drive by buildings or park outside and try to intercept wireless network traffic.

The 802.11 standard specifies the SSID as a form of password for a user's radio network interface card (NIC) to join a particular wireless network. The user's radio NIC

FIGURE 9-2   *Wi-Fi security challenges.*

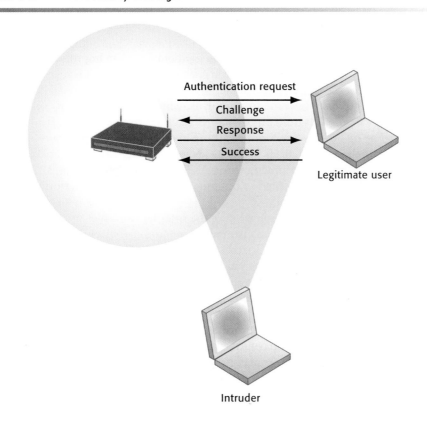

Many Wi-Fi networks can be penetrated easily by intruders using sniffer programs to obtain an address to access the resources of a network without authorization.

Authentication request

Challenge

Response

Success

Legitimate user

Intruder

war driving

must have the same SSID as the access point to enable association and communication. Most access points broadcast the SSID multiple times per second. A hacker can employ an 802.11 analysis tool to identify the SSID. (Windows XP has capabilities for detecting the SSID used in a network and automatically configuring the radio NIC within the user's device.) An intruder that has associated with an access point by using the correct SSID can then obtain a legitimate Internet Protocol (IP) address to access other resources on the network because many wireless LANs automatically assign IP addresses to users as they become active. This enables an intruder who has illicitly associated with a wireless LAN to use the Windows operating system to determine which other users are connected to the network and even to click on other users' devices, locate their documents folders, and open or copy their files. This is a serious problem many end users overlook when connecting to access points at airports or other public locations.

Intruders can also use the information they have gleaned about IP addresses and SSIDs to set up rogue access points on a different radio channel in physical locations close to users to force a user's radio NIC to associate with the rogue access point. Once this association occurs, hackers using the rogue access point can capture the names and passwords of unsuspecting users.

The initial security standard developed for Wi-Fi, called *Wired Equivalent Privacy (WEP)*, is not very effective. WEP is built into all standard 802.11 products, but its use is optional. Users must turn it on, and many neglect to do so, leaving many access points unprotected. The basic WEP specification calls for an access point and all of its users to share the same 40-bit encrypted password, which can be easily decrypted by hackers from a small amount of traffic. Manufacturers of wireless networking products are now beefing up their security by offering stronger encryption and authentication systems.

Malicious Software: Viruses, Worms, Trojan Horses, and Spyware

Malicious software programs referred to as **malware** include a variety of threats such as computer viruses, worms, and Trojan horses. A **computer virus** is a rogue software program that attaches itself to other software programs or data files in order to be executed, usually without user knowledge or permission. Most computer viruses deliver a "payload." The payload may be relatively benign, such as the instructions to display a message or image, or it may be highly destructive—destroying programs or data, clogging computer memory, reformatting a computer's hard drive, or causing programs to run improperly. Viruses typically spread from computer to computer when humans take an action such as sending an email attachment or copying an infected file.

Many recent attacks have come from **worms**, which are independent computer programs that copy themselves from one computer to others over a network. (Unlike viruses, they can operate on their own without attaching to other computer program files and rely less on human behaviour in order to spread from computer to computer. This explains why computer worms spread much more rapidly than computer viruses.) Worms can destroy data and programs as well as disrupt or even halt the operation of computer networks.

Worms and viruses are often spread over the Internet from files of downloaded software, from files attached to email transmissions, or from compromised email messages. Viruses have also invaded computerized information systems from "infected" disks or infected machines. Today email attachments are the most frequent source of infection, followed by Internet downloads and Web browsing.

Now viruses and worms are spreading to wireless computing devices. Mobile device viruses could pose serious threats to enterprise computing because so many wireless devices are now linked to corporate information systems. Table 9-1 describes the characteristics of the some of the most harmful worms and viruses that have appeared.

Over 80 000 viruses and worms are known to exist, with about 25 new ones detected each day. Over the past decade, worms and viruses have cause billions of dollars of damage to corporate networks, email systems, and data. According to the research firm

malware

computer virus

worms

TABLE 9-1 *Examples of Malicious Code*

MyDoom.A	Worm	
Sasser.ftp	Worm	First appeared May 11, 2004. Spreads over the Internet by attacking random IP addresses. Runs a script which downloads the worm by using File Transfer Protocol (FTP).
Klez	Email worm	Most prolific virus of 2002. Delivered in an email containing a random subject line and message body targeting all addresses in the Windows address book, the database of instant messaging program ICQ, and local files. A file from the user's system is randomly selected and sent along with the worm. Klez also attempts to disable antivirus software and drops another virus in the user's system that tries to infect executable files there and across network filing systems.
StartPage.FH	Trojan Horse	First appeared June 15, 2004. Transmitted through infected floppy disks, CD-ROMs, Internet downloads, peer-to-peer (P2P) file sharing. Changes Microsoft Internet Explorer's homepage to display fake messages warning users of spyware infection. Attempts to entice users to visit a Web site where additional malware can be installed.
Netsky.P	Worm	First appeared March 21, 2004. Spreads through email and through P2P file sharing. Deletes entries belonging to several other worms, including MyDoom and Bagle. Activated when the message is viewed in Microsoft Outlook's preview pane.
Sobig.F	Worm	First detected on August 19, 2003. Sends massive amounts of mail with forged sender information. Payload activates on Fridays or Sundays, when it downloads a program and runs it on the infected computer.
Melissa	Macro virus/worm	First appeared in March 1999. At the time, it was the fastest-spreading infectious program ever discovered. Attacked Microsoft Word's Normal.dot global template, ensuring infection of all newly created documents. Mailed infected Word file to first 50 entries in user's Microsoft Outlook address book.

Computer Economics, viruses and worms caused an estimated $16 billion in damage worldwide in 2003 (Hulme 2004).

A **Trojan horse** is a software program that appears to be benign, but then it does something other than expected. The Trojan horse is not itself a virus because it does not replicate, but is often a way for viruses or other malicious code to be introduced into a computer system. The term *Trojan horse* is based on the huge wooden horse used by the Greeks to trick the Trojans into opening the gates to their fortified city during the Trojan War. Once inside the city walls, Greek soldiers hidden in the horse revealed themselves and captured the city.

An example of a modern-day Trojan horse is Trojan.Xombe, which was detected on the Internet in early 2004. It masqueraded as an email message from Microsoft, directing recipients to open an attached file that purportedly carried an update to the Windows XP operating system. When the attached file was opened, it downloaded and installed malicious code on the compromised computer. Once this Trojan horse was installed, hackers could access the computer undetected, steal passwords, and take over the machine to launch denial of service attacks on other computers (Keizer 2004).

Some types of *spyware*, which we introduced in Chapter 4, can also act as malicious software. These small programs install themselves on computers to monitor user Web surfing activity and serve up advertising. Some Web advertisers use spyware to obtain information about users' buying habits and to serve tailored advertisements. Many users find this type of spyware annoying, and some critics worry about its infringement on computer users' privacy.

Other forms of spyware, however, are much more nefarious. *Key loggers* record every keystroke made on a computer to steal serial numbers for software, to launch Internet attacks, to gain access to email accounts, to obtain passwords to protected computer systems, or to pick up personal information such as credit card numbers. Other spyware

Trojan horse

programs reset Web browser home pages, redirect search requests, or slow computer performance by taking up too much memory. Nearly 1000 forms of spyware have been documented.

Hackers and Cybervandalism

A **hacker** is an individual who intends to gain unauthorized access to a computer system. Within the hacking community, the term **cracker** is typically used to denote a hacker with criminal intent, although in the public press, the terms *hacker* and *cracker* are frequently used interchangeably. Hackers and crackers gain unauthorized access by finding weaknesses in the security protections employed by Web sites and computer systems, often taking advantage of various features of the Internet that make it an easy-to-use open system.

Hacker activities have broadened beyond mere system intrusion to include theft of goods and information, as well as system damage and **cybervandalism**, the intentional disruption, defacement, or even destruction of a Web site or corporate information system. Early in 2003, hackers introduced the Slammer worm, which targeted a known vulnerability in Microsoft SQL Server database software. Slammer struck thousands of companies; affected computers at Vancouver's Canaccord Capital; crashed Bank of America cash machines, especially in the southwestern part of the United States; affected cash registers at supermarkets such as the Publix chain in Atlanta, where staff could not dispense cash to frustrated buyers; and took down most Internet connections in South Korea, causing a dip in the stock market there (Tucker 2003). Some hackers, motivated by "hacktivism," launch politically motivated attacks with the same effect. For instance, after the October 12, 2002, terrorist nightclub bombings in Bali, Indonesian hackers hacked or defaced more than 200 Australian Web sites to protest security raids targeting Indonesian families in Australia.

Spoofing and Sniffing Hackers attempting to hide their true identity often spoof, or misrepresent, themselves by using fake email addresses or masquerading as someone else. **Spoofing** can also involve redirecting a Web link to an address different from the intended one, with the site masquerading as the intended destination. Links that are designed to lead to one site can be reset to send users to a totally unrelated site, one that benefits the hacker. For example, if hackers redirect customers to a fake Web site that looks almost exactly like the true site, they can then collect and process orders, effectively

FIGURE 9-3   *Regional distribution of computer viruses and worms worldwide.*

These three charts show the regional distribution of computer viruses and worms worldwide reported by Trend Micro during the past 24 hours, seven days, and 30 days as of October 5, 2004. The virus count represents the number of infected files and the percentage shows the relative prevalence in each region compared to worldwide statistics for each measuring period.

hacker

cracker

cybervandalism

spoofing

stealing business as well as sensitive customer information from the true site. We provide more detail on other forms of spoofing in our discussion of computer crime.

A **sniffer** is a type of eavesdropping program that monitors information travelling over a network. When used legitimately, sniffers can help identify potential network trouble spots or criminal activity on networks, but when used for criminal purposes, they can be damaging and very difficult to detect. Sniffers enable hackers to steal proprietary information from anywhere on a network, including email messages, company files, and confidential reports.

Denial of Service Attacks In a **denial of service (DoS) attack**, hackers flood a network server or Web server with thousands of false communications or requests for services in order to crash the network. The network receives so many queries that it cannot keep up with them and is thus unavailable to service legitimate requests. A **distributed denial of service (DDoS) attack** uses numerous computers to inundate and overwhelm the network from numerous launch points. For example, on June 15, 2004, Web infrastructure provider Akamai Technology was hit by a distributed denial of service attack that slowed some of its customers' Web sites for over two hours. The attack used thousands of "zombie" PCs, which had been infected by malicious software without their owners' knowledge (Thomson 2004). Microsoft, Apple, and Yahoo! were among the sites affected.

Although DoS attacks do not destroy information or access restricted areas of a company's information systems, they can cause a Web site to shut down, making it impossible for legitimate users to access the site. For busy e-commerce sites such as eBay and Buy.com, these attacks are costly; while the site is shut down, customers cannot make purchases.

Figure 9-4 illustrates the estimated worldwide damage from all forms of digital attack, including hacking, malware, and spam between 1997 and 2004.

Computer Crime and Cyberterrorism

Most hacker activities are criminal offences, and the vulnerabilities of systems we have just described make them targets for other types of computer crime as well. We introduce the topic of computer crime and abuse in Chapter 4. The U.S. Department of Justice defines *computer crime* as "any violations of criminal law that involve a knowledge of computer technology for their perpetration, investigation, or prosecution." The computer can be a target of a crime or an instrument of a crime. Table 9-2 provides examples of both categories of computer crime.

No one knows the magnitude of the computer crime problem—how many systems are invaded, how many people engage in the practice, or the total economic damage. While global estimates are in the tens of billions of dollars, many companies are reluctant to

FIGURE 9-4   *Worldwide damage from digital attacks.*

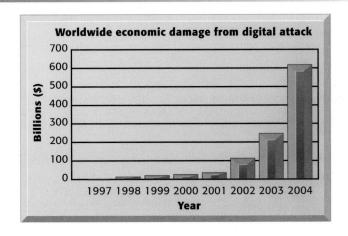

This chart shows estimates of the average annual worldwide damage from hacking, malware, and spam since 1997. Figures for 2004 are estimates based on the historical rate of growth according to data from mi2G and the authors.

sniffer

denial of service (DoS) attack

distributed denial of service (DDoS) attack

report computer crimes because the crimes may involve employees or the company fears that publicizing its vulnerability will hurt its reputation.

The most economically damaging kind of computer crime are DoS attacks, introducing viruses, theft of services, and disruption of computer systems. Traditionally, employees—insiders—have been the source of the most injurious computer crimes because they have the knowledge, access, and, frequently, job-related motives to commit such crimes. However, the Internet's ease of use and accessibility has created new opportunities for computer crime and abuse by outsiders.

With the growth of the Internet and electronic commerce, identity theft has become especially troubling. **Identity theft** is a crime in which an imposter obtains key pieces of personal information, such as social insurance identification numbers, driver's license numbers, or credit card numbers, to impersonate someone else. The information may be used to obtain credit, merchandise, or services in the name of the victim or to provide the thief with false credentials. In Canada, the PhoneBusters National Call Centre received 7629 identity theft complaints in 2002 from Canadians reporting total losses of more than $8.5 million. In 2003, PhoneBusters received 14 526 identity theft-related complaints from Canadians, reflecting reported losses of more than $21.8 million. In just one year complaints increased by 90 percent and reported losses by 156 percent (2005). In addition, two major Canadian credit bureaus, Equifax and Trans Union, indicate that they receive approximately 1400 to 1800 Canadian identity theft complaints per month, the majority of which are from the province of Ontario. The Canadian Council of Better Business Bureaus estimates consumers, banks, credit card firms, stores and other businesses lost $2.5 billion to the perpetrators of identity theft in 2002 (Canadian Bankers Association 2003).

The Internet has made it easy for identity thieves to use stolen information because goods can be purchased online without any personal interaction, and the Internet has also inspired new tactics for stealing personal information. Credit card files are a major target of Web site hackers. Moreover, e-commerce sites are wonderful sources of personal customer information—name, address, and phone number. Armed with this information, criminals can assume a new identity and establish new credit for their own purposes.

identity theft

phishing

One increasingly popular tactic is a form of spoofing called **phishing**. It involves setting up fake Web sites or sending email messages that look like those of legitimate businesses and using them to ask users for confidential personal data. The email message

---

TABLE 9-2 *Examples of Computer Crime*

COMPUTERS AS TARGETS OF CRIME

Breaching the confidentiality of protected computerized data

Accessing a computer system without authority

Knowingly accessing a protected computer to commit fraud

Intentionally accessing a protected computer and causing damage, negligently or deliberately

Knowingly transmitting a program, program code, or command that intentionally causes damage to a protected computer

Threatening to cause damage to a protected computer

COMPUTERS AS INSTRUMENTS OF CRIME

Theft of trade secrets

Unauthorized copying of software or copyrighted intellectual property such as articles, books, music, and video

Schemes to defraud

Using email for threats or harassment

Intentionally attempting to intercept electronic communication

Illegally accessing stored electronic communications, including email and voice mail

Transmitting or possessing child pornography using a computer instructs recipients to update or confirm records by providing social insurance numbers, bank and credit card information, and other confidential data either by responding to the email message or by entering the information at a bogus Web site.

For example, Dan Marius Stefan was convicted of stealing nearly $650 000 by sending email messages that appeared to come from the online auction site eBay to people who were unsuccessful auction bidders. The message described similar merchandise for sale at even better prices. To purchase these goods, recipients had to provide bank account numbers and passwords and wire the money to a fraudulent "escrow site" that Stefan had set up (Hansell 2004).

Phishing appears to be escalating. Visa Canada conducted a survey on phishing, and the results revealed that while most Canadians do not fall victim to phishing scams, 4 percent of phishing email recipients, or approximately 200 000 Canadians, divulged personal information. When phishing was explained, 31 percent of those surveyed had received at least one request for personal or financial information that they believed to be fraudulent (Visa 2004).

Brightmail of San Francisco, a company that filters email for spam, identified 2.3 billion phishing messages in February 2004, representing 4 percent of the email it processed; this figure is up from only 1 percent in September 2003 (Hansell 2004). Phishing scams have posed as PayPal, the online payment service, online service provider America Online (AOL), Barclay's Bank, Citibank, Fleet Bank, American Express, the Federal Deposit Insurance Corporation, the Bank of England, and other banks around the world. British security firm mi2g estimates the worldwide economic damage from phishing scams exceeded $13.5 billion in customer and productivity losses, business interruptions, and efforts to repair damage to brand reputation (Barrett 2004). Almost all financial institutions today have a "phishing" section on their Web site, not only telling their customers how to know if they are being "phished," but telling them how to recognize if an email is actually from the financial institution—such as telling customers that the institution would never ask for personally identifiable information through email.

Most computer crime in Canada is governed by the Criminal Code (Canada) RSC 1985 Chap. C.46, as amended. Of course, case law has interpreted and applied these provisions. There are also various intellectual property laws dealing with copyright, trademarks, passing off, cybersquatting on domain names, negligence causing economic loss, and so forth. Depending on the mischief, these areas of the law may provide a civil action to recover damages or may overlap with various portions of the Criminal Code. Some of the sections of the Criminal Code that deal with computer-related offences include: interception of communications, s. 184; unauthorized use of computer, s. 342.1; mischief in relation to data, s. 430 (1.1); child pornography, s. 163.1; and theft, s. 322(1). As this text is being written, there is a private member's public bill, Bill S-15, to control spam, before Parliament. There are Canadian groups that are trying to limit the amount of spam we receive. CAUCE Canada, the Coalition Against Unsolicited Commercial Email Canada, advocates legislation to eliminate spam in Canada. In 2005, the Honourable David L. Emerson, Minister of Industry, received the final report of the Task Force on Spam, established by Industry Canada, entitled "." The report includes a range of recommendations including more rigorous law enforcement, public education, policy development, and legislation.

Parliament, provincial legislatures, and the various provincial securities commissions have also responded to the threat of computer crime with additional legislation and regulations governing privacy, electronic documents, and corporate governance. The corporate governance regulations and legislation come from Ontario's legislature and the Ontario Securities Commission. Regulations of the Ontario Securities Commission are typically adopted by other provincial securities commissions in Canada.

Cyberterrorism and Cyberwarfare
Concern is mounting that the vulnerabilities of the Internet or other networks could be exploited by terrorists, foreign intelligence services, or other groups to create widespread disruption and harm. These cyberattacks might target the software that runs electrical power grids, air traffic control systems, or networks of major banks and financial institutions. Groups from a number of

countries, including China, have been probing and mapping U.S. networks, and at least 20 countries and are believed to be developing offensive and defensive cyberwarfare capabilities. U.S. military networks and U.S. government agencies suffer hundreds of hacker attacks each year. And in 1999, a 17-year-old American high school student hacked into the Canadian Department of National Defence computer system in less than 10 minutes from his mother's kitchen table. He left instructions at the Web site he had hacked telling the military how to better protect its networks. Still, it took days to safeguard the Web site so it could not be hacked again. It took investigators in Canada and the U.S. a year to build their case against the teen—a painstaking probe into security breaches of government and military computer systems across the continent. This American hacker always hacked into a dozen or more "shell" computers before launching his attacks, making him nearly impossible to track. And he used different aliases, digital alter egos, to claim responsibility. The perpetrator said, "The DND site was an easy target. It was pretty weak. At the time, there were all kinds of patches they could have downloaded for free to fix the problem, but they never did." The American hacker was turned in by a 15-year-old Halifax student who belonged to the same online hackers' group, and he turned him in to be spared from prosecution for hacking. The American hacker also was an online acquaintance of Montreal's infamous hacker Mafiaboy, who brought down many global Web sites in 1999 (Dimmock 2002; *Canadian Firearms Digest* 2002).

The Canadian government has taken some steps to deal with the potential threat. Virtually all of the government's law enforcement agencies have sections or divisions that focus on cybercrime. From the RCMP to CSIS and the military, the federal government is responding to a host of threats to government and private computer resources. In addition, each of the provinces and most Canadian municipalities have their law enforcement agencies focusing on cybercrime as well as more traditional forms of criminal activity.

Internal Threats: Employees

We tend to think the security threats to a business originate outside the organization. In fact, the largest financial threats to business institutions come not from robberies, but from embezzlement by insiders. Some of the largest disruptions to service, destruction of e-commerce sites, and diversion of customer credit data and personal information have come from insiders—once-trusted employees. Employees have access to privileged information, and in the presence of sloppy internal security procedures, they are often able to roam throughout an organization's systems without leaving a trace.

Studies have found that users' lack of knowledge is the single greatest cause of network security breaches. Many employees forget their passwords to access computer systems or allow other coworkers to use them, which compromises the system. Malicious intruders seeking system access sometimes trick employees into revealing their passwords by pretending to be legitimate members of the company in need of information. This practice is called **social engineering**.

Employees—both end users and information systems specialists—are also a major source of errors introduced into an information system. Employees can introduce errors by entering faulty data or by not following the proper instructions for processing data and using computer equipment. Information systems specialists can also create software errors as they design and develop new software or maintain existing programs.

Software Vulnerability

Software errors also pose a constant threat to information systems, causing untold losses in productivity. A major problem with software is the presence of hidden **bugs**, or program code defects. Studies have shown that it is virtually impossible to eliminate all bugs from large programs. The main source of bugs is the complexity of decision-making code. Important programs within most corporations may contain tens of thousands or even millions of lines of code, each with many alternative decision paths. Such complexity is

social engineering

bugs

difficult to document and design—designers may document some reactions incorrectly or may fail to consider some possibilities. Even after rigorous testing, developers do not know for sure that a piece of software is dependable until the product proves itself after much operational use.

Commercial software often contains flaws that create not only performance issues but also security vulnerabilities that can open networks to intruders. These vulnerabilities and bugs can enable malware to slip past antivirus defences. A great deal of malware has been trying to exploit vulnerabilities in the Microsoft Windows operating system and other Microsoft products, but malware targeting the Linux operating system is on the rise as well.

To correct software flaws once they are identified, the software vendor creates lines of code called *patches* to repair the flaw without disturbing proper operation of the software. An example is Microsoft's XP Service Pack 2 (SP2) introduced in 2004, which features added firewall protection against viruses and intruders, capabilities for automatic security updates, and an easy-to-use interface for managing the security applications on the user's computer. It is up to users of the software to track these vulnerabilities, test, and apply all patches. This process is called *patch management.*

Because a company's information technology (IT) infrastructure is typically laden with multiple business applications, operating system installations, and other system services, the process of maintaining patches on all devices and services used by a company can be very time consuming and costly. The Yankee Group consulting firm estimates that a firm with more than 500 PCs spends up to 120 staff hours testing and installing every patch (Foley and Hulme 2004).

The Window on Technology illustrates some of the problems faced by companies trying to practice patch management. Companies are now besieged with numerous malevolent viruses and worms that regularly bring down systems that fail to implement applicable patches. This malevolent software is being created so rapidly that companies have very little time to respond between the time a vulnerability and a patch are announced and the time malicious software appears to exploit the vulnerability. This patch management problem is one reason why Sasser, SQL Slammer, Blaster, SoBig.F, and other worms and viruses have been able to infect so many computer systems so rapidly.

One final issue is that of the growing trend toward peer-to-peer (P2P) computing. This multiplies the potential for vulnerabilities we have just described. P2P downloads and file sharing represent a major area of vulnerability that should be addressed.

9.2 Business Value of Security and Control

Security and control have become a critical, although perhaps unappreciated, area of information systems investment. When computer systems fail to run or work as required, firms that depend heavily on computers experience a serious loss of business function. The longer computer systems are down, the more serious the consequences for the firm. Some firms relying on computers to process their critical business transactions might experience a total loss of business function if they lose computer capability for more than a few days. And with so much business now dependent on the Internet and networked systems, firms are more vulnerable than ever to disruption and harm. Security incidents have been growing at a phenomenal rate (see Figure 9-5).

For example, during the summer of 2003, corporate networks and home computer systems were overwhelmed by attacks from the SoBig.F worm. SoBig.F disguises itself in email, which, once opened, scans a computer for email addresses and then sends scores of messages to the addresses it has collected using its own built-in sending program. SoBig caused an estimated $29.7 billion worldwide during that period, temporarily disabling freight and computer traffic in Washington, D.C., and overwhelming computer systems with the sheer volume of email (*Canadian Business Franchise Magazine* 2005).

FIGURE 9-5 *Security incidents continue to rise.*

This chart shows the growth in the number of security incidents reported to the Computer Emergency Response Team (CERT) between 1996 and 2003.

Source: CERT Coordination Center, **www.cert.org**, accessed July 6, 2004.

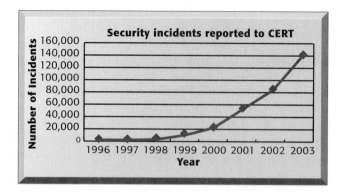

WINDOW ON TECHNOLOGY

The Rush to Patch

Computer viruses and worms appear to be growing smarter and more numerous every day. Fast-spreading worms such as Sasser, SQL Slammer, and Blaster have been able to proliferate rapidly because companies cannot update their software quickly enough to deter them.

A new vulnerability in a software product is not announced until a patch is available. At that point, hackers rush to exploit the vulnerability before the patch has been widely applied. These malicious hackers have become so efficient that they are churning out these powerful new worms faster than corporate security experts can patch their systems. According to Foundstone, Inc., a technology risk-management firm in Mission Viejo, California, the average time between the announcement of a security flaw and the appearance of malicious code to exploit it has declined from 281 days in 1999 to merely 10 days. That means that patch management—tracking and applying updates to fix security flaws—is more challenging today than ever.

The course of the Sasser worm illustrates some of these challenges. A small security firm called eEye Digital Security had informed Microsoft about a vulnerability in the networking feature of the Windows operating system in October 2003. eEye agreed with Microsoft not to disclose vulnerabilities it finds until Microsoft evaluates the risk and creates a software patch. It took six months for Microsoft to release a protective patch. In the meantime, eEye waited, knowing that its network was wide open to being attacked, and there was nothing it could do.

Microsoft finally announced the vulnerability and the availability of a patch in April 2003. Within hours, snippets of "exploitable code" appeared on Internet discussion boards. Sasser's authors then quickly went to work. Only 17 days passed between the time Microsoft announced the flaw and the Sasser worm was released, on April 30, 2004.

Patches can be very time consuming to apply, especially if security updates are needed for client machines as well as servers and larger computers. A large corporation might have hundreds of servers and thousands of desktop client PCs that need to be secured against each virus or worm outbreak, and a separate software patch might need to be installed on each of these machines. For example, Motorola, headquartered in Schaumberg, Illinois, must patch as many as 100,000 computers running the Windows operating system if such updates are required. Station Casinos in Las Vegas has 220 Windows servers running slot machine accounting, player tracking, and restaurant cash register systems that must be patched if necessary. Canaccord Capital, mentioned previously in this chapter, uses a "fly by wire" patch management process. Scott Collins, the company's Vancouver-based manager of technology and infrastructure, worked hard to make patch management a priority. Part of the problem was updating so-called "service packs" first before applying individual patches—a requirement for many software companies' patches.

Moreover, some of these patches are incompatible with the software in some computer systems. Research from AssetMetrix, a Canadian asset-monitoring service provider, found that upgrading to Windows XP Service Pack 2 causes problems in about one in every 10 PCs running the operating system.

Difficulties applying patches explain how the SQL Slammer worm could infect so many computers in such a short period of time. In less than 10 minutes in January 2003 the worm infected tens of thousands of servers running Microsoft SQL Server 2000 database management software, including those supporting the Finnish telephone system, the Davis-Beese nuclear power station outside Toledo, Ohio, Canaccord Capital's 2000 workstations, and 13 000 Bank of America automatic teller machines (ATMs). Microsoft had developed a patch for SQL Server software to deal with this vulnerability six months earlier, but many organizations had been reluctant to apply it, citing concerns that the patch needed more testing and time required to apply it.

If a new vulnerability appears, "anything less than near perfection in patching puts you at risk of substantial downtime," says William Boni, chief information security officer for Motorola. And achieving 100 percent perfection is also difficult because employees are travelling or working remotely. If a system has not been patched, Boni's team removes it from Motorola's network. But that means the system must be updated manually by a technician.

In 2003, Boni was satisfied if his team completed all the patching work for 100 000 computers within 30 days. But the Sasser worm hit the Internet only 17 days after Microsoft disclosed the vulnerability the worm targeted. So, Motorola must respond immediately to new vulnerabilities as if it is already under attack.

System administrators must scramble whenever a new vulnerability is announced. Microsoft, Oracle, SAP, Computer Associates, and other software vendors are trying to make the process more predictable by scheduling disclosure of vulnerabilities and release of patches on a scheduled monthly basis.

To Think About: What management, organization, and technology factors explain why companies have so much difficulty protecting themselves from worms and other malicious software? What steps should they take to deal with this problem more effectively?

Sources: David Bank, "Computer Worm Is Turning Faster," *Wall Street Journal*, May 27, 2004; "Editorial: Time to Apply a Patch," *Federal Computer Week*, June 22, 2004; Gregg Keizer, "Windows XP Service Pack 2: The 10% Problem," *Information Week*, August 31, 2004; Jaikumar Vijayan, "Unprepared Firms Slammed," *Computerworld*, February 3, 2003; Patricia MacInnis, "," *Computing Canada*, April 23, 2004.

Companies have very valuable information assets to protect. Systems often house confidential information about individuals' taxes, financial assets, medical records, and job performance reviews. They can also contain information on corporate operations, including trade secrets, new product development plans, marketing strategies, and customer lists. Government systems may store information on weapons systems, intelligence operations, and military targets. These information assets have tremendous value, and the repercussions can be devastating if they are lost, altered, destroyed, or placed in the wrong hands. A recent study estimates that when the security of a large firm is compromised, the company loses approximately 2.1 percent of its market value within two days of the security breach, which translates into an average loss of $2 billion in stock market value per incident (Cavusoglu, Mishra, and Raghunathan 2004).

Inadequate security and control can also create serious legal liability. Businesses must protect not only their own information assets but also those of customers, employees, and business partners. Failure to do so can open the firm to costly litigation for data exposure or theft. An organization can be held liable for needless risk and harm created if it fails to take appropriate protective action to prevent loss of confidential information, data corruption, or breach of privacy. A sound security and control framework that protects business information assets can thus produce a high return on investment.

Legal and Regulatory Requirements for Electronic Records Management

Recent Canadian legislation has forced companies to take security and control more seriously by mandating the protection of data from abuse, exposure, and unauthorized access. Firms face new legal obligations for electronic records management and document retention as well as for privacy protection. **Electronic records management (ERM)** consists of policies, procedures, and tools for managing the retention, destruction, and storage of electronic records. Much of these policies have been mandated by the Personal Information Protection and Electronic Documents Act (PIPEDA) that went fully into effect in Canada in January 2004. For a further discussion on PIPEDA and other Canadian legislation, see Chapter 4.

In the U.S., the Public Company Accounting Reform and Investor Protection Act of 2002, better known as **Sarbanes-Oxley Act of 2002** after its sponsors, was designed to protect investors after the financial scandals at Enron, WorldCom, and other public companies. It imposes responsibility on companies and their management to safeguard the integrity of the information that is used internally and released externally.

Sarbanes-Oxley requires chief executives and chief financial officers at all publicly traded companies in the United States to certify the accuracy of their organizations'

electronic records management (ERM)

Sarbanes-Oxley Act of 2002

quarterly and annual financial reports and to establish adequate internal controls over their reporting systems. All documents and communications related to these reports and their data must be retained for seven years following an audit. Companies must institute procedures for keeping track of all financial information from the moment it is created, to final submission in annual reports to the Securities and Exchange Commission (SEC). These senior managers face up to 20 years in jail if the firm's financial statements have been falsified.

Sarbanes-Oxley is fundamentally about ensuring that internal controls are in place to govern the creation and documentation of information in financial statements. Because information systems are used to generate, store, and transport such data, the legislation requires firms to consider information systems security and other controls required to ensure the integrity, confidentiality, and accuracy of their data. Each system application that deals with critical financial reporting data requires controls to make sure the data are accurate. Controls to secure the corporate network, prevent unauthorized access to systems and data, and ensure data integrity and availability in the event of disaster or other disruption of service are essential as well.

Sarbanes-Oxley is important to Canadians for several reasons. First, Canadian companies that are publicly traded in the U.S. must, by law, adhere to Sarbanes-Oxley. Second, the Ontario Securities Commission and the Ontario Legislature have passed regulations and legislation that most other provincial bodies are also adopting that mirror the provisions of Sarbanes-Oxley. It is also difficult to attract U.S. investors to Canadian companies unless they follow the U.S. mandates. Finally, since this sort of legislation is undoubtedly coming to Canada where it has not yet been enacted, companies can get ahead of the curve by using Sarbanes-Oxley as a model for their corporate governance and reporting activities.

Electronic Evidence and Computer Forensics

Security, control, and electronic records management have become essential for responding to legal actions. Much of the evidence today for stock fraud, embezzlement, theft of company trade secrets, computer crime, and many civil cases are in digital form. In addition to information from printed or typewritten pages, legal cases today increasingly rely on evidence represented as computer data stored on portable floppy disks, CDs, and computer hard disk drives, as well as in email, instant messages, and e-commerce transactions over the Internet. Email is currently the most common type of electronic evidence.

In a legal action, a firm may have to submit to a discovery request for access to information that may be used as evidence, and the company is required by law to produce those data. The cost of responding to a discovery request can be enormous if the company has trouble assembling the required data or the data have been corrupted or destroyed. Courts now impose severe financial and even criminal penalties for improper destruction of electronic documents.

An effective electronic document retention policy ensures that electronic documents, email, and other records are well organized, accessible, and neither retained too long nor discarded too soon. It also reflects an awareness of how to preserve potential evidence for computer forensics. **Computer forensics** is the scientific collection, examination, authentication, preservation, and analysis of data held on or retrieved from computer storage media in such a way that the information can be used as evidence in a court of law. It deals with the following problems:

- Recovering data from computers while preserving evidential integrity
- Securely storing and handling recovered electronic data
- Finding significant information in a large volume of electronic data
- Presenting the information to a court of law

Electronic evidence can reside on computer storage media in the form of computer files and as *ambient data,* which are not visible to the average user. An example might be a file that has been deleted on a PC hard drive. Data that a computer user may have deleted

computer forensics

on computer storage media can be recovered through various techniques. Computer forensics experts try to recover such hidden data for presentation as evidence.

An awareness of the need for computer forensics should be incorporated into a firm's contingency planning process. The CIO, security specialists, information systems staff, and corporate legal counsel should all work together to have a plan in place that can be executed if a legal need arises.

9.3   Establishing a Management Framework for Security and Control

Technology is not the key issue in information systems security and control. The technology provides a foundation, but in the absence of intelligent management policies, even the best technology can be easily defeated. For instance, experts believe that more than 90 percent of successful cyberattacks could have been prevented by technology available at the time. Inadequate human attention made these attacks so prevalent.

Protection of information resources requires a sound security policy and set of controls. **ISO 17799**, an international set of standards for security and control, provides helpful guidelines. It specifies best practices in information systems security and control, including security policy, business continuity planning, physical security, access control, compliance, and creating a security function within the organization. For example, Alberta Health and Wellness is currently implementing ISO 17799 to meet not only security needs but the dictates of Canadian privacy legislation, including the Health Information Act (2001). Many provinces have passed health information privacy legislation that precedes the jurisdiction of PIPEDA, the federal privacy law.

There are other ISO standards for information security. ISO 13335 provides guidelines for the management of information security, ISO 13569 provides guidelines for banking and other financial services, and ISO 15408 provides evaluation criteria for information security. Canadian organizations, both for-profit and not-for-profit, are implementing these standards.

Types of Information Systems Controls

Protection of information resources requires a well-designed set of controls. Computer systems are controlled by a combination of general controls and application controls. **General controls** govern the design, security, and use of computer programs and the security of data files in general throughout the organization's information technology infrastructure. On the whole, general controls apply to all computerized applications and consist of a combination of hardware, software, and manual procedures that create an overall control environment. **Application controls** are specific controls unique to each computerized application, such as payroll or order processing. They consist of controls applied from the business functional area of a particular system and from programmed procedures.

General Controls General controls include software controls, physical hardware controls, computer operations controls, data security controls, controls over the systems implementation process, and **administrative controls**. Table 9-3 describes the functions of each type of control.

Application Controls Application controls include both automated and manual procedures that ensure that only authorized data are completely and accurately processed by that application. Application controls can be classified as (1) input controls, (2) processing controls, and (3) output controls.

Input controls check data for accuracy and completeness when they enter the system. There are specific input controls for input authorization, data conversion, data editing, and error handling. **Processing controls** establish that data are complete and accurate during updating. Run control totals, computer matching, and programmed edit checks

ISO 17799
general controls
application controls
administrative controls
input controls
processing controls

TABLE 9-3 *General Controls*

TYPE OF GENERAL CONTROL	DESCRIPTION
Software controls	Monitor the use of system software and prevent unauthorized access of software programs, system software, and computer programs. System software is an important control area because it performs overall control functions for the programs that directly process data and data files.
Hardware controls	Ensure that computer hardware is physically secure and check for equipment malfunction. Computer equipment should be specially protected against fires and extremes of temperature and humidity. Organizations that are dependent on their computers also must make provisions for backup or continued operation to maintain constant service.
Computer operations controls	Oversee the work of the computer department to ensure that programmed procedures are consistently and correctly applied to the storage and processing of data. They include controls over the setup of computer processing jobs and computer operations and backup and recovery procedures for processing that ends abnormally.
Data security controls	Ensure that valuable business data files on either disk or tape are not subject to unauthorized access, change, or destruction while they are in use or in storage.
Implementation controls	Audit the systems development process at various points to ensure that the process is properly controlled and managed. The systems development audit looks for the presence of formal reviews by users and management at various stages of development; the level of user involvement at each stage of implementation; and the use of a formal cost-benefit methodology in establishing system feasibility. The audit should look for the use of controls and quality assurance techniques for program development, conversion, and testing and for complete and thorough training and system, user, and operations documentation.
Administrative controls	Formalized standards, rules, procedures, and control disciplines to ensure that the organization's general and application controls are properly executed and enforced.

are used as processing controls. **Output controls** ensure that the results of computer processing are accurate, complete, and properly distributed. Table 9-4 provides more detailed examples of each type of application control.

Not all of the application controls discussed here are used in every information system. Some systems require more of these controls than others, depending on the importance of the data and the nature of the application.

Risk Assessment

Before an organization commits resources to controls, it must know which assets require protection and the extent to which these assets are vulnerable. A risk assessment helps answer these questions and also helps the firm determine the most cost-effective set of controls for protecting assets.

A **risk assessment** determines the level of risk to the firm if a specific activity or process is not properly controlled. Business and risk managers working with information systems specialists can determine the value of information assets, points of vulnerability, the likely frequency of a problem, and the potential for damage. For example, if an event is likely to occur no more than once a year, with a maximum of a $1000 loss to the organization, it may not be feasible to spend $20 000 on the design and maintenance of a control to protect against that event. However, if that same event could occur at least once a day, with a potential loss of more than $300 000 a year, $100 000 spent on a control might be entirely appropriate.

Table 9-5 illustrates sample results of a risk assessment for an online order processing system that processes 30 000 orders per day. The likelihood of each exposure occurring over a one-year period is expressed as a percentage. The next column shows the highest and lowest possible loss that could be expected each time the exposure occurred and an average loss calculated by adding the highest and lowest figures together and dividing by two. The expected annual loss for each exposure can be determined by multiplying the average loss by its probability of occurrence.

output controls
risk assessment

TABLE 9-4 *Application Controls*

Name of Control	Type of Application Control	Description
Control totals	Input, processing	Totals established beforehand for input and processing transactions. These totals can range from a simple document count to totals for quantity fields, such as total sales amount (for a batch of transactions). Computer programs count the totals from transactions input or processed.
Edit checks	Input	Programmed routines that can be performed to edit input data for errors before they are processed. Transactions that do not meet edit criteria are rejected. For example, data might be checked to make sure they are in the right format (for instance, a social insurance number should not contain any alphabetic characters).
Computer matching	Input, processing	Matches input data with information held on master or suspense files and notes unmatched items for investigation. For example, a matching program might match employee time cards with a payroll master file and report missing or duplicate time cards.
Run control totals	Processing, output	Balance the total of transactions processed with total number of transactions input or output.
Report distribution logs	Output	Documentation specifying that authorized recipients have received their reports, checks, or other critical documents.

This risk assessment shows that the probability of a power failure occurring in a one-year period is 30 percent. Loss of order transactions while power is down could range from $5000 to $200 000 (averaging $102 500) for each occurrence, depending on how long processing is halted. The probability of embezzlement occurring over a yearly period is about 5 percent, with potential losses ranging from $1000 to $50 000 (and averaging $25 500) for each occurrence. User errors have a 98 percent chance of occurring over a yearly period, with losses ranging from $200 to $40 000 (and averaging $20 100) for each occurrence. Once the risks have been assessed, system developers can concentrate on the control points with the greatest vulnerability and potential for loss. In this case, controls should focus on ways to minimize the risk of power failures and user errors because anticipated annual losses are highest for these areas.

One problem with risk assessment and other methods for quantifying security costs and benefits is that organizations do not always know the precise probability of threats occurring to their information systems, and they may not be able to quantify the impact of such events accurately. Nevertheless, some effort to anticipate, budget for, and control direct and indirect security costs is needed (Mercuri 2003).

The end product of risk assessment is a plan to minimize overall cost and maximize defenses. To decide which controls to use, information systems developers must examine various control techniques in relation to each other and to their relative cost-effectiveness.

A control weakness at one point may be offset by a strong control at another. It may not be cost-effective to build tight controls at every point in the processing cycle if the areas of greatest risk are secure or if compensating controls exist elsewhere. The

TABLE 9-5 *Online Order Processing Risk Assessment*

Exposure	Probability of Occurrence (%)	Loss Range/Average ($)		Expected Annual Loss ($)
Power failure	30	5000–200 000	(102 500)	30 750
Embezzlement	5	1000–50 000	(25 500)	1275
User error	98	200–40 000	20 100)	19 698

combination of all of the controls developed for a particular application determines the application's overall level of control.

Security Policy

Firms must develop a coherent corporate policy that takes into account the nature of the risks, the information assets that need protecting, and the procedures and technologies required to address the risks, as well as implementation and auditing mechanisms.

A growing number of firms have established a formal corporate security function headed by a **chief security officer (CSO)**. The security group educates and trains users, keeps management aware of security threats and breakdowns, and maintains the tools chosen to implement security. The chief security officer is responsible for enforcing the firm's security policy.

A **security policy** consists of statements ranking information risks, identifying acceptable security goals, and identifying the mechanisms for achieving these goals. What are the firm's most important information assets? Who generates and controls this information in the firm? What existing security policies are in place to protect the information? What level of risk is management willing to accept for each of these assets? Is it willing, for instance, to lose customer credit data once every 10 years? Or will it build a security edifice for credit card data that can withstand the once-in-a-hundred-year disaster? Management must estimate how much it will cost to achieve this level of acceptable risk.

The security organization typically administers acceptable use policies and authorization policies. An **acceptable use policy (AUP)** defines acceptable uses of the firm's information resources and computing equipment, including desktop and laptop computers, wireless devices, telephones, and the Internet. The policy should clarify company policy regarding privacy, user responsibility, and personal use of company equipment and networks. A good AUP defines unacceptable and acceptable actions for every user and specifies consequences for noncompliance.

Authorization policies determine differing levels of access to information assets for different levels of users. **Authorization management systems** establish where and when a user is permitted to access certain parts of a Web site or a corporate database. These systems allow each user access to only those portions of a system that person is permitted to enter, based on information established by a set of access rules.

The authorization management system knows exactly what information each user is permitted to access as shown in Figure 9-6. This figure illustrates the security allowed for two sets of users of an online personnel database containing sensitive information, such as employees' salaries, benefits, and medical histories. One set of users consists of all employees who perform clerical functions, such as inputting employee data into the system. All individuals with this type of profile can update the system but can neither read nor update sensitive fields, such as salary, medical history, or earnings data. Another profile applies to a divisional manager, who cannot update the system but who can read all employee data fields for his or her division, including medical history and salary. These profiles are based on access rules supplied by business groups. The system illustrated in Figure 9-6 provides very fine-grained security restrictions, such as allowing authorized users to inquire about all employee information except that in confidential fields, such as salary or medical history.

Ensuring Business Continuity

As companies increasingly rely on digital networks for their revenue and operations, they need to take additional steps to ensure that their systems and applications are always available. Many factors can disrupt the performance of a Web site, including denial of service attacks, network failure, heavy Internet traffic, and exhausted server resources. Computer failures, interruptions, and downtime translate into disgruntled customers, millions of dollars in lost sales, and the inability to perform critical internal transactions. **Downtime** refers to periods of time in which a system is not operational.

chief security officer (CSO)
security policy
acceptable use policy (AUP)
authorization policies
authorization management systems
downtime

FIGURE 9-6   *Security profiles for a personnel system.*

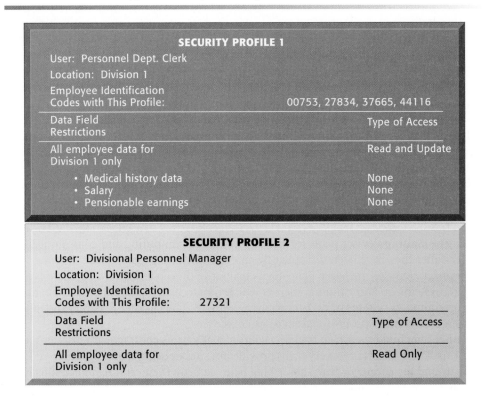

These two examples represent two security profiles or data security patterns that might be found in a personnel system. Depending on the security profile, a user would have certain restrictions on access to various systems, locations, or data in an organization.

Firms such as those in the airline and financial services industries with critical applications requiring online transaction processing have traditionally used fault-tolerant computer systems for many years to ensure 100 percent availability. In **online transaction processing**, transactions entered online are immediately processed by the computer. Multitudinous changes to databases, reporting, and requests for information occur each instant.

Fault-tolerant computer systems contain redundant hardware, software, and power supply components that create an environment that provides continuous, uninterrupted service. Fault-tolerant computers contain extra memory chips, processors, and disk storage devices to back up a system and keep it running to prevent failure. They use special software routines or self-checking logic built into their circuitry to detect hardware failures and automatically switch to a backup device. Parts from these computers can be removed and repaired without disruption to the computer system.

Fault tolerance should be distinguished from **high-availability computing**. Both fault tolerance and high-availability computing are designed to maximize application and system availability. Both use backup hardware resources. However, high-availability computing helps firms recover quickly from a crash while fault tolerance promises continuous availability and the elimination of recovery time altogether. High-availability computing environments are a minimum requirement for firms with heavy electronic commerce processing or for firms that depend on digital networks for their internal operations.

High-availability computing requires an assortment of tools and technologies to ensure maximum performance of computer systems and networks, including redundant servers, load balancing, mirroring, clustering, high-capacity storage, and good disaster recovery and business continuity plans. The firm's computing platform must be extremely robust with scalable processing power, storage, and bandwidth.

Load balancing distributes large numbers of access requests across multiple servers. The requests are directed to the most available server so that no single device is overwhelmed. If one server starts to get swamped, requests are forwarded to another server with more capacity.

online transaction processing
fault-tolerant computer systems
high-availability computing
load balancing

Mirroring uses a backup server that duplicates all the processes and transactions of the primary server. If the primary server fails, the backup server can immediately take its place without any interruption in service. However, server mirroring is very expensive because each server must be mirrored by an identical server whose only purpose is to be available in the event of a failure.

High-availability **clustering** links two computers together so that the second computer can act as a backup to the primary computer. If the primary computer fails, the second computer picks up its processing without any pause in the system. (Computers can also be clustered together as a single computing resource to speed up processing.)

Researchers are exploring ways to make computing systems recover even more rapidly when mishaps occur, an approach called **recovery-oriented computing**. This work includes designing systems that can recover quickly and implementing capabilities and tools to help operators pinpoint the sources of faults in multicomponent systems and easily correct their mistakes (Fox and Patterson 2003).

Business Continuity and Disaster Recovery Planning

Disaster recovery planning devises plans for the restoration of computing and communications services after they have been disrupted by an event such as an earthquake, flood, or terrorist attack. Disaster recovery plans focus primarily on the technical issues involved in keeping systems up and running, such as which files to back up and the maintenance of backup computer systems or disaster recovery services. The Disaster Recovery Institute of Canada even certifies professionals in disaster recovery.

Rather than build their own backup facilities, many firms contract with disaster recovery firms. These disaster recovery firms provide hot sites housing spare computers at locations around the country where subscribing firms can run their critical applications in an emergency. In fact, Canada is becoming disaster recovery central for many U.S. companies. Canadian disaster recovery companies cost U.S. companies less for these services due to the rate of currency exchange, and with the similarities in culture, values, and language, there is little reason for American companies to pay more for having hot sites within U.S. borders (Roberts 2004).

Business continuity planning focuses on how the company can restore business operations after a disaster strikes. The business continuity plan identifies critical business processes and determines action plans for handling mission-critical functions if systems go down.

Business managers and information technology specialists need to work together on both types of plans to determine which systems and business processes are most critical to the company. They must conduct a business impact analysis to identify the firm's most critical systems and the impact a systems outage would have on the business. Management must determine the maximum amount of time the business can survive with its systems down and which parts of the business must be restored first.

The Window on Management describes how business continuity planning is conducted at Deutsche Bank. This global financial institution could not afford to have critical operations disrupted by computer failures. It has both disaster recovery facilities and a business continuity plan in place and prepares employees for its execution.

Security Outsourcing

Many companies such as Wesfarmers, described in the chapter-opening case, lack the resources or expertise to provide a secure high-availability computing environment on their own. They can outsource many security functions to **managed security service providers** (**MSSPs**) that monitor network activity and perform vulnerability testing and intrusion detection. Dynamix Solutions, Bell Security Systems, and IBM are just three providers of MSSP services in Canada.

The Role of Auditing in the Control Process

How does management know that information systems security and controls are effective? To answer this question, organizations must conduct comprehensive and systematic audits. An **MIS audit** identifies all of the controls that govern individual information systems and

mirroring

clustering

recovery-oriented computing

disaster recovery planning

business continuity planning

managed security service providers (MSSPs)

MIS audit

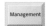

WINDOW ON MANAGEMENT

Deutsche Bank Ties Business Continuity Planning to the Business

Deutsche Bank AG is one of the world's largest banks, with 65 400 employees serving 21 million customers in 74 different countries, including Canada. It has investment banking and asset management businesses throughout Europe, the Pacific Rim, and the Americas. Management is dedicated to protecting the interests of customers, employees, partners, regulators, and shareholders against loss of revenue and reputation, and the company has always treated business continuity planning very seriously.

The bank has a global business continuity and disaster recovery program which addresses data backup and recovery and procedures for minimizing changes in operational, financial, and credit risk exposures. Operational risk focuses on the firm's ability to maintain communications with customers and keep mission-critical systems up and running. Financial risk deals with the firm's ability to continue generating revenue and obtaining adequate financing. Credit risk occurs when investments erode from lack of liquidity in the broader market.

Every six months, Deutsche Bank New York offices test their disaster recovery plan, practicing what they would do if their computer centres went down. The company's data are always backed up on tape. Prior to September 11, 2001, Deutsche Bank had two computer centres: one in the World Trade Center and one in New Jersey. Tragically, Deutsche Bank lost two employees and its New York offices in the World Trade Center terrorist attacks, but the remaining employees were back working within a few days because the company was so well prepared. "One of our data centres was affected, but all applications were recovered from the second site in New Jersey almost immediately," according to Tony Kerrison, Deutsche Bank's head of enterprise services.

Deutsche Bank has a permanent organizational structure to manage and govern business continuity management. Deutsche Bank's Asia Pacific headquarters in Singapore and its bigger locations in Hong Kong, Japan, India, and Australia have full-time teams for this purpose. The bank's business continuity planning (BCP) function brings together various internal units and experts dealing with all aspects of risk—information risk, physical risk, or business risk—to coordinate plans addressing loss of facilities, personnel, or critical systems.

Kenny Seow, head of business continuity management for Deutsche Bank's Asia Pacific Region, heads a team that maintains an 1114 square metre disaster recovery center (DRC) outside the Singapore central business district. The DRC is a "lights-out" facility, meaning that no staff work there during normal operations. It does, however, contain work space to support critical business functions for more than 200 staff and all backup computer and network equipment for disaster recovery, including a generator with a 10-hour refillable fuel tank and smoke detection and sprinkler systems.

The computer centre in the DRC also acts as a backup regional processing hub for Deutsche Bank Asia Pacific so that the Asia Pacific Region would not be affected if there were an outage at its production data centre. Its systems are monitored and controlled remotely from Deutsche Bank's main produc-

tion computer centre or from bank offices where information systems staff work.

Seow's team organizes and conducts interviews with heads of Deutsche Bank businesses to identify what is most critical to them—revenue loss, loss of reputation, loss of customer confidence, or violations of government regulations. Each business then identifies the processes required to minimize the identified risks.

Deutsche Bank has classified critical processes into two major categories: processes for business survival and processes critical to crisis support. Business survival processes are those required for Deutsche Bank to meet its business objectives. An example would be ensuring that traders in money markets and foreign exchange can work continuously because their business is a major revenue stream for the bank. (Deutsche Bank trading amounts to billions of dollars every day.) Deutsche Bank has a trading room in its DRC for this purpose, along with backup back office operations to support trading activity.

An example of processes critical to crisis support is human resources because it looks after staff welfare and staff counselling. Corporate communications are also important in the event of a crisis, but marketing, for example, would receive less priority in a crisis situation.

Seow's group is responsible for ensuring that appropriate processes and resources are in place so that the bank can respond effectively if a catastrophic event occurs. Deutsche Bank's business continuity planning revolves around planning for various scenarios that could affect its operations to make sure business can continue. Worst-case events could be a bomb, an earthquake, or an epidemic such as SARS.

Deutsche Bank communicates its business continuity plan, rehearses it, and keeps it updated to ensure the organization is always prepared. Staff are educated about safety measures, whom to contact in event of emergency, and who is responsible at different stages of an incident. The bank performs power tests on generators to ensure it can switch to backup power at any time. Finally, the bank tests the actual plan. It tests calling trees to ensure that contact numbers are working. It verbally walks employees through the plans so they understand exactly what they should do. Then it brings people to the disaster recovery site to use the systems at the facility to ensure they can work at that location. The bank conducts tests once a year, but some business units test more often if they feel their work is especially critical.

To Think About: Why is business continuity planning so important for a firm such as Deutsche Bank? What management, organization, and technology issues need to be addressed by a business continuity plan?

Sources: Ann Toh, "The Business of Security, *CIO Asia*, January 2004; Kate Pritchard, "Banking on Technology," EMC Corporation, 2004; George Hulme and Jennifer Zaino, "Spring Conference: Leave Complacency Out of Business Plans," *InformationWeek*, March 19, 2002; and Deutsche Bank, "Business Continuity Program," www.deutsche-bank.de, accessed November 24, 2004.

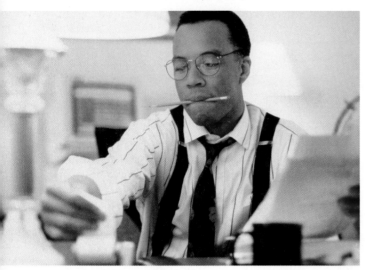

An auditor often traces the flow of sample transactions through an information system and may perform tests using automated audit software. MIS audits help management identify security vulnerabilities and determine whether information system controls are effective.

assesses their effectiveness. To accomplish this, the auditor must acquire a thorough understanding of operations, physical facilities, telecommunications, security systems, security objectives, organizational structure, personnel, manual procedures, and individual applications.

The auditor usually interviews key individuals who use and operate a specific information system concerning their activities and procedures. Security, application controls, overall integrity controls, and control disciplines are examined. The auditor should trace the flow of sample transactions through the system and perform tests, using, if appropriate, automated audit software.

Security audits should review technologies, procedures, documentation, training, and personnel. A very thorough audit will even simulate an attack or disaster to test the response of the technology, information systems staff, and business employees.

The audit lists and ranks all control weaknesses and estimates the probability of their occurrence. It then assesses the financial and organizational impact of each threat. Figure 9-7 is a sample auditor's listing of control weaknesses for a loan system. It includes a section for notifying management of these weaknesses and for management's response. Management is expected to devise a plan for countering significant weaknesses in controls.

9.4 Technologies and Tools for Security and Control

An array of tools and technologies can help firms protect against or monitor intrusion. They include authentication tools, firewalls, intrusion detection systems, antivirus software, and encryption. Tools and methodologies are also available to help firms make their

---

FIGURE 9-7 *Sample auditor's list of control weaknesses.*

Function: Loans Location: Peoria, IL	Prepared by: J. Ericson Preparation date: June 16, 2005		Received by: T. Benson Review date: June 28, 2005	
Nature of Weakness and Impact	**Chance for Error/Abuse**		**Notification to Management**	
	Yes/No	Justification	Report Date	Management Response
User accounts with missing passwords	Yes	Leaves system open to unauthorized outsiders or attackers	5/10/05	Eliminate accounts without passwords.
Network configured to allow some sharing of system files	Yes	Exposes critical system files to hostile parties connected to the network	5/10/05	Ensure only required directories are shared and that they are protected with strong passwords.
Programs can be put in production libraries to meet critical deadlines without final approval from the Standards and Controls group.	No	All production programs require management authorization. Standards and Controls group assigns such cases to a temporary production status.		

This chart is a sample page from a list of control weaknesses that an auditor might find in a loan system in a local commercial bank. This form helps auditors record and evaluate control weaknesses and shows the results of discussing those weaknesses with management, as well as any corrective actions taken by management.

software more reliable; these tools and methodologies are part of a movement toward software quality.

Access Controls

Access controls consists of all the policies and procedures a company uses to prevent improper access to systems by unauthorized insiders and outsiders. To gain access, a user must be authorized and authenticated. **Authentication** refers to the ability to know that a person is who he or she claims to be. Access control software is designed to allow only authorized users to use systems or to access data using some method for authentication.

Authentication is often established by using passwords known only to authorized users. An end user uses a password to log on to a computer system and may also use passwords for accessing specific systems and files. However, users often forget passwords, share them, or choose poor passwords that are easy to guess, which compromises security. Passwords can also be "sniffed" if transmitted over a network or stolen through social engineering.

E-commerce has led to the proliferation of password-protected Web sites. If users employ passwords to access multiple systems and they reuse a password for more than one system, a hacker gaining access to one user account may be able to gain access to others (Ives, Walsh and Schneider, 2004).

Sometimes systems use tokens such as smart cards for access control. A **token** is a physical device similar to an identification card that is designed to prove the identity of a single user.

Biometric authentication represents a promising new technology that can overcome some of the limitations of passwords for authenticating system users. Biometric authentication is based on the measurement of a physical or behavioural trait that makes each individual unique. It compares a person's unique characteristics, such as fingerprints, face, or retinal image, against a stored set profile of these characteristics to determine whether there are any differences between these characteristics and the stored profile. If the two profiles match, access is granted. The technology is expensive, and fingerprint and facial recognition technologies are just beginning to be used for security applications.

Firewalls, Intrusion Detection Systems, and Antivirus Software

Chapter 7 describes the use of *firewalls* to prevent unauthorized users from accessing private networks. As growing numbers of businesses expose their networks to Internet traffic, firewalls are becoming a necessity. A firewall is a combination of hardware and software that controls the flow of incoming and outgoing network traffic. It is generally placed between the organization's private internal networks and untrusted external networks such as the Internet, although firewalls can also be used to protect one part of a company's network from the rest of the network (see Figure 9-8).

The firewall acts like a gatekeeper that examines each user's credentials before access is granted to a network. The firewall identifies names, Internet Protocol (IP) addresses, applications, and other characteristics of incoming traffic. It checks this information against the access rules that have been programmed into the system by the network administrator. The firewall prevents unauthorized communication into and out of the network, allowing the organization to enforce a security policy on traffic *flowing* between its network and other untrusted networks, including the Internet.

In large organizations, the firewall often resides on a specially designated computer separate from the rest of the network so no incoming request can directly access private network resources. There are a number of firewall screening technologies, including static packet filtering, stateful inspection, network address translation, and application proxy filtering. The following techniques are used in combination to provide firewall protection.

Packet filtering examines selected fields in the headers of data packets flowing back and forth between the trusted network and the Internet, examining individual packets in isola-

FIGURE 9-8   *A corporate firewall.*

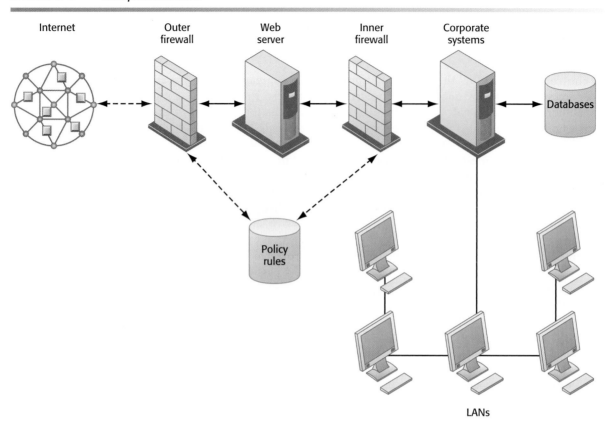

The firewall is placed between the firm's private network and the public Internet or another untrusted network to protect against unauthorized traffic

tion. This filtering technology can miss many types of attacks. **Stateful inspection** provides additional security by determining whether packets are part of an ongoing dialogue between a sender and a receiver. It sets up state tables to track information over multiple packets. Packets are accepted or rejected based on whether they are part of an approved conversation or whether they are attempting to establish a legitimate connection.

Network address translation (NAT) can provide another layer of protection when static packet filtering and stateful inspection are employed. NAT conceals the IP addresses of the organization's internal host computer(s) to prevent sniffer programs outside the firewall from ascertaining them and using that information to penetrate internal systems.

Application proxy filtering examines the application content of packets. A proxy server stops data packets originating outside the organization, inspects them, and passes a proxy to the other side of the firewall. If a user outside the company wants to communicate with a user inside the organization, the outside user first "talks" to the proxy application, and the proxy application communicates with the firm's internal computer. Likewise, a computer user inside the organization goes through the proxy to talk with computers on the outside.

To create a good firewall, an administrator must write and maintain in very fine detail the internal rules identifying the people, applications, or addresses that are allowed or rejected. Firewalls can deter, but not completely prevent, network penetration by outsiders and should be viewed as one element in an overall security plan. To deal effectively with Internet security, broader corporate policies and procedures, user responsibilities, and security awareness training may be required.

Intrusion Detection Systems In addition to firewalls, commercial security vendors now provide intrusion detection tools and services to protect against suspicious network traffic and attempts to access files and databases. **Intrusion detection systems** feature full-time monitoring tools placed at the most vulnerable points or "hot spots" of

stateful inspection
network address translation (NAT)
application proxy filtering
intrusion detection systems

corporate networks to detect and deter intruders continuously. The system generates an alarm if it finds a suspicious or anomalous event. Scanning software looks for patterns indicative of known methods of computer attacks, such as bad passwords, checks to see if important files have been removed or modified, and sends warnings of vandalism or system administration errors. Monitoring software examines events as they are happening to discover security attacks in progress. The intrusion detection tool can also be customized to shut down a particularly sensitive part of a network if it receives unauthorized traffic.

Antivirus Software Defensive technology plans for both individuals and businesses must include antivirus protection for every computer. **Antivirus software** is designed to check computer systems and drives for the presence of computer viruses. Often the software can eliminate the virus from the infected area. However, most antivirus software is effective only against viruses already known when the software was written. To remain effective, the antivirus software must be continually updated.

Securing Wireless Networks

Despite its flaws, WEP provides some margin of security if Wi-Fi users remember to activate it. Corporations can further improve WEP security by using it in conjunction with virtual private network (VPN) technology when a wireless network has access to internal corporate data.

Vendors of Wi-Fi equipment have developed new and stronger security standards. The Wi-Fi Alliance industry trade group issued a Wi-Fi Protected Access (WPA) specification that will work with 802.11i and future wireless LAN products and that can update equipment that uses 802.11b. WPA improves data encryption by replacing the static encryption keys used in WEP with longer, 128-bit keys that continually change, making them harder to crack. To strengthen user authentication, WPA provides a mechanism based on the Extensible Authentication Protocol (EAP) that works with a central authentication server to authenticate each user on the network before the user can join it. It also employs mutual authentication so that a wireless user does not get pulled into a rogue network that might steal the user's network credentials. Data packets can be checked to make sure they are part of a current network session and not repeated by hackers to fool network users.

Encryption and Public Key Infrastructure

Many organizations rely on encryption to protect sensitive information transmitted over the Internet and other networks. **Encryption** is the coding and scrambling of messages to prevent unauthorized access to or understanding of the data being transmitted. A message can be encrypted by applying a secret numerical code, called an encryption key, so that the data are transmitted as a scrambled set of characters. (The key consists of a large group of letters, numbers, and symbols.) To be read, the message must be decrypted (unscrambled) with a matching key.

There are several alternative methods of encryption, but public key encryption has become popular. Public key encryption shown in Figure 9-9 uses two different keys, one private and one public. The keys are mathematically related so that data encrypted with one key can be decrypted using only the other key. To send and receive messages, communicators first create separate pairs of private and public keys. The public key is kept in a directory, and the private key must be kept secret. The sender encrypts a message with the recipient's public key. On receiving the message, the recipient uses his or her private key to decrypt it.

Encryption is especially useful to shield messages on the Internet and other public networks because they are less secure than private networks. Encryption helps protect transmission of payment data, such as credit card information, and addresses the problems of message integrity and authentication. **Message integrity** is the ability to be certain that the message being sent arrives at the proper destination without being copied or changed.

Digital signatures and digital certificates help with authentication. The Personal Information Protection and Electronic Documents Act has given digital signatures the

antivirus software

encryption

message integrity

FIGURE 9-9   *Public key encryption.*

A public key encryption system can be viewed as a series of public and private keys that lock data when they are transmitted and unlock the data when they are received. The sender locates the recipient's public key in a directory and uses it to encrypt a message. The message is sent in encrypted form over the Internet or a private network. When the encrypted message arrives, the recipient uses his or her private key to decrypt the data and read the message.

same federal legal status as those written with ink on paper. Provincial legislation across Canada also provides the same legal status for electronic signatures. A **digital signature** is a digital code attached to an electronically transmitted message that is used to verify the origin and contents of a message. It provides a way to associate a message with a sender, performing a function similar to a written signature. For an electronic signature to be legally binding in court, someone must be able to verify that the signature actually belongs to whoever sent the data and the data were not altered after being digitally signed.

Digital certificates are data files used to establish the identity of users and electronic assets for protection of online transactions (see Figure 9-10). A digital certificate system uses a trusted third party known as a certificate authority (CA) to validate a user's identity. The CA system can be run as a function inside an organization or by an outside company such as VeriSign. The CA verifies a digital certificate user's identity offline. This information is put into a CA server, which generates an encrypted digital certificate containing owner identification information and a copy of the owner's public key. The certificate authenticates that the public key belongs to the designated owner. The CA makes its own public key available publicly either in print or perhaps on the Internet. The recipient of an encrypted message uses the CA's public key to decode the digital certificate attached to the message, verifies it was issued by the CA, and then obtains the sender's public key and identification information contained in the certificate. Using this information, the recipient can send an encrypted reply. The digital certificate system would enable, for example, a credit card user and a merchant to validate that their digital certificates were issued by an authorized and trusted third party before they exchange data. **Public key infrastructure (PKI)**, the use of public key cryptography working with a certificate authority, is becoming the principal technology for providing secure authentication of identity online (Backhouse, Hsu, and McDonnell 2003).

Two primary methods for encrypting network traffic on the Web are SSL and S-HTTP. **Secure Sockets Layer (SSL)** and its successor **Transport Layer Security (TLS)** are protocols used for secure information transfer over the Internet. They enable client and server computers to manage encryption and decryption activities as they communicate with each other during a secure Web session. **Secure Hypertext Transfer Protocol (S-HTTP)** is another protocol used for encrypting data flowing over the Internet, but it is limited to Web documents, whereas SSL and TLS encrypt all data being passed between client and server.

Ensuring Software Reliability

In addition to implementing effective security measures, firms can make systems more reliable by devoting more attention to software reliability and quality. Chapter 10 describes various tools and methodologies that can be used to enforce quality standards as software is being designed and programmed.

Software quality can be improved by expending more resources during the early stages of software design when it is possible to correct errors before the software is actually programmed. Thorough testing further reduces software errors, even though it may be impossible to eliminate them completely. Before software is written, the test normally used is a **walkthrough**—a review of a specification or design document by a small group of carefully selected people. Once programming begins, code must be tested by computer runs. When errors are discovered, the source is found and eliminated through a process called **debugging**.

FIGURE 9-10   *Digital certificates.*

Digital certificates can be used to establish the identity of people or electronic assets.

Electronic commerce and electronic business applications introduce new levels of complexity for testing to ensure high-quality performance and functionality. Behind each large Web site, such as Amazon, eBay, or E*Trade, are hundreds of servers and software programs, creating numerous points of vulnerability. These Web sites must be built and tested to make sure they are secure and that they can withstand unexpected spikes in traffic.

Testing wireless applications poses additional challenges. Many wireless and conventional Web applications are linked to the same back-end systems so the total load on those systems increases dramatically as wireless users are added. Automated load-testing tools that simulate thousands of simultaneous wireless Web and conventional Web browser sessions can help companies measure the impact on system performance.

Management Opportunities, Challenges, and Solutions

Information systems security needs organizational and management resources as well as technologies. Establishing a good framework for security and control requires skillful balancing of risks, rewards, and the firm's operational capabilities.

Opportunities

Information systems security and control are more crucial than ever. Firms today have opportunities to create marvellously secure, reliable Web sites and systems that can support their e-commerce and e-business strategies. On the downside, revenue, liability, reputation, brand image—and even a company's ability to survive—will suffer if a firm is not secure or is unreliable. The stakes have never been higher.

Management Challenges

There are many alternative technologies to help firms achieve security and control, but organizational discipline is required to use these technologies effectively.

Designing Systems That Are Neither Overcontrolled Nor Undercontrolled Although security breaches and damage to information systems still come from organizational insiders, security breaches from outside the organization are increasing because firms pursuing electronic commerce are open to outsiders through the Internet. It is difficult for organizations to determine how open or closed their networks should be to protect themselves. If a system requires too many passwords, authorizations, or levels of security to access information, the system will go unused and therefore will be ineffective. Controls that are effective but do not discourage authorized individuals from using a system are difficult to design.

Implementing an Effective Security Policy Despite increased awareness of worms, denial of service attacks, and computer crime, far too many firms do not pay sufficient attention to security. Controls and security programs are often treated as an afterthought rather than incorporated into the design of key business processes and systems. Research has shown that 75 percent of companies with information security policies do not keep them up-to-date and that only 9 percent of employees understand these security policies. Many firms lack disaster recovery and business continuity plans or fail to patch their software routinely against security vulnerabilities. Managers do not appreciate the value of a sound security strategy. Security threats abound, but they are neither predictable nor finite, making it more difficult to calculate returns on security investments. Unless managers change their thinking about security, security budgets will be inadequate.

Solution Guidelines

One thing is clear: Security and control must become a more visible and explicit priority and area of information systems investment, with greater emphasis on the overall organizational planning process. Coordinating the firm's security plan with its overall business plan shows that security is just as essential to the success of the business as any other business function. Larger firms may merit a formal security function with a chief security officer (CSO). To develop sound security and controls, users may need to change the way they work. Support and commitment from top management is required to show that security is indeed a corporate priority and vital to all aspects of the business.

Security and control will never be a high priority unless there is *security awareness* throughout the firm. Security and control should be the responsibility of everyone in the organization. Users may need special training on how to protect equipment and passwords and how to work with antivirus and other protective software. Key management decisions include determining an appropriate level of control for the organization and establishing standards for system accuracy and reliability. Managers should ask the following questions:

- What firm resources are the most critical to control and secure? How much would it cost to replace these critical assets if they were destroyed or compromised? What would be the legal and business impact if they were accessed by unauthorized parties?

- What level of system downtime is acceptable? How much disruption in business function or financial loss is the business willing to tolerate?

- What is the minimum acceptable level of performance for software and systems? If zero defects are impossible to achieve in large complex pieces of software, what constitutes acceptable, if not perfect, software performance?

- How much is the business willing to invest to protect its information assets?

Summary

1. *Analyze why information systems need special protection from destruction, error, and abuse.*

   With data concentrated in electronic from and many procedures invisible through automation, computerized information systems are vulnerable to destruction, misuse, error, fraud, and hardware or software failures. Corporate systems using the Internet are especially vulnerable because the Internet is designed to be an open system, and this design makes internal corporate systems more vulnerable to actions from outsiders. Hackers can unleash denial of service (DoS) attacks or penetrate corporate networks to cause serious system disruptions. Wi-Fi networks can easily be penetrated by intruders using sniffer programs to obtain an address to access the resources of the network. Computer viruses and worms can spread rampantly from system to system, clogging computer memory or destroying programs and data. Software presents problems because software bugs may be impossible to eliminate and software vulnerabilities can be exploited by hackers and malicious software. End users can introduce errors.

2. *Assess the business value of security and control.*

   Security and control are important but often neglected areas for information systems investment. Firms relying on computer systems for their core business functions can lose sales and productivity. Information assets such as confidential employee records, trade secrets, or business plans lose much of their value if they are revealed to outsiders or if they expose the firm to legal liability. New laws require companies to practice stringent electronic records management and adhere to strict standards for security, privacy, and control. Legal actions requiring electronic evidence and computer forensics also require firms to pay more attention to security and electronic records management.

3. *Evaluate elements of an organizational and managerial framework for security and control.*

   Firms need to establish an appropriate organizational and managerial framework for security and control to use technologies effectively to protect their information resources. They must establish a well-designed set of general and application controls. General controls handle the overall design, security, and use of computers, programs, and files for the organization's information technology infrastructure. Application controls are those unique to specific computerized applications. They focus on the completeness and accuracy of input, updates, and maintenance, and the validity of the information in the system. Application controls consist of (1) input controls, (2) processing controls, and (3) output controls.

   To determine which controls are required, designers and users of systems must identify the most important assets requiring protection and the extent to which these assets are vulnerable. A risk assessment evaluates information assets, identifies control points and control weaknesses, and determines the most cost-effective set of controls.

   Firms must also develop a coherent corporate security policy and plans for continuing business operations in the event of disaster or disruption. The security policy includes policies for acceptable use and authorization. A disaster recovery plan provides procedures and facilities for restoring computing and communication services after they have been disrupted while a business continuity plan focuses on how the company can restore business operations. Comprehensive and systematic MIS auditing can help organizations determine the effectiveness of security and controls for their information systems.

4. *Evaluate the most important tools and technologies for safeguarding information resources.*

   Companies require special measures to support electronic commerce and digital business processes. They can use fault-tolerant computer systems or create high-availability computing environments to make sure that their information systems are always available and performing without interruptions. Firewalls are placed between an organization's private network and external networks such as the Internet to prevent unauthorized users from accessing the private network. Intrusion detection systems monitor private networks to detect suspicious network traffic and to thwart attempts to access corporate systems. Passwords, tokens, and biometric authentication can be used for authenticating system users. Antivirus software can check computer systems for infection by viruses and worms and often eliminate the malicious software. Encryption, the coding and scrambling of messages, is a widely used technology for securing electronic transmissions over the Internet and over Wi-Fi networks. Digital certificates combined with public key encryption provide further protection of electronic transactions by authenticating a user's identity. The quality and reliability of software can be improved by thorough testing procedures and by allocating resources to put more emphasis on secure software design.

5. *Identify the challenges posed by information systems security and control, and propose management solutions.*

   Establishing a good framework for security and control requires skillful balancing of risks, rewards, and the firm's operational capabilities. Designing systems that are neither overcontrolled nor undercontrolled and implementing an effective security policy are major management challenges. Solutions include making security and control a higher management priority and instilling security awareness throughout the firm. Key management decisions include determining an appro-priate level of control for the organization and establishing standards for system accuracy and reliability.

Key Terms

Review Questions

1. Why are computer systems so vulnerable? Describe the most common threats to contemporary information systems.

2. Why are the Internet and Wi-Fi networks so difficult to secure?

3. What is malware? Distinguish between a virus, a worm, and a Trojan horse.

4. What is a hacker? How do hackers create security problems and damage systems?

5. How can software affect system performance and security?

6. What is computer crime? Provide two examples of crime in which computers are a target and two examples in which computers are used as instruments of crime.

7. What is identity theft? Why is it such a big problem today? How does phishing promote identity theft?

8. How can computer systems and networks be used for cyberterrorism and cyberwarfare?

9. What security problems are created by employees?

10. Define security and control. How do they provide business value? How are security and control related to recent government regulatory requirements and to computer forensics?

11. Distinguish between general controls and application controls.

12. What is the function of risk assessment? How is it conducted for information systems?

13. Define and describe the following: security policy, acceptable use policy, and authorization policy.

14. Distinguish between fault-tolerant and high-availability computing and between disaster recovery planning and business continuity planning.

15. How does MIS auditing enhance the control process?

16. Name and describe three authentication methods.

17. Describe the roles of firewalls, intrusion detection systems, and antivirus software in promoting security.

18. How can encryption be used to protect information? Describe the role of encryption and digital certificates in a public key infrastructure.

19. What management challenges are raised by information systems security and control? How can these challenges be addressed?

Discussion Questions

1. *Security is not just a technology issue; it is a business issue. Discuss.*

2. *If you were developing a business continuity plan for your company, where would you start? What aspects of the business would the plan address?*

Application Software Exercise: Spreadsheet Exercise: Performing a Security Risk Assessment

Mercer Paints is a small but highly regarded paint manufacturing company located in Saskatchewan. The company has a network in place linking many of its business operations. Although the firm believes that its security is adequate, the recent addition of a Web site has become an open invitation to hackers. Management requested a risk assessment. The risk assessment identified a number of potential exposures. These exposures, their associated probabilities, and average losses are summarized in the following table.

MERCER PAINTS RISK ASSESSMENT

EXPOSURE	PROBABILITY OF OCCURENCE (%)	AVERAGE LOSS ($)
Virus attack	60	75 000
Data loss	12	70 000
Embezzlement	3	30 000
User errors	95	25 000
Threats from hackers	95	90 000
Improper use by employees	5	5 000
Power failure	15	300 000

In addition to the potential exposures listed, you should identify at least three other potential threats to Mercer Paints, assign probabilities, and estimate a loss range. Using spreadsheet software and the risk assessment data, calculate the expected annual loss for each exposure. Which control points have the greatest vulnerability? What recommendations would you make to Mercer Paints? Prepare a written report that summarizes your findings and recommendations.

Electronic Business Project: Evaluating Security Outsourcing Services

Data and network security are major challenges, and some companies have chosen to outsource the security function rather than train their own staff or hire specialists from outside the company. Finding security outsourcing services can be difficult, although finding sources that help you decide whether to outsource is much easier. In both cases, use several search engines to find sources that can help you decide whether to outsource and to locate computer security companies.

As an information systems expert in your firm, you have been assigned the following tasks. First, present a brief summary of the arguments for and against outsourcing computer security. Second, select two firms that offer computer security outsourcing services, and compare them and their services. Third, prepare a written recommendation to management on whether you believe they should opt for outsourcing computer security and which of the two firms you believe they should select if they do decide to outsource.

Group Project: Analyzing Security Vulnerabilities

A survey of your firm's information technology infrastructure has produced the security analysis statistics that are shown at the top of page 332.

SECURITY VULNERABILITIES BY TYPE OF COMPUTING PLATFORM

PLATFORM	NUMBER OF COMPUTERS	HIGH RISK	MEDIUM RISK	LOW RISK	TOTAL VULNERABILITIES
Windows Server 2003 (corporate applications)	1	11	37	19	
Linux (email and printing services)	1	3	154	98	
Sun Solaris (UNIX) (e-commerce and Web servers)	2	12	299	78	
Windows XP Professional Edition (desktops and laptops with office productivity tools that can also be linked to the corporate network running corporate applications and the intranet)	195	14	16	1237	

High-risk vulnerabilities include unauthorized users accessing applications, guessable passwords, matching of user names and passwords, active user accounts with missing passwords, and unauthorized programs in application systems.

Medium-risk vulnerabilities include users' ability to shut down the system without being logged on, passwords and screen saver settings that were not established for PCs, and outdated versions of software stored on hard drives.

Low-risk vulnerabilities include the inability of users to change their passwords, user passwords not being changed periodically, and passwords smaller than the minimum size specified by the company.

With a group of your classmates, use this information to perform an analysis of this firm's security vulnerabilities that answers the following questions:

1. What is the total number of vulnerabilities for each platform? What is the potential impact of the security problems for each computing platform in the organization?

2. If you have only one information systems specialist in charge of security, which platforms should you address first in trying to eliminate these vulnerabilities? Second? Third? Last? Why?

3. Identify the types of control problems illustrated by these vulnerabilities and explain the measures that should be taken to solve them.

4. What does your firm risk by ignoring the security vulnerabilities identified?

If possible, use electronic presentation software to present your findings to the class.

Web Sites of Interest

There are many interesting Web sites to enhance your learning about information systems security and control. You can search the Web yourself or try to following sites to add to what you have already learned.

Information Security Magazine **www.infosecuritymag.com**
Up-to-date news and technical briefs on information security issues.

AntiOnline E-Magazine **www.antionline.com**
Web magazine for security officers and others interested in preventing information systems security problems.

Information Systems Security Association (ISSA) **www.issa.org**
International association for information systems security professionals. ISSA has three chapters in Canada.

Information Systems Audit and Control Association (ISACA) **www.isaca.org**
International association for those interested in audit and security in information systems, such as internal auditors, CIOs, IS auditors, and others. ISACA has 10 chapters in Canada.

CASE STUDY:
Royal Bank of Canada's Software Woes

Founded in 1864 and chartered in 1869 as the Merchants' Bank of Halifax, Royal Bank of Canada (RBC) took its current name in 1901. In 1941, based on its total assets of $1 billion, RBC became Canada's largest bank. Twenty years later, RBC installed its first computer, making it the first bank in Canada to employ computer technology. In October 2003, the organization had 60 000 employees, a total of $522 billion in assets, and 12 million customers. Including worldwide operations, RBC has spent $1.6 billion on technology.

On Monday, May 31, 2004, the RBC information technology staff made a programming upgrade to what has been described as "key banking software." According to Martin Lippert, RBC's vice chairman and CIO, a glitch in the bank's computer systems "was most likely caused by a single worker entering 'a relatively small number' of incorrect pieces of code during the update." The glitch resulted in a massive computer failure that affected millions of banking customers around the country. Lippert specified that the

incorrect code was related to "transit numbers or field identifiers in a table." The mistakes worked their way through the
bank's systems quickly, but conspicuously. RBC had already
discovered the problem by six o'clock the next morning.
Unfortunately, recognition of the error wasn't even half the
battle.

In fact, RBC fixed the programming error that had been
made on May 31 early on Tuesday, June 1. Still, several days
later, millions of RBC customers were unable to check their
account balances, had not received their paycheques, or had
automatic payments or transfers delayed. The reactions of
customers, as could be expected, were negative. Some customers merely suffered the inconvenience of not having
access to information that they were accustomed to having at
their fingertips all of the time. Other customers, those who
count on their paycheques to get by, had their lives affected
more seriously. One such person, a law firm executive assistant named Andrea Mitchell, was forced to ask her employer
for a cash advance to make up for her temporarily lost pay-
cheque and to meet her personal expenses.

So, if the human programming error was corrected so
swiftly, why did RBC continue to experience problems related
to the glitch over the course of a work week? The glitch put
into motion a chain of management and control procedures
that exacerbated the problem. Procedures that were
intended to fix the problem instead caused a logjam of activity from which the bank could not recover immediately.

The first question that most people asked was: Why
weren't backup systems used to keep business flowing while
the main systems were being fixed? As stated on the bank's
Web site, "Back up facilities exist in case our primary facility is
disabled. As a matter of policy, therefore, all program
changes are implemented simultaneously to both the primary and backup facilities." Therefore, the same error that
compromised the main system also affected the backup
system.

According to Lippert, in addition to the programming code
update being entered incorrectly, the new code was not
tested properly before it was deployed. RBC policy calls for all
new pieces of software to be tested thoroughly before they
are used in production systems.

On Tuesday, June 1, with the knowledge that random
duplications of transactions were occurring in its systems,
RBC decided to suspend its end-of-day processing rather
than let it run with incomplete or inaccurate data. When veri-
fying the health of its systems took longer than expected,
RBC was left with a backlog of transactions to process. All the
while, new transactions were pouring in, as they would on a
normal business day, and these added to the logjam. On
Wednesday, June 2, the IT department was confident that it
could make up the ground lost on Tuesday and remain
current with Wednesday's transactions. The newer transactions were placed at the end of queue because of a sequential numbering system, so the backlog had to be cleared
before RBC could process any new transactions. Also slowing
down the effort was the bank's decision to monitor data processing manually following the glitch to make sure that no
coding errors persisted. Trying to process two days of transactions at once proved to be more difficult than the bank imag-

ined it would be. RBC says it had 245 staff working around-
the-clock shifts to update accounts and verify transactions.

As if the event itself were not bad enough for business,
RBC came under criticism for the way in which it handled the
public relations end of the problem. First, RBC assured that
all systems and accounts would be normalized by Thursday,
June 3. Confident in this assessment, the bank's CEO,
Gordon Nixon, left for Europe on Wednesday, June 2. When
customers were still experiencing difficulties with their
accounts later in the week, the bank appeared weak by not
having its leader available to address customers' concerns.
John Layne, of the crisis management company Contingency
Management Consultants, surmised the common organizational flaw in which lower-level employees are loathe to pass
bad news up the corporate ladder was a possible reason for
Nixon's untimely exit from the scene. In Nixon's absence,
other RBC executives took turns addressing the media and
the public, though the first public comments on the glitch
were not made until late Wednesday afternoon. Having a single representative of the bank to interface with the public
would have inspired more confidence in customers and the
public at large.

Unfortunately for RBC, the cumulative effect of its errors
was widespread. About 62 000 government workers in
Ontario and 10 000 in New Brunswick didn't receive their
automatic deposits even if they didn't do their personal banking at RBC. Their provincial governments used RBC to route
the payroll, so the deposits didn't reach the workers' own
banks. Hundreds of thousands of other workers around
Canada ran into similar delays or difficulties accessing their
deposits. The government of Ontario indicated that it would
issue physical cheques to employees who still had not
received their deposits by the Monday following the initial
computer glitch.

RBC's service disruption had one particularly dangerous
side effect, over which the bank had little control.
Opportunistic scam artists seized on the glitch to unleash a
phishing scam that targeted RBC customers, taking advantage
of the customers' frustrations, security fears, or simply their
naïveté. An email message with the subject line "Official
information from RBC Royal Bank" stated that "due to the
increased fraudulent activity within our site we are undertaking a review of member accounts." The email linked to a
page that looked like RBC's official Web site that instructed
customers to "be sure to enter both client card number or
business card number and password otherwise your account
will not be verified and your access to the account will be
blocked." Once RBC customers entered the requested information at that bogus site, hackers could access their
accounts.

RBC announced that it had resumed normal business
practices during the week beginning June 8, 2004. The bank
continued to resolve discrepancies from service charges and
overdraft interest that resulted from the disruption and indicated that all accounts should be reflected accurately in customers' next statements, by June 30. On June 18, RBC
announced that it had hired Crawford Adjusters Canada as its
"administrator for non-banking-related costs and losses in the
bank's processing disruption." The bank made claim forms

available by phone and on the Internet and set a deadline of September 30, 2004, for customers to file claims. RBC was to handle all claims under $100 itself, leaving larger claims to Crawford. The total loss to RBC was contingent on the number of claims filed. However, that cost could rise significantly based on a class-action suit filed in Quebec that requested damages of $500 for each customer that was affected.

In hindsight, analysts agree that RBC handled the technology portion of its problem effectively. The bank erred mostly in its estimates of how long the recovery period would be. In addition to issuing a formal apology, RBC created an area of its Web site that was devoted to detailed explanations of the problem and updates on the progress of restoring its records. The bank also enlisted IBM Corporation as a consultant to investigate the causes of the problem and provide guidance on how to avoid such problems going forward. RBC offered refunds to its customers for any banking fees that they incurred as a result of the computer problems and agreed to reimburse other financial institutions and their customers for certain expenses that may have resulted from RBC's errors. These moves could go a long way toward restoring faith in customers of the bank, who, in the immediate aftermath, were understandably concerned about the security of their finances. One client said that she didn't intend to leave RBC just then, but, "If it happened again, I may not be so loyal." According to local press reports, the systems problem at RBC cost the bank $9 million, after tax, to fix.

Unfortunately, RBC was not the only Canadian bank hit with a computer glitch in the summer of 2004. At the Canadian Imperial Bank of Commerce (CIBC), customers viewing transactions online in August of 2004 saw many of their transactions listed twice even though they were only listed once when viewed at teller machines or through other means. In July, a computer glitch at CIBC caused transactions

to be billed twice on 60 000 accounts. Also in August of 2004, a software glitch at Toronto Dominion Bank branches prevented some customers from accessing up-to-date account balances.

Sources: Ian Austen, "Bank Software Woes Leave Many Canadians Without Money," *New York Times*, June 7, 2004; "RBC Admits Human Error, Scam Artists Act," *Ottawa Business Journal*, June 10, 2004; Lindsay Bruce, "RBC Glitch Still Not Ironed Out," ITWorldCanada.com, June 7, 2004; Chris Conrath, "Anatomy of a Snafu," ITWorldCanada.com, June 11, 2004; Paul Waldie, "RBC Calls in Help," *Globe and Mail*, **www.theglobeandmail.com**, accessed June 19, 2004; Mel Duvall, "RBC's Account Imbalance," *Baseline Magazine*, July 1, 2004; and *CP*, "RBC Still Making Up for Glitch," *London Free Press*, **www.canoe.ca**, accessed June 19, 2004; "Royal Bank of Canada Computer Glitch Causes Payment Chaos," Finextra, **www.finextra.com/fullstory. asp?id-11948, June 4, 2004**, accessed May 15, 2004; "CIBC Hit by Computer Problem; Westpac Blames Internet Foul-Up on Human Error," Finextra, **www.finextra.com/fullstory.asp?id=12411**.

CASE STUDY QUESTIONS

1. Provide a summary of the security and control problems experienced by the Royal Bank of Canada. How did this problem affect the organization and its clients?

2. What management, organization, and technology factors contributed to the control problems at RBC?

3. What was the most critical flaw in the security and control systems in place at RBC? Explain your answer.

4. How well did RBC respond to its computer problem? What do you think the bank might have done differently to prevent the problem and to handle it once it occurred?

5. If you were a manager at RBC, how would you prevent a problem like this from happening?

CBC ⊛

PART II CANADIAN CASE STUDY:
Wi-Fi in Canada: Many Ways to Access the Internet from Many Places

More than two-thirds of Canadians are connected to the Internet today. It is interesting to note that about 15 percent of Canadians, or 23 percent of those Canadians connected to the Internet, use wireless fidelity, one of the newer standards for telecommunication.

As detailed in Chapter 8, IEEE standard 802.11 governs wireless networking, with three substandards, a, b, and g. 802.11a is not compatible with either 802.11b or 802.11g, but the latter two are compatible with each other. The 802.11b standard has been the most widely used standard for creating wireless LANs and providing wireless Internet access. However, 802.11g may become more popular in the next few years, and dual-band systems capable of handling 802.11b and 802.11g are expected to proliferate. Today most computers are sold with 802.11b or 802.11g networking capability built in, either through a wireless networking card or more recently, with a wireless chip on the motherboard that holds the processing and RAM chips.

How are Canadian businesses and individuals using Wi-Fi? What are the challenges of implementing and using Wi-Fi?

Baycrest Centre for Geriatric Care, headquartered in Toronto, uses Wi-Fi to support its voice-for-nurse call system, supporting hundreds of concurrent users. The more than 200 doctors, nurses, and administrators in Baycrest provide their patients with the highest standard of care. Services such as bedside charting, monitoring, and order entry are carried out using 50 wireless-enabled computers-on-wheels (COWs) to access Baycrest's Meditech System. The doctors, nurses, and administrators needed a single wireless network over which they could transmit voice and data, without making the project costly and complex. IT staff were paid $100 per hour, so keeping costs to a minimum, even after implementation, was critical. Security, of course, was also a paramount concern. The system would need to support myriad wireless devices, from VoIP telephones to laptop computers, handheld personal digital assistants, and voice communication badges. The centre was also considering implementing new applications such as voice over wireless.

Baycrest implemented an Aruba wireless LAN switching system that included a suite of wireless applications. The system was relatively self-configuring, resulting in ease of use and easy addition or movement of the various nodes on the network. It was also simple to add capacity as demand increased. The new wireless network also makes it easy to transmit very large files, such as those in medical imaging. Baycrest implemented data encryption to meet the requirements of the federal Personal Information Protection and Electronic Documents Act. In addition, virtual private networks are hosted on the Aruba wireless network, permitting staff to log in from home to leave patient orders or check on their patients' conditions. Baycrest is one of many companies in the health-care field that are adopting wireless technologies.

The Royal Ottawa Hospital is expected to open to patients in late 2006. There will be a wireless mesh network for telemedicine to serve all of the hospital's facilities and grounds. Doctors, researchers, and hospital staff, numbering over a thousand, will use the Nortel Mobility mesh network to deliver the highest quality of care. "Hospitals tend to be large facilities," says Brian McFadden, chief research officer of Nortel Networks. The mesh network "allows connectivity to a network with broadband capabilities, wirelessly. It allows clinical staff to stay online throughout the facility regardless of the task being undertaken." According to Bruce Swan, CEO, Royal Ottawa Health Care Group, "It builds in flexibility for clinicians." Wireless connectivity, he adds, "makes better use of people's time. It allows information to be recorded at the time of the procedure, rather than having clinicians go back to a workstation to input it."

According to Swan, The design of the Royal Ottawa Hospital building incorporated the ability to install a mesh network. "Positioning of the nodes, required to transmit information, where they will be the most practical is easier than retrofitting a hospital because you don't have to work around existing infrastructure." Wireless-enabled laptops and other handheld devices can help clinical teams to access the hospital's internal network, patient records, the Internet, email, shared files, and other applications. "It is going to drastically reduce the potential for errors," according to McFadden.

Wi-Fi is also coming to consumers at their favourite places of business through Wi-Fi "hot spots." A Wi-Fi hot spot is an area where consumers can log on to the Internet wirelessly, typically for a charge. Via Rail Canada is set to utilize Wi-Fi mobile that will offer Wi-Fi connectivity on certain trains between Montreal and Toronto for Via 1 (Via's first class) passengers. Via hopes to extend Wi-Fi passenger connectivity to the Quebec City–Windsor corridor. Already, Via Rail offers Wi-Fi connectivity to Via 1 and sleeper class passengers in its Panorama Lounges in four stations: Dorval, Kingston, Toronto, and Montreal. In Dorval and Kingston, Wi-Fi connectivity will soon be available throughout the stations. Wireless service does not come cheaply for passengers. Via 1 passengers can select from three different payment plans. They can select the pay-per-use plan, for which the first 15 minutes cost $3.99, and each additional minute cost $0.30, the daily access plan with a flat rate of $8.95 for a 24-hour period, or the monthly access plan, which costs $46.

Guy Faulkner, product manager for corridor service at Via, considers Wi-Fi access to give the company a potential advantage over its competition. Faulkner anticipates a growing interest among Via's passengers in onboard Internet service. Bell Canada, a division of BCE, Inc. in Montreal, is working with Via to provide this service. Technically, the satellite signals are fed into an onboard server and then to a wireless access point in the first-class car that users can then access from their laptops or handhelds. The return signal from user devices is fed from the access point in the car to the server and then over Bell's terrestrial CDMA network, with an average data rate of about 70 Kbs.

But you don't have to ride the rails or fly the skies to have mobile access to wireless Internet service. Hot spots are appearing in any number of retail outlets, primarily coffee shops and restaurants. In the U.S., Schlotzsky's Deli chain offers Wi-Fi access to its customers for free in 30 of its 600 locations. According to Schlotzsky's CEO John Wooley, the free Wi-Fi access results in an additional 15 000 visits per restaurant per year by customers who spend an average of $7 per visit. That means Wi-Fi service brings in more than $117 000 CDN per year per outlet in return for an investment of under $10 000 CDN. Experts speculate that once free Wi-Fi access is universal, the return on investment for that type of service will decrease.

In the United States, Starbucks was one of the first retail companies to incorporate Wi-Fi hot spots into their outlets. Today many Second Cup locations in Canada offer Wi-Fi access through Rogers Wireless, Inc.; Second Cup customers can read their email or surf the Web while drinking their cup of coffee. Rogers is rolling out their brand new Wi-Fi service through Second Cup, starting in Second Cup shops in Toronto. Rogers, along with its competitors Bell Mobility and Telus Mobility, is creating a national standard to make roaming between competing hot spot locations possible. With the Rogers Connect plan, subscribers who have cellular phone service with Rogers can use the Wi-Fi service and charge the cost to their cell phone bill.

You have only to travel the 401 between Toronto and Kitchener to find hot spots at Tim Hortons and Wendy's. Many hotels are offering Wi-Fi access in their meeting rooms or conference areas, where conference attendees can connect during conference breaks. Some hotels are even offering Wi-Fi service—for a fee—from hotel rooms.

After the outbreaks of SARS and West Nile virus and a 30 percent drop in business, Toronto's Forest Hills' Business Improvement Area created a two-block long stretch of wireless Internet access to try to lure customers. Wireless Internet access is available from any store or even outside on Spadina Road. The "village" uses an outdoor Wi-Fi access point with 20 times the regular range using a single business DSL connection. Before customers can actually surf the Web, though, they must sit through one minute of ads—a small price to pay for free access.

Canadian municipalities have rolled out Wi-Fi networks to make themselves more attractive to businesses and technology-savvy citizens. In Ontario, hydro companies are looking at Wi-Fi as a potential backhaul system for the smart meters mandated by the provincial government. With WiMax, a new standard for wireless telecommunication, and its promise of high-speed links over longer distances than Wi-Fi, wireless access may be possible from almost anywhere. One of the key barriers to these advances is the billing dilemma: how do you bill customers for Wi-Fi or WiMax access that is carried through cellular phone carriers? There is little incentive for cellular carriers to permit their customers to make calls over Wi-Fi since they do not bill for those calls. Somehow, a compromise must be reached in the area of billing to converge cellular and wireless broadband technologies.

There are even Web sites that list hot spots around the world, such as **www.wi-fihotspotlist.com**. A user can simply enter the address where they wish to access a hot spot, and the Web site returns a list of hot spots that are available, with the actual address of the hot spot, and a further link detailing a little more about the type of store (if the hot spot is hosted by a store), the type of link, and other potentially useful information.

The dual advantages of the fast data transfer rate of Wi-Fi type technology and the broad range of a cellular phone network are brought together by WiMax, also known as IEEE standard 802.16. The first WiMax-enabled commercial products are planned to be released in late 2005. WiMax, an Internet Protocol (IP)-based technology, makes it posssible to move all types of communication, from voice to data to video, as packets over the same network. According to experts, WiMax will offer potential rates of 75 megabits per second over a distance of more than 50 kilometres. However, as the range of WiMax is extended, the speed of transmission is reduced.

But sometimes the technology is ready—even before the applications are ready. A Windows Pocket PC device turned into a dual-mode phone with capabilities to send and receive both cellular and Wi-Fi calls through the same dialler has been created by Cicero Softphone. With Wi-Fi service, the Softphone routes calls across the Internet, or it defaults to the cellular connection. Skype, the free VoIP provider, now offers a mobile version, permitting Pocket PC devices with Wi-Fi access to make phone calls for free or for very low charges (for example, $.03 CDN to almost anywhere in the world).

In addition to the billing dilemma, most experts feel that security of wireless networks is difficult to establish and manage. It has become so simple to install wireless routers that almost anyone can do it. In fact, many people installing their own home wireless networks never even refer to the user's manual for their wireless routers. They use the default setups found in the installation wizards and feel that they are connected throughout their homes. That's the problem. As the CBC video that accompanies this case study shows, wireless access is accessible over a specific geographic area, meaning that war-walkers, war-bikers, and war-drivers can steal your wireless signal to log on to the Internet.

Many computer aficionados feel that all wireless service should be free. If you have paid to have wireless access in your home, where's the harm if someone else also uses it since it's already there? But accessing your wireless signal means that these interlopers can hack into your home network, perhaps stealing your files, your data, or just logging on to the Internet as you and downloading pornography or other objectionable material. Security on wireless networks is not

that hard to establish: network installers simply need to read the installation manual and follow the instructions to restrict access to your wireless network, including using logon IDs and passwords that are unique to your network.

Whether someone is gaining illegal wireless access while walking, biking, or driving, they are stealing a valuable service. According to Wartalking.com, someone was arrested for hacking into a court's wireless network just to prove that the court's network could be hacked.

What is the future of Wi-Fi? Perhaps it will eventually give way to newer, faster technologies with a broader geographical reach, such as WiMax. But for now, Wi-Fi will be here for several years as the newer technologies mature and applications become available to make use of them.

Sources: Brian Eaton, "Ottawa – A Hospital Built for Mesh," *IT World Canada*, August 2, 2005, available **www.techworld.com/features/index.cfm?featureID=1607**, accessed September 24, 2005; "Secure Voice and Data over Wi-Fi Moves Baycrest to Switch to Aruba," April 2004, available **www.arubanetworks.com/pdf/baycrest_cs.pdf**, accessed September 24, 2005; "Wireless Internet in Via 1 Class," available **www.viarail.ca/wirelessinternet/en_index.html**, accessed September 24, 2005; Bob Brewin, "All Aboard with Wi-Fi on Via Rail Canada," *Computerworld Canada*, July 10, 2003, available **www.computerworld.com/printthis/2003/0,4814,82940,00.html**, accessed September 24, 2005; "Computerworld: Free Hot Spots Pay Dividends," October 22, 2003, available **www.bmannconsulting.com/node/614**, accessed September 24, 2005; Tyler Hamilton, "Wi-Fi 'Hotspots' Coming to a Coffee Shop Near You," *Toronto Star*, February 18, 2005, available **www.thestar.com/NASApp/cs/ContentServer?pagename=thestar/Layout/Article_Type1&c=Article&cid=1108680612792&call_pageid=968350072197&col=Columnist971715454851&DPL=IvsNDS%2f7ChAX&tacodalogin=yes**, accessed September 24, 2005; Michael Martin, "The Wi-Fi/Cell Conundrum," *Network World*, September 16, 2005, available **www.itworldcanada.com//Pages/Docbase/ViewArticle.aspx?ID=idgml-b2e4cb03-ddff-4c06-9aec-ad8679abf822**, accessed September 24, 2005; Peter Judge, "Converged Softphone Cuts Bill," *IT World Canada*, September 8, 2005, available **www.itworldcanada.com/a/search/e10c3e79-22ad-4c3d-a8d4-47e0c1dc6123.htm**l, accessed September 24, 2005; Dan McLean, "Bluetooth and WiFi, Meet WiMAX Technology," *IT World Canada*, August 4, 2005, available **www.itworldcanada.com/a/search/6fa973d9-511a-4d6c-a3e3-c9209578f0df.html**, accessed September 24, 2005; Rosie Lombardi, "Canadian Researchers Uncover New 'Wireless' Possibilities," *IT World Canada*, July 29, 2005, available **www.itworldcanada.com/a/search/a8dd82dc-62b6-46d1-846f-6a50e74b24bf.html**, accessed September 24, 2005; Sean Carruthers, "Forest Hills Cuts the Cords," November 6, 2003, available **www.huba-canada.com/story_10783_4**, accessed September 26, 2005.

Video Resource

"Wireless Internet (WI-FI)," Venture 883 (June 8, 2003).

CASE STUDY QUESTIONS

1. What are the implications of having competing wireless standards, such as three 802.11 standards and WiMAX? Do you see convergence of these standards, one standard winning the battle for users, or a newer standard coming forward in the next three to five years?

2. Do you think that the advent of wireless hot spots will change the way people compute? If people change the way they use their computers (e.g., the place, the time),

do you think that the hardware (e.g., the type of computers people use) will change? How will they change?

3. Looking at the health-care industry, what are some of the ways, in addition to those mentioned above, that you think health-care professionals can make use of wireless technology? Are there any uses of information technology for which wireless is not an appropriate telecommunications method?

4. What are some of the privacy and security considerations in examining wireless technologies? How can these concerns be addressed?

PART III

Systems Development and Management

Part III   Canadian Case Study:
In Tech We Trust: The Story of SAP in Canada

Chapter 10

Systems Development

OBJECTIVES

After completing this chapter, you will be able to:

1. Demonstrate how developing new systems produces organizational change.
2. Explain how a company can develop information systems that fit its business plan.
3. Identify and describe the core activities in the systems development process.
4. Evaluate alternative methods for developing information systems and alternative methodologies for modelling systems.
5. Assess the challenges of developing information systems, and propose management solutions.

Opening Case: Australia's Victoria Country Fire Authority Responds with New Systems

The Victoria Country Fire Authority (CFA) is one of the world's largest volunteer emergency services, with 63 000 volunteer members, more than 1200 fire stations, and 850 permanent support and administrative staff in the state of Victoria, Australia. It is responsible for 2.5 million people in 980 000 homes and 150 182 square kilometres of land. In 2001–2002, CFA brigades responded to 34 139 incidents. CFA's ability to communicate effectively with its volunteer force can be a matter of life and death.

Until recently, CFA was struggling to manage multiple technologies and applications with overlapping processes and functionality. These systems were maintaining a great deal of redundant—and often inconsistent—data that were getting out of hand. The data in CFA systems could not be trusted and were affecting CFA's ability to provide emergency management and ensure community safety.

CFA management contracted with consultants to develop a Web site called Brigades Online that provides information for volunteers and to develop more integrated business systems. The most critical project was an emergency management system, which provides mission-critical management of people and equipment for combating fires, and a supporting locality information system. The locality information system contains information about a particular location, including local risks such as the existence of dangerous goods in industrial areas, operational pre-plans, and CFA educational activities in that area.

Other important projects include new systems for finance, asset management, and human resources; interactive portals for staff and volunteers and for the community; a portal for communicating with local government authorities, utilities, and other state agencies; a performance management system; and a multimedia corporate database. CFA was able to use finance modules of the SAP enterprise system developed for another agency, the Metropolitan Fire brigade.

For each project, CFA researched information requirements, evaluated alternative solutions, reviewed business processes, and developed a business case and implementation schedule to ensure they were aligned with its business goals. Brigade volunteers as well as information systems specialists provided input on how the systems should be designed. Although not all systems could be immediately implemented, CFA emerged with a clear idea of what it needed and a strategy to move forward.

Sources: Sue Bushell, "Blazing a Strategy Trail," *CIO Australia*, June 2, 2004; and www.cfa.vic.gov.au, accessed September 24, 2004.

The Victoria Country Fire Authority's system-development program illustrates the many factors at work in the development of a new information system. Developing the new system entailed analyzing the organization's problems with existing information systems, assessing people's information needs, selecting appropriate technology, and redesigning business processes and jobs. Management had to monitor the system-development effort and to evaluate its benefits and costs. The new information system represented a process of planned organizational change.

During your career, you will undoubtedly look for ways to use new information systems to improve the performance of your firm. You may be asked to help your organization develop a new information system. In this chapter, you will learn how new information systems are conceived, developed, and installed, and how they change the way the organization works. The chapter describes the core systems development activities, alternative approaches for developing systems, and alternative methodologies for modelling systems.

10.1 | Systems as Planned Organizational Change

Developing a new information system is one kind of planned organizational change. The introduction of a new information system involves much more than new hardware and software. It also includes changes in jobs, skills, management, and organization. When we design a new information system, we are redesigning the organization. System developers must understand how a system will affect the organization as a whole.

Linking Information Systems to the Business Plan

Deciding which new systems to develop should be an essential part of the organizational planning process. Organizations need to develop an information systems plan that supports their overall business plan and incorporates strategic systems into top-level planning. Once specific projects have been selected within the overall context of a strategic plan for the business and the systems area, an **information systems plan** can be developed. The plan serves as a road map indicating the direction of systems development (the purpose of the plan), the rationale, the current systems situation, new developments to consider, the management strategy, the implementation plan, and the budget (see Table 10-1).

TABLE 10-1 Information Systems Plan

1. Purpose of the Plan
    Overview of plan contents
    Current business organization and future organization
    Key business processes
    Management strategy

2. Strategic Business Plan Rationale
    Current situation
    Current business organization
    Changing environments
    Major goals of the business plan
    Firm's strategic plan

3. Current Systems
    Major systems supporting business functions and processes
    Current infrastructure capabilities
        Hardware
        Software
        Database
        Telecommunications and Internet
    Difficulties meeting business requirements
    Anticipated future demands

4. New Developments
    New system projects
        Project descriptions
        Business rationale
        Applications' role in strategy
    New infrastructure capabilities required
        Hardware
        Software
        Database
        Telecommunications and Internet

5. Management Strategy
    Acquisition plans
    Milestones and timing
    Organizational realignment
    Internal reorganization
    Management controls
    Major training initiatives
    Personnel strategy

6. Implementation Plan
    Anticipated difficulties in implementation
    Progress reports

7. Budget Requirements
    Requirements
    Potential savings
    Financing
    Acquisition cycle

information systems plan

The plan contains a statement of corporate goals and specifies how information technology will support the attainment of those goals. The plan shows how general goals will be achieved by specific information systems projects. It identifies specific target dates and milestones that can be used later to evaluate the plan's progress in terms of how many objectives were actually attained in the time frame specified in the plan. The plan indicates the key management decisions concerning hardware acquisition; telecommunications; centralization/decentralization of authority, data, and hardware; and required organizational change. Organizational changes are also usually described, including management and employee training requirements; recruiting efforts; changes in business processes; and changes in authority, structure, and management practice.

Establishing Organizational Information Requirements

To develop an effective information systems plan, the organization must have a clear understanding of both its long- and short-term information requirements. Two principal methodologies for establishing the essential information requirements of the organization as a whole are enterprise analysis and critical success factors.

Enterprise Analysis (Business Systems Planning)

Enterprise analysis (also called business systems planning) argues that the firm's information requirements can be understood only by examining the entire organization in terms of organizational units, functions, processes, and data elements. Enterprise analysis can help identify the key entities and attributes of the organization's data.

The central method used in the enterprise analysis approach is to take a large sample of managers and ask them how they use information, where they get their information, what their objectives are, how they make decisions, and what their data needs are. The results of this large survey of managers are aggregated into subunits, functions, processes, and data matrices. Data elements are organized into logical application groups—groups of data elements that support related sets of organizational processes.

Figure 10-1 is an output of enterprise analysis conducted by the U.S. Social Security Administration as part of a massive systems redevelopment effort. It shows what information is required to support a particular process, which processes create the data, and which use them. The shaded boxes in the figure indicate a logical application group. In this case, actuarial estimates, agency plans, and budget data are created in the planning process, suggesting that an information system should be developed to support planning.

The weakness of enterprise analysis is that it produces an enormous amount of data that is expensive to collect and difficult to analyze. The questions frequently focus not on management's critical objectives and where information is needed but rather on what existing information is used. The result is a tendency to automate whatever exists. But in many instances, entirely new approaches to how business is conducted are needed, and these needs are not addressed.

Strategic Analysis or Critical Success Factors

The strategic analysis, or critical success factors, approach argues that an organization's information requirements are determined by a small number of managerial **critical success factors (CSFs)** of managers. If these are easily identifiable, operational goals can be attained and the success of the firm or organization is assured (Rockart 1979; Rockart and Treacy 1982). CSFs are shaped by the industry, the firm, the manager, and the broader environment. New information systems should focus on providing information that helps the firm meet these goals.

The principal method used in CSF analysis is personal interviews—three or four—with a number of top managers identifying their goals and the resulting CSFs. These personal CSFs are aggregated to develop a picture of the firm's CSFs. Then systems are developed to deliver information on these CSFs. (See Table 10-2 for an example of CSFs. For the method of developing CSFs in an organization, see Figure 10-2.)

The strength of the CSF method is that it produces less data to analyze than enterprise analysis. Only top managers are interviewed, and the questions focus on a small number

enterprise analysis

critical success factors (CSFs)

TABLE 10-2 *Critical Success Factors and Organizational Goals*

EXAMPLE	GOALS	CSF
Profit concern	Earnings/share Return on investment Market share New product Energy standards	Automotive industry Styling Quality dealer system Cost control
Nonprofit	Excellent health care Meeting government regulations Future health needs	Regional integration with other hospitals Improved monitoring of regulations Efficient use of resources

Source: Rockart (1979).

FIGURE 10-1 *Process/data class matrix.*

LOGICAL APPLICATION GROUP	PROCESSES	Actuarial estimates	Agency plans	Budget	Program regulations/policy	Administrative regulations/policy	Labour agreements	Data standards	Procedures	Automated systems documentation	Educational media	Public agreements	Intergovernmental agreements	Grants	External	Exchange control	Administrative accounts	Program expenditures	Audit reports	Organization/position	Employee identification	Recruitment/placement	Complaints/grievances	Training resources	Security	Equipment utilization	Space utilization	Supplies utilization	Workload schedules	Work measurement	Enumeration I.D.	Enumeration control	Earnings	Employer I.D.	Earnings control	Claims characteristics	Claims control	Decisions	Payment	Collection/waiver	Notice	Inquiries control	Quality appraisal
PLANNING	Develop agency plans	C	C	C	U	U									U																												
PLANNING	Administer agency budget	C	C	C	U	U						U	U	U		U	U	U		U	U					U	U	U			U		U		U		U			U		U	U
PLANNING	Formulate program policies	U	U		C			U							U			U		U													U										U
PLANNING	Formulate administrative policies		U		U	C	C	U							U			U	U	U																							
PLANNING	Formulate data policies		U	U		U		C	U	U																					U	U	U	U									
PLANNING	Design work processes		U		U	U		C	C			U	U							U																		U					U
GENERAL MANAGEMENT	Manage public affairs		U		U	U		U			C	C	C																														
GENERAL MANAGEMENT	Manage intrgovernment affairs	U	U		U	U		U			U	C	C	C												U	U		U	U			U				U						
GENERAL MANAGEMENT	Exchange data			U				U				U	U	U	U	C	U	U													U												
GENERAL MANAGEMENT	Maintain administrative accounts			U		U		U				U	U			C				U						U	U	U									U			U			
GENERAL MANAGEMENT	Maintain program accounts		U	U				U				U	U					C													U	U		U		U	U	U	U		U		
GENERAL MANAGEMENT	Conduct audits			U	U			U	U							U	U	C		U									U														
GENERAL MANAGEMENT	Establish organizations		U		U			U												C	U								U	U													U
GENERAL MANAGEMENT	Manage human resources		U		U	U	U	U												C	C	C	C	C																			
GENERAL MANAGEMENT	Provide security			U	U		U	U	U																C	C	C	C		U													
GENERAL MANAGEMENT	Manage equipment		U		U		U	U	U																C	C	C	C															
GENERAL MANAGEMENT	Manage facilities		U		U			U																	U	U	C																
GENERAL MANAGEMENT	Manage supplies		U		U			U																	C	U	U	C															
GENERAL MANAGEMENT	Manage workloads	U		U	U	U		U						U											U	U	U	U	C	C		U		U		U						U	U
PROGRAM ADMINISTRATION	Issue Social Security numbers							U				U		U																	C	C											
PROGRAM ADMINISTRATION	Maintain earnings							U				U	U	U																	U		C	C	C	C	U						
PROGRAM ADMINISTRATION	Collect claims information				U	U		U					U																		U	U				C	C	U	U	U			
PROGRAM ADMINISTRATION	Determine eligibility/entitlement							U																							U	U	U			U		C	U	U			
PROGRAM ADMINISTRATION	Compute payments				U			U										U													U		U			U		U	C	C			
PROGRAM ADMINISTRATION	Administer debt management				U			U										U																					U	C			
SUPPORT	Generate notices							U							U																U		U			U		U	U	U	C		
SUPPORT	Respond to program inquiries				U			U		U																					U		U	U		U		U	U	U	U	C	
SUPPORT	Provide quality assessment				U	U		U	U																						U		U			U		U				U	C

KEY: C = creators of data   U = users of data

This chart depicts which data classes are required to support particular organizational processes and which processes are the creators and users of data.

FIGURE 10-2 *Using CSFs to develop systems.*

of CSFs and require a broad inquiry into what information is used in the organization. This method explicitly asks managers to examine their environments and consider how their analyses shape their information needs. It is especially suitable for top management and for the development of decision-support systems (DSS) and executive support systems (ESS). Unlike enterprise analysis, the CSF method focuses organizational attention on how information should be handled.

The method's primary weakness is that the aggregation process and the analysis of the data are art forms. There is no particularly rigorous way in which individual CSFs can be aggregated into a clear company pattern. Second, interviewees (and interviewers) often become confused when distinguishing between *individual* and *organizational* CSFs. These types of CSFs are not necessarily the same. What may be considered critical to a manager may not be important for the organization as a whole. This method is clearly biased toward top managers although it could be extended to elicit ideas for promising new systems from lower-level members of the organization (Peffers and Gengler 2003).

Systems Development and Organizational Change

Information technology can promote various degrees of organizational change, ranging from incremental to far-reaching. Figure 10-3 shows four kinds of structural organizational change that are enabled by information technology: automation, rationalization, reengineering, and paradigm shifts. Each carries different rewards and risks.

The most common form of IT-enabled organizational change is **automation**, using computers to speed up the performance of existing tasks. The first applications of information technology involved assisting employees with performing their tasks more efficiently and effectively. Calculating paycheques and payroll registers, giving bank tellers instant access to customer deposit records, and developing a nationwide network of airline reservation terminals are all examples of early automation.

A deeper form of organizational change—one that follows quickly from early automation—is **rationalization of procedures**. Automation frequently reveals new bottlenecks in production and makes the existing arrangement of procedures and structures painfully cumbersome. Rationalization of procedures is the streamlining of standard operating

automation

rationalization of procedures

procedures. For example, the Victoria CFA's new emergency management system described in the chapter-opening case is effective not only because it uses computer technology but also because its design enables the organization to operate more efficiently. The procedures of the Victoria CFA, or any organization, must be rationally structured to achieve this result. CFA needed standard identification codes for emergency equipment, fire brigades, and localities and standard rules for routing brigades and equipment to the appropriate emergency location. Without a certain amount of rationalization in the CFA's organization, its computer technology would have been useless.

A more powerful type of organizational change is **business process reengineering**, in which business processes are analyzed, simplified, and redesigned. Using information technology, organizations can rethink and streamline their business processes to improve speed, service, and quality. Business reengineering reorganizes work flows, combining steps to cut waste and eliminating repetitive, paper-intensive tasks (sometimes the new design eliminates jobs as well). It is much more ambitious than rationalization of procedures, requiring a new vision of how the process is to be organized.

A widely cited example of business reengineering is Ford Motor Company's invoiceless processing, which reduced headcount in Ford's North American accounts payable organization (500 staff) by 75 percent. Accounts payable clerks used to spend most of their time resolving discrepancies between purchase orders, receiving documents, and invoices. Ford reengineered its accounts payable process so that when the purchasing department enters a purchase order into an online database, it can be checked by the receiving department when the ordered items arrive. If the received goods match the purchase order, the system automatically generates a cheque for accounts payable to send to the vendor. There is no need for vendors to send invoices (Hammer and Champy 1993).

Rationalizing procedures and redesigning business processes are limited to specific parts of a business. New information systems can ultimately affect the design of the entire organization by transforming how the organization carries out its business or even the nature of the business. For instance, the long-haul trucking and transportation firm TransX, headquartered in Manitoba, used new information systems to change its business model. TransX created a new business managing logistics for other companies. Baxter International's stockless inventory system (described in Chapter 3) transformed Baxter into a hospital partner and manager of its customers' supplies. This more radical form of business change is called a **paradigm shift**. A paradigm shift involves rethinking the nature of the business and the nature of the organization.

Paradigm shifts and reengineering often fail because extensive organizational change is so difficult to orchestrate (see Chapter 11). Why, then, do so many corporations contemplate such radical change? Because the rewards are equally high (see Figure 10-3). In many instances, firms seeking paradigm shifts and pursuing reengineering strategies achieve stunning, order-of-magnitude increases in their returns on investment (or productivity). Some of these success stories, and some failure stories, are included throughout this book.

10.2 Business Process Reengineering and Process Improvement

Many companies today are focusing on developing new information systems that will improve their business processes. Some of these system projects represent radical restructuring of business processes while others entail more incremental process change.

Business Process Reengineering

If organizations rethink and radically redesign their business processes before applying computing power, they can potentially obtain very large payoffs from their investments in information technology. We now look at how the home mortgage industry in the United States accomplished this goal.

business process reengineering

paradigm shift

FIGURE 10-3   *Organizational change carries risks and rewards.*

The most common forms of organizational change are automation and rationalization. These relatively slow-moving and slow-changing strategies present modest returns but little risk. Faster and more comprehensive change—such as reengineering and paradigm shifts—carries high rewards but offers substantial chance of failure.

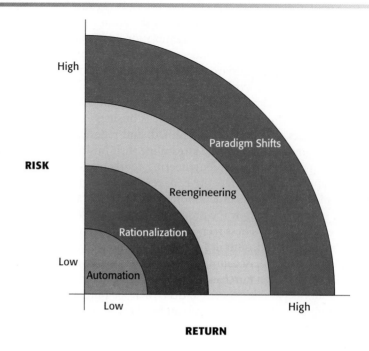

The application process for a home mortgage currently takes about six to eight weeks and costs about $38 000. The goal of many mortgage banks is to reduce that cost to $1250 and the time to obtain a mortgage to about one week. Leading U.S. mortgage banks, such as BankBoston, Countrywide Funding Corporation, and Banc One Corporation, have redesigned the mortgage application process to reduce the cost to $1000 and the time to obtain a mortgage to about one week (see Figure 10-4).

In the past, a mortgage applicant filled out a paper loan application. The bank entered the application into its computer system. Specialists, such as credit analysts and underwriters from perhaps eight different departments, accessed and evaluated the application individually. If the loan application was approved, the closing was scheduled. After the closing, bank specialists dealing with insurance or funds in escrow serviced the loan. This "desk-to-desk" assembly-line approach might take up to 17 days.

The banks replaced the sequential desk-to-desk approach with a speedier "work cell" or team approach. Now, loan originators in the field enter the mortgage application directly into laptop computers. Software checks the application transaction to make sure that all of the information is correct and complete. The loan originators transmit the loan applications over a network to regional production centres. Instead of working on the application individually, the credit analysts, loan underwriters, and other specialists convene electronically, working as a team to approve the mortgage.

After closing, another team of specialists sets up the loan for servicing. The entire loan application process can take as little as two days. Loan information is easier to access than before, when the loan application could be in eight or nine different departments. Loan originators also can dial into the bank's network to obtain information on mortgage loan costs or to check the status of a loan for the customer.

By radically rethinking their approaches to mortgage processing, mortgage banks have achieved remarkable efficiencies. They have not focused on redesigning a single business process, but instead they have re-examined the entire set of logically connected processes required to obtain a mortgage.

To support the new mortgage application process, the banks have implemented work flow and document management software. **Work flow management** is the process of streamlining business procedures so that documents can be moved easily and efficiently. Work flow and document management software automates processes such as routing documents to different locations, securing approvals, scheduling, and generating reports.

work flow management

FIGURE 10-4   *Redesigning mortgage processing in the United States.*

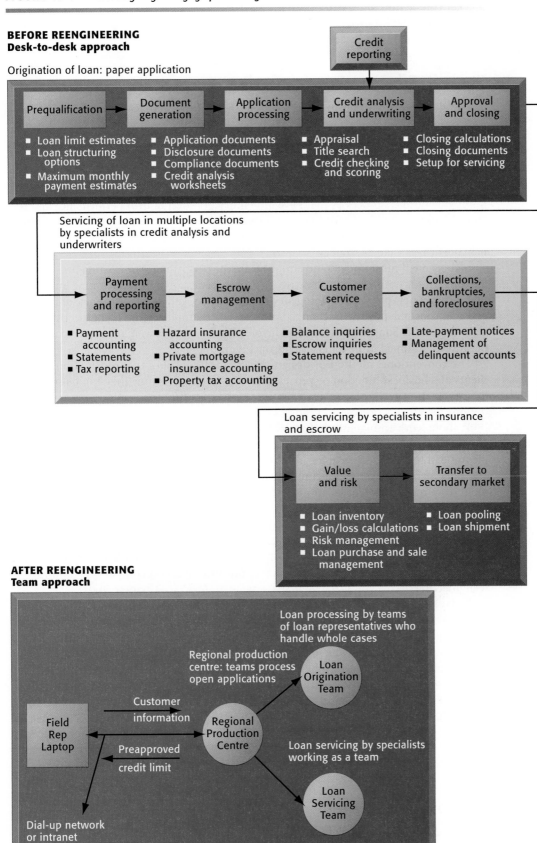

BEFORE REENGINEERING
Desk-to-desk approach

Origination of loan: paper application

Credit reporting

Prequalification → Document generation → Application processing → Credit analysis and underwriting → Approval and closing

- Loan limit estimates
- Loan structuring options
- Maximum monthly payment estimates

- Application documents
- Disclosure documents
- Compliance documents
- Credit analysis worksheets

- Appraisal
- Title search
- Credit checking and scoring

- Closing calculations
- Closing documents
- Setup for servicing

Servicing of loan in multiple locations by specialists in credit analysis and underwriters

Payment processing and reporting → Escrow management → Customer service → Collections, bankruptcies, and foreclosures

- Payment accounting
- Statements
- Tax reporting

- Hazard insurance accounting
- Private mortgage insurance accounting
- Property tax accounting

- Balance inquiries
- Escrow inquiries
- Statement requests

- Late-payment notices
- Management of delinquent accounts

Loan servicing by specialists in insurance and escrow

Value and risk → Transfer to secondary market

- Loan inventory
- Gain/loss calculations
- Risk management
- Loan purchase and sale management

- Loan pooling
- Loan shipment

AFTER REENGINEERING
Team approach

Loan processing by teams of loan representatives who handle whole cases

Regional production centre: teams process open applications

Loan Origination Team

Field Rep Laptop — Customer information → Regional Production Centre

Preapproved credit limit

Loan servicing by specialists working as a team

Loan Servicing Team

Dial-up network or intranet

By redesigning their mortgage processing systems and mortgage application process, mortgage banks will be able to reduce the costs of processing the average mortgage from $3800 to $1250 and reduce the time of approval from six weeks to one week or less. Some banks are even preapproving mortgages and locking interest rates on the same day the customer applies.

Two or more people can work simultaneously on the same document, allowing much quicker completion time. Work need not be delayed because a file is out or a document is in transit. And with a properly designed indexing system, users will be able to retrieve files in many different ways, based on the content of the document.

Steps in Effective Reengineering

One of the most important strategic decisions that a firm can make is not deciding how to use computers to improve business processes but rather understanding what business processes need improvement. When systems are used to strengthen the wrong business model or business processes, the business can become more efficient at doing what it should not do (Hammer 2002). As a result, the firm becomes vulnerable to competitors who may have discovered the right business model. Considerable time and cost can also be spent improving business processes that have little impact on overall firm performance and revenue. Managers need to determine what business processes are the most important to focus on when applying new information technology and how improving these processes will help the firm execute its strategy.

Management must understand and measure the performance of existing processes as a baseline. If, for example, the objective of process redesign is to reduce time and cost in developing a new product or filling an order, the organization needs to measure the time and cost consumed by the unchanged process. For example, before reengineering, it cost C. R. England & Sons $6.45 to send an invoice; after processes were reengineered, the cost per invoice dropped to 19 cents (Davidson 1993).

The conventional method of designing systems establishes the information requirements of a business function or process and then determines how they can be supported by information technology. However, information technology can create new design options for various processes because it can be used to challenge long-standing assumptions about work arrangements that used to inhibit organizations. For example, the mortgage processing application we just described shows that it is no longer necessary for people to be in the same physical location to work together on a document. Using networks and document management technology, people can access and work on the same document from many different locations. Information technology should be allowed to influence process design from the start.

Following these steps does not automatically guarantee that reengineering will always be successful. The majority of reengineering projects do not achieve breakthrough gains in business performance because the organizational changes are often very difficult to manage. Managing change is neither simple nor intuitive, and companies committed to reengineering need a good change management strategy (see Chapter 11).

Today's digital firm environment involves much closer coordination of a firm's business processes with those of customers, suppliers, and other business partners than in the past. Organizations are required to make business process changes that span organizational boundaries. These inter-organizational processes, such as those for supply chain management, not only need to be streamlined but also coordinated and integrated with those of other business partners. In such cases, reengineering will involve many companies working together to jointly redesign their shared processes. Reengineering expert James Champy calls the joint redesign of inter-organizational business processes *X-engineering,* and it is even more challenging to implement successfully than reengineering processes for a single company (Champy 2002). We examine the organizational change issues surrounding reengineering more carefully in Chapter 11.

Process Improvement: Business Process Management, Total Quality Management, and Six Sigma

Business process reengineering (BPR) is primarily a one-time effort, focusing on identifying one or two strategic business processes that need radical change. BPR projects tend to be expensive and organizationally disruptive. But organizations have many business processes and support processes that must be constantly revised to keep the business competitive. Business process management and quality improvement programs provide opportunities for incremental and ongoing types of business process change.

Business Process Management Mergers and acquisitions, changes in business models, new industry requirements, and changing customer expectations all pose multiple process-related problems that continually confront organizations. Business process management (BPM), which we also discuss in Chapter 14, enables organizations to manage incremental process changes that are required simultaneously in many areas of the business. It provides a methodology and tools for dealing with the organization's ongoing need to revise—and ideally optimize—its numerous internal business processes and processes shared with other organizations. It enables organizations to make continual improvements to many business processes simultaneously and to use processes as the fundamental building blocks of corporate information systems.

BPM includes work flow management, business process modelling, quality management, and change management. It also includes tools for recasting the firm's business processes into a standardized form where they can be continually manipulated. Companies practicing business process management use process-mapping tools to identify and document existing processes and to create models of improved processes that can then be translated into software systems. The process models might require entirely new systems or could be based on existing systems and data. BPM software tools automatically manage processes across the business, extract data from various sources and databases, and generate transactions in multiple related systems (see Figure 10-5).

BPM also includes process monitoring and analytics. Organizations must be able to verify that process performance has been improved and measure the impact of process changes on key business performance indicators. A number of commercial software vendors, including IBM, BEA Systems, Vitria, Intalio, FileNet, TIBCO, Fuego, and Vancouver's ACL Services Ltd. supply business process management products.

Oil refiner Tesoro Petroleum set up a business process office with six full-time employees to oversee process improvements. This group recently used Fuego BPM software to

FIGURE 10-5   *BPM software tools.*

TIBCO Business Process Management software provides a graphical interface that lets users model, monitor, and modify process flows.

create—in six weeks—a sales order entry process that interacts with SAP enterprise software. It is also using the software to automate mission-critical processes, such as order-to-cash (sales and invoicing), purchase-to-pay (accounts receivable), and capital budgeting to asset retirement. Tesoro's management reports that business process management has helped the company improve cycle times and reduce non-value-added activities and errors. Transactions that previously took four days are instantaneous and more accurate because the data are verified. Employees who previously spent most of their time entering data can now devote themselves to analyzing data and handling exceptions. By making processes easier to perform, the company has also lowered support costs (Lunt 2003).

Total Quality Management and Six Sigma Quality management is another area of continuous process improvement. In addition to increasing organizational efficiency, companies must fine-tune their business processes to improve the quality in their products, services, and operations. Many are using the concept of **total quality management (TQM)** to make quality the responsibility of all people and functions within an organization. TQM holds that the achievement of quality control is an end in itself. Everyone is expected to contribute to the overall improvement of quality—the engineer who avoids design errors, the production worker who spots defects, the sales representative who presents the product properly to potential customers, and even the secretary who avoids typing mistakes. TQM derives from quality management concepts developed by American quality experts such as W. Edwards Deming and Joseph Juran, but it was popularized by the Japanese.

Another quality concept that is being widely implemented today is six sigma. **Six sigma** is a specific measure of quality, representing 3.4 defects per million opportunities for defects. Most companies cannot achieve this level of quality but use six sigma as a goal to implement a set of methodologies and techniques for improving quality and reducing costs. Studies have repeatedly shown that the earlier in the business cycle a problem is eliminated, the less it costs the company. Thus, quality improvements not only raise the level of product and service quality, but they can also lower costs.

How Information Systems Support Quality Improvements The implementation of TQM and six sigma are considered to be more incremental processes than business process reengineering. TQM typically focuses on making a series of incremental continuous improvements rather than dramatic bursts of change. Six sigma uses statistical analysis tools to detect flaws in the execution of an existing process and make minor adjustments. Sometimes, however, processes may have to be fully reengineered to achieve a specified level of quality. Information systems can help firms achieve their quality goals by helping them simplify products or processes, make improvements based on customer demands, reduce cycle time, improve the quality and precision of design and production, and meet benchmarking standards.

Benchmarking consists of setting strict standards for products, services, and other activities and then measuring performance against those standards. Companies may use external industry standards, standards set by other companies, internally developed high standards, or some combination of the three. L.L. Bean, the Freeport, Maine, outdoor clothing company, used benchmarking to achieve an order-shipping accuracy of 99.9 percent. Its old batch order fulfillment system could not handle the surging volume and variety of items to be shipped. After studying German and Scandinavian companies with leading-edge order fulfillment operations, L.L. Bean carefully redesigned its order fulfillment process and information systems so that orders could be processed as soon as they were received and shipped within 24 hours. You can find other examples of systems promoting quality improvements throughout this text.

10.3 Overview of Systems Development

total quality management (TQM)
six sigma
benchmarking

Whatever their scope and objectives, new information systems are a result of organizational problem solving. A new information system is developed as a solution to some type of problem or set of problems the organization perceives it is facing. The problem may be one in which managers and employees realize that the organization is not performing as well as expected, or it may come from the realization that the organization should take advantage of new opportunities to perform more successfully.

The activities that go into producing an information system solution to an organizational problem or opportunity are called **systems development**. Systems development is a structured kind of problem solving with distinct activities. These activities consist of systems analysis, systems design, programming, testing, conversion, and production and maintenance.

Figure 10-6 illustrates the systems development process. The systems development activities depicted here usually take place in sequential order. But some of the activities may need to be repeated, or some may take place simultaneously, depending on the approach to system development that is being employed (see section 10.4).

Systems Analysis

Systems analysis is the analysis of a problem that the organization will try to solve with an information system. It consists of defining the problem, identifying its causes, specifying the solution, and identifying the information requirements that must be met by a new or improved system.

The systems analyst creates a road map of the existing organization and systems, identifying the primary owners and users of data along with existing hardware and software. The systems analyst then details the problems of existing systems. By examining documents, work papers, and procedures; observing system operations; and interviewing key users of the systems, the analyst can identify the problem areas and objectives a solution would achieve. Often the solution requires developing a new information system or improving an existing one.

When a system needs upgrading, it is important to identify the gaps between the user requirements and what the current system actually does. It is also important to have user input in identifying what the problem really is, not just its symptoms. For example, users might identify the problem as a screen that is hard to read because the data isn't properly lined up and important data is hard to find; the real problem might be that the actual data they need to examine is not even displayed on that screen.

The systems analysis includes a **feasibility study** to determine whether the solution is feasible, or achievable, from a financial, technical, and organizational standpoint.

A feasibility study determines whether the proposed system is a good investment, whether the technology needed for the system is available and could be handled by the firm's information systems specialists, and whether the organization can handle the changes introduced by the system.

FIGURE 10-6   *The systems development process.*

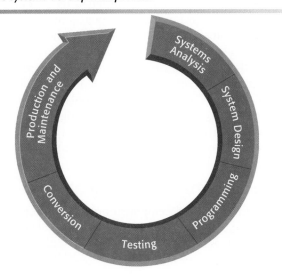

Building a system can be broken down into six core activities.

Normally, the systems analysis process identifies several alternative solutions that the organization can pursue. The process then assesses the feasibility of each. A written systems proposal report describes the costs and benefits, advantages, and disadvantages of each alternative. It is up to management to determine which mix of costs, benefits, technical features, and organizational impacts represents the most desirable alternative.

Establishing Information Requirements Perhaps the most challenging task of the systems analyst is to define the specific information requirements that must be met by the system solution selected. At the most basic level, the **information requirements** of a new system involve identifying who needs what information, where, when, and how. Requirements analysis carefully defines the objectives of the new or modified system and develops a detailed description of the functions that the new system must perform. Faulty requirements analysis is a leading cause of systems failure and high systems development costs (see Chapter 11). A system designed around the wrong set of requirements will either have to be discarded because of poor performance or will need to undergo major modifications. Section 10.4 describes alternative approaches to eliciting requirements that help minimize this problem.

Some problems do not require an information system solution but instead need an adjustment in management, additional training, or refinement of existing organizational procedures. If the problem is information related, systems analysis may still be required to diagnose the problem and arrive at the proper solution.

Systems Design

Systems analysis describes what a system should do to meet information requirements, and **systems design** shows how the system will fulfill this objective. The design of an information system is the overall plan or model for that system. Like the blueprint of a building or house, it consists of all the specifications that give the system its form and structure.

The systems designer details the system specifications that will deliver the functions identified during systems analysis. These specifications should address all of the managerial, organizational, and technological components of the system solution. Table 10-3 lists the types of specifications that would be produced during systems design.

Like houses or buildings, information systems may have many possible designs. Each design represents a unique blend of all technical and organizational components. What makes one design superior to others is the ease and efficiency with which it fulfills user requirements within a specific set of technical, organizational, financial, and time constraints.

The Role of End Users User information requirements drive the entire system-development effort. Users must have sufficient control over the design process to ensure that the system reflects their business priorities and information needs, not the biases of the technical staff. Working on design increases users' understanding and acceptance of the system. As we describe in Chapter 11, insufficient user involvement in the design effort is a major cause of system failure. However, some systems require more user involvement in design than others, and section 10.4 shows how alternative systems development methods address the user participation issue.

One final issue is the difference in user involvement and user participation. Involvement is a perception of having input into the process while participation is actually having to attend meetings, review most materials, etc. Most users want to feel involved; fewer want to participate in terms of devoting significant time and effort to systems projects. Finding the ideal degree of user involvement and participation can be a significant challenge. There are no easy answers to this challenge.

Completing the Systems Development Process

The remaining steps in the systems development process translate the solution specifications established during systems analysis and design into a fully operational information system. These concluding steps consist of programming, testing, conversion, production, and maintenance.

information requirements

systems design

TABLE 10-3 *Design Specifications*

OUTPUT Medium Content Timing	**CONTROLS** Input controls (characters, limit, reasonableness) Processing controls (consistency, record counts) Output controls (totals, samples of output) Procedural controls (passwords, special forms)
INPUT Origins Flow Data entry	**SECURITY** Access controls Catastrophe plans Audit trails
USER INTERFACE Simplicity Efficiency Logic Feedback Errors	**DOCUMENTATION** Operations documentation Systems documents User documentation
DATABASE DESIGN Logical data model Volume and speed requirements File organization and design Record specifications	**CONVERSION** Transfer files Initiate new procedures Select testing method Cut over to new system
PROCESSING Computations Program modules Required reports Timing of outputs	**TRAINING** Select training techniques Develop training modules Identify training facilities
MANUAL PROCEDURES What activities Who performs them When How Where	**ORGANIZATIONAL CHANGES** Task redesign Job design Process design Organization structure design Reporting relationships

Programming During the **programming** stage, system specifications that were prepared during the design stage are translated into software program code. Today, many organizations no longer do their own programming for new systems. Instead, they purchase the software that meets the requirements for a new system from external sources such as software packages from a commercial software vendor, software services from an application service provider, or outsourcing firms that develop custom application software for their clients (see section 10.4).

Testing Exhaustive and thorough **testing** must be conducted to ascertain whether the system produces the right results. Testing answers the question, "Will the system produce the desired results under known conditions?"

The amount of time needed to answer this question has been traditionally underrated in systems project planning (see Chapter 11). Testing is time consuming: Test data must be carefully prepared, results reviewed, and corrections made in the system. In some instances, parts of the system may have to be redesigned. The risks resulting from glossing over this step are enormous.

Testing an information system can be broken down into three types of activities: unit testing, system testing, and acceptance testing. **Unit testing**, or program testing, consists of testing each program separately in the system. It is widely believed that the purpose of such testing is to guarantee that programs are error free, but this goal is realistically

programming

testing

unit testing

Building successful information systems requires close cooperation among end users and information systems specialists throughout the systems development process.

impossible. Testing should be viewed instead as a means of locating errors in programs. Testing should focus on finding all the ways to make a program fail. Once these problems are pinpointed, they can be corrected.

System testing tests the functioning of the information system as a whole. It tries to determine whether discrete modules will function together as planned and whether discrepancies exist between the way the system actually works and the way it was conceived. Among the areas examined are performance time, capacity for file storage and handling peak loads, recovery and restart capabilities, and manual procedures.

Acceptance testing provides the final certification that the system is ready to be used in a production setting. System tests are evaluated by users and reviewed by management. When all parties are satisfied that the new system meets their standards, the system is formally accepted for installation.

The systems development team works with users to devise a systematic test plan. The **test plan** includes all of the preparations for the series of tests we have just described.

Figure 10-7 shows an example of a test plan. The general condition being tested is a record change. The documentation consists of a series of test-plan screens maintained on a database (perhaps a microcomputer database) that is ideally suited to this kind of application.

Conversion **Conversion** is the process of changing from the old system to the new system. Four main conversion strategies can be employed: the parallel strategy, the direct cutover strategy, the pilot study strategy, and the phased approach strategy.

In a **parallel strategy** both the old system and its potential replacement are run together for a time until everyone is assured that the new system functions correctly. This is the safest conversion approach because, in the event of errors or processing disruptions, the old system can still be used as a backup. However, this approach is very expensive, and additional staff or resources may be required to run the extra system.

The **direct cutover** strategy replaces the old system entirely with the new system on an appointed day. It is a very risky approach that can potentially be more costly than running two systems in parallel if serious problems with the new system are found. There is no other system to fall back on. Dislocations, disruptions, and the cost of corrections may be enormous.

FIGURE 10-7   *A sample test plan to test a record change.*

When developing a test plan, it is imperative to include the various conditions to be tested, the requirements for each condition tested, and the expected results. Test plans require input from both end users and information systems specialists.

system testing

acceptance testing

test plan

conversion

parallel strategy

direct cutover

Procedure	Address and Maintenance "Record Change Series"		Test Series 2		
	Prepared By:	Date:	Version:		
Test Ref.	Condition Tested	Special Requirements	Expected Results	Output On	Next Screen
2.0	Change records				
2.1	Change existing record	Key field	Not allowed		
2.2	Change nonexistent record	Other fields	"Invalid key" message		
2.3	Change deleted record	Deleted record must be available	"Deleted" message		
2.4	Make second record	Change 2.1 above	OK if valid	Transaction file	V45
2.5	Insert record		OK if valid	Transaction file	V45
2.6	Abort during change	Abort 2.5	No change	Transaction file	V45

The **pilot study** strategy introduces the new system to only a limited area of the organization, such as a single department or operating unit. When this pilot version is complete and working smoothly, it is installed throughout the rest of the organization, either simultaneously or in stages.

The **phased approach** strategy introduces the new system in stages, either by functions or by organizational units. If, for example, the system is introduced by functions, a new payroll system might begin with hourly workers who are paid weekly, followed six months later by adding salaried employees (who are paid monthly) to the system. If the system is introduced by organizational units, corporate headquarters might be converted first, followed by outlying operating units four months later.

Moving from an old system to a new one requires that end users be trained to use the new system. Detailed **documentation** showing how the system works from both a technical and end-user standpoint is finalized during conversion time for use in training and everyday operations. Lack of proper training and documentation contributes to system failure, so this portion of the systems development process is very important.

Production and Maintenance After the new system is installed and conversion is complete, the system is said to be in **production**. During this stage, the system will be reviewed by both users and technical specialists to determine how well it has met its original objectives and to decide whether any revisions or modifications are in order. In some instances, a formal **post-implementation audit** document is prepared. After the system has been fine-tuned, it must be maintained while it is in production to correct errors, meet requirements, or improve processing efficiency. Changes in hardware, software, documentation, or procedures to a production system to correct errors, meet new requirements, or improve processing efficiency are termed **maintenance**.

Studies of maintenance have examined the amount of time required for various maintenance tasks (Lientz and Swanson 1980). Approximately 20 percent of the time is devoted to debugging or correcting emergency production problems; another 20 percent is concerned with changes in data, files, reports, hardware, or system software. But 60 percent of all maintenance work consists of making user enhancements, improving documentation, and recoding system components for greater processing efficiency. The amount of work in the third category of maintenance problems could be reduced significantly through better systems analysis and design practices. Table 10-4 summarizes the systems development activities.

TABLE 10-4 *Systems Development*

CORE ACTIVITY	DESCRIPTION
Systems analysis	Identify problem(s) Specify solutions Establish information requirements
Systems design	Create design specifications
Programming	Translate design specifications into program code
Testing	Unit test Systems test Acceptance test
Conversion	Plan conversion Prepare documentation Train users and technical staff
Production and maintenance	Operate the system Evaluate the system Modify the system

pilot study
phased approach
documentation
production
post-implementation audit
maintenance

Modelling and Designing Systems: Structured and Object-Oriented Methodologies

There are alternative **development methodologies**, or approaches, for developing systems. Part of such a methodology is the modelling and designing of systems. These methodologies are a collection of methods, one or more for every activity within every phase of a development project. Structured methodologies and object-oriented development are the most prominent.

Structured Methodologies Structured methodologies have been used to document, analyze, and design information systems since the 1970s. **Structured** refers to the fact that the techniques are step by step, with each step building on the previous one. Structured methodologies are top-down, progressing from the highest, most abstract level to the lowest level of detail—from the general to the specific.

Structured development methods are process-oriented, focusing primarily on modelling the processes, or actions that capture, store, manipulate, and distribute data as the data flow through a system. These methods separate data from processes. A separate programming procedure must be written every time someone wants to take an action on a particular piece of data. The procedures act on data that the program passes to them.

The primary tool for representing a system's component processes and the flow of data between them is the **data flow diagram (DFD)**. The data flow diagram offers a logical graphic model of information flow, partitioning a system into modules that show manageable levels of detail. It rigorously specifies the processes or transformations that occur within each **module**, or logical unit of a program that performs one or several functions, and the interfaces that exist between them.

Figure 10-8 shows a simple data flow diagram for a mail-in university course registration system. The rounded boxes represent processes, which portray the transformation of data. The square box represents an external entity, which is an originator or receiver of information located outside the boundaries of the system being modelled. The open rectangles represent data stores, which are either manual or automated inventories of data. The arrows represent data flows, which show the movement between processes, external entities, and data stores. They always contain packets of data with the name or content of each data flow listed beside the arrow.

This data flow diagram shows that students submit registration forms with their name, identification number, and the numbers of the courses they wish to take. In process 1.0, the system verifies that each course selected is still open by referencing the university's course file. The file distinguishes courses that are open from those that have been cancelled or filled. Process 1.0 then determines which of the student's selections can be accepted or rejected. Process 2.0 enrols the student in the courses for which he or she has been accepted. It updates the university's course file with the student's name and identification number and recalculates the class size. If maximum enrolment has been reached, the course number is flagged as closed. Process 2.0 also updates the university's student master file with information about new students or changes in address. Process 3.0 then sends each student applicant a confirmation-of-registration letter listing the courses for which he or she is registered and noting the course selections that could not be fulfilled.

The diagrams can be used to depict higher-level processes as well as lower-level details. Through levelled data flow diagrams, a complex process can be broken down into successive levels of detail. An entire system can be divided into subsystems with a high-level data flow diagram. Each subsystem, in turn, can be divided into additional subsystems with second-level data flow diagrams, and the lower-level subsystems can be broken down again until the lowest level of detail has been reached.

Another tool for structured analysis is a data dictionary, which contains information about individual pieces of data and data groupings within a system (see Chapter 6). The data dictionary defines the contents of data flows and data stores so that systems developers understand exactly what pieces of data they contain. **Process specifications** describe the transformation occurring within the lowest level of the data flow diagrams. They express the logic for each process.

development methodologies

structured

data flow diagram (DFD)

module

process specifications

FIGURE 10-8 *Data flow diagram for mail-in university registration system.*

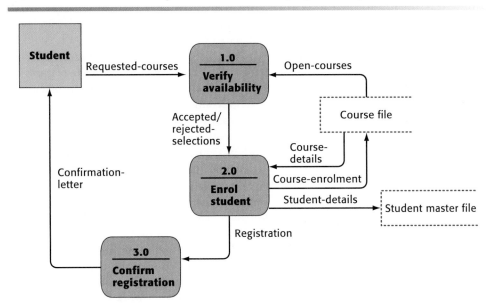

The system has three processes: Verify availability (1.0), Enrol student (2.0), and Confirm registration (3.0). The name and content of each of the data flows appear adjacent to each arrow. There is one external entity in this system: the student. There are two data stores: the student master file and the course file.

In structured methodology, software design is modelled using hierarchical structure charts. The **structure chart** is a top-down chart, showing each level of design, its relationship to other levels, and its place in the overall design structure. The design first considers the main function of a program or system, then breaks this function into subfunctions, and decomposes each subfunction until the lowest level of detail has been reached. Figure 10-9 shows a high-level structure chart for a payroll system. If a design has too many levels to fit onto one structure chart, it can be broken down further on more detailed structure charts. A structure chart may document one program, one system (a set of programs), or part of one program.

Object-Oriented Development Structured methods are useful for modelling processes, but they do not handle data modelling well. They also treat data and processes as logically separate entities while in the real world, such separation seems unnatural. Different modelling conventions are used for analysis (the data flow diagram) and for design (the structure chart).

Object-oriented development and **object-oriented programming** deal with these issues. They use the **object** as the basic unit of systems analysis and design. An object combines data and the specific processes that operate on those data. Data encapsulated in an object can be accessed and modified only by the operations, or methods, associated with that object. Instead of passing data to procedures, programs send a message for an object

structure chart
object-oriented development
object-oriented programming
object

FIGURE 10-9 *High-level structure chart for a payroll system.*

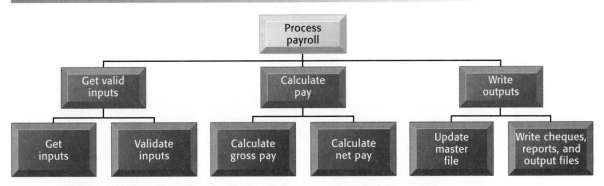

This structure chart shows the highest or most abstract level of design for a payroll system, providing an overview of the entire system.

to perform an operation that is already embedded in it. The system is modelled as a collection of objects and the relationships among them. Because processing logic resides within objects rather than in separate software programs, objects must collaborate with each other to make the system work.

Object-oriented modelling is based on the concepts of *class* and *inheritance*. Objects belonging to a certain class, or general categories of similar objects, have the features of that class. Classes of objects in turn can inherit all the structure and behaviours of a more general class and then add variables and behaviours unique to each object. New classes of objects are created by choosing an existing class and specifying how the new class differs from the existing class, instead of starting from scratch each time.

We can see how class and inheritance work in Figure 10-10, which illustrates the relationships among classes concerning employees and how they are paid. Employee is the common ancestor, or superclass, for the other three classes. Salaried, Hourly, and Temporary are subclasses of Employee. The class name is in the top compartment, the attributes for each class are in the middle portion of each box, and the list of operations is in the bottom portion of each box. The features that are shared by all employees (id, name, address, date hired, position, and pay) are stored in the Employee superclass while each subclass stores features that are specific to that particular type of employee. Specific to Hourly employees, for example, are their hourly rates and overtime rates. A solid line from the subclass to the superclass is a generalization path showing that the subclasses Salaried, Hourly, and Temporary have common features that can be generalized into the superclass Employee.

The phases of object-oriented development are similar to those of conventional systems development, consisting of analysis, design, and implementation. However, object-oriented development is more iterative and incremental than traditional structured development. During analysis, systems developers document the functional requirements of the system, specifying its most important properties and what the proposed system must do. Interactions between the system and its users are analyzed to identify objects, which include both data and processes. The object-oriented design phase describes how the objects will behave and how they will interact with one other. Similar objects are grouped together to form a class, and classes are grouped into hierarchies in which a subclass inherits the attributes and methods from its superclass.

FIGURE 10-10 *Class and inheritance.*

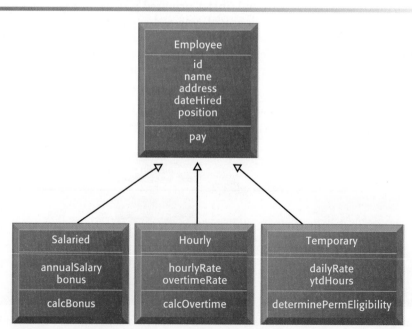

This figure illustrates how classes inherit the common features of their superclass.

The information system is implemented by translating the design into program code, reusing classes that are already available in a library of reusable software objects, and adding new ones created during the object-oriented design phase. Implementation may also involve the creation of an object-oriented database. The resulting system must be thoroughly tested and evaluated.

Because objects are reusable, object-oriented development could potentially reduce the time and cost of writing software because organizations can reuse software objects that have already been created as building blocks for other applications. New systems can be created by using some existing objects, changing others, and adding a few new objects. Object-oriented frameworks have been developed to provide reusable, semicomplete applications that the organization can further customize into finished applications.

Unified Modeling Language (UML) has become the industry standard for representing various views of an object-oriented system using a series of graphical diagrams. The underlying model integrates these views to promote consistency during analysis, design, and implementation. UML uses two principal types of diagrams: structural diagrams and behavioural diagrams.

Structural diagrams are used to describe the relationship between classes. Figure 10-9 is an example of one type of structural diagram called a class diagram. It shows classes of employees and the relationships between them. The terminators at the end of the relationship lines in this diagram indicate the nature of the relationship. The relationships depicted in Figure 10-9 are examples of *generalization*, which is a relationship between a general kind of thing and a more specific kind of thing. This type of relationship is sometimes described as "is a relationship." Generalization relationships are used for modelling class inheritance.

Behavioural diagrams are used to describe interactions in an object-oriented system. Figure 10-11 illustrates one type of behavioural diagram called a use case diagram. A use case diagram shows the relationship between an actor and a system. The actor (represented in the diagram as a stick man) is an external entity that interacts with the system, and the use case represents a series of related actions initiated by the actor to accomplish a specific goal. Several interrelated use cases are represented as ovals within a box. Use case modelling is used to specify the functional requirements of a system, focusing on what the system does rather than how it does it. The system's objects and their interactions with each other and with the users of the system are derived from the use case model.

UML was developed by Grady Booch, Ivar Jacobson and James Rumbaugh to provide a single complete notation for describing object models. They turned their efforts to the development process. They came up with the rational unified process (RUP), which is a general framework that can be used to describe specific development processes. The RUP process consists of 4 processes: inception, elaboration, construction, and transition, each of which has steps that must be performed. RUP is iterative, that is, each phase or portion of a phase can be repeated as needed to fine-tune the outcome. More detail on RUP can be found on the Companion Website.

Computer-Aided Software Engineering Computer-aided software engineering (CASE)—sometimes called computer-aided systems engineering—provides software tools to automate the methodologies we have just described to reduce the amount of repetitive work the developer needs to do. CASE tools also facilitate the creation of clear documentation and the coordination of team development efforts. Team members can share their work easily by accessing each other's files to review or modify what has been done. Modest productivity benefits can also be achieved if the tools are used properly. Many CASE tools are PC-based, with powerful graphical capabilities.

CASE tools provide automated graphics facilities for producing charts and diagrams, screen and report generators, data dictionaries, extensive reporting facilities, analysis and checking tools, code generators, and documentation generators. In general, CASE tools try to increase productivity and software quality by doing the following:

- Enforce a standard development methodology and design discipline
- Improve communication between users and technical specialists
- Organize and correlate design components and provide rapid access to them using a design repository

Unified Modeling Language (UML)

computer-aided software engineering (CASE)

- Automate tedious and error-prone portions of analysis and design
- Automate code generation and testing and control rollout

Many CASE tools have been classified in terms of whether they support activities at the front end or the back end of the systems development process. Front-end CASE tools focus on capturing analysis and design information in the early stages of systems development while back-end CASE tools address coding, testing, and maintenance activities. Back-end tools help convert specifications automatically into program code.

CASE tools automatically tie data elements to the processes where they are used. If a data flow diagram is changed from one process to another, the elements in the data dictionary would be altered automatically to reflect the change in the diagram. CASE tools also contain features for validating design diagrams and specifications. CASE tools thus support iterative design by automating revisions and changes and providing prototyping facilities. A CASE information repository stores all the information defined by the analysts during the project. The repository includes data flow diagrams, structure charts, entity-relationship diagrams, data definitions, process specifications, screen and report formats, notes and comments, and test results.

To be used effectively, CASE tools require organizational discipline. Every member of a development project must adhere to a common set of naming conventions and standards as well as to a development methodology. The best CASE tools enforce common methods and standards, which may discourage their use in situations where organizational discipline is lacking.

FIGURE 10-11   *A UML use case diagram.*

Use case diagrams model the functions of a system, showing how objects interact with each other and with the users of the system. Illustrated here is a use case diagram for credit card processing that was created with SmartDraw software.

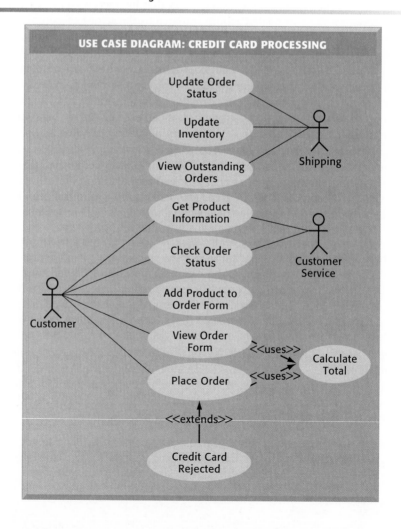

10.4 Alternative Systems-Development Approaches

Systems differ in terms of their size and technological complexity and in terms of the organizational problems they are meant to solve. A number of systems-development approaches have been developed to deal with these differences. This section describes these alternative methods: the traditional systems life cycle, prototyping, application software packages, end-user development, and outsourcing.

Traditional Systems Life Cycle

The **systems life cycle** is the oldest method for developing information systems. The life cycle methodology is a phased approach to developing a system, dividing systems development into formal stages. Systems development specialists have different opinions on how to partition the systems-development stages, but they roughly correspond to the stages of systems development that we have just described.

The systems life cycle methodology maintains a very formal division of labour between end users and information systems specialists. Technical specialists, such as system analysts and programmers, are responsible for much of the systems analysis, design, and implementation work; end users are limited to providing information requirements and reviewing the technical staff's work. The life cycle also emphasizes formal specifications and paperwork, so many documents are generated during the course of a systems project.

The systems life cycle is still used for developing large complex systems that require a rigorous and formal requirements analysis, predefined specifications, and tight controls over the systems-development process. However, the systems life cycle approach can be costly, time consuming, and inflexible. Although systems developers can go back and forth among stages in the life cycle, the systems life cycle is predominantly a "waterfall" approach in which tasks in one stage are completed before work for the next stage begins. Activities can be repeated, but volumes of new documents must be generated and steps retraced if requirements and specifications need to be revised. This encourages freezing of specifications relatively early in the development process. The life cycle approach is also not suitable for many small desktop systems, which tend to be less structured and more individualized.

Prototyping

Prototyping consists of developing an experimental system rapidly and inexpensively for end users to evaluate. By interacting with the prototype, users can get a better idea of their information requirements. The prototype endorsed by the users can be used as a template to create the final system.

The **prototype** is a working version of an information system or part of the system, but it is meant to be only a preliminary model. Once operational, the prototype will be further refined until it conforms precisely to users' requirements. Once the design has been finalized, the prototype can be converted to a polished production system.

The process of developing a preliminary design, trying it out, refining it, and trying again has been called an **iterative** process of systems development because the steps required to develop a system can be repeated over and over again. Prototyping is more explicitly iterative than the conventional life cycle, and it actively promotes system design changes. It has been said that prototyping replaces unplanned rework with planned iteration, with each version more accurately reflecting users' requirements.

Steps in Prototyping Figure 10-12 shows a four-step model of the prototyping process, which consists of the following:

> **Step 1:** *Identify the user's basic requirements.* The system designer (usually an information systems specialist) works with the user only long enough to capture the user's basic information needs.

systems life cycle

prototyping

prototype

iterative

Step 2: *Develop an initial prototype.* The system designer creates a working prototype quickly, using tools for rapidly generating software.

Step 3: *Use the prototype.* The user is encouraged to work with the system to determine how well the prototype meets his or her needs and to make suggestions for improving the prototype.

Step 4: *Revise and enhance the prototype.* The system developer notes all changes the user requests and refines the prototype accordingly. After the prototype has been revised, the cycle returns to step 3. Steps 3 and 4 are repeated until the user is satisfied.

When no more iterations are required, the approved prototype then becomes an operational prototype that furnishes the final specifications for the application. Sometimes the prototype is adopted as the production version of the system.

Advantages and Disadvantages of Prototyping Prototyping is most useful when there is some uncertainty about requirements or design solutions. Prototyping is especially useful in designing an information system's **end-user interface** (the part of the system with which end users interact, such as online display and data-entry screens, reports, or Web pages). Because prototyping encourages intense end-user involvement throughout the systems development life cycle, it is more likely to produce systems that fulfill user requirements.

However, rapid prototyping can gloss over essential steps in systems development. If the completed prototype works reasonably well, management may not see the need for reprogramming, redesign, or full documentation and testing to develop a polished production system. Some of these hastily constructed systems may not easily accommodate large quantities of data, a large number of users in a production environment, or may not provide a secure enough environment. In addition, the non-production prototype system may not run fast enough in production mode.

FIGURE 10-12 *The prototyping process.*

The process of developing a prototype can be broken down into four steps. Because a prototype can be developed quickly and inexpensively, systems developers can go through several iterations, repeating steps 3 and 4, to refine and enhance the prototype before arriving at the final operational one.

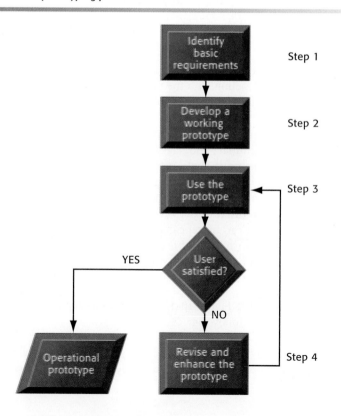

end-user interface

End-User Development

Some types of information systems can be developed by end users with little or no formal assistance from technical specialists. This phenomenon is called **end-user development**. A series of software tools categorized as fourth-generation languages makes this possible. **Fourth-generation languages** are software tools that enable end users to create reports or develop software applications with minimal or no technical assistance. Some of these fourth-generation tools also enhance professional programmers' productivity.

Fourth-generation languages tend to be nonprocedural, or less procedural, than conventional programming languages. Procedural languages require specification of the sequence of steps, or procedures, that tell the computer what to do and how to do it. Nonprocedural languages need only specify what has to be accomplished rather than provide details about how to carry out the task.

Table 10-5 shows that there are seven categories of fourth-generation languages: PC software tools, query languages, report generators, graphics languages, application generators, application software packages, and very high level programming languages. The table shows the tools ordered in terms of ease of use by nonprogramming end users. End users are most likely to work with PC software tools and query languages. **Query languages** are software tools that provide immediate online answers to requests for information that are not predefined, such as "Who are the highest-performing sales representatives?" Query languages are often tied to data management software and database management systems (see Chapter 6).

On the whole, end-user developed systems can be completed more rapidly than those developed through the conventional systems life cycle. Allowing users to specify their own business needs improves requirements gathering and often leads to a higher level of user involvement and satisfaction with the system. However, fourth-generation tools still cannot replace conventional tools for some business applications because they cannot easily handle the processing of large numbers of transactions or applications with extensive procedural logic and updating requirements.

end-user development
fourth-generation languages
query languages

TABLE 10-5 *Categories of Fourth-Generation Languages*

PC software tools	General-purpose application software packages for PCs.	WordPerfect Microsoft Access
Query language	Languages for retrieving data stored in databases or files. Capable of supporting requests for information that are not predefined.	SQL
Report generator	Extract data from files or databases to create customized reports in a wide range of formats not routinely produced by an information system. Generally provide more control over the way data are formatted, organized, and displayed than query languages.	Crystal Reports
Graphics language	Retrieve data from files or databases and display them in graphic format. Some graphics software can perform arithmetic or logical operations on data as well.	SAS Graph Systat
Application generator	Contain preprogrammed modules that can generate entire applications, including Web sites, greatly speeding development. A user can specify what needs to be done, and the application generator will create the appropriate program code for input, validation, update, processing, and reporting.	FOCUS PowerBuilder Microsoft FrontPage
Application software package	Software programs sold or leased by commercial vendors that eliminate the need for custom-written, in-house software.	PeopleSoft HCM SAP R/3
Very high-level programming language	Generate program code with fewer instructions than conventional languages, such as COBOL or FORTRAN. Designed primarily as productivity tools for professional programmers.	APL Nomad2

End-user computing also poses organizational risks because it occurs outside of traditional mechanisms for information systems management and control. When systems are created rapidly, without a formal development methodology, testing and documentation may be inadequate. Control over data can be lost in systems outside the traditional information systems department (see Chapter 6). In addition, two people in an organization may develop similar systems, duplicating effort and wasting resources. End-use systems frequently cannot easily be integrated with other systems.

To help organizations maximize the benefits of end-user applications development, management should control the development of end-user applications by requiring cost justification of end-user information system projects and by establishing hardware, software, and quality standards for user-developed applications.

Application Software Packages and Outsourcing

Chapter 5 points out that the software for most systems today is not developed in-house but is purchased from external sources. Firms can rent the software from an application service provider, they can purchase an **application software package** from a commercial vendor, or they can have a custom application developed by an outside outsourcing firm.

The Window on Technology describes a company that is using multiple approaches to obtain better systems. Canadian National Railway (CN) is using software packages to develop new systems. CN is also using prototyping as a methodology with its vendor-supplied development tools. By combining all of these approaches, CN came up with a powerful set of systems and tools that increased operational efficiency and the ability to take advantage of market trends while allowing the firm to concentrate on its core competency—transloading.

application software package

WINDOW ON TECHNOLOGY

Technology

CN Railway Modernizes Inventory Control System Rapidly

Canadian National Railway (CN), is a $4.1 billion transportation firm headquartered in Montreal. As a part of CN's Transload Group, CN CargoFlo is a network of bulk distribution terminals that provides value-added, state-of-the-art transfer facilities, designed to extend CN's customers' market reach and to create new import/export opportunities.

When products arrive at CN CargoFlo facilities by rail, they are usually held for a period requested by customers and then shipped by truck to them—a process known as break-bulking. This process has the advantages of both the economical long-distance rail hauling to or from break-bulk facilities and flexible short-haul truck delivery.

At present, there are 21 CargoFlo break-bulk facilities in the CN network, serving markets in Canada and the United States. CargoFlo terminals handle a wide variety of commodities, such as chemicals (hazardous and non-hazardous), plastics, fertilizers, construction materials, grain and grain products, bulk foods, and liquids (flammable and non-flammable).

The CN Transload Group positions products for just-in-time deliveries to markets outside their existing service areas, reduces or eliminates a customer's capital expenditures and corporate risk, provides state-of-the-art transfer and transportation services, and reduces or eliminates a customer's need for on-site storage. In other words, the Transload Group permits their customers to reduce their costs while expanding their markets.

For a considerable time, CN relied on a PC Unix-based inventory control system at its Toronto CargoFlo terminal. What began as a single-user system soon increased to 16 users in Toronto, Montreal, and Warren, Manitoba. By early 1994, the limitations of the PC-based system architecture became obvious: the numerous system hardware failures, the data integrity concerns, and the limited networking capabilities of the architecture.

"The old system was simply not capable of supporting the expanding operations," Joe Mangoni, a project officer in the marketing, safety, and RAD systems group at CN explains. "Additionally, management wanted an easier way to obtain a complete picture of the entire operation. The Unix systems were not integrated, which meant reports had to be printed at each terminal and then manually consolidated at headquarters."

The development team wanted to create a more cohesive inventory control system spanning all 21 sites, which would automate a number of manual functions and could be scaled as operations grew. Their first option was a distributed network architecture to extend the existing Unix-based system. However, further analysis led them to realize that a centralized, host-based architecture would be more effective. Many possibilities were considered, but a centralized system offered many more benefits than a distributed system.

The developers planned to interface the new inventory control system with many of CN's other business systems, such as electronic data interchange (EDI), email, and billing. These systems ran on an IBM 3090 mainframe computer at headquarters. The new system would have to facilitate addition of new users and sites while maintaining consistent service levels to existing users.

"Most of these prerequisites proved to be difficult to meet in a distributed environment," Mangoni adds. "We also had to consider our primary expertise in operating systems, networking, communications, security, system backups, and disaster recovery. All of these things pointed to the mainframe."

There is no question that client/server systems have reshaped our corporate information systems. But for large processing tasks, centralized architectures anchored by a powerful host computer are still the order of the day.

"The power of the mainframe, coupled with its security, controlled access, reliability, and mature system utilities are difficult to duplicate in a client/server environment," says Mangoni. For updating the inventory control system at their CN CargoFlo facilities, the developers had to make complex architectural decisions. The team opted for a mainframe-based system that used vendor-supplied development software.

The new inventory control system, dubbed CargoFlo Inventory Management System (CIMS), was to be built using Information Builders' Mainframe FOCUS product with the Multi Session Option (MSO). Large CargoFlo facilities would access the centralized system through the existing SNA-TCP/IP backbone network, and smaller sites would be provided with dial-in access on dedicated telephone lines. (IBM's systems network architecture (SNA) is an architecture reference model similar to OSI.)

"We had experience with FOCUS on two other major applications and had become proficient with its development capabilities," Mangoni says. "There were other tools we could have used, but not if we were to get the job done in the allotted time frame. The Unix system was on its last leg. We had serious problems that demanded fast solutions."

CIMS was quickly completed in just eight months. The close partnership among Mangoni, Bob Singer (systems manager of marketing and traffic information systems), Gabriel Marchitto (a senior programmer/analyst), Jim Brian (a technical support specialist), and Patrice Berube (a third-party FOCUS consultant) produced a complete inventory control and distribution system to monitor and control transfer, delivery, and billing at all CN CargoFlo facilities.

"The beauty of FOCUS is that it allows us to build robust applications very quickly using a simple yet powerful methodology," Mangoni says. "We can mock up a prototype, get immediate user feedback, and then progress in an iterative fashion until the application is completed."

FOCUS's rapid application development (RAD) methodology enabled CN to reduce development time and the users can now include a variety of features designed to meet their requirements. Thus, a bilingual, high-quality computer system,

closely coupled with CargoFlo's operations and procedures, was created.

"It wasn't obvious at the outset just how the system might evolve," Singer recalls. "The tools and techniques we used allowed us to respond to new ideas from the customer, iterating until we had developed the final product. FOCUS supports a cyclical methodology, which means we didn't have to define all the specifications in advance. We had a low up-front cost for prototyping."

In March 1995, two weeks prior to the scheduled target date, the first CIMS site was implemented in Montreal. The new system was well-received among users. "Having users participate in the original prototypes helped considerably," Singer says. "Our management is also extremely satisfied with the system and the cost of its development."

With CIMS, there has been significant expansion. "Our rapid growth is partly due to the new efficiencies brought on by CIMS," Singer says. "We're seeing significantly higher transfer volumes, without the need to increase terminal staff." Centralization of CN CargoFlo's data through CIMS, Singer adds, has enabled senior managers to get a consolidated view of all facilities, at the same time maintaining a reliable and easily supportable environment.

When phase one—the deployment to the major facilities—had been completed, phase two of CIMS was started, and additional capabilities which further increase CN CargoFlo terminal productivity were created. They not only automated 90 percent of the billing function but also centralized all billing activities in Mississauga. Additional automated functions, such as advanced warning of expected cars, routing faxes automatically to customers, and more extensive EDI capabilities, were all created using the existing mainframe infrastructure and programs. "We have grown with FOCUS significantly," Mangoni says. "We are able to reuse a lot of existing code and have done many things to push the technology envelope. It has been very successful."

The most important benefit of CIMS has been to help CN close the loop on its billing procedures. Previously, at each terminal, clerks used to deal with local billing, which would then be sent to headquarters for processing. Now, system-to-system EDI links automate 90 percent of the billing; the clerks to handle only miscellaneous charges while the majority of the billing is done according to predefined rate contracts.

Today CargoFlo's industry-leading inventory management system has EDI capabilities for instantaneous computer-to-computer information exchange. CargoFlo also offers a total quality system to ensure product inspection and testing, product integrity, and security.

To Think About: How did CN CargoFlo benefit from using a vendor solution to develop their inventory control system? What role did prototyping play in development, and why was prototyping used? What management, organization, and technology issues had to be addressed to use these tools effectively?

Sources: "Canadian National Railway Turns to FOCUS to Modernize Inventory Control System," www.informationbuilders.com/applications/cn-rail.html, accessed May 19, 2005; "Transloading Services," www.cn.ca/specialized/transloading/en_KFTransloading.shtml, accessed May 19, 2005; "CNCargoFlo," www.cn.ca/productsservices/transloading/en_KFCargoFlo.shtml, accessed May 19, 2005.

Application Software Packages During the past several decades, many systems have been developed on an application software package foundation. Many applications are common to all business organizations—for example, payroll, accounts receivable, general ledger, or inventory control. For universal functions with standard processes that do not change a great deal over time, a generalized system will fulfill the requirements of many organizations.

If a software package can fulfill most of an organization's requirements, the company does not have to write its own software. The company can save time and money by using the prewritten, predesigned, pretested software programs from the package. Package vendors supply much of the ongoing maintenance and support for the system, including enhancements to keep the system in line with ongoing technical and business developments.

If an organization has unique requirements that the package does not address, many packages include capabilities for customization. **Customization** features allow a software package to be modified to meet an organization's unique requirements without destroying the integrity of the package software. If a great deal of customization is required, additional programming and customization work may become so expensive and time consuming that they negate many of the advantages of software packages.

Figure 10-13 shows how package costs in relation to total implementation costs rise with the degree of customization. The initial purchase price of the package can be deceptive because of these hidden implementation costs. If the vendor releases new versions of the package, the overall costs of customization will be magnified because these changes will need to be synchronized with future versions of the software.

When a system is developed using an application software package, systems analysis will include a package evaluation effort. The most important evaluation criteria are the functions provided by the package, flexibility, user friendliness, hardware and software resources, database requirements, installation and maintenance efforts, documentation, vendor quality, vendor support, and cost. The package evaluation process often is based on a **request for proposal (RFP)**, which is a detailed list of questions submitted to packaged-software vendors. RFPs must be specific as they typically form part of the contract between the vendor and the firm. RFPs list specific deadlines for both the RFP to be submitted as well as milestones in the project and an acceptance sign-off date for the end of the project.

FIGURE 10-13   *The effects on total implementation costs of customizing a software package.*

As the number of modifications to a software package rise, so does the cost of implementing the package. Savings promised by the package can be whittled away by excessive changes.

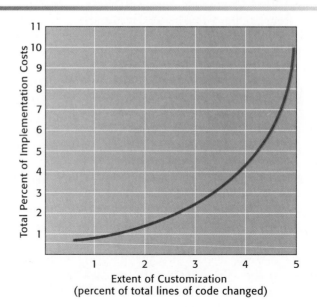

customization

request for proposal (RFP)

When a software package solution is selected, the organization no longer has total control over the system design process. Instead of tailoring the system design specifications directly to user requirements, the design effort will consist of trying to mould user requirements to conform to the features of the package. If the organization's requirements conflict with the way the package works and the package cannot be customized, the organization will have to adapt to the package and change its procedures. Even if the organization's business processes seem compatible with those supported by a software package, the package may be too constraining if these business processes are continually changing (Prahalad and Krishnan 2002).

Outsourcing If a firm does not want to use its internal resources to develop or operate information systems, it can outsource the work to an external organization that specializes in providing these services. An application service provider (ASP), which we describe in Chapter 5, is one form of outsourcing. Subscribing companies would use the software and computer hardware provided by the ASP as the technical platform for their systems. In another form of outsourcing, a company could hire an external vendor to design and create the software for its system, but that company would operate the system on its own computers. Alternatively, the outsourcing vendor could run the system on its computers as an application service provider. The outsourcing vendor might be domestic or in another country, and we discuss the special issues raised by offshore outsourcing in Chapter 12.

Outsourcing has become popular because some organizations perceive it as providing more value than an in-house computer centre or information systems staff. The provider of outsourcing services benefits from economies of scale and complementary core competencies that would be difficult for a firm that does not specialize in information technology services to replicate (Levina and Ross 2003). The vendor's specialized knowledge and skills can be shared with many different customers, and the experience of working with so many information systems projects further enhances the vendor's expertise. Outsourcing enables a company with fluctuating needs for computer processing to pay for only what it uses rather than develop its own computer centre, which would be underutilized when there is no peak load. Some firms outsource because their internal information systems staff cannot keep pace with technological change or innovative business practices or because they want to free up scarce and costly talent for activities with higher paybacks.

Not all organizations benefit from outsourcing, and the disadvantages of outsourcing can create serious problems for organizations if they are not well understood and managed (Lacity and Willocks 1998; Earl 1996). Many firms underestimate costs for identifying and evaluating vendors of information technology services, for transitioning to a new vendor, and for monitoring vendors to make sure they are fulfilling their contractual obligations. These hidden costs can easily undercut anticipated benefits from outsourcing (Barthelemy 2001). When a firm allocates the responsibility for developing and operating its information systems to another organization, it can lose control over its information systems function. If the organization lacks the expertise to negotiate a sound contract, the firm's dependence on the vendor could result in high costs or loss of control over technological direction or even loss of data (Lacity, Willcocks, and Feeny 1996).

Firms should be especially cautious when using an outsourcer to develop or to operate applications that give it some type of competitive advantage. A firm is most likely to benefit from outsourcing if it understands exactly how the outsourcing vendor will provide value and can manage the vendor relationship using an appropriate outsourcing strategy (Lee, Miranda, and Kim 2004). Table 10-6 compares the advantages and disadvantages of each of the systems-development alternatives.

The Window on Organizations describes how some financial services firms deal with the issue of selecting systems-development alternatives. Some firms opt to purchase the technology for new wealth management systems from outside vendors because they believe their strategic advantage lies in their knowledge of clients and investment selection. Other firms believe that the technology is a source of competitive differentiation as well and choose to develop their systems in-house.

TABLE 10-6 Comparison of Systems-Development Approaches

APPROACH	FEATURES	ADVANTAGES	DISADVANTAGES
Systems lifecycle	Sequential step-by-step formal process Written specification and approvals Limited role of users	Useful for large, complex systems and projects	Slow and expensive Discourages changes Massive paperwork to manage
Prototyping	Requirements specified dynamically with experimental system Rapid, informal, and iterative process Users continually interact with the prototype	Rapid and relatively inexpensive Useful when requirements uncertain or when end-user interface is very important Promotes user participation	Inappropriate for large, complex systems Can gloss over steps in analysis, documentation, and testing
Applications software package	Commercial software eliminates need for internally developed software programs	Design, programming, installation, and maintenance work reduced Can save time and cost when developing common business applications Reduces need for internal information systems resources	May not meet organization's unique requirements May not perform many business functions well Extensive customization raises development costs
End-user development	Systems created by end users using fourth-generation software tools Rapid and informal Minimal role of information systems specialists	Users control systems development Saves development time and cost Reduces application backlog	Can lead to proliferation of uncontrolled information systems and data Systems do not always meet quality assurance standards
Outsourcing	Systems developed and sometimes operated by external vendor	Can reduce or control costs Can produce systems when internal resources are not available or are technically deficient	Loss of control over the information systems function Dependence on the technical direction and prosperity of external vendors

Management Opportunities, Challenges, and Solutions

System developers today have more alternatives and tools at their disposal than ever before as they confront new challenges posed by the digital firm environment.

Opportunities

New information systems enable organizations to redesign their structure, scope, power relationships, work flows, products, and services. In many instances, developing a new system creates an opportunity to redefine how the organization conducts its business, leading to higher levels of productivity and performance.

Management Challenges

Electronic commerce, electronic business, and the emerging digital firm intensify the challenges of systems development.

Application Development in the Digital Firm Era There is greater demand than ever for information systems solutions under ever-tightening deadlines (Chiang and Mookerjee 2004). Advances in computer software have not kept pace with the breathtaking productivity gains in computer hardware and networking. Despite the gains from fourth-generation languages, personal desktop software tools, object-oriented methods, and software tools for the Web, many businesses face backlogs in developing the information systems they need.

WINDOW ON ORGANIZATIONS

Wall Street Firms Grapple with Build Versus Buy

One of the big growth areas for financial services firms is the wealth management business, which specializes in high-end services to wealthy clients. A financial adviser works with clients to create individualized financial plans, suggest investments for achieving the client's goals, and discuss the likelihood of success. These affluent investors expect the highest level of service and sophisticated advice, so information systems serving these clients merit special scrutiny.

Typically, a financial services firm develops an overall plan for these clients on how to manage their various assets rather than just providing advice on stock and bond transactions. Most of the systems at these firms were developed over the years for transaction-based businesses rather than a wealth management business model. At many financial services firms, new systems are required for wealth management.

Should these systems be developed in-house or acquired from external vendors? Do wealth management businesses gain any competitive advantage from developing their own systems in-house? Jaime Punishill, a senior analyst at Forrester Research, believes that they don't. "You don't gain any differentiation by running your own back office," he observes, and the same may be true of front-office applications dealing with clients. He believes that expertise, investment selection, and strategy differentiate one financial services firm from another, not the technology they use.

RBC Dominion Securities agrees. "Our first choice is to buy, rather than build. We look for strategic partners" says John Truman, senior vice president of technology for RBC Investments, part of Royal Bank Financial Group. In 2001 RBC Dominion decided to focus on better front-office systems for dealing with its wealth-management clients. The company had used off-the-shelf software for its back-office applications, and it sought similar tools for the front office. "The competitive advantage in wealth management is about product offerings and how you service the client, not necessarily being the best software in the world," said John Tracy, RBC Dominion's manager of strategic initiatives.

RBC Dominion replaced six different legacy systems serving 3000 desktops with contact management and portfolio management software supplied by x.eye Inc. RBC did decide to keep the integration software linking its front- and back-office systems in-house, however, because it believed it had superior knowledge of its data.

Wachovia Securities likewise opted to use an external service provider. Wachovia enlisted Thomson Financial to provide its 19 000 financial advisers with front- and back-office tools that would be useful for wealth management. The solution called for replacing their desktop systems based on Reuters workstations with Thomson's new broker workstation using the Thomson ONE Advisor Financial Planning software. Thomson ONE features real-time market data, client portfolio management capabilities, and powerful decision-support applications that enable advisers to create concise financial plans and demonstrate the probability of success using various financial models. It also has powerful prospecting tools for advisers to open discussions with clients. Thomson also supplied Wachovia with back-office processing and software for integrating front- and back-office systems.

UBS, a leading global investment bank and provider of wealth management services, opted to keep its wealth management systems in-house. Several years ago UBS decided it had too much invested in its own wealth management systems to discard them in favour of solutions from an external vendor. UBS felt it could more easily manage integration between the systems. It internally enhanced its systems to add the new functions it needed. UBS's 7700 advisers can perform an array of functions, such as entering orders, conducting research, reviewing client accounts, and taking notes without having to navigate through separate applications. Information from UBS's back-office record keeping and transaction processing systems is immediately available to its front-office desktop systems for working with clients.

In addition to improving integration among multiple systems, UBS also developed its own contact management system called Relationship Manager, which went live in March 2004. Normally, financial services firms use commercial contact management software packages, but UBS chief technology officer Scott Abbey believes that his firm's existing wealth management platform already has most of the functionality of commercial high-end customer relationship management (CRM) systems. The cost of adding a few missing CRM functions to UBS's own system was much less than implementing an off-the-shelf solution.

UBS also believes technology can provide a competitive edge in wealth management. Even if a third-party vendor was willing to create the right software for the company, UBS management would not want a vendor to develop something it could resell to UBS rivals. According to Abbey, UBS has unique requirements and would not want to give its know-how to competitors.

To Think About: What management, organization, and technology issues did these companies have to consider in determining whether to develop their wealth management systems in-house or buy them from external software and service vendors?

Sources: Jessica Pallay, "Build versus Buy on Wall Street," *Information Week*, April 26, 2004; Jim Middlemiss, "Financial Institutions Tackle Wealth-Management Technology," *Wall Street & Technology*, April 8, 2002, www.wstonline.com/story/supp/WST20020408S0003, accessed May 19, 2005; www.thomson.com, accessed September 23, 2004; and http://financialservicesinc.ubs.com, accessed September 23, 2004.

Technologies and business conditions are changing so rapidly that agility and scalability have become critical success factors and primary goals of systems design. Businesses need software components that can be added, modified, replaced, or reconfigured to enable the firm to respond rapidly to new opportunities. Systems must be scalable to accommodate growing numbers of users and to deliver data over multiple platforms—client/server networks, desktop computers with Web browsers, cell phones, and other mobile devices. E-commerce and e-business systems may also need to be designed so that they can run in hosted environments as well as on the company's own hardware and software platforms. To remain competitive, some firms feel pressured to design, develop, test, and deploy Internet or intranet applications in a matter of weeks or months (Earl and Khan 2001).

The development methods we described earlier often take months or years and were ill suited to the pace and profile of Internet or intranet projects (Avison and Fitzgerald 2003). Traditional methods do not address the new features of Internet-based applications, which might have multiple tiers of clients and servers with different operating systems linked to transaction processing systems, as well as business processes that had to be coordinated with those of customers or suppliers.

New Interorganizational System Requirements E-commerce and e-business also call for systems development based on a very broad view of the organization, one that encompasses business processes extended beyond firm boundaries (Fingar 2000). Firms can no longer execute their business and system plans alone because they need to forge new electronic relationships with suppliers, distributors, and customers. Traditional IT infrastructures in which a single firm manages and owns its own infrastructure and applications are giving way to networks of applications that are owned and managed by many different business partners. Systems development will therefore need to address more interorganizational processes and requirements than in the past, with applications capable of integrating business processes within a single enterprise or across multiple enterprises.

Solution Guidelines

In the digital firm environment, organizations need to be able to add, change, and retire their technology capabilities very rapidly. Companies are adopting shorter, more informal development processes for many of their e-commerce and e-business applications, processes that provide fast solutions that do not disrupt their core transaction processing systems and organizational databases. In addition to using software packages, application service providers, and other outsourcing services, they are relying more heavily on fast-cycle techniques such as joint application design (JAD), prototypes, and reusable standardized software components that can be assembled into a complete set of services for e-commerce and e-business.

Rapid Application Development (RAD) Object-oriented software tools, reusable software, prototyping, and fourth-generation language tools are helping systems developers create working systems much more rapidly than they could using traditional systems development methods and software tools. The term **rapid application development (RAD)** is used to describe this process of creating workable systems in a very short period of time. RAD can include the use of visual programming and other tools for developing graphical user interfaces, iterative prototyping of key system elements, the automation of program code generation, and close teamwork among end users and information systems specialists (see Figure 10-14). Simple systems often can be assembled from pre-developed components. The process does not have to be sequential, and key parts of development can occur simultaneously.

Sometimes a technique called **joint application design (JAD)** is used to accelerate the generation of information requirements and to develop the initial systems design. JAD brings end users and information systems specialists together in an interactive session to discuss the system's design. Properly prepared and facilitated, JAD sessions can significantly speed up the design phase and involve users at an intense level.

Component-Based Development We have already described some of the benefits of object-oriented development for developing systems that can respond to rapidly changing business environments, including Web applications. To further expedite software creation, groups of objects have been assembled to provide software components for common functions such as a graphical user interface or online ordering capability that can be combined to create large-scale business applications. This approach to software development is called **component-based development**, and it enables a system to be developed by assembling and integrating existing software components. Businesses are using component-based development to create their e-commerce applications by combining commercially available components for shopping carts, user authentication, search engines, and catalogues with pieces of software for their own unique business requirements.

Web Services and Service-Oriented Computing Chapter 5 introduced Web services as loosely coupled, reusable software components deliverable using Extensible Markup Language (XML) and other open protocols and standards that enable one application to communicate with another with no custom programming required to share data and services. In addition to supporting internal and external integration of systems, Web services can be used as tools for developing new information system applica-

FIGURE 10-14 *ClearNova's ThinkCAP RAD tool.*

ClearNova's ThinkCAP is a powerful RAD tool for simplifying and accelerating Web-based business application development. Illustrated here is a template for rapidly designing data entry forms and linking them to relational or non-relational data and objects. RAD tools enable businesses to create system solutions quickly without extensive programming.

rapid application development (RAD)

joint application design (JAD)

component-based development

tions or enhancing existing systems. Web services can create software components that are deliverable over the Internet and provide new functions for an organization's existing systems or create new systems that link an organization's systems to those of other organizations. Because these software services use a universal set of standards, they promise to be less expensive and less difficult to weave together than proprietary components.

Web services can perform certain functions on their own, and they can also engage other Web services to complete more complex transactions, such as checking credit, procurement, or ordering products. By creating software components that can communicate and share data regardless of the operating system, programming language, or client device, Web services can provide significant cost savings in systems development while opening up new opportunities for collaboration with other companies (Ferris and Farrell 2003; Hagel and Brown 2001; Patel and Saigal 2002).

Summary

1. *Demonstrate how developing new systems produces organizational change.*

Developing a new information system is a form of planned organizational change that involves many different people in the organization. Because information systems are sociotechnical entities, a change in information systems involves changes in work, management, and the organization. Four kinds of technology-enabled change are automation, rationalization of procedures, business reengineering, and paradigm shift, with far-reaching changes carrying the greatest risks and rewards. Many organizations are attempting business process reengineering to redesign work flows and business processes in the hope of achieving dramatic productivity breakthroughs. Information systems can also be used to support business process management, total quality management (TQM), six sigma, and other initiatives for incremental process improvement.

2. *Explain how a company can develop information systems that fit its business plan.*

Organizations should develop information systems plans that describe how information technology supports the attainment of their business goals. The plans indicate the direction of systems development, the rationale, the implementation strategy, and the budget. Enterprise analysis and critical success factors (CSFs) can be used to elicit organization-wide information requirements that must be addressed by the plans.

3. *Identify and describe the core activities in the systems development process.*

The core activities in systems development are systems analysis, systems design, programming, testing, conversion, production, and maintenance. Systems analysis is the study and analysis of problems of existing systems and the identification of requirements for their solutions. Systems design provides the specifications for an information system solution, showing how its technical and organizational components fit together.

4. *Evaluate alternative methods for developing information systems and alternative methodologies for modelling systems.*

There are a number of alternative methods for developing information systems, each suited to different types of problems. The oldest method for developing systems is the systems life cycle, which requires that information systems be developed in formal stages. The stages must proceed sequentially and have defined outputs; each requires formal approval before the next stage can commence. The system life cycle is useful for large projects that need formal specifications and tight management control over each stage of systems development. However, this approach is very rigid and costly and is not well suited for unstructured, decision-oriented applications for which requirements cannot be immediately visualized.

Prototyping consists of developing an experimental system rapidly and inexpensively for end users to interact with and evaluate. The prototype is refined and enhanced until users are satisfied that it includes all of their requirements and can be used as a template to create the final system. Prototyping encourages end-user involvement in systems development and iteration of design until specifications are captured accurately. The rapid creation of prototypes can result in systems that have not been completely tested or documented or that are technically inadequate or not secure enough for a production environment.

Developing an information system using an application software package eliminates the need for writing software programs when developing an information system. Using a software package reduces the amount of design, testing, installation, and maintenance work required to develop a system. Application software packages are helpful if a firm does not have the internal information systems staff or financial resources to custom develop a system. To meet an organization's unique requirements, packages may require extensive modifications that can substantially raise development costs.

End-user development is the development of information systems by end users, either alone or with minimal assistance from information systems specialists. End-user-developed systems can be created rapidly and informally using fourth-generation software tools. The primary benefits of end-user development are improved requirements determination; reduced application backlog; and increased end-user participation in, and control of, the systems development process. However, end-user development, in conjunction with distributed computing, has introduced new organizational risks by propagating information systems and data resources that do not necessarily meet quality assurance standards and that are not easily controlled by traditional means.

Outsourcing consists of using an external vendor to develop (or operate) a firm's information systems. The work is done by the vendor rather than by the organization's internal information systems staff. Outsourcing can save application development costs or enable firms to develop applications without an internal information systems staff. However, firms risk losing control over their information systems and becoming too dependent on external vendors.

Selection of a systems-development approach can have a big impact on the time, cost, and end product of systems development. Managers should be aware of the strengths and weaknesses of each systems-development approach and the types of problems for which each is best suited. The impact of application software packages and of outsourcing should be carefully evaluated before they are selected because these approaches give organizations less control over the systems-development process.

5. **Assess the challenges of developing information systems, and propose management solutions.**

Businesses today are often required to develop e-commerce and e-business applications very rapidly to remain competitive. New systems are likely to have more interorganizational requirements and processes than in the past. Companies are turning to rapid application development (RAD), joint application design (JAD), and reusable software components to improve the systems development process. Rapid application development (RAD) uses object-oriented software, visual programming, prototyping, and fourth-generation tools for very rapid creation of systems. Component-based development expedites application development by grouping objects into suites of software components that can be combined to create large-scale business applications.

Web services enable firms to obtain software application components delivered over the Internet for developing new systems or integrating existing systems. Web services provide a common set of standards that enable organizations to link their systems regardless of their technology platform through standard plug and play architecture.

Key Terms

Acceptance testing, 354	Fourth-generation languages, 363	Prototyping, 361
Application software package, 364	Information requirements, 352	Query languages, 363
Automation, 344	Information systems plan, 341	Rapid application development (RAD), 371
Benchmarking, 350	Iterative, 361	Rationalization of procedures, 344
Business process reengineering, 345	Joint application design (JAD), 371	Request for proposal (RFP), 366
Component-based development, 371	Maintenance, 355	Six sigma, 350
Computer-aided software engineering (CASE), 359	Module, 356	Structure chart, 357
	Object, 357	Structured, 356
Conversion, 354	Object-oriented development, 357	System testing, 354
Critical success factors (CSFs), 342	Object-oriented programming, 357	Systems analysis, 351
Customization, 366	Paradigm shift, 345	Systems design, 352
Data flow diagram (DFD), 356	Parallel strategy, 354	Systems development, 351
Development methodologies, 356	Phased approach, 355	Systems life cycle, 361
Direct cutover, 354	Pilot study, 355	Test plan, 354
Documentation, 355	Post-implementation audit, 355	Testing, 353
End-user development, 363	Process specifications, 356	Total quality management (TQM), 350
End-user interface, 362	Production, 355	Unified Modeling Language (UML), 359
Enterprise analysis, 342	Programming, 353	Unit testing, 353
Feasibility study, 351	Prototype, 361	Work flow management, 346

Review Questions

1. Why can an information system be considered planned organizational change?

2. What are the major categories of an information systems plan?

3. How can enterprise analysis and critical success factors be used to establish organization-wide information systems requirements?

4. Describe each of the four kinds of organizational change that can be promoted with information technology.

5. What is business process reengineering? What steps are

required to make it effective? How does it differ from business process management?

6. *How do information systems support process changes that promote quality in an organization?*

7. *What is the difference between systems analysis and systems design? What activities does each process comprise?*

8. *What are information requirements? Why are they difficult to determine correctly?*

9. *Why is the testing stage of systems development so important? Name and describe the three stages of testing for an information system.*

10. *What role do programming, conversion, production, and maintenance play in systems development?*

11. *Compare object-oriented and traditional structured approaches for modelling and designing systems.*

12. *What is the traditional systems life cycle? Describe each of its steps and its advantages and disadvantages for systems development.*

13. *What do we mean by information system prototyping? What are its benefits and limitations? List and describe the steps in the prototyping process.*

14. *What is an application software package? What are the advantages and disadvantages of developing information systems based on software packages?*

15. *What is meant by end-user development? What are its advantages and disadvantages? Name some policies and procedures for managing end-user development.*

16. *What is outsourcing? Under what circumstances should it be used for developing information systems?*

17. *Describe the management challenges posed by developing systems and suggest some solutions.*

Discussion Questions

1. *Why is selecting a systems development approach an important business decision? Who should participate in the selection process?*

2. *Some have said that the best way to reduce systems development costs is to use application software packages or fourth-generation tools. Do you agree? Why or why not?*

Application Software Exercise:
Database Exercise: Designing a Customer System for Auto Sales

Ace Auto Dealers specializes in selling new vehicles from Subaru. The company advertises in local newspapers and is also listed as an authorized dealer on the Subaru Web site and other major Web sites for auto buyers. The company benefits from a good local word-of-mouth reputation and name recognition and is a leading source of information for Subaru vehicles in the Halifax, Nova Scotia area.

When a prospective customer enters the showroom, he or she is greeted by an Ace sales representative. The sales representative manually fills out a form with information such as the prospective customer's name, address, telephone number, date of visit, and model and make of the vehicle in which the customer is interested. The representative also asks where the prospect heard about Ace—whether it was from a newspaper ad, the Web, or word of mouth—and this information is also noted on the form.

If the customer decides to purchase an auto, the dealer fills out a bill of sale form and enters the following information into Ace's sales information system: the vehicle identification number, vehicle make and model, colour, options selected, the list price, the final price, and the date of the sale, along with the purchaser's name, address, and telephone number. (The final price is the list price minus any dealer discounts.) Files for this system can be found on the Companion Website for Chapter 10.

Ace does not believe it has enough information about its customers. It cannot easily determine which prospects have made auto purchases or the percentage of prospects who have been converted into buyers. Nor can it identify which customer touch points have produced the greatest number of sales leads or actual sales so it can focus advertising and marketing more on the channels that generate the most revenue. Are purchasers discovering Ace from newspaper ads, from word of mouth, or from the Web? Additionally, the firm cannot tell whether its customers are more interested in no-frills cars or those with luxury options.

Prepare a systems analysis report detailing Ace's problem and a system solution that can be implemented using PC database management software. Then use database software to develop a simple system solution. Your systems analysis report should include the following:

1. Description of the problem and its organizational and business impact.

2. Proposed solution, solution objectives, and solution feasibility.

3. Costs and benefits of the solution you have selected. The company has a PC with Internet access and the full suite of Microsoft Office desktop productivity tools.

4. Information requirements to be addressed by the solution.
5. Management, organization, and technology issues to be addressed by the solution, including changes in business processes.

On the basis of the requirements you have identified, design the database and populate it with at least 10 records per table. Consider whether you can use or modify the existing customer database in your design. Print out the database design. Then use the system you have created to generate queries and reports that would be of most interest to management. Create several prototype data input forms for the system, and review them with your instructor. Then revise the prototypes.

Electronic Business Project: Redesigning Business Processes for Web Procurement

You are in charge of purchasing for your firm and would like to use the Grainger.com (**www.grainger.com**) business-to-business e-commerce site for this purpose. Find out how to place an order for painting supplies by exploring the Catalog, Order Form, and Repair Parts Order capabilities of this site. Do not register at the site. Describe all the steps your firm would need to take to use this system to place orders online for 30 gallons of paint thinner. Include a diagram of what you think your firm's business process for purchasing should be and the pieces of information required by this process.

In a traditional purchase process, whoever is responsible for making the purchase fills out a requisition form and submits it for approval based on the company's business rules. When the requisition is approved, a purchase order with a unique purchase order identification number is sent to the supplier. The purchaser might want to browse supplier catalogues to compare prices and features before placing the order. The purchaser might also want to determine whether the items to be purchased are available. If the purchasing firm were an approved customer, that company would be granted credit to make the purchase and would be billed for the total cost of the items purchased and shipped after the order was shipped. Alternatively, the purchasing company might have to pay for the order in advance or pay for the order using a credit card. Multiple payment options might be possible. How might this process have to change to make purchases electronically from the Grainger site?

Group Project: Preparing Web Site Design Specifications

With three or four of your classmates, select an information system described in this text that uses the Web, such as Manitoulin Transport's supply chain management system described in Chapter 7. Review the Web site for the system you select. Use what you have learned from the Web site and the description in this book to prepare a report describing some of the design specifications, such as input, output, and interface, for the system you select. If possible, use electronic presentation software to present your findings to the class.

Web Sites of Interest

There are many interesting Web sites to enhance your learning about information systems development. You can search the Web yourself or try the following sites to add to what you have already learned.

Sybase **www.sybase.com**
Sybase has products used in RAD and JAD development.

EDS Canada **www.eds.com/about/locations/canada/**
One of the largest consulting firms in Canada. EDS Canada is the result of the merger of Canada's SHL Systemhouse and the United States' EDS.

Affinity Systems **www.affsys.com**
Toronto-based outsourcer of software development solutions.

CASE STUDY:
Scotiabank Develops Systems to Restructure Its Business Processes

Today we expect more from banking than a smile from a teller. We expect to be able to access banking services 24/7, and we expect banking to be available on most devices, such as computers, laptops, PDAs, and even cell phones. We also expect fairly instantaneous service. If we apply for a loan or a mortgage or a credit card, we expect the answer to our request within a few minutes. Banking customers are becoming better informed, too. We shop around for the best rates and banking packages. The technological advances in banking have put enough information in a user-friendly format to enable us to educate ourselves as to where we should bank for which services. Because of these factors, financial institutions of all kinds—not just banks—are trying to discover what customers want and how best to fulfill customers' wishes. In order to attract and keep customers, banks are trying to respond to customer demands more quickly and efficiently.

Scotiabank is one of Canada's top five banks, offering a wide range of financial services, including corporate capital investment and international online banking. Scotiabank has $290 billion in assets and does business in 50 countries. "We do more business internationally than any of the other large Canadian banks and provide a full range of services to meet the needs of our Canadian personal banking customers," says Glenda Hummel, senior vice president of domestic banking operations at Scotiabank.

In today's market, banks must strive to keep up with banking innovations. "Our domestic operations are extensive, serving seven million customers across Canada through almost 1000 branches, four call centres, 2200 ABMs [automated banking machines], and the Internet," says Hummel. "To help us continue to deliver excellent customer service, all of our employees and offices need to interact reliably, efficiently, and effectively with one another as well as with our back-office systems."

It took Scotiabank a number of years to develop and update its business processes. "We were undertaking improvement projects constantly to revise our processes without adding new technology. For example, we overhauled and consolidated all of the various paper forms in our branches," says Hummel. "But we realized that we had done this to the point of diminishing returns. Scotiabank has the best productivity ratio among the major Canadian banks, and in order to get to the next level of efficiency, we were going to need some new tools to automate and streamline our processes enterprise wide."

Hummel and her team began investigating a variety of companies to determine which might provide Scotiabank with the right automation and reengineering tools. "After we narrowed the field to three top-tier providers, we gave each one three weeks to solve a specific, real-world problem that involved both process integration and integration of employee workflows with one of our existing systems," recalls Sue Harrison, senior vice president of retail systems development for Scotiabank. "The vendors had to grapple

with both application-to-application as well as application-to-people interactions."

"For Scotiabank, our biggest integration challenges continue to be in the areas of scalability and reliability. We were confident that IBM WebSphere MQ Workflow was an appropriate product to connect our 1000-plus Canadian branches and processing centres," says Harrison.

IBM's consultants worked with the Scotiabank team in two locations to develop the bank's first workflow solution. Scotiabank decided to Web-enable the project using IBM's WebSphere family of development tools.

"IBM Global Services provided project management, WebSphere MQ Workflow, and WebSphere MQ expertise, and Java development skills, and helped our technical team pick up the expertise it needed during the project," says Harrison. "As part of the project, we formalized a coach-to-student mentoring process. This has enabled our team to conduct subsequent implementations with minimal IBM support." This way, Scotiabank's team will be able to handle most of the updates and modifications, as well as new systems, without input from the IBM consultants.

Service-oriented architecture (SOA), which is an enterprise-level approach to organize application programs, is the tool that Scotiabank used to integrate its software components. SOA utilizes middleware, a process/workflow engine, and other related systems services, such as directory and security. By using this architecture, the networked enterprise can create, integrate, and manage large-scale, distributed applications in heterogeneous environments. "Our biggest integration challenges continue to be in the areas of scalability and reliability," says Harrison.

SOA also makes it possible for Scotiabank to leverage its existing investments. The bank's intranet environment provides business services to its employees through a server farm that runs IBM's WebSphere Application Server. Directory integration that automates synchronization of workflow users with Scotiabank's corporate directory is leveraged by WebSphere MQ Workflow. Scotiabank's corporate database server, which runs IBM's DB2 information management software, houses the MQ Workflow. WebSphere MQ also provides clustering for load balancing and failover capability to optimize server availability (see Chapter 9). Failover capability means using a failover algorithm if the primary operating system fails to start. The failover algorithm makes the server "failover" to another operating system. The algorithm must detect a start failure and then start the server appliance from another partition or volume.

In terms of improving business processes, and not just managing reliability and scalability, Scotiabank is continuing to use the SOA model to apply WebSphere MQ Workflow technology to deploy end-to-end, policy-based, automated business processes for some of its mortgage fulfillment and loan-underwriting support processes, with additional applications under development.

With the introduction of the automated workflow solution, branch personnel no longer need to manually fill out mortgage requests and fax them to Scotiabank's back-office mortgage-processing centre, the Central Mortgage Unit (CMU), where data had to be entered into a centralized database. If the requests sent to the CMU were incomplete in any respect, the entire process had to be repeated. This caused a labour-intensive process and extended customer response times.

With WebSphere MQ Workflow, Scotiabank and IBM established a mortgage fulfillment workflow, allowing branch personnel to input, edit, and confirm mortgage data while they were with their customers. They were also able to send the data electronically to the CMU processing system. As Hummel explains, "The new workflow virtually eliminates rework and duplicate data entry from the process."

Before the new system was introduced, branch sales staff had to email the nearest back-office loan development centre (LDC) whenever an automated credit decision had to be reviewed. The LDC staff then had to print out the request and personally hand it over to an underwriter, who reviewed the application and emailed a response to the branch.

With their new tools, Scotiabank automated its LDC request process, enabling branch personnel to submit requests to a universal queue supported by all six of the bank's LDCs across the country. "The immediate result was load balancing across all our LDCs. Before, each branch worked with only a single centre, but now we have a seamless national system," explains David Clattenburg, vice president of shared services lending support for Scotiabank. "If the Halifax LDC is at capacity, the Hamilton LDC can pick up the slack to minimize turnaround."

Responsiveness and efficiency increased enterprise-wide because labour-intensive and time-consuming paperwork had been replaced by an efficient system that eliminated redundant data entry, faxing, and other manual processes. "During surveys of our pilot branches, 77 percent of our pilot participants reported that business collaboration between our branches and back offices has improved," says Hummel. "And 68 percent felt that the solution created capacity to focus on generating new sales." According to Hummel, WebSphere MQ Workflow has also given Scotiabank new statistical reporting capabilities to determine how many responses fall within, above, or below targeted service levels.

Sources: "Scotiabank Streamlines Business Processes Using IBM Software," IBM Case Study, **www-306.ibm.com/software/success/ cssdb.nsf/csp/bloz-5qzqa8**, accessed May 23, 2005; "WebSphere MQ Workflow for z/OS," **www-306.ibm.com/software/ integration/wmqwf/editions/zos.html**, accessed May 23, 2005.

CASE STUDY QUESTIONS

1. Why did Scotiabank need to restructure its business processes? Why did they need to bring in consultants and to use tools to accomplish their restructuring?

2. Look at the IBM WebSphere Web site. What additional WebSphere applications might interest Scotiabank? Why?

3. What management issues would surface as this project unfolded? How do you think Scotiabank should handle these issues?

4. Is there a downside to restructuring business processes? If so, how did Scotiabank avoid the downside? What do you think made this project work at Scotiabank?

Chapter 11

Information Resource Management

OBJECTIVES

After reading this chapter, you will be able to:

1. Understand the various components of information resource management and the issues involved in each component.

2. Evaluate models for understanding the business value of information systems.

3. Analyze the principal causes of information system failure.

4. Assess the change management requirements for developing successful systems.

5. Select appropriate strategies to manage the system implementation process.

6. Identify the challenges posed by developing new systems, and propose management solutions.

Opening Case:
HSBC Malaysia: Master of Change Management

HSBC Malaysia Berhad is one of the oldest banks in Malaysia. It is a wholly owned subsidiary of HSBC Holdings, headquartered in London, which is one of the largest financial services companies in the world.

This bank has been a leader in introducing Internet banking and short message service (SMS)- based banking in Malaysia, as well as new value-added banking services for businesses. HSBC's V-Banking (Value Banking) provides new electronic services to retail customers while its Automate@HSBC initiative provides e-business and collaborative commerce technologies to local Malaysian small- and medium-sized businesses.

V-Banking provides retail customers with over 30 telebanking and Internet banking services, consolidated portfolio summaries, and detailed account reconciliation. Customers can receive SMS Smart Alert notifications of returned cheques, credit card payment details, and birthday greetings.

These initiatives have made the bank's business processes more digital, with 96 percent of its transactions now handled online. In changing the way the bank delivers services to retail and corporate customers, these systems have naturally changed the way the bank works.

HSBC restructured bank branches across Malaysia to become personal financial services (PFS) centres. These PFS centres offer 24-hour electronic banking machines with more self-service options and fewer counters manned by tellers. Counter activities focus more on providing personal customer service rather than traditional cash banking functions such as accepting cheques and deposits. A portion of the HSBC Malaysia workforce had to change their job responsibilities from manual, labour-intensive tasks to working more closely with customers as "personal bankers." HSBC's customer relationship management systems and call centres were enhanced to handle the new customer demand for information across a variety of touch points.

Chief information officer Chu Hong Keong and his staff had to sell this new way of doing business to the rest of the organization. They tried to enlist support for the new business processes through meetings, demonstrations, and strategy discussions. The team ran retraining exercises to promote more customer-oriented attitudes among banking staff. To train customers in new banking habits, Chu's group stationed V-Banking ambassadors at key branches to demonstrate how the new electronic banking services and Internet banking kiosks would save customers time and money. V-Banking succeeded because Chu and his managers understood the importance of changing the organization along with the technology. Chu and his Automate@HSBC/V-Banking initiative won several awards, but the initiative did not spread to other countries' HSBC subsidiaries; it has not yet reached Canada, where HSBC has 77 offices and several subsidiaries in addition to straight banking offices.

Sources: Raoul LeBlond, "Time as a Strategic Tool," *CIO Asia*, March 2004; **www.hsbc.com.my**, accessed July 11, 2004; **www.hsbc.ca/hsbc**, accessed May 22, 2005; "eBario Wins AFACT's eASIA Award, University Malaysia Sarawak, **www.unimas.my/ebario/award4.htm**, accessed May 21, 2005; A. Asohan, "MDC launches two new APICTA initiatives, August 2, 2003, **www.unrealmind.com/press_release_7.htm**, accessed May 21, 2005.

Organizations today rely on their information systems to stay in business. The proper functioning of these systems—and their contribution to the bottom line—has become critically important to most organizations. Ensuring that appropriate personnel are properly trained, evaluated, and paid, ensuring that systems development projects are well managed, ensuring that proper planning at all levels has been conducted—these are the main issues involved in managing information and information systems as a critical resource for the organization.

One of the principal challenges posed by information systems is ensuring they can deliver genuine business benefits. There is a very high failure rate among information systems projects because organizations have incorrectly assessed their business value or because firms have failed to manage the organizational change process surrounding the introduction of new technology.

Chu Hong Keong and his team at HSBC Malaysia realized this challenge and took special pains to prepare the bank and its customers for the changes brought about by its new systems and business processes. They had to get the systems right, too.

At many points during your career, you will be involved in projects to develop new information systems. You will need to know how to measure the business benefits of these investments and how to make sure that these systems work successfully in your organization. In this chapter, you will learn about alternative ways of measuring the business value provided by information systems. You will also learn about the role of change management in successful system implementation and strategies for reducing the risks in systems projects. You will first learn how the information systems department manages its own processes and information, a function called information resource management.

11.1 | Information Resource Management

Information resource management (IRM) is the process of managing information systems—including hardware, software, data and databases, telecommunications, people, and the facilities that house these information systems (IS) components—as a critical asset or resource. As recently as 30 years ago, the information systems department was thought of as an "ivory tower" peopled by "pointy-headed geeks" who spoke "technobabble." Running the IS department as though it were any other business function was considered impossible by non-IS managers. What a difference 30 years makes!

Today IS departments are well-managed, with personnel regulations and budgets, just like every other department. Like all departments, appropriate, well-thought-out management principles should be used to maximize the value of the IS department. That is the heart of IRM. In the following subsections, we review the basic components of IRM. While we assume that IS managers need to know these components, we also feel strongly that all managers should understand IRM in order to interact effectively and efficiently with the IS department. The IS department is a service provider to other departments and should be held accountable for the level of service provided. Managers who understand the components of IRM can accurately evaluate the level of service the IS department provides to their department.

The Information Systems Department

Almost every organization today has a computer. Whether there is only one computer and only one individual who uses it or whether there are thousands of computers located around the world, the duties and functions of the IS department are vested in one or more individuals. Whether these duties are explicit, as they are in middle- to large-sized organizations, or implicit, as in a "mom-and-pop" shop, these duties must be handled. The IS department has the following duties and functions:

- Manage computer operations
- Manage systems development and systems development projects
- Manage IS personnel
- Budget for the department and others in the organization who use computers
- Plan for strategic, tactical, and operational level systems and for the IS department's operations.
- Justify financial investment in information systems.

IS departments are structured like other departments; they have managers at all levels and a division of duties and reporting responsibilities. A typical IS department will have several divisions, such as systems development, telecommunications, e-commerce/Web, database management, user relations/support, and operations. Each of these divisions might have subdivisions; for example, systems development might have two subdivisions, such as new development and maintenance. Each of the divisions would have a manager to whom those IS staff members assigned to that division would report. Division managers would report to the IS department manager. Figure 11-1 shows a typical IS department structure.

The IS department manager may or may not be the **chief information officer (CIO)**. The CIO is the strategic level manager for information systems. As a member of senior management, the CIO is responsible for strategic level IS planning and for ensuring that all IS plans, systems, and operations support the organization's overall strategy. Some

chief information officer (CIO)

FIGURE 11-1 *A typical information systems department structure.*

Each division has subdivisions to manage the overall departmental responsibilities.

organizations have begun calling the CIO a chief technology officer (CTO) or chief knowledge officer (CKO).

In addition to the CIO at the strategic level, the organization may also make use of a management information system (MIS) steering committee. The **MIS steering committee** sets policy and priorities for the IS department, including approving budgets for major projects and hearing progress reports on those major projects. The MIS steering committee is usually composed of the CIO and other members of senior management. In the best case scenario, the organization's CEO is also a member of the MIS steering committee. It is the responsibility of the CIO to represent the IS department on the MIS steering committee and to communicate effectively with the committee's membership, "selling" them and other top managers on the IS department's plans and projects.

Managing Planning, Strategy, and External Relations

Again, like every other department, the IS department should conduct periodic planning at all levels. Strategic IS plans describe, from a broad perspective, the major strategic information systems that support or will support the organization's strategy. These are long-range plans that have a huge impact on the organization and on the IS department. Tactical IS plans have a shorter focus and concentrate on breaking down the strategic IS plan into more detailed plans that middle level managers can focus on implementing. Finally, operational level IS plans detail how the strategic IS plan will be implemented during the coming short term, usually one year. Specific goals and objectives permit measurement of how the IS department is performing in supporting the organization's strategy. Each of these sets of IS plans—strategic, tactical, and operational—should be *aligned* with the organization's strategy and with the organization's strategic, tactical, and operational level plans (see Figure 11-2).

The CIO is responsible for ensuring that these plans are developed and aligned with the organization's plans. The CIO is also the major link to external parties, such as senior level managers at vendor organizations and strategic partners' CIOs. While many CIOs have been promoted from the ranks of the IS department, because of the communication-intensive nature of the position, many CIOs come from other areas of the organization, such as finance or human resources.

MIS steering committee

FIGURE 11-2 *How information systems strategy and planning are aligned with organizational strategy and planning.*

Figure 11-2A Model of Organizational Strategic Vision and Planning

Figure 11-2B Model of Information Technology Strategic Vision and Planning

Figure 11-2A represents the organization's strategy and planning steps and levels while Figure 11-2B represents the IS department's strategy and planning steps and levels. The dashed lines represent alignment between the organizational and IS strategies and plans at all steps and levels.

Source: Mary Brabston, Robert Zmud, and John Carlson, "Strategic Vision for Information Technology," in *Strategic Information Technology: Opportunities for Competitive Advantage*, edited by Raymond Papp, Idea Group Publishing, 2000.

Managing Systems Development

Systems development has many facets or perspectives. In Chapter 10, we looked at the systems development life cycle and at systems development as organizational change. In this chapter, we continue that discussion and look at systems development in terms of managing the implemented system and in terms of personnel assignments to develop systems.

In Chapter 9, we discussed information systems quality, security, and control in detail. These topics are also part of information resource management. Once a system has been implemented, it is the IS department's responsibility to ensure that policies, guidelines, and decisions about the implemented systems are followed. These responsibilities include ensuring that backups are made, that IS audits are conducted when and where appropriate, that appropriate security processes and appropriate controls, such as passwords and locked doors, are maintained and followed. Included in this are network, database, and Web management, which ensure that organizational and department policies are followed in each of these areas and that these parts of the organization's information systems are secure, reliable, available, and accessible as needed.

In previous chapters, we briefly discussed the role of systems analysts and programmers. IS departments also employ **systems operators** who run the hardware, typically for a minicomputer or mainframe computer, including loading tape and disk drives, starting and stopping computer "jobs," and ensuring that backups are carried out as dictated by policy. **Data entry operators** enter data in computer-readable format and are managed by database managers. **Network managers** supervise networks while **Web masters** handle the organization's Web-based presence. Every organization organizes its IS department and information system components differently. Every organization also calls people who hold these generic positions by different names. A network manager in one organization may be a LAN coordinator in another, but the employee's function is the same.

Many organizations centralize their information systems so that most of the information systems components (hardware, software, etc.) are located centrally and managed by a central IS department. In centralized IS departments, most decisions about information

systems operators
data entry operators
network managers
Web masters

systems are made in the IS department. Other organizations choose to decentralize their information systems, permitting organizational departments or divisions to make their own decisions about what information systems to develop or purchase, frequently housing their own networks, hardware, and software. Many of these decentralized organizations also employ extra IS staff who report to the decentralized unit.

Today, the trend is toward information service units and information centres. Figure 11-1 depicts this modern type of IS department structure. An information service unit is an IS group located within a non-IS department, such as marketing. The information service unit is employed by and reports to the IS department; the IS unit handles requests for systems development, training, or assistance from their assigned department, serving as an interface to the IS department. An information centre, also known as user support, is housed in the IS department but handles requests for support, training, assistance, and guidance from other departments. If the marketing department needs to determine whether to upgrade the operating system their desktop computers use, they could call the information centre for advice.

Assigning Personnel to Develop Systems How does an IS manager decide who will be assigned to a particular systems development project? Should an experienced person be assigned to new projects or to maintaining those projects on which he or she has already worked? Should less experienced personnel be assigned to maintenance projects so that they may gain experience?

New systems development is considered to be creative and more desirable than maintenance, which is viewed similarly to semi-annual dental checkups. It has to be done, but you'd rather not have to do it. Every organization handles the assignment of programmers and analysts to individual projects differently. Frequently, rotation is used, so that personnel may be assigned to new development for a project and, when that project is completed, move on to a maintenance project. Just as frequently, less experienced IS staff are partnered with more experienced staff on projects, who act as mentors and help them to gain higher levels of expertise.

Finally, the IS department is a service department, providing systems development and other services to other departments. Many businesses have implemented *service level agreements*, in which the IS department signs an agreement with a department for which they are developing a system. The service level agreement specifies milestones and deadlines, the budget, the level of service to be achieved, and other requested benchmarks. The IS department agrees to these terms and is held accountable by corporate management for meeting these benchmarks.

Managing Personnel

We mentioned that IS staff were viewed as "pointy-headed geeks." Previous generations of hardware and software required a high level of technical knowledge and expertise. Today's systems permit lower levels of technical knowledge, enabling those with a middle level of technical expertise to succeed as programmers and analysts. This trend has opened IS career tracks to non-computer science majors.

While computer science focuses more on the technical side of information systems, the MIS field focuses on the needs of business that can be met by computer-based information systems. Today's IS departments hire both computer science and MIS staff to fulfill their personnel requirements. In addition, yesterday's pointy-headed geeks receive education and training in business applications and how to communicate effectively without using technobabble. More and more, the language of the IS department is "business-ese" instead of technobabble.

Regardless of whether IS staff members were hired with a computer science or MIS background, like all other organizational employees, they must be evaluated periodically. Determining metrics on which to base IS staff evaluation is a difficult task. Should a programmer be evaluated on the number of lines of code generated? The code could be inefficient and time consuming to run. Should function points be used instead? Function points define where an actual function has been performed, but some functions are complex while others are not. Do you evaluate an analyst on how well the assigned user area is satisfied with their analyst? Or how well the analyst works with his or her programming teams? Determining what criteria should be used in evaluating IS staff is a difficult task because each staff member's job presents a different mix of the technical and behavioural elements; the variation within the technical or behavioural elements and the mixing of the two, depending on the specific job, makes it difficult to develop and use evaluation criteria over a long period of time. A detailed discussion of this topic is beyond the scope of this text, but IS personnel must be evaluated and counselled on their performance on a periodic basis.

The last ten years have seen the salaries of IS staff increase rapidly. How does an organization recruit and retain IS staff when they cannot afford to give periodic raises that are as high as the local rate of increase? Some organizations have taken to giving bonuses based on work done, projects completed, or tenure in the organization. For example, NorthWest Company has on occasion given a "signing bonus" to new employees, accompanied by a retention bonus after one year on the job. Other organizations, such as the City of Winnipeg, have given their IS staff a year-end bonus, up to several thousand dollars, to those employees who have been there for several years. These loyalty bonuses serve to defuse the natural desire of IS staff to "follow the money." How does that fit the company's salary policy?

We hear in Canada about a "brain drain" to the South—skilled Canadians being hired by U.S. companies at inflated salaries. Interestingly, there are experts on each side of the brain-drain issue—those who feel Canada is losing its best and brightest to the U.S. and those who disagree, arguing that the "brain drain" is only based on almost mythical anecdotal evidence. Regardless of which opinion is correct, the bottom line for IRM is that IS managers must attempt to keep their employees happy. In a time when IS jobs are going unfilled, this approach makes sense. The slowing economy of several years ago (particularly following the terrorist attacks on September 11, 2001, in the United States), combined with dot-com failures to reduce the number of available IS jobs. At least in this regard, perhaps the brain drain—if there ever was one— subsided. Today, however, with Canada's dollar gaining ground, the number of IS jobs available in North America has also increased. In fact, many feel that in the long term, there will be a shortage of qualified personnel to fill the IS jobs available in North America and particularly in Canada.

With technology advancing so rapidly, how do IS staff keep their skills up to date? IS departments need to develop policies for staff to receive training and to upgrade their skills. IS training policies need to address the following issues: funding and time off to attend seminars, workshops, and courses; eligibility for funding and time off; the number of courses that can be taken in a given period; and the locus of the decision (who decides which courses employees will take) about continuing education.

In addition to keeping employees' skills up to date, providing training opportunities is an excellent way to motivate employees and retain them. The flip side of the coin is, of course, that the employees will now have advanced skills with which to seek other jobs. Maintaining a challenging, positive environment with a few "perks" such as casual day (now more of a norm than an exception) or an on-site day-care service also helps to retain employees.

Managing Budgets

How can an IS manager know what the budget for the IS department should be for the coming year? A detailed analysis of projects that are ongoing and projects that may come forward during the next year is required, along with an analysis of potential technology upgrades. The IS department must also examine the potential for extraordinary raises or bonuses for exceptional performance to retain key IS staff. These calculations are not easy. IS projects are notorious for running over budget (see the discussion on change management later in this chapter.).

How do you know when you should upgrade hardware or software? What do you do when your most productive and effective analyst comes to you with a job offer in hand for a 10 percent raise and requests only a 5 percent raise to stay in your organization? How does that fit within the budget? Every IS organization handles their budgeting issues differently.

Many IS departments receive *revenue* from other departments in the form of *charge-backs*, or internal transfers of funds to reflect payment for services rendered. Chargebacks for a department can be calculated based on the department's computer usage, the number of nodes the department maintains on the LAN, the department's size in terms of number of employees or revenues generated, or myriad other ways. It is important that the method of chargeback is well communicated to department heads so that they understand the process and the charges.

Taken together, the topics discussed above comprise the major components of IRM. Being able to justify financial investments in information systems is also part of planning at all levels. The IS department must be able to explain and demonstrate that their budget and systems are worth the organization's financial commitment.

11.2 Understanding the Business Value of Information Systems

Before considering the business value of systems, it is important to understand that firms make two kinds of information systems investments. Firms invest in information systems projects that have very specific objectives and that will be implemented in 12 to 24 months. Firms also invest in information technology (IT) infrastructure; these investments often take place over longer periods of time. Infrastructure investments may include upgrading desktop client machines to the latest version of the Windows operating system, doubling the number of corporate servers, converting all telephones to Voice over IP (VoIP), or upgrading the firm's international bandwidth to speed up communication with offshore subsidiaries. Firms also make infrastructure investments by outsourcing.

Understanding the business value of information systems investments is relatively straightforward, and most systems projects can be easily justified using traditional accounting methods. IT infrastructure investments are more difficult, but not impossible, to rationalize using newer techniques of valuation discussed later in this section.

All information technology investments—whether systems projects or infrastructure— produce value for firms primarily in two ways. The most obvious contribution to value is through improvement in existing business processes or the creation of entirely new business processes, the net result of which is to increase firm efficiency. Second, information systems contribute to improvements in management decision making by increasing the speed of decision making and enhancing the accuracy of decision making. Improvements in both business processes and management decision making can be measured using traditional capital budgeting methods described in this section.

Information systems can also create value by strengthening the firm strategically. The value to the firm may not be an immediate superior return on investment, but instead a longer-term return on investment that results in a better strategic position in the industry. Systems may help a firm achieve differentiable and sustainable advantages by strengthening ties to customers and suppliers, differentiating products and services, and increasing flexibility and adaptability over longer periods.

First movers pay high costs for being the first to invest in a new technology, and they often fail while fast followers can often imitate an innovation. But in the case of complex technology investments typical of firms such as Dell and Wal-Mart, it is unclear that imitators can follow or follow quickly. For instance, Dell's efficient manufacturing capabilities and direct Internet marketing operation have helped it achieve record profits and growth in an industry where its competitors are struggling to break even. Wal-Mart appears to have achieved a long-lived logistics advantage through its investment in supply chain systems and related business processes. No other firms have yet been able to copy Dell or Wal-Mart's business models.

A consistently strong information technology infrastructure can, over the long term, play an important strategic role in the life of the firm. In the long term of five to 10 years, IT infrastructure investments have option value by making it possible for the firm to implement new technologies (and launch new products) in the future. We discuss the real option value of information systems later in this section.

It is also important to realize that systems can have value but the firm may not capture all or even some of the value. Although systems projects can result in firm benefits, such as profitability and productivity, some or all of the benefits can go directly to the consumer in the form of lower prices or more reliable services and products (Hitt and Brynjolfsson 1996). Society can acknowledge firms that enhance consumer surplus by allowing them to survive or by rewarding them with increases in business revenues. But from a management point of view, the challenge is to retain as much of the benefit of systems' investments for the firm itself.

The value of systems from a financial perspective essentially revolves around the issue of return on invested capital. Does a particular IS investment produce sufficient returns to justify its costs?

Traditional Capital Budgeting Models

Capital budgeting models are one of several techniques used to measure the value of investing in long-term capital investment projects. The process of analyzing and selecting various proposals for capital expenditures is called **capital budgeting**. Firms invest in capital projects to expand production to meet anticipated demand or to modernize production equipment to reduce costs. Firms also invest in capital projects for many non-economic reasons, such as installing pollution control equipment, converting to a human resources database to meet government regulations, or satisfying non-market public demands. Information systems are considered long-term capital investment projects.

Six capital budgeting models are used to evaluate capital projects:

The **payback method**: A measure of the time required to pay back the initial investment of a project

The **accounting rate of return on investment (ROI)**: A measure that calculates the rate of return from an investment by adjusting the cash inflows produced by the investment for depreciation

The **net present value**: A measure of the amount of money an investment is worth, taking into account its cost, earnings, and the time value of money

The **cost-benefit ratio**: The ratio of benefits to costs

The **profitability index**: A measure that is calculated by dividing the present value of the total cash inflow from an investment by the initial cost of the investment

The **internal rate of return (IRR)**: The rate of return or profit that an investment is expected to earn, taking into account the time value of money

Capital projects generate cash flows into and out of the firm. Capital budgeting methods rely on measures of cash flows into and out of the firm. The investment cost is an immediate cash outflow caused by the purchase of the capital equipment. In subsequent years, the investment may cause additional cash outflows that will be balanced by cash inflows resulting from the investment. Cash inflows take the form of increased sales of more products (for reasons such as new products, higher quality, or increasing market share) or reduced costs in production and operations. The difference between cash outflows and cash inflows is used for calculating the financial worth of an investment. Once the cash flows have been established, several alternative methods are available for comparing different projects and deciding about the investment.

Financial models assume that all relevant alternatives have been examined, that all costs and benefits are known, and that these costs and benefits can be expressed in a common metric, specifically, money. When one has to choose among many complex alternatives, these assumptions are rarely met in the real world, although they may be approximated. Table 11-1 lists some of the more common costs and benefits of systems. **Tangible benefits** can be quantified and assigned a monetary value. **Intangible benefits**, such as more efficient customer service or enhanced decision making, cannot be immediately quantified but may lead to quantifiable gains in the long run.

capital budgeting

payback method

accounting rate of return on investment (ROI)

net present value

cost-benefit ratio

profitability index

internal rate of return (IRR)

tangible benefits

intangible benefits

TABLE 11-1 Costs and Benefits of Information Systems

COSTS

Hardware
Telecommunications
Software
Services
Personnel

TANGIBLE BENEFITS (COST SAVINGS)

Increased productivity
Lower operational costs
Reduced workforce
Lower computer expenses
Lower outside vendor costs
Lower clerical and professional costs
Reduced rate of growth in expenses
Reduced facility costs

INTANGIBLE BENEFITS

Improved asset utilization
Improved resource control
Improved organizational planning
Increased organizational flexibility
More timely information
More information
Increased organizational learning
Legal requirements attained
Enhanced employee goodwill
Increased job satisfaction
Improved decision making
Improved operations
Higher client satisfaction
Better corporate image

Chapter 5 introduced the concept of total cost of ownership (TCO), which is designed to identify and measure the components of information technology expenditures beyond the initial cost of purchasing and installing hardware and software. However, TCO analysis provides only part of the information needed to evaluate an information technology investment because it does not typically deal with benefits, cost categories such as complexity costs, and "soft" and strategic factors discussed later in this section.

Limitations of Financial Models Many well-known problems emerge when financial analysis is applied to information systems. Financial models do not express the risks and uncertainty of their own costs and benefits estimates. Costs and benefits do not occur in the same time frame—costs tend to be up-front and tangible while benefits tend to be back loaded and intangible. Inflation may affect costs and benefits differently. Technology—especially information technology—can change during the course of the project, causing estimates to vary greatly. Intangible benefits are difficult to quantify. These factors wreak havoc with financial models.

The difficulties of measuring intangible benefits give financial models an application bias: Transaction and clerical systems that displace labour and save space always produce more measurable, tangible benefits than management information systems, decision-support systems, and computer-supported collaborative work systems (see Chapters 15 and 16). Traditional approaches to valuing information systems investments tend to assess the profitability of individual systems projects for specific business functions. These approaches do not adequately address investments in IT infrastructure, testing new business models, or other enterprise-wide capabilities that could benefit the organization as a whole (Ross and Beath 2002).

The traditional focus on the financial and technical aspects of an information system tends to overlook the social and organizational dimensions of information systems that may affect the true costs and benefits of the investment. Many companies' information systems investment decisions do not adequately consider costs from organizational disruptions created by a new system, such as the cost to train end users, the impact of users' learning curves have on productivity, or the time managers need to spend overseeing new system-related changes. Benefits, such as more timely decisions from a new system or enhanced employee learning and expertise, may also be overlooked in a traditional financial analysis (Ryan, Harrison, and Schkade 2002).

There is some reason to believe that investment in information technology requires special consideration in financial modelling. Capital budgeting historically concerned itself with manufacturing equipment and other long-term investments, such as electrical generating facilities and telephone networks. These investments had expected lives of more than one year and up to 25 years. However, information systems differ from manufacturing systems because—among other differences—their life expectancy is shorter. The very high rate of technological change in computer-based information systems means that most systems are seriously out of date in five to eight years. The high rate of technological obsolescence in budgeting for systems means that the payback period must be shorter and the rates of return higher than typical capital projects with much longer useful lives. The bottom line with financial models is to use them cautiously and to put the results into a broader context of business analysis. The Companion Website contains a case example of capital budgeting for a new supply chain management system that details how each of these measures is calculated.

Against traditional financial analysis, you might ask what other investments would be better from an efficiency and effectiveness standpoint. Also, you must ask if all the benefits have been calculated. It may be that this investment is necessary for the survival of the firm or necessary to provide a level of service demanded by the firm's clients. What are competitors doing? In other words, there may be other intangible and strategic business factors to consider.

Strategic Considerations

Other methods of selecting and evaluating information systems investments involve strategic considerations that are not addressed by traditional capital budgeting methods. What would happen if the firm did not make the investment? Would competitors gain a strategic advantage?

Additional material on financial models can be found on the Companion Website.

When the firm has several alternative investments from which to select, it can employ portfolio analysis and scoring models. It can apply real options pricing models to IT investments that are highly uncertain or use a knowledge value-added approach to measure the benefits of changes to business processes. Several of these methods can be used in combination.

Portfolio Analysis A second way of selecting among alternative projects is to use portfolio analysis. **Portfolio analysis** helps the firm develop an overall understanding of where it is making information technology investments by inventorying all information systems projects and assets, including infrastructure, outsourcing contracts, and licenses. This portfolio of information systems investments can be described as having a certain profile of risk and benefit to the firm (see Figure 11-3) similar to a financial portfolio.

Each information systems project carries its own set of risks and benefits. (Section 11.3 describes the factors that increase the risks of systems projects.) Firms would try to improve the return on their portfolios of IT assets by balancing the risk and return from their systems investments. Although there is no ideal profile for all firms, information-intensive industries (e.g., finance) should have a few high-risk, high-benefit projects to ensure that they stay current with technology. Firms in non-information-intensive industries should focus on high-benefit, low-risk projects.

portfolio analysis

FIGURE 11-3   *A system portfolio.*

Companies should examine their portfolio of projects in terms of potential benefits and likely risks. Certain kinds of projects should be avoided altogether and others developed rapidly. There is no ideal mix. Companies in different industries have different profiles.

Once strategic analyses have determined the overall direction of systems development, the portfolio analysis can be used to select alternatives. Obviously you can begin by focusing on systems of high benefit and low risk. These promise early returns and low risks. Second, high-benefit, high-risk systems should be examined; low-benefit, high-risk systems should be totally avoided; and low-benefit, low-risk systems should be reexamined for the possibility of redeveloping and replacing them with more desirable systems having higher benefits. By using portfolio analysis, management can determine the optimal mix of investment risk and reward for their firms, balancing riskier high-reward projects with safer lower-reward ones. Firms where portfolio analysis is aligned with business strategy have been found to have a superior return on their IT assets, better alignment of information technology investments with business objectives, and better organization-wide coordination of IT investments (Jeffrey and Leliveld 2004).

Scoring Models A quick and sometimes compelling method for arriving at a decision on alternative systems is a **scoring model**. Scoring models give alternative systems a single score based on the extent to which they meet selected objectives. Using Table 11-2 as an example, a firm must decide among two alternative enterprise resource planning (ERP) systems. The first column lists the criteria that decision makers will use to evaluate the systems. These criteria are usually the result of lengthy discussions among the decision-making group. Often the most important outcome of a scoring model is not the score but agreement on the criteria used to judge a system. Table 11-2 shows that this particular company attaches the most importance to capabilities for sales order processing, inventory management, and warehousing. The second column in Table 11-2 lists the weights that decision makers attached to the decision criteria. Columns 3 and 5 show the percentage of requirements for each function that each alternative ERP system can provide. Each vendor's score can be calculated by multiplying the percentage of requirements met for each function by the weight attached to that function. ERP System B has the highest total score.

As with all objective techniques, there are many qualitative judgments involved in using the scoring model. This model requires experts who understand the issues and the technology. It is appropriate to cycle through the scoring model several times, changing the criteria and weights, to see how sensitive the outcome is to reasonable changes in criteria. Scoring models are used most commonly to confirm, to rationalize, and to support decisions, rather than as the final arbiters of system selection. If a firm had alternative systems projects from which to select, it could have used the portfolio and scoring models as well as financial models to establish the business value of its systems solution.

Real Options Pricing Models Some information systems projects are highly uncertain. Their future revenue streams are unclear and their up-front costs are high. Suppose, for instance, that a firm is considering a $20 million investment to upgrade its information technology infrastructure. If this upgraded infrastructure were available, the organization would have the technology capabilities to respond to future problems and opportunities. Although the costs of this investment can be calculated, not all of the

scoring model

TABLE 11-2 Example of a Scoring Model for an ERP System

CRITERIA	WEIGHT	ERP SYSTEM A %	ERP SYSTEM A SCORE	ERP SYSTEM B %	ERP SYSTEM B SCORE
1.0 Order Processing					
1.1 Online order entry	4	67	268	73	292
1.2 Online pricing	4	81	324	87	348
1.3 Inventory check	4	72	288	81	324
1.4 Customer credit check	3	66	198	59	177
1.5 Invoicing	4	73	292	82	328
Total Order Processing			1370		1469
2.0 Inventory Management					
2.1 Production forecasting	3	72	216	76	228
2.2 Production planning	4	79	316	81	324
2.3 Inventory control	4	68	272	80	320
2.4 Reports	3	71	213	69	207
Total Inventory Management			1017		1079
3.0 Warehousing					
3.1 Receiving	2	71	142	75	150
3.2 Picking/packing	3	77	231	82	246
3.3 Shipping	4	92	368	89	356
Total Warehousing			741		752
Grand Total			3128		3300

benefits of making this investment can be established in advance. But if the firm waits a few years until the revenue potential becomes more obvious, it might be too late to make the infrastructure investment. In such cases, managers might benefit from using real options pricing models to evaluate information technology investments.

Real options pricing models (ROPM) use the concept of options valuation borrowed from the financial industry. An option is essentially the right, but not the obligation, to act at some future date. A typical call option, for instance, is a financial option in which a person buys the right (but not the obligation) to purchase an underlying asset (usually a stock) at a fixed price (strike price) on or before a given date.

For instance, on July 12, 2005, for $4.40 you could purchase the right (a call option) maturing in January 2007 to buy a share of Hudson's Bay Company common stock for $15. If, by the end of January 2006, the price of Hudson's Bay Company stock did not rise above $15, you would not exercise the option, and the value of the option would fall to zero on the strike date. If, however, the price of Hudson's Bay Company common stock rose to, say, $30 per share, you could purchase the stock for the strike price of $15 and retain the profit of $15 per share minus the cost of the option. (Because the option is sold as a 100-share contract, the cost of the contract would be 100 × $4.40 before commissions, or $440, and you would be purchasing and obtaining a profit from 100 shares of Hudson's Bay Company.) The stock option enables the owner to benefit from the upside potential of an opportunity while limiting the downside risk.

ROPMs value information systems projects similar to stock options, whereby an initial expenditure on technology creates the right, but not the obligation to obtain the benefits associated with further development and deployment of the technology as long as management has the freedom to cancel, defer, restart, or expand the project. Real options

real options pricing models (ROPM)

involving investments in capital projects are different from financial options in that they cannot be traded on a market and they differ in value based on the firm in which they are made. Thus, an investment in an enterprise system will have very different real option values in different firms because the ability to derive value from even identical enterprise systems depends on firm factors, for example, prior expertise, skilled labour force, market conditions, and other factors. Nevertheless, several scholars have argued that the real options theory can be useful when considering highly uncertain IT investments, and potentially the same techniques for valuing financial options can be used (Benaroch and Kauffman 2000; Taudes, Feurstein, and Mild 2000).

ROPMs offer an approach to thinking about information technology projects that takes into account the value of management learning over time and the value of delaying investment. In real options theory, the value of the IT project (real option) is a function of the value of the underlying IT asset (present value of expected revenues from the IT project), the volatility of the value in the underlying asset, the cost of converting the option investment into the underlying asset (the exercise price), the risk-free interest rate, and the option time to maturity (length of time the project can be deferred).

The real options model addresses some of the limitations of the discounted cash flow models described earlier, which essentially call for investing in an information technology project only when the value of the discounted cash value of the entire investment is greater than zero. The ROPM enables managers to consider systematically the volatility in the value of IT projects over time, the optimal timing of the investment, and the changing cost of implementation as technology prices or interest rates rise or fall over time.

This model gives managers the flexibility to stage their IT investment or test the waters with small pilot projects or prototypes to gain more knowledge about the risks of a project before investing in the entire implementation. Briefly, the ROPM places a value on management learning and the use of an unfolding investment technique (investing in chunks) based on learning over time.

The disadvantages of this model are primarily in estimating all the key variables affecting option value, including anticipated cash flows from the underlying asset and changes in the cost of implementation. Models for determining option value of information technology platforms are being developed (Fichman 2004; McGrath and MacMillan 2000). The ROPM can be useful when there is no experience with a technology and its future is highly uncertain.

Knowledge Value-Added Approach A different approach to traditional capital budgeting involves focusing on the knowledge input into a business process as a way of determining the costs and benefits of changes in business processes from new information systems. Any program that uses information technology to change business processes requires knowledge input. The value of the knowledge used to produce improved outputs of the new process can be used as a measure of the value added. Knowledge inputs can be measured in terms of learning time to master a new process, and a return on knowledge can be estimated. This method makes certain assumptions that may not be valid in all situations, especially product design and research and development, where processes do not have predetermined outputs (Housel et al. 2001).

Information Technology Investments and Productivity

Information technology now accounts for about 35 to 50 percent of total business expenditures on capital equipment in North America. Whether this investment has translated into genuine productivity gains remains open to debate, although most of the evidence suggests that the answer is positive. Productivity is a measure of the firm's efficiency in converting inputs to outputs. It refers to the amount of capital and labour required to produce a *unit of output*. For more than a decade, researchers have been trying to quantify the benefits from information technology investments by analyzing data collected at the economy level, industry level, firm level, and information systems application level. The results of these studies have been mixed, and the term *productivity paradox* was coined to describe such findings.

Information technology has increased productivity in manufacturing, especially the manufacture of information technology products, as well as in retail. Wal-Mart, which dominates North American retailing, has experienced increases in both productivity and profitability during the past decade through managerial innovations and powerful supply chain management systems. Competitors, such as Sears, Zellers, and Costco, try to emulate these practices. A 2002 study estimated that Wal-Mart's improved productivity alone accounted for more than half of the productivity acceleration in U.S. general merchandise retailing (Johnson 2002).

However, the extent to which computers have enhanced the productivity of the service sector remains unclear. Some studies show that investment in information technology has not led to any appreciable growth in productivity among office workers. The banking industry, which has been one of the most intensive users of information technology, did not experience any gains in productivity throughout the 1990s (Olazabal 2002). Corporate downsizings and cost-reduction measures have increased worker efficiency but have not yet led to sustained enhancements signifying genuine productivity gains (Roach 2003). Cell phones, home fax machines, laptop computers, and information appliances enable highly paid knowledge workers to get more work done by working longer hours and bringing their work home, but these workers are not necessarily getting more work done in a specified unit of time.

Researchers have not made a systematic effort to measure the impact of these devices on unit output or quality of product or service. For instance, university professors who answer their students' email queries within set office hours are clearly communicating with their students more than in the past, and in that sense, the service of higher education has improved. Measuring the value of this improvement is a challenge.

The contribution of information technology to productivity in information and knowledge industries may be difficult to measure because of the problems of identifying suitable units of output for information work (Panko 1991). How do you measure the output of a law office? Should productivity be measured by examining the number of forms completed per employee (a measure of physical unit productivity) or by examining the amount of revenue produced per employee (a measure of financial unit productivity) in an information- and knowledge-intense industry?

Other studies have focused on the value of outputs (essentially revenues), profits, ROI, and stock market capitalization as the ultimate measures of firm efficiency. A number of researchers have found that information technology investments have resulted in increased productivity and better financial performance, including higher stock valuations (Banker 2001; Brynjolfsson and Hitt 1999, 1993; Brynjolfsson, Hitt, and Yang 1999; Chatterjee, Pacini, and Sambamurthy 2002; Davamanirajan, Mukhopadhyay, and Kriebel 2002; Hitt, Wu, and Zhou 2002).

Information technology investments are more likely to improve firm performance if they were accompanied by complementary investments in new business processes, organizational structures, and organizational learning that could unleash the potential of the new technology. In addition to this "organizational capital," complementary resources, such as up-to-date IT infrastructures, have been found to make e-commerce investments more effective in improving firm performance (Zhu 2004; Zhu and Kraemer 2002). Firms that have built appropriate infrastructures—and view their infrastructures as sets of services providing strategic agility—have faster times to market, higher growth rates, and more sales from new products (Weill and Broadbent 1998; Weill, Subramani, and Broadbent 2002).

In addition to reducing costs, computers may increase the quality of products and services for consumers or may create entirely new products and revenue streams. These intangible benefits are difficult to measure and consequently are not addressed by conventional productivity measures. Moreover, because of competition, the value created by computers may primarily flow to customers rather than to the company making the investments (Brynjolfsson 1996).

For instance, the investment in automatic teller machines (ATMs) by banks has not resulted in higher profitability for any single bank although the industry as a whole has prospered and consumers enjoy the benefits without paying higher fees. Productivity gains may not necessarily increase firm profitability. Hence, the returns of information technology investments should be analyzed within the competitive context of the firm, the industry, and the specific way in which information technology is being applied.

11.3 The Importance of Change Management In Information Systems Success and Failure

Benefits from information technology investments are reduced if firms do not engage in the organizational change associated with a particular new system or make these changes effectively (Irani and Love 2000–2001; Ryan and Harrison 2000). The introduction or alteration of an information system has a powerful behavioural and organizational impact. It transforms how various individuals and groups perform and interact. Changes in the way that information is defined, accessed, and used to manage the organization's resources often lead to new distributions of authority and power. This internal organizational change breeds resistance and opposition and can lead to the demise of an otherwise good system.

A very large percentage of information systems fail to deliver benefits or solve the problems for which they were intended because the process of organizational change surrounding system development was not properly addressed. Successful system development requires careful change management.

Information System Problem Areas

The problems causing information **system failure** fall into multiple categories, as illustrated in Figure 11-4. The major problem areas are design, data, cost, and operations.

Design The actual design of the system may fail to capture essential business requirements or improve organizational performance. Information may not be provided quickly enough to be helpful; it may be in a format that is impossible to digest and use; or it may represent the wrong pieces of data.

FIGURE 11-4   Information systems problem areas.

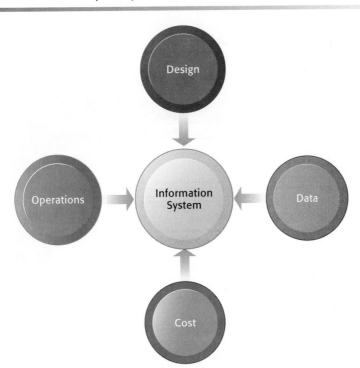

Problems with an information system's design, data, cost, or operations can be evidence of a system failure.

system **failure**

The way in which nontechnical business users must interact with the system may be excessively complicated and discouraging. A system may be designed with a poor user interface. The **user interface** is the part of the system with which end users interact. For example, an input form or an online data entry screen may be so poorly arranged that no one wants to enter data. The procedures to request online information retrieval may be so unintelligible that users are too frustrated to make requests, or the requested data may be displayed in a format that is too difficult to comprehend (Speier and Morris 2003).

Web sites may discourage visitors from exploring further if the Web pages are cluttered and poorly arranged, if users cannot easily find the information they are seeking, or if it takes too long to access and display the Web page on the user's computer (Palmer 2002). This is what happened to Quixtar.com, a major e-commerce sales channel for the Amway Corporation, a company that has a major presence in Canada. This site is considered highly successful, but it is not providing as much value as it could because of poor design (see Figure 11-5). The Window on Organizations explains how Quixtar.com's design affected its ability to convert Web site visitors to buyers and how Quixtar fixed these problems.

An information system can be deemed a failure if its design is not compatible with the structure, culture, and goals of the organization as a whole. Historically, information systems design has been preoccupied with technical issues at the expense of organizational concerns. The result has often been information systems that are technically excellent but incompatible with their organization's structure, culture, and goals. Without a close organizational fit, these systems create tensions, instability, and conflict.

Data The data in the system may have a high level of inaccuracy or inconsistency. The information in certain fields may be erroneous or ambiguous, or it may not be organized properly for business purposes. Information required for a specific business function may be inaccessible because the data are incomplete, or not up to date.

Cost Some systems operate quite smoothly, but their costs to implement and run on a production basis may be way over budget. Other system projects may be too costly to complete. In both cases, the excessive expenditures cannot be justified by the demonstrated business value of the information they provide.

Operations The system does not run well. Information is not provided in a timely and efficient manner because the computer operations that handle information

FIGURE 11-5   Quixtar.com registration form.

This registration form pops up when a visitor to the Quixtar.com Web site places his or her first item in the site's electronic shopping cart, interrupting the shopping process. This feature could discourage some potential buyers from completing their purchases.

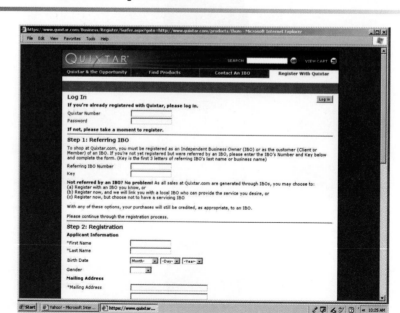

user interface

processing break down. Jobs that abort too often lead to excessive reruns and delayed or missed schedules for delivery of information. An online system may be operationally inadequate because the response time is too long.

Some of these problems can be attributed to technical features of information systems, but most stem from organizational factors (Keil, Cule, Lyytinen, and Schmidt 1998). System developers need to understand these organizational issues and learn how to manage the change associated with a new information system.

Organization   WINDOW ON ORGANIZATIONS

What's Wrong with Quixtar.com?

Amway is the largest multilevel marketing organization in the world, selling billions of dollars a year of products such as soap, water purifiers, vitamins, and cosmetics. Amway runs its business through a network of independent business owners, or IBOs. The IBOs sell Amway products to retail customers, recruit other sellers, and are paid a percentage of sales booked by newcomers.

Amway no longer sells face-to-face in North America. In September 1999, it set up a Web site called Quixtar.com to enable its IBOs to sell over the Web to new IBOs or retail customers. In Canada, Quixtar's Web site, www.quixtar.ca, runs off the company's U.S. server; any purchases made are logged by the www.quixtar.com Web site. Quixtar's brands include Nutrilite nutritional supplements, Artistry skin care and cosmetics, XS Sports Nutrition, and eSpring water purifiers. Through its Store for More, Quixtar also offers products from leading brands such as Maytag, Adidas, and Calvin Klein.

Sales at Quixtar.com have surpassed $1 billion, making Quixtar one of the top online retailers in North America. In June 2004, *Internet Retailer* ranked Quixtar.com first in its online Drug/Health and Beauty category and twelfth among all e-commerce sites in its annual "Top 300 Guide" to the Web.

Quixtar.com works hard at making its Web site available and reliable. It takes in about $3 million in sales each day, spiking to $10 million on the last day of each month. It uses RealiTea software from TeaLeafTechnology in San Francisco to monitor the activities of its visitors to help it pinpoint application failures or bottlenecks. RealiTea tracks every click and keystroke, and these data are captured in a two-terabyte database that can store 10 days worth of user activity. When a problem occurs, Quixtar staff can pinpoint the error by accessing the database to play back specified user sessions. The TeaLeaf replay highlights the visitor's session history to help Quixtar staff see every field a customer typed in or link that a customer clicked.

But something is not quite right. Quixtar's Web site is not as good as it could be because it has usability problems. Mark Hurst, president of Creative Good, an Internet consultancy, estimates that fixing Quixtar's design flaws could produce another $100 million annually.

Both IBOs and individual shoppers who are not part of the Quixtar network can use the site to place orders. Veteran IBOs were able to muddle through because they're very familiar with the Quixtar lingo and procedures. But most retail shoppers back away, creating lost sales because Quixtar wants very much to sell to the general public, and the Web site's confusing interface thwarts sales. Let's see how.

Claudia Case, a usability consultant at Keynote Systems, a Web measurement company, found that Quixtar.com lacked a consistent look and was organized to reflect how Quixtar works rather than how customers shop. Quixtar itself encountered problems with its checkout procedure. In the fall of 2003, the site automatically filled out an incorrect shipping address for 14 online orders without customers' knowledge. Quixtar called the affected customers, and its technicians then fixed the software problem.

Keynote Systems found several design flaws in Quixtar.com's purchasing process that prevented the system from converting as many visitors as it could to buyers of its products. For instance, every time a customer puts his or her first item in a shopping cart, a registration form pops up, interrupting the shopping process before it is completed. The form does not acknowledge that the shopper has chosen any items and could annoy a visitor before that person has committed to spending money at that site. If a user makes a mistake while filling out this or other forms, there is no easy way to correct the errors during the checkout process. These problems could be avoided if Quixtar.com asked for registration or identification information when the customer was ready to pay and if it introduced a process to correct forms on the spot.

Quixtar.com assigns each customer a 9- to 11-digit account number that is required for shopping at the site. The account number is not meaningful to the customer and obviously is difficult to remember. Customers can change their passwords by themselves but they cannot change their account numbers. Hard-to-remember account numbers can slow down or even deter customers from shopping. Quixtar could remedy the situation by providing a capability for customers to personalize their passwords.

Quixtar.com's order history page contains confusing language. Customers who want to view past and pending orders have to decipher unclear terminology. For example, the page contains a "hint" to the customer to "Select a display option. Your current selection is all orders in the current month." Customers would have to work to understand the meaning. If a drop-down bar was labelled "View open and past orders," a hint would not be necessary.

To Think About: How does the design of Quixtar.com's Web site affect the way it runs its business? Evaluate the features that both enhance and impede its performance.

Sources: Kim S. Nash, "Cleaning Up," *Baseline Magazine*, June 2004; www.quixtar.com, accessed May 22, 2005; www.quixtar.ca, accessed May 22, 2005; and www.tealeaf.com, accessed July 14, 2004.

Change Management and the Concept of Implementation

To manage the organizational change surrounding the introduction of a new information system effectively, you must examine the process of implementation. **Implementation** refers to all organizational activities working toward the adoption, management, and routinization of an innovation, such as a new information system. In the implementation process, the systems analyst is a **change agent**. The analyst not only develops technical solutions but also redefines the configurations, interactions, job activities, and power relationships of various organizational groups. The analyst is the catalyst for the entire change process and is responsible for ensuring that all parties involved accept the changes created by a new system. The change agent communicates with users, mediates between competing interest groups, and ensures that the organizational adjustment to these changes is complete.

One model of the implementation process is the Kolb/Frohman model of organizational change. This model divides the process of organizational change into a seven-stage relationship between an organizational *consultant* and his or her *client*. (The consultant corresponds to the information systems designer, and the client to the user.) The success of the change effort is determined by how well the consultant and client deal with the key issues at each stage (Kolb and Frohman 1970). Other models of implementation describe the relationship as one among designers, clients, and decision makers, who are responsible for managing the implementation effort to bridge the gap between design and utilization (Swanson 1988).

Causes of Implementation Success and Failure

Implementation outcome can largely be determined by the following factors:

- The role of users in the implementation process
- The degree of management support for and commitment to the implementation effort
- The level of complexity and risk of the implementation project
- The quality of management of the implementation process

These are largely behavioural and organizational issues and are illustrated in Figure 11-6.

User Involvement and Influence User involvement in the design and operation of information systems has several positive results. First, if users are heavily involved in systems design, they have more opportunities to mould the system according to their priorities and business requirements, and more opportunities to control the

FIGURE 11-6 *Information systems success or failure factors.*

The implementation outcome can be largely determined by the role of users, the degree of management support, the level of risk and complexity of the implementation project, and the quality of management of the implementation process. Evidence of the information system's success or failure can be found in the areas of design, cost, operations, and data.

implementation

change agent

outcome. Second, they are more likely to react positively to the completed system because they have been active participants in the change process. They feel a sense of ownership of the new system. Incorporating user knowledge and expertise leads to better solutions.

Thanks to widespread use of the Internet and fourth-generation tools, today's users are assuming more of a leadership role in articulating the adoption, development, and implementation of information technology innovations (Kettinger and Lee 2002). However, users often take a very narrow and limited view of the problem to be solved and may overlook important technology issues or alternative information systems solutions. The skills and vision of professional systems designers are still required much the same way that the services of an architect are required when building a new house (Markus and Keil 1994).

The relationship between consultant and client has traditionally been a problem area for information systems implementation efforts. Users and information systems specialists tend to have different backgrounds, interests, and priorities. This is referred to as the **user-designer communications gap**. These differences lead to divergent organizational loyalties, approaches to problem solving, and vocabularies.

Information systems specialists, for example, often have a highly technical, or machine, orientation to problem solving. They look for elegant and sophisticated technical solutions in which hardware and software efficiency is optimized at the expense of ease of use or organizational effectiveness. Users prefer systems that are oriented toward solving business problems or facilitating organizational tasks. Often the orientations of both groups are so at odds that they appear to speak different languages.

These differences are illustrated in Table 11-3, which depicts the typical concerns of end users and technical specialists (information systems designers) regarding the development of a new information system. Communication problems between end users and designers are a major reason why user requirements are not properly incorporated into information systems and why users are driven out of the implementation process.

Systems development projects run a very high risk of failure when there is a pronounced gap between users and technicians and when these groups pursue different goals. Under these conditions, users are often driven out of the implementation process. Because they cannot comprehend what the technicians are saying, users conclude that the entire project is best left in the hands of the information specialists alone. With so many implementation efforts guided by purely technical considerations, it is no wonder that many systems fail to serve organizational needs.

Management Support and Commitment If an information systems project has the backing and commitment of management at various levels, it is more likely to be perceived positively by both users and the technical information services staff. Both groups will believe that their participation in the development process will receive higher-level attention and priority. They will be recognized and rewarded for the time and effort they devote to implementation. Management backing also ensures that a systems

TABLE 11-3 The User-Designer Communications Gap

USER CONCERNS	DESIGNER CONCERNS
Will the system deliver the information I need for my work?	How much disk storage space will the master file consume?
How quickly can I access the data?	How many lines of program code will it take to perform this function?
How easily can I retrieve the data?	How can we cut down on CPU time when we run the system?
How much clerical support will I need to enter data into the system?	What is the most efficient way of storing these data?
How will the operation of the system fit into my daily business schedule?	What database management system should we use?

user-designer communications gap

project receives sufficient funding and resources to be successful. Furthermore, to be enforced effectively, all the changes in work habits and procedures and any organizational realignments associated with a new system depend on management backing. If a manager considers a new system a priority, the system will more likely be treated that way by his or her subordinates (Doll 1985; Ein-Dor and Segev 1978).

Level of Complexity and Risk

Systems differ dramatically in their size, scope, level of complexity, and organizational and technical components. Some systems development projects are more likely to fail or suffer delays because they carry a much higher level of risk than others. The level of project risk is influenced by project size, project structure, and the level of technical expertise of the information systems staff and project team.

- *Project size.* The larger the project—as indicated by the dollars spent, the size of the implementation staff, the time allocated for implementation, and the number of organizational units affected—the greater the risk. Very large scale systems projects have a failure rate that is 50 to 75 percent higher than that for other projects because these projects are complex and difficult to control. The organizational complexity of the system—how many units and groups use it and how much it influences business processes—contribute to the complexity of large-scale systems projects just as much as technical characteristics, such as the number of lines of program code, length of project, and budget (Xia and Lee, 2004; Concours Group 2000; Laudon 1989).

- *Project structure.* Some projects are more highly structured than others. Their requirements are clear and straightforward, so outputs and processes can be easily defined. Users know exactly what they want and what the system should do; there is almost no possibility of the users changing their minds. These projects run a much lower risk than those with relatively undefined, fluid, and constantly changing requirements; with outputs that cannot be fixed easily because they are subject to users' changing ideas; or with users who cannot agree on what they want.

- *Experience with technology.* The project risk rises if the project team and the information systems staff lack the required technical expertise. If the team is unfamiliar with the hardware, system software, application software, or database management system proposed for the project, it is highly likely that the project will experience technical problems or take more time to complete because of the need to master new skills.

The Sun Life intranet described in the Window on Management is an example of a complex systems project. Fortunately, Sun Life planned how to best implement their global corporate intranet and succeeded where many others, including IBM, had failed.

 WINDOW ON MANAGEMENT

When It Comes to Intranet Governance, Sun Life Shines

Sun Life Financial is a Canadian financial services company. One of its competitors was Clarica, formerly Mutual Life of Canada. When Sun Life Financial merged with Clarica in 2002, the combined Canadian operations of the merged company held a leading position in most of the Canadian markets served. After the merger, Sun Life Financial established the Sun Life Online Communications Steering Strategy Council to guide the development of a new, worldwide employee portal. "We wanted to break down communications barriers that can sometimes exist between a head office and national operations," says

Cheryl Ficker, manager, corporate affairs, responsible for Sun Life's online communications strategy. "The main driver for establishing a council was to break down the barriers that existed between the corporate group (head office) and the various operations of the business."

Ficker says the council members are also the intranet's key ambassadors and advocates. "The stakeholders are very passionate about their work, and often view their efforts as personal achievements. It's helpful to have diverse views and opinions at the table to ensure buy-in at the start and over the longer-term."

After reading this chapter, you may believe that the biggest obstacles to successful intranet implementation would be technology experience, budget, or change management issues. But, as Sun Life recognized, two of their biggest obstacles to successful implementation of a firm-wide intranet were politics and ownership. A 2001 study of more than 500 intranet managers found that 74 percent felt that content management—the creation, publishing, and management of content on the intranet—was the top intranet management issue. "Insufficient control and ownership" of the intranet was cited by 46 percent of managers, making this the sixth ranked issue. Number eight on the list, with 43 percent, was politics. ("Survey data: Management of the intranet and issues companies face," *Melcrum Research Report: Managing and Developing Intranets for Business Value*, 2001.)

It is the immaturity of intranet technology that causes most of these problems. A number of departments and stakeholders—such as corporate communications, human resources, IT, and various business units—are having to cross their organizational boundaries and cooperate as a single unit with a single intranet home page because of the consolidation of intranet sites and services in a central site or portal. This "forced" cooperation naturally gives rise to politics and competition for ownership.

The first intranets went online in the early to mid-1990s. In essence, they presented an electronic version of a brochure, much like Internet sites through the late 1990s, when companies elected to first present a "company brochure" electronically before evolving to e-commerce and full content management systems. Each department posted its own intranet site, resulting in intranet sprawl. For example, at one time, IBM had 9000 intranet sites, each separately governed, with duplicated effort to develop the intranet, duplicate technologies (e.g., servers), and frequently duplicated content.

Eventually senior managers, including heads of the information systems department, realized what a waste this overlap was and began efforts to consolidate all corporate intranet content into one corporate intranet portal. Soon IT, human resources, corporate communications, and many other departments and business units had to cooperate under a single intranet structure.

Terry Lister, partner and leader of IBM Canada's business consulting services, says, "It's ironic. We wouldn't have these difficulties in a building where you have different groups existing together in the same space. But partly because of the way the intranet grew up, we didn't create a corporate view, and you have to struggle to pull the intranet back and find something better."

In order to resolve political and ownership issues, a defined governance model—a structure outlining the ownership and decision-making process—has to be created. "If you don't have structure, you're going to constantly run into politics," says Lister. "Without a governance structure with standards, different silos try to do something in parallel (their own thing), and it costs more... and will lessen the user experience." There are three governance models that are significant: decentralized, centralized, and collaborative or federated.

Single ownership consolidated in a single department characterizes a centralized governance model, which is more common in early-stage intranets or smaller companies. Decentralized intranet ownership, more common in larger organizations, generates the "wild west" or "intranet sprawl" approach to development and management.

A collaborative or federated model—most often taking the form of a steering committee representing the major functional stakeholders in communications, human resources, operations, IT, and business units—is the next-generation intranet goverance model. It is most successful when the committee membership is made up of one or two key executives, often the CIO or the head of communications or human resources. A collaborative team operates the intranet by applying policies, standards, and templates. The collaborative model, however, uses the far slower and more bureaucratic committee approach to decision-making than the centralized and decentralized models.

The steering committee at Sun Life plays a conflict resolution role, offering a forum for minimizing the politics of ownership. The collaborative model makes sure that all the stakeholders consider the needs of the organization rather than their specific functional silo and facilitates the development of general standards and policies.

"There is no doubt the council was the way to go in terms of establishing a forum for best practices, knowledge sharing, and collective evolution," says Sun Life's Ficker. "Through the council, members have established solid, meaningful, and trusting relationships. At any time, any member can pick up the phone and connect with their colleagues internationally to brainstorm, share a story, or ask a question."

In intranet management, politics and the issues of control, ownership, and standards are inevitable; perhaps it is these issues that have made the defining of governance models a must. As IBM's Lister says, "The key thing is hassle elimination." Even though a governance model may not fully eliminate intranet politics, it may lessen the problems for the overworked intranet managers.

To Think About: What management, organizational, and technology factors caused Sun Life to establish the Sun Life online communications steering strategy council? Be specific and consider IRM, financial justification, and change management. How did the council manage these issues? Could these issues have been handled differently and successfully?

Sources: Toby Ward, "The Politics of Intranet Ownership," *Prescient Digital*, available www.prescientdigital.com/Prescient_Research/Articles/Governance_Articles/The_Politics_of_Intranet_Ownership.htm, accessed May 25, 2005; Toby Ward, "Collaborative Governance (Intranet Politics Part II)," *Prescient Digital*, available www.prescientdigital.com/Prescient_Research/Articles/Governance_Articles/Collaborative_Governance__Intranet_Politics_Part_II_.htm, accessed May 25, 2005; Sun Life Financial Canada, available www.sunlife.ca/canada/cda/homepage_v2, accessed May 25, 2005.

Management of the Implementation Process The development of a new system must be carefully managed and orchestrated, and the way a project is executed is likely to be the most important factor influencing its outcome (Wallace and Keil 2004). Often basic elements of success are forgotten. Training to ensure that end users are comfortable with the new system and fully understand its potential uses is often sacrificed or forgotten in systems development projects. If the budget is strained at the very beginning, toward the end of a project, there will likely be insufficient funds for training and documentation (Bikson et al. 1985).

The conflicts and uncertainties inherent in any implementation effort are magnified when an implementation project is poorly managed and organized. As illustrated in Figure 11-7, a systems development project without proper management will most likely suffer these consequences:

- Costs that vastly exceed budgets
- Unexpected time slippage
- Technical shortfalls resulting in performance that is significantly below the estimated level
- Failure to obtain anticipated benefits

How badly are projects managed? On average, private sector projects are underestimated by one-half in terms of budget and time required to deliver the complete system promised in the system plan. A very large number of projects are delivered with missing functionality (promised for delivery in later versions). The Standish Group International found that only 9 percent of all technology investments were completed on time, on budget, or within scope. Between 30 and 40 percent of all software projects are "runaway" projects that far exceed the original schedule and budget projections and fail to perform as originally specified (Keil, Mann, and Rai 2000). Why are projects managed so poorly, and what can be done about it? Here we discuss some possibilities.

- *Ignorance and optimism.* The techniques for estimating the length of time required to analyze and design systems are poorly developed. Most applications are "first time" (i.e., there is no prior experience in the application area). The larger the scale of systems, the greater the role of ignorance and optimism. The net result of these factors is that estimates tend to be optimistic, "best case," and wrong. It is assumed that all will go well when in fact it rarely does.

- *The mythical man-month.* The traditional unit of measurement used by systems designers to project costs is the **man-month**. Projects are estimated in terms of how many man-months are required. However, adding more workers to projects does not necessarily reduce the elapsed time needed to complete a systems project (Brooks 1974). Unlike cotton picking—when tasks can be rigidly partitioned, communication between participants is not required, and training is unnecessary—developing systems often involves *tasks that are sequentially linked, cannot be performed in isolation, and require extensive communications and training.* Adding labour to software projects where there are many task interdependencies can slow down delivery as the communication, learning, and coordination costs escalate and detract from the output of participants (Andres and Zmud 2001–2002). For comparison, imagine what would happen if five amateur spectators were added to one team in a championship professional basketball game. The team composed of five professional basketball players would probably do much better in the short run than the team with five professionals and five amateurs.

man-month

Without proper management, a systems development project takes longer to complete and most often exceeds the allocated budget. The resulting information system most likely is technically inferior and may not be able to demonstrate any benefits to the organization.

FIGURE 11-7 *Consequences of poor project management.*

Cost overruns
Time slippage
Technical shortfalls impairing performance
Failure to obtain anticipated benefits

- *Falling behind: Bad news travels slowly upward.* For projects in all fields, slippage in projects, failure, and doubts are often not reported to senior management until it is too late (Keil and Robey 2001; Smith, Keil, and Depledge 2001). The CONFIRM project, a very large scale information systems project to integrate hotel, airline, and rental car reservations, is a classic example. It was sponsored by Hilton Hotels, Budget Rent-A-Car, and the Marriott Corporation and developed by AMR Information Services, a subsidiary of American Airlines Corporation. The project was very ambitious and technically complex, employing a staff of 500. Members of the CONFIRM project management team did not immediately come forward with accurate information when the project began encountering problems coordinating various transaction-processing activities. Clients continued to invest in a project that was faltering because they were not informed of problems with database, decision-support, and integration technologies (Oz 1994).

Change Management Challenges for Business Process Reengineering, Enterprise Applications, and Mergers and Acquisitions

Given the challenges of innovation and implementation, it is not surprising to find a very high failure rate among enterprise application and business process reengineering (BPR) projects. These projects typically require extensive organizational change and may require replacing old technologies and legacy systems that are deeply rooted in many interrelated business processes. A number of studies have indicated that 70 percent of all business process reengineering projects fail to deliver promised benefits. Likewise, a high percentage of enterprise applications fail to be fully implemented or to meet the goals of their users even after three years of work.

Many enterprise application and reengineering projects have been undermined by poor implementation and change management practices that failed to address employees' concerns about change. Dealing with fear and anxiety throughout the organization; overcoming resistance by key managers; changing job functions, career paths, and recruitment practices; and training have posed greater threats to reengineering than the difficulties companies faced visualizing and designing breakthrough changes to business processes. All of the enterprise applications require tighter coordination among different functional groups as well as extensive business process change (see Chapter 14).

System Implications of Mergers and Acquisitions

Mergers and acquisitions (M&A) have been proliferating because they are major growth engines for businesses. Potentially, firms can cut costs significantly by merging with competitors, reduce risks by expanding into different industries (e.g., conglomerating), and create larger pools of competitive knowledge and expertise by joining forces with other players. There are also economies of time: A firm can gain market share and expertise very quickly through acquisition rather than building over the long term.

Although some firms, such as CanWest Global Communications, are quite successful in carrying out mergers and acquisitions, research has found that more than 70 percent of all M&A result in a decline in shareholder value and often lead to divestiture at a later time (Frank and Sidel 2002; Lipin and Deogun 2000). Many deals suffer from poor planning and from unrealistic expectations about the synergies that could result from merging companies.

Architects of mergers and acquisitions often fail to appreciate the difficulty of integrating the systems of different companies. Mergers and acquisitions are deeply affected by the organizational characteristics of the merging companies as well as by their information technology (IT) infrastructures. Combining the information systems of two different companies usually requires considerable organizational change and complex systems projects to manage. If the integration is not properly managed, firms can emerge with a tangled hodgepodge of inherited legacy systems developed by aggregating the systems of one firm after another. Without successful systems integration, the benefits anticipated from the merger cannot be realized, or, worse, the merged entity cannot execute its business processes and loses customers.

Once a company targeted for acquisition has been identified, information systems managers need to identify the realistic costs of integration; the estimated benefits of economies in operation, scope, knowledge, and time; and any problematic systems that require major investments to integrate. In addition, IT managers can critically estimate any likely costs and organizational changes required to upgrade the IT infrastructure or make major system improvements to support the merged companies.

11.4 | Managing Implementation

Not all aspects of the implementation process can be easily controlled or planned. However, anticipating potential implementation problems and applying appropriate corrective strategies can increase the chances for system success. Various project management, requirements gathering, and planning methodologies have been developed for specific categories of problems. Strategies have also been devised for ensuring that users play appropriate roles throughout the implementation period and for managing the organizational change process.

Controlling Risk Factors

The first step in managing project risk involves identifying the nature and level of risk confronting the project (Schmidt et al. 2001). Implementers can then handle each project with the tools, methodologies, and risk-management approaches geared to its level of risk (Iversen, Mathiassen, and Nielsen 2004; Barki, Rivard, and Talbot 2001; McFarlan 1981).

Managing Technical Complexity Projects with *challenging and complex technology* to master benefit from **internal integration tools**, a project management technique that ensures the implementation team operates as a cohesive unit. The success of these complex projects depends on how well their technical complexity can be managed. Project leaders need both heavy technical and administrative experience. They must be able to anticipate problems and develop smooth working relationships among a predominantly technical team. The team should be under the leadership of a manager with a strong technical and project management background, and team members should be highly experienced. Team meetings should take place frequently. Essential technical skills or expertise not available internally should be secured from outside the organization.

internal integration tools
formal planning tools
formal control tools

Formal Planning and Control Tools Large projects benefit from appropriate use of **formal planning tools** to structure and sequence tasks and **formal control tools** to help monitor the progress toward the completion of tasks and goals. With project management techniques, such as Program Evaluation and Review Technique (PERT) or Gantt charts, a detailed plan can be developed. A PERT chart lists the specific activities that make up a project, their duration, and the activities that must be completed before a specific activity can start. A Gantt chart, such as the example in Figure 11-8, visually represents the sequence and timing of different tasks in a development project as well as their resource requirements. Tasks can be defined and resources budgeted.

These project management techniques can help managers identify bottlenecks and determine the impact that problems will have on project completion times. They can also help systems developers partition implementation into smaller, more manageable segments with defined, measurable business

This project team of professionals is using computing tools to enhance communication, analysis, and decision making.

FIGURE 11-8 *Formal planning and control tools help to manage information systems projects successfully.*

HRIS COMBINED PLAN–HR	Da	Who	2005 Oct Nov Dec	2006 Jan Feb Mar Apr May Jun Jul Aug Sep Oct Nov Dec	2007 Jan Feb Mar
DATA ADMINISTRATION SECURITY					
QMF security review/setup	20	EF TC			
Security orientation	2	EF JA			
QMF security maintenance	35	TC GL			
Data entry sec. profiles	4	EF TC			
Data entry sec. views est.	12	EF TC			
Data entry security profiles	65	EF TC			
DATA DICTIONARY					
Orientation sessions	1	EF			
Data dictionary design	32	EF WV			
DD prod. coordn-query	20	GL			
DD prod. coordn-live	40	EF GL			
Data dictionary cleanup	35	EF GL			
Data dictionary maint.	35	EF GL			
PROCEDURES REVISION					
DESIGN PREP					
Work flows (old)	10	PK JL			
Payroll data flows	31	JL PK			
HRIS P/R model	11	PK JL			
P/R interface orient. mtg.	6	PK JL			
P/R interface coordn. 1	15	PK			
P/R interface coordn. 2	8	PK			
Benefits interfaces (old)	5	JL			
Benefits interfaces (new flow)	8	JL			
Benefits communication strategy	3	PK JL			
New work flow model	15	PK JL			
Posn. data entry flows	14	WV JL			

RESOURCE SUMMARY

Name		Who	Oct	Nov	Dec	Jan	Feb	Mar	Apr	May	Jun	Jul	Aug	Sep	Oct	Nov	Dec	Jan	Feb	Mar
Edith Farrell	5.0	EF	2	21	24	24	23	22	22	27	34	34	29	26	28	19	14			
Woody Vinton	5.0	WV	5	17	20	19	12	10	14	10	2							4	3	
Charles Pierce	5.0	CP		5	11	20	13	9	10	7	6	8	4	4	4	4	4			
Ted Leurs	5.0	TL		12	17	17	19	17	14	12	15	16	2	1	1	1	1			
Toni Cox	5.0	TC	1	11	10	11	11	12	19	19	21	21	21	17	17	12	9			
Patricia Knopp	5.0	PC	7	23	30	34	27	25	15	24	25	16	11	13	17	10	3	3	2	
Jane Lawton	5.0	JL	1	9	16	21	19	21	21	20	17	15	14	12	14	8	5			
Akshay Duggal	5.0	AD	4	4	5	5	5	2	7	5	4	16	2							
Diane O'Neill	5.0	DO	6	14	17	16	13	11	9	4										
Joan Albert	5.0	JA	5	6			7	6	2	1				5	5	1				
Marie Marcus	5.0	MM	15	7	2	1	1													
Don Stevens	5.0	DS	4	4	5	4	5	1												
Casual	5.0	CASL		3	4	3			4	7	9	5	3	2						
Kathy Mendez	5.0	KM		1	5	16	20	19	22	19	20	18	20	11	2					
Anna Borden	5.0	AB					9	10	16	15	11	12	19	10	7	1				
Gail Loring	5.0	GL		3	6	5	9	10	17	18	17	10	13	10	10	7	17			
UNASSIGNED	0.0	X										9			236	225	230	14	13	
Co-op	5.0	CO		6	4				2	3	4	4	2	4	16			216	178	
Casual	5.0	CAUL								3	3	3								
TOTAL DAYS			49	147	176	196	194	174	193	195	190	181	140	125	358	288	284	237	196	12

The Gantt chart in this figure was produced by a commercially available project management software package. It shows the task, person-days, and initials of each responsible person, as well as the start and finish dates for each task. The resource summary provides a good manager with the total person-days for each month and for each person working on the project to manage the project successfully. The project described here is a data administration project.

results (Fichman and Moses 1999). Standard control techniques can successfully chart the progress of the project against budgets and target dates, so deviations from the plan can be spotted.

Increasing User Involvement and Overcoming User Resistance

Projects with relatively *little structure and many undefined requirements* must involve users fully at all stages. Users must be mobilized to support one of many possible design options and to remain committed to a single design. **External integration tools** consist of ways to link the work of the implementation team to users at all organizational levels. For instance, users can become active members of the project team, take on leadership roles, and take charge of installation and training. The implementation team can demonstrate its responsiveness to users by promptly answering questions, incorporating user feedback, and showing their willingness to help (Gefen and Ridings 2002). E-business initiatives that require rapid system responses to emerging opportunities may benefit from using special "organizational architects" with skills and expertise to bridge communication gaps between business users and technology specialists (Sauer and Willcocks 2002).

Unfortunately, systems development is not an entirely rational process. Users leading design activities have sometimes used their positions to further private interests and to gain power rather than to promote organizational objectives (Franz and Robey 1984). Users may not always be involved in systems projects in a productive way.

Participation in implementation activities may not be enough to overcome the problem of user resistance. The implementation process demands organizational change. Change may be resisted because different users may be affected by the system in different ways. While some users may welcome a new system because it brings changes they perceive as beneficial to them, others may resist these changes because they believe the shifts are detrimental to their interests (Joshi 1991).

If the use of a system is voluntary, users may choose to avoid it; if use is mandatory, resistance may take the form of increased error rates, disruptions, turnover, and even sabotage. Therefore, the implementation strategy must not only encourage user participation and involvement, but it must also address the issue of counterimplementation (Keen 1981). **Counterimplementation** is a deliberate strategy to thwart the implementation of an information system or an innovation in an organization.

Strategies to overcome user resistance include user participation (to elicit commitment as well as to improve design), user education and training, management edicts and policies, and better incentives for users who cooperate. The new system can be made more user friendly by improving the end-user interface. Users will be more cooperative if organizational problems are solved prior to introducing the new system.

Designing for the Organization

Because the purpose of a new system is to improve the organization's performance, the systems development process must explicitly address the ways in which the organization will change when the new system is installed, including installation of intranets, extranets, and Web applications (Chatterjee, Grewal, and Sambamurthy 2002). In addition to procedural changes, transformations in job functions, organizational structure, power relationships,

TABLE 11-4 *Organizational Factors in Systems Planning and Implementation*

Employee participation and involvement
Job design
Standards and performance monitoring
Ergonomics (including equipment, user interfaces, and the work environment)
Employee grievance resolution procedures
Health and safety
Government regulatory compliance

external integration tools

counterimplementation

and behaviour should be carefully planned. Table 11-4 lists the organizational dimensions that must be addressed for planning and implementing many systems.

Although systems analysis and design activities are supposed to include an organizational impact analysis, this area has traditionally been neglected. An **organizational impact analysis** explains how a proposed system will affect organizational structure, attitudes, decision making, and operations. To integrate information systems successfully with the organization, thorough and fully documented organizational impact assessments must be given more attention in the development effort.

Allowing for the Human Factor The quality of information systems should be evaluated in terms of user criteria rather than the criteria of the information systems staff. In addition to targets such as memory size, access rates, and calculation times, systems objectives should include standards for user performance. For example, an objective might be that data entry clerks learn the procedures and codes for four new online data entry screens in a half-day training session.

Areas where users interface with the system should be carefully designed, with sensitivity to ergonomics issues. **Ergonomics** refers to the interaction of people and machines in the work environment. It considers the design of jobs, health issues, and the end-user interface of information systems. The impact of the system on the work environment and job dimensions must be carefully assessed.

Sociotechnical Design Most contemporary systems development approaches tend to treat end users as essential to the systems development process but as playing a largely passive role relative to other forces shaping the system, such as the systems designers and management. A different tradition rooted in the European social democratic labour movement assigns users a more active role, one that empowers them to codetermine the role of information systems in their workplaces (Clement and Van den Besselaar 1993).

This tradition of participatory design emphasizes participation by the individuals most affected by the new system. It is closely associated with the concept of sociotechnical design. A **sociotechnical design** plan establishes human objectives for the system that lead to increased job satisfaction. Designers set forth separate sets of technical and social design solutions. Social design plans explore different workgroup structures, allocation of tasks, and the design of individual jobs. The proposed technical solutions are compared with the proposed social solutions. Social and technical solutions that can be combined are proposed as sociotechnical solutions. The alternative that best meets both social and technical objectives is selected for the final design. The resulting sociotechnical design is expected to produce an information system that blends technical efficiency with sensitivity to organizational and human needs, leading to high job satisfaction (Mumford and Weir 1979). Systems with compatible technical and organizational elements are expected to raise productivity without sacrificing human and social goals.

Management Opportunities, Challenges, and Solutions

Given the relationship between systems and firm performance, investing in systems that provide the most benefit to the firm is one of the most important decisions managers can make—and perhaps one of the most difficult to execute successfully.

Opportunities

By changing business processes and the culture of management decision making, new information systems can produce extraordinarily high returns if system developers can effectively manage the change process and accurately calculate the costs and benefits of their investments.

organizational impact analysis

ergonomics

sociotechnical design

Management Challenges

Successful systems development requires the ability and the desire to measure the business value of systems and to pay serious attention to change management. You should be aware of the following management challenges.

Determining System Benefits and Costs When They Are Difficult to Quantify Many costs and benefits of information systems are difficult to quantify. The impact of a single technology investment may be difficult to ascertain if it is affected by interrelated systems and multiple layers of hardware, software, and database and networking technology in the firm's IT infrastructure. Managers may have difficulty measuring the social costs of implementing new technology in the organization.

As the sophistication of systems grows, the systems produce fewer tangible and more intangible benefits. By definition, there is no solid method for pricing intangible benefits. Organizations could lose important opportunities if they only use strict financial criteria for determining information systems benefits. However, organizations could make very poor investment decisions if they overestimate intangible benefits.

Dealing with the Complexity of Large-Scale Systems Projects Large-scale systems, including enterprise systems that affect large numbers of organizational units and staff members and have extensive information requirements and business process changes, are difficult to oversee, coordinate, and plan. Implementing these systems, which have multiyear development periods, is especially problematic because the systems are so complex. In addition, there are few reliable techniques for estimating the time and cost to develop large-scale information systems.

Solution Guidelines

To meet these challenges, organizations need to find ways of measuring the business value of their information systems and ensuring that systems actually deliver the benefits they promise. Here are some additional recommendations for obtaining more value from information technology investments and for managing large, complex projects.

Obtaining More Value from Information Technology Investments Several studies have shown that very few organizations are obtaining the full value of their systems investments. A sizable percentage of firms do not have central oversight over their IT budgets and lack a process for ranking and managing their technology investments. They typically chose their investments ad hoc, favouring pet projects of powerful managers. Many also lack criteria for defining project success, or they fail to measure fully the returns on their projects after they have been completed. IT investments at these firms are not well integrated into corporate strategy, and senior management is not sufficiently involved in IT planning.

Firms can take a number of steps to obtain more benefits and returns from their systems investments. They can start by fully documenting the firm's applications and IT infrastructure and conducting periodic reviews of the firm's IT portfolio. They should make sure they have appropriate metrics for monitoring project outcomes and information systems investments are closely linked to the most important business objectives of the firm. Project risks and returns should be clearly identified. Real options analysis should be conducted to identify projects that will enable future opportunities. Managers should measure business value throughout the duration of new system projects and should not hesitate to weed out underperforming projects if necessary.

For projects in which benefits involve improved decision making, managers should try to identify the decision improvements which would provide the greatest additional value to the firm. They should then develop a set of metrics to quantify the value of more timely and precise information on the outcome of the decision.

New Approaches to Project Management Traditional techniques for managing projects deal with problems of size and complexity by breaking large projects into subprojects; assigning teams, schedules, and milestones to each; and focusing primarily on project mechanics rather than business results. These techniques are inadequate for enterprise systems and other large-scale systems projects with extremely complex problems of organizational coordination and change management, complex and sometimes unfamiliar technology, and continually changing business requirements. A new set of project management techniques is emerging to address these challenges.

In this model, project planning assumes an enterprise-wide focus, driven by the firm's strategic business vision and technology architecture. Project and subproject managers focus on solving problems and meeting challenges as they arise rather than simply meeting formal project milestones. They emphasize learning as well as planning, seeking ways to adapt to unforeseen uncertainties and chaos that, if properly handled, could provide additional opportunities and benefits (DeMeyer, Loch, and Pich 2002; Markus and Benjamin 1997; Orlikowski and Hofman 1997). It may be useful for organizations to establish a separate program office to manage subprojects; coordinate the entire project effort with other ongoing projects; and coordinate the project with ongoing changes in the firm's business strategy, information technology architecture and infrastructure, and business processes (Concours Group 2000).

Summary

1. **Understand the various components of information resource management and the issues involved in each component.**

   The IS department may be structured in any of several ways: centralized as its own department, decentralized within other departments, or with personnel located both centrally and in various information service units and information centres The CIO and MIS Steering Committee set IS policies and prioritize and review major projects. IS planning takes place at the strategic, tactical, and operational levels and should be aligned with organizational strategy at each level.

   Systems development actually involves a number of IS personnel roles and includes the staff assignments to various projects as well as ensuring that security issues are addressed. IS personnel must be recruited, hired, and retained and must be permitted to keep their skill sets up to date. Like every other department in an organization, the IS department must set a budget, which is difficult at best given the trend toward rapidly changing technology and escalating IS personnel salaries.

2. **Evaluate models for understanding the business value of information systems.**

   Information systems can provide business value for a firm in many different ways, including increased profitability and productivity. Some, but not all, of these business benefits can be quantified and measured.

   Capital budgeting models are used to determine whether an investment in information technology produces sufficient returns to justify its costs. The principal capital budgeting models are the payback method, accounting rate of return on investment (ROI), net present value, cost-benefit ratio, profitability index, and internal rate of return (IRR).

   Other models for evaluating information systems investments involve nonfinancial and strategic considerations. Portfolio analysis and scoring models can be used to evaluate alternative information systems projects. Real options pricing models, which apply the techniques for valuing financial options to systems investments, can be useful when considering highly uncertain IT investments.

   Although information technology has increased productivity in manufacturing, especially the manufacture of information technology products, the extent to which computers have enhanced the productivity of the service sector remains under debate. In addition to reducing costs, computers may increase the quality of products and services for consumers or may create entirely new products and revenue streams. These intangible benefits are difficult to measure and consequently are not addressed by conventional productivity measures.

3. **Analyze the principal causes of information system failure.**

   A very large percentage of information systems fail to deliver benefits or solve the problems for which they were intended because the process of organizational change surrounding system development was not properly addressed. The principal causes of information system failure are insufficient or improper user participation in the systems development process, lack of management support, high levels of complexity and risk in the systems development process, and poor management of the implementation process. There is a very high failure rate among business process reengineering and enterprise application projects because they require extensive organizational change that is often resisted by members of the organization. Enterprise applications as well as system changes resulting from mergers and acquisitions are also difficult to implement successfully because they usually require far-reaching changes to business processes.

4. **Assess the change management requirements for developing successful systems.**

Developing an information system is a process of planned organizational change that must be carefully managed. The term *implementation* refers to the entire process of organizational change surrounding the introduction of a new information system. One can better understand system success and failure by examining different patterns of implementation. Especially important is the relationship between participants in the implementation process, notably the interactions between system designers and users. Conflicts between the technical orientation of system designers and the business orientation of end users must be resolved. The success of organizational change can be determined by how well information systems specialists, end users, and decision makers deal with key issues at various stages in implementation. Eliciting user support and maintaining an appropriate level of user involvement at all stages of system development are essential.

5. **Select appropriate strategies to manage the system implementation process.**

Management support and control of the implementation process are essential, as are mechanisms for dealing with the level of risk in each new systems project. Some companies experience organizational resistance to

change. Project risk factors can be brought under some control by a contingency approach to project management. The level of risk in a systems development project is determined by three key dimensions: project size, project structure, and experience with technology. The risk level of each project determines the appropriate mix of external integration tools, internal integration tools, formal planning tools, and formal control tools to be applied.

Appropriate strategies can be applied to ensure the correct level of user participation in the systems development process and to minimize user resistance. Information systems design and the entire implementation process should be managed as planned organizational change. Participatory design emphasizes the participation of the individuals most affected by a new system. Sociotechnical design aims for an optimal blend of social and technical design solutions.

6. **Identify the challenges posed by developing new systems, and propose management solutions.**

Developing successful systems is something of an art form. It is becoming increasingly difficult to determine the costs and benefits of systems, especially those in which benefits are primarily intangible or those which are interrelated with other systems and pieces of technology in the firm. Implementing large-scale systems and obtaining benefits from these investments are especially challenging. Management solutions include developing metrics and processes to make sure information systems investments provide business value and using more dynamic approaches to project management.

Key Terms

Accounting rate of return on investment (ROI),   386
Capital budgeting,   386
Change agent,   396
Chief information officer (CIO),   380
Cost-benefit ratio,   386
Counterimplementation,   404
Data entry operators,   382
Ergonomics,   405
External integration tools,   404
Formal control tools,   402

Formal planning tools,   402
Implementation,   396
Intangible benefits,   386
Internal integration tools,   402
Internal rate of return (IRR),   386
Man-month,   400
MIS steering committee,   381
Net present value,   386
Network managers,   382
Organizational impact analysis,   405
Payback method,   386

Portfolio analysis,   388
Profitability index,   386
Real options pricing models (ROPM),   390
Scoring model,   389
Sociotechnical design,   405
System failure,   393
Systems operators,   382
Tangible benefits,   386
User interface,   394
User-designer communications gap,   397
Web masters,   382

Review Questions

1. *Name and describe the components involved in information resource management.*

2. *Compare the role of the CIO with that of the MIS steering committee.*

3. *Name and describe the types or levels of IS planning.*

4. *Name and describe the various roles IS personnel have in the IS department.*

5. *Name and describe the principal capital budgeting methods used to evaluate information system projects.*

6. *What are the limitations of financial models for establishing the value of information systems?*

7. *Describe how portfolio analysis and scoring models can be used to establish the worth of systems.*

8. *How can real options pricing models be used to help evaluate information technology investments?*

9. *Have information systems enhanced productivity in businesses? Explain your answer.*

10. *Why do developers of new information systems need to address change management?*

11. *What kinds of problems provide evidence of information systems failure?*

12. *Why is it necessary to understand the concept of implementation when managing the organizational change surrounding a new information system?*

13. *What are the major causes of implementation success or failure?*

14. *What is the user-designer communications gap? What kinds of implementation problems can it create?*

15. *Why is there such a high failure rate among enterprise*

application implementations and business process reengineering (BPR) projects? What role do information systems play in the success or failure of mergers and acquisitions?

16. *What dimensions influence the level of risk in each systems development project?*

17. *What project management techniques can be used to control project risk?*

18. *What strategies can be used to overcome user resistance to systems development projects?*

19. *What organizational considerations should be addressed by information systems design?*

20. *What challenges are posed by trying to determine the business value of systems and manage system-related change? Suggest some solutions.*

Discussion Questions

1. *It has been said that when we design an information system we are redesigning the organization. What are the ramifications of this statement?*

2. *It has been said that most systems fail because systems developers ignore organizational behaviour problems. Why might this be so?*

Application Software Exercise:
Spreadsheet Exercise: Capital Budgeting for a New CAD System

Your company would like to invest in a new computer-aided design (CAD) system that requires purchasing hardware, software, and networking technology, as well as expenditures for installation, training, and support. The Companion Website for Chapter 11 contains tables showing each cost component for the new system as well as annual maintenance costs over a five-year period. You believe the new system will produce annual savings by reducing the amount of labour required to generate designs and design specifications, thus increasing your firm's annual cash flow. Using the data provided and instructions at the Companion Website for this chapter, create a worksheet that calculates the costs and benefits of the investment over a five-year period and analyzes the investment using the six capital budgeting models presented in this chapter. Is this investment worthwhile? Why or why not?

Electronic Business Project: Buying and Financing a Home

You have found a new job in London, Ontario, and would like to purchase a home in that area. Ideally, you would like to find a single-family house with at least three bedrooms and one bathroom that costs between $150 000 and $225 000 and finance it with a 30-year fixed-rate mortgage. You can afford a down payment that is 20 percent of the value of the house. Before you purchase a house, you would like to find out what homes are available in your price range, find a mortgage, and determine the amount of your monthly payment. You would also like to see how much of your mortgage payment represents principal and how much represents interest. Use the Yahoo! Canada site (realestate.yahoo.ca) to help you with the following tasks:

1. Locate homes in your price range in London, Ontario. Find out as much information as you can about the houses, including the real estate

listing agent, condition of the house, number of rooms, and school district.

2. Find a mortgage for 80 percent of the list price of the home. Compare rates from at least three sites (use search engines to find sites other than Yahoo!).

3. After selecting a mortgage, calculate your closing costs.

4. Calculate the monthly payment for the mortgage you select.

5. Calculate how much of your monthly mortgage payment represents principal and how much represents interest, assuming you do not plan to make any extra payments on the mortgage.

When you are finished, evaluate the whole process. For example, assess the ease of use of the site and your ability to find information about houses and mortgages; the accuracy of the information you found; the breadth of choice of homes and mortgages; and how helpful the whole process would have been for you if you were actually in the situation described in this project.

Group Project: Identifying Implementation Problems

Form a group with two or three other students. Write a description of the implementation problems you might expect to encounter for one of the systems described in the Window boxes or chapter-ending cases in this text. Write an analysis of the steps you would take to solve or prevent these problems. If possible, use electronic presentation software to present your findings to the class.

Web Sites of Interest

There are many interesting Web sites to enhance your learning about information resource management. You can search the Web yourself or try to following sites to add to what you have already learned.

International Federation of Accountants **www.ifac.org**
Full of information to planning and project managers.

Project Management Institute **www.pmi.org**
Information for project management professionals.

Canadian Risk Management Council **http://rimscanada.rims. org/website/websiteDisplay.cfm?WTID=93**
Information about risk management in Canada.

Information Resource Management Association of Canada **www.irmac.ca**
Information related to IRM in Canada.

CASE STUDY:
Air Cargo Portal Services Brings Competitors Together

We have seen how UPS, Federal Express, and several other companies have taken advantage of the World Wide Web and the Internet to improve customer service and lower customer costs. By permitting customers to book online—and even be billed online—these companies have offered smaller shipping customers greatly improved service while lowering their own and their customers' costs.

Another company that is using the Web and Internet to its advantage is Cargo Portal Services (CPS), a company owned and run by Unisys, the computer manufacturer and consulting firm. CPS is an electronic booking and shipment management service for the air cargo industry. It was designed in cooperation with major carriers and forwarders. Access to CPS is free for forwarders through the Internet and through secure system-to-system connections. CPS serves more than 3333 branch offices of 1635 forwarding companies in 67 countries.

CPS is the first full-service Internet portal for the air cargo industry. CPS opened for business in 2003 with only three carriers (Air Canada, United, and Northwest). To date, CPS offers transportation services from 430 cities in 117 countries through the global cargo networks of Air Canada, Austrian Airlines, KLM, Northwest Airlines, United Airlines, Continental Airlines, and American Airlines. CPS provides neutral multi-carrier booking facilities with agreed rates and allotments; Cargo 2000 proactive shipment event management and tracking in-line with industry best practice; and

computer system-to-system communications for better integration between forwarders and carriers. Cargo 2000, an interest group of the International Air Transport Association, brings together some 30 major airlines, freight forwarders and ground handling agents with the unique goal of implementing a new quality management system for the worldwide air cargo industry. Their objective is simple: to implement processes, backed by quality standards, that are measurable and supported by data, thereby improving the efficiency of air cargo, enhancing customer service levels, and reducing operational costs (IATA, 2001). CPS uses Cargo 2000 standards to implement services, such as proactive shipment event management, which permits shippers and receivers to be notified of "events," such as delays, during shipping.

Entering the Internet age has not been easy for Air Cargo. Complex IT integration issues have caused the Web-based solutions for booking space and managing shipments to be slow in implementation, or to fail because of unrealistic planning. Airlines and their freight forwarder customers use widely differing legacy systems, and also booking procedures vary from airline to airline. Personal relationships, rather than new technology, are given more importance in business operations. These are some of the major reasons for this problem.

Setting aside their competition, Northwest Airlines, United Airlines, and Air Canada made a decision to overcome this problem by agreeing on a common approach for a Web-based booking and shipment management system. They brought in Unisys in May 2002 to translate their vision into practice. Unisys worked closely with these carriers and their customers, using XML interfaces and a modular approach to deliver a flexible and easy-to-use system, which was quickly accepted by the market.

The Unisys aircargo system was already used by two of the three carriers, and Unisys also had the advantage of Web development and integration expertise gained from other projects. This in-depth experience, plus the determination of Unisys to make the system work, was the force behind the success of the aircargo system.

The three carriers had to act fast and bring their new approach to market since competing platforms were already up and running and cost had to be kept in mind as well. Following the events of September 11, 2001, investments in the airline industry were drastically reduced. With its solid foundation of world-class expertise drawn from the solutions it had developed for other business operations, Unisys was able to provide a faster and more cost-effective solution that went live in just six months.

Unisys had to create a system that would work with the various legacy systems and the differing procedures used by airlines. This involved dealing with divergent booking and pricing practices. Since rates for most shipments are determined through negotiations, Unisys decided not to bother with developing a price quotation system. Unisys thus circumvented one of the serious errors of the failed dot-com solutions—using auction models of selling capacity.

The solution had to be acceptable to forwarders as well as to other carriers. According to Mark Haeussler, director of cargo strategic planning and business development at United Airlines, "Forwarders don't want to go to a large number of carrier sites; they want one portal they can use to book across airlines." Therefore, the site had to satisfy the requirements of the three launch carriers and also make it easy for other carriers to adopt after the portal went live.

CPS's technology decisions were simple enough. It decided on XML for the flexibility of its interfaces, its ability to connect the portal with the diverse systems in the air cargo industry, and its potential for future customization. "There is now recognition among carriers that XML is the way forward, even if they are progressing at different speeds," said Steve Schuppenhauer, Unisys technical architect. "We are taking advantage of that trend and driving it forward."

Unisys also decided on an object-oriented approach to reuse existing modules from its other projects: key technologies such as a Weblogic server and a multitier architecture using J2EE. This approach was significant because it allowed the development team to use an internally developed cargo system in one of the three launch carriers, United Airlines Cargo, as an important test bed for their interface solutions.

What aided the swift and successful development of the system was the synchronized efforts of the airlines and Unisys. Throughout the project, the three carriers continued to work closely and played important roles in the project; they also kept themselves in the loop by holding weekly development meetings with Unisys. At all stages, they also involved the users of the system and the forwarders, who were vital to the project's success or failure. "A key factor for success is that early on we focused on a clear set of requirements," said Jim Friedel, president of Northwest Airlines Cargo. "We hammered down our different wish lists to something achievable. That is a key reason why the project was able to succeed."

With Unisys on board, the process of refining the requirements was intensified. The original broad design had to be broken down into detailed specifications, which took three months and required the three carriers to set aside all of their competitive issues and differences. Thus, they managed to define the precise functionality of the portal even before a single line of code was written. "This was the most challenging aspect of the project," said Unisys project manager Dave Fischer. "But I have to hand it to the carriers. They really came together, and we merged three perspectives into a common approach so the objectives were very clear."

The forwarders were involved from the onset of the project. The three carriers had consulted with a group of nine forwarders of varying sizes and scope when the original plans were developed. The involvement with the forwarders continued through the specification and development phases in the form of a series of meetings and test sessions, which minimized the amount of rework needed during the test phase. The final design reflected all of the customer views since all the glitches had been sorted out early on in the project.

The forwarders provided very useful input which resulted in several enhancements to the CPS, for example, a function to load multiple bookings into the portal that reflected how business is transacted. These ideas were incorporated into the launch version.

The value of forwarder participation was evident when the system went live in January 2003. A major resistance to CPS in the industry at large was from the front line staff in forwarder offices who preferred traditional booking methods, such as phone and fax, and who were not enthusiastic about the new technology. Exhaustive testing of CPS' functionality throughout the development process with an advisory group of 10 forwarders allowed CPS to ensure that the portal met the needs of the booking staff in a satisfactory manner.

Reducing the learning curve of forwarder staff would save costs and speed up adoption. "If you put the system in front of them, they should be able to use it straightaway," said Air Canada's manager of cargo marketing, sales planning and support, Gerald Simpson, who took charge of training for the portal. Early tests were successful. "After demonstration sessions in October and November 2002, we asked forwarders what training they needed," recalls Simpson. "They said that they were comfortable, after one viewing, that they could tell the rest of their staff how it worked."

CPS's success was based on its usability. Sam Racine, the Unisys usability expert with a doctorate in interface design, remained the advisor of the project throughout its course. Racine focused on making sure the system would enable users to do their jobs quickly and simply, keeping costs down by eliminating potential glitches at an early stage, and reducing the amount of future testing and rework.

One of the usability issues that came up during testing was the elimination of the mouse in site navigation. To avoid clicking through multiple screens, screens were made as comprehensive as possible. Complete information was provided under help buttons to enable new and existing users to be self-sufficient.

"The feedback we got is that the system is easy to understand and simple to use. People are at ease with it," said Simpson. When asked how he will determine the effectiveness of a site, he added: "When forwarders start ringing up other carriers and saying 'get on this system, too.'" Friedel considers CPS a case study in successful project management. "Success was all about the people on the project team and the way they took decisions. We avoided transformational technology. We did not try and rebuild institutions—just to substitute technology for what is currently done by phone. Most of all, we kept the design simple for users. With a vision that simple and the team approach to the technical aspects, the odds of success were 100 percent."

Since opening the portal in 2003, CPS continues to increase functionality. In 2004, CPS added waybill (a receipt for shipped goods) processing and a reusable template for recurring bookings to its services.

Following the new United States Customs and Border Patrol's four-hour ruling, CPS introduced house waybill services. Airlines and forwarders now have to provide the house waybill details of shipments no later than four hours prior to flights arriving into the United States. Failure to provide this information to U.S. Customs will cause shipments to be delayed. Frequently, this would create a domino effect because more than one flight segment may be involved before a shipment arrives at its final destination.

The airlines mostly receive house waybill data electronically via the industry standard consolidation list (FHL) message. Alternatively, they manually enter the data into their cargo operational system on documents given to them by the forwarder. Carriers and forwarders, especially small- to medium-sized forwarders which do not have the facility to send FHL messages, can reduce this effort by using the new house waybill service in one of three ways offered by CPS: via the Web; through an XML system-to-system interface with

forwarder systems; or through an EDI-Internet interface with forwarder systems using the FHL message.

Users can submit their permanent or recurring bookings with "recycle booking" launched by CPS. Before this, booking data needed to be re-entered from scratch even when the same booking was done on a daily or weekly basis. With the CPS recycle booking service, the user can store booking data in a template to create single recurring bookings or an entire week of recurring bookings. Thus, a forwarder can get confirmations for its consolidation allocations in a fast and accurate way.

CPS continues to add airline partners and freight forwarder clients to its portal. As can be seen by the recent introduction of additional service. CPS is attempting to be the "go-to" air cargo portal.

Sources: "Cargo Portal Services Launches Two New Services," Enterprise Networks and Servers, October 2004; "Multi-carrier Web-Based Booking for Air Cargo," available **www.unisys.com/transportation/ clients/featured_case_studies/northwest_airlines_c0_ united_airlines_and_air_canada_case_study.htm** (accessed May 22, 2005); "American Airlines Cargo to Join Unisys-Operated Cargo Portal Services," Logistics Management, May 2, 2005.

CASE STUDY QUESTIONS

1. How important are information systems for the air cargo industry?

2. Classify and describe the problems CPS faced in trying to develop and launch its systems, using the categories described in this chapter on the causes of system failure.

3. What management, organization, and technology factors caused those problems?

4. Evaluate the risks of the air cargo portal project and key risk factors.

5. Originally, Air Canada was the only non-U.S. airline involved in CPS. Do you think it was a wise decision for Air Canada to proceed with the CPS project, or should they have let others be the guinea pigs for this project? Why do you feel that way?

6. What financial measures and justification do you think were used in deciding how to proceed with this project?

Chapter 12

Managing Global Systems

OBJECTIVES

After completing this chapter, you will be able to:

1. Identify the major factors driving the internationalization of business.

2. Compare strategies for developing global businesses.

3. Demonstrate how information systems can support different global business strategies.

4. Evaluate the issues and technical alternatives to be considered when developing international information systems.

5. Identify the challenges posed by global information systems and management solutions.

- Set standards
- Design global business processes

- Standardize intercompany processes
- Standardize worldwide data model

- Implement Oracle 9i DBMS and Adapter
- Implement PointOut software for standard global interface

Management

Organization

Technology

Business Challenges
- Rapid expansion through aquisitions
- Decentralized systems
- Localized order processes

Information System
- Track orders automatically worldwide
- Manage global inventory

Business Solutions
- Reduce costs
- Increase revenue

Opening Case:
Dräger Safety Creates a Global Supply Chain

Dräger Safety, based in Luebeck, Germany, develops and sells a wide range of safety products, including protective suits, breathing equipment, and gas detection systems. The company has mushroomed from a two-person shop in 1889 to a network of more than 40 subsidiaries and is considered one of the world's most innovative safety-product companies.

As the number of Dräger subsidiaries grew during the last decade, the company lost revenue and faced higher costs. Dräger could not rapidly take and fulfill orders among 40 companies spread across Europe, Asia, and North America. Every order had to be handled manually because each Dräger subsidiary maintained its own set of information systems. Dräger had no way to link sales, production, storage, and shipping across all of its units worldwide.

For example, the company might take an order in Canada, generate a purchase order in Germany, source the product in the United States, and then ship it to Canada. The salesperson taking the order would create a purchase order on paper and mail it to a production hub. There the order would be input, assembled, stored, and shipped back to the originating sales office, which would then ship it out to the customer. This cumbersome manual system created delays and poorly managed inventory.

For a solution, Dräger selected Oracle9i Database and Oracle 9i Application Server (Oracle9iAS) Interconnect Adapter with standardized enterprise resource planning (ERP) interfaces. The Interconnect Adapter middleware enabled Dräger to link the systems from all its subsidiaries easily because it did not require programming point-to-point connections between the various systems and it could connect a broad range of enterprise systems to the same data platform.

Dräger did have to standardize intercompany processes, including planning, reporting, and product and inventory management to use the common database effectively. The company also had to create a single worldwide data model with standard codes and definitions for customer items, vendor items, production orders, and bills of materials. A software program called PointOut developed by Munich software firm mSE provided a desktop data interface with the same look and functionality at each company.

Today, Dräger's entire order process is fully automated and can track orders worldwide. Dräger can cen-

tralize inventory in each region and ship products directly to customers from the closest regional warehouse. Orders that used to take weeks to fulfill can now be processed in minutes. Dräger has been able to reduce its global inventory by 40 percent, slash inventory at sales locations by 95 percent, and lower process costs by 30 percent.

Sources: Shari Caudron, "Safety in Numbers," *Profit Magazine*, February 2004; and **www.drager-safety.com**, accessed June 4, 2004.

Dräger Safety's efforts to create global supply chain processes is an example of some of the changes in international information systems architecture—the basic systems needed to coordinate worldwide trade and other activities—that organizations need to consider if they want to operate across the globe.

As a manager, you will want to know what issues must be addressed when developing and managing international information systems. To be effective, you will need a global perspective on business and an understanding of the information systems needed to conduct business on an international scale. This chapter shows you how to organize, manage, and control the development of international information systems.

12.1 The Growth of International Information Systems

In earlier chapters, we described the emergence of a global economic system and global world order driven by advanced networks and information systems. The new world order is sweeping away many national corporations, national industries, and national economies controlled by domestic politicians. Many localized firms will be replaced by fast-moving networked corporations that transcend national boundaries. The growth of international trade has radically altered domestic economies around the globe. Over $1.25 trillion worth of goods, services, and financial instruments changes hands each day in global trade.

Today, the production and design of many high-end electronic products is parceled out to a number of different countries. Consider the path to market for Hewlett-Packard's (HP) ProLiant ML150 server, which is illustrated in Figure 12-1. The idea for the product was hatched in Singapore, where the initial design work was

FIGURE 12-1   *Global product development and production.*

A new HP server's path to market:

❶ Idea for product hatched in Singapore.

❷ Concept approved in Houston.

❸ Concept design done in Singapore.

❹ Engineering design in Taiwan, where many computer components are made; initial manufacture by a Taiwanese contractor.

❺ Final assembly in Singapore, Australia, China, and India. Products made in Australia, China, and India are primarily for those markets; machines made in Singapore go to all of Southeast Asia.

Hewlett-Packard and other electronics companies assign distribution and production of high-end products to a number of different countries.

Source: © *New York Times*. Used with permission.

done. HP headquarters in Houston approved the concept. Contractors in Taiwan created the machine's engineering design and initial manufacture. Final assembly of the server takes place in Singapore, China, India, and Australia (Buckman 2004). None of this would be possible without powerful international information and communication systems.

Developing an International Information Systems Architecture

This chapter describes how to go about building an international information systems architecture suitable for your international strategy. An **international information systems architecture** consists of the basic information systems required by organizations to coordinate worldwide trade and other activities. Figure 12-2 illustrates the reasoning we follow throughout the chapter and depicts the major dimensions of an international information systems portfolio.

The basic strategy to follow when developing an international system is to understand the global environment in which your firm is operating. This means understanding the overall market forces, or business drivers, that are pushing your industry toward global competition. A **business driver** is a force in the environment to which businesses must respond and a force that influences the direction of the business. Likewise, examine carefully the inhibitors or negative factors that create *management challenges*—factors that could scuttle the development of a global business. Once you have examined the global environment, you will need to consider a corporate strategy for competing in that

international information systems architecture

business driver

FIGURE 12-2   *International information systems architecture.*

The major dimensions for developing an international information systems architecture are the global environment, the corporate global strategies, the structure of the organization, the management and business processes, and the technology platform.

International Information Systems Architecture

environment. How will your firm respond? You could ignore the global market and focus on domestic competition only, sell to the globe from a domestic base, or organize production and distribution around the globe. There are many in-between choices.

After you have developed a strategy, it is time to consider how to structure your organization so it can pursue that strategy. How will you accomplish a division of labour across a global environment? Where will production, administration, accounting, marketing, and human resources functions be located? Who will handle the information systems function?

Next, you must consider the management issues in implementing your strategy and making the organization design come alive. The key here will be the design of business procedures. How can you discover and manage user requirements? How can you induce change in local units to conform to international requirements? How can you reengineer on a global scale, and how can you coordinate systems development?

The last issue to consider is the technology platform. Although changing technology is a key driving factor leading toward global markets, you need to have a corporate strategy and structure before you can rationally choose the right technology.

After you have completed this process of reasoning, you will be well on your way toward an appropriate international information systems portfolio capable of achieving your corporate goals. Let us begin by looking at the overall global environment.

The Global Environment: Business Drivers and Challenges

Table 12-1 lists the business drivers in the global environment that are leading all industries toward global markets and competition. The global business drivers can be divided into two groups: general cultural factors and specific business factors. Easily recognized general cultural factors have driven internationalization since World War II. Information, communication, and transportation technologies have created a *global village* in which communication (by telephone, television, radio, or computer network) around the globe is no more difficult and not much more expensive than communication down the block. The cost of moving goods and services to and from geographically dispersed locations has fallen dramatically.

The development of global communications has created a global village in a second sense: A **global culture** created by television and other globally shared media now permits different cultures and peoples to develop common expectations about social norms such as right and wrong, desirable and undesirable, heroic and cowardly. The collapse of the Eastern bloc has accelerated the growth of a world culture enormously, increased support for capitalism and business, and reduced the level of cultural conflict considerably.

global culture

TABLE 12-1 *Global Business Drivers*

GENERAL CULTURAL FACTORS
Global communication and transportation technologies
Development of global culture
Emergence of global social norms
Political stability
Global knowledge base

SPECIFIC BUSINESS FACTORS
Global markets
Global production and operations
Global coordination
Global workforce
Global economies of scale

A last factor to consider is the growth of a global knowledge base. At the end of World War II, knowledge, education, science, and industrial skills were highly concentrated in North America, western Europe, and Japan, with the rest of the world euphemistically called the *Third World*. This is no longer true. Latin America, China, southern Asia, and eastern Europe have developed powerful educational, industrial, and scientific centres, resulting in a much more democratically and widely dispersed knowledge base.

These general cultural factors leading toward internationalization result in specific business globalization factors that affect most industries. The growth of powerful communications technologies and the emergence of world cultures create the condition for *global markets*—global consumers interested in consuming similar products that are culturally approved. Coca-Cola, American sneakers (made in Korea but designed in Los Angeles), Canada's Molson Beer, Denmark's Carlsberg Beer, and Cable News Network (CNN) programming can now be sold around the world.

Responding to this demand, global production and operations have emerged with precise online coordination between far-flung production facilities and central headquarters thousands of miles away. At Sealand Transportation, a major global shipping company based in Newark, New Jersey, shipping managers in Newark can watch the loading of ships in Rotterdam online, check trim and ballast, and trace packages to specific ship locations as the activity proceeds. This is all possible through an international satellite link.

The new global markets and pressure toward global production and operation have called forth whole new capabilities for global coordination of all factors of production. Not only production but also accounting, marketing and sales, human resources, and systems development (all the major business functions) can be coordinated on a global scale.

Frito Lay, for instance, can develop a marketing sales force automation system in the United States and may try the same techniques and technologies in Spain. Micromarketing—marketing to very small geographic and social units—no longer means marketing to neighbourhoods in the United States, but to neighbourhoods throughout the world. These new levels of global coordination permit, for the first time in history, the location of business activity according to comparative advantage. Design should be located where it is best accomplished, as should marketing, production, and finance.

Finally, global markets, production, and administration create the conditions for powerful, sustained global economies of scale. Production driven by worldwide global demand can be concentrated where it can best be accomplished, fixed resources can be allocated over larger production runs, and production runs in larger plants can be scheduled and estimated more efficiently and precisely. Lower cost factors of production can be exploited wherever they emerge. The result is a powerful strategic advantage to firms that can organize globally. These general and specific business drivers have greatly enlarged world trade and commerce.

Not all industries are similarly affected by these trends. Clearly, manufacturing has been much more affected than services— they still tend to be domestic and relatively inefficient. However, the localism of services is evolving in telecommunications, entertainment, transportation, financial services, and general business services, including law. Clearly, those firms within an industry that can understand the internationalization of the industry and respond appropriately will reap enormous gains in productivity and stability.

Business Challenges Although the possibilities of globalization for business success are significant, fundamental forces are operating that inhibit a global economy and disrupt international business. Table 12-2 lists the most common and powerful challenges to the development of global systems.

At a cultural level, **particularism**, making judgments and taking action on the basis of narrow or personal characteristics, in all its forms (religious, nationalistic, ethnic, regional, and geopolitical position) rejects the very concept of a shared global culture and rejects the penetration of domestic markets by foreign goods and services. Differences among cultures produce differences in social expectations, politics, and ultimately legal rules. In certain countries, such as the United States, consumers expect domestic name-brand products to be built domestically and are disappointed to learn that much of what they thought of as domestically produced is in fact foreign made.

Different cultures produce different political regimes. Among the many different countries of the world are different laws governing the movement of information, information privacy of citizens, origins of software and hardware in systems, and radio and satellite telecommunications. Even the hours of business and the terms of business trade vary greatly across political cultures. These different legal systems complicate global business and must be considered when building global systems.

For example, European countries have very strict laws concerning transborder data flow and privacy. **Transborder data flow** is defined as the movement of information across international boundaries in any form. Some European countries prohibit the processing of financial information outside their boundaries or the movement of personal information to foreign countries. The European Union Data Protection Directive, which went into effect in October 1998, restricts the flow of any information to countries (such as Canada) that do not meet strict European laws on personal information. Financial services, travel, and health-care companies could be directly affected. In response, most multinational firms develop information systems within each European country to avoid the cost and uncertainty of moving information across national boundaries.

Cultural and political differences profoundly affect organizations' business processes and applications of information technology. A host of specific barriers arise from the general cultural differences, everything from varying reliability of the telephone networks to the shortage of skilled consultants (Steinbart and Nath 1992).

National laws and traditions have created disparate accounting practices in various countries which affect the way profits and losses are analyzed. German companies generally do not recognize the profit from a venture until the project is completely finished, and

TABLE 12-2 *Challenges and Obstacles to Global Business Systems*

GENERAL

Cultural particularism: Regionalism, nationalism, language differences

Social expectations: Brand-name expectations, work hours

Political laws: Transborder data and privacy laws, commercial regulations

SPECIFIC

Standards: Different electronic data interchange (EDI), email, telecommunications standards

Reliability: Telephone networks not uniformly reliable

Speed: Different data transfer speeds, many slower than Canada

Personnel: Shortages of skilled consultants

particularism

transborder data flow

they have been paid. Conversely, British firms begin posting profits before a project is completed, when they are reasonably certain they will get the money.

These accounting practices are tightly intertwined with each country's legal system, business philosophy, and tax code. British, Canadian, and Dutch firms share a predominantly Anglo-Saxon outlook that separates tax calculations from reports to shareholders to focus on showing shareholders how fast profits are growing. Continental European accounting practices are less oriented toward impressing investors, focusing rather on demonstrating compliance with strict rules and minimizing tax liabilities. These diverging accounting practices make it difficult for large international companies with units in different countries to evaluate their performance.

Language remains a significant barrier. Although English has become a kind of standard business language, this is truer at higher levels of companies and not throughout the middle and lower ranks. Software may have to be built with local language interfaces before a new information system can be successfully implemented.

Currency fluctuations can play havoc with planning models and projections. A product that appears profitable in Mexico or Japan may actually produce a loss because of changes in foreign exchange rates. Some of these problems will diminish in parts of the world when the euro becomes more widely used.

These inhibiting factors must be taken into account when you are designing and developing international systems for your business. For example, companies trying to implement "lean production" systems spanning national boundaries typically underestimate the time, expense, and logistical difficulties of making goods and information flow freely across different countries.

State of the Art

One might think, given the opportunities for achieving competitive advantages and the interest in future applications, that most international companies have rationally developed marvellous international systems architectures. Nothing could be further from the truth. Most companies have inherited patchwork international systems from the distant past, often based on concepts of information processing developed in the 1960s—batch-oriented reporting from independent foreign divisions to corporate headquarters, with little online control or communication. Corporations in this situation increasingly face powerful competitive challenges in the marketplace from firms that have rationally designed truly international systems. Still other companies have recently built technology platforms for international systems but have nowhere to go because they lack global strategy.

As it turns out, there are significant difficulties in building appropriate international architectures. The difficulties involve planning a system appropriate to the firm's global strategy, structuring the organization of systems and business units, solving implementation issues, and choosing the right technical platform. Let us examine these problems in greater detail.

12.2 | Organizing International Information Systems

Three organizational issues face corporations seeking a global position: choosing a strategy, organizing the business, and organizing the systems management area. The first two are closely connected, so we discuss them together.

Global Strategies and Business Organization

Four main global strategies form the basis for global firms' organizational structure: domestic exporter, multinational, franchiser, and transnational. Each of these strategies is pursued with a specific business organizational structure (see Table 12-3). For simplicity's sake, we describe three kinds of organizational structure or governance: centralized (in the home

TABLE 12-3 *Global Business Strategy and Structure*

BUSINESS FUNCTION	DOMESTIC EXPORTER	MULTINATIONAL	FRANCHISER	TRANSNATIONAL
Production	Centralized	Dispersed	Coordinated	Coordinated
Finance/Accounting	Centralized	Centralized	Centralized	Coordinated
Sales/Marketing	Mixed	Dispersed	Coordinated	Coordinated
Human Resources	Centralized	Centralized	Coordinated	Coordinated
Strategic Management	Centralized	Centralized	Centralized	Coordinated

country), decentralized (to local foreign units), and coordinated (all units participate as equals). Other types of governance patterns can be observed in specific companies (e.g., authoritarian dominance by one unit, a confederacy of equals, a federal structure balancing power among strategic units, and so forth; Keen 1991).

The **domestic exporter** strategy is characterized by heavy centralization of corporate activities in the home country of origin. Nearly all international companies begin this way, and some move on to other forms. Production, finance/accounting, sales/marketing, human resources, and strategic management are set up to optimize resources in the home country. International sales are sometimes dispersed using agency agreements or subsidiaries, but even here, foreign marketing is totally reliant on the domestic home base for marketing themes and strategies. The U.S.'s Caterpillar Corporation and other heavy capital-equipment manufacturers, including Canada's New Flyer, fall into this category.

The **multinational** strategy concentrates financial management and control out of a central home base while decentralizing production, sales, and marketing operations to units in other countries. The products and services on sale in different countries are adapted to suit local market conditions. The organization becomes a far-flung confederation of production and marketing facilities in different countries. Many financial service firms, such as TD Bank Financial Group, along with a host of manufacturers, such as Nortel General Motors, Chrysler, and Intel, adhere to this strategy.

Franchisers are an interesting mix of old and new. On the one hand, the product is created, designed, financed, and initially produced in the home country, but for product-specific reasons the company must rely heavily on foreign personnel for further production, marketing, and human resources. Food franchisers such as Ontario's Firkin Pubs, McDonald's, Mrs. Fields Cookies, and KFC follow this structure. McDonald's created a new form of fast-food chain in the United States and continues to rely largely on the United States for new products, strategic management, and financing. Nevertheless, because the product must be produced locally—it is perishable—extensive coordination and dispersal of production, local marketing, and local recruitment of personnel are required.

Generally, foreign franchisees are clones of the mother country units, but fully coordinated worldwide production that could optimize factors of production is not possible. For instance, potatoes and beef generally cannot be bought where they are cheapest on world markets but must be produced (and bought) reasonably close to the area of consumption.

Transnational firms are the stateless, globally managed firms that may represent a larger part of international business in the future. Transnational firms have no single national headquarters but instead have many regional headquarters and perhaps a world headquarters. In a **transnational** strategy, nearly all the value-adding activities are managed from a global perspective without reference to national borders. The firm optimizes sources of supply and demand wherever they appear and takes advantage of local competitive advantages. Transnational firms take the globe, not the home country, as their management frame of reference. The governance of these firms has been likened to a federal structure with a strong central management core of decision making, but consid-

domestic exporter

multinational

franchisers

transnational

erable dispersal of power and financial muscle throughout the global divisions. Few companies have actually attained transnational status, but Citicorp, Sony, Ford, and others are attempting this transition.

Information technology and improvements in global telecommunications are giving international firms more flexibility to shape their global strategies. Protectionism and a need to serve local markets better encourage companies to disperse production facilities and become multinational. At the same time, the drive to achieve economies of scale and take advantage of short-term local advantage moves transnationals toward a global management perspective and a concentration of power and authority. Hence, there are forces of decentralization and dispersal, as well as forces of centralization and global coordination.

Global Systems to Fit the Strategy

Information technology and improvements in global telecommunications are giving international firms more flexibility to shape their global strategies. The configuration, management, and development of systems tend to follow the global strategy chosen (Roche 1992; Ives and Jarvenpaa 1991). Figure 12-3 depicts the typical arrangements. By *systems* we mean the full range of activities involved in developing information systems: conception and alignment with the strategic business plan, systems development, and ongoing operation.

For the sake of simplicity, we consider four types of systems configuration. *Centralized systems* are those in which systems development and operation occur totally at the domestic home base. *Duplicated systems* are those in which development occurs at the home base but operations are handed over to autonomous units in foreign locations. *Decentralized systems* are those in which each foreign unit designs its solutions and systems. *Networked systems* are those in which systems development and operations occur in an integrated and coordinated fashion across all units.

As can be seen in Figure 12-3, domestic exporters tend to have highly centralized systems in which a single domestic systems development staff develops worldwide applications. Multinationals offer a direct and striking contrast. Here, foreign units devise their own systems solutions based on local needs with few, if any, applications in common with headquarters (the exceptions being financial reporting and some telecommunications applications). Franchisers have the simplest systems structure. Like the products they sell, franchisers develop a single system usually at the home base and then replicate it around the world. Each unit, no matter where it is located, has identical applications. Finally, the most ambitious form of systems development is found in the transnationals. Networked systems are those in which there is a solid, singular global environment for developing and operating systems. This usually presupposes a powerful telecommunications backbone, a culture of shared applications development, and a shared management culture that crosses cultural barriers. The networked systems structure is the most visible in financial services where the homogeneity of the product—money and money instruments—seems to overcome cultural barriers.

FIGURE 12-3   *Global strategy and systems configurations.*

SYSTEM CONFIGURATION	Strategy			
	Domestic Exporter	Multinational	Franchiser	Transnational
Centralized	X			
Duplicated			X	
Decentralized	x	X	x	
Networked		x		X

The large Xs show the dominant patterns, and the small Xs show the emerging patterns. For instance, domestic exporters rely predominantly on centralized systems, but there is continual pressure and some development of decentralized systems in local marketing regions.

Reorganizing the Business

How should a firm organize itself for doing business on an international scale? To develop a global company and information systems support structure, a firm needs to follow these principles:

1. Organize value-adding activities along lines of comparative advantage. For instance, marketing/sales functions should be located where they can best be performed, for least cost and maximum impact; likewise with production, finance, human resources, and information systems.

2. Develop and operate systems units at each level of corporate activity—regional, national, and international. To serve local needs, there should be *host country systems units* of some magnitude. *Regional systems units* should handle telecommunications and systems development across national boundaries that take place within major geographic regions (European, Asian, American). *Transnational systems units* should be established to create the linkages across major regional areas and to coordinate the development and operation of international telecommunications and systems development

3. Establish a single office at world headquarters responsible for development of international systems and a global chief information officer (CIO).

Many successful companies have devised organizational systems structures along these principles. The success of these companies relies not only on the proper organization of activities, but also on a key ingredient—a management team that can understand the risks and benefits of international systems and devise strategies for overcoming the risks. We turn to these management topics next.

12.3 | Managing Global Systems

Table 12-4 lists the principal management problems posed by developing international systems. It is interesting to note that these problems are the chief difficulties managers experience in developing ordinary domestic systems as well! But these are enormously complicated in the international environment

A Typical Scenario: Disorganization on a Global Scale

Let us look at a common scenario. A traditional multinational consumer-goods company based in Canada and operating in Europe would like to expand into Asian markets and knows that it must develop a transnational strategy and a supportive information systems structure. Like most multinationals, it has dispersed production and marketing to regional and national centres while maintaining a world headquarters and strategic management in Canada. Historically, it has allowed each of the subsidiary foreign divisions to develop its own systems. The only centrally coordinated system is financial controls and reporting. The central systems group in Canada focuses only on domestic functions and production.

The result is a hodgepodge of hardware, software, and telecommunications. The email systems between Europe and Canada are incompatible. Each production facility uses a different manufacturing resources planning system (or a different version with local variations) and different marketing, sales, and human resources systems. Hardware and database platforms are wildly different. Communications between different sites are poor, given the high cost and low quality of European intercountry communications. The central systems group at headquarters recently was decimated and dispersed to the Canadian local sites in the hope of serving local needs better and reducing costs.

What do you recommend to the senior management leaders of this company, who now want to pursue a transnational strategy and develop an information systems architecture to support a highly coordinated global systems environment? Consider the problems you face by re-examining Table 12-4. The foreign divisions will resist efforts to agree on common user requirements; they have never thought about much other than their own units' needs. The systems groups in Canadian sites, which have been enlarged recently and told to focus on local needs, will not easily accept guidance from anyone recommending a transnational strategy. It will be difficult to convince local managers anywhere in the world that they should change their business procedures to align with other units in the world, especially if this might interfere with their local performance. After all, local managers are rewarded in this company for meeting local objectives of their division or plant. Finally, it will be difficult to coordinate development of projects around the world in the absence of a powerful telecommunications network and, therefore, difficult to encourage local users to take on ownership in the systems developed.

Global Systems Strategy

Figure 12-4 lays out the main dimensions of a solution. First, consider that not all systems should be coordinated on a transnational basis; only some core systems are truly worth sharing from a cost and feasibility point of view. **Core systems** are systems that support functions that are critical to the organization. Other systems should be partially coordinated because they share key elements, but they do not have to be totally common across national boundaries. For such systems, a good deal of local variation is possible and desirable. A final group of systems is peripheral, truly provincial, and needed to suit local requirements only.

Define the Core Business Processes How do you identify *core systems*? The first step is to create a short list of critical core business processes. Business processes are defined and described in Chapter 2, which you should review. Briefly, business processes are sets of logically related tasks to produce specific business results, such as shipping out correct orders to customers or delivering innovative products to market. Each business process typically involves many functional areas, communicating and coordinating work, information, and knowledge.

The way to identify these core business processes is to conduct a work-flow analysis. How are customer orders taken, what happens to them once they are taken, who fills the orders, and how are they shipped to the customers? What about suppliers? Do they have access to manufacturing resource planning systems so that supply is automatic? You should be able to identify and set priorities in a short list of 10 business processes that are critical for the firm.

Next, can you identify centres of excellence for these processes? Is the customer order fulfillment superior in Canada, manufacturing process control superior in Germany, and human resources superior in Asia? You should be able to identify some areas of the company, for some lines of business, where a division or unit stands out in the performance of one or several business functions.

When you understand the business processes of a firm, you can rank-order them. You then can decide which processes should be core applications, centrally coordinated, designed, and implemented around the globe, and which should be regional and local. At the same time, by identifying the critical business processes, the really important ones, you have gone a long way toward defining a vision of the future for your firm.

TABLE 12-4 *Management Challenges in Developing Global Systems*

Agreeing on common user requirements
Introducing changes in business processes
Coordinating applications development
Coordinating software releases
Encouraging local users to support global systems

core systems

Agency and other coordination costs increase as the firm moves from local option systems toward regional and global systems. However, transaction costs of participating in global markets probably decrease as firms develop global systems. A sensible strategy is to reduce agency costs by developing only a few core global systems that are vital for global operations, leaving other systems in the hands of regional and local units.

Source: Adapted from *Managing Information Technology in Multinational Corporations* by Edward M. Roche, © 1993.

FIGURE 12-4 *Local, regional, and global systems.*

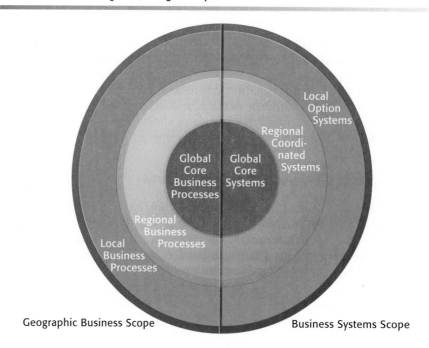

Geographic Business Scope   Business Systems Scope

Identify the Core Systems to Coordinate Centrally

By identifying the critical core business processes, you begin to see opportunities for transnational systems. The second strategic step is to conquer the core systems and define these systems as truly transnational. The financial and political costs of defining and implementing transnational systems are extremely high. Therefore, keep the list to an absolute minimum, letting experience be the guide and erring on the side of minimalism. By dividing off a small group of systems as absolutely critical, you divide opposition to a transnational strategy. At the same time, you can appease those who oppose the central worldwide coordination implied by transnational systems by permitting peripheral systems development to progress unabated, with the exception of some technical platform requirements.

Choose an Approach: Incremental, Grand Design, Evolutionary

The third step is to choose an approach. Avoid piecemeal approaches. These surely will fail for lack of visibility, opposition from all who stand to lose from transnational development, and lack of power to convince senior management that the transnational systems are worth it. Likewise, avoid grand design approaches that try to do everything at once. These also tend to fail because of an inability to focus resources. Nothing gets done properly, and opposition to organizational change is needlessly strengthened because the effort requires huge resources. An alternative approach is to evolve transnational applications from existing applications with a precise and clear vision of the transnational capabilities the organization should have in five years.

Make the Benefits Clear

What is in it for the company? One of the worst situations to avoid is to develop global systems for the sake of developing global systems. From the beginning, it is crucial that senior management at headquarters and foreign division managers clearly understand the benefits that will come to the company as well as to individual units. Although each system offers unique benefits, the overall contribution of global systems lies in four areas.

Global systems—truly integrated, distributed, and transnational systems—contribute to superior management and coordination. A simple price tag cannot be put on the value of this contribution, and the benefit will not show up in any capital budgeting model. It is the ability to switch suppliers on a moment's notice from one region to another in a crisis, the ability to move production in response to natural disasters, and the ability to use excess capacity in one region to meet raging demand in another.

A second major contribution is vast improvement in production, operation, and supply and distribution. Imagine a global value chain, with global suppliers and a global distribution network. For the first time, senior managers can locate value-adding activities in regions where they are most economically performed.

Third, global systems mean global customers and global marketing. Fixed costs around the world can be amortized over a much larger customer base. This change will unleash new economies of scale at production facilities.

Finally, global systems enable the firm to optimize the use of corporate funds over a much larger capital base. For instance, capital in a surplus region can be moved efficiently to expand production of capital-starved regions and cash can be managed more effectively within the company.

These strategies will not by themselves create global systems. You will have to implement what you strategize.

12.4 Technology Issues and Opportunities for Global Value Chains

Once firms have defined a global business model and systems strategy they must select hardware, software, and networking standards along with key system applications to support global business processes. Many companies today are using teams in other countries to develop and run their software and hardware, so they will need to address the challenges of managing global technology services as well.

Global Systems Technology Challenges

Hardware, software, and networking pose special technical challenges in an international setting. One major challenge is finding some way to standardize a global computing platform when there is so much variation from operating unit to operating unit and from country to country. Another major challenge is finding specific software applications that are user friendly and that truly enhance the productivity of international work teams. The major networking challenge is making data flow seamlessly across networks shaped by disparate national standards. Overcoming these challenges requires systems integration and connectivity on a global basis.

Computing Platforms and Systems Integration The development of a transnational information systems architecture based on the concept of core systems raises questions about how the new core systems will fit in with the existing suite of applications developed around the globe by different divisions, different people, and for different kinds of computing hardware. The goal is to develop global, distributed, and integrated systems to support digital business processes spanning national boundaries. Briefly, these are the same problems faced by any large domestic systems development effort. However, the problems are magnified in an international environment. Just imagine the challenge of integrating systems based on the Windows, Linux, Unix, or proprietary operating systems running on IBM, Sun, Hewlett-Packard, and other hardware in many different operating units in many different countries.

Moreover, having all sites use the same hardware and operating system does not guarantee integration. Some central authority in the firm must establish data and other technical standards, with which sites are to comply. For instance, technical accounting terms such as the beginning and end of the fiscal year must be standardized (review the earlier discussion of the cultural challenges to building global businesses), as well as the acceptable interfaces between systems, communication speeds and architectures, and network software.

Connectivity Truly integrated global systems must have connectivity—the ability to link together the systems and people of a global firm into a single integrated network just like the telephone system but capable of voice, data, and image transmissions. However, integrated global networks are extremely difficult to create (Lai and Chung 2002). For example, many countries cannot fulfill basic business telecommunications needs such as obtaining reliable circuits, coordinating among different carriers and the regional telecommunications authority, obtaining bills in a common currency standard, and obtaining standard agreements for the level of telecommunications service provided. Table 12-5 lists the major challenges posed by international networks.

Despite moves toward economic unity, Europe remains a hodgepodge of disparate national technical standards and service levels. Although most circuits leased by multinational corporations are fault-free more than 99.8 percent of the time, line quality and service vary widely from the north to the south of Europe. Network service is much more unreliable in southern Europe. Existing European standards for networking and electronic data interchange (EDI) are very industry and country specific.

Firms can provide international connectivity by building their own international private network using proprietary standards or by using Internet technology. The firm can put together its own private network based on leased lines from each country's post, telegraph, and telephone (PTT) authorities and services from the major global telecommunications providers. Each country, however, has different restrictions on data exchange, technical standards, and acceptable vendors of equipment. These problems magnify in certain parts of the world.

An increasingly attractive alternative is to create global networks based on the Internet and Internet technology. Companies can create global intranets for internal communication or extranets to exchange information more rapidly with business partners in their supply chains. They can use the public Internet to create global networks using virtual private networks (VPNs) from Internet service providers, which provide many features of a private network using the public Internet (see Chapter 7). However, VPNs may not provide the same level of quick and predictable response as private networks, especially during times of the day when Internet traffic is very congested, and they may not be able to support large numbers of remote users.

Moreover, the Internet is not yet a worldwide tool because many countries lack the communications infrastructure for extensive Internet use. Countries face high costs, government control, or government monitoring. Many countries also do not have the speedy and reliable postal and package delivery services that are essential for electronic commerce.

Western Europe faces both high transmission costs and lack of common technology because it is not politically unified and because European telecommunications systems are still in the process of shedding their government monopolies. The lack of an infrastructure and the high costs of installation are even more widespread in the rest of the world. Only about one-third of the world's households have basic telephone service.

Low penetration of PCs and widespread illiteracy limit demand for Internet service in India and other developing countries (see Figure 12-5). Where an infrastructure exists in less-developed countries, it is often outdated, lacking digital circuits and with very noisy lines. The purchasing power of most people in developing countries makes access to Internet services very expensive. Many countries monitor transmissions. Governments in

TABLE 12-5 *Problems of International Networks*

Costs and tariffs
Network management
Installation delays
Poor quality of international service
Regulatory constraints
Changing user requirements
Disparate standards
Network capacity

FIGURE 12-5   *Internet population in selected countries.*

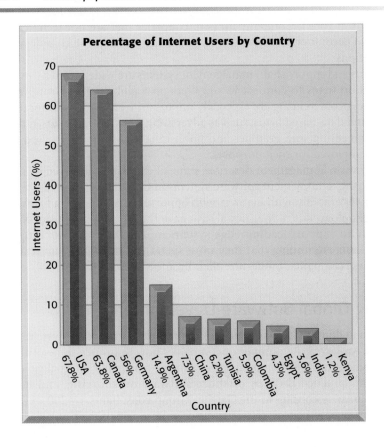

The percentage of the total population using the Internet in developing countries is much smaller than in Canada, the United States, and Europe.

Source: Internetworldstats.com, accessed June 5, 2005.

China, Singapore, Tunisia, Iran, and Saudi Arabia monitor Internet traffic and block access to Web sites considered morally or politically offensive (McFarquhar, 2004).

Global networking will increase as wireless networking services described in Chapter 8 fall in price and gain in power. *Communicate and compute any time, anywhere* networks based on satellite systems, digital cellular telephones, and mobile handheld devices will make it even easier to coordinate work and information in many parts of the globe that cannot be reached by existing ground-based systems.

Software The development of core systems poses unique challenges for application software: How will the old systems interface with the new? Entirely new interfaces must be developed and tested if old systems are kept in local areas (which is common). These interfaces can be costly and messy to develop. If new software must be created, another challenge is to develop software that can be realistically used by multiple business units from different countries given that these business units are accustomed to their unique business processes and definitions of data.

Aside from integrating the new with the old systems, there are problems of human interface design and functionality of systems. For instance, to be truly useful for enhancing productivity of a global workforce, software interfaces must be easily understood and mastered quickly. Graphical user interfaces are ideal but they presuppose a common language—often English. When international systems involve knowledge workers only, English may be the assumed international standard. But as international systems penetrate deeper into management and clerical groups, a common language may not be assumed, and human interfaces must be developed to accommodate different languages and even conventions.

What are the most important software applications? Many international systems focus on basic transaction and management reporting systems. Increasingly, firms are turning to supply chain management and enterprise systems to standardize their business processes on a global basis and to create coordinated global supply chains. However, these cross-functional systems are not always compatible with differences in languages, cultural heritages, and business processes in other countries (Martinsons 2004; Liang et al. 2004; Davison 2002). Company units in countries that are not technically sophisticated may also encounter problems trying to manage the technical complexities of enterprise applications.

EDI systems and supply chain management systems are widely used by manufacturing and distribution firms to connect to suppliers on a global basis. Groupware systems, email, and videoconferencing are especially important worldwide collaboration tools for knowledge- and data-based firms, such as advertising firms, research-based firms in medicine and engineering, and graphics and publishing firms. Internet-based tools will be increasingly employed for such purposes.

The Window on Management describes some of the challenges faced by multinational companies trying to implement software systems in China. China is a vast country that is modernizing very rapidly, with many growth opportunities for foreign firms. It welcomes advanced technology, but it does not always have the appropriate business processes or infrastructure to support leading-edge system applications. Global companies doing business in China are finding that they must spend additional time on training and on helping Chinese companies modernize their business processes.

Managing Global Software Development

Many global and domestic firms are managing their hardware and software resources using global teams. An increasing number of companies now outsource some of their new systems development work or maintenance of existing systems to external vendors in other countries. This practice is called **offshore software outsourcing**, and it has become extremely popular. According to the Gartner Group consultants, by 2004, eight out of 10 CIOs had already been instructed to outsource at least part of their firm's technology services offshore.

The arguments for offshore outsourcing are very compelling: A skilled programmer in India or Russia earns about \$12 500 per year, compared to \$25–45 000 per year for a comparable programmer in Canada. The Internet and low-cost communications technology have drastically reduced the expense and difficulty of coordinating the work of global teams in faraway locations. In addition to cost savings, outsourcing provides firms with access to world-class complementary technology assets and skills.

FIGURE 12-6   *Internet translation tools.*

This Web page from the Pearson Education Canada Web site for this text was translated into Russian using AltaVista's translation tools. Web sites and software interfaces for global systems may have to be translated into multiple languages to accommodate users in other parts of the world.

offshore software outsourcing

Getting Systems to Work in China—Slowly

China looks like the world's hottest market: It has nearly 1 billion consumers between the ages of 15 and 65 with more disposable income than at any other time in the country's history. Economic growth is sizzling. By 2006, China will have more broadband Internet and mobile phone users than any nation on earth. But not so fast. Most of the Chinese population is still poor, and China's communication, transportation, and technology infrastructures are still underdeveloped. Companies seeking to grow their businesses in China must make special efforts to adapt.

General Motors (GM) found this out the hard way when it tried to implement a customer relationship management (CRM) system using Siebel Systems software at its operational centres in Shanghai. GM is trying to overtake Volkswagen as the leading foreign auto brand in China, hoping to sell 1.3 billion vehicles by 2007. GM sells most of its vehicles in China through its joint venture partner Shanghai Automotive Industry Corporation. The company wanted to use the CRM system to develop a more sophisticated view of Chinese car buyers.

Unfortunately, local dealers had never heard of customer relationship management and had little incentive to provide GM with the sales data it needed to make the system work. To encourage dealer participation, GM built a portal that makes it easier for dealers to order vehicles. To use this portal, dealers must supply the customer data that GM needs. When GM receives a vehicle order, it gets the customer data at the same time.

GM is trying to control costs by replicating key aspects of its global technology platform within Shanghai Automotive, much like a franchiser would. It is using SAP software to coordinate sales and shipping information between its factories and its warehouse and trading unit. GM is helping Shanghai Automotive adopt the consistent image of all of GM operations worldwide. GM provided Shanghai Automotive with the specifications but is relying on its partner's information systems staff for implementation. Shanghai Automotive has the local knowledge and can implement new systems for GM at a much lower cost. "Moreover," says Addons Wu, CIO for GM China, "in China, we put more time into getting consensus…. You can order people to do things once or twice, but you lose your influence after that."

United Parcel Service (UPS) has been able to profit from China's poor transportation infrastructure and complicated import and export requirements. Multinational companies operating in China are relying on UPS because it can provide integrated shipping and logistics services to deal with these challenges. UPS focuses on serving multinationals and local businesses partly through Sinotrans, its joint venture partner.

UPS is training its own drivers as well as Sinotrans drivers to make sure they understand English and they can upload the correct shipping information into UPS systems using tools such as its handheld delivery information acquisition device (DIAD). Equally important is the need to train Chinese small businesses

to use automated shipping technology. (Again, this is much like the franchiser, duplicating domestic systems globally.) According to Edward Choi, UPS marketing director for China, "There's a huge group of mom-and-pop shops where business is still done by fax and phone." UPS cannot ignore this market segment because these small businesses supply the big distributors that in turn supply the big multinational companies.

UPS has deployed Chinese language versions of its WorldShip, QuantumVie, and CampusShip shipping-management systems and made them accessible to customers on the Web. UPS installs Web terminals at smaller companies with a large volume of business. Sometimes UPS even purchases the equipment for these businesses to make sure they will use its systems. UPS also runs seminars and conferences to educate business owners about how the technology works and the benefits it provides.

Making UPS systems work in China requires Chinese businesses to standardize their shipping data. In other countries, business clients might clean up their shipping data to verify addresses and avoid duplicates, but Chinese companies sometimes expect UPS to do this work for them.

Other companies operating in China have found they must provide extensive training and collaboration to prepare their business partners for effective deployment. MasterCard trains its business partners in e-commerce. China still does not have central credit-rating agencies, but it does have regional credit bureaus that profile the banking and payment histories of residents in metropolitan areas such as Beijing and Guangzhou. MasterCard provides consulting services to regional banks to help them automate processes such as credit scoring and credit reviews.

Although about 60 million Chinese people have MasterCard debit cards, very few actually have true credit cards. MasterCard's goal is to have 100 million Chinese credit card customers by 2009. To reach this goal, MasterCard needs to persuade small merchants to accept credit cards. (It is primarily the large hotels and other businesses catering to international travellers that accept MasterCard in China right now.) Small merchants may need to wait years before they have the telecommunications capability and technology to link to MasterCard's payment network, so MasterCard offers these small businesses offline transaction processing services. Merchants can send paper receipts to processing centres if they wish to use MasterCard.

Robert Mao, Nortel Networks President and CEO of Greater China, says: "We've been doing business here for more than 30 years." Nortel has more than 1500 employees in China, not counting joint ventures, and 98 percent of those employees are local. "We have four manufacturing facilities in China that support our business and customers in China," Mao says.

Nortel has two research and development (R&D) centres, one in Beijing and one in Guangzhou and, in the next three years, will invest more than $250 million in R&D, mostly at a new R&D centre in Beijing. These R&D centres focus on Internet Protocol-based multimedia and voice services, 3G wireless services, and next generation networking.

According to Mao, "That's a good foundation for winning, but it's not all. China is a good market and any good market invites a crowd. Competition is very keen with major global companies and, increasingly, with local Chinese companies. The local companies are doing well and growing fast but, because of our many years in the country, we compete with them on an equal basis and we win more than our fair share of business."

Nortel must adapt its information systems, not only so they can be used by their Chinese employees, but so the company can integrate the Chinese business and research data with its global data. This is an ongoing challenge for any organization doing business globally.

To Think About: What management, organization, and technology factors explain why global companies must make special efforts to implement their systems in China? Describe some of the steps companies can take to get their systems to work in China.

Sources: Paul McDougall, "The Place to Be," *Information Week*, April 5, 2004; Bruce Einhorn, "China.Net," *BusinessWeek*, March 15, 2004; Keith Bradsher, "G.M. to Speed Up Expansion in China," *The New York Times*, June 8, 2004; Laurie Sullivan, "Road Work in China," *Information Week*, August 30, 2004; and Elaine Kurtenbach, "GM to Spend $3B in China Over Next 3 Yrs," Associated Press, June 7, 2004; "Nortel Networks to Strengthen R&D Capabilities in China," September 16, 2003, available www.nortelnetworks.com/corporate/news/newsreleases/2003c/09_16_03_china_investment.html, accessed June 5, 2005; Wendy Herman, "China on the Move," available www.nortelnetworks.com/corporate/pressroom/feature_article/2004b/04_12_04_mao_china.html, accessed June 5, 2005.

There is a very strong chance that at some point in your career, you will be working with offshore outsourcers or global teams. Thus, it is very important to understand how offshore resources can best be managed. Not all work can be exported, special managerial and organizational issues must be addressed, and the savings are not as great as simple wage comparisons suggest (Krishna, Sahay and Walsham 2004).

Your firm is most likely to benefit from outsourcing if it takes the time to evaluate all the risks and makes sure outsourcing is appropriate for its particular needs. Any company that outsources its applications must thoroughly understand the project, including requirements, method of implementation, source of expected benefits, cost components, and metrics for measuring performance.

Offshore outsourcing can reduce software development costs, but companies will not save as much as they initially think. There are hidden costs to offshore outsourcing, and these costs can increase the total cost of ownership (TCO) of offshore-developed software by over 50 percent. These are the major cost components of offshore software development:

General Motors partners with Shanghai Automotive Industry Corporation to produce and sell automobiles for the Chinese market. It had to take special steps to implement its information systems in China.

1. *Contract cost.* Most of this cost is for labour required by the project—programmers, software engineers, systems analysts, network specialists, and project team managers.

2. *Vendor selection costs.* With any outsourced service, the expense of selecting a service provider can run from 0.1 percent to 10 percent in addition to the cost of the contract. Companies will need to allocate resources for documenting requirements, sending out requests for proposal (RFPs), travel expenses, negotiating contracts, legal fees, and project management. A project leader may be assigned to work full time on these tasks, with others contributing, and these tasks are lost labour costs. The entire process can take three months to a year.

3. *Transition management and knowledge transfer costs.* It takes from three months to a full year to completely transfer work to an offshore partner and make sure the vendor thoroughly understands your business. Users should be prepared to spend even more time with the offshore team than an in-house group to make sure the team fully understands their requirements. A certain number of outsourcer staff must travel to the client company to analyze the client's technology and applications before they can begin the actual work. The client company's systems and specifications have to be thoroughly documented. The offshore employees have to work in parallel with costly

in-house employees, and neither can produce very much during the training period. If not included in the outsourcing contract, additional travel costs and visa costs must be figured in. Companies should expect to spend an additional 2 to 3 percent of their contracts on transition costs.

4. *Domestic human resources costs.* If your company has to lay off domestic employees as a result of the offshore outsourcing, you may have to pay laid-off workers severance pay and retention bonuses to keep them working long enough to share their knowledge with their offshore replacements. Layoffs can also adversely affect employee morale and productivity. The firm's staff may resist working with the outsourcer and resign, taking valuable knowledge with them. Layoffs and related costs can add an extra 3 to 5 percent.

5. *Costs of improving software development processes.* If a company does not have solid in-house processes for software development, it will take much longer to coordinate work with the vendor.

   Both parties should agree on the processes to be used. If the outsourcer has to follow your standards, make sure the offshore team thoroughly understands them.

   Canadian firms often use rather informal methods for documenting and analyzing software projects. They may need to formalize their software development processes and adopt the methodology used by the offshore vendor. For example, many Indian companies use the capability maturity model (CMM) developed by Carnegie-Mellon as their software development methodology, and their clients may need to come up to speed in CMM to work effectively with them. The ability to write clear specifications is critical as well, and creating a good set of specifications is very time consuming.

   Quality assurance testing also must be beefed-up in an offshore arrangement. There must be a dedicated group of people in the client organization who are always available to develop test plans and review results as they are generated by the offshore team. Companies outsourcing software development to external vendors should anticipate spending an additional 1 to 10 percent on the improvement of software development processes.

6. *Costs of adjusting to cultural differences.* Cultural differences can drain productivity. A seasoned Canadian employee cannot automatically be replaced by an offshore worker. Their values and attitudes are different. Canadian workers tend to feel much more comfortable about speaking up and making suggestions. If something doesn't make sense or does not appear workable, they will voice concerns. But offshore programmers may keep these feelings to themselves, believing that their aim is to please, and that this is what the client wants. The work then may take more time and money to complete and require extensive rework. Likewise, an application that makes sense to a Canadian worker such as automating consumer credit cards may be a foreign concept offshore. Lags in productivity can add as much as 20 percent of additional costs to the offshore contract during the first two years. There will probably be a need for more face-to-face interaction than originally anticipated because offshore workers do not interpret things the same way. Productivity lags and adjustments to cultural differences can add an extra 3 to 7 percent to total project costs.

7. *Cost of managing an offshore contract.* Managing the offshore relationship requires additional invoicing, auditing, billing and time-tracking work. It requires additional telecommunications costs as well. Maintaining security merits special attention. Offshore partners must agree on common procedures for data security, data recovery, protection of intellectual property rights, network security, and access control. The European Union (EU) Data Privacy Directive could prohibit an outsourcing agreement from transferring personal data to non-EU countries unless both parties satisfy EU data protection standards. Companies should expect to pay an additional 6 to 10 percent to manage the offshore contract.

Figure 12-7 shows best- and worst-case scenarios for the total cost of ownership of an outsourcing project. It shows how much hidden costs can affect the total cost of an outsourcing project. The best case reflects the lowest estimates for additional costs, and the worst case reflects the highest estimates for these costs. As you can see, hidden costs will increase the total cost of an outsourcing project by an extra 15 to 57 percent.

FIGURE 12-7   *Total cost of outsourcing.*

TOTAL COST OF OFFSHORE OUTSOURCING				
Cost of outsourcing contract			**$10 000 000**	
Hidden Costs	Best Case	Additional Cost ($)	Worst Case	Additional Cost ($)
1. Vendor selection	0.2%	20 000	2%	200 000
2. Transition costs	2%	200 000	3%	300 000
3. Layoffs & retention	3%	300 000	5%	500 000
4. Lost productivity/cultural issues	3%	300 000	27%	2 700 000
5. Improving development processes	1%	100 000	10%	1 000 000
6. Managing the contract	6%	600 000	10%	1 000 000
Total additional costs		1 520 000		5 700 000
	Outstanding Contract ($)	Additional Cost ($)	Total Cost ($)	Additional Cost
Total cost of outsourcing (TCO) best case	10 000 000	1 520 000	11 520 000	15.2%
Total cost of outsourcing (TCO) worst case	10 000 000	5 700 000	15 700 000	57.0%

If a firm spends $10 million on offshore outsourcing contracts, that company will actually spend 15.2 percent in additional costs even under the best-case scenario. In the worst-case scenario, where there is a dramatic drop in productivity along with exceptionally high transition and layoff costs, a firm can expect to pay up to 57 percent in extra costs on top of the $10 million outlay for an offshore contract.

Even with these extra costs, many firms will benefit from offshore outsourcing if they manage the work well. The total cost of doing the software work in-house might run to $18–20 million, so even under the worse-case scenario, the firm could still save about 15 percent.

Although offshore software outsourcing might benefit individual firms, its broader social impact is less clear. Companies that outsource their software work may be eliminating jobs in the domestic software industry. As the practice becomes widespread, will countries whose jobs are going overseas wind up with mass unemployment or higher productivity and better jobs? The Window on Organizations looks at both sides of the debate.

 # WINDOW ON ORGANIZATIONS

Offshore Outsourcing: Good or Bad?

If you're a U.S. customer of E-Loan, an Internet company offering online loan services, you have a choice about where your loan application will be processed. You could have the application processed in India, or you can request to have the loan processed domestically in the U.S. If you choose processing in India, you will have the results two days earlier than if you had the work done in the U.S. E-Loan farmed out loan processing work to Wipro Ltd., a giant Indian outsourcing company, because Indian labour costs are so much lower than in the U.S.

E-Loan's outsourcing of its loan application processing to India is not an isolated phenomenon. It is part of a swelling movement toward *offshore outsourcing*, the movement of white-collar jobs abroad. Many other companies, particularly financial institutions, including Delta Air Lines and American Express, have moved their call centres to India or the Philippines.

Call centre jobs, telemarketing jobs, financial analysts, and

jobs in banking and insurance have been steadily moving offshore. Also threatened are jobs in medical transcription, insurance applications and claims processing, and typesetting, as well as some jobs in accounting and tax preparation. According to a Datamonitor estimate, there are currently more than 250 contact centres and 51 000 agent positions in India devoted to offshore outsourcing. Forrester Research estimates that 3.3 million white-collar jobs will be transferred from the U.S. abroad by 2015. The impact of offshore outsourcing in the information technology industry could be especially severe: According to the Gartner Group, one out of 10 jobs in U.S. computer services may have already shifted to lower-cost countries such as Russia or India. In Canada, Industry Canada's quarterly statistical report in December 2003 showed that services employment in the information technology and communications (ITC) sector fell for the first three quarters of 2003 by a total of 2.6 percent, and this decrease happened during a booming economy. Industry Canada analysts suspect that the drop in employment is the result of Canadian companies beginning to outsource their services off-shore. Even worse, the employment statistics only apply to those in the ITC sector and not those employed at corporations that outsource offshore—meaning that the drop in ITC services employment could be much higher.

While Canadian companies may have begun to offshore, many U.S. companies are offshoring to Canada! In 2002, there were 450 outsourced call centres in Canada. This number is predicted to rise to 600 by 2007. Prominent American call centres currently importing call centre services from Canada include: ACI in Quebec; Dell, Ford Credit and Neiman Marcus in Alberta; and Convergys and eBay in British Columbia. Ontario has attracted such U.S. giants as AmeriCredit, EDS, IBM and Sitel (Buchanan, 2005).

In mid-July 2003, IBM set off a firestorm when news of its plans to move more white-collar and programming jobs overseas was leaked to the press. Hewlett-Packard has 5000 Indian employees in research, software development, and customer support. Many non-technology companies now use offshore programmers for much of their routine programming work.

Critics claim that offshore outsourcing shifts jobs from high-wage countries to low-wage countries, taking jobs away from Canadian workers or pressuring them to take lower pay to remain working. These critics fear that highly trained and educated workers will be ground down by globalization, just as blue-collar workers were in the 1970s and 1980s. In a report released by the Conference Board of Canada, fewer than 40 percent of 132 medium- and large-sized companies the Board had surveyed in 2004 had offshore suppliers or contracts. The report further states that many Canadian companies that have "offshored" have found it difficult, with only 58 percent saying they achieved their stated goals. In the report, 58 percent of responding companies said they were not "offshoring any business or functions." Companies most likely to go offshore were manufacturers (25 percent), high-tech firms, including software development (15 percent), maintenance (15 percent), and user support, such as call centres (13 percent). The size of the offshore investments also appears small, with most at less than $100 000 per contract. But 31 percent of respondents indicated planned investment levels were between $100 000 and $1 million—a potential of more than $40 million in total (Harris 2005). Respondents cited cost savings as the most pressing driver for offshoring while stating that in-house barriers (such as bad publicity) were the prime obstacle to offshoring. But other experts point out that offshore outsourcers often provide better quality work at lower costs. Firms also have a better chance of long-term survival if they can keep their prices competitive. Companies can pass these savings from outsourcing on to consumers or use them to expand the business and create new jobs that provide more value than those replaced. A study by the McKinsey Global Institute estimated that every dollar of costs moved from the U.S. to offshore yields a benefit of US $1.12 to US $1.14 to the U.S. economy.

Another study by economics consulting firm Global Insight, commissioned by the pro-outsourcing Information Technology Association of America, found that the productivity generated by U.S. companies sending computer services work abroad boosted domestic employment by 90 000 jobs in 2003. This study claimed that outsourcing created twice as many U.S. jobs as it displaced and would lead, by 2008, to the creation of 337 000 new jobs in construction, education, health care, and financial services.

The kinds of jobs that are moving overseas are those that can be most easily reduced to a series of rules and performed overseas by another person—or perhaps by a computer. Jobs that will most likely stay in Canada or the United States or that will be newly created in the next decade are those that require human contact or complex analytical skills. In the information systems field, jobs that will remain in North America are those for high-level software designers and people who can apply technology to solve problems in specific businesses such as banking, retailing, or manufacturing. Most at risk are software jobs that involve straightforward coding of software programs, where technical specifications can be handed off to a programmer. These are exactly the technology jobs where wages have fallen since 2002.

Oddly enough, Canada can also benefit from U.S. offshoring. With the value of the Canadian dollar less than the U.S. dollar, American companies can offshore to Canadian companies with few of the cultural, geographic, or language barriers that exist in offshoring to India or the Philippines. In 2002, there were 450 outsourced call centres in Canada. That number is expected to rise to 600 by 2007. These call centres are located throughout Canada, in Ontario, British Columbia, Manitoba, Quebec, and Alberta. Datamonitor estimates that the U.S. will lose about 3000 call centres and 133 000 agent positions by 2008, with a good portion of the contracts being outsourced to Canada. So while some Canadian firms are offshoring and others intend to follow, Canada is also reaping the benefits of the U.S. trend toward off-shoring.

To Think About: Does offshore outsourcing create an ethical dilemma? Why or why not? What are the barriers to offshore outsourcing? Is offshore outsourcing a "double-edged" sword for national economies?

Sources: David Wessel, "The Future of Jobs: New Ones Arise, Wage Gap Widens," *Wall Street Journal*, April 2, 2004; Michael Schroeder, "Outsourcing May Create U.S. Jobs," *Wall Street Journal*, March 30, 2004; Kris Maher, "Next on the Outsourcing List," *Wall Street Journal*, March 23, 2004; Stephen Baker and Manjeet Kripalani, "Software: Will Outsourcing Hurt America's Supremacy?" *BusinessWeek*, March 1, 2004; Jesse Drucker and Ken Brown, "Press 1 for Delhi, 2 for Dallas," *Wall Street Journal*, March 9, 2004; Reuters, "Offshore Outsourcing Set to Hit U.S. Job Market," www.itweb.co.za, accessed July 30, 2003; Stephanie Armour and Michelle Kessler, "USA's New Money-Saving Export: White-Collar Jobs," *USA Today*, August 9, 2003; and Bob Evans, "Business Technology: Offshore Outsourcing: A Means to an End," *InformationWeek*, July 28, 2003; Terri-Sue Buchanan, "Call Centres: Ringing in Profits," *Exportwise*, Winter 2005, www.edc.ca/corpinfo/pubs/exportwise/winter05/p11_e.htm, accessed June 6, 2005; Harris Anwar, "Canadian Firms Cool on Offshore, Board Says," *The Globe and Mail*, April 18, 2005; "Canadian Companies Slow to Embrace Offshore Outsourcing," *Ottawa Business Journal*, April 15, 2005; "International Outsourcing of Call Centre Operations," Canadian Marketing Association, March 2004, www.the-cma.org/council/downloads/InternationalOutsourcingMarch2004.pdf, accessed June 6, 2005; David Ticoll, "Offshoring Will Soon Be Making Waves," *The Globe and Mail*, February 19, 2004.

Management Opportunities, Challenges, and Solutions

When firms operate in many different countries, creating an appropriate organizational and technology infrastructure for conducting international business is very challenging.

Opportunities

Firms have extraordinary opportunities to lower costs through global scale economies by developing international systems that enable them to produce as well as sell goods and services in different regions of the world.

Management Challenges

Developing and managing global systems raise challenges about finding the right global business strategy, managing change in a multicultural enterprise, and achieving sufficient connectivity and integration.

Finding the Right Global Business Strategy If a company wishes to operate internationally, it is essential to determine the right global business model. Should some or all of the business be managed on a global basis using a transnational model? How much local autonomy should be allowed? Which way of organizing the business best fits the company's strategic direction? There are some lines of business in which local variations are slight, and the possibility exists to reap large rewards by organizing globally. It is likely that firms with many lines of business will have to maintain a mixed organizational structure.

Difficulties of Managing Change in a Multicultural Firm Although engineering change in a single corporation in a single nation can be difficult, costly, and a long-term process, bringing about significant change in large-scale global corporations can be daunting. Cultural, political, and language diversity magnifies differences in organizational culture and standard operating procedures when companies operate internationally. These differences create barriers to the development of global information systems that transcend national boundaries.

Difficulties of Achieving Global Connectivity and Integration Choices of technology, platforms, networks, hardware, and software are the final elements in building transnational information systems infrastructures. The Internet and Internet technology will increasingly be used to provide global connectivity and to serve as a foundation for global systems, but many companies will still need proprietary systems for certain functions, and, therefore, international standards. Even with the proper organizational structure and appropriate management choices, it is still possible to stumble over technological issues.

Solution Guidelines

We now can reconsider how to handle the most vexing problems facing managers developing the global information systems architectures that were described in Table 12-4.

Agreeing on Common User Requirements Establishing a short list of the core business processes and core support systems will begin a process of rational comparison across the many divisions of the company, develop a common language for discussing the business, and naturally lead to an understanding of common elements (as well as the unique qualities that must remain local).

Introducing Changes in Business Processes Your success as a change agent will depend on your legitimacy, your actual raw power, and your ability to involve users in the change design process. **Legitimacy** is defined as the extent to which

legitimacy

your authority is accepted on grounds of competence, vision, or other qualities. The selection of a viable change strategy, which we have defined as evolutionary but with a vision, should assist you in convincing others that change is feasible and desirable. Involving people in change, assuring them that change is in the best interests of the company and their local units, is a key tactic.

Coordinating Applications Development Choice of change strategy is critical for this problem. At the global level, there is far too much complexity to attempt a grand design strategy of change. It is far easier to coordinate change by making small incremental steps toward a larger vision. Imagine a five-year plan of action rather than a two-year plan of action, and reduce the set of transnational systems to a bare minimum to reduce coordination costs.

Coordinating Software Releases Firms can institute procedures to ensure that all operating units convert to new software updates at the same time so that everyone's software is compatible.

Encouraging Local Users to Support Global Systems The key to solving this problem is to involve users in the creation of the design without giving up control over the development of the project to parochial interests. Recruiting a wide range of local individuals to transnational centres of excellence helps send the message that all significant groups are involved in the design and will have an influence. These centres draw heavily from local national units, are based on multinational teams, and must report to worldwide management—their first line of responsibility is to the core applications.

The overall tactic for dealing with resistant local units in a transnational company is cooptation. **Cooptation** is defined as bringing the opposition into the process of designing and implementing the solution without giving up control over the direction and nature of the change. As much as possible, raw power should be avoided. Minimally, however, local units must agree on a short list of transnational systems, and raw power may be required to solidify the idea that transnational systems of some sort are truly required.

cooptation

Summary

1. **Identify the major factors driving the internationalization of business.**

   There are general cultural factors and specific business factors to consider. The growth of cheap international communication and transportation has created a world culture with stable expectations or norms. Political stability and a growing global knowledge base that is widely shared contribute also to the world culture. These general factors create the conditions for global markets, global production, coordination, distribution, and global economies of scale.

2. **Compare strategies for developing global businesses.**

   There are four basic international strategies: domestic exporter, multinational, franchiser, and transnational. In a domestic exporter strategy, all factors of production are managed at headquarters. In a multinational strategy, various global offices manage the factors of production independent of the home office. In a franchiser strategy, factors of production are duplicated on a global scale. In a transnational strategy, all factors of production are coordinated on a global scale. However, the choice of strategy is a function of the type of business and product.

3. **Demonstrate how information systems can support different global business strategies.**

   There is a connection between firm strategy and information systems design. Transnational firms must develop networked system configurations and permit considerable decentralization of development and operations. Franchisers almost always duplicate systems across many countries and use centralized financial controls. Multinationals typically rely on decentralized independence among foreign units with some movement toward development of networks. Domestic exporters typically are centralized in domestic headquarters with some decentralized operations permitted.

4. **Evaluate the issues and technical alternatives to be considered when developing international information systems.**

   Implementing a global system requires an implementation strategy that considers both organization design and technology platforms. Typically, global systems have evolved without a conscious plan. The remedy is to define a small subset of core business processes and focus on developing systems that could support these processes. Tactically, co-opting widely dispersed foreign units allows them to participate in the development and operation of these systems while being careful to maintain overall control.

The main hardware and telecommunications issues are systems integration and connectivity. The choices for integration are to go with either a proprietary architecture or open systems technology. Global networks are extremely difficult to develop and operate. Firms can build their own global networks, or they can create global networks based on the Internet (intranets or virtual private networks). The main software issue concerns developing interfaces to existing systems and selecting applications that can work with multiple cultural, language, and organizational frameworks.

5. *Identify the challenges posed by global information systems and propose management solutions.*

Global information systems pose challenges because cultural, political, and language diversity magnifies differences in organizational culture and business processes and encourages proliferation of disparate local information systems that are difficult to integrate. Businesses may have to struggle to find the right global business strategy. Management solutions include identifying a common set of user requirements for the entire global enterprise; coordinating applications development and software releases; and using legitimacy and cooptation to enlist user support in the change process.

Key Terms

Business driver, 415	Global culture, 416	Offshore software outsourcing, 428
Cooptation, 435	International information systems	Particularism, 418
Core systems, 423	architecture, 415	Transborder data flow, 418
Domestic exporter, 420	Legitimacy, 434	Transnational, 420
Franchisers, 420	Multinational, 420	

Review Questions

1. What are the five major factors to consider when developing an international information systems portfolio?

2. Describe the five general cultural factors leading toward growth in global business and the four specific business factors. Describe the interconnection among these factors.

3. What is meant by a global culture?

4. What are the major challenges to the development of global systems?

5. Why have firms not planned for the development of international systems?

6. Describe the four main strategies for global business and organizational structure.

7. Describe the four different system configurations that can be used to support different global strategies.

8. What are the major management issues in developing international systems?

9. What are three principles to follow when organizing the firm for global business?

10. What are three steps of a management strategy for developing and implementing global systems?

11. What is meant by cooptation, and how can it be used in developing global systems?

12. Describe the main technical issues facing global systems.

13. What is offshore software outsourcing? What challenges does it pose? What are the cost components of offshore software development?

14. What are the challenges posed by global systems? How can these challenges be addressed?

Discussion Questions

1. If you were a manager in a company that operates in many countries, what criteria would you use to determine whether an application should be developed as a global application or as a local application?

2. Describe ways the Internet can be used in international information systems.

Application Software Exercise:
Database and Web Page Development Tool Exercise:
Building a Job Database and Web Page for an International Consulting Firm

KTP Consulting operates in various locations around the world. KTP specializes in designing, developing, and implementing enterprise systems for medium- to large-size companies. KTP offers its employees opportunities to travel, live, and work in various locations throughout North America, Europe, and Asia. The firm's human resources department has a simple database that enables its staff to track job vacancies. When an employee is interested in relocating, she or he contacts the human resources department for a list of KTP job vacancies. KTP also posts its employment opportunities on the company Web site.

What type of data should be included in the KTP job vacancies database? What information should not be included in this database? Based on your answers to these questions, develop a job vacancies database for KTP. Populate the database with at least 20 records. You should also develop a simple Web page that incorporates job vacancy data from your newly created database. Submit a disk containing a copy of the KTP database and Web page to your professor.

Electronic Business Project: Conducting International Marketing and Pricing Research

You are in charge of marketing for a Canadian manufacturer of office furniture that has decided to enter the international market. You have been given the name of Sorin SRL, a major Italian office furniture retailer, but your source had no other information. You want to test the market by contacting this firm to offer it a specific desk chair that you have to sell at about $125. Using the Web, locate the information needed to contact this firm and to find out how many euros you would need to charge for the chair in the current market. One source for locating European companies is the Europages

Business Directory (**www.europages.com**). In addition, consider using the Universal Currency Converter Web site (**www.xe.net/ucc**), which determines the value of one currency expressed in other currencies. Obtain both the information needed to contact the firm and the price of your chair in their local currency. Then locate and obtain customs and legal restrictions on the products you will export from Canada and import into Italy. Finally, locate a company that will represent you as a customs agent and gather information on shipping costs.

Group Project: Identifying Information Technology for Global Business Strategies

With a group of students, identify an area of information technology, and explore how this technology might be useful for supporting global business strategies. For instance, you might choose an area such as digital telecommunications (e.g., email, wireless communications, value-added networks), enterprise systems, collaborative software, or the Internet. It will be necessary to choose a business scenario to

discuss the technology. You might choose, for instance, an automobile parts franchise or a clothing franchise, such as Nygård, as example businesses. Which applications would you make global, which core business processes would you choose, and how would the technology be helpful? If possible, use electronic presentation software to present your findings to the class.

Web Sites of Interest

There are many interesting Web sites to enhance your learning about international information systems. You can search the Web yourself or try the following sites to add to what you have already learned.

International Systems Security Association **www.issa.org/**
This not-for-profit, international organization of information security professionals and practitioners has 66 chapters in 10 countries, including Canada.

Global IT Management Association **www.gitma.org**
The Global Information Technology Management Association's mission is to promote the careful examination and dissemination of IT management issues in all parts of the world.

Journal of Global IT Management **www.uncg.edu/bae/people /palvia/jgitm.htm**
An academic journal that contains interesting articles about real-world scenarios around the world.

CASE STUDY:
Celanese Recentralizes with a New Enterprise System

At the end of 2003, Celanese AG, a global chemical company, had about $5 billion in annual sales and about 9500 employees. Celanese is headquartered in Kronberg, Germany, and has 30 facilities in 11 countries on six continents although most of its facilities are located in North America. Celanese had been part of Hoechst AG pharmaceuticals since 1979. However, it was spun off in 1999 when Hoechst merged with Rhône-Poulenc to create a new pharmaceutical company, Aventis.

Celanese is a rather complex multinational organization with five main businesses: Celanese Chemicals, consisting of Acetyl Products, which processes natural gas and ethylene used in products for manufacturing industries, and Chemical Intermediates, which produces specialty chemicals for paints, coatings, agrochemicals, and textiles; Celanese Acetate Products, which manufactures cellulose acetate filament and tow (used in cigarette filters); Ticona Technical Polymers, which makes chemical products for the electronics, telecommunications, automotive, and medical industries; Performance Products, which produces ingredients for food products, such as the Nutrinova sweetener used in Pepsi One; and Celanese Venturs, specializing in research and development, including artificial fibres and alternative energy.

Celanese, like many large corporations, had focused on decentralization during the 1980s and 1990s, and, as a result, its corporate headquarters operated largely like a holding company. Its highly independent units implemented enterprise systems from SAP, the leading enterprise software company. Each unit had its own separate system, and each felt free to modify the SAP package software to meet its own requirements. To complicate matters even further, Celanese had grown during those 20 years partly by purchasing smaller companies, many of which already had their own enterprise systems. Altogether, Celanese had 13 enterprise systems by 2000 (reduced to 10 by 2002 when Celanese sold one of its business units) that were housed in five different computer centres.

By 2000, as the world economies began weakening, many companies began to look for ways to reduce their expenses in the face of declining sales. Centralizing these companies became popular as a way to reduce costs once the expenses of centralization had been absorbed. This approach was very popular in the chemical industry, partly because its raw materials costs were rising at the same time as sales were dropping. When Celanese was spun off, its management set a formidable goal of doubling its sales in five years. To enable the company to achieve that goal, some of the increased sales would have to come from acquisitions, and that meant its stock price would have to go higher for it to afford such purchases.

How could centralization help Celanese reduce its costs? There were numerous ways. The most obvious one was to make the various units of Celanese use the same version of SAP. Celanese units varied from version 3.1 to version 4.6. It was expensive to obtain so many different versions. However, the expense was even higher when so many of the IT staff had first to learn and then to support all of these versions at different Celanese units. Having only one version running on one computer for the whole company would mean far smaller IT staffs within the various units.

But there were other, less obvious, costs that could be significantly reduced. Under the decentralized approach, collecting all the financial information corporate managers needed was not only time consuming, and, therefore, expensive, but it also increased the likelihood of errors in that data. In addition, different units used different names for what were really the same pieces of data. For example, price in one system might be *cost* or *purchase price* in another. Furthermore, many of the units often failed to take advantage of some of the useful new features of their SAP systems. For example, one new function in SAP in 2003 was its supply chain event management (SCEM), an ERP component that enables a company to better forecast its supply needs and better manage its supply chain while reducing inventory costs. The problem in a decentralized environment is that some units adopt that feature while others do not. And some that do adopt it might use it to benefit their own needs rather than using it to benefit the organization as a whole. Another hidden cost of separate ERP systems was that they prevented the company from obtaining a single company-wide view of customers that might indicate opportunities to cross-sell and up-sell customers between business units.

In late 1999, when Hoechst spun off Celanese, company management initiated a new project to recentralize the company, which it named One Celanese. They then began searching for a new global CIO who could reduce the company's costs by integrating many of its information systems. Karl Wachs was hired and given a simple instruction—cut costs. Wachs quickly decided to roll up all the units' disparate enterprise systems into a single system, and he named the project OneSAP. With the aid of 70 people, Wachs began the process of initiating the project, saying, "This is not a four-week decision cycle. It should take a year for approval." In fact, it took 11 months. The project was not cheap. According to Wachs, at the height of the project, it was costing Celanese between $125 000 and $250 000 a day. One of the project managers said the overall cost would be about $75 million. However, Celanese's management concluded OneSAP would pay for itself in two years once the project was completed.

How did Wachs and the Celanese information systems unit go about rolling up the various SAP systems into one? The technical aspects—installing new SAP software so that the various units could begin to use it—were far from the most difficult. Much greater challenges were posed by the organizational cultures of the disparate Celanese operating units. Employees were comfortable using enterprise systems, and they were not necessarily ready to change their way of working to fit a standard set of business processes. The various units were intensely independent; they were not used to thinking of Celanese first but rather of the needs of their own units. According to the employees' old way of thinking, if something went wrong with a transaction that was not in their own unit, it was someone else's responsibility. That thinking had to change.

Moreover, in the past, the Celanese culture had been one of

building consensus, an approach that cannot work in a situation where people are told to make changes they do not want to make. "If we tolerate business units explaining why their outputs are different so that they don't have to change their inputs," Wachs concluded, "then we have lost. The mistake of the past was trying to adapt software to the business." Now the company would have to adapt the business to the software. To accomplish these cultural changes required a lot of explanation, a lot of education, and clear and absolute orders from the very top.

The project was divided into seven tracks, including finance, supply chain management, manufacturing, "order-to-cash," business intelligence reporting, technology, and change management. Each track had several functional stakeholders who were given the responsibility for that track's progress. Each track also had one person responsible for working at a higher level. For example, the finance track had one person assigned to work with the chief financial officer and the controllers "to design the business processes for that organization," as Wachs explained. The project leadership also demanded that Celanese employees follow the six sigma philosophy of "total quality management," which meant that every person was responsible for quality.

The project certainly had its problems. The U.S. and German human resources systems (and several other small systems) were allowed to keep their own SAP systems for "legitimate business reasons." However, by the end of the project, 7 out of 10 of the old SAP systems, representing 90 percent of the business, were shut off. When Celanese was ready to install the SCEM software, Wachs learned that SAP did not have the software ready. Another problem was that in early 2003

Celanese spent $186 million to purchase the emulsion businesses from Clariant, a very old Basel, Switzerland, chemistry company. That meant that the Clariant unit had to be included in OneSAP. Another problem the project team had to face was cleaning and integrating the data from the various existing SAP systems into OneSAP so the new system is reliable and accurate.

Sources: www.celanese.com, accessed June 4, 2004; Rick Mullin, "The Age of Interoperability," **www.e-chemmerce.com**, accessed March 28, 2003; Scott Berinato, "A Day in the Life of Celanese's Big ERP Rollup," *CIO Magazine*, January 15, 2003; Celanese, "1000 Days in Five (Not So) Easy Steps," *CIO Magazine*, January 15, 2003; Celanese Project Team, "The Top Eight Risks to the OneSAP Project," *CIO Magazine*, January 15, 2003; Celanese, "A Brief Tale of a Long History," *CIO Magazine*, January 15, 2003; and OSISoft Case Study, "Celanese Corporation", **www.osisoft.com**, accessed April 1, 2003.

CASE STUDY QUESTIONS

1. Analyze Celanese using the competitive forces and value chain models.

2. How important is Celanese's centralized enterprise system to its business strategy? Why? What is its business value to the company?

3. What management, organization, and technology challenges did Celanese face as it tried to implement OneSAP? Which were the most difficult?

4. How successful was Celanese in meeting these challenges? What problems did it solve? How? Which problems remained unsolved?

Part III CANADIAN CASE STUDY:
In Tech We Trust: The Story of SAP in Canada

The road to ERP success is littered with the corpses of many a company and many a CIO who tried and failed at this complex and demanding undertaking. Why do ERP implementations go wrong? What steps can be taken to help put them on the right track?

Are there certain factors about an organization—for example, its type (e.g., retail, utility, manufacturing), size, or geographical dispersion—that make it harder or easier to implement an enterprise resource planning system, and specifically to implement SAP? Morrie Baker and Gary Lackstein plan to take their franchise operation from three to more than 100 Ben and Jerry's ice cream "Scoop Shops" in just a few years. Operating a handful of ice cream shops may seem like small potatoes (or scoops of ice cream), but multiply those shops by more than 30, and you have the makings of a small empire of frozen treats. With at least 18 flavours per mini-store, the logistics, inventory, human resources, and other service delivery aspects of this business could become overwhelming. Would SAP help to resolve these issues and make managing the Canada-wide operation easier? Let's look at some Canadian and other companies that have experienced problems—and successes—with SAP implementations before returning to the Ben and Jerry's question.

Let us examine NOVA Chemicals, a Calgary-based commodity chemical firm that has reached a level of ERP maturity. NOVA produces styrenics and olefins/polyolefins at 18 locations in Canada, the United States, France, the Netherlands, and the United Kingdom.

By the mid-1990s, NOVA had made a number of acquisitions and had gone through several reorganizations, resulting in myriad outdated legacy systems and a variety of systems running different parts of its business. The company was ripe for significant business process reengineering. Seeing some of its competitors already going the ERP route, NOVA decided to head in that direction as well.

In retrospect, some of NOVA's initial reasons for embarking on its ERP journey may not have been the right ones. As senior vice president and CIO John Wheeler observed, "NOVA is a commodity chemical company. We're not as big or as diverse as some of our competitors. But because of the commonality of our business, one of the things we can do is focus on best practices. So over time, it became apparent that ERP was not about technology. It wasn't even about information systems. It was really about building a company that could leverage best practices. It was about business process." But when NOVA first embarked on ERP, that realization was still years away.

NOVA'S INITIAL IMPLEMENTATION

NOVA first took the ERP plunge in 1995 when it decided to implement SAP's new distributed R3 Version 2.2. SAP is the third-largest software company in the world and specializes in client/server enterprise application software modules. That first plunge into ERP can be like taking a dip in a northern lake on a windy January day. NOVA attempted to do a pilot installation in a small U.S.-based styrenics business, but the project faltered and was abandoned, causing the company to step back and regroup.

During that first installation, NOVA did not have a CIO. But after that initial setback, it was decided that a CIO was necessary, and the company's vice president and controller, Larry MacDonald, was given that responsibility.

Reflecting on the company's early experiences with ERP, MacDonald pointed to the newness of the SAP/R3 product and its integrated nature as two early stumbling blocks. "The distributed R3 version was brand new, and people weren't used to the complexity of SAP implementations," he said. "Having something that was so broad and touched on the business from beginning to end—the total supply chain—was something that we did not understand well. We didn't understand the complexities that integration brought to an implementation."

As a result, NOVA underestimated the scope of the business process improvement and the need to get key people from across the business involved. It also underestimated what it would take to deliver the project and learn the software.

Complicating matters was the reluctance by many people on the business side to embrace SAP. NOVA was implementing all modules, so SAP was being installed virtually "wall to wall" throughout the business. First, the company had to learn how to do the implementation, and then it had to learn how to bring it into the culture of the organization. A lot of people resisted the early implementations, because they weren't receiving much value from them in those days.

"The change that this was bringing to how people did their work was tremendous," noted MacDonald. "We really had to work on the cultural piece, the education piece, and then the technical piece of it."

Consulting firm Deloitte and Touche was NOVA's main implementation partner, bringing a strong change-management capability, as well as strong project- and IT-management methodologies and good knowledge of SAP. According to Wheeler, NOVA's strong operations and change-management capability today can be attributed to practices introduced by its consulting partner.

THE TURNAROUND

Rallying line management was crucial to the success of the implementation. Recalled MacDonald, "Once providing resources to support the implementation became part of line management's job expectations and was clearly embedded in their performance requirements, we started to see a lot of progress. In the initial stages, it wasn't high on the priority list. It had to come from the president that this was important—we had to pay attention to it, and we had to dedicate resources to making this successful."

When newly-appointed CIO Wheeler arrived, business support for ERP was still an issue. His goal was to strengthen support by moving ownership for the system toward the business. A significant measure of management's commitment to the success of NOVA's IT program was current CEO Jeff Lipton's appointment of Wheeler to the company's executive leadership team. Says Wheeler, "Being part of the senior team provides a clear understanding of the expectations of business leaders and an important forum to ensure that we work together to achieve the company's strategic goals."

"In the early days, the criticism is usually that ERP is an IT implementation. You need to move that ownership toward the business and make IT the enabler. To the extent you can do that earlier rather than later, you'll be more successful," he said. "The truly mature IT program is the one in which the business owns the process, the system, the costs, and the value. IT's role is to be in partnership with the business, using technology to enable business needs."

Wheeler believes that ERP projects require full-time commitment from business people. And those full-time people should be quality people. "Sometimes the people you get turn out to be the people who are available, rather than the best people. And that's a mistake," he cautioned. "When you're changing your business process in a fundamental way, you cannot afford not to have your best people—and to have them relatively full time."

SAP: THE COMPANY

Founded in 1972 by four former IBM employees, SAP (Systems, Applications, and Products in Data Processing—pronounced S - A - P) is a dynamic, German-based company that creates client/server enterprise application software modules. Today more than 12 million users employed in more than 20 000 companies in over 100 countries run more than 96 400 installations of SAP software. The company has subsidiaries in more than 50 countries. SAP CEO Hasso Plattner is the company's "visioneer," who sees all departments becoming one, not only across an organization, but across its environment as well. He calls this the "City of E."

SAP Canada Inc. was established in 1989 and is the fourth-largest company subsidiary of the parent SAP with offices in Toronto, Montreal, Ottawa, Calgary, and Vancouver. The Canadian SAP subsidiary is not just interested in making sales. State-of-the-art software products are created by SAP Labs Canada for the mySAP Business Suite family of solutions. This research centre in Montreal is an integral part of SAP's global development network. Developers in SAP Labs Canada are constantly engaged in designing applications for our CRM, Retail and Manufacturing, and Mobile Business solutions.

The two main versions of SAP are R3 (Release 3) and mySAP, the latest Web-enabled version. Companies can buy entire ERP packages for their particular industry, such as SAP Retail, SAP Mining, or SAP Banking, or they can buy individual modules, such as human resources or financial applications. Implementation of SAP can run into the tens of millions of dollars, including hardware, software, networking, personnel, and consulting components. SAP will not permit a company to adopt its software unless there are SAP-certified programmers and consultants on board for the project. SAP's latest "version" is called Accelerated SAP and is targeted at companies below

$250 million in sales. Accelerated Solutions are pre-configured, scaled-down versions of R3. Accelerated SAP claims to have a four-month implementation schedule and is offered at a fixed cost, rather than a per-user cost.

SAP's ERP software can translate foreign currencies and languages and handle taxes that vary worldwide. It is a birth-to-grave application that can cover the life of a product from financing the production plant to payment from the customer after the product has arrived. But SAP does so in its own individual fashion.

SAP software implements "best practices" of companies it has studied, including its customers. Any organization—for profit, not-for-profit, governmental agency—that implements SAP must change its business processes to reflect those found in the way SAP's applications operate. Failure to do so is asking for implementation failure.

Just look at Sobeys, Canada's second-largest supermarket chain, which in early 2001 pulled the plug on its SAP implementation after writing off an after-tax loss of about $50 million. Bill McEwan, president and CEO of Nova Scotia-based Sobeys Inc. said that the two-year-old project had "systemic problems of a much more serious nature" than the growing pains they had been led to expect. SAP implementation—after two years—resulted in "unprecedented" stockouts in December 2000 throughout eastern Canada according to McEwan. He continued, "The SAP Retail software couldn't effectively deal with the extreme, high number of transactions in our retail operating environment." Business operations were affected for four to five weeks while problems were reconciled.

Related to the story of Sobey's, though, is the story of Indigo Books & Music. When the retailer was considering adopting SAP to improve its merchandise assortment planning, Indigo chief technical officer (CTO) Doug Caldwell called an old friend of his—who worked as an executive at Sobey's—to get his opinion on the problems Sobey's had experienced with SAP. The Sobey's executive admitted that many of the problems had been Sobey's problems, rather than problems with SAP. After talking with his friend, Caldwell decided to implement SAP at Indigo. SAP even sponsors a users' conference annually, partly to let SAP customers talk with each other.

Enterprises need to look to software vendors for support, says Michael Moreia, senior technical consultant, IS architecture at ATI Technologies Inc., a graphics equipment manufacturer based in Markham, Ontario. ATI did precisely that to overcome the obstacles in its SAP implementation. Moreia, however, criticized SAP and its experts for failing to bring more support people to Canada. The SAP advisors did help ATI, but they made the calls to Germany rather late by Eastern Standard Time. If they had utilized local help, it would have afforded more reasonable work hours for the ATI staff.

Staffers channelled their anger toward Deidre Stirling, the City of Ottawa's manager of business application management, and the SAP software her team was trying to install across the city's IT infrastructure. What added fuel to the fire was the municipal amalgamation process that was being undertaken in the national capital region at the same time. The implementation was a lengthy and difficult process, but Stirling said, "I survived." Her project did, too. Ottawa spent $40 million on SAP software, but it has already saved $2 million in operational costs. It is expected that the new financial, HR, and property applications will save the city $8 million a year.

For employees of companies that have implemented SAP, one of the major changes is that they work mostly with data and software, rather than with people, according to Barry Hasler of Sony Canada. Another change is that they cannot get the exact reports and information they were used to getting; SAP reports are standard and do the job, but staff must change the information they need as well as what they do with it in the SAP environment.

But for those who are willing to exercise appropriate change management initiatives including changes to their policies and procedures, reporting relationships, and training, SAP does its job well. In other words, it's "The SAP Way, or No Way." Organizations that successfully implement SAP spend about one-third of their SAP budget on change management initiatives—training, communicating, consulting, and selling.

Returning to Ben and Jerry's expanding Canadian operation, should Baker and Lackstein examine whether or not they should use an ERP system? Should they consider SAP?

Sources: David Carey, "Surviving the ERP Journey," *CIO Canada*, May 1, 2001; Rebecca Maxwell, "Rayovac Gets a Charge from Accelerated SAP," *ComputerWorld Canada*, September 10, 2000; Curtis Cook and Michelle Schoffro, "SAP Not Just for Big Companies," *Canada Computes*, October 9, 1999; Lucas Mearlan, "Sobeys Says Goodbye to SAP," *ComputerWorld Online*, February 2, 2001; "mySAP.com to Power Canada's National Newspaper, *The Globe and Mail*," SAP Press Release, **www.sap.com**, accessed August 13, 2001; SAP Web site, **www.sap.com**, accessed October 1, 2005; SAP Canada Web site, **www.sap.com/Canada/ company**, accessed October 1, 2005; Chris Conrath, "SAP is Sold on the Internet," *Network World Canada*, July 28, 2000; Stefan Dubowski, "Book Retailer Spins Its Tale of SAP Tips," *ComputerWorld Canada*, June 10, 2005, **www.itworldcanada.com/a/search/6edebed9-0d6c-4909 -b41a-204441899dcc.html**, accessed October 1, 2005.

Video Resource

"In Tech We Trust," CBC UNDERcurrents 113 (October 31, 1999).
"Ben & Jerry's Ice Cream Moves into Canada 'The Frozen Empire,'" CBC Venture 935 (January 30, 2005)

CASE STUDY QUESTIONS

1. What sort of businesses should invest in SAP's ERP applications? Should a company adopt all of the SAP modules? How does a company decide that it needs an ERP solution?

2. What specific change management actions might a company adopting SAP take to ensure implementation success?

3. Why does SAP consider it necessary for SAP-certified programmers and consultants to work with companies implementing SAP?

4. It has been said that SAP is a change management program or philosophy. Do you agree or disagree? Why? What might happen to implementation if a company chose to try to adapt SAP to its own processes rather than adapting its processes to SAP?

5. Do you believe that Ben and Jerry's Canadian operation should implement SAP? Why or why not?

PART IV

Applications for the Digital Firm

Part IV   Canadian Case Study

Businesses Rely on Loyalty Cards for Decision Making

Chapter 13

Electronic Business and Electronic Commerce

OBJECTIVES

After completing this chapter, you will be able to:

1. Analyze how Internet technology has changed value propositions and business models.

2. Define electronic commerce and describe how it has changed consumer retailing and business-to-business transactions.

3. Compare the principal payment systems for electronic commerce.

4. Evaluate the role of Internet technology in facilitating management and coordination of internal and interorganizational business processes.

5. Assess the challenges posed by electronic business and electronic commerce, and propose management solutions.

Opening Case: Canadian Investor Protection Fund Uses Extranet to Save Time and Improve Service

The Canadian Investor Protection Fund (CIPF) is a not-for-profit corporation established by Self Regulatory Organizations (SROs) to protect customers in the event of member insolvency. The SROs include the Investment Dealers Association of Canada, Bourse de Montréal Inc., and the TSX Group of Companies.

Investment dealer bankruptcy doesn't happen very often because each of CIPF's sponsors, the Securities Commissions, and CIPF require that CIPF members comply with regulatory procedures. CIPF offers protection to investors in the event of bankruptcy. Claims of about $37 million have been paid to eligible customers of 17 insolvent members by CIPF since its beginning in 1969.

Currently, Canadian investment firms are required to file financial statements with CIPF on a monthly or yearly basis to prove their financial "health." Previously, the firms had to use a PC- or Mac-based application to create files that were then exported to CIPF. CIPF then created aggregate totals, which were mailed back to the users. Efficiency was poor since the process could not be sustained among the more than 200 member firms.

Agora Consulting Partners of Toronto and CIPF developed a secure, member-based extranet for member firm users for online creation and review of financial filings. The sophisticated workflow of the application allows the submission of the filing from the individual firm's CFO to the reviewing manager at the SRO to the reviewing manager at CIPF. The application also facilitates reverting to earlier steps at any stage in the workflow if corrections or modifications are needed.

The developers of the application used Windows 2000 Server, Internet Information Server 5.0, Microsoft SQL Server 2000, and COM technologies to create the extranet. Microsoft Visual InterDev 6.0 and Visual Basic 6.0 were employed as developmental tools. More than 50 reports were required in the system, and they were created using the Microsoft Solutions Framework as well as Agora's Reporting Framework with Crystal Reports.

Member firms, SROs, and CIPF users benefited greatly in terms of time saved using the extranet solution. The examiners in these organizations can thus dedicate more time for examining the financial filings. Firms can access their financial filings from any computer's Web browser without having to install a new application.

Sources: "Case Study: Canadian Investor Protection Fund," Agora Consulting Partners, available **www.agorainc.com/casestudies/cs_cipf.htm**, accessed June 7, 2005; Canadian Investor Protection Fund Web site, available **www.cipf.ca**, accessed June 7, 2005.

CIPF's extranet is an example of how organizations are using Internet technology to both streamline their business processes and integrate them with customers and suppliers. CIPF is a small organization, yet it is able to produce a sophisticated system for receiving a large volume of filings and fine-tuning their business processes. This system is both an e-commerce site for member companies to file and review their papers and an e-business system for managing the flow of filings and examining them through the extranet. It is an innovative example of how companies are using Internet technology to transform the way business is conducted.

As a manager, you will want to know how your firm can benefit from e-business and e-commerce. In this chapter, we explore how the Internet is creating a universal technology platform for buying and selling goods and for driving important business processes inside the firm. We describe some new ways of organizing and managing based on Internet technology. In addition to describing new benefits and opportunities, we also identify the management challenges raised by electronic business and electronic commerce and suggest strategies for dealing with them.

13.1 Electronic Business, Electronic Commerce, and the Emerging Digital Firm

Throughout this edition, we emphasize the benefits of integrating information across the enterprise, creating an information technology infrastructure in which information flows seamlessly from one part of the organization to another and from the organization to its customers, suppliers, and business partners. The emerging digital firm requires this level of information integration, and companies increasingly depend on this type of infrastructure to remain efficient and competitive. Internet technology has emerged as the key enabling technology for digital integration.

Internet Technology and the Digital Firm

For a number of years, companies used proprietary systems to integrate information from their internal systems and to link to their customers and trading partners. These systems were expensive and based on technology standards that only a few companies could follow.

The Internet is rapidly becoming the infrastructure of choice for electronic commerce because it offers businesses an even easier way to link with other businesses and individuals at a very low cost. It provides a universal and easy-to-use set of technologies and technology standards for all organizations, no matter which computer system or information technology platform the organizations are using.

Trading partners can communicate directly with each other, bypassing intermediaries and inefficient multilayered procedures. Web sites are available to consumers 24 hours a day. Some information-based products, such as software, music, and videos, can actually be physically distributed over the Internet. Vendors of other types of products and services use the Internet to distribute information about their wares, such as product pricing, options, availability, and delivery time. The Internet can replace existing distribution channels or extend them, creating outlets for attracting and serving customers who otherwise would not patronize the company. For example, Web-based discount brokerages have attracted new customers who could not afford paying the high commissions and fees charged by conventional brokerage and financial services firms.

Internet technology is helping companies radically reduce their transaction costs. Chapter 3 introduced the concept of transaction costs, which include the costs of searching for buyers and sellers, collecting information on products, negotiating terms, writing and enforcing contracts, and transporting merchandise. Information on buyers, sellers, and prices for many products is immediately available on the Web. For example, manually processing a single customer order costs $15. Using a Web-based system, the cost drops to 80 cents per transaction.

Table 13-1 provides other examples of transaction cost reductions made possible by the Internet and Internet technology. Handling transactions electronically reduces transaction costs and delivery time for some goods, especially those that are purely digital (such as software, text products, images, or videos) because these products can be distributed over the Internet as electronic versions.

What's more, Internet technology is providing the infrastructure for running the entire business because its technology and standards enable information to flow seamlessly from one part of the organization to another. Internet technology provides a much less expensive and easier to use alternative for coordination activities than proprietary networks.

Managers are using email and other Internet communication capabilities to oversee larger numbers of employees, to manage many tasks and subtasks in projects, and to coordinate the work of multiple teams working in different parts of the world. Internet standards can link disparate systems, such as those for order processing and logistics tracking, which previously could not communicate with each other. The Internet also

TABLE 13-1 *How the Internet Reduces Transaction Costs*

TRANSACTION	TRADITIONAL	INTERNET
Checking an account balance	$1.08	$0.13
Answering a customer question	$10–$45	Answering an email query: $1–$5
Web self-service:		$0.10–$0.20
Trading 100 shares of stock	$100	$9.95
Correcting an employee record	$128	$2.32
Processing an expense report	$36, 22 days	$4–$8, 72 hours
Sending an advertising brochure	$0.75–$10.00	$0–$0.25
Paying a bill	$2.22–$3.32	$0.65–$1.10

reduces other agency costs, such as the cost to coordinate activities of the firm with suppliers and other external business partners. The low-cost connectivity and universal standards provided by Internet technology are the driving force behind the explosion of electronic business and the emergence of the digital firm.

New Business Models and Value Propositions

The Internet has introduced major changes in the way companies conduct business. It has created a dramatic decline in the cost of developing, sending, and storing information while making that information more widely available. Millions of people are able to exchange massive amounts of information directly, instantly, and almost for free.

In the past, information about products and services was usually tightly bundled with the physical value chain for those products and services. If consumers wanted to find out about the features, price, and availability of a refrigerator or an automobile, for instance, they had to visit retail stores that sold those products. The cost of comparison shopping was very high because people had to physically travel from store to store.

The Internet has changed that relationship. Once everyone is connected electronically, information about products and services flows on its own directly and instantly to consumers. The traditional link between the flow of the product and the flow of product-related information is broken. Information is not limited to traditional physical methods of delivery. Customers can find out about products on their own on the Web and buy directly from product suppliers instead of using intermediaries, such as retail stores.

This unbundling of information from traditional value chain channels is having a disruptive effect on old business models and is also creating new business models. A **business model** describes how the enterprise produces, delivers, and sells a product or service, showing how the enterprise delivers value to customers and how it creates wealth (Magretta 2002). Some of the traditional channels for exchanging product information have become unnecessary or uneconomical, and business models based on the coupling of information with products and services may no longer be necessary.

For example, in pre-Internet retailing days, people who wanted to purchase books had to go to a physical bookstore to learn which titles were available, the contents, and prices. The bookstore had a monopoly on this information. When Amazon.com opened as an online bookstore, it provided Web site visitors with a vast electronic catalogue containing close to 3 million titles, along with tables of contents, reviews, and other information about those titles. People could order books directly from their desktop computers. Amazon.com was able to sell books at lower cost because it did not have to pay rent, employee salaries, warehousing, and other overhead to maintain physical retail bookstores. Selling books and other goods directly to consumers online without using a physical storefront represents a new business model.

The Changing Economics of Information
The Internet and the Web have vastly increased the total amount and quality of information available to all market participants, consumers and merchants alike. Customers benefit from lower **search costs**—the effort to find suitable products and to find all the suppliers, prices, and delivery terms of a specific product anywhere in the world (Bakos 1998). Merchants benefit from using the same technology to find out much more about consumers than they previously could and to provide more accurate and detailed information to target their marketing and sales efforts.

The Internet shrinks information asymmetry, making it easy for consumers to find out the variety of prices in a market and to discover the actual costs merchants pay for products. An **information asymmetry** exists when one party in a transaction has more information that is important for the transaction than the other party. That information helps determine their relative bargaining power.

For example, until auto retailing sites appeared on the Web, there was a pronounced information asymmetry between auto dealers and customers. Only the auto dealers knew the manufacturers' prices, and it was difficult for consumers to shop around for the best price. Auto dealers' profit margins depended on this asymmetry of information.

Today's consumers have access to a legion of Web sites providing competitive pricing information, and, according to MSN's Autos Canada, three-fourths of Canadian auto buyers use the Internet to shop around for the best deal (see Figure 13-1). Thus, the Web has reduced the information asymmetry surrounding an auto purchase. The Internet has also helped businesses seeking to purchase from other businesses reduce information asymmetries and locate better prices and terms.

Before the Internet, businesses had to make trade-offs between the richness and reach of their information. **Richness** refers to the depth and detail of information—the amount of information the business can supply to the customer, as well as information the business collects about the customer. **Reach** refers to how many people a business can connect with and how many products it can offer those people. Rich communication occurs, for example, when a sales representative meets with a customer, sharing information that is very specific to that interaction. This type of rich interaction is very expensive for a business because it can take place only with a small audience.

Newspaper and television ads can reach millions of people quite inexpensively, but the information they provide is much more limited. It used to be prohibitively expensive for traditional businesses to have both richness and reach. Few, if any, companies could afford to provide highly detailed, customized information to a large mass audience. The Internet has transformed the richness and reach relationships (see Figure 13-2). Using the Internet and World Wide Web multimedia capabilities, companies are able to provide detailed product information quickly and inexpensively and specific detailed information to very large numbers of people simultaneously (Evans and Wurster 2000).

Internet Business Models The Internet helps companies create and capture profit in new ways by adding extra value to existing products and services or by providing the foundation for new products and services. Table 13-2 describes some of the most important Internet business models that have emerged. In one way or another, all add value: They provide the customer with a new product or service, they provide additional information or service along with a traditional product or service, or they provide a product or service at a lower cost than traditional means.

Some of these new business models take advantage of the Internet's rich communication capabilities. eBay is an online auction forum that uses email and other interactive features of the Web. People can make online bids for items, such as computer equipment, antiques and collectibles, wine, jewellery, rock-concert tickets, and electronics, which are posted by sellers from around the world. The system accepts bids for items entered on the

---

FIGURE 13-1 *MSN's Autos Canada Web site.*

Visitors to MSN's Autos Canada Web site can research the price, availability, and features of most models of new and used cars and find the best prices and terms for auto purchases. The Internet can reduce search costs and information asymmetry.

richness

reach

FIGURE 13-2   *The changing economics of information.*

In the past, companies have had to trade off between the richness and reach of their information. Internet connectivity and universal standards for information sharing radically lower the cost of providing rich, detailed information to large numbers of people, reducing the trade-off.

Internet, evaluates the bids, and notifies the highest bidder. eBay collects a small commission on each listing and sale. eBay has become so popular that its site serves as a huge trading platform for other companies, hosting around 225 000 "virtual storefronts."

Business-to-business auctions are proliferating as well. GoIndustry, for instance, features Web-based auction services for business-to-business sales of industrial equipment and machinery. Online bidding, also known as **dynamic pricing**, is expected to grow rapidly because buyers and sellers can interact so easily through the Internet to determine what an item is worth at any particular moment.

The Internet has created online communities where people with similar interests exchange ideas from many different locations. Some of these virtual communities are providing the foundation for new businesses. iVillage.com provides an online community for women sharing similar interests, such as diet and fitness, pregnancy, parenting, home and garden, and food. Members post their personal Web pages, participate in online discussion groups, and join online "clubs" with other like-minded people.

A major source of revenue for these communities involves providing ways for corporate clients to target customers, including the placement of banner ads and pop-up ads on their Web sites. A **banner ad** is a graphic display on a Web page used for advertising. The banner is linked to the advertiser's Web site so that a person clicking the banner is transported to a Web page with more information about the advertiser. **Pop-up ads** work in the opposite manner. They automatically open up when a user accesses a specific Web site, and the user must click the ad to make it disappear. These ads have become so annoying that the latest browser versions feature pop-up ad blockers.

Social networking sites are a type of online community that have become increasingly popular. Social networking is the practice of expanding the number of one's business or social contacts by making connections through individuals. Social networking sites link people through their mutual business or personal connections, enabling them to mine their friends (and their friends' friends) for sales leads, job-hunting tips, or new friends. Web sites dedicated to social networking include Friendster, Linkedin, Spoke, Evite, Meetup, Tribe, and ZeroDegrees (see Figure 13-3).

The Web's information resources are so vast and rich that *portals* have emerged as an Internet business model to help individuals and organizations locate information more efficiently. In Chapter 2, we defined a portal as a Web interface for presenting integrated personalized information from a variety of sources. As an e-commerce business model, a portal is a "supersite" that provides a comprehensive entry point for a huge array of resources and services on the Internet.

Yahoo! is an example of a portal. It provides capabilities for locating information on the Internet along with news, sports, weather, telephone directories, maps, games, shopping, email, chat, discussion boards, and links to other sites. Also, specialized portals help users with specific interests. Canoe.ca and Canada.com are other examples of portals. StarMedia is a portal customized for Latin American Internet users, and the portal Sina.com is customized for Chinese users.

Yahoo! and other portals and Web content sites often combine content and applications from many different sources and service providers. Other Internet business models use

dynamic pricing

banner ad

pop-up ads

social networking sites

TABLE 13-2 Internet Business Models

CATEGORY	DESCRIPTION	EXAMPLES
Virtual storefront	Sells physical products directly to consumers or to individual businesses.	Chapters.Indigo.ca EPM.com
Information broker	Provides product, pricing, and availability information to individuals and businesses. Generates revenue from advertising or from directing buyers to sellers.	Edmunds.com Kbb.com, Insweb.com, Ehealthinsurance.com
Transaction broker	Saves users money and time by processing online sales transactions, generating a fee each time a transaction occurs. Also provides information on rates and terms	BayStreet.ca TDWaterhouse.com
Online marketplace	Provides a digital environment where buyers and sellers can meet, search for products, display products, and establish prices for those products. Can provide online auctions or reverse auctions in which buyers submit bids to multiple sellers to purchase at a buyer-specified price as well as negotiated or fixed pricing. Can serve consumers or B2B e-commerce, generating revenue from transaction fees.	eBay.ca Priceline.com ChemConnect.com Pantellos.com
Content provider	Creates revenue by providing digital content, such as digital news, music, photos, or video, over the Web. The customer may pay to access the content, or revenue may be generated by selling advertising space.	FinancialPost.com Yahoo.ca Canada.com MP3.com
Online service provider	Provides online service for individuals and businesses. Generates revenue from subscription or transaction fees, advertising, or collecting marketing information from users.	@Backup.com Xdrive.com Employease.com Salesforce.com
Virtual community	Provides an online meeting place where people with similar interests can communicate and find useful information.	Kidshelp.sympatico.ca FROGnet (a list server for French speaking researchers in non-French-speaking countries) Friendster.com
Portal	Provides initial point of entry to the Web along with specialized content and other services.	iVillage.com Canoe.ca MSN.ca

syndication as well to provide additional value. For example, E*TRADE, the discount Web trading site, purchases most of its content from outsider sources, such as Reuters (news), Bridge Information Systems (quotes), and BigCharts.com (charts). Online **syndicators**, who aggregate content or applications from multiple sources, package them for distribution, and resell them to third-party Web sites, have emerged as another variant of the online content provider business model (Werbach 2000). The Web makes it much easier for companies to aggregate, repackage, and distribute information and information-based services.

Chapter 5 describes application service providers, such as Employease.com or Salesforce.com, that feature software that runs over the Web. They provide online services to subscribing businesses. Other online service providers offer services to individual consumers, such as remote storage of data at Xdrive.com. Service providers generate revenue through subscription fees or from advertising.

Most of the business models described in Table 13-2 are called **pure-play** business models because they are based purely on the Internet. These firms did not have an

syndicators

pure-play

FIGURE 13-3 *A social networking Web site.*

Friendster.com is an Internet business based on creating an online community for social networking. The company generates revenue from advertising sponsors.

existing *bricks-and-mortar* business when they designed their Internet business. However, many existing firms such as udson's Bay Company, Canadian Tire, Office Depot and the *Globe and Mail* have developed Web sites as extensions of their traditional bricks-and-mortar businesses. These businesses represent a hybrid **clicks-and-mortar** business model.

13.2 Electronic Commerce

Although most commercial transactions still take place through conventional channels, rising numbers of consumers and businesses are using the Internet for electronic commerce. Projections show that by 2006, total e-commerce spending by consumers and businesses could surpass $6 trillion (eMarketer 2004).

Categories of Electronic Commerce

There are many ways to classify electronic commerce transactions. One way is by looking at the nature of the participants in the electronic commerce transaction. The three major electronic commerce categories are business-to-consumer (B2C) e-commerce, business-to-business (B2B) e-commerce, and consumer-to-consumer (C2C) e-commerce.

clicks-and-mortar

business-to-consumer (B2C) electronic commerce

business-to-business (B2B) electronic commerce

consumer-to-consumer (C2C) electronic commerce

- **Business-to-consumer (B2C) electronic commerce** involves retailing products and services to individual shoppers. Chapters.Indigo.ca, which sells books, software, and music to individual consumers, is an example of B2C e-commerce.

- **Business-to-business (B2B) electronic commerce** involves sales of goods and services among businesses. Milacron's Web site for selling machinery, mould bases, and related tooling, supplies, and services to companies engaged in plastics processing is an example of B2B e-commerce.

- **Consumer-to-consumer (C2C) electronic commerce** involves consumers selling directly to consumers. For example, eBay, the giant Web auction site, enables people to sell their goods to other consumers by auctioning the merchandise off to the highest bidder. eBay has a Canadian Web site, where consumers can restrict their bids to Canadian-based products.

Another way of classifying electronic commerce transactions is in terms of the participants' physical connection to the Web. Until recently, almost all e-commerce transactions took place over wired networks. Now mobile phones and other wireless handheld digital appliances are Internet enabled to send text messages, access Web sites, and make purchases. Companies are offering new types of Web-based products and services that can be accessed by these wireless devices. The use of handheld wireless devices for purchasing goods and services from any location has been termed **mobile commerce** or **m-commerce**. All B2B, B2C, and C2C e-commerce transactions can take place using m-commerce technology. Chapter 8 discusses m-commerce and wireless technology in detail.

Customer-Centred Retailing

Despite the many failures of early dot-com retail companies, online retailing continues to grow at a brisk pace. The Internet provides companies with new channels of communication and interaction that can create closer, more cost-effective relationships with customers in sales, marketing, and customer support. Companies can use the Web to provide ongoing information, service, and support, creating positive interactions with customers that can serve as the foundations for long-term relationships and repeat purchases.

Direct Sales Over the Web Manufacturers can sell their products and services directly to retail customers, bypassing intermediaries such as distributors or retail outlets. Eliminating intermediaries in the distribution channel can significantly lower purchase transaction costs. Operators of virtual storefronts, such as Puretracks.com or EPM.com, do not have large expenditures for rent, sales staff, and the other operations associated with a traditional retail store. Airlines can sell tickets directly to passengers through their own Web sites or through travel sites such as Destina.ca without paying commissions to travel agents.

To pay for all the steps in a traditional distribution channel, a product may have to be priced as high as 135 percent of its original cost to manufacture (Mougayar 1998). Figure 13-4 illustrates how much savings can result from eliminating each of these layers in the distribution process. By selling directly to consumers or reducing the number of intermediaries, companies can achieve higher profits while charging lower prices. The removal of organizations or business process layers responsible for intermediary steps in a value chain is called **disintermediation**.

The Internet is accelerating disintermediation in some industries and creating opportunities for new types of intermediaries in others. In certain industries, distributors with warehouses of goods, or intermediaries such as real estate agents may be replaced by new intermediary services that specialize in helping Internet business and retail users reduce search costs, tailor offerings more precisely to their needs, obtain assurances about quality and reliability, handle product complexity, or preserve anonymity while conducting online transactions (Bhargava and Choudhary, 2004; Andal-Ancion, Cartwright, and Yip 2003; Anderson and Anderson 2002; Gallaugher 2002; Hagel III and Singer 1999). The information brokers listed in Table 13-2 are examples of one type of service for which such intermediaries can provide value. The process of shifting the intermediary function in a value chain to a new source is called **reintermediation**.

Interactive Marketing and Personalization Marketers are using the interactive features of Web pages to hold consumers' attention or to capture detailed information about consumer tastes and interests for one-to-one marketing (see Chapter 3). Web sites have become a bountiful source of detailed information about customer behaviour, preferences, needs, and buying patterns that companies can use to tailor promotions, products, services, and pricing.

Some customer information may be obtained by asking visitors to "register" online and provide information about themselves, but many companies also collect customer information using software tools that track the activities of Web site visitors.

Clickstream tracking tools collect data on customer activities at Web sites and store them in a log. The tools record the site that users visited prior to coming to a particular Web site

mobile commerce (m-commerce)

disintermediation

reintermediation

clickstream tracking

FIGURE 13-4   *The benefits of disintermediation to the consumer.*

The typical distribution channel has several intermediary layers, each of which adds to the final cost of a product, such as a sweater. Removing layers lowers the final cost to the consumer.

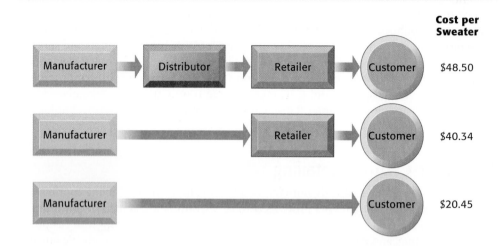

and where these users go when they leave that site. They also record the specific pages visited on the particular site, the time spent on each page, the types of pages visited, and what the visitors purchased (see Figure 13-5). Firms can analyze this information about customer interests and behaviour to develop precise profiles of existing and potential customers.

Communications and product offerings can be tailored precisely to individual customers. Firms can create unique personalized Web pages that display content or ads for products or services of special interest to each user, improving the customer's experience and creating additional value (see Figure 13-6 and Figure 13-7). By using **Web personalization** technology to modify the Web pages presented to each customer, marketers achieve the benefits of using individual salespeople at dramatically lower costs. Personalization can also help firms form lasting relationships with customers by providing individualized content, information, and services.

One technique for Web personalization is **collaborative filtering**, which compares information gathered about a specific user's behaviour at a Web site to data about other customers with similar interests to predict what the user would like to see next. The

FIGURE 13-5   *Web site visitor tracking.*

E-commerce Web sites have tools to track a shopper's every step through an online store. Close examination of customer behaviour at a Web site selling women's clothing shows what the store might learn at each step and what actions it could take to increase sales.

Web personalization
collaborative filtering

FIGURE 13-6   *Web site personalization.*

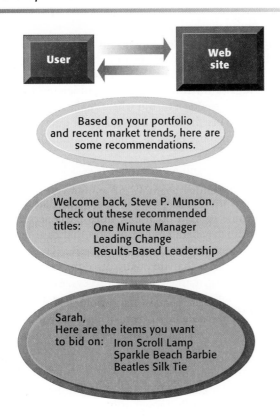

Firms can create unique personalized Web pages that display content or ads for products or services of special interest to individual users, improving the customer experience and creating additional value.

software then makes recommendations to users based on their assumed interests. For example, Chapters.Indigo.ca and Amazon.ca use collaborative filtering software to prepare personalized book recommendations: "Customers who bought this book also bought..."

Blogs have emerged as another promising Web-based tool for marketing. As discussed in Chapter 7, a **blog**, the popular term for a Web log, is an informal yet structured Web site where individuals can publish stories, opinions, and links to other Web sites of interest.

FIGURE 13-7   *A personalized Subaru Web page.*

Web sites can tailor their content to the specific interests of individual visitors. The Subaru Web site will create personalized Web pages for individual Subaru auto owners where they can access their vehicle's service history, request parts, schedule appointments with Subaru dealers, view the owner's manual, and find other valuable information about their cars.

blog

Many users subscribe to a blog site, post their views and opinions, and create links to and from other blogs or Web sites. Most blogs are published by individuals, but corporate blogs have emerged as useful marketing tools.

Blogs provide a more personal way of presenting information to the public and prospective customers about new products and services. For example, Macromedia, which makes Flash, Dreamweaver, Fireworks and Cold Fusion software for multimedia applications, uses Web logs to nurture ties with customers and introduce them to new software features. The blogs provide a forum where managers can discuss the new products, show developers how to use the new features, answer questions, and obtain customer feedback. Some companies also use blogs internally to communicate and exchange ideas about projects and company news.

The cost of customer surveys and focus groups is very high. Learning how customers feel or what they think about products or services by examining customer visits to Web sites and online feedback is much cheaper. Customer information that can be acquired over the Internet has become so useful that new third-party services have arisen to provide businesses with customer-generated information that cannot be obtained by interacting directly with customers on the company Web site. These services monitor customer discussions about products that are taking place through online communities and message boards, conduct online market research surveys, or monitor the online surfing and buying behaviour of large numbers of customers at many different Web sites (Sawhney, Prandelli, and Verona 2003).

Customer Self-Service The Web and other network technologies are inspiring new approaches to customer service and support. Many companies are using their Web sites and email to answer customer questions or to provide customers with helpful information. The Web provides a medium for customers to interact with the company, at the customers' convenience, and find information that previously required a human customer-support expert. Automated self-service or other Web-based responses to customer questions cost only a fraction of what a live customer service representative on the telephone costs.

Companies are realizing substantial cost savings from Web-based customer self-service applications. For instance, Air Canada, KLM, and other major airlines have created Web sites where customers can review flight departure and arrival times, seating charts, and airport logistics; check frequent-flyer miles; and purchase tickets online (see Figure 13-8). Chapter 1 describes how UPS customers can use its Web site to track shipments, calculate shipping costs, determine time in transit, and arrange for a package pickup. FedEx, DHL, and other package delivery firms provide similar Web-based services.

FIGURE 13-8   *Customer self-service on KLM's Web site.*

Visitors to the Web sites of KLM and its partner, Northwest, can find flight schedules and gates, select seats, print boarding passes, and check themselves in for flights. Web sites for customer self-service are convenient for customers and help firms lower their customer service and support costs.

New software products are even integrating the Web with customer call centres, where customer service problems have been traditionally handled over the telephone. A **call centre** is an organizational department responsible for handling customer service issues by telephone and other channels. For example, visitors can click on a "push to talk" link on the Lands' End Web site that lets a user request a phone call. The user enters his or her telephone number and a call-centre system directs a customer service representative to place a telephone call to the user's phone. Some systems also let the customer interact with a service representative on the Web while talking on the phone at the same time.

Business-to-Business Electronic Commerce: New Efficiencies and Relationships

Today, about 80 percent of B2B e-commerce is based on proprietary systems for electronic data interchange (EDI). **Electronic data interchange (EDI)** enables the computer-to-computer exchange between two organizations of standard transaction documents, such as invoices, bills of lading, shipment schedules, or purchase orders. Transactions are automatically transmitted from one information system to another through a network, eliminating the printing and handling of paper at one end and the inputting of data at the other. Each major industry in much of the world has EDI standards that define the structure and information fields of electronic documents for that industry.

EDI originally automated the exchange of documents such as purchase orders, invoices, and shipping notices. Although some companies still use EDI for document automation, firms engaged in just-in-time inventory replenishment and continuous production use EDI as a system for continuous replenishment. Suppliers have online access to selected parts of the purchasing firm's production and delivery schedules and automatically ship materials and goods to meet prespecified targets without intervention by firm purchasing agents (see Figure 13-9).

Although many organizations still use private networks for EDI, companies are increasingly turning to the Internet for this purpose because it provides a much more flexible and low-cost platform for linking to other firms. Using the Internet, businesses can extend digital technology to a wider range of activities and broaden their circle of trading partners.

Take procurement, for example. **Procurement** involves not only purchasing goods and materials but also sourcing, negotiating with suppliers, paying for goods, and making delivery arrangements. Businesses can now use the Internet to locate the lowest-cost supplier, search online catalogues of supplier products, negotiate with suppliers, place orders, make payments, and arrange transportation. They are not limited to partners linked by traditional EDI networks because they can use the Web to work with any other business that is linked to the Internet. *E-procurement* over the Internet provides new opportunities for lowering costs and improving service because Internet technology enables businesses to cast their nets more widely.

The Internet and Web technology enables businesses to create new electronic storefronts for selling to other businesses with multimedia graphic displays and interactive features similar to those for B2C commerce. Alternatively, businesses can use Internet technology to create extranets or electronic marketplaces for linking to other businesses for purchase and sale transactions. *Extranets*, which we introduced in Chapter 1, are private intranets extended to authorized users outside the company.

call centre

electronic data interchange (EDI)

procurement

FIGURE 13-9   *Electronic data interchange (EDI).*

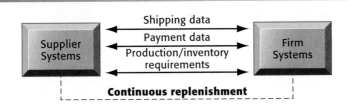

Companies use EDI to automate transactions for B2B e-commerce and continuous inventory replenishment. Suppliers can automatically send data about shipments to purchasing firms. The purchasing firms can use EDI to provide production and inventory requirements and payment data to suppliers.

Private industrial networks are B2B extranets that focus on continuous business process coordination between companies for collaboration and supply chain management. A private industrial network typically consists of a large firm using an extranet to link to its suppliers and other key business partners (see Figure 13-10). The network is owned by the buyer, and it permits the firm and designated suppliers, distributors, and other business partners to share product design and development, marketing, production scheduling, inventory management, and unstructured communication, including graphics and email. Another term for a private industrial network is a **private exchange**. Private exchanges are currently the fastest growing type of B2B commerce.

Net marketplaces, which are sometimes called *e-hubs*, provide a single digital marketplace based on Internet technology for many different buyers and sellers (see Figure 13-11). They are industry-owned or operate as independent intermediaries between buyers and sellers. Net marketplaces are more transaction oriented (and less relationship oriented) than private industrial networks, generating revenue from purchase and sale transactions and other services provided to clients. Participants in Net marketplaces can establish prices through online negotiations, auctions, or requests for quotations, or they can use fixed prices. Customers benefit from lower search costs, lower transaction costs, and wider selection.

There are many different types of Net marketplaces and ways of classifying them. Some Net marketplaces sell direct goods, and some sell indirect goods. *Direct goods* are goods used in a production process, such as sheet steel for auto body production. *Indirect goods* are all other goods not directly involved in the production process, such as office supplies or products for maintenance and repair. Some Net marketplaces support contractual purchasing based on long-term relationships with designated suppliers, and others support short-term spot purchasing, where goods are purchased based on immediate needs, often from many different suppliers. Some Net marketplaces serve vertical markets for specific industries, such as automobiles, telecommunications, or machine tools while others serve horizontal markets for goods and services that can be found in many different industries, such as office equipment or transportation.

Ariba bundles extensive e-commerce services with a Net marketplace for long-term contractual purchasing of both indirect and direct goods. It provides both buyers and sellers with software systems and Net marketplace services, aggregating hundreds of catalogues into a single marketplace and customizing procurement and sales processes to work with their systems. For buyers, Ariba automates sourcing, contract management, purchase orders, requisitions, business rules enforcement, and payment. For sellers, Ariba provides services for catalogue creation and content management, order management, invoicing, and settlement.

FedEx uses Ariba's e-procurement system for $10 million in purchases. Employees use Ariba to order from more than 32 maintenance, repair, and operations (MRO) suppliers

FIGURE 13-10 *A private industrial network.*

A private industrial network, also known as a private exchange, links a firm to its suppliers, distributors, and other key business partners for efficient supply chain management and other collaborative activities.

Suppliers   Distributors

private industrial networks

private exchange

Net marketplaces

FIGURE 13-11   A Net marketplace.

Net marketplaces are online marketplaces where multiple buyers can purchase from multiple sellers.

and catalogues. The system automatically invokes FedEx's business rules for purchasing to route, review, and approve requisitions electronically. By using this Net marketplace, FedEx has reduced the cost of processing purchases by 75 percent and the prices paid for MRO supplies by 12 percent, and it has cut parts delivery time from an average of seven days to two days.

Industry-owned Net marketplaces focus on long-term contract purchasing relationships and on providing common networks and computing platforms for reducing supply chain inefficiencies. Buyer firms benefit from competitive pricing among alternative suppliers, and suppliers benefit from stable long-term selling relationships with large firms.

Exostar is another example of a Net marketplace. This aerospace and defense industry-sponsored Net marketplace was founded jointly by BAE Systems, Boeing, Lockheed Martin, Raytheon, and Rolls-Royce PLC to connect these companies to their suppliers and facilitate collaboration on major projects. More than 16 000 trading partners in the commercial, military, and government sectors around the world, including Canada, use Exostar's sourcing, e-procurement, and collaboration tools for both direct and indirect goods. Exostar includes capabilities for auctioning, purchase forecasting, issuing electronic payments and receipts, and linking to participants' internal corporate systems. Also featured are capabilities for collaboration on joint development projects and sharing engineering product data.

Other industry-owned Net marketplaces include ChemConnect.com, for the chemical industry, Transora.com, for the food industry, and Pantellos.com for the energy services and utilities industries.

Exchanges are independently owned third-party Net marketplaces that can connect thousands of suppliers and buyers for spot purchasing (see Figure 13-12). Many exchanges provide vertical markets for a single industry, such as food, electronics, or industrial equipment, and they primarily deal with direct inputs. For example, FoodTrader.com automates spot purchases among buyers and sellers from over 170 countries, including Canada, in the food and agriculture industry.

Exchanges proliferated during the early years of e-commerce, but many have failed. Suppliers were reluctant to participate because the exchanges encouraged competitive bidding that drove prices down and did not offer any long-term relationships with buyers or services to make lowering prices worthwhile. Many essential direct purchases are not conducted on a spot basis because they require contracts and consideration of issues such as delivery timing, customization, and quality of products (Laudon 2004; Wise and Morrison 2000).

The Window on Technology sheds light on these issues. The Volkswagen Group opted for a private industrial network (private exchange) instead of an industry-sponsored Net marketplace or exchange precisely because it wanted to preserve its control over supplier relationships and its unique business processes for supply chain management. VWGroupSupply.com has become one of Europe's most successful Net marketplaces and a model for the global automobile industry.

exchanges

FIGURE 13-12 *Grainger's exchange Web site.*

Grainger.com provides a single online source from which customers can make spot purchases of maintenance, repair, and operations products from many different companies.

WINDOW ON TECHNOLOGY

Volkswagen Revs Up Its B2B Network

Volkswagen AG is Europe's largest car manufacturer, producing 5 million cars, trucks, and vans each year. VW owns luxury car makers such as Audi, Lamborghini, and Bentley and family car makers such as SEAT in Spain and Skoda in the Czech Republic. The company has 300 000 employees and operates plants in Europe, Africa, the Asia/Pacific Rim, and the Americas, including Ontario, Canada. Vehicles produced by Volkswagen Group account for over 12 percent of the world market.

VW companies purchase annually 60 billion euros, or about $92 billion, in components, automotive parts, and indirect materials. These purchases represent more than 70 percent of VW's annual revenue. Obviously, the procurement process and relationships with suppliers are critical to Volkswagen's success.

The VW Group was looking for ways to create more efficient relationships with its suppliers and reduce the cost of paper-based procurement processes. However, the company did not want to automate procurement using a public exchange or an industry-sponsored Net marketplace because it would have had to adapt its own business processes to a common framework that could be used by many different organizations. It decided not to participate in Covisint, the giant industry consortium Net marketplace set up by Ford, General Motors, and DaimlerChrysler, which provides procurement and other supply chain services for these companies, other automotive manufacturers, and their suppliers.

Instead, VW opted for a private platform that would enable it to integrate its suppliers more tightly with its own business processes. Operating as a private industrial network,

VWGroupSupply.com enabled the VW Group to design a system that optimized its business processes.

During the summer of 2002, VW began implementing this massive private B2B extranet for the Volkswagen Group and its suppliers. VWGroupSupply.com handles 90 percent of all global purchasing for VW, including all automotive and parts components. It is one of the most comprehensive private exchanges in the global automotive industry.

The online Web-based platform can handle requests for quotations (RFQs), contract negotiations, catalogue purchases, purchase order management, engineering change management, vehicle program management, and payments. This B2B private industrial network was developed using technology from a number of vendors, including Ariba, IBM, and i2 Technologies.

Suppliers of all sizes can access VWGroupSupply.com with standard Web browser software. The Web site is limited to suppliers that have done business with one or several companies in the Volkswagen Group and potential new suppliers that go through an authorization process. The system maintains a common data repository with details on each supplier concerning procurement, logistics, production, quality, technical design, and finance.

The extranet also features an online catalogue with 1.37 million items from 750 global suppliers. The catalogue uses the eCl@ss standard to classify its contents. All suppliers who participate in the catalogue ordering process classify their products using this standard.

Online negotiations involve multiple bids by suppliers for

various purchasing contracts. VWGroupSupply.com ensures that all participants meet its technical and commercial qualifications. Before an online solicitation begins, the system informs vendors about the data and precise rules governing the negotiations.

Shifts in market demand have a drastic impact on VW's production activities and affect the ability of suppliers to deliver. Production bottlenecks can result if suppliers are unprepared for a sudden upsurge in demand. If suppliers stock too much inventory, they may incur excess costs from running over capacity. VWGroupSupply.com has an application called Electronic Capacity Management (eCAP) to alert both VW and its suppliers to changes in trends in advance.

eCAP enables suppliers to track VW's continually updated production plans and materials requirements in real time online. This capability captures information about participating suppliers' planned maximum and minimum capacities. If VW production requirements go beyond these limits, the system sets off an alarm so both parties can react quickly. eCAP maintains information on over 200 suppliers and 4000 critical parts.

During its first three years of operation, the material cost reductions and productivity gains from VWGroupSupply.com produced more than 100 million euros ($153 million) in cost reductions.

As of mid-2004, VWGroupSupply.com had handled more than 500 000 transactions with more than 5500 suppliers. More than 4200 contract negotiations involving 26 000 suppliers were conducted online, with a value of 42 billion euros ($64 billion). More than 13 200 people used the online catalogue and placed orders totalling 150 million euros ($229 million).

To Think About: What are the benefits to Volkswagen from using a private industrial network instead of a more open exchange? How does this system change how VW and it suppliers do business? What value does VWGroupSupply.com provide to Volkswagen and to its suppliers?

Sources: Martin Hoffman, "Best Practices: VW Revs Up Its B2B Engine," *Optimize Magazine*, March 2004; www.vwgroupsupply.com, accessed August 23, 2004; and www.hoovers.com, accessed August 24, 2004.

Electronic Commerce Payment Systems

Special **electronic payment systems** have been developed to pay for goods electronically on the Internet. Electronic payment systems for the Internet include systems for credit card payments, digital cash, digital wallets, accumulated balance digital payment systems, stored value payment systems, peer-to-peer payment systems, electronic cheques, and electronic billing presentment and payment systems.

Credit cards account for 80 percent of online payments in Canada and the U.S. and about 50 percent of online purchases outside Canada and the U.S. The more sophisticated electronic commerce software (see Chapters 7 and 8) has capabilities for processing credit card purchases on the Web. Businesses can also contract with services that extend the functionality of existing credit card payment systems. **Digital credit card payment systems** extend the functionality of credit cards so they can be used for online shopping payments. They make credit cards safer and more convenient for online merchants and consumers. They provide mechanisms for authenticating the purchaser's credit card to make sure it is valid and arrange for the bank that issued the credit card to deposit money for the amount of the purchase in the seller's bank account.

Digital wallets make paying for purchases over the Web more efficient by eliminating the need for shoppers to enter their address and credit card information each time they buy something. A **digital wallet** securely stores credit card and owner identification information and provides that information at an electronic commerce site's "checkout counter." The digital wallet enters the shopper's name, credit card number, and shipping information automatically when invoked to complete the purchase. Amazon.com's 1-Click Shopping uses electronic wallet technology. Gator, MSN Wallet, MasterCard Wallet, and America Online's Quick Checkout are other digital wallet systems.

Micropayment systems have been developed for purchases of less than $10, such as downloads of individual articles or music clips that would be too small for conventional credit card payments. Accumulated balance digital payment systems or stored value payment systems are useful for such purposes.

Accumulated balance digital payment systems enable users to make micropayments and purchases on the Web, accumulating a debit balance that they must pay periodically on their credit card or telephone bills. IPIN has been widely adopted by Web sites that sell music tracks for 99 cents. It invoices customers through existing consumer billing services such as telephone and wireless service companies, Internet service providers, and banks.

electronic payment systems

digital credit card payment systems

digital wallet

micropayment

accumulated balance digital payment systems

PaymentOne and Trivnet enable consumers to charge small purchases to their monthly telephone bill.

Stored value payment systems enable consumers to make instant online payments to merchants and other individuals based on value stored in a digital account. Online value systems rely on the value stored in a consumer's bank, chequing, or credit card account, and some of these systems require the use of a digital wallet. Ecount offers a prepaid debit account for online purchases, and RocketCash is a new online stored value system aimed at teenagers.

Smart cards are another type of stored value system used for micropayments. A **smart card** is a plastic card the size of a credit card that stores digital information. The smart card can store health records, identification data, or telephone numbers, or it can serve as an "electronic purse" in place of cash. The Mondex (now part of MasterCard) and American Express Blue smart cards contain electronic cash and can be used to transfer funds to merchants in physical storefronts and to merchants on the Internet. Both are contact smart cards that require use of special card-reading devices whenever the cards need to transfer cash to either an online or offline merchant. (Internet users must attach a smart card reader to their PCs to use the card. To pay for a Web purchase, the user would swipe the smart card through the card reader.)

Digital cash (also known as electronic cash or e-cash) can also be used for micropayments or larger purchases. **Digital cash** is currency represented in electronic form that moves outside the normal network of money (paper currency, coins, cheques, credit cards). Users are supplied with client software and can exchange money with another e-cash user over the Internet or with a retailer accepting e-cash. eCoin.net is an example of a digital cash service. In addition to facilitating micropayments, digital cash can be useful for people who do not have credit cards and wish to make Web purchases. Debit cards fall into this category; in Canada, the Interac network surpassed cash as the predominant retail payment method in 2000.

New Web-based **peer-to-peer payment systems** have sprung up to serve people who want to send money to vendors or individuals who are not set up to accept credit card payments. The party sending money uses his or her credit card to create an account with the designated payment at a Web site dedicated to peer-to-peer payments. The recipient "picks up" the payment by visiting the Web site and supplying information about where to send the payment (a bank account or a physical address). PayPal has become a popular peer-to-peer payment system. Montreal-based AlertPay aims to compete with PayPal by enabling any business or consumer with email to send and receive internet payments securely. AlertPay can use the sender's credit card or chequing account for payment.

Digital chequing payment systems, such as Western Union MoneyZap and eCheck, extend the functionality of existing chequing accounts so they can be used for online shopping payments. Digital cheques are less expensive than credit cards and much faster than traditional paper-based chequing. These cheques are encrypted with a digital signature that can be verified and used for payments in electronic commerce. Electronic cheque systems are useful in business-to-business electronic commerce.

Electronic billing presentment and payment systems are used for paying routine monthly bills. They enable users to view their bills electronically and pay them through electronic fund transfers from bank or credit card accounts. These services support payment for online and physical store purchases of goods or services after the purchase has taken place. They notify purchasers about bills that are due, present the bills, and process the payments.

Canada Post sponsors epost, an online service for bill presentment and payment. When subscribers sign up with epost, they receive private and secure epost boxes (electronic mailboxes), where their bills and other documents are delivered electronically. Using a variety of helpful online tools, subscribers can pay, organize and store bills from more than 65 Canadian companies—when they want, how they want—from any computer with Internet access. The Royal Bank (RBC) has added Webdoxs to its online banking services. This enables RBC customers to receive electronic bills from a variety of organizations as well as pay most of their bills electronically. Currently, the list of Webdoxs companies that will send their bills to RBC customers is limited.

stored value payment systems

smart card

digital cash

peer-to-peer payment systems

digital chequing

electronic billing presentment and
 payment systems

TABLE 13-3 Examples of Electronic Payment Systems for E-commerce

PAYMENT SYSTEM	DESCRIPTION	COMMERCIAL EXAMPLE
Digital credit card payment systems	Secure services for credit card payments on the Internet protect information transmitted among users, merchant sites, and processing banks	eCharge
Digital wallet	Software that stores credit card and other information to facilitate payment for goods on the Web	MSN Wallet MasterCard Wallet AOL Quick Checkout
Accumulated balance payment systems	Accumulates micropayment purchases as a debit balance that must be paid periodically on credit card or telephone bills	Trivnet PaymentOne
Stored value payment systems	Enables consumers to make instant payments to merchants based on value stored in a digital account	Ecount American Express Blue smart card MasterCard One Smart card
Digital cash	Digital currency that can be used for micropayments or larger purchases	eCoin.net Paystone.ca
Peer-to-peer payment systems	Sends money using the Web to individuals or vendors who are not set up to accept credit card payments	PayPal Yahoo PayDirect
Digital chequing	Electronic cheque with a secure digital signature	Western Union MoneyZap ECheck
Electronic billing presentment and payment systems	Supports electronic payment for online and physical store purchases of goods or services after the purchase has taken place	CheckFree Yahoo Bill Pay MSN Bill Pay epost

Some of these services, such as CheckFree, consolidate American subscribers' bills from various sources so that they can all be paid at one time. Table 13-3 summarizes the features of some of these payment systems. The process of paying for products and services purchased on the Internet is complex and merits additional discussion. We discuss electronic commerce security in detail in Chapter 9.

13.3 Electronic Business and the Digital Firm

Businesses are finding that some of the greatest benefits of Internet technology come from applications that lower agency and coordination costs. Although companies have used internal networks for many years to manage and coordinate their business processes, intranets are quickly becoming the technology of choice for electronic business.

An intranet typically centers on a portal that provides a single point of access to internal systems and documents using a Web interface. These corporate portals provide a single, consolidated view of the information resources on the intranet and can be customized to suit the information needs of specific business groups and individual users if required. They may also feature email, collaboration tools, and tools for searching for internal corporate systems and documents.

The Window on Organizations describes two intranets used by CARE, the global humanitarian relief organization. CARE has a global staff of 12 000 operating in more than 70 different countries who can benefit from immediate access to other staff members and critical information. These intranets feature portals to provide access to information from many different sources as well as group collaboration tools. Portions of these intranets have been extended to authorized outsiders.

How Intranets Support Electronic Business

While most companies, particularly larger ones, must support a multiplicity of computer platforms that cannot communicate with each other, intranets provide instant connectivity, uniting all computers into a single, virtually seamless, network system. Web software presents a uniform interface, which can be used to integrate many different processes and systems throughout the company. Companies can connect their intranets to internal company transaction systems, enabling employees to take actions central to a company's operations.

Internal corporate applications based on the Web page model can be made interactive using a variety of media, text, audio, and video. A principal use of intranets has been to create online repositories of information that can be updated as often as required. Product catalogues, employee handbooks, telephone directories, corporate policies, and benefits information can be revised immediately as changes occur. This event-driven publishing enables organizations to respond more rapidly to changing conditions than traditional paper-based publishing while eliminating paper, printing, and distribution costs.

For instance, Rogers Communications, a major telecommunications provider with more than 100 locations across Canada, had several problems with its intranet: multiple sites in each of its operating companies, rough or out-of-date content, and duplication of information. To solve these issues, Rogers created a new enterprise human resources portal called HR Xpress. The new portal is used more often by employees, has increased awareness of other intranet sites, and saved Rogers more than $100 000 in annual administrative costs.

Intranets and Group Collaboration Intranets provide a rich set of tools for creating collaborative environments in which members of an organization can exchange ideas, share information, and work together on common projects and assignments regardless of their physical location. Information from many different sources and media, including text, graphics, video, audio, and even digital slides can be displayed, shared, and accessed across an enterprise through a simple common interface. The intranet for CARE Canada, described in the Window on Organizations, has some of these capabilities.

The Mitre Corporation, which conducts research and development work for the U.S. federal government, set up a collaborative environment called Mitre Information Infrastructure for sharing personnel, planning, and project information. This intranet includes a corporate directory with names, telephone numbers, and resumes of Mitre employees; a Lessons Learned Library with best practices and lessons learned from 10 years of Mitre projects; and capabilities for filing human resources reports, such as time sheets, service requests, and property inventory and tracking forms. Chapter 16 provides additional detail about intranets in knowledge-sharing and collaborative work.

Intranet Applications for Electronic Business

Intranets are springing up in all the major functional areas of businesses, enabling organizations to manage more business processes electronically. Figure 13-14 illustrates some of the intranet applications that have been developed for finance and accounting, human resources, sales and marketing, and manufacturing and production.

Finance and Accounting Many organizations have extensive transaction processing systems (TPS) that collect operational data on financial and accounting activities, but their traditional management reporting systems, such as general ledger systems and spreadsheets, often cannot bring this detailed information together for decision making and performance measurement. Intranets are valuable for finance and accounting

WINDOW ON ORGANIZATIONS

Organization

CARE's Humanitarian Intranets

CARE International is a nonprofit and nonsectarian charitable agency that manages both disaster relief and long-term development programs in 74 countries. Ensuring its global staff of 12 000 can communicate and access the information they need on the spot is absolutely critical to its success. In times of disaster, access to accurate, relevant information can literally mean the difference between life and death.

CARE is actually a federation of 11 relief agencies, the largest being CARE Canada, CARE Australia, and CARE US. This decentralized structure makes CARE's communication problems somewhat greater than those of other large organizations. Additionally, about 80 percent of the staff works in the field providing assistance to local communities, and most CARE workers are in the field in Latin America, Asia, and Africa, which lack robust communication infrastructures.

Much of the information and knowledge used by CARE is housed in disparate systems in over 70 locations around the world. Critical information was often difficult to access when it was urgently needed. CARE is trying to supply its workers with the information and communication capabilities they need by using two closely linked intranet portals. CARE Canada implemented an intranet for collaboration and storing documents that has evolved into a global portal with more than 1000 users throughout the entire CARE federation (see Figure 13-13).

This intranet uses OpenText Livelink groupware software for streamlined collaboration. It is accessible directly from the Web using standard Web browser software, so relief teams can use this tool wherever they are located without installing any special software on their computers.

OpenText Livelink provides more than 380 project teams from multiple organizations with access to information and tools for analyzing data. Livelink captures and indexes data entered by users in memos, online discussions, and project log reports, providing users with tools to help them retrieve specific information and view it in report format.

Integrated with Livelink is a data-gathering application from MODEL Technologies called MERlite. MERlite provides a set of tools for monitoring and evaluating project results so users can perform sophisticated analyses such as comparing emergency needs to available global materials and resources.

This is how the intranet helps. A CARE staff member working on a water and sanitation project in Indonesia, for example, might put a note into a Livelink shared workspace where it could be immediately accessed by other CARE staff in the Indonesian country office, in the Ottawa office, and in the field. CARE Canada's water and sanitation specialist could access the documents and make comments while traveling in Ghana. The ability to access documents and the threads of a discussion and make comments immediately is much more efficient than using email. As Carl Frappaolo, executive vice president of the Delphi Group Consultants, points out, "The more geographically dispersed the community is, the greater value you're going to find from the portal."

CARE's second intranet portal, called GYST, was rolled out in 2002 to provide better federation-wide data gathering and reporting. GYST collects and reports on performance management data for over 800 global relief projects run by CARE and its agencies. Field workers around the globe supply the performance management system with data collected through surveys, evaluations, and informal means. These data are centralized and consolidated so that CARE management can evaluate performance on an organization-wide level and also by country or individual project.

When CARE analyzes performance, it tries to measure intangible benefits related to social change as well as hard-core numbers about how many wells were dug or how many tons of food were distributed. For example, it will try to determine if its programs enabled X number of people to attend school and how that might relate to better health care.

GYST also links to the Livelink intranet and other internal finance and human resources applications. Today GYST has over 800 management-level users and is available in multiple language versions—French, English, and Spanish.

With the exception of human resources data, the data and documents on CARE portals are accessible to all CARE users. Some portions of the CARE intranets have been made accessible to members of other humanitarian and relief organizations, such as CARE's e-library with final evaluations of programs and lessons learned.

Because CARE operates in many remote areas, pages are designed so that people with low-capacity Internet access can access information. Network connections have improved considerably in Asia and Latin America, but those in Africa are still problematic.

To Think About: Why are intranets useful for a global organization such as CARE? How do they provide value?

Sources: Kathleen Reidy, "Global Relief," *Portals Magazine*, February 1, 2004; "CARE Canada—Tackling World Problems" and "CARE Canada—CAREing Enough to Manage World Problems," Open Text Corporation, 2003; www.opentext.com, accessed August 25, 2004.

because they can provide an integrated view of financial and accounting information online in an easy-to-use format. For example, Charles Schwab's SMART reporting system provides managers with a comprehensive view of Schwab's financial activities, including a

FIGURE 13-13 *CARE Canada's intranet portal.*

Care Canada's intranet portal provides access to documents from many different sources for authorized CARE staff members throughout the world.

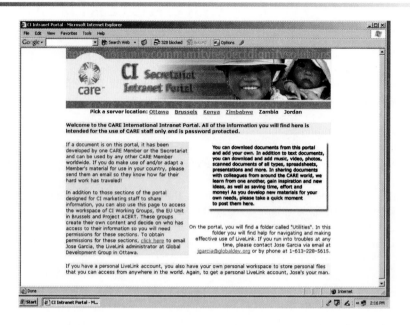

template to help them evaluate nine categories of risk. The Schwab intranet also delivers general ledger reporting in an easy-to-digest format.

Human Resources Principal responsibilities of human resources departments include keeping employees informed of company issues and providing information about employees' personnel records and benefits. The human resources function often uses intranets for online publishing of corporate policy manuals, job postings and internal job transfers, company telephone directories, and training classes. Employees can use an intranet to enrol in health care, employee savings, and other benefits plans if the intranet is linked to the firm's human resources or benefits database, or employees can use it to take online competency tests. Human resources departments are able to deliver information about upcoming events or company developments to employees rapidly using newsgroups or email broadcasts. For example, TransCanada Pipeline employees use the company intranet to process timesheets and expense reports as well as to manage their own pension and benefit accounts.

FIGURE 13-14 *Functional applications of intranets.*

Intranet applications have been developed for each of the major functional areas of business.

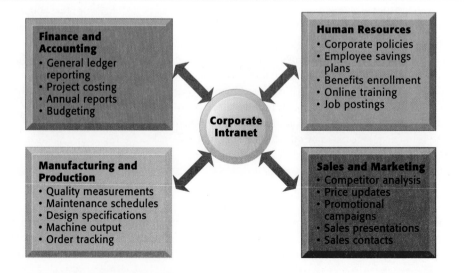

Sales and Marketing Earlier we described how the Internet and the Web are used for selling to individual customers and to other businesses. Internet technology is also useful for the internal management of the sales and marketing function. One of the most popular applications for corporate intranets involves overseeing and coordinating the activities of the sales force. Sales staff consult the intranet for updates on pricing, promotions, rebates, or customers or to obtain information about competitors. They can access presentations and sales documents and customize them for customers. For example, email marketing company Yesmail.com uses a sales intranet for sharing tools and documents about contacts, sales leads, and prospects. The application includes tools for measuring the company's progress in different stages of the sales process.

Manufacturing and Production In manufacturing, information management issues are highly complex, involving massive inventories, capturing and integrating real-time production data flows, changing relationships with suppliers, and volatile costs. The manufacturing function typically uses multiple types of data, including graphics as well as text, which are scattered in many disparate systems. Manufacturing information is often time sensitive and difficult to retrieve because files must be continuously updated. Developing intranets that integrate manufacturing data under a uniform user interface is more complicated than in other functional areas.

Despite these difficulties, companies are launching intranet applications for manufacturing. Intranets coordinating the flow of information between lathes, controllers, inventory systems, and other components of a production system make manufacturing information more accessible to different parts of the organization, increasing precision and lowering costs. For example, Sony Corporation operates an intranet that provides data on production quality measurements, such as defects and rejects, along with maintenance and training schedules.

Business Process Integration

In the pre-Internet environment, business process integration was hampered by the difficulties of making information flow smoothly among many different kinds of systems servicing different functional areas and parts of the organization. Some of this integration can be supplied relatively inexpensively using Internet technology. Firms are using intranets to improve coordination among their internal business processes, and they are deploying extranets to coordinate processes shared with their customers, business partners, and other organizations.

The Internet and Collaborative Commerce In some industries, Internet technology is helping companies collaborate more closely with customers, suppliers, and other firms to improve planning, production, and distribution of goods and services. The use of digital technologies to enable multiple organizations to design, develop, move, and manage products collaboratively through their life cycles is called **collaborative commerce.**

The development of a new product usually involves collaboration among different departments in a single firm and, increasingly, among several different firms. Internet technology provides communication and collaboration tools to connect designers, engineers, and marketing and manufacturing staff in different locations or even different organizations. Internet-based tools help companies coordinate work with suppliers or contract manufacturers as they make and deliver their products.

Firms are using the customer feedback from Web sites or online communities to improve product design. Equipped with appropriate software tools, customers can actually help companies design and develop some types of products. For example, GE Plastics provides its customers with Web-based tools to help them design better plastic products (Thomke and von Hippel 2002). A firm engaged in collaborative commerce with its suppliers and customers can achieve new levels of efficiency in reducing product design cycles, minimizing excess inventory, forecasting demand, and keeping partners and customers informed (see Figure 13-15).

collaborative commerce

FIGURE 13-15 *Collaborative commerce.*

Collaborative commerce is a set of digitally enabled collaborative inter-actions between an enterprise and its business partners and customers. Internet technology helps the collaborative community share data and processes that were once considered interna

Table 13-4 provides examples of how companies are using Internet technology for collaborative commerce.

TABLE 13-4 *How the Internet Facilitates Collaborative Commerce*

APPLICATION	EXAMPLE
Product service and support	Celestica, a Toronto-based electronics manufacturing services provider, has an extranet for its 1000 suppliers. These suppliers use the extranet to pull production planning information from Celestica's supply chain systems. When Celestica gets demand forecast data from one of its large customers, suppliers can view the data through Celestica's corporate portal and let Celestica know how quickly they can deliver the required materials.
Collaborative product design across multiple locations	Engineers at Johnson Controls and DaimlerChrysler used a Web-based design and collaboration system to design part of the Jeep Liberty interior together.
Customer service	Quebec-based Bombardier Aerospace uses its Business Aircraft Customer Support's extranet for their clients. This extranet includes a number of communication tools for Bombardier as well as a proprietary part ordering tool (with over 20 000 parts), that allows their clients to order plane parts online. Using their extranet, Bombardier technicians not only learn how to repair or overhaul a certain item but also can order the necessary parts online.
Supply chain coordination	Hudson's Bay Company's subsidiary Zellers implemented a wireless, integrated replenishment and stockroom management system (called LID for Listed Inventory Database) that provides shift productivity reporting. This system saves Zellers $5 million per year.
Collaborative sourcing	B2B Net marketplace Exostar provides a collaboration tool for multiple suppliers to collaborate on the design and performance of products they jointly develop and sell to companies in the aerospace and defense industries.

Management Opportunities, Challenges, and Solutions

Internet technology has provided businesses with powerful new tools to innovate and to execute much more efficiently, and it has also created a new series of management challenges.

Opportunities

The Internet and Internet technology have created extraordinary opportunities for new and traditional businesses to exploit digital technology. Firms are using these technologies to create new products and services, new channels for sales and marketing, and even entirely new businesses. These technologies have also strengthened traditional business models by helping firms reduce supply chain costs, increase production efficiency, and tighten relationships with customers. No company can afford to ignore the Internet and Internet technology, even if it does not do business online.

Management Challenges

Although digitally enabling business processes and relationships with other organizations can help companies achieve new levels of competitiveness and efficiency, it poses challenges for managers. Many new Internet business models have yet to prove enduring sources of profit. Web-enabling business processes for electronic commerce and electronic business requires changing the way the organization works. The legal environment for electronic commerce has not yet solidified, and companies pursuing electronic commerce must be vigilant about establishing trust, security, and consumer privacy.

Finding a Successful Internet Business Model The Internet has clearly changed business models in a number of key industries, including the media (the press, books, and music), financial services, travel, and automobile retailing. But not all Internet business models have been successful. Hundreds of retail dot-com firms, including Kozmo.com, Webvan, Garden.com, Chinese Books Cyberstore, Productopia.com, and Pets.com, have closed their doors. Only a fraction of the independent exchanges that were operating in the spring of 2000 survive today. "Canada was never infected by the same kind of venture capital disease [as the US]," says K.K. Campbell, a Canadian Internet business consultant who sold his web-development firm several years ago when the price was right. "We have fewer dot-coms, and many that exist are privately held, so we don't get much insight about what's going on" (Stewart 2001).

Doing business over the Internet is not necessarily more efficient or cost effective than traditional business methods. Virtual retailers may not need to pay for costly storefronts and retail workers, but they require heavy outlays for warehousing, customer service call centres, and customer acquisition.

Challenges also confront businesses that are trying to use the Web to supplement or enhance traditional business models. Businesses that are unclear about their online strategy—and its relationship to their overall business strategy—can waste thousands and even millions of dollars building and maintaining Web sites that fail to deliver the desired results (Pinker, Seidmann, and Foster 2002). Introducing a Web site with self-service technology may undermine the business model—and competitive advantage—of a firm that relies on traditional sales representatives to provide unique personalized services to customers (Schultze and Orlikowski, 2004). And even if a company has a viable Internet business model, it can fail if that business model is poorly executed.

Organizational Change Challenges E-business and e-commerce often require new organizational designs and management processes to take advantage of Internet technology. Companies may need to redesign entire business processes rather than trying to graft new technology on existing business practices. Companies must consider a different organizational structure, changes in organizational culture, a different support structure for information systems, different procedures for managing employees and networked processing functions, and, perhaps, a different business strategy.

Traditional boundaries between departments and divisions and companies and distributors may be impediments to collaboration and relationship building. Companies with traditional retail outlets or sales forces can expect **channel conflict**—competition between two or more different distribution channels used to sell the products or services of the same company—if they use the Web for online sales and marketing. Their sales force and distributors may fear that their revenues will drop as customers make purchases directly from the Web or that they will be displaced by this new channel.

Trust, Security, and Privacy Electronic commerce cannot flourish unless there is an atmosphere of trust among buyers, sellers, and other partners involved in online transactions. Because online relationships are more impersonal perhaps than those in bricks-and-mortar commerce, some consumers remain hesitant to make purchases over the Web from unfamiliar vendors. Consumers also worry about the security and confidentiality of the credit card number and other personal data that they supply over the Internet. Internet-based systems are even more vulnerable to penetration by outsiders than private networks because the Internet was designed to be open to everyone.

The Web provides an unprecedented ability to learn about and target customers. But the same capability can also undermine individual privacy. By using Web site monitoring software and other technology for tracking Web visitors, companies can gather detailed information about individuals without their knowledge. In other instances, Web site visitors knowingly supply personal information, such as their names, addresses, email addresses, and special interests, in exchange for access to the site without realizing how the organization owning the Web site may use the information. For companies collecting detailed customer information over the Web, the challenge is balancing the desire to profit from such information with the need to safeguard individual privacy.

Solution Guidelines

Digitally enabling the enterprise with Internet technology requires attention to these issues and careful management planning.

Determining How Internet Technology Can Provide Value for the Business Managers need to understand precisely how Internet technology can provide value for their company. Companies need to think carefully about whether they can create a genuinely workable business model on the Internet and how the Internet relates to their overall business strategy. Internet technology alone is not a substitute for an effective business strategy (Subramanian and Adner 2001; Willcocks and Plant 2001).

Managing Business Process Changes Before embarking on e-commerce or e-business initiatives, managers will need to identify the organizational changes required to make them work. They should then put in place a change management plan for dealing with affected groups within the firm as well as with suppliers and other business partners in the company's network of value creation. Also essential are well-defined policies and procedures for sharing data with other organizations, including specifications for the type, format, level of precision, and security of the data to be exchanged (Barua et al. 2001).

Channel conflict merits special attention. One way to deal with this problem is to compensate sales representatives for online sales in their territories even if they do not work on the sale or meet the buyer. Another solution is to offer only a portion of the company's full product line on the Web. The importance of traditional channels and the level of resistance to Web sales will help determine the appropriate response.

Safeguarding Security and Privacy Both electronic commerce and electronic business require companies to be both more open and more closed at the same

channel conflict

time. Companies need to be open to outsiders such as customers, suppliers, and trading partners, yet these systems also must be closed to hackers and other intruders and protective of customers. Firms engaging in e-commerce and e-business need a new security culture and infrastructure that enables them to straddle this fine line. They also need to reexamine corporate privacy policies to make sure they are properly respecting the privacy of customers and Web site visitors. Chapters 4 and 9 provide more detail on how Internet privacy and security can be safeguarded.

Summary

1. *Analyze how Internet technology has changed value propositions and business models.*

    The Internet is rapidly becoming the infrastructure of choice for electronic commerce and electronic business because it provides a universal and easy-to-use set of technologies and technology standards that can be adopted by all organizations, no matter which computer system or information technology platform they use. Internet technology provides a much lower cost and easier-to-use alternative for coordination activities than proprietary networks. Companies can use Internet technology to radically reduce their transaction and agency costs.

    The Internet radically reduces the cost of creating, sending, and storing information while making that information more widely available. Information is not limited to traditional physical methods of delivery. The unbundling of information from traditional value chain channels is having a disruptive effect on old business models, and it is creating new business models as well. Business models based on the coupling of information with products and services may no longer be necessary. By using the Internet and other networks for electronic commerce, organizations in some industries can exchange purchase and sale transactions directly with customers and suppliers, eliminating inefficient intermediaries.

    The Internet shrinks information asymmetry and has transformed the relationship between information richness and reach. The Internet can help companies create and capture profit in new ways by adding extra value to existing products and services or by providing the foundation for new products and services. Many different business models for electronic commerce on the Internet have emerged, including virtual storefronts, information brokers, transaction brokers, Net marketplaces, content providers, online service providers, virtual communities, and portals.

2. *Define electronic commerce and describe how it has changed consumer retailing and business-to-business transactions.*

    Electronic commerce is the process of buying and selling goods electronically with computerized business transactions using the Internet or other digital network

technology. It includes marketing, customer support, delivery, and payment. The three major types of electronic commerce are business-to-consumer (B2C), business-to-business (B2B), and consumer-to-consumer (C2C). Another way of classifying electronic commerce transactions is in terms of the participants' physical connection to the Web. Conventional e-commerce transactions, which take place over wired networks, can be distinguished from mobile commerce, or m-commerce, which is the purchase of goods and services using handheld wireless devices.

    The Internet provides a universally available set of technologies for electronic commerce that can be used to create new channels for marketing, sales, and customer support and to eliminate intermediaries in buy-and-sell transactions. Interactive capabilities on the Web can be used to build closer relationships with customers in marketing and customer support. Firms can use various Web personalization technologies to deliver Web pages with content geared to the specific interests of each user. Companies can also reduce costs and improve customer service by using Web sites, as well as email and even telephone access to customer service representatives, to provide helpful information.

    B2B e-commerce generates efficiencies by enabling companies to locate suppliers, solicit bids, place orders, and track shipments in transit electronically. Businesses can use their own Web sites to sell to other businesses or use Net marketplaces or private industrial networks. Net marketplaces provide a single digital marketplace based on Internet technology for many buyers and sellers. Private industrial networks link a firm with its suppliers and other strategic business partners.

3. *Compare the principal payment systems for electronic commerce.*

    The principal electronic payment systems for electronic commerce are digital credit card systems, digital wallets, accumulated balance digital payment systems, stored value payment systems, digital cash, peer-to-peer payment systems, digital chequing, and electronic billing presentment and payment systems. Accumulated balance systems, stored value systems (including smart cards), and digital cash are useful for small micropayments.

4. Evaluate the role of Internet technology in facilitating management and coordination of internal and interorganizational business processes.

Private, internal corporate networks called intranets can be created using Internet connectivity standards. Extranets are private intranets that are extended to selected organizations or individuals outside the firm. Intranets and extranets are forming the underpinnings of electronic business by providing a low-cost technology that can run on almost any computing platform. Organizations can use intranets to create collaboration environments for coordinating work and information sharing and to make information flow between different functional areas of the firm.

Extranets help coordinate business processes shared with customers, suppliers, and other external organizations. Collaborative commerce builds on extranets to enable multiple organizations to collaboratively design, develop, build, move, and manage products through their life cycles. A firm engaged in collaborative commerce with its suppliers and customers can achieve new efficiencies by reducing product design cycles, minimizing excess inventory, forecasting demand, and keeping partners and customers informed.

5. Assess the challenges posed by electronic business and electronic commerce, and propose management solutions.

Many new business models based on the Internet have not yet found proven ways to generate profits or reduce costs. Implementing electronic commerce and electronic business requires far-reaching organizational change, including redesign of business processes; recasting relationships with customers, suppliers, and other business partners; and new roles for employees. Channel conflicts may erupt as the firm turns to the Internet as an alternative outlet for sales. Security, privacy, and legal issues pose additional electronic commerce challenges. Before embracing e-commerce and e-business, firms should understand exactly how Internet technology provides value to the business and relates to their overall business strategy. They should also anticipate making organizational changes, including changing business processes and developing a plan for managing channel conflict. Finally, they will need corporate policies and tools for promoting security and privacy within an e-business environment.

Key Terms

Accumulated balance digital payment systems, 459

Banner ad, 448

Blog, 453

Business model, 446

Business-to-business (B2B) electronic commerce, 450

Business-to-consumer (B2C) electronic commerce, 450

Call centre, 455

Channel conflict, 468

Clicks-and-mortar, 450

Clickstream tracking, 451

Collaborative commerce, 465

Collaborative filtering, 452

Consumer-to-consumer (C2C) electronic commerce, 450

Digital cash, 460

Digital chequing, 460

Digital credit card payment systems, 459

Digital wallet, 459

Disintermediation, 451

Dynamic pricing, 448

Electronic billing presentment and payment systems, 460

Electronic data interchange (EDI), 455

Electronic payment systems, 459

Exchanges, 457

Information asymmetry, 446

Micropayment, 459

Mobile commerce (m-commerce), 451

Net marketplaces, 456

Peer-to-peer payment systems, 460

Pop-up ads, 448

Private exchange, 456

Private industrial networks, 456

Procurement, 455

Pure-play, 449

Reach, 447

Reintermediation, 451

Richness, 447

Search costs, 446

Smart card, 460

Social networking sites, 448

Stored value payment systems, 460

Syndicators, 449

Web personalization, 452

Review Questions

1. What are the advantages of using the Internet as the infrastructure for electronic commerce and electronic business?

2. How is the Internet changing the economics of information and business models?

3. Name and describe six Internet business models for electronic commerce. Distinguish between a pure-play Internet business model and a clicks-and-mortar business model.

4. Name and describe the various categories of electronic commerce.

5. How can the Internet facilitate sales and marketing to individual customers? Describe the role played by Web personalization.

6. How can the Internet help provide customer service?

7. How can Internet technology support business-to-business electronic commerce?

8. What are Net marketplaces? Why do they represent an important business model for B2B e-commerce? How do they differ from private industrial networks?

9. *Name and describe the principal electronic payment systems used on the Internet.*

10. *Why are intranets so useful for electronic business?*

11. *How can intranets support organizational collaboration?*

12. *Describe the uses of intranets for electronic business in sales and marketing, human resources, finance and accounting, and manufacturing.*

13. *How can companies use Internet technology for integrating business processes? How does Internet technology facilitate collaborative commerce?*

14. *What is channel conflict? Why is it becoming a problem in electronic commerce?*

15. *Describe the management challenges posed by electronic commerce and electronic business on the Internet, and suggest some solutions.*

Discussion Questions

1. *How does the Internet change consumer and supplier relationships?*

2. *The Internet may not make corporations obsolete, but they will have to change their business models. Do you agree? Why or why not?*

Application Software Exercise:
Spreadsheet Exercise: Analyzing a Dot-Com Business

Pick one e-commerce company on the Internet, for example, The Financial Post, Yahoo.ca, Ashford.com, Buy.com, or Priceline.com. Study the Web pages that describe the company, and explain its purpose and structure. Look for articles at Web sites such as Sedar.com, Globeinvestor.com, or strategis.ic.gc.ca that comment on the company. Use a Web search engine to find out about the company's Web site by looking at press releases, reviews, and company annual reports. Create a simplified spreadsheet of the company's balance sheets and income statements for the past three years.

Is the company a dot-com success, borderline business, or failure? What information forms the basis of your decision?

Why? When answering these questions, pay special attention to the company's three-year trends in revenues, costs of sales, gross margins, operating expenses, and net margins. See the Companion Website for Chapter 13 for definitions of these terms and how they are calculated. Prepare an overhead presentation (minimum of five slides), including appropriate spreadsheets or charts, and present your work to your professor and/or classmates. If the company is successful, which additional business strategies could it pursue to become even more successful? If the company is a borderline or failing business, which specific business strategies (if any) could make it more successful?

Electronic Commerce Project: Comparing Online Storefront Hosting Services

You would like to set up a Web site to sell towels, linens, pottery and tableware from Portugal and are examining services for hosting small business Internet storefronts. Your Web site should be able to take secure credit card payments and to calculate shipping costs and taxes. Initially you would like to display photos and descriptions of 40 different products. Visit Yahoo! Canada's Geocities Web hosting service (**ca.geocities.yahoo.com**) and Webserve.ca, and compare

the range of e-commerce hosting services they offer to small businesses, their capabilities, and costs. Also examine the tools they provide for creating an e-commerce site. Compare both of these services and decide which of the two you would use if you were actually establishing a Web store. Write a small report indicating your choice and explaining the strengths and weaknesses of both.

Group Project: Performing a Competitive Analysis of E-commerce Sites

Form a group with three or four of your classmates. Select two businesses that are competitors in the same industry that use their Web sites for electronic commerce. Visit their Web sites. You might compare, for example, the Web sites for virtual banking created by Bank of Montreal (BMO) and Royal Bank of Canada (RBC), or the Internet trading Web sites of BayStreet.ca and TDWaterhouse.com.

Prepare an evaluation of each business's Web site in terms of its functions, user friendliness, and ability to support the company's business strategy. Which Web site does a better job? Why? Can you make some recommendations to improve these Web sites?

Web Sites of Interest

There are many interesting Web sites to enhance your learning about e-commerce and e-business. You can search the Web yourself or try the following sites to add to what you have already learned.

Ecommerce Times **www.ecommercetimes.com**
The latest on e-commerce technologies, businesses, models, and companies

Internet Week **www.internetweek.com**
A weekly publication of the latest happenings on the Internet

Chapters.Indigo.Ca **www.chapters.indigo.ca**
Canada's alternative to Amazon

CASE STUDY:
Can the Music Industry Change its Tune?

Would you pay $15.99 for a CD of your favourite recording artist if you could get it for free on the Web? This question has shaken the music industry to its foundations. A tremendous number of Internet users have taken advantage of online file-sharing services where they can download digitized music files from other users free of charge. We will look first at the situation in the U.S. and then see how Canada deals with the same situation.

The first such file-sharing service to be widely used was Napster. Its Web site provided software and services that enabled users to locate any of the 1 billion digitized MP3 music files on the computers of other online Napster members and copy them onto their own computers for free. Napster's computers did not store any music files, but instead they acted as a matchmaker. To obtain a specific music file, you would sign on to the Napster Web site and type in the name of the desired song. Napster's central title index would display the connected computers with that specific song. Napster then established a direct connection between the requesting computer and the one storing the desired music file. Your Napster software then would download that file onto your computer. You could play the song on your computer and copy it onto CDs. If you stored it on your computer, others could copy it from you. Napster quickly became so popular that when it was shut down in 2001, it had more than 80 million users worldwide.

Napster users could legally copy and trade uncopyrighted material, but reproducing copyrighted files without permission is illegal because the recipient does not compensate the owner for the use of the intellectual property. In December 1999, the Recording Industry Association of America (RIAA), representing the five major music recording companies (Universal Music, Sony Music, Warner Music, BMG, and EMI), which together were responsible for 80 percent of recorded music, sued Napster for violating copyright laws. U.S. courts ordered Napster to stop allowing users to share copyrighted music files, and the site closed down in July 2002 when it declared bankruptcy. It has since been transformed into a legal, fee-based online digital music service.

Napster was held liable for the illegal copying of copyrighted songs because it maintained a central index of members' music on its central computer. Its closure did not stop widespread illegal music file sharing. Alternative peer-to-peer approaches to free downloading were developed that did not require a centralized computer to manage the file swapping. Services using this approach include Kazaa (KaZaA), Morpheus, and Grokster. Many of the estimated 37 million Americans who have downloaded music have done so using Kazaa. According to research firm BigChampagne LLC, users download more than 1 billion songs per week from Kazaa, Morpheus, and other file-sharing programs.

Kazaa's corporate headquarters are located in Vanatu, a tiny independent island near Australia. Kazaa's software is stored on individual computers, enabling anyone to locate servers where individuals have stored music files available to be copied. Once the software locates the desired song, it establishes a direct peer-to-peer link between the two computers and downloads the desired song file, with no one paying any fees. Distributors of the software claim that their software has valuable legal uses, and they are not responsible if millions of people use it illegally.

To profit from its software, Kazaa allows pop-up advertisements and unsolicited email from vendors who pay for the service. Because the free trading of digitized materials does not go through a centralized computer, no one knows what or how many songs are being downloaded or by whom. But Kazaa reported that, by June 2003, its Media Desktop software for computer-to-computer file sharing had been downloaded 270 million times.

The courts have been unable to shut down sites that only make the peer-to-peer software available. On October 2, 2001, through RIAA, the major record label firms filed suit against Kazaa, Morpheus, and other peer-to-peer services, alleging copyright infringement against all firms that use Media Desktop and similar software to swap copyrighted materials. However, because the exchange of music files is strictly between two individuals, Kazaa claims it is breaking no laws and cannot be shut down. Instead, individual users of Kazaa's software are breaking laws and can be punished.

A big blow against the recording companies came on April 25, 2003, when a suit brought by the major record labels, movie studios, and music publishers against Grokster Ltd. (Grokster software) and StreamCast Networks Inc. (Morpheus software) was decided in favour of the file-sharing services. The U.S. District Court in Los Angeles ruled that the two companies could not be held responsible for illegal music swapping using their software because they cannot monitor or control users of their software exchange files, and so they were not breaking any laws by making their software available. A subsequent ruling on August 19, 2004, by the U.S. Court of Appeals, Ninth District in San Francisco upheld this earlier ruling.

RIAA started to prosecute first students and then other individuals who use the Internet for illegal music downloading. The effort began in the autumn of 2002 with 2300 "cease and desist" letters to colleges, warning them to stop their students from downloading music. RIAA then filed a suit against four individual students in an attempt to stop students from downloading free popular songs illegally and making them available for other students to copy. In an out-of-court settlement on April 30, 2003, the students agreed to cease their music downloading activities and pay RIAA more than US$10 000 each. Immediately after the agreement, a number of similar file-sharing networks on other campuses were pulled down.

In the spring of 2003, RIAA started sending Kazaa and Grokster users millions of instant messages which said, "When you break the law, you risk legal penalties. There is a simple way to avoid that risk: DON'T STEAL MUSIC." Then on September 8, 2003, RIAA filed lawsuits against 261 American computer users whom it believed were using Internet file-sharing services to distribute and download large amounts of copyrighted music illegally. RIAA launched additional suits against users of online file-sharing networks, targeting 532 people in January 2004 and 744 people in August 2004. Legal experts expect most of these lawsuits to be settled in favour of RIAA, but these suits are unlikely to halt illegal music file sharing.

Although RIAA's legal campaign has frightened some illegal music downloaders, many individuals continue to believe that there is nothing wrong with downloading and distributing copyrighted music. This widespread attitude cannot be easily changed. The music industry believes that widespread music file sharing on the Internet has caused music CD sales to plummet and that Internet downloading is costing them billions of dollars in lost sales each year.

In 2000, CD sales were about $44.4 billion; in 2001, sales fell to $42.1 billion, a decrease of 5 percent. According to Nielsen SoundScan, CD music sales fell another 8.8 percent in 2002. In 2003, U.S. recorded music sales only fell 0.8 percent from 2002, but worldwide, sales fell around 10 percent.

Critics of the recording industry claimed that sales slipped only a little in the falling economy. A Jupiter Research report of May 2002 and a report by Professor Felix Oberholzer-Gee of Harvard Business School and Koleman Strumpf of University of North Carolina found that those who use free Internet file-sharing networks, such as Kazaa, to download songs are more likely to increase their spending on music than other music CD purchasers. These reports concluded that free downloading increases music CD sales by making people enthusiastic about new and catalogue music.

Critics pointed out that the number of industry releases

has fallen sharply, from a record 38 900 titles in 1999 to 31 734 in 2001, a 20.3 percent drop. Nielsen also reported that although the 2002 releases rose to 33 443, that was still a 14 percent drop from 1999. "The music industry's [approach] is to throw things against the wall and see what sticks," said Nathan Brackett, *Rolling Stone*'s senior editor. "If they're throwing 20 percent less stuff out there, there's less chance something will stick." Also, the average CD price rose 7.2 percent between 1999 and 2001 from $16.31 to $17.75 while consumer prices rose barely at all.

Critics believe that new forms of competition for entertainment dollars have also contributed to the drop in CD sales. For example, 35 percent of U.S. homes had DVD players in 2002 versus none in 1999. DVDs, video games, and the Internet are becoming strong competitors for entertainment dollars.

Observers emphasize that those who continue to download songs for free actually do face costs. First, users must spend time downloading the music. Then, to play it anywhere but on their computers, they must "burn" it onto compact discs. Moreover, specific songs can be hard to locate. And users have to endure technological problems, including pop-up advertising to pay for the "free" services. Also, prior to downloading, users cannot tell if the song contains a computer virus, is only a virus, or is otherwise a phony or incomplete song. The quality may even be poor, including scratching and popping sounds. Students may have time to experiment, but most people with full-time jobs do not.

The recording industry now realizes that it must change the way it does business if it is to survive. Some industry analysts believe it must find ways to cut costs. Michael Nathanson, the music analyst for Sanford C. Bernstein, said the biggest costs (about 36 percent) were talent and marketing.

Some analysts recommend that recording companies consider signing fewer artists. According to Michael Wolff of McKinsey & Company, "The revenues today can't support such a broad number of releases." Others believe the only way to cut these costs is through consolidation, perhaps cutting the major recording companies from five to three. However, because overhead amounts to only one-third of recorded music costs, the savings would be limited and inadequate. Some claim the underlying problem is that entertainment executives compete with each other for a limited pool of talent. Nathanson suggests the companies need to rely on other sources of revenue. For example, he believes they should get a portion of artists' earnings for concerts, sponsorships, and merchandise sales, all of which are currently kept by the artists themselves.

For years, the recording companies balked at licensing their songs for legal sale online. Most of them burdened the music with unwieldy technical safeguards that prevented consumers from recording songs onto CDs or transferring them to portable music players. These services often required monthly subscription fees, offering too few songs at too high a price per song. They were not very successful.

In 2002, the major labels did a turnaround and started to embrace online music sales. They began experimenting with alternative pricing structures for music delivered legally over the Internet. Some executives believed that the industry should not sell songs individually because people will purchase a whole CD to get one or two songs. However, with the proper price, individual songs could be effectively sold. Tests showed that above US$1 per song, sales fell off rather quickly. John Rose, executive vice president of EMI, concluded, "If all consumers who pirate tracks today bought them for a buck, that would be a US$5 billion a month business."

On April 29, 2003, Apple Computer announced a new Web site for downloading music named the iTunes Music Store. It was an immediate success, selling 1.4 million songs in its first week, and 100 million by August 2004. It stunned the industry. The site charges US99 cents per song and at first offered more than 200 000 songs. Apple has a licensing agreement with all five of the big recording companies and now offers all the songs in their catalogues.

Users do not subscribe to this site, making it less expensive than other sites. The person purchasing the songs can burn as many as 10 compact discs with the same list of songs so the whole family can use them. The site is easy to use. Songs can be located by genre, artist, or album, and they can be downloaded at the click of a single button. Album covers are downloaded with each song or album. Moreover, users can play a 30-second preview of each song for free. Most complete albums cost between $10 and $14, with the majority priced at $12.50. The songs belong to the purchaser who is able to copy them to as many as three computers (a restriction demanded by the big labels).

iTunes has inspired a new wave of similar online music services, including Puretracks, Napster 2.0 (a legal version owned by Roxio Inc.), Sony Connect, RealNetworks, and BuyMusic.com. Microsoft and Yahoo! have entered this market, and Viacom's MTV and Virgin Group have similar plans. As in many other industries, this intense competition is commoditizing the digital music market. Outside of sales or limited promotions, there is very little variation among the major music sites in price or tune selection. iTunes recently opened its music store to Canadians. Previously, the only way for a Canadian to purchase a song from iTunes (or many of the other virtual music stores) was to use an email address that didn't end in .ca. Today not only iTunes, but also many other of these virtual music shops, are open for business to Canadians.

Online distribution of individual songs is still an unproven business model, and profits are very thin—usually about 10 percent at best. Some believe that these sites are useful more as loss leaders to help companies sell related products, such as portable music players or subscription services.

Like other countries, Canada is struggling to deal with advancing technology and its ethical and ownership issues. In Canada, 7 million people download music files, with the market for downloading music estimated at $100 million, according to the Canadian Independent Record Production Association. Several years ago, a tax was levied on blank CDs and other recording media with the proceeds to go to Canadian artists and music companies. The Copyright Board of Canada then levied a tax on MP3 players, between $2 and $25 per player based on storage capacity, but the Canadian Federal Court of Appeal ruled that the levy was illegal. "While

the Copyright Board of Canada is indeed permitted by Canada's Copyright Act to tax sales of blank media, the terms of the Act do not allow it to levy a similar fee from MP3 player makers," Justice Marc Noël said. Judge Noël said he understood the Board's need to compensate artists and copyright holders for potential lost revenue by distributing the levies it receives from sales of blank media, but the authority to impose a levy on an MP3 player still has to be found in the Copyright Act. The Canadian Private Copying Collective, which distributes the proceeds of the levies to artists and recording companies, may attempt to have the Act changed to extend the right to levy a tax to MP3 players as well as more traditional recording media.

In addition, the Canadian Recording Industry Association (CRIA) has tried repeatedly through the courts to obtain access to Internet service provider data about individuals and the sites they visit for the express purpose of tracking those who download music. To date, the CRIA has been unsuccessful. The courts have even ruled that downloading music files from peer-to-peer (P2P) sites such as Kazaa is not illegal in Canada, but that uploading such files is in fact illegal under Canadian law.

As this text is being written, legislation has been tabled in Parliament that would make it illegal to hack or break into the digital locks often used to prevent the copying of movies and software although it will remain perfectly legal in Canada to copy a CD for personal use. The legislation also sets up what is called a notice-and-notice regime to handle complaints of copyright infringement. Under this system, an Internet service provider would receive a notice from a copyright holder complaining about violations from its provider's customers. The ISP would then send a notice to that customer. But industry stakeholders say the legal action is still not tough enough. "Not only is it not as tough as we would like, it doesn't provide the adequate legal framework that we would like," says Graham Henderson, of the Canadian Recording Industry Association. "If a father or mother gets a notice from their ISP that they might be sued because of the activities of their teenaged son or daughter, you could be pretty well assured that that activity is going to change," says Jay Thomson of the Canadian Association of Internet Providers. Whether the legislation passes and how it is implemented once passed remain to be seen.

Will reduced CD prices and Apple's model be the solution for which the music industry as been searching? Will Canada's new legislation be the solution? Or will the illegal downloading of copyrighted music continue to grow? The motion picture industry is anxiously watching because, as high-speed Internet connections become more popular, it may face the same fate as the recording industry. Will the living room become a war zone for digital entertainment or a thriving marketplace shared by the creators of content and the makers of the machines that deliver it?

Sources: Nick Wingfield and Sarah McBride, "Green Light for Grokster," *Wall Street Journal*, August 20, 2004; Nick Wingfield, "Price War in Online Music," *Wall Street Journal*, August 17, 2004, and "Online Music's Latest Tune," *Wall Street Journal*, August 27, 2004; Sarah McBride, "Stop the Music!" *Wall Street Journal*, August 23, 2004; Thomas Claburn, "Feds Target Scofflaws and Spammers," *Information*

Week, August 30, 2004; Alex Veiga, "Recording Industry Sues 532 Over Swapping," Associated Press, March 23, 2004; David McGuire, "Study: File-Sharing No Threat to Music Sales," *Washington Post*, March 30, 2004; Sue Zeidler, "Sony Unveils Music Service, Mulls iPod Killer," Reuters, May 4, 2004; John Schwartz and John Markoff, "Power Players: Big Names Are Jumping into the Crowded Online Music Field," *New York Times*, January 12, 2004; Martin Peers, "Buddy Can You Spare Some Time?" *Wall Street Journal*, January 26, 2004; Ethan Smith, "Music Industry Sounds Upbeat as Losses Slow," *Wall Street Journal*, January 2, 2004; Nick Wingfield and Ethan Smith, "With the Web Shaking Up Music, a Free-for-All in Online Songs," *Wall Street Journal*, November 19, 2003, and "New Ways to Pay 99 Cents for Music," *Wall Street Journal*, October 9, 2003; Cade Metz, "The Changing Face of Online Music," *PC Magazine*, September 24, 2003; Mike France, "Music Pirates, You're Sunk," *Business Week*, August 29, 2003; Amy Harmon, "Despite Suits, Music File Sharers Shrug Off Guilt and Keep Sharing," *New York Times*, September 19, 2003; Amy Harmon, "Industry Offers a Carrot in Online Music Fight," *New York Times*, June 8, 2003; "Kazaa Stays on Track to Be Most Downloaded Program," **news.yahoo.com**, May 25, 2003; Amy Harmon, "Music Swappers Get a Message on PC Screens: Stop It Now," *New York Times*, May 19, 2003; Jane Black, "Big Music: Win Some, Lose a Lot More?" *Business Week Online*, May 5, 2003; Amy Harmon, "Suit Settled for Students Downloading Music Online," *New York Times*, May 2, 2003; Pui-Wing Tam, "Apple Launches Online Store Offering Downloadable Music," *Wall Street Journal*, April 29, 2003; Anna Wilde Mathews and Nick Wingfield, "Entertainment Industry Loses Important File-Sharing Battle," *Wall Street Journal*, April 28, 2003; Jane Black, "Digital Music: Still Scores Left to Settle," *Business Week Online*, April 22, 2003; Jane Black, "Web Music Gets Its Act Together," *Business Week Online*, April 22, 2003; Sarah D. Scalet, "The Pirates Among Us," *CIO Magazine*, April 15, 2003; David Pogue, "The Internet as Jukebox, at a Price," *New York Times Circuits*, March 6, 2003; Saul Hansell, "E-Music Settle on Prices. It's a Start," *New York Times*, March 3, 2003; Julia Angwin and Nick Wingfield, "AOL Brings Online Music to the Masses, for a Price," *Wall Street Journal*, February 26, 2003; Anne Wilde Mathews and Charles Goldsmith, "Music Industry Faces New Threats on Web," *Wall Street Journal*, February 21, 2003; Jane Black, "Big Music's Broken Record," *Business Week Online*, February 13, 2003; Laura M. Holson and Geraldine Fabrikant, "Music Industry Braces for a Shift," *New York Times*, January 13, 2003; and Matt Richtel, "Access to Free Online Music Is Seen as a Boost to Sales," *New York Times*, May 6, 2002; John Borland, "Canada Deems P2P Downloading Legal, Levies MP3 Players," December 15, 2003, ZDNet, available **www.zdnet.com.au/news/business/0,39023166, 20281795,00.htm**, accessed June 9, 2005; John Borland, "Canadian MP3 Player Tax Challenged," January 13, 2004, available **http://news.com.com/2102-1027_3-5140374.html?tag =st.util.print**, accessed June 9, 2005; "File-sharing law to be tabled next week," CTV, June 9, 2005, available **http://www.ctv.ca/servlet/ ArticleNews/story/CTVNews/1118271756635_30/?hub=SciTech**, accessed June 11, 2005.

CASE STUDY QUESTIONS

1. Apply the value chain and competitive forces models to the music recording industry.

2. What role did the Internet play in changing value propositions and the competitive environment? To what extent has it been responsible for declining CD sales? Explain your answer.

3. Analyze the response of the music recording industry to these changes. What management, organization, and technology issues affected this response?

4. What is the current business strategy of the music industry? Do you think it is viable? Is the strategy different in Canada where downloading is legal? Explain your answers.

Chapter 14

Enterprise Applications and Business Process Integration

OBJECTIVES

After completing this chapter, you will be able to:

1. Assess how enterprise systems provide value for businesses, and describe how they work.

2. Assess how supply chain management systems provide value for businesses, and explain how they work.

3. Assess how customer relationship management systems provide value for businesses, and describe how they work.

4. Describe how enterprise applications can be used in platforms for new cross-functional services.

5. Identify the challenges posed by enterprise applications, and propose management solutions.

Opening Case: Manitoba Telecom Uses CRM to make the Customer Number One

The service that Winnipeg-based Manitoba Telecom Services, Inc. (MTS) offers business and residential customers in Manitoba includes a full suite of services—from wireline voice and high-speed data services to next-generation wireless services and digital MTS TV service. Following the acquisition of Allstream (formerly AT&T Canada Long Distance Services) by MTS, a division was created to serve national business customers with connectivity, infrastructure management, and IT services. Being Canada's third largest national communications provider, MTS has revenues of approximately $2 billion and more than 7000 employees. Among Canada's communications carriers, MTS has the broadest reach with its fibre-optic broadband network extending more than 18 000 kilometres.

At the start of the twenty-first century, the telecommunications industry in Canada was undergoing significant changes, as was the rest of the world. In spite of being a leader in the Manitoba market, in 2002, MTS began to face increasing competition. Its customers could be lured away by other providers with tempting offers. MTS had to find ways to utilize the vast amount of information in its various computer systems more effectively.

Jack Riediger, business program manager for Customer One, MTS' customer relationship management (CRM) program, says, "Our main issue was that we had customer information sitting in a lot of different places. Although this situation is pretty typical of most telecom companies, our vision was to become a much more customer-focused organization."

While MTS had an excellent business sales staff, it was difficult for sales staff to obtain the information they needed to develop targeted customer solutions. Salespeople and call centre representatives had to access a variety of different legacy systems and paper files to gather the information they needed. Important information might be missed due to varying customer identification keys across systems. "We missed key cross-sell or up-sell opportunities due to incomplete information," according to Riediger. "We simply didn't have a complete view of the customer. Our salespeople had no consistent place to record information about each customer call to build the 360-degree view we needed."

MTS made a thorough analysis of a number of CRM solutions and finally, in late 2002 and early 2003, chose Siebel Systems, a leading global vendor of CRM systems. Before proceeding with the CRM solution, MTS ran models of expense reduction and revenue enhancements and calculated the net present value, rate of return on capital, and rate of return on equity.

The first phase of the CRM project was launched to approximately 350 people in its sales, marketing, and customer care divisions in early 2004, with IBM as the systems integrator. "For qualifying opportunities in corporate sales, our people are now able to easily look up a customer in only one application," Riediger states. "The sales team can be confident that they're seeing all revenue- and sales-related customer information available. This has resulted in significantly improved lead and opportunity management."

MTS's "customer master" solution contains complete profiles of its business customers. These profiles can be compared with those of the typical business customer in a specific industry, and MTS is thereby able to improve market segmentation and identify and target specific customers for additional business services. "Feedback from field salespeople and call centre reps has been positive," says Riediger. "Precall planning is significantly easier—so is opportunity qualification and after-the-fact analysis."

Not satisfied with what they have already accomplished, MTS is implementing additional CRM solutions. It integrated the CRM solution with eight legacy systems, including four that handle ordering and two for billing. Now MTS has begun using its CRM system to manage promotional campaigns. In the past, MTS could not track campaign results. Today MTS managers can see how effective a particular campaign is, adjust the campaign if time permits, and determine how well field sales and call centre representatives are performing. MTS is also assessing whether to use the CRM system to automate quotes and proposals, including product configuration. Finally, MTS is considering taking their CRM system into the realm of their consumer markets.

Sources: "Manitoba Telecom Creates Unified Customer View and Improves Campaign Effectiveness," available www.siebel.com/common/includes/pdf_frame.shtm?pdfUrl=/downloads/case_studies/manitoba.pdf, accessed May 27, 2005; www.mts.mb.ca, accessed May 27, 2005.

Manitoba Telecom Services found it could improve customer service and expand its cross-selling and up-selling offerings by implementing a customer relationship management system. It had been storing customer data in multiple systems, which made it difficult to know all the customer's interactions with the company. The system enabled MTS to integrate customer data from multiple accounts and analyze that data to provide customers with additional service and products. MTS also used the CRM system for ordering, billing, and promotional campaigns.

As a manager, you will need to know how customer relationship management and the other major enterprise applications can provide value for your organization. You will also want to know how these systems can create enterprise-wide platforms for the delivery of new services. This chapter helps you learn about customer relationship management, supply chain management, and enterprise systems, identifying the key decisions and challenges you will face in implementing and using them.

14.1　Enterprise Systems

Around the globe, companies are becoming more connected, both internally and with other companies. They want to be able to react instantaneously when a customer places a large order or when a shipment from a supplier is delayed. Managers want to know the impact of these events on every part of the business and how the business is performing at any point in time. Enterprise systems provide the integration to make this possible. Let us look at how they work and what they can do for the firm.

What Are Enterprise Systems?

Chapter 2 introduced enterprise systems, which focus on integrating the key internal business processes of the firm. These systems, which are known as *enterprise resource planning (ERP)* systems, are based on a suite of integrated software modules and a common central database. The database collects data from and feeds the data into numerous applications that can support nearly all of an organization's internal business activities. When new information is entered by one process, the information is made immediately available to other business processes (see Figure 14-1).

If a sales representative places an order for tire rims, for example, the system would verify the customer's credit limit, schedule the shipment, identify the best route, and reserve the necessary items from inventory. If inventory stock were insufficient to fill the order, the system would schedule the manufacture of more rims and order the needed materials and components from suppliers. Sales and production forecasts would be immediately updated. General ledger and corporate cash levels would be automatically updated with the revenue and cost information from the order. Users could tap into the system and find out where that particular order was at any minute. Management could obtain information at any point in time about how the business was operating. The system could also generate enterprise-wide data for management analyses of product cost and profitability.

How Enterprise Systems Work

Both the value—and the challenge—of enterprise systems can be found in the integration they force on firms' information and business processes. **Enterprise software** consists of a set of interdependent software modules that support basic internal business processes for finance and accounting, human resources, manufacturing and production (including logistics and distribution), and sales and marketing. The software enables data to be used by multiple functions and business processes for precise organizational coordination and control. Table 14-1 describes some of the business processes supported by enterprise software.

enterprise software

FIGURE 14-1   *Enterprise system architecture.*

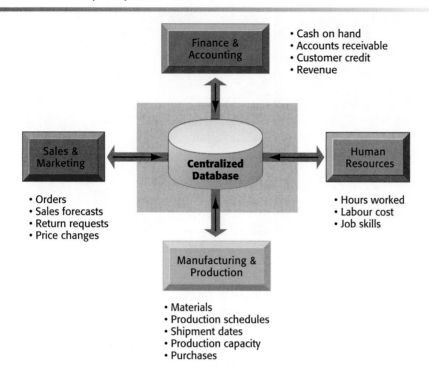

- Cash on hand
- Accounts receivable
- Customer credit
- Revenue

- Orders
- Sales forecasts
- Return requests
- Price changes

- Hours worked
- Labour cost
- Job skills

- Materials
- Production schedules
- Shipment dates
- Production capacity
- Purchases

Enterprise systems feature a set of integrated software modules and a central database that enable data to be shared by many different business processes and functional areas throughout the enterprise.

The software is developed around thousands of predefined business processes, such as those illustrated for equipment procurement in Figure 14-2. Organizations implementing this software would have to first select the functions of the system they wished to use and then map their business processes to the predefined business processes in the software.

Figure 14-2 shows a process map illustrating the procurement process for a new piece of equipment used by SAP, the leading enterprise software vendor. These process maps, or reference models, provided by enterprise software vendors are based on business process knowledge and best practices. **Best practices** are the most successful solutions or problem-solving methods for consistently and effectively achieving a business objective.

The process illustrated here is for procuring new equipment. The process map shows the steps that would need to be performed to complete the process and the roles played by the firm's maintenance engineer, material manager, and asset accountant. The SAP software automates most of the process steps, integrating the work of plant maintenance, materials management, and asset accounting.

best practices

TABLE 14-1   *Business Processes Supported by Enterprise Systems*

Financial and accounting processes, including general ledger, accounts payable, accounts receivable, fixed assets, cash management and forecasting, product-cost accounting, cost-centre accounting, asset accounting, tax accounting, credit management, and financial reporting

Human resources processes, including personnel administration, time accounting, payroll, personnel planning and development, benefits accounting, applicant tracking, time management, compensation, workforce planning, performance management, and travel expense reporting

Manufacturing and production processes, including procurement, inventory management, purchasing, shipping, production planning, production scheduling, material requirements planning, quality control, distribution, transportation execution, and plant and equipment maintenance

Sales and marketing processes, including order processing, quotations, contracts, product configuration, pricing, billing, credit checking, incentive and commission management, and sales planning

FIGURE 14-2 *Process map for procuring new equipment.*

Procurement of New Equipment
This C-Business Map illustrates the procurement process for a new piece of equipment. Through the high measure of integration between Plant Maintenance, Materials Management, and Asset Accounting, all process steps run with optimal system support and are largely automated. This guarantees a smooth process flow, as well as big time savings.

Business Benefits	Value Potentials
Automatic data comparison between assets and equipment through serialization	Up to 100% reduction in workload
Linking of material and equipment data through serialization	Up to 100% higher transparency
Depreciation of assets right from goods receipt	Up to 100% prompter postings
Automatic distribution of relevant data to all involved	Up to 60% time savings

	Maintenance Engineer	Material Manager	Asset Accountant

Inspect and process requirement modification

Select material and create order

Create purchase order

Enter asset number in purchase order

Automatic asset archiving

Receive goods: serialization and equipment created

Synchronization between equipment and asset

Withdraw goods of serialized equipment

Install and maintain equipment

Source: "Discussions with Customers"
The value potentials shown in this table have been reported by selected SAP customers or independent third parties as referenced herein. However, there is no guarantee that such value potentials can be realized in any particular customer-specific business processes, and SAP does not make any representations and disclaims any liability as to the appropriateness of the referenced value potentials for any specific customer situation.
Copyright ©SAP AG 2003.

Value Potentials	Business Benefits
Up to 50% improvement in control over costs	Integration of cost-bearing department through integrated approval process
Up to 75% more effective workflows	Comprehensive workflow connections for optimization of process flows
Up to 60% decrease in maintenance expenditure	High degree of automation for data maintenance
Up to 50% reduction in bad purchases	Direct selection of material required in maintenance order through integration with Materials Management

The process map shows how SAP enterprise software can integrate different enterprise areas into one smooth process flow for the procurement of a new piece of equipment for a maintenance engineer.

Source: © 2004 SAP AG. Used with permission. All rights reserved.

Companies could use configuration tables provided by the software to tailor a particular aspect of the system to the way it does business. For example, a firm could use these tables to select whether it wants to track revenue by product line, geographical unit, or distribution channel. SAP has more than 3000 configuration tables for its enterprise software. Identifying the organization's business processes to be automated by the system and mapping them to the processes in the enterprise software can take a great deal of effort.

If the enterprise software does not support the way the organization does business, companies can rewrite some of the software to support the way their business processes work. However, enterprise software is unusually complex, and extensive customization may degrade system performance, compromising the information and process integration that are the main benefits of the system. (In Chapter 10, we discuss in greater detail the issues raised by customizing application software packages.) If companies want to reap the maximum benefits from enterprise software, they must change the way they work to conform to the business processes in the software.

Major enterprise software vendors include SAP (see Figure 14-3), Oracle and its acquisition PeopleSoft, and Baan. There are versions of their software packages that are designed for small businesses and versions that can be obtained through application service providers over the Web. The small- and medium-sized editions of this software frequently carry price tags that are affordable for these smaller businesses while implementing these systems in larger organizations can run into the millions of dollars. Enterprise systems use a client/server architecture but have been redesigned to take advantage of the Web. Users can now access these systems through a Web browser to link to the systems of other companies. Although initially designed to automate the firm's internal "back-office" business processes, enterprise systems have become more externally oriented and are now capable of communicating with customers, suppliers, and other organizations (see Section 14.4).

Business Value of Enterprise Systems

Enterprise systems promise to integrate diverse internal business processes of a firm into a single information architecture, and that integration can have a very large payback if firms install and use enterprise software correctly. Enterprise systems can produce value both by increasing organizational efficiency and by providing firm-wide information to help managers make better decisions.

FIGURE 14-3   *SAP solution maps.*

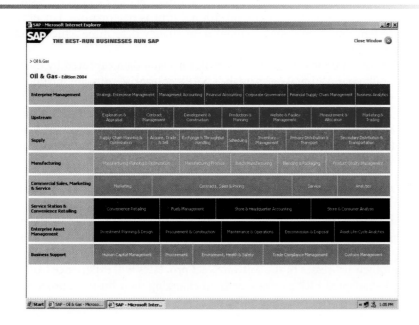

SAP, a leading enterprise software vendor, provides solution maps showing business processes supported by its software that are appropriate for specific industries. Illustrated here is a solution map for the oil and gas industry.

A More Uniform Organization Companies can use enterprise systems to support organizational structures that were not previously possible or to create a more disciplined organizational culture. For example, they might use enterprise systems to integrate the corporation across geographic or business unit boundaries or to create a more uniform organizational culture in which everyone uses similar processes and information. An enterprise-enabled organization does business the same way worldwide.

Nestlé SA, for instance, installed a SAP R/3 enterprise system as a way of standardizing and coordinating its business processes in 500 facilities in 80 countries. Nestlé management had found that decentralized management and lack of standard business processes and information technology prevented the company from leveraging its worldwide buying power to obtain lower prices for raw materials and from measuring the effectiveness of its promotional activities.

More Efficient Operations and Customer-Driven Business Processes

Enterprise systems can help create the foundation for a more customer-driven organization. By integrating discrete business processes in sales, production, finance, and logistics, the entire organization can more efficiently respond to customer requests for products or information, forecast new products, and produce and deliver them as demand requires. Manufacturing is better informed about producing only what customers have ordered, procuring exactly the right amount of components or raw materials to fill actual orders, staging production, and minimizing the time that components or finished products are in inventory.

For example, after installing an Oracle enterprise system in 1999, Lucent Microelectronics Group reduced processes that used to take 10 or 15 days to less than eight hours. It can deliver an order of silicon chips used in cell phones to customers such as Ericsson about 56 hours after that order has been received. If a plant cannot operate because of a power shortage or natural catastrophe, Lucent can shift production to another plant within eight hours. The system has helped Lucent lower its logistics costs (including warehousing, stocking, transportation, and personnel) from 1.5 percent of revenue to less than 1 percent of revenue (Laudon and Laudon 2002).

Firm-wide Information for Improved Decision Making

In addition to monitoring operational activities such as tracking the status of orders and inventory levels, enterprise systems can also improve organization-wide reporting and decision making. Enterprise systems create a single, integrated repository of data for the entire firm. The data have common, standardized definitions and formats that are accepted by the entire organization.

Performance figures mean the same thing across the company and can be provided automatically without human intervention. Senior management can more easily find out at any moment how a particular organizational unit is performing. For example, an enterprise system might help management immediately determine which products are most or least profitable.

Enterprise software includes analytical tools for using data captured by the system to evaluate overall organizational performance. SAP's enterprise software includes analytics for profitability management, product and service cost management, overhead cost management, risk management, balanced scorecard, value-based management investment planning, and other tools for giving managers a comprehensive view of firm performance. (Additional detail on performance management capabilities of enterprise systems can be found in Chapter 15.)

Issues and Challenges in Implementing Enterprise Resource Planning Systems

Enterprise-wide systems provide so many significant advantages that it is easy to overlook the many challenges and obstacles to implementing these systems. Enterprise resource planning (ERP) systems are developed for specific ways of conducting business processes, such as production or inventory control. Businesses that do not adapt their processes to the software's set processes will experience trouble. Those businesses that adapted ERP software without changing their business processes to align with the ERP system are firms that quit using ERP software or went on to develop their own—or finally changed their processes. Sobey's, the Canadian grocer, and Hershey's, one of the world's leading chocolate and candy manufacturers, are just two companies with failed ERP implementation.

ERP systems cross organizational boundaries—between departments, divisions, and even business units. They may also cross interorganizational boundaries. Each organizational unit is likely a little territorial about the way they conduct their processes and business, and each also probably wants to make decisions about what software it uses. Managing change in the face of these issues is a difficult task. For these reasons, as well as the scope and complexity of the implementation, implementing ERP systems is very difficult to do well.

14.2 Supply Chain Management Systems

Today's competitive business environment calls for companies to pay much more attention to how they manage their supply chains. Customers are insisting on greater value, faster order fulfillment, and more responsive service when they make purchases. Shorter product life cycles, global sourcing, and greater product variety have increased supply chain costs and complexity. The value chains of so many businesses are linked together that competitive advantage may be based on entire supply chains rather than individual firms. Supply chain management (SCM) today is not limited only to order fulfillment but is tied to strategic issues such as the ability to create and deliver new products or to create and implement new business models (Kopczak and Johnson 2003).

The Supply Chain

Supply chain management (SCM) is the close linkage and coordination of activities involved in buying, making, and moving a product. SCM integrates business processes to speed information, product, and fund flows up and down a supply chain to reduce time, redundant effort, and inventory costs.

The **supply chain** is a network of organizations and business processes for procuring raw materials, transforming these materials into intermediate and finished products, and distributing the finished products to customers. It links suppliers, manufacturing plants, distribution centres, retail outlets, and customers to supply goods and services from source through consumption. Materials, information, and payments flow through the supply chain in both directions. Goods start out as raw materials and move through logistics and production systems until they reach customers. Returned items flow in the reverse direction from the buyer back to the seller.

Figure 14-4 provides a simplified illustration of a supply chain, showing the flow of information and material among suppliers, manufacturers, distributors, retailers, and customers. The *upstream* portion of the supply chain includes the organization's suppliers and their suppliers and the processes for managing these relationships. The *downstream* portion consists of the organizations and processes for distributing and delivering products to the final customers. The manufacturer also manages *internal supply chain* processes for transforming the materials, components, and services furnished by suppliers into finished goods and for managing materials and inventory.

Materials flow downstream from raw material sources through manufacturing facilities that transform the raw materials into intermediate products (also referred to as components or parts). These are assembled on the next level to form finished products. The products are shipped to distribution centres and from there to retailers and customers.

The supply chain illustrated in Figure 14-4 has been simplified. Most supply chains, especially those for large manufacturers such as automakers, are multitiered, with many thousands of primary (Tier 1), secondary (Tier 2), and tertiary (Tier 3) suppliers. DaimlerChrysler, for instance, has more than 20 000 suppliers of parts, packaging, and technology. Its primary suppliers are its principal suppliers, which furnish chassis, engines, and other major automotive components. These suppliers have their own

supply chain management (SCM)
supply chain

FIGURE 14-4   *A supply chain.*

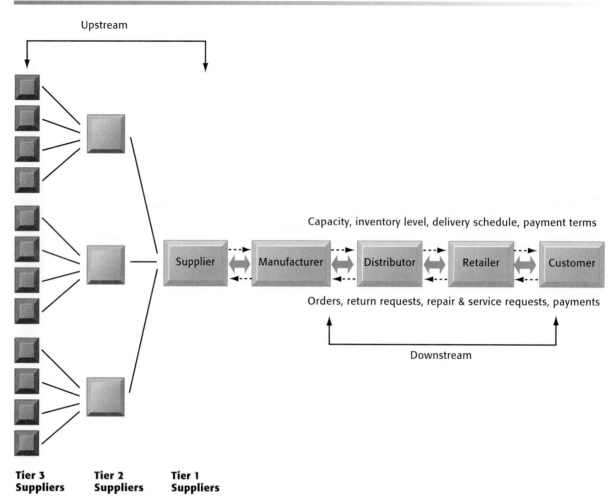

This figure illustrates the major entities in the supply chain and the flow of information upstream and downstream to coordinate the activities involved in buying, making, and moving a product. The wide arrows show the flow of materials between supply chain members, and the dotted line and arrows show the flow of information. Suppliers transform raw materials into intermediate products or components, and then manufacturers turn them into finished products. The products are shipped to distribution centres and from there to retailers and customers.

suppliers (secondary suppliers), who in turn may have their own set of suppliers (tertiary suppliers.)

Supply Chain Processes Many processes and subprocesses are involved in managing the supply chain to expedite this flow of information and materials. The Supply Chain Council (SCC) developed a supply chain operations reference model (SCOR) as a cross-industry process reference model for supply chain management. (SCC members are organizations interested in applying and advancing state-of-the-art supply chain management systems and practices.) SCOR defines a common set of supply chain processes to help companies better understand supply chain management issues and set goals for supply chain improvement. SCOR identifies five major supply chain processes: plan, source, make, deliver, and return (see Figure 14-5).

Plan: Consists of processes that balance aggregate demand and supply to develop a course of action to meet sourcing, production, and delivery requirements

Source: Consists of processes that procure goods and services needed to create a specific product or service

Make: Consists of processes that transform a product into a finished state to meet planned or actual demand

Deliver: Consists of processes that provide finished goods and services to meet actual or planned demand, including order management, transportation management, and distribution management

Return: Consists of processes associated with returning products or receiving returned products, including post-delivery customer support

Logistics plays an important role in these processes, dealing with the planning and control of all factors that will have an impact on transporting the correct product or service to where it is needed on time and at the least cost. (Logistics accounts for 12 to 14 percent of a typical manufacturer's cost of goods sold.) Supply chain management provides an opportunity to optimize the movement of materials and goods among different members of the supply chain.

To manage the supply chain, a company tries to eliminate redundant steps, delays, and the amount of resources tied up along the way as it manages relationships with other supply chain members. Information systems make supply chain management more efficient by providing information to help companies coordinate, schedule, and control procurement, production, inventory management, and delivery of products and services.

Information and Supply Chain Management

Inefficiencies in the supply chain, such as parts shortages, underutilized plant capacity, excessive finished goods inventory, or runaway transportation costs, are caused by inaccurate or untimely information. For example, manufacturers may keep too many parts in inventory because they do not know exactly when they will receive their next shipment from their suppliers. Suppliers may order too few raw materials because they do not have precise information on demand. These supply chain inefficiencies can waste as much as 25 percent of a company's operating costs.

If a manufacturer had perfect information about exactly how many units of product customers wanted, when they wanted them, and when they could be produced, it would be possible to implement a highly efficient **just-in-time** strategy. Components would arrive exactly at the moment they were needed, and finished goods would be shipped as they left the assembly line.

FIGURE 14-5 *Key supply chain management processes.*

The five supply chain management processes consist of many sub-processes performed by members of the supply chain.

logistics

just-in-time

In a supply chain, however, uncertainties arise because many events cannot be fore-seen—uncertain product demand, late shipments from suppliers, defective parts or raw material, or production process breakdowns. To satisfy customers, manufacturers often deal with such uncertainties and unforeseen events by keeping more material or products in inventory than they think they may actually need. The *safety stock* acts as a buffer for the lack of flexibility in the supply chain. Although excess inventory is expensive, low fill rates are also costly because business may be lost from cancelled orders.

One recurring problem in supply chain management is the **bullwhip effect**, in which information about the demand for a product gets distorted as it passes from one entity to the next across the supply chain (Lee, Padmanabhan, and Whang 1997). A slight rise in demand for an item might cause different members in the supply chain—distributors, manufacturers, suppliers, secondary suppliers (suppliers' suppliers), and tertiary suppli-ers (suppliers' suppliers' suppliers)—to stockpile inventory so each has enough "just in case." These changes ripple throughout the supply chain, magnifying what started out as a small change from planned orders, creating excess inventory, production, warehousing, and shipping costs (see Figure 14-6).

For example, Procter & Gamble (P&G) found it had excessively high inventories of its Pampers disposable diapers at various points along its supply chain because of distorted information. Although customer purchases in stores were fairly stable, orders from distrib-utors would spike when P&G offered aggressive price promotions. Pampers and Pampers' components accumulated in warehouses along the supply chain to meet demand that did not actually exist. To eliminate this problem, P&G revised its marketing, sales, and supply chain processes and used more accurate demand forecasting (Lee et al. 1997).

bullwhip effect

The bullwhip can be tamed by reducing uncertainties about demand and supply when all members of the supply chain have accurate and up-to-date information. If all

FIGURE 14-6   *The bullwhip effect.*

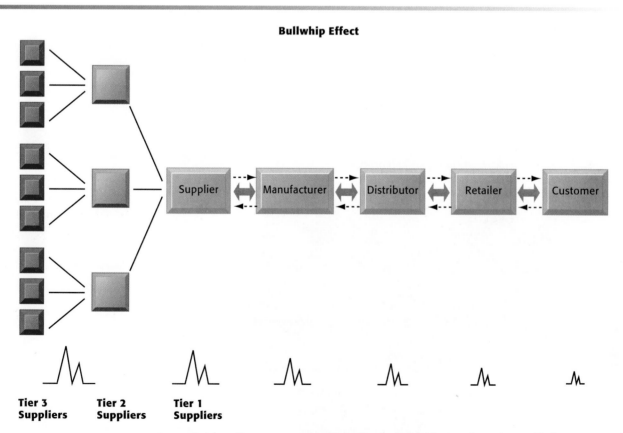

Bullwhip Effect

Supplier — Manufacturer — Distributor — Retailer — Customer

Tier 3 Suppliers   **Tier 2 Suppliers**   **Tier 1 Suppliers**

Inaccurate information can cause minor fluctuations in demand for a product to be amplified as one moves fur-ther back in the supply chain. Minor fluctuations in retail sales for a product can create excess inventory for dis-tributors, manufacturers, and suppliers.

members of the supply chain could share dynamic information about inventory levels, schedules, forecasts, and shipments, they would have a more precise idea of how to adjust their sourcing, manufacturing, and distribution plans. Supply chain management systems provide the kind of information that can help members of the supply chain make better purchasing and scheduling decisions.

Supply Chain Management Applications

The central objective of supply chain management systems is information visibility—open and rapid communication and information sharing between members of the supply chain. Correct movement of accurate information makes it possible to time orders, shipments, and production properly to minimize stocking levels and expedite deliveries to customers. Supply chain management systems automate the flow of information between a company and its supply chain partners so they can make better decisions to optimize their performance.

In essence, supply chain software can be classified as either software to help businesses plan their supply chains (supply chain planning) or software to help them execute the supply chain steps (supply chain execution). **Supply chain planning systems** enable the firm to generate demand forecasts for a product and to develop sourcing and manufacturing plans for that product. These systems help companies make better operating decisions, such as determining how much of a specific product to manufacture in a given time period; establishing inventory levels for raw materials, intermediate products, and finished goods; determining where to store finished goods; and identifying the transportation mode to use for product delivery.

For example, if a large customer places a larger order than usual or changes that order on short notice, it can have a widespread impact throughout the supply chain. Additional raw materials or a different mix of raw materials may be needed from suppliers. Manufacturing may have to change job scheduling. A transportation carrier may have to reschedule deliveries. Supply chain planning software makes the necessary adjustments to production and distribution plans. Information about changes is shared among the relevant supply chain members so that their work can be coordinated. One of the most important—and complex—supply chain planning functions is **demand planning**, which determines how much product a business needs to make to satisfy all of its customers' demands (see Figure 14-7).

Additional material on health care supply chain management can be found on the Companion Website.

FIGURE 14-7   *PeopleSoft Demand Forecasting software.*

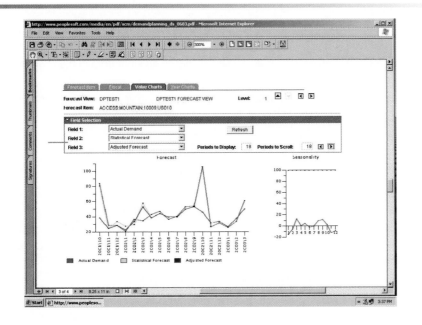

PeopleSoft Demand Forecasting software enables users to create forecasts based on statistical analyses of demand history, causal factors such as promotional events and new product introductions, and input from other members of the organization or trading partners.

supply chain planning systems

demand planning

FIGURE 14-8   *PeopleSoft Supply Planning software.*

PeopleSoft Supply Planning software enables users to view ongoing material requirements and available capacity data to help quickly identify potential shortages or capacity issues and respond in a timely manner.

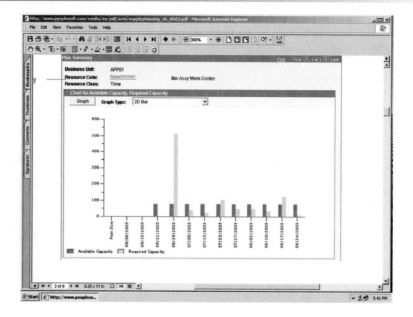

Supply chain execution systems manage the flow of products through distribution centres and warehouses to ensure that products are delivered to the right locations in the most efficient manner (see Figure 14-8). They track the physical status of goods, the management of materials, warehouse and transportation operations, and financial information involving all parties. Table 14-2 provides more details on supply chain planning and execution systems.

supply chain execution systems

TABLE 14-2 *Supply Chain Planning and Execution Systems*

CAPABILITIES OF SUPPLY CHAIN PLANNING SYSTEMS

Order planning: Select an order fulfillment plan that best meets the desired level of service to the customer given existing transportation and manufacturing constraints.

Advanced scheduling and manufacturing planning: Provide detailed coordination of scheduling based on analysis of changing factors, such as customer orders, equipment outages, or supply interruptions. Scheduling modules create job schedules for the manufacturing process and supplier logistics.

Demand planning: Generate demand forecasts from all business units using statistical tools and business forecasting techniques.

Distribution planning: Create operating plans for logistics managers for order fulfillment, based on input from demand and manufacturing planning modules.

Transportation planning: Track and analyze inbound, outbound, and intracompany movement of materials and products to ensure that materials and finished goods are delivered at the right time and place at the minimum cost.

CAPABILITIES OF SUPPLY CHAIN EXECUTION SYSTEMS

Order commitments: Enable vendors to quote accurate delivery dates to customers by providing more real-time detailed information on the status of orders from availability of raw materials and inventory to production and shipment status.

Final production: Organize and schedule final subassemblies required to make each final product.

Replenishment: Coordinate component replenishment work so that warehouses remain stocked with the minimum amount of inventory in the pipeline.

Distribution management: Coordinate the process of transporting goods from the manufacturer to distribution centres to the final customer. Provide online customer access to shipment and delivery data.

Reverse distribution: Track the shipment and accounting for returned goods or remanufactured products.

Supply Chain Performance Measurement Companies need to be able to measure the performance of their supply chain management efforts using objective performance information. A number of metrics can be used to evaluate the performance of supply chain processes, and supply chain management systems can provide the data for them. A **metric** is a standard measurement of performance. Important metrics for measuring supply chain performance include the fill rate (the ability to fill orders by the due date), the average time from order to delivery, the number of days of supply in inventory, forecast accuracy, and the cycle time for sourcing and making a product. (Cycle time is the total elapsed time to complete a business process.)

Companies may not necessarily excel in all these areas, but management should choose the operations that are most critical for the success of the firm and focus on metrics that measure their performance. Although large software vendors have tools for automating many of the most important supply chain processes, no software package or set of tools does everything. The specific supply chain management objectives for each company should determine which supply chain management package or set of software tools to use.

Supply Chain Management and the Internet

In the pre-Internet environment, supply chain coordination was hampered by the difficulties of making information flow smoothly among disparate internal supply chain systems for purchasing, materials management, manufacturing, and distribution. It was also difficult to share information with external supply chain partners because the systems of suppliers, distributors, and logistics providers were based on incompatible technology platforms and standards. Enterprise systems could supply some integration of internal supply chain processes, but they were not designed to deal with external supply chain processes.

Some supply chain integration can be supplied inexpensively using Internet technology. Firms can use *intranets* to improve coordination among their internal supply chain processes, and they can use *extranets* to coordinate supply chain processes shared with their business partners (see Figure 14-9).

Using intranets and extranets, all members of the supply chain can instantly communicate with each other, using up-to-date information to adjust purchasing, logistics, manufacturing, packaging, and schedules. A manager can use a Web interface to tap into

FIGURE 14-9 *Intranets and extranets for supply chain management.*

Intranets can be used to integrate information from isolated business processes within the firm to help them manage their internal supply chains. Access to these private intranets can also be extended to authorized suppliers, distributors, logistics services, and, sometimes, to retail customers to improve coordination of external supply chain processes.

metric

suppliers' systems to determine whether inventory and production capabilities match demand for the firm's products. Business partners can use Web-based supply chain management tools to collaborate online on forecasts. Sales representatives can access suppliers' production schedules and logistics information to monitor customers' order status. The low cost of providing this information with Web-based tools instead of costly proprietary systems encourages companies to share critical business information with a greater number of suppliers.

Global Supply Chain Issues As more and more companies outsource manufacturing operations, obtain supplies from other countries, and sell abroad, they must operate supply chains extending across multiple countries and regions. Global supply chains typically span greater geographic distances and time differences than domestic supply chains, with participants from many different countries. The Internet provides a standard set of tools that can be used by companies all over the world to coordinate overseas sourcing, transportation, communications, financing, and compliance with customs regulations.

Demand-Driven Supply Chains: from Push to Pull Manufacturing and Efficient Customer Response Internet-based supply chain management applications are clearly changing the way businesses work internally and with each other. In addition to reducing costs, these supply chain management systems facilitate efficient customer response, enabling the workings of the business to be driven more by customer demand. (Efficient customer response systems were introduced in Chapter 3)

Earlier supply chain management systems were driven by a push-based model (also known as *build-to-stock*). In a **push-based model**, production master schedules are based on forecasts or best guesses of demand for products, and products are "pushed" to customers. With new flows of information made possible by Web-based tools, supply chain management can more easily follow a **pull-based model**. In a pull-based model, also known as a *demand-driven model* or *build-to-order*, actual customer orders or purchases trigger events in the supply chain. Transactions to produce and deliver only what customers have ordered move up the supply chain from retailers to distributors to manufacturers and eventually to suppliers. Only products to fulfill these orders move back down the supply chain to the retailer. Manufacturers would use only actual order demand information to drive their production schedules and the procurement of components or raw materials, as illustrated in Figure 14-10. Wal-Mart's continuous replenishment system and Dell Computer's build-to-order system, both described in Chapter 3, are examples of the pull-based model.

FIGURE 14-10 *Push- versus pull-based supply chain models.*

The difference between push- and pull-based models is summarized by the slogan "Make what we sell, not sell what we make."

Push-Based Model

Supplier	Manufacturer	Distributor	Retailer	Customer
Supply to forecast	Production based on forecasts	Inventory based on forecasts	Stock based on forecasts	Purchase what is on shelves

Pull-Based Model

Supplier	Manufacturer	Distributor	Retailer	Customer
Supply to order	Produce to order	Automatically replenish warehouse	Automatically replenish stock	Customer orders

push-based model
pull-based model

The Internet and Internet technology make it possible to move from sequential supply chains, where information and materials flow sequentially from company to company, to concurrent supply chains, where information flows in many directions simultaneously among members of a supply chain network. Members of the network can immediately adjust to changes in schedules or orders. Ultimately, the Internet could create a "digital logistics nervous system" throughout the supply chain. This system would permit simultaneous, multidirectional communication of information about participants' inventories, orders, and capacities and would work to optimize the activities of individual firms and groups of firms interacting in e-commerce marketplaces (see Figure 14-11).

Business Value of Supply Chain Management Systems

Supply chain management systems enable firms to streamline both their internal and external supply chain processes and provide management with more accurate information about what to produce, store, and move. By implementing a networked and integrated supply chain management system, companies can match supply to demand, reduce inventory levels, improve delivery service, speed product time to market, and use assets more effectively. Companies that excel in supply chain management have been found to produce higher rates of growth in their market value than the average for their industries (D'Avanzo, von Lewinski, and Van Wassenhove 2003). Effective supply chain management systems enhance organizational performance in the following areas:

1. *Improved customer service and responsiveness.* If a product is not available when a customer wants it, that customer will likely try to purchase it from someone else. Having the right product at the right place at the right time can increase sales.

2. *Cost reduction.* Supply chain management can help companies contain, and often reduce, some or all of the costs associated with moving a product through the supply chain. These costs include material acquisition, inventory carrying, transportation, and planning costs. (Inventory carrying costs may amount to 30 or 40 percent of the value of the entire inventory.) Total supply chain costs represent the majority of operating expenses for many businesses and in some industries approach 75 percent of the total operating budget (Handfield and Nichols 1999). Reducing supply chain costs can thus have a major impact on firm profitability.

FIGURE 14-11   *The future Internet-driven supply chain.*

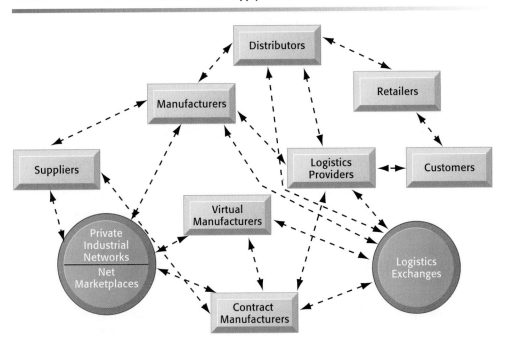

The future Internet-driven supply chain operates like a digital logistics nervous system. It provides multidirectional communication among firms, networks of firms, and e-marketplaces so that entire networks of supply chain partners can immediately adjust inventories, orders, and capacities.

3. *Cash utilization.* The sooner a company delivers a product, the sooner that company will get paid. Companies leading in supply chain efficiency have cash available two to three months faster than companies that do not have this capability.

14.3 Customer Relationship Management Systems

Businesses have always valued their customers, but today there is much greater appreciation of the importance of customers for the profitability of the enterprise. Because competitive advantage based on an innovative new product or service can be very short lived, companies are realizing that their only enduring competitive strength may be their relationships with their customers. Some say that the basis of competition has switched from who sells the most products and services to who "owns" the customer and those customer relationships represent the firm's most valuable asset.

Customer Relationship Management and Partner Relationship Management

Many firms are turning to **customer relationship management (CRM)** to maximize the benefits of their customer assets. Customer relationship management is both a business and technology discipline for managing customer relationships to optimize revenue, profitability, customer satisfaction, and customer retention. It uses information technology to track all of the ways in which a company interacts with its customers and to analyze these interactions to maximize the lifetime value of customers for the company while simultaneously maximizing satisfaction for the customers. The three primary objectives of CRM are acquiring new customers, retaining current customers, and enhancing the profitability of current customers.

Different customers represent different levels of profit for the firm. Some customers cost a great deal to attract and to service while others cost very little to service and to attract for large purchases. Customer relationship management helps organizations identify customers who cost little to attract and keep and who provide the greatest revenues for every marketing or customer service dollar spent. These "good" customers represent about 80 to 90 percent of a company's profits, but they represent only 10 to 20 percent of the company's customer base.

CRM also focuses on ways of retaining profitable customers and maximizing lifetime revenue from them. It can cost up to six times as much to acquire a new customer as to keep an old customer. These figures vary by industry, but higher customer retention rates generally increase revenues and reduce costs for the firm.

Customer relationship management extends to a firm's business partners, which are responsible for selling to customers. **Partner relationship management (PRM)** uses many of the same data, tools, and systems as customer relationship management to enhance collaboration between a company and its selling partners. If a company does not sell directly to customers but rather works through distributors or retailers, PRM helps these channels sell to customers directly. It provides a company and its selling partners with the ability to trade information and distribute leads and data about customers, integrating lead generation, pricing, promotions, order configurations, and availability. It also provides a firm with tools to assess its partners' performance so it can make sure its best partners receive the support they need to close more business.

customer relationship management (CRM)

partner relationship management (PRM)

Customer Relationship Management Applications

Although companies have always talked about putting customers first, until recently, their information systems could not help them with this goal. Pieces of customer data were often fragmented in isolated systems serving finance, distribution, sales, service, and marketing or organized around a product line, line of business, or communication channel. E-commerce generated massive amounts of data about customers and prospects that could not be integrated with the data in compartmentalized information systems.

Customer relationship management (CRM) systems were designed to address these problems by providing information and tools to deliver superior customer experience and to maximize customer lifetime value for the firm. CRM systems capture and integrate customer data from all over the organization, consolidating the data, analyzing the data, and then distributing the results to various systems and customer touch points across the enterprise. A **touch point** (also known as a contact point) is a method of interaction with the customer, such as telephone, email, customer service desk, conventional mail, Web site, or retail store.

Well-designed CRM systems can provide a single enterprise view of customers that can be used for improving both sales and customer service. CRM systems can likewise provide customers with a single view of the company regardless of what touch point the customer uses.

Customer Relationship Management (CRM) Software

Commercial customer relationship management (CRM) software packages can range from niche tools that perform limited functions, such as personalizing Web sites for specific customers, to large-scale enterprise applications that capture myriad interactions with customers, analyze them with sophisticated reporting tools, and link to other major enterprise applications, such as supply chain management and enterprise systems. The more comprehensive CRM packages contain modules for partner relationship management (PRM) and **employee relationship management (ERM)**. Employee relationship management software deals with employee issues that are closely related to CRM, such as setting objectives, employee performance management, performance-based compensation, and employee training.

Major CRM application software vendors include Siebel Systems, Clarify, and Salesforce.com. Enterprise software vendors such as SAP, Oracle, and Baan are also active in customer relationship management and feature tools for integrating their enterprise system modules with their customer relationship management modules.

Customer relationship management systems typically provide software and online tools for sales, customer service, and marketing. Their capabilities include the following:

Sales Force Automation (SFA)   Sales force automation modules in CRM systems help sales staff increase their productivity by focusing sales efforts on the most profitable customers, those who are good candidates for sales and services. CRM systems provide sales prospect and contact information, product information, product configuration capabilities, and sales quote generation capabilities. SFA software can assemble information about a particular customer's past purchases to help the salesperson make personalized recommendations. CRM software enables customer and prospect information to be shared easily among sales, marketing, and delivery departments. It increases each salesperson's efficiency in reducing the cost per sale as well as the cost of acquiring new customers and retaining old ones. CRM software also has capabilities for sales forecasting, territory management, and team selling.

Customer Service   Customer service modules in CRM systems provide information and tools to make call centres, help desks, and customer support staff more efficient. They have capabilities for assigning and managing customer service requests.

One such capability is an appointment or advice telephone line: When a customer calls a standard phone number, the system routes the call to the correct service person, who inputs information about that customer into the system only once. Once the customer's data are in the system, any service representative can handle the customer relationship. Improved access to consistent and accurate customer information can help call centres handle more calls per day and decrease the duration of each call. Thus, call centres and customer service groups can achieve greater productivity, reduced transaction time, and higher quality of service at lower cost. The customer is happier because he or she spends less time on the phone restating his or her problem to customer service.

touch point

employee relationship management (ERM)

CRM systems may also include Web-based self-service capabilities; the company Web site can be set up to provide inquiring customers personalized support information as well as the option to contact customer service staff by phone for additional assistance.

Marketing   Customer relationship management systems support direct-marketing campaigns by providing capabilities for capturing prospect and customer data, for providing product and service information, for qualifying leads for targeted marketing, and for scheduling and tracking direct-marketing mailings or email. Marketing modules would also include tools for analyzing marketing and customer data—identifying profitable and unprofitable customers, designing products and services to satisfy specific customer needs and interests, and identifying opportunities for cross-selling, up-selling, and bundling.

Cross-selling is the marketing of complementary products to customers. (For example, in financial services, a customer with a chequing account might be sold a money market account or a home improvement loan.) **Up-selling** is the marketing of higher-value products or services to new or existing customers. (An example might be a credit card company persuading a good customer to upgrade from a conventional credit card to a "platinum" card with a larger credit line, additional services—and a higher annual fee.)

Bundling is one kind of cross-selling in which a combination of products is sold as a bundle at a price lower than the total cost of the individual products. For example, Rogers Communications sells bundled services that include wireless telephone service, cable television service, and cable access to the Internet. CRM tools also help firms manage and execute marketing campaigns at all stages, from planning to determining the rate of success for each campaign.

Figure 14-12 illustrates the most important capabilities for sales, service, and marketing processes that would be found in major CRM software products. Like enterprise software, this software is business-process driven, incorporating hundreds of business processes thought to represent best practices in each of these areas.

FIGURE 14-12   *CRM software capabilities.*

The major CRM software products support business processes in sales, service, and marketing, integrating customer information from many different sources. Included are support for both the operational and analytic aspects of CRM.

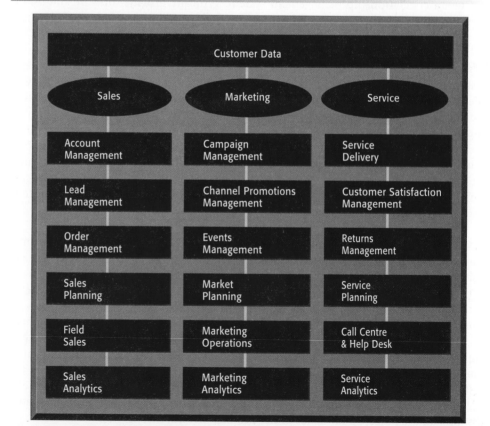

cross-selling
up-selling
bundling

Siebel Systems, the market-leading vendor of customer relationship management software, provides both generic and industry-specific best practices for its software. In addition to codifying best practices for sales, marketing, and service processes that are common across all industries, Siebel has identified and modelled business processes representing best practices for more than 20 specific industries and industry segments, including best practices in finance, consumer goods, and communication and media. To achieve maximum benefit from implementing Siebel software, companies would revise and model their business processes to correspond to the best practice business processes for CRM in the Siebel system.

Figure 14-13 illustrates how a best practice for increasing customer loyalty through customer service might be modelled by CRM software. Directly servicing customers provides firms with opportunities to increase customer retention by singling out profitable long-term customers for preferential treatment. CRM software can assign each customer a score based on that person's value and loyalty to the company and provide that information to help call centres route each customer's service request to agents who can best handle that customer's needs. The system would automatically provide the service agent with a detailed profile of that customer that included his or her score for value and loyalty. The service agent could use this information to present special offers or additional service to the customer to encourage the customer to keep transacting business with the company. Table 14-3 describes other best practice business processes in the Siebel CRM system.

Operational and Analytical CRM

All of the applications we have just described support either the operational or analytical aspects of customer relationship management. **Operational CRM** includes customer-facing applications such as tools for sales force automation, call centre and customer service support, and marketing automation. **Analytical CRM** includes applications that analyze customer data generated by operational CRM applications to provide information for improving business performance management. Table 14-4 provides more specific examples of operational and analytical CRM functions.

Analytical CRM applications are based on data warehouses that consolidate the data from operational CRM systems and customer touch points for use with online analytical processing (OLAP), data mining, and other data analysis techniques (see Chapters 6 and 15). Customer data collected by the organization might be combined with data from other sources, such as customer lists for direct marketing campaigns purchased from

operational CRM
analytical CRM

FIGURE 14-13   Customer loyalty management process map

This process map shows how a best practice for promoting customer loyalty through customer service would be modelled by customer relationship management software. The CRM software helps firms identify high-value customers for preferential treatment.

TABLE 14-3 Examples of Best Practice Business Processes in the Siebel CRM System

BUSINESS PROCESS	DESCRIPTION
Priority-based lead qualification and distribution	Evaluates and scores leads, providing scripted assessment guides to enable sales agents to focus on the leads with the highest potential value.
Integrated customer order management	Automates the workflow for order management, including designing a customer solution, developing a detailed product configuration, applying correct pricing and contract terms, and entering and shipping the order.
Real-time offer optimization	Ensures that the optimal marketing offer is presented to a customer.
Value-based customer segmentation	Enables marketing organizations to deliver different offers and services based on current and potential customer value.
Contact strategy-based targeting	Enables marketing organizations to define and consistently enforce across the enterprise policies governing the types and frequencies of communications with customers. Ensures compliance with customer privacy and communication preferences.
Rules-based service order fulfillment	Ensures that service orders are fulfilled in an order based on the lifetime value of the customer and the specific details of that customer's service agreement.
Value-based service coverage	Ensures that an organization's highest-value customers are routed to the most-qualified customer service agents.

other companies or demographic data. This data could be analyzed to identify buying patterns, to create segments for targeted marketing, and to pinpoint profitable and unprofitable customers (see Figure 14-14). Analytical CRM could also create individual customer profiles showing each person's accounts, transactions with the business, and known interests or preferences.

Retailers could use the customer knowledge gleaned from analytical CRM to make recommendations across sales channels. Multichannel customers are known to have a higher lifetime value than single-channel customers. With multichannel customer data analysis, businesses can identify patterns, such as customers who like to use the Web to view products but then visit a retail store to purchase the product. To sell to this type of customer, businesses might email a coupon to be redeemed at a physical store. Conversely, retailers could use knowledge of multichannel customers' offline purchases to tailor promotions that enhance their online shopping.

TABLE 14-4 Examples of Operational Versus Analytical CRM

OPERATIONAL CRM	ANALYTICAL CRM
Campaign management	Develop customer segmentation strategies
E-marketing	Develop customer profiles
Account and contact management	Analyze customer profitability
Lead management	Analyze product profitability
Telemarketing	Identify cross-selling and up-selling opportunities
Teleselling	Select the best marketing, service, and sales channels for each customer group
E-selling	Identify trends in sales cycle length, win rate, and average deal size
Field sales	Analyze service resolution times, service levels based on communication channel, and service activity by product line and account
Field service dispatch	Analyze leads generated and conversion rates
Customer care and help desk	Analyze sales representative and customer service representative productivity
Contract management	Identify churn problems

FIGURE 14-14   *Analytical CRM data warehouse.*

Analytical CRM uses a customer data warehouse and tools to analyze customer data collected from the firm's customer touch points and from other sources.

Business Value of Customer Relationship Management Systems

Companies with effective customer relationship management systems can realize many benefits, including increased customer satisfaction, reduced direct marketing costs, more effective marketing, and lower costs for customer acquisition and retention. Information from CRM systems can increase sales revenue by identifying the most profitable customers and segments for focused marketing, cross-selling, and up-selling.

Customer churn is reduced as sales, service, and marketing better respond to customer needs. The **churn rate** measures the number of customers who stop using or purchasing products or services from a company. It is an important indicator of the growth or decline of a firm's customer base.

The Window on Organizations illustrates how customer relationship systems have provided value for automotive dealers. Both Mercedes-Benz Canada and Saab Cars U.S.A. invested in customer relationship management systems to help them compete for customers in the crowded premium automotive market. Both had been hampered by fragmented customer data and uncoordinated processes for dealing with customers.

FIGURE 14-15   *Customer relationship management software.*

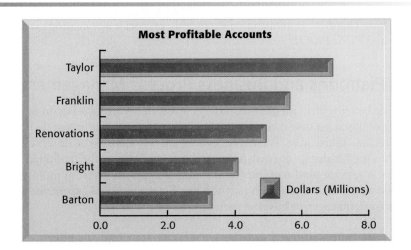

Customer relationship management software provides analytical tools to help firms identify their most important customers, predict future buying patterns, and position the correct resources to increase sales.

churn rate

The Importance of CRM Performance Measurement A company's decision about which customer-related activities to measure, how costs are assigned to the activities, and the manner in which the activities are assigned back to customers can have a huge impact on profitability calculations. Some companies that invest in CRM have little or no idea of their return on investment (ROI). They fail to create measurements of current performance or set targets for improved performance with the new CRM system. Successful CRM implementations require that financial and operational goals and the metrics to evaluate them be clearly defined at the beginning of the project. Metrics for customer relationship management might include the cost per lead, cost per sale, number of repeat customers, reduction of churn, or sales closing rate.

Another important metric is the **customer lifetime value (CLTV)**. CLTV is based on the relationship between the revenue produced by a specific customer, the expenses incurred in acquiring and servicing that customer, and the expected life of the relationship between the customer and the company (Sabri 2003). CLTV represents the difference between revenues and expenses minus the cost of promotional marketing used to retain an account; the value of this amount is expressed in today's dollars. (See the discussion of net present value in Chapter 11.)

14.4 Enterprise Integration Trends

Businesses are now pursuing even greater degrees of cross-functional process integration than that supplied by the traditional enterprise applications. They want to make customer relationship management, supply chain management, and enterprise systems work closely with each other, and they want to link these systems tightly with those of customers, suppliers, and business partners. Businesses also want to obtain more value from enterprise applications, Web services, and other integration technologies by using them as platforms for new enterprise-wide services.

Extending Enterprise Software

Enterprise software has become more flexible and capable of integration with other systems. The major enterprise software vendors have developed Web-enabled software for customer relationship management, supply chain management, decision support, enterprise portals, and other business functions that integrate with their enterprise software to create what they call "enterprise solutions," "business suites," "enterprise suites," or "e-business suites." SAP's mySAP and Oracle's e-Business Suite are examples. The enterprise vendors also provide middleware and tools that use XML and Web services for integrating enterprise systems with older legacy applications and systems from other vendors (see Chapters 5 and 10).

Enterprise software vendors are refashioning their architectures to be more Web-centric so that core systems can work with the Internet, and extended supply chains, CRM systems, and new business-to-business (B2B) and business-to-consumer (B2C) e-commerce models. This new generation of extended enterprise applications is sometimes referred to as *XRP* or *ERP II.*

Service Platforms and Business Process Management

Firms seeking better returns on their technology investments are focusing on ways to create entire services based on new or improved business processes that integrate information from multiple functional areas. These services are built on enterprise-wide service platforms that provide a greater degree of cross-functional integration than the traditional enterprise applications. A **service platform** integrates multiple applications from multiple business functions, business units, or business partners to deliver a seamless experience for the customer, employee, manager, or business partner.

CRM Drives Sales at Mercedes-Benz Canada and Saab USA

Mercedes-Benz and Saab are both premium automobile brands, with large followings of loyal customers. However, both operate in a highly competitive market space with larger rivals launching aggressive marketing campaigns, price incentives, and inexpensive financing offers. Generating showroom traffic is a constant challenge. Instead of spending more on advertising, Mercedes-Benz Canada and Saab U.S.A. turned to customer relationship management to fight back.

Toronto-based Mercedes-Benz Canada, with a network of 55 dealers, believed it did not know enough about its customers. Dealers provided customer data to the automaker on an ad hoc basis. Mercedes did not force dealers to report this information, and its process for tracking dealers that failed to report was cumbersome.

Georgia-based Saab U.S.A., a subsidiary of the Swedish company Saab Automobile AB, imports and distributes more than 37 000 Saab sedans, wagons, and convertibles to 200 U.S. dealerships. Saab had been engaging customers through three channels: its dealer network, a customer assistance centre dealing with service inquiries from Saab owners, and a lead management centre handling marketing and information requests from prospective customers.

Each of Saab's channels maintained customer data in its own database, leaving the company with a splintered view of its customers. The customer assistance centre relied on a SQL server database to manage customer information; dealers kept customer data in their own lead management systems; and Saab stored lead data in other internal systems as well as in systems run by third-party vendors. The company had about 3 million records and 55 files at three different vendors.

Fragmentation of customer data meant that a prospective customer might receive a direct mail offer from Saab one week and an email with an unrelated offer from a third-party marketing vendor the next week. The local dealer might not know about either of these offers and consequently deliver an ineffective pitch when the prospect visited the showroom.

Saab had no integrated lead management process. Saab salespeople received leads from Saab's lead management centre by fax. The leads then had to be manually reentered into the dealership's own lead management systems, a time-consuming and error-prone process. Lead quality was highly variable so many dealers simply ignored the leads. Follow-up to leads was often slow, and the company had no way of tracking leads faxed to its dealers.

Mercedes-Benz Canada sought a solution that would increase customer loyalty through personalized service and targeted marketing campaigns. The company chose Napoleon CRM software for automotive dealers sold by Strategic Connections.

Using its new CRM system, Mercedes-Benz Canada can determine, for example, which customers purchased earlier diesel cars and can send those buyers information about its new E Class diesel vehicle. The system helps salespeople at the dealerships create personalized brochures of vehicles for customers. If the customer does not want to purchase on the first showroom visit, that person can take home leasing, finance, and product specifications for the car that is of interest. The information is stored and made available on the Mercedes Web site for the prospective customer as well. The system also notifies salespeople to follow up with a potential customer in a set number of days or weeks.

Saab U.S.A. implemented three CRM applications from Siebel Systems' Automotive Dealer Integration Set. In January 2002, Saab implemented Siebel Call Center for 45 employees in a new customer interaction centre, which combined the former customer assistance centre and lead management groups. This application provides the customer interaction centre staff with a full view of each customer, including prior service-related questions and all the marketing communication they have received.

In July 2002, Saab rolled out Siebel Dealer to its 220 U.S. dealers. This application provides Saab dealers with a Web-based solution for coordinating sales and marketing activities. Sales leads generated by the customer interaction centre are delivered rapidly by this system to the right salespeople at the right dealerships. Saab salespeople now receive qualified leads through Siebel Dealer rather than faxes.

The system provides detailed information to evaluate each lead more effectively. Saab can track the status of referred leads by monitoring events such as the salesperson's initial call to the customer and the scheduling and completion of a test drive. Saab can use this information to measure the sales results of specific leads, recommend better selling techniques, and target leads more precisely. Since the CRM system was implemented, Saab's follow-up rate on sales leads has increased from 38 to 50 percent, and customer satisfaction has risen from 69 percent to 75 percent.

To Think About: How did CRM systems provide value for both of these companies? What management, organization, and technology issues had to be addressed when these companies implemented their CRM systems?

Sources: Lisa Picarille, "Planes, Trains, and Automobiles," *Customer Relationship Management Magazine*, February 2004; "Saab Cars USA Increases Lead Follow-Up from 38 Percent to 50 Percent with Siebel Automotive," www.siebel.com, accessed May 4, 2004; and Ginger Conlon, "Driving Sales," *Customer Relationship Management Magazine*, July 1, 2003.

For instance, the order-to-cash process involves receiving an order and seeing it all the way through to obtaining payment for the order. This process begins with lead generation, marketing campaigns, and order entry, which are typically supported by CRM systems. Once the order is received, manufacturing is scheduled, and parts availability is verified— processes that are usually supported by enterprise software. The order then is handled by processes for distribution planning, warehousing, order fulfillment, and shipping, which are usually supported by supply chain management systems. Finally, the order is billed to the customer, which is handled by either enterprise financial applications or accounts receivable. If the purchase at some point required customer service, customer relationship management systems would again be invoked.

A service such as order-to-cash requires data from enterprise applications and financial systems to be further integrated into an enterprise-wide composite process. To accomplish this goal, firms need a business process management plan and application integration software that ties the various pieces together. **Business process management** is a methodology for dealing with the organization's need to change its business processes continually to remain competitive. It includes tools for creating models of improved processes that can be translated into software systems. Because most companies are unlikely to jettison their existing customer relationship management, supply chain management, enterprise, and home-grown legacy systems, software tools that could use existing applications as building blocks for new cross-enterprise processes would also be required (see Figure 14-16).

The major enterprise application vendors now have tools for creating cross-application sets of services from existing systems. SAP's version of cross-application services is called xApps. xApps enables businesses to develop and automate new cross-functional, end-to-end processes atop existing applications, regardless of the technology platform they use. xApps uses Web services standards to pull together data from the firm's SAP software suite, from internal legacy systems, or from external systems for use in new business processes that span multiple functions and application areas. The software synchronizes with the existing business processes embedded in these systems. (Chapters 5 and 10 provide more detail on Web services and how the technology supports enterprise integration.) SAP now has prepackaged xApps for mergers and acquisitions, new product launches, and resource and program management. Similar tools from other enterprise vendors include Siebel's Universal Application Network and PeopleSoft's AppConnect.

FIGURE 14-16 *Order-to-cash service.*

Order-to-cash service is a composite process that integrates data from individual enterprise systems and legacy financial applications. The process must be modelled and translated into a software system using application integration tools.

business process management

Increasingly, these new services will be delivered through portals. Today's portal products can provide frameworks for building new composite services. Portal software can integrate information from enterprise applications and disparate in-house legacy systems, presenting it to users through a Web interface so that the information appears to be coming from a single source.

Management Opportunities, Challenges, and Solutions

Implementing an enterprise application is above all a business decision rather than a technology decision. Companies need to be sure that they are defining a problem that a customer relationship management, supply chain management, or enterprise system can solve. It is also critical for organizations to know how much integration they want and what the organization will look and feel like when it is achieved. These systems can provide enormous value if managers understand—and can deal with—their challenges.

Opportunities

Both the promise and the peril of enterprise applications lie in their power to fundamentally change the way the organization works. Over time, most firms obtain extraordinary business value from enterprise applications because of their power to improve process coordination and management decision making. Promises of dramatic reductions in inventory costs and order-to-delivery time, as well as more efficient customer response and higher product and customer profitability make these applications very attractive. But to obtain this value, firms must clearly understand how their business has to change to use these systems effectively.

Management Challenges

Although enterprise applications can improve organizational coordination, efficiency, and decision making, they are difficult to develop and use successfully. A very high percentage (as much as 70 percent) of companies investing in enterprise systems or systems for supply chain management or customer relationship management have not realized the promised benefits on schedule or have spent much more on these systems than originally anticipated. Enterprise applications involve complex pieces of software and large investments of time, money, and expertise. These systems pose multiple challenges: high total cost of ownership (TCO), extensive organizational change, and difficulty realizing strategic value. Managers who are aware of these challenges at the outset can plan accordingly.

High Total Cost of Ownership Enterprise systems, supply chain management, and customer relationship management systems are very expensive to purchase and implement. It might take a large company three years to fully implement all of the organizational and technology changes required by a large-scale enterprise system, supply chain management system, or customer relationship management system. The total implementation cost, including hardware, software, database tools, consulting fees, personnel costs, and training, might amount to five to six times the software package purchase price. Costs run even higher for organizations with global operations, which must manage organizational and technology changes in many different languages, time zones, currencies, and regulatory environments.

A Meta Group study of the TCO of enterprise systems, including hardware, software, professional services, and internal staff costs, found that the average TCO was $19 million (the highest was $376 million and the lowest $500 000). The median initial investment in a CRM application is approximately $535 000, but the cost can run as high as $125 million for a large and complex CRM implementation, and many do not generate the financial returns that justify these expenditures (Schneider 2004; Ebner, Hu, Levitt, and McCrory 2002). Large supply chain management systems have similar costs.

Organizational Change Requirements Enterprise applications require not only deep-seated technological changes but also fundamental changes in the way the business operates. Business processes change dramatically, as do organizational structure and culture. Organizations that do not understand the need for these changes or that are unable to make them will have problems implementing enterprise applications and using them effectively (Agarwal, Harding, and Schumacher 2004).

Employees must accept new job functions and responsibilities. They will have to learn how to perform a new set of processes and understand how the information they enter into the system can affect other parts of the company. New organizational learning is required for organizational members to acquire complex new knowledge about new business rules and business processes (Robey, Ross, and Boudreau 2002).

Most firms embracing CRM systems need to transform their focus from a product-centric view to a customer-centric view in which retaining a customer is a priority. These changes require more interdepartmental cooperation. If a firm's sales, marketing, support systems, back-office systems, and data warehouses exist in isolation, the cross-functional information sharing, integration, and business intelligence to optimize the customer experience cannot occur. Companies typically underestimate the time and cost of cleaning up customer data from disparate sources and of organizing customer data in a company-wide format.

Supply chain management raises implementation hurdles because it extends beyond the walls of the company. Business managers have been accustomed to thinking about their firms, the best interests of their firms, and business process improvements that benefit the entire firm. But in an interorganizational supply chain, they may be asked to redesign the way they work to optimize the performance of the supply chain as a whole.

Unless enterprise application investments are accompanied by improvements in the firm's business processes, they are unlikely to improve the flow of information and goods. If enterprise application software is implemented atop flawed processes, the software could actually make matters worse (Day 2003; Rigby, Reichheld, and Schefter 2003).

The Window on Management addresses this issue. Novartis Pharmaceuticals was experiencing problems paying invoices on time because of incompatibilities between its SAP R/E enterprise software and the company's business processes for initiating purchase requisitions and paying suppliers. It decided to simplify the process, but chose to use other software instead of enterprise software.

 # WINDOW ON MANAGEMENT

Why Novartis Backed Off from Enterprise Software

Novartis A.G. is a leading global pharmaceutical and health-care company headquartered in Basel, Switzerland. It operates in more than 140 countries around the world, employing about 77 200 people and producing nearly $31.5 billion in revenue in 2003. Novartis does business in Canada as Novartis Canada; the products they offer in Canada include Maalox, exlax, Triaminic cough syrup, Clearvue contact lenses, and Clearplan early pregnancy test kits.

Novartis is replacing legacy systems at Novartis offices in more than 50 countries with SAP enterprise software for human resources, supplier relationship management, and supply chain management. Management believes the SAP software will help the company cut down system integration costs as well as standardize and streamline administrative processes, work flow, and reporting in its worldwide operations. The SAP software will also help the company comply with U.S. Food and Drug Administration regulations on electronic records and signatures for the pharmaceutical industry.

Because SAP is recognized as the dominant ERP and SCM vendor for the global pharmaceuticals industry (ranked by a Frost and Sullivan consulting company survey), Novartis had already adopted SAP's R/3 enterprise resource planning and financial modules for many of its operating units. Given the company's enthusiasm for enterprise systems and SAP, it was surprising to learn that the accounts payable department at Novartis Pharmaceuticals, the U.S. arm of the company, was having problems with its SAP enterprise system. Somewhere in the process of paying invoices, payments were being held, and a backlog of overdue bills was building. A few vendors even withheld credit from the company.

The accounts payable and strategic sourcing departments pointed to a recent upgrade to the SAP R/3 financial modules as the source of their financial crisis. Novartis insisted that SAP be its global standard, but the software just wasn't working for these departments. In frustration, these groups met to figure out a way to redesign their requisition-to-pay process, even if it meant scrapping SAP modules that did not meet their needs. They did not want to work with the Novartis information systems department.

Novartis's information systems staff, on the other hand, believed the unpaid invoices were not entirely caused by the SAP software. The company's existing process for invoicing was inefficient, requiring manual approvals from many different managers. It was not a truly integrated requisition-to-pay process. Work was still structured into silos, and no one knew what was going on.

The information systems staff thought a recent implementation of the SAP R/3 software would solve the problem. It believed that if it let the SAP software handle as many business processes as possible, it would not have to deal with so many interfaces between different information systems. The information systems department had assigned special staff members to serve as business information managers (BIMs) who could work more closely with end user departments to clarify and support business goals. Nevertheless, because of tight deadlines and limited budget, information systems specialists scrimped on training and did not pay sufficient attention to the new system's impact on business processes.

Something had to be done to get user and information systems groups to cooperate. Ray Pawlicki, Novartis's vice president for information and chief information officer, invited accounts payable and information systems groups to a six-month program to foster joint leadership. The groups met many times. Eventually, both groups started listening to each other and committed to two outcomes.

One outcome was to create a new way for the information sys-

tems, accounts payable, and strategic sourcing departments to work together to facilitate rapid business transformation. The other outcome was a proposal to improve the purchasing process for Novartis departments so that they would no longer make independent purchases. Instead, all requisitions would be channeled through the strategic sourcing department. By centralizing purchases, the company would be able to obtain larger discounts from suppliers because it would buy in larger quantities. About $5 million to $6 million could be saved annually this way.

The BIMs from the information systems department emerged with a deeper appreciation of business requirements and how these matched up with SAP and other software providers. In the end, the information systems group agreed to what accounts payable and strategic sourcing had originally requested: a solution that was the "best of breed," irrespective of the software vendor that would best support the company's redesigned purchasing process.

In May 2003 the information systems department agreed to update an old system from Ariba that would reduce late payments by automatically reconciling sourcing and accounts payable. The Ariba upgrade improved Novartis's purchasing process so much that $5 to $6 million in savings were achieved within six months.

To Think About: Why was Novartis having trouble with its requisition-to-pay process? What management, organization, and technology factors were involved? Was the solution to this problem a good one? Why or why not?

Sources: Stephanie Overby, "Can't We All Just Get Along?" *CIO Australia*, March 10, 2004 and "SAP Chosen by Novartis as a Major Building Block," *EETimes*, June 16, 2003; www.novartis.ca, accessed May 28, 2005.

Realizing Strategic Value Companies may fail to achieve strategic benefits from enterprise applications if the generic processes enforced by enterprise applications prevent the firm from using unique business processes that had been sources of advantage over competitors. Enterprise systems promote centralized organizational coordination and decision making, which may not be the best way for some firms to operate (Davenport 2000, 1998). Enterprise applications that are state-of-the-art today could bind firms to outdated business processes and technologies tomorrow.

Solution Guidelines

Successful implementation of enterprise applications requires knowledge of how the business works today as well as how it wants to work tomorrow. Learning how enterprise applications work and how the business would have to change to use these systems effectively represents a major research and development effort. In a nutshell, it takes a lot of work to get enterprise applications to work properly. Everyone in the organization must be involved.

Look at Business Objectives First A customer relationship management, supply chain management, or enterprise system is not merely a technology change—it represents a fundamental change in the way the company conducts its business. Many managers contemplating these systems focus too much on the technology and not enough on business goals. Managers must understand the business objectives they want to achieve with enterprise applications before buying any software. They must determine whether an enterprise application will actually help the company meet these objectives. Identifying the key business processes the company is trying to improve and how much these processes must change with an enterprise application should always be the first step.

Attention to Data and Data Management

Enterprise applications require that information that was previously maintained in different systems and different departments or functional areas be integrated and made available to the company as a whole. Firms implementing enterprise applications must develop organization-wide definitions of data. Understanding how the organization uses its data and how the data will be handled in a customer relationship management, supply chain management, or enterprise system is a large-scale research effort.

Managers and employees will have to study the enterprise application software very carefully to make sure they understand the definitions of the data elements in the system, how they relate, and how they can be used for decision making and operational support. They will need to examine their organization's existing data model and see how much it needs to be changed to work with the new software.

The firm must make sure that the data elements needed for decision making are in a form that can be used throughout the organization and that the data are accurate and complete. If, for instance, a firm has data available on product sales but the data cannot be linked back to data on sales promotions or to data on which retailer purchased which item, the system will not be able to link product sales to promotions. Analytic insights from the system will be limited.

Senior Management Commitment and Employee Support

Support and backing from the CEO are critical for ensuring that all the changes required by enterprise applications will be adopted by the entire company. People are much more willing to take on different job responsibilities or change the way they work if senior management is firmly behind the effort.

Rank-and-file employees—the people who actually are going to use the system on a day-to-day basis—should not be overlooked. They need to be involved in some of the decisions about the system as well as implementation and training. Support for the system can be encouraged by clearly demonstrating the business value that comes with the enterprise application project and how everyone can contribute to its success.

Education and Training

Education and training are always essential for successful information system implementation, but even more so for enterprise applications. Managers must learn how the system can change key processes, organizational structure, and the information they use. Employees will need to learn exactly how the system supports the work they perform and how it affects the broader organization each time it is used.

Summary

1. *Assess how enterprise systems provide value for businesses, and describe how they work.*

Enterprise systems integrate the key business processes of a firm into a single software system so that information can flow seamlessly throughout the organization, improving coordination, efficiency, and decision making. Enterprise software is based on a suite of integrated software modules and a common central database. The database collects data from and feeds the data into numerous applications that can support nearly all of an organization's internal business activities. When new information is entered by one process, the information is made available immediately to other business processes. Organizations implementing enterprise software would have to adopt the business processes embedded in the software and, if necessary, change their business processes to conform to those in the software.

Enterprise systems can support organizational centralization by enforcing uniform data standards and business processes throughout the company and a single unified technology platform. The firm-wide data generated by enterprise systems can help managers monitor organizational performance. By integrating business processes in sales, production, finance, and logistics, the entire organization can more efficiently respond to customer requests for products or information, forecast new products, and develop and deliver them as demand appears.

2. *Assess how supply chain management systems provide value for businesses, and explain how they work.*

Supply chain management systems automate the flow of information between members of the supply chain so they can use it to make better decisions about when and how much to purchase, produce, or ship. More accurate information from supply chain management systems reduces uncertainty and the impact of the bullwhip effect. The correct movement of information makes it possible to time orders, shipments, and production properly to minimize inventory levels and expedite deliveries to customers.

Supply chain management software includes software for supply chain planning and for supply chain execution. Supply chain planning systems enable the firm to generate demand forecasts for a product and to develop sourcing, manufacturing, and distribution plans. Supply chain execution systems manage the flow of products through the final stages of production, distribution, and delivery. Supply chain management systems provide data such as fill rates, inventory turns, or source/make cycle time for evaluating the performance of supply chain processes. Firms can use intranets to improve coordination among their internal supply chain processes, and they can use extranets to coordinate supply chain processes shared with their business partners. Internet technology facilitates the management of global supply chains by providing the connectivity for organizations in different countries to share supply chain information. Improved communication among supply chain members also facilitates efficient customer response and movement toward a demand-driven model.

3. *Assess how customer relationship management systems provide value for businesses, and describe how they work.*

Customer relationship management (CRM) systems integrate and automate many customer-facing processes in sales, marketing, and customer service, providing an enterprise-wide view of customers. These systems track all of the ways in which a company interacts with its customers and analyze these interactions to maximize customer lifetime value for the firm. CRM systems capture and integrate customer data from all over the organization, analyzing the data and distributing the results to customer-related systems and customer touch points across the enterprise. Companies can use this customer knowledge when they interact with customers to provide them with better service or to sell new products and services. These systems can also identify profitable or non-profitable customers or opportunities to reduce the churn rate. The major customer relationship management software packages integrate customer-related processes in sales, marketing, and customer service and provide capabilities for both operational CRM and analytical CRM.

They often include modules for managing relationships with selling partners (partner relationship management) and for employee relationship management.

If properly implemented, CRM systems can help firms increase customer satisfaction, reduce direct marketing costs, and lower costs for customer acquisition and retention. Information from CRM systems can increase sales revenue by identifying the most profitable customers and segments for focused marketing, cross-selling, and up-selling. Customer churn can be reduced as sales, service, and marketing better respond to customer needs.

4. *Describe how enterprise applications can be used in platforms for new cross-functional services.*

Enterprise applications can serve as building blocks for new cross-functional services for customers, suppliers, or business partners based on enterprise-wide business processes by using service platforms and enterprise portals. Service platforms integrate data and processes from the various enterprise applications (customer relationship management, supply chain management, and enterprise systems), as well as from disparate legacy applications to create new composite processes. The new composite process is modelled using business process management tools, and application integration software ties various systems together. The new services are delivered through enterprise portals, which can integrate disparate applications so that information appears to be coming from a single source.

5. *Identify the challenges posed by enterprise applications, and propose management solutions.*

Enterprise applications are very difficult to implement successfully. They require extensive organizational change, large new software investments, and careful assessment of how these systems will enhance organizational performance. Management vision and foresight are required to take a firm- and industry-wide view of problems and to find solutions that realize strategic value from the investment. Enterprise applications create new interconnections among myriad business processes and data flows inside the firm (and in the case of supply chain management systems, between the firm and its external supply chain partners) to streamline operations and to make better management decisions. Employees are often unprepared for new procedures and roles. Enterprise applications cannot provide value if they are implemented atop flawed processes or if firms do not know how to use these systems to measure performance improvements.

Companies can meet these challenges by putting business objectives first, securing top management support, paying attention to data and data management, and providing education and training.

Key Terms

Analytical CRM,   495

Best practices,   479

Bullwhip effect,   486

Bundling,   494

Business process management,   500

Churn rate,   497

Cross-selling,   494

Customer lifetime value (CLTV),   498

Customer relationship management (CRM), 492

Demand planning,   487

Employee relationship management (ERM), 493

Enterprise software,   478

Just-in-time,   485

Logistics,   485

Metric,   489

Operational CRM,   495

Partner relationship management (PRM),   492

Pull-based model,   490

Push-based model,   490

Service platform,   498

Supply chain,   483

Supply chain execution systems,   488

Supply chain management (SCM),   483

Supply chain planning systems,   487

Touch point,   493

Up-selling,   494

Review Questions

1. What is an enterprise system? How does enterprise software work?

2. How do enterprise systems provide value for a business?

3. What is a supply chain? What entities does it comprise? What is supply chain management?

4. List and describe the five major supply chain processes.

5. What is the bullwhip effect? How can supply chain management systems deal with it?

6. What are supply chain planning systems and supply chain execution systems? What functions do they perform?

7. How can the Internet and Internet technology facilitate supply chain management?

8. How do supply chain management systems provide value for a business?

9. What is customer relationship management? Why are customer relationships so important today?

10. How is partner relationship management (PRM) related to customer relationship management (CRM)?

11. Describe the tools and capabilities of customer relationship management software for sales, marketing, and customer service.

12. Distinguish between operational and analytical CRM.

13. How do customer relationship management systems provide value for a business?

14. What are service platforms? How can they be used with enterprise applications to provide more cross-functional process integration?

15. What are the challenges posed by enterprise applications? How can these challenges be addressed?

Discussion Questions

1. Supply chain management is less about managing the physical movement of goods and more about managing information. Discuss the implications of this statement.

2. If a company wants to implement an enterprise application, it had better do its homework. Discuss the implications of this statement.

Application Software Exercise:
Database Exercise: Managing Customer Service Requests

Prime Service is a large service company that provides maintenance and repair services for close to 1200 commercial businesses in Ontario, Quebec, and British Columbia. Its customers include businesses of all sizes. Customers with service needs call into its customer service department with requests for repairing heating ducts, broken windows, leaky roofs, broken water pipes, and other problems. The company manually tracks the date each service request was made and assigns each request a service request number. The service requests are handled on a first-come-first-served basis. After the service work has been completed, Prime calculates the cost of the work and bills the client.

Management is not happy with this arrangement because the most important and profitable clients—those with

accounts over $70 000—are treated no differently from its clients with small accounts. They would like to find a way to provide their best customers with better service. Management would also like to know which types of service problems occur the most frequently so that it can make sure it has adequate resources to address them.

Prime Service has a small database with client account information, which can be found on the Companion Website for Chapter 14. It includes fields for the account ID, company (account) name, street address, province, postal code, account size (in dollars), contact last name, contact first name, contact telephone number, and contact fax number. The contact is the name of the person in each company who is responsible for contacting Prime about maintenance and repair work. Use your database software to design a solution that would enable Prime's customer service representatives to identify the most important customers so that they could receive priority service. Your solution will require more than one table. Populate your database with at least 20 service requests. Create several reports that would be of interest to management, such as a list of the highest- and lowest-priority accounts or a report showing the most frequently occurring service problems. Create another report showing customer service representatives which service calls they should respond to first on a specific date.

Electronic Business Project: Evaluating Supply Chain Management Services

Trucking companies no longer merely carry goods from one place to another. They can also provide supply chain management services to their customers and help them manage their information. Investigate the Web sites of two companies, TransX (**www.transx.ca**) and Schneider Logistics (**www.schneiderlogistics.com**) to see how these companies' services can be used for supply chain management. Then answer the following questions:

1. What supply chain processes can each of these companies support for their clients?

2. How can customers use the Web site of each company to help with supply chain management?

3. Compare the supply chain management services provided by these companies. Which company would you select to help your firm manage its supply chain? Why?

Group Project: Analyzing Enterprise Process Integration

Management at your agricultural chemicals corporation has been dissatisfied with production planning. Production plans are created using best guesses of demand for each product, which are based on how much of each product has been ordered in the past. If a customer places an unexpected order or requests a change to an existing order after it has been placed, there is no way to adjust production plans. The company may have to tell customers it cannot fill their orders, or it may accumulate extra costs maintaining additional inventory to prevent stockouts.

At the end of each month, orders are totalled and manually keyed into the company's production planning system. Data from the past month's production and inventory systems are manually entered into the firm's order management system. Analysts from the sales department and from the production department analyze the data from their respective systems to determine what the sales targets and production targets should be for the next month. These estimates are usually different. The analysts then get together at a high-level planning meeting to revise the production and sales targets to take into account senior management's goals for market share, revenues, and profits. The outcome of the meeting is a finalized production master schedule.

The entire production planning process takes 17 business days to complete. Nine of these days are required to enter and validate the data. The remaining days are spent developing and reconciling the production and sales targets and finalizing the production master schedule.

With a group of three or four students, prepare an analysis of this scenario:

1. Draw a diagram of the existing production planning process.

2. Analyze the problems this process creates for the company.

3. How could an enterprise system solve these problems? In what ways could it reduce costs? Create a diagram of what the production planning process might look like if the company implemented enterprise software.

4. If possible, use electronic presentation software to present your findings to the class.

Web Sites of Interest

There are many interesting Web sites to enhance your learning about information resource management. You can search the Web yourself or try the following sites to add to what you have already learned.

SAP **www.sap.com**
The leading ERP vendor worldwide

Siebel Systems, Inc. **www.siebel.com**
The leading CRM vendor worldwide

Sales Force **www.salesforce.com**
A relatively new, but cutting edge, online CRM and sales force automation vendor; data is kept at salesforce.com rather than on company computers.

CASE STUDY:
TransAlta and Its "Single Portal Strategy"—Is One Portal Enough?

Calgary-based TransAlta, founded in 1911, is Canada's largest nonregulated power generation and wholesale marketing company. With annual revenues of more than $2.5 billion, TransAlta has operations in Canada, Australia, Mexico, and the United States. In 1995, TransAlta replaced 40 separate applications with a single, unified view of enterprise-wide information and business processes using enterprise software from SAP. It migrated its SAP systems in 2000 to IBM pSeries servers that were configured in a high-availability clustered multi-processing environment with the aim of developing a single portal through which all users could access almost all applications. According to John McGrath, program manager on the TransAlta Enterprise Portal project, "SAP R/3 has been a great success, and we also use collaborative technologies such as Lotus Domino, QuickPlace, and SameTime. We could clearly see the benefits of integrating these technologies with our core SAP systems."

TransAlta's solution to this was to create a single business portal so that users could access SAP, Lotus Domino, and standard desktop office applications, all from the same single-user environment and sign-on. However, portal access had to be available for a diverse range of data and applications. In a dual-portal strategy, TransAlta used both IBM WebSphere Portal and SAP Enterprise Portal supported by multiple IBM WebSphere integration technologies. "With IBM, TransAlta is delivering both SAP and other applications in a friendly, consistent and efficient way. Integrating people, processes, technology, and information is our core mission statement," says John McGrath. "During deployment, we ran into a few problems, and IBM Software Services were excellent in delivering the solution in a timely fashion so we didn't have to hold anything up. IBM Global Services managed the Enterprise Portal project to ensure we implemented successfully, even given our ambitious timeline." What proved to be immensely valuable during the architectural design phase of the portal project was the support of the IBM SAP collaboration technology support centre (CTSC).

TransAlta's Enterprise Portal project's developers used IBM Global Services, IBM Software Services, the CTSC and IBM Business Partner Sandbox Systems. TransAlta was assured of the viability of the dual portal approach when Sandbox produced a dual portal proof-of-concept in three weeks. TransAlta was certain that the plan was practicable when the speed of production and low maintenance cost of the WebSphere Portal reduced the number of support staff assigned to the project from about 20 to about 5. Alan Wong, portal architect on the TransAlta portal, says, "WebSphere technologies provide all the back-end integration technologies we need to provide a single login and user experience. When we introduce new software, training costs are lower, and the IT team is able to respond faster to new application requirements."

With portal technology, all that users require is browser access in order to view, manage, and enter data into SAP,

Domino, and many other applications. Because this technology offers a consistent interface for multiple programs, training costs are reduced and ease of use and, therefore, productivity are increased. It was, however, not an easy task to integrate SAP R/3 data, Lotus Domino collaboration and teamwork applications, and office productivity programs data.

As John McGrath explains, "There is no more efficient way to deliver SAP content than through SAP Enterprise Portal, and this was used for what we term the vertical SAP applications. For enterprise-wide team tools, we implemented IBM WebSphere Portal." The WebSphere Portal integrates the Lotus Domino and collaboration applications into a single user environment. The WebSphere Portal resembles the SAP Enterprise Portal so closely that users see the dual portal as a single interface. TransAlta's dual portal enables users to reach all their relevant SAP applications and also to log in to Notes, email, calendaring, QuickPlace, SameTime, and other Domino applications. A single user login spans the WebSphere Portal, the SAP Enterprise Portal and all SAP applications; users thus have access to relevant application areas without the need to re-authenticate from system to system. They also get a consistent interface whatever application they are using.

The integration framework consolidates two complex landscapes into one integrated, simplified platform. It combines both technologies into one presentation layer, and the end-user is therefore able to achieve seamless integration. With the WebSphere Portal, users do not need to switch from application to application to search for data, send faxes, or make calls. The smooth movement between underlying applications while inside the portal enables users to find relevant information and act on it in a more timely fashion. Businesses can save costs when they reduce keeping hardcopy information about events, news, staff directory, self-serve human resources materials, procedure manuals, and reference documents.

TransAlta plans to move on to combining portal access to information with workflow capabilities, which would make it possible for end users to carry on their business processes through the portals. They could then tap into operational systems and provide information directly to the portal. "The high-level plan is to integrate operations and data everywhere. Our vision for the future is to turn the portal into the single source for all information and user needs; in order to do that we need to be able to connect to different systems," says John McGrath. He concludes, "Our CIO, Greg Wilson, is a proponent of leveraging TransAlta's strategic vendor partnerships with IBM and SAP. TransAlta plans to exploit the capabilities of both IBM WebSphere and SAP NetWeaver for better business solutions and value for the corporation."

Additional plans for TransAlta's use of SAP included the use of SAP to facilitate and enhance maintenance at TransAlta power plants in both North America and Australia. Creating a separate maintenance portal that could be accepted by maintenance workers and engineers is key to this initiative. Because of the way portals are justified, executive sponsors are often seen as the most important people to sell on projects, or even build functionality for, as opposed to creating a solution that meets the needs of users.

While many might feel that a single portal for all employees is a worthwhile goal, some jobs really require a separate portal, such as the maintenance portal being implemented at TransAlta. One of the keys to good portal implementation is to know when to implement a separate portal versus expanding the current portal. A company as large as TransAlta might need several portals, with links on the desktop to those portals needed by users of that desktop machine.

Sources: "TransAlta powers up with IBM WebSphere Portal and SAP Enterprise Portal," IBM Case Study, available **www-306.ibm.com/software/success/cssdb.nsf/CS/FWAS-6B7C3X?OpenDocument&Site=wsmq**, accessed May 28, 2005; Jim Ericson, "Working Man's Portal," *Portals Magazine*, January 1, 2003; John Cox, "TransAlta Uses Wireless Technology to Get More Competitive," *Network World Fusion*, April 13, 2005.

CASE STUDY QUESTIONS:

1. Evaluate how TransAlta is making use of SAP as its ERP application and using the concept of single portal. How many portals do you think TransAlta may actually need?

2. How does the use of the single portal strategy fit with TransAlta's business strategy? Do you think users buy into that strategy? Why or why not?

3. What management, organization, and technology factors do you think influenced the decisions made at TransAlta?

4. What issues arose during the various implementations described at TransAlta that involved users, designers, and management? What could be done to resolve those issues?

Chapter 15

Enhancing Decision Making in the Digital Firm

OBJECTIVES

After completing this chapter, you will be able to:

1. Describe different types of decisions and the decision-making process.

2. Evaluate the role of information systems in helping people working both individually and in a group to make decisions more efficiently.

3. Demonstrate how executive support systems can help senior managers make better decisions.

4. Assess how systems that support decision making can provide value for the firm.

5. Identify the challenges posed by decision-support systems, group decision-support systems, and executive support systems, and propose management solutions.

- Monitor schedules and costs

- Schedule delivery trucks
- Schedule rail cars

- Implement TESYS software

Management

Organization

Technology

Business Challenges

- Just-in-time production delivery system
- Numerous assembly stations over large area

Information System

- Optimize delivery assignments

Business Solutions

- Improve quality
- Reduce costs

Opening Case: Daimler's Bremen Plant Optimizes Deliveries with DSS

The automotive plant of DaimlerChrysler in Bremen, Germany, has 13 000 employees and produces more than 800 cars per day. Each day, 70 rail cars and 500 trucks transport parts, components, and materials to the factory, which occupies an area of about 1 million square metres. This plant uses a just-in-time delivery system: All of the parts and components must be delivered to the plant's various assembly stations just at the moment when they are needed.

Nearly 20 years ago, Daimler management realized that the intraplant transport capacity was not utilized efficiently because there was no way to manage plant deliveries effectively. When they arrived at the plant, drivers moved their trucks to their loading points, not knowing if they would arrive there in the right order or if the loading point would be free. The trucks were not always able to deliver the required material during the agreed time frame. Material on the trucks might arrive too soon, or urgently needed material might not be available because the truck was waiting in line. Daimler needed a better way to make decisions about organizing its in-plant deliveries.

The company decided to use the Transportation Efficiency Support System (TESYS) to solve this problem. TESYS is a decision-support and optimization software system developed by INFORM GmbH of Aachen, Germany. It synchronizes deliveries with the capacities of loading points within the area of a plant and with the current needs of production. TESYS is currently used at multiple intermodal hubs, ports, and other logistic centres throughout the world.

When a delivery arrives at the DaimlerChrysler plant, requests for unloading are submitted to the plant's control board using either an automated order reception model or the telephone. The system optimizes the assignment, showing the shortest routes and quickest on-time completion of all transport orders. New delivery instructions are transmitted to the appropriate driver using two-way radio.

The system handles most time-critical operations automatically although the software does allow human controllers to handle important special deliveries. Optimal use of resources cuts costs and increases the quality and productivity of the entire plant logistics system. The plant's logistics operations became much more efficient, with utilization of plant transport capacity increasing from 60 percent to 94 percent.

Sources: Hans Jurgen Zimmermann, "Online Optimization," *OR/MS Today*, April 2004; and **www.inform-ac.com/tess/en/02_08.htm**, accessed May 9, 2004.

Daimler's plant delivery optimization system is an example of a decision-support system. It helps managers make decisions about the most efficient way to stage deliveries to loading points given production requirements, routes, and time frames. These systems have powerful analytical capabilities that support managers during the process of arriving at decisions.

As a manager, you will want to know how you can use information systems to improve your decision making, whether you are working alone or in a group. Just as important, you will be responsible for the decisions made by the people who work under you, and you will want systems to help them make better decisions as well.

This chapter focuses on the specialized systems that firms use to achieve better decision making: management information systems (MIS), decision support systems (DSS), group decision-support systems (GDSS), and executive support systems (ESS). You'll learn how these systems work, how they provide value for the business, and the challenges of developing and using them wisely.

15.1 Decision Making and Decision-Support Systems

Chapter 1 pointed out that information systems have business value when they enable more efficient business processes and improve management decision making. As organizations flatten and push decision making to lower levels to include non-management employees, information systems make significant contributions to the overall quality of decision making for the entire firm.

For instance, a service firm such as EchoStar Communications, one of the world's largest television satellite firms, receives millions of calls at the company's call centres each year. If a customer service representative has the right information about a customer calling into the call centre, the employee can decide to offer the customer special services that could encourage the customer to stay with the company or perhaps purchase additional services, thus contributing to the firm's value.

On a larger scale, there are 16.2 million workers in the Canadian labour force producing $1.2 trillion in gross domestic product (GDP). If the decision-making quality of these employees could be improved by just 1 percent in a year, then the GDP might expand by a substantial amount, perhaps equivalent to 1 percent, or $12.2 billion, annually, perhaps far more. For both small and large firms the ability of managers and employees to make the right decision at the right time with the right information can have extraordinary business value.

Business Intelligence and Decision Support

Because of the importance of high-quality decision making, firms are investing heavily in **business intelligence** systems, which consist of technologies and applications designed to help users make better business decisions. When we think of *intelligence* as applied to humans, we typically think of people's ability to combine learned knowledge with new information and change their behaviour in such a way that they succeed at their task or adapt to a new situation. Likewise, business intelligence provides firms with the capability to amass information, develop knowledge about operations, and change decision-making behaviour to achieve profitability and other business goals.

Figure 15-1 illustrates the major applications and technologies used for business intelligence. They include supply chain management, customer relationship management, and enterprise systems; systems for knowledge management; and technologies such as data mining and online analytical processing (OLAP) for obtaining knowledge and insight from analyzing large quantities of data. These systems work with specialized systems for management decision making (MIS, DSS, ESS) that focus on the specific decision needs of managers and employees.

Business Value of Improved Decision Making

Let us try to measure the business benefits of improved decision making and link these improvements to firm profitability. Table 15-1 describes an example of a small manufacturing firm operating in Canada with $280 million annual revenue and 140 employees. The firm has identified a number of key decisions where new systems investments might improve the quality of decision making. Analysts have estimated the value to the firm of improving each decision. The table provides selected estimates of the annual value (either in cost savings or revenue enhancement) of improved decision making in selected areas of the firm.

FIGURE 15-1 *Systems and technologies for business intelligence.*

Each of the major enterprise applications provides support for decision making or "business intelligence" at all levels of the firm in addition to processing daily transactions. Specialized systems such as MIS, DSS, and ESS described in this chapter work with these systems and technologies for data mining and online analytical processing (OLAP) to focus on the specific decision needs of managers and employees.

TABLE 15-1 *Business Value of Enhanced Decision Making*

EXAMPLE DECISION	DECISION MAKER	NUMBER OF ANNUAL DECISIONS	ESTIMATED VALUE TO FIRM OF A SINGLE IMPROVED DECISION	ANNUAL VALUE
Customer Relationship Management (CRM)				
Allocate support to most valuable customers	Accounts manager	12	$100 000	$1 200 000
Predict call centre daily demand	Call centre management	4	$150 000	$600 000
Supply Chain Management (SCM)				
Decide parts inventory levels daily	Inventory manager	365	$5 000	$1 825 000
Identify competitive bids from major vendors	Senior management	1	$2 000 000	$2 000 000
Enterprise System				
Schedule production to fill orders	Manufacturing manager	150	$10 000	$1 500 000
Allocate labour to complete a job	Production floor manager	100	$4000	$400 000
Knowledge Management (KM)				
Determine testing procedure for a new chemical compound	Project team of scientists and engineers	3	$800 000	$3 200 000

Table 15-1 shows that decisions are made at all levels of the firm and that some decisions are very common and routine, but exceptionally valuable. Although the value of improving any single one of these decisions may be small, improving hundreds of thousands of these small decisions adds up to a large annual value.

Business Decision Making and the Decision-Making Process

Before making improvements in corporate decision making with system investments, you must understand more about the nature of decisions and the decision-making process. There are different information requirements at different levels of responsibility in the organization which affect the types of decisions made at each level.

Decision-Making Levels Chapter 2 showed that there are different levels in an organization. Each of these levels has different information requirements for decision support and different constituencies or groups that information systems need to serve (see Figure 15-2). The four different decision-making constituencies in a firm are the following:

- *Senior management.* Senior management is concerned with general yet timely information on changes in the industry and society at large that may affect both the long-term and near-term future of the firm, the firm's strategic goals, short-term and future performance, specific bottlenecks and trouble affecting operational capabilities, and the overall ability of the firm to achieve its objectives.

- *Middle management and project teams.* Middle management is concerned with specific, timely information about firm performance, including revenue and cost reduction targets, and with developing plans and budgets to meet strategic goals established by senior management. This group needs to make important decisions about allocating resources, developing short-range plans, and monitoring the performance of departments, task forces, teams, and special project groups. Often the work of middle managers is accomplished in teams or small groups of managers working on a task.

- *Operational management and project teams.* Operational management monitors the performance of each subunit of the firm and manages individual employees. Operational managers are in charge of specific projects and allocate resources within the project budget, establish schedules, and make personnel decisions. Operational work may also be accomplished through teams.

- *Individual employees.* Employees try to fulfill the objectives of managers above them, following established rules and procedures for their routine activities. Increasingly, however, employees are granted much broader responsibilities and decision-making authority based on their best judgment and information in corporate systems. Employees may be making decisions about specific vendors, customers, and other employees. Because employees interact directly with the public, how well they make their decisions can directly affect the firm's revenue streams.

Types of Decisions Decisions can be classified as structured, semistructured, and unstructured. **Unstructured decisions** are those in which the decision maker must provide judgment, evaluation, and insight into the problem definition. Each of these decisions is novel, important, and non-routine, and there is no well-understood or agreed-on procedure for making them.

Structured decisions, by contrast, are repetitive and routine, and decision makers can follow a definite procedure for handling them to be efficient. Many decisions have elements of both and are considered **semistructured decisions**, in which only part of the problem has a clear-cut answer provided by an accepted procedure.

The characteristics of decisions faced by managers at different levels are quite different. In general, structured decisions are made more prevalently at lower organizational levels while unstructured decision making is more common at higher levels of the firm. Senior executives tend to be exposed to many unstructured decision situations that are open ended and evaluative and that require insight based on many sources of information and personal experience. For example, a CEO in today's music industry might ask, "Whom

unstructured decisions

structured decisions

semistructured decisions

FIGURE 15-2 *Information requirements of key decision-making groups in a firm.*

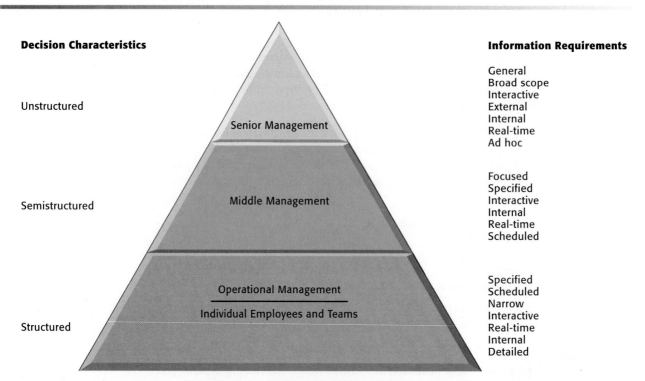

Various levels of management in the firm have differing information requirements for decision support because of their different job responsibilities and the nature of the decisions made at each level.

should we choose as a distribution partner for our online music catalogue—Apple, Microsoft, or Sony?" Answering this question would require access to news, government reports, and industry views as well as high-level summaries of firm performance. However, the answer would also require senior managers to use their best judgment and poll other managers for their opinions.

Middle management and operational management tend to face more structured decision scenarios, but their decisions may include unstructured components. A typical middle-level management decision might be "Why is the order fulfillment report showing a decline over the last six months at a distribution centre in Thunder Bay?" The middle manager could obtain a report from the firm's enterprise system or distribution management system on order activity and operational efficiency at the Thunder Bay distribution centre. This is the structured part of the decision. But before arriving at an answer, the middle manager will have to interview employees and gather more unstructured information from external sources about local economic conditions or sales trends.

Rank-and-file employees tend to make more structured decisions. For example, a sales account representative often has to make decisions about extending credit to customers by consulting the firm's customer database that contains credit information. In this case, the decision is highly structured, it is a routine decision made thousands of times each day in most firms, and the answer has been preprogrammed into a corporate risk management or credit reporting system.

The types of decisions faced by project teams cannot be classified neatly by organizational level. Teams are small groups of middle and operational managers and perhaps employees assigned specific tasks that may last a few months to a few years. Their tasks may involve unstructured or semistructured decisions such as designing new products, devising new ways to enter the marketplace, or reorganizing sales territories and compensation systems.

Systems for Decision Support There are four kinds of systems used to support the different levels and types of decisions just described (see Table 15-2). We introduced some of these systems in Chapter 2. *Management information systems (MIS)* provide routine reports and summaries of transaction-level data to middle and operational-level managers to provide answers to structured and semistructured decision problems. *Decision-support systems (DSS)* are targeted systems that combine analytical models with operational data and support interactive queries and analysis for middle

TABLE 15-2 *Organizational Level and Systems for Decision Support*

ORGANIZATIONAL LEVEL	DECISION TYPE	TYPE OF DECISION-SUPPORT SYSTEM	EXAMPLES
Senior management	Unstructured	Executive support systems (ESS)	Decide entrance or exit from markets Approve capital budget Decide long-term corporate objectives
Middle management/project teams	Semistructured	Management information systems (MIS) Decision-support systems (DSS) Group decision-support systems(GDSS)	Allocate resources to managers and departments Design a new corporate Web site Develop a marketing plan Design a departmental budget
Operational management/project teams Employees	Semistructured Structured	Decision-support systems (DSS) Management information systems (MIS) Group decision-support systems (GDSS)	Evaluate employee performance Restock inventory Routine credit decisions Determine special offers to customers

managers who face semistructured decision situations. *Executive support systems (ESS)* are specialized systems that provide senior management, making primarily unstructured decisions, with a broad array of both external information (news, stock analyses, industry trends) and high-level summaries of firm performance. Group decision-support systems (GDSS) are specialized systems that provide a group electronic environment in which managers and teams can collectively make decisions and design solutions for unstructured and semistructured problems.

Stages in the Decision-Making Process

Making decisions consists of several different activities. Simon (1960) described four different stages in decision making: intelligence, design, choice, and implementation (Figure 15-3).

Intelligence consists of discovering, identifying, and understanding the problems occurring in the organization—why is there a problem, where, and what effects it is having on the firm. Traditional MIS that deliver a wide variety of detailed information can help identify problems, especially if the systems report exceptions.

Design involves identifying and exploring various solutions to the problem. Decision-support systems (DSS) are ideal in this stage for exploring alternatives because they possess analytical tools for modelling data, enabling users to explore various options quickly.

Choice consists of choosing among solution alternatives. Here, DSS with access to extensive firm data can help managers choose the optimal solution. Also group decision-support systems can be used to bring groups of managers together in an electronic online environment to discuss different solutions and make a choice.

Implementation involves making the chosen alternative work and continuing to monitor how well the solution is working. Here, traditional MIS come back into play by providing managers with routine reports on the progress of a specific solution. Support

FIGURE 15-3 *Stages in decision making.*

The decision-making process can be described in four steps that follow one another in a logical order. In reality, decision makers frequently circle back to reconsider the previous stages and through a process of iteration eventually arrive at a solution that is workable.

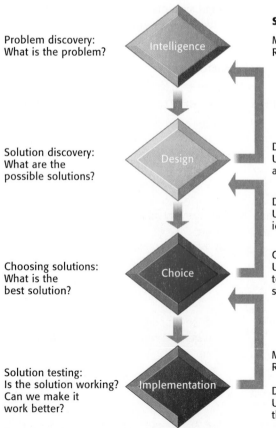

Stages in Decision Making

System Support

Problem discovery: What is the problem? — Intelligence

Management Information Systems (MIS): Routine reports and exception reporting

Solution discovery: What are the possible solutions? — Design

Decision-Support Systems (DSS): Using analytical models and spreadsheets to analyze data and design possible solutions

Decision-Support Systems (DSS): Using analytical models and larger data sets to identify the "optimal" solution

Choosing solutions: What is the best solution? — Choice

Group Decision-Support Systems (GDSS): Using online meeting and collaboration tools to choose the most acceptable and widely supported solution

Management Information Systems (MIS): Routine reports and exception reporting

Solution testing: Is the solution working? Can we make it work better? — Implementation

Decision-Support Systems (DSS): Using analytical models and data to fine-tune the solution

intelligence

design

choice

implementation

systems can range from full-blown MIS to much smaller systems, as well as project-planning software operating on personal computers.

In the real world, the stages of decision making described here do not necessarily follow a linear path. You can be in the process of implementing a decision, only to discover that your solution is not working. In such cases, you will be forced to repeat the design, choice, or perhaps even the intelligence stage.

For instance, in the face of declining sales, a sales management team may strongly support a new sales incentive system to spur the sales force on to greater effort. If paying the sales force a higher commission for making more sales does not produce sales increases, managers would need to investigate whether the problem stems from poor product design, inadequate customer support, or a host of other causes, none of which would be "solved" by a new incentive system.

Decision Making in the Real World The premise of this book and this chapter is that investments in systems to support decision making produce better decision making by managers and employees in the firm, above average returns on investment for the firm, and ultimately higher profitability. Unfortunately, in the real world, for some firms, investments in decision-support systems do not always work out this way for three reasons: data quality, management filters, and organizational culture. Review the discussion on organizations in Chapter 3 as well.

Information Quality

High-quality decisions require high-quality information regardless of information systems. You should consider seven dimensions of information quality when designing decision-support systems:

Accuracy: Do the data represent reality?

Integrity: Are the structure of data and relationships among the entities and attributes consistent?

Consistency: Are data elements consistently defined?

Completeness: Are all the necessary data present?

Validity: Do data values fall within defined ranges?

Timeliness: Are data available when needed?

Accessibility: Are the data accessible, comprehensible, and usable?

Chapter 6 has shown that corporate databases and files have varying levels of inaccuracy and incompleteness, which in turn can degrade the quality of decision making. When the underlying data are poor, the quality of decision making suffers. For instance, until recently, the United Kingdom's Royal Navy was plagued by inaccuracies and inconsistent data for the 510 770 items of supply in its inventory systems. It found 56 035 incorrect or missing entries for the attribute "Packaging Code" alone. Management could not make accurate decisions on what items needed to be ordered or how many items should be kept in inventory (Data Warehouse Institute 2004).

Management Filters

Even with timely, accurate information, some managers make bad decisions. Managers (like all human beings) absorb information through a series of filters to make sense of the world around them. Managers have selective attention, focus on certain kinds of problems and solutions, and have a variety of biases that isolate them from reality. They filter by turning off information they do not want to hear because it does not conform to their prior conceptions.

For instance, Cisco Systems Corporation, one of the most advanced users of online decision-support systems, nevertheless was forced to write off as a loss $3.4 billion in excess inventory in 2001. Cisco's managers built inventory in response to the output from the company's online sales order entry system, which throughout 1999 and 2000 showed exceptionally strong orders. Unfortunately, Cisco managers did not pay attention to the quality of those orders. Customers, perceiving a shortage of routers and other networking equipment, were placing orders with multiple manufacturers, awarding the business to the first one who could deliver, and cancelling other orders. Cisco's systems were recording high levels of order cancellation, but management ignored this "bad news" and emphasized the "good news": new orders were piling up (Laudon and Laudon 2003).

Organizational Inertia   Chapter 3 shows that organizations are bureaucracies with limited capabilities and competencies for acting decisively. When environments change and businesses need to adopt new business models to survive, strong forces within organizations resist making decisions calling for major change. Decisions taken by a firm often represent a balancing of the firm's various interest groups rather than the best solution to the problem.

Consider the record label industry. Despite declining sales since 2000 and the explosion of songs downloaded for free over the Internet (for more about this, see Chapter 13), major recording companies did not move quickly into online music retailing. This change required a much leaner business model. The recording companies resisted selling music over the Internet for years. Until very recently, nearly all executives and most employees at record label companies continued to believe that music should be distributed on physical devices (records, tapes, or CDs) and sold through retail record stores.

Studies of business restructuring find that firms tend to ignore poor performance until threatened by outside takeovers, and they systematically blame poor performance on external forces beyond their control such as economic conditions (the economy), foreign competition, and rising prices, rather than blaming senior or middle management for poor business judgment (Kose, Lang, and Netter 1992).

Trends in Decision Support and Business Intelligence

Systems supporting management decision making originated in the early 1960s as early MIS that created fixed, inflexible paper-based reports and distributed them to managers on a routine schedule. In the 1970s, the first DSS emerged as standalone applications with limited data and a few analytic models. ESS emerged during the 1980s to give senior managers an overview of corporate operations. Early ESS were expensive, based on custom technology, and suffered from limited data and flexibility.

Client/server computing, the Internet, and Web technologies have had a major impact on systems that support decision making. Many decision-support applications are now delivered over corporate intranets. We see six major trends:

- *Detailed enterprise-wide data.* Enterprise systems create an explosion in firm-wide, current, and relatively accurate information, supplying end users at their desktops with powerful analytic tools for analyzing and visualizing data.

- *Broadening decision rights and responsibilities.* As information becomes more widespread throughout the corporation, it is possible to reduce levels of hierarchy and grant more decision-making authority to lower-level employees.

- *Intranets and portals.* Intranet technologies create global, company-wide networks that ease the flow of information across divisions and regions and delivery of near real-time data to management and employee desktops.

- *Personalization and customization of information.* Web portal technologies provide great flexibility in determining what data each employee or manager sees on his or her desktop. Personalization of decision information can speed up decision making by enabling users to filter out irrelevant information.

- *Extranets and collaborative commerce.* Internet and Web technologies permit suppliers and logistics partners to access firm enterprise data and decision-support tools and work collaboratively with the firm.

- *Team support tools.* Web-based collaboration and meeting tools enable project teams, task forces, and small groups to meet online using corporate intranets or extranets. These new collaboration tools borrow from earlier GDSS and are used for both brainstorming and decision sessions.

15.2 Systems for Decision Support

Exactly how have these trends affected systems for business decision making? What can today's decision-support systems do for the firm? Let us look more closely at how each major type of decision-support system works and provides value.

The Difference between MIS and DSS

Management information systems (MIS) provide information on the firm's performance to help managers monitor and control the business. They typically produce fixed, regularly scheduled reports based on data extracted and summarized from the firm's underlying transaction processing systems (TPS). The formats for these reports are often specified in advance. A typical MIS report might show a summary of monthly sales for each of the major sales territories of a company. Sometimes MIS reports are exception reports, highlighting only exceptional conditions, such as when the sales quotas for a specific territory fall below an anticipated level or employees have exceeded their spending limits in a dental care plan. Traditional MIS produced primarily hard-copy reports. Today, these reports are available online through an intranet, and more MIS reports can be generated on demand. Table 15-3 provides some examples of MIS applications.

Decision-support systems support decisions in a different way. While MIS primarily address structured problems, DSS support semistructured and unstructured problem analysis. An MIS provides managers with reports based on routine flows of data and assists in the general control of the business while DSS emphasizes change, flexibility, and rapid response. With DSS, there is less of an effort to link users to structured information flows and a correspondingly greater emphasis on models, assumptions, ad hoc queries, and display graphics.

Types of Decision-Support Systems

Earliest DSS primarily used small subsets of corporate data and were heavily model driven. Recent advances in computer processing and database technology have expanded the definition of DSS to include systems that can support decision making by analyzing vast quantities of data, including firm-wide data from enterprise systems and transaction data from the Web.

Today, there are two basic types of decision-support systems, model driven and data driven (Dhar and Stein 1997). **Model-driven DSS** are primarily standalone systems isolated from major corporate information systems that used some type of model to perform "what-if" and other kinds of analyses. Their analysis capabilities are based on a strong theory or model combined with a good user interface that make the model easy to

model-driven DSS

TABLE 15-3 *Examples of MIS Applications*

COMPANY	MIS APPLICATION
Cartier Kitchens	Brampton, Ontario firm that uses an MIS system to generate a report every morning on sales until they are completed, flagging any service issues or other reasons for incomplete installations.
Shoppers Drug Mart	Healthwatch MIS contains the pharmaceutical profiles of all the patients and informs the pharmacist who carries out the ordinance of any allergic reaction or possible interaction.
Environment Canada	National Enforcement Management Information System and Intelligence System allows tracking and management of pollution and wildlife enforcement activities and actions relating to legislation enforced by Environment Canada.
Taco Bell	Total Automation of Company Operations (TACO) system provides information on food, labour, and period-to-date costs for each restaurant.

use. The patient assessment DSS described in Chapter 2 and DaimlerChrysler's TESYS described in this chapter's opening case are examples of model-driven DSS.

The second type of DSS is **data-driven DSS**. These systems analyze large pools of data found in major corporate systems. They support decision making by enabling users to extract useful information that was previously buried in large quantities of data. Often data from transaction processing systems are collected in data warehouses for this purpose. Online analytical processing (OLAP) and data mining can then be used to analyze the data. Companies are starting to build data-driven DSS to mine customer data gathered from their Web sites as well as data from enterprise systems.

Traditional database queries answer such questions as, "How many units of product number 403 were shipped in November 2003?" OLAP, or multidimensional analysis, supports much more complex requests for information, such as, "Compare sales of product 403 relative to plan by quarter and sales region for the past two years." We describe OLAP and multidimensional data analysis in Chapter 6. With OLAP and query-oriented data analysis, users need to have a good idea about the information for which they are looking.

Data mining, which we introduced in Chapter 6, is more discovery driven. Data mining provides insights into corporate data that cannot be obtained with OLAP by finding hidden patterns and relationships in large databases and inferring rules from them to predict future behaviour (see Figure 15-4). The patterns and rules then can be used to guide decision making and forecast the effect of those decisions. The types of information that can be obtained from data mining include associations, sequences, classifications, clusters, and forecasts:

- *Associations* are occurrences linked to a single event. For instance, a study of supermarket purchasing patterns might reveal that when corn chips are purchased, a cola drink is purchased 65 percent of the time, but when there is a promotion, cola is purchased 85 percent of the time. With this information, managers can make better decisions because they have learned about the profitability of a promotion.

- In *sequences*, events are linked over time. We might find, for example, that if a house is purchased, a new refrigerator will be purchased within two weeks 65 percent of the time, and an oven will be bought within one month of the home purchase 45 percent of the time.

- *Classification* recognizes patterns that describe the group to which an item belongs by examining existing items that have been classified and by inferring a set of rules. For example, businesses such as credit card or telephone companies worry about the loss of

FIGURE 15-4　　*Advizor Solutions software to detect data patterns.*

Advizor Solutions software can help businesses detect patterns in their data. Each dot in this example represents items purchased at one supermarket, with lines drawn between purchases of individual shoppers. The software shows links between different purchase items, such as cookies and milk.

steady customers. Classification can help discover the characteristics of customers who are likely to leave and can provide a model to help managers predict who they are so that they can devise special campaigns to retain such customers.

- *Clustering* works in a manner similar to classification when no groups have yet been defined. A data-mining tool can discover different groupings within data, such as finding affinity groups for bank cards or partitioning a database into groups of customers based on demographics and types of personal investments.

- Although these applications involve predictions, *forecasting* uses predictions in a different way. It uses a series of existing values to forecast what other values will be. For example, forecasting might find patterns in data to help managers estimate the future value of continuous variables such as sales figures.

Data mining uses statistical analysis tools as well as neural networks, fuzzy logic, genetic algorithms, and rule-based and other intelligent techniques (described in Chapter 16). It is an important aspect of *knowledge discovery*, which includes selection, preparation, and interpretation of the contents of large databases to identify novel and valuable patterns in the data.

The Window on Organizations describes a data-driven decision-support system used for analyzing customer and sales data at WH Smith PLC. This massive system mines customer data gathered by WH Smith stores when people buy books, supplies, and other materials. WH Smith carefully analyzes these data to identify each store's likely best-selling books and place them in high-profile locations within each store.

WINDOW ON ORGANIZATIONS

Data Driven Insights at WH Smith PLC

WH Smith PLC, headquartered in Swindon, England, is the number one book and magazine retailer in the United Kingdom, carrying 60 000 items such as reading material, stationery, music, computer games, and gifts at its retail outlets and Web site. It runs approximately 542 retail stores, 190 stores in European airports and train stations, and more than 500 stores in North American airports and hotels. On average, 1.2 million people visit a Smith store each day. In 2001, sales reached $5.66 billion with a profit of $273 million.

Several years ago, Smith's management saw that the company was running into trouble in that it was not as profitable as it could be. At that time, its corporate executives were "only able to monitor sales and stock at the central office," explained Trevor Dukes, Smith's head of information strategy. He pointed out that "senior store managers were sending us tons of paperwork about their stores," more than they could usefully handle. Using paper-based methods, communications were very slow and information in printed reports was already out of date. Moreover, the stores needed to share information with other stores about what is profitable and what is not and how trends are changing. Stores could not even obtain information about the profitability of individual items. Even directives on promotions and incentives that were sent to the stores were not integrated with the stores' products. Management believed that employees, particularly store and area managers, needed a stronger focus on improving profitability.

Company management initiated a project to provide managers with tools and information to help them make better merchandise and stocking decisions. One major goal was to reduce the immense amount of paper being passed back and forth. Another was to help store managers better understand what was happening within their own stores and within other stores in the company. A third goal was to improve managers' ability to recognize customer buying patterns and anticipate trends so they could align their inventory.

The company adopted a business intelligence software package from MicroStrategy Inc. of McLean, Virginia. The system relies on sales and inventory data from each and every purchase, which are automatically sent to a central data warehouse where store managers and corporate staff can access this information via the Web. The system contains report templates and wizards, enabling managers to customize the information as needed, identifying, for example, the highest-margin items, which can then be ranked by sales.

Barrie Stewart, the manager of a store in Dunbartonshire, Scotland, says the new system "allows me to ask several questions, such as, "Is the performance down due to poor display standards, poor stock availability, or incorrect location?" He also asks such questions as whether the product is right for his store and does it earn enough profit for the space it uses. Stewart even shares this information with his employees so, for example, they can display their best-selling products in high visibility locations. He finds that his staff now gives him helpful feedback including ideas on increasing profit. Stewart even says "if we see that a high-margin book is selling particularly well in, say, a tourist location, we can add a display at a shop that has high tourist traffic." Dukes points out that "when we see one store selling out of a particular item, we can shift inventory from a store where it isn't selling as well and take advantage of customer demand." The company even has taken the time to train its employees on the system so they can use it themselves.

To Think About: List the ways this decision-support system helps WH Smith employees make decisions. How has it pro-

vided value for the firm? Suggest other ways the system can help them make decisions and increase profits.

Sources: Pimm Fox, "Insights Turn Into Profits," *ComputerWorld*, February 10, 2002; MicroStrategy Incorporated, "WH Smith PLC Selects Microstrategy to Anchor BI Initiatives," *DSstar*, accessed August 15, 2002, www.tgc.com/dsstar; and WH Smith PLC corporate Web site, www.whsmithplc.com, accessed June 12, 2005.

Components of DSS

Figure 15-5 illustrates the components of DSS. They include a database of data used for query and analysis; a software system with models, data mining, and other analytical tools; and a user interface.

The **DSS database** is a collection of current or historical data from a number of applications or groups. It may be a small database residing on a PC that contains a subset of corporate data that has been downloaded and possibly combined with external data. Alternatively, the DSS database may be a massive data warehouse that is continuously updated by major corporate TPS (including enterprise systems and data generated by Web site transactions). The data in DSS databases are generally extracts or copies of production databases so that using DSS does not interfere with critical operational systems.

DSS software system contains the software tools that are used for data analysis. It may contain various OLAP tools, data-mining tools, or a collection of mathematical and analytical models that can easily be made accessible to the DSS user. A **model** is an abstract representation that illustrates the components or relationships of a phenomenon. A model can be a physical model (such as a model airplane), a mathematical model (such as an equation), or a verbal model (such as a description of a procedure for writing an order). Each decision-support system is developed for a specific set of purposes and makes different collections of models available depending on those purposes.

Perhaps the most common models are libraries of statistical models. These libraries usually contain the full range of expected statistical functions, including means, medians,

FIGURE 15-5   *Overview of a decision-support system.*

The main components of DSS are the DSS database, the DSS software system, and the user interface. The DSS database may be a small database residing on a PC or a massive data warehouse.

DSS database

DSS software system

model

deviations, and scatter plots. The software has the ability to project future outcomes by analyzing a series of data. Statistical modelling software can be used to help establish relationships, such as relating product sales to differences in age, income, or other factors between communities. Optimization models, often using linear programming, determine optimal resource allocation to maximize or minimize specified variables, such as cost or time. A classic use of optimization models is to determine the proper mix of products within a given market to maximize profits.

Forecasting models often are used to forecast sales. The user of this type of model might supply a range of historical data to project future conditions and the sales that might result from those conditions. The decision maker could vary those future conditions (entering, for example, a rise in raw materials costs or the entry of a new, low-priced competitor in the market) to determine how new conditions might affect sales. Companies often use this software to predict the actions of competitors. Model libraries exist for specific functions, such as financial and risk analysis models.

Among the most widely used models are **sensitivity analysis** models that ask what-if questions repeatedly to determine the impact on outcomes of changes in one or more factors. What-if analysis—working forward from known or assumed conditions—allows the user to vary certain values to test results in order to better predict outcomes if changes occur in those values. What happens if we raise the price by 5 percent or increase the advertising budget by $100 000? What happens if we keep the price and advertising budget the same? Desktop spreadsheet software, such as Microsoft Excel or Lotus 1-2-3, is often used for this purpose (see Figure 15-6). Backward sensitivity analysis software is used for goal seeking: If I want to sell 1 million product units next year, how much must I reduce the price of the product?

The DSS user interface permits easy interaction between users of the system and the DSS software tools. A graphical, easy-to-use, flexible user interface supports the dialogue between the user and DSS. The DSS users can be managers or employees with no patience for learning a complex tool, so the interface must be relatively intuitive. Many DSS today are being developed with Web-based interfaces to take advantage of the Web's ease of use, interactivity, and capabilities for personalization and customization. Developing successful DSS requires a high level of user participation to make sure the system provides the information managers need.

Business Value of DSS

DSS can be used in many ways to support decision making. Table 15-4 lists examples of DSS in well-known companies. Both data-driven and model-driven DSS have become very powerful and sophisticated, providing fine-grained information for decisions that enable the firm to coordinate both internal and external business processes much more precisely. Some of these DSS are helping companies with decisions in supply chain management or customer relationship management. Some take advantage of the company-wide data provided

sensitivity analysis

FIGURE 15-6 *Sensitivity analysis.*

Total fixed costs	19000					
Variable cost per unit	3					
Average sales price	17					
Contribution margin	14					
Breakeven point	1357					
			Variable Cost per Unit			
Sales	1357	2	3	4	5	6
Price	14	1583	1727	1900	2111	2375
	15	1462	1583	1727	1900	2111
	16	1357	1462	1583	1727	1900
	17	1267	1357	1462	1583	1727
	18	1188	1267	1357	1462	1583

This table displays the results of a sensitivity analysis of the effect of changing the sales price of a necktie and the cost per unit on the product's break-even point. It answers the question, "What happens to the break-even point if the sales price and the cost to make each unit increase or decrease?"

by enterprise systems. DSS today can also harness the interactive capabilities of the Web to provide decision-support tools to both employees and customers.

To illustrate the range of capabilities of DSS, the following sections describe some successful DSS applications. DaimlerChrysler's TESYS, described in the chapter-opening case, is an example of a model-driven decision-support system. The customer analysis systems used by W.H. Smith is an example of data-driven DSS. Sweden's Laps Care system for managing elderly home care is an application of geographic information systems (GIS), a special category of DSS for visualizing data geographically.

Some of these DSS use data gathered from the Web. Chapter 13 describes how each action a visitor takes when visiting a particular Web site can be captured on that Web site's log. Companies can mine these data to answer questions about what customers are purchasing and what promotions are generating the most traffic. The results can help companies tailor marketing programs effectively, redesign Web sites to optimize traffic, and create personalized buying experiences for Web site visitors. Other DSS combine Web site transaction data with data from enterprise systems.

Data Visualization and Geographic Information Systems

Data from information systems can be made easier for users to digest and act on by using graphics, charts, tables, graphs, maps, digital images, three-dimensional presentations, animations, and other data visualization technologies. By presenting data in graphical form, **data visualization** tools help users see patterns and relationships in large amounts of data that would be difficult to discern if the data were presented as traditional lists of text and numbers. Some data visualization tools are interactive, enabling users to manipulate data and see the graphical displays change in response to the changes they make.

Geographic information systems (GIS) are a special category of DSS that use data visualization technology to analyze and display data for planning and decision making in the form of digitized maps. The software can assemble, store, manipulate, and display geographically referenced information, tying data to points, lines, and areas on a map. GIS have modelling capabilities, enabling managers to change data and automatically revise business scenarios to find better solutions.

GIS can thus be used to support decisions that require knowledge about the geographic distribution of people or other resources in scientific research, resource management, and development planning. For example, GIS might be used to help state and local governments calculate emergency response times to natural disasters, retail chains identify profitable new store locations, or banks identify the best locations for installing new branches or automatic teller machine (ATM) terminals. GIS tools have become affordable even for small businesses, and some can be used on the Web.

This type of decision-support system enables companies to segment their customer base with a high level of precision where it can be used to drive a marketing campaign. Based on the results of data mining, a firm can develop specific marketing campaigns for each customer segment. For example, it could target frequent customers living near a store with coupons for products of interest and rewards for frequent shoppers.

TABLE 15-4 *Examples of Decision-Support Systems*

ORGANIZATION	DSS APPLICATION
General Accident Insurance	Customer buying patterns and fraud detection
Canadian National Railway	Train dispatching and routing
Frito-Lay, Inc.	Price, advertising, and promotion selection
Burlington Coat Factory	Store location and inventory mix
Royal Bank of Canada (RBC)	Customer profiles
Air Canada	Flight scheduling and passenger demand forecasting

data visualization

geographic information systems (GIS)

FIGURE 15-7   *A geographic information system.*

The City of Hamilton uses a geographic information system to examine West Nile Virus risk assessment within the city.

Source: City of Hamilton, Public Health Services, Health Protection Branch, West Nile Virus Program.

The Window on Management shows how GIS are being used in Sweden to help plan the assignment of home health aides who assist elderly people. Planners of elderly home care must deal with a complex set of variables that include multiple tasks, many different caregivers and clients, and limited time frames for both care giving and travel. This particular problem lends itself to geographic information system software because the locations of both elderly clients and home caregivers must be considered when planning daily schedules.

Web-Based Customer Decision-Support Systems

The growth of electronic commerce has encouraged many companies to develop DSS where customers and employees can take advantage of Internet information resources and Web capabilities for interactivity and personalization. DSS based on the Web and the Internet can support decision making by providing online access to various databases and information pools along with software for data analysis. Some of these DSS are targeted toward management, but many have been developed to attract customers by providing information and tools to assist their decision making as they select products and services. Companies are finding that deciding which products and services to purchase has become increasingly information intensive. People are now using more information from multiple sources to make purchasing decisions (such as purchasing a car or computer) before they interact with the product or sales staff. **Customer decision-support systems (CDSS)** support the decision-making process of an existing or potential customer.

People interested in purchasing a product or service can use Internet search engines, intelligent agents, online catalogues, Web directories, newsgroup discussions, email, and other tools to help them locate the information they need to help with their decision. Information brokers are also sources of summarized, structured information for specific products or industries and may provide models for evaluating the information. Companies also have developed specific customer Web sites where all the information, models, or other analytical tools for evaluating alternatives are concentrated in one location. Web-based DSS have become especially popular in the financial services area because so many people are trying to manage their own assets and retirement savings. Table 15-5 lists some examples.

customer decision-support systems (CDSS)

WINDOW ON MANAGEMENT

GIS Help the Elderly in Sweden

Caring for elderly people when they are too old to care for themselves is a growing concern in Canada, the United States, Europe, Japan, and other countries. In Sweden, elderly people in need of daily care can move to retirement homes, or they can remain in their own home with home assistance provided by the state. Today the trend is to encourage the elderly to stay in their own homes as long as possible.

To bring support services into the home, an assessor working with Swedish local authorities determines what type of assistance and how much assistance the client needs. A typical care plan might call for two showers per week, weekly laundry, weekly cleaning, monthly doctor's visit, and 20 hours of additional care per month.

All of this information serves as input into a visit plan stating when and where each visit should be performed. The visit plan can be administered by either the local government or, more commonly, by a private contractor.

The schedule for home health aide visits is normally planned several days in advance. However, plans may need to be revised if staff members become ill or the clients have to be taken to the hospital. Some visits may need to be shortened or postponed or have extra staff allocated. Last-minute changes are made to the plan each morning. Making these last-minute changes might consume 30 to 45 minutes per day, delaying the departure of staff members until everyone's daily assignments are finalized.

Ideally, planning for elderly care should be as efficient as possible and distribute the workload evenly among the staff. Each visit has a window of time and requires a set of skills that must be met by a staff member. Sufficient travel time between visits must be allocated, and each staff member must be given planned breaks for meals. Each elderly client has one or several preferred staff members who visit, and certain visits require multiple staff members.

This problem is similar to vehicle routing problems, which have been popular applications for geographic information systems. Planning must consider many different variables, including skills, time frame, locations, and the number of staff.

The Home Care Department of the Swedish city of Danderyd, Linkoping University, and Linkoping-based software company Optimal Solutions AB came up with a solution. They created a staff planning system called Laps Care that enables rapid and efficient planning of home care staff schedules. Laps Care has been used daily for elderly home care planning since November 2002.

Here's how the system works. The user inputs data about home health care employees, their clients, and the visits that are to be performed, as well as data about the time staff members must spend in transit to reach each client. Maps are included based on map data from Navigation Technologies, which contains a detailed description of the local road network. Using address matching, the system positions each customer on the map. The system uses these data to calculate travel time between visits, generating a plan that represents an optimal solution where the right person with the right skills provides the right care at the right time.

The resulting solution can be viewed as a text grid, in a Gantt chart, or on a map displaying the route of each staff member and the assigned visits. It takes the system about two minutes to generate each alternative solution. Users often use the system to create alternative solutions to evaluate, so within half an hour, they can easily test five to 10 scenarios.

When the city of Danderyd started using Laps Care, it found that the system dramatically cut down the time to develop a daily visit plan. One person could create the plan within 15 minutes, and home health staff could leave for their assignments much earlier, saving about 7 percent of total working time. The system divides the workload much more evenly among caregivers than the earlier manual system and uses staff members' special skills more effectively. Although travel times have been reduced, the system is valued more for producing accurate travel time estimates and good working schedules that leave enough time for travelling. There is much less early morning chaos.

Did the system provide an answer for everything? Not quite. There were some cases for which the system could not come up with a feasible solution even though there were manual plans for home health care. Some home health aides were combining several tasks into one (e.g., doing laundry for three people at once).

Senior staff members initially posed problems by trying to keep the more desirable tasks for themselves, leaving harder work for their newer colleagues. Laps Care eliminated this inequitable situation by creating the fairest possible schedule for everyone. Laps Care was so successful that it won the EURO Award 2003 for Excellence in Practice in Operations Research. Other organizations have since adopted the system.

To Think About: How does Laps Care help home health care services make decisions? What problems does it solve? How does it provide value for these organizations and for their clients?

Sources: Patrik Eveborn, Patrik Flisberg, and Mikael Ronnqvist, "Home Care Operations," *OR/MS Today*, April 2004; www.math.liu.se, accessed May 5, 2004; www.optimalsolutions.com, accessed May 5, 2004; and Optimal Solutions, "Laps Care," 2002.

TABLE 15-5 *Examples of Web-Based DSS*

DSS	DESCRIPTION
Nikon Optical Canada	Web site allows a wide range of employees, including senior managers, marketing analysts, and sales representatives, to track sales activity of optical lenses purchased by practitioners, distributors, and optical laboratories across the Canadian territories. This enables Nikon to identify profitable customers for future sell-up opportunities, to track margins and areas of profitability, and to more effectively execute marketing campaigns.
General Electric Plastics	Web site provides a design solutions centre with a Web-based suite of online engineering tools for materials developers in the plastics industry. Visitors can select plastics materials, perform production cost estimates, search for product-specification information, and get online training.
T.D. Waterhouse	Web site features online, interactive tools application to help clients make decisions about bond investments. It provides information about bonds as investments and an interactive tool to show the effect of price and yield changes.
Bank of Montreal	Web site enables queries to run against the enterprise-wide database each day and delivers intuitive, drillable reports to senior executives, financial service managers, line-of-business managers, branch employees, and HR personnel. The BMO MIND (Management Information-New Directions) CRM system can also perform CRM analyses to highlight accounts with low performance rates.

15.3   Group Decision-Support Systems

The DSS we have just described focus primarily on individual decision making. However, so much work is accomplished in groups within firms that a special category of systems called group decision-support systems (GDSS) has been developed to support group and organizational decision making.

What are Group Decision-Support Systems?

Group decision-support systems (GDSS) are interactive computer-based systems used to facilitate the solution of unstructured problems by a set of decision makers working together as a group (DeSanctis and Gallupe 1987). Groupware and Web-based tools for videoconferencing and electronic meetings described earlier in this text can support some group decision processes, but their focus is primarily on communication. GDSS, however, provide tools and technologies geared explicitly toward group decision making. GDSS were developed in response to a growing concern over the quality and effectiveness of meetings. The underlying problems in group decision making have been the explosion of decision-maker meetings, the growing length of those meetings, and the increased number of attendees. Estimates on the amount of a manager's time spent in meetings range from 35 to 70 percent.

Components of GDSS GDSS make meetings more productive by providing tools to facilitate planning, generating, organizing, and evaluating ideas; establishing priorities; and documenting meeting proceedings for others in the firm. GDSS consist of three basic elements: hardware, software tools, and people. *Hardware* refers to the conference facility itself, including the room, the tables, and the chairs. A facility for group decision making must be physically laid out in a manner that supports group collaboration. It must also include some electronic hardware, such as electronic display boards and audio-visual, computer, and networking equipment.

Chapters 7 and 16 describe groupware tools for collaborative work that can be used to support group decision making. In addition specific GDSS *software tools* support group meetings. These tools were originally developed for meetings in which all participants are in the same room, but they also can be used for networked meetings in which participants are in different locations. Specific GDSS software tools include the following:

group decision-support systems (GDSS)

- *Electronic questionnaires* aid the organizers in pre-meeting planning by identifying issues of concern and by helping to ensure that key planning information is not overlooked.
- *Electronic brainstorming tools* enable individuals, simultaneously and anonymously, to contribute ideas on the topics of the meeting.
- *Idea organizers* facilitate the organized integration and synthesis of ideas generated during brainstorming.
- *Questionnaire tools* support the facilitators and group leaders as they gather information before and during the process of setting priorities.
- *Tools for voting or setting priorities* make available a range of methods from simple voting, to ranking in order, to a range of weighted techniques for setting priorities or voting.
- *Stakeholder identification and analysis tools* use structured approaches to evaluate the impact of an emerging proposal on the organization and to identify stakeholders and evaluate the potential impact of those stakeholders on the proposed project.
- *Policy formation tools* provide structured support for developing agreement on the wording of policy statements.
- *Group dictionaries* document group agreement on definitions of words and terms central to the project.

People refers not only to the participants but also to a trained facilitator and often to staff who support the hardware and software. Together, these elements have led to the creation of a range of different kinds of GDSS, from simple electronic boardrooms to elaborate collaboration laboratories. In a collaboration laboratory, individuals work on their own desktop PCs or workstations. Their input is integrated on a file server and is viewable on a common screen at the front of the room; in most systems, the integrated input is also viewable on the individual participant's screen.

Overview of a GDSS Meeting

In a GDSS electronic meeting, each attendee has a workstation. The workstations are networked and are connected to the facilitator's console, which serves as the facilitator's workstation and control panel, and the meeting's file server. All data that the attendees forward from their workstations to the group are collected and saved on the file server. The facilitator is able to project computer images onto the projection screen at the front of the room. The facilitator also has an overhead projector available. Whiteboards are visible on either side of the projection screen. Many electronic meeting rooms have seating arrangements in semicircles and are tiered in legislative style to accommodate a large number of attendees. The facilitator controls the use of tools during the meeting.

Attendees have full control of their desktop computers. An attendee is able to view the agenda (and other planning documents), look at the integrated screen (or screens, as the session progresses), use ordinary desktop PC tools (such as a word processor or a spreadsheet), tap into production data that have been made available, or work on the screen associated with the current meeting step and tool (such as a brainstorming screen).

During the meeting, all input to the integrated screens is saved on the file server and participants' work is kept confidential. When the meeting is completed, a full record of the meeting (both raw material and resultant output) is available to the attendees and can be made available to anyone else who needs access. Figure 15-8 illustrates the sequence of activities at a typical electronic meeting along with the types of tools used and the output of those tools.

Business Value of GDSS

Studies show that in traditional decision-making meetings without GDSS support the optimal meeting size is three to five attendees. Beyond that size, the meeting process

FIGURE 15-8   *Group system tools.*

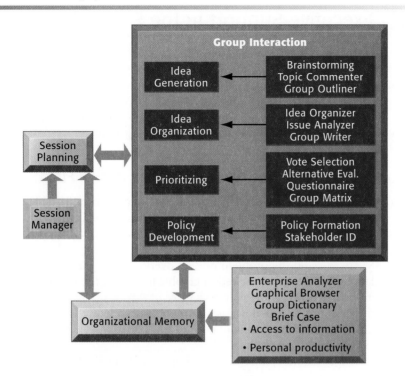

The sequence of activities and collaborative support tools used in an electronic meeting system facilitate communication among attendees and generate a full record of the meeting.

Source: From Nunamaker et al., "Electronic Meeting Systems to Support Group Work," *Communications of the ACM*, July 1991. Reprinted by permission.

begins to break down. Using GDSS software, studies show the number of attendees at a meeting can increase while productivity also increases. One reason for this increase is that attendees contribute simultaneously rather than one at a time, which makes more efficient use of meeting time.

GDSS contribute to a more collaborative atmosphere by guaranteeing contributors' anonymity so that attendees can focus on evaluating the ideas themselves. Attendees can contribute without fear of being personally criticized or of having their ideas rejected because of the identity of the contributor. GDSS software tools follow structured methods for organizing and evaluating ideas and for preserving the results of meetings, enabling non-attendees to locate needed information after the meeting. The documentation of a meeting by one group at one site can also be used as input to another meeting on the same project at another site.

If properly designed and supported, GDSS meetings can increase the number of ideas generated and the quality of decisions while producing the desired results in fewer meetings in both face-to-face and distributed meeting environments (Anson and Munkvold 2004). When used by project teams for frequent meetings, GDSS can lead to more participative and democratic decision making (Dennis and Garfield 2003). However, GDSS outcomes are not necessarily better than face-to-face meetings, and electronic brainstorming has not been widely adopted (Dennis and Reinicke 2004). GDSS seem most useful for tasks involving idea generation, complex problems, and large groups (Fjermestad and Hiltz 2000–2001, 1998–1999).

One problem with understanding the value of GDSS is their complexity. GDSS can be configured in an almost infinite variety of ways, and the nature of electronic meeting technology is only one of a number of factors that affect meeting processes and output. The outcome of group meetings depends on the composition of the group, the manner in which the problem is presented to the group, the facilitator's effectiveness, the organization's culture and environment, the quality of the planning, the cooperation of the attendees, and the appropriateness of tools selected for different types of meetings and decision problems (Dennis and Wixom 2001–2002; Dennis, Wixom, and Vandenberg 2001; Hender, Dean, Rodgers, and Nunamaker 2002).

15.4 Executive Support in the Enterprise

Executive support systems (ESS), which we introduced in Chapter 2, help managers with unstructured and semistructured problems by focusing on the information needs of senior management. Combining data from internal and external sources, ESS create a generalized computing and communications environment that can be focused and applied to a changing array of problems. ESS help senior executives monitor organizational performance, track activities of competitors, spot problems, identify opportunities, and forecast trends.

The Role of Executive Support Systems in the Firm

Contemporary ESS can bring together data from all parts of the firm and enable managers to select, access, and tailor them as needed with easy-to-use desktop analytical tools and online data displays. Use of the systems has migrated down several organizational levels so that the executive and his or her subordinates are able to look at the same data in the same way.

Today's ESS try to avoid the problem of data overload so common in paper reports because the data can be filtered or viewed in graphic format (if the user so chooses). ESS have the ability to **drill down**, moving from a piece of summary data to lower and lower levels of detail. The ability to drill down is useful not only to senior executives but also to employees at lower levels of the firm who need to analyze data. OLAP tools for analyzing large databases provide this capability.

A major challenge of developing executive support systems has been to integrate data from systems designed for very different purposes so that senior executives can review organizational performance from a firm-wide perspective. In the traditional firm, which typically had hundreds or even thousands of incompatible systems, pulling such information together and making sense out of it was a major task. Today, properly configured and implemented enterprise systems can provide managers with timely, comprehensive, and accurate firm-wide information. ESS based on firm-wide data can be considered logical extensions of enterprise system functionality.

External data, including data from the Web, are now more easily available in many ESS as well. Executives need a wide range of external data, from current stock market news to competitor information, industry trends, and even projected legislative action. Through their ESS, many managers have access to news services, financial market databases, economic information, and whatever other public data they may require.

Contemporary ESS include tools for modelling and analysis. With only a minimum of experience, most managers find they can use these tools to create graphic comparisons of data by time, region, product, price range, and so on. (While DSS use these tools primarily for modelling and analysis in a fairly narrow range of decision situations, ESS use them primarily to provide status information about organizational performance.)

ESS must be designed so that high-level managers and others can use them without much training. One area that merits special attention is the determination of executive information requirements. ESS need to have some facility for environmental scanning. A key information requirement of managers at the strategic level is the ability to detect signals of problems in the organizational environment that indicate strategic threats and opportunities (Walls et al. 1992). The ESS need to be designed so that both external and internal sources of information can be used for environmental scanning purposes.

Business Value of Executive Support Systems

Much of the value of ESS is found in their flexibility. ESS put data and tools in the hands of executives without addressing specific problems or imposing solutions. Executives are free to shape the problems as necessary, using the system as an extension of their own thinking processes.

The most visible benefit of ESS is their ability to analyze, compare, and highlight trends. The easy use of graphics enables the user to look at more data in less time with

drill down

greater clarity and insight than paper-based systems can provide. In the past, executives obtained the same information by taking up days and weeks of their staffs' valuable time. By using ESS, staff and executives are freed for the more creative analysis and decision making. ESS capabilities for drilling down and highlighting trends may also enhance the quality of analysis and can speed decision making (Leidner and Elam 1993–1994).

Executives are using ESS to monitor performance more successfully in their own areas of responsibility. Some companies are using these systems to monitor key performance indicators for the entire firm and to measure firm performance against changes in the external environment. The timeliness and availability of the data result in needed actions being identified and carried out earlier than previously could have been done. Problems can be handled before they become too damaging; opportunities can also be identified earlier. These systems can thus help businesses move toward a "sense-and-respond" strategy.

Well-designed ESS could dramatically improve management performance and increase upper management's span of control. Immediate access to so much data enables executives to better monitor activities of lower units reporting to them. That very monitoring ability could enable decision making to be decentralized and to take place at lower operating levels. Executives are often willing to push decision making further down into the organization as long as they can be assured that all is going well. Alternatively, executive support systems based on enterprise-wide data could potentially increase management centralization, enabling senior executives to monitor the performance of subordinates across the company and direct them to take appropriate action when conditions change.

Executive Support Systems and the Digital Firm

To illustrate the different ways in which ESS can enhance management decision making, we now describe important types of ESS applications for gathering business intelligence and monitoring corporate performance, including ESS based on enterprise systems.

ESS for Business Intelligence Today, customer expectations, Internet technology, and new business models can alter the competitive landscape so rapidly that managers need special capabilities for competitive intelligence gathering. ESS can help managers identify changing market conditions, formulate responses, track implementation efforts, and learn from feedback.

BP Sony NV, the Netherlands branch of the multinational electronics giant, wanted more insight from the marketplace to drive its competitive strategy. Until recently, its management reports were based primarily on financial and administrative data that took at least 24 hours to generate. Management wanted to be able to make meaningful decisions based on marketing and sales data as well so it could respond quickly to marketplace changes. Sony Netherlands constructed a data warehouse and executive information system for this purpose.

The system is now available to 78 users in management, marketing, and sales. They can use the system to help them define strategies, search for opportunities, identify problems, and substantiate actions. Using a drill-down function, they can examine the underlying numbers behind the total result. For instance, while senior management can obtain sales results by business unit or product group, a marketing manager can use the system to look only at his or her group of products. The manager can produce a report to indicate exactly which products are strong or weak performers or to rank dealers by performance. The system is flexible, easy to use, and can provide much of this information to the user online (Information Builders 2000).

Corset Shop, a highly regarded intimate apparel retailer for more than 37 years, implemented a suite of applications from Montreal's Gemmar Systems International. Corset Shop operates stores under the name Bare Necessities and also operates leased departments coast-to-coast with more than 35 000 SKUs of lingerie, sleepwear, loungewear, legwear, and accessories. Gemmar's Retail-1 EIS gives Corset Shop executives the ability to drill down, look at category, department, or class statistics, rank their best and worst products, and season and age their products and vendors. They can also examine store performance and refunds, analyze inventory sell through, and a host of other types of analysis.

Monitoring Corporate Performance with Digital Dashboards and Balanced Scorecard Systems

ESS can be configured to summarize and report on key performance indicators for senior management in the form of a **digital dashboard** or "executive dashboard." The dashboard displays all of the critical measurements for piloting a company on a single screen, similar to the cockpit of an airplane or an automobile dashboard. The dashboard presents key performance indicators as graphs and charts in a Web browser format, providing a one-page overview of all the critical measurements necessary to make key executive decisions (Few 2004).

Companies have traditionally measured value using financial metrics, such as return on investment (ROI), which we describe in Chapter 11. Many firms are now implementing a **balanced scorecard** model that supplements traditional financial measures with measurements from additional perspectives, such as customers, internal business processes, and learning and growth. Managers can use balanced scorecard systems to see how well the firm is meeting its strategic goals. The goals and measures for the balanced scorecard vary from company to company. Companies are setting up information systems to populate the scorecard with the data needed for management.

At Nova Scotia Power, Inc., the balanced scorecard (BSC) has been linked to many critical systems. For example, the annual business planning and budgeting process is now driven by the balanced scorecard. This new system is called "Strategic Resource Allocation" because it provides the opportunity to display how resource allocation decisions directly influence the achievement of strategy. The scorecard is also linked to the incentive compensation system and has been cascaded throughout the company to ensure goal alignment at every level. Finally, and perhaps most importantly, the BSC is a powerful communication tool, signalling to everyone in the organization key success measures and how they can influence them.

Amsterdam-based ING Bank, which is part of the ING Group global financial services firm, adopted a balanced scorecard approach when it reorganized. Management wanted to shift from a product to a client orientation and develop appropriate performance indicators to measure progress in this new direction. In 1997, the bank built a Web-based balanced scorecard application using SAS tools for data warehousing and statistical analysis to measure progress with 21 indicators. Data from the scorecard, from sources such as financial ledger applications and client retention and market penetration ratios, feed a central data warehouse. The data come from systems running on Lotus Notes, Microsoft Excel spreadsheets, and Oracle and DB2 databases. The data warehouse and balanced scorecard software run on IBM RS/6000 servers. ING initially made the balanced scorecard system available only to midrange executives in sales, but later extended it to 3000 users, including people at nearly every level of its relationship management group. Users regularly check progress with the scorecard. For example, by comparing how many visits they have made to different clients, sales people can make better decisions about how to allocate their time (McCune, 2000).

Roadway Express: Enterprise-Wide Reporting and Analysis

Enterprise application vendors are now providing capabilities to extend the usefulness of data captured in operational systems to give management a picture of the overall performance of the firm. Some provide reporting of metrics for balanced scorecard analysis as well as more traditional financial and operating metrics. For example, SAP offers a Web-enabled mySAP strategic enterprise management module featuring corporate performance metrics, simulation, and planning tools. Managers can model and communicate key performance indicators for a balanced scorecard. Another measurement tool called the Management Cockpit can be used to monitor strategic performance indicators using internal and external benchmarks.

Companies can use these new enterprise-reporting capabilities to create measures of firm performance that were not previously available, including activity-based costing. **Activity-based costing** is a budgeting and analysis model that identifies all the resources, processes, and costs, including overhead and operating expenses, required to produce a specific product or service. It focuses on determining firm activities that create costs rather than on merely tracking what has been spent. It enables managers to ascertain

digital dashboard

balanced scorecard

activity-based costing

which products or services—or customers—are profitable and those that are not profitable so they can determine the changes required to maximize firm profitability. Instead of reporting in terms of product and income, the system can focus on contribution margins and customer accounts, with the ability to calculate the current and lifetime value of each account.

Roadway Express, headquartered in Akron, Ohio, uses activity-based costing to analyze every step in the process of customer service. The company specializes in less-than-truckload freight hauling in North America, handling 50 000 to 60 000 shipments per day. Labour constitutes 60 percent of its operating expenses and average profit margins for the industry are only 2.5 percent. In 1997, Roadway built an Oracle data warehouse and installed Business Objects data analysis software to analyze information about the size, content, number of shipments, and the time and cost for each step in moving goods from source to destination. The system also captures time and cost data for activities associated with settling claims for damaged freight. This system calculates exactly how much each activity costs and even the actual costs of specific activities for a particular customer. It can identify which customer and which shipment types are the most and least profitable and which are associated with the most damage claims. Better understanding its costs helps Roadway reduce fixed costs, identify profitable customers, and price its services to maximize operating margins (Cone and Carr 2002).

Management Opportunities, Challenges, and Solutions

DSS, GDSS, and ESS are systems for managers, and they create a special set of challenges and opportunities.

Opportunities

Systems for decision support provide extraordinary opportunities for increasing the precision, accuracy, and speed of decisions made by both managers and employees. These systems can have a significant impact on organizations if these DSS equip all decision makers in the firm to make better decisions.

Management Challenges

DSS, GDSS, and ESS can provide information to help managers make better decisions that will enhance organizational performance, but they do not necessarily create additional value. It is not always easy to understand a managerial decision problem if it is unstructured. Managers may not be able to change their thinking to harness the power of these systems. Systems to support managerial decision making raise the following challenges:

Building Systems that Can Actually Fulfill Executive Information Requirements Even with the use of critical success factors and other information requirements determination methods, it may still be difficult to establish information requirements for ESS and DSS serving senior management. Many decisions made by high-level managers are unstructured, and information systems may not be able to support them. Even if a problem can be addressed by an information system, senior management may not fully understand its actual information needs. For instance, senior managers may not agree on the firm's critical success factors, or the critical success factors they describe may be inappropriate or outdated if the firm is confronting a crisis requiring a major strategic change.

Changing Management Thinking to Make Better Use of Systems for Decision Support Enterprise systems and data warehouses have made it much easier to supply DSS and ESS with data from many different systems than in the past. The remaining challenge is changing management thinking to use the data that are available to maximum advantage, to develop better reporting categories for measuring firm performance, and to inform new types of decisions. Many managers use the new capabilities in DSS and ESS to obtain the same information as before. Major changes in management thinking will be required to encourage managers to ask better questions about the data.

Organizational Resistance ESS potentially could give top executives the capability of examining other managers' work without their knowledge, so there may be some resistance to ESS at lower levels of the organization. Implementation of ESS should be carefully managed to neutralize such opposition (see Chapter 11).

Solution Guidelines

Users of DSS, GDSS, and ESS are middle and high-level managers who are pressed for time. The system must be one that the executive can learn very rapidly. Developers must be certain the system will work before they demonstrate it to high-level users, or it will be rejected.

Flexible Design and Development Building DSS, GDSS, or ESS is different from building TPS or MIS, which are based on a specific set of information requirements. The information requirements for DSS or ESS are more unstructured and fluid and require a much greater level of user participation to develop. Users must work with information systems specialists to identify a problem and a specific set of capabilities that will help them arrive at decisions about the problem. The system must be flexible and evolve as the sophistication of users grows. Developing management support systems should therefore use a method such as prototyping (see Chapter 10) that enables users to experiment with evolving versions of the design.

Training and Management Support Several studies have noted that user training, involvement, and experience; top management support; and length of use are the most important factors in the success of management support systems. Success was measured as perceived improvement in decision making and overall satisfaction with the system (Alavi and Joachimsthaler 1992). These success factors are not very different from those for other types of systems (see Chapter 11).

Summary

1. *Describe different types of decisions and the decision-making process.*

The different levels in an organization (strategic, management, operational) have different decision-making requirements. Decisions can be structured, semistructured, or unstructured, with structured decisions clustering at the operational level of the organization and unstructured decisions at the strategic level. Decision making can be performed by individuals or groups and includes employees as well as operational, middle, and senior managers. There are four stages in decision making: intelligence, design, choice, and implementation. Systems to support decision making do not always produce better management and employee decisions that improve firm performance because of problems with information quality, management filters, and organizational inertia.

2. *Evaluate the role of information systems in helping people working both individually and in a group to make decisions more efficiently.*

Specialized systems for business intelligence are specifically designed to help managers and employees make better decisions. Business intelligence includes management information systems (MIS), decision-support systems (DSS), group decision-support systems (GDSS), and executive support systems (ESS) and makes use of data from enterprise applications and technologies such as data mining and online analytical processing (OLAP).

Management information systems (MIS) provide information on firm performance to help managers monitor and control the business, often in the form of fixed regularly scheduled reports based on data summarized from the firm's transaction processing systems. MIS support structured decisions and some semistructured decisions.

Decision-support systems (DSS) combine data, sophisticated analytical models and tools, and user-friendly software into a single powerful system that can support semistructured or unstructured decision making. The components of DSS are the DSS database, the DSS software system, and the user interface. There are two kinds of DSS: model-driven DSS and data-driven DSS. DSS can help support decisions for pricing, asset utilization, supply chain management, and customer relationship management as well model alternative business scenarios. DSS targeted toward customers as well as managers are becoming available on the Web. A special category of DSS called geographic information systems (GIS) uses data visualization technology to analyze and display data for planning and decision making with digitized maps.

People working together in a group can use group decision-support systems to help them in the process of arriving at a decision. Group decision-support systems have hardware, software, and people components. Hardware components consist of the conference room facilities, including seating arrangements and computer and other electronic hardware. Software components include tools for organizing ideas, gathering information, ranking and setting priorities, and documenting meeting sessions. People components include participants, a trained facilitator, and staff to support the hardware and software.

GDSS help decision makers arrive at a decision more efficiently and is especially useful for increasing the productivity of meetings of more than four or five people. However, the effectiveness of GDSS is contingent on the composition of the group, the task, appropriate tool selection and meeting support, and the organizational context of the meeting.

3. Demonstrate how executive support systems can help senior managers make better decisions.

Executive support systems (ESS) help senior managers with unstructured problems that occur at the strategic level of the firm. ESS provide data from both internal and external sources and provide a generalized computing and communications environment that can be focused and applied to a changing array of problems. ESS help senior executives monitor firm performance, spot problems, identify opportunities, and forecast trends. These systems can filter out extraneous details for high-level overviews, or they can drill down to provide senior managers with detailed transaction data if required. ESS are starting to take advantage of firm-wide data provided by enterprise systems.

ESS help senior managers analyze, compare, and highlight trends so that the managers may more easily monitor organizational performance or identify strategic problems and opportunities. They are very useful for environmental scanning, providing business intelligence to help management detect strategic threats or opportunities from the organization's environment. ESS can increase the span of control of senior management, allowing them to oversee more people with fewer resources.

4. Assess how systems that support decision making can provide value for the firm.

DSS, GDSS, and ESS are starting to take advantage of more accurate firm-wide data provided by enterprise systems and the new information technology infrastructure to support very fine-grained decisions for guiding the firm, coordinating work activities across the enterprise, and responding rapidly to changing markets and customers. DSS can be used to guide company-wide decisions in supply chain management, customer relationship management, and business planning scenarios. ESS can be used to monitor company-wide performance using both traditional financial metrics and the balanced scorecard model. The ability to explore the outcomes of alternative organizational scenarios, use precise firm-wide information, and provide tools to facilitate group decision processes can help managers make decisions that help the firm achieve its strategic objectives.

5. Identify the challenges posed by decision-support systems, group decision-support systems, and executive support systems, and propose management solutions.

Systems to support decision making do not always lead to better decisions or improved organizational performance. It is not always easy to understand a managerial decision problem if it is unstructured. Managers may not be able to change their thinking to harness the power of these systems, to ask better questions of their data, or to interpret system output accurately. There may be some resistance to ESS at lower levels of the organization if senior management is using them to monitor performance. These systems are more likely to be successful if they are designed and developed with flexibility and if they have adequate management support and training programs.

Key Terms

Activity-based costing, 532
Balanced scorecard, 532
Business intelligence, 512
Choice, 516
Customer decision-support systems (CDSS), 525
Data visualization, 524
Data-driven DSS, 520

Design, 516
Digital dashboard, 532
Drill down, 530
DSS database, 522
DSS software system, 522
Geographic information systems (GIS), 524
Group decision-support systems (GDSS), 527
Implementation, 516

Intelligence, 516
Model, 522
Model-driven DSS, 519
Semistructured decisions, 514
Sensitivity analysis, 523
Structured decisions, 514
Unstructured decisions, 514

Review Questions

1. What is business intelligence? What applications and technologies does it include?

2. What are the different decision-making levels and decision-making constituencies in organizations? How do their decision-making requirements differ?

3. What is the difference between an unstructured, semi-structured, and structured decision?

4. List and describe the stages in decision making.

5. What is the difference between a decision-support system and a management information system?

6. What is the difference between data-driven DSS and model-driven DSS? Give examples.

7. What are the three basic components of DSS? Briefly describe each.

8. How can DSS help firms with supply chain management and customer relationship management? How do DSS provide value for a business?

9. What is a geographic information system? How does it use

10. What is a customer decision-support system? How can the Internet be used for this purpose?

11. What is a group decision-support system? How does it differ from DSS? What underlying problems in group decision making led to the development of GDSS?

12. Describe the three elements of GDSS and five GDSS software tools.

13. How can GDSS provide value for a business?

14. Define and describe the capabilities of an executive support system.

15. How can the Internet and enterprise systems provide capabilities for executive support systems?

16. How do ESS enhance managerial decision making? How do they provide value for a business?

17. What are the challenges posed by systems to support decision making? How can these challenges be addressed?

data visualization technology? How can it support decision making?

Discussion Questions

1. As a manager or user of information systems, what would you need to know to participate in the design and use of DSS or ESS? Why?

2. If businesses used DSS, GDSS, and ESS more widely, would they make better decisions? Explain your answer.

Application Software Exercise:
Spreadsheet Exercise: Performing Break-Even Analysis and Sensitivity Analysis

Selmore Collectible Toy Company (SCTC) makes toy sets consisting of collectible trucks, vans, and cars for the retail market. The firm is developing a new toy set that includes a battery-powered tractor-trailer, complete with cab and trailer; a sports car; and a motorcycle. Each set sells for $100. Table 1 shows the major components of SCTC's annual fixed costs for the toy set. Each component includes the cost of purchases, depreciation, and operating expenses. Table 2 shows the major components of SCTC's variable costs. Prepare a spreadsheet to support the decision-making needs of SCTC's managers. The spreadsheet should show the fixed costs, variable costs per unit, the contribution margin, and the break-even point for this product. How many sets does SCTC have to sell before it can start turning a profit? Include a data table to show alternative break-even points, assuming variations in insurance costs and labour costs. How would increasing the sale price to $125 affect the break-even point? The Companion Website for Chapter 15 provides more detail on the range of costs to include in your sensitivity analysis and on the calculations required for a simple break-even analysis.

TABLE 1   SCTC Fixed Costs

Category	Amount
Land	$ 42 500
Buildings	332 500
Manufacturing machinery	532 000
Office equipment	212 800
Utilities	30 500
Insurance	99 700
Total	**$1 250 000**

TABLE 2   SCTC Variable Costs

Category	Amount
Labour	$15.00
Advertising	1.00
Shipping and receiving	5.00
Total	**$21.00**

Electronic Commerce Project: Using Web-based DSS for Retirement Planning

The Web site for TD Waterhouse (**www.tdcanadatrust.com/ planning/yrs.jsp**) provides Web-based DSS for financial planning and decision making. Use the site to determine how much you need to save to have enough income for your retirement. Assume that you are 50 years old and plan to retire in 16 years. You have one dependent and $100 000 in savings. Your current annual income is $85 000. Your goal is to be able to generate an annual retirement income of $60 000, including all pension benefit payments. Use the Web site to determine how much money you need to put away to help you achieve your retirement goal. Then critique the site—its ease of use, its clarity, the value of any conclusions reached, and the extent to which the site helps investors understand their financial needs and the financial markets.

Group Project: Designing University GDSS

With three or four of your classmates, identify several groups in your university that could benefit from GDSS. Design GDSS for one of those groups, describing its hardware, soft ware, and people elements. Present your findings to the class.

Web Sites of Interest

There are many interesting Web sites to enhance your learning about decision support systems. You can search the Web yourself or just try the following sites to add to what you have already learned.

Hyperion **www.hyperion.com/ca**
Company specializing in digital dashboard applications.

Balanced Scorecard.com **www.balancedscorecard.com**
Company specializing in balanced scorecard applications; this site has links to other balanced scorecard information.

Microstrategy **www.microstrategy.com**
Company specializing in business intelligence software, including Web-based DSS

CASE STUDY:
Optimizing Operations at UPS

United Parcel Service (UPS) is the world's largest air and ground package-distribution company, with annual sales of about $43 billion. It is also a leading provider of specialized transportation and logistics services. Following its nearly 100-year promise of the "best service and lowest rates," this company currently delivers over 13.6 million parcels and documents every business day within Canada, the United States and more than 200 other countries and territories.

UPS's primary business is time-definite delivery of packages and documents worldwide. It has established a global transportation infrastructure and comprehensive set of guaranteed delivery services, including integrated supply chain solutions for major companies. UPS is the industry leader in the delivery of goods purchased over the Internet.

UPS operates a ground fleet of more than 88 000 vehicles, including its famous brown delivery trucks and large tractors and trailers. In the United States, UPS manages 27 large package operating facilities as well as more than 1000 additional smaller package operating facilities. The smaller facilities have vehicles and drivers stationed for the pickup of packages and for the sorting, transfer, and delivery of packages. UPS owns or leases nearly 600 facilities to support its international package operations and more than 750 facilities that support non-package operations.

This vast ground delivery system is integrated with express air services that use 600 airplanes. UPS operates the ninth largest airline in North America and the eleventh largest in the world. UPS aircraft operate in a hub-and-spokes pattern in the United States with a primary air hub in Louisville, Kentucky, and six other regional air hubs in various cities throughout the United States. These hubs house facilities for the sorting, transfer, and delivery of packages. UPS estimates that this integrated door-to-door delivery system carries goods worth more than 2 percent of the world's gross domestic product.

The company faces relentless competition from other organizations such as Canada Post, FedEx, DHL Worldwide Express, the United States Postal Service, and TNT Post Group. Although UPS is the overall leader, the company is not number one in every way. For example, FedEx, with about $34 billion in annual sales, leads the market in overnight deliveries while DHL is the leader in cross-border (international) express deliveries.

To meet competitors head on, UPS long ago started investing heavily in advanced information systems. Technology powers virtually every service the company offers and every operation it performs. UPS offers many choices: overnight air versus low-cost ground delivery, simple shipping or a panoply of supply chain and warehousing services. Customers can choose the delivery option or service that is most cost-effective and appropriate for their requirements.

UPS has been using its automated package-tracking system to monitor all packages throughout the delivery process, collecting electronic data on 93 percent of the packages that move through U.S. systems each day. Its customers can track their parcels and letters using the UPS Web site, and many customers can also track their items on their computers using a UPS system that the customers embed into their Web sites.

However, UPS's competition now uses much of this same tracking technology and is moving into areas where UPS has been dominant. FedEx, for instance, is trying to become a player in ground palletized-freight and international shipping. It wants to funnel package data from all of its operations into a single transparent system. Fierce competition has stimulated UPS to find even more innovative ways of servicing customers while reducing its costs.

UPS management believes the company is still a leader in reliable package delivery and that its unmatched integrated air and ground network provides it with a level of service quality and economies of scale that differentiate it from competitors. The company's strategy emphasizes increasing core domestic revenues by cross-selling its existing and new services to a large and diverse customer base. It hopes to grow its package business by offering services for synchronized commerce, helping customers manage the flow of goods, information, and funds throughout their supply chains. For example, UPS developed Web-based software for DaimlerChrysler AG to manage centrally all parts moving to and from more than 4500 dealerships. While expanding these services, UPS hopes to limit the rate at which expenses are growing. It is counting on information technology–driven efficiencies to increase its operating profit.

In 2003, UPS announced plans to invest $750 million to simplify and optimize its package-sorting and delivery systems. Management believes that this systems investment will produce significant gains in efficiency, reliability, and flexibility. Once fully deployed in 2007 in more than 1000 UPS package-sorting facilities, these systems are expected to reduce operating costs by approximately $750 million each year. In 2003, UPS domestic operating profit declined $381 million, caused by both slow growth in revenue coupled with higher operating expenses. Higher costs for fuel and higher rents both played major roles in expense increases. More efficient dispatching and loading of delivery trucks could reduce the distance covered by UPS drivers by about 100 million miles, saving as much as 14 million gallons of fuel per year.

The project began when, in the mid-1990s, the company recognized it needed a new software program to map its core operations in the United States, including its pickups and deliveries, its sorting facilities, and its delivery centres. In the past, distribution centre delivery truck loaders had to remember which trucks were headed where, then take the package off the conveyor belt, see the street on the shipping label of the package, and place it on the correct truck. "It was very chaotic," said Bob Sylsbury, a Mount Olive, New Jersey, loader.

Originally, to map every pickup and delivery option in order to select the best was thought to be impossible by Jack Levis, portfolio manager in the UPS industrial engineering division. There would be more than 15.5 trillion options for calculating every possible route using just 25 points. At that time (about 1995), UPS estimated that computing this information would require 500 000 years with the fastest computers in existence. So, the project turned to developing optimization software to assess the most-feasible options for selecting the least-expensive and shortest delivery routes.

Meanwhile, during those years, hardware and software also became more powerful, the necessary computing time fell from years to months, then to days, and then to hours, and it is still dropping today. UPS now has optimization software for both its ground and air delivery services. Systems use the real-time information produced by UPS's package-tracking system, including bar-code labels with all the data the company needs to deliver packages on time. Logistics software aggregates zip code information and uses the data supplied by the bar codes to map out how packages should be loaded onto trucks for the most efficient deliveries.

Lou Rivieccio, a UPS division manager, says the new system is improving delivery from its Mount Olive delivery centre, enabling drivers to increase their daily deliveries from 130 stops to 145 stops while reducing their average route by eight miles. While in the past loaders could load only 2.5 trucks, with the new system each loader can load between 3 and 4 trucks. Moreover, the past confusion during loading resulted in an annual loader turnover rate of 45 percent. That has now been reduced to 8 percent at the 95 distribution centres where the new system is already operating.

The client/server system for optimizing hub operations and delivery fleets of the UPS ground network is called Hub and Feeder Network Optimization. Five full-time planners set up problems using data on package origination, destination, and volume; data on sorting facility location, capacity, and time and distance between sites; and data from a flow file that defines paths packages take between different sortings. Once the problem is set up, it is transmitted to a Unix server, which runs the computations and transmits the results in the form of reports back to the PCs.

Calculations for UPS hub and feeder network optimizations are performed only several times each year. The information they provide helps answer long-range questions such as when UPS will run out of capacity with its current network, where it should expand, or the impact of changing the service level for its ground operations.

By 2006, UPS wants to use software on wireless handhelds so that its drivers, each averaging more than 100 stops per day, can optimize their own routes. Early versions of the system are being tested on leading-edge custom handhelds with local and wide area wireless connectivity and the ability to communicate with peripheral devices, PCs, or global positioning satellites. The software on the handhelds will be synchronized with the dispatch planning optimization systems deployed at UPS delivery centres.

The system for optimizing UPS air operations at the hub in Louisville is called Volcano (standing for Volume, Location, and Aircraft Network System). The system takes into account all UPS aircraft delivery routes to optimize fleet assignments, routes, and package allocations within days or hours. Company executives expect the system to save more than $200 million over the next 10 years by improving the planning and scheduling of air deliveries. The company also uses the system to help schedule the pilots and to help determine if UPS should lease or purchase more aircraft, particularly in high-volume periods such as the Christmas season when required flights can jump by 45 percent. Preventing the company from leasing just one aircraft can save the company $3.8 million in costs.

UPS ran 1500 optimizations to help determine where and how it should build sites as it expands its European operations. So, for example, it selected the site for a new sorting facility in Germany, and it also calculated how large the facility should be. It actually had selected the Louisville, Kentucky, site for its Worldport air hub in 1999 and projected the price tag to be $1.25 billion. The software selected the Louisville site over many other possible sites because expanding that site rather than building a new one would be both quicker and less costly than other possibilities. In 1986, when UPS was considering a new facility in the Chicago area, it took four people three months to run a single optimization calculation. "Today you can make a much more fine-tuned decision with fewer people," Levis points out.

Optimization software has also helped so much in improving customer service, according to UPS, that the company has been able to cut at least a day from the guaranteed delivery time for certain shipments. For example, the company now can guarantee that ground shipment time between New York and Los Angeles will be no more than four business days rather than the five days it used to be.

Sources: Beth Bacheldor, "Breakthrough," *Information Week*, February 9, 2004; Anna Maria Virzi, "United Parcel Service: Sticky Fix," *Baseline Magazine*, February 5, 2004; United Parcel Service, "Annual Report for Fiscal Year Ending December 31, 2003," Form 10-K, United States Securities and Exchange Commission; Steve Berez and Chris Zook, "UPS Links to Customers," *Optimize Magazine*, February 2004; and Paul McDougall, "Load 'Em Up," *Information Week*, September 29, 2003.

CASE STUDY QUESTIONS

1. Analyze UPS using the competitive forces and value chain models.

2. What is UPS' business strategy? How do information systems support that strategy?

3. Why was a decision-support system to optimize delivery routes so important for UPS? What decisions did it support?

4. How successful are these DSS for helping UPS achieve a competitive advantage? Explain your answer.

Chapter 16

Managing Knowledge in the Digital Firm

OBJECTIVES

After completing this chapter, you will be able to:

1. Assess the role of knowledge management and knowledge management programs in business.

2. Define and describe the types of systems used for enterprise-wide knowledge management and demonstrate how they provide value for organizations.

3. Define and describe the major types of knowledge work systems and assess how they provide value for firms.

4. Evaluate the business benefits of using intelligent techniques for knowledge management.

5. Identify the challenges posed by knowledge management systems and propose management solutions.

- Approve product specifications
- Redesign approval process

- Run production plants
- Design products and packaging
- Research new products

- Manage product approval forms using Documentum eRoom

Management

Organization

Technology

Business Challenges
- Rapid product development cycle
- Multiple groups to coordinate

Information System
- Collaborate simultaneously on product approvals

Business Solutions
- Reduce time
- Reduce cost

Opening Case: Cott Struggles to Manage Unstructured Information

Cott Corporation is the world's leading supplier of store-brand soft drinks and juices, with beverage manufacturing facilities in the United States, Canada, Mexico, and the United Kingdom and a concentrate production plant and research and development centre in Columbus, Georgia. Like other companies in its industry, Cott is under pressure to bring out new products very quickly.

Cott had been using email to route product approval forms with details such as a new product's flavour formula or the artwork for a bottle label to managers of various groups involved in the product development process. Difficulties controlling this unstructured information delayed efforts to get new soda and juice products onto store shelves. Because of time lags in routing email from one person to another, it took an average of 60 days for a form to obtain all the necessary approvals. People would begin various production activities before the approval was finalized, and changes were required. The art department might start working on a product label based on an approval form and later learn that they needed to modify the design because of a change in equipment that affected the label's dimensions. Production of the new product might be moved to a different plant.

Cott solved this problem by adopting Documentum eRoom software to manage product approval forms. The software enables employees to set up online project work spaces to create and share documents. The documents are preserved in a company-wide document repository where they can be easily shared and accessed by everyone working on a new product. Each time a new product order triggers the creation of a new product approval form, the system sets up a work space for that product. Managers of various groups involved in product development can track the form, view any changes to the form, and work jointly with others on changes that affect multiple areas of production. By managing product approval information more effectively, Cott's product approval process takes only two to three days, and production is much more efficient.

Sources: Tony Kontzer, "Content Overload," *Information Week*, January 19, 2004; "New Product Development," **www.documentum.com**, accessed June 12, 2004; and **www.cott.com**, accessed June 12, 2004.

Cott Corporation's experience shows how organizational performance can benefit by making organizational knowledge more easily available. Collaborating and communicating with practitioners and experts, creating new knowledge, facilitating access to knowledge, and using that knowledge to improve business processes and decision making have become vital to organizational innovation and survival. As a manager, you will want to know how your firm can benefit from information systems for knowledge management.

In this chapter, we look at information systems that are specifically designed to help organizations create, capture, distribute, and apply knowledge and information. First, we discuss how knowledge has become such an important organizational asset and the series of processes that transform data into useful knowledge. Next, we describe the major types of systems for knowledge management. We conclude by discussing the steps that can be taken by managers to ensure knowledge management systems provide value for the firm.

16.1 The Knowledge Management Landscape

There has been a surge of interest in knowledge management, and knowledge management systems have become one of the fastest-growing areas of corporate and government software investment. Canadian companies realize that knowledge is one of their most important but least efficiently utilized assets. With this realization, the knowledge management (KM) industry—sometimes referred to as content management or information management—has grown by leaps and bounds. While difficult to measure, expert estimates on the size of the worldwide KM industry range from $5 billion to $18.5 billion annually. Over 50 percent of the worldwide market is in North America. North America is also the main force behind the 22.6 percent annual growth rate of this market. According to IDC Canada, database and knowledge management within the software sector, is the second-fastest growing market in Canada, experiencing 44 percent annual growth. The past decade has likewise shown an explosive growth in research on knowledge and knowledge management in the economics, management, and information systems fields (Alavi and Leidner 2001; Cole 1998; Spender 1996).

Why all the interest in knowledge management? Chapter 1 describes the emergence of the information economy and the digital firm. In the digital firm, the major source of wealth and prosperity is the production and distribution of information and knowledge, and the firm increasingly relies on digital technology to enable business processes. At least one study showed that less than 2 percent of an organization's knowledge is actually utilized (Canadian Knowledge Management Software (KMS) Market 2004). Knowledge management has, therefore, become an important theme at many large firms as managers realize that much of their firm's value depends on the firm's ability to create and manage knowledge. Studies have found that a substantial part of a firm's stock market value is related to its intangible assets, of which knowledge is one important component, along with brands, reputation, and unique business processes. (Gu and Lev 2001). Well-executed knowledge-based projects have been known to produce extraordinary returns on investment although knowledge-based investments are difficult to measure (Blair and Wallman 2001).

Important Dimensions of Knowledge

There is an important distinction between data, information, knowledge, and wisdom. Chapter 1 defines *data* as a flow of events or transactions captured by an organization's systems that, by itself, is useful for transacting but little else. To turn data into useful *information,* a firm must expend resources to organize data into categories of understanding, such as monthly, daily, regional, or store-based reports of total sales. To transform information into **knowledge**, a firm must expend additional resources to discover patterns, rules, and contexts where the knowledge works. Finally, **wisdom** is thought to be the collective and individual experience of applying knowledge to the solution of problems. Wisdom involves where, when, and how to apply knowledge.

Knowledge is both an individual attribute and a collective attribute of the firm. Knowledge is made up of concepts, experience, and insight that provide a framework for creating, evaluating, and using information. Knowledge is a cognitive, even a physiological, event, that takes place inside a person's head, but it is also stored in libraries and records; shared in lectures; and stored by firms in the form of business processes and employee know-how. Knowledge residing in the minds of employees that has not been documented is called **tacit knowledge** while knowledge that has been documented is called **explicit knowledge**. Knowledge can reside in email, voice mail, graphics, and unstructured documents as well as structured documents. Knowledge is generally believed to have a location, either in the minds of humans or in specific business processes. Knowledge is "sticky" and not universally applicable or easily moved. Finally, knowledge is thought to be situational and contextual. For example, you must know when to perform a procedure as well as how to perform it. Table 16-1 reviews these dimensions of knowledge.

We can see that knowledge is a different kind of firm asset from, say, buildings and financial assets; that knowledge is a complex phenomenon; and that there are many aspects to the process of managing knowledge. We can also recognize that knowledge-based core competencies of firms—the two or three things that an organization does best—are key organizational assets. Knowing how to do things effectively and efficiently in ways that other organizations cannot duplicate is a primary source of profit and competitive advantage that cannot be purchased easily by competitors in the marketplace.

For instance, having a unique build-to-order production system or customer relationship management system constitutes a form of knowledge and can be a unique asset that other firms cannot copy easily. With knowledge, firms become more efficient and effective in their use of scarce resources. Without knowledge, firms become less efficient and less effective in their use of resources and ultimately fail. Organizations differ in their abilities to apply knowledge, and firms that apply knowledge more effectively than competitors are more successful.

Organizational Learning and Knowledge Management

How do firms obtain knowledge, and how do firms manage knowledge? Like humans, organizations create and gather knowledge using a variety of organizational learning mechanisms. Through collection of data, careful measurement of planned activities, trial and error

knowledge

wisdom

tacit knowledge

explicit knowledge

TABLE 16-1 *Important Dimensions of Knowledge*

KNOWLEDGE IS A FIRM ASSET

Knowledge is an intangible asset.

The transformation of data into useful information and knowledge requires organizational resources.

Knowledge is not subject to the law of diminishing returns as are physical assets, but instead experiences network effects (law of expanding returns). Its value increases as more people share it.

KNOWLEDGE HAS DIFFERENT FORMS

Knowledge can be either tacit or explicit (codified).

Knowledge involves know-how, craft, and skill.

Knowledge involves knowing how to follow procedures.

Knowledge involves knowing why, not simply when, things happen (causality).

KNOWLEDGE HAS A LOCATION

Knowledge is a cognitive event involving mental models and maps of individuals.

There is both a social and an individual basis of knowledge.

Knowledge is "sticky" (hard to move), situated (enmeshed in a firm's culture), and contextual (works only in certain situations).

KNOWLEDGE IS SITUATIONAL

Knowledge is conditional: Knowing when to apply a procedure is just as important as knowing the procedure (conditional).

Knowledge is related to context: You must know how to use a certain tool and under what circumstances.

(experiment), and feedback from customers and the environment in general, organizations gain experience. Organizations that learn then adjust their behaviour by creating new business processes and by changing patterns of management decision making. This process of change is called **organizational learning**. Arguably organizations that can sense and respond to their environments rapidly will survive longer than organizations that have poor learning mechanisms. What has been learned by an organization must also be able to be remembered. **Organizational memory** is the stored learning from an organization's history that can be used for decision making and other purposes. Knowledge management includes the storage and categorization techniques and technologies that enable organizational memory.

The Knowledge Management Value Chain

Knowledge management refers to the set of business processes developed in an organization to create, store, transfer, and apply knowledge. Knowledge management is, in this sense, an enabler of organizational learning. Knowledge management increases the ability of the organization to learn from its environment and to incorporate knowledge into its business processes. Figure 16-1 illustrates the five value-added steps in the knowledge management value chain. Each stage in the value chain adds value to raw data and information as they are transformed into usable knowledge.

In Figure 16-1, a shaded box divides information systems activities and related management and organizational activities, with information systems activities on the top of the graphic and organizational and management activities below. One apt slogan of the knowledge management field is: "Effective knowledge management is 80 percent managerial and organizational, and 20 percent technological."

In Chapter 1 we define *organizational and management capital* as the set of business processes, culture, and behaviours required to obtain value from investments in information systems. In the case of knowledge management, as with other information systems investments, supportive values, structures, and behaviour patterns must be built to maximize the return on investment in knowledge management projects. In Figure 16-1, the management and organizational activities in the lower half of the diagram represent the investment in organizational capital required to obtain substantial returns on the information technology (IT) investments and systems shown in the top half of the diagram.

organizational learning

organizational memory

knowledge management

FIGURE 16-1　*The knowledge management value chain.*

Knowledge management today involves both information systems activities and a host of enabling management and organizational activities.

Knowledge Acquisition Organizations acquire knowledge in a number of ways, depending on the type of knowledge they seek. The first knowledge management systems sought to build corporate libraries of documents, reports, presentations, and best practices and encouraged employees to create documents based on their experiences. These efforts have been extended to include unstructured documents (such as email). In other cases, organizations acquire knowledge by developing online expert networks so that employees can "find the expert" in the company who has the knowledge in his or her head.

In other cases, firms must create new knowledge by discovering patterns in corporate data or by using knowledge workstations where engineers can discover new knowledge. These various efforts are described throughout this chapter. A coherent and organized knowledge system also requires systematic data from the firm's transaction processing systems that track sales, payments, inventory, customers, and other vital data, as well as data from external sources such as news feeds, industry reports, legal opinions, scientific research, and government statistics.

Knowledge Storage Once they are discovered, documents, patterns, and expert rules must be stored so they can be retrieved and used by employees. Knowledge storage generally involves the creation of a database. *Document management systems* that digitize, index, and tag documents according to a coherent framework are large databases adept at storing collections of documents. Communities of expertise and expert systems also help corporations preserve the knowledge that is acquired by incorporating that knowledge into organizational processes and culture. Each of these systems has been discussed in the previous chapter or will be discussed later in this chapter.

Management must support the development of planned knowledge storage systems, encourage the development of corporate-wide schemas for indexing documents, and reward employees for taking the time to update and store documents properly. For instance, management might reward the sales force for submitting names of prospects to a shared corporate database of prospects where all sales personnel can identify each prospect and review the stored knowledge.

Knowledge Dissemination Portal, email, instant messaging, and search engine technology have resulted in an explosion of "knowledge" and information dissemination. These technologies have added to an existing array of groupware technologies and office systems for sharing calendars, documents, data, and graphics (see Chapter 7). Rather than a shortage of information and knowledge, contemporary technology seems to have created a deluge of information and knowledge. What is in short supply are coping mechanisms and understanding. How can managers and employees discover, in a sea of information and knowledge, that which is really important for their decisions and their work? Here, management and organizational activities play a critical role. Training programs, informal networks, and shared management experience communicated through a supportive culture help managers focus their attention on the important knowledge and information.

Knowledge Application Regardless of what type of knowledge management system is involved, knowledge that is not shared and applied to the practical problems facing firms and managers does not add business value. To provide a return on investment, organizational knowledge must become a systematic part of management decision making and become situated in existing and new decision-support systems (described in the previous chapter). Ultimately, new knowledge must be built into a firm's business processes and key application systems, including enterprise applications for managing key internal business processes and relationships with customers and suppliers. Management supports this process by creating— based on new knowledge—new business practices, new products and services, and new markets for the firm. More important, management helps create a cultural environment where decisions and processes are based on informed knowledge, not guesswork.

Building Organizational and Management Capital: Collaboration, Communities of Practice, and Office Environments

Knowledge management is as much about building organizational and management capital as it is about technology. The role of managers is to develop a knowledge culture, where the acquisition, discovery, and application of knowledge are esteemed and rewarded. Managers can also help by developing new organizational roles and responsibilities for the acquisition of knowledge, including the creation of chief knowledge officer executive positions, dedicated staff positions (knowledge managers), and communities of practice. The **chief knowledge officer (CKO)** is a senior executive who is responsible for the firm's knowledge management program. The CKO helps design programs and systems to find new sources of knowledge or to make better use of existing knowledge in organizational and management processes (Earl and Scott 1999; Flash 2001).

Communities of practice (COP) are informal social networks of professionals and employees within and outside the firm who have similar work-related activities and interests. The activities of these communities include self and group education, conferences, online newsletters, and day-to-day sharing of experiences and techniques to solve specific work problems. Many large corporations such as IBM and the World Bank have encouraged the development of thousands of online communities of practice. Natural resources company RioTinto set up 30 active communities of practice for business improvement covering topics such as environmental standards, underground safety, and dragline operation. Health Canada, Hill and Knowlton Canada (a large communications firm), the Creative City Network of Canada, and many others have set up communities of practice to enable them to find and share knowledge and expertise.

There are four areas in which COP can make a difference for knowledge management. COP can make it easier for people to reuse knowledge by pointing community members to useful documents, creating document repositories, and filtering information for newcomers. Members of communities can act as facilitators, encouraging contributions and discussion. COP can also reduce the learning curve for new employees by providing contacts with subject matter experts and access to a community's established methods and tools. Finally, COP can act as a spawning ground for new ideas, techniques, and decision-making behaviour.

chief knowledge officer (CKO)

communities of practice (COP)

Types of Knowledge Management Systems

There are essentially three major types of knowledge management systems: enterprise-wide knowledge management systems, knowledge work systems, and intelligent techniques. Figure 16-2 shows the knowledge management system applications for each of these major categories.

Enterprise-wide knowledge management systems are general-purpose firm-wide efforts to collect, store, distribute, and apply digital content and knowledge. These systems provide databases and tools for organizing and storing structured and unstructured documents and other knowledge objects, directories, and tools for locating employees with expertise in a particular area, and, increasingly, Web-based tools for collaboration and communication. Section 16.2 discusses enterprise-wide knowledge management systems in more detail.

The development of powerful networked workstations and software for assisting engineers and scientists in the discovery of new knowledge has led to the creation of knowledge work systems such as computer-aided design (CAD), visualization, simulation, and virtual reality systems. **Knowledge work systems (KWS)** are specialized systems developed for engineers, scientists, and other knowledge workers charged with discovering and creating new knowledge for a company. We discuss knowledge work applications in detail in Section 16.3.

Knowledge management also includes a diverse group of **intelligent techniques**, such as data mining, expert systems, neural networks, fuzzy logic, genetic algorithms, and intelligent agents. These techniques have different objectives, from a focus on discovering knowledge (data mining and neural networks), to distilling knowledge in the form of rules for a computer program (expert systems and fuzzy logic), to discovering optimal solutions for problems (genetic algorithms). Section 16.4 provides more detail about these intelligent techniques.

16.2 Enterprise-Wide Knowledge Management Systems

Figure 16-3 provides an overview of the technologies and capabilities found in enterprise-wide knowledge management systems. They include capabilities for storing both structured and unstructured data; tools for locating employee expertise within the firm; and capabilities for obtaining data and information from key transaction systems, such as enterprise

knowledge work systems (KWS)

intelligent techniques

FIGURE 16-2   *Major types of knowledge management systems.*

Enterprise-Wide Knowledge Management Systems	Knowledge Work Systems	Intelligent Techniques
General purpose, integrated, firm-wide efforts to collect, store, disseminate, and use digital content and knowledge	Specialized workstations and systems that enable scientists, engineers, and other knowledge workers to create and discover new knowledge	Tools for discovering patterns and applying knowledge to discrete decisions and knowledge domains
Structured knowledge systems		Data mining
Semistructured knowledge systems	Computer-aided design (CAD)	Neural networks
Knowledge network systems	3D Visualization	Expert systems
	Virtual reality	Case-based reasoning
	Investment workstations	Fuzzy logic
		Genetic algorithms
		Intelligent agents

There are three major categories of knowledge management systems, and each can be broken down further into more specialized types of knowledge management systems.

FIGURE 16-3 *Enterprise-wide knowledge management systems.*

Enterprise-wide knowledge management systems use an array of technologies for storing structured and unstructured documents, locating employee expertise, searching for information, disseminating knowledge, and using data from enterprise applications and other key corporate systems.

applications and Web sites. They also include supporting technologies such as portals, search engines, and collaboration tools (including email, instant messaging, and groupware) to help employees search the corporate knowledge base, communicate and collaborate with others inside and outside the firm, and apply the stored knowledge to new situations. Systems for managing employee learning are emerging as another supporting technology for enterprise-wide knowledge management.

Managers and firms must deal with many different kinds of knowledge and knowledge issues. There are three major categories of enterprise-wide knowledge management systems for dealing with these different kinds of knowledge. Some knowledge exists already somewhere in the firm in the form of structured text documents and reports or presentations, and the central problem is organizing this existing structured knowledge into a library and making it accessible throughout the firm. We will call this type of knowledge **structured knowledge**, and we can refer to these types of systems as **structured knowledge systems**.

The first knowledge management systems that appeared in the late 1980s and 1990s focused on this type of knowledge. Managers may also need information that may exist somewhere inside the firm in the form of less-structured documents, such as email, voice mail, chat room exchanges, videos, digital pictures, brochures, or bulletin boards. We can call this knowledge **semistructured knowledge**, and we can refer to the systems that focus on this type of knowledge as **semistructured knowledge systems** (the industry name is *digital asset management systems*).

Systems for structured and semistructured knowledge function as knowledge repositories. A **knowledge repository** is a collection of internal and external knowledge in a single location for more efficient management and utilization by the organization. Knowledge

structured knowledge
structured knowledge systems
semistructured knowledge
semistructured knowledge systems
knowledge repository

repositories are accessed through enterprise portals and search engine technology and may include tools for accessing information from corporate databases.

In still other cases, there are no formal or digital documents of any kind, and the knowledge resides in the minds of experienced employees somewhere in the company. Much of this knowledge is *tacit knowledge* and is rarely written down. Here, the problem faced by managers is building a network that connects knowledge demand with knowledge supply. **Knowledge network systems**, also known as *expertise location and management systems*, attempt to perform this function. Knowledge network systems provide an online directory of corporate experts in well-defined knowledge domains and use communication technologies to make it easy for employees to find the appropriate expert in a company. Some knowledge network systems go further by systematizing the solutions being developed by experts and then storing the solutions in a knowledge database as a best practices or frequently asked questions (FAQ) repository. Table 16-2 compares the major categories of enterprise-wide knowledge management systems.

Structured Knowledge Systems

Structured knowledge is explicit knowledge that exists in formal documents as well as in formal rules that organizations derive by observing experts and their decision-making behaviours. The essential problems of structured knowledge are the creation of an appropriate database schema that can collect and organize the information into meaningful categories and the creation of a database that can be easily accessed by employees in a variety of situations. Once the schema is created, each document needs to be "tagged," or coded, so that it can be retrieved by search engines. *Structured knowledge systems* perform the function of implementing the coding schema, interfacing with corporate databases where the documents are stored, and creating an enterprise portal environment for employees to use when searching for corporate knowledge.

All the major accounting and consulting firms have developed structured document and engagement-based (case-based) repositories of reports from consultants who are working with particular clients. The reports typically are created after the consulting engagement is completed and include detailed descriptions of the consulting objective, participants, and the practices used to achieve the client's objectives. These reports are placed in a massive database to be used later for training new consultants in the company's *best practices* and for preparing new consultants joining an existing on-site consulting team. Accounting firms, for instance, have created large tax law accounting databases that store information on tax policy, the application of that policy to specific client companies, and the advice of in-house tax experts on how local laws work.

Perhaps one of the largest private-sector structured knowledge repositories is KPMG's KWorld. KPMG International is an international tax and accounting firm with 95 000 professionals serving clients through 1100 offices in 820 cities and 150 countries (KPMG 2003). With this large global base of employees and clients, KPMG faced a number of problems in sharing knowledge, preventing the loss of knowledge as consultants retired

knowledge network systems

TABLE 16-2 Categories of Enterprise-Wide Knowledge Management Systems

TYPE OF KNOWLEDGE	KNOWLEDGE CONTENT	CATEGORY OF ENTERPRISE KNOWLEDGE MANAGEMENT SYSTEM
Structured knowledge	Formal documents	Structured knowledge systems
	Email, voice mail, memos, brochures, digital pictures, bulletin boards, and other unstructured documents	
Semistructured knowledge	Digital asset management systems	Semistructured knowledge systems
Network (tacit) knowledge	Expertise of individuals	Knowledge networks

or left the firm, disseminating best practices, and coping with the information overload of individual consultants.

In 1995, KPMG began developing a Web-based knowledge environment known as "Knowledge Web," or KWeb. KWeb contained databases organized around internal and external knowledge domains of interest to its consultants and partners. In 1999, KPMG rolled out an extension of KWeb called KWorld, which features an integrated set of knowledge content and collaboration tools that can be used worldwide. Figure 16-4 provides an abstract overview of the complex nature of knowledge stored by KWorld.

KWorld is an online environment for gathering, sharing, and managing knowledge. Although it is primarily a document repository, KWorld also provides online collaboration capabilities for the firm's consultants and an internal reporting system. KWorld stores white papers, presentations, best practice proposals, articles, presentations, internal discussions, marketing materials, engagement histories, news feeds, external industry research, and other intellectual capital. The content is organized into nine levels by KPMG products and market segments. Within each of these domains are many subcategories of knowledge. For instance, the client knowledge domain includes entries on financials, *industry dynamics, change* dynamics, client organization, client products and customers, and KPMG's history of engagements (KPMG 2003). Consultants use KWorld to coordinate their work as a team with a client, and the client is allowed access to the collaboration environment as well. Figure 16-5 illustrates the system processes used by KPMG to capture and organize content for this system.

KPMG has invested heavily in the organizational and management capital required to make use of the millions of documents stored in KWorld. KPMG has also created a division of knowledge management, headed by a chief knowledge officer. An extensive staff of analysts and librarians assess the quality of incoming information, ensure its proper categorization, assess its value, and provide some analysis of its importance.

Another example of a structured knowledge system is Roche Labs' Global Healthcare Intelligence Platform, which integrates documents from multiple sources to provide its professional services group with up-to-date information and expertise relating to new Hoffman-La Roche pharmaceutical products. The system gathers relevant information from global news sources, specialty publishers, health-care Web sites, government sources, and the firm's proprietary internal information systems, indexing, organizing, linking, and updating the information as it moves through the system. Users can search

FIGURE 16-4   *KPMG knowledge system processes.*

KPMG's KWorld is organized into nine levels of content that are further classified by product, market segment, and geographic area.

FIGURE 16-5 *KPMG knowledge system processes.*

Internal Content
• Work products
• Practice specific

• Quality assessment
• Value assessment
• Taxonomy assignment
• Channel assignment
• Security

Filter, sort, aggregate

• Content screen
• Rules, guidelines, process flow

• Aggregate, focus, direct, order
• Internal & external commentary
• Insights, interpretation, analysis

KWorld
External Web site
Collaboration

External Content
• Industry research
• News feeds

KPMG systems classify, filter, and organize content from both internal and external sources for use internally in KWorld and externally on the company Web site.

multiple sources and drill down through layers of detail to see relationships among pieces of data.

Semistructured Knowledge Systems

Semistructured information is all the digital information in a firm that does not exist in a formal document or a formal report that was written by a designated author. It has been estimated that at least 80 percent of an organization's business content is unstructured—information in folders, messages, memos, proposals, emails, graphics, electronic slide presentations, and even videos created in different formats and stored in many locations. In many cases firms have no idea what semistructured content has been created, where it is stored, or who is responsible for it.

It might be convenient or cost effective not to know this information, but compliance with the law or governmental regulations forces companies to know and report a variety of information from a variety of sources and technologies. Ignorance is not legal or effective defence under such laws such as the U.S. Sarbanes-Oxley Act of 2002, which requires financial services firms to keep records on the origins of all material corporate documents, including emails, brochures, and presentations, and strict internal controls governing their storage. While the Sarbanes-Oxley Act applies to U.S. companies, it also applies to Canadian subsidiaries of U.S. firms, as well as those Canadian companies that are listed on the U.S. stock markets. The health-care industry in Canada has been similarly affected by the Personal Information Protection and Electronic Documents Act (PIPEDA), which requires virtually all institutions (other than those of the federal government), including health-care providers and insurers, to track the flow of all personal information, including health information, meticulously. (In terms of health information, provincial privacy legislation takes precedence, meaning that PIPEDA does not apply in most provinces.)

Firms such as Coca-Cola need to keep track of all the images of the Coca-Cola brand that have been created in the past at all their worldwide offices both to avoid duplicating efforts and to avoid variation from a standard brand image. Without the appropriate tools, a firm may have thousands of content centres located in offices around the world where employees often know only about the materials they create themselves. Searching across departments and offices—from corporate legal to technical engineering to customer correspondence to records, or from Toronto to New York to London to Tokyo—can be a daunting, if not impossible, task. As a result, semistructured documents are continually reproduced and recreated, knowledge is forever lost, and costs climb ever higher.

The essential problem faced by managers is building a database and technical infrastructure that can collect semistructured information and organize it in a coherent fashion. A number of vendors have responded to this need with systems that can track, store, and organize semistructured documents as well as more structured traditional documents.

One of the largest players in this marketplace is Hummingbird, a Canadian software company specializing in "integrated knowledge management systems" (see Figure 16-6). In addition to providing document management in the form of centralized repositories, Hummingbird's Business Intelligence module pulls data from the firm's enterprise systems and makes it available firm-wide through a portal. A more recent addition to the product line is a rules-based email management program that automatically profiles incoming and outgoing email messages using rules developed by line managers.

One user of Hummingbird's enterprise knowledge management system is Aird and Berlis (A&B), a Toronto-based law firm. A&B represents some of the world's largest

FIGURE 16-6 *Hummingbird's integrated knowledge management system.*

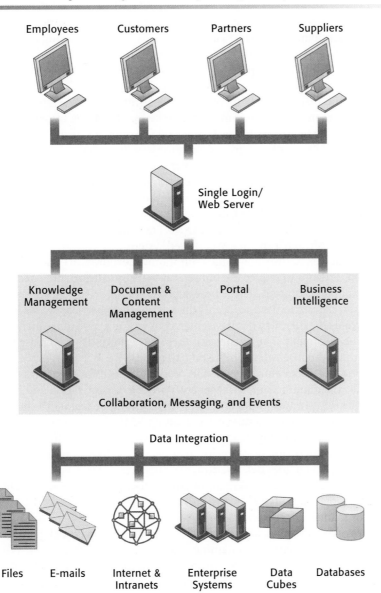

Hummingbird's enterprise solution combines document management, knowledge management, business intelligence, and portal technologies and can be used for managing semistructured as well as structured knowledge.

Source: © Hummingbird Ltd. All rights reserved.

corporations, as well as a variety of entrepreneurial and small firms, government agencies, and individuals. A&B chose Hummingbird Portal and Hummingbird Document Management applications to offer clients access to a multitude of frequently requested legal documents. A&B can offer clients secure access to not only the documents they need but collaborative features and applications also offered by the firm. Previously, A&B's lawyers and clients communicated mostly through email, potentially not the most secure mechanism for communication. Hummingbird offers the ability to integrate dynamic information, such as email, into the portal. Clients can not only access their documents, they can change them when needed, including updating templates they provide the law firm. A&B employees can also access content on the portal from anywhere in the world, another plus (Hummingbird 2005).

Another Hummingbird user is Cuatrecasas, a leading Spanish law firm described in the Window on Management. Cuatrecasas implemented Hummingbird Enterprise to provide a standard platform for organizing and managing both structured and semistructured information. Cuatrecasas maintains many offices in many different locations, and each office used to have its own information systems. The only way information could be shared among offices was by email, and that was also difficult to manage because of version control problems. These problems were solved by adopting a single platform for enterprise-wide knowledge management.

Organizing Knowledge: Taxonomies and Tagging

One of the first challenges that firms face when building knowledge repositories of any kind is the problem of identifying the correct categories to use when classifying documents. It is, of course, possible simply to "dump" millions of documents into a large database and rely on search engine technology to produce results for users. However, a brute search engine approach produces far too many results for the user to cope with and evaluate.

Firms are increasingly using a combination of internally developed taxonomies and search engine techniques. **Taxonomy** is a scheme for classifying information and knowledge in such a way that it can be easily accessed. Taxonomy is like a table of contents in a book or like the Library of Congress system for classifying books and periodicals according to subject matter and author. A business firm can access information much more easily if it devises its own taxonomy for classifying information into logical categories. The more precise the taxonomy, the more relevant are the search engine results. Once a knowledge taxonomy is produced, documents are all *tagged* with the proper classification. Generally, Extensible Markup Language (XML) tags are used for this purpose so the documents can be easily retrieved in a Web-based system.

Products such as ActiveKnowledge (Autonomy Corporation) and Taxonomy (Semio Corporation) attempt to reduce the burden on users by categorizing documents using an existing corporate taxonomy. These products consider the user's prior searches, the context of the search term in the document (the relationships between words in a document), related concepts the user may not have entered, as well as keyword frequency and the popularity of the document. The purpose of these newer tools is to increase the probability that the correct response will be in the first 10 results.

Several tools perform auto tagging and reduce the need for managers to develop their own unique taxonomies. Semio's Tagger software is a categorization and indexing engine that identifies key phrases in documents, assigns relevance factors to these phrases, and organizes the documents into categories, creating XML-based document tags using rules that users can see and modify. Tagger can access more than 200 different document types stored in legacy, enterprise, or other intranet databases. Users can integrate existing taxonomy categories and add, delete, or merge categories after examining how the system responds. Semio claims that its semiautomatic system can achieve 95 percent of the accuracy obtained by manually reviewing and tagging documents in a fraction of the time required for manual efforts (www.semio.com).

One user of Semio's auto-tagging tools is Stanford University's HighWire Press, which publishes 298 online journals containing more than 12 million articles. When the company expanded its collection in 2001 from 1 million to 12 million articles, it needed a way to automate and expand its indexing process. It also needed to provide researchers with better browsing and searching capabilities to support the discovery of unexpected

taxonomy

FIGURE 16-7 *The problem of distributed knowledge.*

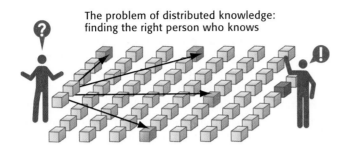

The problem of distributed knowledge: finding the right person who knows

In many organizations, essential knowledge is not available even though someone in the firm many have the information. The problem is finding the right person or group.

relationships, to link articles from a variety of disciplines, to identify concepts in articles, and to link these concepts in logical categories. Currently, the system has developed 22 000 categories and more than 300 000 concepts. The system supports 84 million hits each week with a database of 6 terabytes (Semio 2003). The system requires some active management. HighWire Press reviews its classification scheme every month and makes changes based on user feedback and management insight.

Knowledge Network Systems

Knowledge network systems address the problem that arises when the appropriate knowledge is not in the form of a digital document but instead resides in the memory of expert individuals in the firm. According to a survey by KPMG, 63 percent of employees in Fortune 500 firms complain of the difficulty in accessing undocumented knowledge. Because the knowledge cannot be conveniently found, employees expend significant resources rediscovering knowledge. An International Data Corporation (IDC) study estimated that the average cost of redundant effort in Fortune 500 companies exceeds $60 million per year per firm (AskMe 2003). Figure 16-7 illustrates the problem of "collective ignorance," a situation in which someone in a firm knows the answer, but that knowledge is not collectively shared.

WINDOW ON MANAGEMENT

An Enterprise-Wide Knowledge Management System Pays Off for Cuatrecasas

Cuatrecasas is one of Spain's largest independent law firms, specializing in all areas of business law, including corporate and finance, litigation, tax, and labour. The firm has 600 attorneys and 17 offices in the principal cities of Spain and Portugal, New York City, Brussels, and Sao Paulo. Many Cuatrecasas clients are the largest businesses in Spain, and the firm is especially active in foreign investments in Spain and in counselling Spanish companies expanding abroad.

Cuatrecasas desperately needed to improve collaboration, information exchange, and reuse of knowledge assets among its far-flung employees. Each office had its own file system, so lawyers and other employees had no common medium other than email for searching, accessing, or sharing the firm's collective knowledge assets. Even information in email could not be used efficiently because of problems with version control. Very few internal announcements, documents, and other content were published on the firm's home-grown intranet because the available tools were too difficult to use. The existing infrastructure prevented Cuatrecasas from effectively creating online

communities where attorneys could obtain information about best practices.

In May 2002, Cuatrecasas chose Hummingbird Enterprise portal and knowledge management solutions. Hummingbird provided a broad range of capabilities and allowed for ongoing customization. Cuatrecasas started with two pilot projects and a select group of end users in March 2002. The firm's information systems team spent the period from April through June defining user profiles and standardizing taxonomies for classifying information. By mid-January 2003, nearly 1000 Cuatrecasas employees in 10 global offices had been trained to use the system.

Cuatrecasas used Hummingbird to create a standardized platform for centralized document management, collaboration, and information sharing using a single Web-based desktop interface. Employees across all global office locations can easily and rapidly locate and share information and reuse best practices, regardless of where they work. The new system helped Cuatrecasas reduce the time formerly spent on document management by 10 percent.

The firm can publish nearly three times as much content as in the past, and it can publish this volume of content three to four times more rapidly than before. Publishing the same volume and quality of content with the same speed would have required one full-time dedicated information systems employee, so Cuatrecasas saved $40 000 annually with its new publishing capability.

Standardizing on a single knowledge management platform has reduced infrastructure costs. Current Cuatrecasas offices have been able to reuse file servers that were formerly required to support disparate file systems. Some of these file servers can be deployed in new offices that the firm expects to open over the next three years. Cuatrecasas can also save on its costs for information systems staff. Before Hummingbird was implemented, information systems personnel spent almost 10 percent of their time maintaining disparate file systems and infrastructures at individual offices. A standardized system reduced the time that information systems staff had to spend on all of Cuatrecasas' disconnected systems.

Cuatrecasas subsequently implemented an extranet that permits its clients to access and retrieve documents related to their cases electronically without contacting administrative staff. As use of this extranet expands, the firm anticipates lower administrative costs for client support.

How much value did Cuatrecasas obtain from its new knowledge management system? Nucleus Research was assigned to find out. Nucleus quantified the benefits provided by the system and Cuatrecasass total investment in software, hardware, consulting, personnel, training, and other expenditures over a three-year period. Software costs for the initial Hummingbird licenses and annual license maintenance fees amounted to 42 percent of overall costs. Consulting costs in

the first year made up over one-fifth of total costs. Time spent by Cuatrecasas information systems staff on the initial implementation of the system amounted to 15 percent of costs while hardware costs were only 7 percent of total costs. The remaining costs were for training. Direct and indirect benefits far outweighed the costs of the system, producing a net cash flow after taxes of nearly $566 000 each year.

Cuatrecasas was able to reduce infrastructure costs by deploying existing hardware and by using Hummingbird publishing capabilities to eliminate the need for a full-time information systems employee. Additional savings came from increased productivity of both users and information systems staff. Users did not need to spend as much time searching for and sharing documents. Information systems staff no longer had to maintain so many disparate systems. Nucleus did not put a price tag on the decreased administrative costs that the company expects to achieve in the future once its client extranet is widely adopted.

Nucleus used various capital budgeting models (see Chapter 11) to analyze Cuatrecasas's return on its Hummingbird knowledge system investment. It found that over a three-year period, the new system produced an annual rate of return on investment (ROI) of 84 percent and achieved a payback of the initial investment in only 1.2 years.

To Think About: Why would a knowledge management system be especially useful for a law firm such as Cuatrecasas? What problems did the Hummingbird system solve for this firm? How did the Hummingbird system provide value for this company?

Sources: "A Law Firm's Nucleus of Knowledge," *KM World*, February 2004; and Nucleus Research, "ROI Case Study: Hummingbird Cuatrecasas," www.hummingbird.com, accessed June 10, 2004.

Knowledge network systems seek to turn tacit, unstructured, and undocumented knowledge into explicit knowledge that can be stored in a database. Solutions that are developed by experts and others in the firm are added to the knowledge database. This new knowledge can be stored as recommended best business practices or as an answer in a database of frequently asked questions. Table 16-3 lists some of the key features of enterprise knowledge network systems.

AskMe, Inc., produces a widely adopted enterprise knowledge network system. Its users include Procter & Gamble and Intec Engineering Partnership, a project management company with more than 500 employees worldwide serving the global oil and gas industry. The software, AskMe Enterprise, enables firms to develop a database of employee expertise and know-how, documents, best practices, and FAQs, and then to share that information across the firm using the firm's portal technology.

Figure 16-8 illustrates how AskMe Enterprise works. An Intec engineer with a question, for instance, could access relevant documents, Web links, and answers to previous related questions by initiating a keyword search. If the answer could not be found, that person could post a general question on a Web page for categories such as Pipeline or Subsea for other engineers accessing that page to answer. Alternatively, the person could review the profiles of all company engineers with relevant expertise and send a detailed email query to experts who might have the answer. All questions and answers are automatically incorporated into the knowledge database.

TABLE 16-3 *Key Features of Enterprise Knowledge Network Systems*

FEATURES	DESCRIPTION
Knowledge exchange services	Support for interactive Q&A sessions
	Ability to identify qualified firm experts
	Publish and share documented knowledge with all employees
Community of practice support	Ability to connect experts across functions and units
	Ability to push information to communities
	Strong collaborative tools for communities, such as scheduling, document retrieval, and communication
Autoprofiling capabilities	Ability to profile employee experts automatically
	Ability to permit individuals to manage their own profiles
Knowledge management services	Automatically manage the nomination, approval, and dissemination of best practices and solutions
	Ensure business knowledge and rules conform to regulations and support business processes

FIGURE 16-8 *AskMe Enterprise knowledge network system.*

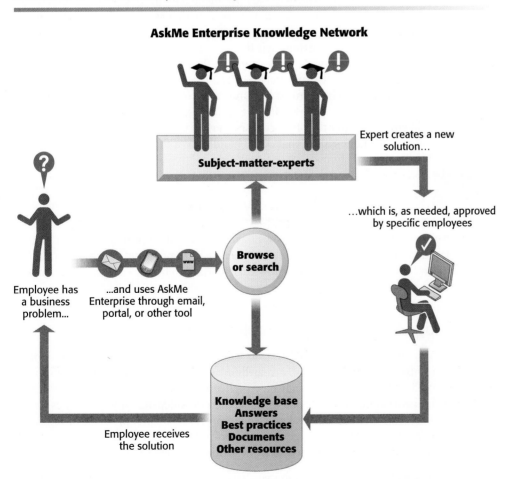

AskMe Enterprise Knowledge Network

Subject-matter-experts

Expert creates a new solution...

...which is, as needed, approved by specific employees

Browse or search

Employee has a business problem...

...and uses AskMe Enterprise through email, portal, or other tool

Knowledge base
Answers
Best practices
Documents
Other resources

Employee receives the solution

A knowledge network maintains a database of firm experts, as well as accepted solutions to known problems and then facilitates the communication between employees looking for knowledge and experts who have that knowledge. Solutions created in this communication are then added to a database of solutions in the form of FAQs, best practices, or other documents.

Supporting Technologies: Portals, Collaboration Tools, and Learning Management Systems

The major commercial knowledge management system vendors are integrating their content and document management capabilities with powerful portal and collaboration technologies. Enterprise knowledge portals can provide access to external sources of information, such as news feeds and research, as well as to internal knowledge resources along with capabilities for email, chat/instant messaging, discussion groups, and video-conferencing. Users can, for example, easily add a collection of documents obtained through a portal to a collaborative work space. The Gartner Group consulting firm uses the term *smart enterprise suites* for this leading-edge knowledge management software.

Learning Management Systems Companies need ways to keep track of and manage employee learning and to integrate it more fully into their knowledge management and other corporate systems. A **learning management system (LMS)** provides tools for the management, delivery, tracking, and assessment of various types of employee learning and training. A robust LMS integrates with systems from human resources, accounting, and sales so that the business impact of employee learning programs can be more easily identified and quantified.

The first learning management systems primarily automated record keeping in instructor-led training. These systems have been enhanced to support multiple modes of learning, including CD-ROM, downloadable videos, Web-based classes, live instruction in classes or online, and group learning in online forums and chat sessions. The LMS consolidates mixed-media training, automates the selection and administration of courses, assembles and delivers learning content, and measures learning effectiveness. If a company had a customer relationship management (CRM) system that kept track of call-handling time, for instance, a sophisticated learning management system might be able to correlate performance data with training data to see whether training correlated with on-the-job performance. Recent versions of learning management systems with open architectures have capabilities for exporting their data to other systems.

The Window on Organizations describes some of the benefits of learning management systems. Knowing how to use the products they sell is a must for sales representatives at Staples, and their product training must be conducted on a very large scale in many different locations. Trainees have many different aptitudes, skills, and sales areas. Trainees must be tested before and after they take courses. Staples Canada was able to implement a single learning management system that could handle all of these requirements.

16.3 Knowledge Work Systems

The enterprise-wide knowledge systems we have just described provide a wide range of capabilities that can be used by many if not all the workers and groups in an organization. Firms also have specialized systems for knowledge workers to help them create new knowledge for the firm.

Knowledge Workers and Knowledge Work

Knowledge workers, at term we introduced in Chapter 1, include researchers, designers, architects, scientists, and engineers who primarily create knowledge and information for the organization. Knowledge workers usually have high levels of education and memberships in professional organizations and are often asked to exercise independent judgment as a routine aspect of their work. For example, knowledge workers create new products or find ways of improving existing ones. Knowledge workers perform three key roles that are critical to the organization and to the managers who work within the organization:

learning management system (LMS)

- Keeping the organization current in knowledge as it develops in the external world—in technology, science, social thought, and the arts

- Serving as internal consultants regarding the areas of their knowledge, the changes taking place, and opportunities
- Acting as change agents, evaluating, initiating, and promoting change projects

Most knowledge workers rely on office systems, such as word processors, voice mail, email, videoconferencing, and scheduling systems, which are designed to increase worker productivity in the office. However, knowledge workers also require highly specialized knowledge work systems. These knowledge work systems (KWS) are specifically designed to promote the creation of knowledge and to ensure that new knowledge and technical expertise are properly integrated into the business. Moreover, knowledge work is segmented into many highly specialized fields, and each field has a different collection of knowledge work systems that are specialized to support workers in that field.

Requirements of Knowledge Work Systems

Knowledge work systems have characteristics that reflect the special needs of knowledge workers. First, knowledge work systems must give knowledge workers the specialized tools they need, such as powerful graphics, analytical tools, and communications and document management tools. These systems require great computing power to handle the sophisticated graphics or complex calculations necessary for knowledge workers such as scientific researchers, product designers, and financial analysts. Because knowledge workers are so focused on knowledge in the external world, these systems also must give the worker quick and easy access to external databases.

 WINDOW ON ORGANIZATIONS

InsightU Trains Staples' Sales Force with E-learning

InsightU (www.insightu.org) is an online 'university' with a mission to provide support for people interested in applying technology to improve their supply chains. The company's mission statement is: "To reignite the human spirit at the workplace so that everyone is passionately contributing to the bottom line." The people at InsightU believe that the best way to accomplish this lofty goal is through e-learning for product training. The InsightU philosophy is that giving the sales force the right tools and the right information at the right time will help the sales personnel work with customers more effectively. Research group IDC agrees with this philosophy—forecasting that the e-learning market would soon reach $28 billion.

Staples, Business Depot (also operating as Bureau En Gros), a wholly owned unit of Staples, Inc. is Canada's largest supplier of office supplies, business machines, computers, office furniture and business services for the small business and home office customer. Staples has more than 200 stores in Canada. Staples chose InsightU to implement new online product training for its entire chain of Canadian Business Depot retail stores. InsightU worked with Staples' manufacturing vendors to create courseware for their products. The sales associates benefit from anytime access to self-paced product training, making them more knowledgeable and confident, in essence enhancing their jobs as well as their profitability.

Kevin Dixon, vice president of business development at InsightU, recalls: "The biggest challenge in implementing Staples, Business Depot's vision for online product training was finding a software platform capable of supporting the sheer scope of the plan. We needed robust interactivity, but also massive scalability. We tried other management systems, but we were impressed with the way Intralearn performed." InsightU used Intralearn to offer e-PK, product training via the Internet or intranet, delivering online training, new product information, product launches, and sales training, not only to inside sales representatives, but also to external dealers and retailers.

IntraLearn products have built-in e-commerce, remote registration, content creation and delivery, multimedia, exams and assessments features. IntraLearn can launch and track standards-based courses, and it can automatically generate reports on learner progress and skill attainment. Interactivity and collaboration are built-in with chat, threaded discussions, email, white boards, Internet links, and group/mentor rooms with file sharing.

Says Dixon, "Fortunately for us and the 8000 Staples, Business Depot associates, we found in Intralearn everything we needed in a learning management system. Intralearn possesses comprehensive and unique back-end database features

A user-friendly interface is very important to a knowledge worker's system. User-friendly interfaces save time by enabling the user to perform needed tasks and get to required information without having to spend a lot of time learning how to use the computer. Saving time is more important for knowledge workers than for most other employees because knowledge workers are highly paid—wasting a knowledge worker's time is simply too expensive, and knowledge workers can easily fall prey to information overload (Farhoomand and Drury 2002). Figure 16-9 summarizes the requirements of knowledge work systems.

Knowledge workstations often are designed and optimized for the specific tasks to be performed; for example, a design engineer requires a different workstation setup than a financial analyst. Design engineers need graphics with enough power to handle three-dimensional computer-aided design (CAD) systems. However, financial analysts are more interested in access to a myriad of external databases and optical disk technology for efficiently storing and accessing massive amounts of financial data.

Examples of Knowledge Work Systems

Major knowledge work applications include computer-aided design (CAD) systems, virtual reality systems for simulation and modelling, and financial workstations. **Computer-aided design (CAD)** automates the creation and revision of designs, using computers and sophisticated graphics software. Using a more traditional physical design methodology, each design modification requires a mould to be made and a prototype to be tested physically. That process must be repeated many times, which is a very expensive and time-consuming process. Using a CAD workstation, the designer need only make a physical prototype toward the end of the design process because the design can be easily tested and changed on the computer. The ability of CAD software to provide design specifications for the tooling

FIGURE 16-9   *Requirements of knowledge work systems.*

Knowledge work systems require strong links to external knowledge bases in addition to specialized hardware and software.

computer-aided design (CAD)

and the manufacturing processes also saves a great deal of time and money while producing a manufacturing process with far fewer problems.

For example, architects from Skidmore, Owings, & Merrill LLP used a three-dimensional design program called Revit to work out the creative and technical details of the design for the Freedom Tower at the site of the former World Trade Center. The software enabled the architects to strip away the outer layer to manipulate the shape of the floors. Changes appeared immediately in the entire model, and the software automatically recalculated the technical details in the blueprints (Frangos 2004).

Hawkes Ocean Technology used Autodesk's Inventor three-dimensional design and engineering program to create and manipulate flowing shapes when designing the revolutionary Deep Flight Aviator submarine for the U.S. Navy. The software allowed Hawkes to create and manipulate flowing shapes, test their stress points, and refine them without ever having to touch a lathe or mould. The system also enabled Hawkes to cut design costs by one-third, reduce engineering staff from 10 to 3, and bypass the prototyping stage when developing new products (Salkever 2002).

Virtual reality systems have visualization, rendering, and simulation capabilities that go far beyond those of conventional CAD systems. They use interactive graphics software to create computer-generated simulations that are so close to reality that users almost believe they are participating in a real-world situation. In many virtual reality systems, the user dons special clothing, headgear, and equipment, depending on the application. The clothing contains sensors that record the user's movements and immediately transmit that information back to the computer. For instance, to walk through a virtual reality simulation of a house, you would need garb that monitors the movement of your feet, hands, and head. You also would need goggles containing video screens and sometimes audio attachments and feeling gloves so that you can be immersed in computer feedback.

Virtual reality is just starting to provide benefits in educational, scientific, and business work. For example, Royal LePage, a Canadian real estate firm, uses virtual reality to host online tours of their listed properties. A visitor to the Royal LePage Web site can take an online tour of various rooms in houses they may wish to consider purchasing—without visiting the property.

Virtual reality applications developed for the Web use a standard called **Virtual Reality Modeling Language (VRML)**. VRML is a set of specifications for interactive, three-dimensional modelling on the World Wide Web that can organize multiple media types, including animation, images, and audio to put users in a simulated real-world environment (see Figure 16-10). VRML is platform independent, operates over a desktop computer, and requires little bandwidth. Using their Web browsers, users can download a three-dimensional virtual world designed using VRML.

FIGURE 16-10   *Lands' End's VRML virtual model.*

Users can create a VRML "virtual model" that approximates their physical proportions to help them visualize how they will look in clothing sold at the Lands' End Web site. This digitized image can be rotated to show how the outfits will look from all angles, and users can click to change the colour of the clothes.

virtual reality systems

Virtual Reality Modeling Language (VRML)

TABLE 16-4 *Examples of Knowledge Work Systems*

KNOWLEDGE WORK SYSTEM	FUNCTION IN ORGANIZATION
CAD/CAM (computer-aided design/computer-aided manufacturing)	Provides engineers, designers, and factory managers with precise control over industrial design and manufacturing
Virtual reality systems	Provide drug designers, architects, engineers, and medical workers with precise, photorealistic simulations of objects
Investment workstations	High-end PCs used in the financial sector to analyze trading situations instantaneously and facilitate portfolio management

CAD systems improve the quality and precision of product design by performing much of the design and testing work on the computer.

DuPont, the Wilmington, Delaware, chemical company, created a VRML application called HyperPlant, which enables users to access three-dimensional data over the Internet using Web browser software. Engineers can go through three-dimensional models as if they were physically walking through a plant, viewing objects at eye level. This level of detail reduces the number of mistakes they make during construction of oil rigs, oil plants, and other structures.

The financial industry is using specialized **investment workstations** to leverage the knowledge and time of its brokers, traders, and portfolio managers. Firms such as TD Canada Trust and Assante have installed investment workstations that integrate a wide range of data from both internal and external sources, including contact management data, real-time and historical market data, and research reports. Previously, financial professionals had to spend considerable time accessing data from separate systems and piecing together the information they needed. By providing one-stop information faster and with fewer errors, the workstations streamline the entire investment process from stock selection to updating client records. Table 16-4 summarizes the major types of knowledge work systems.

16.4 Intelligent Techniques

Artificial intelligence and database technology provide a number of intelligent techniques that organizations can use to capture individual and collective knowledge and to extend their knowledge base. Expert systems, case-based reasoning, and fuzzy logic are used for capturing tacit knowledge. Neural networks and data mining are used for **knowledge discovery**. They can discover underlying patterns, categories, and behaviours in large data sets that could not be discovered by managers alone or simply through experience. Genetic algorithms are used for generating solutions to problems that are too large and complex for human beings to analyze on their own. Intelligent agents can automate routine tasks to help firms search for and filter information for use in electronic commerce, supply chain management, and other activities.

Data mining, which we introduced in Chapter 6, helps organizations capture undiscovered knowledge residing in large databases, providing managers with new insight for improving business performance. It has become an important tool for management decision making, and we provide a detailed discussion of data mining for management decision support in Chapter 15.

investment workstations
knowledge discovery

The other intelligent techniques discussed in this section are based on **artificial intelligence (AI)** technology, which consists of computer-based systems (both hardware and software) that attempt to emulate human behaviour. These systems would be able to learn languages, accomplish physical tasks, use a perceptual apparatus, and emulate human expertise and decision making. Although AI applications do not exhibit the breadth, complexity, originality, and generality of human intelligence, they play an important role in contemporary knowledge management.

Capturing Knowledge: Expert Systems

Expert systems are an intelligent technique for capturing tacit knowledge in a very specific and limited domain of human expertise. These systems capture the knowledge of skilled employees in the form of a set of rules in a software system that can be used by others in the organization. The set of rules in the expert system adds to the memory, or stored learning, of the firm.

Expert systems lack the breadth of knowledge and the understanding of fundamental principles of a human expert. They typically perform very limited tasks that can be performed by professionals in a few minutes or hours, such as diagnosing a malfunctioning machine or determining whether to grant credit for a loan. Problems that cannot be solved by human experts in the same short period of time are far too difficult for an expert system. However, by capturing human expertise in limited areas, expert systems can provide benefits, helping organizations make high-quality decisions with fewer people. Today expert systems are widely used in business in discrete, highly structured decision-making situations.

How Expert Systems Work Human knowledge must be modelled or represented in a way that a computer can process. The model of human knowledge used by expert systems is called the **knowledge base**. A standard structured programming construct is the IF–THEN construct, in which a condition is evaluated. If the condition is true, an action is taken. For instance,

IF INCOME > $45 000 (condition)

THEN PRINT NAME AND ADDRESS (action)

A series of these rules can be a knowledge base. A software program for an expert system may have 200 to 10 000 of these rules, which are much more interconnected and nested than in a traditional software program (see Figure 16-11).

Could you represent the knowledge in the *Encyclopaedia Britannica* this way? Probably not, because the **rule base** would be too large, and not all the knowledge in the encyclopedia can be represented in the form of IF–THEN rules. In general, expert systems can be efficiently used only in those situations in which the domain of knowledge is highly restricted (such as in granting credit) and involves no more than a few thousand rules.

The **AI shell** is the programming environment of an expert system. In the early years of expert systems, computer scientists used specialized artificial intelligence programming languages, such as LISP or Prolog, that could process lists of rules efficiently. Today, a growing number of expert systems use AI shells that are user-friendly development environments. AI shells can quickly generate user-interface screens, capture the knowledge base, and manage the strategies for searching the rule base.

The strategy used to search through the rule base is called the **inference engine**. Two strategies are commonly used: forward chaining and backward chaining (see Figure 16-12).

In **forward chaining**, the inference engine begins with the information entered by the user and searches the rule base to arrive at a conclusion. The strategy is to fire, or carry out, the action of the rule when a condition is true. In Figure 16-12, beginning on the left, if the user enters a client's name with income greater than $100 000, the engine will fire all rules in sequence from left to right. If the user then enters information indicating that the same client owns real estate, another pass of the rule base will occur and more rules will fire. Processing continues until no more rules can be fired.

In **backward chaining**, the strategy for searching the rule base starts with a hypothesis and proceeds by asking the user questions about selected facts until the hypothesis is

artificial intelligence (AI)

expert systems

knowledge base

rule base

AI shell

inference engine

forward chaining

backward chaining

FIGURE 16-11 *Rules in an AI program.*

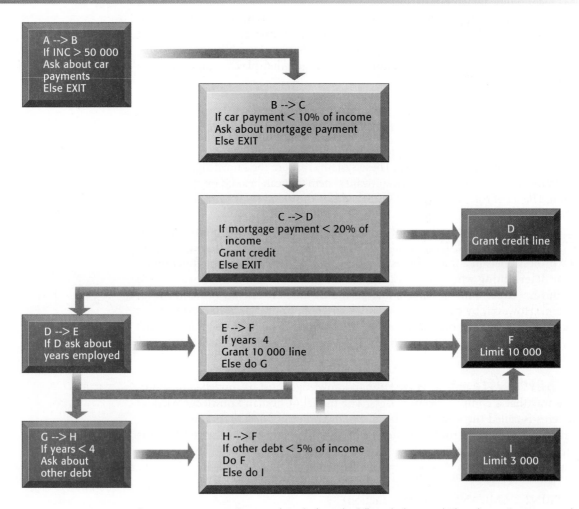

An expert system contains a number of rules to be followed when used. The rules are interconnected; the number of outcomes is known in advance and is limited; there are multiple paths to the same outcome; and the system can consider multiple rules at a single time. The rules illustrated are for simple credit-granting expert systems.

either confirmed or disproved. In our example, in Figure 16-12, ask the question, "Should we add this person to the prospect database?" Begin on the right of the diagram, and work toward the left. You can see that the person should be added to the database if a sales representative is sent, term insurance is granted, or a financial adviser visits the client.

Developing an expert system requires input from one or more experts, who have a thorough command of the knowledge base, and one or more knowledge engineers, who can translate the knowledge (as described by the expert) into a set of rules. A **knowledge engineer** is similar to a traditional systems analyst but has special expertise in eliciting information and expertise from other professionals.

An expert systems development project balances potential savings from the proposed system against the cost. The team members develop a prototype system to test assumptions about how to encode the knowledge of experts. Next, they develop a full-scale system, focusing mainly on the addition of a very large number of rules. The complexity of the entire system grows with the number of rules, so the comprehensibility of the system may be threatened. Generally, the system is pruned to achieve simplicity and power. The system is tested by a range of experts within the organization against the performance criteria established earlier. Once tested, the system is integrated into the data flow and work patterns of the organization.

knowledge engineer

FIGURE 16-12 *Inference engines in expert systems.*

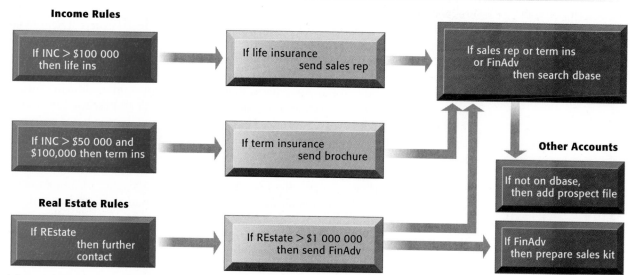

An inference engine works by searching through the rules and "firing" those rules that are triggered by facts gathered and entered by the user. Basically, a collection of rules is similar to a series of nested IF statements in a traditional software program; however, the magnitude of the statements and degree of nesting are much greater in an expert system.

Examples of Successful Expert Systems The following are examples of expert systems that provide organizations with an array of benefits, including reduced errors, reduced costs, reduced training time, improved decisions, and improved quality and service.

The Learning Edge, a Toronto-based company, developed the IBM AS/400 Development Software Advisor as a marketing aid to help IBM's prospective customers better understand their application development needs and options. First the expert system gathers environmental and business process information; then it analyzes the data and recommends a programming language.

Countrywide Funding Corporation in Pasadena, California, is a loan-underwriting firm with about 400 underwriters in 150 offices around the country. The company developed a PC-based expert system in 1992 to make preliminary creditworthiness decisions on loan requests. The company had experienced rapid, continuing growth and wanted the system to help ensure consistent, high-quality loan decisions. Countrywide's Loan Underwriting Expert System (CLUES) has about 400 rules. Countrywide tested the system by sending every loan application handled by a human underwriter to CLUES as well. The system was refined until it agreed with the underwriters in 95 percent of the cases.

Countrywide does not rely on CLUES to reject loans because the expert system cannot be programmed to handle exceptional situations, such as those involving a self-employed person or complex financial schemes. An underwriter must review all rejected loans and makes the final decision. CLUES has other benefits. Traditionally, an underwriter could handle six or seven applications a day. Using CLUES, the same underwriter can evaluate at least 16 per day. Countrywide now is using the rules in its expert system to answer inquiries from visitors to its Web site who want to know if they qualify for a loan.

Galeria Kaufhof, a German superstore chain, uses a rule-based system to help it manage more than 120 000 deliveries of goods that it receives each day, ranging from clothing to complex electronics and fine china. Inspecting each delivery is time consuming and expensive, but the company wants to make sure that it is receiving goods that are not damaged or defective. Kaufhof implemented a rule-based system that identifies high-risk deliveries and passes along lower-risk ones automatically. The system scans delivery labels and identifies each delivery in terms of its size, type of product, whether the product is a new product, and the supplier's past history of deliveries. Deliveries of large numbers of complex products that are new or that have suppliers with unfavourable delivery histories are carefully inspected while other deliveries are passed on without inspection (Booth and Buluswar 2002).

The investment banking firm Goldman Sachs uses a rule-based expert system to keep unwanted stocks out of individual portfolios. Almost all of its client portfolios have restrictions specified by owners on which stocks or even entire sectors to exclude. Goldman wants to make sure its global network of financial advisers respect these restrictions so they do not make any purchases that clients do not want. Goldman's business managers, compliance officers, and private wealth managers all play roles in deciding which stocks to purchase for a portfolio. The company developed a rule-based system that maintains rules for keeping a particular stock from entering a client's portfolio. By creating a centralized portfolio-filtering system, Goldman is better able to catch mistakes before erroneous trades go through (Guerra 2001).

Although expert systems lack the robust and general intelligence of human beings, they can provide benefits to organizations if their limitations are well understood. Only certain classes of problems can be solved using expert systems. Virtually all successful expert systems deal with problems of classification in which there are relatively few alternative outcomes and in which these possible outcomes are all known in advance. Many expert systems require large, lengthy, and expensive development efforts. Hiring or training more experts may be less expensive than developing an expert system. Typically, the environment in which an expert system operates is continually changing so that the expert system must also continually change. Some expert systems, especially large ones, are so complex that in a few years the maintenance costs equal the development costs.

The applicability of expert systems to managerial problems is very limited. Managerial problems generally involve drawing facts and interpretations from divergent sources, evaluating the facts, and comparing one interpretation of the facts with another; they are not limited to simple classification. Expert systems based on the prior knowledge of a few known alternatives are unsuitable to the problems managers face on a daily basis.

Organizational Intelligence: Case-Based Reasoning

Expert systems primarily capture the tacit knowledge of individual experts, but organizations also have collective knowledge and expertise that they have built up over the years. This organizational knowledge can be captured and stored using case-based reasoning. In **case-based reasoning (CBR)**, descriptions of past experiences of human specialists, represented as cases, are stored in a database for later retrieval when the user encounters a new case with similar parameters. The system searches for stored cases with problem characteristics similar to the new one, finds the closest fit, and applies the solutions of the old case to the new case. Successful solutions are tagged to the new case, and both are stored together with the other cases in the knowledge base. Unsuccessful solutions also are appended to the case database along with explanations as to why the solutions did not work (see Figure 16-13).

Expert systems work by applying a set of IF–THEN–ELSE rules against a knowledge base, both of which are extracted from human experts. Case-based reasoning, in contrast, represents knowledge as a series of cases, and this knowledge base is continuously expanded and refined by users. One can find case-based reasoning in diagnostic systems in medicine or customer support where users can retrieve past cases whose characteristics are similar to the new case. The system suggests a solution or diagnosis based on the best-matching retrieved case.

Fuzzy Logic Systems

Most people do not think in terms of traditional IF–THEN rules or precise numbers. Humans tend to categorize things imprecisely using rules for making decisions that may have many shades of meaning. For example, a man or a woman can be *strong* or *intelligent*. A company can be *large, medium,* or *small* in size. Temperature can be *hot, cold, cool,* or *warm*. These categories represent a range of values.

case-based reasoning (CBR)

FIGURE 16-13 *How case-based reasoning works.*

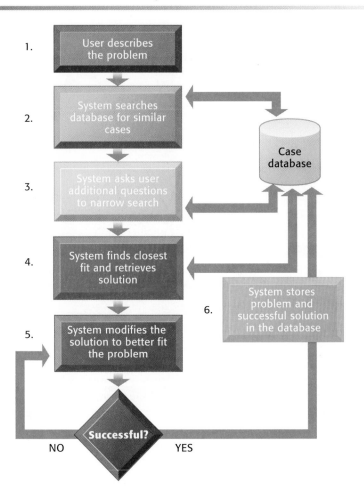

Case-based reasoning represents knowledge as a database of past cases and their solutions. The system uses a six-step process to generate solutions to new problems encountered by the user.

Fuzzy logic is a rule-based technology that can represent such imprecision by creating rules that use approximate or subjective values. It can describe a particular phenomenon or process linguistically and then represent that description in a small number of flexible rules. Organizations can use fuzzy logic to create software systems that capture tacit knowledge where there is linguistic ambiguity.

For example, Ford Motor Company developed a fuzzy logic application that backs a simulated tractor-trailer into a parking space. The application uses the following three rules:

IF the truck is *near* jackknifing, THEN *reduce* the steering angle.

IF the truck is *far away* from the dock, THEN steer *toward* the dock.

IF the truck is *near* the dock, THEN point the trailer *directly* at the dock.

This logic makes sense to us as human beings because it represents how we think as we back that truck into its berth. To see how such logic would be translated into a software system, let us look at the way fuzzy logic would represent various temperatures in a computer application to control room temperature. The terms (known as membership functions) are imprecisely defined so that, for example, in Figure 16-14, cool is between 50 degrees and 70 degrees although the temperature is most clearly cool between about 60 degrees and 67 degrees. Note that cool is overlapped by cold or norm. To control the room environment using this logic, the programmer would develop similarly imprecise definitions for humidity and other factors, such as outdoor wind and temperature. The rules might include one that says: "If the temperature is cool or cold and the humidity is low

fuzzy logic

FIGURE 16-14 *Implementing fuzzy logic rules in hardware.*

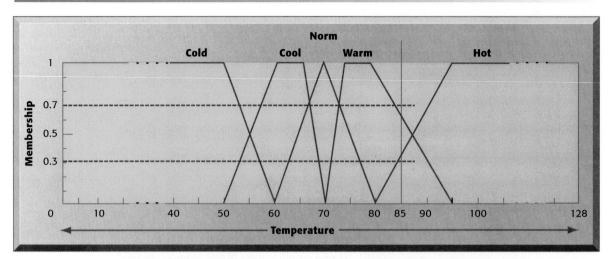

The membership functions for the input called temperature are in the logic of the thermostat to control the room temperature. Membership functions help translate linguistic expressions such as *warm* into numbers that the computer can manipulate.

Source: James M. Sibigtroth, "Implementing Fuzzy Expert Rules in Hardware," *AI Expert*, April 1992. © 1992 Miller Freeman, Inc. Reprinted with permission.

while the outdoor wind is high and the outdoor temperature is low, raise the heat and humidity in the room." The computer would combine the membership function readings in a weighted manner and, using all the rules, raise and lower the temperature and humidity.

Fuzzy logic provides solutions to problems requiring expertise that is difficult to represent in the form of crisp IF–THEN rules. In Japan, Sendai's subway system uses fuzzy logic controls to accelerate so smoothly that standing passengers don't need support. Mitsubishi Heavy Industries in Tokyo has been able to reduce the power consumption of its air conditioners by 20 percent by implementing control programs in fuzzy logic. The autofocus device in cameras is only possible because of fuzzy logic. Many stores sell rice steamers made in Japan that use fuzzy logic. A variable heat setting detects the amount of grain, cooks it at the preferred temperature, and keeps the food warm up to 12 hours. In these instances, fuzzy logic allows incremental changes in inputs to produce smooth changes in outputs instead of discontinuous ones, making it useful for consumer electronics and engineering applications.

Fuzzy logic can be used to express relationships very generally and compactly, requiring fewer IF–THEN rules than traditional software programs. Compact software programs require less computer capacity, enabling, for example, Sanyo Fisher USA to implement fuzzy logic for camcorder controls without adding expensive memory to its product. In Canada, a proposal has been made to the Meteorological Service of Canada to use fuzzy logic to ingest and intelligently combine orthogonal "interest fields," such as observations, climatology, classification-system-based predictors, and radar, satellite, and lightning data.

Management also has found fuzzy logic useful for decision making and organizational control. A Wall Street firm created a system that selects companies for potential acquisition, using the language stock traders understand. Recently, a system has been developed to detect possible fraud in medical claims submitted by health care providers anywhere in the United States.

Neural Networks

Neural networks are used for modelling complex, poorly understood problems for which large amounts of data have been collected. They are especially useful for finding patterns and relationships in massive amounts of data that would be too complicated and difficult for a human being to analyze. **Neural networks** discover this knowledge by using hardware and software that emulate the processing patterns of the biological brain. Neural networks "learn" patterns from large quantities of data by sifting through data, searching for relationships, building models, and correcting over and over again the model's own mistakes.

A neural net has a large number of sensing and processing nodes that continuously interact with each other. Figure 16-15 represents one type of neural network comprising an input layer, an output layer, and a hidden processing layer. Humans "train" the network by feeding it a set of training data for which the inputs produce a known set of outputs or conclusions. This helps the computer learn the correct solution by example. As the computer is fed more data, each case is compared with the known outcome. If it differs, a correction is calculated and applied to the nodes in the hidden processing layer. These steps are repeated until a condition, such as corrections being less than a certain amount, is reached. The neural network in Figure 16-15 has learned how to identify a good credit risk. Also, self-organizing neural networks can be trained by exposing them to large amounts of data and allowing them to discover the patterns and relationships in the data.

While expert systems seek to emulate or model a human expert's way of solving problems, neural network builders claim that they do not model human intelligence, do not program solutions, and do not aim to solve specific problems per se. Instead, neural network designers seek to put intelligence into the hardware in the form of a generalized capability to learn. In contrast, the expert system is highly specific to a given problem and cannot be retrained easily.

Neural network applications are emerging in medicine, science, and business to address problems in pattern classification, prediction, financial analysis, and control and optimization. In medicine, neural networks applications are used for screening patients for coronary artery disease, for diagnosing patients with epilepsy and Alzheimer's disease, and for performing pattern recognition of pathology images. The financial industry uses neural networks to discern patterns in vast pools of data that might help investment firms predict the performance of equities, corporate bond ratings, or corporate bankruptcies. Visa International is using a neural network to help detect credit card fraud by monitoring all Visa transactions for sudden changes in the buying patterns of cardholders.

Unlike expert systems, which typically provide explanations for their solutions, neural networks cannot always explain why they arrived at a particular solution. Moreover, they cannot always guarantee a completely certain solution, arrive at the same solution again with the same input data, or always guarantee the best solution. They are very sensitive and may not perform well if their training covers too little or too much data. In most current applications, neural networks are best used as aids to human decision makers instead of substitutes for them.

neural networks

FIGURE 16-15 *How a neural network works.*

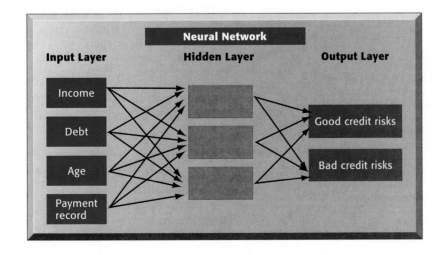

A neural network uses rules it "learns" from patterns in data to construct a hidden layer of logic. The hidden layer then processes inputs, classifying them based on the experience of the model.

Source: Herb Edelstein, "Technology How-To: Mining Data Warehouses," *InformationWeek*, January 8, 1996. Copyright © 1996 CMP Media, Inc., 600 Community Drive, Manhasset, NY 12030. Reprinted with permission.

Genetic Algorithms

Genetic algorithms (also referred to as adaptive computation) are used for finding the optimal solution for a specific problem by examining a very large number of possible solutions for that problem. Their problem-solving techniques are conceptually based on the method that living organisms use to adapt to their environments—the process of evolution. They are programmed to work the way populations solve problems—by changing and reorganizing their component parts using processes such as reproduction, mutation, and natural selection.

Thus, genetic algorithms promote the evolution of solutions to particular problems, controlling the generation, variation, adaptation, and selection of possible solutions using genetically based processes. As solutions alter and combine, the worst ones are discarded and the better ones survive to go on to produce even better solutions. Genetic algorithms breed programs that solve problems even when no person can fully understand their structure

A genetic algorithm works by representing information as a string of 0s and 1s. A possible solution can be represented by a long string of these digits. The genetic algorithm provides methods of searching all possible combinations of digits to identify the right string representing the best possible structure for the problem.

In one method, the programmer first randomly generates a population of strings consisting of combinations of binary digits (see Figure 16-16). Each string corresponds to one of the variables in the problem. One applies a test for fitness, ranking the strings in the population according to their level of desirability as possible solutions. After the initial population is evaluated for fitness, the algorithm then produces the next generation of strings, consisting of strings that survived the fitness test plus offspring strings produced from mating pairs of strings, and tests their fitness. The process continues until a solution is reached.

Many business problems require optimization because they deal with issues such as minimization of costs, maximization of profits, efficient scheduling, and use of resources. If these situations are dynamic and complex, involving hundreds or thousands of variables or formulas, genetic algorithms can expedite the solution because they can evaluate many different solution alternatives quickly to find the best one.

For example, General Electric engineers used genetic algorithms to help optimize the design for jet turbine aircraft engines, where each design change required changes in up to 100 variables. The supply chain management software from i2 Technologies uses genetic algorithms to optimize production-scheduling models incorporating hundreds of thousands of details about customer orders, material and resource availability, manufacturing and distribution capability, and delivery dates. International Truck and Engine used this software to iron out snags in production, reducing costly schedule disruptions by 90 per-

genetic algorithms

FIGURE 16-16 *The components of a genetic algorithm.*

	Colour	Speed	Intelligence	Fitness
1	White	Medium	Dumb	40
2	Black	Slow	Dumb	43
3	White	Slow	Very dumb	22
4	Black	Fast	Dumb	71
5	White	Medium	Very smart	53

A population of chromosomes   **Decoding of chromosomes**   **Evaluation of chromosomes**

This example illustrates an initial population of "chromosomes" each representing a different solution. The genetic algorithm uses an iterative process to refine the initial solutions so that the better ones, those with the higher fitness, are more likely to emerge as the best solution.

Source: Dhar, Stein, SEVEN METHODS FOR TRANSFORMING CORPORATE DATA INTO BUSINESS INTELLIGENCE (Trade Version) 1st © 1997. Electronically reproduced by permission of Pearson Education, Inc., Upper Saddle River, New Jersey.

FIGURE 16-17 *Ward Systems' optimizing software.*

Illustrated here is a sample application from Ward Systems' Gene Hunter for optimizing a portfolio of securities by minimizing risk while simultaneously maximizing return. The trader picks a number of stocks that he or she believes will offer a high rate of return. The genetic algorithm is used to minimize the risk by helping to adjust the portfolio so that it behaves more like the Standard & Poors (S&P) 500 index. The S&P 500 portfolio is considered less risky because it is much larger and more diversified than just a handful of stocks.

cent in five of its plants. Genetic algorithms have helped market researchers perform market segmentation analysis. (Kuo, Chang and Chien 2004; Burtka 1993; Wakefield 2001).

Hybrid AI Systems

Genetic algorithms, fuzzy logic, neural networks, and expert systems can be integrated into a single application to take advantage of the best features of these technologies. These systems are called **hybrid AI systems**. Hybrid applications in business are growing. In Japan, Hitachi, Mitsubishi, Ricoh, Sanyo, and others are starting to incorporate hybrid AI in products such as home appliances, factory machinery, and office equipment. Matsushita has developed a "neurofuzzy" washing machine that combines fuzzy logic with neural networks. Nikko Securities has been working on a neurofuzzy system to forecast convertible-bond ratings.

Intelligent Agents

Intelligent agent technology can help businesses navigate through large amounts of data to locate only information that is considered important and, in some cases, act on that information on behalf of the user. **Intelligent agents** are software programs that work in the background without direct human intervention to carry out specific, repetitive, and predictable tasks for an individual user, business process, or software application. The agent uses a limited built-in or learned knowledge base to accomplish tasks or make decisions on the user's behalf. Intelligent agents can be programmed to make decisions based on the user's personal preferences—for example, to delete junk email, schedule appointments, or travel over interconnected networks to find the cheapest airfare to California. The agent can be likened to a personal digital assistant collaborating with the user in the same work environment. It can help the user by performing tasks on the user's behalf, training or teaching the user, hiding the complexity of difficult tasks, helping the user collaborate with other users, or monitoring events and procedures.

There are many intelligent agent applications today in operating systems, application software, email systems, mobile computing software, and network tools. For example, the wizards found in Microsoft Office software tools have built-in capabilities to show users how to accomplish various tasks, such as formatting documents or creating graphs, and to anticipate when users need assistance.

Of special interest to businesses are intelligent agents for cruising networks, including the Internet, in search of information. For example, Chapter 7 describes how *shopping*

hybrid AI systems

intelligent agents

FIGURE 16-18   *Intelligent agents in P&G's supply chain network.*

Intelligent agents are helping Proctor & Gamble shorten the replenishment cycles for products such as a box of Tide.

1. Software agents schedule deliveries from suppliers. If a supplier can't deliver on time, agents negotiate with other suppliers to create an alternative delivery schedule.

2. Software agents collect real-time sales data on each P&G product from multiple retail stores. They relay the data to P&G production for replenishing orders and to sales and marketing for trend analysis.

3. Software agents schedule shipments from distributors to retailers, giving priority to retailers whose inventories are low. If a shipment to a retailer is delayed, agents find an alternative trucker.

bots can help consumers find products they want and assist them in comparing prices and other features. Because these mobile agents are personalized, semiautonomous, and continuously running, they can help automate several of the most time-consuming stages of the buying process and thus reduce transaction costs.

Agent technology is finding applications in supply chain management for improving coordination among different members of the supply chain in response to changing business conditions (Sadeh, Hildum, and Kjenstad 2003; Cavalieri, Cesarotti, and Introna 2003). Figure 16-18 illustrates the use of intelligent agents in Procter & Gamble's supply chain network. The network models a complex supply chain as a group of semiautonomous "agents" representing individual supply chain components, such as trucks, production facilities, distributors, or retail stores. The behaviour of each agent is programmed to follow rules that mimic actual behaviour, such as "dispatch a truck when it is full." Simulations using the agents enable the company to perform what-if analyses on inventory levels, in-store stock-outs, and transportation costs.

Using intelligent agent models, P&G discovered that trucks should often be dispatched before being fully loaded. Although transportation costs would be higher using partially loaded trucks because of both driver time and fuel to deliver fewer goods, the simulation showed that retail store stockouts would occur less often, thus reducing the amount of lost sales, which would more than make up for the higher distribution costs. Agent-based modelling has saved P&G $300 million annually on an investment of less than 1 percent of that amount (Anthes 2003). Table 16-5 shows how other companies are using intelligent agent technology.

TABLE 16-5 *How Businesses Are Using Intelligent Agents*

ORGANIZATION	INTELLIGENT AGENT APPLICATION
Merck & Co.	Agents help it find more efficient ways to distribute anti-HIV drugs in Zimbabwe.
Southwest Airlines	Agents help optimize cargo routing.
Ford Motor Co.	Agents are used to simulate buyer preferences to recommend packages of car options that optimize the trade-off between production costs and customer demands.
Edison Chouest Offshore LLC	Offshore service company in Galliano, Louisiana, uses agents to optimize its deployment of service and supply vessels in the Gulf of Mexico.

Management Opportunities, Challenges, and Solutions

Successful deployment of knowledge management systems requires a very clear understanding of how the firm creates and uses knowledge. Organizations need to determine precisely how they can benefit from knowledge management programs and whether the benefits are realistic.

Opportunities

Businesses armed with proprietary knowledge about their customers and operations have what could be called an "invisible competitive advantage" if this knowledge is not available to competitors and cannot be purchased by others in the marketplace. For that reason, knowledge management systems can be a source of tremendous value if they enable firms to further leverage that knowledge.

Management Challenges

Proving the quantitative benefits of knowledge management projects that deal with intangibles such as "knowledge" and "collaboration" is often more challenging than other information systems projects (Davenport, DeLong, and Beers. 1998; Davenport and Prusak 1998). Information systems that truly enhance the productivity of knowledge workers may be difficult to develop because the manner in which information technology can enhance higher-level tasks, such as those performed by managers and professionals, is not always clearly understood. Some aspects of organizational knowledge are tacit, unstructured, and not easily captured or codified. Only certain kinds of information problems are appropriate for intelligent techniques.

Research conducted in the past five years on knowledge management projects has uncovered a number of difficulties in implementing knowledge management systems. Among these difficulties are the following:

- Insufficient resources are available to structure and update the content in repositories.
- Poor quality and high variability of content quality results from insufficient validating mechanisms.
- Content in repositories lacks context, making documents difficult to understand.
- Individual employees are not rewarded for contributing content, and many fear sharing knowledge with others on the job or fear that their jobs may be replaced by the new systems
- Search engines return too much information, reflecting lack of knowledge structure or taxonomy.

Solution Guidelines

There are both managerial and technological solutions to these challenges. Communities of practice are useful in providing motivation to employees and help provide context to knowledge. Properly designed knowledge taxonomies are also helpful in organizing knowledge. Firms can revise their employee compensation systems to reward knowledge sharing.

Proper planning and rollout can increase the chances of success for knowledge management projects. There are five important steps in developing a successful knowledge management project that has measurable results:

- Develop in stages
- Choose a high-value business process
- Choose the right audience

FIGURE 16-19 *Implementing knowledge management projects in stages.*

Knowledge management projects have a greater chance of succeeding if they are implemented in stages with clearly defined ways of measuring results.

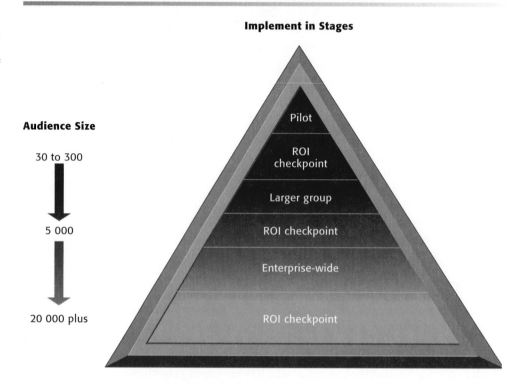

- Measure ROI during initial implementation
- Use the preliminary ROI to project enterprise-wide values

Staged implementation and choice of business process or group to impact are perhaps the most critical decisions (see Figure 16-19). At each stage in the implementation process, somewhat different metrics can be used to evaluate a project.

In general, pilot projects should have 30 to 500 people involved. Knowledge management projects produce value by sharing knowledge among a large number of users and developing a large, useful knowledge repository or knowledge network. Measures of value will change as the project moves from the pilot stage through the group and enterprise stages (see Table 16-6).

In the early stages, bottom-up reports and evaluations from users can be gathered. Users can be asked to assign a value (either a dollar value or minutes and hours saved during work) to the various uses they make of the knowledge management system:

- Number of conversations viewed
- Number of visits
- Number signed on to system
- Number of answers found in the knowledge base

TABLE 16-6 *Stages for Measuring Value of Knowledge Management Systems*

STAGE	APPROACH	REQUIRED TIME	DATA AVAILABILITY	ACCURACY
Pilot project	Bottom up	Short	Usually available	Good
Group implementation	Evaluation metrics	Moderate	Easily gathered	Better
Enterprise-wide implementation	Group utilization data (e.g., demand) Process improvement	Lengthy	Requires effort	Best

TABLE 16-7 Example of Savings from a Knowledge Management System

METRIC	ASSIGNED VALUE	FIRST 90 DAYS RESULTS	TOTAL VALUE
Documents shared	$450	172	$77 400
Answers viewed	$10	6103	$61 030
New answers	$30	486	$14 580
Best practices	$3000	18	$54 000
FAQs	$225	80	$18 000

- Number of answers received from expert providers
- Average rating of answers (on a scale of 1 to 5)
- Number of FAQs requested

In the group implementation stage, a different set of top-down measures can be used. Here, managers need to assign a value to answers viewed, improvements in business processes, new unexpected answers, the number of documents shared (as opposed to reinvented), and the number of FAQs accessed. The emphasis in these stages is on establishing a dollar value for the system's benefits based on reasonable assumptions and reports from users developed in the pilot stage.

Table 16-7 illustrates one set of results of using these measures for 1000 users during a 90-day period. The total savings produced by all of these improvements during that period amounted to $225 010, or an average savings of $225.01 per user. If we projected these benefits for an entire year, total savings would amount to $900 040 (or $900.04 per user). If the system cost $700 000 to implement and $100 000 annually to maintain after the first year, the total benefits would amount to $200 040 in the first year and $800 040 each succeeding year. Chapter 11 describes the various capital budgeting models that can then be used to calculate the actual return on investment.

In the enterprise-wide implementation stage, other enterprise business process metrics become more important, such as response time to customers, speed of new product development, reductions in head count, reduction in procurement costs, and reductions in management decision-making intervals.

Summary

1. **Assess the role of knowledge management and knowledge management programs in business.**

   Knowledge management is a set of processes to create, store, transfer, and apply knowledge in the organization. Businesses need knowledge management programs because knowledge has become a central productive and strategic asset in today's information economy and a potential source of competitive advantage. Much of a firm's value depends on its ability to create and manage knowledge. Knowledge management promotes organizational learning by increasing the ability of the organization to learn from its environment and to incorporate knowledge into its business processes. Effective knowledge management systems require organizational and management capital to promote a knowledge culture and programs for knowledge management, including the creation of a chief knowledge officer. There are three major types of knowledge management systems: enter-

   prise-wide knowledge management systems, knowledge work systems, and intelligent techniques.

2. **Define and describe the types of systems used for enterprise-wide knowledge management and demonstrate how they provide value for organizations.**

   Enterprise-wide knowledge management systems are firm-wide efforts to collect, store, distribute, and apply digital content and knowledge. Structured knowledge systems provide databases and tools for organizing and storing structured documents while semistructured knowledge systems provide databases and tools for organizing and storing semistructured knowledge, such as email or rich media. Knowledge network systems provide directories and tools for locating firm employees with special expertise who are important sources of tacit knowledge. Often these systems include group collaboration tools, portals to simplify information access, search tools, and tools for classifying information based on a taxonomy that is appropriate for the organization. Enterprise-wide knowledge management systems can provide considerable value if they are well designed and enable employees to locate, share, and use knowledge more efficiently.

3. *Define and describe the major types of knowledge work systems and assess how they provide value for firms.*

Knowledge work systems (KWS) support the creation of new knowledge and its integration into the organization. KWS require easy access to an external knowledge base; powerful computer hardware that can support software with intensive graphics, analysis, document management, and communications capabilities; and a user-friendly interface. These capabilities can increase the productivity of highly paid knowledge workers. KWS often run on workstations that are customized for the work they must perform. Computer-aided design (CAD) systems and virtual reality systems, which create interactive simulations that behave like the real world, require graphics and powerful modelling capabilities. KWS for financial professionals provide access to external databases and the ability to analyze massive amounts of financial data very quickly.

4. *Evaluate the business benefits of using intelligent techniques for knowledge management.*

Artificial intelligence lacks the flexibility, breadth, and generality of human intelligence, but it can be used to capture, codify, and extend organizational knowledge. Businesses can use artificial intelligence to help them capture and preserve tacit knowledge, for knowledge discovery, to generate solutions to specific problems that are too massive and complex to be analyzed by human beings on their own, and to help firms search for and filter information.

Expert systems capture tacit knowledge from a limited domain of human expertise and express that knowledge in the form of rules. The strategy to search through the knowledge base, called the inference engine, can use either forward or backward chaining. Expert systems are most useful for problems of classification or diagnosis. Case-based reasoning represents organizational knowledge as a database of cases that can be continually expanded and refined. When the user encounters a new case, the system searches for similar cases, finds the clos-

est fit, and applies the solutions of the old case to the new case. The new case is stored with successful solutions in the case database.

Fuzzy logic is a software technology for expressing knowledge in the form of rules that use approximate or subjective values. Fuzzy logic has been used for controlling physical devices and is starting to be used for limited decision-making applications.

Neural networks consist of hardware and software that attempt to mimic the thought processes of the human brain. Neural networks are notable for their ability to learn without programming and to recognize patterns that cannot be easily described by humans. They are being used in science, medicine, and business primarily to discriminate patterns in massive amounts of data.

Genetic algorithms develop solutions to particular problems using genetically based processes such as fitness, crossover, and mutation. Genetic algorithms are beginning to be applied to problems involving optimization, product design, and monitoring industrial systems where many alternatives or variables must be evaluated to generate an optimal solution.

Intelligent agents are software programs with built-in or learned knowledge bases that carry out specific, repetitive, and predictable tasks for an individual user, business process, or software application. Intelligent agents can be programmed to navigate through large amounts of data to locate useful information and in some cases act on that information on behalf of the user.

5. *Identify the challenges posed by knowledge management systems and propose management solutions.*

Knowledge management systems are difficult to implement successfully, and they do not always provide value after they are put in place. Firms can provide appropriate organizational and management capital to make these systems successful by rewarding knowledge sharing, promoting communities of practice and a knowledge culture, and designing appropriate taxonomies for organizing knowledge. Proper planning, development of appropriate measurements of benefits, and staged rollout can increase the chances of success for knowledge management projects. Key management decisions include identifying business processes for which knowledge management systems can provide the most value.

Key Terms

Review Questions

1. What is knowledge management? How does it promote organizational learning? Why is it of great interest to business?

2. Describe the important dimensions of knowledge. Distinguish between data, knowledge, and wisdom and between explicit and tacit knowledge.

3. Describe the stages in the knowledge management value chain that add value as data and information are transformed into useful knowledge.

4. Describe the role played by organizational and management capital in knowledge management.

5. What are structured knowledge systems? Describe their capabilities.

6. What are semistructured knowledge systems? Describe their capabilities.

7. How do taxonomies and tools for tagging facilitate knowledge management?

8. Describe the capabilities of knowledge network systems.

9. Describe the role of the following in facilitating knowledge management: portals, collaboration tools, and learning management systems.

10. What are knowledge work systems? What role do they play in knowledge management? What are the generic requirements of knowledge work systems?

11. Describe how the following systems support knowledge work: computer-aided design (CAD), virtual reality, and investment workstations.

12. What are intelligent techniques? Why are they of interest to businesses for knowledge management? How does artificial intelligence differ from human intelligence?

13. Define an expert system, describe how it works, and explain how it can contribute to knowledge management.

14. What is case-based reasoning? How does it differ from an expert system? How does it support knowledge management?

15. What is a neural network? How can neural networks help companies with knowledge management?

16. Define and describe fuzzy logic. For what kinds of applications is it suited?

17. What are genetic algorithms? How can they help organizations solve problems? For what kinds of problems are they suited?

18. What are intelligent agents? How can they be used to benefit businesses?

19. What management challenges are raised by knowledge management systems? How can businesses obtain value from their knowledge management investments?

Discussion Questions

1. Knowledge management is a business process, not a technology. Discuss.

2. Describe various ways that knowledge management systems could help firms with sales and marketing or with manufacturing and production.

Application Software Exercise:
Expert System Exercise: Building a Simple Expert System for Retirement Planning

When employees at your company retire, they are given cash bonuses. These cash bonuses are based on the length of employment and the retiree's age. To receive a bonus, an employee must be at least 50 years of age and have worked for the company for five years. The following table summarizes the criteria for determining bonuses.

Using the information provided, build a simple expert system. Find a demonstration copy of an expert system software tool on the Web that you can download (see the recommendations at the Companion Website). Alternatively, use your spreadsheet software to build the expert system. (If you are using spreadsheet software, we suggest using the IF function so you can see how rules are created.)

LENGTH OF EMPLOYMENT BONUS

<5 year	No bonus
6-10 years	20 percent of current annual salary
11-15 years	30 percent of current annual salary
16-20 years	40 percent of current annual salary
20-25 years	50 percent of current annual salary
26 or more years	100 percent of current annual salary

Electronic Commerce Project: Using Intelligent Agents for Comparison Shopping

You have decided it is time to supplement your old film camera with a new digital camera, but you do not know what to purchase. So, prior to buying one, you want to find sites that review digital cameras and explain them. Begin your search using a popular search engine. Certain sites, such as Imaging Resource, also enable you to see the quality of the photographs, which is necessary for you to make your final choice. Several other sites, such as dpreview.com or dcresource.com enable you to compare features and prices. Having read material on the cameras and compared the quality of the photographs on these sites, select a digital camera you might want to purchase.

You would now like to purchase the camera as inex-

pensively as possible. Try several of the shopping bot sites, which do the price comparisons for you. Visit My Simon (**www.mysimon.com**), BizRate.com (**www.bizrate.com**), and CNet.com (**www.cnet.com**). Compare them in terms of their ease of use, number of offerings, speed in obtaining information, thoroughness of information offered about the product and seller, and price selection. Note that with some of the shopping bot sites, you are able to sort the results by model number or price by clicking the column title. Which site or sites would you use and why? Which camera would you select and why? How helpful were these sites for making your decision?

Group Project: Rating Knowledge Network Systems

With a group of classmates, select two knowledge network system products, such as AskMe, Tacit Knowledge Systems, Kamoon Connect, or Sopheon. Compare their features and capabilities. To prepare your analysis, use articles from com-

puter magazines and the Web sites for the knowledge network software vendors. If possible, use electronic presentation software to present your findings to the class.

Web Sites of Interest

There are many interesting Web sites to enhance your learning about knowledge management, artificial intelligence, and expert systems. You can search the Web yourself, or just try the following sites to add to what you have already learned.

Fuzzy Clips **http://ai.iit.nrc.ca/IR_public/fuzzy/fuzzyClips/ fuzzyCLIPS/Index.html**
Describes the evolution of fuzzy clips and links to freeware downloads of fuzzy clips (easy-to-use fuzzy logic modules

developed by the National Research Council of Canada and the U.S. National Space and Aeronautics Administration)

Open Text's LiveLink **www.opentext.com/products/**
Web-based enterprise knowledge management and collaboration software

CompInfo's AI Index **www.compinfo-center.com/tpai-t.htm**
Links to interesting AI Web sites

CASE STUDY:
Scotiabank Uses KMS to Boost Customer Satisfaction

Since it first opened its doors for business in 1832, Scotiabank has provided a broad range of banking services to consumers and commercial investors. Today, Scotiabank is one of North America's leading financial institutions and Canada's most international bank, employing 48 000 people to serve approximately 10 million customers in 50 countries. Catering to the specific needs of its global customers can be challenging, given that Scotiabank offers more than 169 different financial products and services.

To provide better customer service, Scotiabank wanted to integrate its three major Canadian contact centres in Calgary, Toronto, and Halifax, which handle millions of customer calls 24 hours a day, seven days a week, and ensure that each of its 1000 agents were equipped to answer as many inquiries as possible. "I don't expect each individual agent to know the answer to every question, but I expect them to know

how to find the answer," says Mike Hayes, senior vice president, call centre, Scotiabank.

For years, call-centre agents routinely sifted through 30 different Web sites and a series of hard-copy documents stored in binders in order to find relevant customer service information. The lack of a single, central data repository hindered their ability to give customers answers in a timely manner. Furthermore, it was impossible for agents to determine whether the data they found was in its most current form. Without this information, agents were less likely to sell additional bank products—only 3 percent of calls led to further selling.

Scotiabank's contact centres tried tackling this issue with a custom-developed Web solution, Daily News, which acted as a central repository for daily customer information updates, pushing each customer service update to agents when they became available. However, the updates were not organized according to service type. Reading the updates was strictly voluntary, and with an average of 150 messages per day being pushed through the system, few representatives were able to find the most current information.

Scotiabank considered further automating its call-centre workflow by employing more interactive voice response (IVR) software. While automation would help speed call times, it would come with a price: customer care agents encourage customers to do additional business, and this ability to sell would be put at risk if customer service agents were not speaking to customers directly.

Having discounted that idea, Scotiabank's IT team prepared to build another in-house solution, convinced that packaged software would take too long to customize. But the team first evaluated the packaged solutions that were in the market—if only as a benchmark for their in-house development.

To ensure it delivers optimal customer service, Scotiabank needed a solution that was customizable and easy to use. It had to store information so that documents could be located with minimal searching. The solution also needed an intuitive user interface. "Some customer calls take follow-up and special information, but we were really looking to empower our reps to be able to satisfy the customer the first time they call 85 percent of the time," says Hayes.

After looking at a number of alternative package software solutions, Scotiabank chose Microsoft SharePoint® Portal Server 2000 to provide the central data repository for its three call centres. "SharePoint-based technologies fit our needs very, very well. It did much of what we needed right off the shelf, and we did some custom programming just to see if it would do what we wanted. We ran a pilot project, and it was very successful," says Peter Bennet, technical specialist, call centre, Scotiabank.

Relying on the help and expertise of Microsoft consulting services, the Scotiabank IT team planned and conducted the rollout of SharePoint Portal Server, using Microsoft Office XP Developer Edition and Microsoft Office XP Web Components with Microsoft Windows® XP as the operating system, to provide the portal's foundation. The Digital Dashboard interface in SharePoint Portal Server helped reduce the cost and time of development. Together, Scotiabank and Microsoft consulting services had a functioning solution ready in just 45 days.

As any downtime could seriously affect Scotiabank's ability to serve its customers, the call centres chose to run the SharePoint Team Services on the Microsoft Windows 2000 Advanced Server-based platform, which helped to ensure infrastructure stability through compatibility. Microsoft SQL Server 2000 was also implemented to help speed up the turnaround of call centre queries. "We put the SharePoint-based solution in place very quickly, and it was all done well within a budget that was small to begin with," says Hayes.

The positive impact of SharePoint Team Services and SharePoint Portal Server on Scotiabank's call centres was immediate. Data search times were reduced. Agents were now able to navigate more easily using the intuitive interface and find information with just a few mouse clicks once the old, numerous stores of customer service information were consolidated on the SharePoint portal. Agents can still use

the Daily News application, but the SharePoint portal can give agents the confidence that the customer service data they see is current.

Customer service broadcasts can be tailored to specific call centre reps, as opposed to the blanket broadcasts that were sent to all 1000 employees with the previous in-house solution. The new system also allows managers to learn how specific service documents are being read—and by whom. With this data, call centre managers also know which documents have to be rewritten for clarity or gauge which are more important to customers and, as a result, should be placed in a priority position on the team site.

"When you've got a customer on the phone, you don't want to be hitting 25 mouse clicks to get where you want. A lot of thought is put into surfacing the most important information first, and the SharePoint system helps make this a simple process," says Dennis Migel, vice president, Toronto call centre, Scotiabank.

The impact of this knowledge management system can also be seen on Scotiabank's bottom line. As a result of these workflow changes, customer up-sell rates have jumped from 3 percent to 13 percent. "On one Saturday, an inbound sales agent was able to turn a simple, day-to-day banking call into a cross-sell of six services using SharePoint. It's an amazing thing when that happens—and on a Saturday," says Migel.

In the world of banking, time literally is money, and the shortened customer call times the KMS has afforded Scotiabank have saved the organization an estimated $130 000 since migrating to SharePoint in 2003. "SharePoint-based technology has helped us keep our call volumes and times at a relatively flat growth pace. My budget has not increased over the past four years within the call centre, and yet this solution is helping us provide quality service, which we have branched off into our sales aspect as well," says Hayes.

SharePoint Portal Server and SharePoint Team Services supports the Microsoft.NET framework and as a result, the bank's IT staff were not required to learn any other product-specific development languages. "Team sites using SharePoint are very easy to maintain. There's not a whole lot of operational maintenance," Bennet says. "Not only did this save us time and money, it's helped our call centres better serve our customers and fulfill Scotiabank's service mandate."

Scotiabank's business products and customer service and support contact centre has been rated "world class" in a customer survey conducted by Service Quality Measurement Group Inc. (SQM). "World class recognition is especially impressive in Scotiabank's case as call complexity is higher than the average centre," said Mike Desmarais, president, service quality measurement group. "Scotiabank has the highest customer satisfaction ratings for help desk call centres and one of the highest customer satisfaction ratings for all call centres surveyed."

Sources: "Scotiabank Helps Boost Customer Satisfaction with Microsoft Sharepoint-Based Technology," Microsoft Case Study, **www.microsoft. com/Canada/casestudies/scotiabank.mspx**, accessed July 8, 2005; "Scotiabank Call Centre Rated 'World Class' by SQM," **www.newswire. ca/en/releases/archive/January2005/05/c9885.html**, accessed July 8, 2005.

CASE STUDY QUESTIONS:

1. Analyze Scotiabank's call centre business strategy using the competitive forces and value chain models.

2. How important are knowledge management systems at Scotiabank's call centres? How do they provide value to the company? How do they support the call centre's business strategy?

3. Evaluate Scotiabank's call centres' use of the knowledge management system. How effective has it been?

4. How successful do you think Scotiabank will be in using its current knowledge management systems in the future? Do you think this type of knowledge management system should be deployed in other areas at Scotiabank? Which areas and why?

PART IV CANADIAN CASE STUDY:
Shoppers Drug Mart Relies on Loyalty Cards for Decision Making

Loyalty cards were introduced decades ago in the form of "Buy 9, Get the 10th free." This type of "loyalty" or discount card still exists and is still extremely useful in getting customers to increase their purchases. But today, another type of loyalty card, computerized and used for a variety of purposes has replaced most of the former types of loyalty cards.

Today's loyalty card—like debit and credit cards—has a magnetic stripe on it that carries information about the cardholder. Information such as customer number and name can be encoded on the magnetic stripe and used to identify a customer, the products he or she buys, the store he or she buys from, and the date and time of day of the sale. This wealth of data can then be filtered through transaction processing systems and data mining systems to assist management in making decisions about staffing personnel at busier times of the day or week, about how much inventory to order of a popular product, and even about opening or closing store locations.

Depending on the company's marketing information systems, loyalty cards can even yield data that indicate how successful a company's most recent advertising or promotional campaign was—or how successful product placement in the store was. This type of data, once processed into useful information, can help a company target its advertisements or judge the success of a new store opening.

Shoppers Drug Mart is an excellent example of a Canadian company using loyalty cards for decision support of various business functions. Shoppers is Canada's leading drugstore group and health-care products and services provider. Toronto pharmacist Murray Koffler founded Shoppers in 1962. In a little more than 40 years, Shoppers has grown to more than 900 Shoppers and Pharmaprix drug stores and Shoppers Home Health Care stores, operating in every province and two territories. Each store is owned and operated by a local pharmacist. Shoppers' annual sales total more than $4.1 billion.

This massive operation obviously requires centralized computer support, including computer support for all of its stores, across time zones and including a number of Shoppers' stores that operate 24/7. Fifteen years ago, information and communications technology (ICT) was not considered to be a vital part of Shoppers' operations. In the mid 1990s, though, with the advent of the Internet and the ubiquity of the PC, Shoppers' computer strategy changed.

Management began to realize that Shoppers could make money from utilizing ICT and not just consider ICT as an expense. Today Shoppers is now considered to be a leading user of ICT in the Canadian retail sector.

Shoppers has built its reputation and growth on the strategy of delivering the highest level of service to customers. Toward that end, several years ago, Shoppers began its Optimum Rewards Card program. Every time a customer makes a purchase at Shoppers, the Shoppers staff swipes the customer's Optimum card through a credit card reader. The system notes the purchase and adds a certain number of Optimum points to the customer's Optimum point balance. Optimum points are awarded based on the total amount of the purchase, the type of purchase, or specials that Shoppers offers if customers buy a certain product during a certain period of time. Pharmacy purchases are automatically recorded to the customer's Optimum Points balance. It is possible for a customer to earn $75 worth of free merchandise by spending only $200—a twenty-five percent incentive.

Backing up the loyalty card program is an information system that starts with Shoppers data warehouse where all customer transactions are archived. In 2004 Shoppers contracted with Netezza Corporation, headquartered in the U.S., to provide the data warehouse server that anchors the whole operation. Using business intelligence software and data from the warehouse, Shoppers can obtain deeper insight into customer and market trends as well as configure their Optimum card bonus point products to meet Shoppers market needs—whether to promote a new product or promote their own in-store brand.

The Optimum program paints a profile of customer purchasing habits. It plays a vital role in how Shoppers manages its overall inventories and inventories at each location, as well how best to market to customers. Part of implementing a loyalty card program is making the customers aware of the program and getting them to subscribe it, typically through a sign-up sheet. Optimum Rewards reached its one-year target for number of cardholders within the first six months of operation. The loyalty card program uses an application called Base24-frequent shopper to manage the points that are accumulated or redeemed. Even with the rapid growth of the program, the Base24 system managed to operate efficiently. The Base24 system provides comprehensive authorization capabilities and captures complete customer demographic and purchase data; it can also support a variety of marketing programs that interact with the system.

Today Shoppers customers, as well as those at many other organizations with loyalty programs, such as RBC with its RBC Rewards program, can even donate their loyalty card points to worthwhile charities, such as Hope Air, which uses the points (or the rewards from the points) for ongoing fundraising and volunteer support activities.

Other loyalty programs are equally impressive. In the U.S., Corner Grocers had been collecting customer data from use of its loyalty card for several years but had not used that data effectively. Corner Grocers implemented a data mining customer relationship management system by MapInfo and to assimilate the loyalty card data with point-of-sale data and reconcile the data into pointed marketing questions that could yield useful answers. Using MapInfo, Corner Grocers compared data from problem store locations with data from successful locations to identify the characteristics that were most critical to successful locations.

The result was surprising: amenities are critical to customer satisfaction. In other words, it's not all location, but amenities that affect customers' shopping habits. Offering 24-hour pharmacies, one-hour photo services, or ready-to-go dinners could be more important than factors such as population density or competitor proximity. As a result, according to Corner's CEO Gary Walters, "In certain markets, we increased the size and visibility of our pre-cooked meals and added three self-checkout aisles. Sales went up dramatically." Use of this data can even help determine what products should be on the shelves and how much of a product to stock."

Another large company making use of loyalty cards is Profil Optik, a chain of retail opticians in Denmark offering a national name and international standards of service. Its 92 operations, each owned and run by individual opticians, are supported by a central marketing and buying group. Because each of Profil Optik's stores is independently owned and operated, the company needed a simple solution to print the loyalty cards and hand them over on-the-spot to customers while they were shopping at the store. Using Windows operating system drivers and Windows-based software, the store can print a loyalty card using a small, inexpensive Javelin card printer. These personalized plastic cards offer competitive benefits, such as free eyeglass insurance, discounts for repeat orders, and extended warranties.

Similar to loyalty cards, some companies offer extra benefits or "rewards" with use of their credit card. In response, cardholders expect rewards that are commensurate with their preferences and level of loyalty. RBC Royal Bank began using Ernex's real-time marketing solutions in early 2000 to attract and retain more customers, as well as to maintain and strengthen relationships with their existing clientele. Since the implementation, this system has evolved to become the central nervous system for RBC Royal Bank's national card services group.

Using the campaign management capabilities of the Ernex applications, cardholders now receive recognition, promotions, and instant gratification with rewards at the point of sale. Standard campaigns that use the Ernex applications include Swipe 'N Win, Custom Coupons, Custom Messaging, Bonus Points, Instant Email and Points Multiplier.

RBC Royal Bank is also piloting real-time redemption functionality to permit cardholders to instantly redeem their points at the merchant point of sale towards their in-store purchase. Real-time redemption gives cardholders instant reward fulfillment and cuts back on administration costs, overhead, and long fulfillment cycles previously required to order and ship rewards. Using real-time redemption, RBC Royal Bank now has the ability to implement their program at over 200 000 points of sale locations.

But the problem is that loyalty card points then become a liability for the sponsoring company. For example, it is possible that if customers waited a long time to redeem their Optimum Reward points, Shoppers would have a liability for the amount of all the redemptions not yet redeemed.

If you look at airlines with their frequent flyer programs, this problem becomes even more obvious. It is possible for Air Canada to owe every member of AeroPlan the equivalent of a trip to Hawaii. If all the AeroPlan members redeemed their miles in the same reporting period, Air Canada would have a tremendous liability in the form of the fares that would be used but not collected. How companies account for these liabilities in their accounting records and to investors is a problem that has not yet been satisfactorily addressed, in that different companies account for these liabilities in different ways.

As we can see above and in the CBC video that accompanies this case, loyalty cards have become a competitive factor in challenging competition but also a means toward the end of increasing sales and profits. Customers who feel they are receiving real benefits from loyalty cards will not only be more loyal to the company that offers the loyalty card, but they will probably spend more money, too.

Sources: Fabrice Taylor, "Trust me," *The Globe and Mail*, August 19, 2005, available **www.theglobeandmail.com/servlet/story/ RTGAM.20050819.rmtayl0918/BNStory/specialROBmagazine/**, accessed September 17, 2005; "RBC Royal Bank Accelerates Cardholder Value," available **www.ernex.com/loyalty_program_clients/ RBC_Royal_Bank_summary.asp**, accessed September 17, 2005; "Compaq NonStop Servers Fill the Prescription for Mission-Critical Applications," available **http://ztxaawspro03.ztx.compaq.com/ NonStopComputing/downloads/ShoppersDrugMart.pdf**, accessed September 17, 2005; "Shoppers Drug Mart Selects Netezza to Analyze Growing Volumes of Data," available **www.netezza.com/releases/ shoppers.htm**, accessed September 27, 2005; "Shoppers Drug Mart: Case Study," available **www.getronics.com/global/en-b/industries/ retail_transport/cases/shoppers_drug_mart.htm**, accessed September 17, 2005; "Shoppers Drug Mart Manages Rapid Growth by Implementing Base24," available **www.aciworldwide.com/ casestudies/casestudydetail.asp?casestudies_id=41**, accessed September 17, 2005; "Getting You to Getting Better," available **www.hopeair.org/pages/help/help1_loyalty.html**, accessed September 17, 2005; "MapInfo Case Study: Corner Grocers," available **resource.mapinfo.com/static/files/document/1074626936250/ CornerGrocers_CS.pdf**, accessed September 17, 2005; and "Profil Optik Case Study," available **www.nbstech.co.uk/pdfs/ Profil%20Optik%20Case%20Study%2014.11.02.pdf**, accessed September 17, 2005.

Video Resource

"Loyalty Cards Rant," Marketplace 13 (February 4, 2003).

CASE STUDY QUESTIONS

1. How does Shoppers use its loyalty card to increase sales? To promote particular products? To learn about its customers?

2. What does Shoppers do with the data it collects about customers? What additional uses could you foresee for this data?

3. Do you think loyalty programs like the one at Profil Optik are similar to the ones at Shoppers, RBC Royal Bank, and Corner Grocers? Why or why not?

4. Do you think the real-time redemption feature that is being introduced on RBC Royal Bank's Visa Rewards card is likely to be successful? Why or why not?

5. Do you feel that loyalty programs create financial liabilities for companies? How do you think these liabilities should be communicated to shareholders and others interested in the companies' financial health?

References

Chapter 1

Aldrich, H. E. "Technology and Organizational Structure: A Reexamination of the Findings of the Aston Group." *Administrative Science Quarterly* 17 (March 1972).

Allen, Brandt R., and Andrew C. Boynton. "Information Architecture: In Search of Efficient Flexibility." MIS Quarterly 15, no. 4 (December 1991).

Aponovich, David. "No Medal, But IT Integrator Still Scores at Salt Lake Games." *CIO Update* (February 27, 2002).

Avison, David. "Information Systems in the MBA Curriculum: An International Perspective." Communications of the Association for Information Systems 11, Article 6 (January 2003).

Baskerville, Richard L. and Michael D. Myers. "Information Systems as a Reference Discipline." *MIS Quarterly* 26, no. 1 (March 2002).

Bautsch, Holly, et. al. "An Investigation of Mobile Phone Use: A Sociotechnical Approach." Department of Industrial Engineering, University of Wisconsin, Madison (2001).

Bebasat, Izak, and Robert W. Zmud. "The Identity Crisis Within the Discipline: Defining and Communicating the Discipline's Core Properties." *MIS Quarterly* 27, no. 2 (June 2003).

Brynjolfsson, Erik. "The IT Productivity Gap." *Optimize Magazine* 21 (July 2003).

Brynjolfsson, Erik, and Lorin M. Hitt. "Beyond Computation: Information Technology, Organizational Transformation, and Business Performance." *Journal of Economic Perspectives* 14, no. 4 (2000).

Brynjolfsson, E. T., T. W. Malone, V. Gurbaxani, and A. Kambil. "Does Information Technology Lead to Smaller Firms?" *Management Science* 40, no. 12 (1994).

Carr, Nicholas. "IT Doesn't Matter." *Harvard Business Review* (May 2003).

Davis, Gordon B., and Margrethe H. Olson. *Management Information Systems: Conceptual Foundations, Structure, and Development,* 2nd ed. New York: McGraw-Hill (1985).

Davern, Michael J., and Robert J. Kauffman. "Discovering Potential and Realizing Value from Information Technology Investments." *Journal of Management Information Systems* 16, no. 4 (Spring 2000).

Dedrick, Jason, Vijay Gurbaxani, and Kenneth L. Kraemer. "Information Technology and Economic Performance: A Critical Review of the Empirical Evidence." Center for Research on Information Technology and Organizations, University of California, Irvine (December 2001).

eMarketer. "B2C E-Commerce in the U.S." eMarketer.com. http://www. emarketer.com/Report.aspx?b2c_us_jul04 (accessed July, 2004).

eWeek. "Olympics Testing Labs Opened." (November 11, 2002).

Feeny, David E., and Leslie P. Willcocks. "Core IS Capabilities for Exploiting Information Technology." *Sloan Management Review* 39, no. 3 (Spring 1998).

Foust, Dean. "Big Brown's New Bag." *BusinessWeek* (July 19, 2004).

———. "Online Extra: UPS's Eskew on 'the Next Logical Step.'" *BusinessWeek* (July 19, 2004).

Galliers, Robert D., and Maureen Meadows. "A Discipline Divided: Globalization and Parochialism in Information Systems Research." *Communications of the Association for Information Systems* 11, Article 5 (January 2003).

Gallupe, R. Brent. "Images of Information Systems in the Early 21st Century." *Communications of the Association for Information Systems* 3, no. 3 (February 2000).

Gould, Larry. "Effectively Managing Inventory in the Supply Chain." *Automotive Design & Production.* http://www.autofieldguide.com (accessed September 3, 2004).

Greenspan, Alan. "The Revolution in Information Technology." Boston College Conference on the New Economy (March 6, 2000).

Gruman, Galen. "UPS vs. FedEx: Head-to-Head on Wireless." *CIO Magazine.* (June 1, 2004).

———. "New Technologies Hit Mainstream." *CIO Magazine.* (June 1, 2004).

Hacki, Remo, and Julian Lighton. "The Future of the Networked Company." *McKinsey Quarterly* 3 (2001).

Hadoulis, John. "Fixing Games Glitches Before They Happen." Athens News (April 4, 2003).

Hartman, Amir. "Why Tech Falls Short of Expectations." *Optimize Magazine* (July 2002).

Hoffman, Donna L., Thomas P. Novak, and Alladi Venkatesh. "Has the Internet Become Indispensable?" *Communications of the ACM* 47, no. 7 (July 2004).

Ives, Blake, Joseph S. Valacich, Richard T. Watson, and Robert W. Zmud. "What Every Business Student Needs to Know about Information Systems." *Communications of the Association for Information Systems* 9, Article 30 (December 2002).

Jorgenson, Dale W. "Information Technology and Economic Performance: A Critical Review of Empirical Evidence." Center for Research on Information Technology and Organizations, University of California, Irvine (December 2001).

King, John. "Centralized vs. Decentralized Computing: Organizational Considerations and Management Options." *Computing Surveys* (October 1984).

Lamb, Roberta, Steve Sawyer, and Rob Kling. "A Social Informatics Perspective on Socio-Technical Networks." http://lamb.cba.hawaii.edu/pubs (2004).

Laudon, Kenneth C. *Computers and Bureaucratic Reform.* New York, NY: Wiley (1974).

Lee, H. "Broadband and Mobile Opportunities: A Socio-Technical Perspective." *Journal of Information Technology* 18 (2003).

Leonard-Barton, Dorothy. *Wellsprings of Knowledge.* Boston: Harvard Business School Press (1995).

Lev, Baruch. *Intangibles: Management, Measurement and Reporting.* Washington, D.C.: Brookings Institution Press (2001).

Lyons. John. "Expensive Energy? Burn Other Stuff, One Firm Decides." *Wall Street Journal* (September 1, 2004).

———. "Cemex Cements Its Position with Agreement to Buy RMC." *Wall Street Journal* (September 28, 2004).

Marchand, Donald A. "Extracting the Business Value of IT: It Is Usage, Not Just Deployment That Counts!" *Copco Institute Journal of Financial Transformation* (2004).

Marchand, Donald A., William J. Kettinger, and John D. Rollins. *Making the Invisible Visible: How Companies Win with the Right Information, People and IT.* Chichester: Wiley (2001).

———. *Information Orientation: The Link to Business Performance.* Oxford: Oxford University Press (2001).

Mayor, Tracy. "The Supple Supply Chain." *CIO Magazine* (August 15, 2004).

McFarlan, F. Warren, James L. McKenney, and Philip Pyburn. "The Information Archipelago—Plotting a Course." *Harvard Business Review* (January–February 1983).

———. "Governing the New World." *Harvard Business Review* (July–August 1983).

McKenney, James L., and F. Warren McFarlan. "The Information Archipelago—Maps and Bridges." *Harvard Business Review* (September–October 1982).

MCN Direct Newswire. "Atos Origin warms up for winter Olympics." http://www.conferencepage.com/mcndirect/issues2005/mcndirect280605.asp. (accessed. July 19, 2005).

Metz, Cade. "Athens Apps Up and Running." *PC Magazine* (December 23, 2002).

———. "Olympian Technology Powers the Games." *PC Magazine* (February 22, 2002).

Mumford, Enid. "Socio Technical Design: An Unfulfilled Promise or a Future Opportunity." In *The Social and Organizational Perspective on Research and Practice in Information Technology,* edited by R. Baskerville, et al. London: Chapman-Hall (2000).

———. "Assisting Work Restructuring in Complex and Volatile Situations." In *Developing Organizational Consultancy,* edited by J. Neuman et al. London: Rutledge (1997).

Newsome, Melba. "The Cement Mixer." *Context* (December 2001/January 2002).

Orlikowski, W.J. (1992). "The duality of technology: Rethinking the concepts of technology in organizations." *Organization Science* 3(3), 398-427.

Orlikowski, Wanda, and D. C. Gash. "Technological Frames: Making Sense of Information Technology in Organizations." *ACM Transactions in Information Systems* (April 1994).

Orlikowski, Wanda J., and Stephen R. Bailey. "Technology and Institutions: What Can Research on Information Technology and Research on Organizations Learn from Each Other?" *MIS Quarterly* 25, no. 2 (June 2001).

Orlikowski, Wanda J., and Jack J. Baroudi. "Studying Information Technology in Organizations: Research Approaches and Assumptions." Information Systems Research 2, no. 1 (March 1991).

Pettigrew, Pierre. "Address at a Plenary Hosted by the Canadian Chamber of Commerce in Northern Mexico on a New Approach to Business Development http://w01.international.gc.ca/minpub/Publication.asp?publication_id=379348&Language=E (accessed July 19, 2005).

Quinn, James Brian. "Strategic Outsourcing: Leveraging Knowledge Capabilities." *Sloan Management Review* 40, no. 4 (Summer 1999).

Roche, Edward M. "Planning for Competitive Use of Information Technology in Multinational Corporations." Paper presented at AIB UK Region Conference, Brighton Polytechnic, Brighton, U.K. (March 1992.) Edward M. Roche, W. Paul Stillman School of Business, Seton Hall University.

Ross, Jeanne W., and Peter Weill. "Six IT Decisions Your IT People Shouldn't Make." *Harvard Business Review* (November 2002).

RoundUPS. "Paper Trail." (Fall 2004).

Rowsell-Jones, Andrew. "The Best of Both Worlds," *CIO Australia* (July 12, 2004).

Sambamurthy, V., and Robert W. Zmud. "Research Commentary: The Organizing Logic for an Enterprise's IT Activities in the Digital Era— A Prognosis of Practice and a Call to Research." *Information Systems Research* 11, no. 2 (June 2000).

Sawyer, S., and J. P. Allen. "Broadband and Mobile Opportunities: A Socio-Technical Perspective." *Journal of Information Technology* 18 (June 2003).

Slywotzky, Adrian J., and David J. Morrison. *How Digital Is Your Business?* New York: Crown Business (2001).

Stiroh, Kevin. "The Economic Impact of Information Technology." Federal Reserve Bank of New York (2001).

Teece, David. *Economic Performance and Theory of the Firm: The Selected Papers of David Teece.* London: Edward Elgar Publishing (1998).

Tornatsky, Louis G., J. D. Eveland, and David Wessel. "NASA Explores Future of Software." The Technological Innovation: Reviewing the Literature." Washington, D.C.: National Science Foundation (1983).

Triplett, Jack E., and Barry P. Bosworth. "Productivity in Services Industries: Trends and Measurement Issues." Washington D.C.: The Brookings Institution (2003).

Tuomi, Ilkka. "Data Is More Than Knowledge." *Journal of Management Information Systems* 16, no. 3 (Winter 1999–2000).

Weiss, Todd R. "UPS Delivers New Package Check-in System for Customers." *Computerworld* (April 9, 2003).

Williams, R., and D. Edge. "The Social Shaping of Technology." *Research Policy* 25 (1996).

Zhu, Kevin, Kenneth L. Kraemer, Sean Xu, and Jason Dedrick. "Information Technology Payoff in E-Business Environments: An International Perspective on Value Creation of E-business in the Financial Services Industry." *Journal of Management Information Systems* 21, no. 1 (Summer 2004).

Chapter 2

Anthony, R. N. *Planning and Control Systems: A Framework for Analysis.* Cambridge, Mass.: Harvard University Press (1965).

Aronovich, Hanna. "Ready Made Couture." *U.S. Business Review* (March 2005).

Bacheldor, Beth. "Deeper Than Designs." *Information Week* (August 9, 2004).

———. "Product Life-Cycle Management Market Ramps Up." *Information Week* (July 19, 2004).

Barrett, Stephanie S. "Strategic Alternatives and Interorganizational System Implementations: An Overview." *Journal of Management Information Systems* (Winter 1986–1987).

Bensaou, M. "Portfolios of Buyer–Supplier Relationships." *Sloan Management Review* 40, no. 4 (Summer 1999).

Choi, Soon-Yong, and Andrew B. Whinston. "Communities of Collaboration." *IQ Magazine* (July–August 2001).

Concours Group. "ESII: Capitalizing on Enterprise Systems and Infrastructure." (1999).

Cox, Butler. *Globalization: The IT Challenge.* Sunnyvale, Calif.: Amdahl Executive Institute (1991).

Culnan, Mary J. "Transaction Processing Applications as Organizational Message Systems: Implications for the Intelligent Organization." Working paper no. 88-10, 22nd Hawaii International Conference on Systems Sciences (January 1989).

D'Agostino, Debra. "PLM: The Means of Production." *eWeek* (February 7, 2004).

Dassault Systems. "Nissan Diesel Develops Vehicle Configuration Management System with PLM Solutions from IBM and Dassault Systems." (July 12, 2004).

Davenport, Tom. *Mission Critical: Realizing the Promise of Enterprise Systems.* Boston: Harvard Business School Press (2000).

———. "Putting the Enterprise into Enterprise Systems." *Harvard Business Review* (July–August 1998).

Ferdows, Kasra, Michael A. Lewis, and Jose A. D. Machuca. "Rapid-Fire Fulfillment." *Harvard Business Review* (November 2004).

Houdeshel, George, and Hugh J. Watson. "The Management Information and Decision Support (MIDS) System at Lockheed Georgia." *MIS Quarterly* 11, no. 1 (March 1987).

Huber, George P. "Organizational Information Systems: Determinants of Their Performance and Behavior." *Management Science* 28, no. 2 (1984).

Johnston, Russell, and Michael J. Vitale. "Creating Competitive Advantage with Interorganizational Information Systems." *MIS Quarterly* 12, no. 2 (June 1988).

Kalakota, Ravi, and Marcia Robinson. *e-Business2.0: Roadmap for Success.* Reading, Mass.: Addison-Wesley (2001).

Keen, Peter G. W. *The Process Edge.* Boston: Harvard Business School Press (1997).

Keen, Peter G. W., and M. S. Morton. *Decision Support Systems: An Organizational Perspective.* Reading, Mass.: Addison-Wesley (1978).

Malone, Thomas M., Kevin Crowston, Jintae Lee, and Brian Pentland. "Tools for Inventing Organizations: Toward a Handbook of Organizational Processes." *Management Science* 45, no. 3 (March 1999).

McAfee, Andrew. "Do You Have Too Much IT?" *MIT Sloan Management Review* (Spring 2004).

O'Leary, Daniel E. *Enterprise Resource Planning Systems: Systems Life Cycle, Electronic Commerce, and Risk.* New York: Cambridge University Press (2000).

Parks Canada. "Campground Reservation Service: Frequently Asked Questions." http://www.pc.gc.ca/voyage-travel/reserve/faq_E.asp (accessed July 11, 2005).

Parks Canada. "Full Implementation of the New Campground Reservation Service in National Parks of Canada." http://pc.gc.ca/apps/

cp-nr/release_e.asp?id=860&andor1=nr (February 18, 2005, accessed July 11, 2005).

"Product Life-Cycle Management Market Ramps Up." *Information Week* (July 19, 2004).

Rockart, John F., and Michael E. Treacy. "The CEO Goes On-line." *Harvard Business Review* (January–February 1982).

Rohwedder, Cecilie. "Making Fashion Faster." *Wall Street Journal* (February 28, 2004).

Sprague, Ralph H., Jr., and Eric D. Carlson. *Building Effective Decision Support Systems.* Englewood Cliffs, N.J.: Prentice Hall (1982).

Tibbett & Britten. "Case Study: Canada—Alberta LGC." http://tibbett-britten.com/cs/algc-can.php (accessed July 8, 2005).

Tibbett & Britten. "Case Study: North America: Demand Management Services (DMS). http://www.tibbett-britten.com/cs/dms-na.php (accessed July 8, 2005).

Tri-Media. "National Campground Reservation Service." http://www.tri-media.com/en/experience/case_study_archive/details.php?id=21 (accessed July 11, 2005).

White, Erin. "For Retailer Mango, Frenzied 'Fast Fashion' Proves Sweet." *Wall Street Journal* (May 28, 2004).

Chapter 3

Allison, Graham T. *Essence of Decision—Explaining the Cuban Missile Crisis.* Boston: Little, Brown (1971).

Ancona, Deborah, Henrik Breaman, and Katrin Kaufer. "The Comparative Advantage of X-Teams." *Sloan Management Review* 43, no. 3 (Spring 2002).

Attewell, Paul, and James Rule. "Computing and Organizations: What We Know and What We Don't Know." *Communications of the ACM* 27, no. 12 (December 1984).

Bakos, J. Yannis, and Michael E. Treacy. "Information Technology and Corporate Strategy: A Research Perspective." *MIS Quarterly* (June 1986).

Beer, Michael, Russell A. Eisenstat, and Bert Spector. "Why Change Programs Don't Produce Change." *Harvard Business Review* (November–December 1990).

Bikson, T. K., and J. D. Eveland. "Integrating New Tools into Information Work." The Rand Corporation (1992). RAND/RP-106.

Blau, Peter, and W. Richard Scott. *Formal Organizations.* San Francisco: Chandler Press (1962).

Brancheau, James C., Brian D. Janz, and James C. Wetherbe. "Key Issues in Information Systems Management: 1994–1995 SIM Delphi Results." *MIS Quarterly* 20, no. 2 (June 1996).

Bresnahan, Timothy F., Erik Brynjolfsson, and Lorin M. Hitt. "Information Technology, Workplace Organization, and the Demand for Skilled Labor." *Quarterly Journal of Economics* 117 (February 2002).

Camuffo, Arnaldo, Pietro Romano, and Andrea Vinellie. "Benetton Transforms Its Global Network." *Sloan Management Review* 43, no. 1 (Fall 2001).

Cash, J. I., and Benn R. Konsynski. "IS Redraws Competitive Boundaries." *Harvard Business Review* (March–April 1985).

CBC Business News. "Shopping on the Web Up 25%: StatsCan." (September 23, 2004).

Chan, Yolande E., Sid L. Huff, Donald W. Barclay, and Duncan G. Copeland. "Business Strategic Orientation, Information Systems Strategic Orientation, and Strategic Alignment." *Information Systems Research* 8, no. 2 (June 1997).

Chen, Pei-Yu (Sharon), and Lorin M. Hitt. "Measuring Switching Costs and the Determinants of Customer Retention in Internet-Enabled Businesses: A Study of the Online Brokerage Industry." *Information Systems Research* 13, no. 3 (September 2002).

Christensen, Clayton. "The Past and Future of Competitive Advantage." Sloan Management Review 42, no. 2 (Winter 2001).

Claburn, Thomas. "Recipe for a Better Winery." *Information Week* (September 20, 2004).

Clemons, Eric K. "Evaluation of Strategic Investments in Information Technology." *Communications of the ACM* (January 1991).

Clemons, Eric K., and Michael Row. "McKesson Drug Co.: Case Study of a Strategic Information System." *Journal of Management Information Systems* (Summer 1988).

———. "Limits to Interfirm Coordination through IT." *Journal of Management Information Systems* 10, no. 1 (Summer 1993).

———. "Sustaining IT Advantage: The Role of Structural Differences." *MIS Quarterly* 15, no. 3 (September 1991).

Clemons, Eric K., and Bruce W. Weber. "Segmentation, Differentiation, and Flexible Pricing: Experience with Information Technology and Segment-Tailored Strategies." *Journal of Management Information Systems* 11, no. 2 (Fall 1994).

Coase, Ronald H. "The Nature of the Firm." 1937. In *The Economic Nature of the Firm: A Reader*, edited by Louis Putterman and Randall Kroszner. Cambridge University Press (1995).

Cohen, Michael, James March, and Johan Olsen. "A Garbage Can Model of Organizational Choice." *Administrative Science Quarterly* 17 (1972).

Davenport, Thomas H., and Keri Pearlson. "Two Cheers for the Virtual Office." *Sloan Management Review* 39, no. 4 (Summer 1998).

Davenport, Thomas H., Keri Pearlson, Jeanne G. Harris, and Ajay K. Kohli. "How Do They Know Their Customers So Well?" *Sloan Management Review* 42, no. 2 (Winter 2001).

Drucker, Peter. "The Coming of the New Organization." *Harvard Business Review* (January–February 1988).

Eastern Michigan University. "Best Prospects in the ICT Market." (revised April 24, 2004).

Eisenhardt, Kathleen M. "Has Strategy Changed?" *Sloan Management Review* 43, no. 2 (Winter 2002).

Elliott, Christopher. "Hotels Get Pushy About Their Loyalty Programs." *New York Times* (June 1, 2004).

Enns, Harvey G., Sid L. Huff, and Christopher A. Higgins. "CIO Lateral Influence Behaviors: Gaining Peer' Commitment to Strategic Information Systems." *MIS Quarterly* 27, no. 1 (March 2003).

Erasala, Naveen, and John "Skip" Benamati. "Understanding the Electronic Commerce Cycles of Change." *Journal of Organizational Computing and Electronic Commerce* 13, no. 1 (2003).

Etzioni, Amitai. *A Comparative Analysis of Complex Organizations.* New York: Free Press (1975).

Farhoomand, Ali, and Pauline S. P. Ng. "Creating Sustainable Competitive Advantage through Internetworked Communities." *Communications of the ACM* 46, no. 9 (September 2003).

Fayol, Henri. *Administration industrielle et generale.* Paris: Dunods (1950). First published 1916.

Feeny, David. "Making Business Sense of the E-Opportunity." *Sloan Management Review* 42, no. 2 (Winter 2001).

Feeny, David E., and Blake Ives. "In Search of Sustainability: Reaping Long-Term Advantage from Investments in Information Technology." *Journal of Management Information Systems* (Summer 1990).

Fine, Charles H., Roger Vardan, Robert Pethick, and Jamal E-Hout. "Rapid-Response Capability in Value-Chain Design." *Sloan Management Review* 43, no. 2 (Winter 2002).

Fisher, Marshall L., Ananth Raman, and Anne Sheen McClelland. "Rocket Science Retailing Is Almost Here: Are You Ready?" *Harvard Business Review* (July–August 2000).

Freeman, John, Glenn R. Carroll, and Michael T. Hannan. "The Liability of Newness: Age Dependence in Organizational Death Rates." *American Sociological Review* 48 (1983).

Fritz, Mary Beth Watson, Sridhar Narasimhan, and Hyeun-Suk Rhee. "Communication and Coordination in the Virtual Office." *Journal of Management Information Systems* 14, no. 4 (Spring 1998).

Fulk, Janet, and Geraldine DeSanctis. "Electronic Communication and Changing Organizational Forms." *Organization Science* 6, no. 4 (July–August 1995).

Gallaugher, John M., and Yu-Ming Wang. "Understanding Network Effects in Software Markets: Evidence from Web Server Pricing." *MIS Quarterly* 26, no. 4 (December 2002).

Garvin, David A. "The Processes of Organization and Management." *Sloan Management Review* 39, no. 4 (Summer 1998).

Gilbert, Clark, and Joseph L. Bower. "Disruptive Change." *Harvard Business Review* (May 2002).

Gurbaxani, V., and S. Whang. "The Impact of Information Systems on Organizations and Markets." *Communications of the ACM* 34, no. 1 (January 1991).

Hinds, Pamela, and Sara Kiesler. "Communication across Boundaries: Work, Structure, and Use of Communication Technologies in a Large Organization." *Organization Science* 6, no. 4 (July–August 1995).

Hitt, Lorin M. "Information Technology and Firm Boundaries: Evidence from Panel Data." *Information Systems Research* 10, no. 2 (June 1999).

Hitt, Lorin M., and Erik Brynjolfsson. "Information Technology and Internal Firm Organization: An Exploratory Analysis." *Journal of Management Information Systems* 14, no. 2 (Fall 1997).

Holweg, Matthias, and Frits K. Pil. "Successful Build-to-Order Strategies Start with the Customer." *Sloan Management Review* 43, no. 1 (Fall 2001).

Hopper, Max. "Rattling SABRE—New Ways to Compete on Information." *Harvard Business Review* (May–June 1990).

Huber, George P. "Cognitive Style as a Basis for MIS and DSS Designs: Much Ado About Nothing?" *Management Science* 29 (May 1983).

———. "The Nature and Design of Post-Industrial Organizations." *Management Science* 30, no. 8 (August 1984).

———. "Organizational Learning: The Contributing Processes and Literature." *Organization Science* 2 (1991): 88–115.

Iansiti, Marco, and Roy Levien. "Strategy as Ecology." *Harvard Business Review* (March 2004).

Information Builders. "WebFOCUS and iWay Deliver Front-Line Efficiency Improvements at Telus." http://www.informationbuilders.com/applications/telus.html (accessed July 14, 2005).

Isenberg, Daniel J. "How Senior Managers Think." *Harvard Business Review* (November–December 1984).

Ives, Blake, and Gabriele Piccoli. "Custom Made Apparel and Individualized Service at Land's End." *Communications of the Association for Information Systems* 11 (2003).

Jasperson, Jon (Sean), Traci A. Carte, Carol S. Saunders, Brian S. Butler, Henry J. P. Croes, and Weijun Zheng. "Review: Power and Information Technology Research: A Metatriangulation Review." *MIS Quarterly* 26, no. 4 (December 2002).

Jensen, M. C., and W. H. Meckling. "Specific and General Knowledge and Organizational Science." In *Contract Economics,* edited by L. Wetin and J. Wijkander. Oxford: Basil Blackwell (1992).

Jensen, Michael C., and William H. Meckling. "Theory of the Firm: Managerial Behavior, Agency Costs, and Ownership Structure." *Journal of Financial Economics* 3 (1976).

Kanter, Rosabeth Moss. "The New Managerial Work." *Harvard Business Review* (November–December 1989).

Kauffman, Robert J., and Yu-Ming Wang. "The Network Externalities Hypothesis and Competitive Network Growth." *Journal of Organizational Computing and Electronic Commerce* 12, no. 1 (2002).

Keen, Peter G. W. "Information Systems and Organizational Change." *Communications of the ACM* 24, no. 1 (January 1981).

Kettinger, William J., Varun Grover, Subashish Guhan, and Albert H. Segors. "Strategic Information Systems Revisited: A Study in Sustainability and Performance." *MIS Quarterly* 18, no. 1 (March 1994).

King, J. L., V. Gurbaxani, K. L. Kraemer, F. W. McFarlan, K. S. Raman, and C. S. Yap. "Institutional Factors in Information Technology Innovation." *Information Systems Research* 5, no. 2 (June 1994).

King, W. R. "Creating a Strategic Capabilities Architecture." *Information Systems Management* 12, no. 1 (Winter 1995).

Kling, Rob. "Social Analyses of Computing: Theoretical Perspectives in Recent Empirical Research." *Computing Survey* 12, no. 1 (March 1980).

Kolb, D. A., and A. L. Frohman. "An Organization Development Approach to Consulting." *Sloan Management Review* 12, no. 1 (Fall 1970).

Konsynski, Benn R., and F. Warren McFarlan. "Information Partnerships—Shared Data, Shared Scale." *Harvard Business Review* (September–October 1990).

Konsynski, Benn, John Sviokla, and Christopher L. Marshall. "Baxter International: OnCall as Soon as Possible?" *Harvard Business School* 9-195-103 (1994).

Kontzer, Tony. "Data-Driven." *Information Week* (August 2, 2004).

Kopczak, Laura Rock, and M. Eric Johnson. "The Supply-Chain Management Effect." *MIT Sloan Management Review* 44, no. 3 (Spring 2003).

Kotter, John T. "What Effective General Managers Really Do." *Harvard Business Review* (November–December 1982).

Kraemer, Kenneth, John King, Debora Dunkle, and Joe Lane. *Managing Information Systems.* Los Angeles: Jossey-Bass (1989).

Lamb, Roberta, and Rob Kling. "Reconceptualizing Users as Social Actors in Information Systems Research." *MIS Quarterly* 27, no. 2 (June 2003).

Laudon, Kenneth C. *Computers and Bureaucratic Reform.* New York: Wiley (1974).

———. *Dossier Society: Value Choices in the Design of National Information Systems.* New York: Columbia University Press (1986).

———. "Environmental and Institutional Models of Systems Development." *Communications of the ACM* 28, no. 7 (July 1985).

———. "A General Model of the Relationship between Information Technology and Organizations." Working paper, National Science Foundation, Center for Research on Information Systems, New York University (1989).

———. "The Promise and Potential of Enterprise Systems and Industrial Networks." Working paper, The Concours Group. Copyright Kenneth C. Laudon (1999).

Laudon, Kenneth C., and Kenneth L. Marr. "Information Technology and Occupational Structure." (April 1995).

Lawrence, Paul, and Jay Lorsch. *Organization and Environment.* Cambridge, Mass.: Harvard University Press (1969).

Leavitt, Harold J. "Applying Organizational Change in Industry: Structural, Technological, and Humanistic Approaches." In *Handbook of Organizations,* edited by James G. March. Chicago: Rand McNally (1965).

Leavitt, Harold J., and Thomas L. Whisler. "Management in the 1980s." *Harvard Business Review* (November–December 1958).

Levecq, Hugues, and Bruce W. Weber. "Electronic Trading Systems: Strategic Implication of Market Design Choices." *Journal of Organizational Computing and Electronic Commerce* 12, no. 1 (2002).

Lindblom, C. E. "The Science of Muddling Through." *Public Administration Review* 19 (1959).

Machlup, Fritz. *The Production and Distribution of Knowledge in the United States.* Princeton, N.J.: Princeton University Press (1962).

Maier, Jerry L., R. Kelly Rainer Jr., and Charles A. Snyder. "Environmental Scanning for Information Technology: An Empirical Investigation." *Journal of Management Information Systems* 14, no. 2 (Fall 1997).

Main, Thomas J., and James E. Short. "Managing the Merger: Building Partnership through IT Planning at the New Baxter." *MIS Quarterly* 13, no. 4 (December 1989).

Malone, Thomas W. "Is Empowerment Just a Fad? Control, Decision-Making, and IT." *Sloan Management Review* (Winter 1997).

Malone, Thomas W., JoAnne Yates, and Robert I. Benjamin. "Electronic Markets and Electronic Hierarchies." *Communications of the ACM* (June 1987).

March, James G., and G. Sevon. "Gossip, Information, and Decision Making." In *Advances in Information Processing in Organizations,* edited by Lee S. Sproull and J. P. Crecine. Vol. 1. Hillsdale, N.J.: Erlbaum (1984).

March, James G., and Herbert A. Simon. *Organizations.* New York: Wiley (1958).

Markus, M. L. "Power, Politics, and MIS Implementation." *Communications of the ACM* 26, no. 6 (June 1983).

McAfee, Andrew, and Francois-Xavier Oliveau. "Confronting the Limits of Networks." *Sloan Management Review* 43 no. 4 (Summer 2002).

McFarlan, F. Warren. "Information Technology Changes the Way You Compete." *Harvard Business Review* (May–June 1984).

McKenney, James L., and Peter G. W. Keen. "How Managers' Minds Work." *Harvard Business Review* (May–June 1974).

Mendelson, Haim, and Ravindra R. Pillai. "Clock Speed and Informational Response: Evidence from the Information Technology Industry." *Information Systems Research* 9, no. 4 (December 1998).

Mintzberg, Henry. "Managerial Work: Analysis from Observation." *Management Science* 18 (October 1971).

———. *The Nature of Managerial Work.* New York: Harper & Row (1973).

———. *The Structuring of Organizations.* Englewood Cliffs, N.J.: Prentice Hall (1979).

Mintzberg, Henry, and Frances Westley. "Decision Making: It's Not What You Think." *Sloan Management Review* (Spring 2001).

Orlikowski, Wanda J., and Daniel Robey. "Information Technology and the Structuring of Organizations." *Information Systems Research* 2, no. 2 (June 1991).

Pindyck, Robert S., and Daniel L. Rubinfeld. *Microeconomics,* 5th ed. Upper Saddle River, N.J.: Prentice Hall (2001).

Porter, Michael. *Competitive Strategy.* New York: Free Press (1980).

———. *Competitive Advantage.* New York: Free Press (1985).

———. "How Information Can Help You Compete." *Harvard Business Review* (August–September 1985).

———. "Strategy and the Internet." *Harvard Business Review* (March 2001).

Porter, Michael E., and Scott Stern. "Location Matters." *Sloan Management Review* 42, no. 4 (Summer 2001).

Prahalad, C. K., and Venkatram Ramaswamy. "The New Frontier of Experience Innovation." *MIS Sloan Management Review* 44, no. 4 (Summer 2003).

Reich, Blaize Horner, and Izak Benbasat. "Factors That Influence the Social Dimension of Alignment between Business and Information Technology Objectives." *MIS Quarterly* 24, no. 1 (March 2000).

Reinartz, Werner, and V. Kumar. "The Mismanagement of Customer Loyalty." *Harvard Business Review* (July 2002).

Robey, Daniel, and Marie-Claude Boudreau. "Accounting for the Contradictory Organizational Consequences of Information Technology: Theoretical Directions and Methodological Implications." *Information Systems Research* 10, no. 42 (June 1999).

Rogge, Eric. "Move in Sync." *Information Week* (April 1, 2005).

Sauter, Vicki L. "Intuitive Decision-Making." *Communications of the ACM* 42, no. 6 (June 1999).

Schein, Edgar H. *Organizational Culture and Leadership.* San Francisco: Jossey-Bass (1985).

Schwenk, C. R. "Cognitive Simplification Processes in Strategic Decision Making." *Strategic Management Journal* 5 (1984).

Shapiro, Carl, and Hal R. Varian. *Information Rules.* Boston: Harvard Business School Press, 1999.

Shore, Edwin B. "Reshaping the IS Organization." *MIS Quarterly* (December 1983).

Short, James E., and N. Venkatraman. "Beyond Business Process Redesign: Redefining Baxter's Business Network." *Sloan Management Review* (Fall 1992).

Simon, Herbert A. "Applying Information Technology to Organization Design." *Public Administration Review* (May–June 1973).

Simon, Herbert A. *Administrative Behavior —A Study in Decision Making Process in Administrative Organizations.* New York: The Macmillan Company (1947).

Slywotzky, Adrian J., and Richard Wise. "The Growth Crisis, and How to Escape It." *Harvard Business Review* (July 2002).

Songini, Marc L. "Information Builders to Help Measure the Enterprise." *Computerworld* (May 27, 2004).

Starbuck, William H. "Organizations as Action Generators." *American Sociological Review* 48 (1983).

Starbuck, William H., and Frances J. Milliken. "Executives' Perceptual Filters: What They Notice and How They Make Sense." In *The Executive Effect: Concepts and Methods for Studying Top Managers,* edited by D. C. Hambrick. Greenwich, Conn.: JAI Press (1988).

Tedeschi, Bob. "E-Commerce Report." *New York Times* (January 26, 2004).

Teo, H. H., K. K. Wei, and I. Benbasat. "Predicting Intention to Adopt Interorganizational Linkages: An Institutional Perspective." *MIS Quarterly* 27, no. 1 (March 2003).

"The World Fact Book: Mexico," http://www.cia.gov (accessed September 25, 2004).

Turner, Jon A. "Computer Mediated Work: The Interplay between Technology and Structured Jobs." *Communications of the ACM* 27, no. 12 (December 1984).

Turner, Jon A., and Robert A. Karasek Jr. "Software Ergonomics: Effects of Computer Application Design Parameters on Operator Task Performance and Health." *Ergonomics* 27, no. 6 (1984).

Tushman, Michael L., and Philip Anderson. "Technological Discontinuities and Organizational Environments." *Administrative Science Quarterly* 31 (September 1986).

Tversky, A., and D. Kahneman. "The Framing of Decisions and the Psychology of Choice." *Science* 211 (January 1981).

Vandenbosch, Mark, and Niraj Dawar. "Beyond Better Products: Capturing Value in Customer Interactions." *Sloan Management Review* 43, no. 4 (Summer 2002).

Walker, Marlon A. "The Day the E-Mail Dies." *Wall Street Journal* (August 26, 2004).

Weber, Max. *The Theory of Social and Economic Organization.* Trans. by Talcott Parsons. New York: Free Press (1947).

Williamson, Oliver E. *The Economic Institutions of Capitalism.* New York: Free Press (1985).

Wiseman, Charles. *Strategic Information Systems.* Homewood, Ill.: Richard D. Irwin (1988).

Wrapp, H. Edward. "Good Managers Don't Make Policy Decisions." *Harvard Business Review* (July–August 1984).

Zipkin, Paul. "The Limits of Mass Customization." *Sloan Management Review* (Spring 2001).

Chapter 4

Associated Press. "Israeli 'Trojan Horse' Scandal Widens." http://www.msnbc.msn.com/id/8064757/ (June 1, 2005, accessed July 15, 2005).

Association of Computing Machinery. "ACM's Code of Ethics and Professional Conduct." *Communications of the ACM* 36, no. 12 (December 1993).

Australian IT. "Pentagon Tool Records Every Breath." http://australianit.news.com.au (June 3, 2003).

Ball, Kirstie S. "Situating Workplace Surveillance: Ethics and Computer-Based Performance Monitoring." *Ethics and Information Technology* 3, no. 3 (2001).

Bamford, James. "Big Brother Is Tracking You, Without a Warrant." *New York Times* (May 18, 2003).

Barrett, Larry, and Sean Gallagher. "What Sin City Can Teach Tom Ridge." *Baseline* (April 2004).

Bellman, Steven, Eric J. Johnson, and Gerald L. Lohse. "To Opt-in or Opt-out? It Depends on the Question." *Communications of the ACM* 44, no. 2 (February 2001).

Bennett, Colin J. "Cookies, Web Bugs, Webcams, and Cue Cats: Patterns of Surveillance on the World Wide Web." *Ethics and Information Technology* 3, no. 3 (2001).

Berdichevsky, Daniel, and Erik Neunschwander. "Toward an Ethics of Persuasive Technology." *Communications of the ACM 42,* no. 5 (May 1999).

Bergstein, Brian. "Terrorist Scoring System Sparked Investigations and Arrests." *Information Week* (May 20, 2004).

Bhattacharjee, Sudip, Ram D. Gopal, and G. Lawrence Sanders. "Digital Music and Online Sharing: Software Piracy 2.0?" *Communications of the ACM* 46, no. 7 (July 2003).

Black, Jane. "At Justice, NSEERS Spells Data Chaos." *BusinessWeek Online* (May 2, 2003).

———. "Privacy: For Every Attack, a Defense." *Business Week* (July 22, 2003).

Bowen, Jonathan. "The Ethics of Safety-Critical Systems." *Communications of the ACM* 43, no. 3 (April 2000).

Brezezinski, Matthew. "Fortress American." *New York Times* (February 23, 2003).

Broad, William J., and Judith Miller. "Health Data Monitored for Bioterror Warning." *New York Times* (January 27, 2003).

Brod, Craig. *Techno Stress—The Human Cost of the Computer Revolution.* Reading, Mass.: Addison-Wesley (1982).

Bronner, Ethan. "Collateral Damage." *New York Times* (February 22, 2004).

Brown Bag Software vs. Symantec Corp. 960 F2D 1465 (Ninth Circuit, 1992).

Burk, Dan L. "Copyrightable Functions and Patentable Speech." *Communications of the ACM* 44, no. 2 (February 2001).

Carr, David F., and Sean Gallagher. "BofA's Direct-Deposit Debacle." *Baseline* (May 15, 2002).

Cavazos, Edward A. "The Legal Risks of Setting Up Shop in Cyberspace." *Journal of Organizational Computing* 6, no. 1 (1996).

Chowdhary, Sudhir. "Festival Blues: India Inc. Grapples with Spam," *ZDNet India* (December 20, 2004).

Claburn, Thomas. "Anti-Spam Technologies Prove Their Value." *Information Week* (April 26, 2004).

———. "Turning the Tide." *Information Week* (January 17, 2005).

Clarke, Roger. "Internet Privacy Concerns Confirm the Case for Intervention." *Communications of the ACM* 42, no. 2 (February 1999).

Clymer, Adam. "In Fight for Privacy, States Set Off Sparks." *New York Times* (July 6, 2003).

Collins, W. Robert, Keith W. Miller, Bethany J. Spielman, and Phillip Wherry. "How Good Is Good Enough? An Ethical Analysis of Software Construction and Use." *Communications of the ACM* 37, no. 1 (January 1994).

Davis, Ann. "Why a 'No Fly List' Aimed at Terrorists Delays Others." *Wall Street Journal* (April 22, 2003).

Day, George S., Adam J. Fein, and Gregg Ruppersberger, "Shakeouts in Digital Markets." *California Management Review* 45, no. 3 (Winter 2003).

Earp, Julia B., and David Baumer. "Innovative Web Use to Learn About Consumer Behavior and Online Privacy." *Communications of the ACM* 46, no. 4 (April 2003).

Edwards, Randall. "CAPPS II Faces Scrutiny Before Funding." http://www.fce.com (accessed June 19, 2003).

Emery, Brian Gail Repsher. "Patriot Games." Yahoo! News (March 17, 2004).

EPIC USA Patriot Act page. http://www.epic.org/terrorism/usapatriot (accessed July 16, 2005).

Farmer, Dan, and Charles C. Mann. "Give Me Duquesne Minus 7, for a Nickel." *Technology Review* (May 2003).

———. "Surveillance Nation." Pts. I and II. *Technology Review* (April 2003) and (May 2003).

FDA News. "FDA Seeks Injunction against Multidata Systems Intl." (May 7, 2003).

Federman, Josef. "Scandal Jolts Israel's Industrial Elite." *The Winnipeg Free Press* (June 2, 2005).

Flynn, Laurie J. "Internet Giants File 7 Suits Aimed at Stopping Spam." *New York Times* (October 29, 2004).

"4 Rivals Near Agreement on Ways to Fight Spam." *New York Times* (June 23, 2004).

Froomkin, A. Michael. "The Collision of Trademarks, Domain Names, and Due Process in Cyberspace." *Communications of the ACM* 44, no. 2 (February 2001).

Gage, Deborah, and John McCormick. "We Did Nothing Wrong." *Baseline Magazine* (March 2004).

Gattiker, Urs E., and Helen Kelley. "Morality and Computers: Attitudes and Differences in Judgments." *Information Systems Research* 10, no. 3 (September 1999).

Geitner, Paul. "Survey: 36 Percent of Software Pirated." Associated Press (July 7, 2004).

Goo, Sara Kehaulani. "Northwest Gave U.S. Data on Passengers." *Washington Post* (January 18, 2004).

Gopal, Ram D., and G. Lawrence Sanders. "Preventive and Deterrent Controls for Software Piracy." *Journal of Management Information Systems* 13, no. 4 (Spring 1997).

Greenemeier, Larry. "Lawmakers Want Info." *Information Week* (February 25, 2004).

Hagerty, James R., and Dennis K. Berman. "New Battleground in Web Privacy War: Ads That Snoop." *Wall Street Journal* (August 27, 2003).

Hansell, Saul. "Totaling Up the Bill for Spam." *New York Times* (July 28, 2003).

———. "The Internet Ad You Are About to See Has Already Read Your E-Mail." *New York Times* (June 21, 2004).

———. "Junk E-Mail and Fraud Are Focus of Crackdown" *New York Times* (August 25, 2004),

Harrington, Susan J. "The Effect of Codes of Ethics and Personal Denial of Responsibility on Computer Abuse Judgments and Intentions." *MIS Quarterly* 20, no. 2 (September 1996).

Heingartner, Douglas. "Software Piracy Is in Resurgence, with New Safeguards Eroded by File Sharing." *New York Times* (January 19, 2004).

Holland, Jesse J. "Ashcroft Pushes Anti-Terror Law Expansion." Associated Press (June 5, 2003).

Jackson, Linda A., Alexander von Eye, Gretchen Barbatsis, Frank Biocca, Hiram E. Fitzgerald, and Yong Zhao. "The Impact of Internet Use on the Other Side of the Digital Divide." *Communications of the ACM* 47, no. 7 (July 2004).

Jackson, Thomas W., Ray Dawson, and Darren Wilson. "Understanding Email Interaction Increases Organizational Productivity." *Communications of the ACM* 46, no. 8 (August 2003).

Johnson, Deborah G. "Ethics Online." *Communications of the ACM* 40, no. 1 (January 1997).

Johnson, Deborah G., and John M. Mulvey. "Accountability and Computer Decision Systems." *Communications of the ACM* 38, no. 12 (December 1995).

Kapner, Suzanne. "Internet Site, Fearing Suit over Content, Curbs Activity." *New York Times* (March 14, 2003).

Katz, Yaakov. "Trojan Horse Also Hit Major International Firms." *The Jewish Post* (May 30, 2005).

Kling, Rob. "When Organizations Are Perpetrators: The Conditions of Computer Abuse and Computer Crime." In *Computerization and Controversy: Value Conflicts and Social Choices*, edited by Charles Dunlop and Rob Kling. New York: Academic Press (1991).

Kreie, Jennifer, and Timothy Paul Cronan. "Making Ethical Decisions." *Communications of the ACM* 43, no. 12 (December 2000).

Laudon, Kenneth C. *Dossier Society: Value Choices in the Design of National Information Systems.* New York: Columbia University Press (1986).

———. "Ethical Concepts and Information Technology." *Communications of the ACM* 38, no. 12 (December 1995).

Laudon, Kenneth C., and Carol Guercio Traver. *E-Commerce: Business, Technology, Society.* Boston: Addison-Wesley (2004).

Lee, Jennifer S. "State Department Link Will Open Visa Database to Police Officers." *New York Times* (January 31, 2003).

Lee, Jintae. "An End-User Perspective on File-Sharing Systems." *Communications of the ACM* 46, no. 2 (February 2003).

Lenhart, Amanda, John Horrigan, Lee Rainie, Katherine Allen, Angie Boyce, Mary Madden, and Erin O'Grady. "The Ever-Shifting Internet Population." *Pew Internet and American Life Project* (April 16, 2003).

Lewis, Charles, and Adam Mayle. "Justice Department Drafts Sweeping Expansion of Anti-Terrorism Act." The Center for Public Integrity. http://www.publicintegrity.org (February 7, 2003).

Lichtblau, Eric. "Administration Plans Defense of Terror Law." *New York Times* (August 19, 2003).

———. "F.B.I. Said to Lag on Translations of Terror Tapes." *New York Times* (September 28, 2004).

Lohr, Steve. "Software Group Enters Fray over Proposed Piracy Law." *New York Times* (July 19, 2004).

MacDonald, Heather. "The 'Privacy' Jihad." *Wall Street Journal* (April 1, 2004).

Maltz, Elliott, and Vincent Chiappetta. "Maximizing Value in the Digital World." *Sloan Management Review* 43, no. 3 (Spring 2002).

Manjoo, Farhad. "Please Step to the Side, Sir." *Salon.* http://www.salon.com (April 10, 2003).

Mann, Catherine L. "What Global Sourcing Means for U.S. I.T. Workers and for the U.S. Economy." *Communications of the ACM* 47, no. 7 (July 2004).

Marciniak, Sean. "Web Privacy Services Complicate Work of Federal Investigators." *Wall Street Journal* (July 3, 2003).

Martin, David M., Jr., Richard M. Smith, Michael Brittain, Ivan Fetch, and Hailin Wu. "The Privacy Practices of Web Browser Extensions." *Communications of the ACM* 44, no. 2 (February 2001).

Mason, Richard O. "Applying Ethics to Information Technology Issues." *Communications of the ACM* 38, no. 12 (December 1995).

———. "Four Ethical Issues in the Information Age." *MIS Quarterly* 10, no. 1 (March 1986).

Milchen, Jeff. "Fighting Terror Without Losing Our Freedom." Baltimore Sun (June 22, 2003).

Moore, Meg Mitchell. "Serving Up Your Customers." *CSO Magazine* (January 2004).

Moores, Trevor, and Gurpreet Dhillon. "Software Piracy: A View from Hong Kong." *Communications of the ACM* 43, no. 12 (December 2000).

CNN. "Mueller Defends FBI at Civil Liberties Meeting." http://www.cnn.com (June 13, 2003).

Mykytyn, Kathleen, Peter P. Mykytyn Jr., and Craig W. Slinkman. "Expert Systems: A Question of Liability." *MIS Quarterly* 14, no. 1 (March 1990).

Napolitano, Andrew P. "Repeal the Patriot Act." *Wall Street Journal* (March 5, 2004).

Nasaw, Daniel. "Federal Law Fails to Lessen Flow of Junk E-Mail." *Wall Street Journal* (August 10, 2004).

National Telecommunications and Information Administration, U.S. Department of Commerce. "Falling through the Net: Defining the Digital Divide" (July 8, 1999).

Nissenbaum, Helen. "Computing and Accountability." *Communications of the ACM* 37, no. 1 (January 1994).

Okerson, Ann. "Who Owns Digital Works?" *Scientific American* (July 1996).

Oz, Effy. "Ethical Standards for Information Systems Professionals." *MIS Quarterly* 16, no. 4 (December 1992).

———. *Ethics for the Information Age.* Dubuque, Iowa: W. C. Brown (1994).

Pawling, G. Patrick. "Turning Drains into Gains." *Cisco IQ Magazine* (First Quarter 2004).

Payton, Fay Cobb. "Rethinking the Digital Divide." *Communications of the ACM* 46, no. 6 (June 2003).

Pear, Robert. "Survey Finds U.S. Agencies Engaged in 'Data Mining.'" *New York Times* (May 27, 2004).

———. "Panel Urges New Protection on Federal 'Data Mining.'" *New York Times* (May 17, 2004).

Poulsen, Kevin. "FBI Seeks Internet Telephony Surveillance." *BusinessWeek Online* (March 28, 2003).

Business Week Online. "Putting the Blinders Back on Big Brother." (March 27, 2003).

Rainie, Lee, and Dan Packel. "More Online, Doing More." *Pew Internet and American Life Project* (February 18, 2001).

Reagle, Joseph, and Lorrie Faith Cranor. "The Platform for Privacy Preferences." *Communications of the ACM* 42, no. 2 (February 1999).

Redman, Thomas C. "The Impact of Poor Data Quality on the Typical Enterprise." *Communications of the ACM* 41, no. 2 (February 1998).

Reuters. "Judge Rules Against Patriot Act Provision." (September 29, 2004).

Rifkin, Jeremy. "Watch Out for Trickle-Down Technology." *New York Times* (March 16, 1993).

Rigdon, Joan E. "Frequent Glitches in New Software Bug Users." *Wall Street Journal* (January 18, 1995).

Rosen, Jeffrey. "How to Protect America, and Your Rights." *New York Times* (February 6, 2004).

Rotenberg, Marc. "Communications Privacy: Implications for Network Design." *Communications of the ACM* 36, no. 8 (August 1993).

"Royal Assent of Bill C-36, The Anti-Terrorism Act." Department of Justice Canada. http://canada.justice.gc.ca/en/news/nr/2001/doc_28217. html (accessed July 16, 2005).

Rupley, Sebastian. "FBI Petitions for Broad Wiretapping Rights." *PC Magazine* (March 15, 2004).

Samuelson, Pamela. "Computer Programs and Copyright's Fair Use Doctrine." *Communications of the ACM* 36, no. 9 (September 1993).

———. "The Ups and Downs of Look and Feel." *Communications of the ACM* 36, no. 4 (April 1993).

Sanger, David E. "President Urging Wider U.S. Powers in Terrorism Law." *New York Times* (September 11, 2003).

Sewell, Graham, and James R. Barker. "Neither Good, nor Bad, but Dangerous: Surveillance as an Ethical Paradox." *Ethics and Information Technology* 3, no. 3 (2001).

Sharkey, Joe. "When Flying Is Truly the Only Way to Go." *New York Times* (May 25, 2004).

Singel, Ryan. "Secure Flight Gets Wary Welcome." *Wired News* (August 27, 2004).

Sipior, Janice C., and Burke T. Ward. "The Dark Side of Employee Email." *Communications of the ACM* 42, no. 7 (July 1999).

Smith, H. Jeff. "The Shareholders vs. Stakeholders Debate." *MIT Sloan Management Review* 44, no. 4 (Summer 2003).

Smith, H. Jeff, and John Hasnas. "Ethics and Information Systems: The Corporate Domain." *MIS Quarterly* 23, no. 1 (March 1999).

Smith, H. Jeff, Sandra J. Milberg, and Sandra J. Burke. "Information Privacy: Measuring Individuals' Concerns about Organizational Practices." *MIS Quarterly* 20, no. 2 (June 1996).

Sniffen, Michael J. "Pentagon Developing System to Track Every Vehicle in a City." http://www.security-focus.com (July 1, 2003).

Staples, Brent. "The Battle Against Junk Mail and Spyware on the Web." *New York Times* (January 3, 2004).

Stone, Amey. "The Digital Divide That Wasn't." *BusinessWeek* (August 19, 2003).

Straub, Detmar W., Jr., and William D. Nance. "Discovering and Disciplining Computer Abuse in Organizations: A Field Study." *MIS Quarterly* 14, no. 1 (March 1990).

Straub, Detmar W., Jr., and Rosann Webb Collins. "Key Information Liability Issues Facing Managers: Software Piracy, Proprietary Databases, and Individual Rights to Privacy." *MIS Quarterly* 14, no. 2 (June 1990).

Sullivan, Andy. "U.S. to Force Airlines to Provide Traveler Data." Yahoo! News (March 17, 2004).

Swarns, Rachel. "Senator? Terrorist? A Watch List Stops Kennedy at Airport." *The New York Times* (August 20, 2004).

Tam, Pui-Wing. "Fruitcake Debutantes Defined by O, and Other Spam Tricks." *Wall Street Journal* (May 28, 2004).

Tuttle, Brad, Adrian Harrell, and Paul Harrison. "Moral Hazard, Ethical Considerations, and the Decision to Implement an Information System." *Journal of Management Information Systems* 13, no. 4 (Spring 1997).

Urbaczewski, Andrew, and Leonard M. Jessup. "Does Electronic Monitoring of Employee Internet Usage Work?" *Communications of the ACM* 45, no. 1 (January 2002).

U.S. Department of Health, Education, and Welfare. *Records, Computers, and the Rights of Citizens.* Cambridge, Mass.: MIT Press (1973).

Volokh, Eugene. "Personalization and Privacy." *Communications of the ACM* 43, no. 8 (August 2000).

Wald, Matthew L. "Privacy Issue Delays Change in Airport Screening System." *New York Times* (February 13, 2004).

———. "Privacy Issues Slow Updated Airlines Security." *New York Times* (May 11, 2004).

———. "U.S. Wants Air Traveler Files for Security Test." *New York Times* (September 22, 2004).

Wang, Huaiqing, Matthew K. O. Lee, and Chen Wang. "Consumer Privacy Concerns about Internet Marketing." *Communications of the ACM* 41, no. 3 (March 1998).

Webster, T. C. "Government to 'Save' Digital History." http://www. worldnetdaily.com (March 4, 2003).

Weill, Peter, et. al., "Building IT Infrastructure for Strategic Agility." *Sloan Management Review* (Fall 2002).

Welch, Matt. "Get Ready for PATRIOT II." http://www.alternet.org (April 2, 2003).

Wellman, Barry. "Designing the Internet for a Networked Society." *Communications of the ACM* 45, no. 5 (May 2002).

Chapter 5

Acharya, Ravi. "EAI: A Business Perspective." *EAI Journal* (April 2003).

Akin, David. "Canada Sees Future in Grid Computing Projects." *The Globe and Mail* (August 7, 2001).

Aries, James A., Subhankar Banerjee, Marc S. Brittan, Eric Dillon, Janusz S. Kowalik, and John P. Lixvar. "Capacity and Performance Analysis of Distributed Enterprise Systems." *Communications of the ACM* 45, no. 6 (June 2002).

Barry, Douglas K. *Web Services and Service-Oriented Architectures: The Savvy Manager's Guide.* New York: Morgan Kaufman (2003).

Beauchesne, Eric. "Globalization Has Not Yet Cost Canada Well-Paid Jobs." *Edmonton Journal* (January 27, 2005).

Bell, Gordon, and Jim Gray. "What's Next in High-Performance Computing?" *Communications of the ACM* 45, no. 1 (January 2002).

Benamati, John, and Albert L. Lederer. "Coping with Rapid Changes in IT." *Communications of the ACM* 44, no. 8 (August 2001).

Bulkeley, William M. "New IBM Service Will Test Vision of Computing Power as Utility." *Wall Street Journal* (July 1, 2002).

Butler, Steve. "Telecom Spending." *EMarketer* (April 2004).

Champy, James. "Re-examining the Infrastructure." *Optimize* 23 (September 2003).

Chari, Kaushal, and Saravanan Seshadri. "Demystifying Integration." *Communications of the ACM* 47, no. 7 (July 2004).

Conry-Murray, Andrew. "Grid Computing's Promises and Perils." Network Magazine.com (February 5, 2004).

Cuomo, Jerry, et al. "WebSphere Capacity—On Demand: Developing Edge Computing Applications." IBM Corporation and Akamai (2003). http://www.106.ibm.com/developerworks/websphere/library/techarticles/0310_haberkorn/haberkorn.html.

Da Cruz, Frank. *A Chronology of Computing at Columbia University.* Columbia University Computing History http://www.columbia.edu/acis/history/watsonlab.html (December 31, 2004).

David, Julie Smith, David Schuff, and Robert St. Louis. "Managing Your IT Total Cost of Ownership." *Communications of the ACM* 45, no. 1 (January 2002).

Dempsey, Bert J., Debra Weiss, Paul Jones, and Jane Greenberg. "What Is an Open Source Software Developer?" *Communications of the ACM* 45, no. 1 (January 2001).

e.logistics magazine. "Delivering the Drink." http://www.elogmag.com/magazine/31/delivering-drink.shtml. January/February 2004 (accessed February 17, 2005).

Ganek, A. G., and T. A. Corbi. "The Dawning of the Autonomic Computing Era." *IBM Systems Journal* 42, no. 1 (2003).

Gates, Bill, Nathan Myhrvold, Peter Rinearson. *The Road Ahead.* Penguin (1996).

Gerlach, James, Bruce Neumann, Edwin Moldauer, Martha Argo, and Daniel Frisby. "Determining the Cost of IT Services." *Communications of the ACM* 45, no. 9 (September 2002).

Hagel, John, III, and John Seeley Brown. "Your Next IT Strategy." *Harvard Business Review* (October 2001).

HP (Hewlett-Packard). "Success Stories: Canadian Imperial Bank of Commerce (CBC)—with HP Services." http://www.hp.com (accessed September 30, 2004).

Hoovers Online. "Direct Wines Limited." http://www.hoovers.com/direct-wines/—ID__102549—/free-co-factsheet.xhtml. (accessed February 18, 2005).

IBM. "20th Century Disk Storage Technology." http://www-1.ibm.com/ibm/history/exhibits/storage/storage_chrono20.html (accessed July 2004).

———. "Gridlines: The Intersection of Technology and Business." IBM. http://www-1.ibm.com/grid/gridlines/January2004/feature/teamwork.shtml (accessed July 2004).

———. "How Customers Are Making On Demand Real." IBM. http://www.ibm.com/news/us/2003/11/on_demand_real.html (accessed July 2004).

———. "The Mainframe Family Tree and Chronology." IBM. http://www-1.ibm.com/ibm/history/exhibits/mainframe/mainframe_FT1.html (accessed July 2004).

Industry Canada. "Canadian ICT Sector Profile." http://strategis.gc.ca/epic/internet/inict-tic.nsf/PrintableE/h_it07229e.html (accessed April 9, 2005).

———. "Canadian Industry Statistics: Establishments: Canadian Economy." http://strategis.gc.ca/sc_ecnmy/sio/ciseste.html (accessed April 9, 2005.)

Intel Corporation. "Expanding Moore's Law: The Exponential Opportunity." (Fall 2002).

———. "Microprocessor Quick Reference Guide." Intel. http://www.intel.com/pressroom/kits/quickreffam.htm (accessed July 2004).

International Technology Roadmap for Semiconductors Committee. "The International Technology Roadmap for Semiconductors 2003 Edition." http://public.itrs.net/ (accessed July 2004).

Internet World Stats. "Broadband and Consumer E-Commerce in Canada December 2004 Review." http://www.internetworldstats.com/am/ca.htm (accessed April 22, 2005).

Kephart, Jeffrey O., and David M. Chess. "The Vision of Autonomic Computing," *Computer Magazine, IEEE* (2003).

Kern, Thomas, Leslie P. Willcocks, and Mary C. Lacity. "Application Service Provision: Risk Assessment and Mitigation." *MIS Quarterly Executive* 1, no. 2 (2002).

Kerstetter, Jim. "The Linux Uprising." *BusinessWeek Online* (March 2003).

King, John. "Centralized vs. Decentralized Computing: Organizational Considerations and Management Options." *Computing Surveys* (October 1984).

Kontzer, Tony. "Airline Taps IBM for Flexible Pricing Deal." *Information Week* (May 24, 2004).

———. "Qantas Airways Hand Over IT Management to IBM." *Information Week* (May 17, 2004).

Kurzweil, Ray. "Exponential Growth an Illusion?: Response to Ilkka Tuomi." KurzweilAI.net (September 23, 2003).

LeBlond, Raoul, and Ben Worthen. "Taking IT to the Next Level." *CIO Asia*, January 2004.

Lee, Jinyoul, Keng Siau, and Soongoo Hong. "Enterprise Integration with ERP and EAI." *Communications of the ACM* 46, no. 2 (February 2003).

Lohr, Steve. "IBM Helps Promote Linux." *New York Times* (November 11, 2003).

Loo, Alfred W. "The Future of Peer-to-Peer Computing." *Communications of the ACM* 46, no. 9 (September 2003).

Lyman, Peter, and Hal R. Varian. "How Much Information? 2003." School of Management and Systems, University of California at Berkeley (2003).

Markoff, John, and Jennifer L. Schenker. "Europe Exceeds U.S. in Refining Grid Computing." *New York Times,* November 10, 2003.

Marks, Eric A., and Mark J. Werrell. *Executive's Guide to Web Services.* New York: Wiley (2003).

Marshak, David. "Charles Schwab Responds to Market Conditions and Customer Needs: Services-Oriented Architecture Improves Time to Market and Leverages Existing Investments." *Patricia Seybold Group* (December 2003).

McDougall, Paul. "Dow Hires IBM to Take VoIP Project over from EDS." *Information Week* (August 3, 2004).

Miller, Gerry. ".NET vs. J2EE." *Communications of the ACM* 46, no. 6 (June 2003).

Moore, Gordon. "Cramming More Components onto Integrated Circuits." *Electronics* 38, no. 8 (April 19, 1965).

Muscarella, Gregory, M. S. Krishnan, and Harry Ault. "Business Advantages Flow with XML." *Optimize Magazine* (November 2003).

Nasscom Newsline. "In-Focus: Canada." http://www.nasscom.org/newsline/issue40/In-Focus.asp (accessed April 11, 2005).

National Science Foundation. "Revolutionizing Science and Engineering through Cyberinfrastructure: Report of the National Science Foundation Blue-Ribbon Advisory Panel on Cyberinfrastructure." Washington, D.C. (January, 2003).

Niemeyer, Alex, Misok H. Pak, and Sanjay E. Ramaswamy. "Smart Tags for Your Supply Chain." *McKinsey Quarterly* 4 (2003).

Noffsinger, W. B., Robert Niedbalski, Michael Blanks, and Niall Emmart. "Legacy Object Modeling Speeds Software Integration." *Communications of the ACM* 41, no. 12 (December 1998).

Open Source Development Lab. "The Linux Marketplace—Moving From Niche to Mainstream." Prepared by IDC for OSDL http://www.osdl.org/docs/linux_market_overview.pdf. (December 14, 2004).

Pancake, Cherri M., and Christian Lengauer. "High-Performance Java." *Communications of the ACM* 44, no. 10 (October 2001).

Patel, Samir, and Suneel Saigal. "When Computers Learn to Talk: A Web Services Primer." *McKinsey Quarterly*, no. 1 (2002).

Patrick, Ryan B. "City Rolls Out Desktop Linux." OpenCityGov.org, http://www.opencitygov.org. (accessed September 10, 2004).

Phillips, Charles. "Stemming the Software Spending Spree." *Optimize Magazine* (April 2002).

Pickett, Patricia. "City of Calgary Moves to Linux," *ComputerWorld Canada* (March 5, 2004).

Qantas Corporate Communication. "Qantas Faces Significant Challenges." (August 19, 2004).

QAS Customer Case Studies. "Direct Wines—A Case Study" QAS, http://www.qas.com/uk/customers/casestudy.asp?Organisation=DirectWines&Type=Retail, (accessed February 18, 2005).

The Retail Bulletin. "Case Study: Direct Wines Grows with SAP." http://www.theretailbulletin.com/print.php?id=3066 (accessed February 17, 2005).

Ricadela, Aaron. "Living on the Grid." *Information Week* (June 17, 2002).

Salkever, Alex, with Olga Kharif. "Slowly Weaving Web Services Together." *BusinessWeek* (June 24, 2003).

Schmerken, Ivy. "Girding for Grid." *Wall Street and Technology* (April 2003).

Schuff, David, and Robert St. Louis. "Centralization vs. Decentralization of Application Software." *Communications of the ACM* 44, no. 6 (June 2002).

Shankland, Stephen. "IBM: On Demand Computing Has Arrived." CNET News.com, http://news.com/2100-7784-5106577.html (November 12, 2003).

———. "T-Rec Bites into Server Market." CNET News.com (February 27, 2004).

Sibley, Kathleen. "A Tale of Two Open Source Cities." ITBusiness.ca, http://www.itbusiness.ca (accessed April 30, 2004).

SPSS, Inc. "Direct Wines." http://www.spss.com/success/template_view.cfm?Story_ID=66, (accessed February 18, 2005).

Stango, Victor. "The Economics of Standards Wars." *Review of Network Economics* 3, no. 1 (March 2004).

Susarla, Anjana, Anitesh Barua, and Andrew B. Whinston. "Understanding the Service Component of Application Service Provision: An Empirical Analysis of Satisfaction with ASP Services." *MIS Quarterly* 27, no. 1 (March 2003).

Tatemura, Junichi, et al. "Acceleration of Web Service Workflow Execution through Edge Computing." NEC Laboratories America, Inc. (2003).

Tuomi, Ilkka. "The Lives and Death of Moore's Law." *FirstMonday*, col 7, no. 11 (November 2002).

Vaas, Lisa. "Microsoft Pitches New Low-Cost, Entry-Level Database Edition." *eWeek* (February 24, 2005.)

Walsh, Kenneth R. "Analyzing the Application ASP Concept: Technologies, Economies, and Strategies." *Communications of the ACM* 46, no. 8 (August 2003).

Weill, Peter, and Marianne Broadbent. *Leveraging the New Infrastructure.* Cambridge, Mass.: Harvard Business School Press (1998).

———. "Management by Maxim: How Business and IT Managers Can Create IT Infrastructures." *Sloan Management Review* (Spring 1997).

Weill, Peter, Mani Subramani, and Marianne Broadbent. "Building IT Infrastructure for Strategic Agility." *Sloan Management Review* 44, no. 1 (Fall 2002).

Weitzel, Tim. *Economics of Standards in Information Networks.* Springer (2004).

Chapter 6

Barrett, Larry. "FBI: Under the Gun." *Baseline* (September 10, 2003).

Baseline. "NYPD Base Case." (September 10, 2002).

Black, Robert, Gary Fields, and Jo Wrighton. "U.S. 'Terror' List Still Lacking." *Wall Street Journal* (January 2, 2004).

Brown, Doug. "How Homeland Security Budgets Technology." *Baseline* (September 9, 2002).

Bridis, Ted. "Review: FBI Computer Upgrades Inadequate." Associated Press (May 10, 2004).

Cappiello, Cinzia, Chiara Francalanci, and Barbara Pernici. "Time-Related Factors of Data Quality in Multichannel Information Systems." *Journal of Management Information Systems* 20, no. 3 (Winter 2004).

Chen, Andrew N. K., Paulo B. Goes, and James R. Marsden. "A Query-Driven Approach to the Design and Management of Flexible Database Systems." *Journal of Management Information Systems* 19, no. 3 (Winter 2002–2003).

Clifford, James, Albert Croker, and Alex Tuzhilin. "On Data Representation and Use in a Temporal Relational DBMS." *Information Systems Research* 7, no. 3 (September 1996).

Coglin Mill. "AS/400 Data Warehouse Case Study: HSBC Bank Canada." http://www.coglinmill.com/pdf_files/rodrefhsbc.pdf (accessed April 10, 2005).

Computerworld. "FBI Begins Knowledge Management Face-Lift." (April 21, 2003).

———. "Database Woes Thwart Counterterrorism Work." (December 2, 2002).

Cooper, Brian L., Hugh J. Watson, Barbara H. Wixom, and Dale L. Goodhue. "Data Warehousing Supports Corporate Strategy at First American Corporation." *MIS Quarterly* (December 2000).

Coyne, Andrew. "Hamas Is OK, It's You We're Not Sure Of." *The National Post* (November 15, 2002).

D'Agostino, Deborah. "PLM: The Means of Production." *eWeek* (February 27, 2004).

Dignan, Larry. "A Fort Knox for Data." *Baseline* (January 16, 2004).

Eckerson, Wayne W. "Data Quality and the Bottom Line." *Data Warehousing Institute* (2002).

Fayyad, Usama, Ramasamy Ramakrishnan, and Ramakrisnan Srikant. "Evolving Data Mining into Solutions for Insights." *Communications of the ACM* 45, no. 8 (August 2002).

Gage, Debbie. "FBI Bureaucracy Hobbies Tech Adoption." *Baseline* (September 11, 2002).

Gage, Debbie and John McCormick. "The Disconnected Cop." *Baseline* (September 10, 2002).

Gallagher, Sean. "Gotcha! Extending Existing Systems." *Baseline* (September 10, 2002).

Gardner, Stephen R. "Building the Data Warehouse." *Communications of the ACM* 41, no. 9 (September 1998).

Goldstein, R. C., and J. B. McCririck. "What Do Data Administrators Really Do?" *Datamation* 26 (August 1980).

Goodhue, Dale L., Judith A. Quillard, and John F. Rockart. "Managing the Data Resource: A Contingency Perspective." *MIS Quarterly* (September 1988).

Goodhue, Dale L., Michael D. Wybo, and Laurie J. Kirsch. "The Impact of Data Integration on the Costs and Benefits of Information Systems." *MIS Quarterly* 16, no. 3 (September 1992).

Goodhue, Dale L., Laurie J. Kirsch, Judith A. Quillard, and Michael D. Wybo. "Strategic Data Planning: Lessons from the Field." *MIS Quarterly* 16, no. 1 (March 1992).

Grover, Varun, and James Teng. "How Effective Is Data Resource Management?" *Journal of Information Systems Management* (Summer 1991).

Hewitt Associates. "Best Employers in Canada." http://was4.hewitt.com/bestemployers/canada/best.htm (accessed April 13, 2005).

Hirji, Karim K. "Exploring Data Mining Implementation." *Communications of the ACM* 44, no. 7 (July 2001).

IBM. "Axfood Transforms Inventory Management Process with DB2 Data Warehouse." http://www.ibm.com (accessed May 17, 2004).

Jukic, Boris, Nenad Jukic, and Manoj Parameswaran. "Data Models for Information Sharing in E-Partnerships: Analysis, Improvements, and Relevance." *Journal of Organizational Computing and Electronic Commerce* 12, no. 2 (2002).

Kahn, Beverly K. "Some Realities of Data Administration." *Communications of the ACM* 26 (October 1983).

King, John L., and Kenneth Kraemer. "Information Resource Management Cannot Work." *Information and Management* (1988).

Klau, Rick. "Data Quality and CRM." Line56.com (March 4, 2003).

Knowledge Storm. "Virgin Mobile Wins TDWI Award with Oracle Data Warehouse." http://knowledgestorm.co.nz/ksnz/search/viewabstract/71124/index.jsp (accessed April 13, 2005).

Kroenke, David. *Database Processing: Fundamentals, Design, and Implementation*, 9th ed. Upper Saddle River, N.J.: Prentice Hall (2004).

Lamont, Judith. "Law Enforcement Gains Ground in Data Integration and Analysis." *KMWorld* (March 2003).

Lee, Jennifer A. "Threats and Responses: Law Enforcement; State Department Link Will Open Visa Database to Police Officers." *New York Times* (January 31, 2003).

Lee, Yang W., and Diane M. Strong. "Knowing-Why about Data Processes and Data Quality." *Journal of Management Information Systems* 20, no. 3 (Winter 2004).

Low, Lafe. "They Got It Together," *CIO Magazine* (February 15, 2004).

March, Salvatore T., and Young-Gul Kim. "Information Resource Management: A Metadata Perspective." *Journal of Management Information Systems* 5, no. 3 (Winter 1988–1989).

MatrixOne. "Procter & Gamble Awarded Enterprise Value Award by *CIO Magazine* for Work with MatrixOne on Innovative Product Lifecycle Management Application." (February 23, 2004).

———. "Procter & Gamble." http://www.matrixone.com (accessed May 20, 2004).

McCarthy, John. "Phenomenal Data Mining." *Communications of the ACM* 43, no. 8 (August 2000).

McFadden, Fred R., Jeffrey A. Hoffer, and Mary B. Prescott. *Modern Database Management*, 6th ed. Upper Saddle River, N.J.: Prentice Hall (2002).

McGee, Marianne Kolbasuk. "Bigger and Better." *Information Week* (March 22, 2004).

Mintz, John. "DHS Blamed for Failure to Combine Watch Lists." *The Washington Post* (October 2, 2004).

Morrison, Mike, Joline Morrison, and Anthony Keys. "Integrating Web Sites and Databases." *Communications of the ACM* 45, no. 9 (September 2002).

Office of the Auditor General. "National Security in Canada—The 2001 Anti-Terrorism Initiative." http://www.oag-bvg.gc.ca/domino/reports.nsf/html/20040303ce.html (accessed April 17, 2005).

Oracle. "Virgin Mobile Uses Business Intelligence to Achieve Rapid Expansion." http://www.oracle.com (accessed May 17, 2004).

Pictographics Ltd. "Pictographics and Our Web-Enabled Database Solutions." http://www.pictographics.com/databases.lasso (accessed April 14, 2005).

Pierce, Elizabeth M. "Assessing Data Quality with Control Matrices." *Communications of the ACM* 47, no. 2 (February 2004).

Rundensteiner, Elke A., Andreas Koeller, and Xin Zhang. "Maintaining Data Warehouses over Changing Information Sources." *Communications of the ACM* 43, no. 6 (June 2000).

Salkever, Alex. "Spooks, Sleuths, and Data Sharing." Business Week (May 25, 2004).

Truman, Gregory E. "Integration in Electronic Exchange Environments." *Journal of Management Information Systems* 17, no. 1 (Summer 2000).

Tryba, Lynn. "Winning with a Warehouse." *Profit Magazine* (February 2004).

Venetis, Tom. "BMO Uses DB2 to Reach Out to Customers." *Computerworld Canada* (January 21, 2005).

Verton, Dan. "FBI Has Made Major Progress, Former IT Chief Says." *Computerworld* (April 21, 2003).

Watson, Hugh J., and Barbara J. Haley. "Managerial Considerations." *Communications of the ACM* 41, no. 9 (September 1998).

Whitcomb, Christopher. "The Needle in the Database." *New York Times* (May 14, 2004).

Chapter 7

Amor, Daniel. *The E-Business Revolution,* 2nd ed. Upper Saddle River, N.J.: Prentice Hall (2002).

Arnaut, Gordon. "On a Roll with High-Tech Trucks." *Globe Technology,* http://www.globetechnology.com/einsider/robmagazine/stories.roll.html (accessed April 28, 2005).

Banerjee, Snehamay, and Ram L. Kumar. "Managing Electronic Interchange of Business Documents." *Communications of the ACM* 45, no. 7 (July 2002).

Beep Knowledge System. "Case Demonstration: Manitoulin—Transport Online Tracking (Canada)." http://www.beepknowledgesystem.org/ShowCase.asp?CaseTitleID=285&CaseID=649 (accessed April 28, 2005).

Ben Ameur, Walid, and Herve Kerivin. "New Economical Virtual Private Networks." *Communications of the ACM* 46, no 6 (June 2003).

Berners-Lee, Tim, Robert Cailliau, Ari Luotonen, Henrik Frystyk Nielsen, and Arthur Secret. "The World-Wide Web." *Communications of the ACM* 37, no. 8 (August 1994).

Billsus, Daniel, Clifford A. Brunk, Craig Evans, Brian Gladish, and Michael Pazzani. "Adaptive Interfaces for Ubiquitous Web Access." *Communications of the ACM* 45, no. 5 (May 2002).

Brandt, Richard. "Net Assets." *Stanford Magazine* (November–December 2004).

Chatterjee, Samir, and Suzanne Pawlowski. "All-Optical Networks." *Communications of the ACM* 42, no. 6 (June 1999).

Damsgaard Jan, and Kalle Lyytinen. "Building Electronic Trading Infrastructures: A Public or Private Responsibility?" *Journal of Organizational Computing and Electronic Commerce* 11, no. 2 (2001).

Dutta, Amitava, and Rahul Roy. "Anticipating Internet Diffusion." *Communications of the ACM* 46, no. 2 (February 2003).

The Economist. "The 2005 E-readiness Rankings." http://graphics.eiu.com/files/ad_pdfs/2005Ereadiness_Ranking_WP.pdf (2005, accessed July 31, 2005).

Elgin, Ben, with Jay Greene. "Google." *BusinessWeek* (May 3, 2004).

Ewalt, David M. "The New Voice Choice." *Information Week* (March 1, 2004).

Evans, Mark. "VoIP: What Flavour Would You Like?" *The National Post* (June 24, 2004).

Farhoomand, Ali, Pauline S. P. Ng, and Justin K. H. Yue. "The Building of a New Business Ecosystem: Sustaining National Competitive Advantage through Electronic Commerce." *Journal of Organizational Computing and Electronic Commerce* 11, no. 4 (2001).

Federal Networking Council. "Definition of 'Internet.'" October 24, 1995. http://www.hpcc.gov/fnc/Internet res.html (accessed January 7, 2004).

Festa, Paul. "Point, Click and Swap—Digital Photos Go P2P." CNETNews.com (May 17, 2004).

Frauenfelder, Mark. "Sir Tim Berners-Lee." *Technology Review* (October 2004).

Glezer, Chanan, and Surya B. Yadav. "A Conceptual Model of an Intelligent Catalog Search System." *Journal of Organizational Computing and Electronic Commerce* 11, no. 1 (2001).

Glover, Eric J., Steve Lawrence, Michael D. Gordon, William P. Birmingham, and C. Lee Giles. "Web Search—Your Way." *Communications of the ACM* 44, no. 12 (December 2001).

Grant, Peter. "Ready for Prime Time." *Wall Street Journal* (January 12, 2004).

Grote, Brigitte, Thomas Rose, and Gerhard Peter. "Filter and Broker: An Integrated Architecture for Information Mediation of Dynamic Sources." *Journal of Organizational Computing and Electronic Commerce* 12, no. 2 (2002).

Grover, Varun, and Khawaja Saeed. "The Telecommunication Industry Revisited." *Communications of the ACM* 46, no. 7 (July 2003).

Hearst, Marti, Arne Elliott, Jennifer English, Rashmi Sinha, Kirsten Swearinge, and Ka-Ping Yee. "Finding the Flow in Web Search." *Communications of the ACM* 45, no. 9 (September 2002).

Hong, Weiyin, James Y. L. Thong, and Kar Yan Tam. "Does Animation Attract Online Users' Attention? The Effects of Flash on Information Search Performance and Perceptions." *Information Systems Research* 15, no. 1 (March 2004).

Housel, Tom, and Eric Skopec. *Global Telecommunication Revolution: The Business Perspective.* New York: McGraw-Hill (2001).

Industry Canada. "Communications Service Industries Subscribers 1998–2003". http://strategis.ic.gc.ca/epic/internet/insmt-gst.nsf/en/sf06004e.html#figure2-1-3 (accessed April 20, 2005).

Isakowitz, Tomas, Michael Bieber, and Fabio Vitali. "Web Information Systems." *Communications of the ACM* 41, no. 7 (July 1998).

Kanter, Rosabeth Moss. "The Ten Deadly Mistakes of Wanna-Dots." *Harvard Business Review* (January 2001).

Karahanna, Elena, and Moez Limayem. "E-Mail and V-Mail Usage: Generalizing across Technologies." *Journal of Organizational Computing and Electronic Commerce* 10, no. 1 (2000).

Kautz, Henry, Bart Selman, and Mehul Shah. "ReferralWeb: Combining Social Networks and Collaborative Filtering." *Communications of the ACM* 40, no. 3 (March 1997).

Keen, Peter. "Ready for the 'New' B2B?" *Computerworld* (September 11, 2000).

Keen, Peter G. W. *Competing in Time: Using Telecommunications for Competitive Advantage.* Cambridge, Mass.: Ballinger (1986).

Keewaytinook Okimakanak. "IP Video Conference Locations on K-Net's Network." http://services.knet.ca/graphics/CanadaNew2.gif (accessed April 24, 2005).

Kocas, Cenk. "Evolution of Prices in Electronic Markets under Diffusion of Price-Comparison Shopping." *Journal of Management Information Systems* 19, no. 3 (Winter 2002–2003).

Kuo, Geng-Sheng, and Jing-Pei Lin. "New Design Concepts for an Intelligent Internet." *Communications of the ACM* 41, no. 11 (November 1998).

Lieberman, Henry, Christopher Fry, and Louis Weitzman. "Exploring the Web with Reconnaissance Agents." *Communications of the ACM* 44, no. 8 (August 2001).

Maclean, Susan. "Dialing IP for Increased Productivity." *IT Focus.* (January 1, 2004).

MacNeil, David, and Bill St. Arnaud, "CANARIE: CA*net—Canada's National Innovation Infrastructure." CANARIE, http://www.icsti.org/forum/43/macneil_presentation.ppt (accessed May 8, 2005).

Madden, Mary, and Lee Rainie. "America's Online Pursuits." *Pew Internet and American Life Project* (April 25, 2004).

Maes, Patti, Robert H. Guttman, and Alexandros G. Moukas. "Agents That Buy and Sell." *Communications of the ACM* 42, no. 3 (March 1999).

Mangalindan, Mylene, Nick Wingfield, and Robert A. Guth. "Rising Clout of Google Prompts Rush by Internet Rivals to Adopt." *Wall Street Journal* (July 16, 2003).

Manitoulin Transport. "Electronic PickUps." http://www.manitoulin transport.com/service_portfolio/ecommerce.html (accessed April 28, 2005).

Nasaw, Daniel. "Instant Messages Are Popping Up All Over." *Wall Street Journal* (June 12, 2003).

National Research Council. "The Internet's Coming of Age." Washington, D.C.: National Academy Press (2000).

Ngwenyama, Ojelanki, and Allen S. Lee. "Communication Richness in Electronic Mail: Critical Social Theory and the Contextuality of Meaning." *MIS Quarterly* 21, no. 2 (June 1997).

Papazoglou, Mike P. "Agent-Oriented Technology in Support of E-Business." *Communications of the ACM* 44, no. 4 (April 2001).

Pitkow, James, Hinrich Schutze, Todd Cass, Rob Cooley, Don Turnbull, Andy Edmonds, Eytan Adar, and Thomas Breuel. "Personalized Search." *Communications of the ACM* 45, no. 9 (September 2002).

Pogue, Dave. "Video Chat Software Reviewed." *New York Times Circuits* (June 26, 2003).

Ramstad, Evan, and Ken Brown. "China Expands Phone Service via Internet." *Wall Street Journal* (April 22, 2004).

Roush, Wade. "The Internet Reborn." *Technology Review* (October 2003).

Smith, Steve. "Push Back?" *eContent* (July 2003).

Spangler, Todd. "Voice on Data Networks: A Sound Move?" *Baseline* (March 2004).

Statistics Canada. "Survey of Telecommunications Service Providers." http://strategis.ic.gc.ca/epic/Internet/insmt-gst.nsf/rwapj/rt-fig2-1-1e.pdf/$FILE/rt-fig2-1-1e.pdf (accessed April 20, 2005).

Thompson, Marjorie Sarbough, and Martha S. Feldman. "Electronic Mail and Organizational Communication." *Organization Science* 9, no. 6 (November–December 1998).

Totty, Michael, and Mylene Mangalindan. "As Google Becomes Web's Gatekeeper, Sites Fight to Get In" *Wall Street Journal* (February 26, 2003).

Transport Canada. "E-Commerce and the Canadian Trucking Industry — Handbook." http://www.tc.gc.ca/pol/en/report/E-commerce/HandbookEn/menu.htm (accessed April 28, 2005).

Travis, Paul. "Present a United Front." *Information Week* (August 2, 2004).

Valera, Francisco, Jorge E. López de Vergara, José I. Moreno, Víctor A. Villagrá, and Julio Varshney, Upkar, Andy Snow, Matt McGivern, and Christi Howard, "Voice Over IP." *Communications of the ACM* 45, no. 12 (January 2002).

Vara, Vauhini. "High-Speed Surpasses Dial-Up as Top Home Web Access in U.S." *Wall Street Journal,* August 18, 2004.

Varshney, Upkar, Andy Snow, Matt McGivern, and Christi Howard. "Voice Over IP." *Communications of the ACM* 45, no. 1 (January 2002).

Websense. "Websense in Use at Canada Customs and Revenue Agency." http://ww2.websense.com/docs/CaseStudies/Canada%20Customs%20and%20Revenue%20Agency.pdf (accessed April 20, 2005).

Weiser, Mark. "What Ever Happened to the Next-Generation Internet?" *Communications of the ACM* 44, no. 9 (September 2001).

Whitman, Michael E., Anthony M. Townsend, and Robert J. Alberts. "Considerations for Effective Telecommunications-Use Policy." *Communications of the ACM* 42, no. 6 (June 1999).

Wilson, E. Vance. "Email Winners and Losers." *Communications of the ACM* 45, no. 10 (October 2002).

Chapter 8

Anderson, Rick. "Business: Starbucks: Just Getting Started." *Seattle Weekly* (April 30-May 6, 2003).

Brandt, Richard. "Net Assets." *Stanford Magazine* (November–December 2004).

Brandt, Richard, and Ron Vetter. "Emerging Mobile and Wireless Networks." *Communications of the ACM* 42, no. 6 (June 2000).

Carter, Robert. "Six Degrees of Preparation." *Optimize Magazine* 22 (January 2004).

Cho, Cynthia H. "For More Advertisers, the Medium Is the Text Message." *Wall Street Journal* (August 2, 2004).

CIO Magazine. "RFID Adoption Survey: Current and Future Plans." (June 30, 2004).

Claburn, Thomas. "Watching Out." *Information Week* (February 16, 2004).

Cox, John. "Wireless Sparks Enterprise Network Innovation." *Network World Fusion* (April 28, 2005).

Delaney, Karen J. "Inventory Tool to Launch in Germany." *Wall Street Journal* (January 12, 2004).

Dignan, Larry. "RFID: Hit or Myth?" *Baseline* (February 2004).

Dubowski, Stefan. "Jump into Half-Baked RFID Cake." *Computerworld Canada* (April 29, 2005).

Evans, Robert. "Mobile Phone Users Double Since 2000." *Reuters* (December 9, 2004).

Feder, Barnaby J. "Keeping Better Track from Factory to Checkout." *New York Times* (November 11, 2004).

Fedex Corporation. 10-K Report. http://www.fedex.com.

Foust, Dean. "Big Brown's New Bag." *Business* Week (July 19, 2004).

Geek Zone. "More than 3100 Wi-Fi Hotspots in Starbucks Stores." http://www.geekzone.com (accessed July 19, 2004).

George, Tischelle. "Starbucks' Data to Go." *Information Week* (January 20, 2003).

Gruman, Galen. "UPS vs. FedEx: Head-to-Head on Wireless." *CIO Magazine* (June 1, 2004).

———. "New Technologies Hit Mainstream." *CIO Magazine* (June 1, 2004).

Hellweg, Eric. "Tag—You're It." *Technology Review* (July 2004).

Imielinski, Tomasz, and B. R. Badrinath. "Mobile Wireless Computing: Challenges in Data Management." *Communications of the ACM* 37, no. 10 (October 1994).

Intel Corporation. "Wireless LAN Productivity Studies." http://www.intel.com/ business/bss/infrastructure/wireless/ roi/productivity_studies.htm (accessed July 23, 2004).

Kenny, David, and John F. Marshall. "Contextual Marketing." *Harvard Business Review* (November–December 2000).

Kontzer, Tony. "RFID Flies High with Airplane Makers." *Information Week* (June 14, 2004).

Lehr, William, and Lee W. McKnight. "Wireless Internet Access: 3G vs. WiFi?" Center for eBusiness@MIT (August 2002).

Mears, Rena, and Jason Salzetti. "The New Wireless Enterprise." *Information Week* (September 18, 2000).

Mobile Tech News. "Survey Finds 'Explorative Youth' Market Driving Mobile Phone Use in Canada." http://www.mobiletechnews.com/info/ 2004/11/25/002905.html (November 25, 2004, accessed May 4, 2005).

Nicopolitidis, Petros, Georgios Papademitriou, Mohammad S. Obaidat, and Adreas S. Pomportsis. "The Economics of Wireless Networks." *Communications of the ACM* 47, no. 4 (April 2004).

Niemeyer, Alex, Minsok H. Pak, and Sanjay E. Ramaswamy. "Smart Tags for Your Supply Chain." *McKinsey Quarterly*, no. 4 (2003).

Overby, Christine Spivey. "RFID at What Cost?" *Forrester Research* (March 1, 2004).

Palen, Leysia. "Mobile Telephony in a Connected Life." *Communications of the ACM* 45, no. 3 (March 2003).

Pottie, G. J., and W. J. Kaiser. "Wireless Integrated Network Sensors." *Communications of the ACM* 43, no. 5 (May 2000).

Research in Motion. "BlackBerry Expands Leadership in the Legal Sector with Integrated Email, Phone, and Data Applications." (July 25, 2004).

Rothfeder, Jeffrey. "What's Wrong with RFID?" *CIO Insight* (August 1, 2004).

Rush, Susan. "Starbucks Brews Up More Wi-Fi." *Wireless Week* (July 7, 2004).

———. "Starbucks Canada Brews Wi-Fi," *Wireless Week* (October 7, 2005).

Samuels, Mark. "UPS Wireless Plan Reaches Europe." VNU, http://www.vnunet.com (June 30, 2004).

Sandsmark, Fred. "What You Need to Know about Wireless Networking." *CISCO IQ Magazine* (November–December 2002).

Songini, Marc L. "Wireless CRM Takes to the Field." *Computerworld* (July 12, 2004).

TECSYS. "Customer Case Studies: Hospital Logistics Inc." http://www.tecsys. com/resources/casestudies/hli.shtml (accessed May 4, 2005).

Steinert-Threlkeld, Tom. "Make Mine 'To Stay.'" *Baseline Magazine* (April 2003).

Toronto Wireless User Group. "Canadian hospitals make healthy changes with Intermec." http://www.torwug.org/CaseStudies/local/ Intermec_hospitals.asp (accessed May 4, 2005).

Ulfelder, Steve. "Raising an RFID Ruckus." *NewsFactor Top Tech News* (October 7, 2003).

United Parcel Service. 10-K Report. http://www.ups.com.

Varshney, Upkar. "Multicast Over Wireless Networks." *Communications of the ACM* 45, no. 12 (December 2002).

———. "Networking Support for Mobile Computing." *Communications of the Association for Information Systems* 1 (January 1999).

Vetter, Ron. "The Wireless Web." *Communications of the ACM* 44, no. 3 (March 2001).

Wareham, Jonathan, and Armando Levy. "Who Will Be the Adopters of 3G Mobile Computing Devices? A Profit Estimation of Mobile Telecom Diffusion." *Journal of Organizational Computing and Electronic Commerce* 12, no. 2 (2002).

Wingfield, Nick. "Tomorrow's Wi-Fi." *Wall Street Journal*, May 24, 2004.

Chapter 9

Alberts, David S. "The Economics of Software Quality Assurance." Washington, D.C.: National Computer Conference (1976).

Austen, Ian. "Bank Software Woes Leave Many Canadians Without Money." *New York Times* (June 7, 2004).

Austin, Robert D., and Christopher A. R. Darby. "The Myth of Secure Computing." *Harvard Business Review* (June 2003).

Backhouse, James, Carol Hsu, and Aidan McDonnell. "Toward Public-Key Infrastructure Interoperability." *Communications of the ACM* 46, no. 6 (June 2003).

Bank, David. "Computer Worm Is Turning Faster." *Wall Street Journal* (May 27, 2004).

———. "Mydoom Worm Renews Debate on Cyber-Ethics." *Wall Street Journal* (November 11, 2004).

———. "Outbreak!" *Wall Street Journal* (November 15, 2004).

———. "What's That Sneaking into Your Computer?" *Wall Street Journal* (April 26, 2004).

Banker, Rajiv D., and Chris F. Kemerer. "Performance Evaluation Metrics in Information Systems Development: A Principal-Agent Model." *Information Systems Research* 3, no. 4 (December 1992).

Banker, Rajiv D., Robert J. Kaufmann, and Rachna Kumar. "An Empirical Test of Object-Based Output Measurement Metrics in a Computer-Aided Software Engineering (CASE) Environment." *Journal of Management Information Systems* 8, no. 3 (Winter 1991–1992).

Banker, Rajiv D., Srikant M. Datar, Chris F. Kemerer, and Dani Zweig. "Software Complexity and Maintenance Costs." *Communications of the ACM* 36, no. 11 (November 1993).

Barrett, Jennifer. "Phishing Fall-Out." *Newsweek* (April 15, 2004).

Berghel, Hal. "The Discipline of Internet Forensics." *Communications of the ACM* 46, no. 8 (August 2003).

Borzo, Jeannette. "Something's Phishy." *Wall Street Journal* (November 15, 2004).

Brenner, Susan W. "U.S. Cybercrime Law: Defining Offenses." *Information Systems Frontiers* 6, no. 2 (June 2004).

Bruce, Lindsay. "RBC Glitch Still Not Ironed Out." ITWorldCanada.com (June 7, 2004).

Byers, Simon, and Dave Kormann. "802.11b Access Point Mapping." *Communications of the ACM* 46, no. 5 (May 2003).

Cam Winget, Nancy, Russ Housley, David Wagner, and Jesse Walker. "Security Flaws in 802.11b Data Link Protocols." *Communications of the ACM* 46, no. 5 (May 2003).

Canadian Bankers Association. "Identity Theft: An Old Problem Needing a New Approach" (May 2003).

Canadian Business Franchise Magazine. "Internet Education The Best Defense Against Network Security Threats and Spam." http://www.cgb.ca/ wsi/release3.htm (accessed May 13, 2005).

Canadian Firearms Digest 4, no. 470. January 21, 2002.

Canadian Press. "RBC Still Making Up for Glitch." *London Free Press*, http://www.canoe.ca (accessed June 19, 2004).

Cavusoglu, Huseyin, Birendra Mishra, and Srinivasan Raghunathan. "A Model for Evaluating IT Security Investments." *Communications of the ACM* 47, no. 7 (July 2004).

Chipman, Andrea. "Stealing You." *Wall Street Journal* (April 26, 2004).

Choy, Manhoi, Hong Va Leong, and Man Hon Wong. "Disaster Recovery Techniques for Database Systems." *Communications of the ACM* 43, no. 11 (November 2000).

Conrath, Chris. "Anatomy of a Snafu." ITWorldCanada.com (June 11, 2004).

Darby, Christopher. "The Dollars and Cents of Security." *Optimize Magazine* 12 (October 2002).

Datz, Todd. "The Interactive Nightmare." *CSO Magazine* (April 2004).

Dearne, Karen. "Wesfarmers Trusts Security to Specialists." *Australian IT News* (February 10, 2004).

———. "Wesfarmers Limited Protects Its Resources with Symantec Managed Security Services." http://www.riptech.com/region/au_nz (accessed June 19, 2004).

Deutsche Bank. "Business Continuity Program." http://www.deutsche-bank.de (accessed November 24, 2004).

Dimmock, Gary. "How the Hacker's Luck Ran Out." *The Ottawa Citizen* (January 20, 2002).

Di Pietro, Roberto, and Luigi V. Mancini. "Security and Privacy Issues of Handheld and Wearable Wireless Devices." *Communications of the ACM* 46, no. 9 (September 2003).

Duffy, Daintry. "Body of Evidence." *CSO Magazine* (May 2004).

Durst, Robert, Terrence Champion, Brian Witten, Eric Miller, and Luigi Spagnuolo. "Testing and Evaluating Computer Intrusion Detection Systems." *Communications of the ACM* 42, no. 7 (July 1999).

Duvall, Mel. "RBC's Account Imbalance." *Baseline Magazine* (July 1, 2004).

Federal Computer Week. "Editorial: Time to Apply a Patch." (June 22, 2004).

Finextra. "Royal Bank of Canada Computer Glitch Causes Payments Chaos." http://www.finextra.com/fullstory.asp?id=11948 (June 4, 2004, accessed May 15, 2005).

Finextra. "CIBC Hit by Computer Problem; Westpac Blames Internet Foul-Up on Human Error." http://www.finextra.com/fullstory.asp?id=12411 (August 31, 2004, accessed May 15, 2005).

Fitzgerald, Michael. "At Risk Offshore." *CIO Australia* (April 4, 2004).

Foley, John, and George V. Hulme. "Get Ready to Patch." *Information Week* (August 30, 2004).

Fox, Armando, and David Patterson. "Self-Repairing Computers." *Scientific American* (May 2003).

Ghosh, Anup K., and Tara M. Swaminatha. "Software Security and Privacy Risks in Mobile E-Commerce." *Communications of the ACM* 44, no. 2 (February 2001).

Giordano, Scott M. "Electronic Evidence and the Law." *Information Systems Frontiers* 6, no. 2 (June 2004).

Gordon, Lawrence A., Martin P. Loeb, and Tashfeen Sohail. "A Framework for Using Insurance for Cyber-Risk Management." *Communications of the ACM* 46, no. 3 (March 2003).

Gordon, Lawrence A., Martin P. Loeb, William Lucyshyn, and Robert Richardson. "2004 CSI/FBI Computer Crime and Security Survey." Computer Security Institute (2004).

Hansell, Saul. "Online Swindlers Called 'Phishers' Lure the Unwary." *New York Times* (March 24, 2004).

Horowitz, Alan S. "Biting Back." *Computerworld* (January 13, 2003).

Housley, Russ, and William Arbaugh. "Security Problems in 802.11b Networks." *Communications of the ACM* 46, no. 5 (May 2003).

Hulme, George V. "Under Attack." *Information Week* (July 5, 2004).

Hulme, George V., and Thomas Claburn. "Tiny Evil Things." *Information Week* (April 26, 2004).

Hulme, George and Jennifer Zaino. "Spring Conference: Leave Complacency Out of Business Plans." *InformationWeek* (March 19, 2002).

Ives, Blake, Kenneth R. Walsh, and Helmut Schneider. "The Domino Effect of Password Reuse." *Communications of the ACM* 47, no. 4 (April 2004).

Jajoda, Sushil, Catherine D. McCollum, and Paul Ammann. "Trusted Recovery." *Communications of the ACM* 42, no. 7 (July 1999).

Joshi, James B. D., Walid G. Aref, Arif Ghafoor, and Eugene H. Spafford. "Security Models for Web-Based Applications." *Communications of the ACM* 44, no. 2 (February 2001).

Keizer, Gregg. "Windows XP Service Pack 2: The 10% Problem." *Information Week* (August 31, 2004).

———. "Trojan Horse Poses as Windows XP Update." *Information Week* (January 9, 2004).

Klein, Barbara D., Dale L. Goodhue, and Gordon B. Davis. "Can Humans Detect Errors in Data?" *MIS Quarterly* 21, no. 2 (June 1997).

Laudon, Kenneth C. "Data Quality and Due Process in Large Interorganizational Record Systems." *Communications of the ACM* 29 (January 1986).

Littlewood, Bev, and Lorenzo Strigini. "The Risks of Software." *Scientific American* 267, no. 5 (November 1992).

MacInnis, Patricia. "After Slammer, Canaccord Gets Vaccinated: on the Heels of a Virus Attack, The Investment Firm Got Serious about Patch Management and Was Able to Shave." *Computing Canada* (April 23, 2004).

Marer, Eva, and Patrick Thibodeau. "Companies Confront Rising Network Threats." *Datamation* (July 2, 2001).

Mercuri, Rebecca T. "Analyzing Security Costs." *Communications of the ACM* 46, no. 6 (June 2003).

Neumann, Peter G. "Risks Considered Global(ly)." *Communications of the ACM* 35, no. 1 (January 1993).

Newman, Robert. *Enterprise Security.* Upper Saddle River, N.J.: Prentice Hall (2003).

Oppliger, Rolf. "Internet Security, Firewalls, and Beyond." *Communications of the ACM* 40, no. 7 (May 1997).

Orr, Kenneth. "Data Quality and Systems Theory." *Communications of the ACM* 41, no. 2 (February 1998).

Ottawa Business Journal. "RBC Admits Human Error, Scam Artists Act." (June 10, 2004).

Panko, Raymond R. *Corporate Computer and Network Security.* Upper Saddle River, N.J.: Pearson Prentice Hall (2004).

Phonebusters. "Identity Theft Complaints." http://www.phonebusters. com/english/statistics_E03.html (accessed May 13, 2005).

Pritchard, Kate. "Banking on Technology," EMC Corporation (2004).

Rainer, Rex Kelley, Jr., Charles A. Snyder, and Houston H. Carr. "Risk Analysis for Information Technology." *Journal of Management Information Systems* 8, no. 1 (Summer 1991).

Ravichandran, T., and Arun Rai. "Total Quality Management in Information Systems Development." *Journal of Management Information Systems* 16, no. 3 (Winter 1999–2000).

Redman, Thomas. "The Impact of Poor Data Quality on the Typical Enterprise." *Communications of the ACM* 41, no. 2 (February 1998).

Roberts, Mary Lou. "iSeries Disaster Recovery Heads North of the Border." iSeries Network. http://www.iseriesnetwork.com/resources/ artarchive/index.cfm?fuseaction=viewarticle&CO_ContentID=195 36&channel=art&PageView=Search (November 15, 2004, accessed May 14, 2005).

Roche, Edward M., and George Van Nostrand. *Information Systems, Computer Crime and Criminal Justice.* New York: Barraclough (2004).

Russell, Bruce, and Sangit Chatterjee. "Relationship Quality: The Undervalued Dimension of Software Quality." *Communications of the ACM* 46, no. 8 (August 2003).

Sarkar, Pushpak. "A Paragon of Quality." *Intelligent Enterprise* (October 2002).

Schmerken, Ivy. "Offshore Outsourcing: Is Your Data Safe?" *Wall Street and Technology* (May 2004).

Schwerha, Joseph J., IV. "Cybercrime: Legal Standards Governing the Collection of Digital Evidence." *Information Systems Frontiers* 6, no. 2 (June 2004).

Slaughter, Sandra A., Donald E. Harter, and Mayuram S. Krishnan. "Evaluating the Cost of Software Quality." *Communications of the ACM* 41, no. 8 (August 1998).

Stillerman, Matthew, Carla Marceau, and Maureen Stillman. "Intrusion Detection for Distributed Applications." *Communications of the ACM* 42, no. 7 (July 1999).

Straub, Detmar W., and Richard J. Welke. "Coping with Systems Risk: Security Planning Models for Management Decision Making." *MIS Quarterly* 22, no. 4 (December 1998).

Strong, Diane M., Yang W. Lee, and Richard Y. Wang. "Data Quality in Context." *Communications of the ACM* 40, no. 5 (May 1997).

Tayi, Giri Kumar, and Donald P. Ballou. "Examining Data Quality." *Communications of the ACM* 41, no. 2 (February 1998).

Thomson, Iain. "Akamai Investigates Denial of Service Attack." *Personal Computer World,* http://www.pcw.co.uk/news/1155955 (accessed June 17, 2004).

Toh, Ann. "The Business of Security." *CIO Asia* (January 2004).

Totty, Michael. "Business Solutions: The Dangers in Outbound E-Mail" *Wall Street Journal* (April 26, 2003).

Tucker, Bill. "SoBig.F Breaks Virus Speed Records." CNN (August 22, 2003).

Tynan, Craig K., and Joey F. George. "Improving Software Inspections with Group Process Support." *Communications of the ACM* 45, no. 9 (September 2002).

Viega, John, Tadayoshi Koho, and Bruce Potter. "Trust (and Mistrust) in Secure Applications." *Communications of the ACM* 44, no. 2 (February 2001).

Vijayan, Jaikumar. "Unprepared Firms Slammed." *Computerworld* (February 3, 2003).

Visa Canada. "Report Reveals Phishing Attacks are Growing at an Alarming Rate." http://www.visa.ca/en/about/mc_article.cfm?pid=44 (accessed May 13, 2005).

Volonino, Linda, and Stephen R. Robinson. *Principles and Practices of Information Security.* Upper Saddle River, N.J.: Prentice Hall (2004).

Wagstaff, Jeremy. "Gone Phishing: Web Scam Takes Dangerous Turns." *Wall Street Journal* (May 27, 2004).

Waldie, Paul. "RBC Calls in Help." *The Globe and Mail*, http://www.theglobeandmail.com (accessed June 19, 2004).

Wand, Yair, and Richard Y. Wang. "Anchoring Data Quality Dimensions in Ontological Foundations." *Communications of the ACM* 39, no. 11 (November 1996).

Wang, Huaiqing, and Chen Wang. "Taxonomy of Security Considerations and Software Quality." *Communications of the ACM* 46, no. 6 (June 2003).

Wang, Richard. "A Product Perspective on Total Data Quality Management." *Communications of the ACM* 41, no. 2 (February 1998).

Wang, Richard Y., Yang W. Lee, Leo L. Pipino, and Diane M. Strong. "Manage Your Information as a Product." *Sloan Management Review* 39, no. 4 (Summer 1998).

Weber, Ron. *Information Systems Control and Audit*. New York: McGraw-Hill (1999).

Whitman, Michael E. "Enemy at the Gate: Threats to Information Security." *Communications of the ACM* 46, no. 8 (August 2003).

Ye, Nong, Joseph Giordano, and John Feldman. "A Process Control Approach to Cyber Attack Detection." *Communications of the ACM* 44, no. 8 (August 2001).

Zhou, Jianying. "Achieving Fair Nonrepudiation in Electronic Transactions." *Journal of Organizational Computing and Electronic Commerce* 11, no. 4 (2001).

Zviran, Moshe, and William J. Haga. "Password Security: An Empirical Study." *Journal of Management Information Systems* 15, no. 4 (Spring 1999).

Chapter 10

Agarwal, Ritu, Prabudda De, Atish P. Sinha, and Mohan Tanniru. "On the Usability of OO Representations." *Communications of the ACM* 43, no. 10 (October 2000).

Agarwal, Ritu, Jayesh Prasad, Mohan Tanniru, and John Lynch. "Risks of Rapid Application Development." *Communications of the ACM* 43, no. 11 (November 2000).

Alavi, Maryam. "An Assessment of the Prototyping Approach to Information System Development." *Communications of the ACM* 27 (June 1984).

Alavi, Maryam, R. Ryan Nelson, and Ira R. Weiss. "Strategies for End-User Computing: An Integrative Framework." *Journal of Management Information Systems* 4, no. 3 (Winter 1987–1988).

Albert, Terri C., Paulo B. Goes, and Alok Gupta. "GIST: A Model for Design and Management of Content and Interactivity of Customer-Centric Web Sites." *MIS Quarterly* 28, no. 2 (June 2004).

Arinze, Bay, and Murugan Anandarajan. "A Framework for Using OO Mapping Methods to Rapidly Configure ERP Systems." *Communications of the ACM* 46, no. 2 (February 2003).

Avison, David E., and Guy Fitzgerald. "Where Now for Development Methodologies?" *Communications of the ACM* 41, no. 1 (January 2003).

Barthelemy, Jerome. "The Hidden Costs of IT Outsourcing." *Sloan Management Review* (Spring 2001).

Barua, Anitesh, Sophie C. H. Lee, and Andrew B. Whinston. "The Calculus of Reengineering." *Information Systems Research* 7, no. 4 (December 1996).

Baskerville, Richard L., and Jan Stage. "Controlling Prototype Development through Risk Analysis." *MIS Quarterly* 20, no. 4 (December 1996).

Boehm, Barry W. "Understanding and Controlling Software Costs." *IEEE Transactions on Software Engineering* 14, no. 10 (October 1988).

Broadbent, Marianne, Peter Weill, and Don St. Clair. "The Implications of Information Technology Infrastructure for Business Process Redesign." *MIS Quarterly* 23, no. 2 (June 1999).

Bullen, Christine, and John F. Rockart. "A Primer on Critical Success Factors." Cambridge, Mass.: Center for Information Systems Research, Sloan School of Management (1981).

Bushell, Sue. "Blazing a Strategy Trail." *CIO Australia* (June 2, 2004).

Canadian National Railway. "Transloading Services." http://www.cn.ca/productsservices/transloading/en_KFTransloading.shtml (accessed May 19, 2005).

———. "CN CargoFlo." http://www.cn.ca/productsservices/transloading/en_KFCargoFlo.shtml (accessed May 19, 2005).

Champy, James A. *X-Engineering the Corporation: Reinventing Your Business in the Digital Age*. New York: Warner Books (2002).

Chiang, I. Robert, and Vijay S. Mookerjee. "A Fault Threshold Policy to Manage Software Development Projects." *Information Systems Research* 15, no. 1 (March 2004).

Curbera, Francisco, Rania Khalaf, Nirmal Mukhi, Stefan Tai, and Sanjiva Weerawarana. "The Next Step in Web Services." *Communications of the ACM* 46, no. 10 (October 2003).

Davenport, Thomas H., and James E. Short. "The New Industrial Engineering: Information Technology and Business Process Redesign." *Sloan Management Review* 31, no. 4 (Summer 1990).

Davidson, Elisabeth J. "Technology Frames and Framing: A Socio-Cognitive Investigation of Requirements Determination." *MIS Quarterly* 26, no. 4 (December 2002).

Davidson, W. H. "Beyond Engineering: The Three Phases of Business Transformation." *IBM Systems Journal* 32, no. 1 (1993).

Davis, Gordon B. "Determining Management Information Needs: A Comparison of Methods." *MIS Quarterly* 1 (June 1977).

———. "Strategies for Information Requirements Determination." *IBM Systems Journal* 1 (1982).

DeMarco, Tom. *Structured Analysis and System Specification*. New York: Yourdon Press (1978).

Den Hengst, Marielle, and Gert-Jan DeVreede. "Collaborative Business Engineering: A Decade of Lessons from the Field." *Journal of Management Information Systems* 20, no. 4 (Spring 2004).

Earl, Michael, and Bushra Khan. "E-Commerce Is Changing the Face of IT." *Sloan Management Review* (Fall 2001).

Earl, Michael J. "The Risks of Outsourcing." *Sloan Management Review* 37(3), 26-32. (Spring 1996).

Ein Dor, Philip, and Eli Segev. "Strategic Planning for Management Information Systems." *Management Science* 24, no. 15 (1978).

El Sawy, Omar A. *Redesigning Enterprise Processes for E-Business*. New York: McGraw-Hill (2001).

Ferris, C. and Farrell, J. "What are web services?" *Communications of the ACM* Vol. 46, No. 6. 31 (2003).

Fingar, Peter. "Component-Based Frameworks for E-Commerce." *Communications of the ACM* 43, no. 10 (October 2000).

Fischer, G., E. Giaccardi, Y. Ye, A. G. Sutcliffe, and N. Mehandjiev. "Meta-Design: A Manifesto for End-User Development." *Communications of the ACM* 47, no. 9 (September 2004).

Gane, Chris, and Trish Sarson. *Structured Systems Analysis: Tools and Techniques*. Englewood Cliffs, N.J.: Prentice Hall (1979).

Gefen, David, and Catherine M. Ridings. "Implementation Team Responsiveness and User Evaluation of Customer Relationship Management: A Quasi-Experimental Design Study of Social Exchange Theory." *Journal of Management Information Systems* 19, no. 1 (Summer 2002).

Gemino, Andrew, and Yair Wand. "Evaluating Modeling Techniques Based on Models of Learning." *Communications of the ACM* 46, no. 10 (October 2003).

Grant, Delvin. "A Wider View of Business Process Engineering." *Communications of the ACM* 45, no. 2 (February 2002).

Grunbacher, Paul, Michael Halling, Stefan Biffl, Hasan Kitapci, and Barry W. Boehm. "Integrating Collaborative Processes and Quality Assurance Techniques: Experiences from Requirements Negotiation." *Journal of Management Information Systems* 20, no. 4 (Spring 2004).

Hagel III, John, and John Seeley Brown. "Your Next IT Strategy." *Harvard Business Review* (October, 2001).

Hammer, Michael. "Process Management and the Future of Six Sigma." *Sloan Management Review* 43, no. 2 (Winter 2002).

———. "Reengineering Work: Don't Automate, Obliterate." *Harvard Business Review* (July–August 1990).

Hammer, Michael, and James Champy. *Reengineering the Corporation*. New York: HarperCollins (1993).

Hickey, Ann M., and Alan M. Davis. "A Unified Model of Requirements Elicitation." *Journal of Management Information Systems* 20, no. 4 (Spring 2004).

Hirscheim, Rudy, and Mary Lacity. "The Myths and Realities of Information Technology Insourcing." *Communications of the ACM* 43, no. 2 (February 2000).

Hoffer, Jeffrey, Joey George, and Joseph Valacich. *Modern Systems Analysis and Design*, 3rd ed. Upper Saddle River, N.J.: Prentice Hall (2002).

Hopkins, Jon. "Component Primer." *Communications of the ACM* 43, no. 10 (October 2000).

Huizing, Ard, Esther Koster, and Wim Bouman. "Balance in Business Process Reengineering: An Empirical Study of Fit and Performance." Journal of Management Information Systems 14, no. 1 (Summer 1997).

IBM. "Scotiabank Streamlines Business Processes Using IBM Software." http://www-306.ibm.com/software/success/cssdb.nsf/csp/bloz-5qzqa8 (accessed May 23, 2005).

———. "WebSphere MQ Workflow for z/OS." http://www-306.ibm.com/software/integration/wmqwf/editions/zos.html (accessed May 23, 2005).

Information Builders. "Canadian National Railway Turns to FOCUS to Modernize Inventory Control System." http://www.information builders.com/applications/cn-rail.html (accessed May 19, 2005).

Irwin, Gretchen. "The Role of Similarity in the Reuse of Object-Oriented Analysis Models." *Journal of Management Information Systems* 19, no. 2 (Fall 2002).

Ivari, Juhani, Rudy Hirscheim, and Heinz K. Klein. "A Dynamic Framework for Classifying Information Systems Development Methodologies and Approaches." *Journal of Management Information Systems* 17, no. 3 (Winter 2000–2001).

Iyer, Bala, Jim Freedman, Mark Gaynor, and George Wyner. "Web Services: Enabling Dynamic Business Networks." *Communications of the Association for Information Systems* 11 (2003).

Johnson, Richard A. "The Ups and Downs of Object-Oriented Systems Development." *Communications of the ACM* 43, no. 10 (October 2000).

Keen, Peter G.W. *Shaping the Future: Business Design through Information Technology.* Cambridge, Mass.: Harvard Business School Press (1991).

Kendall, Kenneth E., and Julie E. Kendall. *Systems Analysis and Design*, 5th ed. Upper Saddle River, N.J.: Prentice Hall (2002).

Klein, Gary, James J. Jiang, and Debbie B. Tesch. "Wanted: Project Teams with a Blend of IS Professional Orientations." *Communications of the ACM* 45, no. 6 (June 2002).

Lacity, M. C., and Willcocks, L. P. "An Empirical Investigation of Information Technology Sourcing Practices: Lessons from Experience." *MIS Quarterly* 22, no. 3 (September 1998).

Lacity, M.C., Willcocks, L.P., and Feeny, D.F. "The Value of Selective IT Sourcing." *Sloan Management Review*, 37(3). pp. 13-25 (1996).

Lee, Jae Nam, and Young-Gul Kim. "Effect of Partnership Quality on IS Outsourcing Success." *Journal of Management Information Systems* 15, no. 4 (Spring 1999).

Lee, Jae Nam, Shaila M. Miranda, and Yong-Mi Kim. "IT Outsourcing Strategies: Universalistic, Contingency, and Configurational Explanations of Success." *Information Systems Research* 15, no. 2 (June 2004).

Lee, Jae-Nam, Minh Q. Huynh, Ron Chi-wai Kwok, and Shih-Ming Pi. "IT Outsourcing Evolution—Past, Present, and Future." *Communications of the ACM* 46, no. 5 (May 2003).

Levina, Natalia, and Jeanne W. Ross. "From the Vendor's Perspective: Exploring the Value Proposition in Information Technology Outsourcing." *MIS Quarterly* 27, no. 3 (September 2003).

Lientz, Bennett P., and E. Burton Swanson. *Software Maintenance Management.* Reading, Mass.: Addison-Wesley (1980).

Limayem, Moez, Mohamed Khalifa, and Wynne W. Chin. "Case Tools Usage and Impact on System Development Performance." *Journal of Organizational Computing and Electronic Commerce* 14, no. 3 (2004).

Lunt, Penny. "Well-Oiled Machines. BPM Projects Point to Success." *Transform Magazine* (April 2003).

Martin, James. *Application Development without Programmers.* Englewood Cliffs, N.J.: Prentice Hall (1982).

Martin, James, and Carma McClure. *Structured Techniques: The Basis of CASE.* Englewood Cliffs, N.J.: Prentice Hall (1988).

Mazzucchelli, Louis. "Structured Analysis Can Streamline Software Design." *Computerworld* (December 9, 1985).

Middlemiss, Jim. "Financial Institutions Tackle Wealth-Management Technology." *Wall Street & Technology,* http://www.wstonline.com/story/supp/WST20020408S0003 (April 8, 2002, accessed May 19, 2005).

Nerson, Jean-Marc. "Applying Object-Oriented Analysis and Design." *Communications of the ACM* 35, no. 9 (September 1992).

Nidumolu, Sarma R., and Mani Subramani. "The Matrix of Control: Combining Process and Structure Approaches to Managing Software Development." *Journal of Management Information Systems* 20, no. 4 (Winter 2004).

Nissen, Mark E. "Redesigning Reengineering through Measurement-Driven Inference." *MIS Quarterly* 22, no. 4 (December 1998).

Pancake, Cherri M. "The Promise and the Cost of Object Technology: A Five-Year Forecast." *Communications of the ACM* 38, no. 10 (October 1995).

Parker, M. M. "Enterprise Information Analysis: Cost-Benefit Analysis and the Data-Managed System." *IBM Systems Journal* 21 (1982).

Parsons, Jeffrey, and Yair Wand. "Using Objects for Systems Analysis." *Communications of the ACM* 40, no. 12 (December 1997).

Patel, Samir, and Suneel Saigal. "When Computers Learn to Talk: A Web Services Primer." *The McKinsey Quarterly* no. 1 (2002).

Peffers, Ken, and Charles E. Gengler. "How to Identify New High-Payoff Information Systems for the Organization." *Communications of the ACM* 41, no. 1 (January 2003).

Phillips, James, and Dan Foody. "Building a Foundation for Web Services." *EAI Journal* (March 2002).

Pitts, Mitzi G., and Glenn J. Browne. "Stopping Behavior of Systems Analysts During Information Requirements Elicitation." *Journal of Management Information Systems* 21, no. 1 (Summer 2004).

Prahalad, C. K., and M. S. Krishnan. "Synchronizing Strategy and Information Technology." *Sloan Management Review* 43, no. 4 (Summer 2002).

Ravichandran, T., and Marcus A. Rothenberger. "Software Reuse Strategies and Component Markets." *Communications of the ACM* 46, no. 8 (August 2003).

Rivard, Suzanne, and Sid L. Huff. "Factors of Success for End-User Computing." *Communications of the ACM* 31, no. 5 (May 1988).

Rockart, John F. "Chief Executives Define Their Own Data Needs." *Harvard Business Review* (March–April 1979).

Rockart, John F., and Lauren S. Flannery. "The Management of End-User Computing." *Communications of the ACM* 26, no. 10 (October 1983).

Rockart, John F., and Michael E. Treacy. "The CEO Goes On-Line." *Harvard Business Review* (January–February 1982).

Sabherwahl, Rajiv. "The Role of Trust in IS Outsourcing Development Projects." *Communications of the ACM* 42, no. 2 (February 1999).

Scott, Louise, Levente Horvath, and Donald Day. "Characterizing CASE Constraints." *Communications of the ACM* 43, no. 11 (November 2000).

Shank, Michael E., Andrew C. Boynton, and Robert W. Zmud. "Critical Success Factor Analysis as a Methodology for MIS Planning." *MIS Quarterly* (June 1985).

Sharma, Srinarayan, and Arun Rai. "CASE Deployment in IS Organizations." *Communications of the ACM* 43, no. 1 (January 2000).

Sircar, Sumit, Sridhar P. Nerur, and Radhakanta Mahapatra. "Revolution or Evolution? A Comparison of Object-Oriented and Structured Systems Development Methods." *MIS Quarterly* 25, no. 4 (December 2001).

Smith, Howard, and Peter Fingar. *Business Process Management: The Third Wave.* Tampa, Fla.: Meghan-Kiffer Press (2002).

Sprott, David. "Componentizing the Enterprise Application Packages." *Communications of the ACM* 43, no. 3 (April 2000).

Swanson, E. Burton, and Enrique Dans. "System Life Expectancy and the Maintenance Effort: Exploring their Equilibration." *MIS Quarterly* 24, no. 2 (June 2000).

Tam, Kar Yan, and Kai Lung Hui. "A Choice Model for the Selection of Computer Vendors and Its Empirical Estimation." *Journal of Management Information Systems* 17, no. 4 (Spring 2001).

Turetken, Ozgur, David Schuff, Ramesh Sharda, and Terence T. Ow. "Supporting Systems Analysis and Design through Fisheye Views." *Communications of the ACM* 47, no. 9 (September 2004).

Van Den Heuvel, Willem-Jan, and Zakaria Maamar. "Moving Toward a Framework to Compose Intelligent Web Services." *Communications of the ACM* 46, no. 10 (October 2003).

Venkatraman, N. "Beyond Outsourcing: Managing IT Resources as a Value Center." *Sloan Management Review* (Spring 1997).

Vessey, Iris, and Sue Conger. "Learning to Specify Information Requirements: The Relationship between Application and Methodology." *Journal of Management Information Systems* 10, no. 2 (Fall 1993).

Vitharana, Padmal. "Risks and Challenges of Component-Based Software Development." *Communications of the ACM* 46, no. 8 (August 2003).

Watad, Mahmoud M., and Frank J. DiSanzo. "Case Study: The Synergism of Telecommuting and Office Automation." *Sloan Management Review* 41, no. 2 (Winter 2000).

Wulf, Volker, and Matthias Jarke. "The Economics of End-User Development." *Communications of the ACM* 47, no. 9 (September 2004).

Yourdon, Edward, and L. L. Constantine. *Structured Design.* New York: Yourdon Press (1978).

Zachman, J. A. "Business Systems Planning and Business Information Control Study: A Comparison." *IBM Systems Journal* 21 (1982).

Chapter 11

Agarwal, Ritu, and Viswanath Venkatesnh. "Assessing a Firm's Web Presence: A Heuristic Evaluation Procedure for the Measurement of Usability." *Information Systems Research* 13, no. 3 (September 2002).

Aladwani, Adel M. "An Integrated Performance Model of Information Systems Projects." *Journal of Management Information Systems* 19, no. 1 (Summer 2002).

Alleman, James. "Real Options Real Opportunities." *Optimize Magazine* (January 2002).

Alter, Steven, and Michael Ginzberg. "Managing Uncertainty in MIS Implementation." *Sloan Management Review* 20 (Fall 1978).

"American Airlines Cargo to Join Unisys-Operated Cargo Portal Services." *Logistics Management.* May 2, 2005.

Andres, Howard P., and Robert W. Zmud. "A Contingency Approach to Software Project Coordination." *Journal of Management Information Systems* 18, no. 3 (Winter 2001–2002).

Armstrong, Curtis P., and V. Sambamurthy. "Information Technology Assimilation in Firms: The Influence of Senior Leadership and IT Infrastructures." *Information Systems Research* 10, no. 4 (December 1999).

Asohan, A. "MDC launches two new APICTA initiatives." http://www.unreal mind.com/press_release_7.htm (August 2, 2003, accessed May 21, 2005).

Attewell, Paul. "Technology Diffusion and Organizational Learning: The Case of Business Computing." *Organization Science*, no. 3 (1992).

Banker, Rajiv. "Value Implications of Relative Investments in Information Technology." Department of Information Systems and Center for Digital Economy Research, University of Texas at Dallas (January 23, 2001).

Barki, Henri, and Jon Hartwick. "Interpersonal Conflict and Its Management in Information Systems Development." *MIS Quarterly* 25, no. 2 (June 2001).

Barki, Henri, Suzanne Rivard, and Jean Talbot. "An Integrative Contingency Model of Software Project Risk Management." *Journal of Management Information Systems* 17, no. 4 (Spring 2001).

Baudisch, Patrick, Doug DeCarlo, Andrew T. Duchowski, and Wilson S. Geisler. "Focusing on the Essential: Considering Attention in Display Design." *Communications of the ACM* 46, no. 3 (March 2003).

Beath, Cynthia Mathis, and Wanda J. Orlikowski. "The Contradictory Structure of Systems Development Methodologies: Deconstructing the IS-User Relationship in Information Engineering." *Information Systems Research* 5, no. 4 (December 1994).

Benaroch, Michel. "Managing Information Technology Investment Risk: A Real Options Perspective." *Journal of Management Information Systems* 19, no. 2 (Fall 2002).

Benaroch, Michel, and Robert J. Kauffman. "Justifying Electronic Banking Network Expansion Using Real Options Analysis." *MIS Quarterly* 24, no. 2 (June 2000).

Bharadwaj, Anandhi. "A Resource-Based Perspective on Information Technology Capability and Firm Performance." *MIS Quarterly* 24, no. 1 (March 2000).

Bhattacherjee, Ano. "Understanding Information Systems Continuance: An Expectation-Confirmation Model." *MIS Quarterly* 25, no. 3 (September 2001).

Bhattacherjee, Anol, and G. Premkumar. "Understanding Changes in Belief and Attitude Toward Information Technology Usage: A Theoretical Model and Longitudinal Test." *MIS Quarterly* 28, no. 2 (June 2004).

Bikson, Tora K., Cathleen Stasz, and Donald A. Monkin. "Computer-Mediated Work: Individual and Organizational Impact on One Corporate Headquarters." The Rand Corporation (1985).

Boer, F. Peter. "Real Options: The IT Investment Risk Buster." *Optimize Magazine* (July 2002).

Bostrom, R. P., and J. S. Heinen. "MIS Problems and Failures: A Socio-Technical Perspective. Part I: The Causes." *MIS* Quarterly 1 (September 1977); "Part II: The Application of Socio-Technical Theory." MIS Quarterly 1 (December 1977).

Brabston, Mary, Robert Zmud, and John Carlson, "Strategic Vision for Information Technology." in *Strategic Information Technology: Opportunities for Competitive Advantage,* edited by Raymond Papp, Idea Group Publishing (2000).

Brooks, Frederick P. "The Mythical Man-Month." *Datamation* (December 1974).

Brynjolfsson, Erik. "The Contribution of Information Technology to Consumer Welfare." *Information Systems Research* 7, no. 3 (September 1996).

———. "The IT Productivity GAP." *Optimize* 21 (July 2003).

———. "The Productivity Paradox of Information Technology." *Communications of the ACM* 36, no. 12 (December 1993).

Brynjolfsson, Erik, and Lorin M. Hitt. "Beyond the Productivity Paradox." *Communications of the ACM* 41, no. 8 (August 1998).

———. "Information Technology and Organizational Design: Evidence from Micro Data." (January 1998).

———. "Is Information Systems Spending Productive? New Evidence and New Results." Proceedings of the 14th Annual International Conference on Information Systems, Orlando, FL (December, 1993).

———. "Paradox Lost? Firm-Level Evidence on the Returns to Information Systems." *Management Science* 42, no. 4 (1996).

Brynjolfsson, Erik, Lorin M. Hitt, and Shinkyu Yang "Intangible Assets: Computers and Organizational Capital." Brookings Papers on Economic Activity (2002).

Brynjolfsson, Erik, and S. Yang. "Intangible Assets: How the Interaction of Computers and Organizational Structure Affects Stock Markets." MIT Sloan School of Management (2000).

Buss, Martin D. J. "How to Rank Computer Projects." *Harvard Business Review* (January 1983).

Chatterjee, Debabroto, Rajdeep Grewal, and V. Sabamurthy. "Shaping Up for E-Commerce: Institutional Enablers of the Organizational Assimilation of Web Technologies." *MIS Quarterly* 26, no. 2 (June 2002).

Chatterjee, Debabroto, Carl Pacini, and V. Sambamurthy. "The Shareholder-Wealth and Trading Volume Effects of Information Technology Infrastructure Investments." *Journal of Management Information Systems* 19, no. 2 (Fall 2002).

Chau, Patrick Y. K., and Vincent S. K. Lai. "An Empirical Investigation of the Determinants of User Acceptance of Internet Banking." *Journal of Organizational Computing and Electronic Commerce* 13, no. 2 (2003).

Clement, Andrew, and Peter Van den Besselaar. "A Retrospective Look at PD Projects." *Communications of the ACM* 36, no. 4 (June 1993).

Concours Group. "Delivering Large-Scale System Projects." (2000).

Cooper, Randolph B. "Information Technology Development Creativity: A Case Study of Attempted Radical Change." *MIS Quarterly* 24, no. 2 (June 2000).

Datz, Todd. "Portfolio Management: How to Do It Right." *CIO* (May 1, 2003).

Davamanirajan, Prabu, Tridas Mukhopadhyay, and Charles Kriebel. "Assessing the Business Value of Information Technology in Global Wholesale Banking: The Case of Trade Services." *Journal of Organizational Computing and Electronic Commerce* 12, no. 1 (2002).

Davern, Michael J., and Robert J. Kauffman. "Discovering Potential and Realizing Value from Information Technology Investments." *Journal of Management Information Systems* 16, no. 4 (Spring 2000).

Davis, Fred R. "Perceived Usefulness, Ease of Use, and User Acceptance of Information Technology." *MIS Quarterly* 13, no. 3 (September 1989).

De Berranger, Pascal, David Tucker, and Laurie Jones. "Internet Diffusion in Creative Micro-Businesses: Identifying Change Agent Characteristics as Critical Success Factors." *Journal of Organizational Computing and Electronic Commerce* 11, no. 3 (2001).

De Meyer, Arnoud, Christoph H. Loch, and Michael T. Pich. "Managing Project Uncertainty: From Variation to Chaos." *Sloan Management Review* 43, no. 2 (Winter 2002).

Delone, William H., and Ephraim R. McLean. "The Delone and McLean Model of Information Systems Success: A Ten-Year Update." *Journal of Management Information Systems* 19, no. 4 (Spring 2003).

Dempsey, Jed, Robert E. Dvorak, Endre Holen, David Mark, and William F. Meehan III. "A Hard and Soft Look at IT Investments." *McKinsey Quarterly,* no. 1 (1998).

Doll, William J. "Avenues for Top Management Involvement in Successful MIS Development." *MIS Quarterly* (March 1985).

Doll, William J., Xiaodung Deng, T. S. Raghunathan, Gholamreza Torkzadeh, and Weidong Xia. "The Meaning and Measurement of User Satisfaction: A Multigroup Invariance Analysis of End-User Computing Satisfaction Instrument." *Journal of Management Information Systems* 21, no. 1 (Summer 2004).

Dos Santos, Brian. "Justifying Investments in New Information Technologies." *Journal of Management Information Systems* 7, no. 4 (Spring 1991).

Ein-Dor, Philip, and Eli Segev. "Organizational Context and the Success of Management Information Systems." *Management Science* 24 (June 1978).

El Sawy, Omar, and Burt Nanus. "Toward the Design of Robust Information Systems." *Journal of Management Information Systems* 5, no. 4 (Spring 1989).

Enterprise Networks and Servers. "Cargo Portal Services Launches Two New Services." (October 2004).

Fichman, Robert G. "Real Options and IT Platforms Adoption: Implications for Theory and Practice." *Information Systems Research* 15, no. 2 (June 2004).

———. "The Role of Aggregation in the Measurement of IT-Related Organizational Innovation." *MIS Quarterly* 25, no. 4 (December 2001).

Fichman, Robert G., and Scott A. Moses. "An Incremental Process for Software Implementation." *Sloan Management Review* 40, no. 2 (Winter 1999).

Frank, Robert, and Robin Sidel. "Firms That Lived by the Deal in '90s Now Sink by the Dozens." *Wall Street Journal* (June 6, 2002).

Franz, Charles, and Daniel Robey. "An Investigation of User-Led System Design: Rational and Political Perspectives." *Communications of the ACM* 27 (December 1984).

Gefen, David, and Catherine M. Ridings. "Implementation Team Responsiveness and User Evaluation of Customer Relationship Management: A Quasi-Experimental Design Study of Social Exchange Theory." *Journal of Management Information Systems* 19, no. 1 (Summer 2002).

Giaglis, George. "Focus Issue on Legacy Information Systems and Business Process Change: On the Integrated Design and Evaluation of Business Processes and Information Systems." *Communications of the Association for Information Systems* 2 (July 1999).

Ginzberg, Michael J. "Early Diagnosis of MIS Implementation Failure: Promising Results and Unanswered Questions." *Management Science* 27 (April 1981).

Hitt, L. M. and E. Brynjolfsson. "Productivity, Business Profitability, and Consumer Surplus: Three Different Measures of Information Technology Value." *MIS Quarterly* (20) 2 (1996).

Hitt, Lorin, D. J. Wu, and Xiaoge Zhou. "Investment in Enterprise Resource Planning: Business Impact and Productivity Measures." *Journal of Management Information Systems* 19, no. 1 (Summer 2002).

Housel, Thomas J., Omar El Sawy, Jianfang J. Zhong, and Waymond Rodgers. "Measuring the Return on e-Business Initiatives at the Process Level: The Knowledge Value-Added Approach." *ICIS* (2001).

Hunton, James E., and Beeler, Jesse D. "Effects of User Participation in Systems Development: A Longitudinal Field Study." *MIS Quarterly* 21, no. 4 (December 1997).

International Air Transport Association. "Welcome to the Cargo 2000 Web Page." http://www.iata.org/WHIP/Public/frmMain_Public. aspx?WgId=93#3 (accessed October 12, 2005).

Irani, Zahir, and Peter E. D. Love. "The Propagation of Technology Management Taxonomies for Evaluating Investments in Information Systems." *Journal of Management Information Systems* 17, no. 3 (Winter 2000–2001).

Iversen, Jakob H., Lars Mathiassen, and Peter Axel Nielsen. "Managing Risk in Software Process Improvement: An Action Research Approach." *MIS Quarterly* 28, no. 3 (September 2004).

Jeffrey, Mark, and Ingmar Leliveld. "Best Practices in IT Portfolio Management." *MIT Sloan Management Review* 45, no. 3 (Spring 2004).

Jiang, James J., Gary Klein, Debbie Tesch, and Hong-Gee Chen. "Closing the User and Provider Service Quality Gap." *Communications of the ACM* 46, no. 2 (February 2003).

Johnson, Bradford C. "The Wal-Mart Effect: Information technology isn't the whole story behind productivity." *The McKinsey Quarterly* (January 2002).

Joshi, Kailash. "A Model of Users' Perspective on Change: The Case of Information Systems Technology Implementation." *MIS Quarterly* 15, no. 2 (June 1991).

Keen, Peter W. "Information Systems and Organizational Change." *Communications of the ACM* 24 (January 1981).

Keil, Mark, and Ramiro Montealegre. "Cutting Your Losses: Extricating Your Organization When a Big Project Goes Awry." *Sloan Management Review* 41, no. 3 (Spring 2000).

Keil, Mark, and Daniel Robey. "Blowing the Whistle on Troubled Software Projects." *Communications of the ACM* 44, no. 4 (April 2001).

Keil, Mark, Joan Mann, and Arun Rai. "Why Software Projects Escalate: An Empirical Analysis and Test of Four Theoretical Models." *MIS Quarterly* 24, no. 4 (December 2000).

Keil, Mark, Paul E. Cule, Kalle Lyytinen, and Roy C. Schmidt. "A Framework for Identifying Software Project Risks." *Communications of the ACM* 41, no. 11 (November 1998).

Keil, Mark, Richard Mixon, Timo Saarinen, and Virpi Tuunairen. "Understanding Runaway IT Projects." *Journal of Management Information Systems* 11, no. 3 (Winter 1994–1995).

Keil, Mark, Bernard C. Y. Tan, Kwok-Kee Wei, Timo Saarinen, Virpi Tuunainen, and Arjen Waassenaar. "A Cross-Cultural Study on Escalation of Commitment Behavior in Software Projects." *MIS Quarterly* 24, no. 2 (June 2000).

Kettinger, William J., and Choong C. Lee. "Understanding the IS-User Divide in IT Innovation." *Communications of the ACM* 45, no. 2 (February 2002).

Klein, Gary, James J. Jiang, and Debbie B. Tesch. "Wanted: Project Teams with a Blend of IS Professional Orientations." *Communications of the ACM* 45, no. 6 (June 2002).

Kolb, D. A., and A. L. Frohman. "An Organization Development Approach to Consulting." *Sloan Management Review* 12 (Fall 1970).

Laudon, Kenneth C. "CIOs Beware: Very Large Scale Systems." Working paper, Center for Research on Information Systems, New York University Stern School of Business (1989).

LeBlond, Raoul. "Time as a Strategic Tool." *CIO Asia* (March 2004).

Lientz, Bennett P., and E. Burton Swanson. *Software Maintenance Management.* Reading, Mass.: Addison-Wesley (1980).

Lipin, Steven, and Nikhil Deogun. "Big Mergers of 90s Prove Disappointing to Shareholders." *Wall Street Journal* (October 30, 2000).

Lohse, Gerald L., and Peter Spiller. "Internet Retail Store Design: How the User Interface Influences Traffic and Sales." *Journal of Computer-Mediated Communication* 5, no. 2 (December 1999).

Lucas, Henry C., Jr. *Implementation: The Key to Successful Information Systems.* New York: Columbia University Press (1981).

Mahmood, Mo Adam, Laura Hall, and Daniel Leonard Swanberg. "Factors Affecting Information Technology Usage: A Meta-Analysis of the Empirical Literature." *Journal of Organizational Computing and Electronic Commerce* 11, no. 2 (November 2, 2001).

Markus, M. Lynne, and Robert I. Benjamin. "Change Agentry—The Next IS Frontier." *MIS Quarterly* 20, no. 4 (December 1996).

———. "The Magic Bullet Theory of IT-Enabled Transformation." *Sloan Management Review* (Winter 1997).

Markus, M. Lynne, and Mark Keil. "If We Build It, They Will Come: Designing Information Systems That People Want to Use." *Sloan Management Review* (Summer 1994).

Matlin, Gerald. "What Is the Value of Investment in Information Systems?" *MIS Quarterly* 13, no. 3 (September 1989).

McFarlan, F. Warren. "Portfolio Approach to Information Systems." *Harvard Business Review* (September–October 1981).

McGrath, Rita Gunther and Ian C. McMillan. "Assessing Technology Projects Using Real Options Reasoning." *Industrial Research Institute* (2000).

McKinney, Vicki, Kanghyun Yoon, and Fatemeh "Mariam" Zahedi. "The Measurement of Web-Customer Satisfaction: An Expectation and Disconfirmation Approach." *Information Systems Research* 13, no. 3 (September 2002).

Mumford, Enid, and Mary Weir. *Computer Systems in Work Design: The ETHICS Method.* New York: Wiley (1979).

Nambisan, Satish, and Yu-Ming Wang. "Web Technology Adoption and Knowledge Barriers." *Journal of Organizational Computing and Electronic Commerce* 10, no. 2 (2000).

Nash, Kim S. "Cleaning Up." *Baseline Magazine* (June 2004).

Nedda, Gabriela G. Olazabal. "Banking: The IT Paradox." *McKinsey Quarterly*, no. 1 (2002).

Nolan, Richard. "Managing Information Systems by Committee." *Harvard Business Review* (July–August 1982).

Nidumolu, Sarma R., and Mani Subramani. "The Matrix of Control: Combining Process and Structure Approaches to Management Software Development." *Journal of Management Information Systems* 20, no. 3 (Winter 2004).

Olazabal, Nedda Gabriela. "Banking: The IT Paradox." *The McKinsey Quarterly* (January 19, 2002).

Orlikowski, Wanda J., and J. Debra Hofman. "An Improvisational Change Model for Change Management: The Case of Groupware Technologies." *Sloan Management Review* (Winter 1997).

Oz, Effy. "When Professional Standards are Lax: The CONFIRM Failure and Its Lessons." *Communications of the ACM* 37, no. 10 (October 1994).

Palmer, Jonathan W. "Web Site Usability, Design and Performance Metrics." *Information Systems Research* 13, no. 3 (September 2002).

Panko, Raymond R. "Is Office Productivity Stagnant?" *MIS Quarterly* 15, no. 2 (June 1991).

Peffers, Ken, and Timo Saarinen. "Measuring the Business Value of IT Investments: Inferences from a Study of Senior Bank Executives." *Journal of Organizational Computing and Electronic Commerce* 12, no. 1 (2002).

Premkumar, G. "A Meta-Analysis of Research on Information Technology Implementation in Small Business." *Journal of Organizational Computing and Electronic Commerce* 13, no. 2 (2003).

Quan, Jin "Jim," Quing Hu, and Paul J. Hart. "Information Technology Investments and Firms' Performance—A Duopoly Perspective." *Journal of Management Information Systems* 20, no. 3 (Winter 2004).

Rai, Arun, Sandra S. Lang, and Robert B. Welker. "Assessing the Validity of IS Success Models: An Empirical Test and Theoretical Analysis." *Information Systems Research* 13, no. 1 (March 2002).

Rai, Arun, Ravi Patnayakuni, and Nainika Patnayakuni. "Technology Investment and Business Performance." *Communications of the ACM* 40, no. 7 (July 1997).

Reichheld, Frederick E., and Phil Schefter. "E-Loyalty: Your Secret Weapon on the Web." *Harvard Business Review* (July–August 2000).

Roach, S.A. *Making Technology Work.* Economic Research Unit, Morgan Stanley & Co., New York (1993).

Roach, Stephen S. "The Hollow Ring of the Productivity Revival." *Harvard Business Review* (November–December 1996).

———. *Industrialization of the Information Economy.* New York: Morgan Stanley (1984).

———. "Services under Siege—The Restructuring Imperative." *Harvard Business Review* (September–October 1991).

Robey, Daniel, and M. Lynne Markus. "Rituals in Information System Design." *MIS Quarterly* (March 1984).

Robey, Daniel, Jeanne W. Ross, and Marie-Claude Boudreau. "Learning to Implement Enterprise Systems: An Exploratory Study of the Dialectics of Change." *Journal of Management Information Systems* 19, no. 1 (Summer 2002).

Ross, Jeanne W., and Cynthia M. Beath. "Beyond the Business Case: New Approaches to IT Investment." *Sloan Management Review* 43, no. 2 (Winter 2002).

Ryan, Sherry D., and David A. Harrison. "Considering Social Subsystem Costs and Benefits in Information Technology Investment Decisions: A View from the Field on Anticipated Payoffs." *Journal of Management Information Systems* 16, no. 4 (Spring 2000).

Ryan, Sherry D., David A. Harrison, and Lawrence L Schkade. "Information Technology Investment Decisions: When Do Cost and Benefits in the Social Subsystem Matter?" *Journal of Management Information Systems* 19, no. 2 (Fall 2002).

Sambamurthy, V., Anandhi Bharadwaj, and Varun Grover. "Shaping Agility through Digital Options: Reconceptualizing the Role of Information Technology in Contemporary Firms." *MIS Quarterly* 27, no. 2 (June 2003).

Santhanam, Radhika, and Edward Hartono. "Issues in Linking Information Technology Capability to Firm Performance." *MIS Quarterly* 27, no. 1 (March 2003).

Sarkar, Pushpak. "A Paragon of Quality." *Intelligent Enterprise* (October 2002).

Sauer, Chris, and Leslie P. Willcocks. "The Evolution of the Organizational Architect." *Sloan Management Review* 43, no. 3 (Spring 2002).

Schmidt, Roy, Kalle Lyytinen, Mark Keil, and Paul Cule. "Identifying Software Project Risks: An International Delphi Study." *Journal of Management Information Systems* 17, no. 4 (Spring 2001).

Schneiderman, Ben. "Universal Usability." *Communications of the ACM* 43, no. 5 (May 2000).

Siewiorek, Daniel P. "New Frontiers of Application Design." *Communications of the ACM* 45, no. 12 (December 2002).

Sircar, Sumit, Joe L. Turnbow, and Bijoy Bordoloi. "A Framework for Assessing the Relationship between Information Technology Investments and Firm Performance." *Journal of Management Information Systems* 16, no. 4 (Spring 2000).

Smith, H. Jeff, Mark Keil, and Gordon Depledge. "Keeping Mum as the Project Goes Under." *Journal of Management Information Systems* 18, no. 2 (Fall 2001).

Speier, Cheri, and Michael. G. Morris. "The Influence of Query Interface Design on Decision-Making Performance." *MIS Quarterly* 27, no. 3 (September 2003).

Straub, Detmar W., Arun Rai, and Richard Klein. "Measuring Firm Performance at the Network Level: A Nomology of the Business Impact of Digital Supply Networks." *Journal of Management Information Systems* 21, no. 1 (Summer 2004).

Swanson, E. Burton. *Information System Implementation.* Homewood, Ill.: Richard D. Irwin (1988).

Tallon, Paul P., Kenneth L. Kraemer, and Vijay Gurbaxani. "Executives' Perceptions of the Business Value of Information Technology: A Process-Oriented Approach." *Journal of Management Information Systems* 16, no. 4 (Spring 2000).

Taudes, Alfred, Markus Feurstein, and Andreas Mild. "Options Analysis of Software Platform Decisions: A Case Study." *MIS Quarterly* 24, no. 2 (June 2000).

Teng, James T. C., Seung Ryul Jeong, and Varun Grover. "Profiling Successful Reengineering Projects." *Communications of the ACM* 41, no. 6 (June 1998).

Thatcher, Matt E., and Jim R. Oliver. "The Impact of Technology Investments on a Firm's Production Efficiency, Product Quality, and Productivity." *Journal of Management Information Systems* 18, no. 2 (Fall 2001).

Tornatsky, Louis G., J. D. Eveland, M. G. Boylan, W. A. Hetzner, E. C. Johnson, D. Roitman, and J. Schneider. *The Process of Technological Innovation: Reviewing the Literature.* Washington, D.C.: National Science Foundation (1983).

UNISYS. "Multi-carrier Web-Based Booking for Air Cargo." http://www.unisys.com/transportation/clients/featured__case__ studies/northwest__airlines_c0___united__airlines__and__air__ canada__case__study.htm. (accessed. May 22, 2005).

University Malaysia Sarawak. "eBario Wins AFACT's eASIA Award." http://www.unimas.my/ebario/award4.htm (accessed May 21, 2005).

Venkatesh, Viswanath, Michael G. Morris, Gordon B Davis, and Fred D. Davis. "User Acceptance of Information Technology: Toward a Unified View." *MIS Quarterly* 27, no. 3 (September 2003).

Wallace, Linda, and Mark Keil. "Software Project Risks and Their Effect on Outcomes." *Communications of the ACM* 47, no. 4 (April 2004).

Ward, Toby. "The Politics of Intranet Ownership." *Prescient Digital,* http://www.prescientdigital.com/userfiles/HTML/nts_9_1736_1. html (accessed May 25, 2005).

———. "Collaborative Governance (Intranet Politics Part II)." *Prescient Digital,* http://www.prescientdigital.com/userfiles/HTML/nts_9_1967_1. html (accessed May 25, 2005).

Weill, Peter and Marianne Broadbent. *Leveraging the New Infrastructure: How Market Leaders Capitalize on Information Technology.* Cambridge: Harvard Business School Press (1998).

Weill, Peter, Mani Subramani, and Marianne Broadbent. "Building IT Infrastructure for Strategic Agility." *Sloan Management Review* 44, no. 1 (Fall 2002).

Xia, Weidong, and Gwanhoo Lee. "Grasping the Complexity of IS Development Projects." *Communications of the ACM* 47, no. 5 (May 2004).

Yin, Robert K. "Life Histories of Innovations: How New Practices Become Routinized." *Public Administration Review* (January–February 1981).

Zhu, Kevin. "The Complementarity of Information Technology Infrastructure and E-Commerce Capability: A Resource-Based Assessment of Their Business Value." *Journal of Management Information Systems* 21, no. 1 (Summer 2004).

Zhu, Kevin, and Kenneth L. Kraemer. "E-Commerce Metrics for Net-Enhanced Organizations: Assessing the Value of e-Commerce to Firm Performance in the Manufacturing Sector." *Information Systems Research* 13, no. 3 (September 2002).

Zhu, Kevin, Kenneth L. Kraemer, Sean Xu, and Jason Dedrick. "Information Technology Payoff in E-Business Environments: An International Perspective on Value Creation of E-business in the Financial Services Industry." *Journal of Management Information Systems* 21, no. 1 (Summer 2004).

Chapter 12

Agarwal, P. K. "Building India's National Internet Backbone." *Communications of the ACM* 42, no. 6 (June 1999).

Anwar, Harris. "Canadian Firms Cool on Offshore, Board Says." *The Globe and Mail* (April 18, 2005).

Armour, Stephanie and Michelle Kessler. "USA's New Money-Saving Export: White-Collar Jobs." *USA Today* (August 9, 2003).

Baily, Martin N., and Diana Farrell. "Exploding the Myths of Offshoring." *McKinsey Quarterly* (July 2004).

Baker, Stephen and Manjeet Kripalani. Software: Will Outsourcing Hurt America's Supremacy?" *BusinessWeek* (March 1, 2004).

Berinato, Scott. "A Day in the Life of Celanese's Big ERP Rollup." *CIO Magazine* (January 15, 2003).

Blanning, Robert W. "Establishing a Corporate Presence on the Internet in Singapore." *Journal of Organizational Computing and Electronic Commerce* 9, no. 1 (1999).

Bradsher, Keith. "G.M. to Speed Up Expansion in China." *The New York Times* (June 8, 2004).

Buchanan, Terri-Sue. "Call Centres: Ringing in Profits." *Exportwise,* http://www.edc.ca/corpinfo/pubs/exportwise/winter05/p11_e.htm (Winter 2005, accessed June 6, 2005).

Buckman, Rebecca. "H-P Outsourcing: Beyond China." *Wall Street Journal* (February 23, 2004).

Burkhardt, Grey E., Seymour E. Goodman, Arun Mehta, and Larry Press. "The Internet in India: Better Times Ahead?" *Communications of the ACM* 41, no. 11 (November 1998).

Canadian Marketing Association. "International Outsourcing of Call Centre Operations." http://www.the-cma.org/council/downloads/ InternationalOutsourcingMarch2004.pdf (March 2004, accessed June 6, 2005).

Caudron, Shari. "Safety in Numbers." *Profit Magazine* (February 2004).

———. "1000 Days in Five (Not So) Easy Steps." *CIO Magazine* (January 15, 2003).

———. "A Brief Tale of a Long History." *CIO Magazine* (January 15, 2003).

Celanese Project Team. "The Top Eight Risks to the OneSAP Project." *CIO Magazine* (January 15, 2003).

Cox, Butler. *Globalization: The IT Challenge.* Sunnyvale, Calif.: Amdahl Executive Institute (1991).

Davison, Robert. "Cultural Complications of ERP." *Communications of the ACM* 45, no. 7 (July 2002).

Deans, Candace P., and Michael J. Kane. *International Dimensions of Information Systems and Technology.* Boston: PWS-Kent (1992).

Deans, Candace P., Kirk R. Karwan, Martin D. Goslar, David A. Ricks, and Brian Toyne. "Key International Issues in U.S.-Based Multinational Corporations." *Journal of Management Information Systems* 7, no. 4 (Spring 1991).

Drucker, Jesse and Ken Brown. "Press 1 for Delhi, 2 for Dallas." *Wall Street Journal* (March 9, 2004).

Ein-Dor, Philip, Seymour E. Goodman, and Peter Wolcott. "From Via Maris to Electronic Highway: The Internet in Canaan." *Communications of the ACM* 43, no. 7 (July 2000).

Einhorn, Bruce. "China.Net." *BusinessWeek* (March 15, 2004).

Evans, Bob. "Business Technology: Offshore Outsourcing: A Means to an End." *InformationWeek* (July 28, 2003).

Farhoomand, Ali, Virpi Kristiina Tuunainen, and Lester W. Yee. "Barrier to Global Electronic Commerce: A Cross-Country Study of Hong Kong and Finland." *Journal of Organizational Computing and Electronic Commerce* 10, no. 1 (2000).

Herman, Wendy. "China on the Move." http://www.nortelnetworks.com/corporate/pressroom/feature_ article/2004b/04_12_04_mao_china.html (accessed June 5, 2005).

Ives, Blake, and Sirkka Jarvenpaa. "Applications of Global Information Technology: Key Issues for Management." *MIS Quarterly* 15, no. 1 (March 1991).

———. "Global Business Drivers: Aligning Information Technology to Global Business Strategy." *IBM Systems Journal* 32, no. 1 (1993).

———. "Global Information Technology: Some Lessons from Practice." *International Information Systems* 1, no. 3 (July 1992).

Jarvenpaa, Sirkka L., Kathleen Knoll, and Dorothy Leidner. "Is Anybody Out There? Antecedents of Trust in Global Virtual Teams." *Journal of Management Information Systems* 14, no. 4 (Spring 1998).

Jarvenpaa, Sirkka L., Thomas R. Shaw, and D. Sandy Staples. "Toward Contextualized Theories of Trust: The Role of Trust in Global Virtual Teams." *Information Systems Research* 15, no. 3 (September 2004).

Keen, Peter. *Shaping the Future.* Cambridge, M.A.: Harvard Business School Press (1991).

King, William R., and Vikram Sethi. "An Empirical Analysis of the Organization of Transnational Information Systems." *Journal of Management Information Systems* 15, no. 4 (Spring 1999).

Krishna, S., Sundeep Sahay, and Geoff Walsham. "Managing Cross-Cultural Issues in Global Software Outsourcing." *Communications of the ACM* 47, no. 4 (April 2004).

Kurtenbach, Elaine. "GM to Spend $3B in China Over Next 3 Yrs." Associated Press (June 7, 2004).

Lai, Vincent S., and Wingyan Chung. "Managing International Data Communication." *Communications of the ACM* 45, no. 3 (March 2002).

Liang, Huigang, Yajiong Xue, William R. Boulton, and Terry Anthony Byrd. "Why Western Vendors Don't Dominate China's ERP Market." *Communications of the ACM* 47, no. 7 (July 2004).

MacFarquhar, Neil. "Tunisia's Tangled Web Is Sticking Point for Reform." *New York Times* (June 25, 2004).

Maher, Kris. "Next on the Outsourcing List." *Wall Street Journal* (March 23, 2004).

Mann, Catherine L. "What Global Sourcing Means for U.S. I.T. Workers and for the U.S. Economy." *Communications of the ACM* 47, no. 7 (July 2004).

Martinsons, Maris G. "ERP in China: One Package, Two Profiles." *Communications of the ACM* 47, no. 7 (July 2004).

McDougall, Paul. "The Place to Be." *Information Week.* (April 5, 2004).

Mullin, Rick. "The Age of Interoperability." http://www.e-chemmerce.com (accessed March 28, 2003).

Nortel Networks. "Nortel Networks to Strengthen R&D Capabilities in China." http://www.nortelnetworks.com/corporate/news/newsreleases/2003c/09_16_03_china_investment.html (September 16, 2003, accessed June 5, 2005).

OSISoft Case Study. "Celanese Corporation." http://www.osisoft.com (accessed April 1, 2003).

Ottawa Business Journal. "Canadian Companies Slow to Embrace Offshore Outsourcing." (April 15, 2005).

Overby, Stephanie. "The Hidden Costs of Offshore Outsourcing." *CIO* (September 1, 2003).

Petrazzini, Ben, and Mugo Kibati. "The Internet in Developing Countries." *Communications of the ACM* 42, no. 6 (June 1999).

Quelch, John A., and Lisa R. Klein. "The Internet and International Marketing." *Sloan Management Review* (Spring 1996).

Reuters. "Offshore Outsourcing Set to Hit U.S. Job Market." ITWeb, http://www.itweb.co.za (accessed July 30, 2003).

Roche, Edward M. *Managing Information Technology in Multinational Corporations.* New York: Macmillan (1992).

Schroeder, Michael. "Outsourcing May Create U.S. Jobs." *Wall Street Journal* (March 30, 2004).

Soh, Christina, Sia Siew Kien, and Joanne Tay-Yap. "Cultural Fits and Misfits: Is ERP a Universal Solution?" *Communications of the ACM* 43, no. 3 (April 2000).

Steinbart, Paul John, and Ravinder Nath. "Problems and Issues in the Management of International Data Networks." *MIS Quarterly* 16, no. 1 (March 1992).

Straub, Detmar W. "The Effect of Culture on IT Diffusion: E-Mail and FAX in Japan and the U.S." *Information Systems Research* 5, no. 1 (March 1994).

Sullivan, Laurie. "Road Work in China." *Information Week* (August 30, 2004).

Tan, Zixiang, William Foster, and Seymour Goodman. "China's State-Coordinated Internet Infrastructure." *Communications of the ACM* 42, no. 6 (June 1999).

Ticoll, David. "'Offshoring' Will Soon Be Making Waves." *The Globe and Mail* (February 19, 2004).

Tractinsky, Noam, and Sirkka L. Jarvenpaa. "Information Systems Design Decisions in a Global versus Domestic Context." *MIS Quarterly* 19, no. 4 (December 1995).

Watson, Richard T., Gigi G. Kelly, Robert D. Galliers, and James C. Brancheau. "Key Issues in Information Systems Management: An International Perspective." *Journal of Management Information Systems* 13, no. 4 (Spring 1997).

Wessel, David. "The Future of Jobs: New Ones Arise, Wage Gap Widens." *Wall Street Journal* (April 2, 2004).

Chapter 13

Agora Consulting Partners. "Case Study: Canadian Investor Protection Fund." http://www.agorainc.com/casestudies/cs_cipf.htm (accessed June 7, 2005).

Akcura, M. Tolga, and Kemal Altinkemer. "Diffusion Models for B2B, B2C and P2P Exchanges and E-Speak." *Journal of Organizational Computing and Electronic Commerce* 12, no. 3 (2002).

Andal-Ancion, Angela, Philip A. Cartwright, and George S. Yip. "The Digital Transformation of Traditional Business." *MIT Sloan Management Review* 44, no. 4 (Summer 2003).

Anderson, Philip, and Erin Anderson. "The New E-Commerce Intermediaries." *Sloan Management Review* 43, no. 4 (Summer 2002).

Angwin, Julia and Nick Wingfield. "AOL Brings Online Music to the Masses, for a Price." *Wall Street Journal* (February 26, 2003).

Armstrong, Arthur, and John Hagel III. "The Real Value of On-line Communities." *Harvard Business Review* (May–June 1996).

Ba, Sulin, and Paul A. Pavlou. "Evidence of the Effect of Trust Building Technology in Electronic Markets: Price Premiums and Buyer Behavior." *MIS Quarterly* 26, no. 3 (September 2002).

Bakos, Yannis. "The Emerging Role of Electronic Marketplaces and the Internet." *Communications of the ACM* 41, no. 8 (August 1998).

Barua, Anitesh, Prabhudev Konana, Andrew B. Whinston, and Fang Yin. "Driving E-Business Excellence." *Sloan Management Review* 43, no. 1 (Fall 2001).

Bhargava, Hemant K., and Vidyanand Chourhary. "Economics of an Information Intermediary with Aggregation Benefits." *Information Systems Research* 15, no. 1 (March 2004).

Bhattacherjee, Anol. "Individual Trust in Online Firms: Scale Development and Initial Test." *Journal of Management Information Systems* 19, no. 1 (Summer 2002).

Black, Jane. "Big Music: Win Some, Lose a Lot More?" *Business Week Online* (May 5, 2003).

———. "Digital Music: Still Scores Left to Settle." *Business Week Online* (April 22, 2003).

———. "Web Music Gets Its Act Together." *Business Week Online* (April 22, 2003).

———. "Big Music's Broken Record." *Business Week Online* (February 13, 2003).

Borland, John. "Canada Deems P2P Downloading Legal, Levies MP3 Players." ZDNet, http://www.zdnet.com.au/news/business/0,39023166,20281795,00.htm (December 15, 2003, accessed June 9, 2005).

———. "Canadian MP3 Player Tax Challenged." CNet, http://news.com.com/2102-1027_3-5140374.html?tag=st.util.print (January 13, 2004, accessed June 9, 2005).

Brynjolfsson, Erik, Yu Hu, and Michael D. Smith. "Consumer Surplus in the Digital Economy: Estimating the Value of Increased Product Variety at Online Booksellers." *Management Science* 49, no. 11 (November 2003).

Canadian Investor Protection Fund. "Welcome to CIPF: About CIPF." http://www.cipf.ca/c_home.htm (accessed June 7, 2005).

Chaudhury, Abhijit, Debasish Mallick, and H. Raghav Rao. "Web Channels in E-Commerce." *Communications of the ACM* 44, no. 1 (January 2001).

Chiu, Wendy. "Case Study: Rogers Communications." *Federated Press,* http://www.xteric.com/portalevent/resources/1256088_Finding_ROI.pdf (December 2002, accessed June 8, 2005).

Christensen, Clayton M. *The Innovator's Dilemma.* New York: HarperCollins (2000).

Claburn, Thomas. "Feds Target Scofflaws and Spammers." *Information Week* (August 30, 2004).

Clemons, Eric K., Bin Gu, and Karl Reiner Lang. "Newly Vulnerable Markets in an Age of Pure Information Products: An Analysis of Online Music and Online News." *Journal of Management Information Systems* 19, no. 3 (Winter 2002–2003).

CTV. "File-sharing law to be tabled next week." http://www.ctv.ca/servlet/ArticleNews/story/CTVNews/1118271756635_30/?hub=SciTech (June 9, 2005, accessed June 11, 2005).

Devaraj, Sarv, Ming Fan, and Rajiv Kohli. "Antecedents of B2C Channel Satisfaction and Preference: Validating e-Commerce Metrics." *Information Systems Research* 13, no. 3 (September 2002).

Dewan, Rajiv M., Marshall L. Freimer, and Jie Zhang. "Management and Valuation of Advertisement-Supported Web Sites." *Journal of Management Information Systems* 19, no. 3 (Winter 2002–2003).

eMarketer. "B2C E-Commerce in the U.S." (July 2004).

Evans, Philip, and Thomas S. Wurster. *Blown to Bits: How the New Economics of Information Transforms Strategy.* Boston: Harvard Business School Press (2000).

———. "Getting Real about Virtual Commerce." *Harvard Business Review* (November–December 1999).

Fichman, Robert G., and Mary J. Cronin. "Information-Rich Commerce at a Crossroads: Business and Technology Adoption Requirements." *Communications of the ACM* 46, no. 9 (September 2003).

France, Mike. "Music Pirates, You're Sunk." *Business Week* (August 29, 2003).

Gallaugher, John M. "E-Commerce and the Undulating Distribution Channel." *Communications of the ACM* 45, no. 7 (July 2002).

Gefen, David, Elena Karahanna, and Detmar W. Straub. "Trust and TAM in Online Shopping: An Integrated Model." *MIS Quarterly* 27, no. 1 (March 2003).

Grover, Varun, and Pradipkumar Ramanlal. "Six Myths of Information and Markets: Information Technology Networks, Electronic Commerce, and the Battle for Consumer Surplus." *MIS Quarterly* 23, no. 4 (December 1999).

Gulati, Ranjay, and Jason Garino. "Get the Right Mix of Bricks and Clicks." *Harvard Business Review* (May–June 2000).

Hagel, John, III, and Marc Singer. *Net Worth.* Boston: Harvard Business School Press (1999).

Hansell, Saul. "E-Music Settle on Prices. It's a Start." *New York Times* (March 3, 2003).

Harmon, Amy. "Despite Suits, Music File Sharers Shrug Off Guilt and Keep Sharing." *New York Times* (September 19, 2003).

———. "Industry Offers a Carrot in Online Music Fight." *New York Times* (June 8, 2003).

———. "Music Swappers Get a Message on PC Screens: Stop It Now." *New York Times* (May 19, 2003).

———. "Suit Settled for Students Downloading Music Online." *New York Times* (May 2, 2003).

Haskell, Kari. "Do-It-Yourself Design: Just Point and Click." *New York Times*, October 24, 2004.

Hoffman, Martin. "Best Practices: VW Revs Up Its B2B Engine." *Optimize Magazine* (March 2004).

Holson, Laura M. and Geraldine Fabrikant. "Music Industry Braces for a Shift." *New York Times* (January 13, 2003).

Huang, Gregory T. "The Web's New Currency." *Technology Review* (November 2003).

Hui, Kai Lung, and Patrick Y. K. Chau. "Classifying Digital Products." *Communications of the ACM* 45, no. 6 (June 2002).

Iansiti, Marco, F. Warren McFarlan, and George Wessterman. "Leveraging the Incumbent's Advantage." *MIT Sloan Management Review* 44, no. 4 (Summer 2003).

Jones, Sara, Marc Wilikens, Philip Morris, and Marcelo Masera. "Trust Requirements in E-Business." *Communications of the ACM* 43, no. 12 (December 2000).

Kanan, P. K., Ai-Mei Chang, and Andrew B. Whinston. "Marketing Information on the I-Way." *Communications of the ACM* 41, no. 3 (March 1998).

Kaplan, Steven, and Mohanbir Sawhney. "E-Hubs: the New B2B Marketplaces." *Harvard Business Review* (May–June 2000).

Kauffman, Robert J., and Bin Wang. "New Buyers' Arrival under Dynamic Pricing Market Microstructure: The Case of Group-Buying Discounts on the Internet." *Journal of Management Information Systems* 18, no. 2 (Fall 2001).

Kenny, David, and John F. Marshall. "Contextual Marketing." *Harvard Business Review* (November–December 2000).

Koufaris, Marios. "Applying the Technology Acceptance Model and Flow Theory to Online Consumer Behavior." *Information Systems Research* 13, no. 2 (2002).

Lai, Vincent S. "Intraorganizational Communication with Intranets." *Communications of the ACM* 44, no. 7 (July 2001).

Laudon, Kenneth C., and Carol Guercio Traver. *E-Commerce: Business, Technology, Society.* Boston: Addison-Wesley (2004).

Lee, Hau L., and Seungin Whang. "Winning the Last Mile of E-Commerce." *Sloan Management Review* 42, no. 4 (Summer 2001).

Lee, Ho Geun. "Do Electronic Marketplaces Lower the Price of Goods?" *Communications of the ACM* 41, no. 1 (January 1998).

Lee, Younghwa, Zoonky Lee, and Kai R. T. Larsen. "Coping with Internet Channel Conflict." *Communications of the ACM* 43, no.7 (July 2003).

Lightner, Nancy J. "Evaluating E-Commerce Functionality with a Focus on Customer Service." *Communications of the ACM* 47, no. 10 (October 2004).

Lim, Gyoo Gun, and Jae Kyu Lee. "Buyer-Carts for B2B EC: The b-Cart Approach." *Journal of Organizational Computing and Electronic Commerce* 13, nos. 3 and 4 (2003).

Looney, Clayton A., and Debabroto Chatterjee. "Web-Enabled Transformation of the Brokerage Industry." *Communications of the ACM* 45, no. 8 (August 2002).

Magretta, Joan. "Why Business Models Matter." *Harvard Business Review* (May 2002).

Mathews, Anna Wilde and Charles Goldsmith. "Music Industry Faces New Threats on Web." *Wall Street Journal* (February 21, 2003).

Mathews, Anna Wilde and Nick Wingfield. "Entertainment Industry Loses Important File-Sharing Battle." *Wall Street Journal* (April 28, 2003).

Markillie, Paul. "A Perfect Market." *The Economist* (May 15–21, 2004).

McBride, Sarah. "Stop the Music!" *Wall Street Journal* (August 23, 2004).

McGuire, David. "Study: File-Sharing No Threat to Music Sales." *Washington Post* (March 30, 2004).

McKnight, D. Harrison, Vivek Choudhury, and Charlea Kacmar. "Developing and Validating Trust Measures for e-Commerce: An Integrative Typology." *Information Systems Research* 13, no. 3 (September 2002).

McWilliam, Gil. "Building Stronger Brands through Online Communities." *Sloan Management Review* 41, no. 3 (Spring 2000).

Metz, Cade. "The Changing Face of Online Music." *PC Magazine* (September 24, 2003).

Mougayar, Walid. *Opening Digital Markets.* 2nd ed. New York: McGraw-Hill (1998).

Open Text Corporation. "CARE Canada—Tackling World Problems." http://www.opentext.com (accessed August 25, 2004).

———. "CARE Canada— CAREing Enough to Manage World Problems." http://www.opentext.com (accessed August 25, 2004).

Pavlou, Paul A., and David Gefen. "Building Effective Online Marketplaces with Institution-Based Trust." *Information Systems Research* 15, no. 1 (March 2004).

Peers, Martin. "Buddy Can You Spare Some Time?" *Wall Street Journal* (January 26, 2004).

Pinker, Edieal, Abraham Seidmann, and Riginald C. Foster. "Strategies for Transitioning 'Old Economy' Firms to E-Business." *Communications of the ACM* 45, no. 5 (May 2002).

Pogue, David. "The Internet as Jukebox, at a Price." *New York Times Circuits* (March 6, 2003).

Prahalad, C. K., and Venkatram Ramaswamy. "Coopting Consumer Competence." *Harvard Business Review* (January–February 2000).

Rayport, J. F., and J. J. Sviokla. "Managing in the Marketspace." *Harvard Business Review* (November–December 1994).

Reichheld, Frederick E., and Phil Schefter. "E-Loyalty: Your Secret Weapon on the Web." *Harvard Business Review* (July–August 2000).

Reidy, Kathleen. "Global Relief." *Portals Magazine* (February 1, 2004).

Richtel, Matt. "Access to Free Online Music Is Seen as a Boost to Sales." *New York Times* (May 6, 2002).

Rifkin, Glenn, and Joel Kurtzman. "Is Your E-Business Plan Radical Enough?" *Sloan Management Review* 43, no. 3 (Spring 2002).

Riggins, Frederic J. "Market Segmentation and Information Development Costs in a Two-Tiered Fee-Based and Sponsorship-Based Web Site." *Journal of Management Information Systems* 19, no. 3 (Winter 2002–2003).

Rust, Roland T., and P. K. Kannan. "E-Service: A New Paradigm for Business in the Electronic Environment." *Communications of the ACM* 46, no. 6 (June 2003).

Sawhney, Mohanbir, Emanuela Prandelli, and Gianmario Verona. "The Power of Innomediation." *MIT Sloan Management Review* (Winter 2003).

Schlueter-Langdon, Christoph, and Michael J. Shaw. "Emergent Patterns of Interaction in Electronic Channel Systems." *Communications of the ACM* 45, no. 12 (December 2002).

Schwartz, John and John Markoff. "Power Players: Big Names Are Jumping into the Crowded Online Music Field." *New York Times* (January 12, 2004).

Scalet, Sarah D. "The Pirates Among Us." *CIO Magazine* (April 15, 2003).

Schultze, Ulrike, and Wanda J. Orlikowski. "A Practice Perspective on Technology-Mediated Network Relations: The Use of Internet-Based Self-Serve Technologies." *Information Systems Research* 15, no. 1 (March 2004).

Shelfer, Katherine M., and J. Drew Procaccino. "Smart Card Evolution." *Communications of the ACM* 45, no. 7 (July 2002).

Shi, Xinping, and Philip C. Wright. "E-Commercializing Business Operations." *Communications of the ACM* 46, no. 2 (February 2003).

Smith, Ethan. "Music Industry Sounds Upbeat as Losses Slow." *Wall Street Journal* (January 2, 2004).

Smith, Michael Alan. "Portals: Toward an Application Framework for Interoperability." *Communications of the ACM* 47, no. 10 (October 2004).

Smith, Michael D., Joseph Bailey, and Erik Brynjolfsson. "Understanding Digital Markets: Review and Assessment." In *Understanding the Digital Economy,* edited by Erik Brynjolfsson and Brian Kahin. Cambridge, Mass.: MIT Press (1999).

Southard, Peter B., and Keng Siau. "A Survey of Online E-Banking Retail Initiatives." *Communications of the ACM* 47, no. 10 (October 2004).

Stewart, Alan and Paul McLaughlin. "The dirt on dot.cons." *CA Magazine* (June-July 2001).

Strader, Troy J., and Sridhar N. Ramaswami. "Investor Perceptions of Traditional and Online Channels." *Communications of the ACM* 47, no. 7 (July 2004).

Subramanian, Rangan, and Ron Adner. "Profits and the Internet: Seven Misconceptions." *Sloan Management Review* 42, no. 4 (Summer 2001).

Tam, Pui-Wing. "Apple Launches Online Store Offering Downloadable Music." *Wall Street Journal* (April 29, 2003).

Thomke, Stefan, and Eric von Hippel. "Customers as Innovators." *Harvard Business Review* (April 2002).

Torkzadeh, Gholamreza, and Gurpreet Dhillon. "Measuring Factors That Influence the Success of Internet Commerce." *Information Systems Research* 13, no. 2 (June 2002).

Urbaczewski, Andrew, Leonard M. Jessup, and Bradley Wheeler. "Electronic Commerce Research: A Taxonomy and Synthesis." *Journal of Organizational Computing and Electronic Commerce* 12, no. 2 (2002).

Veiga, Alex. "Recording Industry Sues 532 Over Swapping." Associated Press (March 23, 2004).

Venkatraman, N. "Five Steps to a Dot-Com Strategy: How to Find Your Footing on the Web." *Sloan Management Review* 41, no. 3 (Spring 2000).

Werbach, Kevin. "Syndication: The Emerging Model for Business in the Internet Era." *Harvard Business Review* (May–June 2000).

Westland, J. Christopher. "Preference Ordering Cash, Near-Cash and Electronic Cash." *Journal of Organizational Computing and Electronic Commerce* 12, no. 3 (2002).

Wigand, Rolf T., and Robert Benjamin. "Electronic Commerce: Effects on Electronic Markets." *JCMC* 1, no. 3 (December 1995).

Willcocks, Leslie, and Robert Plant. "Pathways to E-Business Leadership." *Sloan Management Review* (Spring 2001).

Wingfield, Nick. "Price War in Online Music." *Wall Street Journal* (August 17, 2004).

———. "Online Music's Latest Tune." *Wall Street Journal* (August 27, 2004).

Wingfield, Nick and Sarah McBride. "Green Light for Grokster." *Wall Street Journal* (August 20, 2004).

Wise, Richard, and David Morrison. "Beyond the Exchange: The Future of B2B." *Harvard Business Review* (November–December 2000).

Yen, Benjamin P.-C., and Elsie O. S. Ng. "The Impact of Electronic Commerce on Procurement." *Journal of Organizational Computing and Electronic Commerce* 13, nos. 3 and 4 (2003).

Yoo, Byungjoon, Vidyanand Choudhary, and Tridas Mukhopadhyay. "A Model of Neutral B2B Intermediaries." *Journal of Management Information Systems* 19, no. 3 (Winter 2002–2003).

Zeidler, Sue. "Sony Unveils Music Service, Mulls iPod Killer." Reuters (May 4, 2004).

Chapter 14

Agarwal, Anupam, David P. Harding, and Jeffrey R. Schumacher. "Organizing for CRM." *The McKinsey Quarterly* no. 3 (2004).

Anderson, James C., and James A. Narus. "Selectively Pursuing More of Your Customer's Business." *MIT Sloan Management Review* 44, no. 3 (Spring 2003).

Bacheldor, Beth. "Implementation Imperative." Information Week (April 28, 2003).

Conlon, Ginger. "Driving Sales." *Customer Relationship Management Magazine* (July 1, 2003).

Cox, John. "Transalta Uses Wireless Technology to Get More Competitive." *Network World Fusion* (April 13, 2005).

D'Avanzo, Robert, Hans von Lewinski, and Luk N. Van Wassenhove. "The Link between Supply Chain and Financial Performance." *Supply Chain Management Review* (November 1, 2003).

Davenport, Thomas H. *Mission Critical: Realizing the Promise of Enterprise Systems.* Boston: Harvard Business School Press (2000).

———. "Putting the Enterprise into Enterprise Systems." *Harvard Business Review* (July–August 1998).

Davison, Robert. "Cultural Complications of ERP." *Communications of the ACM* 45, no. 7 (July 2002).

Day, George S. "Creating a Superior Customer-Relating Capability." *MIT Sloan Management Review* 44, no. 3 (Spring 2003).

Dowling, Grahame. "Customer Relationship Management: In B2C Markets, Often Less Is More." *California Management Review* 44, no. 3 (Spring 2002).

Ebner, Manuel, Arthur Hu, Daniel Levitt, and Jim McCrory. "How to Rescue CRM." *McKinsey Quarterly* 4 (2002).

Ericson, Jim. "Working Man's Portal." *Portals Magazine* (January 1, 2003).

Fayyad, Usama. "Optimizing Customer Insight." *Intelligent Enterprise* (May 13, 2003).

Fisher, Marshall L. "What Is the Right Supply Chain for Your Product?" *Harvard Business Review* (March–April 1997).

Fleisch, Elgar, Hubert Oesterle, and Stephen Powell. "Rapid Implementation of Enterprise Resource Planning Systems." *Journal of Organizational Computing and Electronic Commerce* 14, no. 2 (2004).

Goldenberg, Barton. "Don't Put the Cart Before the Horse." *Customer Relationship Management* (September 2004).

Goodhue, Dale L., Barbara H. Wixom, and Hugh J. Watson. "Realizing Business Benefits through CRM: Hitting the Right Target in the Right Way." *MIS Quarterly Executive* 1, no. 2 (June 2002).

Greenbaum, Joshua. "Build vs. Buy in the 21st Century." *Intelligent Enterprise* (April 22, 2003).

Greenbaum, Joshua, and Peter Graf. "SAP xApps: Maximizing Return on Strategic Assets." White paper. http://www.sap.com (accessed August 1, 2003).

Guptill, Bruce. "Customer Metrics That Matter." *Optimize Magazine* 18 (April 2003).

Handfield, Robert B., and Ernest L. Nichols Jr. *Introduction to Supply Chain Management.* Upper Saddle River, N.J.: Prentice Hall (1999).

Havenstein, Heather. "SAP Aims to Bridge Suites." *InfoWorld* (January 17, 2003).

Hitt, Lorin, D. J. Wu, and Xiaoge Zhou. "Investment in Enterprise Resource Planning: Business Impact and Productivity Measures." *Journal of Management Information Systems* 19, no. 1 (Summer 2002).

IBM Case Study. "TransAlta powers up with IBM WebSphere Portal and SAP Enterprise Portal." http://www-306.ibm.com/software/success/cssdb.nsf/CS/FWAS-6B7C3X?OpenDocument&Site=wsmq (accessed May 28, 2005).

Jaiswal. M. P. "Implementing ERP Systems." *Dataquest* (June 30, 2003).

Kalakota, Ravi, and Marcia Robinson. *E-Business 2.0.* Boston: Addison-Wesley (2001).

———. *Services Blueprint: Roadmap for Execution.* Boston: Addison-Wesley (2003).

Kanakamedala, Kishore, Glenn Ramsdell, and Vats Srivatsan. "Getting Supply Chain Software Right." *McKinsey Quarterly,* no. 1 (2003).

Koch, Christopher. "The ABCs of ERP." CIO Enterprise Resource Planning Research Center. http://www.cio.com/research/erp/edit/erpbasics.html (accessed August 1, 2003).

Kopczak, Laura Rock, and M. Eric Johnson. "The Supply-Chain Management Effect." *MIT Sloan Management Review* 44, no. 3 (Spring 2003).

Kumar, Kuldeep, and Jos Van Hillegersberg. "ERP Experiences and Revolution." *Communications of the ACM* 43, no. 4 (April 2000).

Laudon, Kenneth C., and Jane P. Laudon. *Management Information Systems: Managing the Digital Firm,* 7th and 8th ed. Upper Saddle River, N.J.: Prentice Hall (2002, 2004).

Lee, Hau. "The Triple-A Supply Chain." *Harvard Business Review* (October 2004).

Lee, Hau, L. V. Padmanabhan, and Seugin Whang. "The Bullwhip Effect in Supply Chains." *Sloan Management Review* (Spring 1997).

LoFrumento, Tony. "How Profitable Are Your Customers?" *Optimize Magazine* 18 (April 2003).

Markus, M. Lynne, Conelis Tanis, and Paul C. van Fenema. "Multisite ERP Implementations." *Communications of the ACM* 43, no. 3 (April 2000).

McKie, Stewart. "The Big BAM." *Intelligent Enterprise* (July 18, 2003).

Mearian, Lucas. "Canadian Supermarket Chain Abandons SAP's Retail Software." *Computerworld* (February 2, 2001).

Mello, Adrian. "Global Supply Links." *Cisco IQ Magazine* (May/June 2003).

Myron, David. "6 Barriers to CRM Success." *CRM Magazine* (August 2003).

Norris, Grant, James R. Hurley, Kenneth M. Hartley, John R. Dunleavy, and John D. Balls. *E-Business and ERP: Transforming the Enterprise.* New York: Wiley (2000).

Palaniswamy, Rajagopal, and Tyler Frank. "Enhancing Manufacturing Performance with ERP Systems." *Information Systems Management* (Summer 2000).

Pan, Shan L., and Jae-Nam Lee. "Using e-CRM for a Unified View of the Customer." *Communications of the ACM* 46, no. 4 (April 2003).

Picarille, Lisa. "Planes, Trains, and Automobiles." *Customer Relationship Management Magazine* (February 2004).

Ranganathan, C., Jasbir S. Dhaliwal, and Thompson S. H. Teo. "Assimilation and Diffusion of Web Technologies in Supply-Chain Management: An Examination of Key Drivers and Performance Impacts." *International Journal of Electronic Commerce* 9, no. 1 (Fall 2004).

Reinartz, Werner J., and Pankaj Chugh. "Learning from Experience: Making CRM a Success at Last." *Journal of Call Centre Management* (March–April 2002).

Richebacher, Thomas F. "The Money Shift." *Intelligent Enterprise* (March 20, 2003).

Rigby, Darrell K., Frederick F. Reichheld, and Phil Schefter. "Avoid the four perils of CRM." *Harvard Business Review* 80(2) (February 2002).

Robey, Daniel, Jeanne W. Ross, and Marie-Claude Boudreau. "Learning to Implement Enterprise Systems: An Exploratory Study of the Dialectics of Change." *Journal of Management Information Systems* 19, no. 1 (Summer 2002).

Sabri, Hussain. "CRM: The Power of Prediction." *Intelligent Enterprise* (July 18, 2003).

Schneider, Martin. "ROI Is Increasing among CRM Projects." Destination CRM.com. http://www.destinationcrm.com/articles/default.asp?ArticleID= 3829%20&TopicID=9 (accessed February 2, 2004).

Scott, Judy E., and Iris Vessey. "Managing Risks in Enterprise Systems Implementations." *Communications of the ACM* 45, no. 4 (April 2002).

Siebel Systems, Inc. Case Study. "Manitoba Telecom Creates Unified Customer View and Improves Campaign Effectiveness." http://www.siebel.com/common/includes/pdf_frame.shtm?pdfUrl=/downloads/case_studies/manitoba.pdf (accessed May 27, 2005).

———. "Saab Cars USA Increases Lead Follow-Up from 38 Percent to 50 Percent with Siebel Automotive." http://www.siebel.com (accessed May 4, 2004).

Sinha, Sudhi. "The Smartest Link." *Intelligent Enterprise* (August 10, 2003).

Slone, Reuben E. "Leading a Supply Chain Turnaround." *Harvard Business Review* (October 2004).

"Supply Chain Challenges: Building Relationships." *Harvard Business Review* (July 2003).

Toh, Ann. "Portal Power." *CIO Asia* (August 2003).

Varon, Elena. "Portals Get Down to Business." *CIO* (December 1, 2002).

Welty, Bill, and Irma Becerra-Fernandez. "Managing Trust and Commitment in Supply Chain Relationships." *Communications of the ACM* 44, no. 6 (June 2001).

Winer, Russell S. "A Framework for Customer Relationship Management." *California Management Review* 43, no. 4 (Summer 2001).

Yu, Larry. "Successful Customer Relationship Management." *Sloan Management Review* 42, no. 4 (Summer 2001).

Chapter 15

Alavi, Maryam, and Erich A. Joachimsthaler. "Revisiting DSS Implementation Research: A Meta-Analysis of the Literature and Suggestions for Researchers." *MIS Quarterly* 16, no. 1 (March 1992).

Anson, Rob, and Bjorn Erik Munkvold. "Beyond Face-to-Face: A Field Study of Electronic Meetings in Different Time and Place Modes." *Journal of Organizational Computing and Electronic Commerce* 14, no. 2 (2004).

Apte, Chidanand, Bing Liu, Edwin P. D. Pednault, and Padhraic Smith. "Business Applications of Data Mining." *Communications of the ACM* 45, no. 8 (August 2002).

Bacheldor, Beth. "Beating Down Inventory Costs." *Information Week* (April 21, 2003).

———. "Nimble, Quick Supply Chains in Demand." *Information Week* (March 24, 2003).

———. "Breakthrough." *Information Week* (February 9, 2004).

Barkhi, Reza. "The Effects of Decision Guidance and Problem Modeling on Group Decision-Making." *Journal of Management Information Systems* 18, no. 3 (Winter 2001–2002).

Berez, Steve and Chris Zook. "UPS Links to Customers." *Optimize Magazine* (February 2004).

Briggs, Robert O., Gert-Jan de Vreede, and Jay. F. Nunamaker Jr. "Collaboration Engineering with ThinkLets to Pursue Sustained Success with Group Support Systems." *Journal of Management Information Systems* 19, no. 4 (Spring 2003).

Chidambaram, Laku. "Relational Development in Computer-Supported Groups." *MIS Quarterly* 20, no. 2 (June 1996).

Cone, Edward, and David F. Carr. "Unloading on the Competition." *Baseline* (October 2002).

De Vreede, Gert-Jan, Robert M. Daviso, and Robert O. Briggs. "How a Silvery Bullet May Lose Its Shine." *Communications of the ACM* 46, no. 8 (August 2003).

Dennis, Alan R. "Information Exchange and Use in Group Decision Making: You Can Lead a Group to Information, but You Can't Make It Think." *MIS Quarterly* 20, no. 4 (December 1996).

Dennis, Alan R., and Monica J. Garfield. "The Adoption and Use of GSS in Project Teams: Toward More Participative Processes and Outcomes." *MIS Quarterly* 27, no. 2 (June 2003).

Dennis, Alan R., and Bryan A. Reinicke. "Beta versus VHS and the Acceptance of Electronic Brainstorming Technology." *MIS Quarterly* 28, no. 1 (March 2004).

Dennis, Alan R., and Barbara H. Wixom. "Investigating the Moderators of the Group Support Systems Use with Meta-Analysis." *Journal of Management Information Systems* 18, no. 3 (Winter 2001–2002).

Dennis, Alan R., Jay F. Nunamaker Jr., and Douglas R. Vogel. "A Comparison of Laboratory and Field Research in the Study of Electronic Meeting Systems." *Journal of Management Information Systems* 7, no. 3 (Winter 1990–1991).

Dennis, Alan R., Barbara H. Wixom, and Robert J. Vandenberg. "Understanding Fit and Appropriation Effects in Group Support Systems via Meta-Analysis." *MIS Quarterly* 25, no. 2 (June 2001).

Dennis, Alan R., Jay E. Aronson, William G. Henriger, and Edward D. Walker III. "Structuring Time and Task in Electronic Brainstorming." *MIS Quarterly* 23, no. 1 (March 1999).

Dennis, Alan R., Craig K. Tyran, Douglas R. Vogel, and Jay Nunamaker Jr. "Group Support Systems for Strategic Planning." *Journal of Management Information Systems* 14, no. 1 (Summer 1997).

Dennis, Alan R., Joey F. George, Len M. Jessup, Jay F. Nunamaker, and Douglas R. Vogel. "Information Technology to Support Electronic Meetings." *MIS Quarterly* 12, no. 4 (December 1988).

DeSanctis, Geraldine, and R. Brent Gallupe. "A Foundation for the Study of Group Decision Support Systems." *Management Science* 33, no. 5 (May 1987).

Dhar, Vasant, and Roger Stein. *Intelligent Decision Support Methods: The Science of Knowledge Work.* Upper Saddle River, N.J.: Prentice Hall (1997).

Dutta, Soumitra, Berend Wierenga, and Arco Dalebout. "Designing Management Support Systems Using an Integrative Perspective." *Communications of the ACM* 40, no. 6 (June 1997).

Edelstein, Herb. "Technology How To: Mining Data Warehouses." *Information Week* (January 8, 1996).

El Sawy, Omar. "Personal Information Systems for Strategic Scanning in Turbulent Environments." *MIS Quarterly* 9, no. 1 (March 1985).

El Sherif, Hisham, and Omar A. El Sawy. "Issue-Based Decision Support Systems for the Egyptian Cabinet." *MIS Quarterly* 12, no. 4 (December 1988).

Eveborn, Patrik, Patrik Flisberg, and Mikael Ronnqvist. "Home Care Operations." *OR/MS Today* (April 2004).

Few, Stephen. "Dashboard Confusion." *Intelligent Enterprise* (March 20, 2004).

Fjermestad, Jerry. "An Integrated Framework for Group Support Systems." *Journal of Organizational Computing and Electronic Commerce* 8, no. 2 (1998).

Fjermestad, Jerry, and Starr Roxanne Hiltz. "An Assessment of Group Support Systems Experimental Research: Methodology and Results." *Journal of Management Information Systems* 15, no. 3 (Winter 1998–1999).

———. "Group Support Systems: A Descriptive Evaluation of Case and Field Studies." *Journal of Management Information Systems* 17, no. 3 (Winter 2000–2001).

Forgionne, Giuseppe. "Management Support System Effectiveness: Further Empirical Evidence." *Journal of the Association for Information Systems* 1 (May 2000).

Fox, Pimm. "Insights Turn Into Profits." *ComputerWorld* (February 10, 2002).

Gallupe, R. Brent, Geraldine DeSanctis, and Gary W. Dickson. "Computer-Based Support for Group Problem-Finding: An Experimental Investigation." *MIS Quarterly* 12, no. 2 (June 1988).

George, Joey. "Organizational Decision Support Systems." *Journal of Management Information Systems* 8, no. 3 (Winter 1991–1992).

Ginzberg, Michael J., W. R. Reitman, and E. A. Stohr, eds. *Decision Support Systems.* New York: North Holland Publishing (1982).

Gorry, G. Anthony, and Michael S. Scott Morton. "A Framework for Management Information Systems." *Sloan Management Review* 13, no. 1 (Fall 1971).

Hender, Jillian M., Douglas L. Dean, Thomas L. Rodgers, and Jay F. Nunamaker Jr. "An Examination of the Impact of Stimuli Type and GSS Structure on Creativity." *Journal of Management Information Systems* 18, no. 4 (Spring 2002).

Hilmer, Kelly M., and Alan R. Dennis. "Stimulating Thinking: Cultivating Better Decisions with Groupware through Categorization." *Journal of Management Information Systems* 17, no. 3 (Winter 2000–2001).

Hogue, Jack T. "A Framework for the Examination of Management Involvement in Decision Support Systems." *Journal of Management Information Systems* 4, no. 1 (Summer 1987).

Houdeshel, George, and Hugh J. Watson. "The Management Information and Decision Support (MIDS) System at Lockheed, Georgia." *MIS Quarterly* 11, no. 2 (March 1987).

Kalakota, Ravi, Jan Stallaert, and Andrew B. Whinston. "Worldwide Real-Time Decision Support Systems for Electronic Commerce Applications." *Journal of Organizational Computing and Electronic Commerce* 6, no. 1 (1996).

Keen, Peter G. W., and M. S. Scott Morton. *Decision Support Systems: An Organizational Perspective.* Reading, Mass.: Addison-Wesley (1982).

Kohavi, Ron, Neal J. Rothleder, and Evangelos Simoudis. "Emerging Trends in Business Analytics." *Communications of the ACM* 45, no. 8 (August 2002).

Kose, John, Larry Lang, and Jeffry Netter. "The Voluntary Restructuring of Large Firms in Response to Performance Decline." *Journal of Finance* (July 1992).

Kwok, Ron Chi-Wai, Jian Ma, and Douglas R. Vogel. "Effects of Group Support Systems and Content Facilitation on Knowledge Acquisition." *Journal of Management Information Systems* 19, no. 3 (Winter 2002–2003).

LaCroix, Benoit, and Jacques Desrosiers. "Altitude Manpower Planning." *OR/MS Today* (April 2004).

Laudon, Kenneth C., and Jane P. Laudon. *Management Information Systems: Managing the Digital Firm,* 8th ed. Upper Saddle River, N.J.: Prentice Hall (2003).

Leidner, Dorothy E., and Joyce Elam. "Executive Information Systems: Their Impact on Executive Decision Making." *Journal of Management Information Systems* (Winter 1993–1994).

———. "The Impact of Executive Information Systems on Organizational Design, Intelligence, and Decision Making." *Organization Science* 6, no. 6 (November–December 1995).

Lilien, Gary L., Arvind Rangaswamy, Gerrit H. Van Bruggen, and Katrin Starke. "DSS Effectiveness in Marketing Resource Allocation Decisions: Reality vs. Perception." *Information Systems Research* 15, no. 3 (September 2004).

McCune, Jenny C. "Measuring Value." *Beyond Computing* (July/August 2000).

McDougall, Paul. "Load 'Em Up." *Information Week* (September 29, 2003).

MicroStrategy Incorporated. "WH Smith PLC Selects Microstrategy to Anchor BI Initiatives." Tabor Communications, **http://www.tabor communications.com/dsstar/01/0619/103188.html** (accessed July 5, 2005).

Niederman, Fred, Catherine M. Beise, and Peggy M. Beranek. "Issues and Concerns about Computer-Supported Meetings: The Facilitator's Perspective." *MIS Quarterly* 20, no. 1 (March 1996).

Nunamaker, Jay, Robert O. Briggs, Daniel D. Mittleman, Douglas R. Vogel, and Pierre A. Balthazard. "Lessons from a Dozen Years of Group Support Systems Research: A Discussion of Lab and Field Findings." *Journal of Management Information Systems* 13, no. 3 (Winter 1997).

Nunamaker, J. F., Alan R. Dennis, Joseph S. Valacich, Douglas R. Vogel, and Joey F. George. "Electronic Meeting Systems to Support Group Work." *Communications of the ACM* 34, no. 7 (July 1991).

O'Keefe, Robert M., and Tim McEachern. "Web-Based Customer Decision Support Systems." *Communications of the ACM* 41, no. 3 (March 1998).

Optimal Solutions. "Laps Care: How to Get as Much as Possible Out of Your Home Care Organization." **http://www.optimalsolutions.se/ english/lapscare/Bilder/Laps%20Care_english.pdf** (2002, accessed July 5, 2005).

PeopleSoft. "Spotlight on Performance at Detroit Edison." **http://www.peoplesoft.com** (accessed November 3, 2002).

Pinsonneault, Alain, Henri Barki, R. Brent Gallupe, and Norberto Hoppen. "Electronic Brainstorming: The Illusion of Productivity." *Information Systems Research* 10, no. 2 (July 1999).

Reinig, Bruce A. "Toward an Understanding of Satisfaction with the Process and Outcomes of Teamwork." *Journal of Management Information Systems* 19, no. 4 (Spring 2003).

Rockart, John F., and David W. DeLong. *Executive Support Systems: The Emergence of Top Management Computer Use.* Homewood, Ill.: Dow-Jones Irwin (1988).

Schwabe, Gerhard. "Providing for Organizational Memory in Computer-Supported Meetings." *Journal of Organizational Computing and Electronic Commerce* 9, nos. 2 and 3 (1999).

Silver, Mark S. "Decision Support Systems: Directed and Nondirected Change." *Information Systems Research* 1, no. 1 (March 1990).

Simon, H. A. *The New Science of Management Decision.* New York: Harper & Row (1960).

Sprague, R. H., and E. D. Carlson. *Building Effective Decision Support Systems.* Englewood Cliffs, N.J.: Prentice Hall (1982).

Stodder, David. "True Tales of Performance Management." *Intelligent Enterprise* (June 1, 2004).

Turban, Efraim, and Jay E. Aronson. *Decision Support Systems and Intelligent Systems,* 7th ed. Upper Saddle River, N.J.: Prentice Hall (2005).

United Parcel Service. Annual Report for Fiscal Year Ending December 31, 2003, Form 10-K, United States Securities and Exchange Commission.

Virzi, Anna Maria. "United Parcel Service: Sticky Fix." *Baseline Magazine* (February 5, 2004).

Volonino, Linda, and Hugh J. Watson. "The Strategic Business Objectives Method for EIS Development." *Journal of Management Information Systems* 7, no. 3 (Winter 1990–1991).

Walls, Joseph G., George R. Widmeyer, and Omar A. El Sawy. "Building an Information System Design Theory for Vigilant EIS." *Information Systems Research* 3, no. 1 (March 1992).

Watson, Hugh J., Astrid Lipp, Pamela Z. Jackson, Abdelhafid Dahmani, and William B. Fredenberger. "Organizational Support for Decision Support Systems." *Journal of Management Information Systems* 5, no. 4 (Spring 1989).

Watson, Hugh J., R. Kelly Rainer Jr., and Chang E. Koh. "Executive Information Systems: A Framework for Development and a Survey of Current Practices." *MIS Quarterly* 15, no. 1 (March 1991).

Wrazen, Ed. "UK Forces Cut Supply Chain Costs by $30 Million in 'Dirty Data' Cleanup." TDWI. **http://www.tdwi.org/research/display.aspx?ID=7073** (accessed May 26, 2004).

Yoo, Youngjin, and Maryam Alavi. "Media and Group Cohesion: Relative Influences on Social Presence, Task Participation, and Group Consensus." *MIS Quarterly* 25, no. 3 (September 2001).

Zimmermann, Hans Jurgen. "Online Optimization." *OR/MS Today* (April 2004).

Chapter 16

"A Law Firm's Nucleus of Knowledge." *KM World* (February 2004).

Alavi, Maryam, and Dorothy Leidner. "Knowledge Management and Knowledge Management Systems: Conceptual Foundations and Research Issues." *MIS Quarterly* 25, no. 1 (March 2001).

Allen, Bradley P. "CASE-Based Reasoning: Business Applications." *Communications of the ACM* 37, no. 3 (March 1994).

Anandarajan, Murugan. "Profiling Web Usage in the Workplace: A Behavior-Based Artificial Intelligence Approach." *Journal of Management Information Systems* 19, no. 1 (Summer 2002).

Anthes, Gary H. "Agents Change." *Computerworld* (January 27, 2003).

AskMe Corporation. "Select Customers: P&G Case Study." (August 2003). **http://www.askmecorp.com/customers/default.asp.**

Awad, Elias, and Hassan M. Ghaziri. *Knowledge Management.* Upper Saddle River, N.J.: Prentice Hall (2004).

Balasubramanian, V., and Alf Bashian. "Document Management and Web Technologies: Alice Marries the Mad Hatter." *Communications of the ACM* 41, no. 7 (July 1998).

Bargeron, David, Jonathan Grudin, Anoop Gupta, Elizabeth Sanocki, Francis Li, and Scott Le Tiernan. "Asynchronous Collaboration Around Multimedia Applied to On-Demand Education." *Journal of Management Information Systems* 18, no. 4 (Spring 2002).

Barker, Virginia E., and Dennis E. O'Connor. "Expert Systems for Configuration at Digital: XCON and Beyond." *Communications of the ACM* (March 1989).

Becerra-Fernandez, Irma, Avelino Gonzalez, and Rajiv Sabherwal. *Knowledge Management.* UpperSaddleRiver, N.J.: Prentice Hall (2004).

Bieer, Michael, Douglas Englebart Richard Furuta, Starr Roxanne Hiltz, John Noll, Jennifer Preece, Edward A. Stohr, Murray Turoff, and Bartel Van de Walle. "Toward Virtual Community Knowledge Evolution." *Journal of Management Information Systems* 18, no. 4 (Spring 2002).

Birkinshaw, Julian, and Tony Sheehan. "Managing the Knowledge Life Cycle." *MIT Sloan Management Review* 44, no. 1 (Fall 2002).

Blair, Margaret M., Steven Wallman, and Brookings Task Force on Intangibles. *Unseen Wealth.* Washington, D.C.: Brookings Institution Press (2001).

Booth, Corey, and Shashi Buluswar. "The Return of Artificial Intelligence." *McKinsey Quarterly,* no. 2 (2002).

Burtka, Michael. "Generic Algorithms." *Stern Information Systems Review* 1, no. 1 (Spring 1993).

Busch, Elizabeth, Matti Hamalainen, Clyde W. Holsapple, Yongmoo Suh, and Andrew B. Whinston. "Issues and Obstacles in the Development of Team Support Systems." *Journal of Organizational Computing* 1, no. 2 (April–June 1991).

Canada NewsWire Group. "Scotiabank Call Centre Rated 'World Class' by SQM." **http://www.newswire.ca/en/releases/archive/January2005/05/c9885.html** (accessed July 8, 2005).

Cannataro, Mario, and Domenico Talia. "The Knowledge Grid." *Communications of the ACM* 46, no. 1 (January 2003).

Cavalieri, Sergio, Vittorio Cesarotti, and Vito Introna. "A Multiagent Model for Coordinated Distribution Chain Planning." *Journal of Organizational Computing and Electronic Commerce* 13, nos. 3 and 4 (2003).

Churchland, Paul M., and Patricia Smith Churchland. "Could a Machine Think?" *Scientific American* (January 1990).

Cole, R. E. "Introduction, Knowledge Management Special Issue." *California Management Review* (Spring 1998).

Cross, Rob, and Lloyd Baird. "Technology Is Not Enough: Improving Performance by Building Organizational Memory." *Sloan Management Review* 41, no. 3 (Spring 2000).

Cross, Rob, Nitin Nohria, and Andrew Parker. "Six Myths about Informal Networks—and How to Overcome Them." *Sloan Management Review* 43, no. 3 (Spring 2002).

Davenport, Thomas H., and Lawrence Prusak. *Working Knowledge: How Organizations Manage What They Know.* Boston: Harvard Business School Press (1997).

Davenport, Thomas H., David W. DeLong, and Michael C. Beers. "Successful Knowledge Management Projects." *Sloan Management Review* 39, no. 2 (Winter 1998).

Davenport, Thomas H., Robert J. Thomas, and Susan Cantrell. "The Mysterious Art and Science of Knowledge-Worker Performance." *MIT Sloan Management Review* 44, no. 1 (Fall 2002).

Davis, Gordon B. "Anytime/Anyplace Computing and the Future of Knowledge Work." *Communications of the ACM* 42, no. 12 (December 2002).

Desouza, Kevin C. "Facilitating Tacit Knowledge Exchange." *Communications of the ACM* 46, no. 6 (June 2003).

Desouza, Kevin C., and J. Roberto Evaristo. "Managing Knowledge in Distributed Projects." *Communications of the ACM* 47, no. 4 (April 2004).

Dhar, Vasant. "Plausibility and Scope of Expert Systems in Management." *Journal of Management Information Systems* (Summer 1987).

Dhar, Vasant, and Roger Stein. *Intelligent Decision Support Methods: The Science of Knowledge Work.* Upper Saddle River, N.J.: Prentice Hall (1997).

Du, Timon C., Eldon Y. Li, and An-pin Chang. "Mobile Agents in Distributed Network Management." *Communications of the ACM* 46, no. 7 (July 2003).

Earl, Michael. "Knowledge Management Strategies: Toward a Taxonomy." *Journal of Management Information Systems* 18, no. 1 (Summer 2001).

Earl, Michael J., and Ian A. Scott. "What Is a Chief Knowledge Officer?" *Sloan Management Review* 40, no. 2 (Winter 1999).

Easley, Robert F., Sarv Devaraj, and J. Michael Crant. "Relating Collaborative Technology Use to Teamwork Quality and Performance: An Empirical Analysis." *Journal of Management Information Systems* 19, no. 4 (Spring 2003).

El Najdawi, M. K., and Anthony C. Stylianou. "Expert Support Systems: Integrating AI Technologies." *Communications of the ACM* 36, no. 12 (December 1993).

EMC Documentum. "New Product Development." **http://www.documentum.com** (accessed June 12, 2004).

Farhoomand, Ali, and Don H. Drury. "Managerial Information Overload." *Communications of the ACM* 45, no. 10 (October 2002).

Flash, Cynthia. "Who Is the CKO?" *Knowledge Management* (May 2001).

Frangos, Alex. "New Dimensions in Design." *Wall Street Journal* (July 7, 2004).

Gelernter, David. "The Metamorphosis of Information Management." *Scientific American* (August 1989).

Glushko, Robert J., Jay M. Tenenbaum, and Bart Meltzer. "An XML Framework for Agent-Based E-Commerce." *Communications of the ACM* 42, no. 3 (March 1999).

Goldberg, David E. "Genetic and Evolutionary Algorithms Come of Age." *Communications of the ACM* 37, no. 3 (March 1994).

Gregor, Shirley, and Izak Benbasat. "Explanations from Intelligent Systems: Theoretical Foundations and Implications for Practice." *MIS Quarterly* 23, no. 4 (December 1999).

Griffith, Terri L., John E. Sawyer, and Margaret A Neale. "Virtualness and Knowledge in Teams: Managing the Love Triangle of Organizations, Individuals, and Information Technology." *MIS Quarterly* 27, no. 2 (June 2003).

Grover, Varun, and Thomas H. Davenport. "General Perspectives on Knowledge Management: Fostering a Research Agenda." *Journal of Management Information Systems* 18, no. 1 (Summer 2001).

Gu, Feng, and Baruch Lev. "Intangible Assets: Measurements, Drivers, Usefulness." Baruch Lev's Homepage. http://pages.stern.nyu.edu/~blev/.

Guerra, Anthony. "Goldman Sachs Embraces Rules-Based Solution." *Wall Street and Technology* (May 2001).

Hansen, Morton T., Nitin Nohria, and Thomas Tierney. "What's Your Strategy for Knowledge Management?" *Harvard Business Review* (March–April 1999).

Hayes-Roth, Frederick, and Neil Jacobstein. "The State of Knowledge-Based Systems." *Communications of the ACM* 37, no. 3 (March 1994).

Hinton, Gregory. "How Neural Networks Learn from Experience." *Scientific American* (September 1992).

Holland, John H. "Genetic Algorithms." *Scientific American* (July 1992).

Housel, Tom, and Arthur A. Bell. *Measuring and Managing Knowledge.* New York: McGraw-Hill, 2001.

Hummingbird Ltd. "Conoco Drills into Hummingbird Portal." http://www.hummingbird.com (accessed 2003).

———. "Legal Firm Looks to the Future of Collaboration with Clients." http://www.hummingbird.com (accessed 2005).

Intralearn. "InsightU and Intralearn Redefine Product Training for Staples in Canada." http://www.intralearn.com/4030_SuccessStories.asp (2001, accessed July 7, 2005).

Jarvenpaa, Sirkka L., and D. Sandy Staples. "Exploring Perceptions of Organizational Ownership of Information and Expertise." *Journal of Management Information Systems* 18, no. 1 (Summer 2001).

Jeong, Woo Seok, Sun Gwan Han, and Geun Sik Jo. "Intelligent Cyber Logistics Using Reverse Auction." *Journal of Organizational Computing and Electronic Commerce* 13, nos. 3 and 4 (2003).

Jones, Quentin, Gilad Ravid, and Sheizaf Rafaeli. "Information Overload and the Message Dynamics of Online Interaction Spaces: A Theoretical Model and Empirical Exploration." *Information Systems Research* 15, no. 2 (June 2004).

Kankanhalli, Atreyi, Frasiska Tanudidjaja, Juliana Sutanto, and Bernard C. Y. Tan. "The Role of IT in Successful Knowledge Management Initiatives." *Communications of the ACM* 46, no. 9 (September 2003).

King, William R., Peter V. Marks Jr., and Scott McCoy. "The Most Important Issues in Knowledge Management." *Communications of the ACM* 45, no. 9 (September 2002).

Kontzer, Tony. "Content Overload," *Information Week* January 19, 2004.

KPMG. "Insights from KPMG's European Knowledge Management Survey 2002/2003." KPMG (2003).

———. "Who We Are—Sharing Knowledge." http://www.kpmgcampus.com (accessed 2003).

Kuo, R. J., K. Chang, and S. Y. Chien. "Integration and Self-Organizing Feature Maps and Genetic-Algorithm-Based Clustering Method for Market Segmentation." *Journal of Organizational Computing and Electronic Commerce* 14, no. 1 (2004).

Lee, Kyoung Jun, Yong Sik Chang, Hyung Rim Choi, Hyun Soo Kim, Young Jae Park, and Byung Joo Park. "A Time-Bound Framework for Negotiation and Decision Making of Virtual Manufacturing Enterprise." *Journal of Organizational Computing and Electronic Commerce* 14, no. 1 (2004).

Leonard, Dorothy, and Walter Swap. "Deep Smarts." *Harvard Business Review* (September 1, 2004).

Leonard-Barton, Dorothy, and John J. Sviokla. "Putting Expert Systems to Work." *Harvard Business Review* (March–April 1988).

Lev, Baruch. "Sharpening the Intangibles Edge." *Harvard Business Review* (June 1, 2004).

Lev, Baruch, and Theodore Sougiannis. "Penetrating the Book-to-Market Black Box: The R&D Effect." *Journal of Business Finance and Accounting* (April/May 1999).

Lou, Hao, and Richard W. Scannell. "Acceptance of Groupware: The Relationships among Use, Satisfaction, and Outcomes." *Journal of Organizational Computing and Electronic Commerce* 6, no. 2 (1996).

Maes, Patti. "Agents That Reduce Work and Information Overload." *Communications of the ACM* 38, no. 7 (July 1994).

Maglio, Paul P., and Christopher S. Campbell. "Attentive Agents." *Communications of the ACM* 46, no. 3 (March 2003).

Markus, M. Lynne. "Toward a Theory of Knowledge Reuse: Types of Knowledge Reuse Situations and Factors in Reuse Success." *Journal of Management Information Systems* 18, no. 1 (Summer 2001).

Markus, M. Lynne, Ann Majchrzak, and Less Gasser. "A Design Theory for Systems That Support Emergent Knowledge Processes." *MIS Quarterly* 26, no. 3 (September 2002).

Maryam, Alavi, and Dorothy E. Leidner. "Knowledge Management and Knowledge Management Systems." *MIS Quarterly* 25, no. 1 (March 2001).

McCarthy, John. "Generality in Artificial Intelligence." *Communications of the ACM* (December 1987).

Microsoft Corporation. "KPMG Turns Knowledge into Value with KWorld." Microsoft.com Korea. http://www.microsoft.com/korea/business/downloads/km/kworld.doc (accessed 2003).

———. "Scotiabank Helps Boost Customer Satisfaction with Microsoft Sharepoint-Based Technology." http://www.microsoft.com/Canada/casestudies/scotiabank.mspx (accessed July 8, 2005).

Moravec, Hans. "Robots, After All." *Communications of the ACM* 46, no. 10 (October 2003).

Munakata, Toshinori, and Yashvant Jani. "Fuzzy Systems: An Overview." *Communications of the ACM* 37, no. 3 (March 1994).

Nidumolu, Sarma R., Mani Subramani, and Alan Aldrich. "Situated Learning and the Situated Knowledge Web: Exploring the Ground Beneath Knowledge Management." *Journal of Management Information Systems* 18, no. 1 (Summer 2001).

Nucleus Research. "ROI Case Study: Hummingbird Cuatrecasas." http://www.hummingbird.com (accessed June 10, 2004).

O'Leary, Daniel, Daniel Kuokka, and Robert Plant. "Artificial Intelligence and Virtual Organizations." *Communications of the ACM* 40, no. 1 (January 1997).

Orlikowski, Wanda J. "Knowing in Practice: Enacting a Collective Capability in Distributed Organizing." *Organization Science* 13, no. 3 (May–June 2002).

Perry, Andrew. "KM in Review: Tracing the Value of Knowledge Assets." *KM World* (October 2002).

Piccoli, Gabriele, Rami Ahmad, and Blake Ives. "Web-Based Virtual Learning Environments: A Research Framework and a Preliminary Assessment of Effectiveness in Basic IT Skills Training." *MIS Quarterly* 25, no. 4 (December 2001).

Ranft, Annette L., and Michael D. Lord. "Acquiring New Technologies and Capabilities: A Grounded Model of Acquisition Implementation." *Organization Science* 13, no. 4 (July–August 2002).

Rumelhart, David E., Bernard Widrow, and Michael A. Lehr. "The Basic Ideas in Neural Networks." *Communications of the ACM* 37, no. 3 (March 1994).

Sadeh, Norman, David W. Hildum, and Dag Kjenstad. "Agent-Based E-Supply Chain Decision Support." *Journal of Organizational Computing and Electronic Commerce* 13, nos. 3 and 4 (2003).

Salkever, Alex. "A Whole New World of 3-D Design." *Business Week Online.* http://www.businessweek.com/technology/content/jul2002/tc2002 0716_7915.htm (accessed October 12, 2005).

Schultze, Ulrike, and Dorothy Leidner. "Studying Knowledge Management in Information Systems Research: Discourses and Theoretical Assumptions." *MIS Quarterly* 26, no. 3 (September 2002).

Selker, Ted. "Coach: A Teaching Agent That Learns." *Communications of the ACM* 37, no. 7 (July 1994).

Semio Corporation. "Case Study: Leveraging the World's Largest Repository of Life Science Research with Entrieva's Semio Technology." Entrieva. http://www.entrieva.com/entrieva/downloads/Customer Implementation_HighwirePress_Entrieva.pdf (accessed September 5, 2003).

Spangler, Scott, Jeffrey T. Kreulen, and Justin Lessler. "Generating and Browsing Multiple Taxonomies over a Document Collection." *Journal of Management Information Systems* 19, no. 4 (Spring 2003).

Spender, J. C. "Organizational Knowledge, Learning and Memory: Three Concepts in Search of a Theory." *Journal of Organizational Change Management* 9 (1996).

Starbuck, William H. "Learning by Knowledge-Intensive Firms." *Journal of Management Studies* 29, no. 6 (November 1992).

Strategis. "Canadian Knowledge Management Software (KMS) Market." http://strategis.ic.gc.ca/epic/internet/inimr-ri.nsf/en/ gr116974e.html (accessed October 12, 2005).

Sukhatme, Gaurav S., and Maja J. Mataric. "Embedding Robots into the Internet." *Communications of the ACM* 43, no. 5 (May 2000).

Sviokla, John J. "An Examination of the Impact of Expert Systems on the Firm: The Case of XCON." *MIS Quarterly* 14, no. 5 (June 1990).

Tiwana, Amrit. "Affinity to Infinity in Peer-to-Peer Knowledge Platforms." *Communications of the ACM* 46, no. 5 (May 2003).

Trippi, Robert, and Efraim Turban. "The Impact of Parallel and Neural Computing on Managerial Decision Making." *Journal of Management Information Systems* 6, no. 3 (Winter 1989–1990).

Vandenbosch, Betty, and Michael J. Ginzberg. "Lotus Notes and Collaboration." *Journal of Management Information Systems* 13, no. 3 (Winter 1997).

Wakefield, Julie. "Complexity's Business Model." *Scientific American* (January 2001).

Walczak, Stephen. "An Empirical Analysis of Data Requirements for Financial Forecasting with Neural Networks." *Journal of Management Information Systems* 17, no. 4 (Spring 2001).

Walczak, Steven. "Gaining Competitive Advantage for Trading in Emerging Capital Markets with Neural Networks." *Journal of Management Information Systems* 16, no. 2 (Fall 1999).

Wang, Huaiqing, John Mylopoulos, and Stephen Liao. "Intelligent Agents and Financial Risk Monitoring Systems." *Communications of the ACM* 45, no. 3 (March 2002).

Widrow, Bernard, David E. Rumelhart, and Michael A. Lehr. "Neural Networks: Applications in Industry, Business, and Science." *Communications of the ACM* 37, no. 3 (March 1994).

Wijnhoven, Fons. "Designing Organizational Memories: Concept and Method." *Journal of Organizational Computing and Electronic Commerce* 8, no. 1 (1998).

Wong, David, Noemi Paciorek, and Dana Moore. "Java-Based Mobile Agents." *Communications of the ACM* 42, no. 3 (March 1999).

Yimam-Seid, Dawit, and Alfred Kobsa. "Expert-Finding Systems for Organizations: Problem and Domain Analysis and the DEMOIR Approach." *Journal of Organizational Computing and Electronic Commerce* 13, no. 1 (2003).

Zack, Michael H. "Rethinking the Knowledge-Based Organization." *MIS Sloan Management Review* 44, no. 4 (Summer 2003).

Zadeh, Lotfi A. "Fuzzy Logic, Neural Networks, and Soft Computing." *Communications of the ACM* 37, no. 3 (March 1994).

———. "The Calculus of Fuzzy If/Then Rules." *AI Expert* (March 1992).

GLOSSARY

2.5G networks Wireless digital cellular networks that provide higher-speed data transmission rates ranging from 50 to 144 kilobits per second (Kbps) using the existing cellular network infrastructure.

3G networks Cellular networks based on packet-switching technology with speeds ranging from 144 kilobits per second (Kbps) for mobile users to over 2 megabits per second (Mbps) for stationary users enabling users to transmit video, graphics, and other rich media, in addition to voice.

802.11b Wireless local area network (LAN) standard that can transmit up to 11 megabits per second (Mbps) in the unlicensed 2.4-GHz band and that has an effective distance of 30 to 50 metres.

acceptable use policy (AUP) Defines acceptable uses of the firm's information resources and computing equipment, including desktop and laptop computers, wireless devices, telephones, and the Internet, and specifies consequences for noncompliance.

acceptance testing Provides the final certification that the system is ready to be used in a production setting.

access controls Policies and procedures a company uses to prevent improper access to systems by unauthorized insiders and outsiders.

access point Box in a wireless local area network (LAN) consisting of a radio receiver/transmitter and antennas that link to a wired network, router, or hub.

accountability The mechanisms for assessing responsibility for decisions made and actions taken.

accounting rate of return on investment (ROI) Calculation of the rate of return on an investment by adjusting cash inflows produced by the investment for depreciation. Approximates the accounting income earned by the investment.

accumulated balance digital payment system System enabling users to make micropayments and purchases on the Web, accumulating a debit balance on their credit card or telephone bills.

activity-based costing Model for identifying all the company activities that cause costs to occur while producing a specific product or service. Managers can see which products or services are profitable or losing money and make changes to maximize firm profitability.

administrative controls Formalized standards, rules, procedures, and disciplines to ensure that the organization's controls are properly executed and enforced.

agency theory Economic theory that views the firm as a nexus of contracts among self-interested individuals who must be supervised and managed.

AI shell The programming environment of an expert system.

analytical CRM Customer relationship management (CRM) applications dealing with the analysis of customer data to provide information for improving business performance.

antivirus software Software designed to detect, and often eliminate, computer viruses from an information system.

application controls Specific controls unique to each computerized application.

application proxy filtering Firewall screening technology that uses a proxy server to inspect and transmit data packets flowing into and out of the organization so that all the organization's internal applications communicate with the outside using a proxy application.

application server Software that handles all application operations between browser-based computers and a company's back-end business applications or databases.

application service provider (ASP) Company providing software that can be rented by other companies over the Web or a private network.

application software Programs written for or by users to apply the computer to a specific task.

application software package A set of prewritten, precoded application software programs that are commercially available for sale or lease.

artificial intelligence (AI) The effort to develop computer-based systems that can behave like humans, with the ability to learn languages, accomplish physical tasks, use a perceptual apparatus, and emulate human expertise and decision making.

asynchronous transfer mode (ATM) A networking technology that parcels information into fixed 53-byte cells, enabling data to be transmitted between computers from different vendors at any speed.

attribute A piece of information describing a particular entity.

authentication The ability of each party in a transaction to ascertain the identity of the other party.

authorization management systems Systems for allowing each user access only to those portions of a system or the Web that person is permitted to enter, based on information established by a set of access rules.

authorization policies Policies that determine differing levels of access to information assets for different levels of users in an organization.

automation Using the computer to speed up the performance of existing tasks.

autonomic computing Effort to develop systems that can manage themselves without user intervention.

backbone Part of a network handling the major traffic and providing the primary path for traffic flowing to or from other networks.

backward chaining A strategy for searching the rule base in an expert system that acts like a problem solver by beginning with a hypothesis and seeking out more information until the hypothesis is either proved or disproved.

balanced scorecard Model for analyzing firm performance that supplements traditional financial measures with measurements from additional business perspectives, such as customers, internal business processes, and learning and growth.

bandwidth The capacity of a communications channel as measured by the difference between the highest and lowest frequencies that can be transmitted by that channel.

banner ad A graphic display on a Web page used for advertising. The banner is linked to the advertiser's Web site so that a person clicking the banner is transported to the advertiser's Web site.

behavioural models Descriptions of management based on behavioural scientists' observations of what managers actually do in their jobs.

benchmarking Setting strict standards for products, services, or activities and measuring organizational performance against those standards.

best practices The most successful solutions or problem-solving methods that have been developed by a specific organization or industry.

biometric authentication Technology for authenticating system users that compares a person's unique characteristics, such as fingerprints, face, or retinal image, against a stored set profile of these characteristics.

bit A binary digit representing the smallest unit of data in a computer system. It can have only one of two states, representing 0 or 1.

blade server Entire computer that fits on a single, thin card (or blade) and that is plugged into a single chassis to save space and power and reduce complexity.

blog Popular term for Web log, designating an informal yet structured Web site where individuals can publish stories, opinions, and links to other Web sites of interest.

Bluetooth Standard for wireless personal area networks that can transmit up to 722 kilobits per second (Kbps) within a 10-metre area.

broadband High-speed transmission technology. Also designates a single communications medium that can transmit multiple channels of data simultaneously.

bugs Program code defects or errors.

bullwhip effect Distortion of information about the demand for a product as it passes from one entity to the next across the supply chain.

bundling Cross-selling in which a combination of products is sold as a bundle at a price lower than the total cost of the individual products.

bureaucracy Formal organization with a clear-cut division of labour, abstract rules and procedures, and impartial decision making that uses technical qualifications and professionalism as a basis for promoting employees.

bureaucratic models of decision making Models of decision making in which decisions are shaped by the organization's routines and existing operating procedures.

business continuity planning Planning that focuses on how the company can restore business operations after a disaster strikes.

business driver A force in the environment to which businesses must respond and that influences the direction of business.

business ecosystem Loosely coupled but interdependent networks of suppliers, distributors, outsourcing firms, transportation service firms, and technology manufacturers.

business function Specialized task performed in a business organization, including manufacturing and production, sales and marketing, finance and accounting, and human resources.

business intelligence Applications and technologies to help users make better business decisions.

business model An abstraction of what an enterprise is and how the enterprise delivers a product or service, showing how the enterprise creates wealth.

business process management Methodology for revising the organization's business processes to use business processes as fundamental building blocks of corporate information systems.

business process reengineering The radical redesign of business processes, combining steps to cut waste and eliminating repetitive, paper-intensive tasks to improve cost, quality, and service and to maximize the benefits of information technology.

business processes The set of logically related tasks and behaviours that organizations develop over time to produce specific business results and the unique manner in which these activities are organized and coordinated.

business strategy Set of activities and decisions that determines the products and services the firm produces, the industries in which the firm competes, firm competitors, suppliers, and customers, and the firm's long-term goals.

business-to-business (B2B) electronic commerce Electronic sales of goods and services among businesses.

business-to-consumer (B2C) electronic commerce Electronic retailing of products and services directly to individual consumers.

bus network Network topology linking a number of computers by a single circuit with all messages broadcast to the entire network.

byte A string of bits, usually eight, used to store one number or character in a computer system.

cable modem Modem designed to operate over cable TV lines to provide high-speed access to the Internet or corporate intranets.

call centre An organizational department responsible for handling customer service issues by telephone and other channels.

campus area network (CAN) An interconnected set of local area networks in a limited geographical area such as a college or corporate campus.

capacity planning The process of predicting when a computer hardware system becomes saturated to ensure that adequate computing resources are available for work of different priorities and that the firm has enough computing power for its current and future needs.

capital budgeting The process of analyzing and selecting various proposals for capital expenditures.

carpal tunnel syndrome (CTS) Type of repetitive stress disorder (RSI) in which pressure on the median nerve through the wrist's bony carpal tunnel structure produces pain.

case-based reasoning (CBR) Artificial intelligence technology that represents knowledge as a database of cases and solutions.

cellular telephone (cell phone) A device that transmits voice or data, using radio waves to communicate with radio antennas placed within adjacent geographic areas called cells.

central processing unit (CPU) The part of the computer system where the manipulation of symbols, numbers, and characters occurs, and that controls the other parts of the computer system.

change agent In the context of implementation, the individual acting as the catalyst during the change process to ensure successful organizational adaptation to a new system or innovation.

channel conflict Competition between two or more different distribution chains used to sell the products or services of the same company.

chat Live, interactive conversations over a public network.

chief information officer (CIO) Senior manager in charge of the information systems function in the firm.

chief knowledge officer (CKO) Senior executive in charge of the organization's knowledge management program.

chief security officer (CSO) Person who manages a formal security function for the organization and who is responsible for enforcing the firm's security policy.

choice Simon's third stage of decision making, when the individual selects among the various solution alternatives.

churn rate Measurement of the number of customers who stop using or purchasing products or services from a company. Used as an indicator of the growth or decline of a firm's customer base.

classical model of management Traditional description of management that focused on its formal functions of planning, organizing, coordinating, deciding, and controlling.

clicks-and-mortar Business model where the Web site is an extension of a traditional bricks-and-mortar business.

clickstream tracking Tracking data about customer activities at Web sites and storing them in a log.

client The user point of entry for the required function in client/server computing. Normally a desktop computer, workstation, or laptop computer.

client/server computing A model for computing that splits processing between clients and servers on a network, assigning functions to the machine most able to perform the function.

clustering Linking two computers together so that the second computer can act as a backup to the primary computer or speed up processing.

coaxial cable A transmission medium consisting of thickly insulated copper wire; can transmit large volumes of data quickly.

Code Division Multiple Access (CDMA) Major cellular transmission standard in North America that transmits over several frequencies, occupies the entire spectrum, and randomly assigns users to a range of frequencies over time.

collaborative commerce The use of digital technologies to enable multiple organizations to design, develop, build, and manage products collaboratively through product life cycles.

collaborative filtering Tracking users' movements on a Web site, comparing the information gleaned about a user's behaviour against data about other customers with similar interests to predict what the user would like to see next.

communications technology Physical devices and software that link various computer hardware components and transfer data from one physical location to another.

communities of practice (COP) Informal social networks of professionals and employees within and outside the firm who have similar work-related activities and interests.

competitive forces model Model used to describe the interaction of external influences, specifically threats and opportunities, that affect an organization's strategy and ability to compete.

complementary assets Additional assets required to derive value from a primary investment.

component-based development The development of large software systems by combining preexisting software components.

computer Physical device that takes data as an input, transforms the data by executing stored instructions, and outputs information to a number of devices.

computer abuse The commission of acts involving a computer that may not be illegal but are considered unethical.

computer-aided design (CAD) Information system that automates the creation and revision of designs using sophisticated graphics software.

computer-aided software engineering (CASE) Automation of step-by-step methodologies for software and systems development to reduce the amounts of repetitive work the developer must do.

computer-based information systems (CBIS) Information systems that rely on computer hardware and software for processing and disseminating information.

computer crime The commission of illegal acts through the use of a computer or against a computer system.

computer forensics The scientific collection, examination, authentication, preservation, and analysis of data held on or retrieved from computer storage media in such a way that the information can be used as evidence in a court of law.

computer hardware Physical equipment used for input, processing, and output activities in an information system.

computer literacy Knowledge about information technology, focusing on understanding how computer-based technologies work.

computer software Detailed, preprogrammed instructions that control and coordinate the work of computer hardware components in an information system.

computer virus Rogue software program that attaches itself to other software programs or data files in order to be executed, often causing hardware and software malfunctions.

computer vision syndrome (CVS) Eyestrain condition related to computer display screen use; symptoms include headaches, blurred vision, and dry and irritated eyes.

conceptual schema The logical description of the entire database showing all the data elements and relationships among them.

connectivity The ability of computers and computer-based devices to communicate with each other and share information in a meaningful way without human intervention.

consumer-to-consumer (C2C) electronic commerce Consumers selling goods and services electronically to other consumers.

controls All of the methods, policies, and procedures that ensure protection of the organization's assets, accuracy and reliability of its records, and operational adherence to management standards.

conversion The process of changing from the old system to the new system.

cookie Tiny file deposited on a computer hard drive when an individual visits certain Web sites. Used to identify the visitor and track visits to the Web site.

cooptation Bringing the opposition into the process of designing and implementing a solution without giving up control of the direction and nature of the change.

copyright A statutory grant that protects creators of intellectual property against copying by others for any purpose for a minimum of 50 years.

core competency Activity at which a firm excels as a world-class leader.

core system System that supports functions that are absolutely critical to the organization.

cost-benefit ratio A method for calculating the returns from a capital expenditure by dividing total benefits by total costs.

counterimplementation A deliberate strategy to thwart the implementation of an information system or an innovation in an organization.

cracker Hacker with criminal intent.

critical success factors (CSFs) A small number of easily identifiable operational goals shaped by the industry, the firm, the manager, and the broader environment that are believed to ensure the success of an organization. Used to determine the information requirements of an organization.

cross-selling Marketing complementary products to customers.

customer decision-support systems (CDSS) Systems to support the decision-making process of an existing or potential customer.

customer lifetime value (CLTV) Difference between revenues produced by a specific customer and the expenses for acquiring and servicing that customer minus the cost of promotional marketing over the lifetime of the customer relationship, expressed in today's dollars.

customer relationship management (CRM) Business and technology discipline that uses information systems to coordinate all of the business processes surrounding the firm's interactions with its customers in sales, marketing, and service.

customer relationship management (CRM) system Information system that tracks all the ways in which a company interacts with its customers and analyzes these interactions to optimize revenue, profitability, customer satisfaction, and customer retention.

customization The modification of a software package to meet an organization's unique requirements without destroying the packaged software's integrity.

cybervandalism The intentional disruption, defacement, or even destruction of a Web site or corporate information system.

data Streams of raw facts representing events occurring in organizations or the physical environment before they have been organized and arranged into a form that people can understand and use.

data administration A special organizational function for managing the organization's data resources that is concerned with information policy, data planning, maintenance of data dictionaries, and data quality standards.

data cleansing Activities for detecting and correcting data in a database or file that are incorrect, incomplete, improperly formatted, or redundant. Also known as data scrubbing.

data definition language The component of a database management system that defines each data element as it appears in the database.

data dictionary An automated or manual tool for storing and organizing information about the data maintained in a database.

data element A field.

data entry operators IS personnel who enter data in computer readable format

data flow diagram (DFD) Primary tool for structured analysis that graphically illustrates a system's component processes and the flow of data between them.

data inconsistency The presence of different values for the same attribute when the same data are stored in multiple locations.

data manipulation language A language associated with a database management system that end users and programmers use to manipulate data in the database.

data mart A small data warehouse containing only a portion of the organization's data for a specified function or population of users.

data mining Analysis of large pools of data to find patterns and rules that can be used to guide decision making and predict future behaviour.

data quality audit A survey and/or sample of files to determine accuracy and completeness of data in an information system.

data redundancy The presence of duplicate data in multiple data files.

data visualization Technology for helping users see patterns and relationships in large amounts of data by presenting the data in graphical form.

data warehouse A database with reporting and query tools that stores current and historical data extracted from various operational systems and consolidated for management reporting and analysis.

data workers People such as secretaries or bookkeepers who process the organization's paperwork.

database A group of related files.

database (rigorous definition) A collection of data organized to service many applications at the same time by storing and managing data so that they appear to be in one location.

database administration Refers to the more technical and operational aspects of managing data, including physical database design and maintenance.

database management system (DBMS) Special software to create and maintain a database and enable individual business applications to extract the data they need without having to create separate files or data definitions in their computer programs.

database server A computer in a client/server environment that is responsible for running a database management system (DBMS) to process structured query language (SQL) statements and perform database management tasks.

data-driven DSS Systems that support decision making by enabling users to extract and analyze useful information that was previously buried in large databases.

debugging The process of discovering and eliminating the errors and defects—bugs—in program code.

decision-support systems (DSS) Information systems at the organization's management level that combines data and sophisticated analytical models or data analysis tools to support semistructured and unstructured decision making.

decisional roles Mintzberg's classification for managerial roles in which managers initiate activities, handle disturbances, allocate resources, and negotiate conflicts.

demand planning Determining how much product a business needs to make to satisfy all its customers' demands.

denial of service (DoS) attack Flooding a network server or Web server with false communications or requests for services in order to crash the network.

dense wavelength division multiplexing (DWDM) Technology for boosting transmission capacity of optical fibre by using many different wavelengths to carry separate streams of data over the same fibre strand at the same time.

Descartes' rule of change A principle that states that if an action cannot be taken repeatedly, it is not right to be taken at any time.

design Simon's second stage of decision making, when the individual conceives of possible alternative solutions to a problem.

development methodology A collection of methods, one or more for every activity within every phase of a development project.

digital cash Currency that is represented in electronic form that moves outside the normal network of money.

digital certificate An attachment to an electronic message to verify the identity of the sender and to provide the receiver with the means to encode a reply.

digital chequing Systems that extend the functionality of existing chequing accounts so they can be used for online shopping payments.

digital credit card payment system Secure service for credit card payments on the Internet that protects information transmitted among users, merchant sites, and processing banks.

digital dashboard Displays all of a firm's key performance indicators as graphs and charts on a single screen to provide a one-page overview of all the critical measurements necessary to make key executive decisions.

digital divide Large disparities in access to computers and the Internet among different social groups and different locations.

digital firm An organization in which nearly all significant business processes and relationships with customers, suppliers, and employees are digitally enabled, and key corporate assets are managed through digital means.

Digital Millennium Copyright Act (DMCA) U.S. Legislation that adjusts copyright laws to the Internet Age by making it illegal to make, distribute, or use devices that circumvent technology-based protections of copyrighted materials.

digital signature A digital code that can be attached to an electronically transmitted message to uniquely identify its contents and the sender.

digital subscriber line (DSL) A group of technologies providing high-capacity transmission over existing copper telephone lines.

digital wallet Software that stores credit card, electronic cash, owner identification, and address information and provides this data automatically during electronic commerce purchase transactions.

direct cutover A risky conversion approach in which the new system completely replaces the old one on an appointed day.

disaster recovery planning Planning for the restoration of computing and communications services after they have been disrupted.

disintermediation The removal of organizations or business process layers responsible for certain intermediary steps in a value chain.

distributed database A database that is stored in more than one physical location. Parts or copies of the database are physically stored in one location, and other parts or copies are stored and maintained in other locations.

distributed denial of service (DDoS) attack A denial of service (DoS) attack that uses numerous computers to inundate and overwhelm a network from numerous launch points.

distributed processing The distribution of computer processing work among multiple computers linked by a communications network.

documentation Descriptions of how an information system works from either a technical or end-user standpoint.

domain name English-like name that corresponds to the unique 32-bit numeric Internet Protocol (IP) address for each computer connected to the Internet.

Domain Name System (DNS) A hierarchical system of servers maintaining a database enabling the conversion of domain names to their numeric IP addresses.

domestic exporter Form of business organization characterized by heavy centralization of corporate activities in the home country of origin.

downtime Period of time in which an information system is not operational.

drill down The ability to move from summary data to lower and lower levels of detail.

DSS database A collection of current or historical data from a number of applications or groups. Can be a small PC database or a massive data warehouse.

DSS software system Collection of software tools that is used for data analysis, such as online analytical processing (OLAP) tools, data-mining tools, or a collection of mathematical and analytical models.

due process A process in which laws are well known and understood and there is an ability to appeal to higher authorities to ensure that laws are applied correctly.

dynamic pricing Pricing of items based on real-time interactions between buyers and sellers that determine what an item is worth at any particular moment.

e-business See electronic business

e-commerce See electronic commerce

e-government Use of the Internet and related technologies to digitally enable government and public sector agencies' relationships with citizens, businesses, and other arms of government.

edge computing Method for distributing the computing load (or work) across many layers of Internet computers to minimize response time.

efficient customer response system System that directly links consumer behaviour to distribution, production, and supply chains.

electronic billing presentment and payment system A system used for paying routine monthly bills that enables users to view their bills electronically and pay them through electronic funds transfers from bank or credit card accounts.

electronic business (e-business) The use of the Internet and digital technology to execute all the business processes in the enterprise. Includes e-commerce as well as processes for the internal management of the firm and for coordination with suppliers and other business partners.

electronic commerce (e-commerce) The process of buying and selling goods and services electronically, involving transactions using the Internet, networks, and other digital technologies.

electronic data interchange (EDI) The direct computer-to-computer exchange between two organizations of standard business transactions, such as orders, shipment instructions, or payments.

electronic mail See email.

electronic payment system The use of digital technologies, such as credit cards, smart cards, and Internet-based payment systems, to pay for products and services electronically.

electronic records management (ERM) Policies, procedures, and tools for managing the retention, destruction, and storage of electronic records.

email Application that enables messages to be exchanged from computer to computer, eliminating costly long-distance telephone charges while expediting communication between different parts of the organization. In addition to providing electronic messaging, email software has capabilities for routing messages to multiple recipients, forwarding messages, and attaching text documents or multimedia files to messages.

email handheld Handheld device for wireless data transmission that includes a small display screen and a keypad for typing short email messages.

employee relationship management (ERM) Software dealing with employee issues that are closely related to customer relationship management (CRM), such as setting objectives, employee performance management, performance-based compensation, and employee training.

encryption The coding and scrambling of messages to prevent their being read or accessed without authorization.

end user Representative of departments outside the information systems group for whom applications are developed.

end-user development The development of information systems by end users with little or no formal assistance from technical specialists.

end-user interface The part of an information system through which the end user interacts with the system, such as online screens and commands.

enterprise analysis An analysis of organization-wide information requirements made by looking at the entire organization in terms of organizational units, functions, processes, and data elements; helps identify the key entities and attributes in the organization's data.

enterprise application A system that can coordinate activities, decisions, and knowledge across many different functions, levels, and business units in a firm. Includes enterprise systems, supply chain management systems, and knowledge management systems.

enterprise application integration (EAI) software Software that works with specific software platforms to tie together multiple applications to support enterprise integration.

enterprise software Set of integrated modules for applications such as sales and distribution, financial accounting, investment management, materials management, production planning, plant maintenance, and human resources that allows data to be used by multiple functions and business processes.

enterprise systems Integrated enterprise-wide information systems that coordinate key internal processes of the firm.

entity A person, place, thing, or event about which information must be kept.

entity-relationship diagram A methodology for documenting databases illustrating the relationship between various entities in the database.

ergonomics The interaction of people and machines in the work environment, including the design of jobs, health issues, and the end-user interface of information systems.

ethical "no free lunch" rule Assumption that all tangible and intangible objects are owned by someone else, unless there is a specific declaration otherwise, and that the creator wants compensation for this work.

ethics Principles of right and wrong that can be used by individuals acting as free moral agents to make choices to guide their behaviour.

EV-DO Technology used in Verizon's cellular network service for providing anytime, anywhere broadband wireless Internet access for PCs and other devices at average speeds of 300 to 500 kilobits per second (Kbps). Stands for Evolution Data Optimized.

exchange Third-party net marketplace that is primarily transaction oriented and that connects many buyers and suppliers for spot purchasing.

executive support systems (ESS) Information systems at the organization's strategic level designed to address nonroutine decisions requiring judgment, evaluation, and insight using external data and internal MIS and DSS.

expert system Knowledge-intensive computer program that captures the expertise of a human in a limited domain of knowledge.

explicit knowledge Knowledge that has been documented.

eXtensible Markup Language (XML) General-purpose language that describes the structure of a document and supports links to multiple documents, enabling data to be manipulated by the computer. Used for both Web and non-Web applications.

external integration tools Project management technique that links the work of the implementation team to that of users at all organizational levels.

extranet Private intranet that is accessible to authorized outsiders.

Fair Information Practices (FIP) A set of principles originally set forth in 1973 that governs the collection and use of information about individuals and that forms the basis of most Canadian, U.S. and European privacy laws.

fault-tolerant computer system A system that contains extra hardware, software, and power supply components that can back up a system and keep it running to prevent system failure.

feasibility study As part of the systems analysis process, the way to determine whether the solution is achievable, given the organization's resources and constraints.

feedback Output that is returned to the appropriate members of the organization to help them evaluate or correct input.

fibre-optic cable A fast, light, and durable transmission medium consisting of thin strands of clear glass fibre bound into cables. Data are transmitted as light pulses.

field A grouping of characters into a word, a group of words, or a complete number, such as a person's name or age.

file A group of records of the same type.

File Transfer Protocol (FTP) Specification for retrieving and transferring files from a remote computer.

finance and accounting information systems Systems used to keep track of the firm's financial assets and fund flows.

firewall Hardware and software placed between an organization's internal network and an external network to prevent outsiders from invading private networks.

Firewire Faster port connection on Apple computers and some PCs, known as IEEE1824.

focused differentiation Competitive strategy for developing new market niches for specialized products or services in which a business can compete in the target area better than its competitors.

formal control tools Project management technique that helps monitor the progress toward completion of a task and fulfillment of goals.

formal planning tools Project management technique that structures and sequences tasks, budgeting time, money, and technical resources required to complete the tasks.

formal system A system resting on accepted and fixed definitions of data and procedures, operating with predefined rules.

forward chaining A strategy for searching the rule base in an expert system that begins with the information entered by the user and searches the rule base to arrive at a conclusion.

fourth-generation language A programming language that can be employed directly by end users or less-skilled programmers to develop computer applications more rapidly than conventional programming languages.

frame relay A shared network service technology that packages data into bundles for transmission but does not use error-correction routines. Cheaper and faster than packet switching.

framing Displaying the content of another Web site inside one's own Web site within a frame or a window.

franchiser Form of business organization in which a product is created, designed, financed, and initially produced in the home country, but for product-specific reasons relies heavily on foreign personnel for further production, marketing, and human resources.

fuzzy logic Rule-based artificial intelligence (AI) that tolerates imprecision by using nonspecific terms, called membership functions, to solve problems.

general controls Overall controls that establish a framework for controlling the design, security, and use of computer programs throughout an organization.

General Packet Radio Service (GPRS) 2.5G service that transports data over global system for mobile communications (GSM) wireless networks and improves wireless Internet access.

genetic algorithm Problem-solving method that promotes the evolution of solutions to specified problems using the model of living organisms adapting to their environment.

geographic information systems (GIS) Systems with software that can analyze and display data using digitized maps to enhance planning and decision making.

global culture The development of common expectations, shared artifacts, and social norms among different cultures and peoples.

global positioning system (GPS) Worldwide satellite navigational system.

Global System for Mobile Communications (GSM) Major cellular transmission standard outside North America with strong international roaming capability that operates primarily in the 900-megahertz (MHz) and 1.8-gigahertz (GHz) frequency bands using time division multiple access (TDMA) in which each user is allocated a portion of time on the frequency. This technology is now available from some wireless providers in North America, using the 1.9 Ghz band.

grid computing Applying the resources of many computers in a network to a single problem.

group decision-support systems (GDSS) Interactive computer-based systems to facilitate the solution of unstructured problems by a set of decision makers working together as a group.

groupware Software that provides functions and services that support the collaborative activities of work groups.

hacker A person who gains unauthorized access to a computer system.

hertz Measure of frequency of electrical impulses per second, with 1 hertz equivalent to 1 cycle per second.

hierarchical DBMS One type of logical database model that organizes data in a treelike structure. A record is subdivided into segments that are connected to each other in one-to-many parent-child relationships.

high-availability computing Tools and technologies, including backup hardware resources, that enable a system to recover quickly from a crash.

home page A World Wide Web text and graphical screen display that welcomes the user and explains the organization that has established the page.

hotspot A specific geographic location in which an access point provides public Wi-Fi network service.

hub Very simple device that connects network components, sending a packet of data to all other connected devices.

human resources information system System that maintains employee records; tracks employee skills, job performance, and training; and supports planning for employee compensation and career development.

hybrid AI system Integration of multiple artificial intelligence (AI) technologies into a single application to take advantage of the best features of these technologies.

hypermedia database An approach to data management that organizes data as a network of nodes linked in any pattern the user specifies; the nodes can contain text, graphics, sound, full-motion video, or executable programs.

Hypertext Markup Language (HTML) Page description language for creating Web pages and other hypermedia documents.

Hypertext Transfer Protocol The communications standard used to transfer pages on the Internet. Defines how messages are formatted and transmitted.

identity theft Theft of key pieces of personal information, such as credit card or Social Insurance numbers, to obtain merchandise and services in the name of the victim or to obtain false credentials.

I-mode Standard developed by Japan's NTT DoCoMo mobile phone network for enabling cell phones to receive Web-based content and services.

Immanuel Kant's Categorical Imperative A principle that states that if an action is not right for everyone to take, it is not right for anyone.

implementation All organizational activities working toward the adoption, management, and routinization of an innovation. Also, Simon's final stage of decision making, when the individual puts the decision into effect and reports on the progress of the solution.

industry structure The nature of participants in an industry and their relative bargaining power. Derives from the competitive forces and establishes the general business environment in an industry and the overall profitability of doing business in that environment.

inference engine The strategy used to search through the rule base in an expert system; can be forward or backward chaining.

information Data that have been shaped into a form that is meaningful and useful to human beings.

information appliance Device that has been customized to perform a few specialized computing tasks well with minimal user effort.

information asymmetry Situation in which the relative bargaining power of two parties in a transaction is determined by one party in the transaction possessing more information essential to the transaction than the other party.

information partnership Cooperative alliance formed between two or more corporations for the purpose of sharing information to gain strategic advantage.

information policy Formal rules governing the maintenance, distribution, and use of information in an organization.

information requirements A detailed statement of the information needs that a new system must satisfy; identifies who needs what information, and when, where, and how the information is needed.

information rights The rights that individuals and organizations have with respect to information that pertains to themselves.

information system Interrelated components working together to collect, process, store, and disseminate information to support decision making, coordination, control, analysis, and visualization in an organization.

information systems department The formal organizational unit that is responsible for the information systems function in the organization.

information systems literacy Broad-based understanding of information systems that includes behavioural knowledge about organizations and individuals using information systems as well as technical knowledge about computers.

information systems managers Leaders of the various specialists in the information systems department.

information systems plan A road map indicating the direction of systems development: the rationale, the current situation, the management strategy, the implementation plan, and the budget.

information technology (IT) All of the computer-based information systems used by organizations and their underlying technologies.

information technology (IT) infrastructure The foundation, or platform, on which the firm can develop and run its specific information systems.

informational roles Mintzberg's classification for managerial roles in which managers act as the nerve centres of their organizations, receiving and disseminating critical information.

informed consent Consent given with knowledge of all the facts needed to make a rational decision.

input The capture or collection of raw data from within the organization or from its external environment for processing in an information system.

input controls The procedures to check data for accuracy and completeness when they enter the system.

instant messaging Chat service that enables participants to create their own private chat channels so that a person can be alerted whenever someone on his or her private list is online to initiate a chat session with that particular individual.

intangible benefits Benefits that are not easily quantified.

Integrated Services Digital Network (ISDN) International standard for transmitting voice, video, image, and data to support a wide range of services over public telephone lines.

intellectual property Intangible property created by individuals or corporations that is subject to protections under trade secret, copyright, and patent law.

intelligence The first of Simon's four stages of decision making, when the individual collects information to identify problems occurring in the organization.

intelligent agent Software program that uses a built-in or learned knowledge base to carry out specific, repetitive, and predictable tasks for an individual user, business process, or software application.

internal integration tools Project management technique that ensures the implementation team operates as a cohesive unit.

internal rate of return (IRR) The rate of return or profit that an investment is expected to earn.

international information systems architecture The basic information systems required by organizations to coordinate worldwide trade and other activities.

Internet International network of networks that is a collection of hundreds of thousands of private and public networks.

Internet Protocol (IP) address Four-part numeric address indicating a unique computer location on the Internet.

Internet service provider (ISP) A commercial organization with a permanent connection to the Internet that sells temporary connections to subscribers.

Internet telephony Technologies that use Internet Protocol packet-switched connections for voice service.

Internet2 Research network with new protocols and transmission speeds that provides an infrastructure for supporting high-bandwidth Internet applications.

internetworking The linking of separate networks, each of which retains its own identity, into an interconnected network.

interorganizational systems Information systems that automate the flow of information across organizational boundaries and link a company to its customers, distributors, or suppliers.

interpersonal roles Mintzberg's classification for managerial roles in which managers act as figureheads and leaders for the organization.

intranet An internal network based on Internet and World Wide Web technology and standards.

intrusion detection system Tools to monitor the most vulnerable points in a network to detect and deter unauthorized users.

investment workstation Powerful desktop computer for financial specialists that is optimized to access and manipulate massive amounts of financial data.

ISO 17799 An international set of standards for security and control, provides helpful guidelines. It specifies best practices in information systems security and control, including security policy, business continuity planning, physical security, access control, compliance, and creating a security function within the organization.

iterative A process of repeating over and over again the steps to develop a system.

Java Programming language that can deliver only the software functionality needed for a particular task, such as a small applet downloaded from a network; it can run on any computer and operating system.

joint application design (JAD) Process to accelerate the generation of information requirements by having end users and information systems specialists work together in intensive interactive design sessions.

just-in-time Scheduling system for minimizing inventory by having components arrive exactly at the moment they are needed and finished goods shipped as soon as they leave the assembly line.

key field A field in a record that uniquely identifies instances of that record so that it can be retrieved, updated, or sorted.

knowledge Concepts, experience, and insight that provide a framework for creating, evaluating, and using information.

knowledge- and information-intense products Products that require a great deal of learning and knowledge to produce.

knowledge base Model of human knowledge that is used by expert systems.

knowledge discovery Identification of novel and valuable patterns in large databases.

knowledge engineer A specialist who elicits information and expertise from other professionals and translates it into a set of rules, or frames, for an expert system.

knowledge management The set of processes developed in an organization to create, gather, store, maintain, and disseminate the firm's knowledge.

knowledge management systems Systems that support the creation, capture, storage, and dissemination of firm expertise and knowledge.

knowledge network systems Online directory for locating corporate experts in well-defined knowledge domains.

knowledge repository Collection of documented internal and external knowledge in a single location for more efficient management and utilization by the organization.

knowledge work system (KWS) Specialized system developed for engineers, scientists, and other knowledge workers charged with discovering and creating new knowledge for a company.

knowledge workers People such as engineers or architects who design products or services and create knowledge for the organization.

learning management system (LMS) Tools for the management, delivery, tracking, and assessment of various types of employee learning.

legacy system A system that has been in existence for a long time and continues to be used to avoid the high cost of replacing or redesigning it.

legitimacy The extent to which one's authority is accepted on grounds of competence, vision, or other qualities. Making judgments and taking actions on the basis of narrow or personal characteristics.

liability The existence of laws that permit individuals to recover the damages done to them by other actors, systems, or organizations.

Linux Reliable and compactly designed operating system that is an offshoot of Unix, that can run on many different hardware platforms, and that is available for free or at very low cost. Used as an alternative to Unix and Microsoft Windows NT.

LISTSERV Online discussion groups using email broadcasts from mailing list servers.

load balancing Distribution of large numbers of requests for access among multiple servers so that no single device is overwhelmed.

local area network (LAN) A telecommunications network that requires dedicated channels and encompasses a limited distance, usually one building or several buildings in close proximity.

logistics Planning and control of all factors that will have an impact on transporting a product or service.

mainframe Largest category of computer, used for major business processing.

maintenance Changes in hardware, software, documentation, or procedures to a production system to correct errors, meet new requirements, or improve processing efficiency.

malware Malicious software programs that include a variety of threats such as computer viruses, worms, and Trojan horses.

managed security service provider (MSSP) Company that provides security management services for subscribing clients.

management information systems (MIS) The study of information systems focusing on their use in business and management.

management-level system Information system that supports the monitoring, controlling, decision-making, and administrative activities of middle managers.

managerial roles Expectations of the activities that managers should perform in an organization.

man-month The traditional unit of measurement used by systems designers to estimate the length of time to complete a project. Refers to the amount of work a person can be expected to complete in a month.

manufacturing and production information systems Systems that deal with the planning, development, and production of products and services and with controlling the flow of production.

mass customization The capacity to offer individually tailored products or services using mass production resources.

megahertz (MHz) A measure of cycle speed, or the pacing of events in a computer; one megahertz equals one million cycles per second.

message integrity The ability to ascertain whether a transmitted message has been copied or altered.

metric A standard measurement of performance.

metropolitan area network (MAN) Network that spans a metropolitan area, usually a city and its major suburbs. Its geographic scope falls between a wide area network (WAN) and a local area network (LAN).

microbrowser Web browser software with a small file size that can work with low-memory constraints, tiny screens of handheld wireless devices, and low bandwidth of wireless networks.

micropayment Payment for a very small sum of money, often less than $10.

microprocessor Very large scale integrated circuit technology that integrates the computer's memory, logic, and control on a single chip.

microwave A high-volume, long-distance, point-to-point transmission in which high-frequency radio signals are transmitted through the atmosphere from one terrestrial transmission station to another.

middle managers People in the middle of the organizational hierarchy who are responsible for carrying out the plans and goals of senior management.

middleware Software that connects two disparate applications, enabling them to communicate with each other and to exchange data.

minicomputer Middle-range computer used in systems for universities, factories, or research laboratories that allows decentralized computing, customized to the needs of individual departments.

mirroring Duplicating all the processes and transactions of a server on a backup server to prevent any interruption in service if the primary server fails.

MIS audit Identifies all the controls that govern individual information systems and assesses their effectiveness.

MIS steering committee A strategic-level committee composed of the CIO and other top managers who set IS policy and prioritize and review major IS projects.

mobile commerce (m-commerce) The use of wireless devices, such as cell phones or handheld digital information appliances, to conduct e-commerce transactions over the Internet.

mobile computing Wireless computing that enables Internet-enabled cell phones, personal digital assistants (PDAs), and other wireless computing devices to access digital information from the Internet and other sources from any location.

mobile wallet (m-wallet) Software that stores m-commerce shoppers' personal information and credit card numbers to expedite the purchase process.

model An abstract representation that illustrates the components or relationships of a phenomenon.

model-driven DSS Primarily standalone system that uses some type of model to perform "what-if " and other kinds of analyses.

modem A device for translating a computer's digital signals into analog form for transmission over ordinary telephone lines, or for translating analog signals back into digital form for reception by a computer.

module A logical unit of a program that performs one or several functions.

Moore's Law Assertion that the number of components on a chip doubles each year.

multicasting Transmission of data to a selected group of recipients.

multinational Form of business organization that concentrates financial management and control out of a central home base while decentralizing most other functions and activities.

multiplexing Capability of a single communications channel to carry data transmissions from multiple sources simultaneously.

multitiered (N-tier) client/server architecture Client/server network in which the work of the entire network is balanced over several different levels of servers.

nanotechnology Technology that builds structures and processes based on the manipulation of individual atoms and molecules.

Net marketplace A single digital marketplace based on Internet technology that links many buyers to many sellers.

net present value The amount of money an investment is worth, taking into account its cost, earnings, and the time value of money.

network The linking of two or more computers to share data or resources, such as a printer.

Network Address Translation (NAT) A layer of protection when static packet filtering and stateful inspection are employed. NAT conceals the IP addresses of the organization's internal host computer(s) to prevent sniffer programs outside the firewall from ascertaining them and using that information to penetrate internal systems.

network DBMS Older logical database model that is useful for depicting many-to-many relationships.

network economics Model of strategic systems at the industry level based on the concept of a network where adding another participant entails zero marginal costs but can create much larger marginal gains.

network interface card (NIC) Expansion card inserted into a computer to enable it to connect to a network.

network managers IS personnel who supervise the operations of an organization's networks.

network operating system (NOS) Special software that routes and manages communications on the network and coordinates network resources.

neural network Hardware or software that attempts to emulate the processing patterns of the biological brain.

nomadic computing Wireless computing where users move from wireless hotspot to wireless hotspot to gain network or Internet access.

nonobvious relationship awareness (NORA) Technology that can find obscure hidden connections between people or other entities by analyzing information from many different sources to correlate relationships.

normalization The process of creating small stable data structures from complex groups of data when designing a relational database.

object Software building block that combines data and the procedures acting on the data.

object-oriented DBMS An approach to data management that stores both data and the procedures acting on the data as objects that can be automatically retrieved and shared; the objects can contain multimedia.

object-oriented development Approach to systems development that uses the object as the basic unit of systems analysis and design. The system is modelled as a collection of objects and the relationship between them.

object-oriented programming An approach to software development that combines data and procedures into a single object.

object-relational DBMS A database management system that combines the capabilities of a relational database management system (DBMS) for storing traditional information and the capabilities of an object-oriented DBMS for storing graphics and multimedia.

offshore software outsourcing Outsourcing systems development work or maintenance of existing systems to external vendors in another country.

on-demand computing Firms off-loading peak demand for computing power to remote, large-scale data processing centres, investing just enough to handle average processing loads and paying for only as much additional computing power as the market demands. Also called utility computing.

online analytical processing (OLAP) Capability for manipulating and analyzing large volumes of data from multiple perspectives.

online transaction processing Transaction processing mode in which transactions entered online are immediately processed by the computer.

open source software Software that provides free access to its program code, allowing users to modify the program code to make improvements or fix errors.

Open Systems Interconnection (OSI) reference model Less widely used network connectivity model developed by the International Organization for Standardization for linking different types of computers and networks.

operating system The system software that manages and controls the activities of the computer.

operational CRM Customer-facing applications, such as sales force automation, call centre and customer service support, and marketing automation.

operational-level systems Information systems that monitor the elementary activities and transactions of the organization.

operational managers People who monitor the day-to-day activities of the organization.

optical network High-speed network composed of technologies for transmitting data in the form of light pulses.

opt-in Model of informed consent prohibiting an organization from collecting any personal information unless the individual specifically takes action to approve information collection and use.

opt-out Model of informed consent permitting the collection of personal information until the consumer specifically requests that the data not be collected.

organization (behavioural definition) A collection of rights, privileges, obligations, and responsibilities that are delicately balanced over a period of time through conflict and conflict resolution.

organization (technical definition) A stable, formal, social structure that takes resources from the environment and processes them to produce outputs.

organizational and management capital Investments in organization and management such as new business processes, management behaviour, organizational culture, or training.

organizational culture The set of fundamental assumptions about what products the organization should produce, how and where it should produce them, and for whom the products should be produced.

organizational impact analysis Study of the way a proposed system will affect organizational structure, attitudes, decision making, and operations.

organizational learning Creation of new standard operating procedures and business processes that reflect organizations' experience.

organizational memory The stored learning from an organization's history that can be used for decision making and other purposes.

organizational models of decision making Models of decision making that take into account the structural and political characteristics of an organization.

output The distribution of processed information to the people who will use it or to the activities for which it will be used.

output controls Measures that ensure the results of computer processing are accurate, complete, and properly distributed.

outsourcing The practice of contracting computer centre operations, telecommunications networks, or applications development to external vendors.

packet filtering Examination of selected fields in the headers of data packets flowing back and forth between the trusted network and the Internet, examining individual packets in isolation.

packet switching Technology that breaks messages into small bundles of data; routes them in the most economical way through any available communications channel; and reassembles the bundles of data once they arrive at their destination.

paging system A wireless transmission technology in which the pager beeps when the user receives a message; used to transmit short alphanumeric messages.

paradigm shift Radical reconceptualization of the nature of the business and the nature of the organization.

parallel port Sends a signal multiple bits at a time. Faster than a serial connection.

parallel strategy A safe and conservative conversion approach where both the old system and its potential replacement are run together for a time until everyone is assured that the new one functions correctly.

particularism Making judgments and taking action on the basis of narrow or personal characteristics, in all its forms (religious, nationalistic, ethnic, regionalism, geopolitical position).

partner relationship management (PRM) Automation of the firm's relationships with its selling partners using customer data and analytical tools to improve coordination and customer sales.

patent A legal document that grants the owner an exclusive monopoly on the ideas behind an invention for 17 years; designed to ensure that inventors of new machines or methods are rewarded for their labour while making widespread use of their inventions.

payback method A measure of the time required to pay back the initial investment on a project.

peer-to-peer Network architecture that gives equal power to all computers on the network; used primarily in small networks.

peer-to-peer computing Form of distributed processing that links computers via the Internet or private networks so that they can share processing tasks.

peer-to-peer payment system Electronic payment system for people who want to send money to vendors or individuals who are not set up to accept credit card payments.

personal area network (PAN) Computer network used for communication among digital devices (including telephones and personal digital assistants, or PDAs) that are close to one person.

personal digital assistant (PDA) Small, pen-based, handheld computer with built-in wireless telecommunications capable of entirely digital communications transmission.

pervasive computing Ubiquitous use of computers in every facet of everyday life, including cars, homes, office buildings, tools, and factories, making computers increasingly embedded in people's natural movements and interactions with their environments.

phased approach Introduction of the new system in stages either by functions or by organizational units.

Phishing A form of spoofing that involves setting up fake Web sites or sending email messages that look like those of legitimate businesses and using them to ask users for confidential personal data.

pilot study A strategy to introduce the new system to a limited area of the organization until it is proved to be fully functional; only then can the conversion to the new system take place across the entire organization.

Platform for Privacy Preferences (P3P) Standard for communicating a Web site's privacy policy to Internet users and for comparing that policy to the user's preferences or to other standards. Users can use P3P to select the level of privacy they wish to maintain.

political models of decision making Models of decision making in which decisions result from competition and bargaining among the organization's interest groups and key leaders.

pop-up ad Ad that opens automatically and does not disappear until the user clicks it.

port Used to connect peripheral devices to the central computer unit. Ports determine which devices can be used based on connectors or drivers.

portal Web interface for presenting integrated personalized content from a variety of sources. Also refers to a Web site service that provides an initial point of entry to the Web.

portfolio analysis An analysis of the portfolio of potential applications within a firm to determine the risks and benefits and to select among alternatives for information systems.

postimplementation audit Formal review process conducted after a system has been placed in production to determine how well the system has met its original objectives.

primary activities Activities most directly related to the production and distribution of a firm's products or services.

primary storage Where data and program instructions are stored temporarily during processing while the computer is on. Sometimes called primary or main memory.

privacy The claim of individuals to be left alone, free from surveillance or interference from other individuals, organizations, or the state.

private exchange Another term for a private industrial network.

private industrial network Web-enabled network linking systems of multiple firms in an industry for the coordination of transorganizational business processes.

processing The conversion, manipulation, and analysis of raw input into a form that is more meaningful to humans.

processing controls The routines for establishing that data are complete and accurate during updating.

process specifications Describe the logic of the processes occurring within the lowest levels of a data flow diagram.

procurement Sourcing goods and materials, negotiating with suppliers, paying for goods, and making delivery arrangements.

product differentiation Competitive strategy for creating brand loyalty by developing new and unique products and services that are not easily duplicated by competitors.

product life cycle management (PLM) systems Systems based on a data repository that organizes every piece of information that goes into making a particular product.

production The stage after the new system is installed and the conversion is complete; during this time, the system is reviewed by users and technical specialists to determine how well it has met its original goals.

production or service workers People who actually produce the products or services of the organization.

profiling The use of computers to combine data from multiple sources and create electronic dossiers of detailed information on individuals.

profitability index Used to compare the profitability of alternative investments; it is calculated by dividing the present value of the total cash inflow from an investment by the initial cost of the investment.

program A series of statements or instructions to a computer.

program-data dependence The close relationship between data stored in files and the software programs that update and maintain those files. Any change in data organization or format requires a change in all the programs associated with those files.

programmers Highly trained technical specialists who write computer software instructions.

programming The process of translating the system specifications prepared during the design stage into program code.

protocol A set of rules and procedures that govern transmission between the components in a network.

prototype The preliminary working version of an information system for demonstration and evaluation purposes.

prototyping The process of developing an experimental system quickly and inexpensively for demonstration and evaluation so that users can better determine information requirements.

public key infrastructure (PKI) System for creating public and private keys using a certificate authority (CA) and digital certificates for authentication.

pull-based model Supply chain driven by actual customer orders or purchases so that members of the supply chain produce and deliver only what customers have ordered.

pure-play Business models based purely on the Internet.

push-based model Supply chain driven by production master schedules based on forecasts or best guesses of demand for products, and products are "pushed" to customers.

push technology Method of obtaining relevant information on networks by having a computer broadcast information directly to the user based on prespecified interests.

query language Software tool that provides immediate online answers to requests for information that are not predefined.

radio frequency identification (RFID) Technology using tiny tags with embedded microchips containing data about an item and its location to transmit short-distance radio signals to special RFID readers that pass the data on to a computer for processing.

random access memory (RAM) A computer's internal primary storage. It can directly access any location.

rapid application development (RAD) Process for developing systems in a very short time period by using prototyping, fourth-generation tools, and close teamwork among users and systems specialists.

rational model Model of human behaviour based on the belief that people, organizations, and nations engage in basically consistent, value-maximizing calculations.

rationalization of procedures The streamlining of standard operating procedures, eliminating obvious bottlenecks, so that automation makes operating procedures more efficient.

RDF Site Summary (RSS) A method of describing news or other Web content that is available for distribution or subscription from an online publisher to Web users. An extension of XML.

reach Measurement of how many people a business can connect with and how many products it can offer those people.

read-only memory (ROM) Its contents are present even when the computer is turned off. ROM is nonvolatile and can only be read.

real options pricing models Models for evaluating information technology investments with uncertain returns by using techniques for valuing financial options.

record A group of related fields.

recovery-oriented computing Computer systems designed to recover rapidly when mishaps occur.

reduced instruction set computing (RISC) Computer chips with only the most frequently used instructions embedded in them. Makes the microprocessors faster.

reintermediation The shifting of the intermediary role in a value chain to a new source.

relational DBMS A type of logical database model that treats data as if they were stored in two-dimensional tables. It can relate data stored in one table to data in another as long as the two tables share a common data element.

repetitive stress injury (RSI) Occupational disease that occurs when muscle groups are forced through repetitive actions with high-impact loads or thousands of repetitions with low-impact loads.

request for proposal (RFP) A detailed list of questions submitted to vendors of software or other services to determine how well the vendor's product can meet the organization's specific requirements.

responsibility Accepting the potential costs, duties, and obligations for the decisions one makes.

richness Measurement of the depth and detail of information that a business can supply to the customer as well as information the business collects about the customer.

ring network A network topology in which all computers are linked by a closed loop in a manner that passes data in one direction from one computer to another.

risk assessment Determining the potential frequency of the occurrence of a problem and the potential damage if the problem were to occur. Used to determine the cost-benefit of a control.

Risk Aversion Principle Principle that one should take the action that produces the least harm or incurs the least cost.

router Specialized communications processor that forwards packets of data from one network to another network.

routines Precise rules, procedures, and practices that have been developed to cope with expected situations.

rule base The collection of knowledge in an artificial intelligence (AI) system that is represented in the form of IF-THEN rules.

sales and marketing information systems Systems that help the firm identify customers for the firm's products or services, develop products and services to meet their needs, promote these products and services, sell the products and services, and provide ongoing customer support.

Sarbanes-Oxley Act of 2002 U.S. legislation that imposes responsibility on companies and their management to safeguard the integrity of the information that is used internally and released externally.

satellite The transmission of data using orbiting satellites that serve as relay stations for transmitting microwave signals over very long distances.

scalability The capability of a computer, product, or system to expand to serve a larger number of users without breaking down.

scoring model A quick method for deciding among alternative systems based on a system of ratings for selected objectives.

search-based advertising Payment to a search service to display a sponsored link to a company's Web site as a way of advertising that company.

search costs The time and money spent locating a suitable product and determining the best price for that product.

search engine A tool for locating specific sites or information on the Internet.

Secure Hyptertext Transfer Protocol (S-HTTP) Protocol used for encrypting data flowing over the Internet, limited to Web documents.

Secure Sockets Layer (SSL) Protocol used for secure information transfer over the Internet enabling client and server computers to manage encryption and decryption activities as they communicate with each other during a secure Web session.

security Policies, procedures, and technical measures used to prevent unauthorized access, alteration, theft, or physical damage to information systems.

security policy Statements and policy that ranks information risks, identifies acceptable security goals, and identifies the mechanisms for achieving these goals.

semantic Web Collaborative effort led by the World Wide Web Consortium to make web searching more efficient by reducing the amount of human involvement in searching for and processing Web information.

semistructured decision Decision in which only part of the problem has a clear-cut answer provided by an accepted procedure.

semistructured knowledge Information in the form of less structured objects, such as email, chat room exchanges, videos, graphics, brochures, or bulletin boards.

semistructured knowledge system System for organizing and storing less structured information, such as email, voice mail, videos, graphics, brochures, or bulletin boards. Also known as digital asset management system.

senior managers People occupying the top-most hierarchy in an organization who are responsible for making long-range strategic decisions.

sensitivity analysis Models that ask "what-if " questions repeatedly to determine the impact of changes in one or more factors on the outcomes.

serial port Sends a signal along a cable one bit at a time.

server Computer specifically optimized to provide software and other resources to other computers over a network.

server farm Large group of servers maintained by a commercial vendor and made available to subscribers for electronic commerce and other activities requiring heavy use of servers.

service-oriented architecture Software architecture of a firm built on a collection of software programs that communicate with each other to perform assigned tasks to create a working software application.

service platform Integration of multiple applications from multiple business functions, business units, or business partners to deliver a seamless experience for the customer, employee, manager, or business partner.

shopping bot Software with varying levels of built-in intelligence to help electronic commerce shoppers locate and evaluate products or services they might wish to purchase.

short message service (SMS) Text message service used by digital cell phone systems to send and receive short alphanumeric messages less than 160 characters in length.

Simple Object Access Protocol (SOAP) Set of rules that allows Web services applications to pass data and instructions to one another.

six sigma A specific measure of quality, representing 3.4 defects per million opportunities; used to designate a set of methodologies and techniques for improving quality and reducing costs.

smart card A credit-card-sized plastic card that stores digital information and can be used for electronic payments in place of cash.

smart phone Wireless phone with voice, text, and Internet capabilities.

sniffer A type of eavesdropping program that monitors information travelling over a network.

social engineering Tricking people into revealing their passwords by pretending to be legitimate users or members of a company in need of information.

social networking site Online community for expanding users' business or social contacts by making connections through their mutual business or personal connections.

sociotechnical design Design to produce information systems that blend technical efficiency with sensitivity to organizational and human needs.

sociotechnical view Optimal organizational performance is achieved by jointly optimizing both the social and technical systems used in production.

software package A prewritten, precoded, commercially available set of programs that eliminates the need to write software programs for certain functions.

spam Junk email sent by an organization or individual to a mass audience of Internet users who have not expressed interest in the product or service being marketed.

spoofing Attempting to hide a hacker's true identity by misrepresenting themselves by using fake email addresses or masquerading as someone else. Spoofing can also involve redirecting a Web link to an address different from the intended one, with the site masquerading as the intended destination.

spyware Technology that aids in gathering information about a person or organization without its knowledge.

star network A network topology in which all computers and other devices are connected to a single hub. All communications between network devices must pass through the hub.

stateful inspection Method of packet filtering that provides additional security by determining whether packets are part of an ongoing dialogue between a sender and a receiver. It sets up state tables to track information over multiple packets. Packets are accepted or rejected based on whether they are part of an approved conversation or whether they are attempting to establish a legitimate connection.

storage area network (SAN) A high-speed network dedicated to storage that connects different kinds of storage devices, such as tape libraries and disk arrays, so they can be shared by multiple servers.

storage technology Physical media and software governing the storage and organization of data for use in an information system.

stored value payment system System enabling consumers to make instant online payments to merchants and other individuals based on value stored in a digital account.

strategic information system Computer system at any level of the organization that changes goals, operations, products, services, or environmental relationships to help the organization gain a competitive advantage.

strategic-level systems Information systems that support the long-range planning activities of senior management.

strategic transition A movement from one level of sociotechnical system to another. Often required when adopting strategic systems that demand changes in the social and technical elements of an organization.

structure chart System documentation showing each level of design, the relationship among the levels, and the overall place in the design structure; can document one program, one system, or part of one program.

structured Refers to the fact that techniques are carefully drawn up, step by step, with each step building on a previous one.

structured decision Decision that is repetitive, routine, and has a definite procedure for handling it.

structured knowledge Knowledge in the form of structured documents and reports.

structured knowledge system System for organizing structured knowledge in a repository where it can be accessed throughout the organization. Also known as content management system.

structured query language (SQL) The standard data manipulation language for relational database management systems.

subschema The specific set of data from the database that is required by each user or application program.

supply chain Network of organizations and business processes for procuring materials, transforming raw materials into intermediate and finished products, and distributing the finished products to customers.

supply chain execution system A system to manage the flow of products through distribution centres and warehouses to ensure that products are delivered to the right locations in the most efficient manner.

supply chain management Integration of supplier, distributor, and customer logistics requirements into one cohesive process.

supply chain management systems Information systems that automate the flow of information between a firm and its suppliers to optimize the planning, sourcing, manufacturing, and delivery of products and services.

supply chain planning system A system that enables a firm to generate demand forecasts for a product and to develop sourcing and manufacturing plans for that product.

support activities Activities that make the delivery of a firm's primary activities possible. They consist of the organization's infrastructure, human resources, technology, and procurement.

switch Device to connect network components that has more intelligence than a hub and can filter and forward data to a specified destination.

switching costs The expense a customer or company incurs in lost time and expenditure of resources when changing from one supplier or system to a competing supplier or system.

syndicator A business that aggregates content or applications from multiple sources, packages them for distribution, and resells them to third-party Web sites.

system failure An information system that does not perform as expected, is not operational at a specified time, or cannot be used in the way it was intended.

system software Generalized programs that manage the computer's resources, such as the central processor, communications links, and peripheral devices.

system testing Tests the functioning of the information system as a whole to determine whether discrete modules will function together as planned.

systems analysis The analysis of a problem that the organization will try to solve with an information system.

systems analyst Specialist who translates business problems and requirements into information requirements and systems and who acts as liaison between the information systems department and the rest of the organization.

systems design Details how a system will meet the information requirements as determined by the systems analysis.

systems development The activities that go into producing an information systems solution for an organizational problem or opportunity.

systems life cycle A traditional methodology for developing an information system that partitions the systems development process into formal stages that must be completed sequentially with a very formal division of labour between end users and information systems specialists.

systems operator IS staff member who actually operates the hardware, typically for a minicomputer or mainframe computer.

T lines High-speed data lines leased from communications providers, such as T-1 lines (with a transmission capacity of 1.544 megabits per second).

tacit knowledge Expertise and experience of organizational members that have not been formally documented.

tangible benefits Benefits that can be quantified and assigned a monetary value.

taxonomy Method of classifying things according to a predetermined system.

teamware Group collaboration software that is customized for teamwork.

technology standard Specification that establishes the compatibility of products and the ability to communicate in a network.

technostress Stress induced by computer use; symptoms include aggravation, hostility toward humans, impatience, and enervation.

telematics Wireless services that combine wireless communication with tracking capabilities from the global positioning system.

Telnet Network tool that enables someone to log on to one computer system while doing work on another.

test plan A plan prepared by the development team in conjunction with the users; it includes all of the preparations for the series of tests to be performed on the system.

testing The exhaustive and thorough process that determines whether the system produces the desired results under known conditions.

token A physical device similar to an identification card that is designed to prove the identity of a single user.

topology The way in which the components of a network are connected.

total cost of ownership (TCO) Designates the total cost of owning technology resources, including initial purchase costs, the cost of hardware and software upgrades, maintenance, technical support, and training.

Total Quality Management (TQM) A concept that makes quality control a responsibility to be shared by all people in an organization.

touch point Method of firm interaction with a customer, such as telephone, email, customer service desk, conventional mail, or point-of-purchase.

trade secret Any intellectual work or product used for a business purpose that can be classified as belonging to that business, provided it is not based on information in the public domain.

transaction cost theory Economic theory stating that firms grow larger because they can conduct marketplace transactions internally more cheaply than they can with external firms in the marketplace.

transaction processing system (TPS) Computerized system that performs and records the daily routine transactions necessary to conduct the business; it serves the organization's operational level.

transborder data flow The movement of information across international boundaries in any form.

Transmission Control Protocol/Internet Protocol (TCP/IP) Dominant model for achieving connectivity among different networks. Provides a universally agreed-on method for breaking up digital messages into packets, routing them to the proper addresses, and then reassembling them into coherent messages.

transnational Truly global form of business organization with no national headquarters; value-added activities are managed from a global perspective without reference to national borders, optimizing sources of supply and demand and local competitive advantage.

Transport Layer Security (TLS) Protocols used for secure information transfer over the Internet. They enable client and server computers to manage encryption and decryption activities as they communicate with each other during a secure Web session.

Trojan horse A software program that appears legitimate but contains a second hidden function that may cause damage.

tuple A row or record in a relational database.

twisted wire A transmission medium consisting of pairs of twisted copper wires; used to transmit analog phone conversations but can be used for data transmission.

unified messaging System combining voice messages, email, and fax so that all messages can all be obtained from a single system.

Unified Modeling Language (UML) Industry-standard methodology for analysis and design of an object-oriented software system.

Uniform Resource Locator (URL) The address of a specific resource on the Internet.

unit testing The process of testing each program separately in the system. Sometimes called program testing.

Universal Description, Discovery, and Integration (UDDI) A framework that enables a web service to be listed in a directory of Web services so that it can be easily located by other organizations and systems.

universal serial bus A port that permits up to 128 devices to be "daisy chained" through only one USB port by use of USB hubs.

Unix Operating system for all types of computers that is machine independent and supports multiuser processing, multitasking, and networking. Used in high-end workstations and servers.

unstructured decision Nonroutine decision in which the decision maker must provide judgment, evaluation, and insights into the problem definition; there is no agreed-upon procedure for making such a decision.

up-selling Marketing higher-value products or services to new or existing customers.

Usenet Forums in which people share information and ideas on a defined topic through large electronic bulletin boards where anyone can post messages on the topic for others to see and to which others can respond.

user-designer communications gap The difference in backgrounds, interests, and priorities that impede communication and problem solving among end users and information systems specialists.

user interface The part of the information system through which the end user interacts with the system.

Utilitarian Principle Principle that assumes one can put values in rank order and understand the consequences of various courses of action.

utility computing Model of computing in which companies pay only for the information technology resources they actually use during a specified time period. Also called on-demand computing or usage-based pricing.

value chain model Model that highlights the primary or support activities that add a margin of value to a firm's products or services where information systems can best be applied to achieve a competitive advantage.

value web Customer-driven network of independent firms that use information technology to coordinate their value chains to collectively produce a product or service for a market.

virtual organization An organization that uses networks to link people, assets, and ideas to create and distribute products and services without being limited to traditional organizational boundaries or physical locations.

virtual private network (VPN) A secure connection between two points across the Internet used to transmit corporate data. Provides a low-cost alternative to a private network.

Virtual Reality Modeling Language (VRML) A set of specifications for interactive three-dimensional modelling on the World Wide Web.

virtual reality system Interactive graphics software and hardware that create computer-generated simulations that provide sensations that emulate real-world activities.

Voice over IP (VoIP) Facilities for managing the delivery of voice information using the Internet Protocol (IP).

voice portal Capability for accepting voice commands for accessing Web content, email, and other electronic applications from a cell phone or standard telephone and for translating responses to user requests for information into speech for the customer.

walkthrough A review of a specification or design document by a small group of people who have been carefully selected based on the skills needed for the particular objectives being tested.

war driving The activity whereby eavesdroppers drive by buildings or park outside and try to intercept wireless network traffic without legitimate access to the network.

Web browser An easy-to-use software tool for accessing the World Wide Web and the Internet.

Web bugs Tiny graphic files embedded in email messages and Web pages that are designed to monitor online Internet user behaviour.

Web hosting service Company with large Web server computers used to maintain the Web sites of fee-paying subscribers.

Web log (blog) See blog.

Web master The person in charge of an organization's Web site.

Web personalization The tailoring of Web content directly to a specific user.

Web server Software that manages requests for Web pages on the computer where they are stored and that delivers the page to the user's computer.

Web services Set of universal standards using Internet technology for integrating different applications from different sources without time-consuming custom coding. Used for linking systems of different organizations or for linking disparate systems within the same organization.

Web Services Description Language (WSDL) Common framework for describing the tasks performed by a Web service so that the service can be used by other applications.

Web site All of the World Wide Web pages maintained by an organization or an individual.

Web site performance monitoring tools Software tools for monitoring the time to download Web pages, perform Web transactions, identify broken links between Web pages, and pinpoint other Web site problems and bottlenecks.

wide area network (WAN) Telecommunications network that spans a large geographical distance. May consist of a variety of cable, satellite, and microwave technologies.

Wi-Fi Standards for Wireless Fidelity and refers to the Institute of Electrical and Electronics Engineers (IEEE) 802.11 family of wireless networking standards.

WiMax Popular term for Institute of Electrical and Electronics Engineers (IEEE) Standard 802.16 for wireless networking over a range of up to 31 miles with a data transfer rate of up to 75 megabits per second (Mbps). Stands for Worldwide Interoperability for Microwave Access.

Windows Microsoft family of operating systems for both network servers and client computers.

Wintel PC Any computer that uses Intel microprocessors (or compatible processors) and a Windows operating system.

Wireless Application Protocol (WAP) System of protocols and technologies that enables cell phones and other wireless devices with tiny displays, low-bandwidth connections, and minimal memory to access Web-based information and services.

Wireless Markup Language (WML) Markup language for wireless Web sites; based on Extensible Markup Language (XML) and optimized for tiny displays.

wireless NIC An add-in card (network interface card) that has a built-in radio and antenna to enable wireless transmission.

wireless portal Portal with content and services optimized for mobile devices to steer users to the information they are most likely to need.

wireless sensor network (WSN) Network of interconnected wireless devices with built-in processing, storage, and radio-frequency sensors and antennas that are embedded into the physical environment to provide measurements of many points over large spaces.

wisdom The collective and individual experience of applying knowledge to the solution of problems.

work flow management The process of streamlining business procedures so that documents can be moved easily and efficiently from one location to another.

World Wide Web (WWW) A system with universally accepted standards for storing, retrieving, formatting, and displaying information in a networked environment.

worm Independent software program that propagates itself to disrupt the operation of computer networks or destroy data and other programs.

XML See eXtensible Markup Language.

ZigBee Protocol that handles application-level communication between devices in a wireless sensor network. Determines the content of messages transmitted by each node in the network.

Photo and Screen Shot Credits

Index

Name Index

A

Abbey, Scott, 370
Agassi, Shai, 508
Albrecht, Katherine, 289
Anderson, Rick, 278n
Andreessen, Marc, 243
Angwin, Julia, 475n
Anwar, Harris, 433n
Aponovich, David, 34n
Arnaut, Gordon, 264n
Aromour, Stephanie, 433n
Aronovich, Hanna, 36n
Asohan, A., 379n
Austen, Ian, 334n

B

Bacheldor, Beth, 48n, 539n
Baker, Stephen, 433n
Baldwin, Howard, 223n
Baliour, Fiona, 168
Bamford, James, 142n
Bank, David, 313n
Barnea, Amir, 105
Barrett, Larry, 221n
Beese, Davis, 312
Bennet, Peter, 577
Bennett, Michael, 189
Berez, Steve, 539n
Bergstein, Brian, 141n
Bergstrom, Dan, 223
Berinato, Scott, 439
Berners-Lee, Tim, 243
Berube, Patrice, 364
Black, Jane, 142n, 475n
Black, Robert, 221n
Blatan, Harald, 274
Boni, William, 313
Booch, Grady, 359
Borland, John, 475n
Brabston, Mary, 382n
Brackett, Nathan, 473
Bradsher, Keith, 430
Branswell, Brenda, 257n
Brewin, Bob, 334n
Brezezinksi, Matthew, 142n
Bridis, Ted, 221n
Broad, William J., 142n
Bronner, Ethan, 141n
Brown, Doug, 221n
Bruce, Lindsay, 334n
Brynjolfsson, Erik, 23n
Buchanan, Terri-Sue, 433n
Burke, Robert, 90
Bush, George W., 139, 140
Bushell, Sue, 340
Busser, Dave, 33

C

Campbell, Andrew, 62
Campbell, K.K., 467
Carey, David, 439n
Carlson, John, 382n
Carr, Nicholas, 5, 6
Carruthers, Sean, 336n
Carter, Robert, 299n
Case, Claudia, 395
Casey, Jim, 15
Caudron, Shari, 414
Champy, James, 348
Chapman, Graham, 142
Chowdhary, Sudhir, 133n
Claburn, Thomas, 66n, 133n, 289n, 474n
Clark, Jim, 243
Clattenburg, David, 376
Clymer, Adam, 141n
Collins, Scott, 312
Conlon, Ginger, 499n
Conrath, Chris, 334n
Cox, John, 508
Coyne, Andrew, 221n

D

D'Agostino, Debra, 48n, 199n
Davenport, Tom, 102
Davis, Ann, 142n
Dearne, Karen, 301n
Delaney, Karen J., 289n
Deming, W. Edwards, 350
Desmarais, Mike, 577
Dignan, Larry, 221n
Dixon, Kevin, 557, 558
Dohler, Artie, 278
Dubowski, Stefan, 441n
Dukes, Trevor, 521
Duvall, Mel, 334n

E

Eaton, Brian, 334n
Ebbers, Bernie, 108
Edelstein, Herb, 567n
Edwards, Randall, 142n
Einhorn, Bruce, 430
Elliott, Christopher, 90n
Emerson, David Lo., 309
Emery, Repsher, 141n
English, Larry, 141
Ericson, Jim, 508
Evans, Bob, 433n
Eveborn, Patrik, 526n

F

Fabrikant, Geraldine, 475n
Farmer, Dan, 142n
Faulkner, Guy, 334
Fayol, Henri, 81
Federman, Josef, 105
Ficker, Cheryl, 398

F (continued)

Fields, Gary, 221n
Fischer, Dave, 410
Fischer, Stanley, 105
Flisberg, Patrik, 526n
Flynn, Laurie J., 133n
Foust, Dean, 16n, 299n
Fox, Pimm, 522
France, Mike, 475n
Frappaolo, Carl, 463
Friedel, Jim, 411–412

G

Gage, Deborah, 129n, 221n
Gail, Brian, 141n
Gallagher, Sean, 221n
Garcia, Victor, 128
Geist, Michael, 142
George, Tischelle, 278n
Gertzen, Jason, 257n
Gianni, Ben, 219
Goldsmith, Charles, 475n
Goo, Sara Kehaulani, 141n
Gosling, James, 175
Gould, Larry, 3n
Green, Sean, 254
Greenemeir, Larry, 141n
Gruman, Galen, 16n, 299n

H

Hadoulis, John, 32n
Haephrati, Michael, 105
Haephrati, Ruth, 105
Haeussler, Mark, 410
Hamilton, Tyler, 336n
Hansell, Saul, 133n, 475n
Harmon, Amy, 475n
Harrison, Sue, 376
Hasler, Barry, 439
Hayes, Mike, 576, 577
Henderson, Graham, 474
Herman, Wendy, 430
Hill, Jason, 291n
Hitt, Lorin M., 23n
Hoffman, Martin, 459n
Holland, Jesse J., 142n
Holson, Laura M., 475n
Horton, Mike, 291n
Hulme, George, 321n
Hummel, Glenda, 376
Hurst, Mark, 395

I

Idle, Eric, 142
Indyk, Piotr, 141
Iniguez, Gelacio, 12

J

Jacobson, Ivar, 359
Jacont, Amnon, 105

Organization Index

Subject Index

knowledge repository, 547–548
knowledge revolution, 9
knowledge value-added approach, 391
knowledge work, 556–557
knowledge work systems (KWS)
    computer-aided design (CAD), 558
    described, 546
    examples of, 558–560, 560*t*
    requirements of, 557–558, 558*f*
    Virtual Reality Modeling Language
      (VRML), 559–560, 559*f*
    virtual reality systems, 559
knowledge workers, 19, 556–557

L

large-scale systems projects, 406
Law of Mass Digital Storage, 160
learning management system (LMS), 556
legacy systems, 166
legal issues
    see also political issues
    computer-related liability problems, 126–127
    described, 107
    due process, 112
    electronic records management
      (FRM), 313–314
    liability, 112, 126–127
legitimacy, 435
liability, 112, 126–127
Linux, 163, 172–174, 175
LISTSERV, 251
load balancing, 319
local area networks (LANs), 224–226, 234–235
location-based mobile services, 282
logistics, 485
loyalty programs, 90

M

m-commerce
    applications, 280–282, 281*t*
    challenges of, 284
    described, 451
    digital payment systems, 283–284
    global revenue, 280*f*
    mobile wallets, 284
    services, 280–282, 281*t*
    solution guidelines, 293
    voice portals, 283
    Web access, 282–283
    wireless portals, 283, 283*f*
m-wallets, 284
main memory, 148
mainframe, 155
maintenance, 355
maintenance of boundaries, 130
malicious code, 305*t*
malicious software, 304–305
malware, 304–305
man-month, 400
managed security service providers (MSSPs), 320
management
    behavioural models, 81–82
    challenge of information systems, 26–28
    classical model of management, 81
    decisional role, 82
    enterprise-wide integration, 58–59
    filters, 517–518
    implementation, role in, 397

and information systems, 20
    informational role, 82
    interpersonal roles, 82
    middle managers, 20, 513
    operational management, 513
    operational managers, 20
    project teams, 513
    role of, 81–82
    senior management, 513
    senior management committee, 504
    senior managers, 20
management capital, 22–23, 23*f*, 545
management challenges
    accounting for costs and benefits, 59
    application development in digital firm
      era, 369–370
    choice and coordination of infrastructure
      components, 182
    competitive advantages, sustainability
      of, 97–98
    control issues, 328
    corporate ethics policies, 135
    data management, 213–214
    decision-support systems, 533–534
    demand for systems, 59
    employee training, 59
    enterprise applications, 501–503
    enterprise-wide integration, 58–59
    ethical and social issues, 135
    global systems management, 423*t*, 434
    governance, 183
    information resource management (IRM), 406
    information technology (IT)
      infrastructure, 182–183
    infrastructure change, 182
    Internet technology, 467–468
    knowledge management systems, 571
    loss of management control, 257–258
    moral risks, understanding, 135
    multicultural firms, 434
    networking, 257–258
    organizational change requirements, 258, 502
    organizational performance, 97–98
    privacy issues, 293
    reliability issues, 258
    scalability, 258
    security issues, 258, 293, 328
    system-related change, 98
    systems development, 369–370
    whole firm view, 58
    wireless technology, 292–293
    wise infrastructure investments, 182
management decision making
    see also decision-making process
    bureaucratic models of decision making, 83
    business intelligence, 512
    business value of, 512–513, 513*t*
    decision-making process, 513–518
    design implications, 84
    impact of information technology (IT), 80–84
    information technology, effect of, 80
    models, 82–83
    organizational models of decision making, 83
    political models of decision making, 83
    rational model, 83
management information systems (MIS)
    vs. decision-support systems, 519, 519*t*
    described, 25, 40–41, 515
    sample report, 42*f*

and TPS data, 42*f*
management-level systems, 38
management opportunities
    data management, 213
    decision-support systems, 533
    enterprise applications, 501
    enterprise-wide integration, 58
    ethical and social issues, 135
    global systems management, 434
    information resource management (IRM), 405
    information technology (IT)
      infrastructure, 182
    Internet technology, 467
    knowledge management systems, 571
    networking, 257
    security and control, 327
    systems development, 368
    wireless technology, 292
management opportunity
    organizational performance, 97
managerial roles, 82, 82*t*
manufacturing, 465
manufacturing and production information
    systems, 45–46, 47*t*
market niche, 88–89
marketing, 465, 494
mass customization, 78
mass digital storage, 160
megahertz, 150
mergers, 401–402
message integrity, 325
Metcalfe's law, 160, 228, 228*f*
metric, 489
metropolitan area network (MAN), 235, 241*f*
microbrowser, 273
micropayment, 459
microprocessing power, 157–159
microprocessors, 149–150
Microsoft .NET, 181
microwave, 269
middle managers, 20, 513
middleware, 176
minicomputers, 155
mirroring, 320
MIS audit, 320
MIS steering committee, 381
mobile banking services, 282
mobile bill payment, 281–282
mobile commerce. *See* m-commerce
mobile computing, 280
    see also m-commerce
mobile entertainment, 282
mobile financial services, 282
mobile games, 282
mobile portals, 283
mobile technology. *See* m-commerce; wireless
    technology
mobile wallets, 284
mobile wireless standards for Web access, 273
model, 522–523
model-driven DSS, 519
modem, 232, 233*f*
module, 356
Moore's law, 157–159
moral dimensions
    accountability, liability and control, 126–127
    described, 109
    information rights, 115–121
    intellectual property, 121–126